THE CULTURES AND GLOBALIZATION SERIES ②

THE CULTURAL ECONOMY

Edited By

HELMUT K. ANHEIER
YUDHISHTHIR RAJ ISAR

ANNIE PAUL, ASSOCIATE EDITOR
STUART CUNNINGHAM, GUEST EDITOR

$SAGE

Los Angeles • London • New Delhi • Singapore

First published 2008

SAGE Publications Ltd
1 Oliver's Yard
55 City Road
London EC1Y 1SP

SAGE Publications Inc.
2455 Teller Road
Thousand Oaks, California 91320

SAGE Publications India Pvt Ltd
B 1/I1 Mohan Cooperative Industrial Area
Mathura Road, Post bag 7
New Delhi 110 044

SAGE Publications Asia-Pacific Pte Ltd
33 Pekin Street #02-01
Far East Square
Singapore 048763

British Library Cataloguing in Publication data

A catalogue record for this book is available from the British Library

ISBN 978-1-4129-3473-2
ISBN 978-1-4129-3474-9 (pbk)

Library of Congress Control Number 2006928698

Typeset by C&M Digitals (P) Ltd., Chennai, India
Printed and bound by Zrinski d.d. Croatia
Printed on paper from sustainable resources

CONTENTS

Foreword, by Gilberto Gil   x
Acknowledgements   xiii
Contributors   xv
List of boxes, figures, photos/illustrations and tables   xxiv

Introducing the *Cultures and Globalization Series* and *the Cultural Economy*,
Helmut K. Anheier and Yudhishthir R. Isar   1

PART I: THE CULTURAL ECONOMY TODAY   **13**

Cultural Economy: The Shape of the Field
Stuart Cunningham, John Banks and Jason Potts   15

Issues   **27**

Globalization and Localization   **27**

1   Globalization and the Cultural Economy: a Crisis of Value?   29
    David Throsby

2   Locating the Cultural Economy   42
    Andy C. Pratt

3   The Global Cultural Economy: Power, Citizenship and Dissent   52
    Daniel Drache and Marc D. Froese

4   Strange Bedfellows: Law and Culture in the Digital Age   67
    Mira T. Sundara Rajan

Actors and Forms   **83**

5   Free Culture and Creative Commons   85
    Frances Pinter

6   Cultural Entrepreneurs: Producing Cultural Value and Wealth   92
    Thomas H. Aageson

7   The Intergovernmental Policy Actors   108
    Yudhishthir Raj Isar

Regional Realities   **121**

8   Globalization and the Cultural Economy: Africa   123
    Francis B. Nyamnjoh

9   Globalization and Crafts in South Asia   135
    Jasleen Dhamija

10 East Asia: the Global–Regional Dynamic 141
Michael Keane

11 The New Korean Wave of U 148
Jaz Choi

12 The Impact of Globalization on the Cultural Industries of Central Asia 155
Florent Le Duc

13 European Cultural Systems in Turmoil 163
Xavier Greffe

14 Countries in Transition: Which Way to Go? 172
Kirill Razlogov

15 Southeastern Europe: Emergences and Developments 178
Nada Švob-Dokić, Jaka Primorac and Krešimir Jurlin

16 Impact and Responses in Latin America and the Caribbean 185
Ana Carla Fonseca Reis and Andrea Davis

17 The Local Creative Economy in the United States of America 199
Margaret Jane Wyszomirski

Fields and Genres **213**

18 Spatial Dynamics of Film and Television 215
Michael Curtin

19 Anyone For Games? Via the New International Division of 'Cultural' Labour 227
Toby Miller

20 Digital Media 241
Gerard Goggin

21 Creative Industries: The Case of Fashion 253
Sabine Ichikawa

22 Festivals: Seeking Artistic Distinction in a Crowded Field 260
Dragan Klaic

23 The Bahia Carnival 270
Paulo Miguez

24 Making Material Cultural Heritage Work: From Traditional Handicrafts to 274
Soft Industrial Design
Martha Friel and Walter Santagata

25 Australian Indigenous Art: Local Dreamings, Global Consumption 284
Mark David Ryan, Michael Keane and Stuart Cunningham

26   New York's Chelsea District: a 'Global' and Local Perspective on Contemporary Art   292
     David Halle and Elisabeth Tiso

27   Cultural Economy: Retrospect and Prospect   307
     Allen J. Scott

PART II: INDICATOR SUITES   **325**

Cultural Indicator Suites   327
Helmut K. Anheier

     Cultural values   334
     Digest: cultural values   340

     Cultural participation   341
     Digest: cultural participation   350

     Cultural consumption   352
     Digest: cultural consumption   354

     Heritage preservation   356
     Digest: heritage preservation   364

     The internet + the cultural commons   366
     Digest: the internet & the cultural commons   372

     Transnational cultural corporations   374
     Digest: transnational cultural corporations   385

Cultural ingos + foundations   **388**
Employment + professions   **398**

     Cultural employment + professions   404
     Digest: government cultural expenditures   406

     Government expenditure on education   408
     Digest: government expenditures on culture and education   416

     Trade   418
     Digest: Trade   424

     Global Branding   425
     Digest: Global Branding   429

     Creation, Innovation & Protection   431
     Digest: Creation, Innovation & Protection   436

     Dissemination & Storage   438
     Digest: Dissemination & Storage   442

     Traditional & Indigenous Knowledge   443
     Digest: Traditional Knowledge   445

Cultural Industries & Fields   **446**

     News (offline, online)   447
     Digest: News (offline, online)   448

TV 450
Digest: TV 453

Radio 455
Digest: Radio 457

Print Media 459
Digest: Print Media 461

Books 462
Digest: Books 464

Movies 466
Digest: Movies 468

Music 470
Digest: Music 472

Sports 474
Digest: Sports 476

Computer Games 478
Digest: Computer Games 480

Fashion 482
Digest: Fashion 484

Advertising 486
Digest: Advertising 488

Architecture 490
Digest: Architecture 492

Global Arts Market **493**

Art Auctions & Galleries 493
Digest: Art Auctions & Galleries 494

Global Performance Art 495
Digest: Global Performance Art 497

Prizes & competitions 498
Digest: Prizes & competitions 500

The Internet **503**

The Internet 503
Digest: The Internet 505

Global Sites & Events **507**

Global Cultural Centers & Cities 508
Digest: Global Cultural Centers & Cities 534

Global Events 538
Digest: Global Events 544

Educational Exchange 546
Digest: Educational Exchange 556

Cultural Tourism 558
Digest: Cultural Tourism 565

Global Concert Tours 566
Digest: Global Concert Tours 573

Regulatory Frameworks & Policy 575

International Standards 576
Digest: International Standards 578

National and Regional Cultural Policy 580
Digest: National and Regional Cultural Policy 584

International Regulatory Frameworks 585
Digest: International Regulatory Frameworks 595

References & Source Materials **597**

Heritage & the Cultural Commons **599**

Cultural Preservation & Destruction 599
Digest: Cultural Preservation & Destruction 600

The Internet & the Cultural Commons 601
Digest: The Internet & the Cultural Commons 603

Global Sites & Events **634**

Global Cultural Centers & Cities 634
Digest: Global Cultural Centers & Cities 636

Global Events 637
Digest: Global Events 641

Movements & Flows **641**

Educational Exchange 641
Digest: Educational Exchange 642

Cultural Tourism 643
Digest: Cultural Tourism 644

Global Concert Tours 644
Digest: Global Concert Tours 645

Regulatory Frameworks & Policy **645**

International Standards 645
Digest: International Standards 646

National and Regional Cultural Policy 646
Digest: National and Regional Cultural Policy 648

International Regulatory Frameworks 648
Digest: International Regulatory Frameworks 649

POLITICIZING THE NEW ECONOMY
Gilberto Gil

This book is an opportunity to get to know and analyse the blossoming of a new and stimulating terrain in global politics. The notion of a 'cultural economy' has developed over the last few decades, but I believe that today we can formulate and understand the significance of this novelty. Cultural policy is on the contemporary agenda for many reasons: judging from my own experience and from what I have seen around the world, I believe cultural policy as it has recently returned to the forefront offers a promising new axis for the rehabilitation of political life in general, as an agenda for the necessary transformation of institutional practices. The premise of the 'right to culture' is at the heart of this transformation, both as a symbolic system and as an economic activity. The latter is the specific focus of this volume.

The perspectives of the different authors allow us to see how the economic, conceptual, institutional, technological and legal issues mesh. To enter into the pages of this book is to dive headfirst into one of the most captivating debates of our time: on the role of culture at the center of our development strategies. The volume arrives at an opportune moment to update the debate on public policies for culture and to reveal how far we have reached at the start of this millennium in consolidating thought and coordinated action for this purpose at the international level.

From the heated debates in post-war Europe about the presence of Hollywood movies to similar discussions in our own time, we have evolved both institutionally and politically in constructing a world culture policy that favors cultural diversity. In our countries and in the United Nations System, a complex institutional design has been created that is the result of more progress than steps backward – and the volume provides in-depth analysis of the political reasons for both. It shows how we have constructed not only defences and protections, but proactive strategies and agendas to promote diversity as the heritage of humanity. As the co-editors invite us to do, we can already look back to a history of struggle, of both defeats and victories in the defense of a public responsibility. This book recounts the most recent pages of that recent history, yet the gaze of the authors looks also to the future.

While we have indeed taken great steps forward, the journey ahead of us will be very long. Here the challenges we stil face are clearly highlighted by revealing numbers and comparisons. On one hand, the figures show that culture produces wealth like never before. We have celebrated and pragmatically used such information to broaden the space for culture in our development models, probably much more than most economists expected. The book also reveals the many forms of economic expression of culture, its extraordinary diversity from one region to another. All this data will help governments and societies to believe that their economies depend on a policy for cultural diversity even more closely today than in the past. On the other hand, the same figures show that we are producing not just considerable wealth but considerable inequities as well. They show how poorly this cultural wealth is distributed. They show that instead of culturally developed countries, there are nations that know how to make property rights the fountainhead of a dominant economy and technology. They show that some countries were quicker than others to consolidate a global position. How can we transform this picture in the future, in search of fair trade and the balanced development of all regions in the world? How can we take advantage of multiple mutations: in digital culture and in geopolitics? How can we bring about a benign repositioning? How can we further the agenda that led to the adoption and ratification of UNESCO's *Convention on the Promotion and Protection of the Diversity of Cultural Expressions* or WIPO's Development Agenda?

Such has been the shift of the contemporary political agenda to which I have committed myself, together with colleagues at Ministries of Culture around the world. This volume provides us with yet another instrument with which to defend and nurture this shared new agenda. As it demonstrates, the need for cultural policies is now recognized in industrialized and developing countries alike, although with different foci. Developing countries have a cultural economy based on informality; a great part of this diverse field has not been absorbed in more complex production systems, and sometimes not even in educational systems. In these countries, public institutions and the State undoubtedly play an essential role. The challenges of countries like Brazil are more geared towards social inequities, while rich nations have more solid cultural institutions and a favorable balance of payments in intellectual property yet face greater challenges of cultural cohesion and dialogue in view of the diversity of populations that form their social dynamics. For all countries, the imperatives of cultural diversity must trump the commodification of the marketplace, leading to the integration of a global society, not a global casino.

Our concepts and categories challenge old presuppositions. Perhaps because twentieth century attitudes die hard, we still identify development with industrialization. In many circles, the wisdom of the indigenous peoples, their linguistic heritage and their environmental consciousness are only rhetorically respected. But the very title of this book, which evokes 'economy' rather than 'industry' may help us decode the real meaning of 'development': as a form of collective social well-being the search does not seem to be given to all the peoples on the planet.

At the end of the Cold War, a feeling of historical and political emptiness took hold across the world. The very idea of government lost its credibility, either because of an authoritarian stance inward towards society, or outwards in the guise of 'civilization' as expressed by expansionist and imperial policies. Ideas of the supposed end of the State and public policies may no longer be in vogue today, but I recall that twenty years ago such notions were taken up by governments that then proceeded to eliminate cultural institutions and deregulate markets. The result was the erosion of cultural diversity and the emergence of monopolies that have made our economic and social life poorer. States and institutions were disassembled rather than updated and improved. This 'cultural non-policy' produced its own perverse policy outcomes. It gave us cultural groups excluded from productive processes, it jeopardized work, it reduced incomes and threw the intellectual property regime out of balance. The challenge facing us today is to reinvent policies on new foundations, to recover from the apathy that accompanied the end of the twentieth century, to reinstate the democratic state in its role as a guarantor of rights.

Time magazine recently published an ironical report on French cultural policy. Clearly, its target was not exclusively France and its cultural life, as dynamic today as they always have been. Instead, the real target was clearly the global movement for institutional action – of which this book is a part. As more and more countries become aware of the wealth of their cultural diversity, and the need to prepare policies for the cultural economy of the twenty-first century, the idea of a global cultural policy takes on a new reality.

Some forty years separate the beginning of my career as a musician and my years as Brazil's Minister of Culture. Those years seem to separate not only two phases of my life as an artist and activist, but two worlds and two radically different ways of experiencing culture in our time. From Bahia in those early years, I can well recall one of the first cultural policies I ever encountered, that of Dean Edgar Santos at the Federal University of Bahia. The institution assumed its responsibility as a mentor, betting on the direct engagement of a generation of students and citizens with different forms of knowledge, esthetic experience and instruction from Africa, Europe, and the rest of the world. Those were years of intense cultural life in the city, creating conditions for what would later be a rebirth of Bahian culture, in which I participated as an artist. This policy did not create or replace the rich culture of my state: it merely expanded and strengthened contacts and exchanges that otherwise would have been much more limited. In this sense, cultural policies are an instrument of social emancipation, global articulation and human freedom in the twenty-first century. Seen in this light, the notion of the 'cultural economy' is a welcome politicization of economic debate for the contemporary world.

ACKNOWLEDGEMENTS

The *Cultures and Globalization Series* has benefited from the advice, support, and contributions of many individuals and organizations. We endeavour to acknowledge and thank all of them here. In the ultimate analysis, however, the co-editors alone are responsible for this final version of the publication.

International Advisory Board

Hugo Achugar (Uruguay)
Arjun Appadurai (India/USA)
Benjamin Barber (USA)
Hilary Beckles (Barbados)
Tony Bennett (United Kingdom)
Craig Calhoun (USA)
George Corm (Lebanon)
Mamadou Diouf (Senegal)
Yehuda Elkana (Israel/Hungary)
Yilmaz Esmer (Turkey)
Sakiko Fukuda-Parr (Japan/USA)
Mike Featherstone (United Kingdom)
Anthony Giddens (United Kingdom)
Salvador Giner (Spain)
Xavier Greffe (France)
Stuart Hall (Jamaica/United Kingdom)
David Held (United Kingdom)
Vjeran Katunaric (Croatia)
Nobuku Kawashima (Japan)
Arun Mahizhnan (Singapore)
Achille Mbembe (Cameroon/South Africa)
Candido Mendes (Brazil)
Catherine Murray (Canada)
Sven Nilsson (Sweden)
Walter Santagata (Italy)
James Allen Smith (USA)
Prince Hassan bin Talal (Jordan)
David Throsby (Australia)
Jean-Pierre Warnier (France)
Margaret Wyszomirski (USA)
Yunxiang Yan (China/USA)
George Yúdice (USA)

Additional Support

Research Coordination for Indicator Suites
Tia Morita

Design and Production
Willem Henri Lucas with assistance from David Whitcraft

Researchers
Meghan Corroon, Amber Hawkes, Ielnaz Kashefipour, Aiha Nguyen, Dustianne North, Hoda Gamal Osman, Sarah A. Simons, Mai Truong, Fei Wu, David Zimmer

Artwork
Emilia Birlo

Administration
Jocelyn Guihama

Financial Support

We gratefully acknowledge the financial support of the following institutions:

ARC Center of Excellence for Creative Industries and Innovation
Aventis Foundation
The Bank of Sweden Tercentenary Foundation
Calouste Gulbenkian Foundation
Compagnia di San Paolo
The J. Paul Getty Trust
The London School of Economics
The Prince Claus Fund for Culture and Development
The Sasakawa Peace Foundation
Swedish International Development Agency
UCLA School of Public Affairs

We would also like to acknowledge the support of:

Josephine Ramirez of the Music Center of Los Angeles County; the Walt Disney Concert Hall; Henrietta Moore and the faculty and staff of LSE's Center for the Study of Global Governance; the UCLA International Institute; Dean Christopher Waterman and the UCLA School of the Arts and Architecture.

CONTRIBUTORS

Thomas H. Aageson is the Executive Director of the Museum of New Mexico Foundation (MNMF) in Santa Fe, New Mexico and former Director of Aid to Artisans. Aageson is a cultural entrepreneur who created the successful Maritime Art Gallery at Mystic Seaport Museum along with a print and book publishing venture. He led the development of *New Mexico Creates*, an award winning economic development initiative that markets the work of New Mexico artists and artisans in the MNMF's museum shops and on their Internet shops. Aageson advises the UNESCO Division of Cultural Expressions and Creative Industries, created the Santa Fe Cultural Leaders group and led the economic development planning for Santa Fe's arts and cultural industries in 2003–2004.

Helmut K. Anheier is Professor of Public Policy and Social Welfare at the University of California, Los Angeles (UCLA), and Director of the Center for Civil Society, and the Center for Globalization and Policy Research at UCLA. He also serves as Academic Director of the Center for Social Investment at the University of Heidelberg and is Centennial Professor at the Center for the Study of Global Governance, London School of Economics (LSE). His work has focused on civil society, the non-profit sector, organizational studies, policy analysis, sociology of culture, and comparative methodology.

John Banks is a Postdoctoral Research Fellow in the Federation Fellowship program, ARC Center of Excellence for Creative Industries and Innovation, Queensland University of Technology. His research interests focus on the interface between media corporations and consumer co-creators in participatory culture networks. From 2000–2005 John worked in the video games industry (Auran Games) as an online community manager, facilitating the development of user-led content creation networks; he has published widely on research grounded in this industry background. John's current research continues to work at the interface of game developers and gamers as they negotiate these emerging co-creation relations.

Pierre-Jean Benghozi is Professor of Management and Research Director at the National Center for Scientific Research (CNRS), directs the Pole for Research in Economics and Management at the *Ecole polytechnique* in Paris and has established a research group on Information Technology, Telecommunications, Media and Culture. His current research interests include the adoption and use of ITC in large organizations and the structuring of e-commerce and ITC-supported markets and supply chains, notably in the creative industries; he has published widely on these topics. He also teaches at the University of Paris and is a consultant to various public sector bodies and private firms.

Emilia Birlo (artwork) is a visual artist and fashion designer who divides her time between Germany and the United States. Her art designs can be viewed at www.birlos.de.

Jaz Hee-jeong Choi is a doctoral candidate in the Creative Industries Faculty at Queensland University of Technology. Her research interests are in digital communication, particularly the ways in which various forms of digital communication are developed, established and integrated in an Asian context. Her current research is on the *trans-youth* mobile play culture of South Korea at the intersection of play, culture, creativity, technology, HCI (human-computer-interaction), mobility and urban design. Her website is located at www.nicemustard.com.

Clymene Christoforou is a director of ISIS Arts, a visual arts organization in the North of England. She is Vice-Chair of Waygood Gallery and Studios, Newcastle and a board member of Culture North East. In 2007 she was a NESTA Cultural Leadership Awardee with EFAH (the European Forum for Arts and Heritage) in Brussels.

Stuart Cunningham is Professor of Media and Communications, Queensland University of Technology, and Director of the Australian Research Council Center of Excellence for Creative Industries and Innovation. He is president of the national advocacy body CHASS (Council for the Humanities, Arts and Social Sciences). His books include *Framing Culture* (1992), an influential critique of the limits of cultural studies as applied to cultural policy, and a number of studies of the global dimensions of audiovisual culture (written or edited with John Sinclair and Elizabeth Jacka): *New Patterns in Global Television* (1996), *Australian Television and International Mediascapes (1996)*, and *Floating Lives: The Media and Asian Diasporas* (2001). He edits (with Graeme Turner) the standard tertiary media studies text, *The Media and Communications in Australia* (4th edition, 2006). His most recent work is *What Price a Creative Economy?* (2006). A collection of his key essays is forthcoming in 2008.

Michael Curtin is Professor of Communication Arts and Director of Global Studies at the University of Wisconsin-Madison. Previously, he was a faculty member at Indiana University, a visiting professor at the Chinese University of Hong Kong, and a visiting research fellow at Academia Sinica, Taipei and the Center for the Humanities, Wesleyan University. His books include *Playing to the World's Biggest Audience: The Globalization of Chinese Film and TV* (California 2007) and *Redeeming the Wasteland: Television Documentary and Cold War Politics* (Rutgers 1995). He is currently working on *Media Capital: The Cultural Geography of Globalization* (Blackwell) and *The American Television Industry* (co-author, BFI). With Paul McDonald, he co-edits the 'International Screen Industries' book series for the British Film Institute.

Andrea Davis has worked as a consultant with a variety of Jamaican and international public and private entities related to creative industries including Jampro, the Ministry of Tourism and Industry, Jamaica Intellectual Property Office, Ministry of Foreign Affairs and Trade, United Nations Special Unit for South–South Cooperation, World Intellectual Property Organization, as well as with artistes such as Morgan Heritage, Luciano, Junior Kelly and Marcia Griffiths. Ms. Davis has also worked with creative clients Bridget Sandals, East Fest Productions, L'Acadco Dance Company, Studio One 50th Anniversary, Anchor Group, Creative Production & Technical Center and Grizzly's Entertainment. Ms. Davis' company, Jamaica Arts Holdings, currently represents international recording artistes Diana King and Toots & The Maytals as well as produces the annual International Reggae Day Festival.

Jasleen Dhamija is internationally renowned in the fields of Living Cultural Traditions, Rural Non-Farm Development and History of Textiles and Costumes. She pioneered the development of Handicrafts and Handlooms in India in the 1950s. She also works for the United Nations in Iran, Central Asia, in 21 African countries, the Balkans, South Asia and South East Asia and has served as a consultant to the World Bank and

International NGOs. She was Hill Professor at the University of Minnesota and was a faculty member at the National Fashion Technology as well as visiting faculty at the National Institute of Design in India and at three Universities in Australia. She has authored several books on Textiles and Folk Arts, on Women's Employment, Income Generation, and has organized seminars. She has curated exhibitions in India, and abroad. In 2006, she did a major exhibition on 'Textiles of the Commonwealth' for the Commonwealth Games at Melbourne. She has been appointed President of the Jury for UNESCO's Award for Creativity in Textiles and is Editor of a Volume of the World Encyclopedia of Dress and Adornment.

Daniel Drache is Professor of Political Science and Associate Director of the Robarts Center for Canadian Studies, York University. He has written extensively and published more than 15 books on global cultural flows, the WTO, new citizenship practices, border security and North American integration. He has been a visiting professor in Australia, France and Italy. In 2008 he will be a research professor at the North American Center for Transborder Studies, Arizona State University. His latest book is *The Great Reversal: The Defiant Return of Disgruntled Global Publics* (Polity Press, forthcoming 2008). His reports and articles can be accessed at www.yorku.ca/drache.

Martha Friel is a PhD student in the Department of Economics and Marketing of the IULM University in Milan. She is working on a research project on the role of material culture in local economic development processes. She collaborates with the Research Center of the Touring Club of Italy and is a contributing editor to the *Tourism and Culture Yearbook*.

Marc Froese has just defended his political science dissertation *Power, Governance and Dispute Settlement: An Institutional and Legal Analysis of Canadian Membership at the World Trade Organization* in June 2007. His interests include Canadian foreign policy, Canada/US relations, multilateralism, the organization and functioning of international trade institutions and neo-institutional political economy. He has written on the global cultural economy and the culture of dissent. He has held doctoral fellowship from the Social Science and Humanities Research Council of Canada and has been an active research fellow at the Robarts Center for Canadian Studies. He teaches international relations at the Canadian University College in Alberta.

Vasiliki Galani-Moutafi is Associate Professor in the Department of Social Anthropology and History at the University of the Aegean, Mytilene, Greece. She has published articles in *Annals of Tourism Research*, *Journeys: The International Journal of Travel and Travel Writing*, *Journal of Modern Greek Studies* and chapters in collective volumes. She is also the author of *Tourism Research on Greece and Cyprus: An Anthropological Perspective* (Propombos, 2002, in Greek). Her areas of research and teaching include economic anthropology, anthropology of tourism, cultural change and the negotiation of local identities, tourist representations, place identity, locally distinctive products, commodity cultures, the politics of culture and consumption.

Gerard Goggin is Professor of Digital Communication, and Deputy Director of the Center for Social Research in Journalism and Communication, the University of New South Wales, Sydney, Australia. He is author or editor of a number of books on digital media including *Internationalizing Internet Studies* (2008), *Mobile Phone Cultures* (2007), *Cell Phone Culture* (2006), *Virtual Nation: The Internet in Australia* (2004), and *Digital Disability* (2003). Gerard holds an ARC Australian Research Fellowship, and is editor of the journal *Media International Australia*. His chapter was written while in the Department of Media and Communications at the University of Sydney.

Xavier Greffe is Professor of Economics at the University Paris I, where he chairs the cultural economics postgraduate program. He is also Associate Professor at the National Graduate Institute for Public Policies, Tokyo. He has published articles and books in economics of arts and media, the most recent being: *French Cultural Policy* (Bookdom, Tokyo, 2007), *Arts and artists from an economic perspective* (UNESCO, Paris, 2004) and *Managing our Cultural Heritage* (Aryan Books, New Dehli, 2002). Previously he has been Professor in various French and Foreign universities, and General Director for training and apprenticeship at the Ministry of Labour in Paris (1990–1994). He is developing research in the economics of cultural property and the link between culture and development.

Nicolas Gyss is European Affairs Consultant with KEA European Affairs. He deals with research and public affairs issues and specializes in culture, creativity and sport. He took part in the study on the economy of culture in Europe undertaken by KEA for the European Commission.

David Halle is Professor of Sociology at the University of California, Los Angeles. He is the author or editor of several books including *New York & Los Angeles: Politics, Society and Culture* (University of Chicago Press, 2003), *Inside Culture: Art and Class in the American Home* (University of Chicago Press, 1994) and *America's Working Man: Work, Home and Politics Among Blue-Collar Property Owners* (University of Chicago Press, 1984). He is currently working on a book on the economic, political and cultural development of the Far West Side of Manhattan and a book, with Elisabeth Tiso, on Chelsea's Contemporary Art galleries.

Sabine Ichikawa is an independent consultant and has worked for more than 20 years in Italy, New York, Tokyo and Paris for fashion brands such as Elle, Kenzo (LVMH) and Cacharel. She is interested in the multicultural aspects of branding and in training designers and marketers in this international industry, sharing her experience of fashion marketing and of the Japanese market. She holds a degree in fashion Design and an MBA in International Luxury Brand Management. At the University of Paris she is currently working on a doctoral thesis about the evolution of the Asian fashion business and its future perspectives.

Yudhishthir Raj Isar, an anthropologist by training, is Jean Monnet Professor of Cultural Policy Studies at The American University of Paris and also teaches at the *Institut d'Etudes Politiques (Sciences Po)*. He is the President of the European Forum for Arts and Heritage (EFAH), a board member of the Institute of International Visual Arts (*inIVA*) and of the Fitzcarraldo Foundation (Turin), Special Advisor to the World Monuments Fund (New York) and the Sanskriti Foundation (New Delhi). Earlier, at UNESCO, he was Executive Secretary of the World Commission on Culture and Development, Director of Cultural Policies and of the International Fund for the Promotion of Culture.

Krešimir Jurlin, PhD, works as a Senior Research Fellow at the Department for International Economic and Political Relations, Institute for International Relations (IMO), Zagreb, Croatia. His research interests include international competitiveness, foreign trade analysis, analysis of investment, and the analysis of research and development. He has been involved in numerous projects in the area of European integration and regional studies.

Michael Keane is a senior research fellow at the Australian Research Council Center of Excellence for Creative Industries and Innovation. His interests are East Asian media and creative industries, particularly focusing on the People's Republic of China. His most recent book is *Created in China: the Great New Leap Forward* (Routledge 2007).

Dragan Klaic, a Permanent Fellow of Felix Meritis in Amsterdam, teaches arts and cultural policies at Leiden University. Educated in Belgrade and at Yale, he held professorships in Belgrade and Amsterdam and was a Visiting Professor at the Universites of New Mexico, Pennsylvania, and Bologna, and at the Central European University, Budapest. He led Theater Instituut Nederland, co-founded the European Theater Quarterly *Euromaske*, and presided over the European cultural networks ENICPA and EFAH. He is the initiator and Chair of the European Festival Research Project and active across Europe as writer, lecturer, researcher and advisor. Author of several books among which most recently an exile memoir, *Exercises in Exile,* in Dutch and Croatian (2004 and 2006), *Europe as a Cultural Project* (Amsterdam: ECF 2005), *Mobility of Imagination, a companion guide to international cultural cooperation* (Budapest: CAC CEU 2007) and of many articles and contributions to over 40 edited works. He is Contributing Editor of the *Theater* magazine (USA).

Florent Le Duc is a consultant in development through culture who has specialized in Central Asia. He was Culture Officer at the UNESCO Central Asian regional office (Kazakhstan, Kyrgyzstan and Tajikistan) in Almaty from 2001 to 2004. In 2004/2005, he was Director of the Bactria Cultural Center created by the NGO *ACTED*, in Dushanbe, Tajikistan. President of the NGO *Central Asian Initiatives*, he has been implementing a series of projects in the field of Arts and Culture in Central Asia, with a focus on performing arts and regional cultural information and is currently coordinating an EU-funded project aimed at raising awareness of culture and development among local authorities and foundations in Europe.

Willem Henri Lucas (designer) is a Professor of Design/Media Arts at UCLA. He studied at the Academy of Visual Arts in Arnhem in the Netherlands under the guidance of Karel Martens and worked as an intern and apprentice for Max Kisman. He works for clients mostly based in the field of Culture and Art. From 1990 to 2002 he served as a professor and chair of the Utrecht School of the Arts' Graphic Design department. In 1998 he designed holiday postage stamps for the PTT (Dutch post and telecom company). In 2003 and 2004 he won a 'Best Book' award and a nomination from the Art Directors Club in the Netherlands.

Paulo Miguez is a Professor at Centro de Artes, Humanidades e Letras at Universidade Federal do Recôncavo da Bahia in Brazil. Previously, he has served as Secretary of Cultural Polices, Ministry of Culture, Brazil and has worked as a consultant for creative economy for the UNDP Special Unit for South–South Cooperation – SU/SSC, New York. Between 1982 and 1993 he was the Financial Director in the National Company of Telecommunications in Mozambique (Telecomunicações de Moçambique E. P.). He has lectured and presented papers internationally, teaches both graduate and postgraduate courses and has authored many articles and essays in the field of culture and related matters.

Toby Miller is the author or editor of several books on television, film and cultural studies, including: *Globalization and Sport: Playing the World* (Sage Publications, 2001 – with Geoffrey Lawrence, Jim McKay, and David Rowe); *Sportsex* (Temple University Press, 2001); *Global Hollywood* (British Film Institute/Indiana University Press, 2001 – with Nitin Govil, John McMurria, and Richard Maxwell); *Critical Cultural Policy Studies: A Reader* (Basil Blackwell, 2003 – edited with Justin Lewis); *Television Studies: Critical Concepts in Media and Cultural Studies* (Routledge, 2003 – 5 volumes – edited); *Spyscreen: Espionage on Film and TV from the 1930s to the 1960s* (Oxford University Press, 2003); *Cultural Policy* (Tartu Chu Liu Book Company, 2006 – with George Yúdice); and *Cultural Citizenship: Cosmopolitanism, Consumerism, and Television in a Neoliberal Age* (Temple University Press, 2007). He works at the University of California, Riverside.

Raman Minhas studies law at the University of British Columbia and concurrently works for the Intellectual Property Law firm Smart and Biggar. He holds a Bachelor's degree in Biochemistry from the University of British Columbia, as well as a Master's degree in Molecular Oncology from McGill University in Montreal, Quebec, Canada. Raman is also heavily involved in various global citizenship projects.

Francis B. Nyamnjoh is Head of Publications and Dissemination with the Council for the Development of Social Science Research in Africa (CODESRIA). He has taught sociology, anthropology and communication studies at universities in Cameroon, Botswana and South Africa, and has researched and published widely on globalization, citizenship, media and the politics of identity in Africa. His most recent books include *Negotiating an Anglophone Identity* (Brill, 2003), *Rights and the Politics of Recognition in Africa* (Zed Books, 2004), *Africa's Media, Democracy and the Politics of Belonging* (Zed Books, 2005), *Insiders and Outsiders: Citizenship and Xenophobia in Contemporary Southern Africa* (CODESRIA/Zed Books, 2006). Dr Nyamnjoh has also published three novels, *Mind Searching* (1991), *The Disillusioned African* (1995), and *A Nose for Money* (2006), and a play, *The Convert* (2003). Additionally, he has served as Vice-President of the African Council for Communication Education (ACCE) from 1996–2003.

Annie Paul is a writer and critic based at the University of the West Indies, Mona, Jamaica, where she is head of the Publications Section at the Sir Arthur Lewis Institute of Social and Economic Studies (SALISES). A founding editor of *Small Axe* (Indiana University Press) Paul is the recipient of a grant from the Prince Claus Fund (Netherlands) in support of her book project, *Suitable Subjects: Visual Art and Popular Culture in Postcolonial Jamaica'*. She has been published in international journals and magazines such as *Art Journal, Callaloo, South Atlantic Quarterly, Wasafiri* and *Bomb*. She has also been an invited contributor to Documenta11 curated by Okwui Enwezor; the AICA 2000 International Congress & Symposium at the Tate Gallery of Modern Art, Bankside, London; Meridien Masterpieces, BBC World Service; Dialogos Iberoamericanos (Valencia, Spain) and in forums sponsored by Iniva (Institute of International Visual Arts, London).

Frances Pinter has a PhD in International Relations from University College, London. She currently acts as an advisor to Creative Commons and runs a number of research projects on the use of Creative Commons licenses for improved access to knowledge in developing countries. She is the founder of Pinter Publishers, one of the leading Social Science publishers of the late twentieth century. She was also Publishing Director of the Soros

Foundation Network where she established the Center for Publishing Development and the Central European University Press in Budapest. She was recently CEO of International House Trust in London. She is on the board of REDRESS, an NGO that provides legal assistance to victims of torture.

Jason Potts is Principal Research Fellow at the ARC Center of Excellence in Creative Industries and Innovation at Queensland University of Technology. He is also a senior lecturer in the School of Economics at the University of Queensland. Previous work includes *The New Evolutionary Microeconomics* (Edward Elgar), which won the 2000 Schumpeter Prize. His latest book is *The General Theory of Economic Evolution* (with Kurt Dopfer, Routledge, 2008). His current research focuses on the contribution of creative industries to economic growth and evolution.

Andy C. Pratt is Reader in Urban Cultural Economy at LSE and Director of the LSE Urban Research Center. He teaches courses on social and urban geography, and the cultural industries and policy. His current research focus is on the international cultural economy and its social, spatial and economic embeddedness. Andy has written extensively about the film, television, new media, computer games, and advertising industries based upon fieldwork in Japan, Australia, Senegal, Europe and the USA. He has also advised many governments and international agencies on the cultural economy. His latest book (with P. Jeffcutt) is *Creativity and Innovation* (Routledge, 2007).

Jaka Primorac, M.A., works as a Research Fellow at the Department for Culture and Communication, Institute for International Relations (IMO), Zagreb, Croatia. Her research interests include research in the field of creative and knowledge industries, cultural workers, cultural transition and cultural production. She is the winner of the 2005 Cultural Policy Research Award (www.cpraward.org), awarded by the European Cultural Foundation (ECF) and Riksbankens Jubileumsfond.

Kirill Razlogov is Director of the Russian Institute for Cultural Research and author of 15 books and more than 300 articles on cultural history, art history, film and the media, cultural policy and development. He served as Program Director of the Moscow International Film Festival from 1999–2005 and has organized several other festivals and TV programs on film and art. Previously he has held positions as Researcher with the Russian Film Archive (Gosfilmofond); Special Assistant to the President of the State Film Committee; Professor of cultural studies, film history, media studies at the State Film Institute (VGIK); and Academic Secretary of the National Academy of Motion Pictures Arts and Sciences of Russia. He has also taught courses for film directors and script writers at the Institute for European culture in Moscow.

Ana Carla Fonseca Reis holds a Master's Degree in Management and is pursuing a PhD in Architecture and Urbanism. She is the author of three books on cultural sponsorship, management and the economics of culture and writes regularly for newspapers and magazines. She has a marketing background in multinational companies, based in Latin America, Milan and London. Reis is the founder and senior consultant of 'Garimpo de Soluções', and works as a special advisor on the creative economy for the United Nations, the Secretary of Culture to the State of São Paulo and a series of public and private companies, focusing on business opportunities uniting culture, economics and development. She serves as Director of the Economics of Culture at Instituto Pensarte and as curator of the Creative Clusters Conference.

Mark David Ryan is a research associate and PhD candidate at the Queensland University of Technology. His PhD explores the rise of the contemporary Australian horror film gence and the forces driving this production. He has contributed to several reports, articles and book chapters on creative industries and new media policy. Outside of research, Mark produces short films and writes creatively.

Walter Santagata is Professor of Cultural Economics and Public Economics at the University of Torino, Italy, where he also served as Director of the Department of Economics (2001–2004). He has written many essays and books on the economics of democracy and the economics of culture, including *La Mode. Une Economie de la Créativivitè et du Patrimoine* (with Christian Barrere) 2005, and *La fabbrica della Cultura* (*Make Culture Work*), 2007. In 2007 he was appointed to the Italian National Council for Arts and Culture.

Allen J. Scott is Distinguished Professor in the Department of Public Policy and the Department of Geography at UCLA. He was awarded the Prix Vautrin Lud in 2003.

Andrew Senior is the Senior Expert on the Creative Economy at the British Council in London. A lawyer by profession, he has worked in the arts for over 15 years, initially as a consultant working with theater companies, and more recently at the British Council's expert team on the creative industries and creative economy that he established in 1999. As a creative consumer his interests are eclectic, though he has a passion for literature.

J. P. Singh is Associate Professor in the Communication, Culture and Technology Program at Georgetown University and Editor of the Blackwell-Wiley journal *Review of Policy Research*. He has authored three books and over 30 scholarly articles. His latest book is *Negotiating the Global Information Economy* (Cambridge, 2008). Current projects include a forthcoming book on UNESCO commissioned by Routledge for their Key Global Institutions Series.

Mira T. Sundara Rajan currently holds the Canada Research Chair in Intellectual Property Law at the University of British Columbia Faculty of Law, Vancouver. She earned her doctorate specializing in Copyright at St Peter's College, Oxford University, and has published and consulted throughout Western and Eastern Europe, Russia and India, as well as Canada and the United States. Her book, *Copyright and Creative Freedom,* appeared with Routledge in 2006. She has recently been appointed Series Editor for a completely new and expanded version of the Oxford University Press series on *Intellectual Property: Central and Eastern European States.*

Nada Švob-Dokić PhD, is Senior Researcher (Scientific Advisor) at the Department for Culture and Communication, Institute for International Relations (IMO), Zagreb, Croatia. Her research areas and teaching courses include global and national cultural and scientific development, transformations and transitions, as well as development and transitional policies and strategies. She has been particularly involved in problems of multiculturality, intercultural communication, management of cultural differences, cultural industrialization and technologically induced cultural change. She is the author of 300 articles, books and studies, and the editor of *The Emerging Creative Industries in Southeastern Europe* (Zagreb 2005) and *The Creative City. Crossing Visions and New Realities in the Region* (Zagreb 2007).

David Throsby is Professor of Economics at Macquarie University in Sydney, Australia. He is internationally known as an economist specializing in the economics of art and culture. His current research areas include the economic role of artists, theories of value, the economics of cultural heritage, culture in economic development, and cultural policy. His book *Economics and Culture*, published by Cambridge University Press, has been translated into five languages. He is a past President of the Association for Cultural Economics International, and is a member of the Editorial Boards of the *Journal of Cultural Economics*, the *International Journal of Cultural Policy*, and *Poetics*. He is currently working on a book on the economics of cultural policy.

Elisabeth Tiso is an Art History lecturer at Parsons, at The New School for Social History and The School of Visual Arts in New York City. She has written reviews for *ARTnews Magazine* and *Art in America*. She helped establish and run the Niki de Saint Phalle Foundation in Europe.

Indrasen Vencatachellum was born in Mauritius in 1946, completed his Master of Arts at the Sorbonne in Paris and has been involved since 1976 in international cooperation for cultural development. He is currently in charge of UNESCO's Division of Cultural Expressions and Creative Industries. In 1990 he launched the 'Plan of Action for Crafts Development in the World'; in 1995; the 'Design 21' program; he was also the Managing Editor of the practical guide entitled *Designers Meet Artisans*.

Margaret Jane Wyszomirski is Director of the Graduate Progam in Arts Policy and Administration at the Ohio State University where she holds faculty appointments in both the College of the Arts and the John Glenn School of Public Affairs. From 1991–1993, she was Director of the Office of Policy Planning, Research and Budget at the National Endowment for the Arts. She was a member of the executive team for two American Assembly projects on the arts: The Arts and the Public Purpose (1997) and Art, Technology and Intellectual Property (2002). She is a contributing author and editor of five books on the arts and cultural policy. She was commissioned to prepare a background paper on the prospects for cultural policy change by the Columbus City Council and subsequently was a lead author of the city task force report, 'The Creative Economy: Leveraging the Arts, Culture and Creative Community for a Stronger Columbus'.

Sibel Yardımcı, born in Ankara in 1976, is an assistant professor in the Sociology Department of Mimar Sinan Fine Arts University, Ankara, Turkey. She completed her BA at the Middle East Technical University and her MA at the Bosphorus University; her PhD thesis (Lancaster University, 2004) was entitled 'Meeting in Istanbul: Cultural Globalisation and Art Festivals'. Among her publications in Turkish are *Urban Transformation and Festivalism: the Biennale in Globalising Istanbul* (İletişim Publications, 2005) and 'The Invisible Face of Waste Collecting' (*Toplum ve Bilim*, Spring 2007).

LIST OF BOXES, FIGURES, PHOTOS/ILLUSTRATIONS AND TABLES

Boxes

I.1	'The Arts as International Sport' An extract from *The Global Economy of Prestige* by James English	5
I.2	The language of the 'creative industries'	7
3.1	Cultural industries: from national to global governance	56
4.1	Intellectual property rights in the digital age	68
6.1	Missing the link – why creative entrepreneurs matter	93
6.2	The film industry in Nigeria	95
6.3	Opening markets for majority world photographers	97
6.4	Innovative expansion of pan-African book markets	99
6.5	Weaving together preserves traditions and enhances livelihoods	100
6.6	Using the shopping center model to create artisan markets	102
6.7	Creating an art gallery; creating markets for artists; and generating income for a museum	103
6.8	Cultural entrepreneurship takes hold in Central Asia	105
12.1	Central Asia: A space of interaction	155
13.1	The economy of culture in Europe	168
16.1	A new business model	189
16.2:	Fighting illiteracy and the information divide	190
16.3	Jamaica's Reggae music	193
16.4	IBERMEDIA – promoting audio-visual production of Ibero-American countries	194
16.5	Alternative distribution channels	195
16.6	Swimming against the tide – Manos del Uruguay	196
18.1	Bollywood: globalization and the demand for cultural copying	220
19.1	Video game expos: the fall of LA and the rise of Tokyo	233
19.2	Virtual worlds	235
20.1	The Google Books Library Project	248
20.2	The Frankfurt Book Fair	249
21.1	Some luxury industry figures	255
22.1	The Salzburg festival	261
22.2	Globalization and art festivals: the encounter in Istanbul	262
24.1	Building alliances between artisans and designers	277
26.1	The global art auction market boom	302
26.2	The Dashanzi Art District in Beijing	304
27:1	Excerpt from W. Somerset Maugham (1919) *The Moon and Sixpence*	312
27.2	*Mastiha*: from indigenous commodity to post-industrial luxury	319

Figures

2.1	The cultural economy production system – illustrated by the music industry	45
2.2	Contribution of the creative industries to the economy	45
3.1	The demography of cultural identity	61
7.1	The intergovernment policy-making process	115
11.1	Import and export of Korean broadcasting	150
15.1	Share of selected sectors in total value added	179
15.2	Share of selected sectors in total employment	180
16.1	Entertainment and media market growth 2005–09, compound annual growth rate (%)	188
17.1	Creative industries: definitional approaches	204

17.2   Artistic workers: NEA/BLS model   206
17.3   Holistic model of the creative sector: workforce, industries and infrastructure   209
19.1   Game show attendance for E3 and The Tokyo Game Show   233
19.2   Game console market values for the USA and Japan   234
19.3   Game console market growth for the USA and Japan   234
19.4   Global online social world revenues   235
19.5   *Second Life* residents   236
19.6   *Second Life* active residents by country   236
19.7   Lindex currency exchange   237
20.1   Countries represented at the Frankfurt Book Fair   250
26.1   Art gallery areas, Manhattan and Brooklyn, 1987–2007   293
26.2   Total fine arts auctions held by house   303
26.3   Global fine art market auction turnover by house   303

Photos/Illustrations

Illustration 12.1   Map of Central Asia   156
Photo 16.1   Agentes de leitura   191
Illustration 16.1   International Reggae Day Festival poster   193
Photo 16.2   Manos del Uruguay (Hands of Uruguay)   196

Tables

6.1   Financing strategies   105
14.1   Cultural institutions in Russia (01.01.04)   174
14.2   Piracy markets in Central and Eastern Europe   175
15.1   Internet users in SEE region   181
16.1   IIPA estimated trade losses due to copyright piracy (in US$ millions) and estimated levels of copyright piracy   189
16.2   World Internet usage and population statistics   192
16.3   Recorded music sales (retail) – US$ millions   194
16.4   2004 repertoire origin (per cent of music market value, excluding multi-artist product)   194
16.5   Strengths, weaknesses, opportunities and threats   195
17.1   Core vs total copyright industry dimensions   205
17.2   A comparison of creative industries typologies   208
20.1   Selected countries telephone, mobile and Internet use in 2006   243
23.1   Indicators of the Bahian Carnival: 2006   271
26.1   Number of galleries, by country, at key international art fairs   294
26.2   Art Basel 2007: number of galleries represented, per city   295
26.3   Art Basel 2007: United States galleries, by city and by New York City district   295
26.4   Worldwide annual sales of art, by category, location and year, at Christie's auction house   297
26.5   Subject matter of the art shows in the 16 most important ('star') Chelsea galleries   300

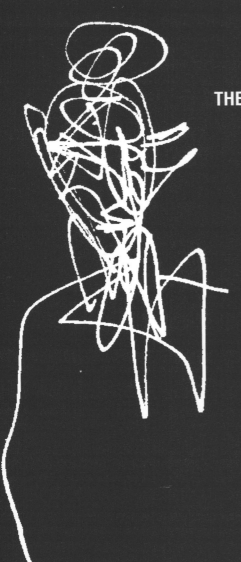

THE CULTURES AND GLOBALIZATION SERIES ②

INTRODUCING *THE CULTURES AND GLOBALIZATION SERIES* AND *THE CULTURAL ECONOMY*

Helmut K. Anheier and Yudhishthir Raj Isar

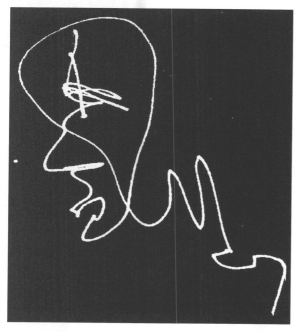

Why the Cultures and Globalization Series?

The relationships between the world's cultures and globalization are inadequately understood. While often reduced to the impacts of globalization on cultures, these relationships are far more complex. For cultural processes themselves affect globalization, changing its patterns and trajectory, manifesting themselves in many other spheres that mould the daily lives of billions (Ray, 2007). The culture of consumerism or the influences of religion are cases in point.

This complex interplay between cultures and globalization is at once unifying and divisive, liberating and corrosive, homogenizing and diversifying. The relationship also crystallizes both positive aspirations and negative anxieties. The interplay transforms patterns of sameness and difference across the world, and modifies the ways in which cultural expression is created, represented, recognized, preserved or renewed. It also contributes to generating powerful new culturalist discourses that evoke 'the power of culture' in domains as diverse as economic development, the fostering of citizenship and social cohesion, human security and the resolution or prevention of conflict.

Yet there remains a major knowledge gap as regards the relationships between cultural change and globalization – a gap that is culturally misleading, politically perilous, socially unsustainable and economically constraining. The *Cultures and Globalization Series* is designed to fill this gap. The first volume of this *Series,* entitled *Conflicts and Tensions,* appeared in 2007. In our Introduction to that volume we spelled out the antecedents and rationale for the project, as well as the conceptual framework we sought to build it upon, and the methods we intended to deploy (Anheier and Isar 2007b). Some of those thoughts need to be reiterated here in order to situate the project as a whole; we refer the reader to that inaugural volume for a fuller treatment of the concepts, frameworks and the core issues.

While a substantial evidence base has been developed on the economic, political and social dimensions of globalization, the cultural dimension continues to be the object of many unsubstantiated generalizations and unquestioned assumptions. The complex mutual relations between cultural change and globalization – the two-way impacts – have remained largely unmeasured and unanalyzed. One reason for the neglect at the global level is that conventional understandings of culture are still connected principally to the sovereign nation-state. However, today, this nexus of culture and nation no longer dominates: the cultural dimension has become constitutive of collective identity at narrower as well as broader levels. As Paul Gilroy reminds us, the idea of culture 'has been abused by being simplified, instrumentalized, or trivialized, and particularly though being coupled with notions of identity and belonging that are overly fixed or too easily naturalized as exclusively national phenomena' (Gilroy, 2004: 6). What is more, cultural processes take place in increasingly 'deterritorialized' transnational, global contexts, many of which are beyond the reach of national policies. Mapping and analysing this shifting terrain, in all regions of the world, as well as the factors, patterns, processes, and outcomes associated with the 'complex connectivity' (Tomlinson, 1999) of globalization, is therefore a main purpose of this *Series*.

The knowledge gap as regards cultures and globalization is also based on an acute paucity of comparative information. In response, each volume of the *Series* includes a significant data section based on innovative 'indicator suites', represented with the help of state-of-the-art information graphics (see Anheier, 2007). We are, of course, aware of the still inchoate state of cultural statistics and, *a fortiori*, of the enormous difficulty of constructing cultural indicators, even at the national level. Using existing cultural statistics just to make cross-national comparisons is more hazardous still, even among closely related countries such as those of the European Union or the United States and Canada. Therefore, in a departure from conventional approaches, we will neither seek to list data by country, nor strive to have a uniform table layout. Instead, we have developed the concept of 'indicator suites' to present data on specific aspects of the relationships between culture and globalization. A basic premise of this approach is that much information on culture and culture-related facets is already 'out there', but is not yet systematically assessed, compiled, analysed and presented. Another is that interpretative presentations using information graphics are better at facilitating understanding of many facets of the relationships between cultures and globalization than 'raw' data in tabular form.

As befits a project of global aspiration, whose genealogy began at UNESCO in the mid-1990s, the *Series* is intended to give voice to different issues and opinions emanating from as many different regions of the world as possible. It is intended to be 'ecumenical' in its embrace of diverse theoretical and disciplinary positions. Although each volume may not be fully 'representative' of the diversity of regional perspectives and points of view, our hope is that the *Series* as a whole will be synoptic in its geo-cultural coverage. And although the project is academy-based, each volume will include contributions by non-academic authors: artists, cultural activists, journalists, etc.

Elements of the conceptual framework[1]

Each volume of the *Series* focuses on a specific set of 'culture and globalization' issues as they are perceived, experienced, analysed and addressed in different geo-cultural regions of the world. Contributions by independent researchers and thinkers, hailing as we have said mainly but not exclusively from academia, will constitute the multiple prisms through which these phenomena will be taken up. Given this collaborative approach, each volume could emerge as little more than a compilation of discrete chapters. To counter this risk, the preparation of each volume is based on a conceptual framework that is discussed and shared with contributors. This conceptual framework in turn borrows from existing as well as emerging 'models' and analyses of cultures and globalization and of the shifting ground on which cultural change is occurring. It not only informs authors, but also guides our thematic choices: in 2007 'conflicts and tensions', this year 'the cultural economy', in 2009 'cultural expression, creativity and diversity' and in 2010 (tentatively) 'heritage, memory and identity'. The framework will also direct us towards a systematic exploration of core themes and critical issues, help build a permanent 'multilogue' across fields, disciplines, countries and regions, so as to provide better conceptual and empirical understandings of how globalization and culture relate to each other. An overriding concern is to provide arguments and perspectives that might be useful to others in developing policy options.

Since 'culture' is directly or indirectly related to virtually every aspect of the human condition, as a concept it is even broader and more capacious than 'economy' or 'society'. Kroeber and Kluckhohn's 281 famous definitions of 1952, a classic reference, come to mind immediately; indeed this is not surprising, since within various disciplines – anthropology and sociology in particular – there have been many attempts to stabilize meanings in the interest of a technical vocabulary (Williams, 1976). Having entirely escaped academic control in recent decades, however, the notion has become even more protean, especially as cultural difference has come to be consciously mobilized in political ways by individuals and groups.

The word 'culture' is thus the object of a complex terminological tangle. With no single definition generally accepted, differences, overlaps and nuances in meaning complicate rather than facilitate rigor and communication in the field. Various disciplines deal with culture and regard it as their 'terrain', however inclusively or exclusively: anthropology, political science, history, sociology, the law, and, of course, the humanities including cultural studies and art history. These disciplines have become institutionalized as such in the academy, and have come to function as rather closed intellectual 'silos', as it were, frequently discouraging multidisciplinary approaches and cross-disciplinary dialogue. Within each discipline, we typically find multiple approaches in terms of focus and methodology, such as the split between quantitative and qualitative sociology, or between cultural and social anthropology. For brevity's sake, we will refer to the sum of academic disciplines concerned with culture as the 'cultural disciplines'.

It is always difficult to avoid such conceptual discontents in these cultural disciplines and so we do not intend to adopt a single set of omnibus concepts, much less a single lens. We know that the many contributors to this collective endeavor will each work with very different concepts of culture – for the reasons already outlined above. Also, the cultural disciplines, as well as cultural operators, activists and policy-makers, tend to oscillate permanently between variants of the 'ways of life' notions of culture and 'arts and heritage' ones. We have nevertheless initiated our work on the *Series* with an agreed understanding of the terms we ourselves shall be using.

Culture in the broad sense we propose to employ refers to the social construction, articulation and reception of meaning. Culture is the lived and creative experience for individuals *and* a body of artifacts, symbols, texts and objects. Culture involves enactment and representation. It embraces art and art discourse, the symbolic world of meanings, the commodified output of the cultural industries as well as the spontaneous or enacted, organized or unorganized cultural expressions of everyday life, including social relations. It is constitutive of both collective and individual identity.

Closely related to culture is the concept of **communication**, which refers to the ways in which meanings, artifacts, beliefs, symbols and messages are transmitted through time and space, as well as processed, recorded, stored and reproduced. Communication requires media of storage and transmission, institutions that make storage and transmission possible, and media of reception.

The notion of **globalization** itself, almost as frustratingly as the term 'culture', is the object of multiple theories and definitions. In this *Series*, we shall use the term to refer to the worldwide interconnections and interdependencies that all have deep origins in world history but today are being increasingly and ever more rapidly brought about through the movement of objects (goods, services, finance and other resources, etc.), meanings (language, symbols, knowledge, identities, etc.) and people across regions and intercontinental space (Warnier, 2004). This notion of globalization as 'time and space compression' is not

a normative concept: not a 'business buzzword', nor a tool for 'miracle growth', nor the result of an evil plot (Chanda, 2007: 268), but simply the global connectivity that characterizes the way we live ever more closely 'bound together' in the world.

The cultural economy

The inaugural theme, 'conflicts and tensions', addressed the broader, 'ways of life' or identity-based understandings of the culture concept as used in the social and human sciences. The exponential growth in affirmations of or claims to cultural difference have given rise to multiple 'conflicts and tensions' in recent years. These loom large in current anxieties. As we put it, 'behind the concern for "culture" that is increasingly evoked in contemporary public debate lurks the specter of conflict: the cultural dimensions of conflict on the one hand, and the conflictual dimensions of culture on the other' (Anheier and Isar, 2007b: 19).

By contrast, the 'cultural economy' topic, for its part, partly embodies anxieties of a different sort, largely related to the specter of cultural domination. For example, the World Commission on the Social Dimension of Globalization, referring to the impact of the global information revolution on local cultures and values across the world, expressed widespread concern at the overwhelming dominance of the cultures and values of the United States, and other Western countries: 'The fear is that constant exposure to the images of Western lifestyles and role models could lead to tensions which would be both culturally and socially divisive' (World Commission on the Social Dimension of Globalization 2004: para. 222).

So how have the terms of debate developed with regard to the 'cultural economy'? How does this debate intersect with our key lines of engagement regarding the cultures and globalization interface? As with practically all the terms associated with the protean notion of 'culture' the notion of 'cultural economy' is umbrella-like, used to embrace a range of different understandings. Our working definition of the cultural economy for the purposes of this volume defines it as an economic system for the production, distribution and consumption of cultural goods and services through market as well as non-market mechanisms. As to what constitutes the 'cultural', we emphasize, as does Allen Scott in Chapter 27, 'all those forms of economic activity producing outputs with significant aesthetic or semiotic content, or what Bourdieu has characterized as symbolic outputs'. In other words, our topic is what Scott refers to as the *cognitive-cultural economy*, meaning an economic order that is intensely focused on mobilizing the knowledge, creativity, cultural attributes, sensibility, and behavioural characteristics of the labour force, in combination with a technological infrastructure based on digital computation and communication.

At the outset, we should acknowledge that, epistemologically speaking, the idea of 'the economy' that underlies our working definition is not without problems. We may well be missing something important by focusing exclusively on a 'separate sphere of social life called "the economy", a sphere … lorded over by distinctive and systemic rules and driven by the imperatives of resource production, allocation, and distribution', as Amin and Thrift (2004: x) put it. They fault conventional economics for 'honing or improving accounts of an un-problematically presented economic realm (e.g., value, profit, distribution, surplus), rather than challenging the ontological status of the economy and the dominance of an economic world-view' (Amin and Thrift, 2004: x). Neoclassical economics does not see the cultural, the social and the economic woven together as a single fabric – recall Karl Polanyi's economy embedded in society – and therefore does not question the significance of economic efficiency seen in isolation. The implications of such views have not been thought through sufficiently, however, and distinguished from various other approaches to the economic that have emerged in the course of the development of economics as a discipline. It is useful, therefore, to review the key features of these other approaches as the two authors have captured them:

- The first approach stresses the centrality of *passions*. Pre-nineteenth-century European economic thought was often concerned with economic principles as a means of overcoming what was seen as a surfeit of passions in the conduct of daily life, while in the course of the nineteenth century, a romantic reaction to this civilizing conception of the economy set in. The economy itself came to be seen as a negative passion for accumulation of the kinds revealed in hoarding by misers and in the theoretical writings of Marx.
- The second approach is loosely related to the first, in that it focuses on *moral sentiments,* an issue explored not only by Adam Smith in connection with moral value, but also present in the trading practices of faith-sensitive Muslim entrepreneurs as well as in a long line of socialist thinkers.

- The third approach identifies *knowledge* as a key motive force, as in the early twentieth-century writings of Thorstein Veblen ('conspicuous consumption'), who argued that because of the strong interdependence between 'habits of thought' and 'habits of life', there can be 'no neatly isolable range of cultural phenomena that can be rigorously set apart under the head of economic institutions' (cited in Amin and Thrift, 2004: xvi).
- The fourth approach, drawing on the work of Darwin, Lamarck, and Spencer, stresses that learning and economic change in general are *evolutionary,* a metaphor with a long history of use and abuse in economic thinking since the mid-nineteenth century. Learning (and learning how to learn) is seen as a means of transmission of culture and processes of evolutionary transmission provide the templates that guide economic behaviour. Evolutionary thinking made it possible to inject a historical dimension into a predominantly equilibrium-based economics, thereby also making a place for the kind of dynamics that included cultural explanations.
- The fifth approach considers the kinds of *disciplines* necessary to produce competent economic actors. It includes the ideas of E.W. Taylor, who was mainly concerned with minute analyses of bodily movement as ciphers for increased productivity and other forms of bodily accountancy that paid more attention to non-quantifiable factors such as worker satisfaction, which, it was argued, were themselves important aspects of productivity.
- The sixth and final approach has read economies as *symptoms* of general economic modes or models that marked cultural life since at least the time of Adam Smith. These readings allowed Marx and Engels, among others, to re-inscribe how cultures see themselves as a single functioning economic system, which, in turn, is returned to these cultures as an established economic and cultural fact. They could thus project nineteenth-century British capitalism – despite all its peculiarities – as a world economic standard and its class culture as the only culture.

As Amin and Thrift again observe:

All these lineages have continued to exist, but as a disorganized field; one that has been marginalized by the weight of marginal [sic] economics and computational knowledge, by political economy and the rationality of structure,

*and by the general neglect of economic
processes within cultural studies. Though certain
organized sub disciplines have emerged as a
partial counterweight – and most notably
economic sociology, economic anthropology,
economic geography, and economic psychology –
they have exerted very little influence on
mainstream economic thought. However,
there is an opening here that might be widened…
(2004: xvii)*

In other words, our apprehension of the economy would be much richer if it could truly encompass the processes of social and cultural relations that accompany, are impacted by or encompass the economic or, as Pratt states in his Chapter 2 as 'the set of socio-economic relations that enable cultural activity'. Seen in this holistic way, then, our exploration would need to embrace the insights of fields such as economic sociology, cultural studies, social studies of finance, business and management studies, economic anthropology and cultural geography, and methodological strategies as diverse as semiotics, ethnography, social studies of science, and theories of practice. Such a broader approach would make it easier to analytically embrace a range of types and regimes of cultural production in all regions of the world, whereas much of the literature on the subject is based on more specifically economic realities in the post-industrial, post-Fordist, 'knowledge economy' contexts of the global North. In other words to explore cultural industries *stricto sensu* (many of which are rather more incipient than developed in the non-Western world) as well as artisanal endeavors in fields such as handicrafts, exploitation of the intangible heritage, communal cultural expression, etc. As well as to understand the field as made up of symbolic production systems of collective representation that are central in forging visions of public identity.

A case in point is the recent work of James English, who, in *The Economy of Prestige* (2005), looks at the economic dimensions of culture in such a plural perspective, when he analyses the contemporary convergence of prizes and cognate awards in literature and the arts – as a new economy of prestige. He addresses the rules or logics of exchange in the market for cultural capital, showing how 'art' has come to be closely related 'to money, to politics, to the social and temporal' (English, 2005: 3) and explores the nature of cultural power and how this form of power is situated in relation to other forms. This cultural economy is now organized at a global level as well (see Box I.1). Without expecting every contributor to subscribe to such an approach, its premises underlay the brief we proposed to authors and we are gratified by the ways in which they have risen to the challenge.

Box I.1   'The Arts as International Sport'

(An extract from Chapter 11, pp. 259–61, of *The Economy of Prestige* by James English)

Today it is more than ever apparent that the economy of cultural prestige is a global one, in which the many local cultural markets and local scales of value are bound into ever tighter relations of interdependence. Not only can we observe the tendency over the past half-century for successful European and American prizes to be reproduced by imitation in one country after another, serving as formal models in an increasingly global process of cultural diffusion and adaptive appropriation ('the Oscars of Taiwan', 'South Africa's Emmy Awards', 'the Catalan Nobel', 'the Russian Booker Prize', and so forth), but, within this McWorld of awards, we can see how the outcome of one prize competition immediately registers as a factor in other, geographically remote ones – the sort of 'action at a distance' that, for Anthony Giddens, characterizes the era of globalization. The decisions of the jury at Cannes or Sundance or FESPACO not only influence the selection of films at other festivals worldwide, but they can alter, within minutes, the odds set by bookmakers on the BAFTAs and the Oscars. The Swedish Academy's choice of a new Nobel laureate is immediately celebrated as a symbolic windfall by those involved in the more local or regional prizes that the laureate can already count among his or her *palmarès,* since it greatly strengthens those prizes' claims to legitimacy.

(Continued)

(Continued)

We can readily observe, too, how the most ambitious prizes are more and more obliged to reach beyond national boundaries both for objects of esteem and for (other) sources of legitimacy. The Praemium Imperiale prizes of Japan are fairly typical of the many international 'super prizes' that have emerged since the 1970s. These prizes have been conceived on the model of the Nobels, and they share the Nobels' pretension to global authority. It is thus no surprise that, in 1995 for example, the Praemium Imperiale prizes were awarded at a Tokyo ceremony to a Chilean-born French painter, two French-born American sculptors, a British composer, a Japanese theater director, and an Italian architect. But whereas the Nobels, at the organizational and ceremonial level, remain a relatively insular Swedish affair, the Praemium Imperiale prizes seize eagerly on symbolic support from extranational sources. In 1995, the board of advisors included former heads of state from three countries; the annual press announcement was made in London; and a reception was hosted by the Queen of England. Such institutional arrangements – more reminiscent of the Olympic Committee than of the Swedish Academy – bespeak the existence of a global economy of cultural prestige deeply interwoven with the international circuits of political, social, and economic power.

While we fault neoclassical economics for either ignoring culture altogether or approaching it in isolation, we are equally critical of popularized buzzwords. For this reason, an important concern has been to question the privileged position occupied by now globalized labels such as 'cultural industries', 'the creative industries', and, most recently, 'creative economy' that appear to have colonized the cultural field in its entirety.

These terms tend to imply that the logic of the market-place reigns supreme – but is the existence of the market all that it takes for the cultural economy to function? For while market forces have a large and important place, nowhere are they able to deliver 'the right and the good' entirely on their own. Sociologists and economists have long pointed out that other social and political Institutions have played a key role in the gradual development of market spheres, just as they have studied the limitations and failures of market mechanisms in terms of efficiency, effectiveness and equity. Placing the entire sweep of cultural practice within the market paradigm also implies an unjustifiable faith in what Robert Hewis on has called the 'pseudo-democracy of supply and demand' that is 'pseudo-democratic because people do not have equal access to the market or equal purchasing power within it. This is both a question of cash, and of cultural capital in terms of education and acculturation.

The vogue terms we use often neglect the very institutional and regulatory aspects that make markets possible. They also defy important nuances, which is why it is wise to be wary of their simplifying power. In this particular case, terms like creative economy or creative industries now drive a bandwagon that many ride for 'fear of being left behind' (Jeffcutt, 2001: 11). Those who join the bandwagon are increasingly both instrumentalizing and instrumentalized; all too often they miss the complexities, the contradictions and the pitfalls of this agenda, as well as the relations of cause and effect that underpin it. At the very least, such terms have to be more precise in delineating how market and non-market forms of creation, production and distribution relate to industrial and non-industrial cultural fields.

Of course, a vast amount of contemporary artistic production, distribution and consumption is industrially, and digitally, mediated. But because there is also much that is not, it does seem increasingly plain that today everything cultural – not just the market-driven forms – is being forced into the procrustean bed of economy-driven paradigms and discourses. Furthermore, since the marriage of culture and economy has been consummated internationally, funding agencies (including, for example, at least five United Nations organizations, international financial institutions and regional development banks – see Chapter 7) are now actively investing in the 'creative economy' as a way of stimulating local economic growth, developing markets for arts and crafts overseas, or generally seeking to improve the quality of life and attractiveness of cities and regions to international investment capital. In other words, the dominance of economic reasoning is driving a growing range of activities, institutions and practices of artistic and creative expression in the same direction, if only to garner recognition and support.

Box I.2   The language of the 'creative industries'

UK artists and cultural organizations have had to learn a new language to successfully secure public funding. It is the language of business. Over the past ten years the growing requirement for the arts to present themselves as a means to solve social and economic problems, has meant adopting new ways of measuring the value and quality of our work. The application forms for European Structural Funds, regional development funds and local authority funds demand a justification for our activity in a language better suited to the creation of a business park, requiring us to present art not as an intrinsic cultural expression but as a measurement of economic activity.

My organization has found a place for arts and culture within this public funding landscape. To do so we have accessed funds for our activity as an 'SME' (Small to Medium-sized Enterprise) with outputs that include the professional development of other SMEs (individual artists). Our success is evaluated on the 'number of paid hours created' and the 'number of training sessions and reports delivered'. We identify 'how many jobs have been created' through our program and 'how many have been safeguarded'. We 'aspire' to a 'full cost recovery model' with our 'overhead costs as integral to project budgets' and we reassure our supporters that our 'exit strategies' are financially robust. We are accordingly described as part of the 'creative industries' – a phrase which neatly encompasses the notion of art as essentially a business to be bracketed with advertising or entertainment or the sale of antiques.

Within this 'climate of enterprise', few questions are asked by those funding bodies about the intrinsic value or quality of our art and we become complicit, trusting that in the gap between the language of the funder and the desire of the artist we can surreptitiously create a space for innovation and risk. The Structural Funds are now disappearing from the UK and the cultural funds are being squeezed to make room for the Olympics. Where policy increasingly views art as a means to another end, I wonder what new languages we will need to learn to create a space for art in the future.

Clymene Christoforou

Should pragmatism lead us to set such qualms aside? To be sure, there is more to the relationship between culture and the economy than semantics or policy fashion. The danger here is similar to what has been observed with regard to the numerous 'economic impact' studies of culture that were launched in the 1980s: even if the evidence is robust (and often it wasn't, the economic case was overstated), surely investment in cultural projects and programs should not be justified on economic criteria alone. In many instances, their contribution to, say, social cohesion or overall quality of life, cannot be measured along the economic calculus alone, if at all in meaningful ways to begin with. If economic performance were the standard, surely other sectors could outperform culture at some point in terms of job creation, value added or multiplier effect. Would culture then have to cede its place? And what about cultural activities and practices that can't deliver economic returns?

Sounding such a note of caution does not mean rejecting the opportunities available to invest in the production, distribution and consumption of cultural goods and services when deemed profitable – and also to increase the flourishing of culture itself as well as human capabilities. This indeed was the main thrust of the original 'cultural industries' concept first used in France and at UNESCO in the late 1970s and then, with more international visibility, by the Greater London Council in the early 1980s (Hesmondhalgh, 2007).[2]

Analysts of this discursive shift have pointed out *inter alia* that the 'cultural industries' included the arts and heritage (including cultural tourism) and the crafts (which are sometimes excluded from the creative industries remit), seen within an agenda of economic as well as social benefits: the subsidized arts with an additional emphasis on applied arts practices in fields such as urban regeneration, audience development, community development and the like. The category has 'tended to be a concatenation of the arts and the established commercial or large-scale public sector media', (Cunningham, 2001: 24) developed mainly for nation-states around the cultures of nation-states. The 'creative industries' category crystallized later, around the new technologies as well as the 'knowledge economy', and focused more on the commercial sector. The key to this paradigm is the argument that while the industries that drove the urban revolution of the nineteenth century were based largely on the use of raw materials, creativity is now based on knowledge and skills, i.e. human capital and its capacity to generate new knowledge from existing knowledge; the ability to generate new ideas that can trigger innovation and its concrete applications.

By the mid-1980s, ideas such as these were strongly at work in the British *zeitgeist* and, in terms of policy debates, the British Government's Department of Culture, Media and Sport that foregrounded the 'creative' industries notion at the end of the decade in its vision and rhetoric (DCMS, 1998, 2001). This concept has since acquired considerable purchase in the English-speaking world, eventually spreading to continental Europe. As noted, however, in a biting recent critique by a leading scholar, herself British:

> ...when the arts and culture per se, become the focal point for capitalisation (the logic of late capitalism as Fredric Jameson famously put it), when culture broadly becomes absolutely imperative to economic policy and planning, when art is instrumentalised so that it begins to provide a model for working lives, and labour processes, and when government opens a Green Paper document as it did in 2001 with the words 'Everyone is creative', then it becomes apparent that what in the past was considered the icing on the cake, has now become a main ingredient of the cake... And what had been in the past left to its own devices, e.g. subculture and style, or black expressive culture or the punk avant garde has been plucked, over the years, from obscurity, and is now promoted with tedious regularity under the prevailing logic of the revival, in the window spaces of Selfridges and Harrods almost every season as a leading edge feature of the UK's contribution to the new global cultural economy. Our imagined community and branded national identity now comes to be constituted through practices which are understood to be creative. (McRobbie, 2006: 2)

The economy-driven notion of creativity was truly popularized internationally, however, in the wake of Richard Florida's 2002 bestseller *The Rise of the Creative Class ... and how it's transforming work, leisure, community & everyday life.* Florida's theses were taken up enthusiastically by many government officials, politicians and cultural activists the world over – and despite the apparent imprecision of the notion of the 'creative class', which stretches across a very broad range of rather different professions and occupations indeed, including scientists, engineers, architects, educators, writers, artists and entertainers. In other words, all those whose economic function is to create new ideas, new technology, and new creative content are now part of the 'creative class', even though the actual economic and social circumstances of the various professions and groups so subsumed varies widely. Florida's argument found such wide and enthusiastic acceptance because of the positive, proactive policy stance implied and the way it presented the creative class as a panacea for local economic problems (Florida, 2002).

It is also clear that the 'branded identity', alluded to earlier, has become an increasingly local affair, but in a setting whose terms have been set by the global. As Allen Scott has observed (see also Chapter 27), 'the geography of culture ... is stretched across a tense force-field of local and global relationships, with the production of culture tending to become more and more concentrated in a privileged set of localized clusters of firms and workers, while final outputs are channelled into ever more spatially extended networks of consumption' (Scott, 2000: 4). Thus city and regional authorities turn increasingly to local *marketing strategies* that rely increasingly on cultural offer, in other words on the presence of artists, creative people and the cultural industries as elements of symbolic capital that exert a strong attraction on international companies and their mobile workforce. Some consider, in fact, that the impact on inward investment that this turn to cultural resources has had is a far more significant outcome than the direct creation of wealth and employment (Bianchini, 1999).

Thus urban 'quality of life' has come to be seen as a key ingredient for 'city marketing' and 'branding', including international strategies to attract mobile external capital and skills. It was thus that public sector-led forms of provision and management began, in some cities and regions, to be accompanied if not replaced by a variety of private, voluntary and semi-public agencies and initiatives. New strategies to mobilize local potential for economic growth began to include actors other than those associated with traditional municipal policies. In these new partnership processes, bargaining systems have emerged which require more cooperative structures and styles of policy-making. Important new sources of funding emerged at this time. Cities and regions now take it increasingly for granted that they must build international competitive advantage in the cultural products sectors.

In all these processes, an important and overarching role is increasingly ascribed to 'identity', i.e. that sense of commonality particular to individual regions or other territorial entities which shapes approaches to and priorities in politics and policy. While sub-national identity has an economic base and also includes such factors as the infrastructure base, administrative traditions, and so on, it is clear that cultural resources express and sustain it, just as they also support social interaction and collective action which is essentially economic in nature. Thus culture has become a core component of self-representation on the part of local authorities, a key element of place branding and marketing and a prop in the search for social cohesion. It is in this sense that local-level cultural policy frameworks, as distinct from those of the central state, are clearly emerging, as the local authorities look at cultural resources ever more systemically, at their inter-connections with economic growth, industry regeneration, tourism, governance and social cohesion.

Yet the practices of 'place marketing' that have emerged as a result present a range of negative symptoms. Thus,

> instead of a dynamic and challenging approach to local character, we are confronted with unrepresentative stereotypes and parodies of the past. Rather than an inclusive methodology that addresses local audiences, it is exclusively outward-looking, thereby ignoring whole sections of the population. Authenticity and reality are substituted for a burlesque caricature of place. The messages follow an insipid formula, which makes it difficult to distinguish one place from

> another... The kinds of identities being projected are at best partial and at worst completely fictitious. (Murray, 2001: 5)

As the spheres of cultural and economic development converge, cultural forms and meanings are becoming critical elements of many different productive as well as discursive strategies. Although the economic importance of cultural goods and services is much greater in some countries (for example in the USA, Western Europe and Japan) than in others, the sector is developing at various speeds and with varying degrees of intensity all over the world (see indicator suites on the cultural economy). This process, initially led by forces mainly in the global North, is now joined by new players in the global South, facilitated by the Internet and the media, cultural tourism, globalizing educational systems, etc. Thus, globally, the capacity to create new ideas and new forms of expression for the so-called 'knowledge economy' is well on the way to becoming a valuable resource base, one that may equal mineral, agricultural and manufacturing assets in importance. This cultural wealth of nations should not be understood principally as a legacy or just a mass distributed industry but as the vitality, knowledge, energy and dynamism in the production of ideas and identities (Venturelli, 2000). For the creative or cultural industries do not simply generate income and employment: they also communicate, reflect and celebrate a diversity of cultural expressions. In an ideal world, therefore, one would expect each society to be able to elaborate goods and services that express its own cultural visions and aspirations and be able to see them compete fairly in domestic, regional and global markets. This is far from being the case, as the relevant indicator suites make clear, for production, distribution and trade flows are dominated by a limited number of countries in the global North.

While these asymmetries obviously affect earnings, they also aggravate historic imbalances in communication exchange, in access to information and entertainment and in civic participation. They hold back cultural development and inter-cultural dialogue. Major asymmetries exist *within* the countries of the South as well. Many people simply cannot afford to pay for the products of recently reconfigured cultural and media industries and their only access to globalized culture is through free, state-run radio and television.

It is in these terms that the question of cultural goods and services has gradually come to the forefront of the international public policy debate on culture at UNESCO, resulting in the 2005 *Convention on the Protection and the Promotion of the Diversity of Cultural Expressions* (Isar, 2006; see also Chapter 7 below). Many see this new international instrument as a 'quantum leap' forward towards world governance in cultural matters. Be that as it may, a key issue in the coming years will be whether and how this legal instrument will effectively alter the way governments make and administer laws and regulations in the arena of culture. Will they recognize the strategic importance of the cultural economy, whether at artisanal or industrial scale, rather than take the increasingly fraught route of protectionist closure?

The perceived threats of globalization have in fact stimulated a whole range of strategies on the part of nations, cities and cultural organizations, as they seek to cope with, counter or facilitate culturally globalizing forces. These include strategies for preserving and protecting inherited cultural forms, for rejuvenating traditional cultures, for resisting cultural imposition, and for processing and packaging – maybe even altering or transforming – local and national cultures for global consumption. 'Local' cultures have not just been destroyed or reconfigured through globalization and regional integration, although most traditional forms of art and craft production continue for their part to express national cultures and to circulate mainly within their country of origin while the intellectual property industries are increasingly organized on transnational lines. Digitalization, television channels, the production of films, discs and videos, opera company tours and music and drama groups are all cases in point. International cultural exchange has seen a significant shift towards international co-productions, joint exhibitions, mutual conferences or festivals which enable cost-sharing, economies of scale and international marketability, all reflected in growing trans-frontier cooperation among film distributors, broadcasting companies, publishers and the music industry. Interdependencies and interconnections such as these, although not always voluntary, make it increasingly less justified to equate globalization with 'Americanization' or 'Westernization': in the cultural economy, as in many other domains, 'we find evidence revealing the phenomenon of

creative adaptation, in which "foreign" solutions are often selected (and modified in the transition) on the basis of rational considerations' and that most imported innovations 'serve as means employed for local purposes or as molds to be filled with local content' (Osterhammel and Petersson, 2003: 149).

With these cultural patterns and trends, that compose a backdrop mixing both threats and opportunities, we asked our contributors to address, in the form most appropriate to their topic, one or more of the following five related sets of critical questions:

1. Does the production of cultural goods and services conform to the patterns of economic globalization? In other words, are the way and extent to which the cultural economy is becoming more globalized similar to what happens in sectors such as machinery, IT services, finance, or travel? Who are the key agents of this globalization? How extensive is globalization *stricto sensu* as opposed to regional groupings in the production of cultural goods and services?

2. What is the relationship between the cultural economy, in which cultural goods and services are becoming increasingly commodified, and the aesthetic realm? How do commercial viability and artistic creativity relate to each other in this context? To what degree do the imperatives of the market threaten (or possibly foster) collaborative or process-based arts activity? How do market-driven phenomena create new figures of the creative artist as a 'motor of innovation' and of the 'creative subject' in increasingly hybrid and precarious working environments?

3. What are the current and emerging organizational forms for the investment, production, distribution and consumption of cultural goods and services? As cultural production becomes part of a mixed economy at the national level, what are the emerging patterns transnationally?

4. Who are the 'winners' and 'losers' as the cultural economy becomes globalized? Are some art forms and genres being marginalized, becoming increasingly excluded, while others move to the center of transnational cultural attention and economic interests? How does the relation between creators, producers, distributors and consumers of culture change in terms of economic positions and cost–benefit considerations? Are the 'business models' of the cultural economy changing?

5. What are the policy implications of the above, and what policy recommendations can be made as a result at local, national and international levels?

Whereas in 2007 the co-editors themselves wrote a second introduction to the volume that explored the 'Conflicts and Tensions' theme, and also provided short introductions to the different parts of the volume, here the multiple strands of specialized findings and reflections are being expertly woven together by two colleagues we have already cited. First, in an introduction to Part I, our Guest Editor, Stuart Cunningham, links the contributors' different lines of inquiry together and connects them to underlying conceptual templates that link culture and the economy.[3] We benefit equally at the close of Part I from the wisdom of the economic geographer Allen Scott, who offers the reader a set of 'retrospect and prospect' reflections on the present and future of the cultural economy and also pulls together some key insights drawn from his careful reading of all the preceding chapters.

Notes

1 For a fuller account of the conceptual approach informing the *Cultures and Globalization Series*, including a discussion of indicator suites, see Volume 1, in particular Anheier and Isar (2007) and Anheier (2007).
2 Cited from the Keynote Address entitled 'Only Connect' Robert Hewison delivered on 8 November, 2007 at the Annual Conference of the European Forum for the Arts and Heritage (EFAH) held in Warsaw.
3 This early usage was cognizant of the Frankfurt School's 'culture industries' ideas (see also the references to the Frankfurt School in Chapters 2, 7 and 27) and contained a degree of apprehension, even disdain in the understanding of culture as mass production for mass society, through forms of industrialization that affected art and popular culture alike and required public cultural institutions and agencies to defend 'art' from the market, while at the same time harnessing the latter (O'Connor, 2007).
4 As Guest Editor, Stuart Cunningham also contributed to the review of our initial 'brief' and significantly to the identification of contributors, particularly in the Asia/Pacific region.

REFERENCES

Amin, A. and Thrift, N. (eds.) (2004) *The Blackwell Cultural Economy Reader.* Oxford: Blackwell.

Anheier, H.K. and Isar, Y.R. (2007a) *Conflicts and Tensions. The Cultures and Globalization Series 1.* London: SAGE Publications.

Anheier, H.K. and Isar, Y.R. (2007b) 'Introducing the Cultures and Globalization Series' in H.K. Anheier and Y.R. Isar (eds.) *Conflicts and Tensions. The Cultures and Globalization Series 1.* London: SAGE Publications.

Anheier, H.K. (2007) 'Introducing Cultural Indicator Suites' in H.K. Anheier and Y.R. Isar (eds.) *Conflicts and Tensions. The Cultures and Globalization Series 1.* London: SAGE Publications.

Bianchini, F. (1999) 'The relationship between cultural resources and urban tourism policies: issues from European debates' in D. Dodd and A. van Hemel (eds.) *Planning Cultural Tourism in Europe: a presentation of theories and cases.* Amsterdam: Boekman Foundation.

Chanda, N. (2007) *Bound Together. How Traders, Preachers, Adventurers amd Warriors Shaped Globalization.* New Delhi: Penguin Viking Books India.

Cunningham, S. (2001) 'From Cultural to Creative Industries. Theory, Industry, and Policy Implications' in Colin Mercer (ed.) *Convergence, Creative Industries and Civil Society. The New Cultural Policy.* Special issue of *Culturelink,* Zagreb: Institute for International Relations.

Department of Culture, Media and Sport (1998) *The Creative Industries Mapping Document.* London: HMSO.

DCMS (2001) *The Creative Industries Mapping Document.* London: HMSO.

English, J. (2005) *The Economy of Prestige: Prizes, Awards, and the Circulation of Cultural Value.* Boston: Harvard University Press.

Florida, R. (2002) *The Rise of the Creative Class.* New York: Basic Books.

Gilroy, P. (2004) *After Empire.* Abingdon: Routledge.

Hesmondhalgh, D. (2007) *The Cultural Industries (Second Edition)*. London: SAGE Publications.

Isar, Y.R. (2006) 'Cultural diversity' in *Theory, Culture and Society*, Special issue on *Problematizing Global Knowledge*, 23(1–2).

Jeffcutt, P. (2001) 'Creativity and Convergence in the Knowledge Economy: Reviewing Key themes and Issues' in *Culturelink*, Special issue on *Convergence, Creative Industries and Civil Society: The New Cultural Policy* (Guest Editor Colin Mercer). Zagreb: IRMO.

Kroeber, A.L. and Kluckhohn, C. (1952) *Culture: A Critical Review of Concepts and Definitions*, Cambridge, MA: The Museum.

McRobbie, A. (2006) 'The Los Angelisation of London: Three Short Waves of Young People's Micro-Economies of Culture and Creativity in the UK'. Unpublished typescript.

Murray, C. (2001) *Making Sense of Place. New approaches to place marketing*. Bournes Green: Comedia.

O'Connor, J. (2007) *The Cultural and Creative Industries: A Review of the Literature*. London: Arts Council of England.

Osterhammel, J. and Petersson, N.P. (2003) *Globalization. A short history*. Princeton, NJ: Princeton University Press.

Ray, L. (2007) *Globalization and Everyday Life*. Milton Park and New York: Routledge.

Scott, Allen J. (2000) *The Cultural Economy of Cities*. London, Thousand Oaks and New Delhi: SAGE Publications.

Tomlinson, J. (1999) *Globalization and Culture*. Cambridge: Polity Press.

Venturelli, S. (2000) *From the Information Economy to the Creative Economy: Moving Culture to the Center of International Public Policy*. Washington: Centre for Arts and Culture.

Warnier, J-P. (2004) *La mondialisation de la culture*, Paris: La Découverte.

Williams, R. (1976) *Keywords: A Vocabulary of Culture and Society*, New York: Oxford University Press.

World Commission on the Social Dimension of Globalization (2004) *A fair globalization: creating opportunities for all*. Geneva: International Labour Office.

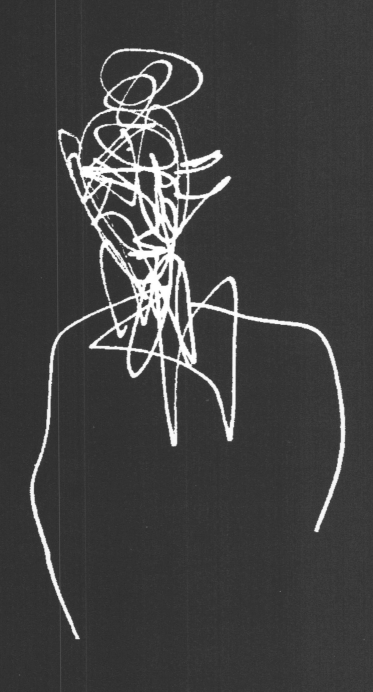

CULTURAL ECONOMY: THE SHAPE OF THE FIELD
Stuart Cunningham, John Banks and Jason Potts

Introduction

Raymond Williams (1976) famously remarked that culture was one of the most complex words in the English language. While not an economist, nor especially interested in the question of the relation between culture and economy that preoccupies us in this volume, Williams made a powerful contribution to its understanding by offering a basic typology of culture – in his foundational text *Culture* (1981: 204) – as *residual*, *dominant* or *emergent*. This is simple but powerful, and emphasizes the dynamic, overlapping and contesting nature of culture and its role in economies globally. The value of Williams' typology is that it embeds the insight that culture is always in process, always propagating (meanings, experiences, identities) rather than only preserving that which is gone, it is becoming rather than begotten, and that it is important to understand its place in relation to the forces that are shaping it and that it is shaping.

We propose to adapt Williams in order to lay out a hopefully useful heuristic by which to introduce the diverse range of approaches to the relation between culture and economy presented in this volume. We start from (but will not stay only with) the position of what does economics make of culture? To address this deceptively simple question adequately, as John Holden points out, we would need to traverse macro- and microeconomics, labour economics, international economics, law (IP, moral rights, freedom of expression, contract theory), spatial economics, and the services innovation literature, to name an indicative few (2007: 4–5). And this is only to name approaches from the standpoint of economics.

When attempting to survey a field as vast as cultural economy, we suggest that it is useful to decompose it into broader sets of relations, and that a natural basis for this is the dynamic relation between the cultural economy and the rest of the economy, i.e. how a change in one affects the other. We can hypothesize four models of this relation, which are the four possible answers to this question, namely: (1) negatively, (2) competitively, (3) positively or (4) in an emergent manner. We call these, respectively, the *welfare model*, the *competitive model*, the *growth model* and the *innovation model*. These map onto Williams' residual = (1), dominant = (2) and emergent crossing over (3) and (4). But it is not a simplistic linear set of relations: there are trends and potentials that see model 1 and model 4 recursively turning toward each other. Each of these four hypotheses suggest different possible economic policy responses: in the first case a welfare subsidy is required; in the second, standard industry policy; in the third, investment and growth policy; and in the fourth, innovation policy is best.

Our reason for emphasizing these different dynamical relations is that the study of the cultural economy has been dominated by models 1 and 2: either the 'negative' model in which the cultural economy produces cultural value but this is rarely economically viable in the market, and thus requires public transfer for support; or the 'competitive' model in which large, industrial-scale and often multinational businesses parlay culture as a commodity and behave just like the rest of the market-capitalist economy.

The first feature we note, in introducing the chapters in Part 1 of this volume, is a decreasing weight of attention to the fields of culture and creativity most readily associated with each successive model. This is consistent with Williams and reflects the fact that most supportive attention has been placed on the 'residual' (those most vulnerable, and often most valued, parts of the cultural continuum, arts, crafts and heritage), and most critical attention placed on the 'dominant' (those large, consolidated industrial-scale fields such as film, music and broadcasting). For this reason, we shall spend some time 'filling the gap', as it were, with exposition of emergent fields of culture and creativity.

Naturally, there are issues we will touch on which complicate the picture this heuristic paints. But the value of a relatively simple model like this is that it allows some measure of organization of the global range and perspective that this volume's contributors bring to bear, if only so that it provides a target for debate and criticism! Are culture and economy in a state of permanent tension, embodying irreconcilably and constitutively different notions of value? Does culture, at this level of organization, obey the iron laws of capitalist industry, especially through the economically contentious optic of labour theories of value? Do the geospatial configurations of cultural industry organization under conditions of globalization betray increasing degrees of structural asymmetry, inequity and exploitation? Does the creative industries' discourse represent a neo-liberal take-over of the cultural debate, or does it offer a pathway to the future shape of cultural activity and markets? Issues such as these seem to us to capture some of the vigour of the debates, evidence and approaches that make the cultural economy so vibrant a topic of attention today.

Four models of culture and the economy

A detailed description of the four models of the dynamic relation between the cultural economy and the rest of the economy can be found in Potts and Cunningham (2007). While the rest of the economy is normally taken to mean the national economy, these models extend to consideration of a global economy in which cultural goods and services are traded globally and in which the new technologies and business models developed within the cultural economy can be adopted and used in a global economic context. These four models can be summarized as follows.

Model 1 (the **welfare model**) is the argument that the arts, broadly considered, are economically successful to the extent that they can extract rents from the rest of the economy. (This may also be called the 'subsidy model', but we prefer the term welfare in the standard, politically neutral, sense that it is used in microeconomic theory.) This is typical of what are called 'public' or 'merit' goods, with the economic justification for resource transfers resting on a *market failure* argument. Policy is then calibrated to estimates of their non-market value. In model 1, cultural activities have a net negative impact on the economy, such that they consume more resources than they produce. To the extent that they exist, their value must lie fundamentally beyond market value. This model fits most accurately the (subsidized) arts end of the cultural spectrum, and the sub-discipline of cultural economics has largely been developed to address issues arising from these assumptions.

Model 2 (the **competitive model**) differs from model 1 in presuming that the cultural industries are not economic laggards, nor providers of special goods of higher significance, but are effectively 'just another industry'. The term cultural industries has historically been used for this part of the cultural spectrum. This model might be seen to fit best the established media industry sectors that are mature, experiencing static growth or are in relative decline, and which are being impacted by emergent distribution/aggregation models as, for example, in some parts of publishing and print, broadcasting and mainstream music copyright firms, and perhaps the commercial end of film.

The distinctive features of this large-scale sector – extreme levels of demand uncertainty, power-law revenue models, tendencies toward monopoly, complex labour markets and property rights, endemic hold-up problems, information asymmetries, highly strategic factor markets, and so on (e.g. Caves, 2000; De Vany, 2004) – are held to be addressable under competitive conditions. This is where the neo-Marxist critique concentrates its energies, analysing how large, powerful, industrial-scale and often multinational businesses parlay culture as commodity and behave just like the rest of the market-capitalist economy. Policy responses under model 2 are not about targeted resource re-allocation, but rather about consistent industrial treatment, or, as in the case of multinational and oligopolistic business, for regulation and control of excess market power.

Model 3 (the **growth model**) explicitly proposes a positive economic relation between growth in the creative industries and growth in the aggregate economy. It is for this model we deliberatively use the term 'creative industries'. This is not because cultural forms, such as the established arts and media, cannot be regarded as part of the creative industries – they can and are – but because the term creative industries is more an idea or proposition than a neutral descriptor of an industry sector. The creative industries are a dynamic force and not just another static sector.

The creative industries, in this view, are a growth driver by their new creation of value, which is consistent with the rise of a global market economy. In this model, culture becomes increasingly important because as economies evolve, a larger fraction of income and attention is devoted to it. In model 3, policy should properly treat the creative industries as a 'special sector'. This is not only because it is economically significant in itself, but because it influences the growth of other sectors. This may plausibly lead to intervention, but unlike model 1, the purpose is to *invest* in economic growth and the development of capacity to meet growth in demand. This model thus accommodates design as an input factor into the economy, industrial digital content and applications like games, and also mobile and Internet media. These exemplify input impact, such as games providing models for next generation education and learning paradigms, or for simulation and virtual reality training in aerospace. It is evidenced by the positive correlation between design intensity in firms and their stock market performance (Design Taskforce, 2003; Design Council, 2004). It also is suggested by the growing proportion of creative occupations 'embedded' in the broader economy. But it is perhaps best exemplified by the huge growth of mobile and Internet media use and content creation and the unexpected (on the supply side) uses to which such activity and inventiveness has been put. The creative industries seem to be a driver of economic growth.

Yet rather than thinking of the creative industries as an economic subset 'driving' growth in the economy, as in model 3, the creative industries may not be well characterized as a sector *per se*, but rather as an element of the *innovation system* of the economy. This is model 4 (the **innovation model** or **creative economy model**). The economic value of the creative industries, in this view, does not stem from their relative contribution to economic value (as in models 1–3), but from their contribution to the coordination of new ideas or technologies and thus to the process of economic and cultural change. In this view, the creative industries are mistakenly classified as an industry in the first place; they would be better modelled as a complex system that derives its 'economic value' from the facilitation of economic evolution – a system that manufactures attention, complexity, identity and adaptation though the primary resource of creativity.

If model 4 is true, this renders innovation policy a superior instrument to competition or industry policy. This justifies an 'elitist' aspect to creative industries policy in the same way that traditional versions of cultural policy justified the development of culture as a public good. But unlike a heritage approach to cultural value, creative industries value lies in the development and adoption of new knowledge, and so is focused on experimentation and difference, rather than conservation and equality. Evidence for model 4 would accrue from the emergence of new industries in consequence of creative industries activity as a facilitator of ongoing structural change and adaptation.

Plainly, these four models have, at different times and places, been more or less appropriate. An abstract model, such as the four possible dynamic relations between the cultural economy and the rest of the economy, helps us to see more clearly the nature of our economic characterizations of the cultural economy, and to point toward appropriate policy frameworks. We have elected here to introduce the works in this volume within this framework because it serves to highlight the difference between dominant Keynesian and neo-Marxist analysis, which are based in a static view of the economy that tend to presume no positive connection between the cultural economy and the process of economic growth and development, and emergent Schumpeterian conceptions of the cultural economy, which do recognize such a dynamic (evolutionary) connection.[1] The fact is that much can be elucidated by these dominant neo-Marxian and Keynesian approaches, but little of the emergent dimensions of cultural economy – which are beginning to impact on all sectors of the cultural economy – are captured in these approaches. This is recognized by many contributors to this volume.

Cultural economy in four models

Approaches to model 1 are well represented in this volume. Friel and Santagata (Chapter 24) argue that cultural economics has neglected material cultural heritage as being of too marginal and hyper-local significance. This field of cultural activity is changing through global niche market development and the application of quality control standards based on 'soft industrial design'. Dhamija's contribution (Chapter 9) reinforces this point, showing the strength of crafts in India as an employer (36 million in the cottage industries sector) and exporter (one of the largest exporters of goods after agricultural produce). It attracts no state subsidies – unlike heavy industry – and forms a crucial link between the massive informal economy and the formal, export-oriented sector.

Similarly, Aageson's chapter on cultural entrepreneurship (Chapter 6) reminds us that, particularly in low income countries, publicly provided infrastructure for culture is often too tenuous to suggest that it readily fits the model of the subsidized arts. This is the space where the cultural entrepreneur operates as a core intermediary. This take on the agency-structure dyad is a necessary balance to emphases on institutional, political-economic and similar large-scale perspectives. However, it also begs the question of a broader vision of the cultural entrepreneur which allows for collective action (cf. Leadbeater and Oakley, 2001) and leaves unaddressed the ways in which cultural entrepreneurship operates in complex advanced economies relatively well-provisioned with state-supported infrastructure. The state in this situation runs the risk of 'crowding out' the entrepreneur.

The arts festival would seem prototypical of model 1 as a time-and-space limited form which would not survive without state support. Klaic surveys the global diversity of the form (Chapter 22), showing that there are a wide range of non-state – philanthropic, commercial sponsorship, community-based – sources of support, but the phenomenon remains a sort of shadow economy, propped up by cargo cultish beliefs in economic benefit which somehow are never quite realized. His suspiciousness of claims made for the economic impact of festivals lead to undervaluing the necessity, driven by globalization, as well as cultural benefits which can flow from place branding. There is also the simple fact that countless individual artists and small companies survive on that globalized diet of festival performance – what is the alternative? (The data on the volume of the live arts in festival settings versus fixed locations would be interesting to compare.) His policy focus is on the local, and directly cultural, benefits of festivals, and/or to do more to make them economically sustainable by using the commoditizing logic of globalization against itself, as it were, by recycling on digital platforms and forming strong international alliances.

The case of Australian Indigenous visual art, canvassed by Ryan, Keane and Cunningham (Chapter 25), is somewhat of a category breaker as well. This is work at the borderland between the intensely local (expressions of fundamental spiritual beliefs and codes rendered into paintings often with access to only the most basic of art materials and conditions) and the global, in terms of its uptake in the metropolitan heartlands of New York and Paris. The major challenges this case raises, involving ethics and governance and questions of value and meaning across huge cultural divides, could have been developed further (see Smith, 2008; De Marchi, 2008; Senate Standing Committee, 2007), but it is an outstanding case of the global and the local, and the strengths and weaknesses of state and commercial backing.

It is no surprise that this first model of culture-economy relations should occupy substantial space in this volume. It is where most debate about culture is played out. It is *because* the model is clear that the relation is one of transfers *from* the economy *to* culture that focuses and sharpens the debate. Most of the contributors mentioned thus far accept that this relation needs to be repositioned to become a more dynamic one – thus the stress on a form of Schumpeterian entrepreneurial spirit, on using the forces of globalization 'against itself', of approaching culture of this type as a form of small business activity, as much as a sector that simply seeks transfers. This balances the traditional focus on a form of Keynesian response to market failure which may require (and perhaps deserve – for its sublime, meta-market value) indefinite state transfers for its survival.

The position on publicly supported culture we would proffer is a dynamic one. Given the importance of non-economic/non-market measures of the arts end of the creative industries spectrum, let us widen the scope to position publicly supported culture (emphasizing that the arts share with public broadcasting and many film industries a common posture *vis-à-vis* the state) as having a dynamic and positive interrelation to the broader creative economy on grounds of *enablement*. John Holden has summarized this well:

What is clear is that in a digitised and globalised world the relationship between culture and creativity has become more complex, and in many ways potentially more economically as well as culturally fruitful. Greater numbers of people are engaging with the content and spaces of publicly funded culture, while the working lives of greater numbers of people are taking on the characteristics and processes of cultural practitioners.

...a number of hypotheses can be put forward for the publicly subsidised cultural sector, to the effect that it:

- *can help to theorise the creative industries;*
- *is embedded in networks that interweave with the creative industries;*
- *displays direct linkages with commercial culture and the wider creative industries (sometimes called 'spill-over');*
- *develops human capital skills that are applicable across a wider field, into the creative industries and beyond;*
- *encompasses models of individual practice that can be applied in the creative industries and beyond;*
- *includes organisational models and practices that can be used in the creative industries;*
- *is a vital part of the infrastructure of cities, where creative industries are generally concentrated;*
- *operates as an attractor for the location of creative individuals and businesses;*
- *provides spaces and places for the development of creative industries' networks and serendipitous exchanges;*
- *has outputs that become the stimulus, and sometimes the inputs, for the creativity of others. (Holden, 2007: 8–9)*

What is apparent from this list is that Holden is appealing to aspects of models 2, 3 and even 4 in seeking to connect the residual to the dominant and the emergent.

It is around the *industrialization of culture*, and thus model 2, that most of the major normative debates concentrate, as they do in this volume. As we asked at the start of this discussion, are culture and economy in a state of permanent tension? Can or should 'Big' culture be fundamentally understood in terms of the iron laws of capitalist industry? Do the geospatial configurations of cultural industries under conditions of globalization look more diverse or are they semi-permanently locked into structural inequity?

Throsby lays out the core normative issue of globalization and related technological change

as increasing the tension between economic and cultural value. The tension is here presented in an unambiguous and rigorous way. But it begs the question of whether previous eras, pre-globalization, had enjoyed stable and mutually supportive relations between such values. One doesn't have to agree with the full thrust of Tyler Cowen's *In Praise of Commercial Culture* (1998) to admit of no automatic golden age against which the present globalizing era will appear definitively a poor relation; or that the commercial domain is always already opposed to the cultural. We might pose, as a counterpoint to Throsby's notion of Western commercial power, the ways in which contemporary technologies of potentially near-global reach and near-global popularity have thrown down the gauntlet to business-as-usual models of globalizing capital. To operate globally in capitalist cultural industries today one must engage in a post-imperialist fashion with non-Western economic and strategic power. The challenges of cross-culturalism in a globalizing world are non-negotiable, and will consolidate with the rising power of China (the fourth largest economy in the world, and about to become the third largest) and India. The challenge to US and Japan-led intellectual property regimes posed by cultural production and consumption in East and South Asia (as Sundara Rajan argues in Chapter 4 of this volume) requires serious engagement with legal and regulatory reform and encouragement of sustainable local production capacity rather than just megaphone diplomacy and threats of sanctions.

Another main question posed by Throsby in Chapter 1 is the assumption that there is a loss of cultural value as a consequence of the growth of the economic value of the cultural industries. To question this assumption would require a review of the classically normative popular-versus-high culture debate. But it is perhaps most relevant here to refer to the five varieties of new media culture to which Goggin points in this volume (peer-to-peer networks, blogging, social networking, mobile phone culture, and mobile media and wireless technology) and to pose the question: can all this emergent activity be assumed to have less cultural value than the traditional cultural forms? These emergent cultural forms have far less shape and history – by definition – but that is why it makes more sense to undertake analysis from the perspective of a model 3 or 4 world.

Of course, it is imperative for Throsby (and several other contributors, including most strongly

Nyamnjoh, Chapter 8) to point to the sometimes extreme disparities of access to and involvement in global cultural affordances and opportunities for wealth creation. For these and other writers, the situation is getting worse, not better. In Nyamnjoh's case for African cultural prospects, this may well be the case, in part because, relative to economic development in other global regions outside the West (such as east and south Asia), Africa is increasingly relatively marginalized. This allows, perhaps authorizes, the deeply value-laden dismissal of African cultural and human capital as 'socially inferior and (because?) economically uncompetitive'. But even in strong statements of global asymmetry, such as that of Drache and Froese in Chapter 3, there is a dialectical acknowledgement of immanent developmental potential as:

> [t]he global cultural economy is driven by technological change towards a global, integrated and interactive sphere of communication in which political power is inexorably moving downwards and towards the margins of international civil society because it gives a voice to those who previously did not have one.

While the games industry would be one of the industry sectors that fit in our model 3, Miller's political economic treatment of it in Chapter 19, as 'essentially a rather banal repetition of Hollywood', is another contribution to the volume's debate over the industrialization of culture. A leading voice of labour analysis in the media industries globally, Miller insists that the reality of the games industry is found at the level of its obedience to the iron laws of conglomeration, take-over, and sourcing its labour inputs at the lowest possible level of cost (thus extending what he calls the New International Division of Cultural Labour). Games' characteristics – their post-passive interactivity, their being born digital (thus being the first major new creative industry of this kind), their blurring of the distinction between producer and consumer, their being produced in more widely dispersed centers across the world than other main industrial-strength cultural output, their (re)constitution of (virtual) community and group dynamics – are dismissed as epiphenomena. We would accord such features of game play and production – together with the sheer size and growth rates of the industry over the space of less than a generation – more weight in trying to grasp changes in the nature of value creation in the contemporary cultural economy.

The geospatial dimension of the cultural economy informs a substantial number of perspectives collected here. Pratt is well known for his careful, rigorous work which demonstrates that, far from the digital age pronouncing the 'death of distance', place may indeed matter even more as cities, industries and creative production people and centers seek to respond to the challenges of globalization. In his essay in this volume (Chapter 2), he links this cultural geography to insights on the vexed issue of adequate measurement of the cultural economy when what it embraces is so contestable. Significantly for our perspective in this Introduction, he acknowledges the fading force of market failure arguments as the sheer dynamism of the cultural economy becomes undeniable, and the blurred divide between the formal and informal, and the commercial and not-for-profit sectors, throws up opportunities which equilibrium economics cannot elucidate.

Curtin resumes the history of the media imperialism thesis – which formed a dominant fraction of the media and communication literature for 30 years and strongly influenced international frameworks such those produced by UNESCO – and argues that globalization should not be thought of as an extension of Western soft imperialism but a way of understanding the emergent diversification of media flows, cultural formations, and the forces that are driving particularly non-Western growth and assertion (see Chapter 18). This certainly does not mean walking away from hard-edged analysis of power, concentration and inequity, but taking each (regional) case on its merits; what we might call a middle-range approach between excessive sanguinity and off-the-rack total explanation.

The section in this book on *Regional Realities* puts much flesh on the bones of these normative debates. It is usually assumed that developing and transitional societies have less purpose and priority for the cultural industries as they struggle to feed, clothe and house their citizens and develop more robust economic and political governance. This has been fed by a certain metropolitanism in much debate which tends to think of the creative industries as associated with the vanguard of the most advanced civilizations (and therefore able to 'indulge' their Maslowian upper hierarchy of needs), and in particular with the powerhouses of New York, Tokyo, London and Paris (Hall, 1998). But there is growing evidence that the large developing and transitional economies (pre-eminently the BRIC bloc – Brazil, Russia, India and China) are well aware of the significance of the creative sector's links to economic advancement and have the urban conglomeration to make the co-location in production and the aggregation processes central to industrial-scale activity work. Thus, Beijing and Shanghai increasingly compete to shoulder Hong Kong out of the way of creative and cultural pre-eminence; Bollywood is diasporized and globalized for both hard economic and soft diplomatic purposes; and Brazil is looking to exercise Global South leadership in this field through close links to UNCTAD, as it has done by taking on Western Big Pharma around the issue of generic drugs. If we add the K to the BRIC, we admit the most intensely networked and one of the most innovative in terms of social and cultural embedding of technology – nations in the world, Korea. These trends are covered for East Asia by Keane (Chapter 10) and for Korea by Choi (Chapter 11).

We can classify many of the other regions treated in the book (South-eastern Europe, Central Asia, Africa, Central and Eastern Europe, Latin America and the Caribbean) as seeking to deal with the challenges and opportunities raised by cultural economy without the scale-and-growth economies of BRICK or the traditional advantages enjoyed by the 'advanced' West. In most instances, the under-developed nature of open markets, and the lack of scale and coordination of cultural activity, means that state sector agency remains critical. Where appeals to the state to do more are made, however, it is with an awareness that this often comes with the caveat that the endogenous institutional and governance frameworks are as much to blame for loss of opportunity and marginalization as the Western hegemons. The appeal of a NGO and SME approach to cultural advancement returns regularly, taking into account that globalization, the Internet and associated networked processes (horizontal cooperation), favor flexible entities such as SMEs rather than top-down, administratively regulated and heavily subsidized bodies.

The regions covered are thus located in large part outside the metropolitan West; the chapters by Greffe on Europe (Chapter 13) and by Wyszomirski on the United States (Chapter 17) are two exceptions. Greffe goes to the heart of tensions in (Western) European approaches to cultural economy, a region

'long regarded as the world's principal location of artistic creation and consumption'. However, it (or, more particularly, the EU) is caught between macroeconomic policies which strive to position the EU as a coherent single economic unit – the largest in the world – with progressive innovation, R&D, educational and social contract frameworks, while on the other hand its cultural policies are still captured by backward-looking protectionism. There is increasing strain between normative free market thought driving much else within the Union while cultural leaders champion exceptionalism. In the context of a global economy, Europe's cultural centrality may be decreasing and its traditional interventionist and protectionist policy stances (its cultural exceptionalism) may prevent it from fully benefiting from the globalization of cultural exchanges. Greffe suggests that suspicion of the market by European artists and a tradition in which culture is viewed as autonomous from markets, and where a distinctive European culture is essentially carried on the back of the state, can make adaptation to a global market difficult. However, increasing recognition of the importance of the creative industries suggests a change in this understanding of the relationship between culture and markets. In this context, the understanding of cultural production is shifting towards small, flexible enterprises linked to global networks of exchange and export.

Wyszomirski reminds us that US exceptionalism (paradigmatic hegemony in entertainment) exists normatively at the national level while at the regional, state and local level, policies to support the creative economy struggle for space and acceptance as in most other countries. She shows that the debates around the creative industries (which many have assumed have not been needed or noticed in the US) have indeed made their mark: a language at once more focused than culture as a whole way of life but much broader than the traditional arts has effected a significant change in policy thinking 'from a resource poor, cost diseased sector in need of subsidy to a set of community assets that can be engines of local development'.

Debates around the idea of the creative industries form the nucleus of treatment of model 3. The term is somewhat of a chameleon, not least because the locus of its effective invention (UK's portfolio ministers and department of Culture, Media and Sport) has changed emphasis over the decade since the late 1990s. It has moved from being about the size and rate of growth of a newly constituted sector – which was defined to include the traditional arts, the established media, the new media as well as architecture, design and software – to an emphasis on the creative economy – the degree to which creative inputs are embedded in, and influencing the growth of, the economy as a whole. (We are arguing here that the term can be pushed further, to embrace the idea of creative activity forming an important element of innovation – the growth and embodiment of new ideas in new technologies and social networks.)

This idea has been taken up widely; attracting significant policy attention while also provoking critical scrutiny.[2] It has generally been regarded as playing to the commercial end of the cultural continuum and criticized for that. Isar's essay (Chapter 7) analyses the tensions created by such 'neo-liberal' incursions into the cultural continuum for the major intergovernmental policy actors: UNESCO, WIPO, UNCTAD, ILO, the United Nations Special Unit for South–South Cooperation (and we could add the various development banks). The state of play would seem to be that 'cultural diversity' is the response and that, while acknowledging the potential of the cultural industries as a pathway to cultural democracy, there remains a deep mistrust of the Western-dominated, commercial spirit of Big Media, digital content and their ilk.

But despite critiques – such as that of Nicholas Garnham (2005) that the creative industries idea is a kind of Trojan Horse, secreting the intellectual heritage of the information society and its technocratic baggage into the realm of cultural practice, suborning the latter's proper claims on the public purse and self-understanding, and aligning it with inappropriate bedfellows such as business services, telecommunications and calls for increases in generic creativity – there are marked variations in its adoption as it has been taken up around the world. The constant definitional wrangling and regular recasting of what counts in the creative industries indicates a productive ferment.

We can broadly identify four main global variations on the creative industries theme as it has traveled around the world: US, Europe, Asia, and the global South.

The term creative industries is employed sparingly in the United States and, despite some developments canvassed by Wyszomirski, the broad sectoral field embraced by the UK definition remains resolutely divided into arts and culture on the one hand and the entertainment/copyright industries on the other. And to the extent there is ongoing adoption of the discourse, it is very much in the arts domain. In the major deployment of the term, by Americans for the Arts, for example, there is an explicit exclusion of 'computer programming'.

As might be fully expected of any process of adaptation of a discourse originating in the Anglosphere, European variations on the creative industries tend to stress a greater degree of communitarian benefit and strategies of social inclusion than is evident in UK settings. It is the social and cultural uptake of ICT as much as it's potential as an economic driver that receives attention.

Kong et al. (2006) carefully trace the way creative industries discourse has been adapted to the local contexts of East and South Asia shows that creative industries work in intermittent, sometimes incoherent or contradictory ways, and emphasize especially the role of national socio-economic and political circumstances. This, to us, is a sign of dynamism, not of a failure to attain the standards of a Platonic ideal of a rational-comprehensive policy model. In the light of Garnham's argument, Kong et al. show that only Hong Kong explicitly includes software and computing as a key sector of the creative industries. In Singapore, for example, the discourse has been used to begin to displace, or at least supplement, the prestige of ICT – which has hitherto held unquestioned sway in a city state known for its normative technocracy. 'Creative industries' has come to mean a quite radical emphasis on creative thinking and problem-solving and a challenge to time honoured Confucian educational models and an new inscription of the prestige of the artistic endeavor.

The creative industries discourse in South America, South Africa, the Caribbean and countries like Brazil, is one which must engage with cultural heritage, poverty alleviation and basic infrastructure, as preconditions for gaining leverage. In the global South, the discourse can be used to leverage support for the development of basic infrastructure, both cultural and ICT – the 'unquestioned prestige' of the latter absolutely cannot be taken for granted.

Emergent culture: new, mobile and interactive digital media

As we have signaled earlier, with the exception of Goggin's chapter (Chapter 20), the book leaves under-developed the crucial role which new, mobile and interactive digital media are playing in the contemporary adoption, absorption and retention of new technologies, in challenging and changing the business models of many industries (not just the media industries) and in creating the conditions for what could be broadly called 'social innovation'.

We are already very aware of the potential, and current reality, of the Internet as a platform for next generation cultural production and communication, and the major opportunities it may present for cultural diversity – Allen Scott reinforces this in his concluding overview chapter. One of the key emergent factors is that China has, in 2007, become the second largest user of the Internet globally and is expected to overtake the US in usage volume relatively soon. As the benefits of economic growth in China become more widely spread, there is potentially an expressive future for young people unthinkable less than a generation ago. China's versions of YouTube (Tudou and Yoqoo) and social networking sites (Douban and QQ), in addition to the exponential growth of blogs (to mid 2007: 34 million in PRC), are driving an extraordinary bottom-up culture of communication.

Another major emergent platform is mobile infrastructure. The rapid uptake and near ubiquity of mobile infrastructure is a given in most OECD countries. As one mid-range country indicator, the latest data from Australia (2004–05, see Access Economics and AMTA, 2007) show that the combined industry gross product (IGP) of mobile network carriers and resellers was higher than that for either free-to-air television services, the newspaper, printing and publishing industry or the computer consultancy services sector. It was almost three times as large as that of the automotive, vehicle and component manufacturing sector. In addition to its direct contributions, it drives productivity gains throughout the economy. In this it is not dissimilar to the role of ICT as a driver of industry change in past decades, and should be contrasted with such headline industry sectors in the Australian economy as mining, which makes a significant direct contribution to the economy but much smaller indirect contributions.

But what from a global equity perspective is more remarkable is the way mobile has 'leapfrogged' fixed line telecommunications in many developing countries. 3G and further developments in mobile carriage of rich content make this a platform with yet-to-be-tapped potential for cultural exchange at a local, regional and global level and from sites of traditional disadvantage in the global communications system. Again using the same analysis from Australia, a forward estimate of the economy-wide benefits arising from mobile data use, made possible by the increasing uptake of 3G technology and increase in mobile data traffic, could add an additional $1 billion to GDP by 2010.

The emergent possibilities of mobile content embracing innovative cultural exchange and communication are clear. In China, it is possible to load whole novellas onto mobiles – an affordance unavailable to Western language speakers at present due to the particularity of ideographic Chinese language – indicating the centrality of mobiles to the culture. In Malaysia, the UAE and Saudi Arabia, you can subscribe to an Islamic religious service and 'take your mobile beliefs with you' – 160 million units were sold in its first year of operation. Maori in Aotearoa are seeking to finalize protracted negotiations over control over the spectrum which they assert are part of their air, land and water rights conferred under the Treaty of Waitangi in 1840 (Bell, 2007).

What, though, are the specific affordances for the cultural economy offered by new, mobile and interactive digital media? There is now a veritable wave of proposal, analysis and prognostication addressing this question. Chris Anderson's *The Long Tail* (2006) and Mark Pesce[3] exposit the limitations of the mass market, model 2 mentality that can be addressed by Internet-based harvesting of the 'long tail' and exploitation of 'hyperdistribution'. Charles Leadbeater's (2007) *We-Think: the power of mass creativity*[4] explores diverse domains where the power of socially networked collective creation and communication are at work. Recent studies by Henry Jenkins (2006) and Yochai Benkler (2006) suggest that consumers' participation in new media production practice now generates significant economic and cultural value. Media production may be shifting from a closed industrial model towards a more open network in which consumers are now participatory co-creators of media culture product. Henry Jenkins is careful to remind us that this is not simply a direct outcome of technology but a significant cultural phenomenon in which we're seeing what happens when the means of cultural production and distribution are co-evolving between producer, aggregator and user. He is aware that this 'bottom-up' process plays out in the context of 'an alarming concentration of the ownership of main-stream commercial media, with a small handful of multinational media conglomerates dominating all sectors of the entertainment industry' (Jenkins, 2006: 18); the economic value of user co-creation and social media poses a significant challenge to business-as-usual for the dominant media.

As an example of models 3 and 4 thinking about the cultural economy, Potts et al. (2007) have recently proposed a new definition for the creative industries as the economic space of 'social network markets'. They are the set of activities and industries that facilitate choice over uncertainty when dealing with novelty in a social context. These are not just the information and communication industries, as that just addresses the technology, but more fundamentally the industries that build networks of people to facilitate the social action and structure, across which new ideas can flow. The social network market idea gains traction by positing that these networks have characteristic properties associated with complexity and evolutionary theory. The implication is that this helps us explain why many cultural economic phenomena we observe are properties of models 3 and 4 worlds, not of model 1.

Here we depart from Benkler's analysis to suggest that rather than being a non-market phenomenon, consumer co-creation practice may be understood as emergent market relationships. Here, we aren't proposing that these practices are simply seamlessly appropriated into existing stable market institutions that support a globally rampant industrial media economy. For this is not a static or closed situation in which we can clearly and definitely identify what are market or non-market motivations, incentives or behaviours. Instead, these emerging practices potentially redefine our understanding of what markets are and how they operate in relation to social and cultural networks.

Complex social networks play at least as significant a coordination role as price signals in cultural economy markets. Markets for novelty as social networks are thus moved closer to the center of the economic analysis of innovation and growth. New, mobile and interactive digital media are the principal means by which such social network markets operate. The very act of consumer choice in creative industries is thus governed not just by the set of incentives described by conventional consumer demand theory, but by the choices and participation

of others. An individual's payoff is an explicit function of the actions of others. There is overwhelming evidence that this applies generally to the creative industries. The social network definition of the creative industries proceeds not in terms of individual 'artistic' or creative novelty in a social context, but rather in terms of individual choice in a complex social system of other individual choice. In turn, these social networks function as markets. Thus recognized, it becomes equally apparent that the creative industries are also a crucible of new or emergent markets that, typically, arise from non-market dynamics and that often then stay at the complex borderland between social networks and established markets. For example, *YouTube*'s social networks were then bought by *Google* and thus market conditions were brought to bear; *MySpace* is a similar example, which was recently bought by Rupert Murdoch, but not marketized – at least to date. *Second Life*, however, is being marketized from within, as it were, through the process of many commercial interests not 'buying' the property, but buying into the social space (Castronova, 2006).

The analytic distinctiveness of the creative industries is not their cultural value or sublime nature (i.e. their non-market value, as in model 1), but the fact that the environment of both their production and consumption is essentially constituted by complex social networks (as in model 4). The creative industries rely, to a greater extent than other socio-economic activity, on word of mouth, taste cultures, and popularity, such that individual choices are dominated by information feedback over social networks rather than innate preferences and price signals. User co-creation relations, then, do not so much statically reallocate resources across markets and non-markets, but rather the cultural economics at work concern dynamic, open, self-organizing networks that generate opportunities for growth, change and innovation.

Consumer co-creation in all its uncertainty is perhaps an agent of change that unsettles existent industrial knowledge and cultural production regimes. This may well result in the introduction of novelty and diversity that will also change our understanding of what markets for the exchange of cultural products and experiences are. In many ways, this analysis is in line with Scott's suggestion in the final essay in this book that the digital foundations of this modern cultural economy may well see a 'proliferation of small-and micro-enterprises with the capacity to contest diverse markets' existing alongside the large multinational corporate players in the cultural economy.

Conclusion

In introducing this volume, we have sought to use a fresh analytic framework for understanding the cultural economy. Specifically, we have suggested a taxonomy based on culture's dynamic relation with the rest of the economy. In so doing, we have contrasted Keynesian, neo-Marxist, and Schumpeterian approaches to cultural economy, and have sought to elucidate the debates engaged in by the volume's contributors in the light of this taxonomy, seeking to give shape to the macro-trends and perspectives across a wide variety of authors.

Our underlying critique has been that the dominant explanatory schema, which seeks to address the place of the arts and media in cultural economy, is increasingly incapacitated in understanding the shape of emerging global trends and advancing both theoretically and practically engaging responses. Furthermore, we think that many of the contributions to this book share that view – without, of course, necessarily agreeing with what we have proposed in their place. We think that model 3 points to good evidence of where growth in the cultural economy is occurring. And we propose that model 4 indicates that 'creative disruption' to established business practice at even, and perhaps especially, the highest levels of media capitalism while also drawing on human (i.e. social) technology, via the creation and maintenance of social networks and the markets that evolve from them, shows that these processes can be progressive in a social and even political sense.

Indeed, these are actually trends and potentials that see model 4 approaches recursively turning toward approaches to model 1 content and value. This recursive potential is apparent if we ask the simple question: where are the untapped cultural sources of future economic potential and gain? Asked in this way, the discourses of, for example, Nyamnjoh (Chapter 8), of Pinter (Chapter 5) or Goggin (Chapter 20) are not diametrically apart insofar as they are all addressing future potential sources of value creation and the nature and structure of future markets.

Finally, the policy implications of this framework are also not without significance. Welfare arguments have delivered much in the way of public support for a range of cultural activity, and no doubt will continue to do so. But new rationales for public investment, together with a preparedness to maximize the potential affordances provided by globalization, and technological and social change, offer a wide range of new opportunity for policy-makers to consolidate the value of the cultural economy at a local, regional, national and supranational level. Culture is part of the process of economic change that in turn changes the conditions of culture. Cultural dynamics come first, economic dynamics come second, but then cultural dynamics come third, starting this process again.

Notes

1 In modern economics, the Schumpeterian endogenous growth model has systematically replaced the Keynesian model as an explanation of how economic systems change through time and in turn this has led to a shift in economic policy focus from industry policy and demand management to innovation policy and the facilitation of entrepreneurship and enterprise.

2 An excellent short overview is Flew (2002), Chapter 6 and a more detailed introduction is Hartley (2005). See also Cunningham (2006).

3 http://www.mindjack.com/feature/piracy051305.html

4 http://www.wethinkthebook.net/home.aspx

REFERENCES

Access Economics and the Australian Mobile Telecommunications Association (2007) *Australian mobile telecommunications industry: economic significance and state of the industry*, http://www.amta.org.au/amta/site/amta/downloads/ pdfs_2007/AMTA%20draft%20report%2013July 07.pdf.

Anderson, Chris (2006) *The Long Tail: Why the Future of Business is Selling Less of More*. New York: Hyperion.

Bell, Genevieve (Director of Digital Home User Experience Group, Intel) (2007) '"real men use sms": contextualizing mobile media', Keynote Address, Mobile Media conference, University of Sydney, July.

Benkler, Yochai (2006) *The Wealth of Networks: How Social Production Transforms Markets and Freedom.* New Haven: Yale University Press.

Castronova, E. (2006) *Synthetic Worlds: The Business and Culture of Online Games.* Chicago: University of Chicago Press.

Caves, R. (2000) *Creative Industries: Contracts between Art and Commerce.* Cambridge, MA: Harvard University Press.

Cowen, T. (1998) *In Praise of Commercial Culture.* Cambridge, MA: Harvard University Press.

Cunningham, Stuart (2006) *What Price a Creative Economy?* Platform Papers No 9, Currency House, Sydney.

Design Council (UK) (2004) 'The Impact of Design on Stock Market Performance: An Analysis of UK Quoted Companies 1994–2003', February.

Design Taskforce (2003), *Success by Design NZ: A Report and Strategic Plan*, Design Taskforce in Partnership with New Zealand Government, in support of the Growth and Innovation Framework (GIF), May.

De Vany, A. (2004) *Hollywood Economics.* London: Routledge.

Flew, Terry (2002) *New Media: An Introduction.* Oxford: Oxford University Press.

Garnham, Nicholas (2005) 'From Cultural to Creative Industries: An analysis of the implications of the creative industries approach to arts and media policy making in the United Kingdom', *International Journal of Cultural Policy*, 11: 15–29.

Hall, P. (1998) *Cities in Civilization.* London: Phoenix Giant.

Hartley, John (ed.) (2005) *Creative Industries*, Malden, MA: Blackwell.

Holden, John (2007) *Publicly-funded Culture and the Creative Industries.* London: Demos. http://www.demos.co.uk/files/Publicly_Funded_Culture_and_the_Creative_Industries.pdf.

Jenkins, Henry (2006) *Convergence Culture: where old and new media collide,* New York: New York University Press.

Kong, L., Gibson, C., Khoo, L-M. and Semple, A-L. (2006) 'Knowledges of the creative economy: Towards a relational geography of diffusion and adaptation in Asia', *Asia Pacific Viewpoint*, 47(2): 173–94.

Leadbeater, C. and Oakley, K. (2001) *Surfing the Long Wave: Knowledge entrepreneurship in Britain.* London: Demos.

De Marchi, Neil (2008) 'Confluences of value: Three historical moments', in Michael Hutter and David Throsby, (eds.) *Beyond Price: Value in Culture, Economics, and the Arts.* New York: Cambridge University Press.

Potts, J. and Cunningham, S. (2007) 'Four Models of the Creative Industries', CCI working paper, QUT.

Potts, J., Cunningham, S., Hartley, J. and Ormerod, P. (2007) 'Complex social networks define creative industries', CCI working paper, QUT.

Senate Standing Committee (on Environment, Communications, Information Technology and the Arts) (2007) 'Indigenous Art – Securing the future: Australia's indigenous visual arts and craft sector', Senate Printing Unit, Parliament House, Canberra, June.

Smith, Terry (2008) 'Creating value between cultures: Contemporary Australian Aboriginal Art', in Michael Hutter and David Throsby (eds.) *Beyond Price: Value in Culture, Economics, and the Arts.* New York: Cambridge University Press.

Williams, R. (1976) *Keywords: A Vocabulary of Culture and Society.* New York: Oxford University Press

Williams, Raymond (1981) *Culture.* Glasgow: Fontana.

ISSUES

GLOBALIZATION AND LOCALIZATION

GLOBALIZATION AND THE CULTURAL ECONOMY: A CRISIS OF VALUE?
David Throsby

This chapter argues that the interaction between the economic and cultural consequences of globalization has resulted in a crisis of value. The crisis exists in the contemporary cultural economy at both micro and macro levels, evidenced in the divergences that exist between economic and cultural value as criteria for resource allocation within the sector. The chapter discusses the ways in which value is created, distributed and received in the contemporary cultural economy and how these activities are affected by both the economic and technological aspects of globalization. In the final sections of the chapter, the effects of the crisis of value are considered in relation to cultural policy-making at domestic and international levels.

Introduction and background

It is now well understood that processes of globalization as they are experienced in the contemporary world are being propelled by economic and technological drivers that have significant cultural implications. In this chapter I shall argue that the interaction between the economic and cultural consequences of globalization has resulted in a crisis of value. The crisis arises primarily because the economic values that underlie the inexorable progress of globalization are in many respects at odds with the cultural values that are an indispensable component of the production, consumption and experience of culture.

Consider the following examples. A composer faces a decision: should she write a piece of music in pursuit of her pure artistic vision or should she respond to the incentives provided by the market and produce a more commercially saleable work? Demonstrators shout slogans outside a meeting of the World Economic Forum because they believe that the power of the global marketplace is undermining their cultural identity. An ancient indigenous language is in danger of dying out because its value as a cultural expression is not reflected in the financial resources that would be required to keep it alive. In their different ways these examples illustrate the tensions that can arise between the economic imperatives of the market and the values inherent in the artistic and cultural aspects of human existence. These tensions are exacerbated by globalization.

We shall look at this question in terms of the cultural economy, a concept that can be depicted in the first instance as a value chain portraying the production, distribution and final demand for cultural goods and services such as artworks, music, literary texts, dramatic performances, movies, video games, print and broadcast media, and so on. These are all commodities that require creativity in their making, convey symbolic messages of one sort or another, and embody, at least potentially, some intellectual property. The value chain stretches from creative producers at one end, through various stages of production and value adding, to distribution networks, and onwards to final consumption.

In addition to this goods-and-services interpretation of the cultural economy, the ambit of culture can be broadened to embrace intangible phenomena such as ways of living, beliefs, attitudes, identities and practices. In this context an economy is more an anthropological or sociological construct than an economic one. When considered in these terms, the cultural economy extends to embrace virtually everyone, through their experience of living in a country, a region or a community bound together by shared cultural experience.

Common to all the actors in the cultural economy, however it is interpreted, is an involvement with value, whether it is the creation of value by an artist, the enhancement of value by an entrepreneur, the appreciation of private value by a consumer, or the recognition of public value by a member of the community. Indeed value is a phenomenon that affects us all, every day. As John Fekete (1987: 1) argues:

> No concept of human life is unrelated to values, valuations and validations. Value orientations and value relations saturate our experiences and life practices from the smallest established microstructures of feeling, thought, and behavior to the largest established macrostructures of organizations and institutions.

What is meant by the term *value*? At its most fundamental, *value* can be thought of as the worth, to an individual or group, of a good, a service, an activity or an experience, with an implied possibility of a ranking of value (better to worse, or higher to lower value) according to given criteria.[1] The process by which value is assigned to something is referred to as *valuation* or *evaluation*, i.e. the process of 'estimating, ascribing, modifying, affirming and even denying value' (Connor, 1992: 8). We should also note the occasional use of the word *valorization* to mean a process by which value is imparted to some object as a result of deliberative action or external event, such as the increase in value accorded to sites of cultural heritage when they are added to the World Heritage List.[2]

How then can we say that a crisis of value exists? To answer this question we can simplify the value concepts under discussion by making a broad distinction between economic and cultural value[3] when applied to artistic and cultural phenomena.

Looking first at economic value, we can observe that the notion of value has a long history in economics[4] dating back to well before Adam Smith drew the distinction between value in use and value in exchange. In the neoliberal economics of the contemporary world, the Benthamite concept of utility underlies consumers' formation of value, reflected in due course for particular goods and services in equilibrium prices that emerge in competitive markets and in people's stated willingness to pay for non-market effects. However it arises, value in the economic paradigm is ultimately expressible in financial terms.

In contrast to this well-defined concept of economic value, the interpretation of cultural value in relation to art objects and other cultural phenomena is by no means clear-cut. It has long been a source of controversy within philosophy, aesthetics and art history; indeed a confrontation between absolute and relative theories of value in the post-modern world has provided cultural theory with a crisis of value of its own that shows no signs of being resolved.[5] Whether there is a right or a wrong in this debate is of less relevance for our discussion than the undeniable fact that cultural value is complex, multi-faceted, unstable, and lacking in an agreed unit of account.

Thus the source of a crisis of value for the cultural economy starts to take shape. On the one hand the neatly circumscribed principles of economic evaluation lead to what appear to be unambiguous estimates of the economic value of cultural goods and services, whilst on the other hand cultural value seems to resist precise, objective and replicable means of assessment. The two interpretations pull in different directions, creating uncertainties surrounding a core question in the cultural economy, whether it is asked at an individual, an institutional or a government level: what values should count in decision-making in relation to the production, distribution and consumption of cultural commodities?

Of course in one sense this crisis of value has always been with us. As Lewis Hyde (2006: 160) argues:

> All cultures and all artists have felt the tension between... the self-forgetfulness of art and the self-aggrandizement of the merchant, and how that tension is to be resolved has been a subject of debate since before Aristotle.

But it is a crisis that is heightened by globalization, through its various impacts on value formation and reception. Although, as we shall see, these impacts can be both positive and negative, in the cultural arena it is the inexorable economic drivers in the global economy that have the strongest impact. As Steven Connor (1992: 99) observes, in free-market economies:

the requirement to produce substantial value is paramount... When everything can be produced, sold and exchanged, even (especially) knowledge and the experience of culture, then it is precisely the insistence on the production of value... which cannot avoid serving the interests of... the global market.

Thus far we have been discussing the crisis of value created by the *economic* consequences of globalization. But the *technological* revolution that underpins the globalization phenomenon also has an impact on value creation, shifting the criteria by which cultural value is assessed, introducing new aesthetic concepts to be absorbed into the evaluation process, and eventually expanding the domain of what may be seen as the artistic canon. Again this may be nothing more than a continuation of long-term trends, where aesthetic judgement is constantly being modified by technological change; one has only to think of innovations like the invention of the saxophone or the development of photography. Nevertheless, by its very speed, the technological transformation being witnessed at the present time can be argued to magnify tensions in cultural valuation that would otherwise take a more leisurely time to work themselves out.

This chapter looks at the ways in which value is created, distributed and received in the contemporary cultural economy and how these activities are affected by both the economic and technological aspects of globalization. In the next section we discuss how artists and firms produce cultural goods and services and what the impacts of globalization are in the production sector. We then move to the next stage of the value chain and examine the globalization of distribution. The value placed on the products of the cultural economy by consumers is considered in the following section, with reference to both private and public goods. Finally, the effects of the crisis of value in the arena of cultural policy are considered in the last two sections of the chapter, with regard to policy-making at domestic and international levels respectively.

Impacts of globalization on systems of value creation

There has been a long debate surrounding the question of how value of a cultural commodity such as an artwork actually comes into being. Is value somehow intrinsic to the work and exists whether or not anyone notices it, or does value only arise through the interaction of the viewer, the reader or the listener with the work? Either way there is a question as to whether the intentions of the original creator(s) have an influence on value and, if so, what that influence might be. In this section we examine the production side of the creative economy – the individual artists and the creative enterprises that produce text, sound and image – and ask what impacts globalization has on their work.

Artists and arts organizations such as music ensembles, theater companies, film production houses and so on can be portrayed as being motivated by a desire to maximize an objective function containing both economic and cultural value as arguments. Different artists and groups are likely to attach different weights to the economic and cultural value components of their objective functions. Those in whom the artistic drive is paramount, for whom an artistic vision is all that matters, and who are willing to survive on a minimum of worldly goods, can be interpreted as attaching stronger weight to cultural than to economic value as a motive for production. The opposite will apply to artists interested solely or mainly in the income-producing opportunities of artistic work. The majority of artists and groups will lie somewhere in between, facing a perennial question as to how to trade off pure artistic creativity against hard economic realities.

How is this balance worked out in reality? Individual artists call upon a range of strategies to allow pursuit of artistic ideals at the same time as satisfying minimum income requirements. Such strategies include taking on additional work within the arts (e.g. teaching) or outside the arts altogether (e.g. driving a taxi) in order to support a creative practice, or seeking financial support through awards or grants provided by foundations or government funding agencies.[6] Many artists are obliged by the economic realities of the marketplace to adjust the qualitative nature of the work they produce; for example a playwright may write plays for small casts because there is more chance of having them performed, or a writer may produce novels rather than poems because poetry yields inadequate financial return. In these ways economic necessity affects cultural value measured in qualitative terms as the scope or composition of artistic output. If globalization amplifies these economic pressures, the impact on cultural value will be correspondingly increased.

Turning from individuals to groups, we can observe similar patterns; creative enterprises in the arts are also obliged to adopt strategies coupling the desire for artistic growth with the necessity for financial survival. In the not-for-profit sector, arts enterprises such as opera companies or symphony orchestras can be portrayed as firms maximizing a weighted combination of the quantity and quality of output subject to a financial break-even constraint. In such a model, the desire to produce cultural value is reflected in the objective function, and the need for minimum levels of economic value is expressed via the constraint set. In the commercial arts, on the other hand, the driving motives are more likely to be financial; firms in the commercial sector of the cultural economy are predominantly larger corporate enterprises whose stockholders demand a return on their capital investment. Thus the cultural decisions of such firms tend to be guided by the prospects for commercial success rather than any notions of 'pure' cultural value.

How, then, does globalization influence this picture of the productive sector of the creative economy? A first glance would suggest a two-fold set of effects. First, the economic imperatives and competitive pressures of the global marketplace may cause artists and organizations to shift the balance in their output towards a greater emphasis on creating economic value, and, as noted above, affect the qualitative nature of the cultural value produced. Second, the new technologies available to creators in all fields may alter their concepts of cultural value in either positive or negative directions. But these are simply preliminary observations. The reality is more complex. We can discuss the effects of globalization on cultural production under three headings: the effects of new technologies on the day-to-day operations of cultural producers; the effects of the spread of global markets for inputs and outputs; and the effects of improved international communications.

New technologies

It is by now commonplace to say that the advent of new information technologies has given rise to an enormous array of innovative possibilities for creative artists to express their ideas. Indeed, ever since the advent of the electronic computer almost half a century ago, artists have been keen to exploit the imaginative possibilities of new media.[7] Almost every artform has found ways to take advantage of the creative potential of the new technologies, from computer graphics to electronic music, from holograms to animation. New artforms such as computer games and video art have been opened up,[8] creating entire industries in the cultural sector that were non-existent a mere decade or so earlier.

The impact of these developments on individual artists can be illustrated using recent data from a survey of practicing professional artists across all artforms in Australia. The survey undertaken in 2002 (Throsby and Hollister, 2003: 55, 108) showed that about 80 per cent of artists used a computer in relation to their art practice; about three-quarters of these artists used the computer for record-keeping and administering their career, and around half used it as a creative medium and to run software that facilitates their creative practice. About 70 per cent of the artists surveyed used the Internet, mainly for research; fewer than one-third of these artists used the Internet to promote or market their work. These numbers can be expected to grow as access to the Internet expands.

A further effect of new information technologies on the lives and careers of individual artists is seen in the widening of the skill base of the art professions. Most training programs for professional artists incorporate significant components dealing with new media. Even in traditional institutions such as music conservatoria, the curriculum increasingly embraces new musical forms and means of expression. The benefits of these developments for the working lives of artists are visible in the increased labour market flexibility that they can call upon. Many visual artists, for example, are able to undertake highly skilled and lucrative work in the digital arena (e.g. designing websites) as a means of supporting a core creative practice.

Most of the foregoing observations about the effects of new technologies on the work of individual artists can be applied also to artistic ensembles and groups. Furthermore, the IT revolution has transformed the way in which such enterprises manage their businesses: museums have digitized their collections and are making them accessible on-line; performing companies have introduced efficient booking and ticketing systems; libraries have radically altered the way they catalogue their holdings.

It can be seen from the above that there are many positive effects on value formation arising specifically from the technological aspects of globalization. The production of economic value from the cultural economy is clearly enhanced as a result of the many efficiency gains and productivity improvements that computer-based applications provide, while the expansion of creative scope in the production of artistic and cultural goods and services can also be seen to add to the yield of cultural value across the board. Whether the realignments of economic and cultural value or the shifts in the composition of cultural value produced are regarded as beneficial or otherwise remains a subjective matter and it is probably too early to judge whether any consensus exists one way or the other.

The spread of global markets

The breakdown of barriers to flows of both capital and labour around the world has facilitated the creation of a global marketplace for many commodities, including those produced by the cultural economy. In particular the freeing up of capital movements has encouraged the growth of transnational corporations and has increased competitive pressures on smaller producers. Moreover, the inexorable expansion of reliance on free-market forces as guides to the allocation of resources within and between countries has accelerated a shift in overall economic power from the public to the private sphere; this shift has been felt in the cultural sector, as elsewhere.

These trends have had significant effects on value production in the cultural economy. Take the music industry, for example. Music is one of the oldest and most fundamental artforms. The stock of music inherited from past civilizations is a vital repository of cultural value, and the flow of music, whether it is produced by skilled musicians or by ordinary citizens, is a basic means of creative expression. Globalization has transformed the music industry. In later sections we shall consider the effects on distribution and consumption; here we are concerned with production. One of the observed effects of the spread of global markets on the music industry has been to concentrate power in the hands of an ever-smaller number of music publishers and record companies. Independent producers committed to promoting music associated with a particular musical genre or national origin have been squeezed out of the market or taken over by the ever-growing transnational corporations. The crisis of value engendered by these trends is clear: music production in these circumstances becomes increasingly a process of creating economic value rather than a

cultural expression whose primary importance is as a purveyor of cultural meaning.

Improved international communications

The rise of the Internet has created unprecedented opportunities for cultural dialogue and exchange of ideas. It has also provided artists and arts organizations with scope to diversify their product range, for example via e-commerce. These developments can be seen as beneficial to the production of culture, through their contribution to the flow of information and their stimulus to creativity.

At the same time there are fears that because cultural symbols are more freely transmitted as a result of improved international communication, a global cultural standardization will emerge. The ubiquity of corporate branding, for example, or the ready availability around the world of the cultural messages emanating from Hollywood, would appear to diminish cultural diversity and weaken the distinctiveness of national or subnational cultural identities. In fact, however, fears of a universal cultural homogenization arising as a result of globalization would appear to be exaggerated, at least for now. Such empirical evidence as exists seems to point towards a strengthening of local cultural differentiation against the forces of global standardization, and a resilience of the nation-state against the threat of a borderless world (Holton, 2005: 117). Indeed writers such as Brown (1995: 66) have argued that greater social differentiation is possible under globalization; he suggests that the means by which people can define themselves and their interests has actually increased, creating a 'global multicultural pastiche of social heterogeneity'.

Furthermore, these very same forces have created conditions for the emergence of new global artforms. 'World music' can be cited as an example, representing a range of specific musical genres or styles originating in various parts of the world, from Cuba to the French Antilles, from Greece to India, from Algeria to Pakistan.[9] Another illustration is the extensive discussion as to whether or not there is such a thing as a 'global literature', a notion first articulated in 1827 in Geothe's *Weltliteratur* and given a significant boost in modern times by the advent of new means for international communication and interchange.[10]

To sum up, where does all of this lead in assessing whether or not a crisis of value exists at least on the production side of the cultural economy? The economic impact of globalizing forces on artists and enterprises producing cultural goods does suggest a pressure towards increased emphasis on the economic value of cultural production, a trend that may be accepted willingly by some producers, and reluctantly and inevitably by others. The technological impacts also have a range of effects, from the undoubted benefits of new media for artistic creativity to the more uncertain effects on the interpretation of cultural value in the new technological utopia.

Are there winners and losers? Stuart Hall has suggested that it is easy to overplay the beneficial effects of globalization on artistic production. He argues:

> One of the immediate effects of globalization has been the internationalization of the circuits and circulations of cultural and artistic production... it's now ideologically represented to us as if there's a frictionless cultural universe in which anybody can get on the tramline anywhere, any work of art will be seen anywhere... [But] in reality... you see massive disparities of access, of visibility, huge yawning gaps between who can and who can't be represented in an effective way. (2004: 34)

This remark has particular relevance to the frustrations felt by artists of the South in trying to access the global cultural economy.

Impacts of globalization on systems of value distribution

The economic and cultural value generated in the production of cultural commodities is distributed to those who consume these goods and services by the firms, the media and the communications networks that transport and market cultural product. Distribution systems can be seen as channels by which value is conveyed from producers to consumers. Along the way the value might be transformed, added to or diminished. How does globalization affect the processes of cultural distribution, and what are the positive and negative effects on the economic and cultural value of the goods and services involved? In this section we consider two related aspects of the distribution of culture that are inextricably associated with the mechanisms of globalization: the Internet and cultural trade.

The Internet

It is a truism to say that the World Wide Web has been the greatest single development in national and international communications in the present era. Its effect on the way in which cultural products are promoted, marketed and exchanged has been profound. In regard to economic impacts, the value-adding enabled by the Web in the processing of cultural goods needs no elaboration. Its impact on cultural value may be somewhat less clear, as we shall see further below.

A significant aspect of the Internet's presence in the cultural arena relates to the intellectual property content of cultural goods and services. We have noted already that cultural commodities typically embody some intellectual property, the rights to which properly accrue to the commodities' original creators. The codification of copyright protection for creative works has existed since the original ratification of the Berne Convention in 1886, but the advent of the Web has greatly expanded its scope. At the same time the digital environment also opens up widespread opportunities for subversion of the system through piracy, which enables users to access protected material without payment to rights owners and without fear of penalty for unauthorized use, a matter we shall return to in the next section.

The value implications of the Web in its dealings with intellectual property can be examined in both economic and cultural domains. In regard to economic effects, the Internet clearly provides an efficient means for facilitating access to many types of copyright material and for conveying appropriate payment to its creators. As such it can be seen to promote greater equity in the distribution of remuneration for creative work and to act as a stimulus to the production of further creative output. The mechanisms for tracking usage and enforcing payment for digital material are constantly being improved, to the point where it is possible to imagine, in the foreseeable future, a universal system for detection of use and a means of directly linking users with rightsholders without the need for intermediaries. In these terms, then, the impacts of the Web on the economic aspects of value creation and transmission for cultural goods can be argued to be positive.

In regard to cultural value, however, the effects of the Internet are more difficult to gauge. By providing a means for the wider exercise of intellectual property rights and the more extensive capture of revenue from their use, the net has tended inexorably to transform what were once public goods into private commodities. Although one of the main functions of copyright has always been to provide for public access to protected material, for example via 'fair dealing' or 'fair use' provisions contained in most copyright legislation, the simple fact is that with the advent of the World Wide Web, the private space for accessing intellectual property has expanded and the public access space has shrunk. To the extent that important elements of cultural value are related to principles of freedom of information, shared identities and community participation in cultural experience, these trends could be seen as inimical to cultural value creation.

Nevertheless there are also ways in which the net can contribute to growth rather than contraction of the public space in which ideas are exchanged. Some artists, more concerned about getting their artistic and cultural messages across than in earning revenue from them, will place their music, visual art or text onto the Web, offering free and unrestricted access to anyone who wants to download their creative work. Broader ideas for a 'cultural commons' have been circulating for some time, using the power of the Internet to create a genuine public arena in which cultural interaction can occur (Drache and Froese, 2006). Such initiatives have taken practical shape in a number of areas; in science, for example, the *Public Library of Science* has been in existence for six years, involving a suite of open-access, on-line, peer-reviewed science journals that aim to make high-quality scientific research freely available.

Cultural trade

The international distribution of cultural goods and services occurs through the international trade systems at two levels: trade in tangible goods such as books and music recordings, and trade in digital material such as television programs where payment is for the intellectual property rights involved. In the area of global cultural trade, the balance between trade in goods and trade in services including trade in rights, has shifted inexorably in recent years in favor of the latter.

Cultural goods and services have always proved an irritant in international trade negotiations, providing a paradigmatic case of the conflict between economic and cultural values in decision-making.

Consider the case of the international market for audio-visual product such as film and television programs. On the one hand producers of these goods in countries such as the United States, who have access to scale and other economies in production and who see lucrative markets in many parts of the world, are likely to oppose any intervention in international trading arrangements that will limit their market access. On the other side of the fence, many importing countries see their local culture swamped by foreign product, against which their local cultural industries are unable to compete without some form of protection. Thus the crisis of value becomes apparent: should cultural goods be treated simply as commercial merchandise, with the economic gains from trade being the only concern in trading negotiations, or should the fact that these goods convey cultural messages, with profound quantitative and qualitative effects on the circulation of cultural value, be taken into account? Since, as we have seen, the processes of globalization have greatly facilitated the international movement of cultural goods and services, it can be argued that globalization has contributed to sharpening these tensions between economic and cultural value in the trading arena.

Trade negotiations are traditionally all about economics, whether on a multilateral basis through the World Trade Organization or in the many bilateral free-trade agreements that are appearing at the present time. Any suggestion that cultural value should be taken into account in determining the rules of the game is likely to be dismissed by economists. Yet the fact that cultural identity, self-recognition and self-esteem are important to people, and that cultural trade has an impact on these values, should give pause for thought. Economic policy-making in this area may need to accept that ultimately the goals of different societies extend beyond immediate material concerns, and that cultural considerations might therefore need to be admitted into policy-making processes in this area.[11]

Impacts of globalization on value reception and interpretation

We now reach the final stage in the value chain, where cultural product is consumed and experienced by end-users. It is convenient to divide our consideration into the consumption of culture as private good and as public good. This distinction arises from the fact that cultural goods and services can be categorized as 'mixed goods', having both private (excludable, rival) characteristics and public (non-excludable, non-rival) characteristics.[12] The economic value to consumers of private cultural goods is reflected in the market prices at which these goods are bought and sold. The economic value of public cultural goods can be derived from knowledge of individuals' willingness to pay for such goods, for example through their taxes. The cultural value of private cultural goods can be assessed in terms of expressed cultural benefits accruing to individuals from their own cultural consumption, whilst the cultural value of public cultural goods can be collated from a variety of indicators relating to the benefits of culture to society as a whole.

Culture as private good

The private demand for cultural goods of all types has been widely studied.[13] For goods such as theater performances or movies, the market price paid to secure the cultural experience reflects the expectation rather than the reality of the cultural value to be derived from consumption, since uncertainty surrounds the quality of the good until it is actually consumed. For such goods, demand can be interpreted within a preference space where expected cultural value is set against the monetary cost. For other cultural goods such as artworks, the quality of the goods is known in advance, although uncertainty still attends the other (possibly additional) motive for demand, namely the expectation that the work's monetary value may increase over time. The demand for such goods can be interpreted as both an investment and a consumption demand, the former reflecting economic value in the eyes of the consumer, the latter reflecting the cultural valuation.

Globalization affects the reception of value in the consumption of private cultural goods in two important ways: it affects the array of prices that consumers face, and it affects the technological means by which cultural product is experienced.

In the first instance, it is apparent that technological change and the spread of global markets has greatly reduced the prices of mass-produced cultural goods such as pop songs relative to those of specialized products such as live theater. Such a

trend can be interpreted as an economic impact of globalization that parallels the effects of economic forces on artists and arts organizations discussed earlier; on the supply side the effect is on the production of cultural value, on the demand side the effect is on how cultural value is received and interpreted. In both cases the outcome is a shift in the balance between economic and cultural elements in determining the operation of the cultural economy, and perhaps also a re-alignment amongst components of cultural value itself within that economy.

The latter possibility arises because the cultural value elements attaching to the products whose demand is favored by the economic effects of globalization are different from the elements defining cultural value for products that are relatively disadvantaged, other things being equal. To illustrate, consider the effects of globalization on the consumption of cultural experiences by tourists. Cultural tourism in both mass markets (high volume, low yield) and niche markets (low volume, high yield) is facilitated by the globalization processes we have been discussing, through reductions in the real costs of travel and the increased availability of information, booking services and so on. The cultural value of the experiences sought by mass tourists is qualitatively different from that sought by well-informed and discriminating cultural tourists, and conflicts arise when the two markets intersect. This occurs in destinations such as Venice or Angkor Wat where the economic impact of mass tourism encouraged by the relentless globalization of the tourist industry threatens to overwhelm the reception of the cultural values yielded by these world heritage sites.

The second aspect of the effects of globalization on demand for cultural goods and services relates to the changing technology of cultural consumption. The rise of the Internet and the escalating adoption of mobile telephony and other platforms have changed the means by which cultural messages are received, and have provided consumers with unprecedented power in signalling their demands (Lam and Tan, 2001). One outcome of these processes has been to blur the creative boundaries between producer and consumer; interactive cultural consumption of some digital artworks, computer games, etc. places the consumer in the role of co-creator. Robinson and Halie (2002: 382) describe this as a revolution when they argue that the 'interactive quality of digital formats [is] a unique characteristic that makes it different from other media advances'. In these circumstances the nature of the cultural value yielded by experience of the arts is radically altered, raising issues about creative responsibility, questioning standards of artistic judgement, and even pointing to the McLuhanesque possibility that in some cases the medium becomes the message.

Culture as public good

The public-good nature of cultural products such as the arts has been widely seen as a justification for government intervention in cultural markets, rationalizing support for local creative producers and protection of them from foreign competition.[14] We have already noted the pervasive effects of globalization in shifting the balance of economic power from the public towards the private sector in many countries and to this extent the public interest aspects of the cultural economy might be seen to be threatened. Nevertheless, public perception of the cultural value of the arts appears to remain resilient to these effects. For example, as yet unpublished data from a random sample survey of the Australian adult population undertaken in 2007 indicate that significant majorities of people either agree or strongly agree with propositions such as 'it is important to keep the arts alive for future generations' (88 per cent), 'the arts have an important role in creating our national identity' (79 per cent), and 'the arts help people to appreciate beauty' (84 per cent). These and similar sentiments can be taken as indicative of a broad public consensus as to the cultural value of the arts, a consensus that is translated into majority agreement with the proposition that 'governments should financially assist the arts' (71 per cent). Such results lend support to arguments that governments should take cultural value into account in the formulation of cultural policy, a matter to which we turn in the next section.

Domestic cultural policy issues

Questions of value permeate government policy across the board. Pre-eminent amongst the priorities seen by national governments in all countries, rich and poor, is the task of ensuring the economic health of the nation, looking to the traditional objectives of maximizing economic growth, minimizing unemployment and maintaining price stability and external balance, all within a context of providing equity in the re-distribution of income and wealth. Recent years have witnessed a strengthening of the economic basis for policy formation in a number of countries, evident, for example, in the re-definition of social policy in areas like health, education and welfare in terms of economic performance criteria. These trends are at least partially attributable to globalization, through the economic pressures noted earlier that are exerted on governments by the emergence of a competitive global market-place.

The cultural sector has not been immune from these effects. A sharpening of the focus of cultural policy can be observed, especially in many parts of Europe and Asia, towards a more explicit recognition of the economic dimensions of cultural activity. The value implications of these developments in the context of the cultural economy can be analysed at two levels: the effects on policy towards the cultural industries, and the effects on state support for the arts and culture that we discussed in the previous section.

In regard to the cultural industries, it is no exaggeration to say that globalization has given them an entirely new prominence and has provided new challenges for cultural policy. In earlier times the production and consumption of cultural goods occurred largely within national and regional boundaries. True, there was considerable international trade in cultural product, especially music, film and television, but it has taken the advent of the new information age to open up new means for the production, distribution and consumption of cultural goods and services and to create a global market place in which these products can be bought and sold. As we have noted already, the major drivers of the worldwide growth in the creative industries can be found particularly in the convergence of multimedia and telecommunications technologies that has led to an integration of the means by which cultural content is produced, distributed and consumed. At the same time the deregulation of media and telecommunications industries and the privatization of previously state-owned enterprises in these spheres has opened the way for massive growth in private-sector investment, with consequent effects on output and employment across the board. Underlying these developments has been a more general trend in economic policy-making towards a broadening of the concept of innovation from one concerned only with science and technology into a more wide-reaching appreciation of the role of creativity in the economy. Acceptance of the idea of creativity as a driving force in the knowledge economy pushes the creative industries into the spotlight as a primary source of the skilled workforce that can produce creative ideas and make innovation happen across a wide range of activities from business entrepreneurship to imaginative new social programs.

The value implications of these developments for domestic cultural policy begin to take shape. If the major forces promoting the growth of the cultural industries are economic in nature, it follows that the balance between economic and cultural value production will tend to be shifted in favor of the former, and policy will be under pressure to reflect the economic rather than the cultural content of the goods and services produced. In other words, the revenue potential or employment-creating effects of growth in the cultural industries will tend to dominate in policy decisions, and the cultural messages conveyed by television programs, video games and so on will take a back seat, or be disregarded altogether.

The second aspect of domestic cultural policy to be considered is the effect of the changing policy environment on public support for the arts and culture. Here the crisis in value can be seen very clearly to arise from the tussle between economic and cultural motives for government intervention. As governments become more focused on justifying public expenditure programs in terms of measurable performance outcomes, support for the arts must increasingly be argued by reference to the economic and social benefits that cultural activity bestows on the community through such avenues as employment creation, wealth generation, urban revitalization, increased social cohesion and so on. Valid though these claims may be, publicly-supported theater companies, orchestras, dance ensembles, art galleries etc. may feel that funding authorities look to economic sustainability rather than cultural viability as a basis for continued funding.

These concerns have led to a vigorous debate about how to introduce cultural value alongside economic value into the making of public policy towards the arts and culture. In the United Kingdom, for example, government obsession with laying down performance targets for cultural organizations is argued to have subverted the organizations' cultural purpose; the measurable economic and social benefits that they provide have become more important to policy-making than the artistic or cultural activity itself (Holden, 2004; 2006). In the US, a recent report by the RAND Corporation on reframing the debate in America about the benefits of the arts (McCarthy et al., 2004) discusses the wide range of economic and social benefits that the arts bring to individuals and to communities, but calls the intrinsic value of the arts 'the missing link'. This report argues that the intrinsic benefits of the arts have become marginalized in public discourse, in part because they are difficult to measure. Both of these influential reports call for a new approach to public-policy formulation with respect to the arts and culture, one that makes explicit the full range of value created by these activities.

International cultural policy issues

One of the most significant events of recent times in the international cultural policy arena has been the ratification by member states of the United Nations Educational, Scientific and Cultural Organization (UNESCO) of what has come to be known as the Cultural Diversity Convention that came into operation in March 2007.[15] The forces of globalization played a significant part in establishing a perceived need for such a treaty. Three different pressures were particularly important: the problem of culture in international trade; the perception that globalization is increasingly threatening people's sense of their own cultural identity; and a profound sense that countries of the Third World are losing out in the process of economic and cultural development. We have discussed these matters already; suffice it to say here that these motives underlying the remarkably rapid adoption and ratification of the Cultural Diversity Convention provide a vivid illustration of the essential thesis of this chapter. In other words, globalization has created a crisis of value in cultural policy around the world, reflected in the conflicts being experienced between the desire to enjoy the benefits of economic and technological progress on the one hand, and the need to recognize the role of culture in representing fundamental human values on the other. The Convention provides one forum in which these conflicts can be re-evaluated in an objective way, where the voice of culture can be given space to be heard, and where the quest for policy solutions at both the national and international level can be directed towards finding 'win–win' outcomes, i.e. policy strategies that can harness the beneficial aspects of globalization for economic and cultural development and avoid the harmful effects.

It remains to be seen whether the mechanisms of international cultural policy administration will be capable of realizing these laudable objectives. As the UN agency most directly concerned with culture, UNESCO has a responsibility to oversee the implementation of the Cultural Diversity Convention, in particular to ensure that the treaty's focus on the value of culture is maintained in an environment where an economic agenda tends to dominate policy-making. Other UN organizations, including the United Nations Conference on Trade and Development (UNCTAD) and the United Nations Development Program (UNDP), are devoting priority attention to the encouragement of creative industries in developing countries, linking economic and cultural growth in a sustainable development framework[16] (see also Chapter 7). The World Bank has asserted its interest in incorporating cultural factors into its development programs and strategies (World Bank, 1999), although as a lending institution it has always to be primarily concerned with the economic viability of its projects. Some NGOs such as cultural foundations are also involved in international projects that reflect concern for cultural value in a globalizing world.

Conclusions

This chapter has argued that a crisis of value exists in the contemporary cultural economy at both micro and macro levels, evidenced in the divergences that exist between economic and cultural value as criteria for resource allocation within the sector. Although processes of globalization are by no means the sole source of the pressures that bring this crisis about, they do exacerbate its effects. We have argued that the pressures arise on two points. First, the economic power of the global marketplace has tended to amplify trends already evident in a number of countries that shift the balance in favor of economic rather than cultural value-creation as motives driving the cultural economy. Second, although the technological aspects of globalization have yielded a multitude of beneficial impacts on cultural production, distribution and consumption, they have also raised questions internal to the assessment of cultural value itself, challenging traditional modes of aesthetic evaluation and proposing new approaches to the interpretation of what we understand by culture.

The way forward in confronting the various aspects of the crisis that we have been describing lies in several arenas. In the scholarly discourses concerned with economic or cultural aspects of the cultural economy, much remains to be done in advancing understanding of how value can be interpreted and how different interpretations influence systems of analytical thought. A particular challenge lies in the area of measurement. Techniques for assessment of the economic value of cultural goods and services are constantly being refined, especially in the area of non-market effects where methods used in environmental economics are proving adaptable to application in the cultural field. However, devising appropriate criteria for representing cultural value is a more difficult task, given the complexity and lack of an agreed metric for capturing the impacts of cultural phenomena.

These theoretical and methodological concerns have their counterpart in the practical world of policy-making. Resource allocation decisions are being made every day at all levels in the cultural economy, from the lone artist to the transnational corporation, from the small theater company to the national Culture Ministry. In all cases, the fundamental questions are the same: what values should count in decision-making and how are they to be evaluated? And if the path towards resolving the crisis of value lies in a clearer understanding of the benefits and costs of globalization assessed in both economic and cultural terms, what data are necessary to inform the decision process?

In the arena of public policy, the forces of globalization present particular challenges. Ultimately policy-makers must be guided by the collective will of those whom they represent. In a world where individual enterprise is a key element of the driving economic ideology, asserting the public interest in culture is not always an easy task.

Notes

1 Value in this singular sense is different from the plural noun 'values' which is used in common parlance to mean a moral or ethical position.
2 For further discussion of this phenomenon, see Klamer (2002).
3 This duality between economic and cultural value is the unifying theme for a collection of essays on value in economics, culture and art by a multidisciplinary group involving economists, art historians, anthropologists and cultural theorists; see Hutter and Throsby (2008).
4 For a fuller discussion, see Throsby (2001: Chapter 2).
5 Assertions of the intrinsic value of art have enjoyed something of a resurgence in recent years; see, for example, Etlin (1996), Johnson (2002), Crowther (2007).
6 For a detailed account of the working conditions and career decisions of creative artists, see Alper and Wassall (2006) and Menger (2006).
7 For an early analysis see, for example, Cornock and Edmonds (1973) who foresaw the possibility that computers might in some circumstances replace the artist altogether.

8 For an overview and analysis, see Candy and Edmonds (2002).
9 See Bohlman (2002), Miller and Shahriari (2006). For a critical view focusing on the cultural values involved, see Brennan (2001).
10 See further in Maxwell et al. (2003), Huyssen (2005).
11 See further in Yúdice (2003: 214–86).
12 A non-excludable good is one which, once produced, is available to all, and no-one can be excluded from enjoying its benefit. A non-rival good is one where one person's consumption does not diminish the amount available for others. Examples of non-excludable non-rival public goods are national defence and broadcast television signals.
13 For an overview see, for example, contributions to Towse (2003) and Ginsburgh and Throsby (2006).
14 For discussions of the economic rationale for government support for the arts, see Throsby (1994) and contributions to Towse (1997).
15 The full title of which is Convention on the Protection and Promotion of the Diversity of Cultural Expressions; see www.unesco.org/culture/en/diversity/convention.
16 See, for example, the United Nations Conference on Trade and Development (2004).

REFERENCES

Alper, N.O. and Wassall, G.H. (2006) 'Artists' careers and their labor markets', in V. Ginsburgh and D. Throsby (eds.) *Handbook of the Economics of Art and Culture*. Amsterdam: Elsevier. pp. 813–64.

Bohlman, Philip, V. (2002) *World Music: A Very Short Introduction*. Oxford: Oxford University Press.

Brennan, Timothy (2001) 'World music does not exist', *Discourse,* 23(1): 44–62.

Brown, Doug (1995) 'The urgency of social value theory in postmodern capitalism', in Charles M.A. Clark (ed.) *Institutional Economics and the Theory of Social Value: Essays in Honor of Marc R. Tool*. Boston: Kluwer.

Candy, Lindy and Edmonds, Ernest (2002) *Explorations in Art and Technology*. New York: Springer.

Connor, Steven (1992) *Theory and Cultural Value*. Oxford: Blackwell.

Cornock, Stroud and Edmonds, Ernest (1973) 'The creative process where the artist is amplified or superseded by the computer', *Leonardo,* 6(1): 11–16.

Crowther, Paul (2007) *Defining Art, Creating the Canon: Artistic Value in an Era of Doubt*. Oxford: Clarendon.

Drahe, Daniel and Froese, Marc D. (2006) 'Globalisation, world trade and the cultural commons: identity, citizenship and pluralism', *New Political Economy,* 11(3): 361–82.

Etlin, Richard A. (1996) *In Defense of Humanism: Value in the Arts and Letters*. Cambridge: Cambridge University Press.

Fekete, John (1987) 'Introductory notes for a postmodern value agenda', in John Fekete (ed.) *Life after Postmodernism: Essays on Value and Culture*. New York: St Martin's Press. pp. i–xix.

Ginsburgh, Victor and Throsby, David (eds.) (2006) *Handbook of the Economics of Art and Culture*. Amsterdam: Elsevier.

Hall, Stuart (in conversation with Michael Hardt) (2004) 'Changing states: in the shadow of empire', in Gilane Tawadros (ed.) *Changing States: Contemporary Art Ideas in an Era of Globalisation*. London: Institute of International Visual Arts.

Holden, John (2004) *Capturing Cultural Value: How Culture Has Become a Tool of Government Policy*. London: Demos.

Holden, John (2006) *Cultural Value and the Crisis of Legitimacy: Why Culture Needs a Democratic Mandate*. London: Demos.

Holton, Robert J. (2005) *Making Globalization*. Basingstoke: Palgrave-Macmillan.

Hutter, Michael and Throsby, David (eds.) (2008) *Beyond Price: Value in Culture, Economics, and the Arts*. New York: Cambridge University Press.

Huyssen, Andreas (2005) 'Geographies of modernism in a globalizing world', in Peter Brooker and Andrew Thacker (eds.) *Geographies of Modernism: Literatures, Cultures, Spaces*. London: Routledge.

Hyde, Lewis (2006) *The Gift: How the Creative Spirit Transforms the World*. Edinburgh: Cannongate.

Johnson, Julian (2002) *Who Needs Classical Music? Cultural Choice and Musical Value*. Oxford: Oxford University Press.

Klamer, Arjo (2002) 'Social, cultural and economic values of cultural goods', Rotterdam: Erasmus University, *mimeo*.

Lam, Calvin K.M. and Tan, Bernard C.Y. (2001) 'The Internet is changing the music industry', *Communications of the ACM*, 44(8): 62–8.

Maxwell, Richard et al. (2003) Editors' Preface to Special Issue on World Literature, *Modern Philology*, 100(4): 505–11.

McCarthy, Kevin et al. (2004) *Gifts of the Muse: Reframing the Debate about the Benefits of the Arts*. Santa Monica: RAND Corporation.

Menger, Pierre-Michel (2006) 'Artistic labor markets: contingent work, excess supply and occupational risk management', in V. Ginsburgh and D. Throsby (eds.) *Handbook of the Economics of Art and Culture*. Amsterdam: Elsevier. pp. 765–811.

Miller, Terry E. and Shahriari, Andrew (2006) *World Music: a Global Journey*. New York: Routledge.

Robinson, Laura and Halie, David (2002) 'Digitization, the Internet and the arts: eBay, Napster, SAG and e-Books', *Qualitative Sociology*, 25(3): 359–83.

Throsby, David (1994) 'The production and consumption of the arts: a view of cultural economics', *Journal of Economic Literature*, 32: 1–29.

Throsby, David (2001) *Economics and Culture*. Cambridge: Cambridge University Press.

Throsby, David and Hollister, Virginia (2003) *Don't Give Up Your Day Job: An Economic Study of Professional Artists in Australia*. Sydney: Australia Council.

Towse, Ruth (ed.) (1997) *Cultural Economics: The Arts, the Heritage and the Media Industries*, 2 vols. Cheltenham: Edward Elgar.

Towse, Ruth (ed.) (2003) *A Handbook of Cultural Economics*. Cheltenham: Edward Elgar.

United Nations Conference on Trade and Development (2004) *Creative Industries and Development*. UNCTAD XI Session, São Paulo, 13–18 June; document TD(XI)/BP/13.

World Bank (1999) *Culture and Sustainable Development: A Framework for Action*. Washington, DC: World Bank.

Yúdice, George (2003) *The Expediency of Culture: Uses of Culture in the Global Era*. Durham and London: Duke University Press.

CHAPTER 2

LOCATING THE CULTURAL ECONOMY
Andy C. Pratt

*This chapter argues that culture, and the cultural econ-
omy in particular, have become an important feature of
the national and the international economy as well as
international relations. This chapter is divided into three
main sections. In the first I discuss the core problem of
definitions and measurement of the cultural economy.
Following on from this I review the characteristics of the
cultural economy, stressing the diversity within as well
as between the cultural industries and the rest of the
economy. In the final section I take up the issue of the
location of cultural activities. The cultural economy is
rapidly growing and changing. The paper highlights a
key tension that researchers and policy-makers need to
focus on in the near future formed by the governance
structures of intellectual property rights and distribution;
these are generally controlled by a small number of
gatekeepers whose interests focused on the Northern
developed economies; and, on the other hand the value*

*of diversity and difference upon which the future growth
and development of the cultural economy rely.*

Introduction

This chapter argues that culture, and the cultural
economy in particular, have become an important feature of the national and international economy as well
as international relations. In many respects the term
'cultural economy' is a portmanteau term; later in this
chapter I will offer a more precise definition. However,
I want to remain with common usage in this introduction. Perhaps the defining aspect of debates about
globalization in recent years has been the extent to
which culture has been mobilized as a 'shield'. It is
claimed by many that culture is destroyed, or that differences are levelled and culture homogenized
through economic globalization. Implicitly, such an
outcome is seen as negative both in terms of sustainability, and in terms of the value and vibrancy of
indigenous cultures. Indeed, in part, this is the platform upon which a vibrant debate about the need to
preserve diversity in culture and heritage has taken
place in organizations such as UNESCO (WCCD,
1996; UNESCO, 2001). However, at the supra-
national level there are also agencies such as the
World Trade Organization (WTO), whose policies
seem to inescapably lead to the domination of monetary value over cultural value, and this has led to
strong debates around intellectual property rights
(Vaidhyanathan, 2003; Lessig, 2004). These debates
are coupled to a broader discourse of globalization
underscored by a version of neo-liberal free-trade
(Hirst and Thompson, 1999).

However, whilst global forces, especially the domination of huge multinationals, are very much a reality in the cultural sector (Herman and McChesney,
1997) we cannot simply 'read off' the consequences
as homogeneity; many argue that the current form
of globalization generates heterogeneity (Pieterse,
1995; Robertson, 1995). From a narrower economic
point of view, some argue that cosmopolitanism has
a positive effect on culture and creativity (Ottaviano
and Peri, 2006); others take an opposing view

(Cowen, 2002). Generally, debates about cosmopolitanism have increasingly questioned the simplistic good/bad distinctions of globalization, and with it highlighted a resultant complex hybridity of processes, outcomes and spaces (Hannerz, 1996; Appiah, 2006; Beck, 2006). Thus, culture is either set against globalization, or, against economics. In many respects such dualisms find an echo in the earlier 'high/low'– 'elite/mass' culture distinction popularized by the Frankfurt School (see below). In this chapter I want to question these dualistic conceptions, and in particular the way that they frame processes and empirical events. I will provide a different interpretation to the norm, one that resists such either/or formulations and rejects an easy romantic individualism (Pratt, 2007a); it is an approach that seeks to accept the challenge of power and domination in the control of cultures, but one that offers a nuanced understanding of the processes, and the variable responses to them.

The core of this argument concerns a re-conceptualization of the relationship between culture and economy, and the consequential spatial and structural implications. I intend to show that through an investigation of the cultural-economy relationship, and how it is changing, we can open up a new agenda for discussion. Moreover, we can highlight the fact that the cultural economy is rather unlike other aspects of the economy that we may be familiar with: that the split between commercial and non-commercial activities is not so clear;[1] that there is not a simple homogenization of product and audiences (or, a universal good); and finally, that the production and consumption of culture is very unevenly distributed, thus only benefiting some people.

The recent growth of interest in culture by policy-makers has a distinctly instrumental dimension, one that does not value cultural activity for itself (the more traditional perspective), but rather values culture in terms of what jobs, investment or social welfare it can create (DCMS, 1999). Again, I want to stress that this is not an either/or question, but it is seldom possible or practicable to achieve all (diverse and contradictory) objectives in any given project. Moreover, policy that focuses upon culture for culture's (economy) sake (i.e. not in an instrumental way) has been neglected. In particular I want to outline how it is possible to conceive of the cultural economy in ways that do not simply sustain particular art forms, or engage in instrumentalism, but that can develop the cultural economy in its own terms.

This chapter is divided into three main sections. In the first I discuss the core problem of definitions and measurement of the cultural economy. Following on from this I review the characteristics of the cultural economy stressing the diversity within as well as between the cultural industries and the rest of the economy. In the final section I take up the issue of the location of cultural activities. I show that despite the much discussed 'death of distance' in a digital world, the case of the cultural economy at least (ironically, one of the most digitized industries) seems to highlight the fact that place matters more than ever. However, there are significant forces at play that have the potential to override such specificity: for instance, the governance structures of intellectual property rights and distribution are generally controlled by a small number of gatekeepers whose interests focused on the Northern developed economies (see also Chapter 4). On the other hand, the value of diversity and difference to the growth of the cultural economy is central. Debates about policy in the cultural economy must urgently engage with these issues; in order to do so we will need a more robust evidence base than we currently have.

Defining the cultural economy

It is an often cited fact that 'culture' is one of the most complex words in the English language; it is not complex because it is difficult to define per se; rather, its subject is constantly contested and shifting. My concern here is not so much to define what culture is, as to expand upon the relationship of culture and the economy. The field of economics is, arguably, as cross-cut with debates about its object as culture; however, the discipline of economics has developed around a structure of thought where the divisions between economics and 'the rest' are perceived to be very clear. Hence, the resonance of the chapter title: *locating* the cultural economy.

A common starting point for analysis of the cultural economy builds upon a particular notion of culture developed by the Frankfurt School in the late 1930s (Adorno and Horkheimer, 1977) that rejects commodification on the grounds that it separated art and culture from its 'aura'. It is from this perspective that Adorno (1991) labelled (and defined) the culture industries in such negative terms. At one and the same time he sought to legislate what was culture, and to equate this with the market. Later work by political economists – common in media and communications studies – has carried forward Adorno's moral baggage and added its own critique of power and control (Ferguson and

Golding, 1997; Herman and McChesney, 1997) thus cementing an unhelpful market/non-market equation with art and commerce.

Arguably the longest running debate about the cultural economy can be tracked more precisely to its status as a mode of analysis and to debates about economic sociology that were founded upon a distinction of the economic and the social implicit in neo-classical economics. In the variants of classical economics that preceded this disciplinary watershed what we now consider the social, cultural and political were an integral part of economic and sociological discourse. Neo-classical forms of argumentation sought to concentrate on atomistic, uniquely economic action, and rational calculation. Critically, this created a 'boundary dispute' with respect to (and exclusion of) the social, a debate that also resonated in political economy. Anthropologies of economic activity, especially those such as Polanyi's (1957) which are important antecedents of institutional and evolutionary economic and sociological approaches (Hall and Taylor, 1996), and echo those of Marx and Weber on class, power and organization, were marginalized (Slater and Tonkiss, 2000). Importantly, in Parsons' (1961) and influential formulation of economic sociology, neo-classical economics was left bracketed off from the social: sociology was allocated the task of exploring the social setting for economic action (Pratt, 2004b). Thus the social (and cultural) dimensions of the economy were allocated to context. For many years economic sociology, and geography, maintained this distinction; it is only relatively recently that writers have sought to challenge this dualism (see Granovetter, 1985, in sociology and Massey, 1984, in geography); in so doing they have opened up the field for a reconsideration of the explanation of economic action proper and thus challenged neo-classical economics on its own ground; moreover, it has opened up a space where the cultural economy can be discussed.

Conceptualizations of the cultural economy can be differentiated by how the two terms are joined: as an adjective (*cultural* economy), or, as a compound noun (*cultural economy*) (Pratt, in press-b, Pratt, in press-c). The notion of a *cultural* economy refers to the cultural dimensions of economic activity (the design or marketing of any product or service; or, simply, the social dimensions of the organization of production) (Lash and Urry, 1993). The term *cultural economy* is indicative of a particular subsection of economic activity that is concerned with cultural products and activities (such as music, film and fine art) as opposed to, say, transportation or mining. This is

the sense in which the term is used in this chapter. The problem with the term 'cultural' is that it is used as a general modifier of terms (cultural industries, cultural communication), and it could be argued that everything is 'cultural' in one way or another in the sense that it has a cultural dimension. So, we need to proceed with care in the context of such ambiguous usage, as with the similarly problematic label 'creative' industries (see below).

The aim of the remainder of this section is to resist the dualism of culture and economy. The conceptual lens that I want to suggest has three moments: the making or production of culture, the governance of culture, and the conceptualization of culture. As I have already noted, Adorno, when he coined the term 'culture industry', was seeking to point to those parts of the economy that were mass-producing what he identified as inferior culture. A radical transposition of the notion was developed by French media and communications scholars in the 1980s; they sought to take this cultural economy seriously, to recognize that the *culture industry* is a legitimate expression of culture, and that its production was 'plural' and various: hence the term *the cultural industries* (Miège, 1987). This notion has been popularized in the United Kingdom by Garnham (1987, 2005), and underpins the policies of the 1980s for cultural regeneration pursued by UK metropolitan authorities.

Drawing upon the work of Miège, Garnham, and Becker (Becker, 1984), the production chain approach has been used to explore the 'making of culture' as a process: those activities that are required to produce and use a cultural product (Pratt, 2007b). Critically, this process-based analysis has sought to stress the situated nature of cultural production, in terms of markets, technologies, organization and regulatory regimes (referred to collectively as governance) (Pratt, 1997a; Pratt, 1997b; Pratt, 2004a; Pratt, 2004c). The production chain approach joins both questions of the 'breadth' of culture (which activities should be included: film, television, books computer games, theater, music, etc.), and the 'depth' of cultural production (which activities are required to produce cultural outputs: manufacturing, distribution and consumption) creating a rich field of the cultural economy (Bourdieu, 1993). In contradistinction to some others (Florida, 2002; Markusen, 2006), the production chain approach uses an industry-based ontology,[2] arguing that an occupational ontology offers a partial and fragmentary perspective and fails to capture the social reproduction of labour and knowledge in the cultural industries. Moreover,

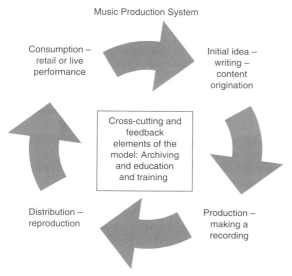

Music Production System

Consumption – retail or live performance

Initial idea – writing – content origination

Cross-cutting and feedback elements of the model: Archiving and education and training

Distribution – reproduction

Production – making a recording

Figure 2.1 The cultural economy production system – illustrated by the music industry

the approach popularized by Florida, mobilized through the agency of the 'creative class', is based upon a central concern with instrumentalism and cultural consumption (Pratt, in press-a). The production

chain approach incorporates production and consumption within the single process.

Various attempts have been made to operationalize measures of the cultural industries. Initial ones, such as those of the early *UK Creative Industries Mapping Document,* used a selective breadth definition – focusing on 13 industries (DCMS, 1998). More recently production chain approaches have been adopted by the policy community (DCMS, 2003; Burns Owens Partnership et al., 2006). These have deployed a more nuanced notion of process that incorporates 'cultural' and 'non-cultural' activities if their end point is cultural production[3] (see Figure 2.1). In order to give some sense of what this data collection has revealed I will present two tables. Figure 2.2 gives a preliminary international coverage; a more consistent definition and data collection for just the EU (KEA_European_Affairs, 2006) shows on average 3.1 per cent of the working population in the cultural sector, accounting for 2.6 per cent of European GDP, on a turnover of 654 billion Euro; some countries such as the UK and Germany are way above these figures. Finally, we can note that the cultural industries are the third most important industry in London (GLA_Economics, 2004).

The challenge for the near future is to create an international agreement on concepts and definitions

Figure 2.2 Contribution of the creative industries to the economy[a]

Country	Proportion of GDP	Proportion of total employment
	(per cent)	(per cent)
United States (2001)	7.8	5.9
United Kingdom (2000)	5.0	5.3
Canada (2000)	5.1	7.0
Australia (2000)	3.3	3.8
Argentina (1993–4)	4.1	3.5
Brazil (1998)	6.7	5.0
Chile (1990–8)	2.0	2.7
Ecuador (2001)	1.8	n.a.
Uruguay (1997)	6.0	5.0
Venezuela (2001)	2.3	n.a.

Notes:

[a] Industries included vary from country to country and percentages are only approximate.

Sources:

Australia and Canada: Wall Communications Inc. (2004), 'The Economic Contribution of the Copyright-Based Industries in Canada', in WIPO (2004), *National Studies on Assessing the Economic Contribution of the Copyright-Based Industries,* Creative Industries Series No. 1 107–208.

UK: DCMS (2001), Creative Industries Mapping Document 2001, Department of Culture, Media and Sport, London.

Other countries: OAS (2004), Culture as an Engine for Economic Growth, Employment and Development, Organization of American States, Washington DC, June.

Source: (Throsby 2007)

of the cultural economy, and then to develop comparative data collection and measurements. Sadly, until this time the picture will be fragmentary.

The organization and performance of the cultural economy

Perhaps the central question for those seeking to analyse the cultural economy concerns its similarity or difference to the 'rest of the economy'. *Sui generis* this also implies the applicability of neo-classical economic analysis to the sector.[4] So, the real question is should the cultural economy be regarded in 'exceptionalist' terms; if so, what is the evidence? This section seeks to highlight the ways in which the cultural economy may be regarded as 'different';[5] clearly this has important consequences for policy-making in terms of identification of processes and the utility of generic approaches. My intention is to provide an overview of ten key research themes of organizational aspects of the cultural economy; clearly this is indicative rather than exhaustive (see, for example, Caves, 2000). These characteristics are shared by all cultural industries, as well as some non-cultural industries, and the manifestation of each is different by different industries that have different market structures: for example, computer games and the film industry, or the theater. There is no space to elaborate these contrasts here.[6]

The first is the general *organizational form*. Most of the cultural industries are dominated by a handful of major international corporations, and sitting below them are many thousands of 'companies' – these companies are very small, indeed micro-enterprises comprising self-employed and two to three person businesses. There is a 'missing middle' or small- and medium-sized enterprises, which leads to some challenges in terms of coordination. On the other hand it develops a network, or rather an interdependent 'ecosystem' of companies that are constantly growing and evolving into other companies, recycling knowledge, expertise and personnel. Like any ecosystem, it is delicately balanced.

Second is the *work process*. The 'life' of products and projects to create them, and the firms that produce them, are short: a matter of weeks or months. These 'firms' are constantly recycling and evolving; they constitute a whole sector of the economy that has a 'project-based' form. As such, traditional analyses that treat the firm as a basic building block

of analysis are not so helpful as those that see the more enduring 'network' or 'institution' as more salient.

Third is the *rapid turnover* of products and sequence of multiple innovations required to sustain activity in the sector; added to which there is incredible uncertainty that when a product reaches a market, or an audience, they will even like it. The critical element of timeliness is crucial. So is the act and coordination of market building through education or publicity. Hence, consumption feeds back into production and both are attenuated by micro-differences.

Fourth, highly competitive markets where both temporal and quality differentiation is small but critical. These types of markets have been well described as '*winner-take-all*' in form (Frank and Cook, 1996); elsewhere, I have referred to them as 'chart' industries (referring to the structure of record or book charts and the sales differential between the top sellers and the 'long tail'; Jeffcutt and Pratt, 2002).

Fifth, the *role of technology* in enabling mass production and the possibility of monopoly profits. Technology is not determining, but it can be deployed under particular governance circumstances to frame products in a way that unlimited rents can be obtained.[7] For example, compare the case of the live singer performing to a limited audience (without amplification), and the same performance in MP3 format.

Sixth, the particularity of *market forms and regulation*. Despite the global nature of cultural production, products are localized via local regulatory regimes and the structure of local markets. For example: the market for imported music in various countries; or the taxation applied to particular goods; or the copyright restrictions enforced. Also, the market structure where it is possible for producers to gain direct access to markets, or that they need to pass through intermediaries and gatekeepers (commonly related to distribution).

Seventh, the relationship between the *formal and informal economies*. Much cultural activity is carried out for self-fulfilment or ceremony. Commonly, even when cultural activities are carried out on a fully costed basis, in the formal economy there is a large degree of 'self-exploitation' associated with participation. Critically, the porous relationship between the formal and informal, and the mutual dependency characterizes much activity.

Eighth, the relationship between, and definition of, the public and commercial/*not-for-profit*, and *for-profit*, spheres. As in the formal–informal relationship, the boundary between these activities is commonly porous, and unacknowledged, or actively ignored, by governance regimes. Likewise, there is a co-dependency of the sectors.

Ninth, the relationship between *production and consumption*. The cultural economy has a very strong, and often institutionalized, feedback system between production and consumption: examples are charts, critics and audiences. Cultural producers really need to engage with this feedback as the cultural market is so competitive, finely differentiated, localized and fast moving.

Tenth, the cultural economy is an *information rich* activity and hence relies upon a highly qualitative and quantitative flow of information, coupled with a finely tuned interpretive and relativistic judgement. There are no absolute and eternal values; they are constantly changing. Shifting information on the precise status of these values at any one point in time, or place, is critical for participants in the cultural economy. For employers, employees and contractors, reputation is a critical quality; as the common saying has it 'you're only as good as your last job'.

These ten (at least) characteristics are interlocking and together they begin to describe the 'force field' within which the cultural economy operates. Moreover, they begin to highlight why 'normal' economics does not seem to apply. Take, for example, film production, where the industry is structured around the principle that over 75 per cent of films will make a loss (Wasko, 2003). There are many more seemingly irrational or contradictory aspects of cultural production, and this is why, at first sight, they may deserve the description of amateurish and incompetent. However, in practice these are very effective industries in terms of earnings, or qualities of outputs (see Vogel, 2001). Not surprisingly, the cultural industries (praised for their flexibility, innovation and ability to manage change) are the current fashion in management studies (Henry, 2001; Bilton, 2007).

Location

These diverse and 'aberrant' characteristics collectively point to a distinct situated dimension of production (in its widest sense). As noted above, informal and qualitative exchanges of information, reputation, market and institutional forms are constitutive practices of the cultural industries. Whilst some of these have an international, or global, form most are of a local and particular nature. One important outcome of this is the geography of the cultural economy, one that is strongly, although not exclusively, articulated to urban areas in the developed world.

At a global scale, the inequalities take on an unsurprising pattern dominated by corporate control in the North, and in cities, and a clustering around market places where consumers have high and growing disposable income. As we have noted, the ownership and control of the cultural industries is less like that of a traditional trans-national corporation and better characterized by a fragmented organizational structure that is controlled via a strong gatekeeper (Negus, 1999). The dimensions of the gatekeeping function are various – but they include controls over (or surrender of) intellectual property rights, and distribution rights. In effect, such a structure weakens the possibility of using the developing world's strength of ownership and innovation of creative ideas. Commonly, the situation is such that creators have to leave their host nation and surrender a proportion of their rights over the product before they gain access to markets. Such a state of affairs limits the flow of income back to the developing world that might otherwise have a beneficial effect (Barrowclough and Kozul-Wright, 2006). Nevertheless, there are significant exceptions; perhaps the best cases are book production and film production that both have a significant non-developed world presence.

Analyses of the social dimensions of economic life have pointed to a range of silences in traditional economic accounts of the localization of the cultural economy in cities. To understand why, it is important to appreciate that a key strand in this work is that of formal neo-classical accounts of agglomeration; these accounts rest on a foundation of the minimization of transactions costs through proximity. From this perspective, agglomeration happens in part as a consequence of the monopoly advantages afforded by space (many want to be in the same position at once). Moreover, it is argued that close proximity produces additional externalities or 'spill-over effects'.

Early classical economic accounts, such as those of Marshall, referred to this externality of industrial districts as 'secrets of business in the air' (1920); others more recently, have pointed to 'trust' (Gambetta, 1988). There is a large debate about the explanation of industrial districts more generally (Amin and Thrift, 1992). The key point made, in particular by those influenced by Flexible Specialization accounts of economic development, stresses the interaction of producers of part-finished goods who not only provide supply and demand (Piore and Sabel, 1984), but also allow ample opportunity to experiment with production and switch suppliers to produce novel/innovative items.

Scott's work exemplifies these issues in relation to what he terms the 'image producing industries' (2000, 2005). Storper points to what he terms 'untraded' dependencies of such local networks (1997). A recent debate has sought to specify such dependencies more clearly first via the notion of the informal exchange of information (buzz) (Bathelt et al., 2004; Storper and Venables, 2004), and through the circulation of reputation (Blair, 2001; Pratt, 2006).

Conclusion

The aim of this chapter has been to develop a more adequate understanding of the cultural economy. I have sought to do this by criticizing a range of common dualisms to which the cultural economy has fallen prey. I introduced the idea of the three moments of cultural production – **concepts, making and governance** – that I have used to situate and specify the cultural economy. I pointed out that significant steps have recently been taken through the application of a more developed concept of cultural production, operationalized in the form of the cultural industries production chain. Whilst such an approach is ultimately flawed owing to the inadequacies of industrial taxonomies and data deficiencies, it does begin to 'visualize' the actually existing cultural economy. In the second part of the chapter I sought to provide some characteristics of the cultural economy. Little research has been carried on in these industries (in part because they were difficult to identify, and in part because they have only really grown in the last 50 years).

I used the outline of ten key characteristics to raise the issue of exceptionalism. Is the cultural economy different to the rest of the economy? If so,

how? And why? Here again, I pointed to the inter-relationship of conceptualization and explanation. However, what evidence is available does point to some significant differences, or more extreme cases, of what might otherwise be regarded as 'business as usual'. As I also noted, this deviation from the norm is commonly, through ignorance, interpreted as inefficiency or incompetence. However, the information that is being collected on the cultural economy does point to the fact that it is one of the most innovative, fastest growing and significant industries in the world. I also pointed out that there is a significant conflict of interest between cultural values and economic values. Clearly, the notion of market failure has been deployed in economic policy-making to address this mismatch (Throsby, 2001). However, given the growth of the cultural economy, and the inter-dependencies between the not-for-profit and for-profit, and the formal and informal, the case for market failure is significantly weakened. Moreover, in an era where state funding for the arts and culture has significantly declined, it is not clear on pragmatic grounds whether such a policy will work. Hence, the need to explore a new form of cultural economy policy-making, and the need for a robust evidence base that I have argued for in this chapter.

Aside from the notion of global distribution and diversity of the cultural industries, there is the local impact. We have seen a huge growth in instrumental policies that involve culture as a 'carrot' for inward investment; indeed, cities feel compelled to market themselves against one another for investment or tourists today (Hall and Hubbard, 1998; Short and Kim, 1998). Setting aside the reasons for this shift we can see that such an approach does little to promote the cultural economy *per se*. Analyses of the structure and organization of the cultural economy, and its embeddedness in place, has revealed a complex process of local effects. In some ways this is also running against expectations: the common notion of the 'death of geography' in the digital age has been answered by 'place matters even more'. This, I take as a positive signal that there is still a place for, and value in, localized production, albeit in a globalizing world.

Overall, this chapter should also be read as a call to rethink culture and cultural policy. What are the relative roles of the formal and informal sectors, the state, the economy, etc.? This is why I have tried to stress the need to comprehend different dimensions of governance (organization and control) of the cultural sector – one that is sensitive to power and control, not simply reduced to an effect of power and control. There is an important space of debate opened up here to discuss alternative models of governance of culture; it is clearly a challenge that will remain in policy-makers', practitioners' and academics' 'inboxes' for a time to come.

Notes

1   The term cultural economy should not be understood as the economy of culture, but rather the set of socio-economic relations that enable cultural activity.
2   The conceptualization of industry or occupation as a fundamental unit of analysis. This concept is operationalized through taxonomies of industry, or of labour markets: that is, measuring workers classified on the basis of the industry they work in, or their occupation.
3   There are three 'fault lines' in debates about the definition of the cultural economy. 1. Whether a number of activities are either 'cultural' or should be included in the cultural economy, the two key areas are tourism and sports. 2. The division between arts, crafts and mass production; these relate more to a residual Frankfurt School concept of culture. 3. Between publicly financed cultural activities and commercial ones: in Western Europe it is common to refer to the former as the cultural industries.
4   The field of cultural economics signals an exceptionalist routeway, e.g., Baumol and Bowen (1966), Throsby (2001).
5   There is another interpretation, namely that the cultural economy is quite similar to the rest of the economy, however, the conceptualization of the 'rest of the economy' is faulty.
6   For example, advertising – Grabher (2001); Grabher (2002); new media – Pratt (2000); film – Scott (2005); music – Hesmondhalgh (1996); computer games – Johns (2006); and, design – Leslie and Reimer (2006).
7   For further elaboration see Pratt and Kretschmer (under submission).

REFERENCES

Adorno, T.W. (1991) 'The schema of mass culture', in J.M. Bernstein (ed.) *The Culture Industry: Selected Essays on Mass Culture*. London: Routledge. pp. 61–97.

Adorno, T. and Horkheimer, M. (1977) 'The culture industry: enlightenment as mass deception', in J. Curran, M.M. Gurevitch and J. Woollacott (eds.) *Mass Communications and Society*. London: Arnold. pp. 349–83.

Amin, A. and Thrift, N. (1992) 'Neo-Marshallian Nodes in Global Networks', *International Journal of Urban and Regional Research*, 16: 571–87.

Appiah, A. (2006) *Cosmopolitanism: Ethics in a World of Strangers*, New York; London: W.W. Norton.

Barrowclough, D. and Kozul-Wright, Z. (eds.) (2006) *Creative Industries and Developing Countries: Voice, Choice and Economic Growth*. London: Routledge.

Bathelt, H., Malmberg, A. and Maskell, P. (2004) 'Clusters and Knowledge: Local Buzz, Global Pipelines and the Process of Knowledge Creation', *Progress in Human Geography*, 28: 31–56.

Baumol, W.J. and Bowen, W.G. (1966) *Performing Arts – The Economic Dilemma: A Study of Problems Common to Theater, Opera, Music and Dance*. New York: Twentieth Century Fund.

Beck, U. (2006) *The Cosmopolitan Vision*. Cambridge, UK; Malden, MA: Polity.

Becker, H.S. (1984) *Art Worlds*. Berkeley, London: University of California Press.

Bilton, C. (2007) *Management and Creativity: From Creative Industries To Creative Management*. Malden, MA; Oxford: Blackwell Publishing.

Blair, H. (2001) '"You're only as good as your last job": the labour process and labour market in the British film industry', *Work, Employment and Society*, 15: 149–69.

Bourdieu, P. (1993) 'The field of cultural production, or: The economic worlds reversed', in R. Johnson (ed.) *The Field of Cultural Production: Essays on Art And Literature*. Cambridge: Polity Press. pp. 29–72.

Burns Owens Partnership, Pratt, A.C. and Taylor, C. (2006) *A Framework for the Cultural Sector: A Report for UIS/ UNESCO*. London: BOP.

Caves, R.E. (2000) *Creative Industries: Contracts between Art and Commerce*. Cambridge, MA: Harvard University Press.

Cowen, T. (2002) *Creative Destruction: How Globalization Is Changing the World's Cultures.* Princeton, NJ: Princeton University Press.

DCMS (1998) *Creative Industries Mapping Document.* London: Department of Culture, Media and Sport, UK.

DCMS (1999) *A Report For Policy Action Team 10: Arts and Sport.* National Strategy for Neighborhood Renewal, London: Department of Culture, Media and Sport/Social Exclusion Unit, UK.

DCMS (2003) *Regional Data Framework for the Creative Industries: Final Technical Report for the Department of Culture, Media and Sport and the Regional Cultural Consortia.* London: Department of Culture, Media and Sport, UK.

Ferguson, M. and Golding, P. (1997) *Cultural Studies In Question.* London: SAGE Publications.

Florida, R.L. (2002) *The Rise of the Creative Class: And How It's Transforming Work, Leisure, Community and Everyday Life.* New York, NY: Basic Books.

Frank, R.H. and Cook, P.J. (1996) *The Winner-Take-All Society: Why the Few at the Top Get So Much More Than the Rest of Us.* New York: Penguin Books.

Gambetta, D. (1988) *Trust: Making and Breaking Cooperative Relations.* Oxford: Basil Blackwell.

Garnham, N. (1987) 'Concepts of culture – public policy and the cultural industries', *Cultural Studies*, 1: 23–37.

Garnham, N. (2005) 'From cultural to creative industries: An analysis of the implications of the "creative industries" approach to arts and media policy making in the United Kingdom', *International Journal of Cultural Policy*, 11: 15–30.

GLA_Economics (2004) *Measuring Creativity: 2004 Update of the GLA's Creative Industry Economic Data.* London: Greater London Authority.

Grabher, G. (2001) 'Ecologies of creativity: the Village, the Group, and the heterarchic organization of the British advertising industry', *Environment and Planning A*, 33: 351–74.

Grabher, G. (2002) 'The project ecology of advertising: Tasks, talents and teams', *Regional Studies*, 36: 245–62.

Granovetter, M. (1985) 'Economic action and social structure: the problem of embeddedness', *American Journal of Sociology*, 91: 481–510.

Hall, P.A. and Taylor, R.C.R. (1996) 'Political science and the three new institutionalisms', *Political Studies*, 44: 936–57.

Hall, T. and Hubbard, P. (1998) *The Entrepreneurial City: Geographies of Politics, Regime, and Representation.* New York: Wiley.

Hannerz, U. (1996) *Transnational Connections: Culture, People, Places.* London: Routledge.

Henry, J.E. (2001) *Creativity and Perception in Management.* London: SAGE Publications.

Herman, E.S. and McChesney, R.W. (1997) *The Global Media: The New Missionaries of Corporate Capitalism.* London; Washington, DC: Cassell.

Hesmondhalgh, D. (1996) 'Flexibility, post-Fordism and the music industries', *Media, Culture & Society*, 18: 469–88.

Hirst, P. and Thompson, G. (1999) *Globalization in Question: The International Economy and the Possibilities of Governance.* Cambridge: Polity.

Jeffcutt, P. and Pratt, A.C. (2002) 'Managing Creativity in the Cultural Industries', *Creativity and Innovation Management*, 11: 225–33.

Johns, J. (2006) 'Video games production networks: value capture, power relations and embeddedness', *Journal of Economic Geography*, 6: 151–80.

KEA_European_Affairs (2006) *The Economy of Culture in Europe.* Brussels: European Commission DG5.

Lash, S. and Urry, J. (1993) *Economies of Signs and Space.* London: SAGE Publications.

Leslie, D. and Reimer, S. (2006) 'Situating design in the Canadian household furniture industry', *Canadian Geographer–Geographe Canadien*, 50: 319–41.

Lessig, L. (2004) *Free Culture: How Big Media Uses Technology and the Law to Lock Down Culture and Control Creativity.* New York: Penguin.

Markusen, A. (2006) 'Urban development and the politics of a creative class: evidence from a study of artists', *Environment and Planning A*, 38: 1921–40.

Marshall, A. (1920) *Principles of Economics: An Introductory Volume.* London: Macmillan.

Massey, D. (1984) *Spatial Divisions of Labour: Social Structures and the Geography of Production.* London: Macmillan.

Miège, B. (1987) 'The logics at work in the new cultural industries', *Media, Culture & Society*, 9: 273–89.

Negus, K. (1999) *Music Genres and Corporate Subcultures.* London: Routledge.

Ottaviano, G.I.P. and Peri, G. (2006) 'The economic value of cultural diversity: evidence from US cities', *Journal of Economic Geography*, 6: 9–44.

Parsons, T. (1961) *The Structure of Social Action: A Study in Social Theory With Special Reference to a*

Group of Recent European Writers. New York: Free Press of Glencoe.

Pieterse, J. (1995) 'Globalization as hybridization', in M. Featherstone, S. Lash and R. Robertson (eds.) *Global Modernities*, London: SAGE Publications. pp. 45–68.

Piore, M.J. and Sabel, C.F. (1984) *The Second Industrial Divide: Possibilities for Prosperity*. New York: Basic Books.

Polanyi, K. (1957) *The Great Transformation*. Boston: GowerBeacon Press.

Pratt, A.C. (1997a) 'Production values: from cultural industries to the governance of culture', *Environment and Planning*, A, 29: 1911–7.

Pratt, A.C. (1997b) 'The cultural industries production system: a case study of employment change in Britain 1984–91', *Environment and Planning A*, 29: 1953–74.

Pratt, A.C. (2000) 'New media, the new economy and new spaces', *Geoforum*, 31: 425–36.

Pratt, A.C. (2004a) 'Creative Clusters: Towards the governance of the creative industries production system?' *Media International Australia* No. 112: 50–66.

Pratt, A.C. (2004b) 'Retail Therapy', *Geoforum*, 35: 519–21.

Pratt, A.C. (2004c) 'The cultural economy: a call for spatialized 'production of culture' perspectives', *International Journal of Cultural Studies*, 7: 117–28.

Pratt, A.C. (2006) 'Advertising and creativity, a governance approach: a case study of creative agencies in London', *Environment and Planning A*, 38: 1883–99.

Pratt, A.C. (2007a) 'Creativity, innovation and urbanization', in J.R. Short, P. Hubbard and T. Hall (eds.) *The Sage Companion to the City*. London: SAGE Publications.

Pratt, A.C. (2007b) 'The state of the cultural economy: the rise of the cultural economy and the challenges to cultural policy making', in *The Urgency of Theory*, Lisbon: Gulbenkian Foundation.

Pratt, A.C. (in press-a) 'Creative accounting? From the creative class to cultural production as the dynamic of urban regeneration', *Geografiska Annaler: Series B, Human Geography*.

Pratt, A.C. (in press-b) 'The cultural economy', in R. Kitchen and N. Thrift (eds.) *International Encyclopedia of Human Geography*. Oxford: Elsevier.

Pratt, A.C. (in press-c) 'The cultural industries', in A. Leyshon, L. McDowell and R. Lee (eds.) *Economic Geography Reader*. London: SAGE Publications.

Pratt, A.C. and Kretschmer, M. (under submission) 'Breaking out of the box: The production of music and copyright', *Information, Communication & Society*.

Robertson, R. (1995) 'Glocalization: time–space and Homogeneity–Heterogeneity', in M. Featherstone, S. Lash and R. Robertson (eds.) *Global Modernities*. London: SAGE Publications. pp. 25–44.

Scott, A.J. (2000) *The Cultural Economy of Cities: Essays on the Geography of Image-Producing Industries*. London: SAGE Publications.

Scott, A.J. (2005) *On Hollywood: The Place, the Industry*. Princeton: Princeton University Press.

Short, J.R. and Kim, Y.-K. (1998) 'Urban crises/urban representations: selling the city in difficult times', in P. Hall and P. Hubbard (eds.) *The Entrepreneurial City: Geographies of Politics, Regime and Representation*. London: John Wiley and Sons. pp. 55–75.

Slater, D. and Tonkiss, F. (2000) *Market Society: Markets and Modern Social Theory*. Malden, Mass.: Polity Press.

Storper, M. (1997) *The Regional World: Territorial Development in a Global Economy*. New York: Guilford Press.

Storper, M. and Venables, A.J. (2004) 'Buzz: face-to-face contact and the urban economy', *Journal of Economic Geography*, 4: 351–70.

Throsby, D. (2001) *Economics and Culture*. Cambridge: Cambridge University Press.

Throsby, D. (2007) *Concept and Context in the World Economy*. Unpublished Mimeo.

UNESCO (2001) *Universal declaration on cultural diversity*. Geneva: UNESCO.

Vaidhyanathan, S. (2003) *Copyrights and Copywrongs: The Rise of Intellectual Property And How It Threatens Creativity*. New York: New York University Press.

Vogel, H.L. (2001) *Entertainment Industry Economics: A Guide for Financial Analysis*. Cambridge: Cambridge University Press.

Wasko, J. (2003) *How Hollywood Works*. London: SAGE Publications.

WCCD (1996) *Our Creative Diversity: Report of the World Commission on Culture and Development (W.C.C.D.)*. Paris: UNESCO.

## CHAPTER 3

THE GLOBAL CULTURAL ECONOMY: POWER, CITIZENSHIP AND DISSENT
Daniel Drache and Marc D. Froese

This chapter examines the complex dynamics of cultural exchange and production. While the narrative of financial globalization privileges system and structure, that of cultural globalization emphasizes the centrality of agency and voice. The first section maps the contours and boundaries of the global cultural economy. The second briefly analyses four industrial sectors in order to illustrate the political economy of cultural production. The third section examines the inherently unequal dynamics of global cultural flows. Finally, we will link the global cultural economy to the growth of political dissent. Dissent is the consequence of power being reallocated downwards and the 'Innisian' and 'Habermasian' power dynamics involved are central to our understanding of the role of agency and voice in the global cultural economy.

The novelty of the global cultural economy

The global cultural economy, as it has come to be termed, is a leviathan in its complexity and market reach. Negotiating the rules of cultural interaction is a complex and often chaotic undertaking in which market power and political influence are always present. Strikingly, there is no consensus on the role that culture plays in the processes of globalization for the very simple reason that culture is a difficult and elusive term to define (Stanley, 2005), and is subject to global pressures and national constraints (Stiglitz and Charlton, 2004). We define culture as a set of ideas and practices embedded in the plural and diverse historical experience of a society. Cultural practices are the markers of public memory. Definitionally, the global cultural economy is an integrated market system of global property rights, mass markets, foreign investment, and multilateral regulation (Paquet, 2005). It also features an extensive commons (see Chapter 5). It includes most media, information and entertainment flows, whether they move through market mechanisms or through the public sphere.

This chapter examines the complex dynamics of cultural exchange and production. We understand that globalization is increasingly a cultural and communicative phenomenon. The narrative of financial globalization privileges system and structure; the narrative of cultural globalization emphasizes the centrality of agency and voice to the social phenomenon of globalization. The first section maps the contours and boundaries of the global cultural economy (Appadurai, 2001). The second section briefly analyses four industrial sectors in order to illustrate the political economy of cultural production (Drache and Froese, 2006). The third section examines the inherently unequal dynamics of global cultural flows.[1] Today, the international market for cultural goods is larger than the markets for steel, automobiles or textiles. Finally, we will link the global cultural economy to the growth of political dissent (Barber, 1995). Dissent is the consequence of two factors: the unequal social relations embedded in cultural flows and the empowerment of individuals and groups through new communications technologies. Power is being reallocated downwards and these Innisian power dynamics are central to our understanding of the role of agency in the global cultural economy.

Mapping the global sphere of interactive communication: a Habermasian/Innisian turn

Market power is frequently theorized as the principal driver of cultural globalization, but we argue that although this power is a central feature of the globalization phenomenon, rapid technological change and activist publics have undermined the political influence and financial might of transnational corporations. A Habermasian reading of the current stage of globalization highlights the growing international public sphere, in which new forms of communication unleash the radical innovative potential of national publics (Habermas, 1989). Habermas (2001) theorized that public reason relied on face-to-face engagement to shape state policy. Today, this dynamic is no longer confined to the agora, but rather takes place through digital means in the global polis (Barney, 2000).

The particular modality of this process within the global interactive sphere of communication was foreseen by Harold Innis (Innis, 2007). Groundbreaking research in the early part of the twentieth century into the origins and possible futures of human communication suggested that in an era of unprecedented technological change, communication technology shifts political power downwards and towards the margins of societies (Innis, 1951). This process has destabilizing effects on traditional patterns of authority (Downing, 2001).

Taken together, Habermas and Innis provide a compelling account of the processes currently underway in the global cultural economy. The global cultural economy is driven by technological change towards a global, integrated, and interactive sphere of communication in which political power is inexorably moving downwards and towards the margins of international civil society because it gives a voice to those who previously did not have one. Innis' grasp of the emancipatory potential of technology hits closer to our current reality than do McLuhan's ideas (McLuhan, 1964). McLuhan thought that the medium of communication eclipses the message it contains, but we see today that his old aphorism, 'the medium is the message', is only true for early adopters of technology in the global North for whom text messaging, for example, was a toy, rather than a communications lifeline.

To be a social actor today, one needs to be patched into the worldwide digital communications network. Do-it-yourself techno-gurus, bloggers, musicians, writers, public intellectuals, counterculture activists, and even knowledge caretakers such as universities, archives and museums, contribute new ideas about what it means to be a citizen in the transnational cultural context (Shaviro, 2003). Benedict Anderson (1991) has argued that in the nineteenth century, print capitalism created the modern citizen and nationalism as the mainstays of the nation-state. In the twenty-first century, hypertext is recreating the modern concept of citizenship through access to new collective identities and new ways of understanding the relationship between local and global.

Hypertext and identity politics

The text messaging phenomenon sweeping Asia, Europe, North America and Africa is a striking example of Innis' primary insight. In the first quarter of 2002, 24 billion messages were sent globally (ITU, 2002). Digital technology is increasingly available to those who have not had access to it in the past, including the poor, children and the disabled, particularly in the global South. The digital divide is in fact shrinking as access to computers and the massive explosion of cell phones in the global South continues to grow at double digit figures annually (Drache and Clifton, 2006). Short Message Service (SMS) technology has been revolutionary for the hard of hearing who now use cellular phones almost as freely as anyone else.

African farmers and fishermen, traditionally excluded from informed participation in the market, are using it to achieve higher prices for the produce they sell. Email and SMS technology were also used to orchestrate mass demonstrations of dissent, such as the 'Battle in Seattle' in 1999 and those in response to the Madrid bombings in 2004 (Summers, 2001). SMS is an ideal instrument for organizing spontaneous public demonstrations in Asia's megacities as well. The anti-Japan demonstrations of 2005 in China were facilitated by text messaging, which was used to mobilize thousands of urban Chinese in Beijing and Shanghai (Yardley, 2005). The instantaneous transmission of photos from Rwanda, the former Yugoslavia and Iraq alerted global publics to human rights abuse and galvanized international condemnation against American imperial ambitions.

The spread of mobile technology occurs unevenly at first, but the effect is often an exponential democratization of communication. The traditional left/right world view imagines that power begets power, and that new information technology empowers corporate intellectual property proprietors. Ownership of the means of communication brings wealth and the ability to control the social agenda. But with the digital communications revolution, the reverse is true. Civil society uses Information and Communication Technologies (ICTs) to strengthen a bottom-up approach to mobilization of the sort necessary for the democratization of the information society (ITU, 2002). Since the mid-1990s, digital technology has been a lynchpin of popular protest and mass dissent. Now, at the dawn of the twenty-first century, it has entered the mainstream of local and regional cultures alongside the other revolutionary media of mass communication, radio and television.[2]

The unique feature of this public sphere of interactive communication is that it is composed of privately owned communications networks. Some writers believe that private ownership removes culture and communication from the public sphere. While many aspects of culture may be privately owned, they are always shared. The quandary facing policy-makers and global governance experts is how can public authorities protect free speech, promote multicultural identities, and simultaneously recognize the property rights of corporate owners? None of these goals triangulate easily with neoliberal intellectual property rights (Appadurai, 1996). Global publics are deeply divided between two visions for the future – a global commodity chain for private economic actors, or a renewed cultural pluralism for global publics. So far, there are no definitive answers, nor any consensus on how to nourish the cultural commons (see Chapter 5).

Principal characteristics of the global cultural economy

The global cultural economy has four main features – its *markets*, *intergovernmental institutions* such as the WTO, WIPO and UNESCO, *norms* such as diversity, accessibility and protection of intellectual property, and *citizenship practices* typified by an often porous divide between public and private:

Global markets
The first feature is a worldwide market system for information and entertainment. The emergence of global markets was a prerequisite for the transnational diffusion of cultural goods and services. Films, books, television, radio and the Internet create a seemingly endless flow of cultural goods and services. These

real and virtual texts create new narratives in privileged spaces about identity, diversity, distraction and transnationality. The explosion of new information technologies has made possible the organization of many different kinds of citizen-accessed outlets and public forums at the local, national and global levels.

Throsby defines cultural production as involving creativity in the production process, the generation, and communication of symbolic meaning, resulting in some form of intellectual property (Throsby, 2001). A final feature is noted by Caves. Cultural products must be experienced in order to be valued. Cultural products are so valuable because they empower the consumer to make their own evaluation of their symbolic power (Throsby, 2001). However, just as the enclosure movement of the eighteenth century fenced off public goods and redefined the rights of investors, so intellectual property rights are primary markers of growth and diffusion of the global cultural economy (Boyle, 2003). The Trade Related Intellectual Property Rights Agreement formalized a formidable series of rights for property owners, particularly in the pharmaceutical and entertainment industries. But enforcement has been logistically complex and compliance remains problematic, not only in the global South, which has emerged as a network of extralegal IP appropriation, but also in the global North where citizens and consumers are not convinced that digital appropriation is a crime on par with the theft of tangible goods.

Millions of citizens worldwide are convinced in a way that even five years ago they were not that the idea of a single global order anchored in the WTO's governance capacity is discredited. Global dissent has its own iconography, popularized by such worldwide best sellers as *No Logo* from Canada's Naomi Klein (2000) and Mark Achbar's surprise documentary hit *The Corporation* (2004). Michael Moore's no-holds-barred books and films attacking the American abuse of power at home and abroad round out this genre. There are dozens of films, books and documentaries in other languages feeding the culture of anti-corporate and democratic dissent.[3]

International organizations
The second feature of the global cultural economy is the newly emergent intergovernmental organizations which provide the necessary regulatory dimension that makes markets possible. The World Trade Organization is the first fully realized institution of international trade governance. It governs the regulations for international exchange of goods

and services. Most important for our discussion are its newest regulatory frames for trade in services and intellectual property. The General Agreement for Trade in Services divides services trade into four modalities, covering everything from the provision of financial services to the movement of service providers.[4] Civil society activists are concerned that the liberalization of services trade will lock in the current unequal division of labour in the global economy (Freedman, 2002).

The Trade Related Intellectual Property Rights Agreement is highly controversial because it creates strict standards for the treatment of intellectual property rights (Mercurio, 2004). Intellectual property is one of the largest growth areas in the global cultural economy and activists are furious that Northern media and entertainment multinationals would attempt to fence in creativity in order to protect corporate profits. The present intellectual property regime is unlikely to enforce compliance because global publics habitually ignore the protestations of transnational corporations that without exclusive property rights, these titans of the global cultural economy will be boarded and scuttled by Southern pirates (Kantor, 2004).

The other major network of intergovernmental regulation is centered at the United Nations and its specialized agencies. The concerns of activists, publics and governments about the subordination of cultural trade to WTO discipline have been taken to the United Nations Educational, Scientific and Cultural Organization (UNESCO), one of whose mandates is to promote cultural diversity and pluralism in artistic expression (UNESCO, 2000). Intense negotiations at UNESCO, with the aim of removing the trade in cultural goods from under the WTO's direct supervision because of national concerns that culture should not be treated like other commodities, led to the 2005 international Convention for the Protection and Promotion of the Diversity of Cultural Expressions (see Chapter 7).

New norms

The third feature of the global cultural economy is its capacity to generate norms that are distinct from the norms that govern conventional commodity trade. The norms of cultural exchange include diversity, accessibility and exclusive rights over creative output. This is not necessarily the same as patent protection as it is conventionally understood. In the realm of culture, rights to the fruit of creativity do not necessarily impinge upon rights to access knowledge (Lessig, 2004). Furthermore, rights are not commodities themselves, but rather they simply guarantee that creators may enjoy the fruit of their labour. Best practice standards in market economies are prescribed by law and regulation, but in the global cultural economy, there are no set standards for diversity and accessibility (Ryan, 1998). Nevertheless, the ideal is a marketplace for goods and services that is supported and sustained by a robust cultural commons. The cultural commons is a public realm for creative sharing, where ideas, not capital, are the primary currency of exchange.

The cultural commons is that portion of culture that remains in the public domain, in which artists, as individuals and citizens, exchange ideas and promote creativity (see again Chapter 5). The idea of the cultural commons has been popularized by the Internet. The anonymity of online interaction facilitated the growth of a libertarian social environment. The rapid growth of the social element of 'virtual reality' was no doubt fueled by the fact that real world public space is encroached upon by omnipresent property rights and aggressive corporate branding. The cultural commons exists partly in the real world of parks, museums and urban streetscapes, but it looms most vividly in our collective 'virtual' reality of unfettered libertarian and hedonistic experience and new citizen practices. As such, it embodies this generation's contradictory longing for collective identity and expectation of individual fulfillment. The boundaries of the cultural commons are constantly shifting and evolving (Drache, 2001). The 'virtual' commons has not yet acquired a formally regulated and protected institutional presence. It is an intensely conflicted space because many governments and international institutions are locked in a dichotomous discourse, unable to grasp how culture can be a commodity and tool of identity at the same time. Culture is central to social relations and building cohesive societies because it intersects with closely held social values, public perceptions and popular sovereignty (Tomlinson, 1999).

Global citizenship

Emergent citizenship practices are the fourth important feature of the global cultural economy. The concept of citizenship untied from a national context became possible with the birth of the Internet. Virtual worlds require an ethic of personal responsibility and standards of appropriate conduct no less than do nations. The notion of transnational citizenship was theorized in the 1990s as a form of cosmopolitanism (Held, 1999). Cosmopolitanism was an all-encompassing creed that denied the importance of locally rooted identities. Theorists of cosmopolitan citizenship failed to grasp the singular importance of the local for the practice of citizenship (Gowan, 2001). In the global cultural economy, the concept of citizenship is not tied to the nation-state, but it does remain rooted in a commitment to the local. And when these global/local publics speak of the Public, it means those actions, policies and practices that are shared by all members of the community and promote its general welfare (Drache, 2004). When they cheer and fight for the integrity of their community, cultural theorists argue that they establish new citizenship practices and new ideals of pluralism.

In a way that mirrors Habermas' idealized account of the global sphere of interactive communication, many theorists believe that the modern ideal of the public is shaped and affirmed through citizenship engagements which build real and virtual networks generating new knowledge and cultural practices around globalization and its potentiality. Earlier research exaggerated the determining role of corporations on consumers and audiences and overstated the passivity of consumer networks. In his influential book on Latinity, Americanness and global consumption, Nestor García Canclini's (2001) central proposition is that consumption has been transformed into 'an arena of competing claims' and 'ways of using it'. Flows of media text and critical ideas help reconstitute a social bond that has been sundered by neoliberal cultural funding cutbacks and mind-numbing appeals to consumer materialism.

Agency and structure in four cultural sectors

To understand the transformative potential of global cultural flows for northern capital and southern development, one needs a sense of their magnitude and intensity. US$1.2 trillion was spent in 2003 on various forms of advertising and entertainment around the world. Many in the global South have been struggling to come to terms with the magnitude of global cultural production (Price Waterhouse Coopers, 2004). But as Singh demonstrates (see box), Southern regional economies grouped around India, China, Mexico and Brazil have become competitors and rivals to the North's ambitious attempt to influence popular culture (Singh, 2007).

Box 3.1 Cultural industries: from national to global governance

There is both irony as well as contradiction in the international discourse about protecting 'national' cultural industries. The irony: the new salience of the national context in global measures follows decades of relative neglect by most governments. The contradiction: many countries seeking 'protection' are among the world's biggest cultural exporters. Cultural industry initiatives in international organizations are now driven forward largely by governments, with some input from civil society and industry initiatives in select cases. The UNESCO *Convention on the Protection and the Promotion of the Diversity of Cultural Expressions* affirms the right of nation-states to formulate cultural policies that promote cultural diversity. International organizations' capacity-building initiatives now target national governments or seek their support to make sure that the cultural industries are targeted. This emphasis is a new challenge to nation-states, who are now expected to engage with this issue after a long period of neglect. Most ministries of culture have hardly been powerhouses. As the issue of cultural industries becomes important globally, it boosts the importance of cultural ministries. Yet what the ministers of culture propose at UNESCO, trade ministers oppose at the WTO. The global culture wars are also national turf wars. The Uruguay Round of trade talks (1986–94) at the General Agreement on Tariffs and Trade galvanized the debate on cultural exports and this has led to the adoption and rapid entry into force of the UNESCO Convention. There are some contradictions here. While the force of the international coalition that achieved this result rested upon the feared onslaught of US cultural exports, those seeking cultural protection are themselves top cultural exporters or seek to become so. According to statistics released by UNESCO in 2005, Canada and France rank among the top ten countries in terms of international trade in cultural products. And while the share of trade for the United States and European Union has declined, that for East Asia has doubled and is increasing for developing countries as well. While UNESCO statistics might well underestimate the scope of US exports by counting customs data and not royalty receipts, the undercounting issue goes beyond the United States in significant ways. For example, these statistics ignore related activities such as information technology, advertising, and architectural services, many of which are now outsourced to developing countries. Similarly, emerging centers of film and television production in Argentina, Brazil, Mexico, Egypt, West Africa, South Africa, India and China are also underestimated. Lastly, if cultural tourism receipts are included, the total 'exports' of those seeking cultural protections rises even more. According to the World Tourism Organization, France tops international tourist arrivals, accounting for 75 million of the 763 million total in 2002.

International efforts to raise the stature of cultural industries politicize this issue in territorial national identity terms. It is not clear how the nation-state, which has a rather patriarchal presence in international relations, can co-exist with or boost cultural and creative industries that thrive on hybridity and extra-territoriality. Hopefully, as more discursive spaces open up for this issue, international rule-making will feature hard deliberation and find a balance between creative expression, cultural identities, and patriarchal nation-states.

J.P. Singh

The following four short sector studies attempt to give some perspective on the complex dynamics between markets, regulatory institutions, norms, and new citizenship practices. Two billion people watch Latin American *telenovelas* (soap operas) and the same number are fans of Indian films. Satellite television and digital video recorders have facilitated this Innisian reallocation of power from the center towards the margins of the political world. The growth of the global communications network has been unprecedented. The combined coverage of broadcast and satellite television, radio and cellular telephones includes approximately 70 per cent of the world's population (Drache et al., 2004). In his pioneering studies, Hall showed that publics are not passive and disinterested spectators. Interpreting text requires engagement and discernment (Hall, 1995). Audiences have become more informed, more focused, and unpredictable as they consume cultural products in increasing amounts.

Film production and distribution

Film is the icon of cultural globalization and one of the dominant contemporary cultural flows. In the USA, the creative industries are central to international trade. The export of movies, TV, music, books and software generates more international revenue than any other single sector, including agriculture, aircraft and automobiles. Further, 'among such drivers of the economy, only the film industry has a positive balance of trade with every country in the world'. In every national jurisdiction, the USA sells more of its foremost cultural product than it buys – an outstanding feat for an industry characterized by such high levels of value added. US movies are distributed in more than 150 countries, a broader market than even the lucrative television market. However, only a fraction of film revenues are taken at the ticket counter.

Most revenues come from overseas distribution and the international markets for releases of films on DVD. The global market for film is worth approximately US$75 billion annually and accounts for almost 10 per cent of the global entertainment sector. The market for television is almost twice as large and, while it is widely acknowledged that Hollywood makes tremendous profits from overseas markets, rival centers of production are flourishing (Pendakur, 2003).

India's 'Bollywood', film production in China, the animation industry in Japan and television production in Mexico, Venezuela and Brazil, where the telenovela enjoys unrivalled popularity, are only a few examples of these competitors. In terms of number of releases, the Mumbai film industry is the largest in the world, releasing more than 1000 films in 2002. On average, no fewer than 900 films are produced annually in India (UK Film Council, 2002). Few experts have stressed this Southern aspect of the picture. The global South is developing rival centers of cultural production in many regions, in ways that nobody could have foreseen even a few decades ago (Canclini, 2001).

Grant and Wood (2004) describe how, when traditional market models are applied to trade in culture, the phenomenon of the film 'blockbuster' often chokes creativity and ultimately starves the market of diverse cultural products. Media companies often bet on the cultural product that seems most likely to sell most quickly, such as blockbuster movies and pop music hits. In the free trade model, producers profit from economies of scale at home and reap massive gains from culture markets abroad. This is the thinking that currently dominates global trade. The goal is to create a virtuous circle between local production, global distribution and the cosmopolitan consumer – an integrated, global commodity chain for culture. For its part, the WTO is a 'dealmaker', creating linkages between copyright protection, market consolidation and corporate expansion. This is accomplished through binding dispute settlement, a much more effective mechanism than old fashioned diplomacy (Weiler, 2000).

Television production and broadcasting

Television is perhaps the most ubiquitous of global cultural products. More people watch television than use any other medium (except radio) (ITU, 2002). New communications technologies are dwarfed in comparison. There are more television sets than people in every part of the world except Africa, where, by recent estimates, there is one for every two people. In the Group of Eight (G8) countries, by comparison, there exist approximately five sets for every person (Drache et al., 2004). While US television is seen in fewer countries than film, it is more profitable, according to the latest research by PriceWaterhouseCoopers.

With television so pervasive, global spending on cable television, new digital cable subscriptions, satellite TV, and pay-per-view movies exceeds US$140 billion per year. Further, the amount spent on television advertising adds another US$120 billion to an already lucrative market. In terms of audience, television remains unrivalled, far outpacing newspapers and the

Internet as the foremost choice for news and entertainment around the world. It is estimated that spending on cable and satellite television will continue to grow at a healthy 7 per cent for the foreseeable future (PriceWaterhouseCoopers, 2004).

Copyrights for television content have been a particular concern for big media companies, as the technology to create high-quality copies for broadcast is widely available. The biggest challenge to property rights for television content comes from small television stations that broadcast without paying associated licensing fees. Part III of the TRIPs agreement, which deals with the enforcement of intellectual property rights, has been an issue in Greece, for example, where US television programming is regularly used without the consent of copyright holders. This sort of theft is often cited as the main reason to tighten national copyright laws, despite the fact that most US cable companies were launched with the re-broadcasting of network programes, which were essentially pirated from NBC, ABC and CBS (Lessig, 2004).

In the history of intellectual property law, there have always been turning points where rights could have been interpreted narrowly by judges and law makers. One such fork in the road occurred in the first half of the twentieth century, when US courts determined that the public good of free culture outweighed the negative externalities for private economic actors. The history of copyright law shows that there are negative consequences to constraining new technologies and ring-fencing small cultural producers because of the threat posed to intellectual property rights. Lawrence Lessig (2004) describes how early producers of film, cable television and radio used pirated content to great commercial success and how their actions were upheld by the US Supreme Court. Cultural creativity is a dynamic process that relies upon an ethic of public sharing. 'The law should regulate in certain areas of culture – but it should regulate culture only where that regulation does good' (Lessig, 2004: 305). Locking up culture in the private sphere of commerce stifles the creative spirit upon which private actors draw in order to create and sell their product.[5]

Books, magazines and newspaper publishing

Books, magazines and newspapers account for almost US$150 billion of annual consumer spending.

As an important set of cultural products, the majority of books are sold in the global North, but Southern markets for newspapers are massive. Cheap newspapers are the primary means of conveying ideas in the mega-cities of the global South such as Rio de Janeiro, New Delhi, Jakarta and Shanghai. The worldwide market for newspapers, both in sales and advertising, was worth US$56 billion in 2003. In every major city across Latin America, Asia and India, there are dozens of daily newspapers in local languages and these are a key venue for advertisers of local goods and services. Print industries are still expanding at a combined average of almost 2 per cent annually, making them attractive for local producers who can find a market niche.

Magazines and newspapers are building blocks for national culture and as such are closely protected by governments. Many governments in both the developed and developing worlds indirectly support publishing through many different kinds of subsidies.[6] The most important cultural protection dispute to date at the WTO involved US magazines sold in Canada. While magazines do not have the profile of audiovisual products, the Internet has revolutionized the publishing process. When a US publisher used the Internet to circumvent Canadian law banning the importation of split-run periodicals — that is, special issues containing advertisements primarily directed at the Canadian market but replicating the editorial content of a foreign issue — the Canadian government imposed a massive excise tax and the USA issued a legal challenge (Canada, 1996).

Article III of the General Agreement on Tariffs and Trade (GATT) states that a country must treat imports in the same way that it treats domestically produced products. The USA argued that Canada's magazine regime unfairly discriminated against imported products (US split-run magazines). The Canadian government responded by declaring that its magazine regime was needed to protect Canadian culture and therefore legal under GATT Article XX, which allows for the protection of public morals, public health and works of artistic or historic value. It argued that Canadian magazines cannot be directly compared to US magazines on the basis of their physical form alone (the dispute settlement panel compared two news magazines, *Time* and *Maclean's*, in terms of size, number of pages and type of paper used). However, physical characteristics are never definitive when comparing cultural products. Canadian magazines carry content important to Canadians; their significance to maintaining Canada's cultural distinctiveness must also be considered (Schwanen, 2001).

The important issue for Canada and the EU, which saw this dispute as an important test case, was whether one was domestically owned and carried domestic news. The panel disagreed, saying that the relative distinctions for the basis of trade are physical — what kind of magazines were these? Are they similar products? The panel's decision stressed that market share should be decided by free competition and not by cultural policy advocacy. Policy experts consider this to be one of the most significant disputes so far because it highlights the institutional incapacity of the WTO to break free from narrow and deterministic legal thinking.[7] Nevertheless, cultural communities see the issue in terms of cultural intangibles, not legal principles such as standard of review or most favored nation. Because freedom of expression is a core value that reflects the plural and diverse experience of many societies, it cannot be treated as a commodity, stripped of its social and creative contexts. WTO jurisprudence does exactly this in most cases. To the policy community, this decision sent a clear signal that the WTO lagged far behind other networks and institutions when it came to thinking about the cultural economy.

The Internet and online connectivity

As the newest form of communication since the introduction of television, the Internet is expected to grow extremely rapidly. But the heyday of the 1990s, when everything was available for free on the Internet, is largely over. User fees and subscriptions have replaced public access. Advertising is a huge source of revenue for most sites with high volumes of 'traffic'. Already a sector with an annual turn-over of $100 billion, combined global spending on Internet access and online advertising is expected to continue its growth spurt of 17 per cent annually into the next decade. Internet growth has been fastest in the North. In G8 countries, the number of people using the Internet exploded from 7.3 million in 1993, to 297 million in 2001. Similarly, in the G20, the number of Internet users rose from 430,000 people in 1993, to more than 25 million in 2001. As of 2005, a billion people are online.

India and China are quickly closing the gap. During the same period, use in Asia grew from 14 million to 74.1 million people. In Africa, where telephone landlines are often a luxury, the proliferation of digital technology has faced obstacles associated with lack of infrastructure. Third generation wireless Internet technology has been slow to penetrate and cheap modems must contend with unreliable phone lines. Nevertheless, Internet usage blossomed from approximately 40,000 people to an estimated 4.25 million in the 1990s and, with the advent of the notebook computer costing US$100, growth undoubtedly will accelerate (Drache et al., 2004). The digital divide in Africa is slowly shrinking, even as HIV/AIDS and crushing poverty ravage the continent (Freedman and Poku, 2005).

Broadband is the next generation of digital communication technology revolutionizing the online experience (Morrison, 2004). Television, movies and even phone calls are now available through a broadband connection. In 2003, China had twice as many broadband Internet subscribers as Canada – 8.6 million to Canada's 3.9 million. The USA leads with almost 22 million broadband subscriptions. However, nowhere in the world has broadband made faster inroads than in Korea, where 70 per cent of all households are connected by broadband. In North America and Europe, price is still a key factor in broadening and deepening diffusion. As prices are expected to fall in the next five years, consumer research groups estimate that the current global market of 100 million broadband subscribers will grow to more than 300 million (Morrison, 2004). Double-digit growth in broadband is projected to continue until 2010, if not longer (PriceWaterhouseCoopers, 2004).

The appeal of broadband for vertically integrated corporations is in the ability to bundle different products and services, which are usually sold separately. The media giants view it as the next technological frontier, with limitless profitability; this is the motor behind many of the new mergers and acquisitions occurring across Europe and North America. Broadband Internet will deliver movies, television and telephone services – all in addition to standard Internet services. Competing in broadband technology requires significant financial reserves, an established market presence, and a ready source of cultural content (Lessig, 2004). Technology makes this bundling possible, but the WTO's expansion of market access and promise of economies of scale makes this opportunity too important to pass up for media giants hungry for the efficiencies found in market consolidation. In the battle for cultural dominance, the media corporations have won the first round.

Global cultural flows: the normative dimension of interactive communication

Global cultural flows are intense transnational movements of people, media, texts and ideas that are disjunctive to financial flows and have unpredictable streaming effects on diasporic communities and cultural diversity. They give rise to agenda-setting publics with new authority structures that are highly normative. Many countries, such as the United States, Canada, Germany, Japan and India, effectively use global markets to produce and promote culture. However, most of the world does not have the resources to sustain the economies of scale required to compete on equal terms with Time Warner. Nevertheless, tourism, entertainment production, art and other forms of media are vital to the gross national product (GNP) of all countries.

Cultural trade in these industries is a significant portion of GNP in Western European, North American and the highly developed Asian economies. 'States are now moving toward either prioritizing cultural industries as a whole at the forefront of their development efforts or singling out priority sectors' (Singh, 2007). For developing countries heavily reliant on international trade, trade in cultural goods has become an important factor in economic development strategies (UNESCO, 2000).

Culture flows as broadly and deeply as it does today because more people can read now than at any other time in the past. Few experts have confronted the transformative potential of the rise in literacy worldwide. According to Emmanuel Todd (2003: 27), this may be the most significant trend of our times, transforming the poorest states from 'least developed' to 'developing' nations, and at the same time raising social, political and economic expectations in the global South. The growth of civil society and social movements, even in traditional societies, has been accelerated by rising educational standards and media literacy. With so many new political actors, the information age has moved from rhetoric to reality. All too frequently, a narrow economic focus

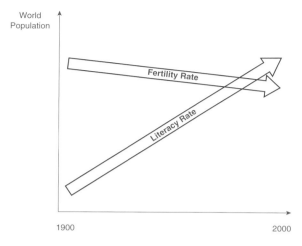

Figure 3.1   The demography of cultural identity

on globalization misses the transformative effects of technology, liberalization and new forms of public administration (Held et al., 1999).

Developing skills for the cultural economy requires raising literacy rates with a greater investment in education – an area of primary importance for developing nations. As literacy levels rise, cultural policy becomes part of a strategy for social cohesion and inclusion. Over the past 20 years, fertility rates have fallen in almost every country across the globe (Todd, 2003). As societies redefine gender roles, corresponding values, rules, institutions and family practices are transformed in new ways. Identity becomes a strategic resource to facilitate the active participation of both genders in the public life of Southern societies. Having soared in the past 20 years, literacy rates are closely associated with this process. Even in such places as Afghanistan, torn by poverty, civil war and violent religious oppression, literacy rates have more than doubled (from 18 to 47 per cent; Todd, 2003: 23).

US cultural industries and the US State Department have found themselves increasingly on the defensive. The US-backed corporate agenda for global free trade in culture consists of a single ambitious goal – bigger national markets for American cultural products. Growing the market requires convincing consumers to spend more. US consumers spend the most, accounting for at least 35 cents of every dollar spent on media and entertainment worldwide, and are willing to spend larger portions of

their wages for entertainment (PriceWaterhouse Coopers, 2004). Capitalizing on this demand is of first-order importance. Concentration of ownership in the Anglo-American market is a natural outgrowth of this drive to capture the lucrative home audience. Media conglomerates eye the global South as the next logical frontier. China and India are especially important to this strategy because of their emerging middle class, not to mention the fact that these two domestic markets account for a third of the world's population. The aim is to consolidate international markets with a focus on the global South. Expansion in the South is less predictable and profits are less assured than many companies assumed when they began forays into Asia and post-communist Eastern Europe in the 1990s.

In a world dominated by global cultural flows, states often equate protection of identity with their continued political viability. Culture flows often produce disjunctive outcomes for producers who are not part of the Anglo-American circuit for English-speaking culture. If we were to map global cultural flows, three features predominate – the sheer commercial intensity of media and entertainment, the asymmetrical movement of people and capital, and a dualistic tension between the commercial and private and the popular and public. As a result, regulating the political economy of culture presents new opportunities and risks for international policy makers.

Three policy strategies for regulating global cultural flows

Governments play a critical role in developing the global cultural commons and channeling the flow of culture across national boundaries. Paradoxically, the global cultural commons is rooted in national cultural policies and local citizenship practices. As cultural goods production has increased in economic importance, Canada, the USA and the EU have developed contrasting and competing views on the role of the state in cultural protection and promotion. The EU looks to build linkages and networks between state regulatory policy, Brussels and cultural producers (Burt, 2005). This tripartite approach is difficult at the best of times, but has been quite effective nonetheless. The EU is linguistically and socially diverse and its internal stability depends upon a pluralistic approach to the global commons. It regards freedom of expression as important to protect as part of its commitment to the social market. The EU is very proactive at the supranational level and recognizes that culture is a public good to be nurtured, much like the environment, for its 450 million citizens.

The Anglo-American model is sharply contrasting in its regulatory and market dimensions. It should be noted that, despite the fact that Britain is a member of the EU, its elites share many ideas with their US counterparts. Simply put, this model views diversity as a function of competition and not the other way round. Consumers choose their cultural diet from a buffet of options. Just like many buffets, portion size is more important than quality and breadth of choice. The Anglo-American model requires super-size profits and relies on regulators to create an environment conducive to corporate growth. US media conglomerates are aggressively promoting the US State Department's objectives to broaden copyright law and deepen trade liberalization. In contrast, policy-makers in the EU understand that the culture/trade interface cannot be one-dimensional and trade must accommodate diversity (EU, 2003).

The model that Canada has pioneered is one of public–private partnerships with a large role for public broadcasters and an even larger role for private actors. The result is a 70/30 mix with public institutions and broadcasters not as well funded as their European counterparts, but offering Canadians a more robust public alternative than is available in the United States. The model is held together through a program of public advocacy and accountability that often promises more than it delivers (Grant and Wood, 2004). Nevertheless, it has been a prominent nation-building strategy and is still broadly supported by all of Canada's diverse regions. It has declined in the past decade, as a result of the federal government's obsession with fiscal austerity. Yet it remains an important feature of Canada's institutional superstructure. Its selling point for the global South is that it protects social diversity while promoting market competition.

This hybrid works for proactive national standards while emphasizing the linkages between domestic cultural producers and transnational cultural and economic actors (Zemans, 2004). One result is that Japan and Germany, not the most obvious markets for Canadian literature and television, are two of the largest consumers of Canadian cultural products in the world. The ubiquitous *Anne of Green Gables* series of books and television programs set in Prince Edward Island are extremely popular in Japan (Allard, 2002). Canadian literary icon Margaret Atwood has a significant following in Germany.

Canada is open to forming alliances with multicultural countries and others in the global South that are skeptical about the willingness of US entertainment industries to use their dominant market position for good.[8] Under WTO governance, trade in cultural goods has accelerated and many local industries have been swamped by US cultural imports. They face new dangers such as corporate concentration of ownership in the cultural industries and the growing dominance of English language entertainment. These challenges have highlighted the corresponding need to safeguard language rights and defend local cultures from predatory trade practices.

The worldwide interest in cultural policy has become one of the new frames for our age. The Canadian magazine *Adbusters* has posted an online Media Carta for individuals to sign, demanding that the right to communicate, including the right for citizens and civil society to buy radio and television airtime under the same rules and conditions as advertising agencies, be enshrined in the Universal Declaration on Human Rights.[9] New ideas about the importance of culture to human freedom and social empowerment have created a dialogue between policy-makers and global publics on the future of cultural diversity in an age of free trade.

Of course, the UNESCO cultural diversity Convention, referred to earlier, is soft law at best, and with no enforcement teeth. Furthermore, it is easy to sign on to an international instrument that promises to buttress state authority in an era when it seems that the legal authority of states is increasingly under challenge. Only time will tell if this interest in cultural pluralism on the part of many countries will balance the asymmetries of present day cultural flows. The fact that there is no single template buttresses continued diversity across contrasting jurisdictions and has become an important constraint on dominant industrial players attempting to impose their vision for regulatory harmonization.

Conclusion: Innisian dissent and the public sphere of interactive communication

New information technologies have made possible the organization of many different kinds of public forums for dissent and political action at the global level. Although it has taken the better part of a decade to get up and running, it is now almost impossible to turn off the global dissenting public's attention-getting activism because so many issues from the environment to the growth in global poverty are linked to the World Trade Organization and its impact on public policy. The recent past underscores the fact that there are many connections between cultural flows that make powerful new claims on the real and symbolic economy – the images, lifestyles and ethnicities – of Innisian dissent. What is the magnitude of these flows? What causes them to surge? Structurally, why are global cultural flows frequent competitors and rivals to global financial flows? For now and into the future, what kinds of institutional pressures are driving global dissent? Where are we in the dissent cycle? Still on the upswing, entering the long plateau, or heading toward the inevitable downturn?[10]

A vast public has been connected in ways that no one could have predicted even a decade ago. More people are informed today about trade politics, environmentalism and social justice than at any other time in the past. Significantly, the lag effects between the awareness and the ability to create a new world of structures, organizations and stable social forms are smaller than a decade ago, but are still demonstrably large. One important development is that today news flows from diverse sources. CNN, Al Jazeera, BBC World and TV5 reach over the heads of the anti-globalization movement and governments to audiences worldwide. Furthermore, new forms of digital dissent are supplementing and perhaps even displacing public protest of the sort that defined the uprisings of 1968. Now, one does not have to wave a placard to be a dissenter. In fact, blogs, MySpace, FaceBook and YouTube are potent tools for expression and dissent with transformative potential for their users.

What is remarkable is that this recent upsurge in interest and public attention has not followed the predictable path that Anthony Downs (1972) wrote about so persuasively, in the early 70s, in his seminal article on the 'issue attention cycle'. Downs explained that with most public issues the 'problem suddenly leaps into prominence', rivets the public's attention and then fades from view, largely unresolved. Downs' theory predicted that consumers of information get bored with big issues such as the environment and governance. Today's global public possesses a longer attention span, which has been revealed to be more committed and less fickle than Downs erroneously predicted.

The reallocation of power that comes with technological change is not a new phenomenon. The industrial revolution brought with it a series of transformative social changes that culminated in the revolutions of 1848. Similarly, scientific revolutions of the twentieth century, including the invention of the birth control pill, fundamentally reorganized the power dynamics of society, freeing women from patriarchal reproductive dynamics and fueling the dissent movement of 1968. Today, the digital communications revolution is also changing the social landscape, with the power to free millions of people from the marginalization that comes from having no voice in global affairs. These three major transfers of power, from market to state, from men to women, and from transnational elites to the global citizen, share a common theme. They have been the great levelers of class relations and have redefined the relationship between agency and structure. None of this has occurred in the way that Marxians had hoped for. Nor has this practice conformed to Hayekian theology, according to which markets operate seamlessly in response to the invariable laws of supply and demand.

This chapter has argued that the agency and voice facilitated by Innisian power dynamics play a crucial role in broadening and deepening cultural flows. In turn, these have fueled new citizenship practices. The democratization of political voice gives global publics the power to change state policy in fundamental ways. Habermas' idea was that citizens can change state policy through acts of assembly. Before the Internet era, he thought that this had to happen through face-to-face interaction. Today, digital technology has facilitated this process in a radical and decentralized way, and communities of unprecedented influence and reach are formed online. The Washington Consensus prioritized system and structure as the key drivers of public policy; Internet, satellite communications, cellular phones, text messaging and even radio and television have turned conventional wisdom on its head. The global cultural economy is instrumental in shaping the fully realized citizen, rooted in the local, but deeply interested in, and able to influence, global issues and events by forming active communities of choice rather disinterested communities of fate.

Notes

1   For a particularly pessimistic view of the ways that structure and system are empowered by new information technologies, see Henning Ziegler (2004).
2   Cell phone manufacturers have begun to cater to Southern consumers, producing handsets for the Muslim world that point in the direction of Mecca and ring the user at prayer time. Mobile providers in India offer services for the Hindu on the go. For a nominal charge, the user can send a prayer over the wireless network, to the appropriate temple. Culture plays an important role in the evolution of technology in different regions (Srivastava, 2004).
3   For a contrarian view see Johnson (2005).
4   For complete texts of WTO agreements see www.wto.org.
5   The US Supreme Court upheld the rights of music companies and cracked down on file-sharing software. Nevertheless, efforts to curb losses were not expected to heal the wound dealt by digital piracy until the end of the 2006 fiscal year. Music publishing is becoming more competitive, as market leaders try to develop and market more effectively their catalogues of music. Apple Computers is the prime example – the iTunes and iPod divisions now account for the bulk of Apple profits, proving to be even more popular than the ubiquitous Macintosh computer. There are profits to be made at the margins by uncoupling music publishing from recording in order to focus on development of markets for existing

work – from bulk sales to radio stations to television commercials, movie soundtracks and even toys. The revenues from these markets are vast and multinationals are moving quickly to exploit the full economic potential of existing copyrights.
6   For example, in France, newspapers are tightly regulated and generously subsidized by the government, to the extent that reporters on assignment receive half-price fares on French railways.
7   Since the GATT came into force in 1947, Article XX has never been successfully used to defend culture. What is most troubling is that WTO agreements contain no effective solution to the problem of public goods in commercial trade. Furthermore, countries attempting to protect culture will be punished in litigation.
8   The International Network for Cultural Policy has been Canada's most critical contribution in this vein. It has become the policy portal for trade and cultural policy ministers across OECD and developing countries (see www.incp-ripc.org). Beside the INCP, cultural activists from the global North and South have created the International Network for Cultural Diversity (INCD) in order to build a popular, non-governmental constituency around many of the key issues being addressed by INCP ministers. There was a vacuum at the global level and these networks of activists and policy experts have begun to fill it, a striking example of an incipient global civil society movement that has concrete policy influence.
9   See www.mediacarta.org.
10   International civil society has acquired legs that were scarcely present a decade earlier. It is not insignificant that according to the most reliable estimates, the NGO global public, an omnibus of groups, civic organizations and coalitions numbering in the ten of thousands, mobilized 25 million people worldwide to march early in 2003, weeks before the US invaded Iraq. Global protests like this one, and many others that are not in the public eye, have taken the dissent movement to new levels of intensity.

REFERENCES

Achbar, Mark (Director) and Abbott, Jennifer (Co-director) (2004) *The Corporation* [Motion picture]. Canada: Big Picture Media Corporation.

Allard, Daniele (2002) 'Taishu Bunka and Anne Clubs in Japan', in Irene Gammel (ed.) *Making Avonlea: L.M. Montgomery and Popular Culture*. Toronto: University of Toronto Press pp. 295–309.

Anderson, Benedict (1991) *Imagined Communities: Reflections on the Origins and Spread of Nationalism*. London/New York: Verso.

Appadurai, Arjun (1996) *Modernity at Large: Cultural Dimensions of Globalization*. Minneapolis: University of Minnesota Press.

Appadurai, Arjun (2001) 'Grassroots Globalization and the Research Imagination', in Arjun Appadurai (ed.) *Globalization*. Durham and London: Duke University Press.

Barber, Benjamin R. (1995) *Jihad vs. McWorld: How Globalism and Tribalism are Reshaping the World*. New York: Ballantine Books.

Barney, David Darin (2000) *Prometheus Wired: The Hope for Democracy in the Age of Network Technology*. Chicago: University of Chicago Press.

Boyle, James (2003) 'Forward: The Opposite of Property', *Law and Contemporary Problems*, 66(1/2).

Burt, Tim (2005) 'Quotas Fail to Save European Producers from an Influx of US Television Shows', *Financial Times of London*, 27 May.

Canada (1996) *Certain Measures Concerning Periodicals*. WT/DS31.

Canclini, Nestor García (2001) *Consumers and Citizens: Globalization and Multicultural Conflicts*. Minneapolis and London: University of Minnesota Press.

Caves, R. (2000) Creative Industries: Contracts between Art and Commerce. Harvard: Harvard University Press.

Downing, John D.H. (2001) *Radical Media: Rebellious Communication and Social Movements*. London: SAGE Publications.

Downs, Anthony (1972) 'Up and Down with Ecology: The Issue-Attention Cycle', *Public Interest*, 28: 38–50.

Drache, Daniel (ed.) (2001) *The Market or the Public Domain: Global Governance and the Asymmetry of Power*. London: Routledge.

Drache, Daniel (2004) 'The Political Economy of Dissent: Global Publics After Cancun'. Retrieved 13 July 2007 from http://www.yorku.ca/robarts/projects/global/ papers/gcf_globalpublicscancun.pdf.

Drache, Daniel and Clifton, David (2006) *The Shrinking Digital Divide: An Empirical and Comparative Analysis of New Information Technology Diffusion of Trends in the Global North and South*. Unpublished report, Robarts Centre for Canadian Studies, York University.

Drache, Daniel, and Froese, Marc D. (2006) 'Globalization and the Cultural Commons: Identity, Citizenship and Pluralism after Cancun', *New Political Economy*, 11(6).

Drache, D., Morra, M. and Froese, M.D. (2004) 'Global Cultural Flows and the Technological Information Grid: An Empirical Examination'. Retrieved www.yorku.ca/drache.

EU (European Union) (2003) 'The Emergence of Collective Preferences in International Trade'. (Internal Memo). Brussels: EU.

Freedman, Des (2002) 'Trade Versus Culture: An Evaluation of the Impacts of Current GATS Negotiations on Audio-Visual Industries'. Retrieved from www.isanet.org/noarchive/freedman.html.

Freedman, Janet and Poku, Nana (2005) 'The Socioeconomic Context of Africa's Vulnerability to HIV/Aids', *Review of International Studies*, 31(4): 665–86.

Gowan, Peter (2001) 'Neoliberal Cosmopolitanism', *New Left Review Second Series*, 11: 79–93.

Grant, Peter S. and Wood, Chris (2004) *Blockbusters and Trade Wars: Popular Culture in a Globalized World*. Toronto: Douglas and McIntyre.

Habermas, Jurgen (1989) *The Structural Transformation of the Public Sphere: An Inquiry into a Category of Bourgeois Society*. Cambridge: Polity Press.

Habermas, Jurgen (2001) *On the Pragmatics of Social Interaction: Preliminary Studies in the Theory of Communicative Action*. Cambridge Mass.: MIT Press.

Hall, Stuart (1995) 'The West and the Rest: Discourse and Power', in D. Held, S. Hall, D. Hubert and K. Thompson (eds.) *Modernity: An Introduction to Modern Societies*. Cambridge: Blackwell pp. 184–227.

Held, David (1999) 'The Transformation of Political Community: Rethinking Democracy in the Context of Globalization', in I. Shapiro and C. Hacker-Cordon (eds.) *Democracy's Edges*. Cambridge: Cambridge University Press. pp. 84–111.

Held, D., McGrew, A., Goldblatt, D. and Perraton, J. (1999) *Global Transformations: Politics, Economics and Culture*. Stanford, CA: Stanford University Press.

Innis, Harold A. (1951) *The Bias of Communication*. Toronto: University of Toronto Press.

Innis, Harold A. (2007) *Empire and Communications* (Voyageur Classics). Toronto: Dundurn Press.

(International Telecommunications Union) (2002) *ITU Strategy and Policy Unit News Update: Policy and Strategy Trends*. Retrieved from www.itu.int/osg/spu/spunews/2002/jul-sep/jul-septrends.html.

Johnson, Steven (2005) *Everything Bad is Good for You: How Today's Popular Culture is Actually Making Us Smarter*. New York: Riverhead Books.

Kantor, Mickey (2004) 'Film Pirates are Robbing Us All', *Financial Times of London*. 18 March.

Klein, Naomi (2000) *No Logo: Taking Aim at the Brand Bullies*. Toronto: Knopf Canada.

Lessig, Lawrence (2004) *Free Culture: How Big Media Uses Technology and the Law to Lock Down Culture and Control Creativity*. New York: The Penguin Press.

McLuhan, Marshall (1964) *Understanding Media: The Extensions of Man*. New York: New American Library.

Mercurio, Bryan C. (2004) 'TRIPS, Patents, and Access to Life Saving Drugs in the Developing World', *Marquette Intellectual Property Law Review*, 8(2): 211–50.

Morrison, Scott (2004) 'Triple Play Shows the Way', *Financial Times of London*. 20 July.

Paquet, Gilles (2005) 'Governance of Culture: Words of Caution', in C. Andrew, M. Gattinger, M.S. Jeannotte and W. Straw (eds.) *Accounting for Culture: Thinking through Cultural Citizenship*. Ottawa: University of Ottawa Press.

Pendakur, Manjunath (2003) *Indian Popular Cinema: Industry, Ideology and Consciousness*. New Jersey: Hampton Press.

PriceWaterhouseCoopers (2004) *Global Media and Entertainment Outlook: 2004–2008*. Retrieved from http://www.pwc.com.

Ryan, Michael P. (1998) *Knowledge Diplomacy: Global Competition and the Politics of Intellectual Property*. Washington, D.C.: The Brookings Institute Press.

Schwanen, Daniel (2001) 'A Room of Our Own: Cultural Policies and Trade Agreements', *Choices*, 7(4), April.

Shaviro, Steven (2003) *Connected, or What it Means to Live in the Network Society, Electronic Mediations*. Minneapolis: University of Minnesota Press.

Singh, J.P. (2007) 'Culture or Commerce? A Comparative Assessment of International Interactions and Developing Countries at UNESCO, WTO and Beyond', *International Studies Perspective*, 8(1): 36–53.

Srivastava, Lara (2004) 'Social and Human Considerations for a more Mobile World', Paper presented at ITU/MIC Workshop on Shaping the Future Mobile Information Society, Seoul, South Korea.

Stanley, Dick (2005) 'The Three Faces of Culture: Why Culture is a Strategic Good Requiring Policy Attention,' in C. Andrew, M. Gattinger, M.S. Jeannotte and W. Straw (eds.) *Accounting for Culture: Thinking through Cultural Citizenship*. Ottawa: University of Ottawa Press.

Stiglitz, Joseph E. and Charlton, Andrew (2004) 'The Development Round of Trade Negotiations in the Aftermath of Cancun: A Report for the Commonwealth Secretariat', New York: Initiative for Policy Dialogue, Columbia University.

Summers, Clyde (2001) 'The Battle in Seattle: Free Trade, Labour Rights, and Societal Values', *University of Pennsylvania Journal of International Economic Law*, 22(1): 61–90.

Todd, Emmanuel (2003) *After the Empire: The Breakdown of American Order*. New York: Columbia University Press.

Throsby, David (2001) *Economics and Culture*. Cambridge: Cambridge University Press.

Tomlinson, John (1999) *Globalization and Change*. Chicago: University of Chicago Press.

UK Film Council (2002) 'The Indian Media and Entertainment Industry', Retrieved 15 October 2004 from www.ukfilmcouncil.org.uk/filmindustry/india/.

UNESCO (2000) 'World Culture Report 2000: Cultural Diversity, Conflict and Pluralism', Paris: United Nations Educational, Scientific and Cultural Organization.

Weiler, J.H.H. (2000, September) 'The Rule of Lawyers and the Ethos of Diplomats: Reflections on the Internal and External Legitimacy of WTO Dispute Settlement', Paper presented at The Jean Monnet Seminar and Workshop on the European Union, NAFTA, and the WTO: Advanced Issues in Law and Policy, Harvard Law School, Cambridge Mass.

Yardley, Jim (2005) 'A Hundred Cellphones Bloom, and Chinese Take to the Streets', *New York Times*. 25 April.

Zemans, Joyce (2004) 'Advancing Cultural Diversity Globally: The Role of Civil Society Movements'. Paper presented at Global Flows, Dissent and Diversity: The New Agenda Conference, York University, Toronto.

Ziegler, Henning (2004) 'Dissent on the Net: Cultures of Electronic Resistance in the United States', *Journal of Hyper(+)drome Manifestation 1*. Retrieved 16 July 2007 from http://journal.hypodrome.net/issues/issue1/ziegler.html.

## CHAPTER 4

STRANGE BEDFELLOWS: LAW AND CULTURE IN THE DIGITAL AGE
Mira T. Sundara Rajan

Among the many changes brought about by globalizing new technologies, the altered relationship between law and culture is among the most significant. Technological developments have generated an entirely novel framework for the interaction of legal principles with cultural movements, signifying both opportunities and challenges for the world of culture. This chapter assesses the impact of law on culture in this new environment. It argues that a new approach to cultural policy is essential for the preservation and encouragement of culture in a technological age. Above all, the cultural law of the future should not fail to consider the human and moral interests implicated in creativity.

Introduction

We live in the era of globalization; it is our catchword. The simplicity of the term is deceptive. Over the years, the efforts of scholars, thinkers, and the media have brought us no closer to a precise definition.[1] Yet its intuitive appeal is undeniable, and we turn to it again and again in order to describe our experience of life in the twenty-first century. It is perhaps most effective, finally, to consider it in metaphorical terms – it is the perfume that imbues the air of our times. Whether or not we can define it, everyone seems to know what it is, its workings are common knowledge, and its essence pervades everything that we do.

On closer examination, at least one thing can be said with certainty about globalization: it is fundamentally a technological phenomenon, driven by information and communications technology. This seems like a narrow and specialized characteristic, so it is especially interesting to observe the vast range of social implications that follow from technology. Change is comprehensive. No sphere of human existence remains untouched by the flavour, or taint, of globalization. No country, culture, group or individual can remain truly untouched. Culture is no exception to this rule. In itself, the idea that culture has a global dimension is not necessarily new. Historical and archeological studies have shown that cultural exchange, in one form or another, has been a reality of human existence since time immemorial.[2] In a sense, ancient man was even more engaged in cultural transformation than we are. He approached culture through aggression and violence, yet ancient societies were keen to discover the improvements offered by cultures with knowledge that was new and different from their own. Countless innovations and products found their way to the Western world through such historical movements, examples ranging from the wars of ancient Greece and Rome, to the enrichment of Western culture with knowledge from the Middle East during the Crusades.

Based on historical experience, we have an intuitive sense for this historical process; this gradual 'cultural globalization' that is now accelerating rapidly. Yet, we can also see that there is something different about the current process of global exchange. As in other areas of globalization, we are at pains to provide a precise description of what is happening. In the realm of culture, though, this lack of clarity is a serious and troubling problem. This chapter argues that cultural globalization, unfortunately, does not refer to mere cultural exchange as it occurred in the past. On the contrary, the marrying of culture with globalization signifies something much larger: the economic dimension that technology has brought to culture. The link between cultural exchange and global economics, although it may well build on an established tradition, represents something completely new, and characteristic of the 'digital age'. It is made possible through the mechanism of intellectual property rights and, in particular, copyright law.[3]

This understanding is crucial to developing a critical appreciation of the process we call cultural globalization. It is often said by intellectual property experts that without international copyright law, there would be no global cultural exchange, or that global cultural opportunities would be significantly reduced. However, this conclusion is far from self-evident. It is true that copyright makes it possible for culture to play a global economic role, but it should also be recognized that copyright law presents obstacles to knowledge that may seriously endanger cultural exchange.

It does so in a number of ways – by imposing terms on access to knowledge, by valuing certain kinds of knowledge over others, and by promoting certain cultural models at the expense of others. Global cultural exchange in a peaceful context – and indeed, in the cause of peace – is probably one of humanity's great opportunities in the coming century. For this reason, copyright policy has an important contribution to make to humanity's future, by helping us to recognize the value of cultural exchange, including the implied need for diversity, and protecting our ability to engage in it.

This study describes how copyright law has transformed culture into an economic phenomenon in the 'digital age'. It analyses the implications of this transformation for society, and seeks to identify both the creative opportunities and critical dangers it presents for the world of culture. The paper concludes with a discussion of how copyright policy can, and should, be used to mitigate the dangers – a goal that can be substantially achieved by re-orienting copyright law towards the human rights of authors and artists.

Box 4.1 Intellectual property rights in the digital age

Intellectual Property Rights (IPR) are emblematic of the transformations brought about by the digital production and delivery of content. Network convergence and the Internet have created radically new market structures. Electronic marketplaces and file-sharing communities greatly expand the means of consuming creation-based products, create original economic transactions, encourage newcomers and transform both competition and the position of firms in the content production and distribution value chain. These developments constitute both threats and opportunities for the creative industries: above all they call for efficient enforcement and regulation of IPR.

A content and a network economy. IPR pose key issues for various converging reasons arising from the characteristics of network and content economics. Firstly, network digital technologies offer users the opportunity to communicate widely and pervasively, making abuses difficult to combat. Digital networks also reduce the cost of strategic integration and widen the role of the technical and telecommunications industries. Software and electronics, telecommunications and Internet providers, now join producers of cultural goods and services. They all strive to possess property rights. Furthermore, dematerialization in a digitized economy undermines the traditional justifications of IPR: low marginal costs of reproduction and distribution do not reflect the cost of the creation process. Exclusive property rights over reproduction and distribution increase the supply of creative works, offering authors a financial incentive to create. Yet IPR hardly produce their usual positive outcomes in the digitalized networks, where free supply is a more efficient way to build reputation than financial incentives, as Open Source and Web 2.0 demonstrate. The music industry was the first – but not the last – to be confronted with the digital revolution. Given the rapid rise of new online music uses, devices and services, consumers now think that music is being sold at an excessive price. Using unauthorized downloads over file-sharing networks, they put copyright protection and traditional sales channels to the test.

Enforcement and regulation at stake. IPR are subject to frequent adaption. In the face of various threats, the public authorities both local and international devise new legal systems and enforcement rules. In consequence, IPR regulation is hampered by a diversity of laws and institutional arrangements across countries and jurisdictions that pertain to the nature and scope of limitations to copyright, duration of protection, liability, fair use, dispute resolution mechanisms, etc. Ongoing regulation as regards both the definition and implementation of rules has thus proven difficult to sustain. This is the reason why content industries such as music have initiated actions simultaneously at the political, legal, technological and economic levels. They seek to increase public awareness through information campaigns; by designing services to compete with file-sharing applications; by taking legal action against infringing companies and individuals; by imposing levies on digital players; by developing technology to prevent copying; or by joining forces with content, broadband and technology providers. This diversity of actions demonstrates the permanent entanglement of legal and judicial concerns (implementing copyright and competition regulation) on the one hand, economic and managerial rationales (emphasis on contractual solutions to the detriment of conventional contracts) on the other.

Hence the permanent tension between property regimes and the public domain. Digital technologies facilitate the circulation of content while enabling restrictive control and traceability. Copyright owners contest the right of consumers to make personal copies and specific uses of copyrighted materials. Meanwhile, consumers deny any right to control and to prevent their individual uses. What is more, users are helped out by other economic agents: file-sharing platforms are neither willing nor able to stop individual file transfers; Internet providers are reluctant to limit breaches of rights and boost their sales while promoting the possibility of unauthorized file-sharing.

Thus new technologies simultaneously globalize markets and segment customers. Facing multi-faceted piracy and dispersion of markets, recent trends are the work of the 'iron hand' of producers, distributors and consumers rather than of legal decisions. A dual movement can be observed: claims to property rights to protect content and competitive positions, but disguising them to decrease costs and to lower entry barriers. Therefore, IPR in the digital age work less and less to protect authors and ensure their 'fair' remuneration and increasingly to protect and stimulate investments in new industries and networks. IPR strategies thus pose risks that go beyond the economic and question the very capacity of consumers to obtain access to a wide range of products. This calls for a flexible, perhaps paradoxical, application of property rights and competition rules – promoting cultural diversity using tools designed to control the behaviour of economic operators. For cultural pluralism can be threatened in a competitive context and, conversely, monopolies may promote a large variety of content. From a strictly economic viewpoint, the result may be the same: the larger the distribution, the greater authors' earnings.

Pierre-Jean Benghozi

Culture in the global economy

Since its development and popularization in the late 1980s, information technology has come to play a central role in the world economy. This has occurred in two parallel streams. Initially, information technology became a major force in the economies of the countries where it was developed, notably spurring growth in the United States and, to an extent, Japan. While this was happening, Americans quickly came to realize that technology held the key to future prosperity on the world stage. By the end of the decade, therefore, American trade negotiators had begun to pursue an unprecedented new agenda in international trade talks. As the Uruguay Round of GATT negotiations progressed, the Americans proposed a new body to deal comprehensively with world trade in all areas of significance. Neither GATT nor any other existing international organization could bear comparison with the size and scope of the proposed new body. This initiative led to the creation of the World Trade Organization (WTO) in 1994 (*Marrakesh Agreement Establishing the World Trade Organization*, 1994). For the first time, the WTO included special provisions dealing explicitly with technology in the global trade arena. These were expressed in an Agreement on Trade-Related Aspects of Intellectual Property Rights, known by the acronym TRIPs (*Agreement on Trade-Related Aspects of Intellectual Property Rights*, 1994).

In order to understand the significance of the WTO arrangements for culture, it is necessary to examine more closely the new technologies themselves. Apart from the joy of pure science, technology has little intrinsic value: rather, it is what can be accomplished through the use of the technology that has social significance. In the case of information technology, its value to society largely depends on its ability to record and transmit knowledge and culture. In other words, it is technology that needs to be fed with 'content', as it has come to be called. Without 'content' to carry, information technology has little potential for growth.

What, exactly, is content? The term refers to information and knowledge of all kinds. From the perspective of cultural globalization, it is important to note that so-called cultural goods, or products, provide a significant proportion of the 'content' that feeds the information circuit. Two aspects of this culture-based trade are striking. First, from a purely economic point of view, trade in cultural goods is among the most significant areas of world trade, and its share is growing consistently.[4] Further, the industries involved in commercializing cultural goods are intensely aware of the potential for further growth generated by information and communications technology, which allows for inexpensive reproduction, virtually instantaneous transmission, and near-universal distribution of cultural products ranging from books and music, to film.

Second, the industry models behind cultural trade deserve mention. The movement of cultural products is almost entirely controlled by corporations which acquire rights to produce and distribute cultural works from their creators. This type of control is acquired by means of contractual arrangements, often highly standardized in the industries in question, or through a provision of copyright laws known as the 'employment rule'. The employment rule is a standard feature of copyright law in common- law countries; it specifies that, where original works are created 'in the course of employment', the employer, rather than the creator, acquires first copyright in those works.[5] The rule permits corporations an important degree of control over different kinds of works, ranging from computer programs to movies. Indeed, the role of corporations is so significant that, in some sectors, they may even be directly responsible for the creation of cultural products in identified market niches – the rise of 'concept groups' in popular music provides an interesting example.[6] Market research and advertising have also attained great prominence in these sectors.

Globalization is thus a double-edged sword: the very factors that lead to outstanding opportunities for growth in the cultural sector threaten to deprive that growth of economic value. In particular, the ease with which cultural products can be transmitted through technology makes it correspondingly difficult to control their movement for the purposes of commercial gain. In economic terms, the conditions of scarcity that are, at least crudely, associated with economic value, do not exist.

Culture can be thought of as a powerful river; in the past, technological limitations were an obstacle interrupting its flow. Technological advances always challenged this natural restraint on the communication of culture, but, with a few minor adjustments, the dam was reasonably able to cope with the increased volume of flow. In the case of current information technologies, however, the dam is near-bursting – if, indeed, it has not already burst. Once a work appears in digitized format, any individual with access to rudimentary information technology facilities – a personal computer and an Internet connection – is in a position to reproduce and transmit the work to others on a virtually limitless basis. There are few practical obstacles, and practically no costs, associated with these activities. In this technological environment, how can anyone hope to extract an economic benefit from a cultural work beyond the date of its first appearance in the public realm?

It is worth noting that creative authors themselves have generally remained in the background of the debate surrounding the impact of technology on culture. Indeed, the structure of the arts industries seems to demand a degree of passivity from them. The primary economic act of the author or artist is to release their work to a publisher; through publication contracts, publishers then undertake the economic risks of publication and collect many of its rewards. For example, authors' royalties remain a relatively small proportion of publishers' overall expenditures, typically ranging from 2.5 to a rare maximum of 15 per cent of sales (see indicator suites in Part II). In this sense, the commercial losses from technology are felt most directly by publishers; and, at a fundamental level, technology also threatens the function that publishers fulfill by publishing works, thereby bringing into question their very *raison d'être*. What need is there for publishers to distribute a work, when it can readily be made available through electronic technologies? It is hardly a surprise that publishers, like music companies and, increasingly, film studios, have faced a fundamental reassessment of their role by the public.

In this environment, the stakeholders in cultural products have found themselves desperately seeking a method of coping with the vast information river made swollen by new technologies. They are at once engaged in a struggle for survival, and in an exploration of unprecedented opportunities for growth. Their struggle is greatly strengthened at the political level by the coincidence of interests between the arts and technology sectors, due simply to the fact that copyright law is now deemed to protect both kinds of products. A closer examination of how copyright assigns value to culture in the digital environment is therefore essential to an in-depth exploration of the current cultural scene.

Copyright and cultural value

Copyright law is closely identified with globalization. This once arcane area of the law seems an unlikely candidate to lead a revolution in cultural concepts. Yet, copyright in the 'digital age' has become so ubiquitous that it may truly be called the legal face of cultural change – its legal counterpart. The newfound prominence of copyright law has its roots in the intimate relationship between copyright and technological change. Copyright originated in technological development: before the invention of printing, there was no need for the concept of authorized reproduction that is the essence of copyright rules, as mere theft was the norm.[7] It is also interesting to note that the technological necessity for copyright, then as now, was matched by a political need. In earlier times, common-law copyright assisted the sovereign to control the appearance of published material in the kingdom. When copyright became a branch of law in its own right, independent of censorship, it did so in the context of a historic drive towards freedom of the press in Great Britain.[8]

In a global environment, value in cultural products depends on two factors: our ability to control the spread of knowledge through technology, and the capacity to do so, not only at a merely local or national level, but also on the global scale. Copyright concepts enable us to respond to the first concern; the internationalization of copyright law through the world trade system now extends the concept of restricting knowledge through copyright rules across most of the globe.

A measurement of cultural value

In the digital age, copyright is instrumental in securing economic returns to culture. Information technology has led to a practical need to reassess the value of cultural products. The new opportunities for growth in the movement of culture lead to interesting consequences: on the one hand, tremendous economic potential, and a degree of temptation, while on the other, the potential for unfettered freedom of use. The tension between wealth and use is potent, and has rapidly become a defining feature of the cultural scene. Yet cultural policies, rather than defusing this antagonism, have actually caused it to intensify to an alarming degree.[9] The reasons behind this are simple: the economic stakes in the cultural sector are so high that the arts and entertainment industries have become active political lobbyists at both the national and international levels. Their lobbying is the most intense in the United States, a country that is known not only for its leadership in technology, but also for the dependence of its national political system on lobby power (Nimmer, 1992). At the same time, American leadership in the international trade arena has meant that the concerns of the US government are championed in international negotiations by the US Trade Representative's (USTR) office, with considerable persuasive power.[10]

In the absence of natural restraints, what force can control the flow of culture when it is borne forward by the powerful currents of technology? This pre-eminent concern of the arts industries receives an age-old response: in lieu of the laws of nature, let us impose moral obligations. In other words, man-made laws replace natural 'laws', and a legal response presents a viable alternative to nature-imposed limitations. Copyright law has come to function as this legal barrier, replacing older, practical restrictions with legal constraints on the ability to use cultural works through digital technology.

It is the role of copyright law in bringing economic value to culture that often leads intellectual property advocates to observe that, in the absence of copyright rules, neither technological growth nor cultural globalization would be possible. Nevertheless, the claim is a normative one: the software industry, now subject to copyright protection, first developed in an environment where regulation of any kind was absent, and although it may be a somewhat speculative point, there is no real necessity to believe that cultural products would behave differently (Ginsburg, 1994: 2559–72).

What is certain is that the economic implications of cultural globalization, in the absence of copyright regulation, would be different. Once again, it is not realistic to say that no economic benefit would be derived from culture in such an environment; but that benefit would probably be felt through some indirect or alternative channel. The implications for the arts industries can hardly be overstated. Copyright law in common-law countries calls itself an author's right, but in practice, nothing could be further from the truth. Through the operation of contracts and the 'employment rule', as described above, corporate entities are often the direct beneficiaries of copyright protection. Accordingly, the structure of the arts industries would be radically transformed by the reality that commercial gain from an intellectual work, after its initial release, would not be realized directly. Fear of this consequence is undoubtedly behind the visceral reaction of major players in the arts industries to new technology. For example, their aggressive strategy has included prominent, and often absurd, lawsuits against parties ranging from private individuals, to artists and authors, and technology companies.[11]

International copyright law: the key to cultural globalization

In the environment of globalization, copyright restrictions would be meaningless unless they were effective on an international scale. Over the past decade, copyright policy in advanced countries, led by the United States, has made the issue of international regulation its primary concern. The establishment of rights at the international level, and their practical enforcement in international jurisdictions, jointly comprise the focus of American copyright policy. Interestingly, and much to the surprise of copyright lawyers and trade officials, the process of extending copyright principles across borders has proven to be highly complex. The experience of the past decade proves that establishing the efficiency of international copyright law is not a simple matter of restating national copyright provisions – for example, the rules in the US Copyright Act – in international instruments. Rather, the approach to copyright in international instruments has arguably led to a shift in the understanding of copyright principles themselves. The underlying reason for this transformation has little to do with law: the complexity of international copyright regulation is due to the complex nature of the cultural phenomena that copyright seeks to control.[12]

It is sometimes said that there is nothing new under the sun, and international copyright law is no exception. The need for international rules was recognized more than a century ago, when in 1886 the adoption of the *Berne Convention for the Protection of Literary and Artistic Works* codified international copyright law for the first time.[13] The Berne Convention was a product of tense circumstances in the publishing trade of the day: European publishers were greatly upset by an upstart nation of 'pirate' publishers, who reprinted *en masse* the works of European authors. That upstart nation was none other than the United States. In contrast to the modern approach to international copyright, the Berne negotiations included, and were in a sense driven by, non-lawyers. A number of celebrated literary figures, including Emile Zola and, as a Russian observer of the proceedings, Ivan Turgenev, were involved in the discussions.[14]

The longevity of Berne is striking. Though it was subject to periodic revisions, the Convention continued to be the primary instrument of international copyright law until 1995, its basic structure remaining unaltered during that time. It was reasonably successful in combining copyright provisions from the different principles of common-law and Continental European traditions, and in bringing developing countries into the international legal arena, first as colonies, and later as independent states. The Berne system operated by setting an international benchmark standard, with which member countries were expected to comply to the best of their ability. Since the Convention was strictly an instrument of international law, without specific 'enforcement' mechanisms that could be effectively invoked in the member countries, the implementation and enforcement of copyright in member states necessarily remained flexible.[15]

The Berne Convention eventually came under the administration of the World Intellectual Property Organization (WIPO), a specialized agency of the United Nations (see also Isar, Chapter 7). The post-War period saw substantial decolonization, which brought new pressures to bear upon the international copyright system as former colonies became gradually aware of their social and cultural distinctness from the West. Accordingly, one of the important aims of WIPO was to provide assistance to developing countries in drafting and implementing modern copyright provisions. Despite, or perhaps because of the pressures exerted by developing countries on the Berne Union, culminating in a serious crisis at the Stockholm conference of 1967,[16] some progress was made in addressing copyright issues of special concern to the developing world. In particular, the improvement of literacy and education, and the protection of cultural heritage, became familiar themes of international copyright discourse.

The adoption of the TRIPs Agreement in 1994 represented a dramatic new direction. TRIPs responded to a number of factors affecting international copyright regulation, including the growing importance of the copyright industries in the United States and other industrialized countries, and their prominence in international trade. Indeed, it may be said that American dissatisfaction with the Berne copyright system, in which the United States controversially refused to participate until 1989, provided the spark for a new international approach to copyright.[17] The TRIPs Agreement brought copyright out of the United Nations system and made it an integral part of the international trade regime at the WTO. In contrast to the Berne Convention, however, the main thrust of the TRIPs Agreement is not to create new copyright norms. Rather, it changes the context of copyright protection, by bringing intellectual property into the broader framework of the general regime for international trade. This structural change means that signatories of the TRIPs Agreement may bring disputes about copyright before the general dispute-settlement mechanism of the WTO, which is empowered to impose economic penalties on nonconforming states. This new power of 'enforcing' intellectual property rights represents a major innovation of the WTO system, and creates a revolutionary new framework for copyright law.[18]

Under TRIPs, copyright industries are now to be treated as any other group of industries included in the series of agreements and structures constituting the WTO. Most importantly, a country's failure to maintain the standards of copyright protection set out in TRIPs could become the subject of dispute-settlement proceedings under the general measures of the WTO. Under the Dispute Settlement Understanding, it had become possible for the Dispute Settlement Body to impose trade sanctions on a country in virtually any area of trade to punish copyright infringement.[19] International lawyers have been quick to point out that the linkage of international trade with dispute settlement unquestionably represents the most significant accomplishment in the creation of the WTO (Dreyfuss and Lowenfeld, 1997).

Over the past decade, the new approach to copyright at the WTO has proven to be highly controversial. Not surprisingly, the main current of dissatisfaction flows from the developing world. Due to the connection between intellectual property and the settlement of international trade disputes, which can allow dissatisfied countries to strike back in sensitive areas of trade, developing countries perceive the TRIPs regime to be coercive in nature. Their concerns seem justified by the fact that the developing world was practically excluded from negotiations for the Agreement, which as a result would presumably tend to prioritize the interests and concerns of the industrialized world – a point that has been noted by legal scholars in industrialized as well as developing countries (Dreyfuss and Lowenfeld, 1997).[20] However, so unusual is the TRIPs framework that the controversy surrounding TRIPs has not been confined to developing countries: it has also resulted in friction between industrialized countries. In particular, the question of 'cultural exception', pitting the United States against France and Canada, has been fraught with contention (Fraser, 1996). The US has argued that 'culture' should be treated as any other area of 'goods', and that trade in culture should not be subject to any exclusive provisions or restrictions. In contrast, France and Canada have persistently argued that culture is, by nature, different from other 'goods', and that the international trading system must recognize this fundamental principle on a par with conventional rules of exchange (Fraser, 1996).

Despite their concerns, most countries of the world, including developing countries, have eagerly embraced the TRIPs Agreement.[21] Renouncing the WTO has not been seen as a realistic economic option by governments in any of these countries. For developing countries, in particular, the demonstrated ineffectiveness of alternative developmental models over the years, as well as the increasingly limited range of ideological options available to support policies restricting trade and economic liberalization, have led to a sense that there is no other choice.[22] Change from within the WTO system may be the hope of many developing countries (*Canada – Certain Measures Concerning Periodicals*, 1997).[23] In the meantime, developing countries have undertaken comprehensive programs of law reform under the TRIPs Agreement, including, of course, copyright provisions.

TRIPs has recently been followed by two international conventions that seek to adapt TRIPs principles specifically to the context of digital technology. Significantly, these conventions were concluded at

WIPO, in the throes of reinventing itself for the post-TRIPs era, and barely recognizable in its new incarnation alongside TRIPs. The WIPO Internet Treaties were drafted as early as 1996, but came into effect only when a minimum number of countries had ratified them, in March and May of 2002 (*WIPO Copyright Treaty*, 1996; *WIPO Performances and Phonograms Treaty*, 1996). Like TRIPs, the Internet Treaties reflect the influence of US trade advisors at the international level, and American legislation implementing them – in particular, the Digital Millenium Copyright Act (DMCA) of 1998 is highly controversial in the United States (*Digital Millennium Copyright Act*, 1998).[24] The DMCA, and the international copyright arrangements which it supports, seem to alienate much of the American public through its emphasis on proprietary control of culture over freedom of access. These attempts to 'reform' American copyright have led to powerful anti-copyright movements, including Open Source and 'Copyleft', a repudiation of the very idea of copyright entitlements.[25] Indeed, the tension between ownership and access encapsulates the debate in the United States over the future of copyright law in a country that is still the unchallenged key player in technological matters.[26]

The cultural implications of international copyright law

The new status of copyright at the international level presents great challenges to cultural diversity. As embodied in the TRIPs Agreement, international copyright rules express a specific model of culture. The cultural perspective of TRIPs is derived from prevailing concepts of culture in Western countries, which are embedded deep within their copyright laws: an understanding of culture that is proprietary in nature, emphasizing ownership over creation or public access; control of cultural works based on the recognition and reward of economic investment; and the importance of material records of culture over its more evanescent forms, such as traditional, oral or folk culture.

A Western perspective has always been inherent in international copyright law – it is a product of copyright history. International norms first developed among industrialized countries, and developing countries, were brought into this system first as subordinate members, and later as outright newcomers.

However, TRIPs represents an entirely new level of cultural domination as a result of two factors, one major – the structural integration of TRIPs into the WTO trade system through dispute-settlement – and one minor – the subtle shift in substantive copyright norms in TRIPs.

This second point, though relatively less impressive than the structural transformation of copyright under TRIPs, deserves a careful look. The relationship between the Berne Convention and the TRIPs Agreement evokes an image of the famous Russian *matryoshka* dolls: the TRIPs Agreement requires all member countries of the WTO to subscribe to Articles 1–17 and the Appendix on Developing Countries of the Berne Convention. These articles contain all of the substantive copyright norms in Berne; the remainder of the Convention deals with procedural matters rather than the substance of copyright protection. TRIPs engulfs the substance of copyright norms in the Berne Convention. However, it should also be noted that TRIPs appends a handful of substantive copyright norms to the provisions of the latter. These few contributions are directly inspired by American law. For example, TRIPs derives from the American copyright statute the requirement that works must be 'fixed' to be protected, excluding non-material forms of cultural expression from recognition, and it provides explicitly for the protection of software through copyright law, on par with other 'literary and artistic works' (TRIPs Agreement: Arts 9.2 10).[27] The cultural approach embodied in the Berne Convention has therefore become further specialized in TRIPs. Through TRIPs, this model of culture is propagated in a strong form: for member states of the WTO, recognizing and honouring it is essential in order to avoid the possibility of punitive action through the international trade dispute-settlement system. At the same time, the scope of TRIPs interpretation remains narrow, and the range of possible 'flexibilities', which could allow the Agreement to be interpreted liberally, is conceded to be quite limited (Matthews, 2005).

The emphasis on legal and, thereby, cultural homogeneity implicit in TRIPs presents a marked contrast to the reality of rapidly increasing cultural diversity in the international copyright arena. It is important to distinguish legal homogeneity from the idea of harmonizing copyright standards throughout the world, a practical necessity in an era of technological fluidity. Harmonization would require consent and cooperation among the world's vastly different copyright jurisdictions. True harmonization would mean, not identical laws, but, actually, different laws that could effectively yield the desired level of recognition for copyright in vastly different jurisdictions. In other words:

> Harmonization finds its natural context, not in law, but in music. In the legal analogy, it seems to have gained currency as meaning a process of revision that makes laws broadly similar to one another. In music, however, this is not what it means. The very notion of harmony depends on difference. Two identical notes cannot 'harmonize' with one another – the essence of harmony has been brilliantly described as a juxtaposition of the disparate. Harmony means that two different notes enjoy a relationship of compatibility within the terms of a defined musical language. What is more, harmony arises when individual notes are colored by the larger context defined by sequences of different notes. If the legal analogy is to be well-drawn, legal 'harmonization' should embrace some concept of a mutually complementary relationship, a level of consensus in the international sphere, however slowly it may be achieved. Harmonized laws will work in concert with other laws, in the context of a wider legal environment. Indeed, introducing 'an identically phrased rule' into two different legal contexts may actually lead to legal differences, rather than the desired effect of sameness. [footnotes omitted] (Sundara Rajan, 2006: 10–11)

Diversity is characteristic of the copyright community; it is reflected in the unprecedented levels of membership in international copyright agreements, the eastward expansion of the European Union, the prominent role of developing countries in technological change, and a growing international awareness of once-remote traditional cultures, including those of aboriginal peoples (Sundara Rajan, 2006). The internationalization of copyright reflects a real and historic need to develop a common basis for diverse cultures to value one another's works and heritage. The need is both economic and social in nature, as many countries and cultures grapple with the question of how to bring recognition and value to traditional culture in the digital era. The compatibility of cultural values with a technological future is by no means assured, and it is increasingly apparent that

the need to develop a means of articulating those values in the digital context may be critically important for the future of cultural heritage.

As reflected in TRIPs, the legal response to this often inarticulate cultural need seems thoroughly inadequate. TRIPs has been called a form of 'cultural imperialism', (Hamilton, 1996; Okediji, 2001) and it is easy to see how the diverse membership of the WTO might resent the Americanization of international copyright rules. The issue is one that will not only disturb developing countries, but also those with cultural preoccupations similar to those of Canada and France (Fraser, 1996).

It is most interesting to note that the 'imperialism' of TRIPs is not only the cultural perspective that the Agreement seems to extend over the world at large; there is also an important element of cultural homogenization within the United States due to TRIPs. Reforms to American copyright law in the TRIPs era have proven to be highly controversial. The problem has intensified due to the adoption of the WIPO Internet Treaties, which powerfully reinforce and update the TRIPs approach. The WIPO Internet Treaties attempt to address the issues surrounding digital reproduction and communication of works directly, defining these new forms of publication and transmission as outright violations of copyright law.[28]

The current situation of international copyright law may therefore be described as a stalemate. International agreements have set in motion a new sequence of copyright developments that have profoundly alienated cultural interests in practically every region of the world. The debate over copyright is sharply polarized, with corporations arguing for ever-tightening copyright restrictions, on the one hand, and public interest organizations pressing for the more or less wholesale elimination of copyright restrictions, on the other. In fact, both solutions are equally unsatisfactory. The corporate insistence on copyright control shows an almost 'willful blindness' to the realities of modern life, its technological and social opportunities and limitations. The anti-copyright movements, despite their nobility of sentiment, fall prey to a curious disregard for the concerns of those who create and propagate culture. They ultimately neglect the question of how to protect cultural interests – in particular, the important issue of protecting creators of culture – in a way that seems analogous to the approach of corporate copyright-owners. They address the problems of access, yet prefer to side-step a serious consideration of the obstacles in the way of creation.

Copyright and human rights: a new policy approach

These considerations point towards the need for a fundamentally new approach to copyright law. In contrast to the approach of Copyleft advocates, I would suggest that the logical place to begin our search for new approaches is actually within copyright law itself. The unprecedented problem confronting twenty-first-century copyright is the compellingly close relationship between copyright and the economic valuation of culture. The connection between copyright and cultural value is magnified through the lens of a global model of trade regulation that embraces cultural products as the way of the future. In this way, copyright and culture have become strange bedfellows, their relationship consecrated through the rites of economic exchange.

However, this perspective on copyright law largely ignores legal history. In fact, copyright, notwithstanding the monolithic terminology, has always been a multi-faceted group of rights and privileges, reflecting many streams of cultural interests and concepts, some of which are even self-contradictory. The impoverishment of copyright concepts to a single, hegemonic idea presents a clear threat to cultural causes in the twenty-first century. In particular, the international copyright system moves twenty-first-century society away from non-economic forms of valuing culture, towards a virtually exclusive focus on economic value.

Can an enlightened cultural policy hope to offer any effective remedy for these ills? Clearly, a cultural policy that will prove to be responsive to the challenges of the digital era must include a coherent rationale for copyright law. As the preceding discussion has sought to show, copyright plays a central role in the globalization of culture. Without copyright, the phenomenon would not exist: culture would move across borders, of course, but its movement would not translate into direct economic benefits.

It is worth noting that copyright's prominence in the digital era is a result of its integral relationship with technology – a contrived relationship, a sort of arranged marriage between law and technology that is largely achieved through political manipulation. Despite much of the current discourse surrounding copyright, there is little that is inevitable about the dominance of technological growth by copyright regulation. This consideration offers much hope for the future. It may come as a surprise to learn that copyright law is almost infinitely malleable – both its strength and its weakness – since this inherent flexibility is what makes copyright concepts vulnerable to manipulation by unscrupulous interests, whether corporations, private individuals, or the governments of states.[29]

The mismanagement of copyright on the global scale not only presents a threat to cultural heritage, but also implies the tragedy of lost opportunity. Cultural policy should therefore seek to address two intertwined questions. First, how can the destructive impact of copyright on culture be minimized? And, secondly, are there strands within the tradition of copyright law that may actually encourage the preservation and transmission of cultural values in the digital environment? The second, often neglected, question is at least as important as the first. As I have sought to demonstrate, globalization, while it offers new opportunities, presents a grave and fundamental challenge to culture, bringing into question its very nature, and its continued relevance for the future.

A comprehensive view of copyright suggests many possible solutions to this quandary. Due to copyright politics, the idea of examining conceptual approaches to copyright that could help re-orient cultural policies is so underdeveloped, that very little discussion of new copyright concepts has occurred over the past decade. However, one new approach is glaringly obvious: the idea that copyright should be re-oriented towards an emphasis on the human rights of authors and intellectuals. They are the creators of culture, and the social re-assessment of authors as 'content providers' in the digital era presents a major threat to culture (see also Chapter 5).

In current debates, it is overwhelmingly important to break down copyright into its constituent parts, rejecting the monolithic approach to copyright questions that dominates international negotiations. In fact, copyright is not a purely economic right: copyright law includes at least two types of rights: not only economic rights, which are the focus of cultural globalization, but also moral rights. Moral rights, an awkward translation from the French legal term *droit moral*,[30] provide legal protection for the personal and artistic interests of authors in their work. They are based on the idea of a special relationship between an author and his or her own creation; this relationship is unbreakable and permanent, since the connection between oneself and one's own work is such. Although they are often portrayed as fundamentally different from economic copyright, this is somewhat inaccurate. Moral rights are simply the reverse side of a single coin; they complement and complete a regime of protection for authors' economic rights.[31] For example, the right of first publication over one's own work is the basis of all economic copyright, but it is also a moral right to choose how and when to 'divulge' your own work to the public.[32] Given the breadth of this underlying rationale, moral rights may include legal protection for a wide range of different rights and interests, but their legal protection is usually limited to the fundamental moral rights of attribution and integrity, incorporated into the Berne Convention in 1928.

Clearly, moral rights are concerned with a different aspect of cultural works, making non-commercial values and priorities the focus of legal principle and practical enforcement. The idea of a moral right makes a valuable contribution to the integrity of creative expression, a basic component of cultural heritage, and the modern basis for cultural diversity.[33] A human rights approach to copyright policy would require a re-examination of the relationship between the economic and moral rights of authors. In most copyright systems of the world, moral rights occupy a place of secondary importance. No doubt this is due to the practical difficulty of protecting moral rights on the one hand, and to the uncertainty, economic and otherwise, that they impose on publishing industries on the other. The global technological revolution has brought more intense pressure to bear on moral rights than ever before, at times making them seem irrelevant, or even dangerous for technological progress (Sundara Rajan, 2004).

However, a strong case can be made for expanding the recognition of moral rights in international copyright law. In contrast to other aspects of copyright law, moral rights have attained widespread international acceptance. In particular, they enjoy virtually universal recognition in developing countries, who have historically resisted Western copyright law on the grounds of culture and tradition, and who are now likely to bear the brunt of cultural globalization upon their own traditions. Developing countries

have seen moral rights as a way of bringing much-needed prestige and protection to national creativity, especially after colonial experiences.[34] Legislators and, especially, judges in developing countries have often developed innovative ways of dealing with moral rights, shaping their legal treatment to reflect different cultural needs and priorities. Moral rights have become applicable to works of folklore;[35] they can apply to any form of the mistreatment of a work, whether or not an author's reputation is damaged;[36] they can protect an artwork against destruction;[37] and they can be vindicated by members of the general public.[38]

The connection between moral rights and human rights is cemented by two basic characteristics of these rights: their inalienability and their potential for unlimited protection. Moral rights are inalienable in the sense that, even after the author has sold the work, or his copyright in it, he continues to retain the moral rights in his work. The legal implications of this assertion can be quite bizarre. Although the author no longer owns his work or has the right to reproduce it, he may object to any failure to attribute the work to him, and he may also sue if the integrity of the work is threatened. Indeed, in the absence of any agreement to the contrary, the author may even sue his own publisher for violation of his moral rights.[39] The rationale behind this feature of moral rights goes back to their origin in the relationship between an author and his work. This relationship is permanent: the author will always be the creator of the work, whoever may acquire rights over the work for whatever purpose. The idea is reflected in Article 6*bis* of the Berne Convention, dealing with moral rights, which stipulates that the rights remain with the author 'even after the transfer of the [author's economic] rights'.[40] Some countries, including Canada and the UK, have chosen to deal with these rights by allowing 'blanket' waivers of moral rights in their copyright laws (*Copyright Act*, 1985: ss. 14–28; *Copyright, Designs and Patents Act 1988*, 1988: s. 87). However, this approach shows a lack of good faith, and it is by no means consistent with the doctrine. Moral rights are, by definition, rights of personal authorship: they cannot be exercized by anyone but the author. Whether corporations or governments, no third party can acquire them by purchase or transfer, or exercize them in lieu of the author.

Similarly, the potential for protection with no limitation in time is a fundamental feature of the author's moral right. Since the author's relationship with his work is permanent, there is no reason to limit protection of the moral rights. After the death of the author, moral rights may be vindicated on his behalf by his descendants, a moral rights executor, or a state or public agency charged with this responsibility.[41] Again, this feature of moral rights presents a striking contrast to economic rights, which are invariably time-limited rights.[42] As in the case of inalienability, however, this implication of the doctrine is often tempered in national legislation: some countries grant perpetual protection, but others prefer to limit the duration of moral rights to the same term as economic copyright.

These features of moral rights reveal the close connection between authors' moral rights and the 'natural' rights of authors. In other words, a human rights theory provides the basis for moral rights. The use of these rights to promote culture, both through the author's personal capacity to act and after his time, represents at least one way in which copyright law contains within itself the seeds of a different approach to culture. A human rights model of copyright may begin with moral rights. In contrast to the dominant thrust of international copyright law, moral rights emphasize the personal interests of authors in their own work, the often non-economic reasons for their creativity, and the broader cultural benefits that may be gained by protecting attribution and integrity interests. Respect for moral rights is essential for the preservation of historical truth.

Conclusion

Without copyright law, cultural globalization would not exist. While technology tends towards ever greater freedom in the creation and communication of knowledge, copyright erects an artificial barrier in its path. This barrier is ostensibly put in place for the public good, but even a cursory examination of the issues reveals that copyright is highly politicized, driven above all by fear of technological change and its economic consequences. A cultural policy that is based on fear can be of little benefit to society. It is time for policy-makers to take a courageous stance, and campaign for the free exploration of copyright concepts. A new model of copyright is essential for the future of culture. Ironically, the very emphasis on over-protection is probably the greatest

threat to copyright's future. As in most areas of human endeavor, a long-term view, and a focus on the eternal, must surely offer the best possible way forward.

Notes

1 See Sundara Rajan (2006: Chapter 1) for some examples of who is concerned with 'globalization'.
2 See, for example, Dissanayake (1992).
3 Trademark may also be implicated in cultural exchange, through the use of images and words in commercial marks that are drawn from cultural contexts. For example, the use of the Inukshuk figure from the Inuit cultures of Canada's far North as a symbol of the Whistler Olympics is but one instance of aboriginal art being used or appropriated for commercial purposes. See Sundara Rajan (forthcoming); Morgan (2004).
4 See, for example, UNESCO Institute for Statistics and UNESCO Sector for Culture (2005).
5 See *Copyright Act* (1985: s. 13); *Copyright Act of 1976* (1976: §§ 201, 101).
6 See *Confetti Records v. Warner Music* (2003). A concept group is a group with a name and a style, but no real members; musicians fill individual sets or engagements on a contract basis, and many different musicians may work under the rubric of a single identity.
7 Colin Tapper, Magdalen College, Oxford, private correspondence.
8 For example, Milton's *Areopagitica* (1644) is considered a seminal text for copyright purposes. See also Tapper (2004: 268). Tapper draws attention to this parallel between ancient and modern in the context of common-law copyright:

> [T]he invention of printing coincided, by no means coincidentally, with the bitter religious and political disputes of the Reformation and the emergence of the nation state, so control was needed to prevent use of the press by potential subversives...
>
> ... However[,] the apparatus of government was still in its infancy, and the very flood of measures designed to quell abuse demonstrates the ineffectiveness of these controls. In an eery precursor of modern attitudes the public sector involved the private so as to achieve its objectives.

In his study of copyright history, L. Ray Patterson (1968: 21) emphasizes, appropriately, that 'copyright was not a product of censorship and press control, as has been sometimes assumed. Censorship was a government policy unrelated to property concepts... In short, copyright was not created because of censorship, nor would the absence of censorship have prevented its creation, but censorship did aid private persons, publishers and printers, in developing copyright in their own interest with no interference from the courts and little from the government. The early censorship regulations thus serve as a prelude to the development of copyright'. Patterson captures the essence of copyright as an unwitting tool of censorship – an observation that is worth reconsidering in the digital age.

9   See, for example, the comments in Sundara Rajan (2005).

10 The 'Special 301' Watch List of IP-renegade countries, whose enforcement of copyright and other intellectual property rights is deemed deficient, is one of the tools used by the USTR in its campaign for stronger enforcement of rights. See online at http://www.ustr.gov.

11 See, for example, *MGM Studios, Inc. v. Grokster, Ltd.* (2005).

12 For a discussion of the ineffectiveness of copyright reform and the reasons behind it, see Sundara Rajan (2006: Chapters 1, 2).

13 *Berne Convention for the Protection of Literary and Artistic Works* (1886). Common-law copyright predates Berne. The Statute of Anne of 1709–10, though not a copyright law in the modern sense, is traditionally considered to be the first UK copyright statute; during the eighteenth century, the English courts also developed some interesting cases on copyright, with their treatment of the issues extending to authors' non-commercial interests. See Rose (1993).

14 For a treatment of the Convention in historical perspective, see Ricketson (1987).

15 Technically speaking, the Berne Convention was, and is, enforceable at the level of complaints by states, through the International Court of Justice (ICJ). However, Berne has yet to give rise to a dispute at the ICJ: Iwasawa (2002: 291).

16 For a discussion of the participation of developing countries in the Berne Union and the problems that arose during the 1967 Stockholm conference, see the detailed treatment in Ricketson (1987: 590–632).

17 For a detailed discussion of these issues, see Gana (1996: 739–42) and Gadbaw and Gwynn (1988: 38, 48).

18 Rochelle Cooper Dreyfuss and Andreas Lowenfeld are even stronger in their assessment of TRIPs; they argue that:

> …completion of the Uruguay Round was a miracle, a package deal with so large an agenda that no state or group of states, and no professional community, could fully grasp the significance of everything that was finally subsumed within the new General Agreement on Tariffs and Trade (GATT).

They go on to identify the inclusion of intellectual property in the WTO as one of 'two major breakthroughs' achieved by the system'. See Dreyfuss and Lowenfeld (1997: 276–77).

19 In the language of international trade, trade concessions can be suspended: see Article 22 of the WTO's *Dispute Settlement Understanding* on 'Suspension of Concessions'. It should be noted that, under Article 64.3 of the TRIPs Agreement, the Council for TRIPs may also have a role to play in dispute settlement; but the implications of this provision remain unclear.

20 A series of essays from India confirms the ambivalence of developing countries towards TRIPs negotiations: for example, see Nair and Kumar (1994: 11).

21 A current list of WTO members can be found on the organization's web site: http://www.wto.org/english/thewto_e/whatis_e/tif_e/org6_e.htm.

22 See Trebilcock and Howse (1995: 301–22): they trace the post-War evolution of theories of development. One of the ironies of the demise of socialism in Eastern Europe, which does not escape their observation, is the current international predominance, verging on exclusivity, of market-based economics, and therefore of trade-based models of development.

23 Some tentative propositions in this regard were advanced by India in the first TRIPs dispute under the DSU, a complaint by the United States against India's pharmaceutical patent provisions. India pointed out that developing countries' understanding of TRIPs requirements should be weighed in the interpretation of the TRIPs Agreement under the DSU, but the panel did not respond to this argument. See *India – Patent Protection for Pharmaceutical and Agricultural Chemical Products (Complaint by the United States)* (1997: para 6.17). The case is cursorily summarized in Adelman and Baldia (1996: 525–29).

24 Note the controversy in Canada surrounding Bill C-60 (2005). For a discussion on the Bill, which was seen as the Canadian equivalent of the DMCA, see generally Geist (2005).

25 See, for example, The Free Software Foundation (online: http://www.fsf.org) and Creative Commons (online: http://creativecommons.org).

26 India presents a disconcerting challenge to US dominance in the field of information technology!

27 Interestingly, this provision is complicated by the fact that patent protection for software is increasingly an accepted legal alternative: see the pioneering US case of *State Street Bank & Trust Co. v. Signature Financial Group* (1998). This leads to the potential difficulty of overlapping intellectual property rights in software arising from copyright and patent.

28 For example, see the 'making available' right in the *WIPO Copyright Treaty* (1996: Art. 6) and *WIPO Performances and Phonograms Treaty* (1996: Art. 8).

29 The manipulation of copyright law by the Soviet government to repress the creative freedom of dissidents is a case in point; the role of the RIAA in US copyright reforms provides a current example. See my discussion of the Siniavskii-Daniel trial and Soviet accession to the UCC in Sundara Rajan (2006: Chapter 9).

30 A more accurate term might be 'personal' or even 'personality' rights, like the German *persönlichkeitsrecht,* which would liberate the English lawyer from the constraints of reconciling law and morality.

31 In civil law systems, however, the status of moral rights is quite different: at least in theory, they are at the origin of all authorship rights, whether economic or personal. See Colombet (1992: 40).

32 *Droit de divulgation:* see Sundara Rajan (2006: 80 and accompanying notes).

33 Moral rights can also be applied to non-traditional works, such as works of folklore or TK (traditional knowledge): see Sundara Rajan (2001a).

34 See the discussion of the rationales supporting copyright in developing countries in Ploman and Hamilton (1980: 23–25).

35 Tunisia was the first country to protect copyright and moral rights in folklore: Ploman and Hamilton (1980: 129–31).

36 Until recently, this was a feature of Indian law: see Sundara Rajan (2001b: 175–6).

37 This, too, was the case in Indian law: see Sundara Rajan (2001a: 84–7). Protection for the moral right of integrity that is not based on the protection of the author's reputation, or which acts to prohibit the outright destruction of a work, are not yet an accepted part of international copyright law. See the discussion in Ricketson (1984: para. 15.57, note 48).

38 The proposed Draft Civil Code provision of the Russian Federation on copyright includes a provision with this effect: see Draft Civil Code (2001: Art. 1287.4).

39 Socialist law saw the conflict between author and publisher as another form of bourgeois exploitation: see the discussion in Sundara Rajan (2006: Chapter 5); 'A Text Writer's Opinion' (1938: 254–5).

40 See Sundara Rajan (2006: Chapter 9, note 86 and accompanying text).

41 Each of these solutions to the problem of moral rights after the author's death may be found in different jurisdictions.

42 Indeed, in some jurisdictions, the notion of 'limited monopoly' is the very essence of the property right into the authors: see the US Constitution.

REFERENCES

'A Text Writer's Opinion' (1938) *Grazhdanskoe Pravo* (Civil Law), Part I, Moscow 1938, 254–55; trans in J.N. Hazard (1947) *Materials on Soviet Law*. New York: Columbia University. p. 35.

Adelman, Martin and Baldia, Sonia (1996) 'Prospects and Limits of the Patent Provision in the TRIPS Agreement: The Case of India', *Vanderbilt Journal of Transnational Law*, 29: 507–33.

Agreement on Trade-Related Aspects of Intellectual Property Rights, Annex 1C to the *Marrakesh Agreement Establishing the World Trade Organization,* 15 April 1994, 33 ILM 1197 (entered into force 1 January 1995), WTO Homepage (Legal Texts), online: http://www.wto. org/english/tratop_e/trips_e/t_agm0_e.htm [TRIPs Agreement]

Agreement on Trade-Related Aspects of Intellectual Property Rights (1994) being Annex 1C to the *Marrakesh Agreement Establishing the World Trade Organization*, 1869 U.N.T.S. 299, 33 I.L.M. 1197, online: http://www.wto.org/English/ docs_e/ legal_e/27-trips.pdf [TRIPs Agreement].

Berne Convention for the Protection of Literary and Artistic Works (1886), 9 September 1886, revised at Paris 24 July 1971, 25 U.S.T. 1341, 828 U.N.T.S. 221, online: http://www. wipo.int/treaties/en/ip/ berne/pdf/trtdocs_wo001.pdf [Berne Convention].

Canada – Certain Measures Concerning Periodicals (1997), WTO Doc. WT/DS31/AB/R (Appellate Body Report).

Colombet, C. (1992) Grands principes du droit d'auteur et des droits voisins dans le monde: Approche de droit compare. 2ième ed. Paris: UNESCO – Libraire de la Cour de cassation.

Confetti Records v. Warner Music (2003) EWCH 1274 (Ch.).

Copyright Act, R.S.C. (1985) c. C-42 [Canadian Copyright Act].

Copyright Act of 1976 (1976) 17 U.S.C. [U.S. Copyright Act].

Copyright, Designs and Patents Act 1988 (1988) c. 48. (U.K.)

Digital Millennium Copyright Act (1998) (1998) Pub. L. No. 105–304, 112 Stat. 2860 [DMCA].

Bill C-60, *An Act to Amend the Copyright Act*, R.S.C. (2005) c. C-60, amending R.S.C. (1985) c. C-42, online: http:// www2.parl.gc.ca/HousePublications/ Publication.aspx?Docid=2334015&file=4.

Dissanayake, Ellen (1992) *Homo Aestheticus: Where Art Comes From And Why*. New York: Free Press.

Draft Civil Code (2001) [OM Kozyr and EV Luchits (tr.)], 30 November.

Dreyfuss, Rochelle Cooper and Lowenfeld, Andreas F. (1997) 'Two Achievements of the Uruguay Round: Putting TRIPS and Dispute Settlement Together', *Virginia Journal of International Law*, 37(2): 275–333.

Fraser, Stephen (1996) 'Berne, CFTA, NAFTA & GATT: The Implications of Copyright *Droit Moral* and Cultural Exemptions in International Trade Law', *Hastings Communications and Entertainment Law Journal*, 18(2): 287–320.

Gadbaw, R. Michael and Gwynn, Rosemary E. (1988) 'Intellectual Property Rights in the New GATT Round', in Timothy J. Richards and R. Michael Gadbaw (eds.) *Intellectual Property Rights: Global Consensus, Global Conflict?* Boulder: Westview Press.

Gana, Ruth L. (1996) 'Prospects for Developing Countries Under the TRIPs Agreement', *Vanderbilt Journal of Transnational Law*, 29(4): 735–75.

Geist, Michael (ed.) (2005) *In The Public Interest: The Future of Canadian Copyright Law*. Toronto: Irwin Law.

Ginsburg, Jane C. (1994) 'Four Reasons and a Paradox: The Manifest Superiority of Copyright over Sui Generis Protection of Computer Software', *Columbia Law Review*, 94(8): 2559–72.

Hamilton, Marci A. (1996) 'The TRIPS Agreement: Imperialistic, Outdated, and Overprotective', *Vanderbilt Journal of Transnational Law*, 29(3): 613–34.

India – Patent Protection for Pharmaceutical and Agricultural Chemical Products (Complaint by the United States), 5 September 1997, WTO Doc. WT/DS50/R (Panel Report), para 6.17, online: http://www.sice.oas.org/DISPUTE/wto/ trips.asp.

Iwasawa, Yuji (2002) 'WTO Dispute Settlement as Judicial Supervision', *Journal of International Economic Law*, 5(2): 287–305.

Marrakesh Agreement Establishing the World Trade Organization (1994) 15 April 1994, 1867 U.N.T.S. 154, 33 I.L.M. 1144 (entered into force 1 January 1995), online: http://www.wto.org/ english/docs_e/ legal_e/04-wto.pdf [WTO Agreement].

Matthews, Duncan (2005) 'TRIPS Flexibilities and Access to Medicines in Developing Countries: The Problem with Technical Assistance and Free Trade Agreements', *European Intellectual Property Review*, 27(11): 420–7.

MGM Studios, Inc. v. Grokster, Ltd., 545 U.S. 913 (2005).

Milton, John (1644) *Areopagitica*. Online: http://www. gutenberg.org/etext/608.

Morgan, Owen (2004) 'Protecting Indigenous Science and Trademarks—The New Zealand Experiment', *Intellectual Property Quarterly*, 1: 58–84.

Nair, K.R.G. and Kumar, Ashok (1994) *Intellectual Property Rights*. UDCCS Seminar Papers Series No. 1. New Delhi: Allied Publishers.

Nimmer, David (1992) 'Conventional Copyright: A Morality Play', *Entertainment Law Review*, 3(3): 94–8.

Okediji, Ruth (2001) 'TRIPs Dispute Settlement and the Sources of (International) Copyright Law', *Journal of the Copyright Society of the U.S.A.*, 49(2): 585–648.

Patterson, L. Ray (1968) *Copyright in Historical Perspective*. Nashville: Vanderbilt University Press.

Ploman, Edward W. and Hamilton, L. Clark (1980) *Copyright: Intellectual Property and Information Age*. London: Routledge & Kegan Paul.

Ricketson, Sam (1987) *The Berne Convention for the Protection of Literary and Artistic Works: 1886–1986*. London: Centre for Commercial Law Studies, Queen Mary College, and Kluwer.

Ricketson, Staniforth (1984) *The Law of Intellectual Property*. Melbourne: The Law Book Company.

Rose, Mark (1993) *Authors and Owners: The Invention of Copyright*. Cambridge, Mass.: Harvard University Press.

State Street Bank & Trust Co. v. Signature Financial Group, 149 F.3d 1368 (Fed. Cir. 1998).

Sundara Rajan, Mira T. (2001a) 'Moral Rights and the Protection of Cultural Heritage: *Amar Nath Sehgal v. Union of India*', *International Journal of Cultural Property*, 10(1): 79–94.

Sundara Rajan, Mira T. (2001b) 'Moral Rights in the Public Domain: Copyright Matters in the Poetical Works of Indian National Poet C. Subramania Bharati', *Singapore Journal of Legal Studies*, 1: 161–95 (pinpoint: 175–6).

Sundara Rajan, Mira T. (2004) 'Moral Rights in Information Technology: A New Kind of "Personal Right"?', *International Journal of Law and Information Technology* 12(1): 32–54.

Sundara Rajan, Mira T. (2005) 'The "New Listener" and the Virtual Performer: The Need for a New Approach to Performers' Rights', in Michael Geist (ed.) *In The Public Interest: The Future of Canadian Copyright Law*. Toronto: Irwin Law.

Sundara Rajan, Mira T. (2006) *Copyright and Creative Freedom: A Study of Post-Socialist Law Reform*. London: Routledge.

Sundara Rajan, Mira T. (forthcoming) 'Moral Rights and Forgery: Can Europe Show the Way?', in Gerte Reichelt (ed.) *Original und Faelschung*. Frankfurt: Manz.

Tapper, Colin (2004) 'Criminality and Copyright', in David Vaver and Lionel Bently (eds.) *Intellectual Property in the New Millennium: Essays in Honour of William R. Cornish*. Cambridge: Cambridge University Press. p. 268.

Trebilcock, Michael J. and Howse, Robert (1995) *The Regulation of International Trade*. London: Routledge.

UNESCO Institute for Statistics and UNESCO Sector for Culture (2005) 'International Flows of Selected Goods and Services, 1994–2003: Defining and capturing the flows of global cultural trade'. Online: http://www.uis.unesco.org/template/pdf/cscl/IntlFlows_EN.pdf.

WIPO Copyright Treaty, 20 December 1996, 36 I.L.M. 65 (entered into force 2 March 2002). Online: http://www.wipo.int/documents/en/diplconf/distrib/94dc.htm [WCT].

WIPO Performances and Phonograms Treaty, 20 December 1996, 36 I.L.M. 76 (entered into force 20 May 2002). Online: http://www.wipo.int/treaties/en/ip/wppt/trtdocs_wo034.html [WPPT].

WTO *Dispute Settlement Understanding*. Online: http://www.wto.org/English/docs_e/legal_e/28-dsu.pdf.

## CHAPTER 5

FREE CULTURE AND CREATIVE COMMONS
Frances Pinter

The concept of free culture arose as a response to the crisis of value as the global drivers of economics and technology came into conflict with non-commercial cultural values. This chapter discusses some of the new models arising out of the confrontation between the traditional economy with ever-tighter copyright regulations and those who promote a 'sharing economy' with more flexible licensing regimes. It looks at alternatives, such as Creative Commons, that have arisen as users of digital technology run up against the dictates of a pre-digital era copyright environment.

A second revolution is occurring around the commoditization of culture. The first revolution occurred when a value that could be traded within the conventional free market began to be attributed to cultural products. The second is only just beginning – arising from the opportunities afforded in the digital realm. New relationships between market and non-market approaches to producing, valuing and distributing the fruits of creativity

are emerging daily. Traditional notions of intellectual property rights sit uncomfortably in this new world and the process of globalization has produced two opposing forces. This chapter will review some of the new models arising out of the confrontation between the traditional economy with ever tighter regulations benefiting multinational corporations, and those who promote a 'sharing economy' with more flexible licensing regimes and new means of remunerating creators and others along the value chain. It looks at creative alternatives arising as users of digital technology run up against the dictates of pre-digital era copyright law. It is too early to say whether David will win out against Goliath, but indicators already show that David is gathering strength. It may well be that at the end of this story there will be not a slain Goliath, but at least a humbled and morphed one.

The concept of free culture arose as a response to the crisis of value as the global drivers of economics and technology came into conflict with non-commercial cultural values. Others in this volume deal with the impact of this conflict and whether it has been exacerbated in the increasingly globalized world. Here we look at how a specific response, enabled by the very technology responsible for some of the conflict in the first place, is provoking a rethink of how we manage culture.

Free culture began with a change of mindset of a few and grew rapidly into several social movements thereby attacking first the fringes and then the core of the conventional business models hitherto governing the production and distribution of cultural goods. The enabler of these alternatives is, of course, the new technology itself. Digitization opened up unprecedented opportunities. At the same time, obstacles stand in the way of adaptations. Vested interests in some of the older practices block the reform of intellectual property laws as established companies are understandably reluctant to take on the risks associated with untested business models. The result is that we are living essentially in two parallel economies. First we have the traditional economy, where everything has an owner and a value, and second, the sharing economy, where more and more creative works are launching their lives in less restricted domains. The motivations vary but often are based on a belief that these means allow creators to reach a wider audience, increase engagement with their readers, listeners and viewers, improve their work through collaborative outputs etc. These works are often licensed utilizing new licensing forms such as Creative Commons (CC) predicated on a 'some rights reserved' principle.

In this chapter we look at the origins of the sharing economy and how it is now finding its way, interfacing with the traditional economy. We will see how this is playing out in a variety of creative sectors, film, music and publishing and how initiatives such as Open Knowledge, Open Access and Open Archives are standing the old business models on their heads. We shall address some of the issues around why this new way of thinking is not only forcing changes in business practices, but may just become one of the most important ideas shaping the free market in the twenty-first century. The Open Source software movement is from where much of the new thinking originates.

Open Source software is source code that is governed not only by conventional copyright, but also by Copyleft, a licensing system invented by Richard Stallman and the Free Software Foundation. Copyleft grants to users of a program the right to alter its source code on condition that they pass on the right to alter the revised code under the same terms (Naughton, 1999: 311).

Furthermore, as Professor Lawrence Lessig states, 'Open Source software is not software in the public domain. The copyright owners of free and open source software insist that the terms of their software license be respected by adopters of free and open software. Free software licensed under the General Public License (GPL) requires that the source code for the software be made available by anyone who modifies and redistributes the software. But that requirement is effective only if copyright governs the software' (Lessig, 2004: 264–5). So, Open Source software is not really free in the sense of not having a copyright holder or value. Indeed many commercial businesses have been built on Open Source software. To understand this we need to grasp how the word 'free' is used in the context of free culture.

Richard Stallman is credited with distinguishing between two types of freedom. Free as in 'freedom of speech' and free as in 'free beer'. While a small number of people are still advocating free beer (without actually understanding the economics of beer-making), the debate has moved on whereby it is acknowledged that goods and services need to be paid for somewhere along the chain. Two questions remain. Who pays? And where in the production/consumption cycle should these payments be made? The answers to these questions assume some sort of intellectual property regime where there is order and understanding of who owns what and how to engage in meaningful contracts that reflect the desired license conditions and expected transactions.

In Chapter 4, Mira Sundara Rajan reminds us that 'the moral credibility of intellectual property rights, an essential foundation for any credible system of law, is increasingly eroded by practices in the cultural industries… the improvement of prospects for culture depends on infusing the law of intellectual property rights with new vitality'. This erosion has occurred for a number of reasons, one notable one being a lack of alignment between the laws that regulate the use of intellectual property (as physical manifestations of creativity) and the new usages enabled by the digitalization of culture. Copyright law, stemming from the early eighteenth century sits poorly in the twenty-first. This has consequences for the fostering of creativity – which was in fact the original intent of copyright law. Indeed when writers in the eighteenth century were first limited to licensing their works for 14 years, it was to protect them against the exploitation of the well-financed printers of the day. Licensing terms now are much longer. Some have argued that, without a fundamental overhaul of the global intellectual property rights regime, creativity will be stifled. Today, as the means of creating culture improve exponentially, the straightjackets produced to restrict the use of creative products grows ever tighter (for example, extensions of copyright terms and application of digital rights management systems). Others have argued that the world economy depends on maximizing the economic value of creative products and culture to fuel global growth and prosperity. While these arguments rage, attempts are being made to work within the existing global copyright regime framework while still advocating reforms that would redefine culture's relationship with the free market. If new rules of the game could be agreed upon there might just be less arguing over free beer and more freedom to build even richer realms of creativity and culture. These new models hint at more, not less, competition on a far more level playing field. However, let us first look at what is meant by 'free culture'.

Lawrence Lessig, in his book *Free Culture* (2004: xvi), defines it as 'a balance between anarchy and control. A free culture, like a free market, is filled with property. It is filled with rules of property and contract that get enforced by the state. But just as a free market is perverted if its property becomes feudal, so too can a free culture be queered by extremism in the property rights that define it'.

Free culture is a call for balanced copyright laws that provide fair recompense for creators and all the intermediaries that help form a creation, bring it to market and exploit its commercial potential in ways that do not limit access unnecessarily. Free culture also allows creators more choice of how they bring their creations to the attention of the public. Thanks to digitization, entry costs to the market place are substantially reduced. Creators, traditionally signing away their copyrights to companies that have the finance and infrastructure to produce and distribute the physical manifestation of the creation (be it book, CD or DVD) are questioning not only the ethics but also the efficacy of these kinds of arrangements. However, copyright laws as they presently stand are impeding this flow of culture. That Lessig and others should think this balance is out of kilter is hardly surprising, given the extension of copyright from an initial 14 years 300 years ago rising to up to 95 years in some instances, with most of those increases having taken place within the last 40 years, coinciding with the centralization of distribution powers through a small number of publishers, record labels and film production companies. Indeed there is an eerie coincidence that every time Mickey Mouse is about to come out of copyright, Disney marches up Capitol Hill demanding an extension of copyright terms.

The governance of intellectual property rights is an international affair under the auspices of the World Intellectual Property Organization (WIPO) that is responsible for copyright, patents and trademarks. It is one of the specialized UN agencies created in 1967 with the stated aim of encouraging creative activity and promoting the protection of intellectual property throughout the world. WIPO currently has 184 member states and administers 23 international treaties. Its role, however, is highly contentious. Because decisions are taken on the basis of each Member having one vote, developing countries were able to block expansions to intellectual property treaties that were not in their interest in the 1960s and 1970s. However, the North's response to this was to move the international standard-setting out of WIPO and into the General Agreement on Tariffs and Trade, which later evolved into the World Trade Organization. In this arena, the North had greater control and it is from here that the Agreement on Trade-Related Aspects of Intellectual Property Rights (TRIPs) emerged.

In 2004, WIPO adopted a 'development agenda' but this has not progressed far enough or fast enough to accommodate the wishes of civil society activists from the various free culture/free knowledge sectors. Indeed, the last 15 years have seen copyright regimes harden in favor of developed countries and the large multinational corporations, whether through WIPO directives or passage of national legislation such as the Digital Millennium Copyright Act in the USA.

And yet, despite this increasing lock down of culture, there has been a growing number of new and smaller independent companies availing themselves of the reduced entry costs to the market afforded by digital media. While they still represent a relatively small part of the monetized market, their influence is increasing. And that is just the picture on the commercial side. The non-commercial opportunities for creators to be seen and heard are growing at a much faster pace. Tools for creation and communication are becoming more ubiquitous, with over 70 million blogs, songwriters uploading their tunes and film-makers releasing their productions online. The UK Arts Council estimates that by 2010, 70 per cent of all content on the web will be user generated. Not surprisingly, corporations with well-known brands are looking for ways and means to fight back. Rupert Murdoch's purchase of MySpace is a spectacular gamble, as is Google's audacious acquisition of YouTube, but these are only two of many attempts underway to marry the free with the for-profit. Web 2.0 offers exponentially more opportunities to mix and match new business models.

There is something quite different in spirit about the culture created for consumption on the web. It has a transformative quality that is hard to pinpoint. According to Yochai Benkler 'new and important cooperative and coordinated action carried out through radically distributed, non-market mechanisms that do not depend on proprietary strategies – plays a much greater role than it did, or could have, in the industrial information economy' (Benkler, 2006: 3). It is the von Hippel notion of 'user-driven innovation' that has begun to expand that focus to thinking about how individual need and creativity drive innovation at the individual level and its diffusion through networks of like-minded individuals (Benkler, 2006: 5). No longer dependent on physical products to carry their works, creators are able to exercise more choice over how they disseminate their products. However, most still have to earn a living and this is where new business models come in, requiring more flexible licensing arrangements.

Magnatune employs an interesting new business model in the music world, adopting Creative Commons licensing and producing revenues for creators and middlemen alike. Founded by John Buckman and his wife Jan, Magnatune is an online record label. Artists submit their music to John who selects what he likes and puts it online. Users can listen for free via their computers; however, to download they are required to pay a minimum of $5 – while Magnatune's recommends a payment of $8. The sum received is shared on a 50–50 basis with the musician. Conventional economics says rational man will pay as little as possible. Yet Magnatune demonstrates this theory to be incorrect under certain circumstances. The average payment per collection is nearly $9.00! The consumer has much greater scope in registering his or her likes and dislikes by deciding how much they wish to pay. Unknown artists have far more exposure on the web than while performing local gigs and waiting for a talent scout to spot them.

Under the Magnatune model, musicians keep their copyright and use a Creative Commons 'some rights reserved' license to protect those rights required to make their music available commercially. Below we discuss how the Creative Commons licensing scheme operates. But before doing so we shall look at a few other developments that have confronted copyright issues.

A few years ago the BBC took the initiative to open up their film and recording archives to the public, for free use and reuse. It would have been an incredible resource to the world (even if only free of charge to the British taxpayer), allowing materials that had been paid for by the public to be used by the public. However, at the time of writing the project is floundering. A review is pending, but not scheduled. The reasons given vary, but at the heart of the matter rests the fact that there is too much third party material involved and the BBC does not have the rights to make it available to the public in this new way. The ever-present problem of rights clearance put paid to an otherwise spectacular project.

Significantly however, in another arena, Open Archiving is beginning to bear fruit. Scholarly research, bought and paid for by public funds, has historically been published by commercial publishers who add value by organizing peer review, editing, marketing and generally providing a branding system that has worked satisfactorily in the print medium. Authors handed over their copyright to publishers in exchange for reaching their intended audience.

Libraries bought the journals and stored them on their shelves. Now most scholarly journals are available online. There is no longer the need to invest in costly paper, distribution and shelving. However, as journal prices in the digital age went up rather than down (justified to some extent by the large investment required for digitization) there was a backlash against commercial publishers. The resulting model has been Open Access, still not definitively tried and tested, but adopted now widely enough to begin monitoring the differences. In the Open Access model, authors pay for publishers to go through the process of peer review, editing etc., when they submit their article. In turn the article is then free to readers online. In reality it is the research funding body that pays, as the fee is usually built into the research grant. Despite these innovations, the prices of journals continue to rise. The reaction of many funding bodies in Europe and North America has been to insist that journal articles be deposited in Open Access archives at some specified period after initial publication (generally around six months). Open Access models are still in transition and funding may move directly from funding body to publishers to streamline the system. However, researchers working outside the prescribed remit of the public research funding bodies may be disadvantaged so other ways of funding their access to peer-reviewed publication will need to be found.

The driving principle behind Open Access and Open Archives has been that publicly funded research and creations should be available to the end user free of charge. A new business model has been born. While copyright principles remain intact, how it is to be licensed is still under review. Taking Open Access one step further, some publishers are now selling collections of e-books to libraries on Creative Commons licenses that step outside the limitations of fair use and fair dealing and allow users to copy, download, cut and paste – all included in the fixed fee paid by the library for the package. Variations of this model are the subject of experimentation. The driving force behind these changes has been a desire, indeed a need, to share more broadly the fruits of creativity and knowledge as well as harness the potential of the Internet. In 2007 the record label EMI announced a deal with Apple to allow unlimited file sharing of music at a premium price ($1.29 per song rather than $0.99 for one user only). Companies are watching the uptake figures anxiously. As Bob Metcalfe said, 'The value of a system grows at approximately the square of the number of users of that system' (Benkler, 2006). This is especially true in the digital world.

Open knowledge is increasingly seen also as a benefit to commercial interests. Even pharmaceutical companies are advocating the open availability of data as a way of speeding up research and avoiding costly and time-consuming duplications of effort. Competitive collaboration, as was the case with the genome project, is of increasing interest. Optimal allocation of resources based on transparency of information is now being sought from various sectors. Governments are now finding themselves grappling with issues surrounding access to public information, taking their mandate as providers seriously while not quite adapting to the role of enablers that the free culture community is demanding of them.

Where does this leave us at the dawn of the twenty-first century? According to Benkler:

> We are in the midst of a technological, economic, and organizational transformation that allows us to renegotiate the terms of freedom, justice, and productivity in the information society. How we shall live in this new environment will in some significant measure depend on policy choices that we make over the next decade or so. To be able to understand these choices, to be able to make them well, we must recognize that they are part of what is fundamentally a social and political choice – a choice about how to be free, equal, productive human beings under a new set of technological and economic conditions. As economic policy, allowing yesterday's winners to dictate the terms of tomorrow's economic competition would be disastrous. As social policy, missing an opportunity to enrich democracy, freedom, and justice in our society while maintaining or even enhancing our productivity would be unforgivable. (Benkler, 2006: 27)

It is with these thoughts that some have turned their minds to addressing the obstacles that stand in the way of fulfilling the web's full potential, without unleashing total anarchy. Addressing intellectual property issues seemed a good starting point for lawyer and Stanford professor Lawrence Lessig. In his quest to balance the interests of creators and the public, he devised the licensing scheme known as Creative Commons (CC). Launched in 2002, this new form of licensing, already tested in courts, has captured the imagination of millions worldwide. Indeed over 150 million items on the web employ CC licenses. The best description of how it works comes from Creative Commons' own website, www.creative commons.org (accessed March 2007):

> A Creative Commons license is based on copyright. So they apply to all works that are protected by copyright law. The kinds of works that are protected by copyright law are books, websites, blogs, photographs, films, videos, songs and other audio & visual recordings, for example. Software programs are also protected by copyright but, as explained below, we do not recommend that you apply a Creative Commons license to software code.

> Creative Commons licenses give you the ability to dictate how others may exercise your copyright rights – such as the right of others to copy your work, make derivative works or adaptations of your work, to distribute your work and/or make money from your work. They do not give you the ability to restrict anything that is otherwise permitted by exceptions or limitations to copyright – including, importantly, fair use or fair dealing – nor do they give you the ability to control anything that is not protected by copyright law, such as facts and ideas.

> Creative Commons licenses attach to the work and authorize everyone who comes in contact with the work to use it consistent with the license. This means that if Bob has a copy of your Creative Commons-licensed work, Bob can give a copy to Carol and Carol will be authorized to use the work consistent with the Creative Commons license. You then have a license agreement separately with both Bob and Carol.

> Creative Commons licenses are expressed in three different formats: the Commons Deed (human-readable code), the Legal Code (lawyer-readable code); and the metadata (machine-readable code). You don't need to sign anything to get a Creative Commons license – just select your license at our 'Publish' page.

> One final thing you should understand about Creative Commons licenses is that they are all

non-exclusive. This means that you can permit the general public to use your work under a Creative Commons license and then enter into a separate and different non-exclusive license with someone else, for example, in exchange for money.

Enthusiasts praise the flexibility of Creative Commons licensing. Sue Charman (2007) says on her blog 'Digitisation and free distribution of content is not an erosion of copyright either. Its an assertion of a different copyright – the right to allow the public to copy freely and legally that which the author and publisher releases for such copying. It is freedom for the author to renounce the extremes of "all rights reserved" and tread instead on the more beneficial middle path of "some rights reserved"'.

The benefits of this approach vary from one type of cultural production to another. There is no doubt that for many it is a political statement, an anti status quo, or an anti big business statement. At the same time it is fostering a sense of community, as more and more people connect through the web and pursue their communal and even commercial interests. This is the case whether one defines culture narrowly as creative products such as film and music, or in the wider sense representing the core values and modes of organizing a society (Moore, 2007). As more and more people turn to the web, not only is the world becoming flatter (a concept made popular by Thomas Friedman, 2005) it is becoming much more connected with communities growing up around specific interest areas.

It is in this new environment that mass culture is competing with niche interests. The web not only allows for a more open and richer public commons, it facilitates people acquiring cultural goods that match their particular tastes. Looking at how this occurs with books we see that the number of titles in print globally has quadrupled from 1.5 million in 1994, to nearly 6 million in 2006 (Anderson, 2006). Some of this apparent growth may be due to better means of tracking titles, but some of this phenomenal increase is distinctly due to lowered costs of entry into the book marketplace. 'Books' can be posted on the web, and then printed on demand for those who want a bound copy (at often lower costs than on a home printer – when accounting for all costs). More importantly, readers can find information about what is available and purchase for even the smallest niche tastes. Means of marketing have changed the profile of book sales. Of the 1.2 million titles in print in the English language, only 15 per cent sell more than 99 copies a year. Without the advent of Amazon and other online retailers (plus the facility of short print runs) the other 85 per cent would be lost to obscurity forever. Indeed 70 per cent of that which is in copyright is out of print and much of that accumulated culture is being lost to posterity as copyright terms increase in line with the life of Mickey Mouse.

So there is now a blur emerging between the commercial and the non-commercial. The main Creative Commons licenses come in six formats, three of which expressly allow commercialization – provided that the user asks permission of the rights holder (thus enabling entering into a contractual/commercial relationship). This interfacing between the commercial and non-commercial was underscored as Professor Lessig stepped down as Chair at CC and passed the baton on to Joichi Ito, a venture capitalist and entrepreneur. Ten years ago it would have been highly improbable that someone who had made millions in the commercial world would chair an organization from which a social movement had been born. But Ito is an example of a growing number of dotcom success stories who are taking an active role in reshaping the world, not just through technology or traditional philanthropy but through active engagement with social and economic policy.

As more dotcom activists enter the arena, alongside a broad range of committed, impatient and clever social entrepreneurs it is likely that the attack on the traditional intellectual property framework will continue. Mainstream foundations such as Ford, MacArthur, Mellon, Open Society Institute and others are funding research and advocacy for change. Multinational corporations intent on suing 12-year-old MP3 file-sharers for billions of dollars in order to 'set an example' have lost the hearts and minds battle and are beginning to seek less draconian ways of preserving their businesses. And while there will remain still a polarization of interests there is nonetheless a recognition that copyright has a role to play in the free market. The issue is how to create a balanced and equitable copyright regime. The thinking behind free culture and the practices of Creative Commons licensing are amongst those that are leading the way.

REFERENCES

Anderson, Chris (2006) *The Long Tail*. London: Random House.

Benkler, Yochai (2006) *The Wealth of Networks*. New Haven: Yale University Press.

Charman, Sue (2007) http://chocnodka.blogware.com/blog-archives/2004/5/24/75489.html (consulted March 2007).

Creative Commons http://www.creativecommons.org (accessed March 2007).

Friedman, Thomas (2005) *The World is Flat*. London: Alan Lane.

Lessig, Lawrence (2004) *Free Culture*. New York: Penguin.

Moore, Henrietta (2007) Global Civil Society seminar, London School of Economics, 13 March.

Naughton, John (1999) *A Brief History of the Future*. London: Weidenfeld & Nicholson.

## CHAPTER 6

CULTURAL ENTREPRENEURS: PRODUCING CULTURAL VALUE AND WEALTH
Thomas H. Aageson

This chapter focuses on cultural enterprises and the cultural entrepreneurs behind them, whether they are found in cultural organizations or independent enterprises. These terms are relatively new and there are important questions that need to be asked and answers developed, such as: What is the role of cultural entrepreneurs? What are the common characteristics of cultural entrepreneurs? What are the essentials for starting a cultural enterprise? How does a cultural entrepreneur finance a cultural enterprise? What does sustainability mean in a cultural enterprise? Who are these cultural enterprises? How can we begin to train future cultural entrepreneurs? Do cultural entrepreneurs play the same role as entrepreneurs do in other parts of the economy that are undergoing globalization? What are the current and emerging organizational forms for the investment, production, distribution and consumption of cultural goods and services?

Cultural entrepreneurs are the bedrock of the cultural economy

In 1987, Stephanie Odegard traveled to Nepal on behalf of the World Bank to help traditional carpet weavers find new markets for their work. One year later, Odegard had transformed this short-term project into Odegard Inc., now a multimillion-dollar business employing 10,000 workers in Nepal (www.odegardinc.com). The company gives back 25 per cent of its profits to further the economic and social development of its workers and their communities, and has helped to create a movement that has successfully eradicated the use of child labour in carpet weaving throughout South Asia.

Cultural entrepreneurship has the power to change an entire community's economic trajectory.

Stephanie Odegard is just one example of a cultural entrepreneur contributing to a dynamic shift in cultural sustainability and economic development. This shift is transforming communities and creating market demand and cultural wealth that might otherwise fade away. The ventures that emerge in the cultural industries by cultural entrepreneurs lead to the development of thriving economic systems that enhance and sustain cultural traditions and values. Stephanie Odegard's story also demonstrates how cultural entrepreneurs add to the artistic world through innovation: Odegard Inc.'s carpets now grace the halls of the J. Paul Getty Museum, The Metropolitan Museum of Art, 70 showrooms in three continents, and the homes of numerous celebrities. Stephanie Odegard's access to these world-class markets has enabled her to build a thriving business. Her leadership has also led to the creation of Rugmark, an independent organization that certifies products that are created under safe, healthy, working conditions.

Behind each cultural enterprise there is an entrepreneur whose vision led to its development. The aggregation of cultural enterprises creates the global cultural economy. The growth of the cultural economy is thus dependent on the vibrancy of these cultural enterprises. Entrepreneurs hold the vision of the enterprise: their passion for cultural traditions provides this vibrancy. Entrepreneurs develop new cultural enterprises and expand existing cultural enterprises with new cultural products and services. Seldom are these innovators recognized for their entrepreneurial skills; globally there are few opportunities for future cultural entrepreneurs to learn from successful cultural entrepreneurs. In order for the growth of the global cultural economy to be enhanced, more innovative entrepreneurs around the world need to be identified; their experiences must be developed into cases for others to learn from; new educational delivery systems are required in order to train the next generation of entrepreneurs; and a network of cultural entrepreneurs needs to be organized and cultural venture funds created to finance new ideas.

Cultural entrepreneurs are change agents who leverage cultural innovation to create thriving economic systems.

Rural entrepreneurs are resourceful visionaries who take risks and generate revenues from cultural activities; their innovative applications of traditions to markets result in economically sustainable cultural enterprises. These enterprises enhance livelihoods and create cultural value for both creative producers and consumers of cultural services and products.

Box 6.1   Missing the link – why creative entrepreneurs matter

How do we build a competitive and sustainable creative economy? One thing is for sure, it's not going to be done on the basis of artists, designers, performers, writers and the like – what we might call 'creative talent' – alone. Whilst they may provide the lifeblood for our enjoyment of culture, design, entertainment and the media, in the context of a functioning economic model they rarely cut it. For every time I've heard an artist say 'I'm a business' (and quite often successful artists are savvy enough to say that), I've heard ten or more decrying the market, expressing disinterest in audience or demanding another government handout. The fact of the matter is that there's an equally important element in the crucible of the creative economy. In an age when we're all led to believe that through the Internet our creativity can get out there and find its own niche market, it's probably the most important element: the creative entrepreneur.

Creative entrepreneurs provide the bridge between creative talent and the market, what we might call 'creative consumers'. They navigate the topography of the business world of creativity; spotting the talent, stimulating the market, negotiating the contracts, ensuring that the revenue comes in. Crucially they sort the wheat from the chaff; they mediate between good and bad in the realm of quality – both quality of content and quality of service. Let's understand that creative entrepreneurs are not something new. Producers, publishers, impresarios, curators, agents and the like have always been there but before they were bit players, a necessary evil taking their percentage. It's only in the context of the creative economy that we've come to understand that they are elemental.

Since 2003 the British Council has been working to identify and raise the profile of young creative entrepreneurs. We've developed a series of programs and awards that create spaces for networking, for showcasing talent, for doing business and which facilitate collaboration and business skills development. The International Young Creative Entrepreneur awards are our leading program, operating in nine areas: communications, design, fashion, interactive, music, performing arts, publishing, screen and visual arts. Ten countries take part in each award. Each country, through a national competition, selects a winner, who then joins their nine fellow winners on a visit to the UK. Over the following two weeks, the finalists get to meet their peers and key players in the UK industry. They attend a major trade fair and are given an opportunity to present work that they believe can find its place in the UK market. It is an incredibly powerful process, establishing them in the context of their peers and helping them to build an international network of individuals with a shared experience: giving them the chance to understand how a developed market

(Continued)

(Continued)

works and making the process of doing business there in the future simpler. Importantly too it promotes South–South trade: finalists leave knowing and understanding their nine fellow finalists, knowing and understanding that they can work together, share ideas and trade with one another. The program doesn't end with an award ceremony. The process is dynamic, stimulating ongoing dialogue and engagement. Based around curated spaces and experiences, mutual trust, need and the potential for economic return, the alumni network is thriving.

We're constantly seeking to innovate, to find new ways of working, test concepts and develop our understanding. In 2006, in India, this included a new program, *Creative Future*; a summer school that sought to build the business skills of 20 young Indian creative entrepreneurs. All had fascinating creative business ideas, but few had the skills to take their idea forward. We worked with Indian and UK partners – the Indian Institute of Management in Bangalore and the Creative Industries Development Agency in Yorkshire – to create the *Creative Future* school. The learning experience for all of us was significant but it also confirmed a shared belief that more and better tailored business training for people in the sector unlocks the potential of the creative economy. These types of experience are essential if we are to energise potential, to make the step changes from the creative idea to managing a creative business to becoming a successful creative entrepreneur.

The programs have highlighted the particular needs of creative entrepreneurs. Every entrepreneur has to deal with people but, in the creative economy, the difference is that the raw material is people with creative talent; people who are possessed of what they do and who, in producing, invest and give enormously of themselves. To work with this raw material, creative entrepreneurs have to have an affinity and understanding of what drives creative talent and the ways in which it works. Creative entrepreneurs are also different in their understanding of the market and the nature of risk. Risk is endemic to the creative process and, consequently, the 'judgement call' on creative entrepreneurs is heightened. Essentially that judgement is about something that the market doesn't know it needs; whether that's a new trend or a new character. With the creative economy we, the creative consumers, are often left saying 'who would have thought that… a book about a boy wizard' or '… a musical about cats'. Creative entrepreneurs have to be a step ahead of us, seeing that potential, backing that talent, taking that risk. Crucially, in this process, they also understand the social contract in the relationship between creativity and society. They recognise that creativity and art are and often have been used as tools – for good and for bad – to assert community, national identity, political truth and religious faith. And they see the role that creativity plays in the sphere of education. They understand how all of these elements of this complex world affect the market.

In our increasingly globalised world, creative entrepreneurs are the bulwark in our defence of cultural diversity. Only a strong, local independent sector will understand the local market and will, in turn, spot the local talent, invest in it and develop it. Increasingly, it is local creative entrepreneurs who will be able to look outwards, understand the global trends and find the right opportunities in that wider market.

Creative entrepreneurs have been the missing link in our understanding of the dynamics of the creative economy. Today their importance is evident. Without them the creative economy simply doesn't exist. But *our* understanding of them and the nature of the creative economy is far from complete. Slowly we're coming to understand this element and recognise that it can enrich us all – culturally, socially and economically. Making, rather than missing, the link – such is the power of creativity.

© Andrew Senior, 2007

(For more information on the British Council's work with young creative entrepreneurs visit www.creativeconomy.org.uk)

As observed in the 2005 UNESCO study *International Flows of Selected Cultural Goods and Services, 1994–2003*:

> The number of products created and sold throughout the world is increasing every year.

Similarly, the growing international trade of these cultural products constitutes an important part of the global economy. According to the United Nations Conference on Trade and Development (UNCTAD) (2004), the global market value of industries with strong creative *and cultural components is estimated at US$1.3 trillion. Since 2000, the industry has grown at an annual compound rate of over 7 per cent.*

Markets are broadening and new markets are being created. Cultural entrepreneurs must be ready to take advantage of these new opportunities. Supporting cultural entrepreneurs is important because they often work in environments where there is little financial or business development assistance available. The knowledge and skills required to develop these enterprises must be made available to entrepreneurs in the field. Most cultural entrepreneurs lack access to the seed capital, market links, information, mentorship and operating experience required to become a successful entrepreneur and business leader. Scores of cultural entrepreneurs could become exponentially more successful given the right management tools, information, access to markets, and financial support or investment. Their successful cultural enterprises are the catalysts that build a vibrant cultural economy.

Globalization has opened cultural markets but displaced others. Exports of film and music from the US threaten to overrun locally produced films and music unless nation-states develop cultural policies and programs to support local creators. Franchised restaurants and hotels threaten the local hospitality industry. Potters have lost markets to inexpensive plastic buckets and local weavers saw their markets disappear to low-cost synthetic textile clothing that has flooded markets. On the other hand, globalization has opened new opportunities for creative people. Potters in Peru and Ghana have converted from utilitarian to decorative, design-based products. Film-makers in India have created the Bollywood phenomenon. San Jolobil weavers in Chiapas have offered their work as folk art and converted to utilitarian products using traditional production techniques. Putumayo created a new class of music with their World Music CDs, while Jamaicans converted the local music into an export and helped build their tourism market and national identity through their music.

Globalization along with economic policy is impacting the cultural economy in other ways as well. The ever more rapid movement of information and people around the world coupled with strong demand in countries with high national income has opened new cultural markets. Professor Phillip Scher maintained in his presentation to the 2006 Arts, Culture and Communities in International Development Conference 'that the decrease of economic options in the region (Caribbean) not only creates a market for culture and tourism; it spawns a form of national identity that measures its success against foreign consumption and recognition. This change in the development of culture is in part spawned by the "marketization" of discrete aspects of social life. These are, in turn, influenced by neoliberal ideology' (Scher 2006: 1). He went on to suggest 'that commodification of cultural forms in the contemporary global climate are not only an imperative of nation-states, they have become synonymous with a nationalist ideology whose agenda has already been set by the growing hegemony of a neoliberal economic order.' (Scher, 2006: 6). Trinidad-Tobago positions itself around Carnival, creating destination events based on the country's cultural traditions. The re-development of Honolulu is an excellent example of a city-state basing its public investment on cultural experiences around Waikiki Beach.

Box 6.2   The film industry in Nigeria

A case in point is the film industry in Nigeria. A few years ago African film was non-existent. The onset of globalization has allowed the African cultural entrepreneur to expose his product to the world. What this has done is to educate the world about the African traditions and practices. The important thing here is that the African film producer has not copied the American producer although he may have been influenced by the Western world in making films in the first place. African films are now the rave in Barbados and some persons are literally watching over five African movies per day! Women especially are so in tune with these films that they have formed informal clubs to exchange movies and have even adopted the dress of Africans.

Sandra Browne

What is a cultural entrepreneur?

The cultural entrepreneur

Cultural entrepreneurs are risk takers, change agents and resourceful visionaries who generate revenue from innovative and sustainable cultural enterprises that enhance livelihoods and create cultural value for both creative producers and consumers of cultural services and products.

'Entrepreneur' comes from the French word, *entreprendre* which means 'to do something' or 'to undertake something'. The word has been traced back to the thirteenth century and was first applied to a business venture in the 1550s; from that point forward, writers have refined the definition. In the early 1700s, Richard Cantillion added the concept that the entrepreneur bears risk, creating a venture without assurance of profit. Jean Baptiste Say, known for Say's Law, developed his thinking around entrepreneurship in the early nineteenth century and observed that the entrepreneur is 'called upon to estimate, with tolerable accuracy, the demand, and the means of production; sometimes to employ a great number of workers, find consumers, to exercise a spirit of order and economy. In the course of such operations there are obstacles to be surmounted, anxieties to be overcome, misfortunes to be repaired, and expedients to be devised' (2005: 87). In the 1940s, Joseph A. Schumpeter added to our understanding of the concept:

> We have seen that the function of entrepreneurs is to reform or revolutionize the pattern of production by exploiting an invention or, more generally, an untried technological possibility for producing a new commodity or producing an old one in a new way, by opening up a new source of supply of materials or a new outlet for products, by reorganizing an industry and so on… This kind of activity is primarily responsible for the recurrent 'prosperities' that revolutionize the economic organism and the recurrent 'recessions' that are due to the disequilibrating impact of the new products or methods… To act

> with confidence beyond the range of familiar beacons and to overcome that resistance requires aptitudes that are present in only a small fraction of the population and that define the entrepreneurial type as well as the entrepreneurial function. This function does not essentially consist of either inventing anything or otherwise creating the conditions, which the enterprise exploits. It consists in getting things done. (1942: 132)

In the 1980s the concept of social entrepreneur began to develop and became popular. It refers to individuals who use their entrepreneurial skills to create social value through social organizations and social enterprises. Today, in the earliest years of the twenty-first century, a new concept is being introduced into the lexicon of entrepreneurship: 'cultural entrepreneur', one who creates cultural value and wealth for the creators and producers of cultural products and services.

Cultural organizations and cultural enterprises

Cultural enterprises

Cultural enterprises are commercial ventures that connect creators and artists to markets and consumers. They create, produce and market cultural goods and services, generating economic, social and cultural opportunities for creators while adding cultural value for consumers. Cultural enterprises are both non-profit and for-profit, that use business approaches; and, deploy financial, human and cultural capital (creativity, talent, cultural traditions, knowledge and intellectual property) in a strategic and entrepreneurial manner.

It is important to be aware of the differences between cultural organizations and cultural enterprises. Cultural organizations are non-profit organizations that earn some of their revenues but also depend on gifts, grants and governmental subsidies to balance their budgets each year.

Examples include operas, museums, performing arts groups, educational institutions, etc. Cultural organizations need financial support over and above their ticket, tuition and other revenues. They enhance the community's quality of life, preserve culture and create important educational opportunities. Often cultural organizations create cultural enterprises to earn needed operating funds. Cultural entrepreneurs are usually the creators of cultural organizations, and as these organizations grow, cultural managers take over the leadership of the organization. They are aptly described as cultural organization entrepreneurs, and they hold a vision and passion just like the enterprise entrepreneur.

Cultural enterprises are commercial ventures that connect creators (artists, writers, artisans, dancers, etc.) to markets and consumers. They create, produce and market cultural goods and services, generating economic, cultural and social opportunities for creators while adding cultural value for consumers. Cultural enterprises can be either non-profit or for-profit; they use business approaches to their ventures but have different measures of return on investment. Cultural enterprises also deploy financial, human and cultural capital in a strategic and entrepreneurial fashion. These enterprises depend on investment and debt financing as well as occasional grants to fund their ventures and are expected to return a profit along with creating cultural value for the community and consumer.

Cultural enterprises are diverse in nature and size and range from micro to small and medium enterprises (SME) to large firms. They operate in a variety of fields including performing arts, visual arts, music, literature, publishing, film, photography, folk art, design, architecture, education hospitality, cultural heritage, creative tourism, new media, etc. Some examples of cultural enterprises are publishing houses, production companies, photo agencies, foundries, bookstores, galleries and museum-related initiatives such as shops and print publications.

Box 6.3   Opening markets for majority world photographers

Shahidul Alam and a partner created *Drik* in order to provide the 'majority world' photographic community with market links into international publishing markets and to establish intellectual property rights. Slowly, international media began to use local photographers. *Drik* has helped with social campaigns through exhibitions and seminars on human rights, particularly working on gender issues and child rights. They set up the first email service in Bangladesh and later a school of photography and the country's first webzine (see www.driknews.com).

The initial investment by Shahidul was a computer and printer; he also gave his personal photographic equipment to *Drik*. He used his personal income as a writer and photographer to support *Drik* at the outset. They produced calendars, postcards and bookmarks that became very successful and helped fund the organization. The major constraint was the need to be socially responsible and financially viable.

Globalization has facilitated the use of media from all sources. *Drik*'s focus is on providing markets for local photographers. They look for areas 'where economic requirements and cultural needs overlap... The most robust and effective organizations will be the ones that can combine the specificity of local situations, like indigenous design and unique cultural attributes, with global distribution mechanisms, such as the Internet'.

'At the production end, organizations and individuals who are networked into the global economy, and have the human and material resources to tap into the system, without diluting their cultural identity will be the winners. Organizations that are unable to cope with the changes or lose their identity in an attempt to be competitive will be the losers.'

Source: Alam, 2007

Cultural capital

Cultural capital is essential to a successful cultural enterprise; it's what makes these businesses unique. Cultural capital is often undervalued or dismissed as something integral to a community but of little economic value. Today, we must understand cultural capital in order to think about entrepreneurial ideas that sustain the uniqueness of a culture and support innovation. Cultural capital can include traditions, music, skills, feasts and celebrations, food and location. Cultural capital is often formed from a legacy of creative talent and traditions. Cultural capital is found in individuals who carry forward the traditions. Museums and libraries serve as repositories of cultural capital; educational organizations foster creativity and advance traditions by building cultural capital amongst students.

Role and characteristics of the cultural entrepreneur

There are cultural creators and cultural workers. They are integrated into a creativity pyramid with the artist-innovator at the peak whose ideas are converted into cultural goods and services that cultural workers produce. (The term artist here broadly encompasses artisan, author, choreographer, film-maker, etc.) The innovator and entrepreneur are sometimes the same person, but more often than not are different individuals. The artist creates the idea, product or service. The cultural entrepreneur creates a vision for a cultural enterprise that bridges a market need with cultural traditions, cultural experiences and cultural innovations, enhancing the livelihoods of cultural creators and workers while at the same time enriching the consumer. The cultural entrepreneur holds the passion to muster the resources and the people to make the enterprise a sustainable reality. The entrepreneur creates the enterprise around the new cultural product or service, then assembles the capital and means of production, which creates employment for cultural workers. The entrepreneur melds cultural capital with human and financial capital. The quality and quantity of each will spell the success of the venture. Commercial franchising creates global homogeneity, while vibrant, local culture creates the diversity that sustains the development of our humanity. Ironically, it is innovation that preserves traditions; entrepreneurs and artists are the catalysts of cultural innovation.

Richard Florida's *The Rise of the Creative Class* (2002) stirred thinking across the globe about regional economic development. In essence, his book used culture and creativity as a measure for attracting innovators that would stimulate the local economy mainly through technological innovation. If a region offers diversity as well as cultural and creative opportunities, then there is a higher probability that the people who tend to be catalysts for innovation leading to economic development, especially in technology-based enterprise, will settle in the region's community. Ironically, Florida paid little attention to the development of cultural enterprises, yet regions and nation-states are finding that 'Cultural and creative industries alone are estimated to account for over 7 per cent of the world's Gross Domestic Product (GDP)' (UNESCO, 2005: 19). In the case of the American city of Santa Fe, New Mexico, nearly 16 per cent of the region's economy is attributable to the arts and cultural industries, one of the highest in the world for a regional economy (BBER, 2004: 11). Discussing the case of Sweden, Florida and Mellander assert that 'the role of talent and creativity in economic development has been a subject of growing interest to social scientists. Human capital is observed both to be an important contributor to growth and to be unevenly distributed geographically... We find that the creative class measures outperform conventional educational measures in accounting for regional development across our sample of Swedish regions' (2007: 3). What is important to Florida's theory of economic development, which depends on innovation, is a vibrant cultural and creative population. Cultural vibrancy is fostered by innovation and the same human talent or 'human capital' required for broader regional economic development.

Cultural entrepreneurs do have common characteristics around the globe that include being *passionate, visionary, innovative, risk takers, networkers* and *leaders*. Their values are similar in terms of their attitudes towards authentic culture. Every entrepreneur has a *passion* for the culture, a community's traditions and talents and especially for the creators, the innovators, as well as cultural workers. Each one cares deeply about cultural traditions and the community and are passionate advocates for preservation. The entrepreneur's focus is on the opportunity and the problem to be solved and she is always committed to innovative solutions and ventures.

Box 6.4 Innovative expansion of pan-African book markets

Paul Brickhill created the Book Café, a multi-disciplinary community arts center in Harare, Zimbabwe, combining bookshop, music, theatre, live poetry, comedy and a restaurant. It also has a strong development program in youth arts, gender, HIV prevention and is starting to develop a film unit. They have financed the arts center through the success of the bookshop and a small grant. Their growth has come about almost entirely from revenue-generating income derived from food and beverages plus rent. The restraints in Zimbabwe include economic deterioration, 1700 per cent real inflation coupled with political intimidation (see www.zimbabwearts.co.zw).

One of Paul's most impressive entrepreneurial initiatives was to work on a pan-African basis to lower the cost of shipping books produced in Africa, therefore broadening the book market and allowing publishers to scale up print runs for their books. 'We approached a courier company on the basis that since there were so few books being couriered between African countries they couldn't possibly lose, they could only gain, by REDUCING rates on books – much like the historic 'printed matter reduced rate' that most post offices used to offer; and deriving value by corporate social responsibility branding as the courier company that is stimulating books and literacy; as well as capturing the entire share of a small but growing trade in books virtually from start-up.'

Paul reports that Zimbabwe has a strong performing arts culture and ethos and that globalization has not impacted much on their activities. However, on the macro-economic level, there is generalized poverty amongst artists and about one third of Zimbabwe's artists have left the country over the last 15 years; their cultural products are being produced outside of Zimbabwe.

In terms of what is needed to strengthen emerging Zimbabwe cultural enterprises and support for local cultural entrepreneurs, the needs are articulated as more pan-African initiatives aimed at intra-African cultural exchange of products and performing arts, that allow for a broader scope, synergy, flow of innovation and bigger regional markets. Also, grant funding and loans, that is, lead funding, that allow enterprise development in the arts aimed entirely at achieving economic vitality is required.

Source: Brickhill, 2007

What distinguishes the implacable preservationist from the entrepreneur is the *vision* that provides the path towards an enterprise that will create both *cultural value* and *wealth*. The cultural entrepreneur has a vision for the enterprise that encompasses the end result and benefit of the enterprise. The entrepreneur sees the problem and the solution, the need and the talent to create the market link as the whole picture. Entrepreneur and opportunity are intermingled in every definition of the cultural entrepreneur. They see the opportunity to make a difference in people's lives, enhance their livelihoods and advance the cultural environment.

The entrepreneur thinks beyond ordinary limits to achieve solutions and build markets while adapting commonly accepted market strategies into the new enterprise. It cannot be stressed enough: *innovation* is the great preservationist of traditions. All traditions in the world today evolved in communities through a series of innovations over the decades and centuries. What we call a tradition today may have never existed generations back. The colourful *alegrijes* of Oaxaca did not exist 50 years ago but today they are synonymous with the region. The multicoloured wire baskets of South Africa made from telephone wire have given birth to an industry providing work to thousands of people yet it is a relatively new tradition that rises out of basket-weaving with fiber.

To recap, the entrepreneur is creative in many ways: he/she creates new products, finds and sometimes creates market niches; he/she is creative in securing resources while not always knowing where they will come from; and he/she engages the right people to help create the vision. Often the cultural entrepreneur has to create new cultural markets rather than enter into an existing market, making the entrepreneurial effort a twofold challenge. The entrepreneur has the facility to create market intelligence through observation and analysis; create analogous scenarios to commercial markets and cultural markets; and adopt and adapt and extrapolate it all into a new cultural enterprise vision. Often a cultural entrepreneur will see demand for a product, such as recorded music, and adapt it to a cultural product like world music, as did Dan Storper at Putumayo that now distributes cultural music worldwide (see www.putumayo.com).

The cultural entrepreneur is like the bow of a ship cutting into new seas. Uncertainty is part of each venture; being able to tolerate *risk* is an essential characteristic of an entrepreneur. The entrepreneur creates new products and services, new ways of producing the work, new ways of distributing and promoting the work. The market is not always obvious and sometimes the demand is latent or not quantifiable, but by instinct and desire, the entrepreneur opens new markets.

Cultural entrepreneurs also maintain a wide *network* of people who will support the vision and create strategic partnerships with investors, opinion makers, market makers and creators. This network can range from financial to marketing to management to production contacts.

The cultural entrepreneur is a *vision-leader* who has the passion to see the vision through to the development of the cultural enterprise. The entrepreneur is persistent, determined, committed to the vision and creates commitment to the vision from others. The entrepreneur has a deep sense of service to the creators and cultural workers as well as to the consumer. There is also a total, selfless dedication to the cultural beneficiaries as a *servant-leader*. Both as visionary and servant, the entrepreneur creates trust amongst everyone the enterprise touches. Most importantly, deviation from a value-based approach will undermine this trust and ultimately the enterprise will fail or wreak havoc on the most vulnerable in the enterprise.

Cultural entrepreneurs are mission-driven and market-focused

In the commercial sphere, the focus of a new enterprise is the creation of wealth for the stockholders. The investors commit their financial resources with the expectation that there will be high returns that are better than their current returns for the capital they have in hand. The cultural entrepreneur has at least dual returns: to create wealth for all involved and build cultural value. The entrepreneur creates an enterprise that is both mission-driven and market-focused. The mission is as important as the return and in fact needs to define the return. The mission and vision also define how the problem will be solved and how opportunities will be taken advantage of through the enterprise. As a commercial venture, the enterprise must also be financially viable which requires staying focused on the market.

Box 6.5   Weaving together preserves traditions and enhances livelihoods

Weavers Studio (www.weaversstudio.com) was established in 1993 by Darshan Shah with a mission to 'Use as many hands as possible'. Young women are trained and employed in the language and aesthetics of India's rich textile heritage. Weavers Studio plays the role of communication, networking and marketing, creating a positive link between the craftspeople at the grass roots and the new emerging discerning buyer in India and abroad. The operations include commercially run handloom weaving, tailoring, hand block printing, screen printing, tie and dye and embroidery centers across India. During Darshan's career in marketing for Apple Computer she traveled her country learning the textile traditions and the situation of the artisans. She trained with master craftsmen to learn the textile techniques and then set up Weavers Studio with a 'few thousand rupees'. The focus of the enterprise is to train women so that they will be more self-sufficient. The key to success for Darshan has been hard work, building her skills in management programs, developing a business relationship of trust and goodwill towards the craftsperson and building a team of dedicated women managers.

In order to build up capital, Darshan saved funds from her work where she continued part-time employment, held sales exhibitions and offered the opportunity for others to sell in her first workshop. She never took out loans and always generated funds internally for any expansion. She kept part of the profits to buy old textiles, books, fund student projects, fund vocational training and fund staff training. As a single mother, Darshan had many personal responsibilities along with those of her enterprise.

Globalization worries Darshan and yet she also sees the opportunities. She commented, 'Though the global economy has grown rapidly, poverty persists and inequality increases among the weaker sections of the society, especially in underdeveloped and developing nations. The cultures of the world have in recent years become more similar, to the point that most of us now share a global, largely Western-dominated culture... With globalization of economic and unrestricted free trade, it is those individuals and organizations with greater financial advantage who benefit more... On the positive side, when the cultural economy goes global, more markets emerge, positive influences and challenges are welcome. The crafts person becomes more exposed, aware, educated, humbled, cost effective, and innovative. Globalization has to be understood in the correct spirit. We can all be winners if we understand and accept that globalization is the larger interest of the society and a prerequisite for growth at all levels.'

Source: Shah, 2007

Sustainability

Sustainability has become an ill-defined cliché. The term is used most often in the environmental development field, and later was incorporated into economics and social sectors. Seldom is it used in the cultural sector. In fact, for cultural enterprises, it is important to use sustainability in a holistic manner. It is like a woven cloth where the weaving must be strong throughout; one weak strand will make the entire work unravel. A cultural enterprise must weave together all aspects of sustainability into a 'whole' cloth. Creating a whole cloth of sustainability, weaving together economic, social, environmental and cultural values defines the set of balances that must always be attended to as the enterprise develops. Jed Emerson is a leader in this line of thinking (see www.blendedvalue.org). He argues that not one value but three (social, economic and environmental) are achieved in any enterprise. What must be added to this equation is cultural value, which is also part of the fabric of a cultural, in fact, any enterprise.

- *Social sustainability* creates wide accessibility to arts and cultural heritage, increases civic participation and social responsibility, enhances the lives of artists and other creators, and creates a positive impact on learning, all resulting in improving quality of life.
- *Economic sustainability* occurs when both creators' and producers' livelihoods are sufficient to meet their essential needs, young people are encouraged to enter the field and the enterprise

is profitable. The enterprise itself is financially sustainable using earnings for reinvestment and depreciation on capital investments to replace capital assets.

- *Environmental sustainability* is achieved when consumption of natural resources does not exceed replenishment cycles nor does it contaminate natural resources. Cultural industries are normally one of the more environmentally sensitive industries.
- *Cultural sustainability* is achieved when the creation and production of cultural products and services results in the continuation and innovation of cultural traditions, creating cultural value in both the local and global community.

Financing a cultural enterprise

'Specifically, there is an abject lack of risk-taking capital. The result is that proven social enterprises are starved of the capital required to grow to an appropriate size. Yet there are also an increasing number of mission-based investors looking for opportunities that go beyond traditional grants and into the realm of debt and equity, and are willing to consider new models of risk and return. However, these two groups are struggling to find one another' (Emerson, 2007: 4). This same situation is true for cultural enterprises, and the dearth of investment capital for these ventures will increase as the numbers of enterprises are created around the globe. Financing a cultural enterprise can be done in

Box 6.6   Using the shopping center model to create artisan markets

Sandra Browne is a unique cultural entrepreneur in that she works for a government agency, the Barbados Investment Development Corporation. Sandra deployed government capital to build Pelican Village (www.barbados.org/pelican_village.htm), a shopping center for Barbados artists and artisans that is centrally located for visitors to reach, especially those coming off the cruise ships. She combines enterprise development work along with marketing of Pelican Village. She works with artists and artisans to develop their products, enhance their retail presentation and services while creating events at the center that draw more foot traffic in the beautiful setting of the retail shops. Sandra comments that 'the most difficult issues relate to the low esteem with which the sector was held and still has that stigma; the artisans too do not see themselves as professionals and allow that reality to affect the quality of their service and interaction with their customers'.

Sandra feels that 'economic globalization may well provide countries with more opportunities to market their cultural goods and services. In fact, the more globalized the world becomes the more in demand the authentic product is... small economies have, through the patterns of economic globalization, the opportunity to spread their cultural products to larger markets... In countries where tourism is the primary money earner, cultural enterprises must be linked in all ways possible to that sector'.

Source: Browne, 2007

different ways; often several sources of capital are combined and deployed in a cultural enterprise. Financial capital comes after the enterprise concept and business plan are developed. The business idea must be viable on paper before capital can be raised to finance the enterprise. Ten of the most common sources of capital are discussed below.

Internally financed capital from the parent cultural organization can be used for investing in a new enterprise. The parent may have cash reserves or an endowment that can be used for an investment. The question for the parent, aside from the mission-related impact, is whether the return will be equal to or greater than what is being currently earned from the reserves or endowment. Also, the parent may use leverage with financial institutions in order to secure debt or donors who will finance the enterprise. If there is a current enterprise that is profitable with a positive cash flow, those funds can be invested in the expansion of an enterprise or to create a new enterprise. Enterprises depreciate their capital assets over time and that non-cash expense is another source of cash flow to reinvest in new capital assets that strengthen the enterprise.

Outside private investments can come from people close to the organization. The enterprise may

have a Board of Directors that can invest in the enterprise or private investors who are prepared to support the new endeavor. For example, a museum store was financed by preferred shares sold to donors who later gave them as a gift to the parent cultural organization. Social venture funds are now beginning to be formed; it is important that cultural enterprises are viewed as having equivalent value as a social enterprise and should be considered for investment by these new funds based on their ability to create cultural value as well as social value. The Ashoka Venture Fund for Leading Social Entrepreneurs is a good example (see www.ashoka.org).

Foundations are developing vehicles for loans and equity investments that are called Program-Related Investments (PRIs) or Mission-Related Investments (MRIs). In the case of a PRI/MRI, a foundation partners with a non-profit in a venture to create new enterprises with a vision that parallels their own vision. Often foundations will blend a grant with a PRI/MRI investment. Even the World Bank's International Finance Corporation (IFC) is making cultural investments alongside their public financing ventures in countries like Peru. There will be a need to create a cultural investment fund soon. New community venture funds are being created that have a goal of creating a 'double bottom line' that gives a return to investors and contributes to the common good. Examples are the Pacific Community Fund and New Mexico Community Capital, Inc. Cultural investments can be strong candidates for these new investment funds. In most cases debt financing will come with an interest cost and equity investments will be made with an expectation of a return. An example of private investment without a return expected are zero-coupon bonds now being issued by banks that guarantee a return of capital in a certain number of years with no interest charged. Another is a community loan fund where social and cultural investors would put their money in the fund and select a return from 0–6 per cent; that money is loaned with an interest charge and the interest income used to operate the loan fund.

By creating a *membership* in the organization to support the endeavor, an enterprise can be financed from start-up through the growth phase. Cooperatives often take this form of financing, with each member contributing their own capital to fund the start-up of an enterprise.

Offering *sponsorships* of a market, a festival or a cooperative can also raise new capital. Sponsorships are often viewed as marketing opportunities by other enterprises that want their name associated with the cultural enterprise. Individual sponsors want to support the endeavor and do not expect a return for their support. This works best with a non-profit where the individual can take advantage of a tax deduction in those countries that allow them.

Governments often have incentives for starting cultural enterprises. These can be marketing funds given by an economic development agency that wants to see the income of cultural workers improve.

Other times there are funds to support development in geographic regions such as rural or depressed urban areas. The entrepreneur can cast the new venture as enterprise development, then the development of a cultural enterprise fits into more categories of governmental support. Unfortunately, it is difficult to find funds for culture alone so one must be creative, innovative and entrepreneurial in developing these sources.

Linking *special events* to the vision of the enterprise can often raise capital. Launches of new products can be done in a fashion that raises funds, as can special-invitation gatherings that have an entrance price. Auctions and lotteries are other creative ways to raise capital for a venture.

Owning property that generates rent can be a source of regular capital to finance a venture. This is called *passive income.* Rather than selling the property, the rental income can be a source of the capital needed to begin the new or next enterprise. Investment income from dividends and interest, should the sponsoring organization hold a portfolio, is also a source of fresh capital.

Debt can be in the form of a bank or private loan as well as by issuing bonds. An established organization of substantial size can float bonds to finance part of a new venture. In some economies, non-profit bonds are tax exempt, which gives the enterprise a favorable rate of interest and tax breaks for the investor.

Personal and family funds, more often than not, are used to start grassroots cultural enterprises. Micro and small enterprises are financed at the beginning with personal funds and/or those of the family. The entrepreneur's passion for the vision is such that initial steps must be taken and created for others to join in the vision.

Box 6.7   Creating an art gallery; creating markets for artists; and generating income for a museum

At Mystic Seaport Museum I came to realize that there were no living artists in the museum's collection and there were just a handful of maritime artists painting at the time that we knew about. There was no market for contemporary work, just auctions of collectible work that would be considered antique. We decided to create a maritime art gallery for the work of living artists and began to look for models in other areas of contemporary art. Our vision was to create an art gallery in the museum shop that would create a market for living maritime artists and generate income to support the museum. It

(Continued)

was difficult to gauge the market easily and build a business plan but we knew we had to support these artists. The market for antique paintings was strong but that information was only partially transferable. We opened the Mystic Maritime Gallery with a juried exhibit that included a distinguished panel of jurors with national reputations. We sent prospectuses out to all of the major maritime museums in the world asking them to pass the word along to artists they knew. When it came time for the jury to meet we had received over 100 works from five countries and the show opened with a beautiful selection of work ranging from paintings, to sculpture, scrimshaw and ship models. We created an exclusive collector's club that was given first viewing and opportunity to purchase work and a party to mix with the artists. We found a market. We found buyers and most importantly we found there were hundreds of maritime artists worldwide seeking a market. The cultural enterprise grew to US$1.5 million in sales and as other entrepreneurs saw the market growing and artists' prices rising, new for-profit galleries opened which expanded the market even more across the country. We remained true to our mission of supporting artists and the museum while managing the enterprise successfully.

Source: Tom Aageson

Each of these strategies needs to be screened as to whether they are long- or short-term and whether they are renewable in the future. Some of these sources of funds can be used for capital and others for operating funds, but before seeking the capital the entrepreneur has to be able to explain the uses of the funds. For example, *Internally Financed* capital is a long-term strategy where the source of capital may be drawn upon intermittently over the years and the return can be set as long term. This type of financing can be used for fixed assets as well as for working capital, in other words for long-term purposes or short-term. The business plan will lay out the sources of capital over a period of time; business plans usually cover a three to five-year projection. Table 6.1 creates a screen to be used when considering the kinds of capital required.

Essentials for starting a cultural enterprise

There are five essentials for starting a cultural enterprise. These are common to every enterprise. Existing enterprises grow by a similar path of development when they introduce new cultural products or services as well as a new enterprise.

1 *Entrepreneur with a vision*: Every new enterprise needs its champion who has the vision and passion for the venture. The entrepreneur sees the connection between the creators and the markets.

2 *Cultural capital*: A rich resource of cultural capital that can be converted into an enterprise. Added to cultural capital must be committed human and financial capital.

3 *A product and a market*: Ultimately, an enterprise serves a need that consumers have realized or not. The enterprise must find that market and fill the need of the consumer. Understanding the potential of the market is first and foremost in the vision yet ultimately it is the end point at which the viability of the enterprise will be determined. By understanding the need, the product or service is created.

4 *Network*: A network of people in the cultural field as well as marketing, production and finance. This includes people who will help fund the enterprise. This team is committed to supporting the development of the cultural enterprise.

5 *Business plan*: The entrepreneur, often with the help of professionals, creates the business plan that lays out the vision, mission and values of the enterprise; defines the product or service; describes the marketing mix strategy of product, pricing, promotion and distribution; outlines the need for human capital; lays out the production and packaging plan; and has a full five-year financial plan that includes profit and loss statements, balance sheet and cash flow and sources of funds.

Table 6.1 Financing strategies

	Short-Term Income Strategy?	Long-Term Income Strategy?	Is it Renewable?	Does it Generate Capital Funds?	Cost of Capital	Does it Generate Operating Funds?
Internally Financed Capital	No	Yes	Yes	Yes	0–10 per cent	Yes
Grants	Yes	No	Seldom	Yes	0 per cent	Yes
Outside Private Support	Yes	Yes	Yes	Yes	0–7per cent	Yes
Membership	Yes	Yes	Yes	Yes	0 per cent	Yes
Sponsorship	Yes	No	Seldom	No	0 per cent	Yes
Government	Yes	No	Seldom	Yes	0 per cent	Yes
Special Events	Yes	Sometimes	Yes	Yes	0 per cent	Yes
Passive Income	No	Yes	Yes	Yes	0–7 per cent	Yes
Debt	Yes	Yes	Yes	Yes	7–12 per cent	No
Personal/Family	Yes	Maybe	Sometimes	Yes	0–7 per cent	Yes

Long-term strategies for a vibrant cultural economy

The growth in nation-state cultural policies has been a catalyst for investment in diverse cultural products and services. This movement, although defensive at first against exports from countries like the USA, has now taken on a positive strategy that is encouraging cultural entrepreneurs to take the risks required for new enterprises to be created locally. Everything must start at the local level in the context of the local culture. Local creativity is an essential ingredient for new cultural enterprises. Countries like Denmark, the UK, Canada, Australia and Latvia have mature cultural policies that can be easily found through a search on the Internet.

Box 6.8 Cultural entrepreneurship takes hold in Central Asia

Raisa Gareeva created her cultural enterprise in her hometown of Bukhara, Uzbekistan and now has a cultural tour business that takes clients throughout Central Asia. She has also developed a folk art export business. 'After the country collapsed I lost my job. I worked as tour guide in the state-run travel company Intourist that had its head office located in Moscow. The only state travel company used to sell tours to different Republics of the Soviet Union. Moscow designed and approved the programs and we had to follow the program, we could not add anything. When the country collapsed, Moscow stopped sending us groups of tourists and guides had no jobs. For several months I looked for a job, worked in the museum, worked as an English teacher. Then I met Peace Corps Volunteers who encouraged me to start my own business. It was not easy but I had no choice. I started my travel business, www.salomtravel.com, in 1994, designed new programs, I was free and no one had to approve my programs; we could arrange meetings with local people, visit schools, show crafts.

'The difference we are making is to revive crafts. Even after 70 years, the Soviet power could not take away the rich culture and the love of the beauty. It was in the blood of people and the roots were too strong. But secrets and skills were lost and thanks to cultural enterprises and development funds

(Continued)

(Continued)

along with help from Aid to Artisans, it was possible to support the artisans. In 1994 there was one woman who embroidered *suzani* and now hundreds of families in the same village do beautiful embroidery. The same happened with wood carving, jewellers, textile weavers, rug weavers, block printers, hat makers and others.'

Raisa states that for her the essential of her success is love. 'I love my country and its rich culture. I love people who create the beauty. I respect hard-working people and want to help them as I can.'

The most difficult restraint in the development of her business was the banking system. 'The banking system changed their laws so many times. It is still hard to withdraw money from our bank to use in our own needs. It is changing very slowly.'

Source: Gareeva, 2007

Cultural policies must include initiatives to train and support the cultural entrepreneur. We need practical educational initiatives led by successful entrepreneurs to pass along their expertise. Training programs need to be both broad in scope and also focused for particular markets, e.g., publishing, film, music, cultural tourism, folk art, etc. Many leading cultural entrepreneurs around the world have been identified and they are willing to share their experience with aspiring cultural entrepreneurs. Educational programs have to be delivered via the Internet and locally in order to reach broadly across the world. New courses are being developed in schools, particularly in the United Kingdom, but they require the student to be nearby to attend classes.

There is also a need for venture capital, whether it is by investors or foundations, to support the development of new cultural enterprises. The effort to start and eventually to scale up an enterprise can only be successful through access to venture funds. New investment tools must be created in order to meet these financial needs.

Cultural entrepreneurs are the catalysts of the cultural economy. Innovators, visionaries and leaders – it is their cultural enterprises that create vibrancy in the cultural economy; create cultural value in the world and enhance the livelihoods of people in the creative sector. If we could train and finance 1000 new cultural entrepreneurs in ten years, who in turn create successful new cultural enterprises, our world would be better for the effort. It is a worthy goal.

REFERENCES

Alam, Shahidul (2007) Director, *Drik*, Bangladesh. Personal Interview.

Ashoka (2007) 'Innovators for the Public Invest in Ashoka'. Online: www.ashoka.org.

Brickhill, P. (2007) Creative Director, Book Café, Harare Zimbabwe. Online: www.zimbabwearts. co.zw. Personal Interview.

Browne, S. (2007) Director, Pelican Village Craft Centre, Barbados Investment Development Corporation. Personal Interview.

(Bureau of Business Economic Research) (2004) 'The Economic Importance of the Arts and Cultural Industries in Santa Fe County'. Online: http://www.unm.edu/~bber/pubs/SFCoArtsPtl. pdf-607.0KB. University of New Mexico.

Emerson, J., Freundlich, T. and Fruchterman, J. (2007) 'Nothing Ventured, Nothing Gained: Addressing the Critical Gaps in Risk-Taking Capital for Social Enterprise'. London: Oxford SAID Business School.

Florida, R. (2002) *The Rise of the Creative Class*. New York: Basic Books.

Florida, R. and Mellander, C. (2007) *The Creative Class or Human Capital? Explaining Regional Development in Sweden*. CESIS Electronic Working Paper Series, 79.

Gareeva, Raisa (2007) Director/Owner, Salom Travel, Bukhara, Uzbekistan. Personal Interview.

Say, Jean Baptiste (2005) *A treatise on political economy: or The production, distribution and consumption of wealth. Tr. from the 4th ed. of the French by C.R. Prinsep. M.A.* Michigan Historical Reprint Series. Scholarly Publishing Office, University of Michigan Library.

Scher, Philip (2006) 'Culture: anthropological perspectives on culture and development after Neoliberalism'. Presentation at the conference 'Culture in Motion. Practice in Contemporary International Development', organized by Arts, Culture and Communities in International Development (ACCID), The New School, New York. Online: http://www.nsaccid.org/Culture%20in%20 Motion%20Report.pdf.

Schumpeter, Joseph A. (1942) *Capitalism, Socialism and Democracy*. New York: Harper and Brothers.

Shah, D. (2007) President/CEO, Weavers Studio, India. Personal Interview. Online: www.weavers studio.com.

UNESCO (2005) *International Flows of Selected Cultural Goods and Services, 1994–2003*. Paris: UNESCO Publishing.

## CHAPTER 7

THE INTERGOVERNMENTAL POLICY ACTORS
Yudhishthir Raj Isar

This chapter will explore some of the ways in which ideas and principles regarding the 'cultural economy' have been promoted by the organizations of the UN system. In analysing these itineraries, it will focus on the agenda-setting processes: how policy issues have been defined, who the different participants and stake-holders have been, what role has been played by individual policy entrepreneurs and how policies and programs have been imagined and implemented. It will also question the coherence of the disparate activities carried out by the different agencies: as vectors of the institutionalized cosmopolitanism that has become integral to globalization, do they 'deliver as one'?

Because they elaborate both norms and instrumental knowledge which have worldwide authority, the specialized agencies of the United Nations system forge the kinds of 'global' perspectives on issues that sociologists include among the concomitants of globalization, e.g. Ulrich Beck's inchoate 'institutionalized cosmopolitanism' (Beck, 2006: 9). Indeed, across a wide range of areas, the United Nations agencies have generated meta-narratives that deeply influence thinking and acting worldwide. Examples include the

UNESCO-generated notions of 'world heritage' or, more recently, 'cultural diversity'.

This cultural economy, however, has assumed its current centrality independently of these organizations. Yet several of them have become active around the discourses of the 'cultural' and/or 'creative' industries (recently enlarged to the 'creative economy'). These actors include UNESCO, the World Intellectual Property Organization (WIPO), the United Nations Conference on Trade and Development (UNCTAD), the International Labour Office (ILO), and, most recently, the United Nations Special Unit for South–South Cooperation.[1] Together they have legitimized and globalized these discourses, mainly by harnessing them to already regnant UN system tropes such as 'sustainable development' and 'poverty alleviation'.

Such an abundance of shared purposes is in itself both exceptional and paradoxical. Exceptional because although only the United Nations Educational, Scientific and *Cultural* (my emphasis) Organization (UNESCO) has a mandate for international cooperation in culture, the four other agencies mentioned are now investing significantly in the cultural industries arena as well. Paradoxical, because although it may appear that at the UN level the 'joined up' approach to cultural policy-making that is still so difficult to obtain at national level is thereby being achieved, the reality is one of distinct if not fragmented approaches that are sometimes overlapping, often rivalrous. Some see the defence of agency turf as a natural occurrence and argue that the complexity of the issues involved provides more than enough space for each organization to contribute meaningfully, without overlap. Yet does this amount to that coherent and cohesive contribution to global human amelioration in which many analysts today place their hopes (Beck, 2006), in view of the unique expertise and resources that the UN agencies bring to global issues? We must recall here that they belong to a UN system designed at the end of the Second World War to be uncentralized and multi-headed, after the idea of a single, centrally coordinated set of organizations had been discussed and discarded.

The primary purpose of this chapter is not to assess the effectiveness of the different agency programs, but rather to delineate their specific genealogies and itineraries.[2] What sorts of ideas launched and shaped the respective institutional histories? Master narratives in international relations? Confrontations of interests and ideologies? Social demand? The production of ideas by scholars and 'experts' (officials have sometimes belonged to both of the latter categories)? The answers vary. Clearly, however, in all the organizations, promoting the cultural economy in the context of the 'development' agenda is an idea 'whose time has come'. Hence the conceptual framework proposed by the political scientist John Kingdon (1995) is suggestive for our purposes. How have *agendas* been set within these bodies and by their authorizing environments? How have policy *problems* been defined, often in the wake of focusing *events?* How have different *participants* or *stakeholders* (secretariat officials; consultants; Member State officials and/or politicians; governing bodies; executive heads, etc.) operated in agenda-setting and choice making? How have *policy entrepreneurs* emerged and in what path-dependent ways have policies and Programs been imagined and implemented?[3]

Yet once such questions are answered, the earlier interrogation remains: can these disparate efforts be coordinated so as to become more than just the sum of the parts? To be sure, the cultural economy as such does not necessarily throw up issues of human survival that can only be tackled globally. And the difficulty of getting institutions to work together is common to many sectors. Yet might it just be possible for this global system of ours to pool its diverse resources, to develop globally concerted action in order to 'deliver as one' (United Nations, 2006)?

The story at UNESCO

Our story must begin at UNESCO, which initiated work on the 'cultural industries' in the early 1980s, pursuing its efforts with varying yet always limited degrees of intensity until the late 1990s, when the synergy between the highly politicized 'cultural exception' agenda and the previously existing 'cultural industries' paradigm began to define a new global agenda in cultural politics. This came to a head in 2005 with the adoption of the *Convention on the Protection and Promotion of the Diversity of Cultural Expressions.*[4]

Almost three decades earlier, in June 1980, the UNESCO secretariat organized in Montreal, at the initiative of the Canadian authorities, a meeting of experts on 'The Place and Role of Cultural Industries in the Cultural Development of Societies'. The Organization's program for that year included 'comparative research… in collaboration with national and international institutions, both public and private, on the place and role of cultural industries in the cultural development of societies'. Given the epoch, the experts' meeting brought together mainly scholars from the industrialized world; the main impetus was Western, albeit in a somewhat uneasy marriage of Frankfurt School disdain for the 'looming eternal sameness and alienating effects of popular culture' (Scott, 2000: 39) and a more pragmatic vision. Opinions were divided 'between those, whose feelings towards cultural industries are those of fundamental and outright distrust, and those for whom cultural industries are the key to cultural democracy and the vehicle for putting it effectively into practice' (UNESCO, 1982a: 22). This ambivalence meshed into two of the international master narratives of the time and it also had a decisive influence in setting the agenda within the Secretariat. The first was the 'New International Economic Order' (NIEO) originating in proposals put forward by developing countries in the 1970s that were designed to recast the international economic system in favor of the 'Third World' and jettison the Bretton Woods-based system. The second was the 'New World Information and Communication Order' (NWICO), an idea elaborated at UNESCO in order to correct the North–South media divide that impaired the 'independent cultural development of the Third World Nations' (Hamelink, 1994: 198).

Both these sets of positions contributed to the crisis of 1984–5 when the United States (the first Reagan administration) and the United Kingdom (under Margaret Thatcher) quit UNESCO, largely as a protest against them. Both were also key subtexts at the World Conference on Cultural Policies held in Mexico City in 1982. *The Mexico City Declaration on Cultural Policies* stressed the importance of the cultural industries 'in the distribution of cultural goods'; observed that 'the absence of national cultural industries may, particularly in developing countries, constitute a source of cultural dependence and give rise to alienation'; and stated that it was 'essential to encourage the establishment of cultural industries in countries where they do not exist, through bilateral and multilateral assistance programs, always ensuring that the production and distribution of cultural goods is in keeping with the integrated development of each society' (UNESCO, 1982b: 44).

Yet UNESCO was far from ready to engage frontally with the real-life market place in which the production of cultural goods and services was beginning to assume such an important place. As recast recently by Pratt, the cultural industries 'sit uneasily within the public policy framework' (Pratt, 2005: 31), given that the latter generally does not concern commercially oriented 'low' culture, but the provision of 'high' culture forms supported and funded as public goods. Thus the mainly *for-profit* cultural industries exist in permanent tension with the mainly *not-for-profit cultural* sector that is the chief object of cultural policy (Isar, 2008). In the Cold War environment of the epoch it was impossible within UNESCO to reconcile a deep mistrust of the commercial sector, in particular the multinational corporations, with the practical imperative of building cultural productive capacity. As a result, work in this domain was given only limited priority and funding; it certainly could not warrant the creation of a unit bearing the name 'cultural industries'. Nevertheless, secretariat official Maté Kovacs (Hungary) and a handful of 'believers' in the division responsible for 'cultural development' kept the flame alive by a modest set of activities centered on awareness-building and the provision of technical expertise. This was done through a series of seminars and workshops organized from the late 1980s onwards, notably a meeting held jointly with the Organization of African Unity in Nairobi in 1992 that drew up the *Dakar Plan of Action* for the development of the cultural industries in Africa (so called because it was endorsed by a Summit of Heads of State and Government held in Dakar later that year). Few of the proposals of this plan of action were ever implemented, however, mainly for want of resources; it should also be said that a close reading reveals a very broad understanding of the notion of 'cultural industries', one that was difficult to make operational: 'Handicrafts and Endogenous Creative Works; art, handicraft, tourism, architecture, dress, hair-style, ornament, gastronomy and African healing art and technology' (UNESCO, 1992: 15).

UNESCO's Medium-Term Plan, drawn up in 1989, recognized the importance of 'the industrial production of cultural goods' and stressed that 'as access to these goods depends on the solvency of the customer, consumption is still very unevenly distributed between industrialized and developing countries'. Yet the Plan envisaged only a rather general boilerplate

agenda (with a very limited financial allocation) under a 'Culture for development' program of 'encouragement… to domestic production, particularly in developing countries' (UNESCO, 1990: 87). It should be said, however, that although recognition of the cultural industries as a distinct domain of intervention was limited in these years, there were certain areas, such as 'book development' in which UNESCO was already professionally involved, and able to make direct technical inputs at various stages of the value chain, e.g., through support to international networks of professionals in the book trade, including independent publishers, and the provision of specialized advice on regional book development strategies. The latter thrust was particularly strong in Latin America, where the Organization helped establish and support the *Centro Regional para el Fomento del Libro en América Latina y el Caribe (CERLALC)*. The Organization has also long lent its support to awareness-building activities such as World Book and Copyright Day and World Book Capital. It has contributed to identifying quality books for children as well as providing books and mobile libraries to develop reading and to promoting the Florence Agreement on the free circulation of educational, scientific and cultural goods (1950) and its Nairobi Protocol (1976).

Copyright has also been an area of concern since long before our present-day awareness of the 'copyright industries': the Universal Copyright Convention was adopted under UNESCO's aegis in 1952.[5] These efforts began to be largely eclipsed in the 1960s by work of the newly established World Intellectual Property Organization (see next section). UNESCO's maintenance of its activities on awareness-raising and capacity-building activities regarding copyright, despite the fact that it can devote only very limited resources to them, is a good example of how programs entrenched in one organization can survive… With the onset of the dotcom era, the focus has shifted to the digital environment in which it is so important to maintain a fair balance between the interests of authors and public access to knowledge and information; and as regards the cultural industries, copyright activities have expanded to cover issues such as piracy.

In the growing 'neo-liberal' atmosphere of the 1990, market forces became somewhat more reputable within UNESCO and the central mediating role of the industrially produced and commodified forms of cultural expression began to be more realistically recognized. Thus, although the Medium-Term Strategy for

1996–2001 (note the semantic shift from a 'Plan', with its statist connotations, to the more business-like term, 'Strategy') stated firmly that 'UNESCO cannot provide direct support to cultural industries, which generally come under the private sector', it nevertheless saw a role for the Organization in encouraging 'those States which so wish, the developing countries in particular, to design national or regional policies conducive to the development of those industries' and declared that 'guided by its experience in the formulation of policies on books and reading, UNESCO will extend its efforts to the other cultural industries involving creative activities protected by copyright' (UNESCO, 1995: 32). At this time also, activities on books and copyright were regrouped with work on the arts, crafts and design, cinema and the music industry to create a larger Division of Creativity, Cultural Industries and Copyright. The new ensemble was conceived by and for a senior official from Spain, Milagros del Corral (already Director of the existing Book and Copyright Division) who had come to UNESCO some years earlier after extensive public as well as private sector experience in book publishing and copyright. Both entrepreneurial and ambitious, del Corral was keenly aware of the potential of the buzzwords in her new division's title.

At this juncture, the 'cultural exception' agenda that France, Canada and other nations had been negotiating for since the end of the Uruguay Round discussions in the mid-1990s, was taking on increasing political salience. When the United States attempted in the GATT–WTO context to make free trade principles apply to all 'cultural goods', principally their own audiovisual exports, in the context of a debate over the European Union's broadcasting directive *Television Without Frontiers*, France countered with the argument that a 'cultural exception' was necessary because culture was not just another type of merchandise. By the time of the Intergovernmental Conference on Cultural Policies for Development held in Stockholm in March–April 1998, the question had become a global issue and was indeed cited in the majority of the ministerial speeches delivered there. The Conference adopted an Action Plan that included the fostering of the cultural industries as a policy objective for Member States, whilst urging them to 'promote the idea that cultural goods and services should be recognized and treated as being not like other forms of merchandise' (UNESCO, 1998: 16).

By this time also, the British government's 'creative industry' rhetoric and practice was beginning to acquire considerable purchase in Europe and beyond. As we now know, Richard Florida's 2002 bestseller *The Rise of the Creative Class* gave an even more decisive push to the enthusiastic espousal of the 'creativity' trope by cultural activists, officials and politicians in many more countries, although the author's 'creative class' category stretched across a very broad range indeed – scientists, engineers, architects, educators, writers, artists and entertainers, in other words all those whose economic function is to create new ideas, new technology, and new creative content. Yet a conceptual bandwagon had been launched in the world, and would soon become a mantra in policy-making circles. The siren song of the 'creative' was gradually to capture imaginations in UNESCO and, as we shall see, in all the other UN agencies. Thus was the ground prepared for the language (and the intentions) of the Medium-Term Strategy for 2002–2009 adopted in 2001.

But another powerful global discourse had now emerged. Soon after the Stockholm Conference, French diplomacy at the highest level, allied with Canada, shifted from the language of 'cultural exception' to that of 'cultural diversity', making the latter term the master concept in an international campaign of influence that led to the elaboration and adoption, also in 2001, of a wide-ranging Universal Declaration on Cultural Diversity, whose core Article 8 was entitled 'Cultural goods and services: commodities of a unique kind'. This in turn informed the drafting of the new Medium-Term Strategy at UNESCO, which set out the objective of 'Safeguarding cultural diversity and encouraging dialogue among cultures and civilizations' and affirmed that 'the protection of diversity requires recognition of the special status of cultural goods and services. Cultural enterprises and creative industries are privileged channels of creativity as well as increasingly important sources of employment and wealth creation' (UNESCO, 2002: 41). Among the program thrusts that were to meet this objective so as to attain the outcome of 'enlarged and diversified cultural offer, in particular from developing countries, contributing to a deceleration of asymmetries at the global level', it was remarkable to see detailed references to monitoring and analysing the workings of the cultural markets, promoting marketing opportunities and business partnerships or exerting influence in the area of trade negotiations.

This, then, was the 'tide in the affairs' of culture at UNESCO that del Corral was determined to take at the flood… Aware of the resource and staff constraints that placed this admirable set of objectives well beyond the Organization's true capacities, e.g., only US$150,000 per year were budgeted for it, she launched in 2002 a scheme intended to realize another goal of the Medium-Term Strategy: 'demonstrating the solidarity of companies in industrialized countries with developing countries, and highlighting the concept of social responsibility by corporations' (UNESCO, 2002: 41). This was a 'Global Alliance for Cultural Diversity' in which developed country actors would help foster and/or open up markets for cultural goods produced in developing countries, whose governments would 'be asked to guarantee appropriate copyright protection and enforcement, both for conventional trade and for e-commerce purposes…' The rationale here was to get away from the 'one-way' model of a benefactor/beneficiary development scheme; the secretariat saw itself as an honest broker for these new partnerships, linking those able to offer services and resources to those in need. Apart from the fact that only US$15,000 per year were allocated initially to this ambitious endeavor, experience has shown that these aims were not realistic, as the secretariat simply does not have the business sector skills required to perform as an honest broker in this way. Perhaps the lacuna could have been overcome by teaming up with a professional body such as a chamber of commerce, but that was not the path adopted. The online database set up as a mechanism to join the scheme today lists some 500 members of the 'Global Alliance'. But most of these are grant- or help-seekers rather than 'donors' or 'sharers'. It would seem, therefore, that the scheme has had a mainly symbolic impact; this hypothesis is to be tested in 2008 when the mechanism will be evaluated.

In October 2005, UNESCO's General Conference adopted the *Convention on the Protection and Promotion of the Diversity of Cultural Expressions* whose Article 14, 'Cooperation for Development', states that 'Parties shall endeavor to support cooperation for sustainable development and poverty reduction, especially in relation to the specific needs of developing countries, in order to foster the emergence of a dynamic cultural sector' and listed means by which the cultural industries may be strengthened, capacity-building enhanced, technology transfer fostered, and financial support increased. This core purpose of the Convention is now being contributed to by a 'Creative Industries for Development Section' in the newly named 'Division of Cultural Expressions and Creative Industries'. The annual budgetary allotment for the Section's activities is in the order of US$200,000 and there are but three professional staff members. These figures do not take into account, however, the significant focusing of policy attention on cultural industry development that is occurring as the Convention, which entered into force in March 2007, is now being implemented.

WIPO: mapping the cultural economy for development

Given its mandate 'to promote the protection of intellectual property throughout the world through cooperation among States and… to harmonize national legislation in this field' (Article 3 of the *Convention Establishing the World Intellectual Property Organization*) this UN agency, set up in 1967, naturally deals with cultural goods and services as well. One of the purposes of intellectual property protection is 'to encourage creative activity'. Unlike its sister agencies, however, WIPO enjoys a great deal of financial ease and independence. It does not have to rely on assessed contributions from its Member States, for as much as 90 per cent of its annual income comes from the fees it collects under the intellectual property application and registration systems which it administers, e.g., the Patent Cooperation Treaty, the Madrid system for trademarks and the Hague system for industrial designs. Again, unlike UNESCO, it interfaces naturally with the private commercial and industrial sectors. It has grown exponentially (now employing some 1300 people) in the last decade, largely as a result of increasing registration requirements. This period has also coincided with the leadership of a Director General from the South, Kamil Idris (Sudan), who has sought to broaden WIPO's political support base and worldwide reach through a resolute developing country agenda (see the issues already discussed in details by Sundara Rajan in Chapter 4 of this volume).

One of the four component units of the organization's Office for the strategic use of intellectual property for development is the Creative Industries Division established recently – in 2005 – and which gestated from initial mapping work in the Mercosur and Caribbean countries, building on previous efforts in copyright and economic development. The efforts of a working group of experts partly supported by the Finnish government resulted in the 2003 *Guide on Surveying the Economic Contribution of the Copyright-Based Industries* prepared with a view to 'outlining a methodology for identifying the contribution of copyright-based industries to the national economy' because 'the often hidden copyright-related components of various industries and activities are generally not clearly identified in statistical and economic terms' (WIPO, 2003: 2). Research was carried out on the basis of recommendations contained in the *Guide* resulting in the 2006 publication entitled *National Studies on Assessing the Economic Contribution of the Copyright-Based Industries*. The five nations studied were Singapore, Canada, the USA, Latvia and Hungary. In the meantime, the Creative Industries Division was established, with a complement of five 'professional' officials (a relatively large number in a UN agency)[6] to run it, with an annual regular budget of US$250,000, to which must be added significant funds-in-trust monies and funds resulting from collaborative arrangements with other units.

Yet demand from member-states already outstrips the resources available to this Division, headed by Dimiter Gantchev, a former Bulgarian diplomat with a doctorate in copyright issues, who has set out the ambitious agenda of engaging directly with creative industry stakeholders; carrying out studies on the creative potential of nations, quantifying the economic contribution of creative activities; developing practical tools for creative enterprises and entrepreneurs; assisting 'creators in benefiting from their intellectual property assets'; advancing 'the development of internationally recognized cultural indicators that measure the broader impact of intellectual property on economic, social and cultural development' and undertaking 'activities aiming at clarifying the negative, direct and indirect impact on the economy, and on society, of non-compliance with intellectual property regimes'.[7] By defining the challenges in these broad terms, the purpose is to reveal the 'human face' of copyright – not to combat piracy in purely legal terms, for example, but in a broader developmentalist perspective. This is particularly important in the context of the North–South divide. There appears to be a growing conviction on the part of developing country IP policy-makers, whose countries are massive net-exporters of copyright-, patent- and trademark-related royalties, that too

many concessions are being made, as regards TRIPs, to the interests of the North.

Work could have been limited to the classic function of promoting intellectual cooperation through studies, but the aim is to be as 'operational' as possible. Thus there are capacity-building activities designed for stakeholders including governments, enterprises, individuals, non-governmental institutions, etc. that provide awareness and skills through seminars, workshops, round tables and other forms of training. There is a specific industry by industry focus as well; a forthcoming technical publication, for example, will be entitled *How to Make a Living From Music*. There is also a series of case studies on 'Creative Clusters' and awareness building campaigns targeting policy-makers, intellectual property rights-holders and users; publications are forthcoming in the fields of publishing, design, film-making and the management of creative enterprises.

The International Labour Office: more and better jobs

The International Labour Office is the secretariat of the International Labour Organization (ILO), founded decades before the present international system, in 1919, as one of the outcomes of the Treaty of Versailles. Thus it even predated the ill-fated League of Nations, and became a member of the UN system at the end of the Second World War. The ILO currently devotes itself 'to advancing opportunities for women and men to obtain decent and productive work in conditions of freedom, equity, security and human dignity. Its main aims are to promote rights at work, encourage decent employment opportunities, enhance social protection and strengthen dialogue in handling work-related issues'.[8] The Organization is governed by representatives of governments, employers and workers who jointly shape its policies and programs. This gives it a 'tripartite' structure that is unique in the UN system and the ILO considers that this gives it a particular edge in incorporating 'real world' knowledge about employment and work.

The ILO has, for many decades, worked on issues of employment and work in the media and entertainment industries since the 1920s, focusing on issues of concern to specific employment groups and industries within the media, culture and graphical sector. These have included changing levels and types of employment, conditions of employment and work, employment relations, intellectual property protection, technological change, skill requirements and training needs, and labour relations. This work eventually led to the adoption of the ILO/UNESCO/WIPO International Convention for the Protection of Performers, Producers of Phonograms and Broadcasting Organisations adopted in 1961. Also typical of its approach (cited by Michael Curtin in Chapter 18) was a 'Tripartite Meeting on the Future of Work and Quality in the Information Society: The Media, Culture, Graphical Sector' held in 2004; the report prepared by the ILO Secretariat cited issues such as 'the concentration of media ownership, restrictions on freedom of expression and information, and concerns about democratic values, diversity and representation of women and minority groups in the media' (ILO, 2004: 2). Similar discussions in fact took place in 2000 (on the impact of information technologies on the media and entertainment industries), 1997 (on multimedia convergence) and 1992 (on conditions of employment and work of performers). The ILO has also provided financial and technical support to performers' organizations through a range of studies.

At a less macro level, the tripartite structure no doubt influenced the manner in which ILO activities, the cultural industries and development goals actually began (the ILO is currently headed by the Chilean Juan Somavia, its first Director-General from the South). This was a grant from the Ford Foundation for a project entitled 'Small Enterprise Development and Job Creation in the Cultural Sector'. Significantly, this grant was decided by the Ford Foundation's then Program Officer for Media, Arts and Culture, Damien Pwono (Democratic Republic of Congo) who was foregrounding cultural enterprise development in his portfolio and was committed to developing strategic relationships with international organizations. The project focused upon countries in Sub-Saharan Africa and was designed to explore 'the possibility that the promotion of cultural entrepreneurship that harnesses local talents, skills and heritage may be especially resistant to the competitive pressures of globalization and may provide innovative possibilities for boosting incomes and generating quality employment in a sector that is normally overlooked by policy-makers or addressed with piecemeal and traditional approaches' (Ambert, 2003: iii). Research was

carried out in five culture sectors: music; performing arts and dance; ethno-tourism; visual arts and crafts; and film and television (published as SEED Working Papers, nos. 49–53, see http://www.ilo.org/dyn/empent/empent.Portal?p_lang=EN). The use of a value chain analysis was found to be a particularly effective tool to identify strengths and weaknesses and help inform policy recommendations for bolstering the weaker 'links' in this chain. A Regional Workshop was held in Cape Town and a National Workshop was held in Zambia in 2002 to disseminate the findings from these studies to stakeholders and plan follow-up activities. The Zambian participants suggested that the strengthening of employment and small enterprise development in the cultural industries be embedded within a national focus upon promoting the tourism industry and developed an Action Plan for Promoting Small Enterprise Development and Job Creation through Cultural Tourism in Zambia, developed in partnership with the Zambian Ministry of Tourism and local associations of artists and stakeholders. An important element of the original project design was the creation of an Advisory Board, which included technical specialists from the ILO itself, as well as the other agencies discussed here. This provided a forum of discussion on broader issues and forged relationships between like-minded officials with similar concerns regarding the developing of the cultural industries, each contributing in terms of their specific agency mandate.

The development of training materials on 'cultural entrepreneurism' had been specified as a key output of the Ford Foundation project, based upon the view that basic business notions such as costing, self-management and marketing adapted to the needs of artists would strengthen their capacity to earn a living from their creative endeavors. Training materials were developed in collaboration with SEED's program on Women's Entrepreneurship (WEDGE), the Start and Improve Your Business (SIYB) Program and received important technical contributions on intellectual property from WIPO and the ILO's Turin Center which has finalized and is now delivering training with these materials. Another international training program has also emerged under the ILO's aegis: its International Training Center in Turin has pooled its resources with the University of Turin to offer a Master program in 'Cultural Projects for Development' that combines essential knowledge of cultural economics and cultural policies with the

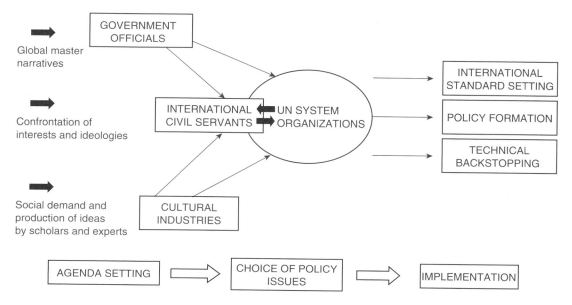

Figure 7.1   The intergovernmental policy-making process
Source: Boris Manev, 2007

competences needed to design projects in the cultural field. Now in its fifth edition, the course is attended by students from across the world (Walter Santagata, a contributor to this volume, is the Scientific Director and David Throsby, also a contributor, is on the faculty).

UNCTAD: a 'positive agenda'

The United Nations Conference on Trade and Development (UNCTAD) was first convened in 1964 to address global trade, investment and development issues: the asymmetries of the international market and between North and South, including the power of multinational corporations. Given the magnitude of the problems at stake, the conference was thereafter institutionalized to meet every four years, with intergovernmental bodies meeting between sessions. It was given a permanent secretariat (numbering some 400 people) in order to 'maximize the trade, investment and development opportunities of developing countries and assist them in their efforts to integrate into the world economy on an equitable basis'. Not surprisingly, it soon became the central locus for the debate on a New International Economic Order (NIEO).

While studies on the economic aspects of the cultural industries had been carried out since 1987, the late 1990s saw the start of more focused initiatives taken by secretariat economist Zeljka Kozul-Wright, for example a 1998 discussion paper 'Becoming a Globally Competitive Player: The Case of the Music Industry in Jamaica' (Ref: UNCTAD/OSG/DP/138, co-authored by Lloyd Stanbury) that was a conceptually sophisticated neo-Schumpeterian application of the concept of a 'National System of Innovation' to the question. The paper closed with a discussion of policy options for music industry development. These explorations came to the attention of Secretary-General Rubens Ricupero, a former Brazilian Minister of Finance and development visionary nominated in 1995, whose priority was to provide capacity-building and policy advice for developing countries as regards multilateral trade negotiations, including in the GATS and TRIPs contexts. Himself sympathetic to the creative industries agenda, he included a focus on them in the 'positive agenda' for developing countries he brought to the UNCTAD X conference held in Bangkok in 2000. This was designed to assist developing countries to better understand the complexity of multilateral trade negotiations, and obtain a mandate to work on audiovisual services. An 'expert meeting on audiovisual services: improving participation of developing countries' was convened in 2002. The previous year, at the UN Third Conference on Least Developed Countries, the Secretariat organized a policy debate emphasizing the opportunities offered by the music industry in diversifying the economies of these nations (UNCTAD/LDC/MISC 82).

Ricupero took a decisive step forward at the eleventh UNCTAD conference held at São Paulo in his home country, Brazil, in June 2004, by using his prerogative to devote one of three cross-cutting informal 'high-level panels' organized at the initiative of the Secretariat to the topic of 'creative industries and development'. He was able thereby to circumvent the likely unwillingness of the most influential member-states to endorse an engagement in this area. The debate involved over 40 experts from diverse cultural domains and regions plus government representatives. For the first time, Ministers of Foreign Affairs, Development, Trade, Technology, Tourism and Telecommunications joined Ministers of Culture in addressing the economic potential of the cultural industries. The key justifications for an UNCTAD investment in this domain were trade gains and wealth creation for development and were deliberately advanced under a broader label: 'creative economy'. The choice of this more general term was determined principally by the international currency it had begun to acquire as a result of John Howkins' book of the same name (it is no accident that Howkins was among the experts at the São Paulo 'High Level Panel') and also because it is 'an evolving and wider concept based on creative assets, embracing economic, technological, social and cultural aspects. It is a set of knowledge-based activities with linkages at macro and micro levels to the overall economy, calling for innovative and concerted public policies' (UNCTAD, 2006: 1). Because it could accommodate many different sorts of activities, it also offered the prospect of obtaining not just a more robust and diversified support base among governments, but also of attracting those artists and cultural operators who still balked at the idea of associating themselves with an 'industry'.

But there was also a UN System inter-institutional imperative: to counter the rising tide of resentment expressed by UNESCO officials at the usurpation of a system-wide monopoly on cultural affairs. The challenge to this monopoly was perceived as all the more galling since the other agencies appeared not only to have more resources, but also interfaced with 'harder' policy-making circles. Aware of this discontent, in 2004 Ricupero pushed for the establishment of a 'UN Multi-Agency Informal Group on Creative Industries' as a way of promoting concertation within the UN family of organizations.

Needless to say, the high-level panel and Conference itself endorsed the 'creative economy' approach; Brazilian Culture Minister Gilberto Gil's direct personal experience and policy interest in the domain contributed of course to this outcome. A mandate was given in paragraph 91 of the declarative segment of the Conference report, which was adopted by 153 member states as the *Sao Paulo Consensus*: 'The international community should support national efforts of developing countries to increase their participation in and benefit from dynamic sectors and to foster, protect and promote their creative industries.' But Ricupero's term of office expired in September 2004. His intention was to create, in 2004, an Inter-Divisional Section/Unit in the Secretariat to reinforce UNCTAD's work in this field. Such a unit was not created, however, as enthusiasm for the cause at the senior-most level did not survive his departure. The staff member responsible, Edna dos Santos, a development economist, now working practically independently as Chief of the 'Creative Economy and Industries Program' (note that the existence of a fully fledged 'division' is the key proof of relevance in these organizations) has continued single-handedly to take the cause forward, astonishing as this may seem, with no dedicated budget for these activities. She has nevertheless worked pro-actively to help share conceptual and policy frameworks, promote research, examine economic and trade indicators to assess the development impact of the creative economy in the developing world and mount awareness-building workshops and seminars – all activities that encompass the classic UN modalities of policy advice, expert services, consensus-building, etc. The main objective is to promote the 'creative economy' as a development strategy, since the creative industries are the most dynamic sector in world trade. UNCTAD also produces and distributes a regular Newsletter reporting on these activities.

The inter-agency tensions already in the air at São Paulo resurfaced in April 2005, when UNCTAD organized, in Salvador de Bahia, an international forum on the proposal to set up an International

Center on Creative Industries (ICCI). The idea had been put forward by the UNCTAD secretariat during UNCTAD XI and Brazilian Culture Minister Gilberto Gil had proposed that the entity be established in Brazil.[9] The Center would serve as a knowledge bank of successful initiatives and create an international network to increase the potential role of these industries in job creation and poverty reduction. At São Paulo a few months earlier, the UNESCO representative objected strongly to this initiative on the grounds that it would duplicate the 'Global Alliance' referred to earlier.[10] It was in this context that the final UN System player appeared on the scene: this was the Special Unit for South–South Cooperation.

The Special Unit for South–South Cooperation: relocating the discourse

This unit, administratively housed at the United Nations Development Program (UNDP), was established a semi-independent entity in 1978 to promote, coordinate and support South–South and triangular cooperation worldwide. Its enterprising director since 2004, Yi Ping Zhou, a former senior trade official for the Chinese government and a UN staffer since 1985, was invited to take part in the international forum in Salvador, and immediately saw the appeal of the 'creative economy' cause. Sensing both a rewarding operational role for his unit as well as a broader opportunity to foster inter-agency collaboration, he agreed to help a cash-poor UNCTAD to push the inter-agency cooperation agenda forward. This led, in December 2005, to a 'Partnership for Technical Assistance for Enhancing the Creative Economy in Developing Countries', which was established at a 'UN Global South–South Creative Economy Symposium' held in his home city, Shanghai. The initiative embraced all the agencies discussed in this chapter, but one could question whether its initial outcomes meant anything more than an agreement among the agencies that each would pursue its own purposes without objections from the others – a kind of Peace of Westphalia at UN System level. This partnership was subsequently mobilized for the preparation of a 'Creative Economy Report', which was launched at UNCTAD XII in April 2008 as a multi-agency effort.

Having brokered an interim peace, the Special Unit began to pursue its own distinctive program of activities, managed by Francisco Simplicio (Brazil), designed principally to redress the marginal contribution that developing countries make to the rapid expansion of the global 'creative' economy, and their almost non-existence in the international flows of cultural goods and services. The Special Unit has made the 'value chain' central to its work of seeking not only to promote and export Southern-based knowledge, talent and creativity, but to substantially build capacity along the entire value chain so that the full benefits of creativity are realized in the South. Hence it strives to promote better understanding of the potential of the creative sector, new opportunities for economic growth, poverty reduction, social inclusion and development. This agenda is now being pushed forward energetically under the 'Creative Economy for Development' program, which has an annual budget of half a million dollars, plus additional resources raised through a wide range of partnerships, and is based upon three mutually supportive 'pillars': 1. better mechanisms to promote and market Southern creative products; 2. promoting networks and cooperation among low- and middle-income countries, so that they can capitalize on their creative resources in ways that contribute to development goals; and 3. broaden and deepen the global knowledge base on the creative economy for development.

The strategy was designed to give substance, theoretical grounding and live examples of how the creative economy can become an effective developmental sector for developing and transition countries. In the short time since its inception, the Special Unit has facilitated a range of forums and dialogues between practitioners, experts, policy-makers and other actors; it has deployed its own strongly branded initiatives whilst piggy-backing high-profile events. For example, the first Shanghai symposium referred to above was quickly followed by another meeting in October 2006, and another four-day meeting organized in conjunction with the World Culture Forum meeting held in Rio de Janeiro in November–December 2006. The series has been called the 'International Forum on Creative Economy for Development'.

The Unit's flagship activity, and the primary means by which it will promote market creation and expansion, will be a 'Global South Creative Economy Expo' planned for Shanghai in 2008, in cooperation with the Shanghai Creative Industries

Association and hosted by the city authorities. This ambitious enterprise is intended to attract more than 10,000 visitors daily and will include a strong private sector engagement. To build momentum for the Expo, smaller-scale regional events targeting practitioners have also been organized or planned. In addition, the Special Unit is developing a capacity-building program based on exchanges and apprenticeships.

The Unit has naturally shown great deference to the work of the Specialized Agencies, billing their activities as efforts to promote, coordinate and facilitate the bringing together of the UN System's substantive expertise on different aspects of the 'creative economy'. Thus its 'Annual Report of Activities and Achievements – 2006' recounts that at the first inter-agency meeting it convened in New York in September 2005, to discuss the project of establishing an International Center on Creative Economy as proposed in the UNCTAD framework, 'it was made clear by UNESCO that they would consider the establishment of an ICCE a challenge to a) the UNESCO exclusive mandate over the cultural field and b) the perceived overlap between the ICCE and the UNESCO "Global Alliance for Cultural Diversity" initiative'. The report goes on to explain how the moderators of the session sought to channel the debate in order to clarify responsibilities, mitigate fears and smooth ruffled institutional feathers. 'In this way, the main concerns expressed by UNESCO were addressed, and the potential for positive partnership between the UN system agencies was made possible' (Special Unit for South–South Cooperation, 2007: 7).

That is good as far as it goes, but now that a laissez-faire working arrangement has been brokered, it begs the question of whether such a 'positive partnership' can actually emerge – a truly cooperative strategy that has the buy-in and active engagement of all of the Agencies and that maximizes constructive synergies and the rational deployment of comparative advantage of all parts of the System, for maximum impact within countries…

Conclusion: joining up the intersecting agendas

In terms of the agenda-setting framework set out initially, the highlights of the story of the cultural industries in the five agencies can be summed up as follows:

- At UNESCO, a 'bottom up' and gradual process, initiated by the influential reasoning of a national policy-maker and subsequently meshing in with global meta-narratives of the early twenty-first century: 'creative industries' discourse and the politically charged 'cultural diversity' platform.
- At WIPO and UNCTAD, a top-down process, driven by chief executives hailing from the developing countries and in a strongly anchored developmental perspective, who recognized a winning game when they saw it.
- At the ILO, a process that began through the encounter between the strategic ambitions of an executive in the Ford Foundation and a secretariat partner.
- At the Special Unit for South–South Cooperation, as a result of entrepreneurial flair exerted at an appropriate moment.

But the existence of these intersecting agendas is in itself emblematic of the kinds of dysfunctional features of the UN as a single system that are beginning to be addressed in response to the *Report of the Secretary-General's High-Level Panel on System-wide Coherence*. As intersecting, if not overlapping, mandates have emerged in the five agencies, the overall picture has come to resemble an unorganized puzzle. The opposite of both is needed at the global level, however, particularly in a sector such as this, in which five agencies compete for limited resources without a clear collaborative framework or reasoned division of labour, each with its legitimate interest, yet lacking a match between their ambitions and the means available. As the *High-Level Panel* believes for the United Nations system as a whole, 'there must be a significant streamlining… so that the United Nations can "deliver as one", reduce duplication and significantly reduce the burdens it currently places on recipient and donor Governments, without diluting the performance and expertise of individual organizations' (United Nations, 2006: 19). It is a good augury for the future, therefore, that the Special Unit for South–South Cooperation is foregrounding this question. It is to be hoped that this is not merely a tactical position but a truly strategic one, and that it will be taken up and acted upon by the other actors. The 'software', as it were, for a shared program of activities that optimizes the comparative advantage of each player is provided by the 2005 *Convention on the Protection and Promotion of the Diversity of Cultural Expressions*.[11] Achieving such a state of things would help ensure that with regard to the cultural economy as well, 'the United Nations development system remains fit for purpose to rise to the challenges of the 21st century' (United Nations, 2006: 11).

Notes

1   There are other players too, who are doing significant work, e.g. financial institutions, such as the Interamerican Development Bank, and regional organizations such as the Convenio Andrés Bello, whose efforts are not discussed here for want of space.

2   The following serving or retired UN agency officials have generously assisted me by providing information and opinions, for which I am most grateful: Milagros del Corral, Edna dos Santos-Duisenberg, Dimiter Gantchev, Maté Kovacs, John Myers, Georges Poussin, Ann Posthuma, Nikolai Rogovsky, Francisco Simplicio and Peter Tomlinson. None of these individuals is responsible, however, for the errors that may remain, nor in any way for the judgements I express in this chapter, which in no way reflect the opinions of these officials (and in some cases contradict them).

3   Kingdon's framework also examined how *alternatives* have been explored; how choices are made between divergent policy options. In the present context, however, but a single choice faced each UN System agency: whether to work in the cultural economy field or not. *How* the organization then did so was not so much a matter of choice but of mandate and of the particular standard-setting and capacity-building modalities available to the different agencies.

4   As far back as 1970, however, at a 'Regional Conference on Ecology, Archaeology and Folk Dance of the Caribbean Region' organized in Jamaica, Edward Seaga, the then Minister of Finance (and later Prime Minister), called for the establishment of 'a Cultural Bank as an arm of UNESCO'. The rationale was that cultural development could not be funded by either the World Bank or the United Nations Development Program (UNDP), whereas the budget of UNESCO, the agency with a mandate for culture was far too limited. Seaga was a free-marketeer and his call for a 'cultural bank' anticipated the notion of venture capitalism for cultural industry. But as nothing in UNESCO's fundamental orientations equipped its staff for market-related activities, the idea of a 'bank' was soon transformed into that of a grant-making body, the 'International Fund for the Promotion of Culture' established in 1974.

5   This international instrument is now more or less moribund, overtaken by many other treaties adopted since then, notably in the WIPO framework.

6   The term 'professional' is used in the UN agencies to refer to the executive cadre of officials, as opposed to clerical and technical service staff in the 'General Service' category.

7   http://www.wipo.int/ip-development/en/creative_industry.

8   ILO website: http://www.ilo.org/global/About_the_ILO/lang—en/index.htm (accessed 30 May 2007).

9   A proposal strongly advocated by the Brazilian delegation was to create an International Center on Creative Economy in Salvador de Bahia, Gil's home city. Despite vigorous efforts by UNCTAD and others since 2004, however, the project has faltered, apparently largely because of political tensions within Brazil.

10   The ILO for its part organized a one-day workshop on the creative industries as part of the international forum, partnering with the Ministry of Culture in financing a set of studies on the employment and enterprise dimensions of the creative industries in Brazil.

11   Article 14 of the *Convention*, Cooperation for Development, sets out a comprehensive array of measures that provide an ideal conceptual framework and activity template for a UN system-wide strategy.

REFERENCES

Ambert, C. (2003) *Promoting the Culture Sector through Job Creation and Small Enterprise Development in SADC Countries: The Music Industry*. SEED Working Paper, 49. Geneva: International Labour Office.

Beck, U. (2006) *Cosmopolitan Vision*. Cambridge: Polity Press.

Florida, R. (2002) *The Rise of the Creative Class*. New York: Basic Books.

Hamelink, C. (1994) *The Politics of World Communication*. London, Thousand Oaks, New Delhi: SAGE Publications.

ILO (2004) *The Future of Work and Quality in the Information Society: The Media, Culture, Graphical Sector*. (Document Tmmcgs/2004). Geneva: International Labour Office.

Isar, Y.R. (2000) 'Cultural Policies for Development: Tilting Against Windmills?' in *Culturelink*, Special

Issue: *Culture and Development vs. Cultural Development*, Kees Epskamp and Helen Gould (eds.) Zagreb: IRMO.

Isar, Y.R. (2008) '"Culture", Conflict and Security: Issues and Linkages' in Björn Hettne (ed.) *Human Values and Global Governance. Studies in Development, Security and Culture*. London: Palgrave Macmillan.

Kingdon, J. (1995) *Agendas, Alternatives and Public Policies*. New York: Harper Collins.

Pratt, A. (2005) 'Cultural industries and Public Policy. An oxymoron' *The International Journal of Cultural Policy*, 11(1): March.

Scott, A. (2000) *The Cultural Economy of Cities*. London: SAGE Publications.

Special Unit for South–South Cooperation (2007) *Annual Report of Activities and Achievements – 2006*. New York: UNDP (unpublished document).

UNCTAD (2004) *São Paulo Consensus*. Final Report of UNCTAD XI. Geneva: Document TD/410.

UNCTAD (2006) *Creative Economy and Industries: Newsletter No. 3*.

UNESCO (1982a) *Cultural industries: a challenge for the future of culture*. Paris: UNESCO.

UNESCO (1982b) *Final Report of the World Conference on Cultural Policies* (document CLT/MD/1). Paris: UNESCO.

UNESCO (1990) *Third Medium-Term Plan, 1990–1995*. Document 25 C/4 Approved. Paris: UNESCO.

UNESCO (1992a) *Final report of the Meeting of Experts on Cultural Industries in Africa organized by OAU and UNESCO, with the support of UNDP, ACI and the EEC/ACP Cultural and Social Foundation*, 20–24 January, 1992, Nairobi (Kenya). UNESCO document, June 1992, no serial number.

UNESCO (1992b) *Cultural and Social Foundation, 20–24 January, 1992, Nairobi (Kenya)*. UNESCO document, June 1992, no serial number.

UNESCO (1995) *Cultural and Social Foundation (1995) Medium-Term Strategy for 1996–2001*. (Document 28 C/4 Approved). UNESCO.

UNESCO (1998) *Cultural and Social Foundation (1998) Final Report of the Intergovernmental Conference on Cultural Policies for Development*. (Document CLT-98/Conf.210/CLD.19). UNESCO.

UNESCO (2002) *Cultural and Social Foundation (2002) Medium-Term Strategy 2002–2007*. (Document 31C/4 Approved). UNESCO.

United Nations (2006) *Delivering as One. Report of the Secretary-General's High-Level Panel on System-wide Coherence*. New York: UN General Assembly. Document A/61/583.

WIPO (2003) *Guide on Surveying the Economic Contribution of the Copyright-Based Industries*. Geneva.

REGIONAL REALITIES

## CHAPTER 8

GLOBALIZATION AND THE CULTURAL ECONOMY: AFRICA
Francis B. Nyamnjoh

The impact of globalization on the cultural economy in and on Africa cannot be understood separately from the hierarchies that continue to shape social and power relations between and among Africans, African diasporas and the rest. Publishing and film-making demonstrate how the logic of profitability impinges on the cultural economy in and on Africa. It argues that African cultural production does not attract sufficient attention from cultural entrepreneurs who are mostly white and located in the global North, unwilling to risk profitability through investing in cultures that are largely perceived to be socially inferior, economically uncompetitive and located in 'hearts of darkness' difficult to penetrate. Even when it ventures into Africa, foreign capital dares not go beyond stereotypical representations. Nor are African investors, intellectuals and political elites, schooled in such negative representations and debasement of Africa, all that keen to develop these sectors in ways that capture their creative encounters with cultural others. Yet there is also growing resistance to the cultural homogenization that reveals how meta-narratives of victimhood obfuscate the

reality of the survival strategies employed by ordinary Africans.

Introduction

Globalization is not only a process of accelerated flows, inclusion and opportunity for global cultural diversity. It is also, and above all, a process of accelerated closures, exclusion and vulnerability for most of the world's cultures. With globalization, cultural hierarchies informed, inter alia, by race, place, class, gender and generation are reproduced even as they are contested. For the entrepreneurs who own and control the global cultural industries (i.e. transnational media, sound recording, publishing, film, news, information and entertainment corporations), whose principal purpose is the pursuit of profit, investing in cultural diversity beyond tokenism is too risky to contemplate. Instead, they are more interested in unregulated commercial exploitation and concentrated ownership and control of the cultural economy. In the interest of the predictability that enables profitability, they aim to streamline, standardize and routinize global cultural production and consumer palates (Golding and Harris, 1997). They are keen to slim all differences down into Barbie-like proportions, on behalf of an idea of culture devoid of complexity, richness and diversity. In the light of such obvious poverty of difference, the tendency is to mistake plurality for diversity, oblivious of the possibility that an appearance of plenty could well conceal a poverty of perspectives (Murdock, 1994).

To minimize investment and maximize returns, global cultural entrepreneurs prefer to target individuals directly as consumers and not as members of cultural communities that mediate what consumer cultural products and values are adopted or rejected. The global cultural entrepreneurs thus present themselves as messiahs of autonomy and desire, with the mission of serving the preferences of individual consumers as hostages and victims of cultures and communities of origin. They exalt the sterile and disembedded accumulation of cultural symbols, and celebrate individuals who sacrifice relationships of sociality and dignity. Hence the slogan: there are no sentiments in business. They privilege statistics over real creativity and community values and find it a lot easier to deal with figures than with the human victims of their Barbie-like idea of culture. With a focus on consumption as the ultimate unifier, a supreme indicator of cultural sophistication and symbol of civilization, global cultural entrepreneurs generally see and treat individuals as autonomous agents glued together by a selfless market that by definition promotes cultural freedom. They downplay the idea that such marginalized cultures could even be worthy of respect and attention and assume that the sociality, interdependence and conviviality of these cultures must be inimical to profitability (Nyamnjoh, 2005: 16–17). Given their particularly powerful position and dual role as players and umpires, global cultural entrepreneurs can afford to ignore calls for ground rules to protect cultural diversity beyond rhetoric or token concessions to 'ethnic minorities', 'first peoples' and 'globalized natives' (McChesney, 2001; Oguibe, 2004). Paradoxically, far from diminishing interest in the consumption of cultural difference in real terms, the indifference demonstrated by the global cultural entrepreneurs in their 'culture game' (Oguibe, 2004) has simply succeeded in driving the cultural products of Africa underground, to the margins or into the arms of illegal dealers, academic researchers, high-level diplomats, celebrities and tourists, thereby further endangering the symbolic and performative value of cultures rendered invisible by commodification and its hierarchies (ICOM, 1995; Kasfir, 1996).

As cautious paymasters and arbiters, global cultural entrepreneurs invest mostly in tastes informed by a narrow understanding of culture. A consequence for cultures and communities that fail the profitability litmus test is reduced recognition of the world's rich creative diversity making the phenomena of cultural imperialism, trivialization and misrepresentation increasingly likely (Walker and Rasamimanana, 1993; Harding, 2003). A parochial Euro-American culture, purportedly global and globalizing, is disproportionately nurtured by the creativity of a particular place, class, gender, generation and language to the detriment of all others amongst whom Africa and Africans occupy the bottom rungs. In this way, culture becomes more contrived than negotiated, and more localized than universal in origin, content and articulation.

Inspired by narrow, individual-centered philosophies of personhood, agency and property rights, this neo-liberalism is aggressive in its sacrifice of community rights and group interests, as it pursues profit through the illusion of promoting the interests of the autonomous individual as a consumer (Brown, 2003; Rowlands, 2004). Old patterns informed by more inclusive philosophies of ownership and control are increasingly giving way to new configurations with a focus on the individual, consumerism and exclusion. National state-owned or public creative industries are yielding to commercial pressure and its emphasis on profit over culture. Furthermore the vision of cultural institutions as public goods, that guarantee cultural pluralism and diversity by providing for groups and social categories that otherwise would be ignored or marginalized by the market, is losing currency. This leaves ordinary consumers, marginal communities, and whole cultures literally at the mercy of the McDonaldized cultural burgers served to them in the interests of profits. It is only natural for content to be uniform regardless of the nationalities or cultural identities of shareholders, as the global cultural entrepreneurs are keener in advancing corporate and commercial interests and values than in valorizing creativity and values that do not guarantee profitability (McChesney, 1998; Thomas and Nain, 2005).

Theorizing the African cultural economy

In this context, the impact of globalization on the cultural economy in and on Africa cannot be understood separately from the dominant hierarchies outside Africa (Walker and Rasamimanana, 1993; Harding, 2003; Magubane, 2007). Elsewhere I have discussed the impact of such hierarchies on cultural attitudes and conflicts (Nyamnjoh, 2006; 2007), and on African writing and scholarship (Nyamnjoh, 2004). Here the focus will be on the African cultural economy and how the reality of profitability shapes it. I argue that the race and geography of African cultural producers and products do not attract sufficient attention from global cultural entrepreneurs who are mostly white and mainly located in the North. The latter are too cautious to risk profitability through investing in cultures that are largely perceived to be inferior socially, uncompetitive economically and located in 'hearts of darkness' difficult to penetrate geographically, politically and ideologically. This, in addition to other factors, has rendered Africa a region invisible to most foreign cultural investors (Ukadike and Ugbomah, 1994). Even when it ventures into Africa, foreign capital is often much too cautious to invest meaningfully in going beyond stereotypical representations to capture and promote the creative negotiation of various encounters and influences in the lives of Africans. Interest in African content is not always inspired by respect for African realities and perspectives, nor articulated in mainstream indigenous African languages recognized as complementary or alternative to dominant European languages (Walker and Rasamimanana, 1993).

It is hardly surprising that African investors, intellectuals and political elites as well, schooled in such negative representations and debasement of Africa, are not that keen to develop and promote marginalized pre-Tarzanic indigenous cultures in ways that capture their creative encounters with cultural others (Soyinka, 1990; Ukadike and Ugbomah, 1994; Harding, 2003). Indeed, as part of a global ecumene for 'the transnationalization of... a supremely local and parochial set of images and values' from the West (Golding and Harris, 1997: 9), the power elite in Africa cannot afford to pay more than lip service to local cultural production and reproduction. Their daily activities and behaviour undermine the very doctrine of the importance of upholding African cultural values (Soyinka, 1990: 114–20). The identity and power conferred by joining the global consumer club explains why, despite much rhetoric about cultural renaissance in many African states, the ruling elites continue to acculturate themselves. They 'progressively take on the look of strangers in their own country due to their daily lifestyle, modeled on that of *homo consumens universalis*' (Amin, 1980: 175; see also Onyeani, 2000). With a ruling elite whose weakness and marginality *vis-à-vis* global capitalism and its institutions of legitimation have been certified, consuming streamlined global cultural products becomes a major way of staking claim to power locally and of further mystifying the disaffected populations with whom they have lost credibility. At best, these elites commission 'traditional dances' and 'praise singing' and other forms of cultural production – poetry, music, art, books, etc. – which they can use for their personal amusement or to entertain foreign friends and visiting counterparts. As Wole Soyinka laments in the case of Nigeria, complex, enriching dimensions of culture are often 'relegated to token, or symbolic, expositions, starved of funds and given scant coverage even in the media' (Soyinka, 1990: 110). In general, performances that were reserved for solemn occasions in the past have been trivialized and in certain cases commodified for consumer tourism, partly for the gratification of the local elite but also because

of the desperate quest by side-stepped cultural communities to survive in a global economy.

Often in their capacity as local subsidiaries or representatives of global cultural entrepreneurs, such 'capitalist niggers' (Onyeani, 2000) are all too keen to jump on the global consumer bandwagon – a situation not helped by the draconian conditionalities imposed by the Structural Adjustment Programs of the World Bank and the IMF since the 1970s (Bgoya, 2005; 2007). They thus seek to streamline the consumer palates of their fellow Africans in tune with cultural menus produced in or inspired by the West. They are ready to entertain African creativity only to the extent that such creativity reproduces stereotypes and internalizes Western-inspired consumer cultural aesthetics. Such mimicry is as true of education, art, writing, cinema, fashion and journalism, as it is of scholarship and publishing (Nyamnjoh, 2004).

Global exclusion, local repression

In most of Africa, threats to cultural diversity are created as much by repressive governments as by the profit motives of global cultural entrepreneurs. The cultural economy in Africa is caught between control by the greedy and aggressive pursuit of profit by global cultural industries on the one hand, and on the other by repression at local levels by states marginalized as global players and reduced to flexing their muscles *vis-à-vis* their own cultural producers (Soyinka, 1990; Assensoh, 2001). Given the reluctance of 'business... to go about its activity totally unprotected', global capital needs public support and regulation as 'an insurance against the full vicissitudes of a turbulent and potentially self-destructive system' (Thompson, 1999: 142). This expectation of public protection is even higher when capital ventures into marginal and highly unpredictable zones of accumulation like Africa, which accounts for barely one per cent of global trade. In Africa more than elsewhere, multinational capital colludes with states at the expense of democracy, equity and social development (Mkandawire, 2002), and in favor of sterile profitability and power without responsibility.

Given the weakness of African states in relation to the interests of rich nations, international financial institutions and multinationals, and their peripheral position in the global economy and politics, the only real authority or semblance of power affordable to African governments is towards their own populations. But the latter in turn are often too poor and too vulnerable to organize and mobilize effectively against cultural exploitation and repression. What neo-liberalism and global cultural entrepreneurs want of African governments are national and regional policies in tune with the profitability expectations of global capital, policies that minimize countervailing traditions, customs, worldviews and expectations of continuity. Once they have guaranteed global capital stability, security and protection from local labour and its needs, African states need do no more than embrace the rhetoric of liberal democracy and the tokenism of its freedoms. All multinational capital really requires of them is not so much a guarantee of democracy and stability, as a dictatorship to ensure that local labour and national interests are kept subservient to the interests of big business. Often it is understood, though not openly stated, that they need do no more than embrace liberal democratic rhetoric, since few seriously believe that it is possible, in practice, for African states or governments to be tolerant both of the demands of global capital and of the clamour for rights and entitlements by their own nationals (Englund and Nyamnjoh, 2004; Englund, 2006). There is trouble only for governments which, like Zimbabwe's Robert Mugabe's, begin to claim national sovereignty beyond rhetoric, thereby impairing the interests of global cultural entrepreneurs and the streamlined consumer culture they represent. With most African governments too conformist to dare, it is hardly surprising that little is done to domesticate the content of cultural menus by the global cultural entrepreneurs, even when their investments are through local subsidiaries headed by Africans armed with an enculturation rhetoric.

If cultural exclusion and repression are the order of the day, what are Africans doing to bypass the structures of repression and exclusion? In what follows, I use publishing and film-making to illustrate the impact of global hierarchies and local repression on the cultural economy in Africa, and the coping strategies developed by Africans.

African publishing

In the economics, culture and politics of publishing and reading in Africa, various hierarchies inform which and how African publications are recognized and represented. In addition, factors such as mediocrity of content and technical quality, language, invisibility, remoteness or the low reputation of the publisher, together with poor marketing and distribution, conspire to ensure that writers and academics perish even when they have published (Currey, 1986; Chakava, 1996; Larson, 2001; Wafawarowa, 2006). If these problems are universal (Mazrui, 1990; Canagarajah, 2002; Altbach, 2002; Waters, 2004), they are also particularly African, thanks especially to the global popularity of negative representations about the continent, its humanity and creativity (Nyamnjoh, 2004). The technical and financial difficulties facing the publishing industry in Africa are well known, as are the repression, censorship and other political challenges by governments less concerned about developing local publishing industries than in ensuring that 'children get books on their desks, regardless of their origin or content [or language]' (Chakava, 1996: 178). Many African writers of fiction and faction, from novelists to academics through poets, playwrights and journalists seeking visibility through publication, cannot but perish, and not always because of poor content. Things are particularly difficult for those writing and publishing in indigenous African languages (Ngugi, 1986; Chakava, 1996; Altbach and Tefera, 1999; Bgoya, 2005). In the social sciences, where objectivity is often distorted by obvious or subtle ideology, African scholars face a critical choice between sacrificing relevance for recognition or recognition for relevance. This is because the political economy of the cultural economy of publishing prevents them from achieving both of these values at the same time (Nyamnjoh, 2004). Yet Africa is afflicted by 'intellectual poverty', caused not only by the fact of 'an academic book famine' (Currey, 1986), but in particular by a famine in books grounded in and of relevance to the cultures of Africa (P'Bitek, 1989; Soyinka, 1990; Taiwo, 1993).

Decisions by publishers are primarily motivated by economic considerations, even if not always by a thirst for profit. Even the most non-commercial, 'progressive' or 'independent' publishers and university presses hesitate to promote plurality and diversity of content because they run the risk of putting themselves out of the business. Reviewers, as arbitrators of taste, standards and knowledge, are readily and uncritically sought after by publishers – regardless of ideological learnings or cultural backgrounds. This implies that publishing is ultimately about policing ideas to ensure that national, regional and global book-markets will be dominated by plurality without diversity.

In reviewing a manuscript or publication, publishers seek to ensure that established traditions and expectations of palatability are maintained. In a world heavy with economic, cultural and political hierarchies informed, *inter alia*, by race, place, class, gender and age, this begs a few questions: Whose traditions? Whose palates? Why traditions and palates? Hence the importance of yet other questions: Who has the power to define, enforce and manage these traditions, tastes and standards? How feasible is it to promote literary or cultural traditions and ideals when they are at variance with economic considerations? If he who pays the piper calls the tune, then the cultural capital most likely to inspire investment is that which is familiar to the paymaster's race, place, class, gender or generation; that into which s/he has been schooled to the point of second nature and which, instinctively, s/he expects every piper worth the name to internalize and reproduce. Yet many of the 'pipers' are just as shaped by their race, place, class, gender and generation as are those who pay them. Inviting them to internalize and reproduce tunes at variance with their own traditions and tastes is to devalue and marginalize their own human experience. Over time, in the interest of convenience and material comfort, many inevitably yield to the wallet and reproduce the cultural expectations of their paymasters. This makes publishing a very conservative industry where, despite rhetoric to the contrary, the emphasis is less on creativity than mimicry, and less on production than reproduction.

Thus socialized into these hierarchies, publishers, editors, peer-reviewers and cultural producers operate in cultural contexts where it is normal to minimize the scientific and creative capabilities of the African mind. Increasingly, for reasons of political correctness, this is true in practice even when it remains unstated. It is hardly surprising then that African artists, writers and scientists continue to face an uphill task convincing publishers about the maturity and validity of their creative endeavors.

The African publishing industry, which contributes a meagre three per cent to the total world publication output and is heavily dependent on school textbook publishing and donor-driven book procurement programs, is still very much in its infancy (Wafawarowa, 2006: 9). Up to 95 per cent of books published in Africa are school textbooks, of which the multinational publishing companies take the biggest share. In South Africa for example, 60 per cent of educational publishing (i.e. 80 per cent of the entire publishing industry) is controlled by multinationals, and the remaining 40 per cent almost exclusively controlled by local white-owned companies (Bgoya, 2005). There is little or no publishing of books of interest and relevance to the African majority, and of those that are published, most are by multinational publishers who target the elite few who can read and write European languages and who – for economic, cultural or political reasons – reproduce work informed by a global hierarchy of creativity in which Africans are perceived to be at the very bottom. Most sub-Saharan African publishers north of the South African Limpopo River might have the will to promote alternative work, but they simply do not have the means to do so – or to survive doing so. Created in the late 1980s and early 1990s to strengthen African writing, publishing and book distribution, networks such as the Pan African Writers Association (PAWA), African Publishers' Network (APNET), Pan African Booksellers Association (PABA) and African Books Collective (ABC) have certainly increased awareness, sensitivity and accessibility, but the challenge of ensuring the visibility and recognition of African publications as vehicles of African creativity and cultural content in Africa and beyond remains (Chakava, 1996; Bgoya, 2005; Wafawarowa, 2006; Mlambo, 2007), and in certain cases requires nothing short of a decolonization of the mind (Ngugi, 1986).

As for the leading publishers and booksellers who are mostly South African, white, and subsidiaries of big names in global publishing, the tunes they call are preponderantly Western even when the stories and scholarship are geographically located in South Africa. Almost systematically, South African publishers reject material from north of the Limpopo, as the following excerpts from my own personal experiences as a novelist with two South African publishers and their manuscript reviewers demonstrate:

Publisher 1

'This is by far the most accomplished of all this author's manuscripts that I have had the privilege of reading. *Dieudonné* has several very interesting strands which come together to form something which is original and entertaining. [...] Over the years,... [name withheld] has found that it is very difficult to sell books that do not have a direct relationship to the experiences of the South African book-buying public. While I am sure this will, and is, changing, it should still be taken into account. [...] At present, despite all the excellent writing that I have found in this manuscript, I do not feel it is of a publishable standard. [...] As stated above, however, of important concern is that a book, even of this quality, may struggle in a South African market that continues to exhibit little interest in literature from elsewhere in Africa.'

Publisher 2

'*Dieudonné* is a further, and more fully realized, contribution to Francis Nyamnjoh's wide-angle critique of Cameroonian society, displaying the same tragicomic impulse seen in *The Forgotten*, with fewer faults of narration and style. The potential of the MS as a work for publication, however, is greatly limited… given the author's (lack of) profile. In short, *Dieudonné* is not a work that will rescue... Nyamnjoh profitably from anonymity, and I recommend that… [name withheld] decline to publish. […] Apart from the fact that today's marketplace makes little space for novellas – even less for those originating from north of the Limpopo – the plain fact is that Nyamnjoh's efforts fall short, in this case, of his ambitious undertaking.'

Fortunately for me, *Dieudonné* and *A Nose for Money* – another novel rejected in South Africa for similar reasons, were accepted by the Nairobi-based East African Educational Publishers, one of the few African publishers that have not neglected fiction altogether. Other rejected writers are, however, not as fortunate, but some refuse to celebrate victimhood. In the domain of scholarly production and creative writing in Cameroon for example, there is little or no interest by the global cultural entrepreneurs who simply do not see a big enough reading market to consider investing in publishing. In addition, the climate of repression since independence has meant a dearth of local publishing in general and of quality in particular. The few publishers that there are have had to steer clear of all controversial material, which, given the sensitivity of government to anything mildly critical, has forced them out of business or reduced them to printers of inoffensive but unprofitable literature. Little of what is published in Cameroon can boast even an ISBN number.

In the 1990s however, a semblance of political liberalization provided some individuals with the opportunity to move into desktop publishing. One of those who have distinguished themselves in this regard is Dr Linus Asong who has taken up self-publishing, starting with his first novel, *Crown of Thorns*, in Canada. His desktop publishing company – Patron Publishing House – has even expanded to publishing other local writers, including a conversational autobiography of Ndeh Ntumazah, an opposition political leader who spent the best part of his life fighting for a new political culture in Cameroon. Although the quality of printing and binding leaves a lot to be desired, Asong's hard work may well have brought to the limelight novels, poetry and books that otherwise would never have made it into print in a situation where

potential authors are either victims of administrative censorship or suffer a high rejection rate at the hands of commercial publishers such as those in South Africa. If and when there is a breakthrough, this is often on the publishers' terms and with scant regard for the official rhetoric and policy of 'African renaissance' in the 'new' South Africa. Asong's efforts may be trivialized and mocked by colleagues published or determined to be published by 'internationally recognized' publishers only, but they tell a story of resistance and hope worthy of emulation.

What is published or not published in South Africa on and from the rest of Africa, plays an important role in perpetuating negative stereotypes between insiders and outsiders, and in undermining the South African contribution to an African renaissance and cultural conviviality. The future of African publishing depends on the extent to which South African publishers and booksellers reach out north of the Limpopo. How effective the manuscript review system remains depends on how receptive to innovative writing and content it is in practice, especially as the merits of reviews cannot be taken for granted. All too often, reviewers use marketability as an excuse to reject what their cultural or ideological palates are uncomfortable with. The inevitable result is that richness and diversity suffer. A future for African publishing will require more than the market, for traditions, like works of fiction, are invented and reinvented. Just as reviewers call upon writers to reinvent and resubmit, marginal voices in South Africa and elsewhere are screaming out for their predicament to be captured by pipers in tune with alternative tunes. It is the place and duty of African publishers to provide for a rainbow continent of multiple identities and cultural conviviality with a unique and powerful voice. This they can achieve partly by taking advantage of e-publishing and print-on-demand technology, which makes it possible to publish books that would otherwise be too costly to print in large quantities where markets are not assured. Creative ways of addressing problems of distribution, the weakest link in African publishing, need to be sought through existing networks and other avenues (Bgoya, 2005; 2007).

Coping with global hierarchies and local repression

An African proverb says: 'Until the lions produce their own historian, the story of the hunt will glorify only the hunter' (Achebe, 2000: 73). The wisdom of this proverb is brought home not only through an analysis of writings on Africa, but also and perhaps more sensationally through the images of Africa captured in the cinematic gaze of the supposedly superior others. As the bottom of the rungs of race and place, Africa has, through the centuries, provided especially Euro-American cultural entrepreneurs with a rich catalogue of stereotypes, prejudices and other negations on which to capitalize. If this is true of publishing, cinema and television have since the twentieth century offered more efficient vehicles for effective traffic in such misrepresentations (Walker and Rasamimanana, 1993; Barlet, 2000; Gugler, 2003; Harding, 2003). In colonial times, while the British government for instance, deplored the showing to "primitive people… of demoralising films, representing criminal and immodest actions by white men and women'" (Smyth, 1979: 437–8), they did not hesitate to commission propaganda films on the exploits of the Empire in Africa. Censorship was strict, especially on American commercial cinema, and South Africa led the way on 'racial discrimination in censorship and segregation in viewing which was adopted in much of East and Central Africa' (Smyth, 1979: 437–8).

In their study of educational films on Africa in American schools, Walker and Rasamimanana (1993) discovered not only the prominence of Tarzan films in the repertoire of 'America's most consistent cinematic denigration of Africans', but also a tendency in Hollywood films to persist in presenting Africa as a continent of negations inhabited by stupid, bloodthirsty savages who are incapable of teaching anyone anything of value, but who must learn all from others to make progress. Such 'inaccurate, misleading, and pejorative' stereotypical films on Africa are 'the worst imaginable and well-documented', and extend beyond Africa and Africans to include people of African ancestry. The study also revealed that films on Africa did not hesitate to overgeneralize, portraying present European involvement on the continent as 'unmitigatedly positive' leading Africans to give up 'their "primitive" lifestyles'. Hardly ever is there mention of the Africans who 'fought determinedly against European aggression and influence to preserve their indigenous and sovereign ways'. Nor do the films recognize 'that many contemporary, well-educated, and cosmopolitan Africans have chosen to maintain their indigenous values and behaviours, or that many others have eclectically adapted or "Africanized" some elements of Western culture while deliberately and consciously rejecting others as inferior to their own'. While consistently positive in their representation of Whites and what Whites have done and are doing for Africa, there is little or nothing on what Whites 'have done to and continue to do to Africa or get from Africa'. Indigenous (pejoratively termed 'traditional' or 'native') African values are caricatured and portrayed as needing to be parted with, and Africans who embrace what passes for Western values are celebrated. 'The stereotypical and often seemingly contrived visual imagery in many of the films viewed reinforces Eurocentric misperceptions about Africa and its people.' If stereotypes and prejudices are this evident in educational films, the situation is worse with commercial films. An effect of feeding school children and adults alike with a consistent menu of misrepresentations about Africa and the African Diaspora is the reproduction of hierarchies that exclude and render invisible African humanity and creativity (Walker and Rasamimanana, 1993: 7–16).

Since colonial times, Africans have been confined largely to consuming (even if creatively) pervasive 'mythic Hollywood screen imagery' (Ambler, 2001), and to feeding the Africa misrepresentation industry (Barlet, 2000; Harding, 2003). In a context like this, where Africans find themselves peripheral to global trends and subjected to the high-handedness and repression of their own governments, it is easy to slip into meta-narratives that celebrate victimhood. While there is genuine reason to be pessimistic and cynical, there is often, on closer observation, also reason to be hopeful. However repressive a government may be and however profound the spiral of silence induced by standardized and routinized global cultural menus, few people are completely mystified or wholly duped. There is always room for initiative or agency at an individual or group level to challenge domination, exploitation and the globalization of indifference to cultural diversity. Histories of struggle in Africa are full of examples in this connection. In cinema, just as in publishing, Africans have found myriad creative ways of participating as active agents in national life and global cultural processes, and of re-imagining their continent, its struggles, victories, challenges and aspirations (Gugler, 2003).

As Eddie Ugbomah, renowned Nigerian filmmaker observes, in Africa, 'There are many trained film-makers who can make films better than Hollywood directors, but they do not have Hollywood money' (Ukadike and Ugbomah, 1994: 157). They are making do with their widow's mite, seeking to fill the cinematic vacuum on the positive contributions of African cultures. In the face of global cinematographic indifference and caricature of their realities, the African lions have sought – despite financial, political and other hurdles – to enrich or contest the accounts of the Euro-American cinematic hunters through films of their own (Medjigbodo, 1980; Ukadike and Ugbomah, 1994; Barlet, 2000; Gugler, 2003; Harding, 2003: 79–83; Ngugi, 2003). Although some African countries are yet to produce a film, quite a significant number are active in cinema, although the aesthetic quality of what is produced sometimes leaves much to be desired. The overriding concern is less with aesthetics than with a message that captures the cultures, predicaments and aspirations of Africans (Ukadike and Ugbomah, 1994: 157–8). However, distribution problems, global indifference and linguistic parochialism mean that few African and non-African consumers of the various country products have a clear and comprehensive picture of the magnitude of the African film industry. This difficulty notwithstanding, worldwide interest in African film is increasing 'as more African feature films and documentaries are being shown outside their countries of origin at film festivals, in art cinemas, and on television' (Schmidt, 1997: 113–18).

One festival that has grown in stature over the years is the Film and Television Festival (FESPACO), a biennial event founded in 1969 to promote the development of the African cinema industry by providing a venue to reflect on, showcase and celebrate achievements in the industry. Held under evolving themes (with the 2007 theme being 'Cinema and Cultural Diversity') FESPACO seeks to contribute African voices and perspectives to the global cinema movement. Since 1972, the festival has been institutionalized and housed within the Burkina Faso Ministry of Culture, with its financing coming mainly from partners such as the French Cultural Center, UNESCO, UNDP, UNICEF and the Prince Claus Fund for Culture and Development. Attended by distributors around the world, this festival in principle plays host to films and documentaries from across Africa. Despite this semblance of cinematographic pan-Africanism, there is an undercurrent of Anglophone and Lusophone African marginalization and dissatisfaction with the preponderance of the French language and influence. To Eddie Ugbomah, a leading Nigerian film-maker, 'FESPACO is a francophone business' which Anglophone film-makers attend 'merely to promote Pan-Africanism, not to advertise or sell their films'. He dislikes the uneven playing field where 'francophone film-makers are subsidized by foundations and governments, [while] anglophone film-makers are subject to heavy

taxation'. He added that it was only after 'intensive lobbying' that the Nigerian government agreed to build the Nigerian Film Corporation and a colour laboratory which nobody is using 'because the government has not been able to convince investors that film is profitable' (Ukadike and Ugbomah, 1994: 152–4).

One look at the list of previous winners of the FESPACO Grand Prix would seem to suggest that but for Kwaw Ansah and Newton Aduaku, there are no good movie producers in Anglophone Africa. Yet the most recognized commercial African film production centers are in Nigeria and South Africa. Differences in perception of investment are apparent between Francophone and Anglophone producers. Francophone producers are often subsidized or sponsored by their own governments or by France which is keen to protect and spread its cultural influence in Africa against the ubiquitous threat posed by the globalization of English and the values it conveys. Meanwhile Anglophone producers seem to seek to put their efforts into self-financing. These modes of financing have different impacts on movie rights and distribution patterns, with consequences for the reception and viewing of African movies by African audiences (Ukadike and Ugbomah, 1994: 152–4). It must be added though that the fact that African cinema continues to be discussed mainly in terms of Francophone, Anglophone, and Lusophone cinemas attests to the weight of the 'heavy burden' of the depredations inflicted on Africa by colonial invaders and their hierarchies of humanity and cultures (Willemen, 1992: 140).

In response to many of these dilemmas, the vibrant Nigerian video-movie industry, with its highly localized locations, settings, dress and narratives, has responded with the direct-to-video marketing, which cuts out theater-going, perceived as not being central to African cultural patterns and practices. The assumption is that, given the tendency for Africans to view movies in the household, movies need not necessarily be distributed mainly for cinema halls, where they would have to compete with Hollywood blockbusters. Through direct-to-video sales, the Nigeria movie industry is making a name for itself locally and internationally, notably amongst Nigerians and Africans in the diaspora (Adejunmobi, 2002: 77–95; Ambler, 2002: 119–20; Harding, 2003: 81–3).

Though sometimes overly dramatic, sensational and stereotypical in their portrayal especially of the occult and ritualized practices drawn largely from ethnic Igbo, Yoruba and Hausa cultures (Okwori, 2003), the Nigerian video-movie industry covers themes and uses language in creative ways relevant to and popular with its African audiences (Adejunmobi, 2002). In Central and West Africa for example, cities are full of shops owned mainly by the Nigerian Igbo business community selling at affordable prices Nigerian-made and pirated films from Hollywood, Bollywood and Nigeria's very own popular Nollywood. Commercial and public television stations throughout Africa feed heavily on Nollywood videos, while from Maputo to Dakar through Harare, Nairobi, Accra and Freetown, pirated latest Hollywood films proliferate at US$5 and less. Indeed, 'video dens and theaters have become ubiquitous features on African landscapes', offering new forms of leisure to urban and rural Africa alike, ranging from establishments where funds are informally collected in exchange for film shows, to more formal movie theaters, through obscure backrooms and home viewing (Ambler, 2002: 119).

Pirating may be a breach of copyright but it is also an indication of the desire to belong by those who are denied firsthand consumption of the cultural products in question. Thanks to dubbing and pirating, Christianity is today more relevant to illiterate urban and village folks in religious Africa, as it is possible for 'Jesus of Nazareth', his white skin notwithstanding, to be betrayed, crucified and resurrected in Pidgin English and local indigenous languages and, above all, to be affordable. Africans in general are benefiting from the Nigerian video-movies industry that has refused to wait until the time it is able to produce high-quality films with sophisticated modern technology. The films may flicker and frustrate even the most accommodating viewers, but their popularity seems to suggest that a poorly produced culturally relevant film is better than none at all (Ukadike and Ugbomah, 1994: 152–4). Using very basic equipment and releasing its products directly on video cassettes and CDs, Nigerian film-makers have captured a large market among Africans at home and in the diaspora, offering films more culturally relevant than even the most sympathetic Hollywood product (Adejunmobi, 2002). It is estimated that the Nigerian movie industry, which produces thousands of video films every year, yields about US$45 million in revenues each year (Ambler, 2002: 119–20). This creativity in African cinema does more than re-imagine Africa and the challenges of being African. It also tells the story of how Africans are actively modernizing their indigeneities and indigenizing their modernities, often in ways not always obvious to those obsessed with cultural hierarchies.

Conclusion

This chapter has demonstrated that race and place are key determinants in the presence or absence of ventures in Africa by global cultural entrepreneurs. Only by adding race and place to the other hierarchies (of class, gender, citizenship, nationality, etc.), are we best able to understand the reality of the relationship between globalization and the cultural economy in and on Africa. Race and place would explain why, as Chika Onyeani argues in his provocative book *Capitalist Nigger* (2000), Africans on the continent and in the diaspora 'consume everything others produce and produce nothing that others could consume'. As he notes among other things, although 'Black people spend more money on purchasing musical equipment than any other group', they do not produce any of these products, and do not even own factories where these musical products are assembled. And 'although Africans consume more Japanese products percentage wise than any other group', from stereos to radios, televisions, cars and other gadgets, 'the Japanese have nothing but scorn for the African', whom two of their former prime ministers have termed 'inferior in intelligence' in public. 'Yet, when you enter the New York Subway, the people you see with Walkmans on their heads and ears are 95 per cent Black people.' In the USA, although more than 88 per cent of the players in the National Basketball Association are Blacks, 'none of the 36 teams are owned by Blacks', and only a handful of coaches are Black, even though the players are most well-paid (Onyeani, 2000: 3–14). Denied visibility even as leading consumers, the Africans' best chance of visibility has, from the times of slavery, colonialism and empire to the present-day celebrity interest in Africa, been as commodities, and seldom as human beings at the center of the production and consumption of their very own cultural realities (Lindfors, 1999; Erlmann, 1997; Magubane, 2007). Even as commodities, there is little to suggest that Africans have competed favorably for the attention of consumers against other commodities such as wildlife, beaches and other natural attractions of their continent. The African is, because of his/her race and place in society or geography, allowed to excel in consumption of cultural products and its vehicles of transmission, but not to harness the technological processes and political economy of the cultural economy. Thus as long as the hierarchies of race and place remain key determinants and profitability the name of the global culture game, the African even as a 'Capitalist Nigger', continues to afford visibility, even as concerns his or her own creativity, mainly as a consumer than as a producer of cultures.

Policy recommendations

Given the centrality of race and place in the African cultural economy, and given the reality of the invisible hand in national and global economies even under globalization, the positive representation of Africans, their cultures and creativity cannot be left to market forces alone. International political mobilization and action are needed to purge the cultural industries of problematic representations based on hierarchies informed less by science and experience than by prejudice. Although the fear of risk makes the global cultural industries settle too easily for stereotypes and caricatures, there is little to suggest that only negative representations of Africa can appeal to non-African consumers. The worldwide popularity of Alexander McCall Smith's 'No.1 Ladies' Detective Agency' novels set in Botswana is evidence that a sensitive and respectful treatment of Africa and Africans is not at variance with profitability. Indeed, as the creative appropriation by Africans of technological innovations such as the Internet and cellphone has demonstrated, far from being inimical to profitability, the sociality, interdependence and conviviality of African cultures are a paradise for investors. This means that the global cultural entrepreneurs have little to fear endorsing calls for ground rules to protect and promote cultural diversity beyond rhetoric and token concessions.

The Nigerian film industry, which yields about US$45 million in revenues each year and is growing in popularity on the continent and amongst the African diaspora, is evidence that Africans are not so much against stereotypical representations as such, but that if stereotypes are the game of the cultural industries, they would rather settle for stereotypes informed by their cultures and real life experiences, and not the figment of the imagination of some pontificating cultural other. Again, this suggests that global cultural entrepreneurs seeking to reach African consumers with their cultural products are more likely to succeed by working in partnership, constant negotiation and interchange

with African cultural producers and consumers. There is thus the need for policies and practices that encourage the formation of collaborative partnerships between producers across cultural lines. The delocalization of cultural production from dominant centers through the creation of culture production centers driven by local realities, demands and imperatives would help in the contextualization of the production process and the commodity which emerges from it. Beyond borrowing African landscapes to caricature the 'exotic', cultural production within the global context would benefit from the complex, nuanced and changing discourses which characterize marginalized African realities. Audiences in Western countries with an appetite for non-Western cinematic and literary products need not be fed grotesque caricatures produced from outmoded stereotypes.

African investors, intellectuals and political elites (on the continent and in the diasporas) need to invest seriously in African cultural production, and their daily activities and behaviour must not undermine the very doctrine of the importance of upholding African cultural values. This includes investment in the training and development of teachers, writers and artists as lenses and the conscience of society, correcting misrepresentations and providing alternative narratives in complex, negotiated and nuanced ways. Although African publishing is heavily reliant on school textbooks, the lion's share of subventions for and business in such projects goes directly to multinational publishers or their local affiliates. Yet these multinational publishers are less keen on investing some of the profit made into developing the local publishing industry, local content and/or promoting publishing in local languages. The disadvantaged African publishers who are interested do not make enough from textbooks to venture into other aspects of publishing. This calls for policies that protect African publishers against uneven competition with established giants driven primarily by profitability. Policies are certainly called for to mitigate these constraints by taking advantage of the possibilities offered by electronic production and consumption. Finally, the invisibility of race and place which Africa suffers means that even when their cultural products are abundantly available, of quality and in demand, conventional arbiters of taste and distribution can still stand in the way of their consumption. This surely requires policy attention.

REFERENCES

Achebe, C. (2000) *Home and Exile*. New York: Anchor Books.

Adejunmobi, M. (2002) 'English and the Audience of an African Popular Culture: The Case of Nigerian Video Film', *Cultural Critique*, 50: 74–103.

Altbach, P.G. (ed.) (2002) *The Decline of the Guru: The Academic Profession in Developing and Middle-Income*. Boston: Boston College.

Altbach, P.G. and Teferra, D. (1999) *Publishing in African Languages: Challenges and Prospects*. Boston: Bellagio Publishing Network.

Ambler, C. (2001) 'Popular Films and Colonial Audiences: The Movies in Northern Rhodesia', *The American Historial Review*, 106(1): 81–105.

Ambler, C. (2002) 'Mass Media and Leisure in Africa', *The International Journal of African Historical Studies*, 35(1): 119–36.

Amin, S. (1980) *Class and Nation: Historically and in the Current Crisis*. London: Heinemann.

Assensoh, A.B. (2001) 'African Writers: Historical Perspectives on Their Trials and Tribulations', *Journal of Black Studies*, 31(3): 348–64.

Barlet, O. (2000) *African Cinemas: Decolonizing the Gaze*. London: Zed Books.

Bgoya, W. (2005) 'Africa and Publishing: Reflections'. Online: http://www.pambazuka.org/en/category/comment/28874.

Bgoya, W. (2007) 'African Publishing', interviewed by Professor Itala Vivan, 5 January, Dar es Salaam, Tanzania.

Brown, M.F. (2003) *Who Owns Native Culture?* Cambridge, MA: Harvard University Press.

Canagarajah, A.S. (2002) *A Geopolitics of Academic Writing*. Pittsburgh: University of Pittsburgh Press.

Chakava, H. (1996) *Publishing in Africa: One Man's Perspective*. Boston: Bellagio Publishing Network.

Currey, J. (1986) 'The State of African Studies Publishing', *African Affairs*, 85(341): 609–12.

Englund, H. (2006) *Prisoners of Freedom: Human Rights and the African Poor*. Berkeley: University of California Press.

Englund, H. and Nyamnjoh, F.B. (eds.) (2004) *Rights and the Politics of Recognition in Africa*. London: Zed Books.

Erlmann, V. (1997) 'Africa civilized, Africa uncivilized: local culture, world system and South African music', in K. Barber (ed.) *Readings in African Popular Culture*. Oxford: James Currey. pp. 170–7.

Golding, P. and Harris, P. (eds.) (1997) *Beyond Cultural Imperialism: Globalization, communication and the New International Order*. London: SAGE Publications.

Gugler, J. (2003) *African Film: Re-Imagining a Continent*. Bloomington: Indiana University Press.

Harding, F. (2003) 'Africa and the Moving Image: Television, Film and Video', *Journal of African Cultural Studies*, 16(1): 69–84.

ICOM (International Council of Museums) (1995) *Le Trafic Illicite des Biens Culturels en Afrique*. Bamako: ICOM.

Kasfir, S.L. (1996) 'Review: African Art in a Suitcase: How Value Travels', *Transition*, 69: 146–58.

Larson, C.R. (2001) *The Ordeal of the African Writer*. London: Zed Books.

Lindfors, B. (ed.) (1999) *Africans on Stage: Studies in Ethnological Show Business*. Bloomington: Indiana University Press.

Magubane, Z. (2007) 'Africa and the New Cult of Celebrity'. Online: http://www.zeleza.com/blogging/popular-culture/africa-and-new-cult-celebrity.

Mazrui, A.A. (1990) *Cultural Forces in World Politics*. London: James Currey.

McChesney, R.W. (1998) 'The Political Economy of Global Media', *Media Development*, XLV(4): 3–8.

McChesney, R.W. (2001) 'Global Media, Neoliberalism, and Imperialism', *Monthly Review* 52(10). Online: http://www.monthlyreview.org/301rwm.htm.

Medjigbodo, N. (1980) 'Afrique Cinématographiée, Afrique Cinématographique', *Canadian Journal of African Studies*, 13(3): 371–87.

Mkandawire, T. (2002) 'Globalization, Equity and Social Development', *African Sociological Review*, 6(1): 115–37.

Mlambo, A. (ed.) (2007) *African Scholarly Publishing: Essays*. Oxford: African Books Collective.

Murdock, G. (1994) 'The New Mogul Empires: Media Concentration and Control in the Age of Divergence', *Media Development*. XLI(4): 3–6.

Ngugi, N. (2003) 'Presenting and (Mis)representing History in Fiction Film: Sembene's "Camp de Thiaroye" and Attenborough's "Cry Freedom"', *Journal of African Cultural Studies*, 16(1): 57–68.

Ngugi wa Thiong'o, (1986) *Decolonising the Mind: The Politics of Language in African Literature*. London: James Currey.

Nyamnjoh, F.B. (2004) 'From Publish or Perish to Publish and Perish: What "Africa's 100 Best Books" Tell Us About Publishing Africa', *Journal of Asian and African Studies*, 39(5): 331–55.

Nyamnjoh, F.B. (2005) *Africa's Media, Democracy and the Politics of Belonging*. London: Zed Books.

Nyamnjoh, F.B. (2006) *Insiders and Outsiders: Citizenship and Xenophobia in Contemporary Southern Africa*. London: CODESRIA/Zed Books.

Nyamnjoh, F.B. (2007) 'Culture, Conflict, and Globalization: Africa', in H.K. Anheier and Y.R. Isar (eds.) *Cultures and Globalization: Conflicts and Tensions*. London: SAGE Publications. pp. 121–32.

Oguibe, L. (2004) *The Culture Game*. Minneapolis: University of Minnesota Press.

Okwori, J.Z. (2003) 'A Dramatized Society: Representing Rituals of Human Sacrifice as Efficacious Action in Nigerian Home-Video Movies', *Journal of African Cultural Studies*, 16(1): 7–23.

Onyeani, C. (2000) *Capitalist Nigger*. Johannesburg and Cape Town: Jonathan Ball Publishers.

P'Bitek, O. (1989) *Song of Lawino*. Nairobi: East African Educational Publishers.

Rowlands, M. (2004) 'Cultural Rights and Wrongs: Uses of the Concept of Property', in K. Verderey and C. Humphrey (eds.) *Property in Question: Value Transformations in the Global Economy*. Oxford: Berg. pp. 302–19.

Schmidt, N.J. (1997) 'Review Essay: Special Issues of Periodicals on African Film', *African Studies Review*, 40(1): 113–19.

Smyth, R. (1979) 'The Development of British Colonial Film Policy, 1927–1939, with Special Reference to East and Central Africa', *The Journal of African History*, 20(3): 437–50.

Soyinka, W. (1990) 'Twice Bitten: The Fate of Africa's Culture Producers', *PMLA*, 105(1): 110–20.

Taiwo, O. (1993) 'Colonialism and Its Aftermath: The Crisis of Knowledge Production', *Callaloo*, 16(4): 891–908.

Thomas, P.N. and Nain, Z. (eds.) (2005) *Who Owns the Media: Global Trends and Local Resistances*, Penang/London: SouthBound/WACC/Zed Books.

Thompson, G. (1999) 'Introduction: Situating Globalization', *International Social Science Journal*, LI(160): 139–52.

Ukadike, N.F. and Ugbomah, E. (1994) 'Toward an African Cinema', *Transition*, 63: 150–63.

Wafawarowa, B. (2006) 'The African Publishing Context and its Relationship with South Africa', *Bookmark: News Magazine of the South African Booksellers' Association*, July–September, pp. 7–10.

Walker, S.S. and Rasamimanana, J. (1993) 'Tarzan in the Classroom: How "Educational" Films Mythologize Africa and Miseducate Americans', *The Journal of Negro Education*, 62(1): 3–23.

Waters, L. (2004) *Enemies of Promise: Publishing, Perishing, and the Eclipse of Scholarship*. Chicago: Prickly Paradigm Press.

Willemen, P. (1992) 'Review: The Making of an African Cinema', *Transition*, 58: 138–50.

## CHAPTER 9

GLOBALIZATION AND CRAFTS IN SOUTH ASIA
Jasleen Dhamija

In traditional societies, crafts play an important role as means of employment and production; they are also a significant aspect of the creative expression of the community, closely tied to its way of life. While many see globalization as a threat to the craft industry, it can in fact be effectively used to reach out to expand markets for the crafts while also increasing craftspersons' earnings. What is needed is a supportive government policy that works in the interest of the craft sector and not against it. This requires greater participation of master craftsmen in the making and implementation of all aspects of crafts promotion policy.

Introduction

In the year 2002, India celebrated 50 years of Handicrafts Development, proud of having been the first nation to deliberately develop this sector as an industry and an avenue for generating employment. This was an occasion to recognize the *Shilp Gurus*, the great masters and teachers, who had maintained and handed down the craft traditions of the subcontinent. A seminar with participants from Asian countries with rich craft traditions was organized. One of the concerns expressed was the adverse impact of globalization on the crafts sector. For example, the import of cheap Chinese silk and the dumping of household goods and objects of everyday use into the local markets was having a negative impact on craft production. The head of a large voluntary organization saw globalization as the end of the crafts sector. The grim situation of the Varanasi weavers was quoted as an example. What stood out in the midst of this discussion was the remark of a young 23-year-old master designer of Varanasi, who specialized in *jala* work, jacquard making: 'It is our fault that Varanasi is in difficulties. It is because we have not globalized'.

This was an extraordinary comment by a descendent of designers who could trace their origins to the great fourteenth century Sufi master of Bokhara, Sheikh Bahaud-e-din Nakshabandi. The young master was actually reminding the seminar that global trading has existed from times immemorial. It was being conducted for example out of the Harappan sea port at Lothal, which has been dated to 2000 BC. This ancient seaport had well-organized facilities, including separate quarters for quarantining incoming travellers; it had two different types of weights and measures for clientele from different regions of the world. It also appeared to have had production centers for cotton weaving and dyeing, as was seen by the presence of a number of implements for spinning, twisting etc. as well as large dye vats, similar to those still being used in Gujarat to make printed and dyed fabrics made for export. In addition, there were kilns for the preparation of agate stones, a speciality of the area which was exported all over the world and have been found in graves in South East Asia, from Myanmar to Laos. Harappan seals possibly used for trading have been found in Mesopotamia.

South Indian archaeological sites have yielded up a number of Greek and Roman coins and a cache of clay amphora, with markings indicating that Italian wine was favored. The large glazed pottery vessels known even today as Martabans came from the port of Martaban. They contained oil, perhaps pickles or was it very strong liquor, which is made side by side with these jars even today.

As many authors now point out, although 'globalization' has become today's buzzword, the phenomenon has long existed and must be seen in terms of a much longer historical perspective. This is also the case with another such term, which has become even more fashionable in the crafts trade sector: 'outsourcing'. But this idea too is old hat. The isolated Maldives Islands, for example, have from the most ancient times been a site for taking on supplies of water and having sailing vessels repaired. While providing these services the islanders also became specialists in fine quality weaving, using materials brought by traders from all over the world to produce quality products that could be sold at good prices and exchanged for their services.

While both globalization and outsourcing may have been around for millennia, the new realities of information technology, the power of the media, rapid transportation and the accelerating pace of competition, now disadvantage the weak and lead to their exploitation. Transfers of capital are taking place for the purpose of quick returns on investment, rather than for trade in ways that would generate income, create employment and distribute wealth. What has been alarming has been the transfer of capital not because of trade, but for greater returns. They have ushered in growing disparities not only between the industrialized countries and many that have only recently emerged from the shadow of colonial domination, but within these very countries, between the wealthy and those who live at subsistence level. India is a glaring example. It is ranked eighth among countries with the largest number of US dollar millionaires; and it is estimated that there will soon be 50 million middle-class and 500 million working-class Indians. And yet the minimum wage for many is less than two dollars a day. A recent study indicated that handloom weavers earn just over one dollar per day and also not throughout the year.

Growing consumerism and expanding markets could benefit all craftspersons, provided they are not exploited and adversely affected by government policies, which actually prevent them from reaching out for the potential benefits, instead of facilitating access to credit, technology and marketing information.

A historical profile of crafts in India

Crafts are created through a highly evolved technology mastered by the hands, the mind, the eye that has produced objects of everyday daily life as well as of ritual and spiritual significance that are among the earliest expressions of human creativity and enrichment. As pointed out by Friel and Santagata in Chapter 24 of this volume, such objects embodied the cultural heritage and were a reflection of the collective psyche of the people. Even when they were created in a repetitive manner, no object was ever the same as another. Yet there has been a misinterpretation of the true nature of craft production, for which semantics have to some extent been responsible. This appears to have stemmed from the increasing use in English of the French notion of *artisanat* to mean crafts, while the word 'artisan' in English actually denotes a worker who performs in a mechanical manner. This is a far cry from the hierarchy of skills and knowledge, the long years of apprentice, of belonging to a guild system that characterized the crafts sector, which was in many countries organized in the same way as the Sufi orders.

Crafts being the very pivot of all the different art forms, the literary, the visual and plastic arts, as well as music, were closely linked and influenced each other. Iranian art created its design from lines, contours, shapes, masses, colours and movement with its varying rhythms. Artistic creation had not only a strong sense of design and rhythm but a lucidity of conception which had its parallel in music and poetry. The thought of the period strongly influenced its art; thus the overall concept of design was not merely decorative but imbued with deeper significance. Thus there was no division between the classical arts and crafts. In fact all art forms were closely linked. For instance, performing arts used a range of crafts for creating an impact on the audience. The maker of a mask for a performance had to know the dance form before he was allowed to create the mask. This was essential, so as to know the angles from which the audience would see the mask. The creator of a musical instrument had to know how to play the instrument. Even the caster of the dancers bells had to know music, so as to cast them in different musical notes, for the most skilled dancers could, by the movement of their calf muscles, create a melody. The master of bells in the remote Rann of Kutch created a range of notes for animal herders, so that they could distinguish each of their cattle; he was also able to create the seven musical notes to create music in the wind.

The artists and poets of Iran and India were versatile and had a deep interest in all the arts. Rudaki, the ninth-century poet, was an expert in a range of art forms, while Mir Ali Shir was a musician, composer, painter, an admirable poet and a distinguished patron of architecture. Ghiyath-ud-Din, the famous designer of the court of Shah Abbas, whose textiles were internationally known and coveted by kings, as we know from Akbar's biography, was a connoisseur of art, a well-known collector, and a witty man, known for his satirical poems. It was in this atmosphere that the crafts developed, where patrons and city dwellers were themselves connoisseurs of art and their discerning taste stimulated higher standards. The master craftsmen too were versatile: the master ebony carver of Nagina was a player of the *sarangi*, and loved to fish; he created poetry as he engraved. Ali Hasan of Varanasi was a distinguished designer of great taste and a connoisseur of poetry and music. The separation of arts and crafts came later as an impact of the colonizers and the setting up of 'arts' and 'crafts' schools.

At different periods, different aspects were emphasized in crafts at all levels because of prevailing influences. This also led to the development of distinctive regional styles expressing the traditions of the area. These traditions were not confined to the court or the urban centers but were a part of the life of all the people, since they actually catered to their daily consumer needs. The varying clientele, however, called for different styles, though there did exist an interchange, and sometimes motifs, forms, and techniques were adopted by rural areas from urban centers and vice versa.

The earliest evolution of a global style can be traced to the ateliers set up by the Caliphate of Baghdad. They began as *Dar-al-Tariz* (or ateliers) for the creation of robes to be worn by the Caliph and his court and later evolved as important ateliers of craftsmanship to serve the Islamic courts. Throughout the Islamic World, from Arabia, the Maghreb, West Asia, Spain and India, the ateliers exchanged designers' patterns and even master craftsmen. It was under discerning and assured patronage that these skills were nurtured. Ideal conditions were provided to the masters to work in unhurried concentration on developing skills and perfecting them. It was in this ambience that some of the finest crafts were developed. The later royal ateliers continued this tradition and provided an opportunity for artists involved in different techniques to work together, and thus create a stylistic unity during a particular period. If a fine Seljuq metal water ewer is closely studied we will see in its sculpturesque fluted form an echo of the fluted tomb towers of the period. A closer examination will show the use of motifs of stylized human and animal figures which are typical of the period. This in turn can be seen in murals and pottery, which are combined with the stylized Kufic lettering, used in the arts and crafts of the period.

In the past, craftsmen were guided by guilds. In India the guild system existed from ancient times and the guild leaders were nominated to the governing body of the city states. It is likely that in Iran as well, besides the workshops which catered to the court, there existed craftsmen's guilds, though there are no records to confirm this. It is an accepted fact that after the thirteenth century in the other Islamic states of the Near East as well as in Egypt, the guild system developed. In Byzantium and late Roman Empire, state organizations existed which regulated the different occupations. The tenth-century work known as *The Book of Perfection* has a detailed account of the guild system in Constantinople. The fact that the organization of the Sufi *khanegahe* appears to be based on the craft guild system also suggests that the system might have existed in Iran earlier than in other Islamic states. Claude Cahen in his study of pre-Ottoman Turkey also mentions that it is possible that Iran and Central Asia did not have exactly the same traditions as those of Egypt and Syria which had formerly been under Roman influence and occupation, and it is likely that the guild system may have existed from pre-Islamic times. These guild systems protected the interests of the craftsmen and guided them at every step. Under colonization and other developments of the modern era, including the establishment of arts and crafts schools, the guild system appears to have collapsed and was replaced by a new system which created the separation of crafts and arts and deprived master-craftsmen of the ability to develop their own responses to changing market needs.

Industrialization

It is well known that industrialization transformed ways of life everywhere. As the machine was seen as an answer to all problems, the artisan was seen as an extension of the machine; and man in turn in early modern theories of behaviour was seen as a push-pull automaton, as B.F. Skinner observed in his 1991 classic *Beyond Freedom and Dignity*. Man himself may be controlled by his environment, but it is an environment which is almost wholly of his own making. The physical environment of most people is largely man-made. The surfaces a person walks on, the walls which shelter him, the clothing he wears, many of the foods he eats, the tools he uses, the vehicles he moves about in, most of the things he listens to and looks at are human products.

Twentieth-century economists saw industrialization as the solution to unemployment and inequality and South Asia was where the first experiments in post-colonial governance were carried out. Western-trained national planners and economists saw industrialization as the panacea. In India, however, the influence of Gandhi on Jawaharlal Nehru led to a dual economy policy: Small scale and 'cottage' industry was to be developed alongside heavy industry. It was recognized that the Cottage Industry or the Handicraft Handloom sector was the largest employer after agriculture and also the largest production activity in the non-formal sector. Its demands on capital and energy were limited. It could respond to the needs of a dispersed rural population, to the lack of facilities, as well as the possibility of working with local resources and local skills; an export market could be built up for it.

The creation of a network of craft organizations where nothing existed previously was the herculean task undertaken by Kamaladevi Chattopadhya appointed by Jawaharlal Nehru, independent India's first Prime Minister. Lack of data and experience did not deter Kamaladevi, a remarkable woman whose organizational skills had been developed during the freedom movement, from taking up the challenge. Despite the fact that the mandarins of the country's Planning Commission saw crafts as an antediluvian activity and the leftists called it slavery of the people, craft activity was revived and also rebuilt; old markets which had been lost were regained and new ones created. One current estimate puts the number of persons involved in this cottage industry sector at 36 million. It is also the largest employer after agriculture and provides subsidiary income for rural populations still tied to the land; it is also one of the largest export sectors after agriculture and is the biggest employer in the non-formal sector, the largest employer in most developing countries. According to

a recent Indian study, the formal sector employs only seven per cent of the work force, the bulk of which is in the non-formal sector, which makes the lowest demands on the government for capital, energy and investment.

The mistaken notion exists that the Indian crafts sector is heavily subsidized. In fact, no subsidies are offered to the sector and industry receives far more financial support for research, capital formation, soft loans, etc. The cottage industry sector is widely dispersed and herein lies its strength, as well as its weakness. The strength is its ability to use local resources and create products which can find an easy access to markets at multiple levels; the weakness is that there is no support group or political organization to make its voice heard, so as to get the government to pay greater heed to its needs. These needs are limited, the most important being direct access to raw materials and credit and a supportive distribution system, instead of the corrupt, lethargic bureaucratic machinery. Most of the support organizations set up by the government are non-functional; despite this, the sector is flourishing and there is a growing demand for quality products both within the country and for export. A number of dynamic masters have emerged, who are running successful businesses in their own villages and towns because they are able to understand market trends, learn and develop new technologies and change their level of operation, and are helped by certain NGOs and even some forward-looking business houses.

India has been a pioneer in this field and set an example for other developing countries. It has been the leader in terms of concentration of skills, range of products and employment, as well as income generation. In countries such as the Philippines, Indonesia, Iran and Central Asia, this sector today employs large numbers of people and is a major source of income and employment as well.

Impacts and unrealized potential of globalization

A number of organizations working with the craft sector consider that globalization exerts a negative impact. They believe that the opening up of the market, which would lead to competition from cheaper products, newer patterns and changed tastes, will shrink the local market. It is also felt that the dislocation of communities, changing labour patterns, as well as changes in ways of life and the rejection of old traditions will also have a negative impact as many craft products are linked with the observance of traditional rites of passage, etc. However, a realistic view would be that globalization *per se* is neither good nor bad. It depends on how we use globalization as a way of opening up and/or tapping new markets. Reaching out to the growing middle class that has entered the consumer market in a big way is important.) However, crafts still need to be supported and protected. At present the adverse impact of globalization on crafts, especially in India, is not just competition from the products of other countries that are dumping cheap goods, but also the fact that the government now allows the export of raw material needed by the handicraft sector. One of the most crucial commodities for the handloom sector that can now be freely exported is hanks of cotton yarn, of which there is a shortage. The mills which produced yarn concentrate for the use of power looms and textile industry cannot produce enough for the handloom sector. Now that they are allowed to export hanks, the shortage has escalated and the price of yarn has increased. Retailers of handlooms are unwilling to increase their prices and the weaver is hence forced to take production short cuts in order to maintain his meagre earnings. The result is that the quality of the woven fabric suffers. This act on the part of the government has a far more adverse effect than the dumping of cheap goods.

There is also encroachment on regional creative expression, for instance the copying of the brocaded silk scarves of Varanasi by local jacquard users as well as the Chinese, or attempts by the latter to make Kanchipuram saris. This needs to be prevented by more effective recourse to the WTO. A Commission of NGOs and Master Craftsmen should be set up to keep a vigilant eye on these dangers. The government's role should be protective and supportive; and it should involve master craftsmen and NGOs in its efforts. Whereas the USA protects its farmers and industrial producers in many different ways, many developing countries are neglecting the needs of the craft sector, and in fact appear to be working against its most basic interests.

If an active NGO sector and government could pool their resources and mobilize the crafts sector, they would be able to capture a large market outside as well as within the country. China, for instance, has, by mechanical production of crafts, lost the intrinsic value of the crafts. They have a treasure house of crafts, which can still be effectively revived and they could develop the skills of 72 ethnic minorities

effectively. Today China has a very limited demand for its crafts locally, but if it tried to develop its production by maintaining the unique quality of its crafted objects, a significant domestic market would open up. India for its part has an essential market amongst Indians and the large and affluent diaspora, which has maintained the rich cultural traditions. It is interesting that Fabindia, a leading private concern known for the sale of handloom products and garments, and which has branches all over India, has opened stores in China at the invitation of the government.

Many business houses dealing in silks, handlooms, matting and crafts are doing very well. They function as large businesses. These certainly benefit the craftsmen, but what is needed even more is the establishment of joint promotional units, which would provide the services needed by the craft communities, so that greater benefit could accrue to them. The initiative of the United Nations Industrial Development Organization (UNIDO) of setting up 'Clusters of Craftspersons' in India was extremely successful. The scheme became popular with the government, who used the nomenclature, but not the modus operandi. Two of the main government craft organizations set up cluster schemes, but these only produced reports and studies, which had no impact on production, technology or designs. Nor did they address the vital questions of credit and marketing. Millions were spent, but for no benefit to the weavers. Rather it was the so-called expert institutions selected to look after the schemes who benefited.

For the long term development of this sector the crafts must be brought into the mainstream of the educational system. There is a need to set up training institutes where the children of the crafts practitioners themselves can participate. This would meet two important needs of the sector: prepare the next generation to become entrepreneurial (cf. Aageson's chapter on entrepreneurship in this volume – Chapter 6) and increase the status of the crafts practitioner. The Design Institutes and Art Colleges have no place for them; indeed most of them are elitist organizations inaccessible to the children of craftsmen. Most professional institutions such as schools of architecture, engineering, or design Institutes all have master craftsmen on their technical staff, but none are members of the faculty. It is important that this sector be given much more adequate recognition and the status of the master craftsmen be brought on a par with all the other creative practitioners. Schools all over the country have music, dance, drama and today even the media, as part of their extra curricular activities;

however, mastery of crafts is not taught – what they teach is a degraded form of craft skill. There are also no institutions except *Shantiniketan,* founded by Rabindranath Tagore, where degree courses are taught for crafts, but even here the latter are kept apart from *Kala Bhawan*, the Art House.

South Asia has the world's richest range of crafts in a highly evolved craft sector yet its master craftsmen and craft practitioners are looked down as they belong to the lower castes. Recently, when a Rajput became a painter and then later a potter, his family felt that he had lost his caste, his status and they were stigmatized because of his taking to pottery, even though it had brought him national and international acclaim and honours. The patronizing attitude towards the practitioners of crafts still exists and many of the organizations and NGOs do not have any masters of crafts as their advisory members, even though they are meant to benefit the crafts people. The most typical attitude is to hold international seminars on topics like the 'Crafts and its Makers' or 'The Crisis of Crafts' but with not a single practitioner of crafts present.

Today the old systems of support have disappeared and no new ones have taken their place.

Instead, we blame globalization for adversely affecting craft traditions. The opening up of the market to the import of goods has indeed affected some sectors, but it could also be a good way of offering competition and thus improve product quality. The other opportunity is to find new markets. We balk at the Chinese for encroaching on our markets and also for imitating our traditional weaves. Yet the dire situation of the weavers of Varanasi is not due to Chinese products, but to the fact that the traditional wedding sari, their mainstay, is now being woven on the power loom, with the use of the jacquard, at one third of the price of the handloom sari. It is the sale of power loom cloth as handloom that is most grievously affecting the handloom weavers. The policy of protection to the handloom sector is not being applied by the government. The proposal to have a handloom mark or a compulsory selvedge for power loom cloth is yet to be applied. Globalization can offer access to newer markets, improved design inputs and technology, in other words, better returns on existing skills. It can also inculcate a sense of self worth, of social justice and the importance of nurturing the rich repertoire of indigenous knowledge and skills.

## CHAPTER 10

EAST ASIA: THE GLOBAL–REGIONAL DYNAMIC
Michael Keane

This chapter argues that there are two ways of reframing the globalization of culture. The first follows the time-honoured model, referred to here as 'the economics of foreign programs'. The emphasis is on the sale of finished cultural goods and services in international markets. The second accounts more for intermediate inputs and the transfer of knowledge about formats, co-productions and franchises. Exploitation of the second model has allowed East Asia to expand its cultural economy, both regionally and internationally. The second model also lends itself to government intervention, not so much in terms of protectionism, but in industry facilitation that allows creative businesses to climb the value chain.

The records of Marco Polo, the legendary Venetian traveller of the fourteenth century, provide an important footnote in the history of globalization.[1] Polo wrote of his journeys from Europe to East Asia, and of the cultural and culinary marvels he witnessed. He wrote about the communication system by which important messages were dispatched, and about merchants who transported goods up and down the Yangzi River in the region surrounding Hangzhou, at that time the capital of the Southern Song Dynasty.

Cultural exchange between the East and West, however, did not begin with Marco Polo. Trade and exchange of ideas took place long before Polo, through the Silk Road and across the Indian Ocean spice routes. However, Polo's records alert us to the importance of Western imaginings of what would become the 'Far East'.

Exchanges of information, ideas, values and technologies have accelerated with the virtually instantaneous reach of modern media. Accordingly, the idea of Western dominance in cultural flows retains support, despite mounting evidence that shows cultural consumption tastes in East Asia to be increasingly regional (Chua, 2004; Iwabuchi et al., 2004; Erni and Chua, 2005; Keane, 2006; Keane et al., 2007; Tunstall, 2007).[2] While Hollywood cinema and gossip about Hollywood stars maintain interest in East Asia, television drama, music, animation, the Internet, video games and mobile content sectors are dominated by local content. By 2002, South Korean movies were accounting for almost 50 per cent of overall box office sales in local cinemas (Shin, 2005: 56). By the late 1990s, Taiwanese and Korean TV dramas were entering into co-productions with mainland Chinese producers, capitalizing on the appeal of East Asian pop culture in China (Chen, 2007; Lee, 2007). A decade earlier Sony's purchase of Columbia in 1989 had paved the way for the internationalization of Japanese anime (animation) and computer games. Even before that, in 1982, Hong Kong's TVB had set up its TVB International (TVBI) to promote the syndication of its programs internationally.

The reassertion of the region in cultural production is a combination of several related factors. The integration of East Asian economies within global markets has created more opportunities for international distribution of cultural goods and services. In addition, increased migration of creative personnel across the East Asian region has generated confidence in a pan-Asian cultural economy.[3] Policies by governments to reward creative enterprise have led to productive interdependencies among investors in the region. In turn, transfer of technologies through joint ventures, co-productions and licensing agreements have created greater efficiencies and communities of interaction. All these factors are complemented by rising cosmopolitanism in East-Asian cities and the decentering of Chinese identity, so much so that multiple dialects (Mandarin, Cantonese, Hokkien) are now utilized without producing cultural confusion (Chua, 2004). The problem of 'cultural discount' – a reduction in the trans-region tradability of works bearing different accents and values – no longer applies.

In the first section of this chapter I offer a brief account of how 'finished' cultural texts are received, absorbed and localized into East-Asian environments, and how these texts influence the creative capabilities of producers, leading to hybrid products and services capable of targeting global markets. In the second section, I examine the internationalization process from a different perspective and propose a cultural economy development model that explains the new face of globalization in East Asia. What are the actual market processes that underpin the reassertion of Asian culture in global markets? What is the role of Western cultural products, services and knowledge? Central to this analysis, therefore, is a re-theorization of cultural exchange. What happens when knowledge and ideas are transferred, whether by open source globalization (the web) or by deliberate processes of cultural exchange (trade shows, seminars, joint ventures, franchises)?

Sending and receiving texts

We conventionally imagine cultural products as pre-formed textual commodities – films, documentaries, TV dramas, books, magazines, artworks, performances, etc. Finished products are the standard measurable outcomes of the field of cultural economics. Very much a static and pre-Internet approach to calibrating the cultural economy, the finished text analysis is beholden to what Bates (1998) calls 'the economics of foreign programs'. The key issue is the value of goods in multiple markets and the key question for the cultural exporter is: will my work translate and have value in foreign markets?

In his study of Russian literature, the semiologist Yuri Lotman argued that national cultures proceed through cycles of importing and exporting texts. Writing about the cross-cultural transferability of finished texts, Lotman proposed a five stage sending– receiving process (Lotman, 1990).[4] His first stage of reception is where the foreign text (or product) exhibits an aura. When television began in Japan in the 1950s, programs such as *I Love Lucy* and *Superman* were attractive to Japanese viewers because the production techniques were superior (Kato, 1998). The 'foreign' television program was more 'beautiful'. Likewise, Taiwanese TV gained a reputation in China during the 1990s for being well made and creative, while tapping into the same structures of feeling as Mainland programs. Japanese trendy dramas achieved similar success in Taiwan during the 1990s (Iwabuchi, 2002).

The second stage of cultural exchange is where the 'imported' texts and the 'home' culture restructure each other: 'translations, imitations and adaptations multiply' (Lotman, 1990: 146). It wasn't long before the American mode of production was incorporated into Japanese television. Watching American programs allowed Japanese producers insights into how to make more sophisticated television. In Taiwan, a similar process occurred. News programs mimicked US formats while TV drama aped Japanese trendy dramas (Liu and Chen, 2004).

In the third stage the format of the imported text is re-versioned to suit the local. More than just imitation, this is a process of stripping away inappropriate foreign elements and inserting the 'pure' values of the locality. TV formats from *Who Wants to be Millionaire*, to *The Weakest Link, Survivor* and *Big Brother* have undergone extensive purification in Hong Kong, Taiwan, China and Japan (Keane et al., 2007). The best example of recombination is perhaps the Taiwanese teen idol drama, *Meteor Garden*. Based on a Japanese *manga* (comic), *Meteor Garden* cashed in on the fascination with Japanese trendy dramas and pop culture. By combining pop idol fascination with serial narrative, the Taiwanese added value to the Japanese formats. The remade 'idol drama' was successfully circulated among Mandarin-speaking Chinese communities in Asia and within diasporic communities in the West (Liu and Chen, 2004).[5] On the other side of the cultural divide, movies conceived in Japan (*The Seven Samurai* 1954/*The Magnificent Seven* 1960; *Ringu* 1998/*The Ring* 2002) have been remade in Hollywood (Xu, 2004).

In the fourth stage, imported texts are entirely dissolved in the receiving culture. For instance, the Korean video game *The Legend of Mir* had become a huge financial success in China by 2002. Drawing on the cultural history of China allowed *Legend of Mir* to claim authenticity. The fifth stage is where the receiving culture becomes a sending culture. The foreign text is absorbed, cleansed and localized. The ignominy – and the economic reality – of paying license fees to the Korean company Actoz impelled the distributor Shanda, itself the leading Chinese game developer, to commission local games that drew directly on the myths and legends of China. Shanda's key product became *The World of Legend*, more than just an imitation of Actoz's version of history. At the same time, another developer called Netease commissioned *Journey to the West (xiyouji)*, a game based on the classic legend of the Ming Dynasty. In effect, authenticity is added to cleanse and claim territory. The host culture then becomes an originator. It can now export the renovated product.

The cultural economy as an economic growth model

The model of finished cultural products is well understood. Naturally, producers and investors covet the sales of products in international markets, whether re-versioned or original. However, there is an ignored distinction between finished cultural products (movies, TV dramas, games, novels) and intermediate inputs into production (finance, talent, technique and management). What is mainly counted in industry data are finished products, the number of units traded: for instance, the revenue earned from box-office sales, ratings of TV and radio shows, subscriptions to magazines or data bases, license and rental fees, sales of products such as artworks, and commissions for performances. Publications such as *Variety* trade in this information and advertisers rely on such throughput industry data to justify rates.

This kind of analysis is often fragmented and static. It tells us about breaking news, mergers, and hits in the marketplace but less about the processes and dynamism that comes with collaboration. While finished products – Western television programs, animation, and pop stars – have waned in popularity in global markets (Kapner, 2003), the international influence is maintained through 'formatting', a term that describes how global production templates, fashions and styles circulate (see Keane et al., 2007). These formats are not 'finished' cultural products as much as recipes. In other words, the crust is international but the important ingredients are local. This model of globalization relies for its utility on the increasing opportunities to produce adaptations. International

flows of content, together with multi-channeling have increased the ease of entry into new markets. Adaptation, however, often requires specialist knowledge. The intermediate input in this case is the professional expertise of how to adapt, manage and shift content into different locations and different formats. This modification of an industrial model – from finished products to intermediate inputs – further destabilizes the cultural imperialism thesis.

In this view, the growth of the cultural economy parallels the 'ordinary economy' in East Asia. In other words, cultural expression, often regarded as essentially intangible and distinctive, can benefit from knowledge transfer comparable to industries such as manufacturing and high-technology. Business writers Ellis and Gadiesh (2006) have proposed three stages of development to describe the rise of Japanese and Korean companies during the past two decades. The first stage saw the building of local manufacturing capacity in order to provide low cost production (including outsourcing) to multinationals; in the second stage, Japanese and Korean companies borrowed capabilities through technology licensing and joint ventures; and finally, they bought assets and brands abroad.

The rise of the East-Asian cultural economy has moved through various stages and political transitions over the past several decades. As I mentioned in the introduction, there are reasons for the recent resurgence, most notably the infrastructure, capital and talent in cultural hubs such as Hong Kong, Japan, Taipei and Seoul. Mainland China has the same aspirations but due to serious restrictions on cultural expression under the pressures of socialist nation-building, has so far failed to capitalize on them. The Chinese cultural economy is now confronting the consequences of decades of cultural restriction in its inability to trade internationally, while absorbing cultural imports from Korea, Taiwan, Hong Kong, and to a much lesser extent, the US and Europe (Keane, 2007). While Taiwan and South Korea progressed through the restrictions of martial law in the 1980s and early 1990s, they eventually opened up cultural production to competition and progressively relaxed import quotas. Hong Kong, on the back of its film industry in the 1980s, took on the role of defining and internationalizing the kung-fu tradition, with the aid of Bruce Lee in Hollywood, and later Jackie Chan. Hong Kong's success as a television center during the 1980s and 1990s has been well documented (Curtin, 2003; 2007). Tokyo has established a reputation as a center for new media, *manga*, animation and electronic entertainment industries, while Seoul has become a production center for video games and film.

The development model of East-Asian cultural economies, with the exception of front-runners Hong Kong and Japan, parallels the rise up the value chain in the general economy. At the base is low-cost production. In other words, much cultural production in recent years has shifted to low-cost destinations. The now ubiquitous 'made in China' brand has replaced 'made in Taiwan' in a range of household manufactured items, but 'made in China' is now applicable to 'trade in tasks' in cultural industries – time-consuming rendering of Japanese and US animation production, the production of fashion outsourced from New York, Paris and Tokyo to sweat shops, and the low-budget film and TV shoots in many parts of China.[6] Outsourcing in cinema is perhaps the most celebrated example. China's biggest studio backlot, the Hengdian World Studios, is situated in coastal Zhejiang province, a few hours from Shanghai. It provides cheap production for East Asian (Korean, Hong Kong and Taiwanese) film and television companies and even international production houses. The chief asset is reserves of surplus low-paid labour and cheap location services (Keane, 2007).

A further rung up the cultural value chain sees the effects of mass imitation, and its darker side, piracy. Cloning someone else's success is a business model that provides short-term rewards, but brings with it the associated problems of intellectual property infringement. Imitation is also an effect of globalization, which simultaneously promotes flows of products and knowledge of how to copy products in different continents. Imitation has obvious benefits. It is a relatively simple matter to make identical or similar products and services, usually at lower cost. This applies to software (content) as much as hardware (applications). Where this activity is unlicensed and opportunistic, it exacerbates a cloning culture. As players recognize the gains to be made in the cultural economy, they will seek the shortest route to market, whether this is fake artifacts to tourists or, in the case of media industries, copying TV format ideas from competitors. However, to see this as completely non-redemptive is misleading. A point eventually arrives when industry associations and consumer advocacy combine to promote the benefits of original creation. This realization often comes through association with international business.

In the mid-stage growth of media industries in China, Taiwan and Korea, industries have moved, and are continuing to move up the value chain by various

forms of 'learning by doing'. In other words, intangible notions about value creation, branding and marketing are brokered through trade shows, joint ventures, partnerships and international communities. The international co-production model constitutes a strategy to build value while promoting local industry development. Pooling of resources, access to foreign government's incentives and subsidies – and to desirable exotic locations – are all advantages associated with co-productions (Miller et al., 2001; Hoskins et al., 2003; Elmer and Gasher, 2005; Goldsmith and O'Regan, 2005). Cinema is where we mostly celebrate successful co-productions but co-productions and other sharing of resources are evident in television. The practice of licensing television formats shows how technologies and ideas can be transferred. In such cases, consultancy and expertise is the valued commodity. Television formats have become templates for low-cost replication across countries and within domestic markets. It is important to note here that intermediate inputs are often traded.

However, while international data is available on the trade in TV formats and consultancies, very little reliable data has been collected in East Asia, even despite Japan's pre-eminence as an exporter of TV formats. Japan has been a leader within Asia in reversing the flow of television programming, most notably through international formats – *Happy Family Plan*, *Iron Chef* and *Future Diary*. TBS, the leading exporter of TV programs and format in Japan, has sold more than 100 program formats to more than 40 countries. TBS started in the format business with its sale of the format *Wakuwaku Animal Land* to the Netherlands in 1987 (Iwabuchi, 2004). In turning the tables on the Americanization of culture thesis, Japan has successfully achieved international distribution through franchising – a business model that according to Iwabuchi (2002) allows Japanese creativity to circulate without overt traits of Japanese-ness that might undermine reception in many parts of East Asia, where the memory of Japanese imperialism remains strong.

Greater access to information via the Internet means that consumers of cultural products and services are increasingly knowledgeable and demanding (Cowen, 2002). Anderson has described how the practice of 'user recommendation' is breaking down the hegemony of the critic and the power of the blockbuster. He has coined the term 'the long tail' to describe both the disintermediation and democratization of cultural production. The end result is that more East-Asian content, from *manga* to flash animation, circulates in the recommendation economy, in the long tail. Much niche content is also appearing on subscription digital channels, where ratings are less important. For broadcasters in East Asia, international channels and distribution through video outlets provide sales income. If these sales are secured in US and European markets, the returns are significant for the seller. Returns from Asian Diaspora video markets are substantial for distributors such as Hong Kong's TVB. However, because it is difficult to police video retailers, much value in these markets is blighted by copyright infringement (Cunningham and Sinclair, 1999). In some cases, access to lucrative international channels is conditional on allowing international broadcasters into the local market. This conditionality clause has been the case in China. Landing rights (that is, permission to broadcast in certain areas) for News Corporation's Star TV platform and its mandarin language channel (*xingkong weishi*) have led to China Central Television's international channels, CCTV-4 and CCTV-9, being carried on some US cable networks.

One of the positive benefits of globalization, however, is increasing trade between regions and the 'discovery' of traditional cultures. The globalization of film and television, and the search for the next breakthrough, provide some confidence for East-Asian cultures. Breakthrough hits occur from time to time, although East-Asian cinema hits are usually a combination of timing, marketing, and financial support from major media investors and studios. Movies such as *Crouching Tiger Hidden Dragon*, directed by Ang Lee (Taiwan) and *Hero* (Zhang Yimou; China) are essentially new versions of old stories, tapping into traditions and folklore. The international development of these 'kung-fu' stories, already well established in East-Asian media markets, has been built on the reputation of directors who have already experienced initial 'breakthroughs'. In the case of Ang Lee, the crossover breakthrough was achieved in the film *Wedding Banquet* (1993). Zhang Yimou, likewise, established a reputation for films that were dazzling in their depiction of an oriental China, playing on the stereotypes and expectations of Western audiences in *Raise the Red Lantern* (1991) and more recently *House of Flying Daggers* (2004). Likewise, the Korean hit of 2001, *My Wife is a Gangster*, is arguably a smarter remake of James Cameron's *True Lies* (1994).

Top-down planning takes two forms as we move up the value chain in the cultural economy. The optimum model for creating high-value cultural exports is agglomeration, whether the transnational media corporation or the creative cluster model. The media corporation organizational form allows content producers to exploit cross-promotion and vertical integration strategies. Mergers and acquisitions deliver further competitive advantages – and, in some cases, deliver monopolies (Schiller, 1999). The metaphor of mother ship and flotilla captures what is at stake here. Large mother ship oligopolies include CBS/Viacom and Vivendi/Universal, Disney, Sony, Viacom and News Corporation with smaller studios and companies such as Dreamworks, HBO and MTV forming an affiliated flotilla.

The clustering of media companies in geographical locations adds to network advantages, even taking into account the tendency to outsource to global locations. Fishing from a clustered pond of talent allows majors to make more informed decisions based on superior project development. Distribution agreements, along with economies of scale and scope, further compound the difficulty faced by small media organizations competing in the same language pond. In other words, large companies can control both content production and content distribution. Being a mega platform owner with global brand awareness or a critical mass of subscribers (for instance, pay TV) also brings 'capital complementarities' – in other words, the ownership of technologies and content, combined with global status, produces cumulative effects. Producers want to get their content on to successful channels. In China, CCTV is the national broadcaster and commands the greatest advertising rates. Elsewhere in East Asia, 'creative clusters' are the policy prescription for leveraging the advantages of talent and capital (see Keane, 2007).

Conclusion

How, then, might new models of production and distribution, typified by formatted or franchised culture, impact upon global media trade? In the first decade of the twenty-first century, a new global model of integration has emerged. The long tail thesis suggests that fewer companies actually control distribution of culture, even if they own the rights to archives. As they are impacted by disintermediation the majors are rethinking their internationalization models. Digital technologies have reduced production costs. This reduced cost, combined with advantages offered by the rapid transfer of information and the long tail effect, allows accelerated catch-up for formerly peripheral cultural economies. Catch-up is facilitated by a proliferation of global and regional production networks, which have, in turn, acted as conduits for knowledge diffusion outside the developed economies. The increase in flows of global ideas – and the growth of inter-regional trade due to falling protection barriers – provide greater opportunities for cultural exchange and local networks of cooperation. This environment of culturally assisted global integration destabilizes media imperialism models. It also sets up opportunities for new players, such as China and Korea, to work their way up the ladder of growth, offsetting the competitive advantages of incumbent media centers such as Hong Kong and Hollywood.

The West–East imperialism model is problematized by these developments and the internationalization of Asian cultural product in world markets. Miller et al. (2001) have written extensively about 'the new international division of cultural labor' whereby Hollywood production is relentlessly outsourced. As I have shown, this becomes part of the growth trajectory of the newcomers. To look at the landscape from a different perspective, Hollywood's re-making of Asia through films such as *The Ring* (2001) and *Shall We Dance* (2004), as well as Hollywood's recruitment of Asian directors including Ang Lee and John Wu, is a form of reverse outsourcing. Asia is now supplying the talent and the narratives to stimulate the longevity of Hollywood. Meanwhile, China's leading director, Zhang Yimou, exploits the low-end production of China while choosing expensive off-shore post-production at Animal Logic in Australia. The new world order of the cultural economy is rising in the East.

For a 'relative' newcomer to the global cultural economy such as China, creating value means learning from the success of its East-Asian neighbors. East Asia has maintained its distinctiveness through heritage preservation even though there are some reservations about theme park preservation 'strategies'.

Over the past decade, East Asia has managed to promote its content into Western markets. China can, and should, take advantage of these successes. The expansion of space for artistic production in Chinese cities over the past few years, particularly evident in the construction of cultural precincts and districts, is extremely significant. Likewise, China's current attention to reversing its 'cultural trade deficit' signals a shift away from propaganda-heavy cultural content towards lighter entertainment-based formats – the kind of successful product that has increasingly expanded into world markets from Japan, South Korea and Taiwan. The important point we need to bear in mind in this analysis, moreover, is that there is still a leading role for government, not as gatekeeper and censor, but as the facilitator of cultural development, education, investment and trade.

Notes

1   Polo's exploits are 'legendary' in the sense that there is no clear evidence that he actually visited the places he wrote about.
2   Media imperialism is re-versioned by Dan Schiller as 'digital capitalism'. See Schiller (1999). For a discussion of how the Western domination of global markets is maintained through the New International Division of Cultural Labour (NICL) see Miller et al. (2001). For a discussion of the limitations of the cultural imperialism thesis see Curtin (2007), Hesmondhalgh (2007), Keane (2006) and Kraidy (2005).
3   These arguments are set out in detail in Iwabuchi et al. (2004).
4   See O'Regan (1999) for a discussion of this in relation to film.
5   *Meteor Garden* was also subtitled for non-Mandarin audiences.
6   For a fascinating account of unbundling of production in the fashion industry, see Rivoli (2005). Also http://www.imf.org/external/np/tr/2005/tr051019.htm.

REFERENCES

Anderson, C. (2006) *The Long Tail: How Endless Choice is Creating Unlimited Demand*, London: Random House Business Books.

Bates, B. J. (1998) 'The economics of transborder video', in A. Goonasekera and P.S.N. Lee (eds.) *TV Without Borders: Asia Speaks Out*. Singapore: AMIC.

Chua, Beng-Huat (2004) 'Gossips about stars: newspapers and pop culture China', *Asia Research Institute, Working Paper Series*, 29, August.

Chen, Yi-Hsiang (2007) 'Looking for Taiwan's Competitive Edge: the Production and Circulation of Taiwanese TV drama', in Ying Zhu, M. Keane and

Ruoyun Bai (eds.) *TV Drama in China Unfolding Narratives of Tradition, Political Transformation and Cosmopolitan Identity*. Hong Kong: HKU Press.

Cowen, T. (2002) *Creative Destruction: How Globalization is Changing the World's Culture*. Princeton, NJ: Princeton University Press.

Cunningham, S. and Sinclair, J. (eds.) (1999) *Floating Lives: The Media and Asian Diasporas*. St. Lucia: University of Queensland Press.

Curtin, Michael (2003) 'Media Capital: Towards the Study of Spatial Flows', *International Journal of Cultural Studies*, 6(2): 202–28.

Curtin, Michael (2007) *Playing to the World's Biggest Audience*. Santa Cruz: University of California Press.

Ellis, S. and Gadiesh, O. (2006) 'Outsmarting China's Start-arounds', *Far Eastern Economic Review*, 169(6): 5–10.

Elmer, G. and Gasher, M. (2005) *Contracting Out Hollywood: Runaway Productions and Foreign Location Shooting*. Lanham, MD: Rowan and Littlefield.

Erni, John Nguyet and Chua, Siew Kang (2005) *Asian Media Studies: Politics of Subjectivities*. Oxford: Blackwell.

Goldsmith, B. and O'Regan, T. (2005) 'The policy environment of the contemporary film studio', in Greg Elmer and Mike Gasher (eds.) *Contracting Out Hollywood: Runaway Productions and Foreign Location Shooting*. Lanham, MD: Rowan and Littlefield.

Hesmondhalgh, D. (2007) *The Cultural Industries*, 2nd edition. London, Thousand Oaks and New Delhi: SAGE Publications.

Hoskins, C., McFayden, S., Finn, A., Zhou, Xiaojuan and Mitchell, D. (2003) 'International Joint Ventures for Television and Film Production: The Role of Cultural Distance and Management Culture', in I. Alon (ed.) *Chinese Culture, Organizational Behavior and International Business Management*. Westport, CONN: Praeger.

Iwabuchi, K. (2002) *Recentering Globalization: Popular Culture and Japanese Transnationalism*. Durham, NC: Duke University Press.

Iwabuchi, K. (2004) 'Feeling glocal: Japan in the global television format business', in A. Moran and M. Keane (eds.) *Television Across Asia: Television Industries, Programme Formats and Globalization*. London: Routledge.

Iwabuchi, K., Muecke, S. and Thomas, M. (eds.) (2004) *Rogue Flows: Trans-Asia Cultural Traffic*. Hong Kong: Hong Kong University Press.

Kapner, S. (2003). 'US TV shows losing potency around the world', *The New York Times*, 2 January.

Kato, H. (1998). 'Japan', in Anthony Smith (ed.) *Television: An International History*. Oxford: Oxford University Press.

Keane, M. (2006) 'Once were peripheral: creating media capacity in East Asia', *Media, Culture & Society*, 28(6): 835–55.

Keane, M., Fung, A. and Moran, A. (2007) *New Television, Globalization and the East Asian Cultural Imagination*. Hong Kong: Hong Kong University Press.

Keane, M. (2007) *Created in China: the Great New Leap Forward*. London: Routledge.

Kraidy, M. (2005) *Hybridity or the Cultural Logic of Globalization*. Philadelphia: Temple University Press.

Lee, Dong-Hoo (2007) 'From the Margins to the Middle Kingdom: Korean TV Drama's Role in Linking Local and Transnational Production', in Ying Zhu, M. Keane and Ruoyun Bai (eds.) *TV Drama in China Unfolding Narratives of Tradition, Political Transformation and Cosmopolitan Identity*. Hong Kong: HKU Press.

Liu, Yu-Li and Chen, Yi-Hsiang (2004) 'Cloning, adaptation, import and originality: Taiwan in the global television format business', in Albert Moran and Michael Keane (eds.) *Television Across Asia: Television Industries, Programme Formats and Globalization*. London: Routledge.

Lotman, Yuri M. (1990) *The Universe of the Mind: A Semiotic Theory of Culture*, translated by Ann Shukman. Bloomington and Indianapolis: Indiana University Press.

Miller, T, Govil, N., McMurria, J. and Maxwell, R. (2001) *Global Hollywood*. London: British Film Institute.

O'Regan, T. (1999) 'Cultural Exchange', in Toby Miller and Robert Stam (eds.) *A Companion to Film Theory*. Oxford: Blackwell.

Rivoli, P. (2005) 'Travels of a T-Shirt in the Global Economy: An Economist Examines the Markets, Power, and Politics of World Trade', Hoboken, N.J.: John Wiley & Sons.

Schiller, D. (1999) *Digital Capitalism: Networking the Global Market System*. Cambridge, MA: Massachusetts Institute of Technology Press.

Shin, Jeeyoung (2005) 'Globalization and new Korean cinema', in Chi-Yun Shin and J. Stringer (eds.) *New Korea Cinema*. Edinburgh: Edinburgh University Press.

Tunstall, J. (2007) *The Media Were American: US Mass Media in Decline*. New York and Oxford: Oxford University Press.

Xu, G. G. (2004) 'Remaking East Asia, Outsourcing Hollywood', *Senses of Cinema*, November. Online: http://www.sensesofcinema.com/contents/05/34/remaking_east_asia.html/ [accessed 17 April 2006].

## CHAPTER 11

THE NEW KOREAN WAVE OF U[1]
Jaz Choi

The Korean Wave is neither a fortuitous phenomenon nor the result of a governmental master-plan, but a complex concoction of actors of various types and strata. This chapter first outlines the development of the Korean Wave in the domain of TV dramas and contextualizes its evolutionary process by examining both macro and micro factors. It then further extrapolates the trajectory of the Korean Wave within the paradigm of convergence and concludes by emphasizing the need to reconceptualize the cultural industries in this era of digital ubiquity, as epitomized by the case of the Korean Wave.

Introduction

Hallyu (Hanryu), otherwise known as the Korean Wave, is a phenomenon that has swept Korean popular culture across Asia and other regions in the past two decades. At its peak in 2004, the phenomenon contributed to a 0.18 per cent increase in the national GDP (Trade Research Institute, 2005). Although Korean media products, particularly TV dramas, were increasingly gaining popularity in neighbor countries such as China and Taiwan in the late 1990s, it was not until the initial years of the

present century that the term came into use to describe its broad effects on various domains nationally and internationally. The nation's import/export ratio for TV programs became reversed at this time, and the situation remains unchanged to date.

It has only been a decade since Saya Shiraishi's claim that 'Japanese popular culture is becoming Asian popular culture' (1997: 236). Around the time this statement was made, the dominance of Japanese popular culture was being fervently experienced across the region, as evidenced by Iwabuchi's statement that Japan's dominant position 'generates [a] positive sense of cultural immediacy' (2002: 50) amongst its intra-Asian consumers; through such 'cultural odourlessness' (2002: 27) – lack of distinctively Japanese representations – consumers are enabled to collectively imagine 'Asian modernity' (2002: 154). At this point, then, two important questions arise: how did the Korean Wave emerge as a global phenomenon, and what makes it different from other similar waves that preceded it?

It could take several volumes to explore the Korean Wave thoroughly. It is a complex phenomenon, which arose from and was sustained by diverse interrelating macro and micro economic sectors. In addition, its increasing multiplicity can be attributed to the emerging paradigm of convergence in recent years, especially the fundamental role the Internet plays in amplifying the momentum and diversity of processes in various aspects of cultural production, consumption and distribution. In fact, considering Korea's status as one of the most connected societies in the world, the hybridity of the Korean Wave comes as no surprise. This, in conjunction with significant non-economic consequences of cultural trade, makes the economic evaluation of the phenomenon, using the existing industrial taxonomy, somewhat problematic. Therefore, although it may be possible to identify specific cases of success and failure within the Korean Wave, to dichotomously identify the 'winners' and 'losers' on a broader level – sectorial or national, for example – would be as complex and ambiguous as the question: 'who won the Korean War?'.

In this chapter, I first outline the development of the Korean Wave in the domain of TV dramas and contextualize its evolutionary process by examining both macro and micro factors. I then further extrapolate the trajectory of the Korean Wave within the paradigm of convergence and conclude with an emphasis on the need for reconceptualizing the cultural industries in this era of digital ubiquity, as epitomized in the case of the Korean Wave.

The Rise of *Hallyu*, the Korean Wave

The Korean Wave began as a less conspicuous regional phenomenon than its current status might suggest. Its initial rise was not a result of strategic government promotion; rather, it emerged from the 'historical juncture of media liberalisation in Asia' (Shim, 2006: 38) that started in the 1990s. In fact, the term *Hallyu* itself was a product of Chinese journalism, describing the Korean pop-cultural inundation (or 'invasion' as some would refer to it) of China, one of the most crucial *Hallyu*-influenced countries – in terms of increased sales and distribution through Chinese diaspora networks. In this respect, CCTV's (China Central Television Station's) initial airing of a Korean TV drama *What is Love All About* in 1997 heralded the beginning of the Korean Wave. It became the first foreign-produced drama to achieve the highest rating of 16.6 per cent in Chinese television (Shin and Lee, 2006: 77), followed by much demanded re-airing of the show in 1998.

Although the Korean Wave was not pragmatically imagined at the time, endogenous revolutions were under way in the Korean media industry in the midst of wide global media liberalization, opening up more opportunities for cultural trade in the early 1990s. 1991 saw the launch of Korea's first private terrestrial broadcasting service, SBS (Seoul Broadcasting System), and the enactment of the Cable TV Act, as well as legislative enforcement of outsourced production (as opposed to in-house production by broadcasting companies). The aim of this legislation was to diversify broadcast media content and enhance content quality through increased market competition. Although the compulsory ratio of outsourced production was initially set to three per cent of total airtime, today it stands at up to 40 per cent for terrestrial broadcasting services. Such fundamental structural and legislative transformations in Korean television animated the industry by inviting new commercial opportunities and creative talents into the home market. The year 1991 was important in Korean media

history because it manifested the paradigmatic shift in the government's understanding of the domestic media industry: that it was 'not only ideological and cultural … but also an economic matter' (Shim, 2002), thus highlighting the fact that increased (though controlled) liberalization was a necessity for its growth.

Three years later, the Korean public experienced the same paradigmatic shift when a government report came out urging then president Young Sam Kim to focus upon the audio-visual sector as a national strategic industry. To support this argument, the report presented an economic comparison between the Hollywood film *Jurassic Park* and Hyundai cars, the proud national symbol of economic growth in the industrial era. *Jurassic Park*, the report claimed, generated revenues greater than 1.5 million Hyundai cars – two years' worth of Hyundai's car exports (Shim, 2002: 340). This is now a well-known anecdote, but its impact was so great that, within months, the Motion Picture Promotion Law was enacted, followed by pragmatic support from the government for media and culture industries in diverse areas such as taxation and education. Of course, such prompt actions and the public's enthusiastic response were not the only results of the report; rather, they were a part of the government's substantial 'top-down reform of the Korean political economy' that was essential, in President Kim's own words, 'to survive and thrive in this age of increasingly fierce, borderless global competition' (Shin, 2003: 10). This was predominantly in response to pushing for global market liberalization as a result of the Uruguay Round of the General Agreement on Tariffs and Trade in 1993 (Shin, 2005: 52); nevertheless, 'no state in the post-Cold War era cast its lot with globalisation as decisively or as publicly as Korea did under the Kim Young Sam administration' (Kim, 2000: 2). Globalization (*Segyehwa*) officially became the national agenda for Korea.

In such an accommodating climate, *chaebol* (large family-owned conglomerates) quickly established multiple businesses in numerous sectors of the local media industry, exploiting, according to Shim, 'Korean nationalism, diverting the public's concern about the possible oligopolistic structure in Korean media/culture industries' (2002: 341). Mobilized in this argument was the trope of David and Goliath: Korea's fight against the giant Hollywood. This ostensibly patriotic fight, however, turned into a war amongst Davids for Goliath's amusement as the *chaebol's* intense competition against one another only led to inflated price tags on

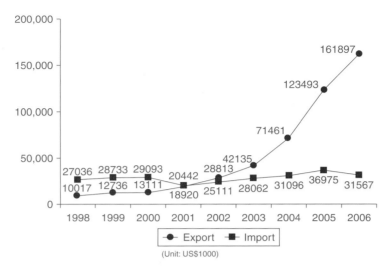

Figure 11.1   Import and export of Korean broadcasting

imported foreign media products, mostly Hollywood films. This fierce and unfortunate fight came to an unexpected end with the Asian economic crisis of 1997. Despite devoted efforts of individual Koreans to save the nation's financial situation – including personal donations of gold jewellry in response to the government's plea, a story covered widely by international media – Korea was unable to alleviate the *chaebol*'s foreign debts and inevitably resorted to a bail-out package from the International Monetary Fund (IMF). The *chaebol*'s involvement in the cultural sector was largely curtailed under the restructuring mandate by IMF (Shim, 2006: 33), and the future of the Korean media industry became very uncertain.

Riding global tides

The continuing rise of the Korean Wave through, or paradoxically because of, the financial crisis in the late 1990s is one of the main reasons why it is viewed as a fortuitous incident. In fact, it would not have been surprising should it have come to an end then. Instead, what came next was an even bigger wave with greater diversity, quality and popularity both in domestic and international markets with an average growth rate of 40.9 per cent in broadcasting export (Korean Broadcasting Institute, 2007: 2) as illustrated in Figure 11.1 (adapted from Korean Broadcasting Institute, 2007).

The span of the Korean Wave has also expanded not only within Asia, but also to countries such as

Mexico and Uzbekistan, where one of the most successful Korean dramas so far, *Winter Sonata*, reached a record rating of 60 per cent when it was first aired in 2004 (Yoon, 2005) with subsequent four re-airings. According to NHK's annual financial report, the same drama generated a total revenue of 3.5 billion yen for the network through licensed broadcasting and sales in other media formats including print and DVD in Japan (Kitamura, 2006: 8).

How did the Korean Wave not only survive but become bigger through one of the toughest financial crises in Korean history? Analysing the literature to date leads to three main inter-relating factors that together form an answer to this question. First, the *chaebol*'s abrupt withdrawal from the cultural sector brought about restructuring of the invested capital – human resources, knowledge and technology – which still remained within Korea at the time. These forms of capital played a key role in revitalizing cultural industries with additional input from the new generation of talents who had completed tertiary education in the field under the globalization (*Segyewha*) regime, as mentioned above. Second, weakening domestic private consumption underlined an imminent need for increased export for economic sustenance; at the same time, those economies affected by the crisis showed a preference for the cheaper Korean programming (Shim, 2006: 28) over that of Japan or USA, making the transaction bilaterally beneficial. Furthermore, the immediate aftermath of the crisis – high rates of unemployment and financial hardship – had psychological ramifications such as escapism

(Yoo and Ahn et al., 2005: 179) and racial/ethnic collectivism (Shin, 2003: 9), which were partly manifested in the consumption of Korean media in Asia. This point is inherently relevant to the third factor: the socio-cultural aesthetics of Korean media. It has been emphasized in many studies that Korean dramas have an 'unashamedly Korean' (Yasumoto, 2006) feel, but they simultaneously render cultural sensibilities common to many Asian societies – for example, collectivism and filial piety – in modern urban scenery through visually sophisticated narrative techniques (see Paik, 2005; Park, 2005; Shin and Lee, 2006). Such 'foreign-yet-alike' traits have enhanced Korean media's aesthetic appeal to societies in close cultural, social and political proximity; this is particularly evident in nations with ideological antagonism against Japan and USA – such as China – where consuming these cultures is viewed with social hostility. For such societies, Cho asserts, Korea became the 'logical choice' for cultural affection (2005: 155).

Inflow of *Hallyu* riders

Socially affirmed preferences for Korean cultural products have consequently expanded to an increase in consumption of Korean products and services, further boosted by effective marketing strategies such as product placement (PPL) and celebrity endorsement. China is one of many countries where not only products themselves but also the 'image' of Korean culture is ardently consumed by young people with its fashionable and accessibly liberal appeal (Onishi, 2006; Shin and Lee, 2006: 80). For many fans of Korean media, interest in the mediated version of Korean culture evolved into a desire to experience aspects that are more intrinsically Korean – or what is *imagined* as real Korean culture – in reality. The Korean Wave, in this respect, cannot be conceptualized as a discrete field of media but a dynamic network of numerous fields. An obvious example is growing *Hallyu* tourism, a trend analogous to the 'Frodo Economy' of New Zealand, which was brought about by the influx of jet-setters following the success of the *Lord of the Rings* trilogy. According to Korea Tourism Organization's *Hallyu* Tourism Status Report (2007: 90), the estimated number of *Hallyu* visitors in 2006 was 1.29 million, generating revenue of US$1.1 billion. The report also suggests the possible receding of the Korean Wave in the 'old markets' – Japan, Taiwan and Hong Kong – as represented in the slow down of *Hallyu* tourism in those countries compared

to the burgeoning 'new markets' – China, Singapore and Thailand. This suggests that a new phase of the Korean Wave is imminent, and thus calls for a contextual change that will cultivate the next phase of the Wave most effectively.

The new wave of convergence

Convergence by definition denotes plurality and negotiation between or amongst the merging entities. It therefore also conveys the notion of decentralization, which is the crux of what Castells (1996) calls the network society, in which nodes of divergent capacities, contexts and categories – be they human, cultural, technological, or economic – are connected via networks at different levels. In the domain of cultural trade, an obvious instance of convergence would be in culture itself by means of appropriation; in the case of the Korean Wave, this can occur tactically as a form of co-production. Attempts at co-production have had mixed results, most of which have failed to achieve the same level of success with all parties involved. This was largely due to the lack of innovative content and adequate consideration of differing organizational and cultural environments (Cho, 2005; Park, 2005). As alluded to earlier, the main appeal of Korean dramas to international audiences is their 'in-betweenness' through which both foreign and familiar values are conveyed. The audience, then, needs to make further efforts to translate content according to multiple discursive facets of their identity such as nationality and gender, all of which together create a cultural experience. Therefore, continued efforts in cultural convergence need to be strongly advocated not only for their advantages in pooling resources or preventing controversial conflicts – as seen in the case of the Japanese manga called *kenkanryu* (which can be translated as 'anti' or 'hate' the Korean Wave) – but also in stimulating the sharing of knowledge and cultures.

Another important sphere of convergence is in the conduit of contemporary cultural content: digital communication technologies. As evidenced in the recent emergence of TPS (Triple-Play-Service) and even QPS (Quadruple-Play-Service) intermixing the Internet, broadcasting, and telecommunications services, ICTs (Information and Communication Technologies) have become an integral part of cultural and social experiences in today's society. For the second time, Korea was ranked at the top of ITU's Digital Opportunity Index (2006); with limited natural resources and continuously susceptible political circumstances, this 'opportunity' is vital to the sustenance of the Korean economy. Recognizing this, the Korean government has initiated the 'Digital Hallyu' project with a twofold intent: 1) amplification of the Korean Wave through integration of ICTs, and 2) promotion of Korean ICTs to the extent that it did for the original Korean Wave. Recent examples include the commercialization and continued research and development of ubiquitous cross/multi-platform multimedia technologies; for example, DMB (Digital Media Broadcasting) and WiBro (Wireless Broadband)-enabled mobile phones and portable devices have been competitively rolled out in the domestic market in the past two years. Here, it should be emphasized that these developments do not only occur on a macro/infrastructural level; more importantly, they encompass – and are essentially based on – micro-level individual networks in which each user has increased autonomy to experience mediated contents in various socio-cultural contexts rather than simply *consume*. Although this is not a new concept – see Pine and Gilmore's *Experience Economy* (1999), for example – it has not been given the amount of consideration that it deserves in understanding the Korean Wave.

U: the future

Time magazine's 2006 Person of the Year was awarded to *YOU*, accentuating that the agency of those formerly known as the audience needs to be reconceptualized in creating the narrative of humanity. As the article suggests, the *audience* has become the *user* who does not 'just sit and watch' but also works 'like crazy' (Grossman, 2006). This is otherwise known as the culture of UCC (user-created-content), *produsage* (Bruns, 2005), and participatory culture (Jenkins and Clinton et al., 2006). In a similar vein, the Korean Ministry of Culture and Tourism's slogan – *creation, community, sharing* – clearly resonates with the spirit of network culture in which the user produces and consumes cultural experiences; in Korea's case, the nation's high level of new media access – not only technological but also social and cognitive (see Bucy and Newhagen, 2003) – allows such involvement to occur by means of ubiquitous media experience via broadband network. In fact, active UCC culture has been one of the main buttresses of the Korean Wave. Within Korea,

ubiquitous broadband access allows more active and varied means for audience participation in consuming and remixing media. Outside, the Internet is used to access Korean popular cultural content – both 'official' (industry-created) and 'unofficial' (user-created) – and to communicate/ re-create such content adaptively to the user's own technological and socio-cultural contexts.

Such flexibility and autonomy afforded by the Internet motivates users' increased media consumption and fortifies their interest by allowing faster circulation and translation of media by transcending 'time-space constraints and official distribution hierarchy' (Hu, 2005). Moreover, these attributes also enhance the quality of media through sharing of critical and creative ideas, as seen in Paik's study (2005: 251–91) on actor Byung-Hun Lee's fan sites. Korean dramas are produced while televised and thus permits instantaneous response to the audiences' feedback about various aspects including the storyline and characters. Therefore, nurturing of the user-driven culture can ground 'the space of creativity... whose occupancy invites other occupancies' (Trinh, 1991: 50). This space of social networks provides rich soil for user-led innovations, the most crucial element of contemporary cultural industries. For this reason, the *user* is and will continue to be the key generator of the Korean Wave.

Reconceptualizing cultural economy

The Korean Wave has been a surprise to the world, including Koreans themselves. Consequently, efforts have been made to understand the phenomenon, but most of the studies do not, unfortunately, go beyond macro-level analysis. At the center of this misinterpretation is the growing confusion in understanding the economic value of creativity, that in today's network society creative outputs are 'not so much mass-produced as mass accessed', one of the main characteristics of creative (as compared to cultural) industries, according to Potts (2006: 340). This is the missing concept, and the situation must be rectified.

This chapter has demonstrated that the Korean Wave is an outcome of non-static exogenous and endogenous convergence processes in an evolving system that is closer to the configuration of a network than a hierarchy. Whether it is between society and technology, foreign and familiar, products and services, or producers and users, the intersection of convergence provides opportunities for collective creativity and innovations. This allows for potential economic growth even for societies with limited tangible resources, unlike the situation in the industrial era. Furthermore, advancement in communication technologies necessitates and augments the individual user's agency in both consuming and producing – or experiencing – cultural products by providing a metamorphic conduit within the network of the creative economy. In the case of the Korean Wave, the audiences – or users – as nodes are linked in translation, actively adopting and adapting cultural values in various inter-related contexts. Through this evolving communication, significant economic value has been produced to the surprise of Korea and the world.

The rapid development of mobile network technologies will only increase the level of complexity to the existing inter-relation between creativity and socio-economic order at local and global levels. The Korean Wave epitomizes the way in which innovations occur through this multifarious and evolutionary convergence process. Therefore, continued effort to understand this convergence is crucial not only in the academic and commercial domains, but also in socio-cultural terms. Especially for the Korean government, encouraging organic growth of convergence networks will not only continue but also raise the Korean Wave to a greater level.

Note

1   The 'U' in this title stands for the notion of ubiquitous, user-led media, etc., in the network society.

REFERENCES

Bucy, E. Page and Newhagen, John E. (2003) *Media Access: Social and Psychological Dimensions of New Technology Use*. Mahwah, N.J.: L. Erlbaum.

Bruns, Axel. (2005) *Anyone Can Edit: Understanding the Producer – Guest Lecture at SUNY, Buffalo/New School, NYC/Brown Univ./Temple Univ.* [Audio recording: mp3].

Castells, Manuel (1996) *The Rise of the Network Society*. Cambridge, MA: Blackwell Publishers.

Cho, Hae-Joang (2005) 'Reading the "Korean Wave" as a Sign of Global Shift', *Korea Journal*, 45(4): 147–82.

Grossman, Lev (2006) '*Time*'s Person of the Year: You'. *Time*. 13 December.

Hu, Kelly (2005) 'The power of circulation: digital technologies and the online Chinese fans of Japanese TV drama', *Inter-Asia Cultural Studies*, 6(2): 171–86.

(International Telecommunication Union) (2006) 'World Information Society Report. I.T. Union'. Geneva, International Telecommunication Union.

Iwabuchi, Koichi (2002) *Recentering Globalization: Popular Culture and Japanese Transnationalism*. Durham: Duke University Press.

Jenkins, H., Clinton, K., et al. (2006) 'Confronting the Challenges of Participatory Culture: Media Education for the 21st Century'. Retrieved 6 November 2006, from http://www.digitallearning. macfound.org/site/c.enJLKQNlFiG/b.2108773/apps/nl/content2.asp?content_id=%7BCD911571-0240-4714-A93B1D0C07C7B6C1%7D&notoc=1.

Kim, Samuel S. (2000) 'Korea and Globalization (*Segyehwa*): A Framework for Analysis', in S.S. Kim *Korea's Globalization*. Cambridge: Cambridge University Press. pp. 1–29.

Kitamura, Kayoko (2006) *The Korean Wave and Korean Image in Japan*. Seoul, Korea Foundation for International Culture Exchange. pp. 1–15.

Korea Tourism Organization (2007) '2006 Second-Half Status of Hallyu Tourism' (2006). Seoul, Korea Tourism Organization. pp. 1–99.

Korean Broadcasting Institute (2007) '2006 Status Report of the Import an Export of Korean Broadcasting'. Seoul, Korean Broadcasting Institute. pp. 1–15.

Onishi, Norimitsu (2006) 'A Rising Korean Wave: If Seoul Sells It, China Craves It', *The New York Times*. 10 January.

Paik, Wondam (2005) *Hallyu: The Culture Choice of East Asia*. Seoul, Pantagram.

Park, Jae-Bok (2005) *Hallyu: Competitive Power of Culture in the Age of Globalisation*. Seoul, Samsung Economic Research Institute.

Pine, B. Joseph and Gilmore, James H. (1999) *The Experience Economy: Work Is Theater & Every Business A Stage*. Boston: Harvard Business School Press.

Potts, Jason (2006) 'How Creative are the Super-Rich?', *Agenda*, 13(4): 339–50.

Shim, Doobo (2002) 'South Korean Media Industry in the 1990s and the Economic Crisis', *Prometheus*, 20(4): 337–50.

Shim, Doobo (2006) 'Hybridity and the rise of Korean popular culture in Asia', *Media, Culture & Society*, 28(1): 25–44.

Shin, Gi-Wook (2003) 'The Paradox of Korean Globalization'. Retrieved 7 April 2007, from http://koreanstudies.stanford.edu/publications/paradox_of_korean_globalization_the/.

Shin, Jeeyoung (2005) 'Globalization and New Korean Cinema', in C.-Y. Shin and J. Stringer. *New Korean Cinema*. New York: New York University Press. pp. 51–62.

Shin, Yoon-Hwan and Lee, Han-Woo (2006) *Hallyu in East Asia*. Seoul, Jeonyewon.

Shiraishi, Saya (1997) 'Japan's Soft Power: Doraemon Goes Overseas', in P. Katzenstein and T. Shiraishi, *Network Power: Japan in Asia*. Ithaca, NY: Cornell University Press. pp. 234–72.

Trade Research Institute (2005) 'Analysis of Economic Effects of the Korean Wave.' Retrieved 11 October 2006, from http://www.culturekorea.org/html/marketList.asp?page=2& tblID=report&col1=&col2=&col3=&col4=&col5=desc&col6=10&sTxt1=&sTxt2 =.

Trinh, T. Minh-Ha (1991) *When the Moon Waxes ed: Representation, Gender, and Cultural Politics*. New York: Routledge.

Yasumoto, Seiko (2006) *The Impact of the 'Korean Wave' on Japan: A case study of the influence of trans-border electronic communication and trans-national programming industry*. 16th Biennial Conference of the Asian Studies Association of Australia, Wollongong.

Yoo, Sangchul and Ahn, Hyeri, et al., (2005) *The Secret of the Hallyu DNA*. Seoul, Seng Gak Ui Namoo.

Yoon, Jae-Shik (2005) 'Current Status of Broadcasting in Uzbekistan', *Trend and Analysis*, Korean Broadcasting Institute.

## CHAPTER 12

THE IMPACT OF GLOBALIZATION ON THE CULTURAL INDUSTRIES IN CENTRAL ASIA
Florent Le Duc

Central Asia is a unique cultural area that benefited from cultural exchanges and traditions inherited from both nomadic and sedentary civilizations, from the ancient Silk Roads and the Soviet Empire. Since the collapse of the USSR, three main cultural sectors have contributed

to the region's rebirth on the world cultural map: cinema, handicrafts and contemporary arts. Beyond these 'success stories', Central Asia faces structural problems such as institutional deficiencies and sharp decreases in public funding, inappropriate cultural policies and regulatory frameworks, lack of independent production and distribution structures, the inexistence of cultural media. If the regions cultural sector is to benefit from globalization, a series of challenges have to be tackled, starting from the development of cultural management curricula and trainings, support to regional and international cultural networks providing a basis for artists' information and mobility, and the development of dedicated media for culture.

Historical background

Central Asia is a unique cultural area (see Box 12.1) that has inherited a great deal of valuable tangible and intangible heritage from both nomadic and sedentary civilizations. Its peoples have espoused a variety of religions and beliefs, such as Buddhism and Islam but also pre-Islamic traditions, Sufism or Shamanism. Its cultural diversity presupposes the existence of a historical process of exchanges, which has encouraged an openness to renewal and innovation along with the transmission of ancient traditions.

Box 12.1   Central Asia: A space of interaction

Central Asia has long been a space of interaction between nomadic and settled peoples, in contact with both Western and Eastern civilizations, as well as the influences of Islam, Buddhism and Christianity. In consequence, the region is characterized by a unique combination of linguistic and cultural factors. In Uzbekistan and Tajikistan, the ancient sedentary cultural life and architectural heritage of the settled civilizations have encouraged the development of sculpture and decorative fine arts. The nomadic cultures prevailing in Kazakhstan, Kyrgyzstan and Turkmenistan developed oral poetic art, textile and crafts as well as applied arts based on complex motifs drawn from space and nature. Despite these differences, fundamental historical and cultural continuities exist throughout the region, chief among them the place it has occupied as an intermediary among cultures and peoples, and which justify considering the region as a unity.

Illustration 12.1   Map of Central Asia

Source: University of Texas Libraries, http://www.lib.utexas.edu/maps/asia/html

The role of two historical moments from the distant and recent past of Central Asia – the Great Silk Road and the Soviet era – is fundamental in understanding the region's cultural evolution in the current context of globalization. At the crossroads of Europe, Asia and the Middle East, Central Asia has benefited from commercial, scientific and cultural exchanges between East and West along the Great Silk Road since the first century AD. As such, globalization is not a new phenomenon for the region. Today, the imagery attached to the ancient 'Silk Road' and the region's historical nature as an intermediary among cultures and peoples, remain key aspects of its cultural identity.

During the twentieth century, the Soviet Union insulated the economies of all its republics from global competition by integrating them into a single economic system. In parallel, the Soviet State aimed at creating a new and unified Soviet identity, and in order to do so dismantled the traditional cultures and sought to limit external cultural influences in the region. Soviet policies introduced massive literacy campaigns and developed modern infrastructures for culture and education, such as schools and universities, public libraries, theaters, science academies, museums and publishing houses. However, at the same time, the Russian leadership also attempted to decrease the role of the region's own religious, political and cultural elites and promoted 'Russification'

among the local populations. Although the Soviet period gave common structural elements to the Central Asian region and promoted regional links in terms of social and cultural policies, it also imposed censorship and ideological restraints to local creativity, while severing the region from its cultural roots and preventing access to international exchanges.

After the collapse of the USSR, the five republics of Central Asia–Kazakhstan, the Kyrgyz Republic, Tajikistan, Turkmenistan, and Uzbekistan emerged overnight as sovereign nations, constituting a newly distinct geopolitical region in which historical conflicts, political rivalries, arbitrarily established borders and different national interests contributed to the disruption of regional cohesion. The status of Central Asian countries changed from membership of a centrally planned Soviet economy to participation in the uncontrolled global market economy (Mandelbaum, 1994; Pomfret, 1995). In this context, the globalization process could arguably have both a negative impact by replacing the 'colonizer's' culture with imported cultural commodities and a positive influence in promoting the renewal of local culture through international flows and exchanges. Although the speed of the liberalization process has differed from one country to another,[1] the historical background of the region and the current circumstances have imprinted both a certain coherence and a mosaic structure onto the contemporary cultural landscape. The newly established nation-states have been using the simultaneous processes of 'desovietization' and globalization to affirm their independence and to rebuild national cultural identities. As a result of their quest for new forms of national consciousness, state policies have focused on the identification and valorization of national heroes, languages and indigenous historical symbols, thus limiting innovation and hampering the positive effects of these countries' opening to the international cultural scene.

(It is important to analyse the consequences and the limits of the globalization process on the Central Asian cultural economy. Which local cultural actors benefit from globalization? What are the main production sectors for the creative economy in Central Asia? How is the current distribution and promotion of cultural goods and services organized? The impact of globalization on local cultural production has been limited to a few specific sectors, while there is still a crucial need for renewed cultural policies and management forms in order for Central Asia to take full advantage of the globalization process.)

The rebirth of Central Asia on the world cultural map

Following their independence and progressive integration into a globalized economic system, these countries have experienced an opening of their cultural markets to international products and an increasing connectivity with the international cultural scene. In the 1990s, a new market for international cultural products emerged in Central Asia, with the massive arrival of audio and video productions, new TV channels,[2] Hollywood blockbusters shown in brand new cinemas, and the latest audio and video productions made available in CD/DVD shops (mainly pirate production). With Internet cafes mushrooming in all the principal cities, more travel opportunities[3] and new forms of cultural and eco-tourism, the region has been opening up to new external influences and is progressively connecting with the rest of the world. Consequently and despite drastic budget cuts and reductions in subsidies to the traditional cultural domains, the globalization process has provided Central Asian creative workers with new sources of inspiration and new opportunities for development. Some specific cultural sectors have clearly benefited from this opening: in particular, contemporary art has been able to play a specific and original role in

situating the identity of modern Central Asia on the world cultural map; Central Asian cinema has also benefited from new international production and diffusion channels, while handicraft production is providing significant opportunities for the local economic sdevelopment of some countries.

As a consequence of the Cold War, Central Asian artists were isolated from international artistic dialogue and trends for over 70 years. The Soviet Union certainly provided in itself a vast space for inspiration and exchange among artists, but the latter had very little (if no) access beyond its borders. Today, while Central Asian artists continue to work within the ex-Soviet regional network of artists and curators, their concern is to increase their global connections to the world cultural market. In particular, **contemporary art** has proved to be a new source of regional and international connections for Central Asia. Thanks to the efforts of a number of dedicated scholars, curators and cultural organizations both in Central Asia and abroad, contemporary artists of the region have been increasingly participating in international exhibitions, master-classes and artists' residencies abroad.[4]

In this context, the year 2001 marked a significant turning point for Central Asian arts in the international realm. Tashkent hosted two contemporary art biennales in 2001 and 2003, and three major exhibitions from Central Asia took place in Europe from 2002 to 2004.[5] The opening of the Afghan and Central Asian Pavilions at the Venice Biennale 2005 was also 'an important event in the cultural life of the region giving a powerful stimulus for integration of Central Asian art in the international arena'.[6] The event not only acknowledged Central Asian artists individually,[7] but also allowed them to represent the region's identity in the global cultural context. In particular, the characteristics of Central Asian video-art and the role of Shamanist traditions in its cultural production should be underlined. Since the opening of the Afghan and Central Asian Pavilions, a series of international exhibitions have included Central Asian contemporary artists,[8] although these international events have had very little or no echo in the region itself. Do artists consider that the Central Asian audience, and above all Central Asian cultural policy-makers, are not ready or mature enough to understand their universe? Obviously, some Central Asian contemporary artists are much more popular abroad than in their own countries.[9]

Experience has shown that often the arts and culture are the first to respond to changes in a society. In Central Asia, **cinema**, as the most dynamic type of art, started to change before the others: along with the entire industry in the Soviet Union, cinema underwent a fundamental mutation. Lenin claimed that it was the most important of all the arts and it was used as a propaganda instrument for the diffusion of Soviet myths. In the 1990s, Central Asian cinema had to adapt to post-Soviet realities in order to correspond to new sources of inspiration and new audiences. A new generation of film-makers appeared in the 1980s and gained world exposure in the 1990s, winning prizes in certain international film festivals: among them, Bakhtiar Khudoinazarov in Tajikistan, with *Luna Papa*; Darejan Omirbaev (Kazakhstan) with *Killer*; and Aktan Abdykalykov with *Beshkempir*, (Kyrgyzstan).[10] Cinematographers proved to be the most realistic communicators of the socio-economic problems that Central Asian societies faced during the transition period. They were the first to offer aesthetic judgements and artistic assessment of their social environment and circumstances.[11] It is important to point out that most of these film directors have been living and working in Europe since independence, while still producing films reflecting the reality of Central Asia.

An interesting new phenomenon is the development of co-productions between Central Asian film studios (with the apparition of private film studios, mainly in Kazakhstan and Kyrgyzstan) and Western studios (notably France, Germany or Italy), producing Central Asian directors with very personal and unique universes. It is clear that these connections with the West are influencing the process of creation in Central Asian cinema. With regard to this new generation of Central Asian film-makers, some Western and Russian critics argue that their mastery of the film industry's dominant genres (i.e. *film noir*, road movie) is proof that recent Central Asian films are directed primarily at an international film-festival audience, not a domestic one, be it regional or national.[12] In terms of diffusion, brand new cinemas in Almaty or Bishkek show almost only American blockbusters, while Indian Bollywood cinema has become popular in Tajikistan. The Kazakh film *Nomads* is the first Central Asian blockbuster to have been shown in its 'home' country.[13]

Although intra-regional film distribution channels on a regular basis do not exist, there has been a revival of film festivals in Central Asia since the early 2000s, some of them reaching an international scale and concretely contributing to improving connections with neighbor countries and regions. *Didor*, the international film festival in Tajikistan,[14] and the *Eurasia Festival* in Kazakhstan[15] are among these flagship events.

During the Soviet era, traditional **craft production** was banned by the Soviets in their push for modernization and pressure for conformity. People were discouraged or prevented from operating private businesses or making hand-crafted products. However, some underground craft production continued. Nowadays it is commonly recognized that traditional arts and crafts have a crucial role to play in the economic and cultural development of any unindustrialized region. In Central Asia, this sector is soon to become one of the success stories of the local cultural economy through its achievements in market development. In less than 15 years, Central Asian craftsmen have managed to successfully revive national and regional crafts markets (through craft fairs[16]), with the assistance of international organizations such as Aid to Artisans, UNESCO and the Eurasia Foundation.

After 11 September 2001, when the narrow but growing Central Asian tourist market abruptly collapsed, artisans were forced to use export markets as a means of diversifying their customer base. Confronted with the realities of the international market, craftsmen realized the need to adapt, and switched from traditional and local-oriented market and tastes, to products suitable for contemporary exposure, whether national or international. The most successful craftsmen have subtly used typical ornamental patterns in textile design and crafts, merging local traditions, motifs, materials and skills with market trends, with the aim of developing products that are more appealing to specific target markets.[17] This has been an integral part of the process of promoting a contemporary or 'modern' identity for Central Asia, and has necessarily come about as a result of international exchanges with Western designers, marketing or fair trade specialists, mostly sponsored by international organizations. Indeed, since 2002, Central Asian artisans have forged significant links with importers in other countries, particularly in the global North. Today, artisans not only benefit regularly from regional sales but also travel at their own expense to fairs in other countries, thus highlighting the possible role of handicraft production in local economic development.

Despite the relative integration of these three sectors – contemporary arts, cinema and handicraft – into the global cultural economy, the impact of globalization on the Central Asian cultural industries has been very limited. These examples can be considered to be exceptions. Other cultural sectors such as theater and performing arts, design and architecture, and music, still suffer from geographical isolation and structural problems,[18] sometimes inherited from the Soviet period, that hamper their development.

Challenges of sustainable development

Over the last ten years in Central Asia, culture, as other social sectors, has been through a difficult transition period. The persistent leftovers of the Soviet period in the institutional and regulatory frameworks as well as in the decision-making process continue to hamper the development of relevant cultural policies in the current context of globalization.

With the current redefinition of the role of culture in social and economic development that has entered global awareness, the acceleration of information flows and the growing centrality of the cultural industries, there is a crucial need for **renewed forms of cultural management** in Central Asia. As culture played a major ideological role in Soviet times, it is still seen by policy-makers as an instrument for the (re-) construction of national identities, in which national 'founding fathers' occupy the vacuum left by Lenin.[19] The cultural policies in these nations focus on heritage preservation and the renovation of Soviet cultural infrastructures, which are not always relevant to modern cultural production. In particular, there is a lack of independent publishers, music recording studios, and artists' residencies. Consequently, the development of the arts (especially new forms of expression) generally takes place in conditions of institutional deficiency, absence of dialogue with the authorities, misunderstandings at the local level resulting in export-oriented art production and the emigration of artists.

Moreover, with the collapse of the USSR, state funding for art practice, cultural institutions and networks disappeared abruptly, and artists or administrators did not have the skills needed to adapt to new structural realities and to seek alternative sources of income.[20] This has of course greatly weakened the whole cultural economy: creative unions ('Soyuz') have modified their activities, competent people have been dismissed and local cultural organizations have been used for new purposes, often far removed from their initial competence. Since then, little has been done to tackle this issue, and almost none of the Central Asian training institutions in the arts and culture provide students or young professionals with decent management training. Some

courageous self-made managers exist, but they are few and far between. Traditionally subsidized cultural sectors (classical theater, classical music, literature or museums) and local structures (isolated from decision-making centers) have suffered the most from the transition to a liberal system and the necessary adaptation to modern management methods.

Another challenge is related to the weak **regulatory framework**, in particular in the field of intellectual property rights. The level of software piracy in the region[21] is one of the highest in the world. With the exception of Kazakhstan, where diffusion of audio, video and software products is gradually being taken over by national companies,[22] Central Asian countries have not been able to update their legislation or implement international treaties on intellectual property rights to which they have adhered.[23] This has had major consequences in terms of copyright protection and other aspects of artists' rights. As put by some artists in the region, 'it will be an efficient globalization when authors, distributors and producers will earn property rights from the region!'

The need for reform also applies to **cultural training and employment policies**. A new legal status for artists needs to be defined and local cultural services and professions need to be developed. There exists almost no cultural press in Central Asia, thus limiting the diffusion of quality information in the field of culture. Some personal and local initiatives should be mentioned, such as the journal *Kurak* at regional level, or *Fonus* in Tajikistan, which both provide analysis on regional cultural life, but their diffusion is minute and irregular, and they are not available on the web. The only cultural media relevant for the region originate in Russia (Moscow newspapers/websites and Russian public channel *Kultura*, accessible via cable television[24]) and rarely cover cultural realities in Central Asia itself.

Globalization, regionalization and civil society

The worldwide importance of civil society has been underlined in the debate on the role of culture and cultural policies in sustainable human development. Participation of both the public and private sectors in the cultural field as well as the creation of new associations and foundations for the promotion of artistic production are now being systematically encouraged across the world. Since the opening of Central Asian economies and the development of the private sector in the early 2000s, new forms of support for cultural projects have begun to emerge, providing new opportunities for creative people in the region. For example, the Central Asian Pavilion at the Venice Biennale in 2005 was mainly supported by a Kyrgyz businessman; in Kazakhstan, some banks have been developing cultural sponsorship[25] while individual businessmen have opened local art galleries. In Almaty, Bishkek, Tashkent and Dushanbe, key personalities have been promoting Central Asian contemporary art through their own international networks, having a clear understanding of what the world can offer to Central Asia in terms of creativity and sources of inspiration, but also with a strong will to promote Central Asian identity. As a consequence, a new cultural geography of the region has taken shape, demarcating countries benefiting from substantial revenues from international trade that are able to invest in dynamic cultural sectors and industries led by self-trained or abroad-trained managers from all the others, who are unable to do so.

As they benefit from increasing international exposure, Central Asian artists are also rebuilding strong regional links. According to artists and creative workers in Central Asia, only a handful of international organizations are committed to supporting cultural projects in the region,[26] which illustrates the still limited understanding of the role of arts and culture in political stability and economic development. Some of these organizations, as well as a few local cultural associations, play a crucial role in the development of regional cultural networks, thus promoting understanding and cooperation within the region. It is worth mentioning that some of the successful sectors in Central Asia, such as contemporary art, cinema and handicraft, have benefited from regional networks and initiatives that have helped to promote them on the world cultural map and strengthened their international visibility.[27] Since inaccessibility, instability and political obstacles have contributed to the region's isolation, it is all the more important to promote a positive image of the region in order for its artists and cultural producers to regain access and acceptance to culture industry markets around the world.

Policy recommendations

By way of conclusion it would seem appropriate to suggest some policy recommendations on the basis of the successful cultural initiatives bridging Central Asia with other regions of the world (notably in the fields of contemporary arts, cinema and handicrafts). It is clear that strategies for the replication of these best practices in other cultural sectors are needed. In particular, there is a special role for regional and international networks in strengthening Central Asia on the world cultural map. In this respect, circulation of cultural information between Central Asia and the rest of the world is essential and necessitates new dedicated media. Since Central Asian artists are often more popular abroad than in their own countries, new forms of public incentives should support national and regional structures for art diffusion in Central Asia. In the same spirit, public authorities should facilitate and support artists' mobility through the creation of a specific (regional?) fund, which could involve private funders. This fund could foster the development of a network of artist residencies in Central Asia. The necessary adaptation to new structural realities in Central Asia also implies the creation of training curricula and structures providing updated skills for cultural management. This process should be reinforced through twinning programs with specialized institutions abroad and the facilitation of exchanges among young cultural managers. The current regulatory framework must also be reconsidered in particular regarding cultural operators' employment, training and legal status.

Notes

1 Since 1991, the Kyrgyz Republic and Kazakhstan have been the quickest to implement liberal trade policies; Uzbekistan's trade policy is less liberal, and keeps tight administrative controls on foreign exchanges. Turkmenistan and Tajikistan have been the slowest to establish frameworks for market-based economies.

2 In addition to dozens of Russian TV channels, many American (MTV, CNN, channels for kids) and European channels (Euronews, MCM, etc.) are now available.

3 There is a growing number of reliable international air connections with Central Asia.

4 Ahmadi L. (2006) *The Taste of Others, research and curatorial project 2005–2006*. Asia Art Archive Martell Contemporary Art Research Grant.

5 'No Mad's Land' in Berlin, 'Reorientation' in Weimar, and 'Trans-Forma' in Geneva.

6 Kurama Art, 'Central Asian Pavilion 2005'.

7 To mention a few key players in Central Asian contemporary art: Soros Center for Contemporary Arts and the NGO 'Asia Art+' in Almaty – Kazakh artists like Erbossin

Meldibekov, Said Atabekov or the artist duo Yelena and Victor Vorobyev; In Bishkek, a trained architect, Ulan Djaparov – together with the internationally active artist duo Gulnara Kasmalieva and Muratbek Djoumaliev (NGO ArtEast); they all constitute the most important motor of the art scene that is working on emancipating itself from the structure of an artists' union that is still, for the most part, clinging both aesthetically and policy-wise to the old USSR patterns.

8　'New countries–new identity–new art' (Istanbul Biennale, 2003); 'From the Red Star to the Blue Dome' (Stuttgart) 2003; 'Pueblos y Sombras' (Mexico) 2004; Venice Biennale, 2005; Istanbul Biennale, 2005; 'Tamerlano's Syndrome: Art and Conflicts in Central Asia', Orvieto, Umbria, Italy (2005); Sydney and Singapore Biennales, 2006; 'The Paradox of Polarity: Contemporary Art from Central Asia', New York City, January 2007.

9　Cf. Auezkhan Kodar: 'For Western artists, defended by all the power of their institutions, it is difficult to understand Asian actionist artists, who try to be modern in a place where only the archaic prevails. They explode into the big world, where they are received with open arms, and then return again to their desert, where they have no status and no chance for growth' in *Art from Central Asia, a contemporary archive* – catalogue of the Central Asian Pavilion, Venice Biennale, 2005.

10　*Luna Papa* notably won the Grand Prix (Nantes, Three Continents Festival, 1999), and the Best Artistic Contribution Award (Tokyo International Film Festival, 1999); *Killer* won the award 'Un certain regard' at the Cannes festival, 1998; *Beshkempir* won numerous international awards including the Silver Leopard Prize at the 1998 Locarno International Film Festival.

11　Gulnara Abikeeva, 'What is the phenomenon of the Central Asian Cinema?' Online: http://www.kinokultura.com/CA/A1centralasia.html.

12　Russian Film Symposium 2002, Global Amnesia 3. Central Asian Cinema and Film Genres, http://www.rusfilm.pitt.edu/2002/ga3/.

13　*Nomads*, a big-budget epic – about US$40 million, financed by the government of Kazakhstan (2005).

14　The first international Film Festival, *Didor* (Dushanbe, October 2004) brought together film-makers from Central Asia, Afghanistan, Azerbaijan, Georgia, Iran and Russia as in the good old days. It has been supported by the Swiss Development and Cooperation Agency (SDC) and organized by the Tajik private company LLC KINOSERVICE. A second edition of the festival took place in 2006.

15　The Second and Third International *Eurasia* Festivals took place in 2005 and 2006 in Almaty, with participation of international cinema players (see www.eurasiaiff.kz).

16　At the November 2002 crafts fair in Almaty, Kazakhstan, 270 artisan groups representing all five Central Asian republics were present and total sales were estimated at $135,000, an average of $500 per group. (*An Artisan Association is Born: a case study of Aid to Artisans in Central Asia, 1994–1999*.)

17　Product differentiation for local versus international markets: Artisans have applied principles of differentiation as they diversified their markets. As examples, a blacksmith generates farm tools for local needs and whimsically decorated scissors for tourists. In a second example, felt artisans in Kyrgyzstan produce felt products for export and for local marriage needs and are exploring expansion of tourism patronage. (*An Artisan Association is born: a case study of Aid to Artisans in Central Asia, 1994–1999*.)

18　These problems, elaborated in the next paragraph, include institutional deficiency and the sharp fall in public funding, lack of independent production and distribution structures, inappropriate cultural policies and regulatory frameworks, and the inexistence of cultural media.

19　Historical figures in Central Asia include Abilay Khan in Kazakhstan, the contemporary figure 'Turkmenbashi' (Previous president Nyazov, self-declared 'father of all the Turkmens' in Turkmenistan), Ismail Samani in Tajikistan, Timur (Tamerlane) in Uzbekistan.

20　The rapid economic growth of some of the Central Asian countries (Kazakhstan mainly) offers new private funding opportunities for the cultural sector.

21　According to Business Software Alliance (BSA) study – http://www.bsa.org.

22　The company Meloman is the first diffusion-sale company with 22 shops in Kazakhstan and Kyrgyzstan – one of the only examples of a regional cultural private company.

23　Link to all treaties administered by the World Intellectual Property Organization (WIPO): http://www.wipo.int/treaties/en/.

24　This is a unique channel, financed by the state of Russian government and free from advertising, which is fully dedicated to cultural events that provide information on Russian, Commonwealth of Independent States and international cultural events and news.

25　On the occasion of the first concert of the Kazakhstan Philharmonic Orchestra 'Turan Alem' held at St. James concert hall in London (March 2007), Mukhtar Ablyazov, Chairman of the Board of Directors of JSC 'Bank Turan Alem' noted: 'The idea of the fist concert of "Turan Alem" orchestra in London is being held following the bank's social responsibility, where BTA is the conductor of state interests in other countries'. Cf. http://bta.kz/en/press/news/2007/03/25/1368/.

26　Among the main organizations supporting cultural projects in/with Central Asia are: *International*: UNESCO; *US*: the Aga Khan Trust for Culture, Christensen Foundation, Soros Foundation Network/ Open Society Institute, Ford Foundation, Eurasia Foundation, Trust for Mutual Understanding, CEC ArtsLink; *Asia*: Japan (JICA); – *Europe*: HIVOS (Netherlands), Swiss Agency for Development and Cooperation, French Embassies, British Council, Goethe Institute.

27 Regional networks exist in various fields such as:

- *Contemporary arts*: informal networks of artists and managers.
- *Cinema*: Central Asian Cinema Academy and the Association of Central Asian Festivals, initiated by central Asian cinema specialists.
- *Handicrafts*: CACSA, Central Asian Crafts Support Association, launched by the international NGO Aid to Artisans.

The regional networking approach, with the creation in 1998 of the first handicraft regional network, CACSA, has played an important role in developing international connections and promoting handicraft as a tool for development of the region. Other initiatives are ongoing, such as the creation of a Central Asian Performing Arts Networks, initiated by the International Network for Contemporary Performing Arts (IETM) (Cf. http://www.ietm.org/index.lasso?p=focus&q=Central%20Asia&l=en).

REFERENCES

Mandelbaum, M. (1994) *Central Asia and the World: Kazakhstan, Uzbekistan, Tajikistan, Kyrgyzstan, and Turkmenistan*. New York: Council on Foreign Relations.

Pomfret, R. (1995) *The Economies of Central Asia*. Princeton: Princeton University Press.

## CHAPTER 13

EUROPEAN CULTURAL SYSTEMS IN TURMOIL
Xavier Greffe

Long devoted to making the best of its cultural wealth, Europe today faces challenges of globalization and digitalization for which it is ill-prepared. European nation-states have tended to protect culture from market forces as a lever of national identity and development. Today, these governments realize that while it is normal to promote specific cultural forms (the cultural diversity argument), simply defending a heritage (in the spirit of 'cultural exception') is less so. Thus support mechanisms are increasingly integrated around the goal of advancing creativity while respecting cultural specificities. These policies progress at different rates, however, and Europe's linguistic fragmentation does not help. Hence European nations need to steer a path between the market regulation of standardized products and the administrative regulation of content, in the process developing synergies among themselves so as to build new synergies with other continents.

Europe has long been regarded as the world's principal location of artistic creation and consumption. Artists from all over the world came to be trained here and Europe set standards for many cultural products. In the global economy, however, this centrality is decreasing rapidly. What is more worrying is that the European landscape is also affected by a number of internal tensions that prevent it from benefiting to the full from the globalization of cultural exchanges. There are paradoxes in this situation that need to be understood (Hartley, 2005), just as important organizational changes brought about by globalization present major challenges (Greffe, 2004), in which the various actors of the cultural system figure as winners or losers (Cunningham, 2002). All these developments interrogate all our public policies for the cultural sector in Europe, questioning their overall vision and in particular making it necessary to rethink traditional interventionist stances. In this picture, does regionalization prepare these public polices to better face the challenges of globalization?

How globalization challenges traditional approaches

Seen globally, the production of cultural goods and services in Europe presents a somewhat paradoxical picture. For centuries Europe has mobilized significant resources for cultural activities and has created the corresponding value chains, beginning with the training of the artists and ending with the export of literary and audio-visual products. European countries should thus have clearly benefited from globalization, but many of them adopted positions *vis-à-vis* trade liberalization that were more than reticent, while suffering from a decreasing and often negative trade balance in cultural goods and services. For example, in 2005, France, the champion of the cultural exception, was able to offset the value of its imports in audio-visual products only by the volume of the classical paintings and sculptures it exported!

Three factors are responsible for this situation.

First, European production remains very fragmented among countries for whom the market for cultural goods was primarily a national one (Sassoon, 2006). Public interventionism always caused the consumption of cultural goods to be perceived as a reinforcement of national awareness among citizens. Central governments tended to make cultural production a lever of unity and a national symbol, notably through civil and military architecture, the collections of the national museums and the like. This phenomenon is compounded by linguistic fragmentation. Hence many cultural products, except in the field of music, are deeply marked by their national context; and their export may well require very high expenditures on adaptation, translation or publication.

Second, the arts developed in Europe through an endogenous artistic rather than a commercial logic (Greffe, 2006). Artists have come to see themselves as far removed from market considerations; they have always preferred a self-identification based on purely aesthetic criteria. This point is far from being a minor one, for far too often difficulties in cultural and artistic productions can be explained by phenomena such as cost disease, or excessive State intervention. But there is also a very strong tradition according to which culture begins where the market stops. Such a position is unsustainable today, and this has become very clear when national or local governments are no longer in a position to finance cultural expenditures as they did in the past. Although there are many variations within Europe, the tradition of a culture that is considered to be autonomous of the market makes adaptation to a global market much more difficult, despite the fact that the variety of consumer preferences the latter represents actually opens many more opportunities.

Finally, Europeans tend to distrust the cultural industries, preferring the visual and live arts. This tendency has been strengthened by artists who are far better positioned in the living arts than in relation to the cultural industries; it is expressed in a very radical way by those for whom 'canned culture' is not culture. Central governments consider the cultural value chain to run from live arts to cultural industries, while the global economy shows more and more the opposite movement occurring. This is now beginning to change, however, particularly as Europeans are increasingly using the Internet for the production and distribution of cultural goods and services (Donnat and Tolila, 2003).

These various elements have created a mismatch as regards the opportunities of globalization, the apex of which has been the narrow interpretation of the so-called 'cultural exception'. Things are beginning to change, as the increasing central place of the creative industries is recognized. But the discourse of cultural tourism is at least as important as a kind of nostalgia for the older paradigm.

New stakeholders

A dual transformation

A twofold transformation is changing European production behaviour. New consumption processes are appearing. Two key elements have to be borne in mind here (McCarthy and Jinnett, 2001; Livingstone, 2002; Allard, 2005). The first is the new form of individualization, which consists of the turn towards domestic consumption of cultural forms such as concerts and films that were previously heard or seen in public spaces. Radio and television largely contributed to intensifying these tendencies towards 'entertainment exit'. This individualization has taken place with different speeds in different media. It is based on a double phenomenon of mechanical reproduction of existing content and, more recently, of the electronic extension of this content by means of peripheral devices. It is thus closely related to technological innovations such as miniaturization, and with economic trends, such as the decreasing cost of electronic equipment. The second major trend is the rise of 'networked culture', based on the strong convergence of cultural and communication practice, especially of remote communication by means of new technologies. This also alters the traditional balance between domestic cultural exchanges and external exchanges. The spectacular development of the Internet has considerably modified cultural consumption in the private sphere. It should be noted also that the development of data processing and Internet have together contributed to promoting the extent of 'amateur' artistic activity, in other words the new 'expressive individualism' in the digital universe.

New forms of cultural creativity have also appeared (Greffe, 2004; Hartley, 2005). Old formulations no longer adequately describe creative practices in an environment where 'competition is the main policy lever and consumer protection rather than cultural development is the social dividend' (Cunningham, 2005: 5). Individual genius gives way to the collective creativity of collaborative teams, and a creator works on many projects simultaneously. Priorities shift away from artists creating unique works of arts towards the needs of creative producers developing content for the digital and networked infrastructure which covers much of the globe. Their works are categorized as being within the arts yet their legitimacy cannot be separated from the commercial and material dimensions. This is a relational and non-hierarchical habitat of symbolic activity in which the arts and the creative industries are realigned and merged under the influence of the digital. The act of creation is also transformed: it is no more focused on a well-defined product but is a cross between various references with retrogressions, disjuncture, etc.: *rip, mix and burn*. Small and flexible enterprises and networks are, in these circumstances, much better equipped for these new perspectives than traditional cultural mammoths.

From traditional to new producers

The result is a very important change in the definition and role of cultural producers. Key institutional actors see their relative importance downsized. The reduction of central government support for culture is another general tendency, with very rare exceptions, such as the case of France. In this country, indeed, the notion that public expenditure under the General Account of the central government in favor of culture must account for at least one per cent of the budget has tended to be respected, and the 2007 budget envisaged an increase in cultural expenditure twice as big as that of the General Account overall. Elsewhere, disengagement has been perceptible since the beginning of the 1990s. Efforts required to comply with the criteria of the Treaty of Maastricht led governments to reduce many subsidies, in particular those in favor of live arts, which actually led in some countries such as Italy to a decline in the number of artists. This reduction of cultural subsidies reflects the 'superior good' dimension of cultural goods, in Veblen's sense, where the consumption of cultural goods decreases when income decreases. This very unfavorable movement was consolidated by the enlargement of the European Union: culture loomed large in the budgets of both central and local governments in the communist-era Member States, but these expenditures have been radically reduced in order to absorb the costs of both transition and privatization.

This disengagement led in certain cases to palliatives. Very likely, the most known is the devolution of cultural functions to local governments (Spain, Italy), or the development of matching grants merging central and decentralized efforts. Another palliative resulted in deriving other sources of funds in favor of cultural activities, such as lotteries (United Kingdom) or the reserves of the banking foundations (Italy). These have all modified the rules of the game for the management of culture. When decentralized funding replaces previously centralized forms, the direct control of taxpayers and users usually increases. Moreover, when the central governments hand over responsibility to local communities, the production of national existence values takes second place to the production of direct use values. This is very clear with regard to the way in which heritage conservation loses funds to the benefit of the development of reading or music.

New cultural SMEs and third sector grassroots organizations are more and more numerous. In many European countries many small companies have appeared, particularly in the production sectors, in both the audio-visual sector and the live arts. This was a logical response to the diversification of demand as well as to the need to produce an increasing number of new products in a continuous flow. This is a true decentralization of production. But distribution remains more concentrated. While the small companies are less fragile than it is thought, they nevertheless face a certain number of challenges. To understand these challenges, it is necessary to analyse the genesis and survival of the new cultural companies. How do they appear, flourish, and/or disappear? What are the variables that explain divergent rates of survival? According to an exhaustive recent French study (Greffe and Simonnet, 2006), the rate of survival of the new cultural SMEs is similar to that of other companies, but it is not stable over time and differs according to the sub-sector considered (it is very unstable for live arts, much less so for heritage institutions). Survival rates are very sensitive to geographical clustering. While a cultural company of a given type may well suffer because of the proximity of another company of the same type (competition effect), it will also profit from the presence of other types of cultural companies (synergy effect). This underlies the logic of both the cultural cluster approach and the 'metropolitanization' of cultural production noted in recent years.

These developments highlight other issues faced by cultural SMEs, such as:

- Imbalances between 'production' and 'commercialization', as their resources are mainly allocated to technical operations and are often very limited for commercialization purposes.
- A lack of information about both the market and the kind of support structures that exist; frequently,

they work in isolation, unaware of the rare mechanisms or organizations that might assist them.

- Not enough specialized professional competencies: creative people find themselves overwhelmed by the wide array of skills needed to run a business and potential entrepreneurs cannot start their own businesses without benefiting from specific training (see Chapter 6 by Aageson in this volume).

Third sector bodies in the form of associations have always been present in this sector and their place is growing rapidly. They have three main roles in Europe today. First, they produce goods and cultural services intended to be sold on the market. In this case they fulfil the same role as production companies, but they adopt the associative form in general to profit from a certain number of flexible regulations and tax advantages. They widen the access to culture to a certain number of traditionally excluded people (rural, old people, disabled) or for whom the costs of access often remain high (young people). They aim also at developing amateur practices, blurring the traditional barriers between users and artists by making actors out of users. This tendency is all the more strong today as it corresponds to the recognition of the extrinsic values of culture.

In this context, non-cultural companies in their patterns of business sponsorship are beginning to behave innovatively, in line with their own policy visions, instead of in the traditional sponsorship mould (Rectanus, 2002). Companies such as LVMH or Dior (both in the French luxury goods sector) are increasingly tending to elaborate a 'cultural policy' of their own, and these may even, in certain cases, substitute for those of central governments. Not content with spending in order to create a positive image, many companies are projecting their own 'corporate culture' by defining a clear relationship between image and product. By seeking to disseminate the values of their own creativity, they replicate the utility function and stances of non-profit institutions. Some observers read more into this program of the business sector to disseminate its own values in the arts. They see this merging of tangible products with intangible ideas as a legitimation of the reigning economic system. By acquiring an influence in the public space of ideas and social dialogue, businesses can henceforth express objectives which largely exceed their commercial role. They can thereby acquire a social legitimacy which is disputed by their market rivals. They are thus installed in the public sphere as central and non-conflictual partners (Greffe, 2002a).

These 'cultural policies' of the business sector also invest in so-called *low culture*, the cultures of minorities, digital culture, etc. For companies, the differences between high and low culture do not count: they are complementary niches and the techniques for reaching them are remarkably similar. They offer the postmodernist possibility, in addition, of breaking down class oppositions in the generalized field of consumption. As they do so, they also mobilize a new lever: the quasi-patronage of their employees. In the 1980s, for example, Margaret Thatcher's 'give as you earn' or 'payroll giving' schemes provided that a business employer could directly match the contributions of its employees to a cultural project. This gave companies a strategic role in information, decision-making and financing. Many laws have been adopted subsequently either to broaden this opportunity or to limit some of the potential excesses.

European winners and losers

The winners are mainly the consumers, the new SMEs and the third sector associations, while the losers are mainly traditional government-subsidized culture, whether public or private, for profit or non-profit. More significant than the numbers of these winners and losers is the way in which the redistribution of costs and benefits involved is the direct consequence of globalization.

In the global economy, cultural creativity is increasingly the result of horizontal cooperation that constantly feeds the cultural field with new references, values and reactions. The Internet or the e2e process has played a very important role here, creating and disseminating both open source and open commons. Only flexible entities or networks can access this informal knowledge and transform it into formal knowledge that can be marketed. It is precisely for this reason that cultural development can no longer be envisaged as a top-down process, administratively regulated or centralized. This is why traditional subsidized bodies face growing difficulties and the new small flexible actors and networks encounter major new development spaces.

But, as in many 'games', the winner positions can be compromised for at least two reasons. The reduction of public subsidies (that results mainly here from more pressure on the financial constraints) undermines all cultural actors. Networks, grassroots organizations and new SMEs suffer from these reductions as well as traditional subsidized organizations. The free access culture that is disseminated through this new model can also destabilize these winners. Peer to peer can harm the big companies as well as the small ones. Potential winners that are close to the audio-visual sector may expect to benefit from the market system in which advertisement revenues compensate for no payment from users. But for many other companies, this creates a real challenge. This is probably why artists as well as SMEs have followed the very restrictive position of the big companies as regards the debate on copyright issues.

Public policies for culture in the age of globalization

In the face of the globalization challenge, some countries in the European Union have adopted the strategy known as 'cultural exception'. Because of the role that works of art and artistic products play in the development of a country's identity and the education of its citizens, these countries wish to shelter such goods and services from market forces, which would inevitably cause original national creative products to be replaced by imported forms, thus diluting the country's image. Although France has only since the late 1990s invoked this strategy explicitly at the international level, it has followed it implicitly for many decades. This strategy, also practiced in varying degrees by Greece, Italy and Spain, first manifested itself clearly during the Uruguay Round and the negotiations on the inception of the WTO. To avoid the abolition of broadcasting quotas for audio-visual products under the European Union's Television Without Borders Directive, France prevailed upon its EU partners in order to exclude audio-visual goods and, by extension, cultural goods in general from the negotiations, so that they would continue to enjoy existing EU or national protection.

Arguments in favor of cultural exception can, of course, mask other motivations such as the interests of lobbies seeking to protect their market positions and revenue from competition. But it cannot be ignored that many countries advocate the strategy of cultural exception that poses problems for market integration. Various international regulations have more or less recognized the specific nature of cultural goods. The GATT acknowledged the need for production quotas for films in 1947 and reiterated it in 1994. It also excludes national treasures of artistic, historical or archaeological value from its regulations (Art. XXf). The General Agreement on Trade in Services (GATS) allows temporary exceptions (the 'positive list' principle), as in the case of film production, for a period of five years. The Agreement on Trade-Related Intellectual Property Rights (TRIPs) renewed existing agreements and proposed new measures to assist their protection. European Union measures include the *Television Without Borders Directive* (STE-132), the Culture 2000 program designed to create a common cultural area, the public broadcasting service proposal, the agreement on co-producers and the agreement on the mobility of artists (1999). More recently, the EU has been a leading player in securing the adoption and rapid entry into force of the 2005 UNESCO *Convention on the Protection and Promotion of the Diversity of Cultural Expressions* (cf. Chapter 7). It has staked out a significantly positive position on this instrument in its 'Communication' of May 2007 'on a European agenda for culture in a globalizing world', given that the 27 member states of the Union will ratify the Convention at very different speeds, and it cannot be excluded that several of them do not envisage ratifying it at this time (Commission of the European Communities, 2007). Furthermore, the recognition of 'cultural diversity' as the organizing principle for cultural markets in the countries of the European Union will have consequences, leading to specific regulations that will modify and filter the effects of competition.

In contrast to the total liberalization of trade – which debars advances on revenues and eliminates quotas, so as not to hinder the circulation of cultural goods and give a free rein to competition – cultural diversity is seen by more and more European countries as a way of guaranteeing the fundamental right to information and freedom of expression and even of enhancing the meaning of competition and integration through the criterion of excellence, in addition to numerous economic benefits. Diversity in this reading is a source of creativity and quality and encompasses goods that are not cultural by definition; it is a form of capital that enriches the development process. This observation is supported by new theories of economic geography and international trade, which argue that the initial endowment of resources is less important than the capacity to obtain increasing yields from them. But it is true as well that cultural diversity is a very slippery concept. It means many things and it can be easily manipulated. Very likely, it can be used here to distinguish between the diversity of contents, which is the most traditional understanding of the term, structural diversity, which is related to the consideration of minorities, and access diversity which is related to the possibility of using various spaces or channels of access.

The time seems to be ripe to stop justifying state intervention in the arts as being necessary because high culture is unable to pay for itself or in order to protect specific economic players such as artists or art dealers. It is in fact the economic, social and territorial implications of artistic goods and industries that are prompting governments to engage in responsible competition because there can be no progress without the development and cross-fertilization of cultures. But the starting positions are too unequal for many countries and territories to do without mechanisms that give different cultures the opportunity to express themselves. As is often the case in the artistic field, distribution, rather than production and retailing, is the key issue since cultural diversity can only be maintained if products are known, i.e. if they can enter the market.

Faced with this issue, we need to adopt modern criteria of competition. There is no shortage of declarations in Europe, where the management of 'containers' is traditionally divorced from the management of their 'contents', whereas in the United States the two are combined. This separation is responsible for maintaining areas of intervention specific to each country. It is likely that different national positions will converge over time, because the different countries realize that cultural diversity is more important than cultural exception. However, this convergence of positions within the EU will depend on developments in the market for 'containers' over the next few years.

The main European defender of the cultural exception, France, still supports the former approach, but it has softened its position. France accepts the idea that cultural exception or cultural diversity may be redefined at the level of the European Union and would agree to change its national regulations, if similar regulations are adopted at the Union level. It is also willing, apparently, to support 'European culture' instead of just French culture if cultural specificity is asserted at Union level. This is a delicate balance to achieve, given the many issues at stake, the variety of national positions and the conflicting interests of the Commission, which is at once the natural and explosive meeting point of free-market dynamics and technocracy. Perspectives therefore vary from sector to sector and the result is more a change in the mode of governance of cultural activities in the EU than a major change in regulations or structures.

Box 13.1 The economy of culture in Europe

In November 2006, the European Commission published a study on the economy of culture in Europe undertaken by the firm KEA European Affairs (www.keanet.eu). The study captured for the first time the direct and indirect socio-economic impact of the cultural and creative sector across Europe. It also made recommendations for a creative Europe to help achieve the Lisbon objective of making the EU, by 2010, 'the most competitive and dynamic knowledge-based economy in the world, capable of sustainable economic growth with more and better jobs and greater social cohesion'.

Main findings in figures

The study confirmed that the cultural and creative sector in Europe is outperforming other sectors. Its turnover was (654 billion in 2003. It contributed to 2.6 per cent of EU GDP, while the food, beverage and tobacco manufacturing sector contributed 1.9 per cent. The growth of the sector between 1999 and 2003 was 19.7 per cent, which was 12.3 per cent higher than that of the economy at large. While over 2 million people work directly for the automotive industry – one of Europe's key industrial sectors – the cultural and creative sector employed close to 6 million people in 2003, representing 3.1 per cent of total EU25 workers. Moreover, whereas total employment in the EU between 2002 and 2004 decreased, employment in the cultural and creative sector increased by 1.85 per cent over the same period. These numbers are evidence that the European cultural and creative sector contributes significantly to the 'Lisbon Agenda'.

Key recommendations

The competences of the European Union in cultural matters date back to the adoption of the Maastricht Treaty in 1993 and focus on the ideas of enhancing heritage and cultural cooperation between Member States. This cultural dimension now deserves to move to a next stage, especially when Europe's competitiveness and influence in a globalized world are at stake. Hence the main recommendations of the study are the following:

- Establish a strong quantitative evidence base for policy-makers.
- Use and make the most of existing EU support programs (FP7 – structural funds – support to SMEs).
- Promote links between creators and technology by clustering the various competences in creativity platforms.
- Maximize the use of financial instruments of the EIB and the EIF in line with the EIB i2010 Initiative.
- Reinforce the internal market for creative people, products and services.
- Promote creativity and business education from schools through to professional levels.
- Integrate the cultural dimension in cooperation and trade agreements between the EU and third countries with a view to develop exchanges and promote cultural diversity.

A first positive step was the decision by the heads of states and governments (Council Summit of March 2007) to recommend that the European Commission should take the creative industries into consideration in its policy for the internal market. In its Communication on a European agenda for culture in a globalizing world (May 2007), the European Commission emphasizes the role of culture as a catalyst for creativity in the framework of the Lisbon Strategy for growth and jobs.

Nicolas Gyss

What kind of public policy?

With cultural diversity as an objective, policies are progressively being transformed to take into account the benefits of exchange while maintaining some support for cultural production. The first step is to try to harmonize the tools used at the European level. The European Union has no special competency in the realm of culture beyond the limited terms of article 151 in the Treaty of Amsterdam. But in certain domains other than the 'cultural' it can take initiatives in conjunction with its Member States by issuing directives. It may act in accordance with competition policy if the recognition and the management of intellectual rights create barriers for the market. Finally, it may intervene in support of the freedom of circulation of goods and persons, known as 'community principles' (acquis communautaires). Moreover, a harmonized legal framework on copyright and neighboring rights, through increased legal certitude and providing a high level of protection for authors' rights, encourages substantial investment in creativity.

From the outset, two radically different positions have been articulated. One is the position adopted by the Commission, largely inspired by unrestrained free-market dynamics, which seeks to impose the principle of a single market across all sectors. The other is the position adopted by most Latin countries, who consider that artistic goods should be exempted from homogenization and solely market-based treatment. In different sectors, this has led to different degrees of pragmatism and different outcomes.

Publishing policy

The book industry is less globalized than the record industry and is characterized by sub-regional issues. Although there are fewer public stakeholders in the French book industry than in other cultural sectors, France put in place a highly symbolic regulation in the context of regional integration and the transition to a single market, viz. the 1983 law on fixed prices for books. By having fixed prices for books with severe restrictions on discounts (a maximum of 5 per cent), the government sought to protect not only the livelihood of independent bookshops, but also the future of numerous books destined to disappear from distribution channels and, over the years, from production. Although the issue owes more to the conventional economic debate (small shops and product lines threatened by mass retailing) than to cultural exception as such, the government's position was determined by the fact that cultural goods were involved. Many countries have followed the example of France in different ways (Greffe, 2002). Some countries have enshrined the principle of fixed prices in law (Belgium, Greece, Italy and Portugal). Others have preferred to achieve the same result through agreements with industry (Austria and Germany). Still others have abandoned this approach after exploring it in some measure (Sweden and the United Kingdom).

The debate was gradually brought before the Commission, at the instigation of private operators – divided in their opinions – and the European Parliament, which sought to protect the specificity of books. The Commission, already opposed to the principle of fixed prices and France's proposed aim of generalizing it, was equally hostile to the proposal of many countries to fix prices across given linguistic areas (or, failing that, in individual countries), because this would hinder cross-border trade. However, since the Commission is unable to impose its views, it continues to allow each country the freedom to pursue its own policy, simply insisting that member states must consult the Commission before effecting any changes in their legislation (Article 81 of the Treaty). As it often happens, there is co-ordination between countries that agree to apply a given principle; but in the absence of unanimity they have not succeeded in transforming it into legislation at the Union level (Ministère de la Culture et de la Communication, 2000).

Circulation of moveable heritage

The problem of the permanent transfer of paintings and sculptures has prompted the question whether art markets in different countries should dissolve into a single art market. Across the continent, the implementation of the single market is changing this system radically. The single-market principle was applied to works of art, but with a major exception at the request of France and other countries with an extensive national heritage. European legislation makes a distinction between national treasures and artistic goods, with the definition of national treasures left to each country. Countries can retain national treasures, but they must allow the free export of other artistic goods, at least temporarily and usually permanently. However, this has raised the problem of some countries divesting the new legislation of all meaning through their definition of national treasures.

Cinema and audio-visual production

This is the most visible area of conflict. Among the many protectionist instruments currently deployed, two play a key role: advances on revenues and quotas. These mechanisms have frequently provoked the ire of the American film industry and 'cultural exception' is traditionally invoked to defend them. In terms of regulations, however, the Commission has not gone further than issuing directives whose application is largely left to the member states. At the instigation of countries that support an interventionist policy, the Commission launched the MEDIA program, which offers various grants for training and for the production, translation and retailing of audiovisual works. Some limited assistance is also provided for retailing films in other European countries. The Commission considers the cinema as a product in a class of its own, but it prefers incentive to regulation although it does not prevent countries from implementing their own legislation.

Copyright

After a long debate, the European Union believes that the harmonization of copyright and related rights must be based on a high level of protection, since such rights are crucial to artistic creation. Their protection helps to ensure the maintenance and development of creativity in the interests of authors, performers, producers, consumers and the public at large (WIPO, 2004). It can thus be said that the European Commission has achieved a synthesis between the two traditional approaches of authors' rights. It has on the one hand confirmed the French tradition of defining, without any ambiguity, the author as the holder of the copyright, yet at the same time it has integrated the Anglo-Saxon tradition by establishing a clear link between the definition of exceptions to the right and economic interests. Therefore member states are given the option of making provisions for certain exceptions and limitations for educational or scientific purposes, for the benefit of public institutions such as libraries and archives, for purposes of news reporting, for quotations, for use by people with disabilities, for public security uses and for uses in administrative and judicial proceedings. When assessing these exceptions, they should be submitted to a *triple test*. The exception should not be permanent. It should not alter the author's rights (such exceptions and limitations should not be applied in a way that damages the legitimate interests of the right-holder or comes into conflict with the exploitation of his work). Finally, it should not weaken economic activity (the provision of such exceptions by member states should duly reflect the increased economic impact that such exceptions may induce in the context of the new electronic environment and make up for it).

Transforming cultural activities into new development assets

In Europe, the opposition between art and economics has often reflected the divide between functional utility and aesthetic value devoid of any utilitarian dimension, or between content and form. Since the primary objective of the economy is to satisfy needs, content takes priority over form. The doctrine of 'art for art's sake' has deepened this divide, to the point of depreciating artisans who, unlike artists, attempt to strike a balance between form and function. Creative workers today seem to have moved beyond this dichotomy by demonstrating the difficulty of separating the substance of content from the substance of form. The satisfaction of needs is compatible with difference in forms, and different forms can become assets in the conquest of new markets. For many European countries, the only hope of benefiting from global competition is to improve the quality and variety of their products. Here, the cultural can contribute in two ways. It offers a ready set of benchmarks for defining new products. By constituting the prototype of productive activity and thus developing a culture (in the anthropological sense of the term) it can disseminate a culture of creativity.

In some European countries, the 'creative' economy or modern cultural economy already marks the new frontier of employment and incomes. By 'modern cultural economy', we mean all those sectors that offer products incorporating a high symbolic meaning or value relative to their utilitarian value (Scott, 2000). For an increasing number of European States and citizens, this cultural economy is in the vanguard of the global knowledge economy.

REFERENCES

Allard L. (2005) 'Express yourself 2.0!', in E. Maigret and E. Macé, (eds.) *Penser les médiacultures. Nouvelles pratiques et nouvelles approches de la représentation du monde*, Paris: Armand Colin.

Commission of the European Communities (2007) *Communication from the Commission to the European Parliament, the Council, the European Economic and Social Committee and the Committee of the Regions on a European agenda for culture in a globalizing world*. Document COM(2007) 242 final.

Cunningham, S. (2002) 'Culture, Services, Knowledge or Is Content King, or Are We Just Drama Queens?' *Communication Research Forum*, October 2–3, 2002. Online: www.dcita.gov.au/crf/papers02/Cunningham.pdf.

Donnat O. and Tolila P. (2003) *Les publics de la culture: politiques publiques et équipements culturels*. Paris: Presses de l'Institut d'Etudes Politiques.

Greffe, X. (2002) *Arts and Artists from an Economic Perspective*. Paris: UNESCO and Brookings (2003).

Greffe, X. (2004) 'Artists in a digital Age', *The Journal of Arts and Management*, Spring, 2: 66–88.

Greffe, X. (2006) *Création et diversité culturelle au miroir des industries culturelles*. Paris: La documentation française.

Greffe, X. and Simmonet, V. (2006) *Les nouvelles entreprises culturelles*. Paris: Ministère de la Culture et de la Communication.

Hartley, J. (ed.) (2005) *Creative Industries*. Oxford: Blackwell Publishing.

Livingstone, S. (2002) *Young People and New Media*. London: SAGE Publications.

McCarthy K.F. and Jinnett, K. (2001) *A New Framework for Building Participation in the Arts*. Santa Monica: Rand Corporation.

Ministère de la Culture et de la Communication (2000) Synthèse du Colloque de Strasbourg sur 'L'économie du livre dans l'espace européen' (held on 29–30 September 2000, during the French presidency of the EU). Online: http://www.culture.gouv.fr/culture/europe/synthese-strasb.htm

Rectanus, M.W. (2002) *Culture Incorporated: Museums, Artists and Corporate Sponsorships*. Minneapolis: University of Minnesota Press.

Sassoon, D. (2006) *The Culture of the Europeans: From 1800 to the Present*. London: Harper.

Scott, A.J. (2000) *The Cultural Economies of Cities: Essays on the Geography of Image-Producing Industries*. London: SAGE Publications.

OECD (2005) *Culture and local development*. Paris: OECD

WIPO (2004) *WIPO Intellectual Property Handbook*. 2nd edition, Geneva.

## CHAPTER 14

COUNTRIES IN TRANSITION: WHICH WAY TO GO?
Kirill Razlogov

This chapter surveys the major transformations in the cultural sphere that have accompanied the transition from Communism to capitalism in Central and Eastern Europe as well as Russia. It reviews the key challenges and issues that have arisen during this still ongoing transition period, as each country (and each community) is obliged to choose its own position in relation to globalization and its path towards (or its reaction against) the postmodern and post-industrial world.

For more than half a century, Central and Eastern Europe has been a privileged space of social and cultural experiments. After the tragic turmoil of the Second World War a large part of the continent was more or less forced to closely follow the Soviet model: authoritarian regimes, subordinated to Moscow, a centrally planned economy and an absolute rule of collective ownership of the means of production. In terms of culture it meant total ideological control, an inflation of national cultural values and under financing of the sector as the lowest priority item in the state budget.

The disintegration of the Soviet Union announced freedom to former 'allies' (Hungary, Poland and Czechoslovakia, later – the Czech Republic and Slovakia) and brought to life new independent states – Latvia, Lithuania and Estonia in the Baltic region, Belarus, Moldova, Ukraine and some think even Russia itself. But it only submitted these countries to new rules: those of the 'market economy' and the European Union on the one hand, and those of globalization (often perceived as 'Americanization') on the other. Culture in the traditional sense (arts and heritage) lost its importance (and a large share of public funding), relinquishing space to the media, the Star System and global mass-culture (usually wrongly perceived in Europe as anti-culture and non-Art).

During the transition period which is still ongoing, each country (and each community) has had to choose its own path towards (or reaction against) the postmodern and post-industrial world, the information, transformation or knowledge society. The world over, intellectuals and artists underline the contradictions between the untrammelled 'capitalism' that reigns in the world and the fundamental cultural values to which most of its peoples still subscribe – in other words, the contradictions between economic and cultural and development. Members of the Russian Academy of Sciences, especially scholars of literature and the arts, are pessimistic about the current trends; they express the view that the marketplace is killing true culture (see 'Ten years that shook culture', 2002). Economists and policy-makers, on the contrary, see no fundamental contradictions between culture and the market economy, both local and global. For most of them, measuring the economy of culture focuses exclusively on the 'value added to the economy', in other words the increase in wealth that is attributable to the cultural and creative sector. In so doing they are putting aside not only intellectual values but most of the human development aspects. The roots of this contradiction go far back in time. The Enlightenment project of modern times put forward culture and education as the ultimate values that are non-measurable economically, and this was true even for Karl Marx. The post-modern age (in fact global mass culture of the twentieth and twenty-first centuries) based upon the entertainment principle, has on the contrary declared the universal supremacy of the economic calculus. A nice lady from the Russian Ministry of Economic Development addressed artists and cultural workers with the following order: 'You have to prove that you can generate profits to get anything from the state.'

The overall context

Different as they have been politically, economically and socially, the cultures of the post-socialist states are all in equally difficult circumstances. They no longer enjoy state protectionism or financial allocations managed by fiat; nor are there adequate instruments of support such as those available in the mature market economies. Inevitably, labour relations, employment and wage levels in the sphere of culture have been affected.

There are two external factors that influence the state of culture: the development of market mechanisms and limitations on the same mechanisms in the form of state aid to culture. By the beginning of the 1990s, both the system of management and the organizational structures of the performing arts, museums, libraries and culture centers had grown obsolete. The problems that had for decades accumulated in the performing arts resulted in the emergence of latent unemployment in culture. The system of egalitarianism had provided equality for both the hard-working and the lazy, the talented and the hacks, guaranteeing that all would receive full wages simply because they belonged to the socially acknowledged vocations. The quality of performance and contribution to the creative process were effectively ignored.

The transition period saw the emergence of new economic relations in culture. The state gave up the strictly centralized system of administration and updated the system of remuneration. The simplified procedure of founding new performing groups with alternative forms of ownership helped create new jobs. The network of theaters, concert halls, circuses, museums and galleries has been supplemented with temporary groups founded expressly for

the purpose of implementing this or that cultural project. While the bright side to the market economy is freedom of choice, the dark side brings tough competition, risks, and inadequate or non-existent guarantees of the right to work and earn. As film director Alexei German pointed out at a professional meeting during this crucial period: 'in the past we [artists] used to live as if in a cage, under strict surveillance, but we were well fed and out of danger. Now we find ourselves in the jungle, free but fighting for food and having the choice between kill or get killed.'

It is the latter side of the market that is the focus of state attention. In effect, culture is a special zone: in 1992–5, the period of radical transformations in the former socialist states, the main aim of state cultural policy was to preserve culture and cultural heritage along with state institutions and organizations. In Russia, thanks to state support, the existing system of cultural organizations has been preserved. Even in 2004 the structures had not changed much (see Table 14.1).

In other countries of Central and Eastern Europe and smaller new independent states, the crisis was more evident. The number of cultural institutions diminished, prices went up and audiences went down. A common recent trend has been a structural shift towards the arts: although the overall number of libraries and culture centers has been diminishing, towards the end of the twentieth century the number of theaters, concert halls, music performing groups, museums and art galleries began to rise. The creative potential and the simplified procedure of founding new artistic institutions tipped the balance of human resources in favor of the 'new', i.e. small theaters, troupes, museums and galleries. The process is reversed in the case of libraries and culture centers: they are becoming fewer but larger.

The share of wages in the overall expenditure of cultural institutions has dropped. Between 1992 and 1994 in the Russian Culture Ministry's system, for example, it had diminished from 38 per cent to 27 per cent, including in the performing arts from 48 to 39 per cent; in museums, from 18 per cent to 13 per cent; and in culture centers and libraries, from 39 per cent to 27 per cent. Calculations indicate that the same is true of the structure of budget allocations: over the three years, the share of wages went down 10 per cent in the performing arts and museums, and 16 per cent in libraries and culture centers. Paying so little for creative labour, the state channels a part of the money thus 'saved' to compensate for the inflationary growth of material expenditures.

Table 14.1   Cultural institutions in Russia (01.01.04)

Types of institutions	Number of institutions		Including	
	Total	Ministry of culture	Regional	Federal
1. Performing arts institutions (total) including:	**913**	**891**	**781**	**110**
Theaters	568	546	521	25
Concert organizations	282	282	257	25
Circuses	63	63	3	60
2. Cultural institutions (total) including:	**10693**	**103210**	**103107**	**103**
Museums	1572	1492	1434	58
Affiliate museums	657	650	614	36
Libraries	50583	48767	48758	9
Leisure institutions	53592	51772	51772	–
Parks	508	508	508	–
Zoos	21	21	21	–
3. Cinema institutions (total) including:	**14586**	**14586**	**14551**	**35**
Film studios	35	35	–	35
Screening facilities	14551	14551	14551	–
TOTAL for culture, arts and cinema	**12243**	**118687**	**118439**	**248**
including publicly financed	10784	104095	103882	213
4. Educational institutions (total) including:	**6107**	**6107**	**6029**	**78**
Universities	73	73	17	56
Specialized high schools	265	265	247	18
Children art schools	5769	5769	5765	4
Research institutions (total)	**6**	**6**	**–**	**6**
Total	**12854**	**124800**	**124468**	**332**

Source: Russian Ministry of Culture Statistical Bureau (GIVZ)

Another face of crisis management has shown itself in the cultural industries, which were supposed to be able to function following strict market rules. The key notion here was privatization.

Climax...

In fact, globalization took over, where regional blocs failed. Market liberalization brought mass cultural products to Western Europe soon after the Second World War – much earlier than to the East. The globalizing of Eastern Europe took place later, but more actively and quickly, bringing about a complete transformation in the understanding of cultural policies. The main problem in the public–media relationship becomes cultural diversity within the mix of global mass culture. From this point of view, external relations change into internal ones and communication processes become much more complex.

The case of cinema: to each his own

Privatization of film and broadcasting in a strict sense is limited to ex-socialist countries. Most cinemas in Western Europe are private and more or less monopolized by national or transnational financial groups. Small and independent owners are being gradually expelled from the scene. Non-profitable cinemas in the West are usually supported (and sometimes owned) by municipalities. In the ex-socialist countries, the state-supported over-extended cinema network has collapsed, and attendance has dropped dramatically (more than 20 times – from 9 per year per habitant in Russia, for example in 1988, to 0.34 in 1996 admissions). Many cinema halls have been given to municipalities, then privatized and reconstructed for a different type of commercial use (from casinos, to furniture or automobile shops). Out of 25 cinemas privatized in Lithuania, not a single one kept its original function, in spite of a legal obligation to do so (Liutkus, 1997: 136–8.) The future of the old cinemas

Table 14.2 Piracy markets in Central and Eastern Europe

	Cinema		Soundtracks		Software, office		Software, leisure		Books	
	Loss	Piracy share	Loss	Piracy share	Loss	Piracy share	Loss	Piracy share	Loss	Total loss
Ukraine	45	90%	125	75%	59	91%	n/a	85%	n/a	229
Russia	275	75%	405	64%	704	87%	n/a	80%	40	1424
Belarus	n/a	n/a	22	74%	n/a	n/a	n/a	n/a	n/a	22
Bulgaria	4	25%	7	80%	16	71%	n/a	n/a	0.3	27.3
Hungary	20	30%	8	30%	55	42%	n/a	n/a	4	87
Latvia	n/a	85%	10	80%	10	57%	n/a	95%	n/a	20
Lithuania	n/a	n/a	13.5	85%	10	58%	n/a	90%	n/a	23.5
Poland	30	30%	34	45%	171	58%	n/a	n/a	5	240
Romania	8	35%	18	80%	28	73%	n/a	n/a	2	56
Slovakia	2	25%	n/a	n/a	24	50%	n/a	n/a	n/a	26

Source: Dolgin, 2006: 495–7

has thus become part of the battle for real estate. The attendance crisis in Eastern and Central Europe took place in parallel with an attendance rise in the West, brought about by the technical revolution of the multiplexes. Constructing a new generation of cinemas is extremely expensive, hence the process started slowly in post-socialist countries. The few existing projects were supported (and sometimes owned) by transnational investors. In the beginning of the twenty-first century the multiplex boom gained big cities in Russia, then in Poland and in the Czech Republic.

The transfer of managerial skills from the West to Eastern and Central Europe from one cultural setting to another, remains a major problem. Methods which are effective in old democracies with a developed middle class usually prove to be ineffective in countries with a very low personal income. If Moscow – where 70 per cent of Russia's capital is concentrated – can afford a film theater with the world's highest ticket price (almost US$50), in other Russian cities the average price drops to US$2, while the costs of exploitation and maintenance are hardly different.

At the same time a completely private (and pirated) video business was generated all over Central and Eastern Europe, as the few state enterprises were completely uncompetitive, due to bureaucratic constraints and copyright issues. Piracy was a principal outcome of the laissez-faire market-oriented mantra (Bennett, 1995: 199–216). New intellectual property rights legislation, implemented in most post-socialist states, reduced the scope of piracy, but only slightly (see Table 14.2).

The only field where the state still has a stake is film production. Privatization involves, of course, the huge technical facilities of the formerly state-constructed, -owned and -managed film studios. Yet some governments (Russia, the Czech Republic, Estonia) are reluctant to give away their film studios and try to keep local film-making alive even if it is not profitable. The experience of the giant Babelsberg film studios in the former East Germany (widely known as UFA [*Universal Film Aktien Gesellschaft*] in pre-war Germany, then DEFA [*Deutsche Film Aktien Gesellschaft*] in the GDR) proves that even in the most favorable conditions, film activity still exists – privatization leads to a massive sell-out of land and real estate.

Except for the obsolete production units of the still state-owned big studios and co-productions with public TV channels, film production in Eastern Europe is mostly handled by private companies, sometimes created especially for one single film. That does not mean that they do not use public money. On the contrary, the Western European system is organized in a way that requires matching grants from different national and supra-national funds and bodies, thereby redistributing what is basically public money. In Eastern Europe the principle of recycling public money works even more clearly. In some countries each sector of film production and distribution is subsidized separately. For example, in Russia, a private distributor might obtain a film, financed by the state, almost for free, then ask for a subsidy for prints and advertising, and sell the film to regional and local distributors (who use money from regional and local budgets). The whole system only works thanks to public money, because low attendance and minimal prices make it impossible for the cinemas to cover even their operating expenses (electricity, heating, water, etc.). As a result, the profit of most private distributors comes exclusively from public sources. The only exception is the revival of the film market in Russia where local blockbusters after year 2000 are more successful than the Hollywood ones.

Denouement

The picture of both the general trends and the local specificity of different transitions is a plural one and therefore it determines scenarios of future development for Central and Eastern European countries that are linked to issues of multiculturalism. The main point here is the problem of cultural adaptation in relation to ethnic conflicts across the region. Sometimes these are seen as a reaction against globalization. Most scholars refuse to acknowledge the cultural roots of the present conflicts, however, concentrating mostly on their economic, political and military aspects. On the contrary, broadcasting transfers all over certain territories project a clearly political and culturally acceptable image of unacceptable wars and conflicts. Traditional majorities and minorities were and are defined by ways of living together. New cultural communities are not only reflected in the media structures, but also in many ways are created by them. Trans-local cultural communities forged and developed by the Internet offer good examples of this latest tendency. Some cultural minorities have newspapers and television channels in their native languages, reflecting new 'multiculturalism' policies. Some are still fighting for the right to enjoy such means of voice and expression. As a rule, these media cannot support themselves and survive on either public money and/or help sent to the diasporas from the 'homeland'.

In the former Soviet Union, the so-called Union Republics (those that became independent states after 1991) had two official languages for press and broadcasting – their own national language and Russian. After independence Russian lost this status in most of them, but survived in a diminished scope in the media. In fact it was replaced by English among the new elites and young people. This last remark is even more applicable to Poland, the Czech Republic, and Slovakia.

What are the relations of these cultures with global mass culture? Few of them stand a chance of invading the global media networks. But sometimes interesting things happen. If we look closely, for example, into the Russian contribution to global mass culture, we encounter adaptations (digests or films and TV series) of classical novels, especially by Leo Tolstoy or Dostoyevsky, the idea of Russian soul, Rasputin, vodka, the tennis player Sharapova… The only entertainment industry example is the *Tatu* group – two very young singers pretending to be teenage lesbians, who cry more than they sing about their passions and pains. Love and sex appeal to young audiences everywhere. But why precisely *Tatu*? There are different kinds of musical groups in Russia, and alongside *Tatu* you can find hundreds and thousands (even millions) of other performers who never wanted to, or succeeded in, joining global mass culture. It just happens that mass culture can adapt itself and find a way to integrate these popular cultural phenomena, and the dialogue between *Tatu*, Reggae, *Rai* and Lambada can happen everywhere, including here, on Central and Eastern European territory. And this kind of dialogue is fundamentally unlike the traditional travels of artists or tourists. In the global networks the expressive forms are not exotic but equal. A different problem is the relation between mass culture and subcultures, including not only regional or national, but also 'high', 'youth', 'minority', etc. cultures. These and other subcultures tend also to become closed worlds; they expressly do not want to be part of the mass media network but rather forge group cultural identities.

Policy options

The consensus is that it is impossible to automatically adapt traditional 'Eastern' values to Western standards. The mis-adaptation or radical refusal of modernization demonstrates the impasse. As for the two other scenarios – selective adaptation and co-adaptation or modernization of a convergent type – their results depend on a specific combination of leading national and minority cultures and their interrelation for each country, which often reveal the pathologies of transition. For each of these cases, different policy options are required. The main issue is the need to adapt modernization policies to local cultural traditions and standards, including majority and minority cultures (see: http//www.culturalpolicies.net). A point repeatedly encountered in scholarly work by Eastern European scholars and even more so in Western publications about the East is the need to import some of the advantages of the state cultural sector of the communist period into the market economy (Bakacsi et al., 2002: 69–80). The economic difficulties of the transition period made necessary a high level of state support not only to traditional and classical culture, but also to the cultural industries and the media. But the basic orientation of cultural and development policies should not be the present state of the so-called developed world, but future stages of the information and even post-information society, where the role of culture is bound to grow enormously.

REFERENCES

Bakacsi, G. et al. (2002) 'Eastern European cluster: tradition and transition', *Journal of World Business*, 37: 69–80.

Bennett, O. (1995) 'Cultural policy in the United Kingdom: collapsing rationales and the end of a tradition', *European Journal of Cultural Policy*, 1(2): 199–216.

http//www.culturalpolicies.net

Liutkus, V. (1997) 'Lithuania', in A. van Hemel and N. van der Wielen (eds.) *Privatization/Désétatisation and Culture: Limitations or Opportunities for Cultural Development in Europe? (Conference Reader)*. Amsterdam: Boekman Foundation/ Twente University. pp. 136–8.

Десять лет, которые потрясли культуру (*Ten years that shook culture*). Очерки культурной жизни России. Moscow: State Art Institute.

Dolgin. A. (2006) Экономика символического обмена (*Economy of Symbolic Exchange*). M.: 2006,pp. 495–7.

## CHAPTER 15

SOUTHEASTERN EUROPE: EMERGENCES AND DEVELOPMENTS
Nada Švob-Đokić, Jaka Primorac and Krešimir Jurlin

In Southeastern Europe, current processes of cultural industrialization have linked particular cultural settings with global cultural trends. A transition towards cultural economy is underway, and new perspectives on cultural development have opened up in the whole region. This is clearly reflected in changing cultural identities and values, in the use of new technologies, in the creation of cultural markets and of cultural development overall. A specific kind of interaction among local cultures and global technological, media, creative and artistic developments is taking place. For the further development of these interactions participatory responses are needed that would connect local cultural values and creativity with global cultural developments.

Analysis of the cultural or creative industries is a rather new field in Southeastern Europe (SEE), the region that is being re-constituted after the conflicts that followed the dissolution of Yugoslavia, the emergence of six new states and the systemic transition of its nine ex-socialist states.[1] Present cultural developments, as well as the state of cultural production and consumption largely reflect the introduction of new social and economic patterns that comply with globalization processes. Cultural identification remains,

however, an important aspect of the overall cultural change and is the backbone of local responses to globalization. Economic globalization is, in practical terms, reflected primarily as the cultural industrialization of the region.

Cultural industrialization

The emergence of cultural/creative industries in this part of Europe appears in the context of Western post-industrialism, post-modernism and an intensive economic globalization. The whole area is characterized by transitional and post-transitional, second modernization[2] developments. Cultural industrialization is strongly and essentially influenced by global cultural markets, the increase in local cultural consumption and the occasional foreign investment in cultural production. The newly emerging cultural economy develops in a social and historical context that is radically different from contexts established within the capitalist free market entrepreneurial systems. It begins in public and state-owned enterprises, with the initial mission to educate and entertain. Privatization has overturned the ownership mode of cultural production, but this has not changed its character and quality instantly. Local social and political contexts are therefore relevant for development and understanding of the SEE cultural economy as much as are global influences and markets. The cultural industrialization of the region is inextricably related to social and political practices that remain discernible and oriented to local cultural identities and ways of life in spite of the growing transnational influences. *The SEE cultural economy thus differs from the established patterns of economic globalization due to the specific role of local agents.*

The transition towards cultural economy

The systemic transition from socialism to capitalism involves establishment of *organizational forms favoring foreign investments* and introducing new types of cultural consumption, production and services.

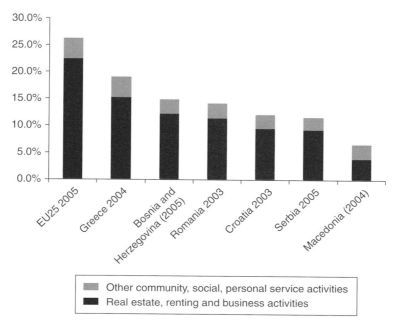

Legend:
- Other community, social, personal service activities
- Real estate, renting and business activities

Figure 15.1   Share of selected sectors in total value added

Source: Eurostat, national statistics offices

Transnational projects, schemes, investments and productions invade local markets and societies. The results of their presence and influence are still rather non-transparent as the regional cultural markets are approached disguised as friendly participation in modernization processes. The small transitional states of the region are unprepared to regulate relations with foreign investors. They cannot define local strategies or clear regional standpoints. They even have problems defining the cultural or media policies[3] that they would like to implement.

The differences in cultural development and industrialization therefore multiply all over the region: the positions of states differ in relation to transnational companies and their agents; the positions of local agents within the states also differ in relation to central states, and in relation to transnational organizations. This is combined with the fact that SEE markets are small and hardly regulated at all, which is not particularly attractive for foreign investors. Organizational forms for investment, production, distribution and consumption of cultural goods and services are almost exclusively developed or transferred by the transnational companies, their sister companies and sometimes (rarely) by local companies or agents that work for transnationals. This produces a double effect on the local scene: a kind of 'foreign' culture enters local societies; local response is weak and disorganized. It may be friendly (willingness to cooperate and participate in promotion of new cultural productions and enhancing consumption), or less friendly (weak resistance from the local level, often disguised as a 'national identity' preservation and strengthening). Nevertheless, cultural industrialization progresses and is influenced by global trends and companies. It is no longer supported or enhanced by states and other local sources, although these have not vanished, but it is relying now more on fragile cultural markets. This trend is shaped by local values and tastes since local production can still, to a certain extent, meet domestic demand, particularly in pop music, local TV series production, festivals, performances, exhibitions, etc.

The present situation

The creative/culture industries are not yet recognized as separate economic activity. They therefore do not appear in national statistics as separate entries, which creates significant obstacles to the analysis of their place and role in national economies. Identification of creative/culture industries has to rely on depicting the activities that best represent the

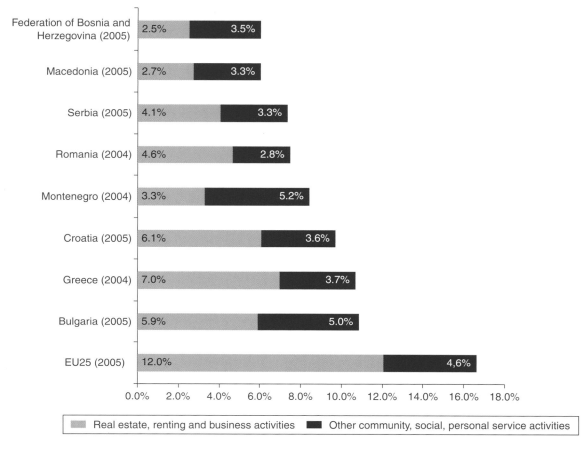

Figure 15.2   Share of selected sectors in total employment
Source: Eurostat, national statistics offices

meaning and content of these industries from the official statistical classification. International data
sources referring to SEE do not include detailed statistics on creative industries, or on investments by
transnational corporations. The present analysis
therefore relies on an effort to consolidate statistical
data. These mostly cover publishing, intellectual personal services, research and development and cultural activities in the narrow sense (theater, film,
music production, etc.). Data needed for the basic
assessment of the share of creative industries in
national SEE countries' GDPs, and their contribution
to the total employment is traced. A rather broad
insight in development and value of creative/cultural
industries in the region may be possible when the
aggregated data (creative activities and simple services) on sectors are presented. A rough estimate
shows that sectors containing creative industries in

SEE countries have a half of the share of the respective industries in the EU25 countries.

The data on employment provide a much better
insight into the development scope of the cultural or
creative industries. These suggest that the share of
the selected industries in total employment in the SEE
countries is half that in the EU countries. Most of this
gap is due to differences in shares of real estate, renting and business activities, while the share of other
community, social and personal services in the SEE
countries does not diverge so much from the EU average. In fact, in Bulgaria and Montenegro, shares of
these services exceed the EU average. However, this
might indicate a large number of persons employed in
simple personal services and service crafts rather
than a higher share of culture/creative industries.

In line with Marxian-inspired theoretical approaches and due to the deeply rooted anthropological

Table 15.1   Internet users in SEE region

		Population (2007 est.)	Internet users, latest data	Population (penetration)	User growth (2000–2007)
	Europe	809,624,686	314,792,225	38.9%	199.5%
1	Albania	3,087,159	188,000	6.1%	7,420.0%
2	Bosnia and Herzegovina	4,672,165	806,400	17.3%	11,420.0%
3	Moldova	3,727,246	550,000	14.8%	2,100.0%
4	Serbia	10,087,181	1,517,000	14.2%	279.3%
5	Bulgaria	7,673,215	2,200,000	28.5%	411.6%
6	Croatia	4,468,760	1,472,400	32,9%	636.2.6%
7	Macedonia	2,056,894	392,671	19.1%	1,208.9%
8	Montenegro	665,734	117,000	14.8%	2,100.0%
9	Romania	21,154,226	4,940,000	23.4%	517.5%
10	Greece	11,338,624	3,800,000	33.5%	280.0%
11	Slovenia	1,962,856	1,090,000	55.5%	263.3%

Source: Inter World Stats (http://www.internetworldstats.com/) accessed on 6 April 2007

interpretation of cultures as either national or class emancipation value systems, industrial and market-oriented cultural production has been understood almost as a negation of cultural values and cultures themselves. However, cultural/creative industries have been developing as part of overall industrialization and the generalized fascination with technological innovation, although the processes that turn cultural creativity into mass industrial production have been insufficiently analysed or theoretically rationalized. Even today, the cultural economy, understood as the economic system for the production, distribution and consumption of cultural goods and services through market as well as non-market mechanisms, is far from being constituted in this region. Its economic and social role remains undefined and unclear. It may be perceived as a source of profits in the production of pop music, distribution of CDs and other video and film prints, and as a contribution to the improvement of personal services. It is also ever-more credited with the fact that it enhances individual choices in cultural consumption. Today consumers appear to be less passive and more demanding when it comes to the quantity and quickness of distribution of cultural goods. Their ever-more active response to consumption of cultural products may incite more active cultural participation, and also willingness to take part in creation or adaptation of cultural goods. The emergence of the cultural economy definitely contributes to the increased influence of consumers on cultural production. In this respect, the 'first' modernity (primary

socialist industrialization) is being overcome by the 'second'. This is visible through the influence of new technologies and their growing usage. The increased technological modernization may be a precondition for enhanced creativity, development of national and regional culture industries, and for their more efficient and diversified inclusion in global cultural production trends. The usage and presence of new technologies in cultural and creative industries may be illustrated by data on Internet users (see Table 15.1).

These numbers illustrate important differences among countries, while all of them remain quite behind the European average.

Markets and aesthetics

Markets that have developed in response to the interests of large audiences (e.g., pop music, film production, etc.) have long existed, but have not been cultivated. Diversification and cultivation of markets is a clear result of global influences, and of producers' interests in raising cultural consumption. As markets and the growing mass production have an ever-more intense influence on cultural values, the aesthetic aspects of the recent cultural industrialization should be mentioned. Mass industrial production fills the gap between high cultures and traditional, already disappearing folk cultures by introducing the usage of new technologies and by creation of new tastes that correspond to the globally spreading creative/culture industries. The role of media and of mediation of cultural values has become crucial.

All the processes that contributed initially to the development of the cultural economy have recently become more expansive. In *the aesthetic realm*, these have included the destruction of elite socialist cultures and cultivated tastes, which has particularly affected culture professionals. Cultural communication in the region has always been diversified and in modern times primarily oriented to European cultures, although it also included exchanges with African, Asian and Latin American cultures. Now it has narrowed and is almost exclusively West (USA and Europe)-focused, which has diminished the choice of aesthetic inspirations and provided for faster and deeper inclusion of local cultures in European cultural trends.

Participation in global cultural developments has become and remains mostly individual. It is exercised through cultural activities and the creativity of individual artists and culture professionals. Many individual success stories testify to the fact that the local level in aesthetic terms remains marginal and that artistic success is first recognized in global frameworks. As prominent artists and other cultural professionals join Western 'cultural circles', tastes and aesthetic influences have come ever closer to globalized art trends. They follow demand in global markets and their inspiration is decreasingly local. Collective self-reflection adjusted to artistic creativity that would be accepted by large social strata has rapidly disappeared. 'World' existential problems, combined with the nausea of individual existence has been clearly present and reflected in recent art works and trends as a concern for survival, often inspired by ecological, violent conflict, peace-building and other global issues, adjusted to the different local settings. At the same time, mass cultural production largely follows explicit global trends, such as low quality mass produced cheap love stories, popular gossip-framed novels (chick-lit), crime TV series and novels, etc.

The position of artists and cultural workers in culture/creative industries is rather diverse and ranges from work in unstable creative industries centered to local markets and state-subsidies (e.g., the book industry, films), to the position in dynamic firms oriented to global markets and branches of global media and advertising companies. Similarly, as their counterparts in Western economies, cultural workers are confined to multiple jobs and to a

diminishing of the boundaries between work and leisure. However, their position differs from their Western counterparts because of the unstable SEE economies and societies, which is reflected in low profits and fees, non-transparent and non-functioning legislatures, unregulated social status, etc. Among the most problematic issues are the unregulated intellectual property rights infringements. Lack of modern professional education and a need for better cultural management in all culture/creative industries is evident.

New interactions of the local and the global

The transition from socialism to capitalism opened up a Pandora's Box containing a non-transparent space of creative/cultural industries, cultural markets and cultural consumption. Foreign trade in cultural goods and their local production provided incentives to study cultural consumption and new cultural tastes. Audiences developed a certain contempt for many mass cultural products, but they were nevertheless easily and largely consumed. Cultural consumption and demand is gradually being standardized and strongly supported by imports. The media, and TV in particular, have been under increased pressure to adopt international formats and foreign ideas and genres. They are organizing and widening local markets by linking them into regional networks. However, regional cultural exchange and cooperation still remain rather questionable. The whole region is exposed to imports of cultural goods and cultural formats, technologies and new values and tastes, but these have not (yet) produced a regional cultural synergy. On the contrary, local societies are losing interest in neighboring cultures, which is particularly seen in the growing language and value barriers. They are all orientated to cultural consumerism and dazzled by so-called 'world culture' products. It remains to be seen whether the widening of markets and the need to connect them through networks will incite changes in regional cooperation and regional identification.

The development of cultural/creative industries is, on the one hand, dependent on national transitional states, which function with difficulty and are unable to solve efficiently most of the problems they encounter, and, on the other, it is led by transnational corporations looking for new markets and who may be ready to invest in professionalized approaches to cultural/creative productions and in standardization of tastes and cultural needs. This may appear to be the classic encounter of national states and international markets, but often it is much more that that: it is in fact the disappearance of traditions, high cultures, prevailing cultural identities, combined with rather widespread dissatisfaction with the newly introduced 'democratization', and introduction of cultural consumerism, spread and domination of low quality cultural products, misuse of cultural values and dissolution of established identities, combined with extreme liberties, absence of social solidarity and inaccessibility of the best cultural achievements.

So far local creative/cultural production remains small scale and diversified. It indicates a positive attitude to creativity, rather than consumption. Cultural production remains artistic and artisan; the fast spread and use of new technologies is mostly confined to small, often private, and dynamic firms operating in different services, book printing industries, pop music recording and distribution, etc. However, the inability to organize local markets, and connect creativity potentials by networks, marginalizes local presence in the economic and cultural life of the region. Local actors often turn to global markets where they can find a niche in the rich and diversified offering. While they try to adapt, the task of creating cultural economy as a system seems to remain with the global actors.

In a situation in which both global influences and local responses are not quite clearly defined, it is difficult to determine 'winners' and 'losers'. Are the main losers local societies whose creative potential is being drained out and largely substituted by the imported cheap trash cultural products? Are the foreign companies that control some types of cultural production and distribution, and thus open up and integrate the local media and other cultural markets, the exclusive winners or just a set of new actors enhancing cultural development in the region? Are the artists and cultural professionals, who have left their countries in order to secure a better existence and working conditions, the winners? Are local societies, forced into cultural transitions and change of cultural identities, the exclusive losers? It would be difficult to answer such questions as long as there is a hope that local responses to the newly created situation might be offered at either the national or the regional level. Such a hope would be based on an effort to integrate, to participate and to create; an effort to preserve the best parts of the cultural heritage, to introduce it to global audiences, to sustain artistic and cultural creativity that originates from specific, discernible traditions and cultures.

A (possible) participatory response

Creative/cultural industries growth in SEE has introduced and almost established the awareness that creativity may be expressed in mass industrial production which distils the values of rich and diversified cultural backgrounds and transforms them. New technologies have enabled an easy access to mass products, but their usage is restricted to limited numbers of people. Consumption nevertheless grows, and markets widen. There is a hope that small-scale cultural industries and productions could be acceptable here both economically and culturally. They would preserve the cultural diversity of the region and the co-existence of different cultural values. Such industries enlarged neighboring markets, and they thus may restore cultural links among different SEE peoples. If organized regionally, creative/cultural industries might function in cooperation and partnership with large-scale cultural industry producers and companies, which may not always be interested in developing and cultivating small, disorganized SEE markets. This would enhance solving a range of so far unsolved problems: ownership and property rights, privatization in culture, cultivation of markets, access to cultural goods, technological and economic convergence, role of the state, extremely sensitive issues of cultural identities and their reconstruction, etc.

All these and many other issues would be best approached through the elaboration of cultural policies and strategies. Currently, however, even when they exist formally, such policies are hardly practiced. If envisaged differently and actually applied, they would represent an effort to define a kind of participatory response that would have to harmonize global and local approaches to cultural/creative industries development and thus provide for cultural change that includes world, regional and local expectations.

Notes

1 Southeastern Europe denotes the region that in recent usage has inherited the name 'Balkans' (referring mainly to countries in the Balkan Peninsula), encompassing the following independent states: Albania, Bosnia and Herzegovina, Bulgaria, Croatia, Former Yugoslav Republic of Macedonia, Greece, Montenegro, Romania, Slovenia and Serbia. Four countries of the region are full members of the EU (Bulgaria, Greece, Romania and Slovenia). The region has hardly been constituted as an entity, however; its states and societies are highly diverse in historical, systemic, cultural and economic terms.

2 The 'first' or 'simple' modernization is interpreted (Beck, 1986) as a social change differentiating industrial from pre-industrial societies. The 'second' or 'late' modernization (Beck, 1986, 2001; Giddens, 1991a and b) differentiates the industrial from the post-industrial societies and opens the way to the constitution of the 'risk' society (Beck, 1986). The second modernization also introduces tolerance for alternative lifestyles, and enhances the role of creativity in production and development of culture/creative industries.

3 Cultural policies have been elaborated and published for all the countries of the region. The incentive and role of the Council of Europe in formulating such policies has been very important. However, general transitional uncertainty and the lack of national and regional development policies have largely prevented the application and implementation of the cultural policies elaborated. Cf. http://www.culturalpolicies.net.

REFERENCES

Adorno, T.W. (1991) *The Culture Industry. Selected Essays on Mass Culture.* London: Routledge.

Beck, U. (1986) *Risikogesellschaft.* Frankfurt/M.

Beck, U. (2001) *Pronalaženje političkoga Prilog teoriji refleksivne modernizacije.* Zagreb: Naklada Jasenski i Turk.

Breznik, M. (2005) 'Slovenian Publishing: Enigma of Local Cultural Industry' in *The Emerging Creative Industries in Southeastern Europe*, Culturelink Joint Publications, 8. Zagreb: Institute for International Relations.

Giddens, A. (1991a) *The Consequences of Modernity.* Stanford: Stanford University Press.

Giddens, A. (1991b) *Modernity and Self-Identity.* Cambridge: Polity Press.

Švob-Đokić, N. (ed.) (2005) *The Emerging Creative Industries in Southeastern Europe*, Culturelink Joint Publications, 8. Zagreb: Institute for International Relations.

Švob-Đokić, N. (ed.) (2004) *Cultural Transitions in Southeastern Europe*, Culturelink Joint Publications Series, 6. Zagreb: Institute for International Relations.

Tomić- Koludrović, I. and Petrić, M. (2005) 'Creative Industries in Transition: Towards a Creative Economy', in *The Emerging Creative Industries in Southeastern Europe*, Culturelink Joint Publications, 8. Zagreb: Institute for International Relations.

## CHAPTER 16

IMPACTS AND RESPONSES IN LATIN AMERICA AND THE CARIBBEAN

Ana Carla Fonseca Reis and Andrea Davis

This chapter analyses some of the principal impacts of the double-edged global sword on the multi-faceted region the United Nations classifies as 'Latin America and the Caribbean'. It will reflect upon the local impacts of globalization as regards key issues, such as intellectual property rights, the digital divide as a cultural divide, funding access and market concentration. Illustrated by practical case studies and assessments, it will explore the region's strengths and limitations vis-à-vis new trends in the global dynamics, and will look for alternative solutions and possibilities which recognize the power of cultural assets as the basis of a development strategy.

Getting started

This chapter seeks to explore how globalization affects the cultural economies of the countries that the United Nations groups together as Latin America and the Caribbean. *Global*, here, assumes that economic activities are globally integrated and work as one unit in real time, around interconnected financial markets, globally organized production of goods and services and are based on a flexible structure of nets (Castells, 2000). Except for the last item, this is particularly true of transnational cultural conglomerates, which tend to operate and transform local and regional markets into one global space, leveraged by financial resources and production that know no geographical boundary or constraint. However, as emphasized by García Canclini (2002), this process does not affect all sectors and countries evenly. Hence we see *globalization* 'not as a simple process of homogenization, but of reordering of the differences and inequalities, without suppressing them' (García Canclini, 2006: 11).

It should be stressed from the outset that no single pattern of globalization, across all cultural sectors, affects all the countries of the region in the same way. Small Latin American countries and the entire Caribbean region face the greatest obstacles in cultural fields where technical requirements and scale production are a must. This is particularly the case for the audio-visual sector, media and, in a way, music. But even in sectors where production could be more scattered yet remain viable, like publishing, heterogeneity is under threat. We shall return to this point later. This pattern of globalization has singular impacts on cultural identities, particularly as societies evolve from the multicultural to the intercultural (García Canclini, 2005) and follows the logic of transnational economies (Yúdice, 2004). Three of its characteristics can be stressed: a) the flows of production, distribution, consumption, capacity and influence overcome national borders; b) their control rests in the hands of a minority; c) the relations between economic, cultural, political and social dimensions are increasingly intricate. Assessing the impacts on culture, therefore, requires that the latter be seen not only as goods and services that embody both economic and symbolic value, but also in terms of social processes (García Canclini, 2005). And, in this logic, a redefinition of development as a multidimensional process is also required.

As we shall argue, the countries of the region have improved their socio-economic standing in recent years according to most of the standard indicators. Nevertheless, their performance is far from satisfactory. As technology speeds up the pace of decision-making and the appearance of new opportunities and as global reach breaks down geographic and industry barriers, *development* – understood as freedom and the expansion of choices (Sen, 2000) – can only be achieved if underpinned by socioeconomic, political and cultural inclusion and rights. Economic and social rights have been on the regional agenda for many years, but it was only after the end of the era of dictatorships in the 1980s that the debate was expanded to include cultural rights. However, the meanings and practice of cultural rights have not yet been broadly accepted and, as Yúdice (2004) reminds us, in most cases are not even adjudicated. The neglect of this fundamental dimension impoverishes the basis on which a broader development paradigm, one that encompasses the recognition of cultural rights, can be elaborated.

This chapter will throw light on these issues from a Latin American and Caribbean perspective. It is composed of four parts. First, it will sketch an outline of the demographic, socioeconomic and entrepreneurial aspects of the region. The second part will tackle three burning issues of globalization: intellectual property rights; the digital divide; and market concentration. A few examples on how these lemons can be turned into lemonade will also be presented, though the latter's ability to quench the regional thirst remains an open question. An assessment of the current situation weighed against future possibilities will lead us to a brief SWOT analysis of where the cultures in this region stand in the face of globalization. Finally, a few conclusions and guiding principles will be offered to policy-makers, cultural activists and development agents.

Latin America and the Caribbean – a cultural patchwork

Every culture is born of mixture, encounter, confrontation. It is isolation that leads to the death of civilisations.

Octavio Paz

Latin America and the Caribbean comprise a fascinating patchwork of cultures, consisting of no less than 33 countries, besides smaller islands and *départements* of the French Republic.[1] Since the nineteenth century, efforts at regional unification in the Caribbean have been on the political agenda. Most attempts have resulted in failure, including the short-lived Federation of the British West Indies, which collapsed in 1961.

From the ashes of this failed political venture emerged, in time, a free trade arrangement (CARIFTA in 1968), a common market (CARICOM in 1973), and in the case of the smaller countries a confederal and functional cooperation apparatus (the Organization of Eastern Caribbean States – OECS – in 1981). Currently, there are three concentric circles of integration in the region, each with points of contact and relevance with the others. The most tightly drawn integration outfit, the OECS, constitutes the innermost concentric circle. CARICOM, under the revised Treaty of Chaguaramas of 2001, with its quest to fashion a single market and economy, is the next concentric ring. Outside of this is the Association of Caribbean States (ACS), a grouping of Caribbean countries and those from Latin America bordering the Caribbean Sea, which focuses its functional integration thrust in the areas of trade, transportation, tourism, and technology.[2]

As a general rule, Latin American and Caribbean cultures are still treated as peripheral by the rest of the world and, regrettably, individual countries within this grouping also have little knowledge of one another. If information and statistics are sometimes hard to obtain at a country level, regional data and debate are far from being abundant. Nevertheless the region is linked by common historical and cultural factors such as a history of colonization, Spanish-Portuguese Catholic values mingled with Indian or African religions and, in the second half of the twentieth century, dictatorships and/or civil wars that devastated many countries. In addition these countries have had to deal with the hegemonic influence of the United States in the region. All this has led to a cultural orientation pointing outwards, first to Europe then to the United States. Miami seems to be not only a hub for most internal flights in Latin America and the Caribbean, but also a symbolic economic and cultural hub. This feeling of insularity and distance despite geographic proximity poses the first challenge in dealing with a regional approach to globalization.

A few attempts to reverse this situation deserve mention. Aiming to foster cultural and commercial exchanges internally, the Latin-American Parliament – Parlatino – was created in 1964, comprising 22 permanent members (including four from the Caribbean).[3] Regional agreements, such as Mercosur, CAN (Andean Nations Community), CARICOM (Caribbean Community), ALADI (Latin American Integration Association) and SICA (System of Centro-American Integration), focus mainly on commercial aspects, such as taxation and free movement of goods and services and only secondarily on social issues. Culture is barely mentioned.[4] Even in the realm of Mercosur, where a few audio-visual co-productions and festivals[5] have surfaced, the lack of priority given to culture in individual countries was, in the words of Mota da Silva (2007), 'multiplied by four and flew into the immense emptiness that characterizes the so-called Cultural Mercosul'.

In a world where regional blocks expand the sense of belonging beyond national boundaries and commercial trade is leveraged by the strength of a small group of countries, a fundamental point is therefore to understand how globalization can help people in the region learn more about its cultures and identities so that it can successfully showcase itself to the rest of the world.

Let's start from an overview of the region through a number of basic indicators. Taken as a whole, the region does not score badly in terms of GDP, which reached US$2.332 million in constant market prices (dollars of 2000, CEPAL 2006). However, the numbers are mostly dominated by Brazil (US$689 million), Mexico (US$666 million) and Argentina (US$340 million), which altogether make up 72.3 per cent of the total. The average annual growth rate was 5.3 per cent in 2000, with huge disparities on a country-to-country basis, from 2.8 per cent (Brazil) to 10 per cent and above (including Venezuela, Dominican Republic, Trinidad and Tobago). According to CEPAL-STAT, the statistical department of the Economic Commission for Latin America, and the Caribbean, the total population of the region was 576 million people in 2006 and is likely to reach 783 million by 2050. Considering that Mexico and Brazil account for 58.1 per cent of the regional GDP and 42.3 per cent of the population, two background questions emerge: first, the imbalance in cultural production in the region. Media concentration is easy to see in the prevalence of soap operas produced in Brazil (Rede Globo), Mexico (Televisa) and Venezuela (Grupo Cisneros). Secondly, the tenuousness of minority cultures in the individual countries.

Though figures are declining, the *Social Panorama of Latin America* (ECLAC, 2006a) indicates that in 2005, no less than 209 million people (39.8 per cent of the population) lived in poverty, of whom 81 million (15.4 per cent) were in *extreme poverty*. The percentage of mean shortfall from the poverty line (the magnitude of poverty, as the result of multiplying the proportion of people who live below the poverty line by the difference between the poverty line and the average income of the population living under the poverty line) is 3 per cent.[6]

In terms of illiteracy, disparities again abound, with highs (Nicaragua, Guatemala, Honduras, Haiti) and lows (Barbados, Trinidad and Tobago, Guyana, Uruguay, Argentina and Chile). On average, the illiteracy rate of populations aged 15 years and over reached 9.5 per cent in 2005. Though declining (11.1 per cent in 2000), this still significant figure poses two sorts of problems. First and more urgently, those less qualified remain in a vicious circle of lower wages, and therefore have little chance to improve their qualifications – especially in the so-called knowledge economy. Second and more importantly, as technologies rapidly evolve, illiterates today are likely to become victims of the digital divide – leading eventually to a cultural divide.

Immigration is another fundamental vector of the way Latin American and Caribbean cultures are perceived around the world. The millions of legal and illegal immigrants in the United States and Europe exceed 10 per cent of the population of many countries, from Mexico to Uruguay. 'Latin America is not complete in Latin America' as García Canclini puts it (2002: 19); neither is the Caribbean. The first wave of Caribbean migration to the UK in the 1950s and 1960s was followed by the exodus of the 1970s and 1980s to the US and Canada which have resulted in strong second, third and now fourth generation niche market strength in these transnational spaces.

Though the presence of transnational conglomerates is massive, the business structure in Latin America and the Caribbean is very much based on micro, small and medium-sized enterprises. In *Mexico* these represented in 1998 no less than 99.7 per cent, out of which 7 per cent were classified as being related to culture.[7] In *Brazil*, the number of micro and small, private, formal, urban

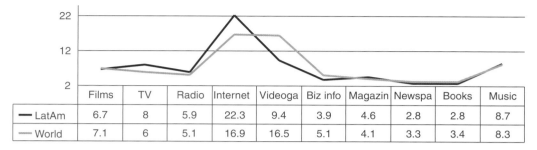

	Films	TV	Radio	Internet	Videoga	Biz info	Magazin	Newspa	Books	Music
— LatAm	6.7	8	5.9	22.3	9.4	3.9	4.6	2.8	2.8	8.7
— World	7.1	6	5.1	16.9	16.5	5.1	4.1	3.3	3.4	8.3

Figure 16.1   Entertainment and media market growth 2005–09, compound annual growth rate (%)

Source: PriceWaterhouseCoopers, 'Global Entertainment and Media Outlook, 2005–2009'

companies reached 99.2 per cent in 2002. However, this number is quadrupled if we add the micro and small enterprises operating in the informal economy and in rural areas.[8] Two main issues need to be tackled in this situation: distribution, as will be discussed later; and access to funding, particularly when the value of intangibles (such as culture) is still hard to prove.[9] As for the cultural market, a PriceWaterhouseCoopers global report (2005) states that developing countries will be the main driver of global spending growth in the entertainment and media market in the coming years. It projects astounding growth in all of the entertainment and media sectors in the period 2005–09, such as filmed entertainment (6.7 per cent compound annual growth rate, to US$2.2 billion) and television networks (8 per cent, the fastest rate of all regions, totaling US$7.2 billion). In Latin America alone (the Caribbean is not assessed) this market will total US$47 billion in 2009, up from US$32 billion in 2004, advancing at a compound annual rate of 8.2 per cent.[10]

The most promising sectors for the global industry of entertainment and media are expected to be Internet, music, TV and radio, where regional growth is estimated to be higher than the global average (see Figure 16.1). The digital music business continues to grow as trade revenues in 2006 doubled to about U$2 billion – around 10 per cent of total sales which is expected to reach 25 per cent of global sales by 2010 according to IFPI Chairman and CEO John Kennedy.[11] The chief winner in the rise of digital music has been the consumer, who can access 24-hour music stores with unlimited shelf space offering content in new formats from downloads to video to ringtones. The long held view that the

knowledge economy is the future means that countries will be more reliant on creative industries for employment, tax revenues, foreign exchange earnings and economic growth.[12] Today there are some 500 legitimate online music services in over 40 countries including two new sites launched in Brazil in 2006 with Terra and UOL joining the established Imusica, bringing to 20 the number of websites offering legal downloads in the country.[13]

Sweetening the lemonade: action and reaction

What happens to those cultures which, because they are excluded from globalisation, lose what they had of local content? Not only do they no longer have economic and social bases; they also lose meaning.

Néstor García Canclini (2002: 87)

One of the commonly acknowledged positives of globalization is assumed to be its demolition of the geographic barriers between ideas, values and cultures, turning the world into a plural, multicultural landscape. But is this really so? Three phenomena would seem to contradict this optimistic image of a democratic, united world. First, the legal framework of intellectual property rights, which limits access to information and cultural expressions to those who can afford it. Suffice it to remember García Canclini's words that cultures flow and mingle much more easily than our legal frameworks permit: '... in the days of the internationalization of national cultures, when you were

Table 16.1 IIPA estimated trade losses due to copyright piracy (in US$ millions) and estimated levels of copyright piracy

	Records and Music		Motion Pictures		Entertainment Software		Books
	Losses	Levels	Losses	Levels	Losses	Levels	Losses
PRIORITY WATCH LIST							
Argentina	69.5	60%	318.0	90%	NA	NA	4.0
Chile	22.7	51%	10.0	35%	NA	NA	1.0
Costa Rica	18.3	60%	2.0	100%	NA	NA	NA
Dominican Republic	10.8	75%	3.0	89%	NA	NA	1.0
Mexico	376.5	65%	483.0	62%	137.7	75%	42.0
Venezuela	33.0	83%	30.0	63%	NA	NA	NA
WATCH LIST							
Brazil	334.5	52%	101.0	22%	120.8	77%	18.0
Colombia	47.7	71%	41.0	75%	NA	NA	6.0
Ecuador	26.3	90%	NA	NA	NA	NA	2.5
Peru	66.0	98%	12.0	63%	NA	NA	9.0
SPECIAL MONITORING							
Paraguay	128.0	99%	2.0	86%	NA	NA	2.0

Source: 'IIPA 2007 "Special 301" Recommendations', www.iipa.com

not satisfied with what you had, you could find an alternative elsewhere... Nowadays what's produced in the entire world is right here and it is difficult to know what is our own'.[14] Second, trade and access are increasingly tied to the digital – a language still unknown to most Latin American and Caribbean people who are now threatened by the digital divide, following their exclusion from the knowledge economy (Reiss, 2006). Third, concentration in distribution prevents free circulation of cultural products, even when the barrier of IPR is overcome and the digital divide is bridged. Though this phenomenon is not exclusive to this region, the lack of recognition of the importance of culture as a cross-cutting dimension for socioeconomic inclusion and development increases national vulnerabilities to global trends.

Globalization, culture and IPR

The first problem faced in Latin America and the Caribbean is that IPR legislation proposes a monolithic approach to culture, without taking into consideration traditional or collective knowledge and creations (see Chapter 4 above). Six years after it first met, the WIPO Intergovernmental Committee on Intellectual Property and Genetic Resources, Traditional Knowledge and Folklore (2001), was still discussing a draft provision against misappropriation and misuse of traditional knowledge.[15] Indeed, the current approach to IPR is incomprehensible to many people in the region to whom it is inconceivable that communally owned cultural knowledge or technology could now be registered as intellectual property. Thus from the perspective of those who aim to protect traditional knowledge, an open market in cultural goods and services is a double-edged sword. But even in the more commercial arena, 70 per cent of Spanish publications are exported to Latin America, while only three per cent of Latin American publications flow the other way. So Spanish publishers now decide which Latin American writers are read in Latin America (García Canclini, 2002), just as five or six majors decide on the sorts of audio-visual and music products that circulate in the region. There is a strange kind of freedom of choice in this system where regional production is strangled in the distribution arena before it reaches the market and recovers costs, while doors are wide open to all sorts of Northern products, which are well paid with IPR.

The problem is not restricted to registration. The current IPR framework also excludes from knowledge consumption those who cannot afford the prices fixed by transnational conglomerates. And there's nothing

Box 16.1   A new business model

In the Amazonian state of Pará, in Brazil, a parallel economic model has emerged. The so-called 'Tecnobrega' (Technotacky) uses the sales of CDs not to boost the copyrights paid to the artists, but as a sales tool. Piracy? Who cares! In this new system, CDs are sold through street vendors, at prices way below the market average (around US$1). As a result DJs, bands and singers are increasingly called on to give live performances. Who benefits from this? Everybody: the public, who pays less for a CD; the artists, who have a busy calendar; the owners of nightclubs, constantly full; the vendors and all the connected economic sectors. The crucial point here is, therefore, that alternative models to the current universe of copyrights may not only be possible, but also profitable.[16]

that authors and creators can do about it, as is daily experienced by professors who cannot make copies of their own writings to give out to their own students (no wonder Creative Commons and other initiatives are becoming so popular in the region).

This leads the debate to another burning issue: piracy. In the absence of more neutral data, it is useful to explore the figures provided by the International Intellectual Property Association, a private coalition formed in the interest of US copyright-based industries (see Table 16.1). Six Latin American countries were classified as 'priority watching countries' in 2005–06 (the Caribbean is not assessed by the Association). Piracy of records and music is higher than 50 per cent in all countries, reaches up to 89–100 per cent in motion pictures (Dominican Republic, Argentina and Costa Rica) and 75–77 per cent in entertainment software (Mexico and Brazil).

According to the International Federation of Phonogram and Videogram Producers (IFPI) more than one third of audio products purchased around the world are pirated goods valued at approximately U$4.5 billion in 2005, when pirate CDs outnumbered legitimate CD sales in 30 markets. Online, nearly 20 billion songs were downloaded illegally in 2005.[17] Latin America and Caribbean digital markets are still in their infancy, limited by low broadband penetration, resistance to online credit card use and high levels of piracy (Brazil and Mexico were included in the IFPI's top 10 priority countries in 2006).[18] The court victory of IFPI over Kaaza, the biggest international brand name in music piracy until July 2006, signals a new legal landscape for digital music as courts act to protect Intellectual Property Rights.[19] It is hard to avoid wondering what kind of piracy is more harmful: that based on illegal copying or the form that allows corporations to register, trade and exclude traditional people who produced that very cultural knowledge.

Box 16.2   Fighting illiteracy and the information divide

First there are the illiterates (9.5 per cent in the region). Then come the 'functional illiterates', incapable of interpreting a text. Not by chance, they live mainly in the poorest areas of the region. They provide the perfect setting for innovative solutions. Each day, 175 bikers carrying 70 books pay a visit to 16 cities with low HDI (Human Development Index) and reach a total of 4375 families in Brazil. They are the *Reading Agents*, sons of those very cities who receive a minimum but fundamental wage to read, make books available and organize roundtables of regional storytelling in those families. Using the book as an instrument to promote human development, results prove very positive. One year after it started, children who had difficulties or no interest in books at school developed a real taste for reading.

There is a similar initiative in Colombia, where four years ago a teacher started taking 80 books across the mountains, using Alpha and Bet, his two donkeys. Targeting mainly the indigenous populations, his walking library works on the weekends, lending books from Saturday to Saturday.[20]

Photo 16.1   Agentes de leitura

The knowledge economy and the digital divide

In the knowledge economy, literacy is a pre-requisite to access social, economic and cultural participation. However, formal education and literacy alone no longer guarantee a place in the 'age of access' (Rifkin, 2001). Digital literacy and Internet access are also required. Digital exclusion not only restricts access to information and the consumption of cultural goods circulating in digital media and on the web, it also limits the ways in which distribution channels for cultural products and services (such as printed books and digital music) can be explored. Further, it erases the Long Tail Effect (Anderson, 2006), by which a large number of relatively small titles can jointly make up a significant market. Finally, it reduces the freedom of cultural creation based on multimedia platforms, which represents a low-cost production, compared to traditional studios. Meanwhile, the digital music market alone expanded in 2005 to approximately 5 per cent of music industry sales

(1.4 per cent in 2004) and estimates indicate a sky-rocketing increase to 24 per cent by 2009.[21] In spite of the region's musical wealth, only two of its countries ranked among the 20 top markets in music sales (physical and digital) in 2005: Brazil (10th place) and Mexico (11th).[22]

The first issue is Internet access. In December 2006, the Latin American and Caribbean Regional At-Large Organisation (LACRALO) signed an agreement with the Internet Corporation for Assigned Names and Numbers (ICANN), becoming the first official regional association of Internet users. According to the Internet World Stats, compiled in Table 16.2, in January 2007 Latin America and the Caribbean had around 89 million Internet users (with 5 million in the Caribbean), representing a 16 per cent penetration, or 8.1 per cent of the Internet population in the world (for 8.5 per cent of the population). More importantly, it reached a usage growth of 391 per cent between 2000 and 2007. Though Brazil has the highest number of users (23 million, or 13.9

Table 16.2   World internet usage and population statistics

World Regions	Population (2007 est.)	% of the world population	Internet usage, latest data	Penetration (% population)	Usage % of world	Usage growth 2000–07
Africa	933,448,292	14.2%	32,765,700	3.5%	3.0%	625.8%
Asia	3,712,527,624	56.5%	389,392,288	10.5%	35.6%	240.7%
Europe	809,624,686	12.3%	312,722,892	38.6%	28.6%	197.6%
Middle East	193,452,727	2.9%	19,382,400	10.0%	1.8%	490.1%
North America	334,538,018	5.1%	232,057,067	69.4%	21.2%	114.7%
Latin America/ Caribbean	556,606,627	8.5%	88,778,986	16.0%	8.1%	391.3%
Oceania/Australia	34,468,443	0.5%	18,430,359	53.5%	1.7%	141.9%
WORLD TOTAL	6,574,666,417	100.0%	1,093,529,692	16.6%	100.0%	202.9%

Source: www.internetworldstats.com

Notes: Internet usage and world population statistics were updated on 11 January 2007.
Demographic (population) numbers are based on data contained in the *world-gazetteer* website.
Internet usage information comes from *Nielsen//NetRatings*, the *International Telecommunications Union*, local NICs and other sources.

per cent of the population), penetration rates are more significant in Barbados (59.8 per cent), Chile (42.4 per cent), Jamaica (39.4 per cent) and Argentina (34 per cent).[23]

The importance of boosting Internet access was already recognized in the Millennium Development Goals.[24] However, while the focus is on the number of personal computers made available, mobile phones may be a complementary instrument to promote digital access, thanks to the fast pace of convergence. As the handset revolution continues, cell phones play an important role in developing the mobile market with audio/video supported handsets becoming the norm. The move to convergence was boosted in early 2007 when Apple made its iPhone available to consumers initially in the US, Europe and Asia. Among mobile phone providers, a dedicated Xpress Music brand will be complemented by a Nokia music store and FM radio as part of their objective to be the market leader in digital music distribution in the next five years.[25]

The hope that digital inclusion may prove more efficient via mobile is supported by the estimates of Wireless World Forum, predicting that over 50 per cent of Latin Americans would own a mobile by the end of 2007,[26] Brazil alone representing the fifth largest mobile population in the world.[27] The second obstacle to digital participation at global level is language, as English is by far the dominant language on Internet pages. As a consequence, most of the information circulating on the web is not understandable to most users.

Diversity at risk – oligopoly and the distribution bottleneck

According to an old UNESCO report, 'by the end of 1998 the flows of trade in cultural goods are unbalanced, heavily weighted in one direction with few producers and many buyers. There are great structural disparities both within and between the various regional trading blocks'.[28] Disparities forecast by UNESCO could be shown in terms of both trade numbers and content. While developing countries imported cultural contents (printed matter, literature, cinema and photography), they exported fast moving goods with no symbolic value (radios, televisions, sporting goods and games). Eight years later, Latin America and Caribbean countries rose from a meager 1.9 per cent to a still insignificant 3.0 per cent of the international flow of cultural goods and services. Not surprisingly, then, Latin American movies are not available in Europe, nor is much Caribbean music heard in Asia and Trinidad and Tobago's famous carnival remains unknown in the United States. Though cultural production is vibrant in Latin America and the Caribbean, its products hardly ever reach mainstream audiences in the rest of the world – as a general rule

Box 16.3   Jamaica's reggae music

The case of Jamaica's reggae music demonstrates the simultaneous vibrancy of the creative product coupled with the inadequate management, which has characterized its organic internationalization over the past 50 years. Reggae music emerged as a genre out of the creative expression and experience of Jamaica's marginalized underclass. It was shaped by the socioeconomic conditions of the newly independent colony inspired by the philosophical movement of Rastafari and exported by small to medium enterprise labels such as Studio One and Island Records and icons like Bob Marley, Jimmy Cliff and others. The first wave of the music's internationalization resulted from the migration of countless Jamaicans, first to the UK and then to the US and Canada in the 1960s and 1970s. These migrants traveled with their homegrown music on vinyl to play at pubs and community dances.

Illustration 16.1   International Reggae Day Festival poster

According to a World Bank Report, 'The Jamaican music industry can significantly widen the range of economic opportunities to individuals and enterprises alleviating problems of unemployment, especially for the large population of Jamaican youth and generate foreign exchange earnings on a sustainable basis'.[29] Despite the global appeal of reggae music, Jamaica has yet to benefit from the potential value added as talent continues to be exploited by external third parties primarily through licenses and artist deals, with 8–14 per cent royalty deals and distribution controlled by overseas middlemen or majors.

Recognized as an evergreen, most strategic music labels own some amount of reggae catalogue, which they periodically repackage and reissue to a new generation of the market. The major independent labels which have distributed the majority of Jamaican music in the past 25 years are New York-based VP Records and London-based Jet Star Records which, although owned by Jamaican migrants, the profits do not directly benefit the Jamaican economy. Despite the proliferation of music studios, the Jamaican music industry still lacks the strength of record company structures required to operate a value-added industry business model. With the advent of digital distribution however, Jamaica could develop a model for the export of cultural products.

Small economies of scale, fragmentation, lagging access to technology and limited institutional capacity require a government policy designed to enable and regulate, where necessary, for a sector based on intellectual property, sensitive to the role of capital, level of risk, institutions required for growth and market dynamics.[30]

Table 16.3 Recorded music sales (retail) – US$ millions

	2002	2003	2004
Brazil	387.7	320.5	374.2
Argentina	35.4	62.8	83.9
Central America	28.3	22.8	21.2
Colombia	63.5	52.5	48.5
Paraguay	0.9	0.7	1.9
Uruguay	1.5	2.9	4.6
Mexico	395.2	331.2	360

Source: IFPI (2005)

Table 16.4 2004 repertoire origin (per cent of music market value, excluding multi-artist product)

	Domestic	International	Classical
Argentina	40%	56%	4%
Brazil	74%	23%	3%
Central America	–	98%	2%
Chile	25%	70%	5%
Colombia	31%	67%	2%
Ecuador	–	98%	2%
Mexico	43%	55%	2%
Uruguay	41%	58%	1%

Source: IFPI (2005)

it does not even circulate in the region, Jamaican music being the exception. An absence of distribution networks causes a growing bottleneck restricting the circulation of Latin American and Caribbean cultural products.

The link between the distribution bottleneck and market concentration is direct. However, not all sectors are affected in the same way. Concentration has increased over the past years in Latin America. In the media field the biggest press conglomerate holds 61 per cent market share in Uruguay and 32 per cent in Colombia, while the main TV channel controls 54 per cent of the market in Brazil and at least 30 per cent in nine other countries.[31] In book publishing the illusion that Latin American authors now reach global markets, based on the presence of a few known names (Paulo Coelho, García Marquez) obscures the fact that it is increasingly difficult for unknown or new authors to get published in their own countries. A similar situation prevails in the audio-visual sector. Given the relatively high costs of production, most countries in Latin America and the Caribbean have difficulty in producing films, as suggested in Luciano Álvarez's *The House with no Mirrors*, which reflects on audio-visual production in Uruguay. The situation in the music sector is particularly enlightening, as can be seen in Tables 16.3 and 16.4. In 2004, recorded music sales in Argentina totaled US$83.9 million and US$374.2 million in Brazil.

However, with the exception of Brazil, where domestic songs represented 74 per cent of the market, in all other countries the domestic repertoire ranged from 25 per cent to 43 per cent. This picture is especially worrying as the four majors (Sony BMG, Warner, Universal and BMI) control 70 per cent of the global market (IFPI).

Box 16.4 IBERMEDIA – promoting audio-visual production of Ibero-American countries

Because of the difficulties of the audio-visual sector, Ibermedia Fund was created in 1997 and ratified by Argentina, Bolivia, Brazil, Chile, Colombia, Cuba, Mexico, Panama, Peru, Puerto Rico, Portugal, Spain, Uruguay and Venezuela. Aiming to solve the bottlenecks in capacity, development, co-production, distribution and promotion, Ibermedia focuses on independent producers and distributors in member countries, establishing specific criteria for access to funding and other activities. In the case of co-production, for instance, all productions are required to be in Portuguese or Spanish; the director, screenwriter, composer, main actors and technical crew also have to be sourced from these countries. In the first six years of Ibermedia's existence, the number of co-productions between Spain and Latin America almost tripled (from 59 to 164).[32]

Box 16.5 Alternative distribution channels

The Tortilleria Editorial, in Mexico, offers another interesting parallel economic model. It works as a kind of underground resistance, created by a group of authors, either professionals or beginners, who felt they did not have any decision-making power when negotiating with publishing houses. In March 2007, the Editorial consisted of 237 authors, sharing 3860 texts on the web. Each is free to print and sell their works and those of the other authors of the project, paying and receiving no copyright for the texts.[33]

Another interesting initiative is Papaya Music, a consortium of musicians, producers and researchers, based in Central America. They focus their works on traditional popular composers, mixed with contemporary performers and sound names and offer an alternative distribution channel to local productions.[34]

It is important to keep the problem of media concentration in the spotlight, as the media not only influence people's world views and mental makeup, filtering information and knowledge, but they also have the power to keep populations informed, or uninformed (Solanas and Vazquez, 1997). Public television in Latin America is not that common and, when it exists, is constantly torn between the imperatives of commercial feasibility and political independence. On the other hand, private channels such as Televisa (Mexico), Globo (Brazil) and Cisneros (Venezuela) have a dominant presence. The decisions on what should be seen therefore depend on a limited number of players, who tend to favor commercial, mainstream productions. Innovation, in an oligopoly, is not a very popular concept.

Where are we in this tiny global world?

It remains to be seen who will be the poor people who continue to contribute to this enrichment and who will be the ones relegated to the passive role of simple consumers of cultural goods. To have or not to have the right to creativity, that is the question.

Celso Furtado (1984: 25)

Having reviewed the weaknesses and strengths of Latin America and Caribbean cultures in the face of globalization we turn our attention now to the opportunities and threats presented (see Table 16.5). With very few exceptions (mainly Chile), there is a historical lack of continuity of public policies and political will in the region. This obviously does not favor the

Table 16.5 Strengths, weaknesses, opportunities and threats

STRENGTHS	OPPORTUNITIES
Cultural diversity/richness	Regional integration
Flexible mindset/creativity	Mobile penetration as a tool for digital inclusion
SMEs	Digital revolution globally
Good examples of successful practices	Convention on Cultural Diversity
Name recognition and brand appeal	Culture as a hook for reviewing development
	Intersectorial linkages
WEAKNESSES	**THREATS**
Weak policy-making	Lack of continuity of public policies
Low education and digital level	Lack of political will
Low export rates of cultural products and services	Lack of recognition of culture as crosscutting
Language (mainly Portuguese/Spanish)	Enforceable international agreements in the
Lack of regional or national statistics	digital realm
High concentration of majors	Digital exclusion
Inadequate distribution control	

Box 16.6   Swimming against the tide – Manos del Uruguay

Photo 16.2   Manos del Uruguay (Hands of Uruguay)

Manos del Uruguay ('Hands of Uruguay') is a cooperative business created in 1968, with a mission to provide traditional artisans with stable incomes and give them the opportunity to live off their production in their original communities. The main problem was the lack of distribution channels, either in the country or abroad. It now employs 100 people and houses 350 producers scattered across 39 communities. Manos' products, made from natural raw materials and strongly identified with their countries of origin, are traded in a chain of stores, established in the poshest areas of Uruguay and also available in Paris, Tokyo and New York.

implementation of long-term strategies. In addition, there is no clear view of culture as a cross-cutting dimension, intimately connected with education, tourism, foreign affairs and the economy. Complementarily, digital exclusion is at the door and finally, enforceable international or bilateral agreements may take a leap in the coming years, superseding the concerns with cultural diversity.

On the other hand, regional integration could propel internal production and market growth, providing better economies of scale and putting Latin America and the Caribbean in a more balanced position *vis-à-vis* the international flow of cultural goods and services. Also, mobile penetration rates are paving the way for a new platform of digital inclusion and the ratification of the *Convention on the Protection and Promotion of the Diversity of Cultural Expressions* provides hope that individual countries will be more empowered to implement cultural policies. Finally, as the importance of culture as a carrier of values, as an economic sector and as a crucial factor for social and political inclusion becomes clearer, the whole concept of development requires revision – including the role that culture plays in the process.

Recommendations and guidelines

Globalization is a double-edged sword, promoting or sweeping away cultural diversity and intensity, depending on how ready a country or region is to face it. In the case of Latin America and the Caribbean, even though civil society and local entrepreneurs have been resourceful in coming up with innovative solutions, public policy is still a significant issue in this debate. Our final words have therefore to be directed to policy-makers.

First, no progress can be made in dealing with globalization unless culture is recognized as a fundamental ingredient of any development strategy. This involves the promotion of synergies between cultural policy and areas such as education, tourism, economy, international affairs and environment. Second, a macroscopic approach to the integrated value chain will favor a balance between cultural production, distribution and consumption, a fundamental step in the promotion of sustainable development. After all, as Yúdice (2004) has observed, taking the public into account is a novelty in Latin American cultural policy, focusing up to now on production while neglecting distribution. Third, producing statistics that illuminate the current state of our cultural production and diversity is key to guiding the planning process in the long term, which would include the funding of micro and small and individual enterprises; the promotion of dialogue with civil society and the private sector, changing a paradigm of corporate involvement with culture from philanthropy to business opportunities; and the fostering of programs such as co-productions, designed to break down cultural barriers in the region. This intertwined perspective will lead to the creation of alternative markets and distribution channels, emphasize the need to assure digital inclusion and generate awareness of the need to adjust the current legal IPR framework.

Notes

1   Following ECLAC's statistics, available data for *Latin America* includes 20 economies: Argentina, Bolivarian Republic of Venezuela, Bolivia, Brazil, Chile, Colombia, Costa Rica, Cuba, Dominican Republic, Ecuador, El Salvador, Guatemala, Haiti, Honduras, Mexico, Nicaragua, Panama, Paraguay, Peru and Uruguay. The *Caribbean* includes 24 economies: Anguilla, Antigua and Barbuda, Aruba, Bahamas, Barbados, British Virgin Islands, Cayman Islands, Cuba, Dominica, Dominican Republic, Grenada, Guadeloupe, Haiti, Jamaica, Martinique, Montserrat, Netherlands Antilles, Puerto Rico, Saint Kitts and Nevis, Saint Lucia, Saint Vincent and the Grenadines, Trinidad and Tobago, Turks and Caicos Islands, and United States Virgin Islands.

2   Citation from a speech entitled 'An appropriate regional governance framework for promoting growth and balanced development in the Caribbean in the twenty-first century', an Address given by Dr. The Honourable Ralph E. Gonsalves, Prime Minister of St. Vincent and the Grenadines, to the Caribbean Forum for Development at Barbados sponsored by the Caribbean Group for Cooperation and Economic Development, 6 May 2005.

3   www.parlatino.org.

4   This is obvious from an examination of the declared purposes and the list of activities and agreements published on the sites www. mercosur.int, www.comunidadandina.org, www.caricom. org, www.aladi.org and www.sica.int.

5   See Florianópolis Audiovisual Mercosul, http://www.oma. recam.org.

6   http://mdgs.un.org/unsd/mdg/Host.aspx?Content=Data/ Trends.htm.

7   The Competitive Intelligence Unit.

8   SEBRAE, based on IBGE and INCRA.

9   *PyMEs de la Cultura: el Desafío de la Competitividad.*

10 The audited countries are Argentina, Brazil, Chile, Colombia, Mexico and Venezuela. The report claims to cover 99 per cent of the total spending in the global entertainment and media marketplace. No Caribbean country is considered.

11 'Digital Music in 2007 – A Brave New World', John Kennedy, IFPI (2007: 3).

12 Digital Market Overview in 2006, IFPI (2006: 7).

13 Digital Market Overview in 2006, IFPI (2006: 8).

14 García Canclini (2006: 32).

15 As published on WIPO's site in April 2007.

16 For detailed information on how Tecnobrega works, please refer to www.overmundo.com.br, a site which is another great example of how to generate alternative business models and to Ronaldo Lemos (2005).

17 'The Many Faces of Music Piracy', IFPI (2006: 4).

18 'The Many Faces of Music Piracy', IFPI (2006: 3).

19 'Progress Against Pirate Operations', IFPI (2007: 20).

20 www.secult.ce.gov.br and www.senderos.gov.co/ experiencias/Articulos/133/Default.aspx.

21 Crédit Suisse (2006).

22 IFPI (2005).

23 www.internetworldstats.com/stats.htm.

24 Goal 8, target 18: 'In cooperation with the private sector, make available the benefits of new technologies, especially information and communications.' Indicator 48: 'Personal computers in use per 100 population and Internet users per 100 population.'

25 'Music on Mobile Grows in Popularity', IFPI (2007: 10).
26 Latin America Datasheet, May 2006.
27 www.w2forum.com.
28 *International Flow of Selected Goods and Services 1980–1998*, p. 3.
29 Compton and Allgrove (1995: 2).
30 Davis (2001: 3) Jamaican Entertainment Policy, Ministry of Tourism and Industry.
31 Becerra and Mastrini (2006).
32 www.programaibermedia.com.
33 http://tortilleria.vientos.info.
34 www.papayamusic.com.

REFERENCES

Anderson, Chris (2006) *The Long Tail – Why the future of business is selling less of more*. New York: Hyperion.

Becerra, Martín and Mastrini, Guillermo (2006) *Periodistas y Magnates – Estructura y concentración de las industrias culturales en América Latina*. Buenos Aires: Prometeo.

Bourne, Compton and Allgrove, S.M. (1995) World Bank Report: 'Prospects for Exports of Entertainment Services from the Caribbean: The Case of Music'. Office of Planning and Development, University of the West Indies.

Castells, Manuel (2000) 'La Ciudad de la nueva economía'. *La Factoría*, 12 Junio–Septiembre. www.lafactoriaweb.com/articulos/castells12.htm.

CEPALSTAT – Estadísticas de América Latina y el Caribe, http://websie.eclac.cl.

Crédit Suisse (2006) *Global Music Industry 'Just the two of us'*. Equity Research.

Davis, Andrea M. (2001) *Jamaican Entertainment Policy*, Kingston, Jamaica: Ministry of Tourism and Industry.

ELAC (Economic Commission for Latin America and the Caribbean) (2005) 'Anuário estadístico de América Latina y el Caribe'.

ELAC (Economic Commission for Latin America and the Caribbean) (2006a) 'Social Panorama of Latin America'.

Furtado, Celso (1984) *Cultura e Desenvolvimento em época de crise*. Rio de Janeiro: Paz e Terra.

García Canclini, Néstor (2006) *Consumidores e Cidadãos*. (6th edition) Rio de Janeiro: UFRJ.

García Canclini, Néstor (2005) *Diferentes, Desiguais e Desconectados*. Rio de Janeiro: UFRJ.

García Canclini, Néstor (2002) *Latinoamericanos buscando lugar en este siglo*. Buenos Aires: Paidós.

García Canclini, Néstor and Piedras Feria, Ernesto (2006) *Las Industrias Culturales y el Desarrollo de México*. Mexico, DF: Siglo XXI Editores.

IPFA (International Federation of Phonogram and Videogram Producers) (2005) *The Recording Industry in Numbers*.

IPFA (International Federation of Phonogram and Videogram Producers) (2006) *The Recording Industry Piracy Report, Protecting Creativity in Music*.

IPFA (International Federation of Phonogram and Videogram Producers) (2007) *Digital Music Report*.

Lemos, Ronaldo (2005) *Direito, Tecnologia e Cultura*. Rio de Janeiro: Editora FGV.

Mota da Silva, Denise (2007) *Vizinhos Distantes – Circulação cinematográfica no Mercosul*. São Paulo: Annablume.

PriceWaterhouseCoopers (2005) *Global Entertainment and Media Outlook 2005–2009. Global Overview*. 6th Annual edition.

Reis, Ana Carla Fonseca (2006) *Economia da Cultura e Desenvolvimento Sustentável – o caleidoscópio da Cultura*. São Paulo: Ed. Manole.

Rifkin, Jeremy (2001) *The Age of Access – The new culture of hypercapitalism, where all of life is a paid-for experience*. New York: Tarcher.

Sen, Amartya (2000) *Development as Freedom*. New York: First Anchor Books Edition.

Solanas, Facundo and Vazquez, Mariana (1997) *Mercosur: Estado, economía, comunicación y cultura*. Buenos Aires: UBA.

UNESCO, 'International Flows of Selected Cultural Goods and Services 1994–2003'.

Yúdice, George (2004) *A Conveniência da Cultura – Usos da cultura na era global*. Belo Horizonte: UFMG.

## CHAPTER 17

THE LOCAL CREATIVE ECONOMY IN THE UNITED STATES OF AMERICA
Margaret Jane Wyszomirski

The US cultural economy itself exhibits multiple models of cultural interaction and experiences many of the tensions that accompany the increasing globalization of culture. However, creative economy initiatives in the US are concentrated at the local level and are taking shape without the benefit of central government leadership, support, or linkage as they are in most other countries. Instead, an informal network consisting of key national professional associations representing local officials as well as national and international scholarly groupings shares knowledge, models and emergent policy tools. Furthermore, the policy impetus tends to come from the non-profit arts community. It requires the development of a new paradigm that accommodates not only the subsidized arts, but also the commercial cultural industries, avocational arts activities and diverse cultural heritages.

Fundamental debates on the following issues are therefore reviewed and synthesized in this chapter: the characterization of related products or goods (i.e., cultural, creative or artistic); the determination of the component parts of the 'creative economy' and the conceptualization of the structure and inter-relationships of the whole (i.e., economy, clusters, or sector).

Other countries often regard the entertainment industries of the United States as a culturally homogenizing and imperialistic force (Isar, 2000). The popular culture goods that America produces in the form of film, television, recorded music, video games, publications, and Internet content has become the nation's leading export. The cultural industries are one of the fastest growing sectors of the American economy. The success of American popular culture industries is attributed to a number of 'natural advantages' – the large and diverse American domestic market, an infrastructure of global distribution channels, production in the English language which is the new lingua franca of the global economy, a cultural integrative capacity that comes, in part, from the immigrant composition of the population.

As cultural globalization proceeds apace, other countries are seeking to capitalize on similar natural advantages and thus become more competitive with the US. For example, over the past decade, the English-speaking nations of the United Kingdom, Australia and Canada have all pursued extensive creative industry development. India's Bollywood not only plays to a large domestic market but is exported to the Indian diaspora around the world. China also has a large domestic market and is seeking to develop its creative industries as both an economic and a diplomatic goal. The European Union has provided incentives for media co-production among its member states and to promote such cultural products within its regional, common market.

The obvious hegemonic effect that American entertainment industries exert internationally often obscures the fact that they are only part of the

American creative economy. Another large and important segment is composed of the subsidized or non-profit arts and culture fields. The United States has a long tradition and an exceptionally large set of civil society institutions in the arts and culture. These include both professional 'high' or elite arts organizations as well as informal institutions that are either community-based or amateur. Over the past half century, this segment of the American creative economy has grown, diversified, and dispersed domestically through a public–private policy partnership that amounted to industrial development of the subsidized arts. Today the commercial and subsidized arts industries are being reconceived as two different but inter-acting parts of the American creative economy.

Thus, the US creative economy itself exhibits multiples models of cultural interaction and experiences many of the cultural tensions that have become evident with the increasing globalization of culture. Mass and elite cultural elements both compete and interact as well as follow specific industrial trajectories. Hybrid cultural content and products both challenge and invigorate the preservation of traditional cultural heritages. Professional artistic creativity and presentation co-exist with a lively amateur, emerging, and pluralistic involvement. Spectator and consumerist relations between arts industries and their market are experiencing an outburst of interactive and participatory involvement that blurs old disciplinary and industrial boundaries while taking advantage of new technological capabilities.

John Hartley (2005: 5) argues with regard to the case in the UK that 'the idea of the creative industries seeks to describe the conceptual and practical convergence of the creative arts… with the Cultural Industries… in the context of new media technologies within a new knowledge economy…'. The flow of this concept along with its translation into policy attention and initiatives around the world, including the US, is another example of cultural globalization. For the United States, the ideas of the creative industries and the creative economy facilitate the repluralization of local cultural policy as each city, state or region seeks to employ the arts and culture in creating its own image and identity. Not every city can be home to a concentration of a commercial entertainment industry. But every city can, and is, home to a particular mix of creative industries and cultural heritages. In other words, each local creative economy can become 'a culture of cultures' (Isar, 2000: 36). Creative economy initiatives in each community allow them to shape their particular 'glocal' responses to cultural globalization pressures and opportunities. Furthermore, most local creative economy initiatives in American localities are feasible only because they can build on the capacities and support systems of the subsidized arts while also drawing on the knowledge and networked resources of national and global talent, presentation, and distribution networks as well as an infrastructure of local ethnic communities, professional associations, public–private funding, and education and training institutions.

In many other countries the impetus for local creative economy initiatives is spurred by public leadership from the national level. This is not the case in the US. Instead, a loosely linked policy community that is also internationally networked has mobilized to design and formulate cultural policies to advance the creative industries, the creative workforce, and to employ cultural development initiatives in community and economic development efforts. American creative economy initiatives can exhibit the entire range of Crane's (2002) models of cultural globalization. Between popular and high culture realms, one may observe a cultural imperialist model where the political interests of commercial entertainment industries seem to overpower those of the subsidized and traditional arts. Cultural capitals like New York City, Los Angeles and San Francisco might be said to exhibit a cultural flow or network model where cross-fertilization is dynamic. Many communities, large and small, display a multicultural reception model. And finally, given this range of concurrent models, there is a common layer of the negotiation and competition model that operates in each locality – one that is often mediated by the local arts agency or the local economic development association.

Much has been written about the American entertainment industries. Similarly, much has been written about the development and public policy support for the subsidized arts. The object here is not to recapitulate this knowledge. Rather it is to understand how cultural policy, prompted by a 'glocal' impulse, has been using the concept of the creative industries to both bridge the heretofore separate domains of the entertainment (cultural) industries and the creative arts field at the local level.

In the United States, policy action regarding the creative economy is concentrated at the local level. An ad hoc series of local and regional initiatives, combined with scholarly interest across a number of disciplines and fields, has informally been developing a conceptual framework, refining a mapping methodology, and gaining field experience without the benefit of federal leadership, support or linkage. Nationally, these dispersed experiences are coalescing into common knowledge, shared modeling and emergent policy through the activities of national professional associations representing local officials and interest as well as through national and international scholarly networks. This chapter is interested in examining how this informal and loosely linked policy community is effecting the evolution of policy-making regarding the local creative economy.

A second focus of this chapter seeks to explain how the subsidized arts fit into the evolving cultural industries and creative economy discourse. Current interest in and initiatives concerning local creative economy policy tend to come from the subsidized arts community and from state and local arts agencies that provide public funding for these arts activities. This is contrary to the situation in many other countries, where the impetus behind creative industry policy tends to come from and focus on the cultural industries. Thus, to understand the dynamics of this policy-making process and its influence on policy substance, it is necessary to explore how the preceding economic impact approach both sets the stage for and differs from the creative economy conceptualization. Furthermore, it is helpful to understand how both policies to prompt and document economic impact of the arts as well as to develop and harness the creative economy for local development fit into the larger frame of cultural policy.

A third theme of this chapter is to understand how local cultural policy initiatives concerning the creative industries and the creative economy fit into the different cultural policy paradigm taking shape in the United States. Key characteristics of this emergent paradigm are:

- a loosely coupled intergovernmental system;
- a broadened definitional scope that encompasses the full spectrum of arts, entertainment, and heritage activity; as well as
- a multiplicity of issues beyond public arts funding;
- diversity in policy goals and instruments; and
- a general shift of policy initiative and innovation to the state and local levels.

Clearly, local creative economy policies epitomize each of these new paradigm characteristics. Local arts interests have taken the lead in exploring the implications of a broadened definition of 'the arts', in pushing creative economy research as a tool for policy planning and decision-making, and in pursuing the link between the arts, creative cities, the creative class, the creative economy and community development.

Residue of the old public patronage paradigm and the economic impact approach

Two deep-running attitudinal streams in the American political culture carry suspicions of cities and of artists. This may help explain why American cities have only recently come to establish public arts agencies on a widespread basis. Continuing advocacy efforts have been necessary to the process of establishing a local cultural policy infrastructure of agencies, laws, funding sources and positive political awareness. Federal support for developing a capacity to conduct and use economic impact of the arts information and arguments was a key component of this local advocacy activity. Between 1976 and 1981, the NEA embarked on a concerted effort to lead and fund the development of useful and credible arts impact studies (NEA, 1981: 5). During this period, the NEA research division supported a five-year series of projects, meetings, case studies, and research reports designed to develop a common methodology primarily for use at the local/city level. It involved the participation of academic researchers from the fields of economics and urban planning, leaders of arts institutions in at least six communities, and a national advisory committee of national service associations[1] (Cwi and Lyall, 1977; NEA, 1981).

By the mid-1980s, the basic form and methodology of arts impact had become fixed and was to be widely replicated across the country. Two characteristics are of particular relevance to this discussion:

1. The definition of the arts was usually confined to non-profit arts organizations and a multiplier was used to estimate total economic impact of these institutions.
2. Economic impact studies of the arts were used primarily for arts advocacy efforts with the principal purpose of improving the effectiveness of arguments for increased financial support for public arts agencies and with private institutional funders (Radich and Foss, 1987: 78).

In addition to articulating the composite economic impact of non-profit arts and cultural institutions in a particular locale, these studies also developed other arguments and strategies for how the arts affected the economies of cities. Harry Chartrand (1987: 8–9) identified three additional impact strategies: *arts centers* drew suburban and tourist audiences into the city and increased neighborhood property values; *concentrations of artists* living in a particular area often helped gentrify it; and artistic facilities and activities serving as *positive amenities* were often a positive factor in industrial (re)location decisions. Commissioning and funding public art projects and programs were a fourth way to create new positive amenities for communities. For example, the NEA and the General Services Administration (GSA) commissioned a total of nearly 800 pieces of public art in an effort to enhance public spaces and buildings, thus adding a valuable amenity asset to each site. In some cases, the public artwork went on to become an important feature of a city's identity and image.

By the early 1990s, undertaking economic impact studies had become so common among cities, countries and other local jurisdictions that the National Assembly of Local Arts Agencies (NALAA) undertook the first national effort to conduct simultaneous and comparable economic impact studies among a number of local communities and to use this information and an input/output model to estimate the national economic impact of the arts (NALAA, 1992). Arts impact studies continue to be undertaken to the present day and have been endorsed by the national service organizations that represent state and local arts agencies as well as major performing arts institutions (NASAA, 2005; PARC, 2004). The National Assembly of State Arts Agencies (NASAA) published a 'best practices' workbook for its members on how to conduct an economic impact study (Barsdate, 1997). NALAA, now known as AFTA (Americans for the Arts) repeated its national, multi-community impact study in 2002 and 2007 with the number of participating communities increasing from the original 33 to 91 to 151 cities, counties and regional groupings (AFTA, 2002; 2007).

We can now see that three decades of public arts funding policy (approx. 1965–95) successfully stimulated the expansion and professionalization of the non-profit arts organizations and their coalescence into specific artistic fields nationally. As the spatial distribution of individual organizational members of these fields developed and matured in communities across the nation, art fields became the non-profit analogues of industries and local collections of non-profit arts organizations became proto-industrial clusters. In the long term, economic impact studies helped to demonstrate the de facto industrial development of the subsidized arts.

But there was also criticism of arts impact studies and advocacy. Economists and policy analysts complained that the arts impact approach had 'little or no public policy utility... [since]... no evidence exists that the studies ever have been used or were even designed to be used by the sponsoring agencies as an aid to their own decision-making (Cwi, 1987: 106–7). Calling them 'a fashionable excess', economist Bruce Seaman argued that economic impact studies of the arts were '...focusing on the wrong issues using an inappropriate tool, and perhaps reaching false conclusions' (1987: 44). Furthermore, the successful use of arts impact studies as an advocacy tool of the public funding paradigm made it difficult for creative economy initiatives to argue that its associated information gathering and mapping activities were credible for planning and policy-making. This duality can be seen in the fact that AFTA is concurrently and quite separately conducting and reporting on two different cultural economics projects: arts impact and creative industries.

The emerging creative economy paradigm and local cultural policy

The development of a policy environment receptive to the idea of creative industries and a creative sector was necessary before operational definitions and research efforts could acquire traction and interest outside the academic community. As long as arts policy remained focused on professional non-profit arts organizations and disconnected from other branches of cultural policy activity, more expansive and inclusive notions of a creative economy fell on deaf policy ears. However, three developments in the mid-1990s began to reset the stage.

1. The scope of the 'cultural wars' that raged during the first half of the 1990s demonstrated that a large range of arts and cultural phenomena were experiencing similar challenges and controversies. Charges that creative goods and services generated negative public impacts because they involved pornography, blasphemy, obscenity and excessive violence were leveled across the arts spectrum, from high to popular art (Wyszomirski, 1995). Thus, previously 'silo' industries and fields across the creative economy discovered that they *faced a common political threat*.
2. The 1980s and 1990s were a period in which national administrations of both Democrats and Republicans pursued *a general policy of decentralization, devolution and reinventing government*.

This general policy tide affected arts and cultural policy both directly and indirectly. The historic budgetary growth trajectory of the NEA stopped, went into decline, then was dramatically reduced. Meanwhile, the combined total of state arts appropriations continued to grow. The intersection of these two trends slowly shifted the balance of power and initiative within the intergovernmental cultural policy system away from the federal level (DiMaggio, 1991a) and to the state and local levels (Lowell and Ondaatje, 2006).

Thus as the decade of the 1990s advanced, these developments led toward creative economy initiatives at the local level. General decentralization shifted greater responsibility for economic policy toward the subnational levels as governors and mayors sought to adapt their communities to the changing economy (Strom, 2003). Concomitantly, economic development agencies began to identify distinct industrial clusters of the emerging knowledge and global economies as investment targets. Meanwhile, local arts communities had at once the resources, the incentive, and their experience with arts impact arguments to advance the case for the arts as an economic development tool. In aggregate, the arts enjoyed more public funding and higher agenda status at the subnational levels, particularly as cities sought ways in which to promote their economic competitiveness, project a 'cool image', and improve their quality of life.

3. *Two seminal national arts policy reports* published in 1997 argued for a fuller spectrum consideration of the arts. The *Creative America* report from the President's Commission for the Arts and Humanities (PCAH), noted that 'In the United States, amateur, non-profit and commercial creative enterprises all interact and influence each other constantly' (PCAH, 1997: 2). It refers to this larger phenomenon as 'the cultural sector'. It asserted that '… the future vitality of American cultural life will depend on the capacity of our society to nourish amateur participation, to maintain a healthy non-profit sector, and to encourage innovation in commercial creative industries' (1997: 4).

The second national report was issued by American Assembly, a non-partisan convener on issues of important national policy. A diverse group of public and private leaders '…defined the arts inclusively – in a spectrum from commercial to not-for-profit to volunteer, resisting the conventional dichotomies of high and low, fine and folk,

professional and amateur, pop and classic' (American Assembly, 1997: 5). It went on to argue that 'all three parts of the arts sector contributed in major and varying ways, to [the] public purposes…', pointed out 'opportunities that could dynamically increase the arts sector's capacity to achieve public purposes…' and offered recommendations on how public and private policies could '…help artists and artistic enterprises both to meet public purposes and to flourish' (1997: 7).

These reports helped cultivate a public perception that the three parts of the cultural economy – the commercial, popular arts and entertainment industries: the professional, subsidized 'high' arts; and a pluralist set of ethnic/informal/amateur arts – could be seen as part of a single conceptual entity. The language of this broadening policy framework now focuses on ideas such as the creative class, the cultural/creative economy, creative and/or cultural industries, the arts and social capital, public value of the arts, how the arts can play a role in city image-building and branding. Such language indicates a fundamental change in policy thinking about the arts and culture – from a resource-poor, cost-diseased sector in need of subsidy, to a set of community assets that can be engines of local development. Furthermore, it inherently expands and links thinking about the subsidized arts with other, related concerns such as creative and knowledge workers, with the entertainment industries, and with the generation of public goods and purposes. In other words, it expands the horizons of cultural policy from a narrow concern with the arts as specific and privileged manifestations of culture, to an awareness of the arts as part of a larger 'signifying system' involved in the production of social meaning in the form of texts and symbols (Hesmondhalgh, 2002: 11–13; Williams, 1981: 11).

Key debates about the creative economy

The shift from an advocacy-based concern with the economic impact of the arts to a policy and planning approach to developing the creative economy is occurring without the benefit of national political leadership. Instead, ideas, information and initiatives are percolating in local, regional and epistemic communities. In turn, these are circulating through the national cultural policy community and beginning to take a discernible shape. A consensus is emerging that the issue of developing the local creative economy is high on the local policy agenda and that it has the potential to reshape the arts and cultural policy

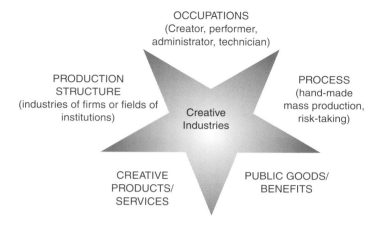

OCCUPATIONS
(Creator, performer,
administrator, technician)

PRODUCTION
STRUCTURE
(industries of firms or fields of
institutions)

PROCESS
(hand-made
mass production,
risk-taking)

Creative
Industries

CREATIVE
PRODUCTS/
SERVICES

PUBLIC GOODS/
BENEFITS

Figure 17.1 Creative industries: definitional approaches

arena because it necessitates forging a truly working coalition across the arts and cultural spectrum. Currently, movement towards a creative economy policy coalition at the sub-national level must contend with four main lines of definitional debate:

1. how to characterize the grouping of related products or goods (i.e., cultural, creative or artistic);
2. how to operationalize the composition of the 'creative economy;
3. how to characterize the structure and inter-relationships of the whole (i.e., economy, clusters or sector), and
4. how to characterize and measure the outcome of cultural development initiatives.

The first three topics of debate will be discussed further. The fourth topic concerning the character and outcome of cultural development initiatives is still at a formative stage and is too big and diverse a subject to treat here (Wyszomirski, 2005).

Definitional Debate #1: Characterizing the overall grouping
The debate over the characterization of the overall grouping finds proponents of both the cultural and creative labels arguing that each term is too inclusive. Some note that being 'creative' is not limited to artistic activities but rather is also manifest in science, technology and even entrepreneurial business activities. Richard Florida has been criticized for such over-breadth in his work on the 'creative class' which 'boils down to those who have received higher education whether or not they are actually doing creative work

and excludes all creative workers without degrees' (Markusen et al., 2006: 5). From this perspective, the cultural economy is the artistic component of a larger creative economy (which still others refer to as the knowledge economy, the information economy, or simply the new economy).

Conversely, others find the term 'cultural' too broad, particularly in its anthropological meaning as encompassing a whole way of life: material, intellectual and spiritual. Under such a definition, cultural phenomena would include not only aesthetic creativity, but other symbol/meaning activities like religion, sports and language. This concern is evident in the San Diego Foundation report on arts and culture which noted that it had adopted 'an expansive, inclusive definition of art and culture... [which] includes high or fine art as well as popular, ethnic, and commercial arts... [but did] not encompass cultural forms such as religion or the environment' (2006: 8). From this perspective, creative is the preferable definitional label with the creative economy being part of a more diffuse cultural realm (Caves, 2000; Mercer, 2001; Wyszomirski, 2003). Both perspectives seem to have rejected the alternative of 'the arts' as simply too narrow.

Definitional Debate #2: Determining inclusion and measuring the dimensions
At the operational level, debate often presumes different criteria for determining what is 'similar' and thus the basis for deciding what is and is not considered to be included in the collectivity. Surveying relevant literature, policy and practice, five definitional approaches come into play. These are illustrated in Figure 17.1 and concern:

Table 17.1   Core vs total copyright industry dimensions

	Earning	% of GDP	# of employees	% of domestic workforce
Core copyright	$819B	6.56%	5.38M	4.03%
Total copyright	$1.38T	11.12%	11.3M	8.49%

Source: Siwek (2006)

1. Products and services
2. Production structures
3. Occupations
4. Key production processes
5. Public goods and benefits.

Analysts typically build off one definitional perspective, then refine this perspective and derive measures for the parameters of the creative economy by reference to other definitional characteristics (see Figure 17.1).

A common starting point to determine similarity and relatedness focuses on products and services and quickly implicates production structures. For example, a 1997 report on the arts in the New England economy defined the creative cluster as 'those enterprises and individuals that directly and indirectly produce cultural products' (Wassall and DeNatale, 1997). In 2000, Richard Caves defined creative industries as those that supply 'goods and services that we broadly associate with cultural, artistic, or simply entertainment value' (2000: 1). In contrast, a 1999 study of Portland, Oregon, focused on the creative services industry noting that these combined design, technology and communications and thus included a cluster of industries and freelancers in advertising, public relations, film and video, design, multi-media and software, and closely related fields. (Scruggs et al., 1999: 19). The 2005 report on 'Creative New York' defined core creative industries as those 'in which the creative element is central to both the cultural and economic values of what they produce... and included both businesses and individuals involved in all stages of the creative process – conception, production and initial presentation...' (Center for an Urban Future, 2005: 6).

Different definitional starting points can result in dimensions that vary significantly. For example, the International Intellectual Property Association (IIPA) publishes a biannual report on the contribution of the copyright industries to the US economy (Siwek, 2006). In this research, the copyright industries (*firms*) are defined as those whose primary task is to produce copyrighted materials (*products*) including

newspapers, periodicals, books; recorded music and music publishing; business and entertainment software; radio and TV broadcasting; and motion pictures. Information on the set of 'core' copyright industries is augmented by an estimated portion of other industries offering products and/or services both up-stream and down-stream in the production chain such as the 'partial copyright industries' (essentially applied design in fashion, jewellry, apparel, etc.); 'copyright distribution industries' (e.g., cable TV, transportation, satellite communications); and 'copyright distribution industries' (e.g., hardware such as computers, radio and TV receivers). This definitional suite is then used to determine dimensions such as earning, per cent of GDP, employment and wages, foreign sales and exports. The difference between looking at only the core or the total set of copyright industries is substantial (see Table 17.1).

Note that the copyright industries approach presents a distorted picture of creative workers because it counts everyone who works in the copyright industries, whatever their specific job responsibilities. This industrial definition also omits the non-profit art fields, as well as mixed fields like theater (both Broadway and non-profit) and visual arts (museums, galleries and auction houses). In addition, public goods and services are largely left out of this picture.

Studies focused in the non-profit arts have tended to begin with an organizational definition which expands and contracts according to local context. Despite strong disciplinary field identities that aggregate at the national level, at the local level, a multi-disciplinary collection of non-profit enterprises produce a group of aesthetic and heritage products and services called 'the arts'. Few cities are home to clusters of artists and non-profit arts enterprises large enough to be considered an 'industry'. Thus, for most cities and regions, the key indicator of their arts 'industry' is non-profit, professional arts organizations. This, in turn, implies that products and services in the live performing arts and in particular genres of visual, literary and musical arts are part of an industrial group of 'similar' products called 'the arts'.

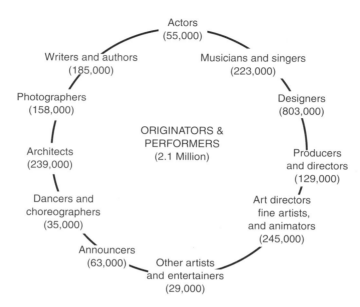

Figure 17.2   Aristic workers: NEA/BLS model
Source: Nichols (2005)

Increasingly both states and city policy-makers are recognizing that any definition of the creative industries must include both non-profit and commercial enterprises. NASAA observed that state arts agencies 'use a variety of terms – arts, culture, creative, or heritage – to describe economic development efforts' concerning the creative economy. Furthermore, NASAA notes that 'Depending on each state's or region's distinctive characteristics, the creative sector may include human, organizational, and physical assets in the performing arts, visual arts, crafts, folklife, culinary arts, science, technology, film design, architecture, history, humanities, popular culture, the natural environment and more.' (NASAA, 2005: 1). Clearly this is a very elastic definitional approach. On the one hand, it maximizes flexibility and ability to contextualize the identification of local cultural assets. On the other hand, such variability hinders the development of a broadly and commonly accepted definitional framework that facilitates comparability and might build toward a national model of American creative industries.

Since 2000 and noticeably since 2004, at least 14 states have undertaken creative economy initiatives with another half dozen focusing on cultural tourism programs. Virtually all of these initiatives begin with research to inventory the state's creative assets and subsequently develop a variety of programs designed to develop creative districts, the creative

workforce, or clusters of creative industries. Often spearheaded by the state arts agency, the state department of development and/or economic growth, the department of trade and commerce or the governor's office, efforts to develop the creative economy may employ community improvement grants, tax incentives, loans, technical and small business assistance, while also creating benchmarks as well as data-gathering and assessment tools like the Creative Vitality Index (Washington state), the New England Cultural Database, and the Cultural Economic Development Online Tool (CEDOT-Michigan) (NASAA, online, May 2007).

Other researchers approach the definitional task from a combined occupational and employment perspective. For over 20 years, the Research Division of the National Endowment for the Arts has been releasing reports on the artistic workforce using data collected by the Bureau of Labor Statistics (BLS) (Nichols, 2006). BLS defines the artistic workforce as comprised of 11 occupational groups drawn from the later category of 'professional speciality occupations' (which also include engineers, scientists, clergy and lawyers). The 11 artistic occupations and the size of the workforce in each is indicated in Figure 17.2. The combined total finds 2.1 million individuals who were employed as artists as their primary job. Note that these figures capture selective and incomplete information on creative workers such as administrative staff of arts organizations and businesses, arts edu-cators and technical workers. It is also widely believed that, because of collection methods, the BLS figures are likely to produce an undercount in many of the 11 artistic occupations that it focuses on. Recent occupational studies have brought new insights to what Ann Markusen calls 'the impover-ished view of the arts and its role in the regional economy' by focusing on artists rather than on arts organizations (Markusen and King, 2003: 3; Markusen et al., 2004; Markusen et al., 2006). She argues that a focus on arts organizations tends to omit or seriously under-estimate the economic con-tribution of individual artists as entrepreneurs, small businesses and contract workers. Another recent study found that 28 per cent of the New York creative workforce is self-employed or works on a freelance basis, thus accounting for a significant component of that city's creative economy (Center for an Urban Future, 2005). Markusen demonstrated that artistic dividends such as value added design activities, touring and export sales outside the community, and supplemental income and public value generation are often omitted from measures of the creative economy. She notes the example of Seattle, where an organizational approach found that only 14 per cent of local performing artists were full-time employ-ees of arts organizations, thus missing both the direct economic effects and the artistic dividend of 86 per cent of the artistic workforce.

The production structure approach is often combined with a product dimension. That is, an orga-nization that presents symphonic music is an orches-tra. The product and the production structure are regarded as virtually synonymous. Perhaps the most challenging definitional approach involves a consid-eration of public goods which are notoriously difficult to identify or to collect information about. With the extensive activities of the multi-state public value pro-ject, this dimension is coming into sharper focus (Moore and Moore, 2005). Furthermore, as creative city initiatives start with the assumption that arts and culture have a substantial effect on city image and quality of life, they are implicitly recognizing some of the public goods, social capital, and public value that the creative/cultural economy produces. Increasingly analysts are coming to agree that cultural goods and products are generally characterized by an unusually high expressive meaning and value in comparison to utilitarian functional value. Many would also concur that the communicative value of cultural products can serve a range of purposes: entertainment, education,

aesthetic, escapism and identity. Historically, different types of cultural products tended to be associated with different expressive value and hence were regarded as dissimilar. This dissimilarity, in turn, con-stituted the basis for separation into different indus-tries and fields. For example, popular culture is mass produced by the media industries of film and broad-casting and valued as entertainment. In contrast, traditional culture and folk arts tend to be hand-made by heritage artisans and are valued for their commu-nication and embodiment of cultural and community identity. Alternatively, the fine and 'high' arts focus on cultural products of high aesthetic quality that are created, presented and preserved by specialized, professional institutions that operate on a patronage, rather than a market-based, financial model. Increasingly, the measurement of the creative economy is moving toward a layered approach that incorporates multiple definitional approaches (Wyszomirski, 2004: 10).

Definitional Debate#3: Characterizing the interrelation of the parts

A third point of contention centers on how to charac-terize the several components of the whole and how the parts interrelate. The most frequently used terms seem to be industry(ies), cluster, sector and econ-omy. Compare the following definitions:

A *Field* is an area of activity, subject or profession; an arena of common purpose where organizations are part of an institutional life where they are con-nected by having the same consumers, being regu-lated by the same agencies, and by producing the same products... [as a recognized area of institu-tional life, a field includes] key suppliers, resource and product consumers, regulatory agencies, and other organizations that produce similar services or products (DiMaggio, 1991b: 64). (Tends to be used with reference to non-profit art fields such as dance, orchestras, museums, etc.)

An *Industry* is a group of related firms supplying a given type of product or service. An *industrial sector* is a group of related industries supplying a given type of product or service. (Tends to be used with refer-ence to commercial art industries like film, entertain-ment, music business, etc.) Hesmondhalgh's (2002) definition of the cultural industries emphasizes the *key production process*, arguing that creative/cultural goods that do not employ an industrial production process – like theater, contemporary crafts, painting – should be classified as 'peripheral' activity rather than as core creative/cultural industries. In other words, a

Table 17.2   A comparison of creative industries typologies

Classification Model	NEC (2000) Clusters (7)	AFTA Business Sectors (6)	Creative NY Industries (9)
	Applied Arts (Architecture; advertising; photography; crafts; graphic, industrial, interior, and webdesign)	**Design**	**Applied Design Advertising Architecture**
	Performing Arts	**Performing Arts**	**Performing Arts**
	Visual Arts	**Visual Arts and Photography**	**Visual Arts** (Incl. dealers and museums)
	Literary Arts	**Publishing**	**Publishing** (books, newspapers and periodicals)
	Media (broadcasting, cable, film, music)	**Film, Radio, TV**	**Film and Video Music Production Broadcasting**
	Heritage	**Museums and Collections**	–
	Advocacy and Support (education, cultural councils, funders)	**Art Schools and Services**	**Other** (Independent artists, writers, performers)

cultural industry is not simply a group of related firms producing similar goods or services, but these firms must produce their goods through an industrial manufacturing process.

A *cluster* shares the following characteristics: closely related product lines (e.g., musical performance and recorded music), shared markets (e.g., museum members and patrons of art galleries), and common resource needs (e.g., actors who work in both non-profit and commercial theatrical venues) (NEC, 2000). 'Surrounding the core cluster of industries... is a rich infrastructure of public and private entities that both supports and benefits from the existence of a vital creative economy' (NEC, 2001: 6). (Tends to be used in describing geographic concentrations of particular industries or fields.)

A societal *sector* includes all organizations within a society supplying a given type of product or service together with their associated organization sets: suppliers, financiers, regulators and the like (Scott and Meyer, 1983). 'The full range of activities from ideas, to primary creation, production distribution and consumption along with ancillary functions such as management, accountancy, legal services, promotion, marketing, etc... as well as informally organized infrastructures of knowledge and expertise... that includes cultural intermediaries and cultural entrepreneurs' (O'Connor, 2000).

Table 17.2 displays a side-by-side comparison of three classification schemes of the creative economy in the United States. All include both non-profit as well as commercial arts and culture activities. Note that each scheme tends to create aggregate categories that encompass a set of fields or industries into industrial sectors. Although there is some variation in how these groupings are constituted and labelled, there is considerable agreement across the three classification schemes. Implicitly, all the classification schemes seem to treat fields and industries as roughly equivalent, thus declining to treat the *key production process* definitional variable as determinative. To the extent that identified industrial sectors also include any support services, ancillary functions or soft infrastructure elements, each industrial sector could be considered a cluster. Putting all the industrial sectors together plus identifying a common set of support, ancillary and infrastructure elements would constitute a societal sector or a model of the overall creative production system. Of course, few cities would exhibit the entire creative sector of the economy. Rather each city will display particular clusters and have the potential to develop some other clusters.

It is also important to notice what is not included in these classification schemes. None recognizes the informally structured parts of the non-profit arts – those

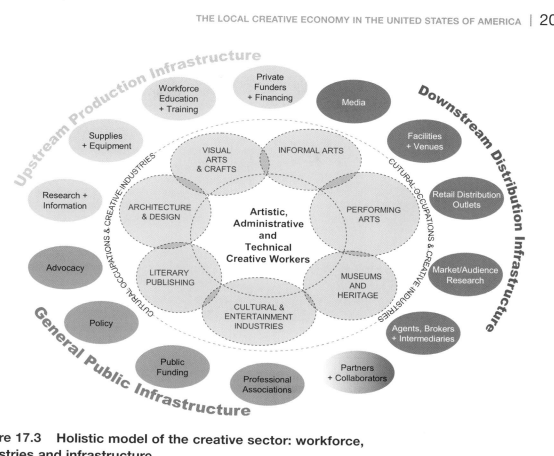

Figure 17.3   Holistic model of the creative sector: workforce, industries and infrastructure

that are volunteer managed, community-specific, and/or amateur. While these 'informal arts' may account for only a small economic component of the creative economy, they provide a significant proportion of the public goods provided by the arts. Unlike the copyright industries classification model mentioned earlier, most local creative industry inventories do not account for distribution activities like movie theaters, video and CD stores, bookstores or presentation venues. Similarly, providers of supplies and equipment for the creative industries are seldom evident. A range of other services and support systems are also missing. These include financial support; policy, legal and advocacy services; professional and trade associations; education, training, and workforce development providers; media and communication services; or research and information systems. Omitting many of these activities may be justified when establishing an economic classification system for measuring the size,

location, productivity and variety of the creative economy. However, if one is mapping the production, delivery and preservation system that propels the creative economy for policy and planning purposes, then including distribution, equipment, workforce development and other support systems are essential components.

Figure 17.3 tries to synthesize these classification schemes plus account for what was omitted to construct a holistic model of the creative sector.

A few concluding thoughts

As noted at the outset, current policy thinking about the creative economy in the United States is part of an emergent policy paradigm characterized by notable differences from the twentieth-century model of public funding patronage of the arts. Indeed, implicit policy experimentation, customization and learning are dispersed among many local communities while conceptual integration and modeling is being shaped by a loosely linked policy community that is both domestically and internationally networked. The resultant explicit policy knowledge is then used by other communities to formulate their own creative economy initiatives and to build a broad public awareness of the role of the arts in the new economy of the twenty-first century. In contrast to the previous cultural policy paradigm, current creative economy initiatives at the local level demonstrate not only a 'glocal' impetus but an inherent recognition of the public value of the arts in the forms of cultural identity, city image and quality of life.

Notes

1   The advisory committee included representatives of the US Conference of Mayors, the National league of Cities, the National Governors' Conference, the National Assembly of State Arts Agencies, and the National Assembly of Community Arts Agencies.

REFERENCES

American Assembly (1997) *The Arts and the Public Purpose: Final Report of the 92nd American Assembly*. New York: American Assembly, June.

AFTA (Americans for the Arts) (2002) *Arts and Economic Prosperity: The Economic Impact of Nonprofit Arts Organizations and Their Audiences*. Washington, DC: AFTA.

AFTA (Americans for the Arts) (2007) *Arts and Economic Prosperity III: The Economic Impact of Nonprofit Arts Organizations and their Audiences*. Washington, DC: AFTA.

Barsdate, Kelly J. (1997) *Measuring Your Arts Economy: Twelve Questions and Answers About Economic Impact Studies*. Washington, DC: National Assembly of State Arts Agencies.

Caves, Richard E. (2000) *Creative Industries: Contracts between Art and Commerce*. Cambridge, Mass: Harvard University Press.

Center for an Urban Future (2005) *Creative New York*. New York: Center for an Urban Future, December.

Chartrand, Harry Hillman (1987) 'The Economic Value of Economic Reasoning and the Arts', in A.J. Radich and S. Schowoch (eds.) *Economic Impact of the Arts: A Sourcebook*. Denver, Colorado: National Conference of State Legislatures, May.

Crane, Diana (2002) 'Cultural Globalization from the Perspective of the Sociology of Culture', paper presented at the Symposium, *Statistics in the Wake of Challenges Posed by Cultural Diversity in a Globalization Context*, UNESCO Institute of Statistics, Montreal, 21–23 October.

Cwi, David and Lyall, Katharine C. (1977) 'Issues in Developing a Model to Assess the Community-Wide Economic Effects of Cultural Institutions', in David Cwi (ed.) *Research in the Arts: Proceedings of the Conference on Policy Related Studies of the National Endowment for the Arts*. Baltimore, MD: Walters Art Gallery in cooperation with the Johns Hopkins University Center for Metropolitan Planning and Research. pp. 54–9.

Cwi, David (1987) 'Economic Impact Studies', in A.J. Radich and S. Schwoch (eds.) *Economic Impact of the Arts: A Sourcebook*. Denver, Colorado: National Conference of State Legislatures, May. pp. 77–110.

DiMaggio, Paul (1991a) 'Decentralization of Arts Funding from the Federal Government to the States', in Stephen Benedict (ed.) *Public Money and the Muse*. New York: W.W. Norton.

DiMaggio, Paul (1991b) 'Constructing an Organizational Field as a Professional Project: U.S. Museums, 1920–1940', in Paul DiMaggio and William Powell (eds.) *The New Institutionalism in Organizational Analysis*. Chicago: University of Chicago Press.

Hartley, John (ed.) (2005) *Creative Industries*, Oxford: Blackwell Publishing Ltd.

Hesmondhalgh, David (2002) *The Cultural Industries*. London: SAGE Publications.

Isar, Yudhishthir Raj (2000) 'Americans in the Global Maze: Perils, Powers and Possibilities', in *Going Global: Negotiating the Maze of International Cultural Interactions*. Proceedings of the 2000

Barnett Symposium on the Arts and Public Policy. Columbus, OH: Ohio State University-Arts Policy & Administration Program. pp. 31–9.

Lowell, Julia F. and Heneghan Ondaatje, Elizabeth (2006) *The Arts and State Governments: At Arm's Length or Arm in Arm?* Santa Monica: Rand Corporation.

Markusen, Ann and King, David (2003) *The Artistic Dividend: The Arts' Hidden Contributors to Regional Development.* Minneapolis: University of Minnesota: Project on Regional and Industrial Economics.

Markusen, A., Schrock, G. and Cameron, M. (2004) *The Artistic Dividend Revisited.* Minneapolis: University of Minnesota: Project on Regional and Industrial Economics.

Markusen, A., Gilmore, S., Johnson, A., Levi, T. and Martinez, A. (2006) *Crossover: How Artists Build Careers across Commercial, Nonprofit, and Community Work.* Minneapolis: University of Minnesota: Project on Regional and Industrial Economics.

Markusen, A., Wassall, G.H., Denatale, D. and Cohen, R. (2006) 'Defining the Cultural Economy: Industry and Occupational Approaches', Paper presented at the North American Regional Science Council Meeting: Toronto, 17 November.

Mercer, Colin (2001) *'Guest Editor Introduction'* in 'Convergence, Creative Industries and Civil Society: The new cultural policy'. *CultureLink*, pp. 3–8.

Moore, Mark and Moore, G.W. (2005) *Creating Public Value Through State Arts Agencies.* Minneapolis, MN: Arts Midwest.

NALAA (National Assembly of Local Arts Agencies) (1992) 'The Impact of the Arts in the Local Economy'. Washington, DC: NALAA.

NASAA (National Assembly of State Arts Agencies) (2005) 'States and the Creative Economy'. (State Policy Brief 1,1) Washington, DC: NASAA.

NASAA (National Assembly of State Arts Agencies) (2007) 'State Arts Agency Creative Economy Initiatives.' Retrieved from www.nasaa-arts.org on 22 May 2007.

NEA (National Endowment for the Arts) (1981) 'Economic Impact of Arts and Cultural Institutions'. Washington, DC: The Research Division, Report #15, January.

NEC (New England Council) (2000) 'The Creative Economy Initiative: The Role of the Arts and Culture in New England's Economic Competitiveness'. Boston: Report Prepared by Mt. Auburn Associates, June.

NEC (New England Council) (2001) 'The Creative Economy Initiative: A Blueprint for Investment in New England's Creative Economy'. Boston: The New England Council, June.

Nichols, Bonnie (2006) 'Research Note #90: Artist Employment, 2005'. Washington, DC: National Endowment for the Arts, July.

O'Connor, Justin (2000) 'The Definition of the Cultural Industries', *The European Journal of Arts Education*, 2(3) (February): 15–27.

PARC (Performing Arts Research Coalition (2004) *The Value of the Performing Arts in Ten Communities: Summary Report.* Washington, DC: Urban Institute, June.

PCAH (President's Committee on the Arts and the Humanities (1997) *Creative America: A Report to the President.* Washington, DC: PCAH, February.

Radich, Anthony J. and Foss, Sonja K. (1987) 'Economic Impact Studies of the Arts as Effective Advocacy', in A.J. Radich and S. Schwoch (eds.) *Economic Impact of the Arts: A Sourcebook.* Denver, Colorado: National Conference of State Legislatures, May, pp. 77–104.

San Diego Foundation (2006) *PARTICIPATE San Diego: The Case for Increased Patronage for Arts and Culture in the San Diego Region.* San Diego, The San Diego Foundation.

Scott, W.R. and Meyer, J.W. (1983) 'The Organization of Societal Sectors', in John W. Meyer and W. Richard Scott (with the assistance of Brian Rowan and Terrance E. Deal). *Organizational Environments: Ritual and Rationality.* Beverly Hills: SAGE Publications.

Scruggs, Patricia C., Cortright, J. and Douglas, M. (1999) *Designing Portland's Future: The Role of the Creative Services Industry.* Portland: Portland Development Commission.

Seaman, Bruce A. (1987) 'Arts Impact Studies: A Fashionable Excess', in A.J. Radich and S. Schwoch (eds.) *Economic Impact of the Arts: A Sourcebook.* Denver, Colorado: National Conference of State Legislatures.

Siwek, S.E. (2006) *Copyright Industries in the U.S. Economy: The 2006 Report.* Washington, DC: International Intellectual Property Alliance.

Strom, Elizabeth (2003) 'Cultural Policy as Development Policy: Evidence from the United States', *International Journal of Cultural Policy* 9(3): 247–63.

Wassall, G.H. and Denatale, D. (1997) *Arts, Cultural and Humanities Organizations in the New*

England Economy, 1996. Boston: New England Foundation for the Arts.

Williams, Raymond (1981) *Culture.* London: Fontana.

Wyszomirski, Margaret Jane (1995) 'The Politics of Arts Policy: Subgovernment to Issue Network', in Kevin V. Mulcahy and Margaret Jane Wyszomirski (eds.) *America's Commitment to Culture.* Boulder: Westview Press. pp. 47–76.

Wyszomirski, Margaret Jane (2003) 'The Creative Industries and Cultural Professions in the 21st Century: A Background Paper'. Columbus, OH: Presented at the 2003 Barnett Symposium on the Arts and Public Policy, 7–9 May.

Wyszomirski, Margaret Jane (2004) 'Defining and Developing Creative Sector Initiatives'. Paper presented at the FOKUS Seminar, Vienna, Austria, March. Retrievable as OSU-APA Working Paper #34 at www.arted.osu.edu/publications/apapaper. php.

Wyszomirski, Margaret Jane (2005) 'Developing the Creative Industries'. Paper presented at the Creative Cities Network Conference, Trois Rivieres, Quebec, Canada. October.

FIELDS AND GENRES

## CHAPTER 18

SPATIAL DYNAMICS OF FILM AND TELEVISION
Michael Curtin

Discussions about globalization commonly suggest that trans-border forces and flows are posing significant challenges for national media institutions, practices and policies. Yet few accounts move beyond national frameworks to provide theoretical models for explaining the spatial dynamics of global media. If not nationally, how might we analyse film and television industries today and in the future? Where in the world might we expect to find centers of creative endeavor? Which institutions will prove most influential? And what factors will shape the patterns of media circulation? Advancing the concept of media capital, this chapter suggests that analysts pay particular attention to logics of accumulation, trajectories of creative migration, and forces of socio-cultural variation. It is argued that these principles can provide a foundation for critical analysis, industry practice and policy intervention.

Economic globalization has engendered new patterns of spatial concentration and dispersion, as a result of dramatic changes in transportation, communication, and trade protocols. In this new environment, 'global cities' (Sassen, 1991) serve as command and control centers for complex, transnational enterprises, while manufacturing has dispersed to low-wage territories, resulting in what Castells (1996) refers to as the 'global assembly line'. Remarkably, few critics have systematically considered the spatial dynamics of the global cultural economy. This is puzzling, since the globalization of the culture industries is a very contentious policy issue. For example, in Europe during the 1980s, some of the most controversial aspects of economic unification revolved around the future of television. How might trade liberalization affect national media industries? Would it foster the cultural dominance of countries such as Germany at the expense of smaller countries like Denmark? Would it sacrifice national distinctiveness for bland continental co-productions, so called 'Euro-pudding'? And would it provide cover for the further encroachment of Hollywood movies and television shows? Similar debates unfolded in many parts of the world as the neo-liberal project of economic integration spread further afield in the aftermath of the Cold War. Central to these deliberations were urgent questions about the fate of local, national and ethnic identities. Such concerns were often framed in terms of media imperialism, a critique that achieved prominence among scholars and policy-makers during the 1960s, suggesting that Western, and especially American, economic dominance relies on the distribution of film and television products to distant markets where they displace local values and cultural institutions.

By the early 1990s, however, the explanatory value of the media imperialism thesis began to be called into question for a number of reasons. Because it was broad and structural in nature, critics claimed that this view failed to account for the diverse ways in which audiences make use of foreign media. It also seemed to overlook the growing influence of domestic media producers and failed to acknowledge the increasing prominence of transnational media production centers in cities such as Mumbai (formerly Bombay), Beirut and Hong Kong. The media imperialism thesis focused on national cinemas and national broadcasting systems, paying little attention to the increasingly complex and trans-border circulations of popular media. It furthermore privileged the United States as a central and organizing actor in the international media economy. Global studies of media on the other hand pointed to the complex and contingent forces and flows at work in the multi-centric cultural economy of television and cinema.

Since the 1980s, the number of media producers, distributors and consumers has grown dramatically, first in Europe and then in Asia, with China and India adding almost two billion new viewers in the past couple of decades. Although powerful global media conglomerates were active contributors to these trends, local, national and regional media firms expanded rapidly as well. In India, Rupert Murdoch's Star TV intruded upon the state's television monopoly only to find itself beleaguered in turn by dozens of new indigenous competitors, many of them telecasting in subaltern languages, all of them commercially driven (Curtin, 1999; Kumar, 2005). As a result, Star TV was forced to localize its programming and institutional practices, so as to adapt to competitive forces on the ground. Though Star's original intention was to penetrate and dominate sub-continental markets with Western technology and Hollywood programming, it nevertheless found itself pulled into lively competition with Indian media enterprises. Such developments complicated media imperialism's structural notions of center and periphery. In many parts of the world, global media corporations were adapting their operations to local conditions at the very same time that local film and television enterprises were becoming more globalized in their perspectives and practices. Rather than exhibiting concrete patterns of domination and subordination, media institutions in places like India seemed to be responding to the push–pull of globalization, as increasing connectivity inspired significant changes in textual and institutional practices.

Globalization of media therefore should not be understood reductively as cultural homogenization or Western hegemony. Instead, it is part of a larger set of processes that operate trans-locally, interactively and dynamically at a variety of levels: economic, institutional, technological and ideological. As John Tomlinson (1991: 175) observes, globalization 'happens as the result of economic and cultural practices which do not, of themselves, aim at global integration, but which nonetheless produce it. More importantly, the effects of globalization are to weaken the cultural coherence of all nation-states, including the economically powerful ones – the 'imperialist powers' of a previous era'. In other words, unlike theories of media imperialism that emphasize the self-conscious extension of centralized power, globalization theories suggest that the world's increasingly interconnected media environment is the outcome of messy and complicated interactions across space. What globalization theorists have failed to produce, however, is a persuasive account of the most significant forces driving these processes and a clear explanation of why some places become centers of cultural production and therefore tend to be more influential in shaping the emerging global system.

A concern with location is perhaps the most significant and enduring continuity between the imperialism and globalization schools of media scholarship. Where and why do certain locations emerge as significant centers of media production? What is the extent of their geographical reach? How do spatial dynamics influence power valences between groups, cultures, institutions, and societies? Whether stated explicitly or implicitly, these are the central concerns that continue to stimulate film and television research. Whereas the media imperialism school analysed these issues through the prism of the international system of nation-states, globalization research has tended to comment upon the erosion of national regulations and national modes of production. Yet globalization studies generally fail to offer compelling models for how we might begin to map the shifting contours and practices of media institutions around the world. In an effort to address these shortcomings, this analysis offers several hypotheses regarding the spatial dynamics of *media capital*.

When describing the terrain of contemporary culture, critics often invoke such adjectives as fractal, disjunctive or rhizomatic; words that aim to characterize a complex terrain of textual circulation, reception and appropriation in the 'postmodern era' (Appadurai, 1996; Deleuze and Guattari, 1987). Even though these adjectives may aptly describe a rupture with prior cultural regimes, screen industries that produce and circulate popular texts have nevertheless followed fairly consistent patterns of operation for almost a century. The amount of textual production may have increased dramatically and the patterns of circulation may have grown ever more complicated, but the spatial dynamics of media capital have remained fairly consistent, playing a structuring role in the film and broadcasting industries since the early twentieth century. Most prominently, media capital operates according to: 1) a logic of accumulation; 2) trajectories of creative migration; and 3) forces of socio-cultural variation.

Logic of accumulation

The logic of accumulation is not unique to the media industries, since all capitalist enterprises exhibit innately dynamic and expansionist tendencies. As David Harvey points out, most firms seek efficiencies through the concentration of productive resources and through the extension of markets, so as to fully utilize their productive capacity and realize the greatest possible return in the shortest amount of time. These tendencies are most explicitly revealed during periodic downturns in the business cycle when enterprises are compelled to intensify production and/or extensify distribution in order to survive. Such moments of crisis call for a 'spatial fix', says Harvey, as capital must on the one hand concentrate and integrate sites of production so as to reduce the amount of time and resources expended in manufacture and on the other hand it must refigure the circuits of distribution in order to reduce the time it takes to bring distant locales into the orbit of its operations (Harvey, 2001). These *centripetal* tendencies in the sphere of production and *centrifugal* tendencies in distribution were observed by Karl Marx (1973: 539) more than a century ago when he trenchantly explained that capital must 'annihilate space with time' if it is to overcome barriers to accumulation.

As applied to contemporary media, this insight suggests that even though a film or TV company may be founded with the aim of serving particular national cultures or local markets, it must over time re-deploy its creative resources and reshape its terrain of operations if it is to survive competition and enhance profitability. Implicit in this logic of accumulation is the contributing influence of the 'managerial revolution' that accompanied the rise of industrial capitalism (Chandler, 1977). Indeed, it was the intersection of capitalist accumulation with the reflexive knowledge systems of the Enlightenment that engendered the transition from mercantile to industrial capitalism (Giddens, 1990). Capitalism became more than a mode of accumulation; it also became a disposition towards surveillance and adaptation, as it continually refined and integrated manufacturing and marketing processes, achieving efficiencies through a concentration of productive resources and through the ongoing enhancement of delivery systems.

The history of the American cinema – the world's most commercial and most intensively studied media industry – provides an instructive example of these core tendencies. During the first decade of the twentieth century, US movie exhibitors depended on small, collaborative film-making crews to service demand for filmed entertainment. Yet as theater chains emerged, as distribution grew more sophisticated, and as competition intensified, movie companies began to centralize creative labour in large factory-like studios with an eye towards improving quality, reducing costs and increasing output. By refiguring the spatial relations of production, managers concentrated the creative labour force in a single location where it could be deployed among a diverse menu of projects under the guidance of each studio's central production office. Inspired by Taylorism – then in vogue among industrial manufacturers – the major film companies furthermore separated the domains of planning and execution, creating a blueprint (or script) for each film that guided the work of specialized craftspeople in lighting, make-up and dozens of other departments. As American cinema entered this factory phase during the 1910s, the intensification of production accelerated output and yielded cost efficiencies, providing theater operators around the country with a dependable flow of quality products (Bordwell et al., 1985; Bowser, 1990).

Similar patterns emerged in the Indian commercial film industry with major studios emerging in the Bombay area by the 1930s (Pendakur, 2003; Prasad, 1998; Rajadhyaksha, 2003). In Chinese cinema, transnational cinema circuits were firmly in place by the 1930s, but the mode of production was initially more dispersed for a variety of reasons. During the post-Second World War era as prosperity returned to the industry, both Cathay and Shaw Brothers established integrated production operations in Hong Kong that rivaled the scope and productivity of their American counterparts (Bordwell, 2000; Curtin, 2007; Fu, 2002; 2003). This capital-intensive factory model prevailed with major movie companies around the world, but it is nevertheless important to note that unlike the auto or steel industries, film-making employees were creating distinctive *prototypes* rather than redundant batches of products with interchangeable parts. Each commodity was relatively unique, even if production routines grew increasingly standardized and even if the films were intended for mass audiences (Bordwell et al., 1985: 93).

Not only was film production distinctive from other forms of industrialized manufacturing but so too was film distribution, since movies are what economists refer to as public goods (Kepley, 1990; Hesmondhalgh, 2002). That is, each feature film is a commodity that can be consumed without diminishing its availability to other prospective customers. And given the relatively low costs of reproducing and circulating a film print when compared to the costs of creating the prototype, it behooves the manufacturer to circulate each artifact as widely as possible, thereby encouraging the establishment of an expansive distribution infrastructure. Unlike other cultural institutions that needed to be close to live audiences or patrons (e.g., vaudeville and opera), and unlike industrial manufacturers who incurred substantial shipping costs for their finished products (e.g., automobiles and washing machines), movie studios could dispatch their feature films expansively and economically. The key aim of the distribution apparatus was therefore to stimulate audience demand and insure access to theaters in far-flung locales. They achieved the latter by establishing theater chains or by collaboration with major exhibitors, both nationally and internationally (Balio, 1993; Gomery, 1986; Thompson, 1985). Film distribution during this period provides a profound example of the centrifugal spatial tendencies of capitalist enterprise.

Trajectories of creative migration

The second principle of media capital emphasizes trajectories of creative migration, since audio-visual industries are especially reliant on creativity as a core resource. Recurring demand for new prototypes requires pools of labour that are self-consciously motivated by aesthetic innovation as well as market considerations. Indeed, attracting and managing talent is one of the most difficult challenges that screen producers confront. At the level of the firm this involves offering attractive compensation and favorable working conditions, but at a broader level it also requires maintaining access to reservoirs of specialized labour that replenish themselves on a regular basis, which is why media companies tend to cluster in particular cities.[1]

Nevertheless it is rare that such centers of creativity emerge strictly as a response to market forces, and history suggests that we should look beyond the logic of accumulation to understand patterns of creative migration. During the pre-modern era, artists

and craftspeople congregated at sites where sovereigns and clergy erected grand edifices or commissioned regular works of art. Patronage drew artists to specific locales and often kept them in place for much of their working lives, and they in turn passed their skills along to succeeding generations and to newly arrived migrants. Rather than market forces, one might imagine that spiritual inspiration and feudal relations of patronage significantly influenced trajectories of creative migration during this period, but it is also important to acknowledge the tendency of artists to seek out others of their kind. In large part, artists are drawn to co-locate with their peers due to the mutual learning effects engendered by such proximity. As the bourgeoisie rose to prominence in the early modern era, commercial cities became new centers of artistic production and exhibition, even though pre-existing centers retained residual prestige among the cognoscenti (DiMaggio, 1986). Industrialists built performance venues, established galleries and subsidized educational institutions, all of which enhanced the cultural capital of the emergent entrepreneurial class and attracted fresh talent to cities such as Berlin, New York and Shanghai.

Popular culture was layered over this topography of the fine arts, further elaborating the trajectories of migration since scarce resources and dispersed populations made it difficult for popular artists and performers to subsist in any one locale. Instead, they established circuits of recurring migration, playing to crowds in diverse towns and villages. These circuits were formalized in the nineteenth century by booking agents who rationalized the scheduling of talent across a regional chain of performance venues. The apex of each circuit was located in a major city that provided exposure to the wealthiest and most discriminating audiences, as well as cross-fertilization with other domains of the creative arts (Allen, 1980; Gilbert, 1940; McLean, 1965). This historical sketch suggests that the spatial circulation of performers and the rise of creative centers were shaped by diverse practices that were increasingly rationalized and commodified during the nineteenth century. Film industries further accentuated these tendencies by yoking the centripetal logic of production to these existing tendencies towards the agglomeration of creative labour. Nevertheless reversals in their respective fortunes brought an end to the studio system in the American (1950s), Indian (1940s) and Chinese (1970s) film industries. Studio artists and labourers found themselves shifting from the security of long-term studio employment to the uncertainties of casual labour at a growing number of independent production houses.

Why then did Hollywood, Mumbai and Hong Kong continue to act as magnets for cultural labour? One might suggest that like prior transitions, the residual aura of the city helped to sustain its status as a center of creative endeavor, but geographers Michael Storper and Susan Christopherson (1987: 113) contend that, more importantly, a disintegrated (or flexible or post-Fordist) mode of production in the movie industry actually encourages and sustains the agglomeration of creative labour due to the fact that constant changes in product output require frequent transactions between contractors, subcontractors and creative talent. Their study of Hollywood shows that the number of inter-firm transactions in the movie business has grown dramatically over the past 50 years at the very same time that the scale of transactions have diminished, indicating that many small subcontractors now provide the studios with crucial services, such as wardrobe, set construction and lighting, as well as key talent, with many stars now incorporated as independent enterprises rather than as contract labour. Storper and Christopherson argue that this pattern of disintegration encourages studios to employ *local* subcontractors and talent because proximity allows directors and managers to oversee outsourced creative labour and to make changes more easily and more frequently as work progresses. As for the workers, they cluster around Hollywood where studios and subcontracting firms are based, since it helps them 'offset the instability of short-term contractual work by remaining close to the largest pool of employment opportunities'.[2]

Geographer Allen J. Scott (see also his concluding overview, Chapter 27) extends this principle of talent agglomeration to industries as diverse as jewellry, furniture and fashion apparel, arguing that manufacturers of *cultural* goods tend to locate where subcontractors and skilled labourers form dense transactional networks. Besides apparent cost efficiencies, Scott points to the mutual learning effects that stem from a clustering of interrelated producers. Whether through informal learning – such as sharing ideas and techniques while collaborating on a particular project – or via more formal transfers of knowledge – craft schools, trade associations and awards ceremonies – clustering enhances product quality and fuels innovation. 'Place-based communities such as these are not just foci of cultural labor in the narrow sense', observes Scott (2000: 33), 'but also are active hubs of social reproduction in which

crucial cultural competencies are maintained and circulated'. This centripetal agglomeration of labour encourages path-dependent evolution such that small chance events or innovations may spark the appearance of a culture industry in a particular location, but clustering engenders a growth spiral, as creative labour migrates to the region in search of work, further enhancing its attraction to other talent. Locales that fail to make an early start in such industries are subject to 'lock-out', since it is difficult to lure talent away from an existing media capital, even with massive government subsidies. Scott suggests that the only way a new cluster might arise is if its producers offer an appreciably distinctive product line.

It seems reasonable to suggest that the centripetal migrations of creative labour are not necessarily specific to post-Fordist regimes of flexible specialization or even to capitalism, but have in fact existed under various regimes of production. In post-Fordist industrial settings, mutual learning effects are no doubt an animating force behind the enduring concentration of creative labour but, just as interestingly, many *Fordist* enterprises self-consciously sought to realize these effects as well.[3] Bordwell, Thompson, and Staiger demonstrate that under the Hollywood studio system of the early twentieth century, a set of creative norms emerged out of complex and extended interactions among employees within a given studio and among the local film-making community. The 'Hollywood style' grew out of collective reflection and discussion regarding various experiments in cinematic representation. As we can see from this example, mutual learning effects prevailed in both the integrated studio era and in the disintegrated studio era.

In general, we can conclude that cultural production is especially reliant upon mutual learning effects and trajectories of creative migration, and that, inevitably, particular locations emerge as centers of creativity. These principles have operated throughout history under various regimes of accumulation, but the modern era is distinctive because the centripetal logic of capitalist production has been married to the centripetal trajectories of creative migration, engendering the rise of transnational film production centers. One might imagine that in today's world of increasing commercial flows and diminishing trade barriers we might be approaching a time when one city would become a dominant global center attracting talent from around the world and producing a majority of the world's popular screen narratives. Yet the complexities of distribution undermine such pretensions to singular dominance, especially when media products rub up against counterparts in distant cultural domains that are often served, even if minimally, by competing media capitals that are centers of creative migration in their own right.

Forces of socio-cultural variation

Cities such as Hollywood, Mumbai and Hong Kong lie across significant cultural divides from each other, which helps to explain why producers in these cities have been able to sustain distinctive product lines and survive the onslaught of distant competitors. These media capitals are furthermore supported by intervening factors that modify and complicate the spatial tendencies outlined above. Consequently, the third principle of media capital focuses on forces of socio-cultural variation, demonstrating that national and local institutions have been and remain significant actors despite the spatial tendencies of production and distribution. Indeed, the early years of cinema

were exceptional in large part because the logic of media capital unfolded relatively unimpeded by national regulation, but as the popularity of Hollywood narratives increased, many countries established cultural policies to address the growing influence of this new commodity form. Motion pictures presented governments with a unique policy challenge since they were distributed even more widely than newspapers, magazines or books, the circulations of which were limited to literate consumers within shared linguistic spheres. By comparison, silent era cinema overcame these barriers and challenged linguistic, class and national boundaries, as well. Films circulated widely within the US and overseas, swelling the size of audiences dramatically and fueling the growth of large-scale enterprises. According to Kristin Thompson (1985), US movie companies became dominant exporters by the mid-1910s, a trend that contributed to a further concentration of resources and talent, and encouraged the refinement of film styles and production values. By the 1920s, however, opinion leaders

Box 18.1   Bollywood: globalization and the demand for cultural copying

Globalization has had profound effects on the psyche of Indian society and the very fabric upon which it is founded. The 'Westernization' of traditional Indian culture, termed 'modernization' by many social commentators, has altered not only the manner in which Indians view the world, but also how they perceive themselves in the global arena. Though some may argue that globalization is merely another influencing force to be added to a long series of 'globalizers' – beginning with the 'Aryans' three millennia ago all the way through, most recently, to the British – who have continuously shaped this pluralistic civilization throughout its long history, few can deny the radical and far-reaching transformations India has undergone in the last 15 to 20 years. From McDonald's, to music, to Microsoft and to the movies, globalization has sunk its claws into almost every facet of Indian society.

Arguably one of the most dominant gateways to the globalization of India is the Mumbai-based Hindi film industry, or 'Bollywood' – a portmanteau of 'Bombay', the former name of the city where the majority of Indian films are produced, and 'Hollywood', the epicentre of the American film industry. The Indian film industry as a whole, which is dominated by Bollywood, but also includes film producing centers from other regions of India, is the largest producer of cinematographic works in the world. The numbers are staggering: as a whole, Indian film studios generate upwards of 1000 films per year, compared to about 400 produced by Hollywood; the United States sells approximately 2.9 billion tickets each year while India sells 3.1 billion, a number predicted to increase to 4 billion by 2009; and Bollywood's gross revenue tops approximately $10 billion annually. Not only are the financial statistics impressive, but the opportunity for the exploitation of Bollywood as a portal for globalization is also enormous, simply based upon its global reach. The year 2004 marked the first time in history that more people globally watched Bollywood than Hollywood movies – 3.8 billion as compared to 3.6 billion. In addition, some analysts predict that the Indian film industry on its own could tap 12 per cent of the global entertainment market by 2008.

Thus, it is indisputable that Indian cinema plays a massive role not only in the life of a resident Indian, but also internationally, where Bollywood films are exported to more than 100 countries across the world. The dominance of Bollywood in Indian culture has placed it on a plane ripe for cultural globalization. In many ways, however, Bollywood itself is not only a powerful current in the flow of Western influence, but also a product of pre-established globalization permeating throughout India. The advent of global communications, satellite TV, the internet, and the rise of a middle class made prosperous by the influx of jobs created by globalization, has fostered a new breed of audience in India – an audience whose expectations and cinematic standards have both become heightened. The result is a demand for a brand of cinema which largely ignores traditional, formulaic plotlines in favor of a new variety of stylistic, narrative and thematic approaches. The rise of these expectations, created by a globalization domino-effect, creates a cinematic environment which now scrambles to feed the insatiable appetite of Indian movie-goers for Western-laced plots. Inevitably, this species of globalization cultivates the 'Indianization' or 'cultural copying' of American movie scripts.

Born of the immense popularity of Indian cinema, cultural copying now runs rampant in Bollywood. The Indianization of Western storylines involves the copying of American movie plots and transposing them on the traditional Bollywood template. Thus, original, creative works in Hollywood are pillaged through direct scene-to-scene or dialogue-to-dialogue translations of films. These translated scripts are subsequently meshed with conventional song-and-dance numbers, grandiose sets, colourful costumes, melodramatic settings, and overall effervescence to create a cinematographic work which is sure to appeal to the Indian masses. The numbers do not lie: eight out of every ten films produced in Bollywood yearly are cultural copies to some degree, and the rate and frequency at which American films are copied continues to rise.

This novel phenomenon, however, has not nurtured a socially static state in the minds of all. Though the benefit of access to, and availability of, Western films has been improved film quality for the average movie-goer in India, endemic Indianization has also led to the introduction of themes, ideas and concepts which India has not only never encountered in the mass media, but also to which it has been traditionally averse. The arrival of images of kissing, lovemaking, nudity and homosexuality has shocked this nation, habitually disinclined to embrace not only on-screen kisses, but also public displays of affection within the family structure and society generally. Quite distinct from the social effects of cultural copying in Bollywood, there is also a prominent legal component to the issue of Indianization. American film producers are protected through international copyright agreements which legally prohibit actions such as the cultural copying seen occurring in Bollywood. Though there are legitimate arguments to be made on both sides of the debate surrounding the detailed legalities of what constitutes cultural copying, the threshold for copyright infringement, etc., what is not up for debate is that Hollywood studios and creators of original works in the US are beginning to recognize both the global span of Bollywood, as well as the potential for legal recourse in cases of cultural copying. Though no Hollywood studio has so far pursued a cause of action against Bollywood for copyright infringement, the recent case of *Bradford v. Sahara* heard in Indian courts suggests that the days of Bollywood copying Hollywood films unscathed may be nearing an end. In *Bradford v. Sahara*, Barbara Taylor Bradford, the best selling author of the novel *A Woman of Substance*, claimed copyright infringement against Sahara Media Entertainment Ltd. for the production of a 260 part mini-series whose plot and characters closely resembled Taylor's novel. Though the Indian courts ruled in favor of Sahara, citing an absence of substantial infringement, the door may now be open for additional copyright infringement claims by American producers.

Globalization has created a fascinating cycle of cause and effect in the Indian film industry. While stimulating a changing Indian landscape, it has created a demand for Western-style themes and plotlines, but only to the extent that it does not offend traditional, societal value systems. That demand for Western-style stories has subsequently led to an incidence of cultural copying by which Bollywood continues to draw upon American film creativity. It is the same reality of globalization, however, that is also allowing Hollywood film studios to become cognizant of these occurrences and potentially pursue legal action. Globalization, therefore, is in many ways a paradigm for cost–benefit analyses; it is filling the Indian cultural landscape with a diversity and richness never seen before. At the same time it can be argued that it is precipitating the loss of a cultural identity in India at a rate which has, again, never before been seen. Though only time will provide a lens through which the effects of globalization in the cultural realm can be accurately measured, one thing is certain: as a result of it, Bollywood will never be the same.

Raman Minhas

and politicians abroad grew wary of Hollywood movies and cultural critics began to clamour for regulation. Many countries imposed import quotas and content regulations on Hollywood films and some set up national film boards to subsidize cinema productions with national themes and talent (Crofts, 1993; Higson, 1989; Jarvie, 1992; O'Regan, 2002).

Most important, however, was state-subsidized radio broadcasting, which in most every country outside the Western hemisphere was established as a public service system and remained so until the 1980s. Britain, which would serve as a model to others, explicitly charged the British Broadcasting Corpo-ration with responsibility to clear a space for the circulation of British values, culture and information (Hilmes, 2003; Scannell, 1991). Radio seemed an especially appropriate medium for intervention, since many of its characteristics helped to insulate national systems from foreign competition. Technologically, radio signals traveled only 30 to 60 miles from any given transmitter. As in Britain, one could interconnect a chain of transmitters that would blanket the countryside, but the only way for foreign competitors to reach one's home audiences was via shortwave radio, a temperamental technology that was comparatively inaccessible to the masses. Such insulation was furthermore insured by an international regulatory regime that allocated radio frequencies on a national basis, thereby minimizing technical as well as cultural interference between countries. Language provided another bulwark, since radio relied on aural competence in the state's official language, helping to distinguish national productions that played in one's domicile, from Hollywood 'talkies' that played at the cinema. Finally, public service radio systems were bolstered by indigenous cultural resources to which the state laid claim. Literary and theatrical works were commonly appropriated to the new medium, as were folk tales and music. State ceremonies and eventually sporting events also filled the airwaves, as the medium participated in self-conscious efforts to foster a common national culture.

Radio also promoted a shared temporality among audiences. Its predecessor, the nineteenth-century newspaper, pioneered this transformation, as it not only directed readers to stories that the editors considered significant but also encouraged them to absorb these stories at a synchronous daily pace. Hegel's reference to the morning ritual of reading the newspaper suggests the ways in which readers partook not only of common narratives but furthermore did so at more or less the same time (Anderson, 1983). Radio extended such rituals to non-literate groups, which expanded the horizon of synchronization, such that programming schedules began to shape daily household routines and create a national calendar of social and cultural events. Radio insinuated itself into the household, interlacing public and private spheres, and situating national culture in the everyday world of its listeners (Hilmes, 1997; Morley, 2000; Scannell, 1991). Even though radio systems were founded under the guiding hand of politicians, educators and cultural bureaucrats, they would over time open themselves up to audience participation, employing yet another distinctive cultural resource as part of their programming repertoire: the voice of the people. In each of these ways, public service radio accentuated national contours of difference in opposition to media capital's desire to operate on a smooth plane of market relations worldwide. Although the British system served as a template for public service radio, national services were diverse and their success varied. All India Radio was quite elitist and consequently developed slowly until the incursions of foreign satellite competitors forced public service radio and television to compete for popular audiences (Robin, 2006). Nigerian state broadcasting was rife with political Favoritism, censorship and corruption until it found itself competing in the 1990s with popular Nigerian video films (Afolabi, 2000; Haynes, 2000; Haynes and Okome, 1998; Larkin, 2004; McCall, 2004). Nevertheless regulation of the airwaves has provided an effective way for governments to refigure the centripetal and centrifugal tendencies of a capitalist regime of accumulation.

Regulation can also act as an influential enabler by establishing institutions and policies that foster the growth of media industries. Intellectual property laws are especially compelling examples in this regard as are media licensing regimes.[4] The commercial development of broadcasting in the United States was facilitated by a regulatory regime that in effect made it possible to 'sell the airwaves' to corporate operators. In so doing, the government created a market-driven system out of an intangible public resource, enabling a national program distribution system that stimulated the growth of national advertising and concentrated creative resources in a handful of urban centers (Streeter, 1996). Just as the British system became a model for public service systems around the world, the commercial licensing regime of American broadcasting became the standard for deployment of satellite transmission allocations, which in turn pressured governments around the world to adapt to commercial models.

Consequently, even though market forces have been primary engines of cultural production and circulation, the boundaries and contours of markets are subject to political interventions that enable, shape and attenuate the dynamics of screen industries. Accordingly, media policy remains an influential force, suggesting that concepts such as 'free flow' and 'market forces' are in fact meaningless without self-conscious state interventions to fashion a terrain for commercial operations. Markets are made, not given. And the logic of accumulation must therefore be interrogated in relation to specific and complex mixtures of socio-cultural forces.

Finally, it should also be pointed out that self-conscious state policies are not the only actors that organize and exploit the forces of socio-cultural variation. Media industries in Mumbai, Cairo and Hong Kong have themselves taken advantage of social and cultural differences in their production and distribution practices. Operating across cultural divides from Hollywood and from other powerful exporters, they have employed creative talent and cultural forms that resonate distinctively with their audiences. These industries have furthermore made use of social networks and insider information to secure market advantages, and they invoke cultural and national pride in their promotional campaigns. Forces of socio-cultural variation provide resources for carving out market niches that are beyond the reach of competitors.

Policy implications

Media capital is a concept that at once highlights the *spatial* logics of capital, creativity, culture and polity without privileging one among them. Just as the logic of capital provides a fundamental structuring influence, so too do trajectories of creative migration and forces of socio-cultural variation shape the diverse contexts in which media are made and consumed. The concept of media capital encourages us to provide dynamic and historicized accounts that delineate the operations of capital and the migrations of talent, while at the same time directing our attention to socio-cultural forces and contingencies that give shape to discourses, practices and spatialities.

It furthermore encourages us to consider new directions for media policy. Over the past few decades, neo-liberal political projects around the world have repeatedly undermined government institutions, investing faith instead in market forces.

Although commercial forces have indeed had salutary effects on film and television in many parts of the world, media policy remains an urgent necessity. Yet it should not be invoked in a defensive manner nor should it be used to prop up political parties or national governments. Nor should policy aim to regulate imports, control access or censor programs. Such restraints, though relatively effective in the past, are nowadays counterproductive due to new technologies of transportation and communication. The Chinese government, for example, strictly limits the number of Hollywood movies imported each year, but this has little effect on the actual consumption of American films in China, since they are widely available through black market video distribution channels (Wang, 2003). Such government restrictions fail to influence personal consumption, but they have a tremendously negative impact on Chinese film and TV industries, since they drive audiences out of the formal media economy.

Media policy should therefore focus on the supply side of the equation, intervening selectively to enhance the productivity of particular media centers and institutions by providing infrastructural, educational and financial resources that might stimulate further growth. Policy-makers cannot create new media capitals out of whole cloth, but they can recognize and support those locales that seem to be gathering talent and resources, and generating innovative programming. They can also promote the enforcement of intellectual property laws, so as to ensure that the distribution revenues flow centripetally to producers and investors. Although the US government is the most vocal proponent of IP enforcement, piracy is in fact having a far more deleterious effect on media industries in Lagos, Mumbai and Hong Kong than it is on Hollywood. IP policies should acknowledge some global standards, while reserving the right to shape those standards to local and national circumstances.

Finally, media policy should acknowledge that although market dynamics and talent migrations will privilege a small number of global media capitals, policy-makers must intervene where the market comes up short. In many cases, governments will need to prioritize and even subsidize media institutions because they provide vital resources for local, national and alternative cultures. Like public parks and libraries, media play a vital role in making particular places worth living. They foster identity, enhance social cohesion, serve local businesses, enhance property values, and provide spaces for public discourse. Some of these functions will be supported by the market, but others will not. The principles of media capital help to explain the spatial tendencies of commercial film and television, and in so doing they provide a rationale for policy interventions that seek to attenuate, shape or modify the logic of the market. As noted earlier, policy makes markets, but it also makes publics. Without the former, media capital will wither; without the latter, it will suffocate.

Notes

1 Although it does not address media industries specifically, an extensive literature discusses the impact of human capital on the clustering of business firms in particular locations (Florida, 2005; Jacobs, 1984; Porter, 1998).

2 Despite the development of new communication technologies that allow creative collaborations across vast expanses, creative labour also needs to congregate so as to build relationships of trust and familiarity that can enable and sustain long-distance collaborations. Giddens' discussion of facework (1990) and Bourdieu's notion of social capital (1986) both point to the importance of physical proximity.

3 For example, Alfred Chandler (2001) observes that large corporations in the information industry internalized and compounded learning effects throughout the twentieth century. Indeed he contends that leading firms in the electronics and computer industries, such as ATT and IBM, were distinguished by their ability to foster continuous paths of organizational learning. Moreover, firms that successfully manage ongoing innovation – i.e., the production of prototypes – tend to concentrate their creative workforce and to establish effective conduits for channeling information among production units and from consumers back to producers. For Chandler, learning effects may take place within a single integrated enterprise or they may extend to a nexus of interconnected and complementary firms that support a core company. In either case, geographic clustering stimulates innovation.

4 In the United States, court rulings during the 1910s provided movie studios with intellectual property rights so that they – rather than their employees – might claim protection for the films they 'authored'. Although copyright laws originally aimed to foster creative endeavor by *individuals*, the courts allowed movie factories to claim artistic inspiration as well. Interestingly, they furthermore ruled that waged and salaried labourers at the major studios were neither creators nor authors but were rather 'work for hire'. In this way, the American legal system profoundly transformed copyright law, facilitating the industrialization of cinematic production and providing expansive legal protection for movie distributors (Bordwell et al., 1985).

REFERENCES

Afolabi, Adesanya (2000) 'From Film to Video', in J. Haynes (ed.) *Nigerian Video Films*. Athens: Ohio University Center for International Studies.

Allen, Robert C. (1980) *Vaudeville and Film: 1895–1915: A Study in Media Interaction*. New York: Arno Press.

Anderson, Benedict (1983) *Imagined Communities: Reflections on the Origin and Spread of Nationalism*. New York: Verso.

Appadurai, Arjun (1996) *Modernity at Large: Cultural Dimensions of Globalization*. Minneapolis: University of Minnesota Press.

Balio, Tino (1993) *Hollywood as a Modern Business Enterprise 1930–1939*. New York: Scribners.

Bourdieu, Pierre (1986) 'The Forms of Capital', in J.G. Richardson (ed.) *Handbook for Theory and Research for the Sociology of Education*. New York: Greenwood. pp. 241–58.

Bordwell, David (2000) *Planet Hong Kong: Popular Cinema and the Art of Entertainment*. Cambridge: Harvard University Press.

Bordwell, D., Staiger, J. and Thompson, K. (1985) *The Classical Hollywood Cinema: Film Style and Mode of Production to 1960*. London: Routledge & Kegan Paul.

Bowser, Eileen (1990) *The Transformation of Cinema: 1907–1915*. New York: Scribner.

Castells, Manuel (1996) *The Rise of Network Society*. Malden: Blackwell.

Chandler, Alfred D. (1977) *The Visible Hand: The Managerial Revolution in American Business.* Cambridge: Belknap.

Chandler, Alfred D. (2001) *Inventing the Electronic Century: The Epic Story of the Consumer Electronics and Computer Industries.* New York: Free Press.

Curtin, Michael (1999) 'Feminine Desire in the Age of Satellite Television', *Journal of Communication,* 49(2): 55–70.

Curtin, Michael (2007) *Playing to the World's Biggest Audience: The Globalization of Chinese Film and TV.* Berkeley: University of California Press.

Crofts, Stephen (1993) 'Reconceptualizing National Cinema/s', *Quarterly Review of Film & Video,* 14(3): 49–67.

DiMaggio, Paul (1986) *Non-Profit Enterprise in the Arts: Studies in Mission and Constraint.* New York: Oxford University Press.

Florida, Richard (2005) *Cities and the Creative Class.* New York: Routledge.

Deleuze, Gilles and Guattari, Felix (1987) *A Thousand Plateaus: Capitalism and Schizophrenia.* Minneapolis: University of Minnesota Press.

Fu, Poshek (2003) *Between Shanghai and Hong Kong: The Politics of Chinese Cinemas.* Stanford: Stanford University Press.

Fu, Poshek (2002) 'Hong Kong and Singapore: A History of the Cathay Cinema', in Ain-ling Wong (ed.) *The Cathay Story.* Hong Kong: Hong Kong Film Archive.

Giddens, Anthony (1990) *The Consequences of Modernity.* Stanford: Stanford University Press.

Gilbert, Douglas (1940) *American Vaudeville: Its Life and Times.* New York: McGraw-Hill.

Gomery, Douglas (1986) *The Hollywood Studio System.* New York: St. Martin's Press.

Haynes, Jonathan (ed.) (2000) *Nigerian Video Films.* Revised edition. Athens: Ohio University Center for International Studies.

Haynes, Jonathan, and Okome, Onookome (1998) 'Evolving Popular Media: Nigerian Video Films', *Research in African Literatures,* 29(3): 106–28.

Harvey, David (2001) *Spaces of Capital: Towards a Critical Geography.* New York: Routledge.

Hesmondhalgh, David (2002) *The Cultural Industries.* London: SAGE Publications.

Higson, Andrew (1989) 'The Concept of National Cinema', *Screen* 30, 4: 36–46.

Hilmes, Michele (1997) *Radio Voices: American Broadcasting 1922–1952.* Minneapolis: University of Minnesota Press.

Hilmes, Michele (2003) 'Who We Are, Who We Are Not: The Battle of Global Paradigms', in L. Park and S. Kuma (eds.) *Planet TV: A Global Television Reader.* New York: New York University Press. pp. 53–73.

Jacobs, Jane (1984) *Cities and the Wealth of Nations.* New York: Random House.

Jarvie, Ian (1992) *Hollywood's Overseas Campaign: The North Atlantic Movie Trade 1920–1950.* Cambridge: Cambridge University Press.

Kepley, Jr., Vance (1990) 'From "Frontal Lobes" to the "Bob-and-Bob" Show: NBC Management and Programming Strategies 1949–65', in T. Balio (ed.) *Hollywood in the Age of Television.* Boston: Unwin Hyman.

Kumar, Shanti (2005) *Gandhi Meets Primetime: Globalization and Nationalism in Indian Television.* Urbana: University of Illinois Press.

Larkin, Brian (2004) 'Degraded Images, Distorted Sounds: Nigerian Video and the Infrastructure of Piracy', *Public Culture,* 16(2): 289–314.

McCall, John C. (2004) 'Juju and Justice at the Movies: Vigilantes in Nigerian Popular Videos', *African Studies Review,* 47(3): 51–67.

McLean, Albert F. (1965) *American Vaudeville as Ritual.* Lexington: University of Kentucky Press.

Marx, Karl (1973) *Grundrisse: Foundations of the Critique of Political Economy.* New York: Vintage.

Morley, David (2000) *Home Territories: Media, Mobility, and Identity.* New York: Routledge.

O'Regan, Tom (2002) 'A National Cinema', in G. Turner (ed.) *The Film Cultures Reader.* New York: Routledge. pp.139–64.

Pendakur, Manjunath (2003) *Indian Popular Cinema: Industry, Ideology, and Consciousness.* Cresskill: Hampton Press.

Porter, Michael E. (1998) 'Clusters and the New Economics of Competition', *Harvard Business Review,* November.

Prasad, Madhava (1998) *Ideology of the Hindi Film: A Historical Construction.* New York: Oxford University Press.

Rajadhyaksha, Ashish (2003) 'The "Bollywoodization" of the Indian Cinema: Cultural Nationalism in a Global Arena', *Inter-Asia Cultural Studies,* 4(1): 25–39.

Robin, Jeffrey (2006) 'The Mahatma Didn't Like the Movies and Why It Matters', *Global Media and Communication,* 2(2): 204–24.

Sassen, Saskia (1991) *The Global City: New York, London, Tokyo.* Princeton, NJ: Princeton U Press.

Scannell, Paddy (1991) *A Social History of British Broadcasting*. Cambridge: Blackwell.

Scott, Allen J. (2000) *The Cultural Economy of Cities*. Thousand Oaks: Sage.

Storper, Michael and Christopherson, Susan (1987) 'Flexible Specialization and Regional Industrial Agglomerations: The Case of the U.S. Motion Picture Industry', *Annals of the Association of American Geographers*, 77(1): 104–17.

Streeter, Thomas (1996) *Selling the Air: A Critique of the Policy of Commercial Broadcasting in the United States*. Chicago: University of Chicago Press.

Thompson, Kristin (1985) *Exporting Entertainment: America in the World Film Market 1907–34*. London: BFI Publishing.

Tomlinson, John (1991) *Cultural Imperialism: A Critical Introduction*. Baltimore: Johns Hopkins University Press.

Wang, Shujen (2003) *Framing Piracy: Globalization and Film Distribution in Greater China*. Lanham: Rowan and Littlefield.

## CHAPTER 19

ANYONE FOR GAMES? VIA THE NEW INTERNATIONAL DIVISION OF CULTURAL LABOUR[1]
Toby Miller

This chapter examines the double-sided nature of global gaming that reappears and circles in on itself in seemingly endless binary iterations: freedom to play against freedom to monitor; creativity versus industrialization; new ideas opposed to intellectual property; and big capital and big government contra cybertarian mythology. This Janus face is on display most obviously in the networked online multi-user environment: everybody's in a focus group and everybody is an active fan, because there's no other way, in a sense, to participate. At the same time, a small number of countries and companies absolutely dominate the games sector.

Theorizing globalization and culture

Today's era of (technical) post-imperialism sees capital move at high velocity, lighting on areas and countries in a promiscuous way. Materials and people are exchanged across the globe in a profoundly asymmetrical manner. Globalization stands for a sense from across time and space that those very categories are in peril, as jobs are undertaken by people on the basis of price and docility rather than locale. And nations are threatened by corporate control, as unelected, far-distant elites displace or instruct local politicians. In the global economic system that has evolved since the mid-1970s, Northern class fractions support a transnational form of capital that has displaced non-capitalist systems elsewhere. Regulatory and other mechanisms have liberalized world trade, contained socialism, promoted legislation favorable to capitalist expansion, and aggregated world markets. What are the cultural corollaries of these developments? Cultural diffusion has always been international, but the velocity and profundity of its processes are increasing. For instance, in material terms, it took 40 years before radio reached 50 million homes; 13 years for television to do so; and four for the Internet (International Labour Office, 2000). And at a conceptual level, an indissoluble link melds the 'ideology of corporate globalization' with the 'ideology of worldwide communication' through decades of European and US government and corporate funding for intellectuals to cultivate the mythology of communications technologies as signs of freedom, even as these innovations enabled 'a world ruled by the logic of social and economic segregation' (Mattelart, 2002: 591–2, 596–9).

Widespread reaction against globalization has foregrounded the US capitalist media as crucial components in the formation of commodities, mass culture, and economic and political organization in the Third World. Examples include the export of Hollywood screen products and infrastructure, and US dominance of international communications technology. Critics claim that the rhetoric of development through commercialism had decelerated economic growth and disenfranchised local culture, with emergent ruling classes in dependent nations exercising local power only at the cost of relying on foreign capital and ideology. But because culture covers aesthetic discrimination as much as monetary exchange, it is simultaneously the key to international textual trade and one of its limiting factors. Ethics, affect, custom and other forms of knowledge both enable and restrict commodification. Africa, the Middle East and Latin America have long-standing debates about local democratic participation and control; the major economic powers of Western Europe argue about the need to build pan-Europeanism in contrast to the homogenizing forces of Americanization; and the former state-socialist polities of Eastern and Central Europe seek to develop independent civil societies with privatized media. Meanwhile, an array of mostly textual critics and neoliberal social scientists argue for the splendid autonomy of audiences to the export of the popular. They stress culture's destination rather than its origin, focusing on the power of interpretation over production.

Rather than adjudicate between these graceless antinomies, which I have long argued need not operate in opposition to one another, I want to get at a much more complex and contradictory approach to games and globalization, via the New International Division of Cultural Labour (NICL). The NICL derives from the idea of a New International Division of Labour (NIDL), which states that developing markets for labour and sales, and the shift from the spatial sensitivities of electrics to the spatial *in*sensitivities of electronics, pushed businesses beyond treating Third World countries as suppliers of raw materials to look on them as shadow-setters of the price of work, competing among themselves and with the First World (Fröbel et al., 1980). As production was split across continents, the prior division of the globe into a small number of industrialized market economies and a majority of under-developed countries was compromised. Whereas the old IDL kept labour costs down through the formal and informal slavery of colonialism (the trade in people and indentureship) and importation of cheap raw materials with value added in the metropole, this eventually produced successful action by the working class at the center to redistribute income away from the bourgeoisie. The response from capital was to export production to the Third World, focusing especially on young women workers. Since that time, any decision by a multinational to invest carries the seeds of insecurity, because it will move on if tax incentives or other factors of production beckon – or at least threaten to do so, thereby eliciting obedience from the state and the proletariat. We shall see the NICL at play with reference to games. But first we must address some of the rhetoric of games analysis.

Theorizing games

Gaming has been around for a long time. In my college bar a quarter of a century ago, I watched as separatist men played *Space Invaders* in one corner, and separatist women shot pool in the other. In the first case, women did not try to join in. In the second, men who did so were told to stay away lest they 'invade our space', with the exception of a retired naval cook who had gone back to school to major in women's studies, the better to understand his teenage daughters. Three decades later, women comprised 39 per cent of US gamers and more than 50 per cent of Korean (Taylor, 2006: 93). The data for pool are less easy to come by, as it doesn't lend itself to consumer surveillance the way gaming does through the purchase of materials and subscriptions.

There is something different about today from the 1970s, isn't there, in this era of the more privatized electronic game, played by so many more people, in so many different environments? Aren't we at a bold new dawn of meaning, where cybertarian technophiles, struck by the 'digital sublime', attribute magical properties to a communication and cultural technology that supposedly obliterates geography, sovereignty and hierarchy – a combination of truth and beauty that has the potential to heal the wound of the division of labour and turn nation-states into memorabilia? Doesn't this promise a perfect global liberation of the mind? The gaming environment makes consumers into producers, frees the disabled from exclusion, encourages new subjectivities, rewards intellect and competitiveness, links people across cultures, and allows millions of flowers to bloom in a post-political cornucopia – or at least, that is what some analysts fantasize. As Vincent Mosco reminds us, these 'myths are important both for what they reveal (including a genuine desire for community and democracy) and for what they conceal (including the growing concentration of communication power in a handful of transnational media businesses)' (2004: 19).

There is a powerful binary in games studies that situates, at one antinomy, an omniscient, omnipotent group of technocrats plotting to control the emotions and thoughts of young people around the world and turn them into malleable consumers, workers and killers; and at the other, all-powerful desiring machines called players, whose wishes are met by producers (Tobin, 2004). In the latter group, new-media *savants* are fond of invoking pre-capitalist philosophers, thereby dodging questions of labour exploitation through wages by heading instead for aesthetics. High aesthetics and high technology are brokered through high neo-liberalism. The dominant discourses on gaming fail to explain, for example, that the first electronic game, *Tennis for Two*, was produced at the US Department of Nuclear Energy (Consalvo, 2006). But the fantasy that innovation comes from supply and demand mechanics is misleading. The state – specifically the military wing – is at the core. They refer to ludology (but ignore the work of professional associations such as The Association for the Study of Play or the North American Society for the Sociology of Sport) and narratology, returning to the non-materialist, non-medium specific work of literary studies (but ignore the media studies parlayed by the International Association for Media and Communication Research or the Union for Democratic Communication). Drawing on the possessive individualism of neo-classical economics, reactionary game analysts study virtual environments as ways of understanding 'whole societies under controlled conditions' (Castronova, 2006), ignoring or caricaturing the discourses of history and ethnography in the process.

Collective struggles between social actors – often drawing on this binary – are at the heart of gaming, as per the fascinating 2007 conflict between Sony and the Church of England and Mothers Against Violence over the depiction of Manchester Cathedral in *Resistance: Fall of Man*. Set in the 1950s, *Resistance* features violent science-fiction battles. It alarmed clerics, given the city's problems with gun violence. They were also perturbed by the use of a religious environment for death and mayhem. Whereas the Church and the Mothers argued for an undue and deliberate realism to the setting that would encourage mimesis and pervert vulnerable minds, the multinational's riposte relied on three arguments: the imagery was 'game-created footage' rather than 'video or photography' (it wasn't documenting staged or naturally occurring events, so it wasn't realistic); the story drew on a fictional genre (there is no relation between narrative and reality); and the company had secured relevant permissions (copyright is central) ('Cathedral Row...', 2007). These often contending areas of analysis – civil-society versus corporate claims about media effects, industrial uses of genre, and the setting provided by legal frameworks – are just as important as the apolitical, ahistorical objects and methods of study that characterize hegemonic games analysis. Hence my stress on political economy in this chapter.

Games and the global

Electronic games have been sold internationally since the mid-1980s, from arcade play to handheld consoles to on-line subscriptions; from imaginary spheres of self-absorption to violent recruitment devices for the military. The overall market of US$30 billion is expected to grow by 16 per cent annually between 2006 and 2009. Games incarnate the centralized labour of production and the decentralized labour of interpretation that constitutes the NICL, as evidenced by Hong Kong participants hybridizing games into local forms of popular culture via references to local films and comic books in the arcade *argot* of play, and by redisposal inside cultural production, with comic-book artists drawing on the games (Consalvo, 2006; 'Console Wars', 2007; Ng, 2006; Withers, 2006).

This multiplicity of purposes has been a boon to corporations and the state. Coca-Cola is diverting money from its TV advertising budget to place products in games, and generating 'advergames' for people to play during brief respites from work. They cost US$50,000, with global applicability, as opposed to US$500,000 for a spot on television. By 2007, interactive advertisements embedded in games and quizzes accounted for a twelfth of online marketing revenue. And institutions such as the Christian Game Developers Conference have emerged alongside hundreds of faith-based companies that target parents overcome with moral panic and superstition. Instead of continuing to denounce the medium, Christians are joining the trend, much as they did with rock music in the 1970s. Slow to catch on and overcome their fears, then competent at capitalizing on means of renewing their media to suit the young of the time – from *Jesus Christ Superstar* on Broadway to *The Bible Game* on PlayStation 2 (Carolipio, 2006; Gaudiosi, 2005). Then there is the US military, the great mismanaged, misdirected, but numerically and technologically masterful behemoth that underpins globalization. It needs to recruit 80,000 new people a year in order to maintain world dominance. The military–diplomatic–fiscal disasters of the 2001–07 period jeopardized the steady supply of new troops, imperiling the army's stature as the nation's premier employer of 17–24 year-old workers. In response, videogames have interpellated the country's youth by situating their bodies and minds firing the same weapons and facing the same issues as in the real world, with TV commercials depicting soldiers directly addressing gamers and urging them to show their manliness by volunteering for the real thing and serving abroad to secure US power. Designed with a multi-million dollar budget, these games have registered seven million users. Daily downloads are at a rate of between 10,000 and 50,000, and just under half of new recruits report having played prior to enlistment. Companies like Pandemic (part-owned by that high-corporate moralist, Bono) invest, along with the University of Southern California's Institute for Creative Technologies. They produce recruitment tools like *Full Spectrum Warrior* ('New Wargames…', 2007; Verklin and Kanner, 2007). On the other hand, we must consider more positive instances of globalization and gaming: *Food Force*, an advergame developed by the World Food Program to highlight global hunger; MTV's *Darfur is Dying*, which drew 700,000 people online in a month; Serious Games Interactive's *Global Conflict: Palestine*, with a journalist protagonist seeking the truth amongst conflicting sources analysing the conflict between Israel and Palestine; and *A Force More Powerful: The Game of Nonviolent Strategy* ('And Now…', 2005; 'Middle-East Conflict Informs Game', 2006; Verklin and Kanner, 2007).

And a sharply critical political-economic approach must account for supposedly cybertarian environments, such as the World Cyber Games or *Second Life*. The latter is a massively multiplayer online game (MMOGs). MMOG virtual worlds provide US$1 billion revenue a year in the US and Europe, and have seen Korea and China surpass Japan as key markets by contrast with the console sector, because companies there favor it as a counter to piracy. Since 2001, women have outnumbered men as participants in these necessarily social and collaborative enterprises (Day, 2005: 454; Malaby, 2006; 'MMO Games…', 2007; Taylor, 2006: 93). Originating primarily through freeware and extra-commercial organization, they are nevertheless increasingly corporatized and governed by end-user license agreements (EULAs), which mean that when players invent new ideas, they add value to corporate property. In three years from its public opening in 2003, *Second Life* – built by residents – attracted well over a million participants from across the globe. But even this utopia was animated by 'pioneering' and suburbanizing discourses of possessive individualism. Far-distant from communal utopias, *Second Life* promises the 'perfect parcel of land to build your house or business' and, of course, a unit of currency that is convertible to Yanqui dollars at online exchanges (secondlife.com/whatis/). It comes as

no surprise that this entrepreneurial fantasy was founded with money from Jeff Bezos (Amazon), Mitchell Kapor (Lotus), and Pierre Omidyar (eBay), or that Wells Fargo bank sports a branded island within the environment. Linden Labs, which owns and operates *Second World*, does software work that permits inventiveness by others (though they must pay to gain real estate) (Taylor, 2006: 21, 124, 130, 134).

More overtly corporate (and a crucial part of audience/player surveillance) is the Hollywood Stock Exchange (HSX), founded in 1996 and sold to Cantor Fitzgerald, a Wall Street firm, in 2001. 'HSX was conceived as a game to take advantage of the public's obsession with box-office numbers', said one of the founders, but the real plan was to sell forecasts based on 'information it has collected on the folks who frequent the site' (founder quoted in Bates, 2000). By 2004, HSX had about a million registered users, mostly affluent young men, who trade stocks of movies and bonds of stars. Music groups are also traded. HSX makes up starting prices based on past performances and sales, then lets trading determine price fluctuations, which it tracks as per a Wall Street exchange. Cantor sells HSX research to film studios as 'a real-time update of consumer opinion… using the predictive market versus going out on the street with a clipboard and asking people questions' (Alster, 2003). It also has a Sports Stock Exchange, which began to coincide with the men's World Cup of association football. The company boasts about potential reuse of 'the data collected from the Exchange as market research to entertainment, consumer product and financial institutions and as original content to radio, television and print media' (hsx.com/about). Players are played – they are made into samples for predicting cultural taste. This type of surveillance has become 'the interactivity that matters', by 'cracking human personality in real time' and turning it into global data (Burke, 2003).

Then there is the more venerable console sector. Half of all console games played across the globe are owned by three corporations: Sony, Electronic Arts and Nintendo. New consoles come on the market every half-decade to build in obsolescence and exclude new entrants. Since the original Sony PlayStation in 1995, the idea has been to preclude outsiders from creating programs for general use beyond a corporate platform – copying the model of the sealed-set transistor that turned radios into receiving rather than transmitting devices decades earlier. This has also led to rapid takeovers of small companies by the major firms. So one might argue that *Grand Theft Auto* was a neat instance of cultural appropriation, since this *ur*-text of US urban dross was actually created in Britain – but it was also a *niche* instance, since the business was quickly taken over by Yanqui capital. Independents must always look to global sales, because most domestic markets are too slight to recoup investment in development and promotion (Green, 2006; Kerr and Flynn, 2003; Thompson, 2006).

In 2000, PlayStation 2 outdid Nintendo's GameCube and Microsoft's Xbox, selling 100 million units and gaining 70 per cent of the international market, while the next phase sees PlayStation 3 pitted against Xbox 360, which came out first and sold six million consoles in its first year, and Nintendo Wii, a cheap alternative designed for easy-going neophytes and casual users rather than needy obsessives. By 2006, global sales of PlayStation 2 stood at 100 million and Xbox, 40 million. PlayStation 3 is designed to promote Sony's Blue-Ray high-definition technology and Internet video downloading. The resources allocated to global marketing stretch even these privileged companies, with Sony profits tumbling by 68 per cent in 2006–07 as a consequence, because the straightforward Wii was becoming more popular in both Europe and the US. Meanwhile, Xbox 360 draws on old-style cybertarian mythology by inviting amateurs to create new texts through use of Game Studio Express – for ultimate ownership by Microsoft. Convergence is not about the dominance of the consumer or of interactivity – it is about corporate planning and intra-class rivalry, but the calculation and management of consumers, and associated intra-class conflict, does not come cheaply. Nor is it cheap for workers – Sony was quick to fire hundreds of employees from its European operations. The only influential group of consumers is the critical mass located in Japan and the US – their tastes determine what is produced for console consumption. Britain is a distant third in market power. Efforts to make Korea a key player are not about new forms of capitalism, but very old ones, with a national Game Academy funded by large multinationals and the state (Butcher, 2006; Hogge, 2006; 'Playing a Different Game', 2006; 'Playing a Long Game', 2006; 'PlayStation Creator…', 2007; 'PS3 Launch…', 2007; Thompson, 2006; Verklin and Kanner, 2007).

Big publishers develop exploitative labour practices as their power increases via the destruction and purchase of small businesses and insertion into the NICL. Rock Star, for instance, is a British company with a studio in Vancouver that made *Grand Theft Auto*. Their game process starts when someone builds a demonstration model and shows it to the company, which previews it to the press. The firm generally decides to ready the game in time for Christmas sales. By March, they only have six months left, and require workers to be present 60 hours a week, promising a bonus when the game is shipped. Then management goes over the game and insists on changes. By June, people are working 80 hours a week. Then the company finds the product won't be available by Christmas. It shifts shipment to March, but keeps everyone working at the same rate. The bonus migrates months into the future.

Workers for a major gaming firm like Electronic Arts (EA), which makes *The Sims*, are under monumental pressure both in terms of the need to create more and more product for the global market and to compete with other workers at home and off-shore. In 2004, the blogger ea_spouse pseudonymously posted a vibrant account of grotesque exploitation experienced by her *fiancé* and others at EA, via *LiveJournal*. She eloquently ripped back the veneer of joyous cybertarianism from games development, noting that EA's claim to blend aesthetics and technology, as per their name and corporate trademark 'Challenge Everything' belied both its treatment of workers and its products. Re labour, she wrote: 'To any EA executive that happens to read this, I have a good challenge for you: how about safe and sane labour practices for the people on whose backs you walk for your millions?' Re texts, she challenged: 'Churning out one licensed football game after another doesn't sound like challenging much of anything to me; it sounds like a money farm' (ea_spouse, 2004). Then she detailed the exploitation: a putatively limited 'pre-crunch' is announced, such that 48-hour weeks are required, with the alibi that months of this will obviate the need for a real 'crunch' at the conclusion of development; the pre-crunch goes on beyond its deadline; then 72-hour work weeks are mandated; that crunch passes its promised end; illness and irritability strike; then a new crunch is announced, whereby everyone must work between 85 and 91-hour weeks, 0900–2200 Monday–Sunday inclusive, with the occasional Saturday evening off after 1830. There is no overtime or leave in return for this massive expenditure of talent and time. The workers discern no measurable impact from the crunch other than on themselves – so many errors are made from fatigue that time is needed to correct them. Turnover amongst engineering workers ran at 50 per cent. In the middle of this, *Fortune* magazine ranked EA among the '100 Best

Companies to Work For'. It was #91 amongst corporations that 'try hard to do right by their staff' as measured by the Great Place to Work® Institute in San Francisco. EA described itself to *Fortune* as 'a one-class society', and its Vice-President of Human Resources announced the following astonishing dictum: 'Most creativity comes at one of two times: When your back is up against the wall or in a time of calm.' In case readers found this firing-squad analogy alarming, *Fortune* reassured them that workers could 'refresh their energy with free espresso or by playing volleyball and basketball'. In 2007, the firm ranked #62 in the magazine's 'List of Industry Stars' (Levering et al., 2003; 'The List...', 2007).

Meanwhile, ea_spouse's brave intervention (as we say in academia) or outburst (as they say elsewhere) generated febrile and substantial responses to *LiveJournal*, such as calls for unionization, appeals to federal and state labour machinery, confirmation that EA was horrendous but by no means aberrant, frustration that the bourgeois press was disinclined to investigate or even report the situation, a series of wonderful denunciations of asinine managerialism and private-sector bureaucracy ('The average game company manager is quite possibly the worst qualified leader of people in the world'), and a recognition of how intellectual-property rights make labour disposable ('I'm beginning to think that EA is really nothing more than a licensing warehouse. [T]hey'll always be able to recruit naïve talent to slave away... alienating talent is not a big problem for them').[2] But labour solidarity remains compromised by job threats from around the world and non-disclosure agreements, which send a chill through conversations across employment silos (Waters, 2007).

Of course, work on games does not end with production. The Political Economy Research Institute's 2004 *Misfortune 100: Top Corporate Air Polluters in the United States* has media owners at numbers 1, 3, 16, 22 and 39. Many of the multinational corporations have denied responsibility for the post-consumption histories of their dangerous products, with recycling programs that corporations sponsor in the US relying on customers paying them to take away these poisonous goods. The Environmental Protection Agency remains stoically silent on the topic, and the US has used the World Trade Organization to counter efforts at diminishing pollution from this equipment. Fortunately, the combination of European market power and the European Union's crucial Restriction of Hazardous Substances legislation, plus other mandates already in place, mean that even US firms specializing in hazardous computer parts must now adhere to strict safety standards in their components, if not their work practices. At the other end of this NICL, those games that are sold physically end up as recycling fodder, along with the materials they are played on. Sixteen-year-old girls leave villages in northern China to work in effectively indentured compounds run by Japanese, Taiwanese and US businesses in the south to build computers used for games. Pre-teen Chinese girls pick away without protection at discarded First-World computers full of leaded glass in order to find precious metals, then dump the remains in landfills. The metals are sold to recyclers, who do not use landfills or labour in the First World because of environmental and industrial legislation *contra* the destruction to soil, water and workers that are caused by the dozens of poisonous chemicals and gases in these dangerous machines. More than 130,000 personal computers a day are thrown out around the world, leading to millions of pounds of toxic waste. PlayStation consoles are illegal in many countries (not the US) because of the deadly levels of cadmium contained in their cables (Basel Action Network, 2004; Basel Action Network and Silicon Valley Toxics Coalition, 2002; 'Electronics...', 2005; Reygadas, 2002: 17, 86–104; 'Europe's Rules...', 2005; 'First Time Unlucky', 2005; 'Give Us...', 2005; Pellow and Park, 2002: 201–2; Tamaki, 2006: C4; Wallach and Woodall/Public Citizen, 2004: 37, 299–300 n. 98).

Conclusion

The global gaming industry is essentially a rather banal repetition of Hollywood history: domination by firms that buy up or destroy small businesses and centralize power in the metropole; decimation of little bedroom concerns in favor of giant conglomerates; a working mythology of consumer power; and massive underwriting by the state (Kerr and Flynn, 2003; Miller et al., 2005). We need to follow the money, follow the labour, follow the high-tech trash. And follow Mosco, when he reminds us that once the utopic/dystopic couplet of new communications technologies and cultural genres has been played out, the real work begins, at that moment when the 'mythic period' of alarm and fantasy has given way to banality and every move is neither hailed nor derided, but silently normalized (2004: 19). Then we can understand whether anyone or everyone is 'for games', and how the NICL operates. Otherwise, we are left with the same tired choice placed before the putatively sovereign rational consumer: 'the freedom to choose after all the major political, economic, and social decisions have already been made' (Mosco, 2004: 60).

Box 19.1 Video game expos: the fall of LA and the rise of Tokyo

The video game industry is entering a new era, an era where technology and creativity will fuse to produce some of the most stunning entertainment of the twenty-first century. Decades from now, cultural historians will look back at this time and say it is when the definition of entertainment changed forever.

Douglas Lowenstein, President, Entertainment Software Association. (Entertainment Software Association, 2006)

Stepping onto the expo's main hall floor, you are overwhelmed by the crowd of people circulating in currents around a sea of booths. The deafening sounds of machine guns, space aliens, boxing matches, and a thousand other storylines being played out by participants fill the air. Humans in fantastical character suits roam about handing out promotional flyers. This is just a snapshot of the 'game show' experience shared by droves of game-lovers and industry members who are increasing in numbers each year around the world.

Video and computer games have become a worldwide consumer phenomenon. From North America to Africa to Asia, children and adults alike purchase and play video games at unprecedented rates. This is illustrated by the impressive overall industry growth rate of 18 per cent experienced in 2005 (Riley, n.d.). In order to further tap into this growing consumer base and to act as a showcase for new products, various members of the industry launched several game fairs throughout the mid-1990s. There are now a plethora of smaller game conventions, fairs and expos. However, two particular shows have emerged as the largest and geographically representational of the two industry sales Meccas: the US and Japan.

The LA Electronic Entertainment Expo (or E3) is organized by the Entertainment Software Association (ESA) and was originally intended to target industry professionals, journalists, developers and guests of exhibitors such as celebrities. However, as time went on, word of the Expo spread and was increasingly infiltrated by Gamers, Bloggers and other members of the quasi-public audience. Due to these additional participants, the attendance numbers for the E3 swelled to 70,000 in 2005 (*E3 Media and Business*

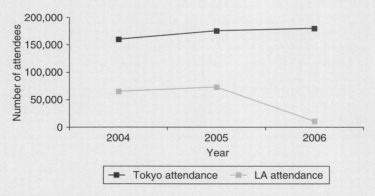

Figure 19.1 Game show attendance for E3 and the Tokyo Game Show

Source: E3 Insider: The Official E3 Website website and Tokyo Game Show 2006 website

(Continued)

(Continued)

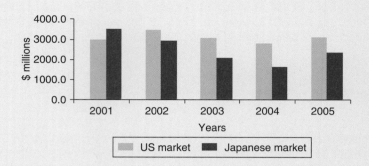

Figure 19.2   Game console market values for the USA and Japan

Source: Datamonitor (Japanese market, 2006) and Datamonitor (US market, 2006)

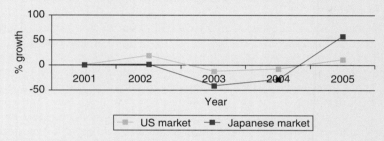

Figure 19.3   Game console market growth for the USA and Japan

Source: Datamonitor (Japanese market, 2006) and Datamonitor (US market, 2006)

Summit website). In October 2006, the ESA shocked the industry by announcing a massive scaling-back of the E3 to be invite-only with attendance projected at about 5,000 people. The ESA changed the name of the event to the E3 Media and Business Summit and is now marketed as a more controlled and business-like event (*E3 Media and Business Summit* website). Critics are concerned about the effects of this lower-profile approach on the US industry's sales as well as the effects on smaller game developers who had used the E3 as their main source of publicity and exposure in the past (see Figure 19.1).

This year Tokyo is being hyped as the rising mega-star of gaming venues with its previous competition, E3, reigning in attendance numbers. From 2004 to 2005, the Tokyo Show went from 117 exhibitors to 131 and attendance rose from 160,000 to 176,000 people (see Figure 19.1). These numbers, while astronomical compared to the E3, are mainly due to the open-door policy Tokyo took in allowing the public to attend. What does this mean in overall sales and the regional economic impact of game expos on the US and Japanese consumer markets?

Game console sales are a common tool used in the video game industry to calculate and project overall revenue. Figure 19.2 depicts the evolution of total US dollar market values for console sales in the US as compared to Japan. Interestingly we see Japan starting out strong in 2001, then showing a substantial decrease through 2002 to 2004 and beginning to make a significant comeback in market value in 2005. Conversely, the US saw a surge in market value in 2002, allowing it to surpass Japan and since that time has leveled off or shown incremental increases. Actual growth rates of both industries show patterns which help to explain overall market values and possible relationships to the major gaming expos. The US console sales growth figures again show a peak in 2002 followed by a subsequent decline and then consistently similar rates through 2005. Japan, on the other hand, shows a significant decline in growth in 2003 but then a remarkable comeback with a growth rate of close to 46 per cent, surpassing the US in 2005. While many external and cultural factors affect the sales of video games and consoles, marketing to the Japanese public has been a powerful tool. The Tokyo Game Show's decision to remain open to the public has provided a visceral cultural and marketing experience to over 176,000 people and most likely contributed to the goliath-like Japanese growth rates.

In contrast, the new professionalized version of E3 targets video game producers rather than focusing on the demand side of the market. This may jeopardize the US industry's growth in two ways. First, through the elimination of the largest US-based video game publicity event, which drew in increasing numbers of consumers with each additional year E3 was in existence. Second, the old E3 format highlighted underground game designers and cutting-edge technology that created an atmosphere of excitement and anticipation with both suppliers and consumers. The loss of the old E3 may not initially lower overall video game console sales in the US; however, it may impede growth rates which are already showing signs of stagnation, thus having a long-term negative effect on the industry.

Meghan Corroon

Box 19.2   Virtual worlds

Massively Multiplayer Online Games (MMOGs) is an umbrella term for web-based games that are capable of supporting thousands of players in a persistent online universe. The evolution of gaming environments towards a more complex web-based, creative, and user-defined emphasis has spurred the popularity of highly interactive virtual worlds. In July 2006, the total number of MMOG players worldwide exceeded 12 million, a 22 per cent increase from 2005 (mmochart.com). In the same year, MMOGs constituted 55 per cent of the market share of all online computer games (DFC Intelligence Group, 2006).

Although fantasy constitutes the bulk of MMOG game genres, the growing popularity and economic utility of Massively Multiplayer Online Social Games (MMOSGs) has drawn much attention in recent years. Through free, downloadable client-software, game publishers allow players' avatars (self-created virtual personas) to simulate real life. No scores are kept, but rather the rules of the game are for players to interact, communicate, trade, create, play, build and live with each other. While initial membership is free, game publishers amass revenues through monthly subscription rates, advertising, and as traders of in-world money (virtual currency). In a recent report by TowerGroup (Aug 2006), online social world revenues reached US$2.5 billion in 2006, and are expected to reach US$9 billion with 40 million users by 2010 (see Figure 19.4).

'Your World, Your Imagination' – Your Second Life

One notable MMOSG is called *Second Life*. Created by the San Francisco-based Linden Lab in 2001, the *Second Life* world (also referred to as a 'society' by the maker) has grown from a handful of residents to almost 4.5 million in February 2007 (see Figure 19.5).

Although a majority of players come from the United States, a large number also represent European countries, followed by Brazil, Canada and others (see Figure 19.6). Residents' *avatars* take on human appearances and can walk, run, fly or teleport through the *Second Life* world.

Figure 19.4   Global online social world revenues

Source: Tower Group (Aug 2006).

(Continued)

(Continued)

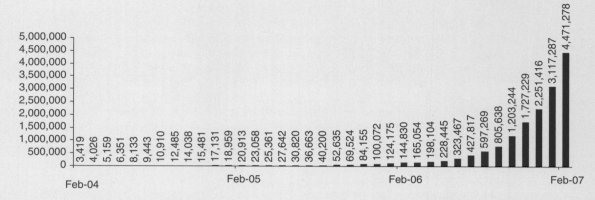

Figure 19.5 *Second Life* **residents**

Source: Linden Lab (Feb 2007)

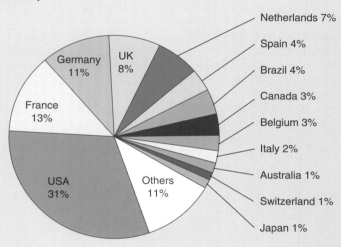

Figure 19.6 *Second Life* **active residents by country**

Source: Linden Lab (Feb 2007)

What sets *Second Life* apart from other MMOSGs is that it allows its users to maintain the intellectual property rights for anything created in-world. The *Second Life* software is available through Open Source, providing residents with the scripting language and tools to develop their virtual environment. In this way, *Second Life* is entirely built and owned by its residents, and dependent upon the creativity of its users. Professor Edward Castronova, a leading scholar on MMORGs and virtual worlds, attributes creativity and property rights to *Second Life*'s growth, '[i]f you let people capture the value of what they create, they're going to create a lot more' (*BusinessWeek*, 2006); thus, in the case of virtual worlds, not only property rights, but creative freedom, are the fundamental elements for longevity and success. In 2006, the annual gross domestic product of *Second Life* was estimated at US$64 million (Newitz, 2006). As the cornerstone of the *Second Life* economy, the Linden dollar (L$) has a current exchange rate of approximately US$1 to L$189. Residents can exchange real money for L$ via Lindenx (the official *Second Life* exchange), other residents or through the growing number of online game currency exchange services. From January 2006 to 2007, the total volume of $US exchanged increased by 89 per cent (see Figure 19.7).

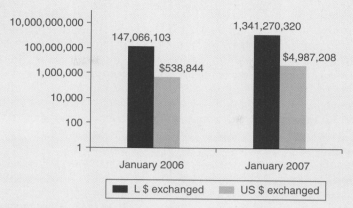

Figure 19.7 Lindenx currency exchange

Source: Linden Lab (May 2007)

Player motivations for becoming residents vary from simple curiosity to socializing, to commercial and economic purposes. Invariably, someone will meet someone with something they need or want: a friend, a date, professional advice, knowledge, a new outfit for their avatar, music, or a lesson in a foreign language. Linden Lab does not track numbers within professions; however, it has a growing list of in-world job titles reported by its residents:

- party and wedding planner
- pet manufacturer
- casino operator
- tattooist
- nightclub owner
- automotive manufacturer
- fashion designer
- aerospace engineer
- custom avatar designer
- jewellry maker
- architect
- XML coder
- freelance scripter
- game developer
- fine artist
- virtual film set designer
- tour guide
- dancer

- musician
- custom animation creator
- lottery operator
- theme park developer
- real estate speculator
- vacation resort owner
- advertiser
- bodyguard
- magazine publisher
- private detective
- writer
- gamer
- landscaper
- publicist
- special effects designer
- gunsmith
- hug maker

Like any real world country, *Second Life* faces issues of accountability, governance and protection of rights for its residents. Linden Lab's strict policy of zero governance has had mixed results. On the one hand, *Second Life* represents a truly free and democratic society where artistic expression, social networking and good will are exercised and promoted; on the other, it represents a world where adults are given a free reign to wreak chaos and showcase pornography, violence and plagiarize ideas from fellow residents. *Second Life's* Open Source platform leaves it vulnerable to cyber-hackers who attempt to steal the personal information on residents from Linden Lab's database or plant bugs in the *Second Life* system in order to shut it down. While *Second Life* is increasingly utilized as a platform for international organizations like the UN and by civil society social movements to organize and

(Continued)

network in-world and beyond, much to the chagrin of its residents, *Second Life* remains open to governments and corporations who see it as a venue for political campaigns, advertising and promotion of transnational corporations such as General Motors, Toyota, IBM and Sony, with others (Wal-Mart, Intel and American Express) waiting at the gates. Finally, the larger question remains for governments when virtual market transactions are clearly entering into real world economics – should these exchanges be taxed and subject to the same rules and regulations as trade in the real world?

Despite these issues, there is no denying that the development of markets for virtual goods, the ability to exercise one's creativity without limit, the possibility of experiencing life outside the bounds of physics (flying) or the threat of death, and the promise of participation in a world where networks bridge the global into a virtual world will continue to capture the attention and imagination of the real world from this day forward. Gartner, an information technology research and consulting company, predicts that 80 per cent of all active internet users and Fortune 500 companies will have an avatar in a virtual world by 2011 (April, 2007). While such predictions are not assured, it is undeniable that virtual worlds are the next large players of the online economy – illustrating the possibility that some emerging markets need not exist in the real world.

Tia Morita

Notes

1 This chapter has benefited greatly from a conversation with Chris Klug and Edna Bonacich and comments from the editors.

2 The string can be found by following the references in ea_spouse, 2004.

REFERENCES

Alster, Norm (2003) 'It's Just a Game, but Hollywood is Paying Attention', *New York Times*: C4, 23 November.

'And Now, a Game from Our Sponsor.' (2005, 11 June). *Economist*: 3–4.

Basel Action Network and Silicon Valley Toxics Coalition (2002) *Exporting Harm: The High-Tech Trashing of Asia*.

Basel Action Network (2004, 4 August). *CRT Glass Recycling Survey Results*.

Bates, James (2000) 'Site Hopes to Put Profitable Spin on Hollywood Fame Game', *Los Angeles Times*: C1, 19 May.

Burke, David (2003) 'Your TV is Watching You', *openDemocracy.net*. 6 March.

BusinessWeek (2006, 1 May) *Virtual Worlds, Virtual Economies*. Retrieved 5/2/07 from http://www.businessweek.com/magazine/content/06_18/b3982010.htm

Butcher, Mike (2006) 'So, You Want a Job in Video Games?', *New Statesman*: 16–17. 13 November.

Carolipio, Redmond (2006) 'What Would Jesus Play?', *Inland Valley Daily Bulletin*. 3 March.

Castronova, Edward (2006) 'On the Research Value of Large Games: Natural Experiments in Norrath and Camelot', *Games and Culture: A Journal of Interactive Media*, 1(2): 163–86.

'Cathedral Row Over Video War Game.' (2007, 9 June). *BBC News* <bbc.co.uk>.

CNET (2006, 9 November) *A Brief History of the Virtual World*. Retrieved 4/16/07 from http://news.com. com/A per cent2Bbrief per cent2Bhistory per cent2Bof per cent2Bthe per cent2Bvirtual per cent2Bworld/2008-1043_3-6134110.html?tag=nefd.lede

Consalvo, Mia (2006) 'Console Video Games and Global Corporations: Creating a Hybrid Culture', *New Media & Society*, 8(1): 117–37.

'Console Wars.' (2007, 24 March). *Economist*: 73–4.

Datamonitor (Japenese market) (2006), 'Game Consoles in Japan: Industry Profile'.

Datamonitor (US market) (2006), 'Game Consoles in the United States: Industry Profile'.

Day, Wan-Wen (2005) 'Being Part of Digital Hollywood: Taiwan's Online Gaming & 3D Animation Industry Under the New International Division of Cultural Labor', *International Journal of Comic Art*, 7(1): 449–61.

DFC Intelligence Group, (2006, 7 March) *Who Will Benefit from the Growth of Online Game Subscription Revenue?* Retrieved 3/9/07 from http://www.dfcint.com/game_article/mar06 article.html

E3 Insider: The Official E3 Website. Available at http://www.e3insider.com/. (3/1/07).

E3 Media and Business Summit. Available at http://www.e3expo.com/. (3/1/07).

ea_spouse (2004) 'EA: The Human Story', *Live Journal*, ea-spouse.livejournal.com/274.html, 11 November.

'Electronics, Unleaded.' (2005, 12 March). *Economist*. 6–7.

Entertainment Software Association (2006) *2006 Sales, Demographic and Usage Data: Essential Facts about the Computer and Video Game Industry*.

'Europe's Rules Forcing U.S. Firms to Clean Up.' (2005, 16 May). *Los Angeles Times*: A1, A6.

'First Time Unlucky.' (2005, 25 February). *Screen International*: 14.

Fröbel, F., Heinrichs, J. and Kreye, O. (1980) *The New International Division of Labour: Structural Unemployment in Industrialised Countries and Industrialisation in Developing Countries*. Trans. P. Burgess. Cambridge: Cambridge University Press; Paris: Éditions de la Maison des Sciences de l'Homme.

Gartner (April 2007) *80 per cent of Users to Get a Second Life*. Retrieved 5/8/07 from eMarketer: http://www.emarketer.com/Article.aspx?1004856 &xsrc=view_article_sitesearchx

Gaudiosi, John (2005) 'Gamers Converting to Christianity', *Hollywood Reporter*, 11. 25 July.

'Give Us Your Tired Computers.' (2005, 29 January). *Economist*: 60.

Green, Chris (2006) 'All Systems Go to Join the Convergence Game', *Screen International*, 4. 17 March.

Hogge, Becky (2006) 'Everyone is a Competitor in a Global Economy', *New Statesman*, 12–14. 13 November.

International Labour Office (2000) *Sectoral Activities Programme: Media; Culture; Graphical*. Geneva.

Kerr, Aphra and Flynn, Roddy (2003) 'Revisiting Globalisation Through the Movie and Digital Games Industries', *Convergence: The International Journal of Research into New Media Technologies*, 9(1): 91–113.

Levering, R., Moskowitz, M., Harrington, A. and Tzacyk, C. (2003) '100 Best Companies to Work For', *Fortune*. 20 January.

'The List of Industry Stars.' (2007). *Fortune*.

Malaby, Thomas (2006) 'Parlaying Value: Capital in and Beyond Virtual Worlds', *Games and Culture: A Journal of Interactive Media*, 1(2): 141–62.

Mattelart, Armand (2002) 'An Archaeology of the Global Era: Constructing a Belief'. Trans. Susan Taponier with Philip Schlesinger. *Media Culture & Society*, 24(5): 591–612.

'Middle-East Conflict Informs Game.' (2006, 18 October). *BBC News* <bbc.co.uk>.

Miller, T., Govil, N., McMurria, J., Maxwell, R. and Wang, T. (2005) *Global Hollywood 2*. London: British Film Institute.

'MMO Games on the Rise.' (2007, 20 March). *BBC News* <bbc.co.uk>.

mmochart.com. Retrieved 3/9/07 from http://www.mmogchart.com/

Mosco, Vincent (2004) *The Digital Sublime: Myth, Power, and Cyberspace*. Cambridge, Mass.: MIT Press.

Murdock, Graham (2005) 'Public Broadcasting and Democratic Culture: Consumers, Citizens, and Communards', in Janet Wasko (ed.) *A Companion to Television*. Malden: Blackwell. pp. 174–98.

'New Wargames for Sir Bono's Profit.' (2007, 6 April). *The Phoenix*: 4.

Newitz, Annalee (2005) 'Your Second Life is Ready', *Popular Science*.

Newitz, Annalee (September 2006) 'Your Second Life Is Ready', *Popular Science*. Retrieved 5/2/07 from http://www.popsci.com/popsci/technology/ 7ba1af8f3812d010vgnvcm1000004eecbccdrcrd/ 3.html

Ng, Benjamin Wai-ming (2006) '*Street Fighter* and *The King of Fighters* in Hong Kong: A Study of Cultural Consumption and Localization of Japanese Games in an Asian Context', *Gamestudies: The International Journal of Computer Game Research*, 6(1).

Pellow, David Naguib and Park, Lisa Sun-Hee (2002) *The Silicon Valley of Dreams: Environmental Injustice, Immigrant Workers, and the High-Tech Global Economy*. New York: New York University Press.

'Playing a Long Game.' (2006, 18 November). *Economist.* 63–4.

'PlayStation Creator to Cut Jobs.' (2007, 18 April). *BBC News* <bbc.co.uk>.

'PS3 Launch Costs Hit Sony Profits.' (2007, 16 May). *BBC News* <bbc.co.uk>.

Reygadas, Luis (2002) *Ensamblando Culturas: Diversidad y conflicto en la globalización de la industria.* Barcelona: Editorial Gedisa.

Riley, David M.I. 'Total Industry Experienced 18 Percent Growth Over 2005', The NDP Group. Available at http://www.npd.com/press/releases/press_070119.html. (3/4/07).

Tamaki, Julie (2006) 'Still Missing the Link', *Los Angeles Times*: C1, C4, 26 March.

Taylor, T. L. (2006) *Play Between Worlds: Exploring Online Game Culture.* Cambridge, Mass.: MIT Press.

Thompson, Bill (2006) 'Video Games Love Affair is 25 Years Old', *New Statesman*, 10–11. 13 November.

Tobin, Joseph (2004) 'Introduction', in Joseph Tobin (ed.) *Pikachu's Global Adventure.* Durham: Duke University Press. pp. 3–33.

Tokyo Game Show 2006. Available at http://expo.nikkeibp.co.jp/tgs/2006/english/exhibitor/. (3/1/07).

TowerGroup (August 2006) *Online Social Worlds as Emerging Markets: A Dose of (Virtual) Reality.* Retrieved 3/9/07 from eMarketer: www.emarketer.com/Chart.aspx?56802

Verklin, David and Kanner, Bernice (2007) 'Why a Killer Videogame is the U.S. Army's Best Recruitment Tool', *MarketingProfs.com.* 29 May.

Wallach, Lori and all, Patrick/Public Citizen (2004) *Whose Trade Organization? A Comprehensive Guide to the WTO.* New York: New Press.

Waters, Darren (2007) 'Videogames Industry "is Maturing"', *BBC News* <bbc.co.uk.> 5 March.

Withers, Kay (2006) 'Intellectual Property Rights are the Lifeblood', *New Statesman*, 24–25. 13 November.

## CHAPTER 20

DIGITAL MEDIA
Gerard Goggin

Digital media are among the most prominent features of the interactions between cultures and globalization, especially when it comes to the cultural economy. Digital media forms are often credited with far-reaching transformations, across West and East, North and South, and hailed for their innovative development of new, hybrid, convergent fields and genres. The problem, however, is that we lack evidence-based, systematic mapping and theorizing about them that is genuinely international in its scope. The thesis of this chapter, therefore, is that digital media forms are novel and highly significant for their contribution to the cultural economy in the context of globalization – but in quite different ways from those assumed in the customary, dominant accounts.

Introduction

While digital media are among the most salient aspects of the interactions between cultures and globalization, they are inadequately understood because they have not been properly theorized and mapped internationally. Consequently, I argue, their place in the globalized cultural economy must be analysed in ways that depart significantly from the conventional wisdom.

In order to elaborate this main argument, and indicate the structure and underpinnings of this chapter, it is helpful to break this thesis down into four sub-theses.

The significance of digital media in cultural economy and globalization

Thesis 1: The novelty of digital media forms

It is a characteristic of media developments especially, but objects and processes of change generally, that their *new* or *revolutionary* character is emphasized. Debate rages on this point, and helpful demystifications abound, especially from literatures of social studies of science and technology. What is difficult, of course is the precise identification of the changes that digital media represent. This is an easier task when it comes to thinking about globalization, as it is clear that important aspects of these contemporary transformations rely upon digital media. Most obviously, the networks and infrastructures that digital media rely upon are now vital to the conduct of economic life – from the digitization of traditional institutions such as stock exchanges, banks, transnational corporations and regulatory institutions, to the important role the Internet plays in information, purchasing and delivery.

What is less well-understood, yet well-established as a process of deep and uncertain transformation, is the way that digital media are reworking previous media and communication. Traditional media companies are still struggling with how to understand the changes to this part of the economy, but we see the following: most newspapers putting significant resources into their online presence; television broadcasters dealing with the expected changes of digital broadcasting, but also the irruption of viewer-led reconfiguration of television through Internet downloading of programs; the slow introduction of digital audio broadcasting, but radio stations quickly responding to the phenomenon of podcasting; advertisers revising their ideas of audience, and the migration of advertising revenues to online sources.

We also see the emergence of new phenomena associated with digital media that do not easily fit traditional media models (at least in their early stages): peer-to-peer (p2p) networks such as music-sharing sites (notably Napster) and video-sharing sites (notably Bittorent); photosharing sites (the proverbial Flickr); new forms of interactive video and televisual networks (most spectacularly Youtube); the personalization and customization of mobile phone culture.

Thesis 2: Digital media are highly significant for their contribution to cultural economy

I would suggest that digital media are highly significant for their contribution to cultural economy in two broad respects. First, digital media have become an important part of the economic system for the production, distribution and consumption of cultural goods and services through market as well as non-market mechanisms. The exact scale of this change is debated. Available data suggests that, while beleaguered and often facing declining consumption and revenue (as in the case of many newspapers for instance), many traditional media, in their non-digital forms, retain their relevance and influence. However, it is the case, as I have suggested, that digital media, notably the Internet, now are responsible for a significant and growing contribution to cultural economy. Second, digital media are associated with new kinds of cultural goods and services, and indeed new sorts of production, distribution and consumption practices and relations. Some of these are most comfortably accounted for by existing market mechanisms: many aspects of mobile phone culture, for instance, such as text messaging, or sales of customizable handsets, or video downloads via cell phone, have been relatively easy to 'commoditize' through the tried-and-tested billing systems of telecommunications carriers and service providers. Other new digital cultural goods and services are not so easy to capture with market mechanisms, or, indeed, arguably are founded on a critical role for non-market mechanisms. User-generated content – as for instance in the consumer-as-producer modification culture of computer gaming or remixing practices of mash-ups or machima – have kicked off furious debate and much commercial interest in what the underlying economic basis of such activity is (Wark, 2007), or to what extent it should be captured and sustained

through market or non-market mechanisms. The debate over the digital or creative commons is one of the key sites for such discussions (Benkler, 2006). Another debate is conducted among economists over whether non-market mechanisms are essential for the character of digital media, or merely a typical feature in the innovation and development processes – that is, evolution – of any new technologies. Here there is disagreement about the political economy associated with digital media, and how it varies or rather conforms to that of other cultural and non-cultural products. A third debate can be seen in the theorizations of the 'new economy', and then the widespread discussions on creativity and innovation (as, for instance, in the creative industries literature).

Thesis 3: That digital forms are also highly significant for the cultural dynamics of globalization

In my second thesis, I have argued that digital media are highly significant for the cultural economy of globalization (while the exact nature of this is still unfolding and currently not well measured or understood). My third thesis is that the forms associated with digital media are also very significant for contemporary cultural dynamics. I imagine there would be broad agreement that through the twentieth century various media took on cardinal importance to cultural dynamics – television, radio, newspapers, magazines, for instance, playing different roles in different societies and contexts. This is documented in a range of media and cultural research, for instance work on media events, or accounts of media and globalization.

Crucial aspects of the new relations and dynamics of culture with contemporary globalization are being played out through new digital forms. The production, transmission and reception of news, for instance, not only involve satellite broadcasting and multi-channel transmission, but also involve a crucial role for website, mobile alerts, blogs, open-source journalism and citizen journalism. Youth culture is both quite local and culturally specific, but also draws upon globally circulating digital media cultures – whether text or instant messaging, games, new forms of website interactivity (Marshall, 2004), and downloading and file exchange practices. The communicative and cultural possibilities of digital media have opened up new public spheres and spaces for cultural diversity and representation, especially for small language groups (Welsh or Catalan, for instance – see Cuncliffe, 2008 and Masip and Mico, 2008), for oppositional groups, or sexual minorities

Table 20.1 Selected countries, telephone, mobile and Internet use in 2006

Countries	Population (millions)	GDP per capita US$ (2005 figure)	Total telephone subscribers per 100 inhabitants	Cellular mobile subscribers per 100 inhabitants	Internet users per 100 inhabitants	Broadband subscribers per 100 inhabitants
Africa						
Ethiopia	79.29	143	2.01	1.09	0.21	–
Tunisia	10.21	2,844	84.30	71.88	12.68	0.43
Americas						
Haiti	8.65	487	7.57	5.87	7.51	–
Mexico	108.33	7,180	70.97	52.63	20.31	3.44
United States	301.03	41,768	134.55	77.40	69.10	19.31
Asia						
China	1,323.64	1,732	62.62	34.83	10.35	3.85
Hong Kong	7.12	25,239	185.53	131.45	52.97	25.24
Korea (Rep.)	47.98	16,309	139.76	83.77	71.11	29.27
Europe						
Turkey	74.17	4,954	85.51	59.58	16.56	3.74
United Kingdom	59.85	37,319	172.54	116.39	56.03	21.71
Oceania						
Australia	20.37	32,512	145.83	97.02	75.12	19.15
Papua New Guinea	6.00	738	2.36	1.27	1.83	–

Source: ITU, 2007a, 2007b, and 2007d

(Berry et al., 2003; McLelland, 2005; O'Riordan and Phillips, 2007). Mobile phone practices, social networking software, and sites such as MySpace or Cyworld, are redrawing the boundaries between private and public spheres, and altering the way we think about the role of 'public' media.

This said, I think there are important caveats to this thesis, which are quite revealing – namely the importance accorded to digital forms varies significantly across social demographics, across countries and regions, and across cultural and linguistic groups, and across class and identity markers (race, disability, gender – for example, Goggin and Newell, 2003; Shade, 2002). Here this points to variances between the production of cultural goods and services and the patterns of economic globalization generally.

Thesis 4: That digital media matters for cultural globalization in ways different from those typically assumed

My fourth thesis implies that we have some way to go before we can grasp the implications of digital media and cultural globalization. There is ground-clearing work still underway to cut through both utopian and dystopian discourses on digital media. There is definitional and conceptual work on the forms and characteristics of digital media. Crucially, I would suggest, there is a need to work along two axes: firstly, to interrelate and reassemble various forms of digital media, as I seek to do here with the Internet and mobiles; secondly, to assemble accounts of digital media that understand how their development, update and logics work, at the same time, in different settings but also transnationally.

In what follows, I develop this argument, and seek to characterize the forms of digital media, by focusing on and broadly contrasting two new technologies and the changes to the relationships among production, distribution and consumption they bring to cultural economy: the Internet and the cellular mobile phone. Following this, I will illustrate and indicate key features of digital media forms, centring on these two cardinal and increasingly related technologies. I will then organize my discussion around five short case studies: p2p technology; blogging; social networking forms; mobile phone culture; and new forms associated with mobile media and wireless devices.

Internet and mobiles

Digital media include a range of potential technologies, applications, genres and forms. There is the threshold difficulty in defining and distinguishing between different instances of digital media. Then there is the lack of reliable, international data on digital media – and especially data and cultural indicators that provide a picture of digital media's place in the cultural economy and globalization.

At the most general level, there are reasonably good statistics relating to Internet access and subscription gathered by many countries that vary in terms of what aspects of the Internet they measure and how rigorously they do so. The International Telecommunications Union (ITU), for example, collects good, relatively reliable world data on Internet and broadband, as well as telephone and mobile subscription.

Since the World Summit on the Information Society, there has been a concerted effort by international agencies to bring together various kinds of statistics and data on digital technologies in order to monitor international progress on meeting objectives on diffusion of ICT: for instance the United Nations 'Partnership on Measuring ICT for Development' has developed core ICT indicators to bring together data on infastructure and access by households, individuals, businesses, as well as economic data on the ICT sector and trade in ICT goods (United Nations Partnership, 2005). The data this has yielded is a good starting point, but has limitations. It is oriented around measuring policy goals of development and basic access to ICTs (ITU, 2007c), and does not contain figures on lucrative and popular aspects of mobile phone and media culture, such as text messaging or multimedia downloads. Such figures on mobile and wireless cultural activity are typically proffered by commercial organizations or industry associations, and at best have only indicative value (the number of text messages being one of the most notorious).

Indeed one of the problems in the data and cultural indicators for assessing digital media is that new Internet-based phenomenon in particular – such as blogging or social software, for instance – are not well covered as yet. The best-known data has come from the US Pew Internet & American Life surveys. In July 2007, to take one instance, Pew reported that:

- 57 per cent of online adults have used the Internet to watch or download video, and that 19 per cent do so on a typical day.

- 74 per cent of broadband users with high-speed connections at home and work watch or download video online.
- 57 per cent of online video viewers share links with others to the video they find. (Madden, 2007)

Also that:

- 55 per cent of online American youth aged 12–17 have created a personal profile online and 55 per cent used social networking sites like MySpace or Facebook. (Lenhart and Madden, 2007)

Excellent country data is now coming from the World Internet Survey partners (www.worldinternetproject.net), such as that released by the University of Southern California-Annenberg Digital Future project (www.digitalcenter.org), or the Oxford Internet Institute (OII; www.oii.ox.ac.uk). The OII survey tells us, for instance, that in 2007:

- 93 per cent of Internet users check their email, 60 per cent do instant messaging, and 29 per cent participate in chat rooms;
- 12 per cent of Internet users write a blog (down from 17 per cent in 2005);
- 17 per cent of Internet users have created a profile on a social networking site;
- 53 per cent of Internet users have downloaded music, 44 per cent played games, and 34 per cent have downloaded video;
- 88 per cent of Britons used a mobile;
- 60 per cent of mobile phone owners use their mobile to take pictures, and 83 per cent text message.

(OII, 2007)

The 2005 Chinese survey forming part of the World Internet project found among those interviewed that:

- Internet Relay Chat (IRC) was the most popular communications tool used on the Internet (68.7 per cent), followed by instant messaging (ICQ or the popular Chinese software QQ) (66.6 per cent), email (63 per cent), bulletin board services (BBS) (44.8 per cent), and blogs (29.5 per cent);
- 62 per cent of Internet users play online games, and 56.7 per cent download music;
- Internet users spend 85 per cent of their time on mainland Chinese content, 8 per cent on overseas Chinese content, 4 per cent on mainland foreign-language content, and 3 per cent on overseas foreign-language content;

- 87.6 per cent of Internet users had a cell phone, compared to 65.6 per cent of non-Internet users. (Liang, 2005)

The World Internet Survey hopes to provide international comparative and longitudinal data on the Internet, however this aspect of the project is still in its early stages. So, while we have good information now available on specific aspects of Internet activity in say Britain and the US, or even Canada and China, there are two major problems from the perspective of trying to understand digital media and cultural globalization. First, we still lack fundamental, detailed, comparative international data on facets of digital media activity. Second, we have very little information that goes further to provide reliable indications of cultural activity and implications of digital media, especially in emerging and new areas of Internet and mobile cultures.

To be sure, there is also quite an amount of other data from organizations that count or estimate Internet hosts, computers and service, as well as figures from market research firms, notably Nielsen. The problem with this information, of course, is that its availability and quality varies, and it is often difficult, when it is publicly available, to scrutinize its methodology. Another threshold problem in mapping digital media is the varying range and quality of information on other digital media, from digital television or radio to mobiles and wireless devices.

Another difficulty with the cultural indicators in this area relates to assessing the economic impact of new aspects of digital media. For example, the nature of new industrial arrangements and work in new kinds of digital media – such as website design, for instance (Gill, 2006) – and what the value of this might be. There is also lack of agreement about the economic value of cultural activity at the intersection of consumption and production. In what sense does the gamer's active construction of computer games add real value to the worth of products and services in this area? Or how do we understand the value that the user's time, creativity and investment in participatory culture (Jenkins, 2006b) adds (for example, to social software and website developments like MySpace or Cyworld or p2p networks)?

Five important digital media forms

1. Peer-to-peer (p2p) networks
A new form that has swiftly challenged existing media arrangements is p2p applications and networks.

Central to these is the notion of sharing between, and using the resources of peers. In computing networking terms, p2p networks move away from topologies based on some powerful computers being designated servers, and many others taking on the subsidiary, passive role of clients. Rather, a p2p network draws upon the computing, data networking power, and resources of all participants.

Currently p2p networks underlie the new digital forms developing in two particular areas of media: music and television (and video). P2p networks rose to prominence with the rise of the music file-sharing technology, Napster. Broadly, Napster allowed users to make their digital music collections available for sharing with millions of other users around the world. During its brief heyday, Napster was a form of what has been called 'disintermediation'. Users bypassed established forms of mediation, and media organizations, institutions and distribution networks (record companies and music stores, for instance) to offer media for consumption by other users. Napster was seen as a threat to the established regimes of copyright and intellectual property, as well as the organized structures of the music industry. Consequently, Napster, and later p2p music file-sharing networks such as Gnutella, Grokster and Kazaa, were vigorously pursued by the international music recording and publishing, and motion picture industries.

While the widespread file-sharing of mainstream, copyrighted material has gone underground, what has emerged is a range of applications and busi-ness models for selling digital music online – something that was not prevalent at the time Napster achieved its popularity. However, what some of these digital music platforms reveal, most controversially Apple's iTunes, is the restrictive guise these corporate forms of digital media can take when compared to the practices of p2p networks. There has been an important struggle globally over the expectations, prices and rights of consumers versus producers and copyright owners when it comes to new digital goods and services. Should consumers be able to copy legitimately purchased digital music onto other computers or devices? Share it with friends? How many times should they be able to listen to it? To what extent can they modify it, and provide it to others?

As well as music, other kinds of files and media content were shared via p2p networks including software, games and video from relatively early on. However, it was not until about 2005 with the diffusion of broadband Internet and widespread adoption of specific p2p applications such as BitTorrent that concern grew about the practices of downloading of television programs over the Internet. Digital personal video recorders made recording of television programs relatively easy and once a digital recording was available it could be easily copied and made available for peer-sharing online (indeed many programs are now copied directly onto a networked computer device). Once acquired via download, the television program could be watched on a range of devices, including laptop computers, handhelds, video iPods or televisions.

Like the new p2p forms of digital music consumption, we can see television downloading as an organic movement of citizens and consumers reconfiguring television. As much as anything this is an impatient response to the slow and disappointing introduction of digital broadcasting and much vaunted digital set-top boxes, not to mention the circumscribed capability of personal video recorders in many countries, tightly controlled by existing television broadcasters and copyright holders.

Space does not permit a full discussion of p2p networks, and their complexities as new forms of cultural and political economies, but it is a crucial site for understanding new forms of digital media.

2. Blogging

Since their beginnings in online diaries in the mid-1990s, blogs (web logs) have now achieved a phenomenal popularity. While the measurement of the number of blogs is far from accurate, the sheer numbers of people blogging is phenomenal. The leading US site Technorati estimated approximately 75 million blogs worldwide. Blogging has developed its own not inconsiderable industry, including software companies (WordPad), hosting sites (such as LiveJournal), and indexing, searching and commentary. Even assuming many people begin blogging enthusiastically, and then their blogging tails off, it is evident that blogs have considerably extended the possibilities of media in a number of directions.

First, the nature of blogs as a dialogical medium – with comment, annotation, tracking and linking being inherent to what have come to characterize them (what has been captured in the idea of the autonomous realm of the blogosphere) – has genuinely added interactivity and a new textual and conversational infrastructure not only to the Internet,

but especially to mainstream media. Consequently, it became commonplace for many well-known media to add blogs to their cross-platform repertoire – the blog of the Manchester *Guardian* newspaper being just one example where considerable thought has gone into how the blog relates to the brand. Second, blogs have wrought significant changes in the construction of news and journalism – over and above the canards that blogs lack credibility, are unreliable and break only the news not fit to print. Third, blogs have been part of the wider phenomenon by which the Internet has enabled communities and groups under-represented or ill-served by traditional media to gain greater presence or access to public spheres. Indeed in some cases they constitute new kinds of public spheres (transnational public spheres, for instance). Fourth, the multimedia possibilities of blogs, crossed with other new developments in digital media, have created new kinds of media production and audience practices. One example of this is podcasting, Internet radio, and audio blogs offered by blind people, historically not well-served by various forms of media culture, especially print culture.

While we still have only few critical accounts of blogs (for instance, see Bruns and Jacobs, 2006; Lovink, 2007; Tremayne, 2007), one concern is that dominant ideas about blogs have been shaped by the early experience of the North American blogosphere. There is little recognition of the thriving blogospheres in Indonesia, for example, or the enormous and distinctive blogging cultures in languages such as Persian. Thus the topic of blogging and cultural globalization is worthy of investigation in its own right.

3. Social networking sites

Another important digital media form centers on what has been called 'social networking' sites (or 'social software' or 'social media'). Like p2p networks and blogs, social networking websites and applications have their antecedents and origins in early Internet cultures. One of the first social networking sites often mentioned is the US classmates.com, launched in 1995. It really did not become widespread until the advent of *Friendster*, then followed by a spate of sites such as *Orkut*, *LinkedIn* (focusing on business networking), then the two most popular to date in North America and other western countries – *Facebook* (especially for the US college community) and *MySpace*.

Each of these social networking sites is imagined on a different model, and uses somewhat different applications and interfaces, but the idea common to all of them is to encourage people to sign up – generally through an invitation from someone they know – to meet new friends and contacts. Social networking sites are thus premised on users sharing their own personal information and identities, and being prepared to have this released to others.

The commercial value of social networking sites and the importance of this digital media form was registered in July 2005 when Rupert Murdoch's News Limited corporation acquired MySpace. MySpace is an extraordinary phenomenon in its own right, because it combines – remediates – various facets of previous digital cultures, upon the architecture of social networking sites. So it is now an imperative for many business, social and cultural organizations, as well as for individuals, to have a MySpace website. MySpace has overtaken many other organizations for the hosting of blogs. While MySpace is a massive presence in the area of digital social networking, it should be kept in perspective. Take, for instance, the hugely popular Korean developments around Cyworld and mini-hompy. Here mobile devices are central to the new personal and communal practices, which are articulated and aggregrated through digital networking into pervasive and important new media forms.

4. Mobile phone culture

My first three case studies have emphasized the Internet, but, as the Korean example reveals, the mobile phone is an important new development in digital media. When first introduced commercially in the late 1970s, first generation mobile cellular phones were analogue-based. However, the second generation mobile standards saw digital systems introduced – notably the European Global Standard for Mobile (GSM) – that were pivotal in the widespread takeup of the technology that saw over one billion subscribers worldwide by 2002.

Mobile phones were important for a number of reasons: their introduction was linked with new political economies of communications, with deregulation and privatization but also the growing importance of data communications; mobiles became an important part of everyday life, and so their implications for the reshaping of the social have been far-reaching; mobile networks and applications provided a key platform for convergent digital media. By the mid-1990s, distinctive mobile phone cultures were established that were shaped globally (by processes of design, innovation and transnational marketing and advertising) but also by national, regional and local setting, and, critically, by user adoption, reworking and domestication. In a number of countries, notably Japan, the spread of the Internet was very much a mobile experience (Gottlieb and McLelland, 2003; Ito et al., 2005). Not only did users access the Internet via portable mobile devices, but new facets of cultural economy sprang up around mobile phone cultures. In Japan, the i-mode cellular mobile system not only saw user homepages browsed but also music and graphic downloads, with a micro-payments system devised.

An important development in mobile phone culture was text messaging (SMS, or short message service), something in which user innovation played a central role. When first conceived, SMS was not seen as a major feature of second-generation digital mobiles, yet it became a new way for people to communicate – especially young people (Kasesniemi, 2003). Then SMS became the basis for grafting aspects of existing media onto mobile phone culture (and vice versa), as in the case of television voting and downloads mentioned above. Another development in mobile phone culture, which also forms part of contemporary cultural dynamics, is the popularity of the camera phone. Mobile camera phones have led to new kinds of photographic practices, as part of the broader field of the reconfiguration of cameras and visual industries with digital photography.

5. Mobile media and wireless technology

With the widespread ownership and use of mobile cellular devices, there has been great interest in the technology that has become integrated in people's lives and identities (Rheingold, 2002). Mobile Internet was not at first successful with the Wireless Access Protocol (WAP) in the late 1990s (though, as I have noted, it was important in Japan), but with the salience of search and improvements in speed and screens, it has become important. Mobile film and video, and then mobile television, have attracted much attention, and are starting to become part of the reckonings of media industry as well as attracting the attention of users themselves. The extension of second generation mobiles, the belated takeup of third generation mobile networks, as well as new compression techniques and applications allow for relatively fast transfer of music, image and video.

These kinds of mobile media seeking to capitalize on the ubiquity, reach and profitability of the cellular phone, should also be related to the multitude of developments in the field of wireless technology. Wireless-equipped laptops (using WiFi and WiMax technologies), portable digital assistants, email via Blackberries and other handheld devices, are increasingly seeing hybrids between wireless Internet and other data networks combined with mobile cellular networks – not to mention positioning, mapping and tagging technologies. Down the track also is the integration into mobile and wireless digital media of technologies such as radiofrequency identification (RFID) tagging.

Conclusion and policy implications

In this chapter I have inevitably had to simplify the dynamic and sprawling field of contemporary digital media, and to greatly abbreviate the analysis needed to do it justice. Nonetheless, I would draw a number of conclusions from my argument here about the significance of digital media for cultural economy and globalization.

First, there is genuine cultural innovation in digital media forms around the world, and significant investment of producer and consumer resources are being made here. Second, we are only at the early stages of understanding many of these new forms, and so careful mapping, analysis and interpretation of these is needed. Third, the task of understanding this aspect of cultural economy is not assisted by legacy thinking, based on culturally, geographically and linguistically specific notions of digital media forms; our ideas need to acknowledge and engage with the diverse realities of digital media use and forms in non-Western societies in particular. Fourth, while 'digital divide' concepts are inaccurate and outmoded – and we are still to appreciate the innovative Internet, telecommunications and other digital media use and cultures in developing countries, and less powerful and influential groupings (especially outside, across, and below nation-states) – there are enormous differences, and significant 'winners' and 'losers', within and across different societies, that scholars are not crediting and policy-makers not addressing.

To my mind there are three key policy implications to these digital media developments. First, that international collaboration at scholarly, industry, regulatory and governmental levels is necessary to provide accurate, detailed and rigorous information on digital media forms, and their role in cultural economy. Second, that scholarly and policy attention needs urgently to shift to understanding the characteristics, consumption and development of digital media forms across the East–West, North–South divides. Third, that priority needs to be given to issues of access, equity, democracy and cultural citizenship, as the developing market and non-market institutions are not going to provide a comprehensive approach to these – despite throwing up many new ideas and mechanisms. For their part, governments are still failing to comprehend and deal adequately with fast-moving developments in digital media – and we badly need to think beyond narrow 'digital divide' concepts and the impasse of the World Summit on the Information Society (WSIS) deliberations.

Box 20.1   The Google Books Library Project

In 2002, Google embarked into two years of project development and testing for what would become one of the world's most ambitious digital book projects. At the Frankfurt Book Fair in 2004, Google officially launched the Google Books Library Project – a collaboration between Google and several well-known libraries and publishers to create a searchable index of digitized books made available to anyone in the world. According to the Google website, the intent of the Library Project is to 'make it easier for people to find relevant books – specifically, books they wouldn't find any other way such as those that are out of print – while carefully respecting authors' and publishers' copyrights'. Although Google does not provide official counts of how many books it has digitized, a recent *NY Times* article (Hafner, 2007) speculates that Google has scanned at least a million books to date.

Google hopes to build what it describes as a 'virtual card catalog of all books in all languages that helps users discover new books and publishers discover new readers', yet for legal reasons stops short of a complete virtual full-text library. While out of print books and books through agreements with publishers will be available in full-text, only bibliographic information of copyrighted books will be displayed along with no more than three snippets *of a few sentences each* surrounding the relevant search term.

Proponents of the Library Project view it as a way to help expand knowledge, making it available more equitably and fairly to people who otherwise do not have access. In the information technology age, some argue that such a vast digital library will help to reduce the educational divide, and in so doing, will increase overall interest in books and book sales. Conversely, critics argue that the project endangers the creative rights of authors and other copyright holders, such as publishers. They fear that the 'unbinding' of books could harm the publishing industry at a time when traditional print forms are increasingly challenged by the Internet, where ownership could eventually become irrelevant in the public domain as books are copied and disseminated without regard to copyright (*Economist*, 2007). Both the American Association of Publishers and the Authors Guild expressed their disapproval of the Project. The Authors Guild and five large publishers filed lawsuits against Google, saying that the company was unlawfully scanning full texts into its search engine (even though these full texts were not available to the Google Library user). In 2005, Google offered an opt-out option for copyright owners; if they do not want their works to be included for reference through snippets, Google will not include the book in its collection. Some critics think that the opt-out policy is insufficient because Google should not scan the books without approval in the first place.

Aside from its legal ramifications, the main challenge of the Google Books Library Project is to reconcile the tensions inherent in the growing digitization of culture (or cultural forms) and globalization. On the one hand it is a major technological advance where momentum history, heritage, creativity and knowledge no longer need to be housed and protected in the vaults of museums, libraries and archives, but in a virtual and digital world that is without limit. At the same time, the Library Project arouses legitimate suspicions of cultural imperialism and causes fears that some literary forms (in this case English language books) will take over the Internet, while others are made less available or obsolete.

So far, no real legal decisions have been made for or against Google and the Library Project. What is certain is that the tensions and suspicions that have followed its launch have spurred other actors to come forward with their own digital library projects, in an effort to protect their cultural and literary traditions. For instance, in April 2006, the National Library of France launched a digital library project called *Gallica*, and has already digitized 80,000 works and 70,000 images ready to be placed online (Reid, 2005). In this way, the digitization of books can be viewed equally as an instrument of cultural globalization as well as cultural preservation.

Tia Morita

Box 20.2   The Frankfurt Book Fair

The Frankfurt Book Fair (FBF) started some 500 years ago as a gathering of local book sellers. Today it is the largest international marketplace for professionals and book lovers to gain insights into the key trends and players in the global book market.

According to the Association of German Trade Fair Industry (AUM, 2006), in 2005, an estimated 285,000 visitors gathered to survey over 380,000 titles and book-related products and services. Exhibitors totaled 7,225, representing 101 countries, a majority from European and English speaking nations (see Figure 1).

Books represent 43.1 per cent of all products sold, however, with the advent of the Internet and online literary services, digital media forms are emerging as featured products. For instance, in 2004, software constituted only 0.5 per cent of all products exhibited (AUM, 2004) compared to 2 per cent in 2005. Although this is a minor amount compared to that of books, exhibits for online services, DVDs,

(Continued)

(Continued)

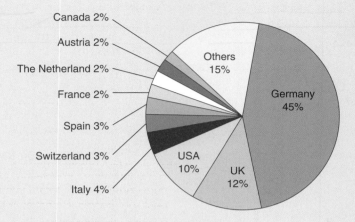

Figure 20.1   Countries represented at the Frankfurt Book Fair

CD-ROMs, Videos and eBooks continue to grow. Recently, representatives from the technology field have utilized the FBF to debut new online and electronic media and services pertinent to the book industry. A prime example is the Google Print Library Project – first introduced to European audiences at FBF in 2004 (see Box 20.1 on the Google Print Library). The promotion and proliferation of digitization has generated great concern over the longevity of traditional print forms, but the size of the global audience that continues to flock to the FBF every October is hardly evidence of the demise of the book.

Internationalization of the Frankfurt Book Fair

In 2005, international publishers represented 44 per cent of all exhibitors. The international draw of the FBF not only makes it *the* venue to negotiate rights and licensing fees for the translation of books into other languages, but for trade in film rights as well. According to AUM, in 2005, the International Agents Center for Adaptations and Screenplays at the FBF attracted 40 international publishing companies and agencies, and 60 international producers from 10 countries. Still, these figures pale in comparison to the 441 literary agents from 27 countries that came in 2005 to trade in book rights and licenses, a majority of these from Germany, the UK and USA – a clear indication of the major players in the global publishing industry.

Each year, the FBF invites a particular country as its guest of honour to highlight its literary traditions, writers, publishers and printing industry. In 2006, India became the first country to be recognized twice as the guest of honour, in part due to the rapid expansion of the Indian publishing industry, as well as the increasing number of German book licenses to India. In 2004, the Arab League was so honoured; in 2005 it was the Republic of Korea; and in 2008 it will be Turkey. In the last few years, the FBF has increased its worldwide activities with the goal of building a global network within the book industry, and to provide support to publishing companies for entry into the market and assistance with rights and license brokering. With German book collective stands organized at over 20 other international book fairs; German Book Information Centers (BICs) in Bucharest, Moscow, Beijing, Warsaw and New York, and recent collaborations between the FBF and the South African Publishers Association and the Abu Dhabi International Book Fair to promote similar publishing fairs in those countries, the FBF strives to imprint the vitality of the book and the German publishing industry in the minds of consumers and industry professionals worldwide.

Tia Morita

REFERENCES

(AUM) Ausstellungs- und Messe-GmbH (2006) *Frankfurter Buchmesse: Facts & Figures*. Retrieved 5 March 2007, from http://www.book-fair.com/en/portal.php.

(AUM) Ausstellungs- und Messe-GmbH (2004) *Frankfurter Buchmesse: Facts & Figures*. Retrieved 5, March 2007, from http://www.book-fair.com/en/portal.php.

Benkler, Yochai (2006) *The Wealth of Networks*. New Haven, CT: Yale University Press.

Berry, Chris, Martin, Fran, and Yue, Audrey (eds.) (2003) *Mobile Cultures: New Media in Queer Asia*. Durham, NC: Duke University Press.

Bruns, Axel and Jacobs, Joanne (eds.) (2006) *Uses of Blogs*. New York: Peter Lang.

Cunliffe, Daniel (2008) 'The "Old Language" in the Internet Age: Welsh on the World Wide Web', in Gerard Goggin and Mark McLelland (ed.) *Internationalizing Internet Studies: Beyond Anglophone Paradigms*. New York: Routledge. In press.

'The future of books: not bound by anything'. *The Economist*, 24–30 March 2007.

Gill, Rosalind (2006) *Technobohemians or the New Cybertariat? New Media Work in Amsterdam a Decade after the Web*. Amsterdam: Institute of Network Cultures. http://www.networkcultures.org/networknotebooks/

Goggin, Gerard and Newell, Christopher (2003) *Digital Disability: The Social Construction of Disability in New Media*. Lanham, MD: Rowman & Littlefield.

Goggin, Gerard (2006) *Cell Phone Culture: Mobile Technology in Everyday Life*. London and New York: Routledge.

Goggin, Gerard and McLelland, Mark (eds.) (2008) *Internationalizing Internet Studies: Beyond Anglophone Paradigms*. New York: Routledge.

Google Books Library Project, an overview. Available at: http://books.google.com/googlebooks/library.html. A historical timeline of the development of the project is available at: http://books.google.com/google-books/newsviews/history.html.

Gottlieb, Nanette and McLelland, Mark (eds.) (2003) *Japanese Cybercultures*. London and New York: Routledge.

Hafner, Katie (2007, 10 March). 'History, Digitized (and Abridged)'. *New York Times*. Retrieved 16 May 2007, from http://www.nytimes.com/2007/03/10/business/yourmoney/11archive.html?ex=1331182800&en=9bf0874841a9d705&ei=5090&partner=rssuserland&emc=rss.

International Telecommunication Union (2007a) *Basic indicators: Population, GDP, total telephone subscribers and total telephone subscribers per 100 people*. Geneva: ITU. http://www.itu.int/ITU-D/icteye/Indicators/

ITU (2007b) *Internet indicators: subscribers, users and broadband subscribers*. Geneva: ITU. http://www.itu.int/ITU-D/icteye/Indicators/

ITU (2007c) *Measuring the Information Society ICT Opportunity Index and World Telecommunication/ICT Indicators – 2007*. Geneva: ITU.

ITU (2007d) *Mobile cellular, subscribers per 100 people*. Geneva: ITU. http://www.itu.int/ITU-D/icteye/Indicators/

Ito, Mizuko, Okabe, Daisuke and Matsuda, Misa (eds.) (2005) *Personal, Portable, Pedestrian: Mobile Phones in Japanese Life*. Cambridge, MA, and London, England: MIT Press.

Jenkins, Henry (2006a) *Convergence Culture: Where Old and New Media Collide*. New York: New York University Press.

Jenkins, Henry (2006b) *Fans, Bloggers, and Gamers: Exploring Participatory Culture*. New York: New York University Press.

Kasesniemi, Eija-Liisa (2003) *Mobile Messages: Young People and a New Communication Culture*. Tampere: Tampere University Press.

Klinenberg, Eric (ed.) (2005) *Cultural Production in a Digital Age*. Thousand Oaks, CA: SAGE Publications.

Lenhart, Amanda, and Madden, Mary (2007) 'Social Networking Websites and Teens: An Overview', project memo, 3 January. http://www.pewinternet.org/pdfs/PIP_SNS_Data_Memo_Jan_2007.pdf

Liang, Guo (2005) *Surveying Internet Usage and Impact in Five Chinese Cities*. Beijing: Research Center for Social Development, Chinese Academy for Social Sciences. http://www.worldinternetproject.net/publishedarchive/China Report 2005.pdf

Lovink, Geert (2007) *Zero Comments: Blogging and Critical Internet Culture*. New York: Routledge.

McLelland, Mark (2005) *Queer Japan from the Pacific War to the Internet Age*. Lanham, MD: Rowman & Littlefield.

Madden, Mary (2007) *Online Video*. 25 July. Washington, DC: Pew Internet & American Life Project. http://www.pewinternet.org/PDFs/PIP_Online_Video_2007.pdf

Marshall, P. David (2004) *New Media Cultures*. London: Arnold.

Masip, Pere, and Mico, Josep Lluis (2008) 'The Fight of a Minority Language against the Weight of Globalization: The Case of Catalan on the Internet', in Gerard Goggin and Mark McLelland (ed.) *Internationalizing Internet Studies: Beyond Anglophone Paradigms*, New York: Routledge. In press.

O'Riordan, Kate and Phillips, David J. (eds.) (2007) *Queer Online: Media Technology and Sexuality*. New York: Peter Lang.

(Oxford Internet Institute) (2007) 'Oxford Internet Surveys'. Oxford: Oxford Internet Institute. http://www.oii.ox.ac.uk/microsites/oxis/

Reid, D. (2005, 25 June). 'French Answer to Google Library'. *BBC News*. Retrieved 18 May 2007 from http://news.bbc.co.uk/2/hi/programs/click_online/4619019.stm.

Rheingold, Howard (2002) *Smart Mobs: The Next Social Revolution*. Cambridge, MA: Basic Books.

Shade, Leslie Regan (2002) *Gender and Community in the Social Construction of the Internet*. New York: Peter Lang.

Tremayne, Mark (ed.) (2007) *Blogging, Citizenship, and the Future of Media*. London: Routledge.

United Nations Partnership on Measuring ICT for Development (2005) *Core ICT Indicators*. Beirut: UNESCWA. www.itu.int/ITU-D/ict/partnership/material/CoreICTIndicators.pdf

Wark, McKenzie (2007) *Gamer Theory*. Cambridge, MA, and London, England: Harvard University Press.

## CHAPTER 21

CREATIVE INDUSTRIES: THE CASE OF FASHION
Sabine Ichikawa

This chapter will illustrate the effects of globalization on creation, production, distribution and communication in the fashion industry. It will give examples of how globalization widens the gap between winners and losers, and show how fashion, located at the crossroads of cultures and at the heart of contemporary exchanges of goods, aesthetics and concepts, can promote understanding between 'developed' countries and those now emerging as major economic players and thereby develop its potential for a positive global impact.

Introduction

Fashion has grown considerably as an international industry in recent decades, and its destinies are connected to several key aspects of globalization. Although it fascinates the general public, and many works by journalists, economists and historians among others have been devoted to it, fashion defies complete understanding, for it is a fast-paced and extremely complex industry, with dozens of facets. It is both actor and acted upon in a changing world. In this chapter I shall try to provide some insights into the multi-dimensional nature of the fashion phenomenon, and its relationship with globalization. In the first part, on how globalization affects the way fashion is developing, through examples of its implications in creation, production, distribution and communication, I will include examples of how globalization widens the gap between winners and the losers in a global economic system that leaves little room for alternative paths. Next, I shall examine emerging forms, and illustrate how fashion, located at the crossroads of cultures and through the exchange of goods, aesthetics and concepts, can promote understanding between emerging and developed countries and thus itself have a positive impact on globalization. Finally, I shall propose some policies to further enhance positive practices and reduce the negative impact of fashion.

The transnational movement of ideas and cultures by means of brands and products can be an opportunity for positive exchange. While goods have always traveled internationally in human history, the pace of these transactions has grown exponentially as a result of the technological revolutions of transportation and the Internet. The interaction between cultures and economies has also increased interdependency for fashion companies, as integral parts of the world economy and world culture. And while fashion is truly a huge money-making business, it is also deeply related to people's identities, both at the individual and national levels. The Armani group sells Italian taste and elegance, Ralph Lauren sells the American way of life, Chanel sells Parisian lifestyle. Brands are deeply rooted in cultural identity and, as such, fashion conveys distinctive identities through the products and images spread around the globe by the increasing power of global media and distribution networks. Globalization also means that brands originating in countries such as Brazil, China, Japan and India will soon become 'global' like Gap or Levi's.

The impact of globalization on fashion

Since fashion has become an international business (in 2006, 91 per cent of the revenues of the French luxury group LVMH's fashion and leather goods branch was earned in international markets) and a high profit source of income, new issues and questions have emerged. What is the relationship between globalization and fashion? In the realm of fashion today we can observe the effect of globalization in the creation, production, distribution and communication processes that companies deal with on a daily basis. To put it simply, fashion companies look for low cost labour to produce competitive products; new foreign designers to develop innovative brands; booming consumer markets to target and communicate dreams to. Because of the sheer size of the fashion industry, for the purposes of this chapter I shall discuss only the well-known brands, rather than the entire apparel and textile industry.

Because the fashion business requires a high level of investment and is international in scale, global brands have emerged at two ends of the market: the luxury industry and mass market retailing. In fact, since the 1990s, heavy investment in fashion brands has been made essentially by multinational luxury groups (e.g., LVMH, Richemont, Gucci Group), or by mass market retailer brands such as H&M (Sweden) which in 2006 owned 1,345 stores in 28 countries (H&M 2006 Annual Report) or Zara, part of the Inditex group (3,186 stores at the group level in 2006), or Benetton, present in 120 countries with 5,540 stores in 2006. There is a direct link between financial clout and the power to open hundreds of outlets across the world, while imposing visual messages on a mass audience worldwide. Managing a fashion business today requires formidable skills in brand and product development of large collections, innovative logistics and supply chains, store management and merchandizing on a worldwide scale.

In the 1950s, the Ready to Wear revolution began to allow everyone to wear fashionable yet inexpensive clothes, and the young designers boom (e.g., Mary Quant in Great Britain) was an alternative to the *haute couture* system. How does it work today? *Haute couture*'s role has changed in the last 20 years; it has become a communication tool to sell accessories and perfumes on a global scale. Creation-driven, ready to wear brands (Vivienne Westwood, Cacharel, etc.) which were launched in local markets in the 1970s are challenged by international retailer brands, today, such as Zara (Spain), H&M (Sweden), Gap (US), Top Shop (GB), Etam (France), Benetton (Italy), and, more recently, Uniqlo (Japan). The result of globalization is that, in a few decades, fashion brands' and creators' only key for survival is to be financially backed by powerful groups. More than ever before, the challenge is to capture world attention through media coverage, and reach millions of customers through thousands of shops. Global communication and global distribution have become essential for expansion.

Creation and the aesthetic realm

In view of these two factors, the process of creation varies according to the positioning of brands in the market. In other words, the role of design and innovation as well as the time and financial input required at Louis Vuitton or Zara to launch a new collection are each totally different, but they are both global brands aiming at global markets. The creation process will differ because of the brand history, the distribution system, the price positioning, the customers they target, social status, and the amount of aspirational values attached to each brand.

How does globalization impact the creation process? Designers at Donna Karan, Armani, Chanel, or Louis Vuitton may well enjoy full freedom of expression but they are also obliged to seek financial and marketing objectives. Outfits photographed on the runways of Milan, Paris, London or New York cannot ensure sustainable growth unless more saleable items are added to the line, and presented to buyers in the showrooms.

Design-oriented luxury and designer brands can afford to be more creative than middle range or mass market ones, as they lead fashion trends, are highly priced, are often status-oriented and need a great deal of visibility for the promotion of perfumes and accessories. Artistic directors such as John Galliano (from Great Britain) at Dior, and Marc Jacobs (from the US) at Louis Vuitton, work with designers of different nationalities. According to the company's design policy, the creative studio takes into consideration the needs of customers from many different countries, and sometimes works with marketing people whose main objective is to make sure products will meet commercial success everywhere in the world. Adaptation to international customers can sometimes be subtle in terms of product assortment and variations, fabric or smaller sizes for Japan for instance, or gorgeous colours for leather goods in Russia or the Middle East. Other brands, such as Burberry, Calvin Klein, Ralph Lauren, Kenzo and Sonia Rykiel, sign licensing contracts with foreign manufacturers and distributors to adapt their products even further to local needs. We may say therefore that the global growth of luxury brands has transformed creation into a mainly commercial tool designed to implement financial objectives.

Market-driven brands such as H&M can have up to 100 designers scan world trends for inspiration, and to ensure their collections will reach a global audience. In comparison to designer brands, the marketing objectives, production speed, cost-cutting and quick delivery are tighter here, as more references are produced and low retail prices reduce the final margin. Globalization also has an impact on the very structure of fashion companies. Ownership, location, production and artistic director may well come from different countries. Christian Dior's designer, John Galliano, is British. Cacharel's designer is Brazilian, based in London, and it manufactures in Japan, China and North Africa. Donna Karan belongs to the French group LVMH. Chanel's designer, Karl Lagerfeld, is German. Fast Retailing in Japan, owns Uniqlo, and two French brands, Comptoir des Cotonniers and Princesse Tam Tam.

How much culture is there in the creative process?

In the fashion realm, the creative process and brand identity (personality) are based on a mix of various factors. Earlier, in the twentieth century, fashion creation was closely related to local culture, a designer's nationality (Balenciaga from Spain, Ferragamo from Italy, Christian Dior from France), the brand or manufacturer's location (DKNY from NY, Armani in Milan, Christian Lacroix from Arles), the raw materials available in a particular place (silk, leather, knitwear, diamonds), and craftsmanship or technical knowhow (gloves at Millau in the south of France). Fashion was a combination of specific people in a specific place and time, catering to the needs of a group of wealthy people.

Production

High creativity, speed, short product life-cycles, risk linked to trends, obsolescence of last season's products – these are all characteristics of fashion production. Nevertheless, high volume and low retail prices require low cost labour, and delocalizing. It can take two to three months for a Chinese or Indian factory to ship goods to the US and Europe. In a fast-running industry, time and distance are key issues, as distance can prevent shops from receiving the goods on time. Therefore North African countries such as Morocco or Tunisia, which are closer to Europe, try to compete against China on the grounds that they can deliver small batches quickly to European companies. The end of the textile quotas in January 2005 had a strong impact on developing country suppliers of fashion, although they had been preparing for years to export competitive apparel in large quantities. The market share of Chinese and Indian products has grown steadily (about 90 per cent of Japanese apparel is already imported from China). But the products imported to the United States, the European Union and Japan are conceived by the importers themselves, sub-contracting to local producers, or using their own delocalized production facilities, bearing their own brand name. When China and India will be able to export their own concepts, under their own brand names, we will observe a new globalized phenomenon.

Some luxury houses such as Louis Vuitton, Hermès or Chanel choose the strategy of vertical integration. This means keeping control of the whole value chain internally from production to distribution in order to increase profit and control the brand image better. Others start globalizing their production, to increase their margin further. As a result it has become easier for counterfeiters to make genuine-looking copies of their designs. For instance, Ermenegildo Zegna group, the Milan men's fashion house, found fabric in China that the company had not produced with the Zegna name woven onto the edge (Covin, 2005).

Distribution

Consumers have more shopping options and shop more often in part because the information available has increased exponentially and trends traverse the globe at great speed. This has led to the standardization of shop windows. From New York to Tokyo, luxury brands and mass market brands alike manage their shops (also called 'flagship stores') in a unified way. For example, H&M advertised Madonna's designs simultaneously in different shops from Paris to Hong Kong because the impact is stronger, global, and one ad reaches more customers at a time with one budget.

The design centers of Paris, Milan, London and New York City are linked more tightly than ever before. The ability to manage an efficient supply chain becomes a key factor of success. The industry recognizes that better control of supply chains is the key to being able to meet changing customer demand worldwide. Moving goods efficiently from design to production centers to stores is where competition is. Therefore fashion retailers are looking for new supply chain strategies and technologies in order to reduce transportation costs and speed products to markets in a faster way. The fashion industry's diversity of products, their short life-cycles and the speed with which products change, combined with the lengthening distance between producers and consumers, means companies are more dependent on transportation. Centralizing decision-making and investing in technology has enabled fashion retailers (such as Zara) to reduce delivery times from six months to a couple of weeks.

Communication

How does global culture impact fashion communication? Communication is a powerful tool used for international brand expansion. In order to add value to their products, Western fashion brands use strong images and symbols (icons), personified by worldwide stars, such as H&M's use of Madonna in 2007. The ads can be perceived as imposing not only international standards but Western images of seduction, lifestyle, beauty and the like on young customers of different cultural backgrounds. The reaction to these images can be quite the opposite to that which is sought. On the one hand, some Japanese women copy the Western standards, by dying their hair blonde or using blue eye lenses. On the other hand, Saudi Arabia fights against these images by imposing strict rules on fashion photographers, often based in Lebanon, in order to have religious beliefs and social order respected. Naked bodies, and Western style glamour are not permitted. Thus campaigns on a worldwide scale always need to be adapted to local habits.

Fashion advertising, more than the products themselves, conveys cultural values and standards. Culture is present in the fashion process through product creation to communication and store design. Advertising uses cultural phenomena to communicate fashion images to the public. In the case of fashion and cosmetics, visual images can have a strong impact on consumption habits. Ads often relate to movie and music stars, or art, in order to create more value in consumers' eyes. A counter example is the scandal that occurred concerning the top model Kate Moss, who lost some contracts because she was photographed using drugs, and her image could no longer be associated with fashion brand images for some time. Another example of the link between art and fashion is the French brand Marithé & François Girbaud, known for its innovative jeans. The ad campaign they launched in 2005, inspired by Leonardo da Vinci's *The Last Supper* was highly criticized and finally banned after pressure from Catholic institutions, who resented this form of association between religion and commerce.

What is artistic about fashion?

Fashion is part of the aesthetic movement, sometimes inspiring design, sometimes being inspired by it. The most artistic pieces are made by the *haute couture* houses and avant-garde designer brands, which have always been closely connected to traditional local craftsmanship. For example, Chanel bought the suppliers they were working with, in order to ensure the availability of production for embroidery, hats and accessories, as well as the transmission of know-how to future generations. The origin of fashion was linked to art, to prestige, to the elite and power. The French designer Paul Poiret worked closely with the artists of the 1920s. Castelbajac today thinks he is more a designer than a fashion designer.

Today, the level of competition between actors of this industry has evolved from producing quality products, into fighting for the position they occupy in customers' minds. Marketing and brand management techniques which emerged in mass market consumer goods, are now used in fashion industries. Therefore branding, communication and distribution strategies have become the main issues. The issue is to communicate the same message to the customers worldwide. It is also to extend presence and visibility in all directions. That means expanding geographically in new unexplored markets, and reaching new potential customers in developing countries. Extension also means increasing the product offer to satisfy customers with different expectations and different cultural backgrounds. Therefore culture-based marketing techniques are increasing.

Winners and losers

This ever-intensifying competition creates new issues and pressures. Who are the 'winners' and the 'losers'? The winners are the international conglomerates, with global brands, investing heavily in production, distribution and advertising. While securing their business in Europe, US and Japan, they target countries with high birth rates and increasing per capita income such as China, India, and to a lesser extent Brazil. In terms of production, companies such as Zara, Gap and H&M can take advantage of low cost labour to compete on price and volume; they have the power to negotiate low prices with manufacturers, because of the volume they order each season. In terms of distribution they are also the winners because they can invest heavily in store openings (more than 150 a year for H&M in 2006) and take full advantage of emerging consumer markets. The target countries have the following characteristics: a high level of economic growth, high birth rates, demographically booming cities, an increase in the average income, and growing demand for consumer goods.

In the luxury industry, some brands such as Balenciaga and Nina Ricci have made a comeback. The job done by Tom Ford for the Gucci brand is one of the best examples in fashion history of what building a global luxury brand entails. Unfortunately some designers are fired after a few seasons. Thus a young

and successful designer can also be a victim of globalization. For instance, Procter and Gamble, owner of the Rochas brand, closed down the 'money-losing fashion house' in July 2006, to concentrate on the fragrance business that was more profitable (Miles, 2006). The Rochas designer, a talented 30-year old Belgian, Olivier Theyskens, became Nina Ricci's new creative director and showed his debut collection in March 2007 in Paris with great success. This designer's talent is so outstanding that Mario Grauso, president of Puig Fashion Group, which owns Nina Ricci, estimated a 70 per cent growth in the first year of his arrival (Miles, 2007). His contract came to an end because of profit-oriented policy, not because of his talent.

Without investors, small brands can hardly go international, and cater to local needs. The investment in logistics, production, distribution and advertising is limited, and they tend to stay local, unless acquired by a larger group. Unless they offer a unique product and use their small size as an advantage for flexibility and fast decision-making, they can hardly survive. The losers will be the businesses that fail to build up internal capabilities to benefit from new global opportunities.

The future of fashion

This second section will offer a glimpse into the new world order that appears to be emerging as regards fashion, made up of new consumption patterns and other phenomena that are likely to transform the industry.

Emerging countries

Countries in the global South will shift from being major locations for manufacturing, to becoming consumer markets, and developing value-added and concept-driven brand-making companies. Significant demographic changes explain that the center of gravity in the economy and perhaps in culture too, is shifting towards Asia. According to many economists, in 2050 China, India and Japan will represent 50 per cent of total world economic output. Falling birth rates in Europe and Japan will result in fashion brands targeting developing countries even more than today. More alternatives are likely to appear from developing countries, with business models and cultural references that will challenge the established ones, as was shown in the 1980s by the impact of Japanese designers – a totally new way of conceiving clothing, body, culture and fabric design astounded Western fashion journalists and professionals. A polycentric development will stimulate creativity and fashion could be used to enhance these emerging countries' individuality and role in the international arena.

Innovation and intellectual property

Innovation-driven economies and creative industries such as fashion have a bright future ahead of them, as creation and innovation will lead the way in all areas. Innovation is also a means of differentiation in a standardized world. As a consequence, the protection of intellectual property rights is strengthening, and is being taught in Japanese primary schools (*Jetro Newsletter*, 2007).

Consumption

Consumers are becoming increasingly sensitive to brands that take a stand on environmental and ethical issues, e.g. that use biological fiber, approved by international eco standards, or that place orders with small manufacturers (Fair Trade) or build a manufacturing process that is environment-friendly and which respects human rights. Even environment-friendly transportation needs to be taken into consideration, as circulation of goods creates pollution. Timberland is an example of an environment-conscious company. The Los Angeles-based brand, American Apparel, sets new standards in terms of ethics in the industry, and competes on new grounds, by choosing not to delocalize and giving good working conditions to their employees. Uniqlo (Japan) launched a recycling program to have customers bring in their old Uniqlo clothes, to be given away to refugees; in September 2006, they were able to collect 140,000 items of apparel, many of which were recyclable or reusable (WWD, 2007). Although the Fair Trade movement is still in its infancy, people in general are more socially conscious. Another example of polycentric influence is the 'J Pop' phenomenon or *Japanese Popular Culture boom*. Western fashion photographers are flocking to Tokyo to observe the street youth culture in trend-setting parts of the city such as Shibuya. Japan has absorbed many foreign influences at different stages of its history and is creating new and breathtaking trends in cultural industries such as fashion, music, *anime* (Japanese animation and cartoons) and video games. It is also strategically using its popular culture to enhance good relationships with the rest of the world.

Can China build a brand with international appeal?

Armani sells Italy, Tommy Hilfiger sells American culture. Chinese companies will have to face many obstacles before they can develop their own global brands that can appeal to Westerners, unless they use foreign concepts, or buy a foreign brand like the French Marionnaud, which was acquired by a Chinese investor. Today's image of China is generally not associated with lifestyle, style, dream, seduction, emotion, sex appeal, intangible factors, taste, sports, innovative fabrics or Fair Trade. Building emotional brands with glamour, seduction and fantasies, and creating desire requires different skills. Being able to launch a cultural phenomenon is even more difficult. They need to make contact with the aspirational values of consumers in other countries. What could Brazilian, American or French consumers associate with China so as to be induced to buy Chinese fashion? Developing international recognition will be part of the process, having people dream of China as much as young Chinese dream of American lifestyle or Europeans of Japanese J Pop through the manga, *anime* or the videos they were brought up with since the 1980s. Thus developing cultural industries (movies, music, food, art) is the next step for China to compete on a worldwide scale, before launching fashion brands. Brands will appeal if related to an imaginary world, conveyed through creative images. Hong Kong movies have such an impact. Will the 2008 Olympics have a positive impact for Chinese brands?

Marketing: differentiation and creating brand value

In a highly competitive market, differentiation has become a key necessity. Since global brands cover the world market in a standardized manner, how can one product attract more than another? By brand-building, creating value, emotion-based purchases, and having customers dream of the products they can possess. Consumption patterns are quite contradictory today. Can 'cultural identity' compete with glamour and VIP lifestyles or environmental and health issues? 'Cultural identity' can certainly be emphasized more strongly in crafted goods and in the luxury goods industry, as well as hand-made and customized products. The mass market brands are cosmopolitan but often lack identity because they hide their origin and follow fashion leaders. An example is provided once again by H&M's strategy of attaching Chanel's designer, Karl Lagerfeld, to their brand image by having him design a collection a few seasons ago, as well as Madonna's name, because H&M itself lacks a strongly defined identity. This enabled the brand to be different from other retailers. A final example is the concept of customization and personalization – products which are mass produced but made to measure at the same time, to make the customer feel unique, as is practiced by Levi's and Nike.

Conclusion

Now that we have looked at some key questions related to globalization in fashion, there are three issues that could have a positive impact in this domain in the years to come: education, culture and free trade.

The *educational challenge* is to nurture cultural understanding and develop intercultural skills alongside purely professional competencies, in developed and developing countries alike, so as to prepare the coming generations to live in a polycentric world. How could this be achieved in fashion? Could we integrate cultural diversity even further in the process of developing fashion itself? Some houses already hire foreign designers, but few of these hail from emerging countries. Then, if we consider production from a more humanitarian point of view, why not envision delocalization as an opportunity to increase economic growth and transfer skills to emerging countries which need to develop their own textile industries? In terms of distribution too, we can see the impact of teaching management techniques to improve the skills of educated staff, and in turn develop their distribution network. Developed countries can see an advantage, if not humanitarian, perhaps in business terms, to help these target future customers achieve a better quality of life. In developed countries, education could strengthen the ability to accept other ways of thinking, working, relating to each other, and accepting ideas,

concepts and brands that emerge as challenges from other parts of the world. This task could be pursued by UN and EU agencies, setting standards to be developed in each country, as well as by private companies, by engaging proactively with societal issues. Interdisciplinarity has been rendered necessary by the vast complexities of globalization. Therefore continuing education is needed to keep up with the changes, and also keep quality human talent within the firm. Human capital is more precious than before. This process of learning, however, is likely to be slow and difficult because it requires far-reaching changes in current ways of thinking and established patterns of thought.

Globalization is developing a process of profound transition potentially leading to the emergence of radically new fashion practices. *Cultural globalization* can be enhanced by fashion, if considered as an opportunity for mutual exchange of cultural forms, styles and customs across different cultures, rather than a unidirectional flow of cultural practices from the West to the rest of the world. Cross-border borrowings are taking place already (Jean Paul Gaultier; Dries Van Noten; Galliano's collections are often inspired by other countries) and will only increase. Sponsoring world culture exhibits is also a way to promote mutual understanding. For example LVMH regularly sponsors art exhibitions.

Further liberalization of *trade* is difficult to implement but it will provide the surest way to give opportunities to fashion brands from the non-Western world to grow and express a greater diversity of cultural identities through products, concepts, communication strategies developed *with a different frame of mind, and with the aim of challenging the established order of things.*

REFERENCES

Covin, Geoffrey (2005) *Fortune*, 6 July, Vol. 151, issue 11 p. 23.
Jetro Newsletter (2007) 'Le Japon à la page,' No. 54. Paris.
Journal du Textile, 26 June 2006.
Miles, Socha (2006) 'When talent is not enough', *Women's Wear Daily*, 12 December.
WWD (*Women's Wear Daily*) (2007) 'In brief', 3 August, Vol. 193.

Miles, Socha (2007) 'Theyskens taking it one step at a time at Ricci', *Women's Wear Daily*, 3 February.

Websites of LVMH, Zara, H&M, Benetton and Xerfi:

- www.lvmh.fr
- www.zara.fr
- www.hm.com
- www.benettongroup.com
- www.xerfi.com

## CHAPTER 22

FESTIVALS: SEEKING ARTISTIC DISTINCTION IN A CROWDED FIELD
Dragan Klaic

This chapter argues that expectations of economic returns from international artistic festivals are highly exaggerated: only a handful among them actually generate such returns, thanks to factors such as location, size, tourist appeal and reputation. The author reviews the economic conditions of festival production in different regions of the world and pleads for public support, rather than tenuous sponsorship arrangements, as the key guarantor of stability and quality. Festivals generate cultural capital but fail to grow it by using digital technology and building client loyalty among audiences. Public authorities rarely develop clear funding policies that set cultural, social and economic objectives for the festivals they support and provide criteria for monitoring, evaluation and funding decisions.

Despite a dizzying diversity of templates, concepts and programming solutions, all international artistic festivals reflect the general patterns of economic globalization in the way they distribute cultural goods and adjust the modalities of their own cultural production. They also play, within certain categories, disciplines and genres, a key role in the formation of perceived cultural value and in the establishment of a prestige hierarchy of cultural goods and their creators.

The recent rapid proliferation of international artistic festivals could in itself be seen as a consequence of globalization, insofar as it signals a pervasive form of imitative behaviour – every self-respecting city nowadays strives to launch its own festival or even a panoply of festivals of different sorts, spread throughout the year (Noordman et al., 2005). If festivals were in the past instigated chiefly by visionary individuals or prestigious cultural institutions, with the purpose of compensating for what the regular cultural season could not offer or to celebrate artistic excellence on an international scale, festivals today are often politically inspired and enter into the political marketing of particular politicians or parties. The prestige, large audiences, media attention and thus high visibility of festivals cater to the self-celebratory needs of politics (Hunyadi et al., 2006).

Excessive economic expectations

Increasingly, political support and public funding are offered to artistic festivals on the expectation of an economic benefit. The first festivals established after the Second World War were envisaged as being beneficial for *cultural life*, even as celebrations of peace and post-war reconciliation (Autissier et al., 2006). Today, they are rationalized predominantly as beneficial for the *local economy*. They are expected to boost employment and inward investment, increase tourist visits, and stimulate additional spending, thus reinforcing the positive *branding* of the city and its destination marketing campaigns. In thus adopting the economic rationale of the prevailing political discourse, festival operators tend to exaggerate the economic impact of their festivals when seeking public subsidies. While they remain dependent on those subsidies, they shift their case from the emancipatory ideology of culture and general welfare state rhetoric to the presumed economic benefits. The reformulation of the expected impact reflects the decentralization of cultural policy, with cities becoming the key public funders of cultural activities instead of national governments, but also escalating competition among cities themselves.

Yet this putative economic impact remains mostly in the murky zone of wishful thinking, belief and speculation. Economic impact studies are unreliable and most often commissioned by the stakeholders themselves in order to provide proof for a predetermined positive conclusion (Vrettos, 2006). If hard data on positive economic impact cannot be obtained, a vague assumption is made that festivals nevertheless *indirectly* generate some economic benefit by boosting the image of the place and supporting its destination marketing strategy. The problem is that even if visitor numbers and spending increase, it is difficult to trace this growth directly to the festival operation and exclude all other variables.

It can well be assumed that many festivals, especially in smaller places, redistribute the existing financial resources within the local economy. They can indeed deliver earnings to local restaurants, cafes, hotels and taxi drivers, printers and designers, for example, but much of the fees and salaries earned actually leaves the locality, as the recipients reside elsewhere. The employment opportunities created by festivals are limited and short-term because most festivals run just for a week or two and increasingly rely on volunteers.

The relationship between artistic festivals and the tourist industry is complex and problematic. In some places, festivals are able to upgrade the tourist offer and attract more affluent tourists who spend more. In cities that are major tourist destinations already, such as London, Paris, Tokyo, Shanghai, Rio de Janeiro or Cairo, holding a festival can have only a limited impact, measured in year-round city turnover from tourism. The visitors these festivals attract are a miniscule part of the overall visitor mass. Some smaller places with a large volume of visitors generate a significant part of their tourist income in the weeks of a festival's duration, for example Avignon, Spoleto or the Dutch island of Terschelling with its Oerol festival (Twaalfhoven et al., 2007). Festivals are in general beneficial for tourism but the tourist boom

Box 22.1   The Salzburg festival

This festival's prestige translates into snob appeal and results in an impressive box office income of €24.27 million, and €6.41 million in 'other' income (merchandizing, royalties, subsidiary rights), against which generous government subsidies of €12.82 million present only 28 per cent of the total budget of €45.8 million. If one assumes that for every euro spent at the *Festspiele* box office an average visitor spends another €4 in town for food, lodging, drinks and shopping, the festival generates at least €97 million on top of the box office income and perhaps much more. This arithmetic makes the cartel of local restaurant and hotel owners a powerful group of stakeholders, ready to unabashedly meddle in the artistic matters of the festival program, fearful that any aesthetic change might alienate the conservative elites on whose spending their income depends. Consequently, they fought Gerard Mortier's programming choices with venom, their apparent cultural traditionalism resting on sound economic self-interest.

The proportions between public subsidy and earned income and between the festival total budget and the economic benefit generated to Salzburg are unique and cannot be replicated elsewhere. Because of the unique socio-cultural value attached to the festival, a very high number of wealthy visitors are willing to come and pay high ticket prices while the same prestige keeps the public authorities willing to continue with a high subsidy. Surprisingly, sponsorship participation in the budget amounts to a meager €2.29 million, or just 5 per cent – less than many smaller and more modest festivals are able to generate. With the public authorities lending a generous subsidy and with the rich queuing to pay for expensive tickets, the *Festspiele* leaders do not have to put much energy in the recruitment of sponsors. At least, not yet.

is not always beneficial for festivals. The recovery of Dubrovnik, Croatia, a decade after the 1991–5 war destruction and isolation, has brought mass tourism, of a kind that is totally indifferent to the programming of the Dubrovnik Summer Festival established in 1950. The summer crowds and their noise push the festival performances outside the medieval urban core, away from those medieval fortresses, squares and palaces that served as their initial inspiration and prime location.

In the case of some festivals, it is simply assumed that they have a significant economic impact, such as Avignon, Edinburgh and Salzburg. For the first two, their non-selective, open programming (Avignon Off with over 700 productions and Edinburgh Fringe with more than 2,000 productions), parallel to the official Program, increases the economic impact due to a large number of participants and not just spectators. Many of Avignon Festival visitors are day trippers who vacation in Provence and come into the town to see one or two performances only, walk around, shop, have a drink or a meal. The regional concentration of this mass of vacationers benefits Avignon but also sustains some 400 smaller festivals held in the south of France every summer, often with just a few thousand tickets sold – in contrast to the 120,000 tickets sold for the official Avignon Festival Program (Festival d'Avignon, 2003).

Many Asian cities are reluctant to reveal any financial information concerning their festivals, whether publicly or privately funded, so that their proportions remain difficult to assess and compare. While in China artistic festivals rely on government support (also in Macao, but not in Hong Kong), in Japan, South Korea and Taiwan private initiative keeps festivals in business (Darmawan et al., 2005). In Australia, veteran festivals in Adelaide, Melbourne, Perth and Sydney originally delivered mainstream European high culture, mostly British, to nostalgic immigrant elites. These festivals were made possible through a combination of private sponsorship and limited public support that nevertheless shifted programming concepts from a post-colonial mode to a celebration of multiculturalism and exploration of cultural diversity, especially among Pacific neighbors. In Latin America, artistic festivals with international programming remain a rarity in comparison to other fiestas and program crowd gathering events such as the Rio de Janeiro Carnival (cf. Chapter 23). Some once well-known festivals continue on stubbornly (Festival Cervantino, Guanajuato) or are now defunct (Caracas, Venezuela). The extensive programming of the International Theater Festival of Bogotá, Colombia, with almost 50 foreign visiting companies in 2006, is exceptional. Its existence in such an impoverished country, ravaged by guerilla and mass kidnappings, with hardly any articulated cultural policy, can be explained only by the convenience it offers to the narco-cartels to combine money laundering with the acquisition of some goodwill among the local people, who are offered free access to lavish events in stadiums and parks.

Artistic festivals remain a rarity in the Arab world because of economic and political factors. The governments are reluctant to invest in them and sponsors are rare, while both official censorship and religious puritanism create additional obstacles. The Cairo and Amman international theater festivals do not engage in their own programming, but ask foreign governments to send (and pay for) productions of

Box 22.2 Globalization and art festivals: the encounter in Istanbul

The cultural sphere in Turkey has been transformed since the country was caught in a moment of tension between the suppression of military rule in 1980 and the new discourse of freedom and choice promised by economic liberalization and global integration. As the latter discourses have gradually prevailed, religious and ethnic affiliations repressed in the making of the modern Turkish nation have also returned. Istanbul has discovered not only artefacts and practices appropriated from other geographies but also those that it has retrieved from its own history, the 'provincial' forms that Anatolians in search of employment brought with them, and finally the public face of political Islam. All these elements have created a unique mixture that draws from sources not necessarily compatible. And yet, contestation has been largely avoided because the re-circulation of these forms, as commodities, was made possible by the extension of market logic into other spheres, which robbed them, simultaneously, of their social-political connotations and allowed them to return as the 'cultural accessories' of a city, which, after a century of decay, was now longing for its erstwhile international prominence.

It is in this cultural context that art festivals have become influential cultural institutions, precisely because of their ability to develop an ethos that fits the emerging order of globalization without challenging the existing order of the modern nation-state. The International Istanbul Festival, for example, which was the first of these, has developed from modest beginnings into a stream of artistic activities, performances and co-productions spread throughout the year, pulling together various economic and strategic resources, and diversifying its audiences. Initially, festivals articulated an educational objective as part of the modernization project of the nation-state, which envisioned cultural transformation in terms of the appropriation of Western cultural forms to create a national culture. The role of educating the 'populace' was thus assigned to elites equipped with cultural capital. As the limitations of the nationalist project were soon recognized, and cultural integration came to be seen as a prerequisite for full economic globalization, the progressive motive behind festivals has been replaced by an instrumental one. Festivals are now instrumentalized in city promotion by different interest groups which believe that a more vibrant culture will enhance the flow of capital, attract tourists and professional workers, and thus boost the economy. Festivals have also been *touristified*. And yet, because they are unable to create difference in their contents, they have been pushed to emphasize, instead, the specificity of the city, in an image of 'Oriental' Istanbul that merges its socio-historical heritage with a Western techno-economic level of material development, familiarity with high culture, and adherence to secularism. Festivals contribute to this picture as a symbol of 'Western', 'high' culture, bridged to local space and tradition. This bridge, however, actually enables but a one-way flow, from the former to the latter, and frequently positions the West as a reference point against which Turkey's success in cultural development can be assessed. Festivals have thus turned from a project of national modernization into a strategy for globalization. To the extent that both take the 'West' as their reference point for further development, there is no conflict between the two purposes...

Sibel Yardımcı
(based on her unpublished PhD Thesis of 2004 entitled
Meeting in Istanbul: Cultural Globalization and Art Festivals)

their choice which they then feature and host without a fee. This minimalism leads to incoherent artistic results but at least in Cairo censorship takes a step back and allows for an evening or two of some foreign productions that it would never permit outside the festival setting. Hence an enormous public interest for things foreign that are just not available at any other time. After the end of the civil war in Lebanon, some rich hoteliers stimulated the renewal of dance and music festivals, in order to re-build quality tourism and appeal to Western visitors. (Johnson and Nelson, 2004). The new hostilities with Israel in the summer of 2006 and the ensuing instability have frustrated these efforts, yet another Baalbek International Festival was announced with an impressive array of local and international sponsors for the summer of 2007. In contrast, the Theater of the Oppressed Season under the title 'Building Bridges… Breaking Barriers', which took place in seven Palestinian cities in April 2007, was a mini-festival with Palestinian, German, Spanish and Brazilian companies, made possible by NGO support. It generated no economic impact but had great cultural and political significance, displaying the other face of globalization: the acceleration

and intensification of exemplary gestures of solidarity with isolated and oppressed communities.

The logic of prestige

Since the 1984 Los Angeles Olympic Games, a rich cultural program has become a standard feature of the Games, as an artistic festival that runs parallel with the sports events. There is little evidence that fans of the sports disciplines favor particular artistic forms but these Olympic festivals are being conceived in the logic of prestige and programmatic overkill, not as part of a marketing strategy. The businessmen who stood behind the Los Angeles Olympics were quick to cancel chunks of the cultural Program when the threat of an overall deficit loomed. Nevertheless, they encouraged other cities hosting the Olympics to stretch their cultural ambitions and set the precedent for the subsequent Peter Sellars' festival adventures (1990–3), celebrating the link between the cultures of the Pacific Rim and their diasporic communities in the Los Angeles area. Coming after a few short-lived international performing arts festivals in Baltimore and

Denver, the Los Angeles event succeeded in lowering the prejudice against foreign language performances in the US and created a climate of curiosity that enabled subsequent international festivals in New York, such as the New Wave in the Brooklyn Academy of Music and the Lincoln Center Summer Festival, to take off and bring in the foremost contemporary artists and their work.

These large events are run on modest local public subsidies and a great deal of sponsorship and private donations but would not be possible at all without the subsidies of the foreign governments that support their artistic ensembles as representatives of the national culture. Because access to the prestigious New York City venues appeared to be crowded and expensive, the Dutch government subsidized, in 2007, an entire summer festival called 'NL: a Season of Dutch Arts in the Berkshires', stretched over the hills of Western Massachusetts, between the Tanglewood music festival and the Jacob's Pillow dance festival, on the assumption that part of the New York cultural elite spends its vacation in the area. The rationale is not just the affirmation of national prestige via culture but is also based on the expectation that this condensed package will create more demand for Dutch arts in the US that will one day be satisfied on more commercial terms and with less need for government support. An illusion, for sure, because the cash-strapped US presenters continue to pay low fees. Yet those working in New York and a few other US cities profit, together with their Moscow, Beijing, Shanghai and São Paolo counterparts, from their prestige status: they are where everyone wants to be, the artists and especially the prestige-hungry governments.

The same prestige obsession, focused locally rather than abroad, has kept alive the European Cultural Capital scheme, initiated by the European Union and premiered in Athens in 1985. Since then, every year, one, later two or three cities (but nine in 2000!) are allowed to carry the label and to organize a year long mega-festival. The EU contribution of roughly 1.5 per cent of the total budget on average pales into insignificance against the huge investment of the national, regional and local authorities (around 80 per cent), modest-earned income and sponsorship in varying amounts. Since Glasgow (1990), this label has been seen as an opportunity for major infrastructural investment (sometimes completed after the end of the festive year!) and consequently the budgets keep rising. In the northern French city of Lille, for example, in 2004, the budget was €74 million. Frequently the promised economic benefits and the expected masses of visitors do not materialize and the slight increase in external expenditure and hotel nights ebbs away in a year or two, while the local audiences quickly tire of the avalanche of international programming (Palmer, 2004). Whatever image-making hocus pocus is attempted, city reputations do not get essentially altered with just one year of heightened cultural life. Paris, Florence, Amsterdam, Prague, Barcelona or even small Weimar retain all the cultural references they had before obtaining the label, while cultural backwaters such as Luxemburg, Patras or Sibiu do not become transformed into favorite visitor destinations or into influential laboratories of cultural production.

Mainstream limitations and alternative responses

The proliferation of artistic festivals adds to the ongoing commodification of artistic works as cultural goods, offered in large programmatic packages, made to create an impression of plenty, diversity and richness, as a seductive bazaar or emporium of artistic creativity and talent, where lesser known names can piggyback the allure of the famous. Regardless of their artistic discipline or the multi/interdisciplinary character of their programming, international artistic festivals embody the art of packaging in the first instance, the mastery of *bricolage*, of composition and fusion in how their programs are put together (De Wend Fenton et al., 2005). Most festival programrs have insufficient travel budgets, so they are forced to program not on the basis of broad insight into new artistic production and their own first-hand experience but more on rumour, gossip and opportunity – in other words according to whether some authority such as a ministry, a government agency, British Council or a Goethe Institute, or a conveniently identified sponsor, is willing to pay for a particular company.

In the dense logistics of artistic festivals, companies and artists move in and out of town or appear at various locations during the same evening, competing for the attention of both spectators and the media, often hardly distinguishable one from the other while they take each other's place. Equally, they are all quite decontextualized from their own original creative circumstances, made dependent on the marketing slang of the festival brochures and framed as exclusive goods that can be consumed only in the limited time allowed by the rhythm of the festival program (Sabate et al., 2004).

In the performing arts, some experts claim to be able to recognize productions specifically made to appear on the festival circuit, in accordance with prevailing fashions and fads – such works are usually made to be quite easy, communicative, appealing, visually rich and less dependent on the spoken language in order to reduce the hassle of translation. At the same time, surtitling has facilitated the touring of language-based productions from one festival to another. Successful theater productions appear sometimes at a dozen festivals within a year or two, provoking complaints by critics that all festivals increasingly resemble each other. They forget, however, that festival audiences are much less mobile than theater professionals and critics.

In the world of feature film festivals, where commercial interests prevail, the presence of stars and their glamour serve to sustain media attention and engineer success, so as to facilitate background business transactions and the packaging of new film co-productions. In the consensual hierarchy of film festivals, their prizes have a specific commercial impact, with Venice and Cannes in the forefront, and Moscow, Toronto, Rotterdam and Chicago following closely behind.

Classical music festivals focus on the rather coherent and static music repertory of the last 200 years, but also on a tacit hierarchy of artists, ensembles and orchestras, derived from a limited set of references: who trained with whom, won which prizes, worked with which conductor or director, appeared on which opera stage or concert hall. These career markers determine the prestige of artists and of the festivals that program them and are also reflected in the appropriate fee scale, sometimes also in the range of ticket prices.

In contrast to those habitually subsidized events, commercial rock and pop music festivals nestle within specific music idioms and seek to capitalize on the groups and musicians who provide clear brand recognition, supported by an extensive line of merchandizing. The growing popularity of 'world music' as a heterogeneous genre has enabled some festivals to shift gradually from non-profit to for-profit logic, with a steep rise in audience numbers that enables more programming. This inevitably turns previously obscure music phenomena and their practitioners, once marketed for their exoticism and supposed authenticity, into stars capable of setting global fashions and covering festival costs without public subsidy.

And yet, there are also festival niches that resist commodification, privilege surprise and excitement over perfect logistics and deliberately seek marginality or liminality against media overexposure. These are small, usually short festivals in remote and not easily accessible locations, in the post-industrial debris of abandoned factories, in slums or in rural areas. These self-styled and self-propelled alternatives shun public support and sponsorship, stage unexpected performances in a zone of temporary autonomy, make underground creativity visible briefly for a relatively small audience of cognoscenti and fellow travellers, alerted via Internet sites and SMS messages. The interest of the audience is to attempt to *step out of globalization* into something very local, very specific and of short duration but meaningful in terms of extraordinary experience, unavailable elsewhere. Even when they feature international artists, such festivals remain deliberately local in their context and impact, creating a cultural opposition to the more globalized spaces of cultural consumption, set in the centers of prestige and public attention.

While official artistic festivals abound in China, endowed with public subsidies of regional and municipal authorities, eager to jump on the globalization bandwagon and propelled by an increased willingness of corporations to sponsor them, small unofficial festivals, lasting only two to three days, pop up in Beijing and Shanghai, on the urban margins, without any visible support, in unconventional and obscure places, offering a sense of adventure to the participating artists, both Chinese and foreign, and small audiences. These occasional events avoid the official scrutiny of cultural programming by the authorities and at the same time counter the growing commercial orientation of both public and private cultural organizations. They leave hardly any traces, stay out of media attention and guard the anonymity of their teams (Klaic, 2007).

Unstable sponsors and under-explored recycling

International artistic festivals differ much in their operating budget, degree of public subsidy vs. own income, duration, number of program features and audience volume. Some are autonomous non-profit organizations; others are spin-offs of permanent cultural institutions that once a year at least aim to produce something different, special and eminently international. Increasingly, municipalities are setting up specialized agencies to invent and run festivals of different format and type on a consistently professional level of production, communication and marketing (Silvanto, 2007).

Those international festivals that have an evident artistic core and primary artistic purpose – in contrast to commercial crowd-gathering events and community celebrations, where artistic work might have a mere decorative and entertainment function – almost inevitably depend on public subsidy to safeguard and advance their artistic ambitions. Even artistic festivals operating in the non-profit logic experience shifts in their economy as they seek to compensate shrinking subsidies with sponsorship and more earned income. Sponsorship deals tend to be short-lasting and in some instances unstable relations with sponsors imperil continuity. Big world brands appear as common festival sponsors, but tend to be led by the logic of local market opportunities. The competition of corporations for chief sponsor's role is rare: the famous rivalry of Sberbank and Nestle for the sponsorship of the Golden Mask festival, won by the former while the latter accepted the role of a secondary sponsor, remains an exception, explainable by specific Moscow circumstances, of a big, hot consumer market with too few prominent large-scale festivals that are suitable for sponsorship. Everywhere, sponsorship is a conceivable option for festivals that are big, have considerable exposure and audience volume and are consequently rather mainstream, if not conventional or elitist in their artistic program. The best strategy of smaller festivals is to turn their business associates and regular providers of goods and services into sponsors in kind, e.g. printers, accountants, lawyers, travel agencies, taxi companies, cafés and caterers etc. In countries where the government occasionally funds but regularly controls cultural productions, festivals that do not receive government subsidy cannot expect to find a sponsor either, while the awarding of government subsidy makes them in principle safe for sponsors, as in Singapore, where the National Art Council appears as the festival organizer, production subsidy distributor, censor and landlord.

As periodically reccurring events, festivals find it difficult to sustain *client loyalty* from one edition to another but most of them still do not use the Internet sufficiently as a platform on which to build a virtual community of hardcore fans and offer them a steady flow of information, services and products to create loyalty. In big cities with rich cultural offerings, most festival goers see only one or two program features – despite festival marketing that seeks to convey the entire program as something exceptional and unique. This signals that festivals are competing with all other culture producers for the limited attention of the public, itself overwhelmed with constantly increased cultural consumption options.

In the performing arts, including music, festivals increasingly appear as producers and not only as presenters. They pool resources and share risks with other producers, festivals and venues in order to make available new artistic work that could hardly be conceivable in the regular production of the theaters, operas and music halls, leading to surprising combinations of artistic talent, and requiring budgets that no producer could provide alone. Such co-productions guarantee a longer series of performances and sufficient exposure for a secondary circuit of programrs to consider programming the production at some later time.

Festivals thus create and not only distribute cultural capital. Yet they do not pursue existing and emerging technological opportunities sufficiently to *recycle it* through digital platforms and reach a secondary audience in protracted time and expanded space. They under-estimate the economic 'window of opportunity' made available by globalization and ICT revolution, as well as the chance to further legitimize public subsidies through digital educational applications derived from the live festival program. Only in the UK does the formulation of educational and outreach programs appear as a mandatory precondition for the granting of public subsidies. One might expect that, with increased competition for subsidies elsewhere, those cultural operators who offer additional educational benefit from their cultural and artistic programming would be more likely to be recipients of public funds. Festivals are always chiefly local endeavors in their cultural, economic and social impact, but digital recycling offers them a chance to achieve a global presence as co-producers and distributors.

Local partnerships and alliances bring sustainability

Despite international programming and globalized reputations, festivals remain quite dependent on local circumstances – audience reception, political support, media coverage and loyalty or hostility of local artistic communities. Increased competition among cities underlines competition among festivals – for prestige, prominent artists, media attention, sponsors and visitors. Locally, it seems that festivals able to forge a wide range of partnerships with domestic stakeholders tend to prosper and in some cases enhance the collaborative attitudes of cultural and educational organizations, the media, businesses and NGOs, thus becoming key contributors to local development. However, this prominent exposure exposes them to the imperative of permanent growth and forces them to prove that they can produce more programs, reach more audiences, secure more sponsorship and generate more minutes of electronic media attention. This unlimited growth is, however, unsustainable and even well-positioned festivals, with many associations and partnerships, could find themselves under the pressure of escalating and mutually incompatible expectations that ultimately engender frustration, disappointment and opposition.

It is conceivable that international artistic festivals will get caught in the cross fire between forces of globalization that seek to mainstream them and make them conform to successful formulae and commercial events, and defenders of the specifically local, and that they will in the process frustrate the expectations of both, thus provoking two-sided hostility. Local cultural elites and artistic communities may perceive a home festival as the importer of dangerous, subversive, contaminating cultural goods and as a peddler of effete foreign ware. At the same time, festivals might be reproached for not doing enough to appreciate, elevate and promote local creative talents and impulses internationally.

Older, established and prestigious festivals have discovered that prestige alone cannot ensure their vitality or guarantee the continuity of high public funding they used to take for granted. Neither can accumulated prestige hide fatigue and routine that undermine their credibility among audiences, always eager to experience something new and different. Fellow professionals, peers and colleagues appear as the most dangerous critics and their impatience with the 'business as usual' attitude could become quite dangerous (Hansen et al., 2004).

Festivals of classical music appear to be increasingly disoriented by rapidly greying audiences, the collapse of the recording industry and the flight of traditional sponsors. Taken together these factors seriously endanger their financial equilibrium, made worse by rising costs, especially in the form of hefty fees for leading artists. It is increasingly difficult to find programming distinction within the constraints of a fairly narrow classical music repertory, whose core is made up of European music composed between 1750 and 1950. Paradoxically, thanks to digital copying and high capacity carriers, more people listen to more music than ever before, but festivals of classical

music are finding it quite difficult to turn this situation to their advantage (Négrier and Jourda, 2006).

That a top of the range MP3 player can contain today the programs of *all* classical music festivals held in the course of a single summer means that an average listener can, with little effort and minimal cost, function as their own programer and secure a broader range of music than any single festival. This should be seen as an alerting signal and prompt programming innovation and genre mixture in order to make festivals profit from the eclectic music taste of the baby boomers, who remain loyal to their formative rock music experiences even as they turn into senior citizens – but invest their cosmopolitanism in the exploration of world music, while their preferences within the classical music repertory remain undifferentiated or, on the contrary, focused on some specific niche. Festivals that stubbornly perpetuate a classic repertory without experimentation, surprising mixtures and commissioning of new music, might end up as the big losers, despite their reputation and tradition. Small classical music festivals, driven by the passion and enthusiasm of a circle of music lovers and developed throughout the summer in unusual settings, such as small village churches in popular vacation regions of France, show growth and good interactions with the local tourist industry.

Many festivals thrive in a clearly defined programming niche and derive their strength from a coherent concept and context, from a local loyalty of volunteers and collaborating partners, from programming that is consistent yet offers participative opportunities. Festivals that phrase their artistic program in terms of a social agenda, referring to gender, migration, exclusion, marginality, and festivals that explore their urban context, making the urbanity both the topic and the context, seem to be successful as well as festivals of new media that test the audience's habits and preferences and challenge it with new capabilities and modes of interactivity.

Those festivals that have avoided being labelled a tacit ally of the forces of globalization but instead bring globalization into their programming philosophy, not as a fatality but as a phenomenon that provokes the articulation of a critical discourse, are, as a rule, doing well and finding partners and allies, locally and internationally. While some festivals complain of rising costs, not matched adequately by public subsidies, sponsorship and ticket sales, in some parts of the world successful festivals are still being put together on a shoestring budget, with much free work and donated services and goods and very little cash expenditure, but with international artists participating without a fee, out of a sense of adventure or solidarity.

The need for festival policies

The rapidly growing number of festivals, often in the same place, creates dilemmas for the public author-ities: which ones to support, why and with how much? Public authorities need therefore to articulate a firm festival policy with precise objectives, goals, funding criteria and monitoring and evaluation pro-cedures. Otherwise, they will continue to dwell in the prevailing practice of incidental and arbitrary deci-sions, serving steady and recurring clients, rich in tradition and prestige, and short-changing new, dis-gruntled applicants who promise more results for less money. Very few cities, regions and national ministries for culture or funding agencies have attempted to develop such policies; private founda-tions, often instrumental in festival funding, have not done so either.

On the international level, there is not much policy-making that could be suggested or expected, espe-cially as national governments jealously consider culture as their exclusive realm of competence. UNESCO, the Asia-Europe Foundation and the Anna Lindh Foundation for Euro-Mediterranean Cooperation, *inter alia*, could develop ways to sup-port festivals not so much for their expected eco-nomic benefits (because they will in most cases not be achieved) but primarily as instruments of artistic, cultural and social development, inclusion through new audience development and innovation in cul-tural practices. They may decide to support festivals that can develop the spirit of partnership and broad local alliance-building and enhance the intercultural competencies of both cultural operators and audi-ences. The European Union has recognized the value of artistic mobility and promotes in its culture program more international co-productions with the participation of different festivals, but frustrates the growing ambitions and productive ingenuity of cul-tural operators by its miniscule budget and heavy-handed administrative requirements.

Conclusions

Artistic festivals remain chiefly a local affair – despite the international component in their programming, success or failure depends on local entrepeneurship, the capability to engage various local constituencies and the capacity to turn the dialectic of the global and local to their advantage rather than against it. The impacts are also chiefly local and lie predomi-nantly in the artistic, cultural and social sphere, not in the generation of economic benefit, as is often assumed. Direct economic impact is a privilege of very few festivals whose programming formulae and public appeal are reinforced by an advantageous location, a certain festival mythology and ample pub-lic subsidies.

Hosting many foreign artists in a condensed pro-gramming frame benefits local artists and audiences and offers opportunities to innovate as regards cul-tural practices, expands the audience base and cre-ates new partnerships among local players. Public authorities that support artists and artistic ensem-bles to travel to foreign festivals are mainly driven by prestige considerations but in fact they support the development of artistic excellence through mobility and ultimately local audiences as well.

Artistic festivals function in a context determined by globalized economic pressures that impose a uni-formization of artistic practices and the commodifi-cation of the cultural goods created and featured. Due to the increased competition of consumer options within limited leisure time, any cluster of events now often calls itself a festival in order to con-vey some exceptional significance. This is often an isolated marketing gimmick rather than a sustained and consistent programming strategy. Yet artistic fes-tivals can respond productively to such pressures: by the flexible modification of programming formulae, or the inclusion of social issues, through international co-productions and the digital recycling of cultural capital, by forging solid local alliances. They can also turn globalization itself into the subject of festival nar-ratives and critical discourse.

Retrenching public authorities see private spon-sorship as a panacea for shrinking public subsidies instead of developing consistent festival funding poli-cies. But festivals will depend increasingly on local subsidies and support bases which they can rein-force through their international reputation and pres-tige. On the international scale, major festivals will probably form consortia to produce exceptional high-budget works, ensure their proper exposure and pro-longed exploitation through digital spin-offs, thus reinforcing their own dominant position in the dense festival jungle.

REFERENCES

Autissier, A-M. et al. (2006) *Still so much to be done. Challenges for Culture in Europe*. Gent: European Festivals Association.

Darmawan, D., Boitano, J. and Liang, Y. (2005) 'The Programmatic Interests and Financing Modalities of Festivals in East Asia'. Leiden University School of Management, MBA thesis.

De Wend Fenton, R., Neal, L. et al. (2005) *The Turning World. Stories from the LIFT*. London: Calouste Gulbenkian Foundation UK.

Festival d'Avignon (2003). *Alternatives théâtrales*. pp. 78–79.

Hansen, K. et al. (2004) *Festivals: Challenges of Growth, Distinction, Support Base and Internationalization*. Tartu: Cultural Department, City of Tartu. Also available at www.tartu.ee/festivalbook.

Hunyadi, Z., Inkei, P. and Szabo, J.Z. (2006) *Festivál-vilag*. Budapest: Kulturpoint iroda/Budapest Observatory.

Johnson, K. and Nelson , K. (eds.) (2004) *Staging Independence. Mutual Strategies for Directors and Theatermakers in Europe and in the Arab World*. London: Directors Guild of Great Britain.

Klaic, D. (2007) 'Chinese performing arts: from communist to globalised kitsch'. IIAS *Newsletter* 44 (summer): 18–9.

Négrier, E. and Jourda, M-T. (with the collaboration of Pierre Négrier) (2006) *Les Nouveaux territoires des festivals. Un état des lieux pour la musique et la danse*. Paris: France Festivals.

Noordman, T.B., Kroes, M. and de Graauw, C.A.H. (2005) *Festivals en gemeentlijk beleid in Nederland*. Rotterdam: RISBO/Erasmus Universiteit.

Palmer, R. (2004) *European Cultural Capitals*. A study for the European Commission. Brussels: Palmer & Rae (www.palmer-rae.com).

Sabate, J., Frenchman, D. and Schuster, J.M. (2004) *LLocs amb esdevenimentes/Event Places*. Barcelona: International Laboratory on Cultural Landscapes.

Silvanto, S. (ed.) (2007) *Festivaalien Helsinki*: Helsinki: HPK/HKK.

Twaalfhoven, A., Schmitz, J. and Deuss, B. (2007) *Luchtig en toch verlicht. Theater maken in de zomer*. Den Haag: FAPK.

Vrettos, A. (2006) *Economic Impact of Arts & Culture Festivals. A Comparative Analysis of 4 Economic Impact Studies*. Maastricht: University of Maastricht MA thesis.

NB. The European Festival Research Project (EFRP), an international consortium, makes festival research outcomes publicly accessible on the website of the European Festival Association: http://www.efa-aef.org/efahome/efrp.cfm.

## CHAPTER 23

THE BAHIA CARNIVAL
Paulo Miguez

The Bahian Carnival is a centenary and large-scale popular event. Since the late 1980s this popular festival has become the catalyst and backbone of a particular type of cultural economy. This chapter analyses the ways in which this Carnival has come to perform as the principal component of an exuberant market of symbolic-cultural goods and services that has come to characterize the city of Salvador de Bahia.

Brazil is the country of the 'many Carnivals' evoked in Caetano Veloso's song, for the Brazilian Carnival is diverse. It has multiple dimensions and distinctive manifestations in different cities: the Carioca Carnival in Rio de Janeiro, the Carnival of Recife and Olinda in Pernambuco, and the Salvador Carnival in Bahia, among others. The Carioca Carnival, for example, is characterized mainly by its appeal as spectacle and its strong links to the tourism economy. In Recife and Olinda, on the other hand, Carnival is more strongly linked to traditional forms of popular expression. The Bahian festival is distinctive in terms of the issues discussed in this volume: it is a large-scale, popular event characterized by cultural hybridization and innovation that has also established itself since the late 1980s as the catalyst and backbone of a robust and multi-faceted cultural economy.

Bahian culture and its Carnival

Bahia has always occupied a special place on the Brazilian cultural scene. This is because of the many Bahian artists and creative people who have marked the process of cultural development in Brazil. Suffice it to cite, for example, João Gilberto, the brilliant creator of the *Bossa Nova*, Glauber Rocha, father of the *Cinema Novo*, and Caetano Veloso and Gilberto Gil, creators of the 'Tropicália Movement' – all three were true cultural revolutions that transformed the Brazilian cultural scene in the second half of the twentieth century.

Carnival does not represent the entire cultural production of the city of Salvador. But it is evident that the Carnival festivities, with its *blocos*,[1] *afoxés*[2] and *trios elétricos*[3] are what construct and support the exuberant market of symbolic-cultural goods and services that has come to characterize the city in the last 25 years. The Bahian Carnival now comprises a range of mercantile practices that, in more recent years, have added definitively to the configuration of what can be called *carnaval-negócio* (business Carnival), a particular type of cultural economy. In effect, it is around the Carnival that Salvador, realigning tradition and contemporaneity, begins to fuse the celebration and the logic of the cultural industry. This new approach results from the conjunction of three important, culturally distinct developments that have occurred in the last 50 years.

The first is the creation/invention at the 1950 Carnival of the *trio elétrico*. An excellent vehicle for advertising and, therefore, a privileged target of sponsorships, the *trio elétrico* carved out the first contours of the Carnival enterprise, opening a space for the diffusion of a mercantile logic that will mark all subsequent efforts of the celebrating parties. A pioneer in the introduction of business practices in this moment of popular satire, the *trio elétrico*'s transforming role was even more significant in that it redefined aesthetic

Table 23.1   Indicators of the Bahian Carnival: 2006

Indicators	Statistics
Duration	7 days
Estimated public	1.5 to 2 million people/day
Occupied urban space	25 km of avenues, streets and squares and 30,000 square meters of alternative spaces for shows and other events
Number of Carnival groups	227 groups
Artists involved	11,750 people
Number of casual employments	169,021 people
Number of tourists (national)	360,307 people
Number of tourists (foreign)	96,401 people
Hotel occupation	100%
Income generated by tourists	US$94 million
Accredited press professionals	2,531

Source: Emtursa (2006)

and organizational aspects and inaugurated thereby the element of popular participation that has since characterized the Carnival.

The next rupture took place in the middle of the 1970s and was characterized by the resurgence of *afoxés* and, particularly, the emergence of the *blocos afro*,[4] a new form of participation of organized negro-mestizo youth. The introduction of these new actors radically transformed the Carnival frame. With a markedly explicit afro-ethnic character, the new organizations gave a hegemonic role to the festivities; from the aesthetic, musical and gestural point of view, they brought culture, politics and the market closer together, providing the aesthetic matrix for the cultural industry boom that has occurred since the 1980s.

The 1980s gave rise to the third and last of the three ruptures, the emergence of the *blocos de trio*.[5] Because they privatize the *trio elétrico*, they have reintroduced social hierarchy in the occupation of the public space of the Carnival and thereby brought a movement that was the inverse of the one registered in 1950 when this same hierarchy was disarticulated by the emergence of the *trio elétrico*. From the aesthetic point of view these organizations constitute a privileged setting for the birth of the so-called *axé music*, the name of a musical genre that, from the Carnival of Bahia, has conquered the entire Brazilian phonographic market. When the *blocos de trio* organized themselves as enterprises privileging the market dimension, they caused an important jump of scale, contributing to the transformation of the Bahian Carnival as a product that exceeds the limits of the Carnival itself and of the city as well. The *blocos de trio* are responsible for the exportation of the Bahian Carnival model to other Brazilian cities that were hitherto used to more traditional practices. This has stimulated other Carnival organizations, particularly the *blocos afro*, to risk similar organizational adventures, particularly in relation to the market.

Apart from these three important Carnival landmarks, which together determine its current configuration, several other elements have turned it into big business: the emergence of recording and publishing firms, FM broadcasting stations, performance venues, etc.; significant technological advances (of the *trio elétrico* and recording studios, etc.); political-administrative actions such as aggressive tourism promotion strategies accompanied by infrastructure arrangements and public service developments; and political-cultural actions carried out by the *blocos afro*. As a result, the afro-electric-Carnival elements turned it into a mega-event in the 1990s and transformed the product as well as the market. With an impressive capacity to generate, to transform and to market its multiple products (music, artists, organizations and the *trio elétrico* itself) and to embed them into the broader cultural industry framework (radio, television, phonographic industry), as well as with the urban leisure, tourism and service economy, the Carnival now began to take on an increasingly complex organizational structure and logic. It began to represent a fully developed, integrated and diversified economy, which would be a significant source of jobs and incomes for the city.

The business Carnival

The Bahian Carnival thus transformed itself into a mega-event, surpassing by far, in all aspects, any other such event in Brazil, as shown by the figures presented in Table 23.1.

As the above figures suggest, the Bahia Carnival has required a transformation of the role and scope of the city government's role as regards organization, planning, training, managements, services, security, etc. It has also involved private sector bodies contracted by the city authorities for services such as electricity supply, telecommunications, sanitation and the like. It is understood that the municipal administration has become the most important actor of the Carnival. Treated as a strategic business by the multiple public and private actors involved, the Bahian Carnival has thus acquired great social and economic importance for the life of the city. It has amplified the business opportunities for many actors.

An important group of activities is directly linked to the event itself. First, those of the *blocos de carnaval*, the biggest symbol of the Carnival business. With a trajectory that confuses itself with the history of the Carnival itself, the *blocos* were transformed from casual clubs to lucrative companies that have led the organizational and technological innovations of the last 25 years. Numbering today about 200, the *blocos* carry out innumerable activities. The great *blocos*, for example, employ about 2,000 people during the Carnival, ranging from the self-employed to an army of sub- and un-employed who serve as musicians, dancers, waiters, health workers, drivers, security personnel, *cordeiros*,[6] stylists, electricians, carpenters, sound and light technicians, etc. To this numerous set of services must be added the services contracted for the *blocos*, from companies responsible, for example, for the construction of the *trios elétricos* and the assembly of support vehicles, to the making of the *abadás*,[7] etc. Even the small *blocos* that are less professional also appeal to a variety of services that mobilize dressmakers, carpenters, painters, electricians, etc. – many of whom live and work within the community of the origin of the *bloco* or *afoxé*. But the great *blocos* are the ones whose 'portfolios' contain a wide range of activities linked to the production and commercialization of specifically Carnival-linked cultural symbolic products such as:

- the sale of *abadás*;
- the acquisition of sponsorships, which in many cases extend to other events connected to the *bloco*, e.g. participation in other Carnivals and in other manifestations throughout Brazil;
- the sale of food and drink during the parade and linked events;
- the ownership of other *blocos*;
- partnerships with singers and bands[8] that result in new ventures such as the so-called 'extemporaneous' carnivals that are now held throughout the year in many Brazilian cities; musical performances; recordings, etc.
- franchises in many of Brazilian cities that organize extemporaneous carnivals.

A second set of activities corresponds to the services and products directly and indirectly linked to the tourism economy: hotels, airlines and travel agencies, tour operators, the hotel and restaurant sector, etc. A third set, equally important, includes the activities of the cultural industries as already mentioned above. Another set of activities is street commerce, with its significant contingents of small vendors. A constant presence in the history and daily life of the old city of Salvador, these activities take on a special colouring during the Carnival. There are the famous traditional *baianas de acarajé*, fixed and ambulatory vendors of all kinds of food and drink, gatherers of paper and aluminum cans for recycling, car guards, etc. In 2006, this small army of vendors totalled around 25,000 people (Emtursa, 2006).

Challenges of the Bahian Carnival

Since there is no methodology in place to track the growth and diversification of the economy of the Bahian Carnival, it has not been possible to transform the survival strategies employed by the local population into a development project defined in post-industrial terms. In any such project, the public authorities would need to occupy a leading position, in view of the reigning patterns of inequality and social exclusion. Beyond the regulatory role, or measures of a repressive character, there are varied mechanisms through which government intervention might maximize the opportunities and alternatives the Carnival offers. In the ultimate analysis, this cultural phenomenon presents a double challenge. It is not only a question of the money economy but also of symbolic-cultural meaning, of the soul of the city and its people. The latter must not be diminished in the name of the former.

Notes

1   The *blocos* are the groups of people who parade while singing and dancing. The origin of the *blocos* precedes the emergence of the Carnival itself. Their probable ancestors were the groups of masked performers known as *cucumbis*, formed by black slaves who participated in the festivities of the *Entrudo* in colonial society. Such groups paraded singing and dancing to the sound of their musical instruments, mainly satirizing the dominant white society. This festive spirit animates the modern *blocos* that represent the popular counterpoint to the remarkably Europeanized masked balls and parades that had characterized the first Carnivals.

2   The *afoxés* are old Carnival groups of the negro-mestiza population explicitly linked with the *candomblé*, the Afro-Brazilian religion.

3   The *trio elétrico*, created by Bahians Dodô and Osmar in the 1950 Carnival, is a platform mounted on a truck equipped with giant speakers on which musicians perform the local genres and people follow the trucks singing and dancing.

4   The *blocos afro*, that parade to the sound of great orchestras basically formed by percussion instruments, have been a symbol of the Bahian Carnival since the 1970s. Among the most famous are the internationally known Olodum.

5   The *blocos de trio* were a creation of the Bahian middle class and are characterized by their use of a *trio elétrico*.

6   The *cordeiros* are the thousands of workers, consisting mainly of blacks and poor people who are responsible for the ropes that delimit the space of the *blocos* during the Carnival parade.

7   The *abadá* is a fancy dress used by the participants in the *blocos*.

8   Deeply associated with the growth of the *blocos* is the artistic success achieved by the singers and musical groups who now occupy a leading place in the mercantile space of the Carnival. Many simple *bloco* singers have entered the market with their own *blocos*, or becoming co-owners of already existing *blocos*, or setting up their *trios elétricos*; many have become great stars, creating their own producers, recording studios and publishing companies for the distribution of hundreds of thousands of records and take part in the so-called 'extemporaneous' carnivals – these are festivities not organized exactly 40 weekdays before Easter, as the Christian calendar requires, but at any and all times during the year.

REFERENCES

Emtursa (2006) *Relatório*. Salvador: Emtursa S. A.

## CHAPTER 24

MAKING MATERIAL CULTURAL HERITAGE WORK: FROM TRADITIONAL HANDICRAFTS TO *SOFT* INDUSTRIAL DESIGN

Martha Friel and Walter Santagata

In many developing countries, the production of material culture-based goods by small and micro firms has become the basis for sustainable endogenous growth. After a brief discussion on the definition of material culture – the special area bordering intangible-oral and tangible-natural cultural heritage – and an historical overview on the sector's evolution, quantitative data on the economic importance of artisanal goods on national and international markets will be analysed. Finally, a new model of the transition from traditional handicraft production to soft *industrial design – based on high quality and high quantity production – will be presented. Both the economic advantages of this*

transformation and the strategies needed for its implementation will be discussed.

Introduction

Mainstream cultural economics largely neglects the anthropological, sociological and economic value of humankind's *material culture*, whose goods and services are beyond any doubt live witnesses to the evolution of every civilization or culture (Keesing, 1958; WIPO/ITC, 2003). Culture is not only made up of Leonardo's paintings – Armani's fashion ware and traditional Chinese silk are real expressions of culture too. *Material cultural heritage*, both tangible and intangible, is made up of the many artefacts and services associated with the traditional culture of a local community, with the way that human group has met its needs or shaped its way of life.

These goods and services are also neglected because of the old stereotype according to which handicrafts and local traditions – the primary products of material culture – are considered to be of low quality or low economic value. Material culture production has therefore been relegated to the region of technological backwardness and its captivating aesthetic qualities under-recognized. As a result, it has been neglected in both cultural programs and economic development strategies (Moreno et al., 2005).

A crucial move away from this low economic profile may be expected, however, in the age of globalization, from traditional handicraft to industrial design. Today there is considerable evidence worldwide that trade in material cultural products is a key factor of local development, especially for micro enterprises and local communities '…allowing them to develop in accordance with their own characteristics, providing them with new economic activities and thus enabling them to become less vulnerable and less dependent on current more erosive development strategies' (Moreno et al., 2005). An increasing number of intersnational organizations and specialized agencies such as UNESCO (2004), UNCTAD (UNESCO/UNCTAD, 1997), ILO (2003) the World Bank or Aid to Artisans are funding and implementing crafts developing projects. Material cultural heritage along with its intangible technical and aesthe traditions provides, in practice, the only endogen dowment of capital for most developing countrie natural resources and agricultural surplus are missing.

International experience has shown that craftsmanship was not always the realm of low quality production: it has attained high aesthetic quality, symbolic value and significant production levels as well. Today, however, handicraft must change to reach these goals. While it must preserve or recover its traditional high quality, it must simultaneously develop greater productive power. By applying the industrial design model to handicrafts, we can coin the term 'soft industrial design', as an appealing perspective for competing in the global markets both in terms of quality and quantity.

According to the rules of modern industrial design, goods based on material culture can become a modern example of sustainable and endogenous growth based on micro-firm clusters, cultural districts or localized cultural industries (Pyke et al., 1990; Santagata, 2001; Becattini et al., 2003; Power and Scott, 2004; Santagata, 2006), because they are the first front of industrialization, closer to local resources and traditional knowledge, less demanding in terms of financial capital and technological innovations and most concerned with intellectual property rights to protect their intellectual value.

Against this background, the aim of this chapter is to tie together three aspects: (1) material cultural heritage; (2) the nexus between traditional crafts and *soft* industrial design, that is a design strategy adapted to micro-enterprises; and (3) the role of collective property rights in buttressing cultural districts and the search for quality in the context of global competition. For this purpose, a model of endogenous local economic development based upon the transformation of the handicraft sector into *soft* industrial design will be proposed. The economic characteristics and advantages of this transformation, as well as the main traits of a policy for its implementation, will be discussed. The first section of the chapter will define the concept of material culture. The second section will sketch the historical background to industrial design and compare it with traditional handicrafts and argue how quantitative data on the economic weight of artisanal products makes it possible to assess their strategic role in developing countries' economies. The third section will present a model on the transition from handicraft to *soft* industrial design. The two main policies which should be addressed for implementing the model are the cultural district formula and the assignment of collective trademarks: these will be explored in the fourth section.

Material cultural heritage: from handicraft to design

Our definition of material culture is, broadly speaking, anthropological rather than artistic or humanistic. We consider material culture as the base of the artefacts with both a function and a form that human beings produce to protect themselves, and get a better life. Because it goes beyond the notion of artisanal products to include technological goods, industrial design and architecture, this definition gives us a rather impressive list of goods. As numerous as they are heterogeneous, these goods and services all represent economic and social answers to the human aspiration to a more comfortable habitat. Furthermore, the geography of material culture shows its worldwide diffusion: defending it means defending cultural diversity. According to the anthropological view of Keesing: 'Material culture has the special distinction of linking the behaviour of the individual with external man-made things: artefacts' (Keesing, 1958).

In this sense, functional handicrafts are distinct from works of art, like paintings or sculptures, that do not have a functional use and are therefore conceived without an intentional functional form. Yet traditional artefacts represent a crucial part of a community's culture and both their physical shape and functional nature are the outcome of many factors: local raw materials, traditional knowledge and practices, specific cultural behaviours and beliefs. Not all of them can be considered exclusively artisanal products. Some are the output of artist–artisan ateliers, but most are produced both by the handicraft and industrial sectors (except that when developing countries are considered, the vision of handicraft production, as we will see later, prevails). On the contrary, industrial design rules are applied mostly by medium and large industries in Western economies. In developing countries, handicraft production shows aesthetic and ornamental qualities, but does not assimilate any modern industrial strategy leading at the same time to serial production and good quality standards.

Evolution of the handicraft: craftsmanship between art and industrial design

From fine arts to industrial design

The production of functional objects began at the dawn of humanity. The only technical input was manual ability. Quality was low and workshops produced limited quantities. This was our material culture for centuries. Two unexpected disjunctures then occurred together in the evolution of handicraft. The first was the search for aesthetic value and the symbolic expression of beauty. The artist appeared alongside the craftsman, his studio alongside the workshop. Quality increased. The work of art became 'use-less'. But for both artists and craftsmen conception and execution were a unique phenomenon.

The second transformation was linked to the appearance of machines. The industrial revolution increased the productive power of the craftsman and transformed him into a modern entrepreneur. Firms appeared beside the shop and the studio and here hosts of workers sold abstract work for executing projects and ideas conceived elsewhere. Conception and execution lost their unity. Work lost its skills.

All over the world the basic starting point of craftsmanship took different paths in accordance with the different local processes involving artists, entrepreneurs and workers.

The industrial design idea can be thought of as the strongest attempt to unify conception and execution, using machines as means, not as ends. It was an intellectual choice that gave rise to the social movement anticipated by John Ruskin (1819–1900) and led by William Morris (1834–96) and others. Indeed, the decline in the importance of handicraft began with the industrial revolution and was accompanied in search of even lower costs, by a serious decrease in product quality. The reaction to this crisis spawned movements such as William Morris' *Arts and Crafts*, the *Guild of Handicrafts* launched by Charles Ashbee in London, the activity of Charles Mackintosh in Glasgow and the *Wiener Werkstätte,* created in Vienna by Hoffmann and Moser.

The two fundamental years for the modern European history of handicraft and for the beginnings of industrial design were 1851, with the London 'Great Exhibition of the Works of all Nations' and April 1919, when at Weimar a leaflet announced the program of a new school, the Public Bauhaus, synthesis of the Academy of Fine Arts and of the school of handicraft. The return to handicraft was seen by the Bauhaus as a way for the artist to realize a new 'unitary work of art' which could include different kinds of individual artistry that would give form at the same time to a popular and collective art.

At the beginning of the twentieth century, the taxonomy of the handicraft sector was the following:

- *traditional handicraft*, which was by now an impoverished sector with low quality products made by craftsmen;
- *art works* based on material culture and made by artists and artists–artisans;
- *serial utilitarian products* made by industrial workers with low quality and low production costs;
- *functional industrial design objects* based on mechanical production and incorporating conceptual, aesthetic and technological advances.

The emergence and main characteristics of industrial design

The Bauhaus experience ended in 1932 for political reasons but gave rise to a new approach. The rationale of industrial design comes in fact from the consciousness that the serial product has the same dignity as the unique object because of the originality and specific individuality of the design conception. The underlying concept of industrial design is that an original and artistic idea conceived for a few can, through serial production, be offered at a lower price and in greater numbers. Applied to artefacts, the process extends the notion of industrial design to popular art and gives rise to the category *design-based goods*. This new class of designed and planned commodities differs from mere industrial products, traditional artefacts and works of art (Giedion, 1948; Bologna, 1972; Dorfles, 1972; Castelnuovo, 1989). A *design-based good* can be defined by four essential characteristics.

- It is a *serial* product, made principally by machines and according to the logic of industrial organization.
- It is a product with a high *intellectual component* embedded into its aesthetic, decoration, shape and technology. The share of the intellectual component as compared with the raw material component and other productive factors is high, dominant and increasing.
- Intellectual property rights are the institutional way to protect a design-based good. It

is a *symbolic* good, according to the intention of both the creator and the consumer. Its symbolic meaning (social, relational, ritual and ideological) goes beyond its functional character. Symbols strengthen beliefs and sentiments shared by the members of a community and, hence, by extension have an influence also on consumer behaviour, when this phenomenon becomes ritual and produces cultural lock-in.

- Its intellectual creation does not follow the incremental path of scientific knowledge, yet it seeks a break with tradition, innovating by opposition and difference. This discontinuity or non-cumulativity is a characteristic trait of Italian design (Branzi, 1999).

Box 24.1   Building alliances between artisans and designers

The issue of design intervention in crafts, in the broader context of globalization, questions the way the crafts and the design industries interact, the way artisans and craftsmanship are perceived, the role they are able to play in local, national and global economies and their capacity to cope with the demands of distant and increasingly competitive markets. Indeed, globalization is often considered to be a threat to the richness, diversity and economic viability of the crafts. As the gap between artisans and consumers is constantly increasing, both literally and metaphorically, it becomes difficult for the former to cater to a distant clientele. Users are more demanding and selective as markets offer a wide range of new products, produced in great quantities, often standardized, and sold at very low prices, from which they can invariably choose and discriminate depending on unpredictable tendencies such as fashion trends. Global brands are also engaged in fierce competition which craft-makers are often unprepared and unable to face.

Yet, several favorable trends speak positively for the role and importance of artisans in today's societies: the growing awareness of public and private actors as well as of regional and international cooperation agencies of the strategic importance of the crafts sector; growing consumer preference for authentic, hand-made and eco-friendly quality products; and the recognition of certain qualities that are often taken for granted in crafts – qualities of timelessness and permanence, the adaptability of artisans and their materials to changing needs as well as the spiritual dimensions. The emergence of global and highly competitive brands has simultaneously created a niche for creativity, innovation and uniqueness, and an increasing demand for well-applied design. Design intervention should therefore be carefully managed so as to guide artisans in directions that enable them to make optimal use of their skills.

How may an effective alliance be formed between artisans and designers? What should be the role of designers and which areas should they focus on in order to support and further develop the crafts sector? How can design intervention mediate between tradition and change? What are the kinds of markets that have opened up to artisans through the medium of design intervention? Does design intervention add value to the artisan's work economically and in terms of creative inputs?

As artisans are caught in the ambiguous position of being pressured to adjust to market demands while also encouraged to remain true to their ancient traditions, designers can become key partners in the preservation of crafts, the marketing of products and the integration of appropriate technology, provided that there is a shared vision and a spirit of mutual respect.

First of all, *their interventions should aim at preserving the diversity and authenticity of crafts.* Researching, documenting, analysing, categorizing and maintaining references on crafts – on traditional skills, techniques, materials, patterns, etc. – especially on languishing or dying forms, helps sustain some of the essential qualities and characteristics which define peoples' identities. The creativity of artisans and the uniqueness of their products are also strong assets to be promoted. Respecting the materials they use, their techniques and vision, designers can guide artisans in the search for new solutions that emerge from their own creativity, innovative patterns that are also adapted to modern life. In addition, mediating between tradition and change requires that designers keep in mind the context in which crafts have emerged; taking an object out of its context objectifies it, and neglects the fact that a craft has

(Continued)

usually been produced to respond to a certain social need. Emphasizing the socio-cultural context in which products have been crafted can increase people's awareness of their value and meaning. Identifying whether crafts have a ritual value and communicate history, myths and beliefs, helps designers and artisans decide if these can and should be used for purposes other than the purely decorative.

Second, *designers can guide artisans in dealing with market demands and sensitize buyers to the qualities of crafts.* Helping artisans combine their traditional crafts with modern techniques, tools and materials to compete with the products of modern industrialized countries helps generate new revenues. Design intervention should thus focus on ways of adapting to changing market demands and design patterns, on choosing and coordinating colours or eco-friendly materials. Focusing on revitalizing and targeting local markets is nevertheless the best way for artisans to secure regular and more predictable incomes than they would by exporting to distant and fleeting markets. Although the relationship between craftspeople and local consumers is not what it used to be – since the artisan is no longer simultaneously the producer, designer and marketer of his products – designers can study the tastes and preferences of local people more easily and renew and strengthen the client base, whilst encouraging continued use of indigenous and local craft products. On the whole, contrary to modern urban and export markets, local markets secure long-term resources, closer and longer customer relationships with local people and more economic independence for the artisan. Also, catering to a less discerning public by providing consumers, local or distant, with more information about the way craft products have been developed, by sensitizing them to the many qualities of crafts, strengthens their economic viability.

Finally, *knowledge transfer and the introduction of appropriate technologies* are fields in which alliances between artisans and designers can be formed. Globalization and the evolution of society's needs call for adapted knowledge transfer, training and equipment to support these changes. In fact, the ability of artisans to seize the new opportunities of global interaction to widen their knowledge of technologies and capacities is greater than generally assumed. Informing them about skills-upgrading, revival of traditional motifs, designs and techniques, and marketing tools such as principles of costing, quality control and product planning, introduction of effective planning and promotional strategies are indispensable. Technological improvement is also a key element; it requires the introduction of appropriate technologies adapted to the community, area, region or country context and that show artisans the easiest, simplest, least expensive and most efficient way of dealing with everyday problems. In other words, they must fit into the socio-economic fabric and environment. Simple and affordable technologies, installed with little training, should be introduced to craftsmen whether by improving traditional technologies or by down-scaling modern technologies.

Indrasen Vencatachellum

The economic importance of handicraft in developing countries

But what is the real economic importance of traditional craft for local development nowadays and what does the economic realm consider as crafts? Given their variety and complexity, measuring the economic role of handicrafts in domestic and international markets is no easy task. Even if export statistics related to craft are provided, craft exports are still quite difficult to measure within the international classification system of trade statistics since most artisan products are not identified in the customs classification system used for trade statistics. In addition, data on production, both in terms of quantities produced and of the labour force involved, are unavailable for many developing countries.

On the one hand it should be interesting therefore to analyse the weight of handicraft as a share of the national GDP or in terms of people employed. On the other hand an effective way to asses the economic importance of handicrafts could be to look at trade in international markets. The main drawback of this perspective is that it ignores the domestic economy: in some countries, while exports or access to international markets are limited, the domestic production for internal consumption may be high. Thus, taking into account the above remarks, some sort of indicator on the economic importance of handicrafts can, in principle, be analysed. Although absolute figures with respect to production, in terms of both quantities produced and labour force involved, are lacking for most developing countries, still it is possible to use some data from the 1997 UNESCO and ITC survey on crafts in the international markets (UNESCO, 1997) even if some figures are only estimates and rules and definitions in data collection vary from country to country. Thus the survey reports revenues from crafts in the Philippines amounting to US$591 million and to US$200 million in Iran; in Peru 200,000 full-time and 1.6 million part-time workers produced US$13 million worth of crafts; India was producing crafts worth more than US$1,400 million and employed two million full-time and 5 million part-time workers in the sector; in Mali US$60 million of crafts were produced involving around 60 per cent of the active population.

Using data from the ITC (International Trade Center) it is also possible to assess the economic importance of handicrafts by analysing the volume of trade in international markets and comparing the countries' quotas of exports in each artisan sector. In the most significant textile categories – handbags, cotton bed/table/toilet/kitchen linen, and other cotton bed linen – which represent about 47 per cent of world textile exports, the role of developing countries is dominant. China, for example, exports 30 per cent, in terms of US$ value, of the world's handbag output, 30 per cent of other kinds of cotton bed linen (another 32 per cent is exported by Pakistan and 9 per cent by India), and 18 per cent of cotton/bed/ table/toilet/kitchen/linen (another 30 per cent is exported by Turkey, India and Poland). In general, for the textile sector, we observe[1] that, in terms of US dollars, developing and emerging countries – above all China and India – play a role of primary importance in world craft exports. But it is possible to find the same evidence for many other craft products such as, for example, basket, wicker and other vegetable fiber works in which developing countries are dominant with respect to world exports: China, Vietnam, Philippines, Indonesia produce more than 80 per cent of basketware and wickerwork of vegetable material, and 75 per cent of the world's artisanal seats of cane, bamboo etc.

The comparison in terms of unit value (US$/unit) is also a useful indicator of the economic value which can be attached to industrial design that is more developed in Western industrialized countries than handicraft. These differences could help in explaining how the industrial design production line is much more productive in terms of monetary value. The unit value is the sum of many components which are difficult to consider separately: symbolic and design value; humanpower value; raw material value, capital cost. The comparison in terms of Country Export/Country GDP is also revealing when trying to measure the leading role of the handicraft sector in developing countries, also for the accumulation of foreign exchange reserves. For example, in 2005, the export value of textile handicrafts from India amounted to more than US$2 billion and jewellry exports were around US$2.6 billion. The Philippines exported, in 2005, US$1,941 million of basketwork crafts and Iran's carpet exports alone reached nearly US$400 million (0.2 per cent of GDP but the whole craft sector amounts to more than 3 per cent). In Vietnam the value of exported crafts – counting only wood, leather, pottery and basket-based crafts – represents nearly 3 per cent of GDP.[2]

From traditional crafts to 'soft industrial design'

In this section we will present a model of the transition from traditional handicraft to *soft* industrial design. This change is mainly linked to the development of local traditional production. To enter knowledge society markets in the context of globalization, traditional production needs to increase both the *quality and quantity* of its own goods and services. If quality or quantity are missing, progress will be limited.

Let's first take the case of lack of quality. The starting point is a kind of commodity expression of a local and old tradition. It is usually supposed that the original quality was high. Excellent artefacts can be found in museums or eco-museums that confirm this view. The problem is that the warped economic trends in the second half of the last century focused on the search for low costs. It seemed that the only way to compete in the global market was by lowering production costs. Yet low costs and low wages are usually connected to low quality. So, pursuing low costs meant accepting a significant lowering of quality at the same time. Low quality became the prerogative of developing and poor countries, while industrialized countries moved toward new and superior levels of quality. Today international competition revolves around the quality issue. A commodity of low quality has a very low economic value and its export does not attain, in volume, the desired effects in terms of export-based models of development. In summary, the lack of quality means both limited penetration capacity in global markets and a low unit value of the product at the limit of the international exploitation of local resources.

Let's now take the case of lack of quantity resulting from normal handicraft production. When a traditional product is appreciated by consumers all over the world, it is considered a real success. Yet on closer examination things can appear different. In fact the success of some kinds of local production, let's say Indian silk or artistic glass, will create space for an increase in international demand. Consumers attracted by the product will be induced to buy it and shopkeepers will be induced to stock it. But if the quantity produced is lower than demand for the product it is possible that instead of an increase in prices, new competitors will enter the market to fill the gap. This can happen when the barriers to entry are low because the technology used for handicraft production is easily acquired or traditional decorations easily copied. The final result will be that new producers will enter the market and occupy the space previously taken by the original firms. This demonstrates that international success in the handicraft sector can be immediately reversed if it is not supported by enough productive power.

So, quality and quantity are always needed simultaneously in the handicraft market.

This is why industrial design can help. But considering the normal size of the firms working in the handicraft sector, the opportunity to develop a special version of industrial design that we call *soft* industrial design should be considered.

Soft industrial design has the same basic characteristics of industrial design, namely serial production, intellectual property, symbolic value and non-cumulativity. What changes is the economic and social context.

- First of all the innovative rules of industrial design must apply to micro and small firms. So the main economic constraints of soft design are the circumstances of local production, its cultural district nature. It has to develop seriality in a context in which there are few employees per firm, shortages of financial capital, primitive technology, a great role for creative ornament, vertical or horizontal integration of firms, strong social links, collective trademarks, and common international outlets.
- Soft industrial design must hold manual and mechanical production together; that means holding mechanical perfection and manual imperfection together. Soft design involves introducing planned imperfections even in a large series.

- Soft design should fit patterns of community or collective labour organization. Networks, families, clans and tribes are special settings the designer has to take care of. In other words the designer should closely consider the local organization of labour.
- Soft design means using raw materials produced locally, ones which are traditionally of good quality or historically suitable for the original version of the products. This should increase the general quality results: natural colours look better, fine wool is dyed in soft elegant colours, etc.
- Often soft design easily generates economies of scale. These are supported by the existing integration of micro firms and the cultural district atmosphere. New products can be developed by designers using the same mechanical and personal abilities in other sectors.
- Soft design can usually develop in a context of micro-finance.

While the traditional handicraft is roughly based on *high quality – low quantity* production or on *low quality – high quantity* production, soft industrial design perspective should allow new production opportunities based on both *high quality* and *high quantity*.

This relatively new model seems to be crucial for entering international markets in a sustainable way, allowing crafts people to succeed in terms of the quality of their production and at the same time allowing them to be present with their commodities in retail outlets and satisfy international demand.

As a result of this transformation, our taxonomy would change, making traditional products:

1. *art works* based on material culture and made by artists and artists–artisans;
2. *serial utilitarian industrial products*;
3. *functional objects from the 'soft industrial design'*.

Policies: cultural districts and collective intellectual property rights

Two policy orientations that can be used to implement such a model are the 'cultural district' perspective and the assignment of collective trademarks. The cultural district is the best context in which to make the evolution from crafts to soft industrial design. The latter can then develop further if collective institutions and a sense of identity assist the community; and product quality is improved, for instance through the management of collective trademarks. Industrial clusters, mostly made by micro firms, and collective intellectual property, can leverage local sustainable development in the less developing countries.

Cultural districts

A *cultural district* corresponds, both in developed and developing countries, to a special industrial formula for the production of traditional goods based on creativity and culture (Santagata, 2001, 2006). A cultural district is grounded on two characteristics: first of all the idiosyncratic nature of culture, which is peculiar to a given place or community and to a specific time, and secondly on the positive externalities generated by the spatial agglomeration of micro firms. In a cultural district a local community rich in cultural traditions and in accumulation of technical and tacit knowledge is found. A Marshallian *industrial atmosphere*, animated by micro and small enterprises, locally involves social capital, agglomeration economies, trust and cooperation. The goods based on material culture, or design-based goods, are usually produced in this special industrial setting made of a spatial agglomeration of micro and small firms. Let's take as an example *the Cultural District of San Gregorio Armeno,* in Naples (Cuccia et al., 2007). This cultural district has been producing the traditional characters of the Neapolitan Christian Crib since the Middle Ages and demonstrates the key components of a cultural district:

- A reputation which goes far beyond the district's borders: domestic and international.
- A community-shared cultural tradition.
- Horizontally integrated micro and small firms.
- Low-grade technology, as is typical of works of art.
- Great creativity.
- Similar firms with common goals: free circulation of information, good relation with institutions, common reputation.
- A strong sense of collective identity.
- The transmission of creativity to the next generations is based on tacit knowledge and learning by doing.
- High tourist attraction capacity.
- Cohabitation of artistic activity and business.

The evolution from crafts to soft industrial design is grounded on some specific traits. First of all the district can act as a magnifier for the reputation of local production. This is due to its greater ability to communicate and develop collective marketing and financial services. The district can satisfy international demand led by growing reputation. Hence the main way to respond to the increased demand is to resort to serial production with high quality and convenient prices. To extend the supply chain for soft industrial design many of its articulations must be developed by transforming a short supply chain into a longer one based on the product department conception, the department of sculptures and casts, the scenography department and the department of artistic decoration.

It is not uncommon in developing countries to find traces of crafts based on clusters of activities variously framed within and linked to the local cultural heritage (Pye, 1988). This is something *less* than a cultural district. There are local economic forces, one or more pioneers in the material culture sector, in arts and crafts manufacturing, local and external demands, labour skills and learning effects, but what is commonly lacking is an incentive system leading the main economic actors towards more efficient ways of investing, trading, communicating and marketing their products. In other words, *institutions* and *good governance* are lacking.

Collective trademarks

The enforcement of a distinctive brand fulfils many economic purposes: it reduces the probability of unfair competition and gives rise to individual efficient incentives to create and produce (Santagata, 2002, 2006; Cuccia and Santagata, 2004, Ghafele and Santagata, 2005). The three main functions of collective trademarks can be summarized as follows:

- *Transformation function.* The creation of collective trademarks transforms traditional knowledge, images and ideas into 'property'. Local knowledge becomes 'intellectual property': it becomes something that could be owned by the local producers who would agree to comply with the minimal requirements of regulated local production.
- *Information function.* Identifying the owner of the brand and signalling his/her reputation contributes to diffusing information about the quality of goods and services. This role acts as a safeguard against the illegal copying of design, ideas, tags, labels or logos.
- *Management function.* The managerial role, namely the collective trademark and certification

mark, is related to the enhancement of the quality of goods and services provided through the introduction of rules, standards, inspections and mechanisms for business development into a local area.

Setting product quality standards implies maintaining a particular level of cooperation, marketing and monitoring among the local micro and small enterprises. If we think, for instance, of the collective trademarks assigned to a local area and a local community, it is easy to observe their role in fostering the local reputation through increases in the quality of locally produced goods and of the services provided. In this sense, collective trademarks can be used to assist the transformation of a potential cultural district based on traditional crafts into a real cultural district based on crafts and soft industrial design. Therefore collective intellectual property rights will be analysed from this unconventional perspective concerning their ability to foster culture-based product quality and move the supply chain towards industrial design. Collective trademarks can be used as tools to forge various activities linked with cultural heritage into effective institutions with good governance (Betting, 1996; World Bank, 2004). A bootstrap procedure has been proposed for managing this tool kit efficiently (Ghafele and Santagata, 2005). It should be implemented by an association of local stakeholders on the basis of the following actions: establishing a local committee, identifying the image for local products and services; filing the selected collective mark; setting the rule of compromise as a decision rule; selecting minimum quality standards; defining the registration and accreditation procedure; and managing royalties.

The case of San Gregorio Armeno (Cuccia et al., 2007) confirms the above characteristics of collective trademarks. They are a safeguard against unfair competition and piracy, a sign of quality certification, they foster deliberative democracy and stakeholder participation, and last but not least, through the procedure of 'Registration & Accreditation', they are a politically friendly means of increasing quality. Looking at the economic value of a collective trademark it can be said that the average value of the trademark (willingness to pay) for local consumers is 10.02 per cent of the price paid. The producers of San Gregorio Armeno are willing to pay on average from 10 cents to 2 Euro for the tag/label, depending on the value of the object.

Conclusions

Developing countries, whose production is largely based on agriculture, handicraft and natural resources are on the cusp of a radical change. The handicraft sector has the potential to increase its quality and quantity and enter the international market. The main strategy for this change is based on the deployment of soft industrial design rules.

Notes

1   Data from ITC creative industries database.
2   Data are based on IMF and ITC, 2005

REFERENCES

Becattini, G., Bellandi, M., Dei Ottati, G. and Sforzi, F. (2003) *From Industrial Districts to Local Development. An Itinerary of Research.* Cheltenham: Edward Elgar.

Betting, R. (1996) *Copyrighting culture. The political economy of Intellectual Property.* Boulder, CO: Westview Press.

Bologna, F. (1972) *Dalle arti minori all'industrial design.* Bari: Laterza.

Branzi, A. (1999) *Introduzione al design italiano. Una modernità incompleta.* Milano: Baldini e Castoldi.

Castelnuovo, E. (1989) *Per una storia del design*, in E. Castelnuovo (ed.) *Storia del disegno industriale.* Milano: Electa.

Cuccia, T. and Santagata, W. (2004) 'Collective Property Rights and Cultural Districts: The Case Study of Caltagirone Pottery in Sicily', in

E. Colombatto (ed.) *Companion to Property Right Economics*. Cheltenham: Edward Elgar.

Cuccia, T., Marrelli, M. and Santagata, W. (2007) 'Collective trademarks and cultural districts: the case of San Gregorio Armeno – Naples', in P. Cooke and L. Lazzeretti (eds.) *Creative cities, cultural cluster and local economic development*. Cheltenham: Edward Elgar.

Dorfles, G. (1972) *Introduzione al disegno industriale. Linguaggio e storia della produzione di serie*. Torino: Einaudi.

Ghafele, R. and Santagata, W. (2005) 'Cultural tourism and collective trademarks: the case of Byblos and Saida, Lebanon', Working paper No. 01/2006, International Centre for Research on the Economics of Culture, Institutions, and Creativity (EBLA CENTER): University of Turin.

Giedion S. (1948) *Mechanisation Takes Command*. Oxford and New York: Oxford University Press.

Greffe, X., Noya, A. and Pflieger, S. (2005) *Culture and local development*. Paris: OECD.

ILO (2003) *Promoting the Culture Sector through Job Creation and Small Enterprise Development in SADC Countries: Craft and Visual Arts*. Geneva: International Labour Office.

IMF (International Monetary Fund): www.imf.org, last accessed march 2007.

ITC (International Trade Centre) Creative Industries Database, last accessed March 2007.

Keesing F. (1958) *Cultural Anthropology: The Science of Customs*. Stanford.

Moreno, Y.J., Santagata, W. and Tabassum, A. (2005) *Material Cultural Heritage and Sustainable Development*, in Working Papers, EBLA Center: University of Turin, N.7.

Power, D. and Scott, A.J. (2004) *The Cultural Industries and the Production of Culture*. London: Routledge.

Pye, E.A. (1988) *Artisans in economic development*. Ottawa: International Development Research Centre.

Pyke, F., Becattini, G. and Sengenberger, W. (1990) *Industrial District and Inter-Firm Co-Operation in Italy*. Geneva: International Labour Office.

Santagata, W. (2001) *Economia creativa e distretti culturali,* in 'Economia della Cultura', N.2.

Santagata, W. (2002) 'Cultural Districts, Property Rights and Sustainable Economic Growth', in *International Journal of Urban and Regional Research*, N.26.

Santagata, W. (2006) 'Cultural Districts and their role in Economic Development', in V. Ginsburg and D. Throsby (eds.) *Handbook on the Economics of Art and Culture*. Elsevier Science: North Holland, Amsterdam.

UNESCO (2004) *Crafts/Tourism Index Report*. Paris: UNESCO.

UNESCO/UNCTAD (1997) *La artesania y el Mercado international: comercio y codificacion aduanera*, acts from the International Symposium, Manila, 6–8 October.

WIPO/ITC (2003) *Marketing Crafts and Visual Arts: The Role of Intellectual Property*. Geneva: ITC/WIPO.

World Bank (2004) *Poor People's Knowledge: Promoting Intellectual Property in Developing Countries*. Washington DC: World Bank.

## CHAPTER 25

AUSTRALIAN INDIGENOUS ART: LOCAL DREAMINGS, GLOBAL CONSUMPTION

Mark David Ryan, Michael Keane and Stuart Cunningham

Indigenous Australian visual art is an outstanding case of the dynamics of globalization and its intersection with the hyper-local wellsprings of cultural expression, and of the strengths and weaknesses of state, philanthropic and commercial backing for cultural production and dissemination. This chapter traces the development of the international profile of Indigenous 'dot' art – a traditional symbolic art form from the Western Desert – as 'high-end' visual art, and its positioning within elite markets and finance supported by key international brokers, collectors and philanthropists.

Indigenous Australian visual art frequently headlines in international auctions. The names of artists such as Clifford Possum Tjapaltjarri and Paddy Bedford (Goowoomji) are synonymous with authentic Indigenous culture. The Western Desert 'brand' attracts affluent aficionados of the arts from across the globe. These paintings, mostly created in third world conditions, finish up adorning first world living spaces and galleries (Altman et al., 2002; Myers, 2002). While critically acclaimed and highly valued, Indigenous Australian 'high art' is mostly made in places with limited basic infrastructure, high rates of unemployment and welfare dependency, poverty, illness, substance abuse and violence (Australia Council for the Arts, 2006; Creative Economy, 2006).

Yet Indigenous visual art has become arguably Australia's most significant cultural export. Terry Smith (2007: 25) captures the terms of this stunning emergence:

> By the mid-1990s, Aboriginal art had become the strongest force in Australian art according to any measure: the quality and challenge of much of the work, as well as its sheer quantity and attractive variety. It had become a contemporary art in its own right, and it was actively setting the terms of its own reception. A cultural movement can, when it gains momentum, force a shift in perception of 'quality,' largely by its own force as an emerging paradigm.

However, as Myers (2002) illustrates in his seminal study *Painting Culture,* public subsidy and support mechanisms – while sustaining production in the 1970s and deepening production capacity in the 1980s – have mostly facilitated the domestic market. International success has been driven by individual agents, drawing finance from private, philanthropic and foundational sources. This is both a strength (private sector passion and entrepreneurship may have achieved more than public sector processes) and a weakness (the market has been subject to unethical, corrupt and exploitative behaviour detrimental to Indigenous benefit and sustainability).

Over the last three and a half decades, Indigenous Australian visual art has become an industry whose turnover is estimated to be as high as AU$500 million per annum (Papunya Tula Artists, 2006), growing strongly from between AU$100 million and AU$300 million per annum in 2002 (Altman et al., 2002; Australia Council for the Arts, 2006). Accurate data in this field is extremely hard to achieve. Most work is produced in very isolated communities, records are often unreliable, and much data is privately held and not subject to mandatory release. It was estimated in 2003 that more than half the total number of Indigenous visual artists are in remote areas of the Northern Territory (see Altman, 2003). Demand for Indigenous visual art has increased dramatically, particularly in international markets. Estimates suggest between 5,000–6,000 artists and painters work in the industry (Altman et al., 2002; Myer, 2002), making up between 25 and 50 per cent of all working Australian visual artists. This is a remarkable figure considering that the Indigenous population comprises about 2 per cent of the Australian population.

This case study examines the international profile of Indigenous 'dot' art – a traditional symbolic art form from the Western Desert – as 'high-end' visual art, and the relationship between its positioning within elite markets and finance. There are multiple ironies and 'category busters' in this story. While Indigenous visual art has enjoyed strong, at times insatiable, international demand, the art of non-Indigenous Australians (a category used to encompass all settlers and migrants, including the white population) struggles in the international marketplace. As the Contemporary Visual Arts and Craft Inquiry (Myer, 2002: 259) observed, it is 'extremely difficult' to sell Australian exhibitions and artwork more generally to galleries outside of Australia – with Indigenous art the only exception. The works circulate as 'mysteriously' symbolic high art, yet they are mostly representations of spiritual knowledge (Dreamings) that document geographical locales with careful precision.

They embody, for many buyers and aficionados, the lure of the primitive, but have been produced in many cases out of sophisticated and reflexive commodification processes which are nevertheless not immune from egregious exploitation. While Indigenous visual art has become a multimillion dollar export industry, the financial returns to Indigenous artists themselves run from the reasonable to the scandalous (the average practising visual artist is estimated to earn a meagre $7,200 per annum (Australia Council for the Arts, 2006). It would be awfully easy to decry the exploitation, the cultural ignorance and the theft of intellectual property and leave it at that, were it not the case that sales provide often the only non-welfare finances in many communities. It would be easy as well to denounce the commodification and reification of an authentic and fragile culture were it not that many artists have managed their careers and reputations deftly and successfully.

The Indigenous Australian value chain

Toby Miller (1994; 1995) offers a brilliant epigram for the importance of Indigenous Australia to the country's place in the world: 'When Australia became modern, it ceased to be interesting.' Before Australia became a sovereign nation (that is, modern) in 1901, Indigenous Australians were of critical importance to much foundational intellectual inquiry seeking to examine questions about origins, authenticity and 'human truths'. Indigenous Australians 'provided Europe with a photographic negative of itself' (Miller, 1995: 7). When Australia became a nation, it eliminated the 'birth right of citizenship from people of colour'. Australia became just another British colony filled with 'white-fellas'; it became 'dull, boring and obvious' to intellectual debate (Miller, 1994: 207). Internationally, Australians were transformed 'from dashing blacks living out of time into dull anglo-celts living out of place' (Miller, 1995: 7). Indigenous Australian visual art now circulates in a postmodern *Zeitgeist*, where its cultural ambassadorial role is again unparalleled.

Culture and knowledge: creating value

A careful comparative examination of the value chain in Indigenous visual art (cf. Keane and Hartley, 2001) highlights key continuities and differences with standard cultural value chains. For Indigenous people in Australia, as elsewhere, the raw material of content creation is culture and knowledge, which is to say their everyday lives, beliefs and practices. Combined with the creative talent of the artist, the performer and the technician, this becomes a unique and distinctive intellectual property that finds its way into several markets (domestic – Indigenous and non-Indigenous – tourist and international) of which the most profitable is the elite international art or 'high art' market.

Indigenous visual arts resemble mainstream creative industries, insofar as they are generally characterized by an over-supply of content-providers clustered around the most profitable links in the chain, notably distribution. The circulation and delivery of

Indigenous art, given the often vast distances – both culturally and geographically – between supply and demand, see cultural intermediaries play a key role, sometimes drawing inappropriately large profits from their activity. Indigenous artists rarely negotiate directly with commercial galleries or retail outlets for the sale of their work. Their work is handled by Indigenous art centers or cooperatives. These organizations are staffed by art coordinators who operate as both commercial and cultural mediators between producers and mainly non-indigenous procurers of indigenous art.

Market demand and tensions for Indigenous artists

The markets for Indigenous art are complex and highly differentiated. The Indigenous market, obviously the most culturally proximate, is also by definition the smallest, least remunerative and most discriminating. There are what we call the domestic consumer market, the particularly international tourist market, the public sector or 'grants' market and breakthrough markets such as international art galleries and museums, and major investors/collectors.

The demands of the international marketplace, while driving and sustaining production, create tensions for Indigenous artists. The United States is a major international market for global visual art exports. It accounts for 41 per cent of the world market and US$3 billion of global annual sales (Australian Trade Commission, 2006). It is a key market for Indigenous visual art exports. However, while US galleries and auction houses generate strong demand for Indigenous Australian 'dot-art', there is little interest in the many other forms of Indigenous art. (Dot-art styles and motifs rode on the back of phenomenal critical acclaim in the 1980s and 1990s, becoming almost synonymous with Indigenous visual art.)

This market segmentation belies the rich diversity of traditional, contemporary and geographic styles that comprise Indigenous visual art. Contemporary artists are forging a variety of styles, most of which have little opportunity to achieve international recognition because of the 'displacement effect' of the dominance of dot painting. Nevertheless, the force of traditional Indigenous art ultimately derives from 'ancestral stories of the land from which Indigenous people draw physical and spiritual strength'. According to Megaw and Megaw, Indigenous artwork has a religious nature – a 'perceived relationship to the dreamtime', ancestral spirits and the

'inextricable links' between individuals, groups and land (2001: 97). And despite temporal and geographic varieties, artworks have 'a certain basic symbolic vocabulary… seen in geometric patterns', the meanings and interpretations of which, for Indigenous artists and in some cases communities, are 'strictly controlled' (2001: 97).

Because of these intrinsic cultural elements, paintings have been used as 'evidence of title' in land claims. Art also acts as an important bridge between generations, contributing to the maintenance of cultural and spiritual knowledge (Australia Council for the Arts, 2006). In central Australia, the *tjukurrpa* (dreaming or story) are essentially overhead maps 'of locations and the journeyings of individual characters in the ancestral dreamtime'. Artworks are therefore a medium for the transmission of knowledge and this is revealed step by step to the young (Megaw and Megaw, 2001: 97–8). Before colonization, there were over 700 Indigenous Australian languages. Now some 200 remain; of these, all but 20 are endangered.[1] Bereft of the transfer of knowledge from generation to generation through forms of cultural expression such as art, many other aspects of the Indigenous way of life are under threat of extinction.

The lure of lucrative sales can encourage artistic compromise – the abandoning of personal or custodial styles to produce popular or 'traditional' styles sought by elite markets. This can have serious ramifications. Artists producing artworks with no relations to custodial ownership or ancestral dreamings, can sever 'the inextricable' links between artist, clan/totem, belief systems and their spiritual connections with the land.

Market trends for Indigenous visual art

As we have seen, the markets for Indigenous Australian visual art are recently established, volatile and complex. The Australian art market, for example, has experienced a dramatic shift over the last two decades, marked by a steep rise in Indigenous Australian art market share and a decline in non-Indigenous Australian auction sales. The following typology, adapted from Keane and Hartley (2001), is a representation of the limitations and potential of markets for Indigenous Australian visual art:

The international tourist market: Tourists seeking to purchase authentic Indigenous Australian cultural artifacts and experiences represent an important market for Indigenous art. Cultural theme parks and general tourist markets provide important outlets for the sale of Indigenous visual art. Popular tourist destinations strongly associated with images/notions of Australia and Indigenous people/culture such as Uluru (Ayers Rock), create opportunities for artists, collectives and communities to sell directly to tourists. Product differentiation is important within the tourism market in order to appeal to different market sections, namely: 'overseas tourists; people interested in learning about Indigenous Australian culture; young people; adventurous people and those interested in reconciliation' (Keane and Hartley, 2001: 31). The darker side of this trade is the high incidence of opportunistic copying and cloning, with value not being returned to the producer.

The domestic consumer market: Indigenous visual art, like many elite forms of traditional culture, often meets with apathy within the domestic market. The problem of disinterest in national cultural treasures is often seen by supporters of such forms to be due to a lack of financial support. However, the relative availability and seeming everydayness of such forms can detract from their value at home. As a recent survey found, 55 per cent of all Australian respondents had no interest in indigenous tourist attractions, products or activities (Colmar Brunton Social Research, 2004: 114).

The public sector market: The government and public sector agencies are a major market for Indigenous art with procurement policies seeing artworks adorning the halls and lobbies of local, state and federal government agencies, educational institutions and universities. The 'grants' market is also a large market for Indigenous art. This is where artists, galleries, collectives and art enterprises compete for a limited supply of government and foundation funds for activities and projects that enhance national or regional identity. Ideally, enterprises which access grants or benefit from procurement policies use these to leverage their ability to meet wider markets. Papunya Tula Artists Pty Ltd is one example where an Indigenous art enterprise, although initially fostered by government funding, has since become a viable and sustainable private enterprise without government assistance for ten years (Papunya Tula Artists, 2006).

Breakthrough market: International elite markets, such as Sotheby's auctions, are an example of breakthrough markets. Product from the developing world finds itself occasionally celebrated as unique and valued. The market for Indigenous art represents a breakthrough into this narrow but lucrative market. It is to this remarkable aspect of Indigenous art history that we now turn.

The international uptake of 'dot' painting

The beginnings
Until about 40 years ago, several Indigenous Australian tribal groups lived in Australia's Western Desert without any involvement in the 'cash economy'. Like many other Aboriginal clans across Australia at the time, the Aranda, Anmatjira Aranda, Warlpiri, Loritja and Pintupi were brought in from their tribal lands by the government during the 1950s and 1960s and settled on a government reserve at Papunya, northwest of Alice Springs. It was here, as one commentator has noted, in 'oppressive, desolate and poverty-stricken conditions… with one sixth of residents dying of treatable disease between 1961–1966' (Allan, 2001) that the Papunya Tula Art movement emerged during the 1970s, giving birth to contemporary acrylic 'dot' painting (see Bardon (1991) for a moving account of this 'birth'). A school teacher posted at Papunya, Geoffrey Bardon was an important figure in these early developments. Before his arrival, Western Desert art was largely confined to Aboriginal ceremonial practices and some small-scale tourist sales (Allan, 2001). In 1971, Bardon submitted several acrylic works to the Alice Springs Caltex Art competition. The competition resulted in AU$1,300 in cash sales and ultimately introduced the Papunya artists to the cash economy and commercial production practices. Bardon encouraged an artist's cooperative at Papunya and in 1972 he helped form the Papunya Tula Artists limited liability company. From this initial success, over 600 paintings and 300 smaller works were produced over the next 18 months (Allan, 2001).

Policy and market development
From 1973–5, Papunya Tula art production increased. The cash market, however, was still small-scale and largely informal. Arts advisors visited painting communities periodically to pay artists for completed paintings and to commission new works. There were small-scale exhibitions and modest sales to museums and art galleries in the Northern Territory but the survival of the Papunya Tula art collective was largely the result of government action.

The principal backers throughout the 1970s were two government bodies: the Aboriginal Arts Board and

Aboriginal Arts and Crafts Pty Ltd. The former was a board of the Australia Council for the Arts – the national arts funding body – and the latter was a federally sponsored retail/wholesale company with an important role to play in marketing and retailing Indigenous art (see Altman (2005) for a historical account of the institutions involved in marketing Indigenous arts). These two bodies had initial success in developing a market for Aboriginal art, but, according to Myers (2002: 134), 'there was a tremendous problem in maintaining a viable stream of circulation between artists' desire to paint and scarce demand'.

A major policy problem that emerged as production increased was the inadequate purchasing procedure of Aboriginal Arts and Crafts. The company was developed to stabilize an income flow, foster production, increase employment and increase economic returns for artists. The company purchased paintings from artists, and acted as a wholesaler selling artworks to metropolitan retail outlets. The company paid for artwork upfront, with the respective artist receiving payment immediately, not on consignment as was the procedure of most commercial galleries. The company, however, failed to match sales – because of limited demand – with production rates, resulting in stock over-accumulation, and the exhaustion of the company's funds – with funds invested in stockpiles not being sold. Consequently, no new paintings could be purchased, leading to prolonged delays between sales, new purchases and thus cash flow back into art collectives. Without start-up capital, arts advisors – important intermediaries between artists and the market – were unable to buy collections for potential exhibitions. Artists regarded the halt in sales 'as a sign of disrespect' and 'failure on the part of the advisor' (Myers, 2002: 138).

In response, Aboriginal Arts and Crafts developed a 60-day system, where artworks would be held for 60 days, allowing time for items to be sold before a payment was made to the artist. However, this system also failed with artists wanting immediate payment in exchange for their work. Soon artists and advisors began selling artwork to sources outside of the company. Private collectors were later to become important buyers. Grants from the Aboriginal Arts Board largely kept the Papunya Tula cooperative operational during the 1970s with its funds purchasing stockpiled paintings for museums and international 'cultural preservation' exhibitions (Myers, 2002: 143). In addition, the policies of the Arts Board led to the establishment of arts and crafts centers throughout the Northern Territory during the 1970s and 1980s, which has been described as 'absolutely vital to the Indigenous arts infrastructure and industry and a positive focal point for the community' (Myers, 2002: 198).

The early stages of this market can be categorized as a *grants market* focused on *domestic demand*. Papunya Tula and other art collectives competed for and became reliant upon limited funds from Aboriginal Arts and Crafts and the Aboriginal Arts Board. Myers comments that public support for the development of a market during this period can be characterized as a 'welfare' approach (2002: 135). Change occurred because, in the words of Altman et al. (2002: 2), recognition that Indigenous arts and crafts policy 'might provide a means to combine cultural maintenance and economic activity for both Indigenous and National benefit' was linked to increases in Indigenous visual art production and 'in part growth in domestic and inbound tourism and a demand for "authentic" indigenous cultural product'.

During the early 1980s, government policy shifted from a focus on cultural preservation to an emphasis on the development of an Aboriginal 'arts and crafts' industry – a broad term encompassing all visual arts, souvenirs, crafts and performing arts. With this policy shift a more structured 'art world' emerged, generating increased journalistic attention, a growth in institutional recognition and acquisition and an expansion of retail galleries, collecting and curatorship. This policy rearticulation with a focus on 'economic enterprise' marked a concerted shift away from public subsidy. In the 1990s, the former Aboriginal and Torres Strait Islander Commission launched the National Arts and Crafts Industry Support Strategy which effectively wound down government-supported wholesaling and retailing operations and invested in fostering 'more substantial and consistent support of… community-based art centers' (Altman et al., 2002: 2). There are now over 106 art and craft centers in operation across Australia. It was during the late 1980s period of policy restructuring and industry development that the international success and development of international markets for Aboriginal 'high art' began to materialize, largely outside of public funding mechanisms.

The 1988 Dreamings exhibition in New York
The 1988 Asia Society exhibition, *Dreamings: The Art of Aboriginal Australia,* held in New York from October to December, was instrumental in the achievement of international critical acclaim and recognition, and the initiation of a commercial export

market. The exhibition drew an attendance of 27,000 people, becoming the most successful event ever to be held at the Asia Society. It elevated Aboriginal art from being 'ethnographic art' to internationally renowned 'high art' sought after by elite up-scale galleries and collectors. The exhibition was important for a number of reasons. It exemplified how a *specific targeted audience* can be reached. The organizers of this exhibition carefully selected the venue. At the time, the Asia Society galleries were important in the mediation of culture and commerce relations between the US and Asia; the art was displayed in ways that corresponded to 'high art' styles, in renowned galleries rather than in museums as it had been in the past (Myers, 2002). The financing of this event was indicative of the move towards new private partnerships and illustrated the use of informal social networks and institutions. The organizers sought to raise private and corporate finance through the Asia Society's numerous networks and connections. Exploitation of the Asia Society's organizational structure was critical as it possessed an extensive business network, trustees and other ancillary connections including 'hired consultants who could make connections to corporations' (Myers, 2002: 243). Indeed, the organization's structure provided triangulation between the US, Asia and Australia, bringing together three spectrums of interest and potential financial support. The strategy was directed at mobilizing informal social connections and elite networks and through the utilization of the Asia Society's private consultants.

Finance eventuated from a range of relatively unexpected sources. The exhibition witnessed the beginnings of US financial interest in Aboriginal art, with funding coming from the National Endowment for the Humanities and the New York-based non-profit funding organizations, the Andrew Mellon and Starr Foundation[s]. Other corporate/private financial support came from the Westpac Banking Corporation and associates of the Asia Society galleries network.

The New York market, private collectors and philanthropy

While there are now a large number of public funding and grant schemes available for Aboriginal artists and arts enterprises through the Australia Council for the Arts, international enthusiasm and most notably the New York market are significant forces driving demand, production and the development of the *high-end* of Indigenous Australian visual arts. In July 2003, Sotheby's in New York sold 560 Aboriginal art works at a total of AU\$A7.5 million (Cho, 2004). Sotheby's percentage of international Indigenous Australian art sales has risen from 20 per cent in 1996 to 70 per cent in 2003 (Reid, 2003). International markets for Indigenous Australian art are now characterized by a growing number of very serious collectors and a large number of occasional buyers (Reid, 2003). New York art galleries are important purchasers of Indigenous Australian art. Since the *Dreamings* exhibition in 1988, the number of up-market galleries specializing in Indigenous Australian art has increased significantly. As well, general galleries now have substantial sections dedicated to Indigenous Australian art. There are now direct linkages between up-scale galleries and 'talented artists' and cooperatives. Galleries foster and encourage artists to produce works either specifically for their galleries or to be auctioned at Sotheby's, New York.[2]

Private collectors and philanthropists have become significant purchasers, and in some cases, sources of finance for the production of Indigenous Australian art. An outstanding example is the private collection of Florida billionaire John W. Kluge. Kluge has amassed one of the largest collections of Indigenous Australian art outside of Australia containing 1,600 works from between the 1940s and 1990s. Kluge reportedly 'fell in love with Australian Aboriginal art' after seeing the *Dreamings* exhibition in New York in 1988 (Genocchio, 2004: 11). He bought his first selection of Indigenous Australian art in 1988 – a total of 130 paintings for US\$500,000. The money from this sale was reported to be used by the 'impoverished reservation style community of some 700 people' to build an arts center to contribute to the development of the region's art communities (Genocchio, 2004: 11). He also commissioned many pieces from individual artists and art collectives providing them with sources of income and investment. In the 1990s, arts agents hired by Mr. Kluge invested in several Aboriginal arts communities in Northern and Western Australia.

Conclusion

This case study exemplifies that a high-growth, high value, export-oriented sector can emerge from severely economically marginal communities. It illustrates key aspects of the dynamics of a globalizing cultural economy. Individual agents can successfully adapt 'traditional elite' cultural forms (without sacrificing cultural uniqueness or integrity) to appeal to the tastes of a specific *targeted* international audience and market. The mobilization and utilization of informal social networks can be a successful method of establishing an international network with linkages to important financial sources. The leverage of institutional networks with formal or informal international networks can be an important means of obtaining finance and establishing financial streams. Finally, philanthropic, foundational and private investment can be important financial sources for the production and distribution of art considered quite marginal. This, of course, is not to the exclusion of public sector contribution: witness the provision of a permanent showcase for some of Australia's most respected Indigenous painters in the iconic *Musée du quai Branly* in Paris which opened in 2006.

The development of Indigenous Australian visual art markets from remote 'outback' beginnings is a truly remarkable achievement considering the obstacles. However, these successes at the same time demonstrate the fragile nature of the Indigenous cultural economy as well as the intrinsic value of visual art to the Indigenous people. It has alerted Indigenous people to the monetary value of their culture and encouraged the use of their culture as a resource. Contemporary Indigenous creative ventures are increasingly characterized by entrepreneurial flair, innovative business models and investment drawn from private partnerships and collaborative ventures.

They might also be making Australia interesting – again.

Notes

1 Australian Museum Online (2004) 'What is Cultural Heritage?', Australian museum: http://www.dreamtime.net.au/indigenous/culture.cfm [accessed: 20/03/2007].

2 'Struck by the beauty of Aboriginal art', *Doncaster Templestowe News,* 3 December 2003.

REFERENCES

Allan, Susan (2001) *Papunya Tula: The birthplace of contemporary Australian Aboriginal Art.* World Socialist Web Site, published by International Committee of the Fourth International.

Altman, J.C. (2003) *Developing an Indigenous Arts Strategy for the Northern Territory: Issues paper for consultations,* Working Paper no. 22, Canberra: Centre for Aboriginal Economic Policy Research.

Altman, J.C. (2005) 'Brokering Aboriginal art: A critical perspective on marketing, institutions, and the state', *Kenneth Myer lecture in arts and entertainment management.* Melbourne: Deakin University, Center for Leisure Management Research, 7 April.

Altman, J.C., Hunter, B.H., Ward, S. and Wright, F. (2002) *Some competition and consumer issues in the indigenous visual arts industry,* no. 235, Discussion Paper, Centre for Aboriginal Economic Policy Research.

Australia Council for the Arts (2006) *Submission to the Senate Inquiry into the Indigenous Visual Arts and Craft Sector,* November, Senate Environment, Communications, Information Technology and the Arts Committee Inquiry into Australia's Indigenous visual arts and craft sector.

Australian Trade Commission (2006) *Visual arts to the USA,* February, Canberra: Australian Trade Commission.

Bardon, Geoffrey (1991) *Papunya Tula: Art of the Western Desert.* Melbourne: McPhee Gribble.

Cho, Ines (2004) 'Aboriginal Art: A Modern Primitivism', *Joins.com,* Dow Jones & Reuters, 29 January.

Colmar Brunton Social Research (2004) *Demand for nature-based and Indigenous tourism product.* Canberra: Department of Industry, Tourism and Resources.

Creative Economy 2006, *Submission for the inquiry into Australia's indigenous visual art and craft sector,* November, Senate Environment, Communications, Information Technology and the Arts Committee Inquiry into Australia's Indigenous visual arts and craft sector.

Genocchio, Benjamin (2004) 'An Artist's Bounty from the Australian Wilderness', *The New York Times*, 7 March, p. 11.

Keane, Michael and Hartley, John (2001) *From Ceremony to CD Rom: Indigenous Creative Industries in Brisbane*. Brisbane: CIRAC.

Megaw, J.V.S. and Megaw, M. Ruth (2001) 'Visual arts', in James Jupp (ed.) *The Australian People: An Encyclopaedia of the Nation, Its People and Their Origins*. Cambridge: Cambridge University Press. pp. 97–101.

Miller, Toby (1994) 'When Australia became modern', *Continuum: The Australian Journal of Media & Culture*, 8(2): 206–14.

Miller, Toby (1995) 'Exporting truth from Aboriginal Australia: portions of our past become present again, where only the melancholy light of origin shines', *Media Information Australia*, 76: 7–17.

Myers, Fred, R. (2002) *Painting Culture: The Making of an Aboriginal High Art*. Durham: Duke University Press.

Myer, R. (chairman) (2002) *Report of the Contemporary Visual Arts and Crafts Inquiry*, Canberra: Department of Communications, Information Technology and the Arts.

Papunya Tula Artists (2006) *Inquiry into the Indigenous Visual Arts sector*, Senate Environment, submission to the Communications, Information Technology and the Arts Committee Inquiry into Australia's Indigenous visual arts and craft sector.

Reid, Michael (2003) 'Aboriginal artworks set the standard', *The Australian*, 13 August.

Smith, Terry (2007) 'Creating value between cultures: Contemporary Australian Aboriginal Art', in Michael Hutter and David Throsby (eds.) (2007) *Beyond Price: Value in Culture, Economics and the Arts*, New York: Cambridge University Press.

## CHAPTER 26

NEW YORK'S CHELSEA DISTRICT: A 'GLOBAL' AND LOCAL PERSPECTIVE ON CONTEMPORARY ART
David Halle and Elisabeth Tiso

This chapter explores the dynamics of the Chelsea art gallery district on Manhattan's Far West Side, which is probably the most important location worldwide for sales of new works of Contemporary Art. The central finding is the major (though not total) irreducibility between, on the one hand, the economic markets in which the art is traded, and on the other, the content of the art and its meaning for the audience as they view it displayed in the galleries. Although the market is crucial in all kinds of ways, neither content nor meaning can be reduced to economics, or usefully analysed primarily in

economic terms. This is not to argue for the 'autonomy of aesthetics', but that the aesthetic domain here is in many ways shaped by, and responds to, a different set of dynamics than the market domain. Both spheres are important for understanding Contemporary Art and modern society; to study one but not the other gives a misleadingly one-sided view.

Chelsea's art gallery district on Manhattan's Far West Side is now probably the most important location worldwide for sales of new works of Contemporary Art (defined here as works produced by artists who are still alive or recently deceased). For example, at Art Basel 2007, the world's leading annual fair for Contemporary Art, there will be 31 galleries from Chelsea. The next largest gallery contingent, way behind, is Berlin with 22, followed by London with 18. Understanding Chelsea is clearly important for the goal of mapping key cultural enterprises across the world.

Chelsea's rise occurred with stunning speed. From 1996 to 2007 (July), the number of Chelsea galleries grew from 12 to at least 260 (almost all commercial rather than non-profit), dwarfing other art districts in the United States and elsewhere. Galleries in SoHo, once New York City's most dynamic gallery neighborhood, fell to about 44 and many former SoHo galleries have re-located to Chelsea (see Figure 26.1).

In this chapter we adopt a dual strategy. We first view Chelsea in the context of the international Contemporary Art market, looking in particular at art fairs and auctions. We then discuss detailed material from Chelsea. This strategy, placing the 'global' in a local context, solves a general dilemma facing research on cultural enterprises. On the one hand it is important to understand the international context, yet to do only this is typically insufficient. In this case of the cultural economy of Contemporary Art, for example, it overlooks a close examination of how a local art market actually functions and especially it overlooks an analysis of the art itself – its content and meaning for the audience. One consequence, especially if discussion focuses on markets and

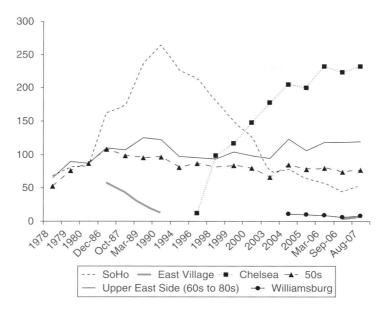

Figure 26.1   Art gallery areas, Manhattan and Brooklyn, 1987–2007

'globalism', is to imply that the art too is primarily about markets and economics. Our Chelsea research suggests that this is often a serious exaggeration and even just wrong. On the contrary, for most of the Chelsea audience the art above all speaks to central themes in the audience's lives (e.g. the modern family, the landscape and environmental threats to it). Indeed, the irreducibility of these two key sectors – the markets (local and 'global') on the one hand and the art's content and meaning for the audience on the other hand – is our central substantive finding in this chapter.

It is important, at the outset, to clarify the concept of 'global'. It is not, for example, fruitful to classify everything with an international dimension as 'global'. Discussing this issue, Michael Mann (2007) has usefully distinguished six geographical/spatial interaction networks, five of which are less than 'global'. These are local (any sub-national network of interaction), national (networks bounded by states, though not necessarily organized by states), international (between national units), macro-regional (transnational but regionally bounded), transnational (transcending the boundaries of the national and potentially global) and global (the extension and intensification of social relations over the globe). In what follows, we will argue, when discussing international art fairs and auction houses and following Mann's typology, that these are actually 'macro-regional' in

character rather than global. We will also often place 'global' in quotes so as not to beg the question of whether what is being discussed is truly 'global'.

International art fairs

The growth of annual international art fairs is one key development underlying the perception that the art world is becoming increasingly international and 'global'. These fairs, composed primarily of commercial art galleries, in principle allow galleries from any country to sell their art abroad, at least for the few days the fair lasts, thereby promoting a gallery's stable of artists in a market/country outside its home base(s). Art fairs, therefore, constitute one suitable terrain for examining 'globalization' in the Contemporary Art market.

Art Basel (Switzerland) bills itself as 'the world's premier modern and contemporary art fair', and few in the art world would disagree. Competition among galleries for selection (by an admissions committee) at Art Basel is ferocious. Ranked behind Art Basel is a group of international fairs including New York's Armory show, Frieze in London, ARCO in Madrid, FIAC in Paris, and Art Basel Miami Beach. These fairs were all basically established in their current forms in the last decade, underlining the rapidity of this international market's growth.

Table 26.1 Number of galleries, by country, at key international art fairs

Country	Art Basel (Switzerland) 2007	Armory Show (NY) 2007	Frieze (London) 2006
United States	61 (25%)	51 (42%)	36 (24%)
Germany	46 (19%)	16 (13%)	26 (17%)
Switzerland	32 (13%)	3 (2%)	7 (5%)
England	20 (8%)	21 (17%)	29 (19%)
France	16 (7%)	–	6 (4%)
Italy	14 (6%)	5 (4%)	8 (5%)
Spain	7	1	3
Austria	6	3	7
Holland	5	2	4
Belgium	4	2	1
Japan	4	5	3
Brazil	3	–	–
Sweden	–	3	–
Scotland	–	1	3
Denmark	–	–	3
Canada, Greece, Mexico, South Korea, Poland, Sweden	2	2 Korea	2 Greece, Brazil
**China, Finland, Ireland, Israel , Norway, Portugal, Russia, Scotland, Slovenia, South Africa, Turkey*	1	1 Turkey, Mexico, India, Israel, South Africa, Ireland, Greece, Romania	1 Sweden, Ireland, Slovenia, Russia, Portugal, Israel, Egypt, China, South Korea
Total	**241**	**123**	**149**

Source: Art 38 Basel (2007), Frieze Art Fair (2007), Armory Show (2007). Although some galleries have locations in more than one country, the art fair websites typically list only one country per gallery, presumably the country the gallery considers its main base.

* This row means that at Art Basel there were two galleries each from Canada, Greece, Mexico, etc, and so on for the other venues.

** This row means there was one gallery from each of the countries named at the respective venues.

Analysis of the geographic origins – by nation, city and neighbourhood – of the galleries selected for Art Basel in June 2007 is illuminating. Considering first national origins, there is a clear concentration of galleries from a handful of countries located in two regions, the United States and Western Europe, which together account for 90 per cent of the 242 galleries selected. Twenty-five per cent of the galleries are from the United States, clearly the most numerous contingent. German galleries are in second place, with 19 per cent, followed by galleries from Switzerland (13 per cent), England (8 per cent), France (7 per cent) and Italy (6 per cent) (see Table 26.1). Although Art Basel's claim to showcase galleries from all five continents is formally correct, representation from Africa is tiny (one gallery from South Africa), small from Latin America

(just two galleries from Mexico and three from Brazil), and modest from Asia despite the burgeoning economies of China and India (four galleries from Japan, two from South Korea, one from China, none from India). Analysis of galleries at The Armory Show and Frieze confirms this picture.

Turning from national to city data, New York City clearly tops the hierarchy. It accounted for 21 per cent of all the galleries accepted at Art Basel 2007, over twice as many as Berlin, the second largest city represented with 9 per cent of all the galleries, followed by London (7 per cent), Zurich (6 per cent) and Paris (5 per cent) (see Table 26.2). Finally, analysis within New York City shows Chelsea's dominance over other gallery districts there. Galleries located in Chelsea account for 63 per cent of all New

Table 26.2   Art Basel 2007: number of galleries represented, per city

New York	51 (21%)
Berlin	22 (9%)
London	18 (7%)
Zurich	16 (6%)
Paris	16 (5%)
Cologne	12 (3%)
Basel	7
Milan	6
Madrid	6
Vienna	5
Los Angeles	4
Geneva	4
Brussels	4
Tokyo	4
Sao Paolo	3
Munich	3
Amsterdam	3
São Francisco	3
Antwerp, Athens, Chicago, Düsseldorf, Seoul, Stockholm, Turin, Verona	2
Barcelona, Bochum, Glarus, Dortmund, Dresden, Dublin, Frankfurt am Main, Glasgow, Hamburg, Helsinki, Istanbul, Johannesburg, Karlsruhe, Krakow, Lausanne, Lisbon, Ljubljana, Lucerne, Lugano, Montreal, Moscow, Oslo, Oxley, Rome, Salzburg, San Gimignano, Santa Monica, St. Moritz, Shanghai, Tel-Aviv, Toronto, Venice, Warsaw	1
Total	**242**

Table 26.3   Art Basel 2007: United States galleries, by city and by New York City district

New York	51
Chelsea	32 (63%)
SoHo	2 (4%)
East 50s	7 (12%)
East 60s	2 (4%)
East 70s	5 (10%)
East 80s	3 (6%)
Los Angeles	4
San Francisco	3
Chicago	2
Santa Monica	1
Total	**61**

York galleries selected for Art Basel. Manhattan's East 50s neighborhood is a distant second, constituting 12 per cent of the New York galleries, followed by the East 70s (see Table 26.3).

To summarize, the world of art fairs basically involves circulation around a select group of fairs by a select number of art galleries, mostly from a few key cities in Western Europe and North America, with New York's Chelsea gallery neighborhood at the apex. In Mann's (2007) spatial typology, these relationships are 'macro-regional' not strictly 'global'. In a superb discussion Quemain (2006) has generalized this point, based on detailed empirical research, beyond art fairs and commercial art galleries. As he put it, despite enormously increased international mobility, '…the world of contemporary art has a center of gravity which revolves around a duopoly formed by the US on the one hand and a small number of Western European countries on the other hand… In contrast to this western center is an "artistic periphery" that consists of the remaining countries – not just third World but Japan, Canada, Spain, etc.'.

International auction houses

Auction houses, the art resale market, are a second key source of the perception that the art market is increasingly 'global'. Auction houses are represented above all by the power houses, Sotheby's and Christie's, each of which has sales operations in multiple locations around the world. We focus here on data from Christie's, the biggest house with overall 2006 sales of US$4.7 billion, in order to answer two questions. First, how important are particular cities/regions in the secondary market for art? Second, how does this vary for specific categories of art? As with art fairs, the results show concentration in a limited number of geographic areas, but with some significant differences. For example, Asia, represented by Hong Kong, is an important secondary market site and Asian Contemporary Art is a significant part of the burgeoning secondary market in Contemporary Art.

City/regional strengths
New York and London dominate the auction market for art, with 45 per cent and 30 per cent of all Christie's 2006 sales revenue respectively. Hong Kong is third, though far back with 8 per cent, followed by France with 5 per cent and a tiny new presence from Dubai (see Table 26.4).

The mostly European absence (except for London and Paris) from the auction market partly reflects a set of European cultural attitudes towards auctions that have a long history. Selling art by auction has never been socially completely accepted in most of Europe and is still often considered somewhat crass and 'too public' a commercial transaction. London is an exception, which, especially since Thatcher, is far more favorable disposed to commerce than most of Europe. In general, the contrast is stark between gallery sales – where the prices that a work has sold for are a carefully guarded

secret linked to the privacy of the buyer/collector – and auction sales. The spectacle that auctions provide is likely more attractive to the American, London-based and Asian collectors, who are often eager to show their wealth in a glamourous auction setting. Distaste for auctions is also tax related. Wealthy Europeans are often eager to avoid government attention and associated taxes – mostly higher than in the United States (or Britain).

Particular artistic genres
Regarding auction sales of particular categories of art, the most lucrative by far was Impressionist/modern with US$1.2 billion or 26 per cent of all sales (see table 26.4). 'Post-war and Contemporary Art' was Christie's second most lucrative area, bringing in US$822m or 18 per cent of all sales. ('Contemporary' and 'post-war' art are merged in the data, as are 'Impressionist' and 'modern'. Recall that, on the whole, 'Contemporary' refers to artists who are alive.) Old Masters lags far behind, with just 5 per cent (US$256m) in 2006.

Artistic genres by cities/regions
Combining the data on types of art and on specific cities/regions, New York is paramount in both largest categories, Impressionist/modern and post-war/ Contemporary, substantially outselling London, the second strongest site for these genres. New York sold 764m of Impressionist/modern, roughly three-and-a-half times London's 221m, and New York sold 565m of post-war/Contemporary art, roughly three times as much as London's 180m (see Table 26.4). London's strength vis-à-vis New York is Old Masters, where it sold 157m – roughly twice as much as New York.

Hong Kong's strength, unsurprisingly, is Asian art. Its 306m overall sales of Asian art were roughly five times more than second placed (for Asian art) London. Traditional Chinese art (e.g. jewellry, jade, ceramics, watches, classical paintings) is the largest component of Hong Kong's Asian sales by far (62 per cent). But 44m of Hong Kong sales are in Contemporary Asian Art (a category consisting of 'Asian Contemporary Art' and 'Modern and Contemporary South East Asian Art'), and a separate category, '20th Century Chinese Art', garnered 74m in sales. Together these categories, Contemporary, modern and 20th century, constituted 39 per cent of all Hong Kong sales, which probably reflects the existence of recently wealthy Asian entrepreneurs interested in new, not just traditional, Asian art. There is also now a lively market for Contemporary

Table 26.4 Worldwide annual in sales in US$ of art, by category, location and year, at Christie's auction house[a]

	2006		2005
Impressionist/modern	1.23 billion (18)*		680m
	New York	764m	
	London	221m	
	Paris	10m	
Post-war and Contemporary Art	822m (23)		560m
	New York	565m	
	London	180m	
	Hong Kong	62m	
	Paris	8m	
Asian art	438m		391m
	Hong Kong	306m	
	New York	66m	
	London	26m	
	Paris	5m	
Jewellry and watches	408m (12–38m H.K.)		283m
Old Master pictures	256m (18)		208m
	London	157m	
	New York	77m	
	Amsterdam	2m	
Other	1.51b		
Total	4.67 billion		3.43 billion
New York	2.1 billion (45%)		1.4 billion
London	1.4 billion (30%)		917m
Hong Kong	355m (8%)		286m
France	250m (5%)		141m
Dubai	8.5m (0.2%)		
Other	1.1 billion (25%)		

[a]Source: Christie's, 2007

*Data in parentheses indicate the number of auction sales that year. A day's sale that is broken into sessions such as morning and evening is counted as two sales.

Asian Art outside Asia (Hong Kong). For example, New York had an 18 million dollar sale of 'Modern and Contemporary Indian Art' in 2006, which reflects the interest of non-Asians in Contemporary Asian Art, just as non-Asians have long been interested in classical Asian art.

To summarize, the auction market and art fairs are more appropriately classified as 'macro-regional' (i.e., transnational but regionally bounded) than 'global'. Each involves a limited number of international sites, with New York leading both markets. An interesting difference is that, while the art fair world remains dominated by galleries from the United States and Western Europe, in the auction market, Asia, represented by Hong Kong, has a significant presence and Asian Contemporary Art is now important in the burgeoning auction market for Contemporary Art.

The local market

The analysis so far shows a world of Contemporary Art dominated by a limited number of players – elite art galleries, and auction houses – focused on a limited number of macro-regional sites. This is correct as an analysis of the international market, but needs to be set alongside the detailed Chelsea material which is not well captured by the idea that the world of Contemporary Art is dominated by elite organizations (galleries, fairs, auction houses) operating in macro-regional markets driven primarily by profit maximization on the part of the audience, producers and distributors. The world of Contemporary Art, when viewed at its most important local site – Chelsea – turns out to be too interesting and complex to be viewed exclusively through a single lens. Because of space limits, and because we have written about some of these Chelsea features elsewhere (Halle Tiso, 2006), the salient features of Chelsea are presented here briefly.

The multiplication and persistence of small galleries

Despite the presence of a sizeable contingent of elite, global galleries, Chelsea would not be the dense art gallery neighborhood that it is without the plethora of small, boutique size galleries, owned by individuals not corporations, that make up the majority of the gallery scene. For the purposes of obtaining an accurate numerical count, the elite galleries can be distinguished from the rest in several ways. These include a ground floor location, which is easily accessible to the public, rather than an upper floor; participation in at least one of the major annual fairs; and having a roster of artists at least one of whose work has an established secondary market, measured by having been resold at Sotheby's or Christie's. Using the first criterion, upper or ground floor location, roughly 60 per cent (210 galleries) of all the galleries in Chelsea are non-elite (having an upper floor location).

This co-existence in the same environment of elite and a plethora of small operations has some parallels to dominant centers in other creative industries such as Sillicon Valley. Thomas Crow (1996: 34) too has commented on the fact that so much of the gallery system exists at the 'artisanal level'. Our interviews in Chelsea also found that gallery owners, often motivated by 'art for art's sake', may be willing to settle for less profit than 'humdrum entrepreneurs', which also helps explain the existence of dense concentrations of small galleries.

The best free show in town

Unlike the established art museums in New York City, which charge admissions (entry to the recently re-opened MoMA is $20), Chelsea galleries impose no entry charge, do not pressure the onlookers to buy, and are open and welcoming. Further, data from our interviews with samples of the audience show that the vast majority (over 95 per cent) of the audience come just to look, with absolutely no intention of purchasing art. The major purchasers (serious collectors) typically attend private showings arranged specially for them and even buy works based on photos (e.g. viewed via the Internet). The rest of the audience are, therefore, viewers but arguably not 'consumers' if that term refers to people whose role is to purchase goods in the market. This absence of an admission charge runs counter to the strong tendency in the modern world towards the 'commercialization of leisure life', whereby a growing proportion of spare time consists of events for which admission is paid. A large commercial locus such as Chelsea offers, ironically, this huge, no-charge benefit for the public.

Further, in other cultural spheres when the 'show' is free, audiences typically pay another price, for example, long lines for admission or second-rate performers. What is interesting, and perhaps even unique about Chelsea, is that it is the elite galleries that make art by the very best of Contemporary artists available in the most easily accessible form. The audience simply step right off the street into these galleries, whereas visiting the majority of (lesser) galleries usually involves ascending to a non-ground level floor. This feature appears to distinguish Chelsea from other key 'cultural enterprises' such as Hollywood and Silicon Valley. Whether this set-up (the free show) is 'rational' for the galleries (e.g. arguing that the non-buying public attending the 'free show' create 'buzz' around the work and artist which in some ways validates the work and encourages the collectors to buy), or something that just emerged, is not yet clear.

Commercial galleries as opportunities for artists

Although nearly every Chelsea gallery is commercial, almost all the artists, whether successful or struggling, say that the Chelsea galleries generally offer them far more freedom and opportunity than do not-for-profit museums and other institutions, in New York or elsewhere. The artists mostly consider that museum directors and curators tend to be more conservative and focused on established art and less open to new art and artists than the typical gallery owner/director. Above all, the artists that we interviewed do not, on the whole, see the gallery system as a structure of dominance or oppression.

An occupational community of 'gallerists'

Chelsea is not a residential community of artists. From its start as a gallery district in the mid-1990s few artists could afford to live there, and they certainly cannot now. (SoHo was, by contrast, an occupational and residential community of artists who produced art from their lofts/homes.) Yet Chelsea has developed into an occupational community of people who work in/run/own galleries, and a special term 'gallerists' has emerged to describe this phenomenon. Indeed, Chelsea's gallerists are not well described as an impersonal set of atomistic units locked in ferocious competition, one stereotype of market relations. Rather, they arguably have many of the positive aspects associated with the idea of 'community'.

The local commercial real estate market: will Chelsea go the way of SoHo?

The local features described so far could not be deduced from a model that stressed a 'global' market of oligopolistic players, although they are not incompatible with that model. Still, some features of Chelsea do fit more closely to such a model. Above all, every Chelsea gallery must deal with Manhattan's ferocious realestate market. Indeed, Chelsea's very rise was real-estate-driven. Rents soared in SoHo from 1995–9, fuelled by an influx of clothing boutiques and forcing a mass exodus to Chelsea of galleries that could not afford the new rents.

Not surprisingly, a much debated topic among Chelsea gallery owners and other observers is whether real estate developments will eventually cause a similar, SoHo-style, debacle. Learning from that, most of those galleries that came to Chelsea with sufficient capital bought their spaces so as to insulate themselves from the commercial rental market. The other galleries, the vast majority, signed leases and are at the mercy of the commercial real estate market, which in Manhattan has no controls. At the end of the typical five-year lease, plus a five-year option to extend, landlords can charge whatever they can get.

Emerging gallery–auction house conflict

Chelsea too is a site to study an emerging challenge by auction houses to the long prevailing division of labour in the art market between art galleries and auction houses. Recently auction houses have begun to move into the galleries' lucrative market for primary works. The brashest, and most successful, such challenger is located in Chelsea. Phillips de Pury, an auction house founded in London in 1796, in 2003 moved its headquarters to Chelsea in a spectacular space just north of the Meatpacking district on 15th Street. What is innovative is that in 2006 Phillips began what it called 'Selling Exhibitions' where it displayed and sold brand new works that had never been on the market before. To stress its new, dual role as both gallery and auction house, Phillips repackaged itself as an 'art company that does auctions' (of Contemporary Art, photography, design and jewellry), not just an auction company.

This intrusion into the gallery world by Phillips de Pury was followed by Christie's February, 2007 purchase of Haunch of Venison, a contemporary art gallery in London and Zürich, with plans announced to open a gallery in New York, in the Rockefeller Center in the Fall of that year. This move was less drastic than Phillips's, since Christie's was not (yet) itself selling new works, and auction houses have owned galleries in the past, though never a successful one. Still, given Christie's size, the move has raised enormous attention, and often anxiety, in the gallery world, alongside Phillips's explicit abandoning of the traditional division of labour.

These intrusions by auction houses merit close study. For example, will the auction houses drive the gallery world towards the kind of concentrations long present in other creative industries such as publishing and movie production and of which the auction world, long dominated by the Sotheby's/Christie's duopoly, is an extreme form?

The content of the art displayed in Chelsea

Content analysis of the art displayed in Chelsea galleries, combined with interviews with the audience about what the art means for them, also suggests a very different set of dynamics than those discussed in the analysis of the 'global' market for Contemporary Art. The art displayed in Chelsea is above all about major, ongoing issues in people's lives. Again, for

Table 26.5 Subject matter of the art shows in the 16 most important ('star') Chelsea galleries[1]

% of all shows(n=32)[2]	Major topics[3,4]
25%	Landscapes
	Classic landscapes (beautiful views) (13%)
	Environmentalist landscapes (landscape is threatened) (9%)
	Political (2%)
25%	Sex
	Sexual activity and/or focus on sex organs (13%)
	Nudes or semi-nudes (without sexual activity or focus on sex organs) (13%)
16%	Decrorative/abstract
16%	Troubled nuclear family
16%	Natural forms/man-made basic materials
	Minor topics
9%	Poor, those in troubles (Poor, addicts, etc)
6%	Mass production/commodites
6%	Political
3%	Religion

reasons of space the analysis is shortened. Five topics dominate the content of the art displayed in Chelsea, to the point of being arguably obsessions. Each of these topics constitutes at least 13 per cent of all the works in the sample (see Table 26.5). (Note that over 70 years ago Schapiro (1936), the distinguished art historian, argued that the entire corpus of 'Western' art could be reduced to five topics. Two of these overlap with those discussed here; the rest are new.)

Depictions of landscapes/nature constitute 25 per cent of all the topics sampled. These landscapes divide into two main kinds. There is the classic 'good stretch of countryside/water/sky' (13 per cent of all the topics). This vision featured prominently in Western landscape art over the last 200 years. It clearly remains immensely popular.

The second type of landscape, 9 per cent of all topics and almost as common among Chelsea landscapes as the first, is 'radical environmental'. These landscapes foreground concern, and often alarm, about the deterioration of the natural environment. This genre is in many ways new since the 1960s and clearly reflects a widespread alarm, and even social

panic, at the possible damage humans have done to their world.

Sex as a topic is just as popular as landscapes, constituting 25 per cent of all the topics of the art displayed. About half of these images depict sexual activity – most often intercourse between male and female. The other half of the images classified as 'sex' here just depict naked or semi-naked people, usually women. These are therefore akin to the classic nude of art history.

Like 'radical environmental art', sexual intercourse is unusual in Western art, at least for the last two millennia. Naked or semi-naked men and women pervade the history of Western art, but they have rarely been depicted as engaged in sexual activity. (There are some exceptions. Indian art, for example, has a well known tradition of eroticism, as did classical Greek pottery.)

A third topic is the nuclear family, but typically depicted with a critical or satirical edge as a troubled institution (16 per cent of all topics). Serenely confident families and individual family members, of the kind depicted by Norman Rockwell, are so rare as to be almost taboo. This topic – the problematic family – is also a new genre in art history. While troubled families have obviously existed in actuality throughout history, artists or patrons did not depict them in a sufficiently systematic way so as to make them a recognizable genre.

The fourth topic (16 per cent of all topics) is the decorative/mostly pure design. Grouped under the umbrella of 'abstract' art, this topic was seen by an 'avant garde' in the twentieth century as the apogee of art, superior in almost every way to other specific topics depicted in representative or figurative art. These claims are now widely seen as exaggerated (e.g. Kleiner and Mamiya, 2005). In Contemporary Art as displayed in Chelsea, the abstract/decorative has settled into a more modest, though still important, position as (just) one of five themes.

A fifth topic is raw/basic materials, either of nature (wood, stone etc.) or man-made (steel I beams, plastic structures), along with a related interest in the basic constituents of our world. This subject also clearly has affinities with the first topic of landscapes as well as with discoveries in modern science especially molecular biology.

The general picture obtained from considering these five topics does not fit the view that the art is primarily about trading and making money in a global market. On the contrary the topics are mostly rooted in modern life and in the varied ways that people (artists and audience) experience today's world. For example, environmental landscapes seem rooted in post-1960s alarm about the deteriorating natural environment. Sexual intercourse seems to mimic current interest in pornography, especially promoted by the web. The troubled nuclear family mimics today's high divorce rate as well as the growing prominence of same-sex relations. Interviews with samples of the audience for particular shows likewise suggest that these themes flourish because they resonate with the audience's lives in an ongoing, creative and interactive way.

It is true that for some of the tiny minority of the audience who intend to purchase, namely the 'collectors', the work may also be a financial investment. But even here a conflation of the market-oriented analysis, with an analysis of the art and its meaning, short-circuits the question of how certain works and artists come to be sufficiently attractive in the first place to constitute a promising investment. The central answer suggested here is that the works resonate with the lives of the audience.

Conclusions

Our conclusions are methodological, substantive and policy related. Substantively, a central finding is the major (though not total) irreducibility between two central spheres, on the one hand the economic markets (and related sectors) in which the art is traded, and on the other hand the content of the art itself, and its meaning for the audience as they view it displayed in the galleries. Although the market is crucial in all kinds of ways, the content of the art that is traded and its meaning for the audience cannot typically be reduced to economics, or usefully be analysed primarily in economic terms. This is not to argue for the 'autonomy of aesthetics' but it is to argue that the aesthetic domain in this case is in many ways shaped by, and responds to, a different set of dynamics than the market domain. Both spheres are important for an understanding of the world of Contemporary Art and modern society and to look at one but not the other gives a misleadingly one-sided view.

Our central methodological conclusion follows from this. We need to look at cultural phenomena both globally and locally and beware of partial analyses that omit salient data. It is hard to adequately research and understand the meaning (including aesthetic meaning) of cultural phenomena without some detailed local/case study research. Hence it seems unlikely that a single theory or perspective can properly capture the complexity of an important component of the cultural economy like Contemporary Art.

A related conclusion is the importance of being open, via empirical research, to the unexpected. For example, despite the existence of a contingent of elite galleries that are active in the ferocious global market, the vast majority of Chelsea galleries are small shops offering a series of opportunities to young artists that are far superior to their chances in the art museum world. Moreover, the elite galleries offer an unparalleled free show of the very best of Contemporary Art to an audience, few of whom intend to buy, and who are therefore viewers but not plausibly 'consumers'. Further, although Chelsea is far too expensive a neighborhood to support a residential community of artists, the dense network of galleries does support an occupational community of 'gallerists'.

Finally, two policy implications. First, Chelsea represents the triumph of the commercial gallery system as a way of nurturing and bringing to prominence artists and their works. Its most obvious contrast is the 'French model', the view that official, usually state-sponsored, competitions judged by impartial experts are the most appropriate way to select meritorious art and artists, whereas the market model sacrifices ('sells out') quality to commerce. Chelsea's success, and the continued relative decline of French art and artists, suggests that the market model has a lot to recommend it.

Needless to say, this topic is complex and needs further research.

A second policy implication results from the popularity of environmentalist art. In the real world, many 'local' environmental issues clearly cannot be solved only on the local level, and this geo-political reality now informs the aesthetic fabric of one crucial component of Contemporary Art, namely environmental art. Here, appropriately, the local and 'global' have also merged — a cause, in this case, for approval, not concern.

Box 26.1   The global art auction market boom

In 2006, the fine art auction market generated total revenue of US$6.2 million, a startling 52 per cent increase over 2005 revenue. According to artprice.com, the number of lots sold for over a million dollars during the year 2005 nearly doubled from 477, to 810 lots. This unprecedented growth was accompanied by marked shifts in consumer demand, both spatially and in terms of genre. In the past, almost all the large auction houses were located in London, Paris and New York. Now they are becoming increasingly present in Hong Kong, Tel Aviv, Dubai and Madrid. These shifts in consumer trends are being closely followed by the major art auction houses, in particular the two most powerful: Christie's and Sotheby's. Together, they hold only 9 per cent of all auctions worldwide, but command an impressive 76 per cent of global auction turnover (See Figures 26.2 and 26.3). Versatility in auction locations and featured genres have made their continued reign possible as the top two grossing art auction institutions possible.

The art market has been growing at about 17 per cent per year as compared to the overall art market at 8 per cent (Mann et al., 2006). The sale of works by living artists at auctions has increased dramatically in the past five years, from 7.9 per cent in 2000 to 17.6 per cent in 2005 (*Artprice,* 2005). This growth far outpaces sale of work from other periods and is an increasingly important trend to watch since the 'art boom' is unequally represented across genres and periods. Auction houses worldwide are being forced to cater to the growing demand of international buyers for contemporary pieces. Some respond more successfully than others. Christie's of New York, the leading auction house in terms of overall turnover, has set a new Contemporary Art sale record with De Kooning's *Untitled XXV* going for US$24.2 million. Christie's and Sotheby's combined have close to a monopoly on Contemporary Art auction sales of a million dollars and above (*Artprice,* 2006).

Chinese art is also experiencing off-the-chart growth and represents an emerging genre as well as new consumer markets. With the liberalization of the Chinese economy, local artists can access the global market much more easily. Private art auctions had been prohibited in China until the late 1990s. With a government that now prioritizes GDP growth, auction houses in and around the mainland have begun catering to a burgeoning market. Illustrating this trend, contemporary Chinese art has seen an overall jump in price of 400 per cent as compared to world prices that have increased 45 per cent. Christie's and Sotheby's were the first international auction houses to open locations in Hong Kong, followed by Bonhams just last year. In November 2006, Christie's continued to set new records with two sales in Hong Kong that grossed 31.5 million Euros, an amount never previously achieved by a Chinese auction. In the autumn of 2006, Christie's of Hong Kong went on to set the Asian market price record for a work of art with US$19.6 million paid for a rare porcelain 'swallows' bowl from the Qianlong period (Christie's, 21 March 2007). Christie's and Sotheby's have also leveraged their presence and connections in Asia to bring more contemporary Chinese art to buyers in Europe and the US, thus successfully catering to consumer genre and location preferences. Because of their ingenuity and versatility, they still top emerging markets for fine art and will continue to dominate the market (see Figure 26.3).

Meghan Corroon

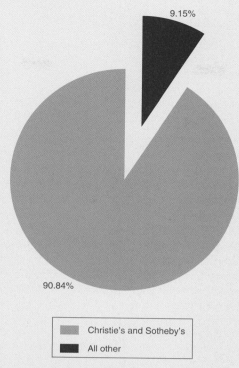

9.15%

90.84%

Christie's and Sotheby's

All other

Figure 26.2   Total fine arts auctions held by house
Source: *Artprice*, 2006

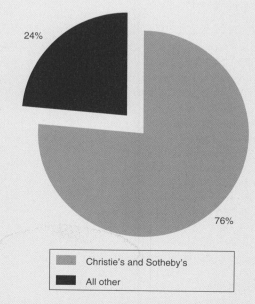

24%

76%

Christie's and Sotheby's

All other

Figure 26.3   Global fine art market auction turnover by house
Source: *Artprice*, 2006

(Continued)

Box 26.2   The Dashanzi Art District in Beijing

In the 1990s, a disapproving Chinese government pushed contemporary avant-garde artists out of Beijing and into the peripheries of the city. Many of these artists relocated to the area of Dashanzi in Chaoyang District – into abandoned warehouses that were once used to produce military grade electronics. The Dashanzi Art District today is now the center of Chinese Contemporary Art and is often compared to New York's Greenwich Village or SoHo. Yet, once again Chinese artists find themselves challenged by government politics, urbanization and grandiose plans for the 2008 Olympics.

Before the Arts District
The architecture of the Dashanzi District is itself unique and lends itself to the space created by resident artists. What is known today as Factory 798 is actually one structure in a complex of many factories constructed in the early 1950s through a joint venture between the Chinese government, East Germany and Russia. Once in operation, these factories were central to Mao's 'Great Leap Forward' campaign in the latter half of the 1950s when significant reforms to create a competitive and productive, yet classless, China were instituted (Tan, 2005). The factories followed in the functional Bauhaus tradition and were designed to foster a communal working environment. Factory workers lived, worked, were educated and trained in the complex of Dashanzi. In the spirit of the Cultural Revolution, the walls and spaces were filled with Maoist party propaganda – the red paint of Maoist slogans can still be seen on the gallery walls of Factory 798 today.

Where function meets form
The factories of the Dashanzi District were rendered obsolete in the late 1980s, having fallen victim to the reforms begun under Deng Xiaoping and waning financial support for large state-owned enterprises. During this same time, the Chinese government evicted artists considered too avant-garde from their enclave near the Old Summer Palace in Beijing. Seeking a new refuge, many of these artists relocated to the deserted factories in Dashanzi, where rent was affordable and the functionality of the complex proved fitting for a living and working art community.

In the time that they have been there, the factories of Dashanzi have flourished into what is commonly referred to as the Dashanzi Art District, where remnants of the Cultural Revolution and Maoist past seem to enhance the flavour of the art galleries and work spaces. Since its establishment, the Dashanzi Art District has attracted the attention of foreign artists, exhibitors, gallery owners and curators interested in the yet undiscovered contemporary artists of China, as well as an opportunity to break into what has certainly become a booming art market (see Box 26.1 on the Global Arts Market). One of the earliest foreigners to set up shop was Mr. Tabata Yukihito from Japan's Tokyo Gallery, who renovated the space of Factory 798 and started the Beijing Tokyo Art Project (BTAP). Starting in 2003, Factory 798 became host to many large and international events, including the first Beijing Biennale and the Dashanzi International Arts Festival.

The growing attention of the Dashanzi Art District has not only attracted visitors, but restaurants, cafes, nightclubs, retail shops, publishing companies, and more. This in turn has spurred the gentrification of what was once a dilapidated industrial area into an increasingly high rent market. In order to pay for raising rent prices, artists and galleries in Dashanzi have turned to commercial activities, such as holding gala events for L'Oreal Paris and Omega watches, and fashion shows for Nike and Christian Dior. No doubt, artists and gallery owners have also come to rely upon a steady stream of tourists, interested in viewing the latest works in Beijing's up and coming cultural arts center.

Threats and challenges
Living on the outskirts of Beijing, the artists of Dashanzi have been able to pursue their art with little fear of censorship. Yet the increasing international attention paid to them in recent years has caught

the eye of the Chinese government which, as recently as in 2006, suddenly banned art pieces or artists deemed too political from exhibiting their work in Dashanzi. Conversely, art work displaying overt nudity, sex, violence or religious themes have been unaffected.

The recent bout of censorship is one in a string of growing threats from a government preoccupied with its public and global image. Not only has it attempted to maintain a positive political image, but also that of an economically strong and modern China. Recent plans for the 2008 Olympics calling for the demolition and redevelopment of Dashanzi, which lies in a high traffic area between the Beijing International Airport and the city, were temporarily scrapped only because of a strong outcry from the international arts world in support of the area. The government has called off the demolition, at least until the conclusion of the Olympics, and hence has acknowledged that growing support for the district makes Dashanzi an important center for the arts in Beijing. Thus, in its continued existence, Dashanzi symbolizes resistance to governmental manipulation of space in order to control people, economics, industry and development, as well as resistance to the government's pursuit of an image of modernization in a global economy.

Tia Morita

Notes

1   The galleries include: Paula Cooper, Matthew Marks, Barbara Gladstone, Larry Gagosian, Metro Pictures, Robert Miller, Marlborough, Mary Boone, Andrea Rosen, Luhring Augustine, James Cohan, Pace Wildenstein, Cheim and Read, Galerie Lelong, Sonnabend, Marianne Boesky. A different group of experts would probably not pick an exactly similar list of 'star' galleries, but we believe there would be agreement on the vast majority in the list.
2   The research is still in progress, with n=32 so far. The plan is to sample each 'star' gallery three times, making a total of 48 shows.
3   Classifying the content of the art is not straightforward. For example, a depiction of a naked female could, in theory, be about at least one or several of the following – classic mythology, anatomy of the nude, eroticism or feminism. So, in classifying the works we supplemented this 'objective' look with a second perspective that considers the artist's intentions. We derived these intentions from the written materials that accompany most shows, since these typically have the artist's approval.
4   Several of the works/shows covered more than one topic. If the topic constituted a third or more of the show it was assigned 1 point. Thus some shows could count for up to 3 points. These 'multi-topic' works/shows therefore have more weight in the overall table than single topic works/shows. We did this because our aim is to understand which topics are most widespread in Contemporary Art, so if a show has three topics that should be recorded. This is why the percentages in Table 26.5 sum to over 100.

REFERENCES

Armory show (2007) www.re-title.com/exhibitions/Armory Show.asp

Artprice (2005) *2005 Art Market Trends/Tendances du marché de l'art.* Artprice: pp. 5, 7, 15.

Artprice (2006) *2006 Art Market Trends/Tendances du marché de l'art.* Artprice: pp. 4, 8.

Art 38 Basel (2007) www.artbasel.com/ca/bt/kh/

Chinese Ceramics & Works of Art. Christie's (n.d).

Available at http://www.christies.com/departments/ccw/overview.asp. (Retrieved 21/3/2007).

Christie's (2007) 'Christie's Annual Global Art Sales Total $4.67 billion, the Highest Results in Art Market History.' Press Release.11 Jan.

Crow, Thomas (1996) *Modern Art in the Common Culture.* New Haven and London: Yale University Press.

Frieze Art Fair (2007) www.friezeartfair.com/

Halle, David and Tiso, Elisabeth (2006) 'Lessons From Chelsea', *International Journal of Humanities, 3.*

Kleiner, Fred and Mamiya, Christin (2005) *Gardner's Art Through the Ages.* Belmont, CA: Wadsworth, 12th edition.

Mann, J., Lake, M., Foster, M. and Quest, R. (2006) 'Contemporary Art', CNN International. 18 Dec.

Mann, Michael (2007) 'Globalizations: an Introduction to the Spatial and Structural Networks of Globality'. Unpublished paper.

Quemain, Alain (2006) 'Globalization and Mixing in the Visual Arts', *International Sociology* (July) 21(4): 522–50.

Schapiro, Meyer (1936) 'The Social Bases of Art', *Proceedings of the First Artists Congress against War and Fascism.* New York. Cited in Crow (1996).

Tan, L. (2005) 'Revolutionary Spaces in Globalization: Beijing's Dashanzi Arts District'. Hybrid Entities. Intersections Conference Journal – Graduate Student Conference of Ryerson/York University. March. Online: www.yorku.ca/topia/docs/conference/Tan.pdf.

## CHAPTER 27

CULTURAL ECONOMY: RETROSPECT AND PROSPECT
Allen J. Scott

This final chapter will provide a broad overview of the logic and dynamics of the cultural economy. I begin by drawing attention to the ways in which economy and culture are increasingly convergent with one another in contemporary capitalism, and I examine what this means for cultural consumption and judgement generally. I proceed to an analysis of the cultural economy as such, paying special attention to its quantitative significance and to its technological and organizational foundations. This is followed by an extended commentary on the ways in which the cultural economy materializes in geographic terms in synergy-laden clusters located above all in large city-regions. If the cultural economy is highly localized in terms of basic production activities, it also participates to a major degree in processes of globalization, and this facet is examined with special reference to questions of cultural diversity. In the subsequent section a series of policy questions are subject to examination, and the relevance of the cultural economy to economic development policy is given special consideration. The conclusion draws attention back to the question of cultural consumption and judgement in the twenty-first century and to the importance of cultural politics as a means of revivifying the democratic energies of modern society.

Introduction

Some time toward the end of the 1970s and the beginning of the 1980s, a number of analysts began to note that a new kind of capitalism seemed to be emerging out of the system of Fordism that had dominated the economically advanced countries over much of the twentieth century, and that was now racked by seemingly permanent crisis. As this new version of capitalism developed, various attempts to understand its basic logic and dynamics were made by reference to formulae such as 'sunrise industries', or 'flexible specialization', or 'post-Fordism', or the 'knowledge economy', or 'cognitive capitalism', or just simply the 'new economy' (cf. Bagnasco, 1977; Esser et al., 1996; Markusen et al., 1986; Piore and Sabel, 1984; Rullani, 2000). As we now enter the twenty-first century, I suggest that perhaps the most effective shorthand way of characterizing this new state of play is by the designation *cognitive-cultural economy*, meaning an economic order that is intensely focused on mobilizing the knowledge, creativity, cultural attributes, sensibility and behavioural characteristics of the labour force, in combination with a technological infrastructure based on digital computation and communication (Scott, 2007). As such, the cognitive-cultural economy coincides with sectors like science-intensive manufacturing, business and financial services, fashion-oriented production, neo-artisanal industries, audio-visual media, publishing, and so on.

Within this overall cognitive-cultural economy, a particular set of sectoral groups that we might label collectively as the *cultural or creative economy* are of special interest in the present context. The cultural economy can be identified broadly as all those forms of economic activity producing outputs with significant aesthetic or semiotic content, or what Bourdieu (1971) has characterized as symbolic outputs.[1] Of course, in this sense, there has always been a degree of cultural production in capitalism. What is new is the scale and variety of this form of production, and, following Engel's Law, the increasingly voracious demands of consumers for cultural products as incomes rise and as discretionary spending becomes a higher and higher proportion of family budgets. One of the peculiarities of modern capitalism, then, is that the cultural economy continues to expand at a rapid pace as a function of the escalating demand for goods and services that provide entertainment and distraction, forms of personal ornamentation, modes of social display, sources of information and self-awareness, and so on, i.e. goods and services whose symbolic value to the consumer is high relative to their purely practical purposes. The same trend reflects what Baudrillard (1968) referred to in a prescient analysis as the ever-increasing incursion of sign-value into the sphere of productive activity. This type of incursion is all the more intense in contemporary capitalism, because many different kinds of firms seek increasingly to intensify the design content and styling of their outputs in the endless search for market share (see also Lawrence and Phillips, 2002). Accordingly, a further significant feature of the cultural economy is its focus on niche marketing, or in a more contrived vocabulary, Chamberlinian or monopolistic competition (Chamberlin, 1933), in which producers seek to imbue their outputs with distinctive qualitative attributes that can certainly always be imitated by competitors but never fully reproduced. The liberal deployment of branding, trade marks and intellectual property rights further reinforces this deepening Chamberlinian aspect of the modern economy. I should stress immediately that there can be no hard and fast line separating sectors that specialize in cultural products from those whose outputs are purely utilitarian. Rather, there is a more or less unbroken continuum of sectors ranging from, say, motion pictures or recorded music at the one extreme, through an intermediate series of sectors whose outputs are varying composites of the cultural and the utilitarian (such as office buildings, cars or kitchen utensils), to say, iron ore and wheat at the other extreme.

Economy and culture in question

One of the defining features of contemporary capitalism, then, is the conspicuous convergence that is occurring between the domain of the economic on the one hand and the domain of the cultural on the other. Vast segments of the output of the modern economy are inscribed with significant cultural content (in the senses given above), while culture itself is increasingly being supplied in the commodity form, i.e. as goods and services produced by private firms in conformity with price signals and profitability criteria. This state of affairs raises a fundamental question – as Throsby and Pratt indicate in the present volume, Chapters 1 and 2 – about possible collisions and inconsistencies between the cultural values and the economic values ascribable to the products of the cultural economy. Greffe (Chapter 13) alludes to a related question when he refers to the common preconception/prejudice to the effect that culture begins only where the market stops. How, we might ask, should we situate and evaluate these questions?

We may begin with the observation that from its very historical beginnings, capitalism, and the commercial values that go with it, have been widely perceived as being fundamentally antithetical to cultural interests, especially when these are identified in specifically artistic and aesthetic terms. This incompatibility never seemed more complete than in the nineteenth century, where the economic order was represented by regimented and often dehumanizing forms of industrialization, while the aesthetic ideals of the period were in large degree enmeshed in an otherworldly romanticism. Ruskin's *The Stones of Venice*, published in the middle of the century, functioned as a paean to the past of Gothic crafts and architecture, and as an indictment of the cultural degradation that he believed was becoming ever more apparent in industrial-urban Britain. Indeed, the very different social imperatives to which industrialization on the one hand and aesthetic practice on the other were subject at this time, not only set them in opposition to one another as a matter of principle, but also established physical barriers between them, as expressed above all in the divergent urban environments where these activities flourished. We might say, in a broad sense, that the lives of the proletariat and the factory owners who employed them were bound up with one set of urban conditions, whereas the lives of artists and their most enthusiastic audiences were bound up with another. Of course, the incompatibility between the two sides was never absolute, and in some cities, various sorts of coexistence, if not interdependence, were worked out, as in the case of Chicago at the turn of the century, with its industrial and commercial bustle combined with a remarkable proclivity to architectural innovation and literary experiment. In certain metropolitan centers, most notably the Paris of Balzac and Zola, the worlds of commerce and culture came directly into contact with one another at selected points of social and spatial intersection. Even so, places like the surging industrial cities of, say, northern England or the German Ruhr on the one hand, and the more traditional historical and cultural centers of Europe on the other, seemed to represent irremediably antithetical universes.

Over much of the twentieth century, this tension between culture and accumulation continued to leave its mark on urban life and form in the advanced capitalist societies. As mass production moved to center stage of economic development, urban centers continued to grow in the Mammon quest, while the pursuit of cultural production became, if anything, yet more ghettoized. The metropolitan areas of the American Manufacturing Belt in particular (Detroit, Cleveland, Pittsburgh, etc.) now became to many commentators the archetypes of the utilitarian, philistine city (Lees, 1985). Indeed, the mass production system carried the manufacturing and consumption of standardized commodities (as well as urban development), to new heights of functional intensity. To begin with, the system flourished on the basis of competitive cost-cutting, and hence (given its machinery-intensive structure), it was focused insistently on the search for internal economies of scale in production and the consequent routinization of manufacturing methods. In addition, much of the output of the system consisted of consumer goods such as cars, domestic appliances and processed foods, designed largely to absorb the wages of the burgeoning blue-collar workers who made up the majority of the urban populace. The system was thus endemically committed to the production of low-cost, undifferentiated and desemioticized outputs, leading to the charges of 'eternal sameness' that Frankfurt School critics were soon to level against its effects as it started to make incursions into popular culture (Adorno, 1991; Horkheimer and Adorno, 1972). The large industrial cities themselves were seen in many quarters as being given over to a syndrome of 'placelessness' that critics like Relph (1976) ascribed to the increasing domination of technical rationality in mass society.

To be sure, Walter Benjamin, writing in the mid-1930s, had already set forth a series of quite hopeful views about the potentially progressive nature of what he called 'mechanical reproduction' in the arts, and especially in the cinema (Benjamin, 1969). By the 1940s, however, the core Frankfurt School theorists were expressing grave concern about the direct application of mass production methods in cultural-products industries like film, recorded music, and popular magazines (see Pratt in Chapter 2 above). To people like Adorno and Horkheimer, these methods,

being driven by capitalistic interests, were aesthetically suspect from the beginning, and they averred that the content of the products to which these methods gave birth were not only devoid of meaningful cultural value but also patently manipulative and depoliticizing in practice. It is nowadays fashionable to criticize the Frankfurt School theorists for their alleged *mitteleuropäischen* elitism, though the charge is blunted, perhaps, when their work is recontextualized within the conjuncture from which they wrote, with its relatively standardized and watered-down forms of commercial popular culture. Where they did err was not so much in the imputation of qualities of meretriciousness and triviality to commodified culture (such qualities are all too evident, then as now) but in their failure to see the possibility that the products of capitalist enterprise might also be capable of accommodating other more positive qualities.

A further important possibility that the Frankfurt School theorists failed to recognize – and they were certainly not alone in this – was that the peculiar version of capitalism they encountered in mid-twentieth-century America might one day be succeeded by another, and that its capacity for cultural expression might be vastly intensified. They failed in particular to see that a quite different system of technology and industrial organization might eventually come to dominate late twentieth and early twenty-first century capitalism, and that out of it would flow streams of goods and services inflected with increasingly higher levels of design variegation and cultural meanings. An alternative form of capitalism has now actually been gathering steam since the early 1980s, bringing with it a strikingly new nexus of economic and cultural outcomes in the advanced capitalist societies. Simultaneously, a sharp intensification of the economic significance and symbolic content of commodified culture has rather clearly been occurring, as well as concomitant transformations in function and form of the places where this culture is produced.

To put the argument in its most dramatic form, art is always produced in the context of definite historical and social conditions that in themselves lie outside the sphere of art but that shape artistic aspirations and practices. Provisionally, then, there is no reason to assert *on principle* that capitalist firms working for a profit are congenitally unable to turn out goods and services with inherent aesthetic and semiotic value (or what Clive Bell (1924), in a rather different context, called 'significant form'), just as

Greek and Roman artisans or Florentine painters, sculptors, architects, goldsmiths, jewellers, etc., working in relation to the definite political and social obligations by which they were bound, could still produce masterworks of transhistorical value (Cowen, 1998). In fact, and even as mass production was moving into high gear, a modernist aesthetic was already trying to come seriously to terms with its driving logic. Thus, as represented perhaps most dramatically by the Bauhaus and the great modernist urban design proposals of architects like Le Corbusier or Oscar Niemeyer, various aesthetic programs were mounted in theory and implemented in actuality in an attempt to give artistic expression to the main thrust of mass-production society (Banham, 1960). With the advent of the new cognitive-cultural economy, this push in the direction of aestheticized outputs from the production system has become ever more pronounced.

The contemporary cultural economy

The cultural industries today produce an enormous range of different goods and services. In previous chapters of this volume, frequent reference has been made to sectors such as film and television-program production (Curtin), music (Choi, Keane, Reis and Davis), games (Miller), fashion industries (Ichikawa), handicraft and artisanal production (Aageson, Dhamija, Friel and Santagata, Ryan et al., Throsby). We might extend the list to include advertising, tourist facilities, architecture, graphic arts, gastronomic food products, and so on, virtually indefinitely. At the same time, events like festivals (Klaic) and sports gatherings, or facilities like museums, concert halls, and libraries – whether privately or publicly controlled – also constitute an important part of the contemporary cultural economy. Yet another manifestation of today's cultural economy is the deepening market for Western and non-Western art, and as Halle and Tiso point out in Chapter 26, the concomitant proliferation of galleries and auction houses serving affluent consumers.

Taken collectively, these sectors and activities constitute a major and generally rising share of output and employment in all advanced capitalist societies (Hall, 2000; Pratt, 1997; Scott, 1996). Given the imperfections of standard industrial classifications and the ambiguities entailed in drawing any strict line separating cultural from other forms of production, it is extraordinarily difficult to make precise quantitative assessments of the full extent of the new cultural economy in any given country. Published studies vary greatly in their definitions and range, but all of them suggest that the cultural economy is of major and increasing quantitative significance in both North America and Western Europe. In one recent study, it was found that in the United States, just over three million workers (2.4 per cent of the total labour force) were employed in 29 cultural-products sectors representing both manufacturing and service activities (Scott, 2000a). In Britain, according to Pratt (1997), a little under one million workers (4.5 per cent of the total labour force) are employed in cultural industries and their main input providers. Both of these sets of figures are almost certainly undercounts. At the same time, employment in cultural-products industries appears to be overwhelmingly located in large cities. Thus, Scott's analysis indicates that in the United States, just over 50 per cent of all workers in cultural-products industries are concentrated in metropolitan areas with populations of one million or more, and of this group of workers the majority is actually to be found in just two centers, namely, New York and Los Angeles. Pratt's data show that London accounts for 26.9 per cent of employment in British cultural-products industries. Power (2002), following Pratt's definitional lead, finds that most workers in the Swedish cultural economy (which accounts for 9 per cent of the country's total employment) are located in Stockholm. Garcia et al. (2003) estimate that 4.5 per cent of Spain's total GDP is generated by the cultural economy, with Madrid being by far the dominant geographic center.

If the cultural economy is especially well developed in the more advanced capitalist countries today, it is nonetheless making significant inroads into the economic profiles of countries in many other parts of the world as well. Thus, Keane, in Chapter 10 above, writes about the rising importance of film, television, games, music fashion and the visual arts in the economies of East Asia. Švob-Đokić et al., in Chapter 15, suggest that the music and film industries are contributing increasingly to economic development in Southeastern Europe. Even Central Asia, according to Le Duc in Chapter 12, is now beginning to produce significantly in sectors such as film, art and handicrafts. And, of course, Latin America and the Caribbean, as Reis and Davis indicate in Chapter 16, are important producers of cultural outputs (including Jamaican reggae and Brazilian, Mexican and Venezuelan television programs) across a wide spectrum. A phenomenon of special interest is described by Choi in Chapter 11 on the rise of the Korean Wave of pop culture (*Hallyu*) since the early 1990s and its rapidly growing levels of export to neighboring Asian countries. Despite these widespread instances of successful achievement in the domain of the cultural economy, we must nevertheless acknowledge that it is very unevenly developed around the globe, and that there is much contention in a number of countries about cultural invasions from outside. Thus, as Nyamnjoh shows in Chapter 8, the modern cultural economy remains at a low ebb over much of the African continent, and this problem is exacerbated by the fact that African markets are saturated with foreign imports that not only undermine local cultural production, but also confront consumers with cultural idioms and models that originate from far outside the region itself. Many of the same predicaments characterize the situation in Latin America today (Reis and Davis, Chapter 16).

In other words, while globalization has vastly extended the market reach and power of cultural producers in some countries, it is also associated with diverse developmental problems, both economic and cultural, in others. This state of affairs has been greatly heightened by the advent of the new digital technologies that make it possible to distribute certain kinds of cultural products, such as videos, musical recordings, written texts, and so on, far and wide at minimal cost (Goggin, Chapter 20). It is therefore unsurprising to note that policy-makers have been extremely active in many different countries in regard to these problems, and have been especially concerned both to encourage the growth of local cultural industries (including, as Aageson shows in Chapter 6, support for small entrepreneurs in poor countries), and to restrict foreign cultural imports in various ways. One consequence of this interventionism has been a rising temperature in the international forum in regard to trade in cultural products. Drache and Foese (Chapter 3) allude to a notable case involving Canada's dispute with the United States over magazine publication. Perhaps the most dramatic illustration of this kind of dispute is presented by the so-called 'cultural exception' rule that was negotiated (under the leadership of France and in direct opposition to the US position) at the time of the GATT/WTO meetings in 1994. The rule exempted audio-visual products from the free trade provisions that were otherwise supposed to be extended to all forms of international exchange under GATT/WTO rules. With the passage of time, the blunt cultural exception argument appears to be evolving into a more nuanced policy stance based on principles of cultural diversity. This position has recently been reinforced by UNESCO's *Convention on the Protection and Promotion of the Diversity of Cultural Expressions*, which was ratified in October 2005 and came into force in March 2007. In any case, unlike many other kinds of goods and services, cultural products are intimately bound up with matters of social identity, consciousness, and self-esteem (Throsby, Chapter 1). Conflicts over these matters as a consequence of cultural products flowing from one country to another are to be expected and need to be dealt with on their own terms. A rhetoric of pure market ideology inevitably misses the crucial point here. Even in the United States, governmental concern is frequently voiced over the portrayal of drugs, sex, violence and other controversial issues in the media, and it is scarcely surprising that other countries should also seek to monitor aspects of the cultural offerings within their own jurisdictions. It might be plausibly argued that direct US governmental engagement with the content of, say, motion pictures has been averted only because of the self-regulation of the industry, dating from the time of the promulgation of the Hays Code in 1930.

The ever more rapid circulation and ease of reproduction (or piracy) of cultural products in the context of globalization has engendered considerable rounds of policy ferment in regard to issues of copyright and intellectual property in general. The intensity of concern for these issues is, of course, as Sundara Rajan points out in Chapter 4, related to the fact that the assertion of intellectual property rights is a basic condition for the appropriation of economic returns to cultural production. In the international arena, the *Agreement on Trade Related Aspects of Intellectual Property Rights (TRIPs)*, promulgated in 1994, and administered by the WTO, regulates trade in intellectual property and provides enforcement procedures for ensuring that copyright, certificates of geographic origin, performers' rights, patents, trade marks, and so on are duly respected (Drache and Froese (Chapter 3), Sundara Rajan (Chapter 4)). The TRIPs arrangements have been strongly supported by large multinational corporations, for they have much to lose in the absence of any meaningful enforcement of intellectual property rights on the international front. By contrast with these attempts to privatize culture and knowledge, there are significant popular movements whose objective is to open up as large a public space as possible in these domains. In her chapter on free culture and the creative commons, Pinter describes a number of these movements and their advocacy of such protocols as Open Knowledge, Open Archives, Open Access, Open Source, and so on. A number of

Italian and French scholars have recently attempted to generalize some of the arguments in support of these tendencies by positing the existence of a creative commons emanating from the labour of a so-called 'cognitariat' (Moulier Boutang, 2007; Rullani, 2000; Vercellone, 2007). The commons represents a socially collective intelligence to which all contribute, and from which all in turn draw. A number of these scholars have then extracted from this notion the proposition that some sort of universal guaranteed income should substitute for the traditional wage relation. Given the power and reach of private interests in contemporary global capitalism, I would contend that not a great deal of confidence can be invested in the likelihood of this sort of advocacy being translated into observable practice. What we probably can expect, as the digital foundations of the modern cultural economy develop in both their intensive and extensive dimensions, is another and much less radical form of democratization in the guise of a continuing proliferation of small and micro-enterprises with the capacity to contest diverse markets through the enabling powers of new production and distribution technologies. This prospective eventuality is not likely to challenge the fundamental importance and power of large multinational corporations in the cultural economy, but it does imply that these entities will find themselves to ever-increasing degree embedded in a long-tailed distribution made up of myriad small-scale niche producers (Anderson, 2006).

Economy, culture, place

One of the most pervasive features of the cultural economy is its tendency to expression in geographic terms in the guise of unique agglomerations or clusters of producers. Various authors in this volume have already alluded to this phenomenon and the ways in which it underpins the social reproduction and competitive advantages of cultural producers (see Chapters 13, 17, 18 and 24). Even in the case of non-commercial artistic activities, the tendency for individuals to come together to form specialized clusters in geographic space is extremely common. We might exemplify this remark by reference to painting in Paris in the 1880s when impressionism was in full flower, or to the development of 'atonal' music in Vienna at the turn of the nineteenth century when Berg, Schönberg and Webern, were creating their revolutionary compositions, or to abstract expressionist painting in Manhattan in the 1950s when Kooning, Motherwell, Pollock, Rothko and others were at work (Lévy, 1999). In these and similar cases, numerous social infrastructures comprising interpersonal networks, professional services and contacts, suppliers of materials, commercial outlets, and so on, help to bring practitioners together in distinctive communities and to sustain their work (see Box 27.1).

Box 27.1   Excerpt from W. Somerset Maugham (1919) *The Moon and Sixpence*, New York: George H. Doran. pp. 21–2

In those days conversation was still cultivated as an art; ... and the epigram, not yet a mechanical appliance by which the dull may achieve a semblance of wit, gave sprightliness to the small talk of the urbane. It is sad that I can remember nothing of this scintillation. But I think the conversation never settled down so comfortably as when it turned to the details of the trade which was the other side of the art we practiced. When we had done discussing the merits of the latest book, it was natural to wonder how many copies had been sold, what advance the author received, and how much he was likely to make out of it. Then we would speak of this publisher and of that, comparing the generosity of one with the meanness of another; we would argue whether it was better to go to one who gave handsome royalties or to another who pushed a book for all it was worth. Some advertised badly and some well. Some were modern and some were old-fashioned. Then we would talk of agents and the offers they had obtained for us; of editors and the sort of contributions they welcomed, how much they paid a thousand, and whether they paid promptly or otherwise. ... It gave me an intimate sense of being a member of some mystic brotherhood.

In the contemporary cultural economy, this proclivity to clustering in identifiable places is especially marked. Irrespective of the locations of final markets, many cultural-products sectors are typified by complex relations on the supply side that induce them to congregate together locationally, often in great masses, and especially within large metropolitan areas. Familiar examples of this tendency are the motion-picture industry of Hollywood, the publishing and media complex of Manhattan, fashion houses in Paris and Milan, and the theater, music and dance companies of London. A full account of the spatial dynamics of these and other cultural-products industries would require considerable time and effort. Fortunately, there is already a large literature on the subject, (see, for example, Becattini, 1987; Scott, 2005; Scott and Leriche, 2005; Storper and Christopherson, 1987), and so only a few brief descriptive strokes are called for here, with special reference to the organization, employment structure and innovative capacities of these industries. Three main points now need to be made:

1. As Caves (2000), among many others, has observed, much of the cultural economy can be described as conforming to a contractual and transactional model of production. As a result, production in the cultural economy is typically carried out within shifting networks of specialized but complementary firms. Such networks can assume many different forms, ranging from heterarchic[2] webs of small establishments to more hierarchical structures in which the work of groups of establishments is coordinated by a dominating central unit, with every possible variation between these two extreme cases. By their nature, these networks are frequently most efficient when a significant proportion of the producers caught up within them are located in close mutual proximity to one another so that the myriad daily interactions out of which they are composed can proceed with relative dispatch. Moreover, the existence of many different kinds of specialized producers all located in close proximity to one another means that networks can be constituted and reconstituted over and over again in varying configurations depending on the nature of the projects and products at issue at any given time.

2. The same producers share collectively in local labour markets, each one of which may comprise tens or even hundreds of thousands of workers. This feature helps to accentuate spatial concentration because (within limits) there are major economic advantages to be obtained by the agglomeration of interrelated producers close to the center of a large local labour market. The economies of scale associated with job search and recruitment activities are among the more significant of these advantages. The unstable project-oriented nature of much work in the modern cultural economy helps to reinforce these advantages of agglomeration (Grabher, 2001a; 2001b). Furthermore, dense communities of specialized firms and workers invariably act as magnets for individuals from other areas, especially for capable and aspiring neophytes who recognize that personal and professional fulfillment in their chosen line of work can best be attained by migration to a center where that sort of work is well developed and highly valued (Menger, 1993; Montgomery and Robinson, 1993). Thus, visual artists are attracted in droves from all parts of the world to Paris and New York, ambitious scriptwriters and film actors to Hollywood, and aspiring country musicians into Nashville, Tennessee. In this manner, new talent is imported into particular agglomerations from outside, and local production capacities are continually refreshed.

3. The entire local system of production, employment and social life makes up a geographically structured field that under appropriate conditions acts as a fountainhead of learning and innovation effects. As extended formal and informal exchanges of information occur in any cluster (e.g. in situations where inter-firm collaboration is proceeding, or in project-oriented work teams) considerable learning and worker sensibilization are liable to go on – much of the time unself-consciously – about different aspects of product design, production technology, the general business environment, and so on. This information, in turn, is often incorporated into streams of innovations and marginal improvements in local productive practices. I have referred elsewhere to the structures within industrial agglomerations that encourage these sorts of learning and innovation effects as a 'creative field' or a structured set of interrelationships that stimulate and channel various kinds of creative energies (Scott, 2006b). At one level, this phenomenon coincides with the networks of firms and workers that make up any given agglomeration, and with the multiple interactions that go on between these different units of decision-making and behaviour. At another level, it is partly

constituted by the social overhead capital, such as local schools, universities, research establishments, design centers, and so on, that complement the innovative capacities of these networks. At yet another level it is an expression of the cultures, conventions and institutions that come into existence in any agglomerated structure of production and work and that help to establish and sustain design archetypes representing the cultural signatures of different places and different collectivities of workers.

These three points signify that selected sets of producers in the cultural economy frequently have the capacity to generate multidimensional flows of agglomeration economies (or localized increasing returns effects), inducing all participants therefore to cluster together, especially in large urban areas. Soja (2000) refers to these kinds of synergies by the term *synekism*. This is the increment above the simple sum of the parts that holds any given urban-industrial structure together as a geographic cluster. With steady improvement in technologies of long-distance transportation and distribution, producers in any given cluster can sell their outputs on increasingly distant markets. By this means, the cluster is able to grow in size, and, by the same token, to become more deeply differentiated internally. In this manner, agglomeration economies are yet further intensified. It is true, of course, that in the absence of corrective action, agglomeration *dis*economies will tend to put limits on the growth and competitiveness of any single center, though urban policy-makers are continually at work to remove the obstacles that in this manner periodically threaten efficient operation.

The marked progress of the cultural economy of capitalism over the last couple of decades is evident not only in the proliferation and expansion of many different centers of production around the globe, but also in significant revitalization of the landscapes of cities where it is most highly developed. This revitalization is both an indirect outcome of the expansion of cultural production (via rising incomes, for example) and a further manifestation of its operation in urban areas as it ramifies through the city in the guise of shopping malls, restaurants and cafes, clubs, theaters, galleries, boutiques, and so on (Zukin, 1995). Architectural and design trades play an important part in this connection, not only because they are flourishing components of cultural production systems themselves, but also because the very urban landscape is one of their main outputs. Often, too, the same transformations involve ambitious public efforts of urban rehabilitation in the attempt to enhance local prestige, increase property values, and attract new investments and jobs (Kearns and Philo, 1993). When the landscape develops in this manner, significant portions of the city (though rarely, if ever, all portions) start to function as an ecology of commodified symbolic production and consumption (cf. Urry 1995), in which, and in contrast to the classical industrial metropolis, the functions of leisure and work seem to be converging to some sort of (historically specific) social equilibrium. Even advertising becomes part of the general spectacle that is one of the important ingredients of this ecology.

In any ecology like this, moreover, there will tend to be powerful and recursively intertwined relations between the meanings that adhere to the urban landscape and the symbologies of the goods and services produced in the local area. Thus, on the one hand, the symbolic forms (films, television programs, recorded music, fashion clothing, and so on) produced for different markets invariably draw to some extent on local images, cultural associations, social traditions, and so on. Indeed, this very process is important in authenticating and differentiating these symbolic forms in the minds of the consumer (Molotch, 1996). On the other hand, the meanings lodged in the same forms create images of their places of origin, and the same images are often re-assimilated in different ways back into the urban landscape of the producing center. Where this relation is especially strongly developed – Hollywood is an outstanding example – the ever-growing fund of symbolic assets that comes to be incarnated in the local environment then functions as a source of inputs to new rounds of cultural production and commercialization, leading in turn to further symbolic enrichment of the urban landscape, and so on. Thus, in terms of both space and dynamics, the role of the city as a creative field fostering innovation and learning effects is greatly magnified.

Local/global dimensions of the cultural economy

The cultural geography of the pre-capitalist landscape can be roughly represented in schematic terms as a patchwork of many different ways of life and forms of symbolic expression. Throughout the history of capitalism there has been a tendency for the erosion of significant parts of this more traditional cultural pattern to occur. However, and notwithstanding the fragility of many traditional cultures, especially as globalization proceeds, (see Nyamnjoh in Chapter 8) they evidently arm those who are socialized into them with a remarkable degree of resilience to the messages and meanings embodied in commodified symbolic forms imported from outside. Individuals in these cultures are sometimes capable of quite imaginative feats of re-interpretation of these forms (Appadurai, 1996). Yet if such acts of re-interpretation do unquestionably occur with much frequency, they are also probably in some retreat as a significant force of resistance before the rising tide of commodified cultural products that is now sweeping through world markets. The central questions that we need to pose in this context are these: Does the steady opening up of world markets to the latter products imply a deepening uniformization and massification of patterns of cultural consumption across the globe? Alternatively, is it conceivable that many different and dissimilar centers of cultural production might thrive in the future, thus providing a more varied palette of offerings (even though 'non-traditional' and commodified) that can be selectively consumed by diverse groups of individuals? And a subsidiary question is, can these offerings, even in the presence of variety, be the instruments of anything but mendacious aesthetic and semiotic experiences?

A plausible argument can be made to the effect that there *are* processes at work in today's world whose terminal point (should it ever be reached) is one dominant center for any given product, cultural or otherwise. The argument here plays on the self-reinforcing effects of agglomeration economies and increasing returns effects in large production centers especially in contexts where competing smaller centers fail to mount viable strategic responses, whether by inaction or miscalculation (e.g. by inadequate or inappropriate differentiation of products). The appearance of one dominant center is all the more predictable in theory where distribution costs to the rest of the world are low, so that in combination with the center's concentrated efficiency and learning effects, local producers can very powerfully contest markets across the globe. The worldwide impact in the immediate post-war decades of popular cultural products fabricated in New York and Los Angeles can probably at least in part be accounted for in terms like these. At the same time, American cultural-products industries benefited enormously, as they still do, from the presence of multinational corporations which aggressively pioneered the modern distribution and marketing of commercialized culture on global markets. Network television in the 1950s and 1960s, with its messages tailored to the lowest common denominator, was a classic early case of this phenomenon (Castells, 1996). Similarly, American cinematic products today represent a special threat in many different parts of the world given their seemingly invincible competitive force based as it is in the potent agglomeration economies and collective power of Hollywood and the unmatched distributive capacities of the US entertainment and media conglomerates.

This reasoning is limited, however, for the very reason that it eliminates the effects of alternative competitive strategies, and especially product differentiation, on the part of producers in non-dominant centers. To be sure, when individual agglomerations come into head-on competition with one another, some will stagnate and decline as their outputs become locked out of markets by centers and countries with superior levels of efficiency and marketing power and with outputs that have high consumer appeal. As suggested earlier, however, others will find it possible to evade the worst effects of this competition by focusing on specialized market niches, and this will notably be the case for cultural-products agglomerations that already enjoy some local monopoly of substance, style or expressiveness. Not all attempts at product differentiation will succeed, but since – over time and space – there are likely to be many different experiments in this regard, at least a few of them may be expected to prosper, especially where they are also associated with successful efforts to organize wider distribution and marketing networks. Thus, in the case of the international high-fashion industry, which was traditionally dominated by the *grands couturiers* of Paris, important complementary centers now also thrive in New York, London, Milan, Tokyo and elsewhere, on the basis of their talented designers and constantly evolving styles, and even centers in parts of the world periphery are now gearing up for attacks on world fashion markets. In the US recorded music industry, Nashville has attained a subsidiary but extremely durable standing (after New York and Los Angeles) by reason of its highly specialized output (Scott, 1999).

With this more extended argument in sight, a developmental scenario that looks toward an increasing rather than a decreasing number and variety of cultural-products agglomerations across the globe has much to commend it. As it happens, the new transportation and communications technologies now available will undoubtedly increase the likelihood of this scenario emerging into reality. These technologies tend to reduce, if not eliminate, economies of scale in distribution systems, thus making it possible for specialized producers in small centers to contest scattered markets around the globe. A clear presentiment of this scenario can be found in the recorded music business where new internet technologies are making it possible for hitherto quite marginal groups of producers (such as the immigrant Vietnamese musicians of Orange County in California) to tap into geographically extended audiences. The Internet also eliminates several layers of intermediary organization between producers and consumers, thus enlarging the discretionary power of the latter, and increasing their ability to command a greater choice of products.

Given the enduring if not augmented significance of agglomeration economies in cultural production systems, it follows that continued reductions of distribution costs are not so much liable to lead to generalized deterritorialization as they are to encourage the rise of a wide variety of relatively small clusters interspersed among a more limited number of larger clusters. In other words, reductions in distribution costs can be expected to enhance economic returns at big centers and to help them maintain their lead, but also to lower the threshold of entry for smaller centers which can survive (i.e. contest markets) where they successfully implement competitive strategies – such as the pursuit of product differentiation and design excellence – to compensate for their relatively weak territorial foundations. Their survival can be further assured where policy-makers at production locales are able to work out effective systems for the provision of coordination and steering services directed to the amplification of agglomeration economies and the correction of time-dependent negative lock-in effects.

Besides the clusters of locally owned firms that generally make up the greater part of productive agglomerations, multinational corporations also play a critical role in the cultural economy. These corporations actually represent an ever greater force in the production and distribution of cultural products. Many such corporations (above all American media and entertainment giants) have acquired considerable control over certain global product markets. At the same time, major multinational corporations with stakes in the cultural economy (some of the largest, for example, being Sony Corp., Disney Co., Daewoo Corp., Time Warner Inc., Bertelsmann AG., L'Oréal SA., Seagram Co., Havas SA., Christian Dior SA., and others) tend nowadays to display a surprising variety of national origins. In addition, they are in numerous cases engaged in active diversification, especially by acquisition of affiliated production units in cultural-products agglomerations all over the world. In parallel with this diversification, large corporations with significant symbolic output have shown a proclivity to engage in micro-marketing of their products, as evidenced in sectors as varied as musical recording and brewing (Negus, 1998). There are countervailing signs, then, to suggest that despite an earlier (Fordist) corporate trend entailing standardization of outputs, diversification nowadays represents a generally more viable productive strategy, and this, in many instances, is probably working to reinforce the incipient geographic differentiation of the global cultural economy described above. Even in the case of cinematic products, the stranglehold of the American media corporations remains by no means unassailable, and it is increasingly coming under attack both from inside and outside the United States as independents and film-makers in places as far afield as Australia, Britain, China, Hong Kong, India and elsewhere seek to cultivate alternative market niches.

A number of broad generalizations can be drawn from this discussion. There was indeed a moment corresponding to the period of internationalization, or what we might call proto-globalization, in the immediate post-war decades, in which American cultural products tended (though never exclusively) to take a lead on world markets and we are by no means yet fully beyond this particular state of affairs. More recently, cultural-products agglomerations in many different parts of the world have been responding to intensified competition but also to increasing market opportunities by means of specialization and product differentiation strategies, if not always successfully. New transportation and communications technologies will probably encourage a further proliferation of specialized production locales, many of which will be able to survive despite their limited size and limited agglomeration economies because they can effectively supply very specific and highly diffuse market niches; and new styles of corporate organization and behaviour appear on the whole to be conducive to increasing diversification rather than standardization of outputs. Accordingly, if at one stage in the recent past there seemed to be much evidence, both empirical and theoretical, in favor of the view that cultural production and consumption throughout the world was becoming more uniform, more massified, and more Americanized, there are now indications to suggest that contrary trends are occurring, and that the further intensification of globalization processes may well be associated with a markedly more polycentric system of cultural production than has been the case in the recent past. The old cultural imperialism argument seems to be losing at least some of its force (Chapter 18), and a new cultural activism, partly aided by the rise of the Internet, is making its appearance in many erstwhile peripheral centers (Chapter 3). Notwithstanding the many cultural clashes that continue to break out as globalization runs its course, we seem to be moving steadily into a world that is becoming more and more cosmopolitan and eclectic in its modes of cultural consumption. Certainly for consumers in the more economically advanced parts of the world, the standard American staples are now but one element of an ever-widening palette of cultural offerings comprising Latin American *telenovelas*, Japanese comic books, Hong Kong kung fu movies, West African music, Korean pop culture, London fashions, Balinese tourist resorts, Australian and Chilean wines, Mexican cuisine and untold other exotic fare. This trend is in significant degree both an outcome of and a contributing factor to the recent, if still incipient, advent of an extensive global system of cultural-products agglomerations. In view of these comments, globalization does not appear to be leading to overall cultural uniformity so much as it is to a polycentric pattern of production on the supply side and increasing variety of options on the demand side.

Cultural economy and economic development policy

The emergence of the cultural economy raises many policy problems in regard to piracy, trade, cultural identity, and so on, and as Isar shows in Chapter 7, a number of international institutions have emerged over the last few decades for the purpose of regulating some of the most difficult of these problems on the global front. Several of the chapters in this volume point as well to the importance of the cultural economy as an instrument of economic development (e.g. Aageson, Pratt, Friel and Santagata, Greffe, Klaic, Ryan et al.), and policy-makers have recently shown a very special interest in the potentialities of the cultural economy in this regard. In view of my earlier remarks about agglomerative tendencies in the cultural economy, this interest has understandably revolved in important ways around the urban and regional dimensions of the issue and on the potentials of cultural production for local economic development. A number of major policy statements on this theme have recently been published by governmental agencies in Britain (British Department of Culture, Media and Sport, 2001), Hong Kong (Hong Kong Central Policy Unit, 2003), Paris (IAURIF, 2006), and Germany (STADTart, 2000), to mention only a few. The growing concern among urban policy-makers for fostering 'creative cities' (Florida, 2004; Landry, 2000; Scott, 2006a) has also greatly contributed to this focus on the local. Moreover, as Wyszomirski points out in Chapter 17, cultural policy as such is frequently (above all in the United States) formulated and implemented in very localized contexts. Thus, in the current conjuncture, there would seem to be increasing possibilities at the municipal or metropolitan levels for devising synergistic economic and cultural development programs.

There are many additional reasons, of course, for presuming that cultural-products industries are, or ought to be, of compelling interest to policy-makers concerned with local economic development. As we have seen, these industries are growing rapidly; they tend (though not always) to be environmentally friendly; and they frequently (though again not always) employ high-skill, high-wage, creative workers. Equally, cultural-products industries generate positive externalities in so far as they contribute to the quality of life in the places where they congregate and enhance the image and prestige of the local area. But they cannot be conjured into existence by simple acts of political will or fiscal prodigality. Just as local governmental authorities all over the United States threw huge sums of money out of the window in the 1980s and 1990s in the quest to build 'the next Silicon Valley', so can we predict parallel miscarriages of policy in years to come as efforts to build various new Hollywoods or the next Silicon Valley materialize.

Careful and theoretically informed assessments of available opportunities and inherent constraints are essential if such miscarriages are to be avoided. Developmental agendas focused on cultural-economy sectors at large need to be especially clear about the character of the dense agglomerations that are one of the primary expressions of these sectors' spatial logic. For any given agglomeration, the essential first task that policy-makers face is to map out the collective order of the local economy along with the multiple sources of the increasing-returns effects that invariably crisscross through it. It is this collective order, more than anything else, that presents possibilities for meaningful and effective policy intervention. Blunt, top-down approaches focused on directive planning are unlikely, in and of themselves, to accomplish much at the local scale, except in special circumstances. In terms of cost–benefit ratios and general workability, the most successful types of policies will, as a general rule, be those that focus on the character of system-wide external economies of scale and scope as public or quasi-public goods. The point here is both to stimulate the formation of useful agglomeration effects that would otherwise be under-supplied or dissipated in the local economy, and to ensure that existing external economies are not subject to serious misallocation. Finely tuned bottom-up measures are essential in situations like this.

The earlier discussion of the underlying dynamics of economic and cultural agglomerations provides important clues about possible domains of intervention where policy can have a positive impact. Thus, policy-makers need to pay special attention to promoting (a) high trust inter-firm relations in order to mobilize local assets to the fullest possible extent, (b) efficient, high skill local labour markets, and (c) local industrial creativity and innovation, especially where market failure mechanisms are present. The means by which these objectives might be achieved are many and various depending on circumstances, but basic institution-building in order to promote collaborative behaviour between different groups of local actors is likely to be of major prominence. Complementary lines of attack involve approaches such as the initiation of labour-training programs (cf. Le Duc Chapter 12), setting up centers for the encouragement of technological upgrading or design excellence, organizing exhibitions and export drives, and so on, as well as socio-juridical interventions like dealing with threats to the reputation of local product quality due to free rider problems (especially in tourist resorts), or helping to defend communal intellectual property. Friel and Santagata in Chapter 24 write

about the importance of collective trademarking for protecting the competitive advantages of regional production systems. In practice, and notwithstanding these broad illustrative guidelines, there can be no standardized or boilerplate approach to the problem of local economic development. Each case needs to be treated on its own merits, paying full attention to the unique historical and geographical conditions that are found at each individual place. This admonition is doubly emphatic in the case of the cultural economy, marked as it is by enormous heterogeneity of production activities and sensitivity to subtle place-specific forces. A simple but sound precept guiding any plan of action in regard to regional economic development based on cultural-products industries is to start off with what already exists, and to build future expectations around whatever latent opportunities this initial position may make available.

I suggested above that the most highly developed and dynamic cultural-products agglomerations today occur for the most part in large metropolitan areas, though not all metropolitan areas are necessarily important centers of cultural production. The great global city-regions of the advanced capitalist countries represent in practice the high-water marks of the modern cultural economy. This proposition refers not only to the many and diverse individual sectors of cultural production that are usually located in these cities, but also to their wider environmental characteristics and global connections. Some sections of great city-regions today display a remarkable systemic unity running from the physical urban tissue, through the cultural production system as such, to the texture of local social life. These features, indeed, are mutually constitutive elements of much of the contemporary urbanization process. One small but telling illustration of this point is the recent transformation of the central garment manufacturing area in Los Angeles from a dispiriting collection of decaying factory buildings into a 'fashion district' that is now a locus of upscale production and showroom activities; and these core commercial functions are complemented by a surrounding street scene with a variegated bazaar-like atmosphere that attracts crowds of tourists. Central Paris with its monumental architectural set pieces, its intimate forms of street life, and its traditional luxury and fashion-oriented industries represents a similar symbiotic convergence of built form, economy, and culture, but on a far grander scale (Scott, 2000b). In cases like these, the role of policy is not so much to stimulate development *ab initio* but to intervene at critical junctures in the production system and the urban milieu in order to release critical collective benefits leading to superior levels of product appeal, innovativeness and competitiveness.

Cities or regions that lack any pre-existing base of cultural production face a more refractory policy problem. Yet even where no obvious prior resources are available, it has occasionally been feasible to initiate pathways of development based on cultural-products industries. Much new development in various old manufacturing areas has focused on building a cultural economy by means of a conscious effort to use the relics of the industrial past as core elements of a reprogramed landscape of production and consumption. The specific cases of Manchester and Sheffield in Britain may be usefully invoked here. In the former city, an area of recycled factories and warehouses on the fringe of the central business district has come to function as a magnet for diverse cultural and economic activities. This Northern Quarter, as it is called, is now a main focus of Manchester's new cultural economy, with its lively club scene, a music industry, and a nascent group of website designers. A very similar urban enclave, known as the Cultural Industries Quarter, has emerged in Sheffield. The Quarter is anchored by the Red Tape Recording Studios established by the local municipality in 1986; and a burgeoning array of clubs, restaurants, theaters, educational institutions and other cultural activities has developed around this point of origin. Neither of these experiments can be said as yet to be much more than provisionally and partially successful, though there is every likelihood that they will continue to evolve further along their current trajectory, especially if they can develop more fully as nuclei of dynamic, conjoint networks of producers. Local authorities right across Europe and North America are striving to revalorize inner city areas on the basis of experiments like these, often in concert with local real estate interests.

Finally, policy-makers have to keep a clear eye on the fact that any industrial agglomeration is dependent not only on the proper functioning of its complex internal relationships, but also on its ability to reach out to consumers in the wider world. Successful agglomerations, in short, must always be possessed of adequate systems for marketing and distributing their outputs. This matter is of special importance in regard to cultural products because they are subject above all to symbolic rather than utilitarian criteria of consumer evaluation, and in many cases are dependent on peculiar kinds of infrastructures and organizations for their transmission. In a situation of intensifying global competition, effective distribution is critical to survival and indispensable for growth. It might be contended, for example, that the poor commercial performance of French films in export markets is not so much due to linguistic barriers – and certainly not to a lack of talent – as it is to the competitive deficiencies of French film marketing and distribution systems outside of France. I have argued elsewhere (Scott, 2000c) that partial redress of these deficiencies might be secured through a shift in policy by the *Center National de la Cinématographie* (the central government-industry body responsible for oversight of the French cinema) toward lower levels of subsidized production and higher levels of subsidized distribution. A clear recognition of the general importance of distribution is expressed in the European Union's Media Plus Program initiated in January 2001 in succession to the earlier Media I and Media II programs. A principal objective of the Program is to build up international distribution systems for European audio-visual products.

Box 27.2 *Mastiha*: from indigenous commodity to post-industrial luxury

Mastiha is a commodity indigenous to the Eastern Aegean island of Chios. Belonging to the botanical family *Pistacia Lentiscus*, the *mastiha* tree thrives and produces its aromatic resin only in an area comprising 24 villages in the southern part of the island. As a 'Product of Regional Origin', *mastiha* has specific attributes and quality characteristics, which are intrinsically embedded in its place of origin. Chios is known because of its *mastiha* but, more importantly, the product has acquired its generic designation by its geographical location. Its producers have been organized since 1938 into a Union of Cooperatives, which has ever since developed into a powerful marketing and distribution organization,

(Continued)

(Continued)

being the only supplier of *mastiha* to foreign markets and to private firms. In recent decades, the Union has intensified its marketing role and has turned to retailing with the establishment of a chain of stores.

Mastiha's status on the global market has changed from a relatively inexpensive indigenous commodity in the past, to a much discussed and high-priced consumer item today. Spanning countries and continents, the commodity regime in which it is embedded is becoming increasingly more global geographically, especially as the natural resource itself is experiencing shifts in its identity. Since the 1980s, while continuing to traverse its old trade paths, *mastiha* has moved into a wholly different economic niche, penetrating into a quasi 'ethnic' cuisine, being included in a wide array of edible and cosmetic products, and entering the market as a self-help medicine. What sets it apart from other commodities is the growth of a domestic (national) market in the face of a history of export promotion. It is within this market – which operates with its own expansive dynamic and shapes the terms of interface with the extra-national one – that *mastiha*'s transformation into a post-industrial commodity has occurred.

One innovation behind its global expansion relates to its consumption as both a named ingredient in a wide range of eatable products and as a substance incorporated into hygienic and luxury, cosmetic items. Yet, despite this expanding trajectory in the realm of circulation and consumption, *mastiha*'s manufacturing and refinement continue to be restricted largely to Chios. Firms that sell and formulate *mastiha*-based products stress their connections to Chios, as the only source of the natural product; this is part of the allure of the commodities they market. In addition, they project a system of knowledge, which is informed on the one hand by a 'local' and historically derived real and imagined discourse and, on the other, endorses or is adapted to modern sensibilities and concerns about purity. These firms direct their commodities to consumers who are global in their own geography and self-awareness, whose outlook is attuned to lifestyles of a middle class, whose consumption is part of a project of status marking, and is cognizant to some degree of the existence of a global market niche oriented to notions of purity and the preservation of natural quality. *Mastiha*'s increasing popularity within the food and cosmetics industry is thus located in a broader set of trends where mass goods are becoming restricted and the mass market crowded with a large variety of products that mark class and status-specific aspirations and identities.

Vasiliki Galani-Moutafi

Conclusion

The many different sectors of the cultural economy that have risen to prominence especially since the early 1980s have unleashed dramatic new rounds of development and expansion in world capitalism. On the demand side, there has been a massive enlargement of the pool of individuals practising the sort of variegated and discretionary expenditure that in classical consumer society had largely been confined to a small minority able to afford luxury goods. Concomitantly, consumption patterns, at least in the advanced capitalist societies, have tended to progress beyond blunt consumerism, in the sense of obsessive preoccupation with quantitative acquisition and self-identification with 'middle class' norms of possession (in terms of a package of housing,

cars, domestic appliances and all the rest) into a series of highly differentiated niches and lifestyle types. This trend has encouraged, in turn, a corresponding intensification and diversification of the symbolic content of final goods and services. Even the symbols of contestatory groups like feminists, gays or ethnic minorities, tend in one way or another to become eventually incorporated into this economic logic.

Contemporary culture theorists have invested considerable energy in attempts to understand the social meaning of the symbolic forms now produced in such profusion by capitalist enterprise. However, few social scientists today appear ready to carry forward the torch of the earlier Frankfurt School theorists with their scathing condemnations of commodified culture.[3] Many would even argue that if the symbolic forms produced by capitalist enterprise today are often in practice devalued and degraded, commodification does not always or necessarily result in the degeneration of cultural expression; indeed, these forms are on occasions at the cutting edge of new artistic movements, and they have been closely associated with various post-modern aesthetic claims (Wollen, 1993). This is not the place to pass judgement on contemporary canons of taste. From a purely sociological point of view, we may in some sense cut through the Gordian knot of this puzzle with the observation that capitalism can be regarded as just another historical site of cultural production, though of course it does not produce just any culture. Nowadays, capitalist firms deliver an extraordinarily varied fare of cultural products and experiences in the effort to meet the growing and ever-mutating volume of demand. Nor are consumers invariably no more than passive vessels at the receiving end of this process. If, as noted, many different kinds of contestatory groups are eventually brought into the demand structure of the new cultural economy of capitalism, there is also much active conflict over the meanings and images contained in the rising flow of goods and services on offer, leading in turn to cultural collisions that are directly related to, though rarely in fundamental opposition to, the commodification of culture. We probably ought not, as Jameson (1998) has argued, to expect anything much in the way of negation of the logic of commodity production by virtue of these trends, but neither should we necessarily expect that it will lead to anything resembling the bleak predictions of an earlier and more pessimistic generation of culture theorists.

Geography, of course, is fundamental to all of these developments. In the first place, as I have argued, there are definite locational transformations at work in contemporary capitalism, involving the growth and spread of cultural-products agglomerations across the globe. In the second place, the expanding worldwide network of cultural-products agglomerations will almost certainly be accompanied by increasing differentiation of outputs as individual centers struggle to mobilize whatever place-specific competitive advantages they may initially possess, and as they build up reputations for particular kinds of product designs and forms of semiotic expression. In the third place, if we can envisage the distinct possibility that some producers and/or agglomerations will be able to establish monopoly powers in certain global market segments, there is also a compensating tendency to geographic diversification of productive efforts and socio-spatial fragmentation of demand. As we enter the twenty-first century, globalization appears less and less to be resulting in a pattern of mass cultural uniformity. To the contrary, we seem to be entering an era where cultural production is becoming increasingly polycentric and polysemic. The most evident expression of this state of affairs is the steady emergence of a worldwide mosaic of cultural production centers tied together in complex relations of competition and collaboration, and where the ultimate viability of each individual center depends closely on its ability to carve out a distinctive market niche for itself. Still, as Reis and Davis point out in Chapter 16, while globalization may not be leading in the direction of overall cultural homogenization, many inequities remain, and these will no doubt continue to generate heated political debate and contestation. At the same time, the increasing commodification of the culture that we consume continues to be the source of many burning questions in the wider context of debates about the meaning and value of culture generally. A purely market driven system of cultural supply can never secure transcendence of these predicaments. By the same token, an energetic but still, in important respects, prospective cultural politics (in the sense of self-conscious contestation of the symbolic content of economic outputs) is one of the conditions of enhanced democratic order in the modern world.

Notes

1 The sense in which I am applying the term 'cultural economy' therefore differs rather sharply from the sense in which it is used by certain culture theorists who use it to denote the ways in which cultural variables and attributes inflect the economic system at large including its organizational and strategic arrangements (cf. Amin and Thrift, 2007).

2 A heterarchic system is one that is configured as a network or fishnet.

3 A noteworthy exception to this remark is Bourdieu, who (notwithstanding his conscientious demystification of the bourgeois cult of art) expresses in his work a deep aversion to the incursion of commercial rationality into the sphere of cultural production. See for example, Bourdieu (1979; 1999).

REFERENCES

Adorno, T.W. (1991) *The Culture Industry: Selected Essays on Mass Culture*. London: Routledge.

Amin, A., and Thrift, N. (2007) 'Cultural economy and cities', *Progress in Human Geography*, 31: 143–61.

Anderson, C. (2006) *The Long Tail: How Endless Choice is Creating Unlimited Demand*. London: Random House Business Books.

Appadurai, A. (1996) *Modernity at Large: Cultural Dimensions of Globalization*. Minneapolis: University of Minneapolis Press.

Bagnasco, A. (1977) *Tre Italie: la Problematica Territoriale dello Sviluppo Italiano*. Bolgna: Il Mulino.

Banham, R. (1960) *Theory and Design in the First Machine Age*. London: The Architectural Press.

Baudrillard, J. (1968) *Le Système des Objets: La Consommation des Signes*. Paris: Gallimard.

Becattini, G. (ed.) (1987) *Mercato e Forze Locali: Il Distretto Industriale*. Bologna: Il Mulino.

Bell, C. (1924) *Art*. London: Chatto and Windus.

Benjamin, W. (1969) *Illuminations: Essays and Reflections*. New York: Schocken.

Bourdieu, P. (1971) 'Le marché des biens symboliques', *L' Année Sociologique*, 22: 49–126.

Bourdieu, P. (1979) *La Distinction: Critique Sociale du Jugement*. Paris: Le Sens Commun.

Bourdieu, P. (1999) 'Une révolution conservatrice dans l'édition', *Actes de la Recherche en Sciences Sociales*, 126/127: 3–28.

British Department of Culture, Media and Sport (2001) *The Creative Industries Mapping Document*. http://www.culture.gov.uk/creative/mapping.html.

Castells, M. (1996) *The rise of the network society*, Information age; 1. Cambridge, Mass.: Blackwell.

Caves, R.E. (2000) *The Creative Industries: Contracts between Art and Science*. Cambridge, Mass.: Harvard University Press.

Chamberlin, E. (1933) *The Theory of Monopolistic Competition*. Cambridge, MA: Harvard University Press.

Cowen, T. (1998) *In Praise of Commercial Culture*. Cambridge, MA: Harvard University Press.

Esser, K., Hillebrand, W., Messner, D. and Meyer-Stamer, J. (1996) *Systemic competitiveness: new governance patterns for industrial development*, GDI book series; no. 7. London: Frank Cass.

Florida, R. (2004) *Cities and the Creative Class*. London: Routledge.

García, M.I., Fernández, Y. and Zofío, J.L. (2003) 'The economic dimension of the culture and leisure industry in Spain: national, sectoral and regional analysis', *Journal of Cultural Economics*, 27: 9–30.

Grabher, G. (2001a) 'Ecologies of creativity: the village, the group, and the heterarchic organization of the British advertising industry', *Environment and Planning A*, 33: 351–74.

Grabher, G. (2001b) 'Locating economic action: projects, networks, localities, institutions', *Environment and Planning A*, 33: 1329–31.

Hall, P. (2000) 'Creative cities and economic development', *Urban Studies*, 37: 639–50.

Hong Kong Central Policy Unit (2003) *Baseline Study on Hong Kong's Creative Industries*. Hong Kong: Centre for Cultural Policy Research, University of Hong Kong.

Horkheimer, M. and Adorno, T.W. (1972) *Dialectic of Enlightenment*. New York: Herder and Herder.

IAURIF (2006) *Les Industries Culturelles en Ile-de-France*. Paris: Institut d'Aménagement et d'Urbanisme de la Région Ile-de-France.

Jameson, F. (1998) 'Notes on globalization as a philosophical issue', in F. Jameson and M. Miyeshi (eds.) *The Cultures of Globalization*. Durham: Duke University Press. pp. 54–77.

Kearns, G. and Philo, C. (eds.) (1993) *Selling Places: The City as Cultural Capital, Past and Present*. Oxford: Pergamon Press.

Landry, C. (2000) *The Creative City: A Toolkit for Urban Innovators*. London: Earthscan.

Lawrence, T.B. and Phillips, N. (2002) 'Understanding cultural-products industries', *Journal of Management Inquiry*, 11: 430–41.

Lees, A. (1985) *Cities Perceived: Urban Society in European and American Thought, 1820–1940*. New York: Columbia University Press.

Lévy, J. (1999) *Le Tournant Géographique: Penser l'Espace pour Lire le Monde*. Paris: Belin.

Markusen, A., Hall, P. and Glasmeier, A. (1986) *High Tech America: The What, How, Where and Why of the Sunrise Industries*. Boston: Allen and Unwin.

Menger, P.M. (1993) 'L'hégémonie parisienne: économie et politique de la gravitation artistique', *Annales: Economies, Sociétés, Civilisations*, 6: 1565–1600.

Molotch, H. (1996) 'LA as design product: how art works in a regional economy', in A.J. Scott and E.W. Soja (eds.) *The City: Los Angeles and Urban Theory at the End of the Twentieth Century*. Berkeley and Los Angeles: University of California Press. pp. 225–75.

Montgomery, S.S. and Robinson, M.D. (1993) 'Visual artists in New York: what's special about person and place?' *Journal of Cultural Economics*, 17: 17–39.

Moulier Boutang, Y. (2007) *Le Capitalisme Cognitif, Comprendre la Nouvelle Grande Transformation et ses Enjeux*. Paris: Editions Amsterdam.

Negus, K. (1998) 'Cultural production and the corporation: musical genres and the strategic management of creativity in the US recording industry', *Media, Culture and Society*, 20: 359–79.

Piore, M. and Sabel, C. (1984) *The Second Industrial Divide: Possibilities for Prosperity*. New York: Basic Books.

Power, D. (2002) 'Cultural industries in Sweden: an assessment of their place in the Swedish economy', *Economic Geography,* 78: 103–27.

Pratt, A.C. (1997) 'The cultural industries production system: a case study of employment change in Britain, 1984–91', *Environment and Planning A*, 29: 1953–74.

Relph, E. (1976) *Place and Placelessness*. London: Pion.

Rullani, E. (2000) 'Le capitalisme cognitif: du déjà vu?' *Multitudes*, 2: 87–94.

Scott, A.J. (1996) 'The craft, fashion, and cultural products industries of Los Angeles: competitive dynamics and policy dilemmas in a multi-sectoral image-producing complex', *Annals of the Association of American Geographers*, 86: 306–23.

Scott, A.J. (1999) 'The US recorded music industry: on the relations between organization, location, and creativity in the cultural economy', *Environment and Planning A*, 31: 1965–84.

Scott, A.J. (2000a) *The Cultural Economy of Cities: Essays on the Geography of Image-Producing Industries*. London: SAGE Publications.

Scott, A.J. (2000b) 'The Cultural Economy of Paris', *International Journal of Urban and Regional Research*, 24: 567–82.

Scott, A.J. (2000c) 'French cinema: economy, policy and place in the making of a cultural products industry', *Theory, Culture and Society*, 17: 1–38.

Scott, A.J. (2005) *On Hollywood: The Place, The Industry*. Princeton: Princeton University Press.

Scott, A.J. (2006a) 'Creative cities: conceptual issues and policy problems', *Journal of Urban Affairs*, 28: 1–17.

Scott, A.J. (2006b) 'Entrepreneurship, innovation and industrial development: geography and the creative field revisited', *Small Business Economics*, 26: 1–24.

Scott, A.J. (2007) 'Capitalism and urbanization in a new key? The cognitive-cultural dimension', *Social Forces*, 85: 1465–82.

Scott, A.J. and Leriche, F. (2005) 'Les ressorts géographiques de l'économie culturelle: du local au mondial', *L'Espace Géographique*, 3: 207–22.

Soja, E.W. (2000) *Postmetropolis: Critical Studies of Cities and Regions*. Oxford: Blackwell.

STADTart (2000) *Culture Industries in Europe. Regional Development Concepts for Private-Sector Cultural Production and Services.* Düsseldorf: Ministry of Economy and Business, Technology and Transport and Ministry for Employment, Social Affairs and Urban Development, Culture and Sport of the State of North Rhine-Westphalia.

Storper, M. and Christopherson, S. (1987) 'Flexible specialization and regional industrial agglomerations: the case of the US motion-picture industry', *Annals of the Association of American Geographers*, 77: 260–82.

Urry, J. (1995) *Consuming Places*. London: Routledge.

Vercellone, C. (2007) 'From formal subsumption to general intellect: elements for a Marxist reading of the thesis of cognitive capitalism', *Historical Materialism*, 15: 13–36.

Wollen, P. (1993) *Raiding the Icebox: Reflections on Twentieth-Century Culture*. Bloomington and Indianapolis: Indiana University Press.

Zukin, S. (1995) *The Cultures of Cities*. Oxford: Blackwell.

CULTURAL

INDICATOR SUITES Helmut K. Anheier

INTRODUCTION[1]

[1] This chapter draws on the detailed introduction to the notion of indicator suites presented in Volume 1 of the Cultures and Globalization Series (Anheier, 2007); the latter also discussed alternative approaches to the construction of cultural indicators.

The purpose of the indicator system provided in this volume is to offer an empirical portrait of key dimensions of the relationships between culture and the economy in the context of globalization, many of which have been finely analyzed by the contributors to Part I.

Figure 1 presents our approach to the development of an indicator system for this purpose. The relationship between cultures and globalization is viewed from a perspective that is both analytical and factual. It is analytical because the globalization of the cultural economy does not take place in isolation from other globalization processes and fields of activity: a book or movie is a cultural, legal, social and economic entity at the same time. The analytical perspective simply emphasizes some aspects of globalization (in this volume it is the economic aspects); other dimensions may be treated as more contextual (e.g., political or social) but nonetheless relevant.

The perspective is factual in the sense that it explores the various globalization processes taking place, which may differ in their strengths, scope, and implications for different cultures and cultural fields. What the factual perspective achieves is to bring in empirical facts about globalization and related processes as they relate to culture. For example, international trade laws may not be written with a focus on cultural matters, but the former certainly influence the latter.

OPERATIONALIZING ECONOMY AND CULTURE IN THE CONTEXT OF GLOBALIZATION

The indicator system here focuses on what we have called the cultural economy: the economic system for the production, distribution and consumption of cultural goods and services through market as well as non-market mechanisms. The links between the present-day cultural economy and globalization are seen in the context of three processes:

– first, economic globalization in terms of trade and the rise of integrated, transnational productions and distribution systems dominated by large transnational corporations and financial markets;

– second, the emergence of a transnational, and increasingly global, civil society that has accelerated since the end of the Cold War, facilitated by the rise of international nongovernmental organizations, activist networks, and civil value patterns; and

– third, the 'thickening' of the international rule of law has continued as well, although unevenly and with persistent enforcement problems and nationalist interpretations of global governance.

The cultural economy shapes and, in a more pronounced way, is shaped by these larger processes. Furthermore, within these contextual processes, we can approach 'culture' in different ways (Figure 1):

– as a system of artistic endeavor and realm of creativity;

– as a social system of meaning and values;

– as an economic system of production, distribution and consumption; and

– as a political system of positions of power and influence.

Each 'lens' or systemic view is equally valid and brings to the fore different questions, leading to different insights and implications.

The relationship between cultures and globalization is not only multi-faceted from a systemic perspective. Each systemic view brings different units of analysis and flows into play. These can be transnational and domestic, individuals, organizations, or professions as well as institutional patterns, communities, and societies, including nation states (Figure 1). These units and flows are often connected, leading to consequences for other units. For example, the rise of the Internet brought wide access to online news, which in turn has changed the business model of the newspaper industry, the role of journalism with the increased popularity of blogs, etc.

Figure 1: **FRAMEWORK FOR EXPLORING**
THE RELATIONSHIP BETWEEN THE CULTURES AND GLOBALIZATION

Context:

| ECONOMIC GLOBALIZATION | POLITICAL - LEGAL GLOBALIZATION | GLOBAL CIVIL SOCIETY |

Descriptive and Analytic Focus:

CULTURES AND GLOBALIZATION

System Focus:

| CULTURES AS A SYSTEM OF MEANING AND VALUES | CULTURES AS AN ECONOMIC SYSTEM | CULTURES AS A SYSTEM OF SITES AND MOVEMENTS | CULTURES AS A POLITICAL ASPECTS SYSTEM |

Unit of Analysis of Entities and Flows:

| PLACES AND EVENTS | COMMUNITIES/ SOCIETIES/ COUNTRIES/ NATIONS | INSTITUTIONS/ ORGANIZATIONS/ PROFESSIONS/ NETWORKS | INDIVIDUALS |

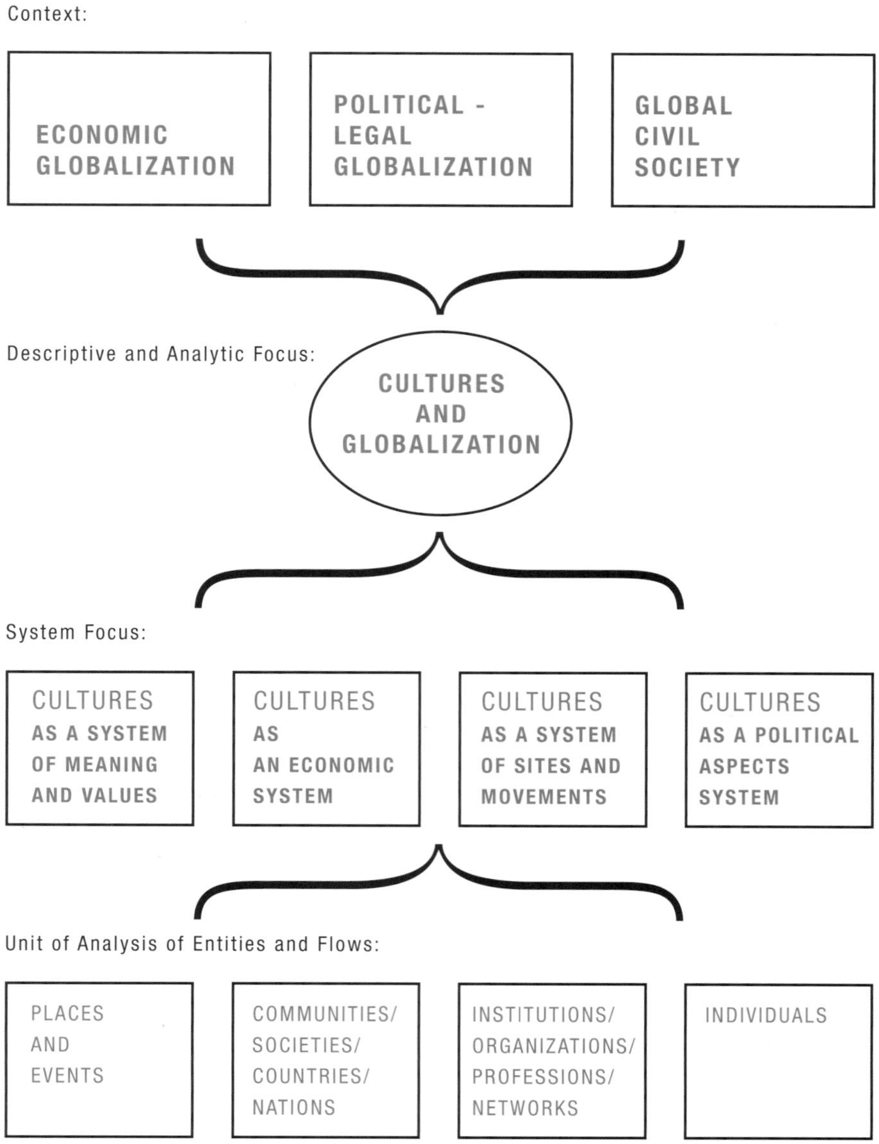

Table 1 presents the implementation of this general framework for the cultural economy. Each 'lens' (i.e., culture as a social, economic, political system, etc.) is broken down into major components and sub-components that make up individual indicator suites. For example, the social aspects of culture are broken down into values, practices and heritage. Culture as an economic system includes indicators of corporations, employment, professions, arts markets, the media and specific fields. The result is an integrated, thematic hierarchy of indicators.

Table 1: INDICATOR SUITES FOR THE CULTURAL ECONOMY

SOCIAL ASPECTS OF CULTURES AS A SYSTEM OF MEANING, VALUES, AND PRACTICES

VALUES, PARTICIPATION, CONSUMPTION
1. Cultural Values
2. Cultural Participation
3. Cultural Consumption

HERITAGE & THE CULTURAL COMMONS
4. Heritage Preservation
5. The Internet & The Cultural Commons

CULTURES AS AN ECONOMIC SYSTEM OF PRODUCTION, DISTRIBUTION, CONSUMPTION, AND COMMUNICATION

CORPORATIONS & ORGANIZATIONS
6. Transnational Cultural Corporations
7. Cultural INGOs & Foundations

EMPLOYMENT & PROFESSIONS
8. Employment & Professions

CULTURAL PRODUCTION & DISSEMINATION
9. Government Cultural Expenditures
10. Trade
11. Global Brands
12. Creation, Innovation & Protection
13. Dissemination & Storage
14. Traditional & Indigenous Knowledge

CULTURAL INDUSTRIES & FIELDS
15. News (offline, online)
16. TV
17. Radio
18. Print Media
19. Books
20. Film
21. Music
22. Sports
23. Video Games
24. Fashion
25. Advertising
26. Architecture & Design

GLOBAL ARTS MARKET
27. Art Auctions & Galleries
28. Global Performance Art
29. Prizes & Competitions

THE INTERNET
30. The Internet

CULTURES AS A SYSTEM OF SITES AND MOVEMENTS

GLOBAL SITES & EVENTS
31. Global Cultural Centers & Cities
32. Global Events

MOVEMENTS & FLOWS
33. Educational Exchange
34. Cultural Tourism
35. Global Concert Tours

CULTURES AS A POLITICAL SYSTEM

REGULATORY FRAMEWORKS & POLICY
36. International Standards
37. National & Regional Cultural Policy
38. International Regulatory Frameworks

INDICATOR SUITES

The notion of indicator suites is informed by Tufte's (1997; 2001) groundbreaking approach to the visual display of quantitative information, and the use of graphics in suggesting interpretations. In a departure from conventional approaches, indicator suites neither seek to list the actual data (typically by country as the primary unit of analysis), nor strive to have a uniform tabular layout; rather for each indicator we would select salient characteristics, patterns and trends that seem appropriate for the purpose at hand, even if the presentation will be different across indicator suites.

The basic idea behind the notion of indicator suites is that indicators of different units of analysis, and even with incomplete data, can still be brought together in a thematic (not statistical) way, and generate insights about relevant aspects of the relationship between culture and globalization. What unites indicators to form a thematic suite is not some statistical rationale but a conceptual, qualitative one.

In methodological terms, we are using (mostly) quantitative information in a (mostly) qualitative way. Indicator suites are a compromise in the sense that they take the inchoate and incomplete state of quantitative cultural indicators as a given, at least for the medium term, while refusing to accept the interpretative limitations this state imposes on descriptive analysis. In other words, indicator suites make do with what is empirically available.

The development of indicator suites is an iterative, almost hermeneutic process, as shown in Figure 2. It begins with the identification of a theme or topic, for example, cultural industries, media, and fields. This is broken down into various dimensions such as news, books, print media, music, film, TV, radio, fashion design, architecture, video games, etc. In each case, the questions become: what do we want to know about this topic in the context of cultural globalization, and why? And, what are some of the key trends and policy implications and issues the data could suggest or illuminate?

For example, for the Heritage and Cultural Commons topic, it was important to examine the distribution of World Heritage Sites by type, over time and across geographic regions; how the expansion of sites is reflected in UNESCO's budgets; and how many sites are listed as endangered, and where. As this example suggests, once we have a conceptual and policy-related justification for a particular topic, an initial operationalization (number of sites, budget allocations, etc.) leads to a search for possible indicators and data, with a continued process of data evaluation, incorporation of data sets, and preparing them for analysis.

To present a different example, the indicator suite for Educational Exchange includes
• A network analysis of flows of students at the tertiary level, with countries being the unit of analysis,
• A list of the top 15 sending and receiving countries overall and by major geographic region,
• The top five fields of study among international students in select countries,
• International students as a share of the total student population in higher education,
• The international student body in leading universities in major regions.

We arrived at the relatively small number of indicators in an iterative fashion by examining alternative measures and data. Taken together, this parsimonious set of indicators points to what seems significant: the centrality of a few countries in sending (China, India, Republic of Korea) and receiving (US, UK, Germany, France, Japan) a relatively large share of the total number of international students, and the limited role of the Arab World, Central Asia, Africa and Latin America in this exchange network.

The indicator suites combine structural and flow measures, and make use of maps, charts and figures rather than long and complex tabular presentations. The various elements of such indicator suites are graphically presented on double page spreads, with text (i.e., Digests) pointing to major findings, showing connections, suggesting interpretations, and providing background and further references.

Figure 2: **DEVELOPING INDICATOR SUITES**

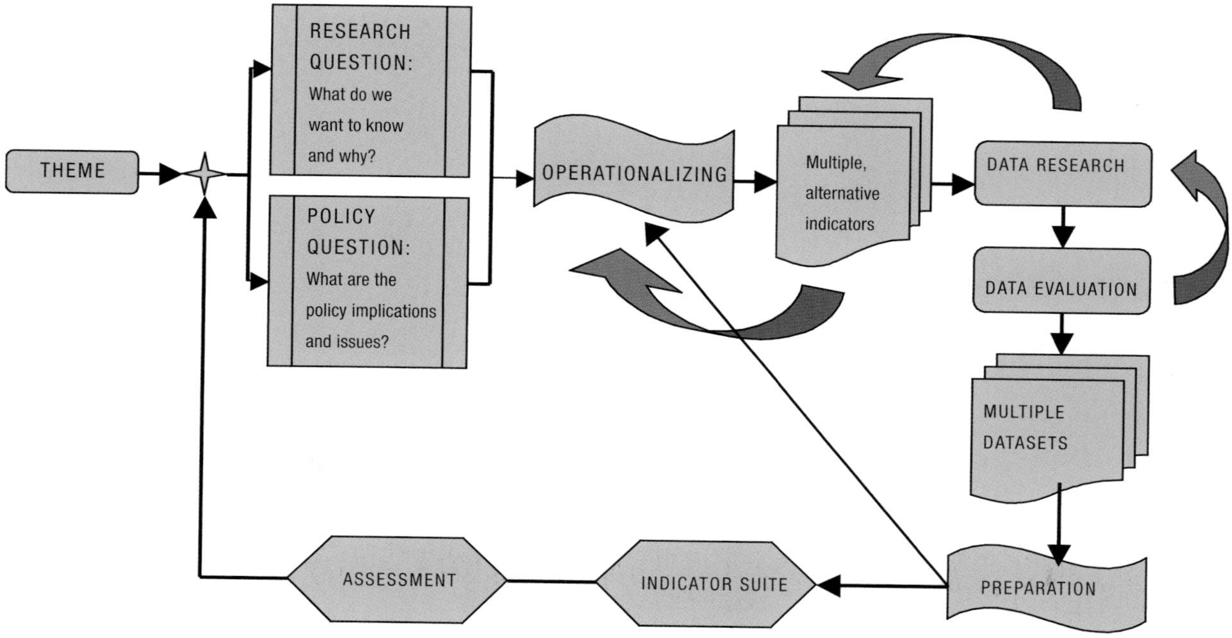

In conclusion, it is useful to point out that the list of indicator suites and indicators, including their operationalization and measurement, is neither fixed nor final, and is expected to develop and improve over time.

- Most of the data collected for the various indicator suites come from sources available on the Internet; and while much information is increasingly available online, much other useful information is not.
- We did not collect original data, and relied on secondary data exclusively.
- Almost all indicator suites have an accompanying Digest that helps readers interpret and understand the information presented. These Digests are typically placed either before or after the relevant suites.
- Complete references to source material are at the end of the indicator suite section, and listed sequentially for each suite and in numerical order for each data element presented.

Anheier, H. (2007). Introducing cultural indicator suites. In H. Anheier & Y.R. Isar (Eds.), The Cultures and Globalization Series: Vol. 1. Conflicts and tensions (pp. 335-347). London: Sage.

Anheier, H., & Y. R. Isar (2007). Introducing the Cultures and Globalization Series. In H. Anheier & Y.R. Isar (Eds.), The Cultures and Globalization Series: Vol. 1. Conflicts and tensions (pp. 3-16). London: Sage.

Tufte, E. (1997). Visual explanations: Images and quantities, evidence and narrative. Cheshire, CT: Graphics Press.

Tufte, E. (2001). The visual display of quantitative information. Cheshire, CT: Graphics Press.

INDICATOR SUITE

SOCIAL ASPECTS
OF CULTURE AS MEANINGS,
VALUES + PRACTICES

VALUES, PARTICIPATION, CONSUMPTION

01. **CULTURAL VALUES**

02. **CULTURAL PARTICIPATION**

03. **CULTURAL CONSUMPTION**

HERITAGE + THE CULTURAL COMMONS

04. **HERITAGE PRESERVATION**

05. **THE INTERNET + THE CULTURAL COMMONS**

CULTURAL VALUES

1. OUR WAY OF LIFE NEEDS TO BE PROTECTED AGAINST FOREIGN INFLUENCE

PLEASE TELL ME WHETHER YOU COMPLETELY AGREE, MOSTLY AGREE, MOSTLY DISAGREE OR COMPLETELY DISAGREE THAT OUR WAY OF LIFE NEEDS TO BE PROTECTED AGAINST FOREIGN INFLUENCE (2003).

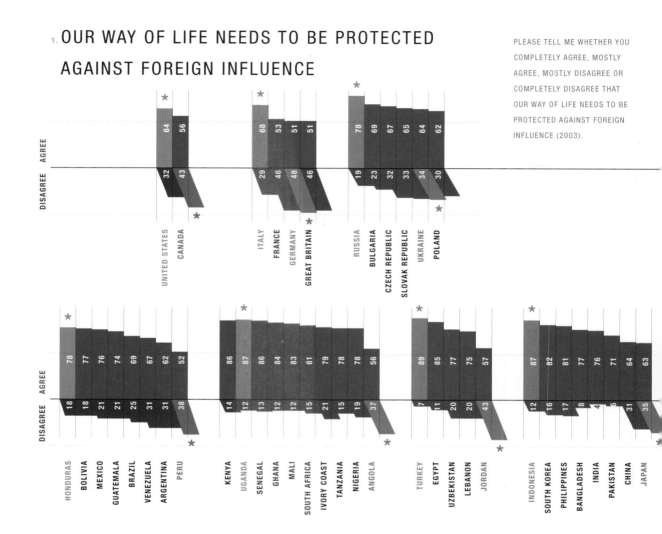

PLEASE TELL ME IF YOU THINK CELLULAR PHONES / INTERNET / TELEVISION HAS BEEN A CHANGE FOR THE BETTER, A CHANGE FOR THE WORSE, OR HASN'T MADE MUCH DIFFERENCE (2003).

% OF POPULATION WHO PERCEIVES A BETTER CHANGE DUE TO
CELLULAR PHONES / INTERNET / TELEVISION

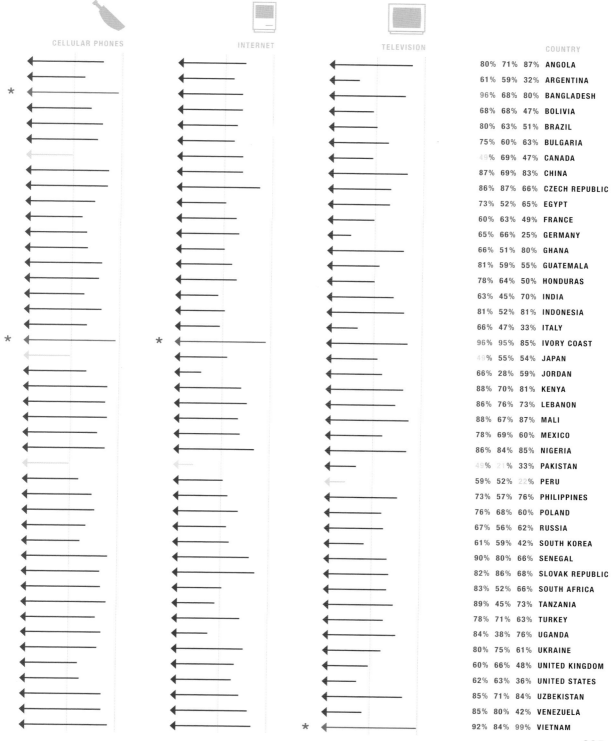

CELLULAR PHONES	INTERNET	TELEVISION				COUNTRY
			80%	71%	87%	ANGOLA
			61%	59%	32%	ARGENTINA
*			96%	68%	80%	BANGLADESH
			68%	68%	47%	BOLIVIA
			80%	63%	51%	BRAZIL
			75%	60%	63%	BULGARIA
			49%	69%	47%	CANADA
			87%	69%	83%	CHINA
			86%	87%	66%	CZECH REPUBLIC
			73%	52%	65%	EGYPT
			60%	63%	49%	FRANCE
			65%	66%	25%	GERMANY
			66%	51%	80%	GHANA
			81%	59%	55%	GUATEMALA
			78%	64%	50%	HONDURAS
			63%	45%	70%	INDIA
			81%	52%	81%	INDONESIA
			66%	47%	33%	ITALY
*	*		96%	95%	85%	IVORY COAST
			49%	55%	54%	JAPAN
			66%	28%	59%	JORDAN
			88%	70%	81%	KENYA
			86%	76%	73%	LEBANON
			88%	67%	87%	MALI
			78%	69%	60%	MEXICO
			86%	84%	85%	NIGERIA
			49%	21%	33%	PAKISTAN
			59%	52%	22%	PERU
			73%	57%	76%	PHILIPPINES
			76%	68%	60%	POLAND
			67%	56%	62%	RUSSIA
			61%	59%	42%	SOUTH KOREA
			90%	80%	66%	SENEGAL
			82%	86%	68%	SLOVAK REPUBLIC
			83%	52%	66%	SOUTH AFRICA
			89%	45%	73%	TANZANIA
			78%	71%	63%	TURKEY
			84%	38%	76%	UGANDA
			80%	75%	61%	UKRAINE
			60%	66%	48%	UNITED KINGDOM
			62%	63%	36%	UNITED STATES
			85%	71%	84%	UZBEKISTAN
			85%	80%	42%	VENEZUELA
		*	92%	84%	99%	VIETNAM

% OF POPULATION WHO HAVE A GREAT DEAL OF CONFIDENCE IN THEIR NATION'S PRESS

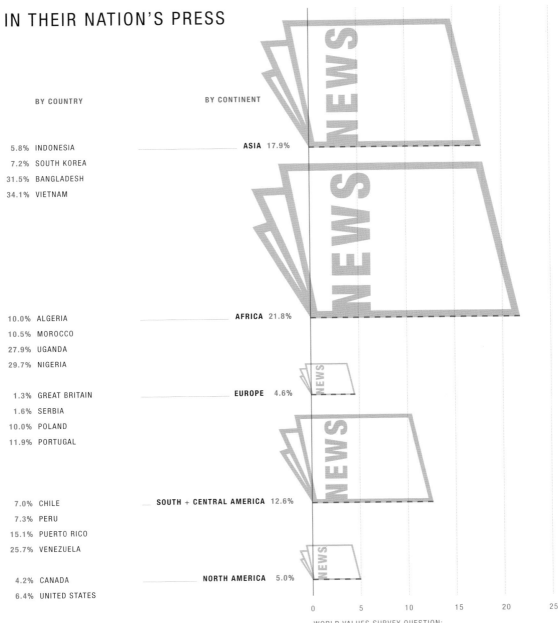

BY COUNTRY

BY CONTINENT

5.8% INDONESIA	
7.2% SOUTH KOREA	**ASIA** 17.9%
31.5% BANGLADESH	
34.1% VIETNAM	

10.0% ALGERIA	
10.5% MOROCCO	**AFRICA** 21.8%
27.9% UGANDA	
29.7% NIGERIA	

1.3% GREAT BRITAIN	**EUROPE** 4.6%
1.6% SERBIA	
10.0% POLAND	
11.9% PORTUGAL	

7.0% CHILE	
7.3% PERU	**SOUTH + CENTRAL AMERICA** 12.6%
15.1% PUERTO RICO	
25.7% VENEZUELA	

4.2% CANADA	**NORTH AMERICA** 5.0%
6.4% UNITED STATES	

0   5   10   15   20   25

WORLD VALUES SURVEY QUESTION:
HOW MUCH CONFIDENCE DO YOU
HAVE IN YOUR NATIONAL PRESS;
A GREAT DEAL OF CONFIDENCE,
QUITE A LOT OF CONFIDENCE,
NOT VERY MUCH CONFIDENCE OR
NONE AT ALL.

NOTE: COUNTRIES WERE SURVEYED
IN DIFFERENT YEARS WITHIN
1999-2004.

AVAILABILITY OF MOVIES, TV, MUSIC FROM AROUND THE WORLD

46% + 27% **CANADA**
40% + 22% **UNITED STATES**

36% + 42% **ITALY**
58% + 19% **GREAT BRITAIN**
42% + 25% **GERMANY**
41% + 23% **FRANCE**

74% + 20% **UKRAINE**
59% + 30% **POLAND**
54% + 34% **RUSSIA**
52% + 28% **BULGARIA**
47% + 22% **SLOVAK REPUBLIC**
39% + 25% **CZECH REPUBLIC**

68% + 24% **LEBANON**
51% + 28% **UZBEKISTAN**
56% + 18% **PAKISTAN**
45% + 24% **TURKEY**
42% + 27% **EGYPT**
26% + 35% **JORDAN**

56% + 30% **MEXICO**
59% + 26% **HONDURAS**
47% + 35% **BRAZIL**
50% + 29% **GUATEMALA**
43% + 34% **BOLIVIA**
45% + 28% **VENEZUELA**
37% + 30% **PERU**
23% + 30% **ARGENTINA**

64% + 25% **NIGERIA**
57% + 31% **SENEGAL**
55% + 30% **MALI**
55% + 27% **ANGOLA**
50% + 30% **KENYA**
58% + 21% **SOUTH AFRICA**
38% + 41% **GHANA**
46% + 29% **UGANDA**
47% + 27% **IVORY COAST**
32% + 26% **TANZANIA**

56% + 36% **VIETNAM**
59% + 31% **INDONESIA**
47% + 39% **SOUTH KOREA**
48% + 35% **PHILIPPINES**
39% + 38% **BANGLADESH**
61% + 13% **INDIA**
34% + 39% **JAPAN**
25% + 40% **CHINA**

IS THE AVAILABILITY OF MOVIES, TV AND MUSIC FROM DIFFERENT PARTS OF THE WORLD HAPPENING A LOT MORE, SOMEWHAT MORE, ONLY A LITTLE MORE, OR NOT MORE THESE DAYS? (2003)

% OF POPULATION STRONGLY AGREEING WITH TV BEING THE MOST IMPORTANT SOURCE OF ENTERTAINMENT

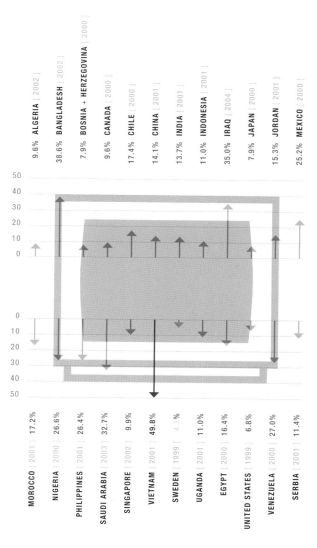

9.6% ALGERIA [2002]
38.6% BANGLADESH [2002]
7.9% BOSNIA + HERZEGOVINA [2000]
9.6% CANADA [2000]
17.4% CHILE [2000]
14.1% CHINA [2001]
13.7% INDIA [2001]
11.0% INDONESIA [2001]
35.0% IRAQ [2004]
7.9% JAPAN [2000]
15.3% JORDAN [2001]
25.2% MEXICO [2000]

MOROCCO [2001] 17.2%
NIGERIA [2000] 26.6%
PHILIPPINES [2001] 26.4%
SAUDI ARABIA [2003] 32.7%
SINGAPORE [2002] 9.9%
VIETNAM [2001] 49.8%
SWEDEN [1999] 4. %
UGANDA [2001] 11.0%
EGYPT [2000] 16.4%
UNITED STATES [1999] 6.8%
VENEZUELA [2000] 27.0%
SERBIA [2001] 11.4%

% OF YOUTH (AGES 18-29) PERCEIVING A GOOD IMPACT FROM THE AVAILABILITY OF CULTURAL IMPORTS

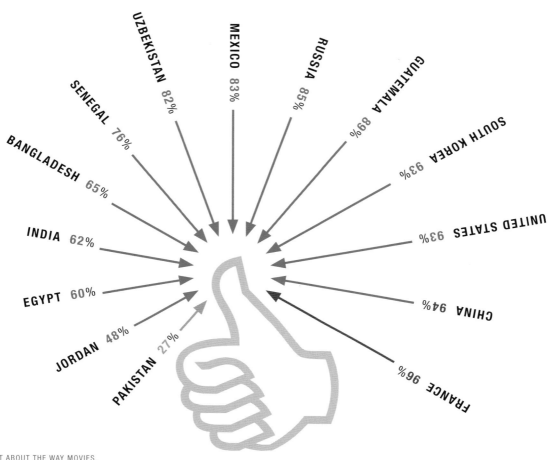

UZBEKISTAN 82%

MEXICO 83%

RUSSIA 85%

GUATEMALA 89%

SENEGAL 76%

SOUTH KOREA 93%

BANGLADESH 65%

UNITED STATES 93%

INDIA 62%

EGYPT 60%

CHINA 94%

JORDAN 48%

PAKISTAN 27%

FRANCE 96%

WHAT ABOUT THE WAY MOVIES, TV AND MUSIC FROM DIFFERENT PARTS OF THE WORLD ARE NOW AVAILABLE (IN SURVEY COUNTRY) —DO YOU THINK THIS IS A VERY GOOD THING, SOMEWHAT GOOD, SOMEWHAT BAD OR A VERY BAD THING FOR YOUR COUNTRY? (2003)

DO YOU THINK COMMUNICATION AND TRAVEL BETWEEN PEOPLE (OF THE SURVEY COUNTRY) AND PEOPLE IN OTHER COUNTRIES IS HAPPENING A LOT MORE, SOMEWHAT MORE, A LITTLE MORE, OR NOT MORE THESE DAYS? (2003)

% POPULATION TRAVELED IN PAST FIVE YEARS 2003

% POPULATION WHO PERCEIVE INTERNATIONAL TRAVEL AND COMMUNICATION TO HAPPEN A LOT MORE 2003

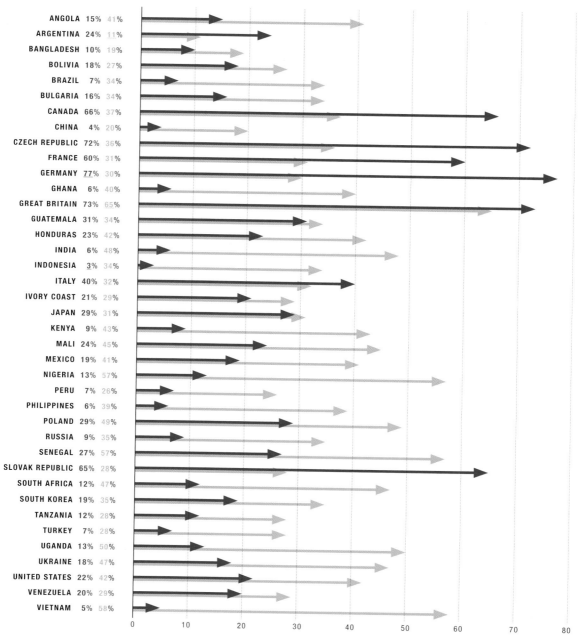

ANGOLA	15%	41%
ARGENTINA	24%	11%
BANGLADESH	10%	19%
BOLIVIA	18%	27%
BRAZIL	7%	34%
BULGARIA	16%	34%
CANADA	66%	37%
CHINA	4%	20%
CZECH REPUBLIC	72%	36%
FRANCE	60%	31%
GERMANY	77%	30%
GHANA	6%	40%
GREAT BRITAIN	73%	65%
GUATEMALA	31%	34%
HONDURAS	23%	42%
INDIA	6%	48%
INDONESIA	3%	34%
ITALY	40%	32%
IVORY COAST	21%	29%
JAPAN	29%	31%
KENYA	9%	43%
MALI	24%	45%
MEXICO	19%	41%
NIGERIA	13%	57%
PERU	7%	26%
PHILIPPINES	6%	39%
POLAND	29%	49%
RUSSIA	9%	35%
SENEGAL	27%	57%
SLOVAK REPUBLIC	65%	28%
SOUTH AFRICA	12%	47%
SOUTH KOREA	19%	35%
TANZANIA	12%	28%
TURKEY	7%	28%
UGANDA	13%	50%
UKRAINE	18%	47%
UNITED STATES	22%	42%
VENEZUELA	20%	29%
VIETNAM	5%	58%

0 10 20 30 40 50 60 70 80

CULTURAL VALUES
One of the most consistent findings of social research on values is the stability of value patterns or 'worldviews' over time as opposed to the greater volatility of attitudes. For example, basic values grounded in religion, and convictions about god, liberty or justice, or notions about family, tolerance, or foreign influence are more stable than attitudes about public institutions, confidence in the press, and the evaluation of cultural imports. At the same time, values shape attitudes and set the boundaries which they can change—changes that, at times, can be quite fickle and even inconsistent.

Shifts in basic value patterns are relatively rare, and if they happen, they are full of consequences and implications—from social and economic behavior and politics to the institutions of society at large. Typically, values change more between than within generations, and research attributes major inter-generational changes to various causal factors: differences in value formation during primary and secondary socialization (parents' economic well-being; changes in the educational system, the role of socializing agents such as religious institutions, etc.); and the impact of major events (wars, recessions, political upheavals) that, as collective experiences, shape individual value dispositions.

Over the last quarter century, and continuing into the first part of the twenty-first, major changes have occurred around three value-related fields: religion, role of government vs. individual responsibilities, and cosmopolitan values. However, these shifts have occurred neither contemporaneously nor equally across regions and cultures. For the so-called developed countries, this value shift took place between 1970 and the late 1980s. Researchers have used several different labels (e.g., materialism vs. postmaterialism) to describe this value shift, and identified a number of sociological correlates (Inglehart et al., 1998; van Deth and Scarborough, 1995):

- Decline in reliance on family, changes in the role of women, greater emphasis on individual responsibility
- Decline in emphasis on material security, less security seeking
- Decline in allegiance to traditional institutions (church, unions, etc.) with other forms of organizing and participation becoming more frequent
- New searches for meaning of life, and greater diversity of life styles
- Rise of cosmopolitan values (more tolerance, less nationalism, appreciation of cultural diversity)
- Preference for democratic forms of governance, and for more participatory organizations

Importantly, however, these shifts are not global. In particular, developing countries appear much less affected by them, and the position in the societies of Central and Eastern Europe remains somewhat unsettled.

As globalization continues to heighten the density and number of transactions and flows among people from very different parts of the world, there is also concern about the impact of 'foreign influences' on local and regional cultures and ways of life. While in some countries such as the United States, this fear may interact with questions of national security and perceived threats of terrorism, people in developing nations particularly see their traditional ways of life as threatened by this foreign influence (see data point 1). While many may cherish the avenues through which the world is becoming more interconnected and coming 'closer' (i.e., travel, cell phones, the Internet, a greater number of television channels, and a wider distribution of movies) there is a distinct feeling of traditional ways of life being lost.

Indeed such fears are widespread as data collected by the Pew Global Attitudes Project indicate. At the same time, youths across many regions and countries seem more positive about the impact of cultural imports (see data point 6), and populations generally expect international travel and communication to intensify in the future. However, African nations seem particularly fearful of their everyday lifestyle being eroded by global influences. Asian nations, with the exception of India and Pakistan, on the other hand, find that their way of life remains strong, despite the plethora of cultural imports from around the world. Unsurprisingly, African nations are among those with the highest percentage of people who believe that their nation needs protection from foreign influences, while Western nations find this protection less necessary (see data point 1). The two countries that find this protection of greatest importance are India and Pakistan; they are also the nations with the greatest amounts of indigenous knowledge and registered traditional practices.

One would think that the notions of commercialism and consumerism, mostly Western-created, would evoke a similar response as the question of foreign influence threatening traditional ways of life, however the data suggest otherwise. In fact, respondents who find that commercialism and consumerism *threaten* cultures are more likely from economically more developed countries: Indeed, France and Italy rank among those with the highest percentage believing that commercialism and consumerism threaten their cultures.

It is interesting to note that countries encouraging youth to expand their intellectual horizon are also those that find traditional ways of life least threatened. Western and many Asian countries see in the foreign and global many positive attributes and therefore encourage children's imagination along those lines. Unsurprisingly, a relatively low percentage of youth from countries less encouraging in this regard perceive a positive impact of cultural imports (see data point 6). This most likely is due to value patterns that equate foreign influence with the negative and unknown.

The general trends emerging from this suite can be summarized as the following:

- People in developing countries fear foreign cultural influence more than their developed counterparts.
- Among developing nations, Africans think that their traditional ways of life are being lost as a result of foreign influences, while most Asian nations find the opposite to be true.
- Young people in those nations who embrace change and foreign imports are more likely to identify a positive impact in cultural imports.

CULTURAL PARTICIPATION

1. GLOBAL INTERNET INDEX CHART

	DEC '06	NOV '06	% CHANGE
SESSIONS/VISITS PER PERSON PER MONTH	34	34	0.00
DOMAINS VISITED PER PERSON PER MONTH	69	70	-1.24
WEB PAGES PER PERSON PER MONTH	1,453	1,493	-2.63
PAGE VIEWS PER SURFING SESSION	42	43	-2.18
PC TIME SPENT PER MONTH	30:30:22	30:24:38	0.31
TIME SPENT DURING SURFING SESSION	00:53:51	00:53:30	0.66
DURATION OF A WEB PAGE VIEWED	00:00:45	00:00:44	1.20
ACTIVE DIGITAL MEDIA UNIVERSE	334,052,947	331,608,691	0.74
CURRENT DIGITAL MEDIA UNIVERSE ESTIMATE	490,577,395	488,865,738	0.35

2. MONTHLY HOME INTERNET AUDIENCE METRICS
(BY SELECT COUNTRY)

	USA DEC '06	BRAZIL DEC '06	UK JUL '06
SESSIONS/VISITS PER PERSON PER MONTH	35	32	31
DOMAINS VISITED PER PERSON PER MONTH	63	57	70
PC TIME SPENT PER MONTH	33:08:12	35:32:59	25:47:17
DURATION OF A WEB PAGE VIEWED	00:00:48	00:00:47	00:00:44
ACTIVE DIGITAL MEDIA UNIVERSE	150,419,613	14,419,335	24,286,031
CURRENT DIGITAL MEDIA UNIVERSE ESTIMATE	211,108,086	22,096,645	33,796,446

	SPAIN OCT '06	FRANCE DEC '06	SWITZERLAND DEC '06
SESSIONS/VISITS PER PERSON PER MONTH	35	42	37
DOMAINS VISITED PER PERSON PER MONTH	69	88	79
PC TIME SPENT PER MONTH	30:17:02	36:52:33	31:50:33
DURATION OF A WEB PAGE VIEWED	00:00:54	00:00:41	00:00:37
ACTIVE DIGITAL MEDIA UNIVERSE	12,714,303	21,183,022	3,753,112
CURRENT DIGITAL MEDIA UNIVERSE ESTIMATE	19,204,771	27,738,125	5,097,822

	GERMANY DEC '06	SWEDEN JAN '06	ITALY OCT '06
SESSIONS/VISITS PER PERSON PER MONTH	36	32	28
DOMAINS VISITED PER PERSON PER MONTH	84	56	61
PC TIME SPENT PER MONTH	33:34:32	27:36:36	24:01:42
DURATION OF A WEB PAGE VIEWED	00:00:37	00:00:34	00:00:44
ACTIVE DIGITAL MEDIA UNIVERSE	33,396,576	4,651,538	16,959,123
CURRENT DIGITAL MEDIA UNIVERSE ESTIMATE	47,543,336	6,324,830	27,943,123

	JAPAN NOV '04	AUSTRALIA DEC '06
SESSIONS/VISITS PER PERSON PER MONTH	25	37
DOMAINS VISITED PER PERSON PER MONTH	76	59
PC TIME SPENT PER MONTH	35:15:00	31:06:13
DURATION OF A WEB PAGE VIEWED	00:00:31	00:00:50
ACTIVE DIGITAL MEDIA UNIVERSE	36,582,978	10,698,764
CURRENT DIGITAL MEDIA UNIVERSE ESTIMATE	67,677,947	13,889,536

3. AVERAGE TIME SPENT ON CULTURAL ACTIVITIES SELECT COUNTRIES

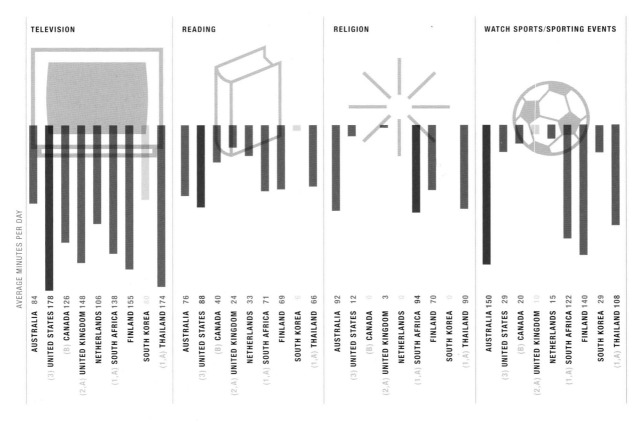

TELEVISION

AVERAGE MINUTES PER DAY

AUSTRALIA 84
(3) UNITED STATES 178
(B) CANADA 126
(2,A) UNITED KINGDOM 148
NETHERLANDS 106
(1,A) SOUTH AFRICA 138
FINLAND 155
SOUTH KOREA 80
(1,A) THAILAND 174

READING

AUSTRALIA 76
(3) UNITED STATES 88
(B) CANADA 40
(2,A) UNITED KINGDOM 24
NETHERLANDS 33
(1,A) SOUTH AFRICA 71
FINLAND 69
SOUTH KOREA 6
(1,A) THAILAND 66

RELIGION

AUSTRALIA 92
(3) UNITED STATES 12
(B) CANADA 0
(2,A) UNITED KINGDOM 3
NETHERLANDS 0
(1,A) SOUTH AFRICA 94
FINLAND 70
SOUTH KOREA 0
(1,A) THAILAND 90

WATCH SPORTS/SPORTING EVENTS

AUSTRALIA 150
(3) UNITED STATES 29
(B) CANADA 20
(2,A) UNITED KINGDOM 10
NETHERLANDS 15
(1,A) SOUTH AFRICA 122
FINLAND 140
SOUTH KOREA 29
(1,A) THAILAND 108

1=USES UN NAS SYSTEM OF TIME USE (SEE UN WEBSITE)

2=TV, VIDEOS, RADIO AND MUSIC FIGURES FROM 2000

3=UNITED STATES READING AVERAGE FOR HOUSEHOLDS WITH AND WITHOUT CHILDREN UNDER 18

A=INCLUDES WATCHING VIDEOS ON TV

B=INCLUDES TIME SPENT ON OTHER CULTURAL ENTERTAINMENT

AUSTRALIA: AVERAGE TIME SPENT, MINUTES PER DAY FOR TOTAL POPULATION 15 AND OVER, 1997

FINLAND: AVERAGE TIME SPENT, MINUTES PER DAY BY PARTICIPANTS AGE 10 AND OVER, 1999

UNITED STATES: AVERAGE TIME SPENT, MINUTES PER DAY FOR TOTAL POPULATION AGE 18 AND OVER, 2005

CANADA: AVERAGE TIME SPENT, MINUTES PER DAY FOR TOTAL POPULATION AGE 15 AND OVER, 2005

SOUTH KOREA: AVERAGE TIME SPENT, MINUTES PER DAY FOR TOTAL POPULATION AGE 10 AND OVER, 2000; NOTE: CINEMA, OTHER ENTERTAINMENT,
AND MUSIC ARE INCLUDED IN THE FIGURE OF 'LEISURE TIME', IN TOTAL IS 208 MINUTES PER WEEK OR APPROXIMATELY 30 MINUTES PER DAY

NETHERLANDS: AVERAGE TIME SPENT, MINUTES PER DAY FOR TOTAL POPULATION AGE 12 AND OVER, 2000

SOUTH AFRICA: AVERAGE TIME SPENT, MINUTES PER DAY FOR TOTAL POPULATION AGE 10 AND OVER, 2002; SPORTS INCLUDES OTHER CULTURAL VENUES
(SUCH AS CONCERTS)

THAILAND: AVERAGE TIME SPENT, MINUTES PER DAY FOR TOTAL POPULATION AGE 15 AND OVER, 2002

UNITED KINGDOM: AVERAGE TIME SPENT, MINUTES PER DAY FOR TOTAL POPULATION, 2005

TIME USE COMPARISON OF 15 EU COUNTRIES SELECT AGES **2005**

0 – 12 MINUTES PER DAY/PER YEAR RELIGIOUS ACTIVITIES
0 – 14 MINUTES PER DAY/PER YEAR TELEPHONE CONVERSATIONS
0 – 14 MINUTES PER DAY/PER YEAR ENTERTAINMENT + CULTURE
0 – 16 MINUTES PER DAY/PER YEAR SPORTS
0 – 04 MINUTES PER DAY/PER YEAR ARTS

0 – 07 MINUTES PER DAY/PER YEAR COMPUTER + VIDEO GAMES
0 – 17 MINUTES PER DAY/PER YEAR READING BOOKS
0 – 12 MINUTES PER DAY/PER YEAR RADIO + MUSIC
0 – 34 MINUTES PER DAY/PER YEAR OTHER READING
0 – 164 MINUTES PER DAY/PER YEAR TV + VIDEO

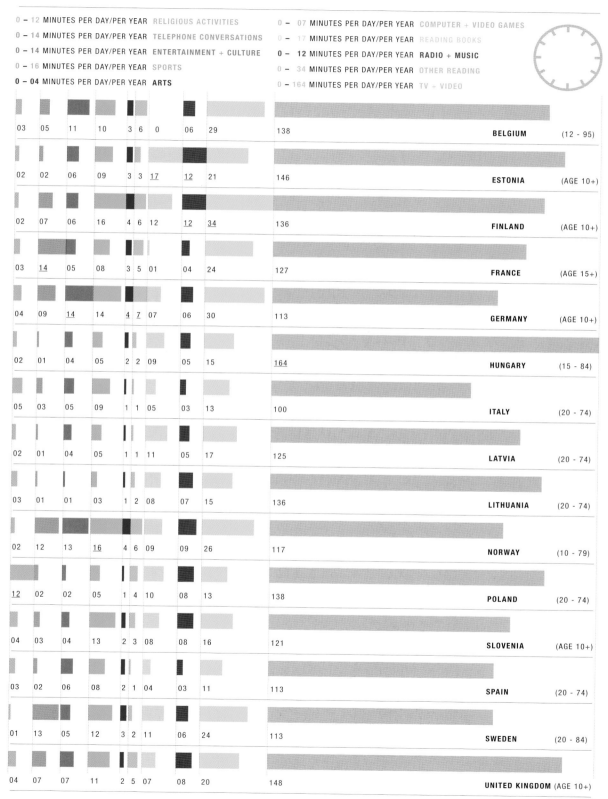

										Country	Age
03	05	11	10	3	6	0	06	29	138	**BELGIUM**	(12 - 95)
02	02	06	09	3	3	_17_	_12_	21	146	**ESTONIA**	(AGE 10+)
02	07	06	16	4	6	12	_12_	_34_	136	**FINLAND**	(AGE 10+)
03	_14_	05	08	3	5	01	04	24	127	**FRANCE**	(AGE 15+)
04	09	_14_	14	_4_	_7_	07	06	30	113	**GERMANY**	(AGE 10+)
02	01	04	05	2	2	09	05	15	_164_	**HUNGARY**	(15 - 84)
05	03	05	09	1	1	05	03	13	100	**ITALY**	(20 - 74)
02	01	04	05	1	1	11	05	17	125	**LATVIA**	(20 - 74)
03	01	01	03	1	2	08	07	15	136	**LITHUANIA**	(20 - 74)
02	12	13	_16_	4	6	09	09	26	117	**NORWAY**	(10 - 79)
_12_	02	02	05	1	4	10	08	13	138	**POLAND**	(20 - 74)
04	03	04	13	2	3	08	08	16	121	**SLOVENIA**	(AGE 10+)
03	02	06	08	2	1	04	03	11	113	**SPAIN**	(20 - 74)
01	13	05	12	3	2	11	06	24	113	**SWEDEN**	(20 - 84)
04	07	07	11	2	5	07	08	20	148	**UNITED KINGDOM**	(AGE 10+)

EU-15: FREQUENCY OF PARTICIPATION IN CULTURAL ACTIVITIES

AVERAGE % OF ALL EU RESPONDENTS, 2001 QUESTION: HOW MANY TIMES IN THE LAST 12 MONTHS DID YOU DO THE FOLLOWING ACTIVITIES?

NEVER 1-3 TIMES 4-6 TIMES 7-12 TIMES > 12 TIMES

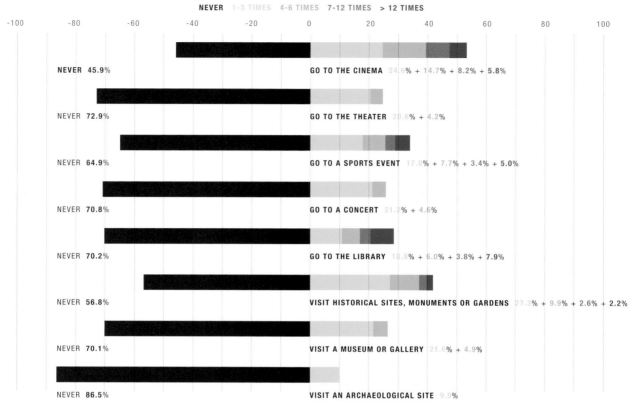

NEVER 45.9% **GO TO THE CINEMA** 24.6% + 14.7% + 8.2% + 5.8%

NEVER 72.9% **GO TO THE THEATER** 20.6% + 4.2%

NEVER 64.9% **GO TO A SPORTS EVENT** 17.8% + 7.7% + 3.4% + 5.0%

NEVER 70.8% **GO TO A CONCERT** 21.2% + 4.6%

NEVER 70.2% **GO TO THE LIBRARY** 10.8% + 6.0% + 3.8% + 7.9%

NEVER 56.8% **VISIT HISTORICAL SITES, MONUMENTS OR GARDENS** 27.3% + 9.9% + 2.6% + 2.2%

NEVER 70.1% **VISIT A MUSEUM OR GALLERY** 21.6% + 4.9%

NEVER 86.5% **VISIT AN ARCHAEOLOGICAL SITE** 9.9%

EU-15: PARTICIPATION IN CULTURAL ACTIVITIES

AVERAGE % OF ALL EU RESPONDENTS, 2001 QUESTION: IN THE LAST 12 MONTHS, HAVE YOU PRACTICED THE FOLLOWING ACTIVITIES?

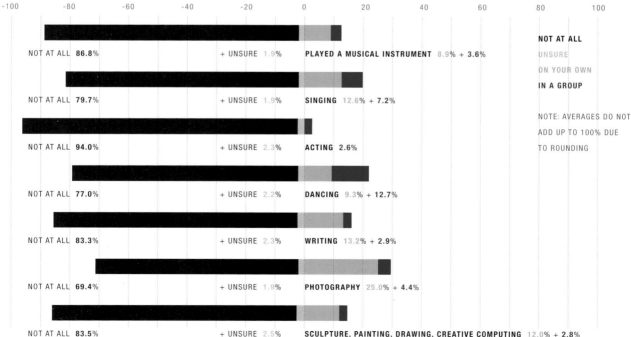

NOT AT ALL 86.8% + UNSURE 1.9% **PLAYED A MUSICAL INSTRUMENT** 8.9% + 3.6%

NOT AT ALL 79.7% + UNSURE 1.9% **SINGING** 12.6% + 7.2%

NOT AT ALL 94.0% + UNSURE 2.3% **ACTING** 2.6%

NOT AT ALL 77.0% + UNSURE 2.2% **DANCING** 9.3% + 12.7%

NOT AT ALL 83.3% + UNSURE 2.3% **WRITING** 13.2% + 2.9%

NOT AT ALL 69.4% + UNSURE 1.9% **PHOTOGRAPHY** 25.0% + 4.4%

NOT AT ALL 83.5% + UNSURE 2.5% **SCULPTURE, PAINTING, DRAWING, CREATIVE COMPUTING** 12.0% + 2.8%

NOT AT ALL
UNSURE
ON YOUR OWN
IN A GROUP

NOTE: AVERAGES DO NOT ADD UP TO 100% DUE TO ROUNDING

TIME USE COMPARISON OF 15 EUROPEAN UNION COUNTRIES

SELECT AGES AVERAGE MINUTES PER DAY 2005

LEISURE TOTAL

SPAIN	UNITED KINGDOM	FRANCE	BELGIUM	NORWAY	SWEDEN	ITALY	POLAND	SLOVENIA	HUNGARY	LATVIA	LITHUANIA	FINLAND	ESTONIA
280	313	263	311	360	306	263	279	307	303	254	240	342	309

SOCIAL LIFE TOTAL

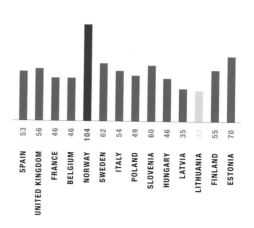

SPAIN	UNITED KINGDOM	FRANCE	BELGIUM	NORWAY	SWEDEN	ITALY	POLAND	SLOVENIA	HUNGARY	LATVIA	LITHUANIA	FINLAND	ESTONIA
53	56	46	46	104	62	54	49	60	46	35	33	55	70

SPORTS TOTAL

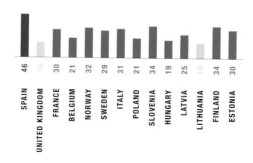

SPAIN	UNITED KINGDOM	FRANCE	BELGIUM	NORWAY	SWEDEN	ITALY	POLAND	SLOVENIA	HUNGARY	LATVIA	LITHUANIA	FINLAND	ESTONIA
46	16	30	21	32	29	31	21	34	19	25	16	34	30

STUDY TOTAL

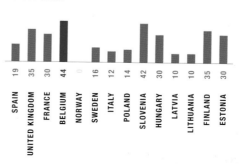

SPAIN	UNITED KINGDOM	FRANCE	BELGIUM	NORWAY	SWEDEN	ITALY	POLAND	SLOVENIA	HUNGARY	LATVIA	LITHUANIA	FINLAND	ESTONIA
19	35	30	44	0	16	12	14	42	30	10	10	35	30

8. EU CC-13 COUNTRIES: IN THE LAST 12 MONTHS HAVE YOU PARTICIPATED IN ANY OF THE FOLLOWING ACTIVITIES?

(MULTIPLE ANSWERS ALLOWED) 2003

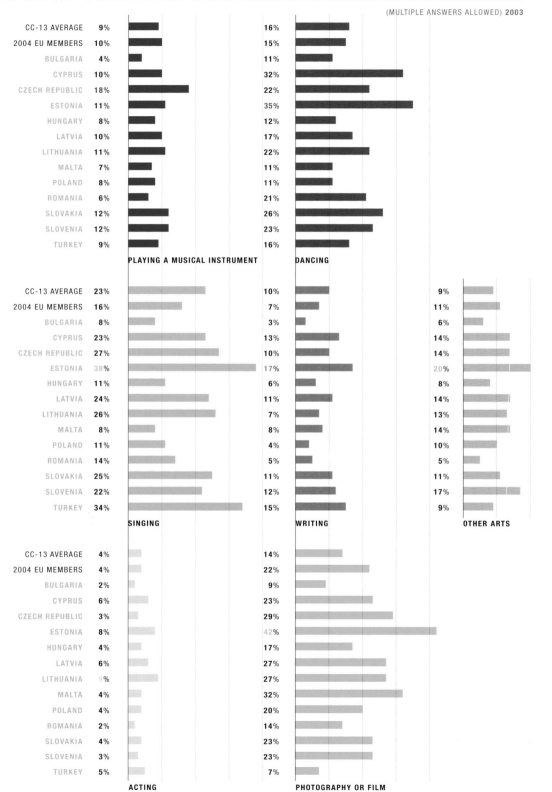

	PLAYING A MUSICAL INSTRUMENT	DANCING
CC-13 AVERAGE	9%	16%
2004 EU MEMBERS	10%	15%
BULGARIA	4%	11%
CYPRUS	10%	32%
CZECH REPUBLIC	18%	22%
ESTONIA	11%	35%
HUNGARY	8%	12%
LATVIA	10%	17%
LITHUANIA	11%	22%
MALTA	7%	11%
POLAND	8%	11%
ROMANIA	6%	21%
SLOVAKIA	12%	26%
SLOVENIA	12%	23%
TURKEY	9%	16%

	SINGING	WRITING	OTHER ARTS
CC-13 AVERAGE	23%	10%	9%
2004 EU MEMBERS	16%	7%	11%
BULGARIA	8%	3%	6%
CYPRUS	23%	13%	14%
CZECH REPUBLIC	27%	10%	14%
ESTONIA	38%	17%	20%
HUNGARY	11%	6%	8%
LATVIA	24%	11%	14%
LITHUANIA	26%	7%	13%
MALTA	8%	8%	14%
POLAND	11%	4%	10%
ROMANIA	14%	5%	5%
SLOVAKIA	25%	11%	11%
SLOVENIA	22%	12%	17%
TURKEY	34%	15%	9%

	ACTING	PHOTOGRAPHY OR FILM
CC-13 AVERAGE	4%	14%
2004 EU MEMBERS	4%	22%
BULGARIA	2%	9%
CYPRUS	6%	23%
CZECH REPUBLIC	3%	29%
ESTONIA	8%	42%
HUNGARY	4%	17%
LATVIA	6%	27%
LITHUANIA	9%	27%
MALTA	4%	32%
POLAND	4%	20%
ROMANIA	2%	14%
SLOVAKIA	4%	23%
SLOVENIA	3%	23%
TURKEY	5%	7%

9. SINGAPORE: TICKETED ARTS ATTENDANCES IN THOUSANDS

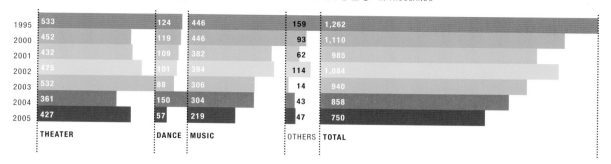

	THEATER	DANCE	MUSIC	OTHERS	TOTAL
1995	533	124	446	159	1,262
2000	452	119	446	93	1,110
2001	432	109	382	62	985
2002	475	101	394	114	1,084
2003	532	88	306	14	940
2004	361	150	304	43	858
2005	427	57	219	47	750

10. MEXICO + CUBA: ATTENDEES AT CULTURAL EVENTS OR VENUES

OF ATTENDEES 2003

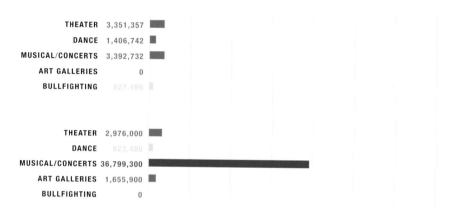

THEATER	3,351,357
DANCE	1,406,742
MUSICAL/CONCERTS	3,392,732
ART GALLERIES	0
BULLFIGHTING	827,496

THEATER	2,976,000
DANCE	923,400
MUSICAL/CONCERTS	36,799,300
ART GALLERIES	1,655,900
BULLFIGHTING	0

11. AUSTRALIA:

ATTENDANCE AT SELECTED CULTURAL VENUES + EVENTS 2002

% ATTENDANCE RATE IN LAST YEAR

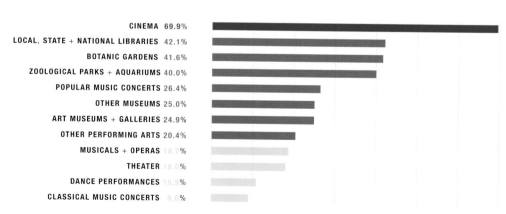

CINEMA	69.9%
LOCAL, STATE + NATIONAL LIBRARIES	42.1%
BOTANIC GARDENS	41.6%
ZOOLOGICAL PARKS + AQUARIUMS	40.0%
POPULAR MUSIC CONCERTS	26.4%
OTHER MUSEUMS	25.0%
ART MUSEUMS + GALLERIES	24.9%
OTHER PERFORMING ARTS	20.4%
MUSICALS + OPERAS	18.7%
THEATER	18.0%
DANCE PERFORMANCES	10.9%
CLASSICAL MUSIC CONCERTS	9.0%

347

12. % OF POPULATION SPENDING TIME WEEKLY AT SPORTS, VOLUNTARY OR SERVICE ORGANIZATIONS

WORLD VALUES SURVEY QUESTION: FOR EACH ACTIVITY, WOULD YOU SAY YOU DO THEM EVERY WEEK, ONCE OR TWICE A MONTH, ONLY A FEW TIMES A YEAR OR NOT AT ALL?

13. % OF POPULATION WHO BELONG TO EDUCATION, ARTS, MUSIC OR CULTURAL ORGANIZATIONS

WORLD VALUES SURVEY QUESTION: OF EDUCATION, ARTS, MUSIC OR CULTURAL ORGANIZATIONS, WHICH DO YOU BELONG TO?

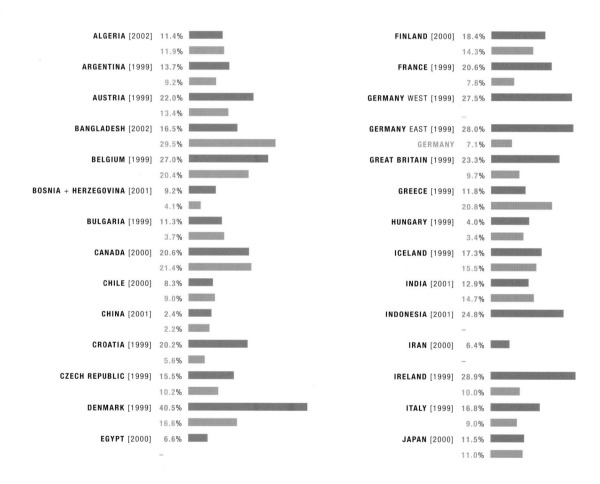

ALGERIA [2002]	11.4%	
	11.9%	
ARGENTINA [1999]	13.7%	
	9.2%	
AUSTRIA [1999]	22.0%	
	13.4%	
BANGLADESH [2002]	16.5%	
	29.5%	
BELGIUM [1999]	27.0%	
	20.4%	
BOSNIA + HERZEGOVINA [2001]	9.2%	
	4.1%	
BULGARIA [1999]	11.3%	
	3.7%	
CANADA [2000]	20.6%	
	21.4%	
CHILE [2000]	8.3%	
	9.0%	
CHINA [2001]	2.4%	
	2.2%	
CROATIA [1999]	20.2%	
	5.6%	
CZECH REPUBLIC [1999]	15.5%	
	10.2%	
DENMARK [1999]	40.5%	
	16.6%	
EGYPT [2000]	6.6%	
	–	

FINLAND [2000]	18.4%	
	14.3%	
FRANCE [1999]	20.6%	
	7.8%	
GERMANY WEST [1999]	27.5%	
	–	
GERMANY EAST [1999]	28.0%	
GERMANY	7.1%	
GREAT BRITAIN [1999]	23.3%	
	9.7%	
GREECE [1999]	11.8%	
	20.8%	
HUNGARY [1999]	4.0%	
	3.4%	
ICELAND [1999]	17.3%	
	15.5%	
INDIA [2001]	12.9%	
	14.7%	
INDONESIA [2001]	24.8%	
	–	
IRAN [2000]	6.4%	
	–	
IRELAND [1999]	28.9%	
	10.0%	
ITALY [1999]	16.8%	
	9.0%	
JAPAN [2000]	11.5%	
	11.0%	

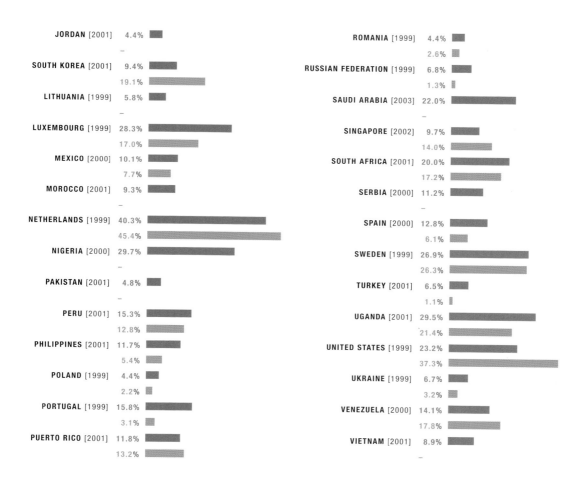

JORDAN [2001]	4.4%	
	–	
SOUTH KOREA [2001]	9.4%	
	19.1%	
LITHUANIA [1999]	5.8%	
	–	
LUXEMBOURG [1999]	28.3%	
	17.0%	
MEXICO [2000]	10.1%	
	7.7%	
MOROCCO [2001]	9.3%	
	–	
NETHERLANDS [1999]	40.3%	
	45.4%	
NIGERIA [2000]	29.7%	
	–	
PAKISTAN [2001]	4.8%	
	–	
PERU [2001]	15.3%	
	12.8%	
PHILIPPINES [2001]	11.7%	
	5.4%	
POLAND [1999]	4.4%	
	2.2%	
PORTUGAL [1999]	15.8%	
	3.1%	
PUERTO RICO [2001]	11.8%	
	13.2%	

ROMANIA [1999]	4.4%	
	2.6%	
RUSSIAN FEDERATION [1999]	6.8%	
	1.3%	
SAUDI ARABIA [2003]	22.0%	
	–	
SINGAPORE [2002]	9.7%	
	14.0%	
SOUTH AFRICA [2001]	20.0%	
	17.2%	
SERBIA [2000]	11.2%	
	–	
SPAIN [2000]	12.8%	
	6.1%	
SWEDEN [1999]	26.9%	
	26.3%	
TURKEY [2001]	6.5%	
	1.1%	
UGANDA [2001]	29.5%	
	21.4%	
UNITED STATES [1999]	23.2%	
	37.3%	
UKRAINE [1999]	6.7%	
	3.2%	
VENEZUELA [2000]	14.1%	
	17.8%	
VIETNAM [2001]	8.9%	
	–	

HONG KONG: DO YOU
DO ANY OF THE FOLLOWING
CREATIVE ACTIVITIES?

% OF 604 RESPONDENTS 2004

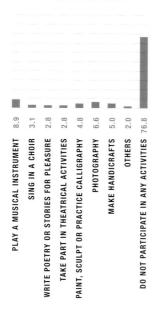

PLAY A MUSICAL INSTRUMENT	8.9
SING IN A CHOIR	3.1
WRITE POETRY OR STORIES FOR PLEASURE	2.8
TAKE PART IN THEATRICAL ACTIVITIES	2.8
PAINT, SCULPT OR PRACTICE CALLIGRAPHY	4.8
PHOTOGRAPHY	6.6
MAKE HANDICRAFTS	5.0
OTHERS	2.0
DO NOT PARTICIPATE IN ANY ACTIVITIES	76.8

15. JAPAN: PARTICIPATION RATE
FOR TOTAL POPULATION 15
AND OVER

% PARTICIPATION 1991 **2001**

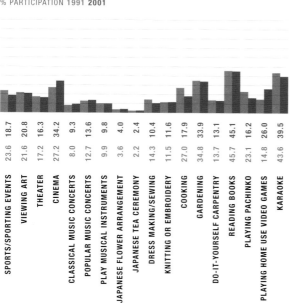

	1991	2001
SPORTS/SPORTING EVENTS	23.6	18.7
VIEWING ART	21.6	20.8
THEATER	17.2	16.3
CINEMA	27.2	34.2
CLASSICAL MUSIC CONCERTS	8.0	9.3
POPULAR MUSIC CONCERTS	12.7	13.6
PLAY MUSICAL INSTRUMENTS	9.9	9.8
JAPANESE FLOWER ARRANGEMENT	3.6	4.0
JAPANESE TEA CEREMONY	2.2	2.4
DRESS MAKING/SEWING	14.3	10.4
KNITTING OR EMBROIDERY	11.5	11.6
COOKING	27.0	17.9
GARDENING	34.8	33.9
DO-IT-YOURSELF CARPENTRY	13.7	13.1
READING BOOKS	45.7	45.1
PLAYING PACHINKO	23.1	16.2
PLAYING HOME USE VIDEO GAMES	14.8	26.0
KARAOKE	43.6	39.5

CULTURAL PARTICIPATION Historically, concepts of what constitutes culture, and therefore cultural activities, have privileged Western culture over all others. The institutionalization of these concepts has permeated relevant theories of cultural participation, and also influenced current thinking about globalization and cultural developments. Scholars have suggested that increased diversity of cultural options due to globalization has given rise to a more globalized cultural economy, opened up avenues, and indeed generated demand for non-Western cultural products and experiences, with the Internet being a prime example. At the same time, cultural participation remains closely linked to inequalities in socio-economic status and life chances generally. These inequalities exist both within and between countries and communities. This suite, although limited largely to the OECD countries for which information is available, offers an overview of the choices people make about the type and level of their cultural participation.

WHAT IS CULTURAL PARTICIPATION AND HOW IS IT MEASURED?

Knowledge about cultural participation has suffered from contested definitions and a poor information base. Some analysts link cultural participation to cultural citizenship, defined as 'the maintenance and development of cultural lineage via education, custom, language, religion, and the acknowledgement of difference in and by the mainstream' (Lewis and Miller, 2003:1). Thus, cultural participation can be seen as the enactment of cultural citizenship. Statistics on cultural participation are also gathered using different definitions across countries, often making comparisons difficult.

A GLIMPSE INTO
CULTURAL PARTICIPATION WORLDWIDE

The suite demonstrates the range of cultural activities and attendances in which the populaces of various nations engage:

- Worldwide, people reported they visited the Internet an average of 34 times per month in 2006 (see data point 1); France (42), Switzerland (37), and Australia (37) are examples of nations whose citizens visit the Internet more often than the global average (see data point 2).
- Japanese (25) and Italians (28) showed less frequent visits to the Internet; in Japan, however, individuals were likely to visit more domains per month (76) than people in many countries.
- As data point 3 shows, television is by far the most common cultural activity across countries selected for inclusion in the suite, in comparison with reading, religious activities, and sports and sporting events (which comes in second).
- In Mexico and Cuba, according to data point 10, cultural events with the highest attendance were musical and concert events (3,392,732 Mexico; 36,799,300 Cuba), as well as theater activities (3,351,357 Mexico; 2,976,000 Cuba).
- Data point 9 shows that in Singapore, in 1995-2005, theater attendance (361-533) consistently exceeded attendance of dance (57-150), music (219-446), and other (14-159) cultural events.
- In Australia, cinemas (69.9 per cent), libraries (42.1 per cent), and botanic gardens (41.6 per cent) enjoyed the greatest attendance in 2002, according to data point 11.

- People in Japan, 1991 and 2001, were more likely to go to the cinema (27.2, 34.2), read a book (45.7, 45.1), or perform Karaoke (43.6, 39.5) than to engage in other similar cultural activities (data point 15). In Hong Kong, as data element 14 illustrates, playing a musical instrument (8.9 per cent) was the most popular creative activity, followed by photography (6.6 per cent); however, the vast majority of people surveyed said that they do not participate in any listed creative endeavors.
- Among populations in 15 selected EU countries in 2001, people were most likely to be involved in photography (31.6 per cent), either alone or in a group, followed by dancing (23 per cent) and singing (20.3 per cent), as shown in data point 6.
- People in 15 EU nations in 2001 were most likely to go to the cinema (54.1 per cent), go to a sporting event (75.1 per cent), or visit historic sites and gardens (34.2 per cent). These individuals consistently spent the greatest amount of the time they were engaged in cultural activities by watching television and videos (range: 100 minutes per day in Italy; 164 in Hungary), reading materials other than books (range: 11 minutes per day in Latvia; 34 in Finland), or sports activities. Generally, people in Europe spent more of their leisure time on their social lives (especially in Norway, Estonia, and Slovenia) than they did engaged in sports or study. Norway, Finland, and Estonia enjoyed the highest levels of leisure time overall.
- The Czech Republic, Estonia, Cyprus, Turkey, Slovenia, and Lithuania showed the highest levels of participation in cultural activities, such as playing musical instruments, dancing and singing, writing, acting and photography.

THE ISSUES:
GLOBALIZATION AND CULTURAL PARTICIPATION

Much contemporary analysis of cultural participation is based upon the formation and cultivation of what Pierre Bourdieu and Jean-Claude Passeron called 'cultural capital' (1977). Bourdieu (1984) theorized that cultural capital was the result of a specific socialization process whereby dominant social classes establish cultural benchmarks in terms of cultural knowledge and expertise, amplified through unequal access to educational institutions. The nurturing of cultural capital in the children of elite families (i.e., the appreciation and consumption of high-art or elite-culture by younger generations) was a way to ensure the reproduction of high social status. Education and the arts, therefore, were crucial to this process and served as signifiers of achievement and cultural attainment. In this light, the evolution of cultural capital is linked to issues of acculturation and participation in activities that influence or shape a so-called 'cultured' individual within society.

Alongside participation in 'fine arts' (by Western standards) is involvement in popular arts, exemplified by Hollywood blockbuster movies, as a highly commodified form of culture. The frequent tension between 'high' culture and 'popular' culture, characteristic of the West, is exported into other cultural systems, and the dominance of popular Western culture increasingly influences cultural participation in many parts of the world. For example, the suite demonstrates that television and video, the cinema, and reading materials are highly consumed worldwide. To the extent, then, that media products 'travel,'

these represent the most likely agents which spread cultural ideas and innovations, influencing what is considered to be 'in' or 'en vogue' culturally.

By contrast, some scholars have pointed to the growing diversity available to individuals within many societies as a result of globalization. This diversity informs and changes people's tastes, preferences, and activities. Globalization of cultural activities has changed participation to include more transnational, perhaps more cosmopolitan, tastes. Advances such as the Internet not only increase worldwide access to participation in shared cultural experiences, but also, through high accessibility and lower cost (compared to more conventional media), provide a platform for both Western and non-Western cultures to find a voice in the global arena. Whereas in Bourdieu's world, one 'elite' culture was privileged among many, today the privileged person is the one who is informed and can participate in many cultures (DiMaggio and Mukhtar, 2004). Globalization therefore both expands cultural production and changes its nature and the balance of power among cultures.

CULTURAL CONSUMPTION

1. % HOUSEHOLD SPENDING ON RECREATION + CULTURE

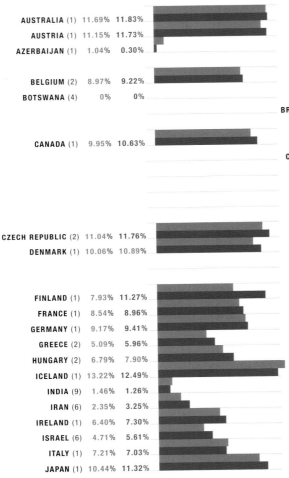

AUSTRALIA (1)	11.69%	11.83%
AUSTRIA (1)	11.15%	11.73%
AZERBAIJAN (1)	1.04%	0.30%
BELGIUM (2)	8.97%	9.22%
BOTSWANA (4)	0%	0%
CANADA (1)	9.95%	10.63%
CZECH REPUBLIC (2)	11.04%	11.76%
DENMARK (1)	10.06%	10.89%
FINLAND (1)	7.93%	11.27%
FRANCE (1)	8.54%	8.96%
GERMANY (1)	9.17%	9.41%
GREECE (2)	5.09%	5.96%
HUNGARY (2)	6.79%	7.90%
ICELAND (1)	13.22%	12.49%
INDIA (9)	1.46%	1.26%
IRAN (6)	2.35%	3.25%
IRELAND (1)	6.40%	7.30%
ISRAEL (6)	4.71%	5.61%
ITALY (1)	7.21%	7.03%
JAPAN (1)	10.44%	11.32%

DATES OF COMPARISON

(1) 1994 + 2004
(2) 1995 + 2004
(3) 1993 + 2001
(4) 1994 + 2002
(5) 1996 + 2000
(6) 1993 + 2003
(7) 1995 + 2003
(8) 1992 + 2001
(9) 1994 + 2000
(10) 1992 + 2002

% HOUSEHOLD SPENDING ON EDUCATION

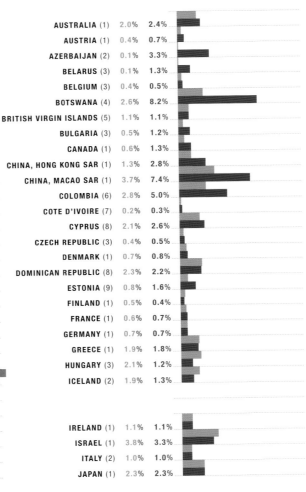

AUSTRALIA (1)	2.0%	2.4%
AUSTRIA (1)	0.4%	0.7%
AZERBAIJAN (2)	0.1%	3.3%
BELARUS (3)	0.1%	1.3%
BELGIUM (3)	0.4%	0.5%
BOTSWANA (4)	2.6%	8.2%
BRITISH VIRGIN ISLANDS (5)	1.1%	1.1%
BULGARIA (3)	0.5%	1.2%
CANADA (1)	0.6%	1.3%
CHINA, HONG KONG SAR (1)	1.3%	2.8%
CHINA, MACAO SAR (1)	3.7%	7.4%
COLOMBIA (6)	2.8%	5.0%
COTE D'IVOIRE (7)	0.2%	0.3%
CYPRUS (8)	2.1%	2.6%
CZECH REPUBLIC (3)	0.4%	0.5%
DENMARK (1)	0.7%	0.8%
DOMINICAN REPUBLIC (8)	2.3%	2.2%
ESTONIA (9)	0.8%	1.6%
FINLAND (1)	0.5%	0.4%
FRANCE (1)	0.6%	0.7%
GERMANY (1)	0.7%	0.7%
GREECE (1)	1.9%	1.8%
HUNGARY (3)	2.1%	1.2%
ICELAND (2)	1.9%	1.3%
IRELAND (1)	1.1%	1.1%
ISRAEL (1)	3.8%	3.3%
ITALY (2)	1.0%	1.0%
JAPAN (1)	2.3%	2.3%

DATES OF COMPARISON

(1) 1993 + 2003
(2) 1994 + 2004
(3) 1995 + 2003
(4) 1994 + 2001
(5) 1995 + 1999
(6) 1994 + 2002
(7) 1996 + 1998
(8) 1992 + 1996
(9) 1994 + 2003
(10) 2000 + 2003

(11) 1994 + 2000
(12) 1992 + 2002
(13) 1996
(14) 1993 + 1996
(15) 1992 + 1997
(16) 1996 + 2004
(17) 1995 + 2004
(18) 1996 + 1999

% HOUSEHOLD SPENDING
ON RECREATION + CULTURE

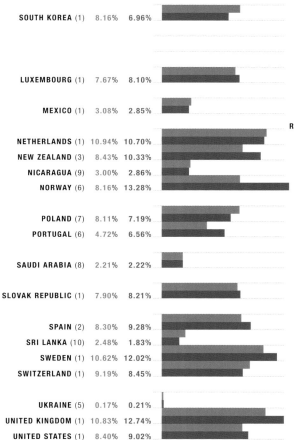

SOUTH KOREA (1)	8.16%	6.96%
LUXEMBOURG (1)	7.67%	8.10%
MEXICO (1)	3.08%	2.85%
NETHERLANDS (1)	10.94%	10.70%
NEW ZEALAND (3)	8.43%	10.33%
NICARAGUA (9)	3.00%	2.86%
NORWAY (6)	8.16%	13.28%
POLAND (7)	8.11%	7.19%
PORTUGAL (6)	4.72%	6.56%
SAUDI ARABIA (8)	2.21%	2.22%
SLOVAK REPUBLIC (1)	7.90%	8.21%
SPAIN (2)	8.30%	9.28%
SRI LANKA (10)	2.48%	1.83%
SWEDEN (1)	10.62%	12.02%
SWITZERLAND (1)	9.19%	8.45%
UKRAINE (5)	0.17%	0.21%
UNITED KINGDOM (1)	10.83%	12.74%
UNITED STATES (1)	8.40%	9.02%

% HOUSEHOLD SPENDING
ON EDUCATION

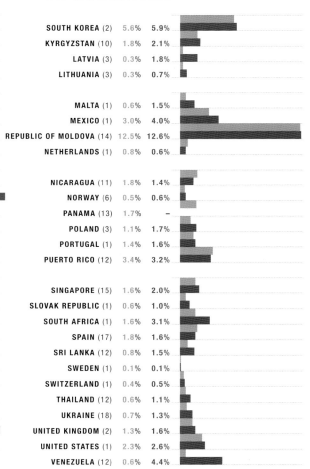

SOUTH KOREA (2)	5.6%	5.9%
KYRGYZSTAN (10)	1.8%	2.1%
LATVIA (3)	0.3%	1.8%
LITHUANIA (3)	0.3%	0.7%
MALTA (1)	0.6%	1.5%
MEXICO (1)	3.0%	4.0%
REPUBLIC OF MOLDOVA (14)	12.5%	12.6%
NETHERLANDS (1)	0.8%	0.6%
NICARAGUA (11)	1.8%	1.4%
NORWAY (6)	0.5%	0.6%
PANAMA (13)	1.7%	–
POLAND (3)	1.1%	1.7%
PORTUGAL (1)	1.4%	1.6%
PUERTO RICO (12)	3.4%	3.2%
SINGAPORE (15)	1.6%	2.0%
SLOVAK REPUBLIC (1)	0.6%	1.0%
SOUTH AFRICA (1)	1.6%	3.1%
SPAIN (17)	1.8%	1.6%
SRI LANKA (12)	0.8%	1.5%
SWEDEN (1)	0.1%	0.1%
SWITZERLAND (1)	0.4%	0.5%
THAILAND (12)	0.6%	1.1%
UKRAINE (18)	0.7%	1.3%
UNITED KINGDOM (2)	1.3%	1.6%
UNITED STATES (1)	2.3%	2.6%
VENEZUELA (12)	0.6%	4.4%

CULTURAL CONSUMPTION

Globalization changes cultural consumption patterns as it increases access to cultural goods and services of many kinds and from many providers. UNESCO and the OECD define private consumption expenditures of culture and recreation as spending on audiovisual equipment, newspapers and books, package holidays, and other recreational services.

However, this definition is problematic as it assumes a strict differentiation between the cultural and the non-cultural in classifying goods and services. Some countries, however, include expenditures on religion and similar activities or services as cultural spending. By contrast, expenditures serving purposes other than their cultural and recreational value, such as vehicles and furniture, tend to be excluded. The case is now being made that certain commodities are really purchased for their recreational or symbolic value and less for their functional value as a means of transport. The conflation of cultural and non-cultural consumption is becoming more frequent as producers of what were essentially non-cultural goods such as furniture or cars increasingly 'aestheticize' them by introducing arts, design and crafts elements to improve sales through product differentiation (see chapter by Scott in this volume). In sum, the definition of what constitutes cultural expenditure on consumption is somewhat imprecise, which impacts the interpretation of the information presented in the suite.

Private spending outweighs public spending on recreation and culture in all industrially developed countries that are included in this analysis (see figure below). While household consumption expenditures are relatively close for the US on the one hand and the three European countries on the other, the higher government expenditures in France, Germany and Italy suggest a greater role of the public sector.

A different picture emerges in spending on education. Government spending in this sector outweighs private spending in all countries in the analysis, including the United States (not shown), as the figure on the next page illustrates.

WHAT ARE THE TRENDS?

There is an increase in the share of cultural and recreational goods in the total private consumption basket among developed countries (see data point 1). With few exceptions, they have increased their share of cultural consumption over the ten-year span. Developing countries display a different trend. India, Azerbaijan, and Mexico, among others, have lowered their share of culture and recreation in total consumption. If sorted by real GDP per capita, the data point on cultural consumption patterns would illustrate a positive relation between real GDP per capita and the share of culture and recreation in consumption. In fact, the correlation coefficient between the percentage of household consumption of culture and real GDP per capita is 0.67.

Combining these patterns and trends, a diverging picture emerges. To some extent, the data suggest that poorer countries consume less culture and recreation privately, and that some are further decreasing their share. By contrast, trends in developed countries generally go in the opposite direction. Hence the global gap in terms of private consumption of culture and recreation is widening.

However, for household spending on education, the trends are not as easily spotted. In particular, the more developed countries are not moving in one single direction. While some, including Norway, Australia, and the United States, have increased their share of education in household expenditure, others, such as The Netherlands, Finland, and Spain, display a decreasing trend. Developing countries are generally increasing their educational shares in household spending with few exceptions. Some of these countries, including Venezuela, Colombia, and Botswana, actually show quite dramatic increases over the time span of the analysis.

WHAT ARE THE ISSUES?

There is disagreement among experts with respect to the private consumption of culture. On the one hand, critics of commercialized culture claim that popular culture leads to commodification and mass production. This then limits choice for the consumer

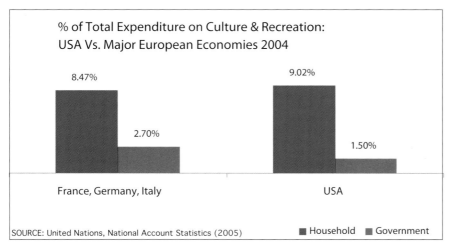

% of Total Expenditure on Culture & Recreation: USA Vs. Major European Economies 2004

8.47%   2.70%   France, Germany, Italy

9.02%   1.50%   USA

SOURCE: United Nations, National Account Statistics (2005)

■ Household   ■ Government

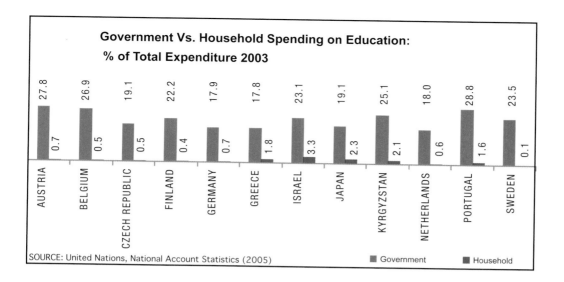

Government Vs. Household Spending on Education: % of Total Expenditure 2003

Country	Government	Household
AUSTRIA	27.8	0.7
BELGIUM	26.9	0.5
CZECH REPUBLIC	19.1	0.5
FINLAND	22.2	0.4
GERMANY	17.9	0.7
GREECE	17.8	1.8
ISRAEL	23.1	3.3
JAPAN	19.1	2.3
KYRGYZSTAN	25.1	2.1
NETHERLANDS	18.0	0.6
PORTUGAL	28.8	1.6
SWEDEN	23.5	0.1

SOURCE: United Nations, National Account Statistics (2005)   ■ Government   ■ Household

as niche markets are ignored because they are not commercially viable. This process, some claim, may lead to cultural dilution and the loss of indigenous cultural heritage.

A more recent counter-argument is that to be commercially viable, goods and services must become increasingly differentiated from competitors. Branding, thus, is essential to ensure the survival of a product in a saturated market. The result is that private markets will support diversity and niche markets, hence providing incentives for the private sector to be creative and to broaden the cultural spectrum.

Another issue that comes up is the effect that culture may have on those citizens who are not involved in the purchasing process. In other words, does culture display characteristics of a public good? If a consumer decides to buy a Play Station for her child, does this have an effect on the neighbor's children? And if so, can policy intervention in the private market help alleviate potential market failure caused by real or imagined negative externalities?

Cultural diversity and the need for protection of regional cultural heritage is a policy issue that arises with this pattern at the cross-national level. If the private sector determines the bulk of what culture is produced and consumed, do some countries run a risk of diluting their cultural heritage via 'Americanization' or 'Japanization'—given the unequal share of market forces involved? Some countries like China, Brazil, and South Africa are responding by creating a system of cultural heritage protection and promotion campaigns that seek to reconcile indigenous cultural and knowledge preservation by capitalizing on economic values and revenue generation.

The 'cultural exemption' in the World Trade Organization (WTO) has become a critical policy issue in this respect. In general, all goods and services to be traded by member countries are subject to policy obligations including that of national treatment, i.e., treating goods and services from other countries equal to those produced domestically, and the 'most favored nation' clause that is meant to ensure equal treatment of all trading partners. However, some European countries argued for a temporary ex-

emption of cultural goods, particularly in the audiovisual sector, from these obligations during the Uruguay round of negotiations of GATS. They did not agree to give cultural goods and services the same treatment as other goods and services, and thus, European audiovisual industries receive preferential treatment domestically.

These issues were also debated in the preparation of the 2005 Convention on the Protection and Promotion of the Diversity of Cultural Expressions (see chapter by Isar in this volume) which recognizes the sovereign right of States to frame and implement public policies to protect and promote cultural diversity. The Convention will no doubt strengthen the EU position in future negotiations, and support Canada's policy of some sort of cultural protection from what could easily become overwhelming market forces originating in the US.

Analysts generally agree more on the 'public good' nature of education. Public school systems have been established in most areas of the world. This may at least partially explain that government spending in the sector dominates private spending. Nevertheless disagreements exist with respect to how much education ought to be provided by the government and what role privately-funded education can play, particularly in the US, Japan and some European countries.

HERITAGE PRESERVATION

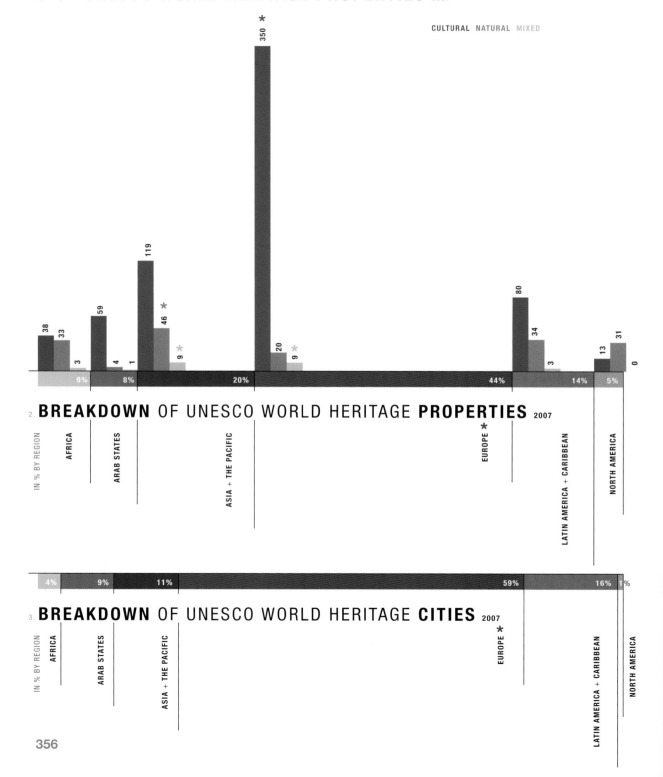

1. # OF UNESCO WORLD HERITAGE **PROPERTIES** 2007

CULTURAL NATURAL MIXED

350 *
119
59
46 *
38
33
20
9 *
80
34
31
13
4
3
1
9 *
3
0

9% 8% 20% 44% 14% 5%

2. **BREAKDOWN** OF UNESCO WORLD HERITAGE **PROPERTIES** 2007

IN % BY REGION

AFRICA | ARAB STATES | ASIA + THE PACIFIC | EUROPE * | LATIN AMERICA + CARIBBEAN | NORTH AMERICA

4% 9% 11% 59% 16% 1%

3. **BREAKDOWN** OF UNESCO WORLD HERITAGE **CITIES** 2007

IN % BY REGION

AFRICA | ARAB STATES | ASIA + THE PACIFIC | EUROPE * | LATIN AMERICA + CARIBBEAN | NORTH AMERICA

4. UNESCO WORLD HERITAGE **EXPENDITURES** v. **INCOME**

TOTAL INCOME TOTAL EXPENDITURE

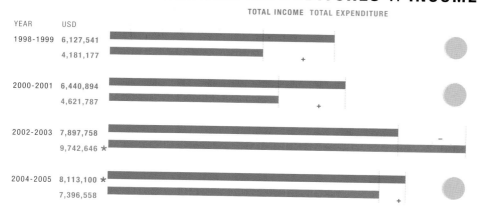

YEAR	USD
1998-1999	6,127,541
	4,181,177
2000-2001	6,440,894
	4,621,787
2002-2003	7,897,758
	9,742,646 ★
2004-2005	8,113,100 ★
	7,396,558

5. # OF ORAL + INTANGIBLE **HERITAGE MASTERPIECES** BY REGION + BY YEAR

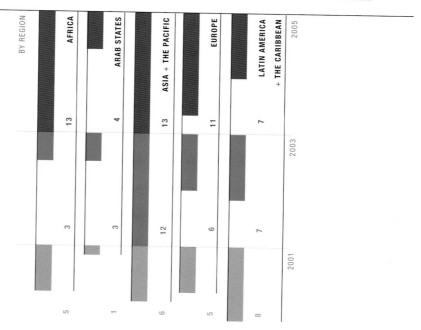

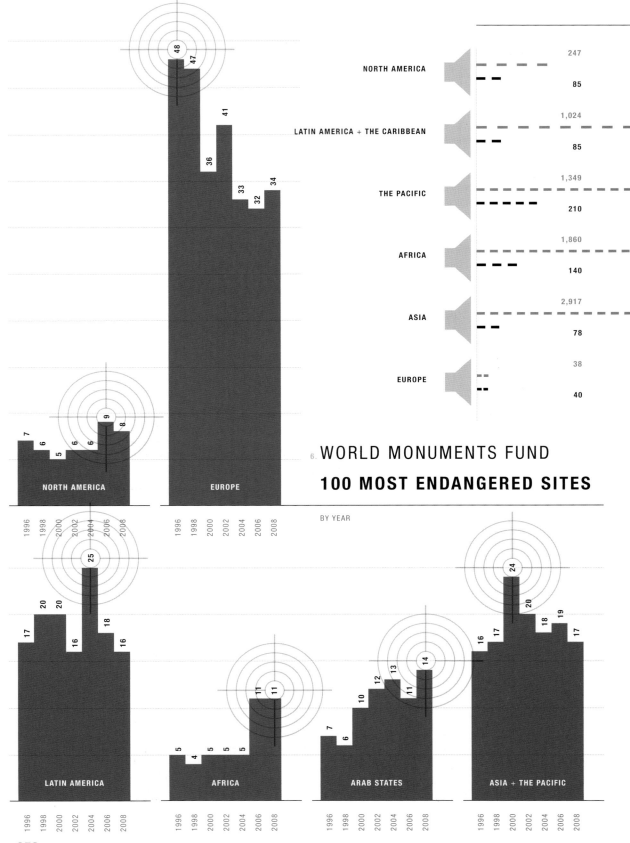

6. WORLD MONUMENTS FUND
100 MOST ENDANGERED SITES

BY YEAR

NORTH AMERICA — 247 / 85

LATIN AMERICA + THE CARIBBEAN — 1,024 / 85

THE PACIFIC — 1,349 / 210

AFRICA — 1,860 / 140

ASIA — 2,917 / 78

EUROPE — 38 / 40

NORTH AMERICA: 7, 6, 5, 6, 6, 9, 8

EUROPE: 48, 47, 36, 41, 33, 32, 34

LATIN AMERICA: 17, 20, 20, 16, 25, 18, 16

AFRICA: 5, 4, 5, 5, 5, 11, 11

ARAB STATES: 7, 6, 10, 12, 13, 11, 14

ASIA + THE PACIFIC: 16, 17, 24, 20, 18, 19, 17

ENDANGERED + LIVING **LANGUAGE COMPARISON** AS OF 2005

BY REGION   NON-ENDANGERED LANGUAGES   **ENDANGERED LANGUAGES***

* ENDANGERED LANGUAGES ARE DEFINED AS HAVING LESS THAN 500 SPEAKERS OR BEING EXTINCT.
YEARS OF DATA COLLECTION VARIED BY LANGUAGE; SEE SOURCE FOR EXACT DATES.

8. GENERAL OVERVIEW 2006-2007 PROGRAM + BUDGET 2006-2007
FOR THE **WORLD HERITAGE CONVENTION**

	WORLD HERITAGE FUND	OTHER UNESCO		OTHER TRUST FUND	TOTAL
		REGULAR BUDGET	SPECIAL ACCOUNT		
COORDINATION OF STATUTORY MEETINGS	2,808,150	651,250	0	411,587	3,870,987
PROMOTION OF A MORE BALANCED AND REPRESENTATIVE WORLD HERITAGE LIST	500,000	289,497	0	4,878,598	5,677,095
STRENGHTENING THE PROTECTION OF THE WORLD HERITAGE PROPERTIES, ESPECIALLY THE ENDANGERED SITES	2,948,686	1,574,100	167,592	30,294,454	34,984,832
SUPPORTING ACTIVITIES & GENERAL OPERATING EXPENSES	0	677,940	0	0	677,940
INTERNATIONAL ASSISTANCE - EMERGENCY	400,000	57,413	123,248	1,500,000	2,080,661
EARMARKED ACTIVITIES	243,915	0	0	0	243,915
TOTAL	6,900,751	3,259,200	290,840	37,084,639	47,535,430

3. **THE**

STATUE

OF ZEUS

THE WORK OF THE ATHENIAN
SCULPTOR PHIDIAS, CONSTRUCTED
INSIDE THE PANTHEON.

★ ITALY

4. **THE**

COLLOSUS

OF RHODES

A GIGANTIC BRONZE STATUE THAT ONCE
STOOD 32 METERS (110 FEET) HIGH ON
A MARBLE PLINTH.

6. **THE**

MAUSOLEUM

OF

HALICARNASSUS

THE MAUSOLEUM STOOD 50 METERS
HIGH AND WAS SURROUNDED BY 36
COLUMNS, STANDING ATOP A MARBLE
PEDESTAL.

★ GREECE

2. **THE**

TEMPLE

OF ARTEMIS

THE GREATEST TEMPLE OF
THE ANCIENT WORLD.

★ TURKEY

METHOD OF SELECTION:
ALL MAN-MADE MONUMENTS,
SELECTED BY PHILON OF BYZANTIUM
IN 200 B.C. TO ACT AS A TRAVEL
GUIDE FOR FELLOW ATHENIANS.

CRITICISMS:
1. NON-INCLUSIVE METHODS OF
CHOOSING THE 7 WONDERS.
2. REGIONALLY NARROW - WONDERS
ARE ONLY LOCATED IN THE
MEDITERRANEAN AND THE MIDDLE
EAST REGIONS.
3. OUTDATED AND DOES NOT
TAKE INTO ACCOUNT MORE
MODERN MAN-MADE WONDERS.

1. **THE**

LIGHTHOUSE

OF ALEXANDRIA

THE ONLY WONDER THAT SERVED
A PURPOSE.

7. **THE**

PYRAMIDS

OF EGYPT

THE ONLY SURVIVING WONDER OF
THE ANCIENT WORLD, THE PYRAMIDS
WERE THE PHENOMENAL ACHIEVEMENT
OF EGYPTIAN CONSTRUCTION
AND ENGINEERING.

★ EGYPT

5. **THE**

HANGING

GARDENS

OF BABYLON

A BOTANICAL OASIS OF BEAUTY AMID
A BLEAK DESERT LANDSCAPE.

★ IRAQ

2. COLOSSEUM IN ROME

THE DESIGN CONCEPT HAS BEEN INTEGRATED IN ALMOST EVERY MODERN SPORTS STADIUM AND STANDS AS A SYMBOL OF THE ROMAN EMPIRE.

★ ITALY

4. GREAT WALL OF CHINA

THE LARGEST MAN-MADE MONUMENT EVER TO HAVE BEEN BUILT.

★ CHINA

7. THE ANCIENT MAYA CITY OF CHICHÉN ITZÁ

THE MOST FAMOUS MAYAN TEMPLE CITY, SERVED AS THE POLITICAL AND ECONOMIC CENTER OF MAYAN CIVILIZATION.

★ MEXICO

METHOD OF SELECTION:
100 MILLION VOTERS FROM THE PUBLIC (THROUGH INTERNET AND PHONE) NOMINATED 77 SITES. NEXT THE N7W PANEL CHOSE 21 FINALISTS AND THESE WERE VOTED ON BY THE PUBLIC.

CRITICISMS:
1. WHILE MORE GEOGRAPHICALLY REPRESENTATIVE, STILL DOES NOT FEATURE ANY SITES FROM AFRICA.
2. THERE WAS NO FOOL-PROOF WAY TO GUARANTEE THAT VOTERS DID NOT VOTE MORE THAN ONCE.
3. NO SCIENTIFIC METHODS OR CRITERIA WERE INVOLVED IN THE NOMINATION OF SITES.
4. THE ORGANIZING FOUNDATION DID NOT TAKE IN ACCOUNT THE PO-TENTIAL THREAT THAT INCREASED TOURISM COULD POSE FOR THE NEWLY NAMED WONDERS.

6. THE INCA RUINS OF MACHU PICCHU

THE FORMER INCA CITY LIES HALFWAY UP THE ANDES PLATEAU, DEEP IN THE AMAZON JUNGLE AND ABOVE THE URUBAMBA RIVER.

★ PERU

1. CHRIST THE REDEEMER

THE STATUE OF JESUS STANDS 38 METERS TALL ATOP CORCOVADO MOUNTAIN OVERLOOKING RIO DE JANEIRO.

★ BRAZIL

5. THE ANCIENT CITY OF PETRA

THE GLITTERING CAPITAL OF THE NABATAEAN EMPIRE OF KING ARETAS IV (9 B.C. TO 40 A.D.)

★ JORDAN

3. TAJ MAHAL

BUILT OUT OF WHITE MARBLE AND STANDING IN FORMALLY LAID-OUT WALLED GARDENS, IT IS REGARDED AS THE MOST PERFECT JEWEL OF MUS-LIM ART IN INDIA.

★ INDIA

## 10

MATRIX OF 2007 **NEW WORLD HERITAGE PROPERTIES**

DATE OF INSCRIPTION 2007

EUROPE:	COUNTRY:	TYPE OF SITE:	CRITERIA:	DESCRIPTION:
BORDEAUX, PORT OF THE MOON	FRANCE	CULTURAL	(II) (IV)	AN INHABITED PORT CITY CREATED DURING THE TIME OF ENLIGHTENMENT.
GAMZIGRAD-ROMULIANA, PALACE OF GALERIUS	SERBIA	CULTURAL	(III) (IV)	A PALACE BUILT IN THE LATE THIRD, EARLY FOURTH CENTURY.
GOBUSTAN ROCK ART CULTURAL LANDSCAPE	AZERBAIJAN	CULTURAL	(III)	AN OUTSTANDING COLLECTION OF OVER 6,000 ROCK ENGRAVINGS OVER 4,000 YEARS OLD.
LAVAUX, VINEYARD TERRACE	SWITZERLAND	CULTURAL	(III) (IV) (V)	A WELL-PRESERVED VINEYARD AND SET OF BUILDINGS ORIGINATING IN THE 11TH CENTURY.
MEHMED PASA SOKOLOVIC BRIDGE OF VISEGRAD	BOSNIA + HERZEGOVINA	CULTURAL	(II) (IV)	A BRIDGE REPRESENTATIVE OF THE CLASSICAL OTTOMAN PERIOD.
OLD TOWN OF CORFU	GREECE	CULTURAL	(IV)	A TOWN LOCATED IN A STRATEGIC POSITION AT THE ENTRANCE OF THE ADRIATIC SEA.
THE PRIMEVAL BEECH FOREST OF THE CARPATHIAN	SLOVAKIA + UKRAINE	NATURAL	(IX)	TEMPERATE FORESTS AND THE MOST COMPLETE ECOLOGICAL PATTERNS OF PURE STANDS OF EUROPEAN BEECH.
TEIDE NATIONAL PARK	SPAIN	NATURAL	(VII) (VIII)	TEIDE NATIONAL PARK COVERS 18,990 HA AND FEATURES THE TEIDE-PICO VIEJO STRATOVOLCANO.
LATIN AMERICA + THE CARIBBEAN:				
CENTRAL UNIVERSITY CITY CAMPUS OF THE UNIVERSIDAD DE NACIONAL AUTÓNOMA DE MÉXICO (UNAM)	MEXICO	CULTURAL	(I) (II) (IV)	A UNIQUE CAMPUS EXAMPLE OF 20TH CENTURY MODERNIST DESIGN.
ASIA + THE PACIFIC:				
IWAMI GINZAN SILVER MINE	JAPAN	CULTURAL	(II) (III) (V)	A CLUSTER OF MOUNTAINS AND RIVER VALLEYS FEATURING THE ARCHAEOLOGICAL REMAINS OF LARGE SCALE MINES.
KAIPING DIAOLOU AND VILLAGE	CHINA	CULTURAL	(II) (III) (IV)	DEFENSIVE VILLA HOUSES THAT DISPLAY A FUSION OF CHINESE AND WESTERN STRUCTURAL FORMS.

	COUNTRY:	TYPE OF SITE:	CRITERIA:	DESCRIPTION:
PARTHIAN FORTRESSES OF NISA	TURKMENISTAN	CULTURAL	(II) (III)	ONE OF THE EARLIEST AND MOST IMPORTANT CITIES OF THE PARTHIAN EMPIRE.
RED FORT COMPLEX	INDIA	CULTURAL	(II) (III) (VI)	CONSIDERED TO REPRESENT THE ZENITH OF MUGHAL CREATIVITY.
SAMARRA ARCHAEOLOGICAL CITY	IRAQ	CULTURAL	(II) (III) (IV)	A POWERFUL ISLAMIC CAPITAL CITY WHICH RULED OVER THE PROVINCES OF THE ABBASID EMPIRE.
SYDNEY OPERA HOUSE	AUSTRALIA	CULTURAL	(I)	A GREAT URBAN SCULPTURE SET IN A REMARKABLE WATERSCAPE. BUILT IN 1973.
JEJU VOLCANIC ISLAND AND LAVA TUBES	REPUBLIC OF KOREA	NATURAL	(VII) (VIII)	FINEST LAVA TUBE SYSTEM OF CAVES ANYWHERE AND MOUNT HALLASAN, THE HIGHEST IN KOREA.
THE SOUTH CHINA KARST	CHINA	NATURAL	(VII) (VIII)	ONE OF THE WORLD'S MOST SPECTACULAR EXAMPLES OF HUMID TROPICAL TO SUB-TROPICAL KARST LANDSCAPES.

AFRICA:

	COUNTRY:	TYPE OF SITE:	CRITERIA:	DESCRIPTION:
RICHTERSVELD CULTURAL AND BOTANICAL LANDSCAPE	SOUTH AFRICA	CULTURAL	(IV) (V)	SUSTAINS THE SEMI-NOMADIC PASTORAL LIVELIHOOD OF THE NAMA PEOPLE.
TWYFELFONTEIN OR /UI-//AES	NAMIBIA	CULTURAL	(III) (V)	ONE OF THE LARGEST COLLECTIONS OF ROCK PETROGLYPHS, OVER 2,000 DOCUMENTED TO DATE.
THE RAINFORESTS OF THE ATSINANANA	MADAGASCAR	NATURAL	(IX) (X)	INSCRIBED FOR THEIR BIODIVERSITY AND THE THREATENED SPECIES THEY SUPPORT ESPECIALLY FOR FAUNA AND PRIMATES.
THE ECOSYSTEM AND RELICT CULTURAL LANDSCAPE OF LOPÉ-OKANDA	GABON	MIXED	(III) (IV) (IX) (X)	INTERFACE BETWEEN DENSE TROPICAL RAINFOREST AND RELICT SAVANNAH ENVIRONMENTS.

NORTH AMERICA:

	COUNTRY:	TYPE OF SITE:	CRITERIA:	DESCRIPTION:
RIDEAU CANAL	CANADA	CUTURAL	(I) (IV)	ONE OF THE FIRST CANALS TO BE DESIGNED SPECIFICALLY FOR STEAM-POWERED VESSELS.

SELECTION CRITERIA:

I.   TO REPRESENT A MASTERPIECE OF HUMAN CREATIVE GENIUS;

II.   TO EXHIBIT AN IMPORTANT INTERCHANGE OF HUMAN VALUES,
OVER A SPAN OF TIME OR WITHIN A CULTURAL AREA OF THE WORLD, ON
DEVELOPMENTS IN ARCHITECTURE OR TECHNOLOGY, MONUMENTAL ARTS,
TOWN-PLANNING OR LANDSCAPE DESIGN;

III.   TO BEAR A UNIQUE OR AT LEAST EXCEPTIONAL TESTIMONY TO
A CULTURAL TRADITION OR TO A CIVILIZATION WHICH IS LIVING OR WHICH
HAS DISAPPEARED;

IV.   TO BE AN OUTSTANDING EXAMPLE OF A TYPE OF BUILDING,
ARCHITECTURAL OR TECHNOLOGICAL ENSEMBLE OR LANDSCAPE WHICH
ILLUSTRATES (A) SIGNIFICANT STAGE(S) IN HUMAN HISTORY;

V.   TO BE AN OUTSTANDING EXAMPLE OF A TRADITIONAL HUMAN
SETTLEMENT, LAND-USE, OR SEA-USE WHICH IS REPRESENTATIVE OF
A CULTURE (OR CULTURES), OR HUMAN INTERACTION WITH THE
ENVIRONMENT ESPECIALLY WHEN IT HAS BECOME VULNERABLE UNDER THE
IMPACT OF IRREVERSIBLE CHANGE;

VI.   TO BE DIRECTLY OR TANGIBLY ASSOCIATED WITH EVENTS
OR LIVING TRADITIONS, WITH IDEAS, WITH BELIEFS, OR WITH ARTISTIC
AND LITERARY WORKS OF OUTSTANDING UNIVERSAL SIGNIFICANCE (THE
COMMITTEE CONSIDERS THAT THIS CRITERION SHOULD PREFERABLY BE
USED IN CONJUNCTION WITH OTHER CRITERIA);

VII.   TO CONTAIN SUPERLATIVE PHENOMENA OR AREAS OF
EXCEPTIONAL NATURAL BEAUTY AND AESTHETIC IMPORTANCE;

VIII.   TO BE OUTSTANDING EXAMPLES REPRESENTING MAJOR STAGES
OF EARTH'S HISTORY, INCLUDING THE RECORD OF LIFE, SIGNIFICANT ON-
GOING GEOLOGICAL PROCESSES IN THE DEVELOPMENT OF LANDFORMS, OR
SIGNIFICANT GEOMORPHIC OR PHYSIOGRAPHIC FEATURES;

IX.   TO BE OUTSTANDING EXAMPLES REPRESENTING SIGNIFICANT
ON-GOING ECOLOGICAL AND BIOLOGICAL PROCESSES IN THE EVOLUTION
AND DEVELOPMENT OF TERRESTRIAL, FRESH WATER, COASTAL AND MARINE
ECOSYSTEMS AND COMMUNITIES OF PLANTS AND ANIMALS;

X.   TO CONTAIN THE MOST IMPORTANT AND SIGNIFICANT
NATURAL HABITATS FOR IN-SITU CONSERVATION OF BIOLOGICAL DIVERSITY,
INCLUDING THOSE CONTAINING THREATENED SPECIES OF OUTSTANDING
UNIVERSAL VALUE FROM THE POINT OF VIEW OF SCIENCE OR CONSERVATION.

THE PROTECTION, MANAGEMENT, AUTHENTICITY AND INTEGRITY OF
PROPERTIES ARE ALSO IMPORTANT CONSIDERATIONS.

SINCE 1992 SIGNIFICANT INTERACTIONS BETWEEN PEOPLE AND THE
NATURAL ENVIRONMENT HAVE BEEN RECOGNIZED AS **CULTURAL LANDSCAPES**.

HERITAGE PRESERVATION

Heritage preservation has become a global phenomenon and, in close alliance with tourism, the 'heritage industry' is now a major player in the cultural economy. The heritage preservation movement was born in Western Europe, where it was driven by social and economic developments over several centuries that transformed the relationships of societies to their pasts (Lowenthal, 1985). Material culture inherited from those pasts gradually became building blocks of collective memory and identity-building—and of deliberate destruction when targeted precisely because it embodies both (cf. Viejo Rose, 2007). In the late twentieth century, the scope of heritage preservation expanded exponentially and the preservationist outlook became a global one.

Both trends were driven by the work of an intergovernmental organization, UNESCO, which in 1972 established the notion of a 'world cultural and natural heritage' of 'outstanding universal value' that is the common property of humankind (http://whc.unesco.org/en/about/). But this was 'heritage' in its tangible forms alone, and the terms in which 'outstanding universal value' was defined were exclusionary in several ways. Burgeoning demand from all quarters for broader recognition of the diversity of heritage led gradually, in 2003, to the adoption at UNESCO of the Convention for the Safeguarding of the Intangible Cultural Heritage, designed to protect and promote '…the practices, representations, expressions, knowledge, skills—as well as the instruments, objects, artefacts and cultural spaces associated therewith—that communities, groups and, in some cases, individuals, recognise as part of their cultural heritage' (Isar, 2004; UNESCO, n.d.).

WHAT DO WE LEARN ABOUT WORLD/INTANGIBLE HERITAGE?

The data suite informs us about these developments rather than about the economic dimensions of heritage preservation worldwide. It confirms that UNESCO-designated World Heritage Sites are located predominantly in Europe while Oral and Intangible Heritage Masterpieces are mostly found in the Asia-Pacific region (see data points 1, 2 and 5).

• Europe is the most represented region on UNESCO's World Heritage List and list of World Heritage Cities, with 44 per cent and close to 60 per cent of the properties respectively; Asia and Latin America follow, but significantly behind.

• Africa has made the greatest advances in the number of Masterpieces of the Oral and Intangible Heritage of Humanity, nearly doubling the number inscribed in 2005 as compared to 2001 and 2003 combined (see data point 5).

• The greatest number of languages, key elements of 'intangible heritage,' is found in Asia (2,995) while the greatest number of endangered languages is located in the Pacific region with 210 (see data point 7).

SOME ISSUES SURROUNDING THE PRESERVATION OF TANGIBLE HERITAGE

Who decides what constitutes tangible heritage; what should be preserved for future generations and what will be forgotten and left unprotected? These are fundamental questions. In the World

Heritage context, the questions have turned on the notion of 'outstanding universal value,' the basis on which a given cultural or natural property is deemed a 'legacy for all.' UNESCO's criteria of excellence were developed by architectural conservators from Western Europe and North America, all working with a largely 'monuments and sites' notion, based on the kinds of properties that in these regions have survived the ravages of time to be recognized as 'heritage.' This led inevitably to a privileging of sites located in Europe and to the neglect of other regions, notably Africa. Awareness of this imbalance was a decisive factor in the elaboration of the 'intangible heritage' concept, one that could be much more broadly inclusive. Although the ideas are now truly global, the process emerged from the nation-state system, at a time when governments are increasingly 'sensitive to the value of publicly asserting the value of their national cultures in various forums that bestow and reflect international prestige' (Kurin, 2004).

UNESCO's World Heritage Committee also maintains a 'World Heritage in Danger' list. While Europe has by far the highest numbers of sites in danger, since 1996 the number of endangered sites has fallen steadily even though the majority of UNESCO heritage sites are still located in Europe. Contrastingly, Africa has had the lowest number of World Heritage properties but has shown a steady increase in the number of endangered sites. Many of these are nature reserves (e.g., all the five sites in the Democratic Republic of the Congo) increasingly threatened by poaching and other incursions resulting from turmoil, conflict and large-scale population movements that impoverished governments cannot combat adequately for sheer lack of resources and manpower. Since inscription on the danger brings a higher level of funding, some governments are quite sanguine about their sites being thus categorized, while others are shamed by such a situation. For its part, the World Monuments Fund, an American not-for-profit organization, has with the support of the American Express Foundation created the 'World Monuments Watch List of 100 Most Endangered Sites.'

Indeed, many of the gravest dangers are man-made. According to ARCH (http://www.arch.at/), a cultural conservation organization, 'negative human impact is directly responsible for the loss of over 50 per cent of the world's cultural heritage during the past century.' According to the World Monuments Fund (see data point 6), almost 70 per cent of its endangered sites are in jeopardy for reasons that are attributable to human impact, with only 10 per cent endangered by natural reasons and the remainder of sites threatened by some combination of the two. Many of the specific human-related dangers cited were related to unsustainable levels of tourism, destruction from other forms of development, both residential and industrial, various states of armed conflict, and insufficient funds for preservation.

The pressure of tourism on heritage sites (see also indicator suite on cultural tourism) is a complex issue addressed by UNESCO, other international bodies, and national governments. Getting local properties listed as World Heritage has become part and parcel of place-marketing and local tourism development. But the blessings are mixed. Chinese officials have expressed concern at the naming of the Great Wall, not only as World Heritage but also as a new 'Wonder' (see below), because the ever larger numbers of tourists who flock to it each year are straining its carrying capacity to the limit. In Mexico, archaeologists are worried about the state of the Mayan ruins at Chichen Itza (BBC News, July 7, 2007).

A recent development that is emblematic of the globalized cult of heritage was the July 2007 announcement of the 'New Seven Wonders of the World.' This initiative, funded by a Swiss private foundation, was touted to be the first ever global election for choosing heritage sites (see data point 9). Mainly because of the lack of a scientific framework guiding the ranking and analysis, UNESCO did not participate in the project (Telegraph.co.uk, July 9, 2007)—but obviously it challenged the primacy of the already state-sponsored World Heritage system. Other critics charged that voting was unregulated, and possibly allowed for multiple votes to be cast by the same voter. There were also reports that certain countries went to great lengths to influence citizens to vote on behalf of their national, nominated 'wonder.' For example, China's Academy of the Great Wall encouraged voters to flood the Seven Wonders website; Brazil promoted votes by printing messages on bus tickets and an Indian singer dedicated a song to the Taj Mahal (Smith, July 8, 2007).

THE INTERNET + THE CULTURAL COMMONS

1. % GROWTH OF VISITORS TO **SOCIAL NETWORKING SITES** 2005-2006

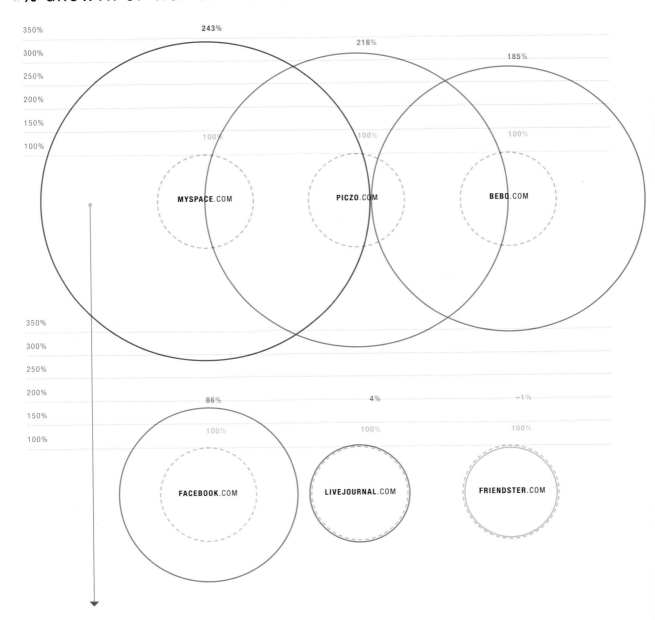

243%

216%

185%

350%
300%
250%
200%
150%
100%

100%   100%   100%

MYSPACE.COM   PICZO.COM   BEBO.COM

350%
300%
250%
200%
150%
100%

86%   4%   −1%

100%   100%   100%

FACEBOOK.COM   LIVEJOURNAL.COM   FRIENDSTER.COM

2. **MYSPACE** BREAKDOWN BY COMPONENT APRIL 2006

71.4% PROFILES   6.0% FORUM POSTS

13.0% BLOGS   1.3% GROUPS

7.0% CLASSIFIED LISTINGS   1.3% BAND PROFILES

OF UNIQUE VISITORS TO **SOCIAL NETWORKING SITES** IN MILLIONS AUGUST 2006

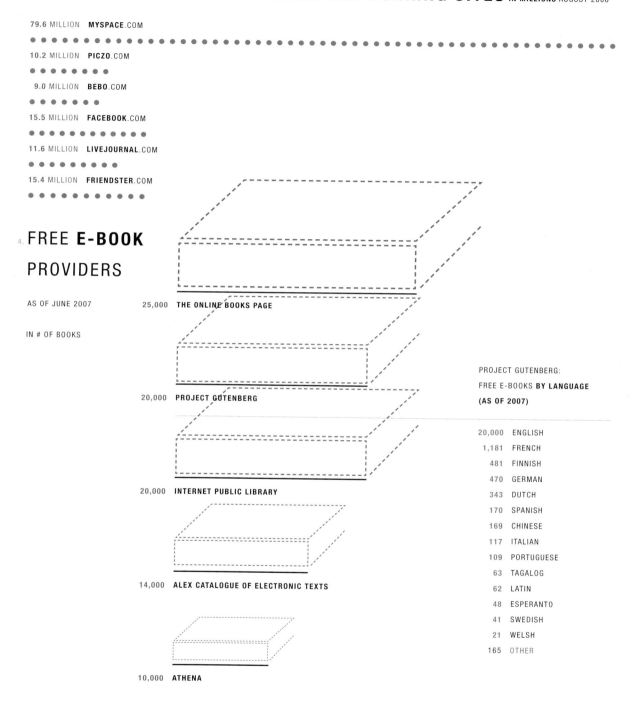

79.6 MILLION **MYSPACE**.COM

10.2 MILLION **PICZO**.COM

9.0 MILLION **BEBO**.COM

15.5 MILLION **FACEBOOK**.COM

11.6 MILLION **LIVEJOURNAL**.COM

15.4 MILLION **FRIENDSTER**.COM

4. FREE **E-BOOK**
PROVIDERS

AS OF JUNE 2007

IN # OF BOOKS

25,000 **THE ONLINE BOOKS PAGE**

20,000 **PROJECT GUTENBERG**

20,000 **INTERNET PUBLIC LIBRARY**

14,000 **ALEX CATALOGUE OF ELECTRONIC TEXTS**

10,000 **ATHENA**

2,100 **UNIVERSITY OF VIRGINIA LIBRARY**

PROJECT GUTENBERG:
FREE E-BOOKS **BY LANGUAGE**
(AS OF 2007)

20,000	ENGLISH
1,181	FRENCH
481	FINNISH
470	GERMAN
343	DUTCH
170	SPANISH
169	CHINESE
117	ITALIAN
109	PORTUGUESE
63	TAGALOG
62	LATIN
48	ESPERANTO
41	SWEDISH
21	WELSH
165	OTHER

5. TOP 50 **YOUTUBE VIDEOS** % BY CATEGORY (AS OF JUNE 2007)

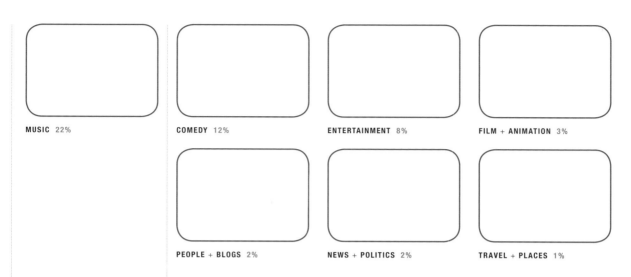

MUSIC 22%

COMEDY 12%

ENTERTAINMENT 8%

FILM + ANIMATION 3%

PEOPLE + BLOGS 2%

NEWS + POLITICS 2%

TRAVEL + PLACES 1%

6. TOP 30 **MOST VIEWED** YOUTUBE VIDEOS

BY **LANGUAGE** + TYPE (AS OF JUNE 2007)

MUSIC VIDEOS		OTHER	
15	FRENCH	15	FRENCH
15	CHINESE	15	CHINESE
7	GERMAN	23	GERMAN
4	JAPANESE	26	JAPANESE
17	SPANISH	13	SPANISH
13	ENGLISH	17	ENGLISH

7. % **P2P USERS** IN TOTAL POPULATION

TOP 10 COUNTRIES (AS OF APRIL 2006)

LUXEMBOURG	11.70%
ICELAND	7.60%
FINLAND	3.70%
NORWAY	2.70%
IRELAND	2.60%
UNITED STATES	2.60%
AUSTRIA	2.50%
HUNGARY	1.90%
BELGIUM	1.60%
CZECH REPUBLIC	1.50%

8. % OF TOTAL **P2P NETWORK USERS**

BY COUNTRY (AS OF APRIL 2006)

1.5%	BELGIUM
1.7%	HUNGARY
1.7%	FINLAND
1.8%	SPAIN
1.8%	AUSTRIA
3.2%	UNITED KINGDOM
3.2%	CANADA
3.5%	FRANCE
4.8%	GERMANY
66.2%	UNITED STATES
10.6%	OTHER

GLOBAL USE OF **PEER-TO-PEER NETWORKS**

BY SIMULTANEOUS AUDIENCE AT PEAK VOLUMES **(IN MILLIONS)**

AUGUST, 2002	3.6334
SEPTEMBER, 2002	4.3459
OCTOBER, 2002	4.9777
NOVEMBER, 2002	5.5134
DECEMBER, 2002	5.3764
JANUARY, 2003	7.0915
FEBRUARY, 2003	7.1458
MARCH, 2003	7.3347
APRIL, 2003	7.1089
MAY, 2003	7.1970
JUNE, 2003	6.8181
JULY, 2003	6.5341
AUGUST, 2003	6.2945
SEPTEMBER, 2003	7.3993
OCTOBER, 2003	8.7591
NOVEMBER, 2003	7.6809
DECEMBER, 2003	8.6711
JANUARY, 2004	8.7672
FEBRUARY, 2004	8.8888
MARCH, 2004	9.4539
APRIL, 2004	9.4738
MAY, 2004	9.2796
JUNE, 2004	8.3243
JULY, 2004	8.2408
AUGUST, 2004	7.7719
SEPTEMBER, 2004	7.9876
OCTOBER, 2004	8.0300
NOVEMBER, 2004	8.8311
DECEMBER, 2004	9.6339
JANUARY, 2005	9.9768
FEBRUARY, 2005	10.0795
MARCH, 2005	10.1030
APRIL, 2005	10.3848
MAY, 2005	10.3271
JUNE, 2005	11.1732
JULY, 2005	12.3553
AUGUST, 2005	12.1258
SEPTEMBER, 2005	12.0096
OCTOBER, 2005	12.0162
NOVEMBER, 2005	11.3051
DECEMBER, 2005	11.2206
JANUARY, 2006	11.6032
FEBRUARY, 2006	11.4849
MARCH, 2006	11.4750

KANEVA.COM

54.1%	UNITED STATES	||||||||||||||||||||||||||||||||||||||||||||||||||||||||||||||||
5.4%	GERMANY	||||||||||||||||||
3.1%	UNITED KINGDOM	||||||||||
2.8%	FRANCE	|||||||||
1.9%	ROMANIA	||||||||
1.8%	AUSTRALIA	||||||||
1.6%	EGYPT	||||||
1.5%	SAUDI ARABIA	||||||
1.0%	CANADA	||||
1.0%	PERU	||||

MOOVE.COM

30.8%	UNITED STATES	||||||||||||||||||||||||||||||||||||||||||||||||||||||||||||||||||
12.3%	GERMANY	|||||||||||||||||||||||||||||
5.4%	BRAZIL	||||||||||||||||||
3.8%	TURKEY	|||||||||||
3.8%	CANADA	|||||||||||
3.1%	CROATIA	||||||||||
2.3%	ISRAEL	|||||||||
2.3%	HUNGARY	|||||||||
2.3%	AUSTRIA	|||||||||
2.3%	UNITED KINGDOM	|||||||||

THERE.COM

30.9%	UNITED STATES	||||||||||||||||||||||||||||||||||||||||||||||||||||||||||||||||
5.7%	UNITED KINGDOM	|||||||||||||||||||||
4.6%	PHILIPPINES	||||||||||||||||||
3.4%	GERMANY	||||||||||||
2.9%	CANADA	|||||||||||
2.3%	AUSTRALIA	|||||||||
2.3%	NETHERLANDS	|||||||||
2.3%	FRANCE	|||||||||
2.3%	MALAYSIA	|||||||||
2.3%	BRAZIL	|||||||||

ACTIVEWORLDS.COM

37.2%	UNITED STATES	||||||||||||||||||||||||||||||||||||||||||||||||||||||||||||||||||||||
19.4%	UNITED KINGDOM	||||||||||||||||||||||||||||||||||||||||||
3.1%	GERMANY	||||||||||
3.1%	CROATIA	||||||||||
2.6%	NETHERLANDS	|||||||||
2.6%	CANADA	|||||||||
2.1%	ISRAEL	||||||||
1.6%	ROMANIA	||||||
1.6%	PORTUGAL	||||||
1.6%	INDIA	||||||

SECONDLIFE.COM

21.0%	UNITED STATES	|||||||||||||||||||||||||||||||||||||||||||||||
9.0%	JAPAN	|||||||||||||||||||||||||||||
8.2%	GERMANY	||||||||||||||||||||||||||
5.3%	FRANCE	||||||||||||||||||
5.3%	UNITED KINGDOM	||||||||||||||||||
4.9%	ITALY	|||||||||||||||
4.3%	SPAIN	|||||||||||||
4.1%	BRAZIL	|||||||||||||
2.5%	PORTUGAL	||||||||||
2.5%	CANADA	||||||||||

VIRTUAL WORLD SITES: BUSINESS MATRIX

NAME / START DATE / BASED IN / CREATOR	BUSINESS MODEL	NOTES
SECOND LIFE 2003 SAN FRANCISCO, CA, UNITED STATES **LINDEN RESEARCH, INC.** **PHILIP ROSEDALE**	SELLS ADVERTISING SPACE AND UPGRADED MEMBERSHIPS, REVENUE ALSO FROM CURRENCY EXCHANGE	_OVER 7 MILLION RESIDENTS _AN AVERAGE OF 302,000 RESIDENTS ARE SPENDING MONEY IN SECOND LIFE
THERE OCTOBER 2003 SILICON VALLEY, CA, UNITED STATES **WILL HARVEY** **JEFFREY VENTRELLA**	SELLS ADVERTISING SPACE, CORPORATE PARTNERSHIPS, SELLS UPGRADED MEMBERSHIPS AS WELL AS FREE BASIC, REVENUE FROM CURRENCY EXCHANGE	_CONTAINS 12 MAJOR ISLANDS, 500,000 INHABITANTS, AND BUSINESSES _USES THEREBUCKS (TBUX) AS CURRENCY _CONTRACT WITH MTV FOR VIRTUAL LAGUNA BEACH _BILLED AS 'ONLINE HANGOUT' _DEVELOPER PROGRAM ALLOWS YOU TO DESIGN AND BUILD YOUR OWN PROJECTS TO SELL
THERE PHILIPPINES **2005-2006** SILICON VALLEY, CA, UNITED STATES **THERE.COM**	SIMILAR TO 'THERE' BUT BUSINESS MODEL STILL TO BE DETERMINED	_OPERATES MAINLY OUT OF CAFES IN THE PHILIPPINES _CAN'T TAKE CREDIT CARDS DUE TO HIGH LEVELS OF FRAUD
MOOVE 2001 COLOGNE, GERMANY **LOTHAR BONGARTZ** **DR. A. BURAK KOZAN**	SELLS ADVERTISING SPACE, SELLS UPGRADED MEMBERSHIP AS WELL AS FREE BASIC	_MAINLY FOR SOCIAL NETWORKING, CHAT, DATING, INTERIOR DESIGN _ SHOPPING BUT NO SELLING
ACTIVE WORLDS 1997 NEWBURYPORT, MA UNITED STATES **RON BRITVICH**	SELLS MEMBERSHIPS TO ACTIVE WORLDS, SELLS SOFTWARE LICENSES TO BUSINESSES, E-COMMERCE	_ACTS AS A MARKETPLACE FOR 3D ART _ALLOWS FOR BUILDING, CHAT, TRAVELLING, AND SHOPPING _CAN BE A TRAVELER, CITIZEN OR A WORLD OWNER
DOTSOUL 2006 _ _ **JOSEPH BERGERON** **LAURA HERRMANN**	DOES NOT RUN ON A REVENUE- PRODUCING MODEL, DONATION BASED	_DESIGNED TO FACILITATE THE RELEASE OF PEOPLE'S SUBCONSCIOUS _GOAL OF THE PARK IS TO CREATE A DREAMSCAPE OR PLAYGROUND OF THE MIND _REFERRED TO AS THE GREENWICH VILLAGE OF THE INTERNET _OPEN ARCHITECTURE SO THAT THE CONTENT IS DEPENDENT ON THE USERS _NO COSTS FOR USERS
KANEVA 2006 ATLANTA, GEORGIA UNITED STATES **CHRISTOPHER KLA**	SELLS ADVERTISING SPACE, IN- WORLD SHOPPING	_FIRST VIRTUAL WORLD TO UNIFY 2D WEB WITH THE 3D GAME EXPERIENCE _COMBINES VIDEO SHARING _CATERS TO MORE MAINSTREAM BRANDING, E.G., FOR BIG COMPANIES
ENTROPIA UNIVERSE _ GOTHEBURG, SWEDEN **MINDARK**	CURRENCY EXCHANGE, IN-WORLD E-COMMERCE, AND LICENSING, NO MEMBERSHIPS OR SOFTWARE FEES	_OVER 580,000 PLAYERS
CHINESE VERSION (BEIJING COMP.—CYBER RECREATION DEVELOPMENT CORP. USING MINDARK'S TECH.) **AUGUST 2008** CHINA **MINDARK**	SIMILAR TO ENTROPIA UNIVERSE	_WILL BE ABLE TO HANDLE 7 MILLION PLAYERS SIMULTANEOUSLY _CONSISTS OF SEVERAL 'CHINESE' PLANETS WITHIN A UNIVERSE

THE INTERNET & THE CULTURAL COMMONS

With the ongoing expansion of Internet usage, accompanied by technological advances in communication, file sharing and storage, the idea of an electronic global commons has become both a reality and a horizon for significant expansion. Never before have cultural creators been able to feature such a wide range of work in a commons that includes visual, written, audio, 2D and 3D—all posted in an electronic forum accessible to a potential audience of millions around the world. The 'emancipatory effect of technology' (see the Drache and chapter by Froese in this volume) increases access to a wide range of Internet-based projects including online libraries, virtual worlds where artists and designers showcase new creations, sites for music file sharing among millions of users, and multilingual video sites.

WHAT IS THE CULTURAL COMMONS?

The concept of the 'commons' refers to spaces that provide unrestricted access to the public. Drache and Froese define the cultural commons as 'that portion of culture that remains in the public domain, in which artists, as individuals and citizens, exchange ideas and promote creativity.' With the development and greater application of copyright law, and international treaties such as the Agreement on Trade Related Aspects of Intellectual Property Rights (TRIPS), private ownership and access to cultural goods have become much more regulated (Gordon-Murnane, 2005). By contrast, the cultural commons is less institutionalized and regulated, and remains as more an aspiration than a reality.

WHAT DO WE KNOW ABOUT THE CULTURAL COMMONS?

While the cultural commons has increased overall access to cultural goods, the data show that different cultural communities are neither represented nor participate in it equally:

• Online free access to full-text e-books is on the rise with projects such as Project Gutenberg and The Online Books Page (see data point 4).
• The US has the highest per cent of P2P users. However, when looking at the per cent of total P2P users within the total population of a country, a different trend emerges, with Luxembourg, Iceland and Finland on top (see data points 7 and 8).
• Despite the legal challenges filed against many P2P file sharing sites global use has been consistently on the rise between 2002 and 2006 (see data point 9). File sharing sites have used various strategies to avoid being shut down, such as conforming (partially) to copyright law or incorporating themselves in countries with less-stringent copyright and enforcement policies.
• Several of the most popular virtual world sites show multiregional representation in global usership across Europe, the Middle East, Latin America, and the Asia-Pacific region (see data point 10). However, Africa is notably absent from the top ten usership countries for any of the sites.
• Seven of the nine virtual world sites profiled originate in Europe or the United States (see data point 11).

WHAT ARE THE ISSUES?

The primary issue that emerges is that of private versus common ownership. This issue has been debated by scholars, economists and historians since the term 'commons' originated (Ostrom and Hess, 2001). The efficient use of resources in cultural commons (due to the free-rider problem) and the maintenance of the commons in the absence of both private and governmental oversight are at the heart of this debate. In the case of the cultural commons, there are specific issues around artist compensation, market-driven cultural creation and the manner in which competition fuels creativity.

The neo-liberal argument for the protection of intellectual property rights advocates paid compensation to creators of cultural goods in order to provide market-driven incentives for increased competition, which would raise the bar in terms of innovation and the quality of goods and services produced. This argument maintains that without market-driven competition, the cultural industries would stagnate. Conversely, the commons argument maintains that cultural goods are created and accessed by the public not just as paid-for commodities, but as integral pieces of information and of identities, thus removing the need for cultural goods to be located within the commercial economy (Lessig, 2004). In fact, the commons provides a space for non-market driven cultural goods and services which allows for increased innovation and creativity that the market would not normally support through demand alone.

However, allowing for unfettered access to cultural goods through the elimination of any form of compensation to artists would only serve to limit the pool of people who are able to create and provide cultural goods/services to those with substantial external resources. One possible solution to the question of culture as a public good or a commodity lies with a more flexible framework for copyright law as pertaining to intellectual property rights that would allow cultural creators to exact compensation but not charge unnecessarily in order to allow for increased public access (see the chapter by Frances Pinter in this volume).

Another major issue emerging from the indicator suite is the heavy use of the Internet as a vehicle to create and maintain space for open and free cultural exchange of ideas, goods and services. Significant barriers still prevent certain populations from participating in this rapidly changing cultural debate. Around the world, people living in rural areas, the urban poor and women and girls are prevented by a lack of resources and by cultural norms from accessing the Internet and, thus, the newly emerging electronic cultural commons.

The *user-generated content* movement, or the *open source* movement, is one of the primary technological underpinnings of the cultural commons. Broadly defined, user-generated content refers to media forms that are created by the audience/end-users. User-generated content forms the basis of 'commons' websites such as YouTube, Project Gutenberg, MySpace, Second Life, and many others. Such virtual worlds' sites take open source to a new level where users create their own virtual worlds, from landscapes to interior design and to forming visual representation of themselves. As shown by the suite, virtual world sites are leading the way in internationally diverse usership as compared to other cultural commons sites.

INDICATOR SUITE

CULTURES AS ECONOMIC SYSTEMS OF PRODUCTION, DISTRIBUTION + COMMUNICATION

CORPORATIONS + ORGANIZATIONS

06. **TRANSNATIONAL CULTURAL CORPORATIONS**

07. **CULTURAL INGOs + FOUNDATIONS**

EMPLOYMENT + PROFESSIONS

08. **EMPLOYMENT + PROFESSIONS**

CULTURAL PRODUCTION + DISSEMINATION

09. **GOVERNMENT CULTURAL EXPENDITURES**

10. **TRADE**

11. **GLOBAL BRANDS**

12. **CREATION, INNOVATION + PROTECTION**

13. **DISSEMINATION + STORAGE**

14. **TRADITIONAL + INDIGENOUS KNOWLEDGE**

CULTURAL INDUSTRIES + FIELDS

15. **NEWS** OFFLINE, ONLINE

16. **TV**

17. **RADIO**

18. **PRINT MEDIA**

19. **BOOKS**

20. **FILM**

21. **MUSIC**

22. **SPORTS**

23. **VIDEO GAMES**

24. **FASHION**

25. **ADVERTISING**

26. **ARCHITECTURE + DESIGN**

GLOBAL ARTS MARKET

27. **ART AUCTIONS + GALLERIES**

28. **GLOBAL PERFORMANCE ART**

29. **PRIZES + COMPETITIONS**

THE INTERNET

30. **THE INTERNET**

TRANSNATIONAL CULTURAL CORPORATIONS

1. FORBES GLOBAL 2000 CORPORATIONS IN **MEDIA** OF 2007

SORTED BY PROFITS

COMPANY	OVERALL FORBES GLOBAL 2000 RANK	COUNTRY	SALES ($ BIL)	PROFITS ($ BIL)	ASSETS ($ BIL)	MARKET VALUE (US$)
TIME WARNER	67	USA	44.22	6.53	131.67	77.99
WALT DISNEY	107	USA	35.16	4.34	60.99	70.16
NEWS CORP	134	USA	26.74	3.34	59.17	71.43
COMCAST	121	USA	24.97	2.53	110.41	80.17
VIVENDI	155	FRANCE	23.03	3.73	50.47	45.57
DIRECTV GROUP	380	USA	14.76	1.42	15.14	27.59
CBS	274	USA	14.32	1.66	43.51	23.73
TOPPAN PRINTING	968	JAPAN	13.18	0.13	14.62	6.64
DAI NIPPON PRINTING	636	JAPAN	12.83	0.55	14.09	10.59
WPP	418	UK	11.56	0.85	28.55	17.95
VIACOM	352	USA	11.47	1.59	21.8	27.3
OMNICOM GROUP	465	USA	11.38	0.86	18.16	17.31
LAGARDÉRE SCA	641	FRANCE	10.44	0.87	10.93	10.92

THE FORBES GLOBAL 2000 LIST ONLY RANKS PUBLIC COMPANIES; THEREFORE BERTELSMANN IS ABSENT FROM THEIR LIST.

2. FORTUNE GLOBAL 500 CORPORATIONS IN **ENTERTAINMENT** OF 2007

SORTED BY REVENUES

COMPANY	OVERALL FORTUNE 500 RANK	COUNTRY	REVENUES	PROFITS (US$ MILLIONS)
TIME WARNER	137	USA	44,788.00	6,552.00
WALT DISNEY	191	USA	34,285.00	3,374.00
NEWS CORP	266	USA	25,327.00	2,314.00
BERTELSMANN	281	GERMANY	24,211.00	2,636.00

TOP 5 COMPANIES IN **GLOBAL CULTURAL INDUSTRIES**

AS LISTED ON HOOVERS.COM 2007

CORPORATION	MEDIA	MUSIC	NEWSPAPER + PERIODICAL PUBLISHING	BOOK PUBLISHING	RADIO + TV BROADCASTING	FILM + VIDEO	INTERNET SEARCH + NAVIGATION SERVICES	INTERNET CONTENT PROVIDERS	# OF INDUSTRIES AS A KEY PLAYER
AMERICAN EXPRESS COMPANY (USA)			3						1
APPLE INC. (USA)		4							1
BRITISH BROADCASTING CORPORATION (UK)				3					1
COX ENTERPRISES, INC. (USA)								4	1
DOGAN SIRKETLER GRUBU HOLDING A.S. (TURKEY)							4		1
GENERAL ELECTRIC (USA)	1				1				2
GOOGLE, INC. (USA)							3	5	2
LVMH MOET HENNESSY LOUIS (FRANCE)			5						1
MCGRAW-HILL COMPANIES, INC. (USA)				4					1
MICROSOFT CORPORATION (USA)							1		1
NEWS CORPORATION (USA)		3	4	2		5		3	5
PROCTER & GAMBLE COMPANY (USA)	5				3				2
SONY CORPORATION (JAPAN)	4					1			2
TELEFONICA, S.A. (SPAIN)	3								1
TIME WARNER INC. (USA)		1			4	2	2	1	5
VERIZON COMMUNICATIONS (USA)	2				2				2
VIVENDI (FRANCE)		2				4			2
WALT DISNEY COMPANY (USA)		1	2	1	5	3		2	6
WOLTERS KLUWER NV (NETHERLANDS)				5					1
YAHOO! INC. (USA)		5						5	2

PROFILES OF THE TOP 5 GLOBAL MEDIA COMPANIES:

TIME WARNER

TOP MEDIA CORPORATIONS RANK	#1
PARENT COMPANY	TIME WARNER
HEADQUARTERS	NEW YORK, NY
REVENUES (2006)	$44.22 BILLION
CEO	RICHARD D. PARSONS (CHAIRMAN + CEO)
TELEVISION	TURNER BROADCASTING SYSTEM INC.
	HBO INC.
	CINEMAX
	CARTOON NETWORK
	COURT TV
	CNN
	TBS
	TCM
	TNT
	WARNER BROS. TELEVISION
	WARNER HORIZON TELEVISION INC.
	TELEPICTURES PRODUCTIONS INC.
	CW NETWORK (50-50 JOINT VENTURE WITH CBS CORPORATION)
CABLE	TIME WARNER CABLE INC.
	ACQUIRED ADELPHIA COMMUNICATIONS CORP. WITH COMCAST
PRODUCTION	WARNER BROTHERS PICTURES
	WARNER INDEPENDENT PICTURES
	CASTLE ROCK
	TELEPICTURES PRODUCTIONS INC.
	WARNER BROS. ANIMATION, INC.
FILM	WARNER BROS. ENTERTAINMENT INC.
	NEW LINE CINEMA CORPORATION
	PICTUREHOUSE (NEW LINE'S JOINT VENTURE WITH HBO)
	HBO INDEPENDENT PRODUCTIONS
MUSIC	WARNER MUSIC GROUP (DISCONTINUED)
MAGAZINES	OVER 120 INCLUDING:

TIME INC.	OXMOOR HOUSE
ENTERTAINMENT WEEKLY	SUNSET
PEOPLE	IPC MEDIA UNIT (UK)
FORTUNE	AMATEUR PHOTOGRAPHER
ALL YOU	HOMES & GARDENS
BUSINESS 2.0	TVTIMES
SPORTS ILLUSTRATED	WALLPAPER
IN STYLE	WOMAN'S WEEKLY
MONEY	DC COMICS
GOLF	E.C. PUBLICATIONS, INC. (MAD MAGAZINE)
ESSENCE	
REAL SIMPLE	
SOUTHERN LIVING	
HEALTH	
SOUTHERN ACCENTS	
COOKING LIGHT	
COASTAL LIVING	

INTERNET SERVICES	AOL LLC
	ADVERTISING.COM
	AIM
	COMPUSERVE
	GAMEDAILY.COM
	ICQ
	LIGHTNINGCAST
	MAPQUEST
	MOVIEFONE
	NETSCAPE
	RELEGENCE
	ROAD RUNNER HIGH SPEED ONLINE
	SPINNER.COM
	TMZ.COM
	TRUVEO
	USERPLANE
	WEBLOGS
	WINAMP
	XDRIVE
	PARTNERSHIP WITH GOOGLE FOR ADVERTISING
BOOK PUBLISHING	TIME INC.
	DC COMICS
	TIME WARNER BOOK GROUP INC. (SOLD IN 2006)
	BOOKSPAN (50% INTEREST IN)
SPORTS	ATLANTA BRAVES - WILL SELL TO LIBERTY MEDIA CORP.
THEME PARKS	WARNER VILLAGE THEME PARKS (50%) - SOLD IN 2006
OTHER	TIME WARNER GLOBAL MEDIA GROUP
	TIME WARNER INVESTMENTS
	TIME WARNER TELECOM (SOLD ALL SHARES IN 2006)
	WARNER BROS. CONSUMER PRODUCTS, INC.
	LICENSE TO RIGHTS TO HANNA-BARBARA CHARACTERS
	LEISURE ARTS, INC. - WILL SELL TO LIBERTY MEDIA CORP.
	DIGITAL PHONE
	WARNER BROS. INTERACTIVE ENTERTAINMENT (VIDEO-GAMES)
	DC COMICS

PROFILES OF THE TOP 5 GLOBAL MEDIA COMPANIES:

WALT DISNEY COMPANY

TOP MEDIA CORPORATIONS RANK	#2
PARENT COMPANY	WALT DISNEY COMPANY
HEADQUARTERS	BURBANK, CA
REVENUES (2006)	$34.29 BILLION
CEO	ROBERT A. IGER (PRESIDENT + CEO)
TELEVISION	ABC TELEVISION NETWORK
	ABC FAMILY
	BUENA VISTA TELEVISION
	ESPN
	DISNEY CHANNEL
	TOON DISNEY
	SOAPNET
	LIFETIME NETWORK
	A&E
	E!
	JETIX EUROPE & JETIX LATIN AMERICA
	THE HISTORY CHANNEL
	THE HISTORY CHANNEL EN ESPANOL
	HISTORY INTERNATIONAL
	MILITARY HISTORY CHANNEL
	THE BIOGRAPHY CHANNEL
	OWNED + OPERATED TV STATIONS:
	WLS (CHICAGO)
	WJRT (FLINT)
	KFSN (FRESNO)
	KTRK (HOUSTON)
	KABC (LOS ANGELES)
	WABC (NEW YORK CITY)
	WPVI (PHILADELPHIA)
	WTVD (RALEIGH, DURHAM)
	KGO (SAN FRANCISCO)
	WTVG (TOLEDO)
PRODUCTION	TOUCHSTONE TELEVISION PRODUCTION & DISTRIBUTION
	WALT DISNEY TELEVISION ANIMATION
	BUENA VISTA TELEVISION
	BUENA VISTA THEATRICAL PRODUCTIONS
	MIRAMAX
FILM	WALT DISNEY PICTURES
	TOUCHSTONE PICTURES
	MIRAMAX FILMS
	BUENA VISTA WORLDWIDE HOME ENTERTAINMENT
	PIXAR ANIMATION STUDIOS

MUSIC	BUENA VISTA MUSIC GROUP
	WALT DISNEY MUSIC PUBLISHING
	WALT DISNEY MUSIC RECORDS
	BUENA VISTA RECORDS
	HOLLYWOOD RECORDS
	LYRIC STREET RECORDS
MAGAZINES	WONDERTIME
	FAMILY FUN
	DISNEY ADVENTURES
INTERNET SERVICES	WALT DISNEY INTERNET GROUP
BOOK PUBLISHING	DISNEY PUBLISHING WORLDWIDE
	DISNEY BOOK GROUP
	HYPERION
	DISNEY PRESS
	DISNEY EDITIONS
	DISNEY LIBRI
	ESPN PUBLISHING
RADIO	RADIO DISNEY NETWORK
	ESPN RADIO
	LOCAL RADIO STATIONS IN 38 U.S. CITIES
THEME PARKS	DISNEYLAND RESORT
	WALT DISNEY WORLD RESORT
	TOKYO DISNEY RESORT
	DISNEYLAND RESORT PARIS
	HONG KONG DISNEYLAND RESORT
	DISNEY VACATION CLUB
	DISNEY CRUISE LINE
	ADVENTURES BY DISNEY
	DISNEY REGIONAL ENTERTAINMENT
OTHER	BUENA VISTA GAMES
	BUENA VISTA WORLDWIDE MARKETING AND DISTRIBUTION
	WORLD OF DISNEY STORES
	DISNEY TOYS & CONSUMER ELECTRONICS
	THE BABY EINSTEIN COMPANY
	DISNEY LIVE FAMILY ENTERTAINMENT (DISNEY ON ICE)
	DISNEY'S VIRTUAL MAGIC KINGDOM
	WALT DISNEY IMAGINEERING
	DISNEY APPAREL, ACCESSORIES & FOOTWEAR
	DISNEY FOOD, HEALTH & BEAUTY
	DISNEY HOME FURNISHINGS AND DÉCOR
	DISNEY STATIONARY
	ESPN ZONE
	ESPN VIDEO GAMES
	ESPN OUTDOORS

PROFILES OF THE TOP 5 GLOBAL MEDIA COMPANIES:

NEWS CORPORATION

TOP MEDIA CORPORATIONS RANK	#3
PARENT COMPANY	NEWS CORPORATION
HEADQUARTERS	NEW YORK, NY
REVENUES (2006)	$25.33 BILLION
CEO	**K. RUPERT MURDOCH** (CHAIRMAN & CEO)
TELEVISION	**FOX BROADCASTING COMPANY**
	TWENTIETH CENTURY FOX TELEVISION
	FOX TELEVISION STUDIOS
	TWENTIETH TELEVISION
	REGENCY TELEVISION (50%)
	35 FOX TELEVISION STUDIOS IN U.S. CITIES
	FOXTEL
	MYNETWORK TV
	FOX SPORTS AUSTRALIA
	CABLE NETWORK PROGRAMMING:
	FOX NEWS CHANNEL
	FOX CABLE NETWORKS
	FOX MOVIE CHANNEL
	FOX REGIONAL SPORTS NETWORKS (15):
	SPEED
	FUEL TV
	FX
	FSN
	FOX REALITY
	NATIONAL SPORTS PARTNERS
	FOX COLLEGE SPORTS
	NATIONAL ADVERTISING PARTNERS
	FOX SPORTS BAY AREA (40%)
	FOX PAN AMERICAN SPORTS (38%)
	FOX SOCCER CHANNEL
	NATIONAL GEOGRAPHIC CHANNEL-INTERNATIONAL (50%)
	NATIONAL GEOGRAPHIC CHANNEL-DOMESTIC (67%)
	NATIONAL GEOGRAPHIC CHANNEL-LATIN AMERICA (67%)
	STATS, LLC (50%)
	STAR (ASIA)-16 SUBSIDIARIES
	DIRECT BROADCAST SATELLITE TV:
	SKY ITALIA
	SKY SPORT
	CALCIO SKY
	SKY CINEMA
	SKY TG 24
	BRITISH SKY BROADCASTING (38%)
	SKY NEWS
	SKY SPORTS
	SKY TRAVEL
	SKY ONE
	SKY MOVIES
	DIRECTV GROUP (US) (38%)
	TATA SKY (ASIA) (20%)

CABLE	FOX CABLE NETWORKS
PRODUCTION	FOX FILMED ENTERTAINMENT
FILM	TWENTIETH CENTURY FOX FILM CORPORATION
	FOX 2000 PICTURES
	FOX SEARCHLIGHT PICTURES
	TWENTIETH CENTURY FOX HOME ENTERTAINMENT
	TWENTIETH CENTURY FOX LICENSING & MERCHANDISING
	BLUE SKY STUDIOS
	PREMIUM MOVIE PARTNERSHIP (AUSTRALIA & NEW ZEALAND) (20%)
	BALAJI TELEFILMS (ASIA) (26%)
	FOX STUDIOS AUSTRALIA
	FOX STUDIOS BAJA
MUSIC	FOX MUSIC
MAGAZINES	THE WEEKLY STANDARD
	GEMSTAR-TV GUIDE INTERNATIONAL, INC. (41%)
	INSIDEOUT (UK)
	TRAVEL MAGAZINE (UK)
	LOVE IT! (UK)
	ALPHA (AUSTRALIA)
	BIG LEAGUE (AUSTRALIA)
	DONNA HAY (AUSTRALIA)
	SUNDAY MAGAZINE (AUSTRALIA)
	INSIDEOUT (AUSTRALIA)
	NEWS AMERICA MARKETING
	IN-STORE
	FSI (SMARTSOURCE MAGAZINE)
	SMARTSOURCE IGROUP
	NEWS MARKETING CANADA
INTERNET SERVICES	MYSPACE
NEWSPAPERS	WALL STREET JOURNAL (U.S.)
	NEW YORK POST (U.S.)
	NEWS OF THE WORLD (UK)
	TSL EDUCATION (UK)
	THE SUN (UK)
	THE SUNDAY TIMES (UK)
	THE TIMES (UK)

AUSTRALIA MORE THAN 100 TITLES, INCLUDING:

WEEKLY TIMES (AUSTRALIA)	THE COURIER-MAIL (AUSTRALIA)
THE AUSTRALIAN (AUSTRALIA)	THE WEEKEND AUSTRALIAN (AUSTRALIA)
DAILY TELEGRAPH (AUSTRALIA)	SUNDAY HERALD SUN (AUSTRALIA)
HERALD SUN (AUSTRALIA)	SUNDAY MAIL (AUSTRALIA)
GOLD COAST BULLETIN (AUSTRALIA)	SUNDAY TASMANIAN (AUSTRALIA)
MX (AUSTRALIA)	THE SUNDAY TELEGRAPH (AUSTRALIA)
THE MERCURY (AUSTRALIA)	SUNDAY TERRITORIAN (AUSTRALIA)
THE ADVERTISER (AUSTRALIA)	FIJI TIMES (FIJI)
NEWSPHOTOS (AUSTRALIA)	SUNDAY TIMES (FIJI)
NEWSPIX (AUSTRALIA)	NAI LALAKAI (FIJI)
NEWSTEXT (AUSTRALIA)	SHANTI DUT (FIJI)
NT NEWS (AUSTRALIA)	POST-COURIER (PAPA NEW GUINEA) (63%)

BOOK PUBLISHING	HARPERCOLLINS PUBLISHERS (AUSTRALIA, CANADA, U.S., EUROPE)
	ZONDERVAN
RADIO	FOX SPORTS RADIO NETWORK

SPORTS	**FOX REGIONAL SPORTS NETWORKS** (15) HAS RIGHTS TO **NHL'S ATLANTA THRASHERS**
	SHARES RIGHTS TO **MLB'S ATLANTA BRAVES**
	SHARES RIGHTS TO **NBA'S ATLANTA HAWKS**
	ACQUISITION OF TURNER SOUTH
	NATIONAL RUGBY LEAGUE
	ACQUISITION OF TGRT (TURKEY)
OTHER	**DOW JONES**
	FOX MOBILE ENTERTAINMENT INTERACTIVE MEDIA
	MYSPACE
	KSOLO
	IGN ENTERTAINMENT
	ASKMEN
	SCOUT
	WHATIFSPORTS
	ROTTENTOMATOES
	FOX.COM
	FOXSPORTS.COM
	AMERICANIDOL.COM
	CHINA NETWORK SYSTEMS (ASIA)
	HATHWAY CABLE AND DATACOMM (ASIA) (26%)
	BROADSYSTEM VENTURES (EUROPE)
	NDS (EUROPE) (74%)
	CONVOYS GROUP (EUROPE)
	LONDON PROPERTY NEWS
	NEWS OUTDOOR GROUP (EUROPE)
	MOSGORREKLAMA (EUROPE) (50%)
	BALKAN NEWS CORPORATION (EUROPE)
	FOX TELEVIZIJA (EUROPE)
	FOXTEL (AUSTRALIA & NEW ZEALAND) (25%)
	SKY NETWORK TELEVISION LIMITED (AUSTRALIA & NEW ZEALAND) (44%)
	NEWS INTERACTIVE (AUSTRALIA & NEW ZEALAND)
	PROPERTYFINDER.COM (AUSTRALIA & NEW ZEALAND)
	REALESTATE.COM (AUSTRALIA & NEW ZEALAND) (58%)

PROFILES OF THE TOP 5 GLOBAL MEDIA COMPANIES:
COMCAST

TOP MEDIA CORPORATIONS RANK	#4
PARENT COMPANY	COMCAST
HEADQUARTERS	PHILADELPHIA, PA
REVENUES (2006)	$24.97 BILLION
CEO	BRIAN L. ROBERTS (CHAIRMAN & CEO)
TELEVISION	CN8 THE COMCAST NETWORK
	E! ENTERTAINMENT
	E! ENTERTAINMENT NETWORK (VIA SATELLITE IN EUROPE, AFRICA, ASIA, PACIFIC, AND THE MIDDLE EAST)
	STYLE NETWORK
	G4-VIDEO GAME TV
	THE GOLF CHANNEL
	AZN TELEVISION
	TV ONE (JOINT VENTURE WITH RADIO ONE)
	PBS KIDS SPROUT (IN PARTNERSHIP WITH HIT ENTERTAINMENT, PBS, AND SESAME WORKSHOP)
	VERSUS
	EXERCISE TV (IN PARTNERSHIP WITH BODY BY JAKE, NEW BALANCE, AND TIME WARNER CABLE)
	FEARNET (JOINT VENTURE WITH SONY PICTURES ENTERTAINMENT AND LIONSGATE ENTERTAINMENT)
	COMCAST SPORTSNET
	COMCAST SPORTS SOUTHEAST-CCS (JOINT VENTURE WITH CHARTER COMMUNICATIONS)
CABLE	COMCAST DIGITAL CABLE (ON DEMAND DVR, HDTV)
	OWNS A 21% SHARE OF **TIME WARNER CABLE**
INTERNET SERVICES	COMCAST HIGH-SPEED INTERNET
SPORTS	COMCAST-SPECTATOR
	PHILADELPHIA FLYERS (NHL)
	PHILADELPHIA 76ERS (NBA)
	PHILADELPHIA PHANTOMS (AHL)
	WACHOVIA CENTER ARENA
	WACHOVIA SPECTRUM ARENA
	4 FLYERS SKATE ZONE COMMUNITY ICE SKATING & HOCKEY RINKS
	COMCAST SPORTSNET PHILADELPHIA
OTHER	COMCAST DIGITAL VOICE
	COMCAST INTERACTIVE MEDIA:
	ZIDDIO
	GAMEINVASION.NET
	COMCAST SPECTATOR OWNS:
	GLOBAL SPECTRUM
	OVATIONS FOOD SERVICES
	NEW ERA TICKETS
	FRONT ROW MARKETING SERVICES
	3601 CREATIVE GROUP
	ANNUALLY PRODUCES **10 NATIONALLY-TELEVISED FIGURE SKATING SPECTACULARS** ON NBC
	(IN PARTNERSHIP WITH DISSON SKATING)
	COMCAST SPOTLIGHT (ADVERTISING)

PROFILES OF THE TOP 5 GLOBAL MEDIA COMPANIES:

VIVENDI

TOP MEDIA CORPORATIONS RANK	#5
PARENT COMPANY	VIVENDI
HEADQUARTERS	PARIS, FRANCE
REVENUES (2006)	20.04 BILLION EURO
CEO	JEAN-BERNARD LEVY (CHAIRMAN & CEO)
TELEVISION	CANAL+ GROUP (100%) MEDIA OVERSEAS (100%) CANAL+ FRANCE (65%) NBC UNIVERSAL (20%) CANAL+ SA (49%) STUDIOCANAL (100%) MULTI-THEMATIQUES (100%) CYFRA+ (75%) CANAL+ DISTRIBUTION (100%) I>TELE (100%) CANALSAT (100%) CANAL+ REGIE (100%) TPS (100%)
PRODUCTION	NBC UNIVERSAL (20%) CANAL+ (100%)
FILM	CANAL+ (100%) STUDIOCANAL (100%) ACQUIRED OPTIMUM RELEASING (UK COMPANY) NBC UNIVERSAL (20%)
MUSIC	UNIVERSAL MUSIC GROUP (100%) ACQUISITION OF VALE MUSIC ANNOUNCEMENT OF ACQUISITION OF BMG MUSIC PUBLISHING GROUP DEAL WITH YOUTUBE TO SHARE ADVERTISING REVENUE ACQUIRED AROUND UMG CONTENT UMG RECORDING LABELS INCLUDE: ISLAND DEF JAM MUSIC GROUP INTERSCOPE GEFFEN A&M RECORDS LOST HIGHWAY RECORDS MCA NASHVILLE MERCURY RECORDS POLYDOR UNIVERSAL MOTOWN RECORDS GROUP DECCA VERVE IMPULSE! MAROC TELECOM (51%)
INTERNET SERVICES	NEUF CEGETEL (40.5%) CANALPLAY NBC UNIVERSAL (20%)
THEME PARKS	MAROC TELECOM (51%)
OTHER	MAURITEL SA (51%) ONATEL (51%) SFR (56%) NEUF CEGETAL (40.5%) IN THE PROCESS OF ACQUIRING FIXED-LINE AND ADSL OPERATIONS OF TELE2FRANCE VIVENDI GAMES (100%) ACQUISITION OF CENTERSCORE, SECRET LAIR STUDIOS, AND CH'IN STUDIO

TRANSNATIONAL CULTURAL CORPORATIONS

Transnational corporations (TNCs) play a central role in shaping and expanding the scope of globalization. Cultural TNCs exist in entertainment, media and publishing, and now there are also web-based conglomerates with a variety of different holdings spanning Internet, publishing, IT, radio, and television mediums. Over the past decade, many giant cultural TNCs have emerged, bringing considerable consolidation and expansion: today, a relatively small number of corporations, typically as diversified holdings, control the majority of the formal cultural industries sector. These parent companies shape media and entertainment offerings and influence the promotion of artistic talent and cultural products according to corporate interests.

Cultural TNCs also have a symbiotic relationship with globalization. At the same time that they perpetuate global interconnectedness they are facilitated by the structures and technologies of a globalized world. Furthermore, many TNCs whose primary industry is not cultural have substantial holdings and/or complete ownership of cultural companies (subsidiaries). For instance, while the primary industry of General Electric is commercial finance, as well as infrastructure and industrial appliances, the corporation also owns 80 per cent of NBC Universal (the other 20 per cent is owned by Vivendi, the fifth largest cultural TNC in the world), through which it also owns a substantial portion of CNBC, MSNBC, Universal Pictures, Focus Features & Rogue Pictures, USA Network, Bravo, Telemundo, and many others.

Data point 3 lists the top five companies (in terms of sales) in the different cultural industries (both primary and secondary industries are taken into account). When the top five and the cultural industries are compared, it becomes apparent that many of the same companies are among the top five in several of the different cultural industries. The companies highlighted are the topmost players in a majority of the categories.

WHAT DO WE KNOW ABOUT CULTURAL TNCS?

Fewer than ten cultural TNCs dominate the global media industry. These include Time Warner, Disney, News Corporation, Comcast, Vivendi, Bertelsmann, CBS Corporation and Viacom, which are ranked the top cultural TNCs in terms of revenues (sales) (see data points 1 and 2). Virtually all of these TNCs have holdings in several media subcategories, including film, television, radio, music recording, publishing, newspapers, magazines, and others. Several, including Time Warner, Disney, Comcast, and Bertelsmann, also have diversified retail and service holdings. Time Warner, which is currently the world's top media conglomerate, had 2006 revenues of $44.2 billion (Hoovers.com) and also has major holdings in cable, Internet services, telecommunications, software, and leisure. News Corporation, with 2006 revenues of US$25.3 billion, through its subsidiary Fox, owns 35 broadcast television stations in the US and 15 regional sports networks; several television networks in Asia; direct broadcast satellite television in the US, the UK, Italy, and Asia; several film production studios; HarperCollins Publishing; hundreds of magazine and newspaper titles; and recently the

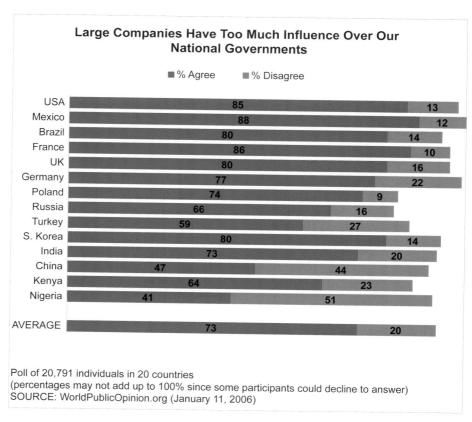

Large Companies Have Too Much Influence Over Our National Governments

■ % Agree   ■ % Disagree

	% Agree	% Disagree
USA	85	13
Mexico	88	12
Brazil	80	14
France	86	10
UK	80	16
Germany	77	22
Poland	74	9
Russia	66	16
Turkey	59	27
S. Korea	80	14
India	73	20
China	47	44
Kenya	64	23
Nigeria	41	51
AVERAGE	73	20

Poll of 20,791 individuals in 20 countries
(percentages may not add up to 100% since some participants could decline to answer)
SOURCE: WorldPublicOpinion.org (January 11, 2006)

Dow Jones and *Wall Street Journal*. In effect, the breadth and diversity in the holdings of this small group of cultural TNCs make it apparent how oligopolistic the global cultural media industry has become.

WHAT ARE THE ISSUES?

The oligopolization of the cultural industries raises questions of diversity, fair competition, and cultural domination. The democratization of nations around the world facilitates global expansion of cultural TNCs because democratization is often accompanied by more open markets, less stringent government controls, and greater flow of foreign direct investment. A recent study evaluated public opinion around the world on whether 'large companies have too much influence over [their] national government' (World Public Opinion, 2006). In many countries, the majority agreed with the above statement (see graphic).

Meanwhile, cultural TNCs have been seeking to loosen government regulations through lobbying, large campaign contributions, and powerful use of intellectual property rights, which includes contracts that limit artists' rights to their creative output. Critics point out that national and international governments and civil society must play new, active roles in monitoring and regulating cultural TNCs.

The market for independent media appears much too competitive for smaller companies to survive as they are rapidly acquired by the large TNCs. The media oligopoly is constantly increasing its ownership of diverse cultural holdings, so that culture is continuously becoming mass-produced and mass-commercialized (Hannaford, 2007). Most recently, the top global media TNC after Time Warner and Disney—Rupert Murdoch's News Corporation—purchased the Dow Jones and *Wall Street Journal*. Here the acquired was not by any means a small company. In this case, critics are worried that the journalistic independence, objectivity, standards, and subsequently the very reputation of the *Wall Street Journal* will be compromised under Rupert Murdoch's control (*The Economist*, August 2, 2007).

While some argue that codes of conduct for TNCs should be voluntary, others believe that they should be enforceable by law. Specific issues surface around the cultural hegemony and homogenizing impact of their oligopoly on countries throughout the world. Their impact on national and regional customs, values, and belief systems are profound (Dunning, 2006). Cultural TNCs continue to consolidate at a rapid pace, and media TNCs in particular control the news that people receive and the cultural outlets and expressions they are exposed to. Cultural TNCs shape their products to appeal to the widest possible market in order to ensure the highest margins of profit. As a result, they create products that are easily consumable, and in the process they promote a global pop culture, which becomes an item for consumption by 'global elites,' 'a global middle class,' and other neatly categorized consumer groups (see chapter by Nyamnjoh in this volume). Non-commercial cultural production cannot compete.

The cultural TNCs are now moving into web-based spheres ('new media'). In fact, the top media TNCs are now referred to as the 'old media' (*The Economist*, January 21, 2006). The Internet offers an opportunity for more equal access to information and cultural production, and sites that offer capabilities to create music, movies, etc., can encourage local production. In addition, 'new media' are increasingly participatory, and this offers huge opportunities for democratic participation in culture and exchange of ideas (see chapter by Goggin, in this volume). Many predict that this could have implications for the control and flow of cultural goods and for the cultural TNCs as well. In fact, it has been shown that the 'old media' could be losing to 'new media'—the rapidly expanding Internet industry. For example, Google's market value is now equivalent to that of Walt Disney, News Corporation, and Viacom combined (see text box on Google's ambitious digital book project in Goggin's chapter in this volume). Furthermore, music and video piracy, online newspapers and magazines, digital video recorders, and the threat of film and television piracy are coming close to threatening the very existence of 'old media' cable, television, film, news, and music businesses, which have increasingly lost consumers to the Internet. All of this said, it is still predicted that 'old media' will catch on and catch up quickly and very likely come to dominate the Internet and digital media industry as have the 'old' media industry (*The Economist*, January 21, 2006).

CULTURAL INGOs

NUMBER OF INTERNATIONAL ORGANIZATIONS

BY CULTURAL SUBJECT AREA 2000-2004

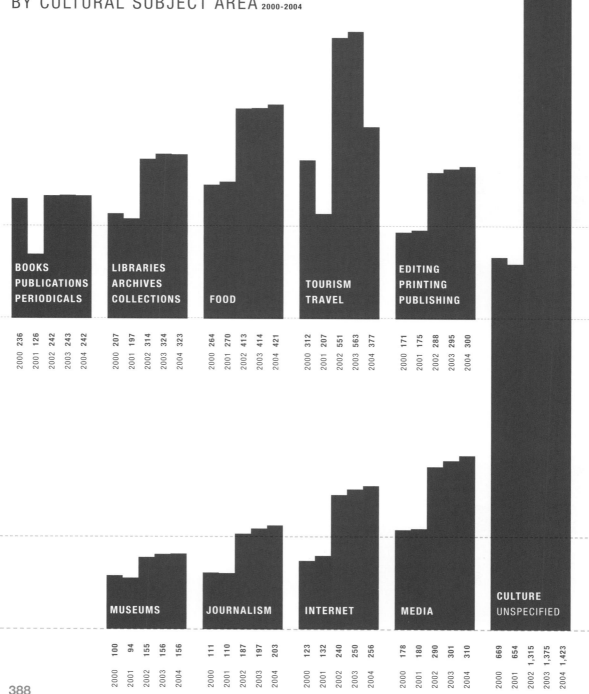

BOOKS
PUBLICATIONS
PERIODICALS

2000	236
2001	126
2002	242
2003	243
2004	242

LIBRARIES
ARCHIVES
COLLECTIONS

2000	207
2001	197
2002	314
2003	324
2004	323

FOOD

2000	264
2001	270
2002	413
2003	414
2004	421

TOURISM
TRAVEL

2000	312
2001	207
2002	551
2003	563
2004	377

EDITING
PRINTING
PUBLISHING

2000	171
2001	175
2002	288
2003	295
2004	300

MUSEUMS

2000	100
2001	94
2002	155
2003	156
2004	156

JOURNALISM

2000	111
2001	110
2002	187
2003	197
2004	203

INTERNET

2000	123
2001	132
2002	240
2003	250
2004	256

MEDIA

2000	178
2001	180
2002	290
2003	301
2004	310

CULTURE
UNSPECIFIED

2000	669
2001	654
2002	1,315
2003	1,375
2004	1,423

+ FOUNDATIONS

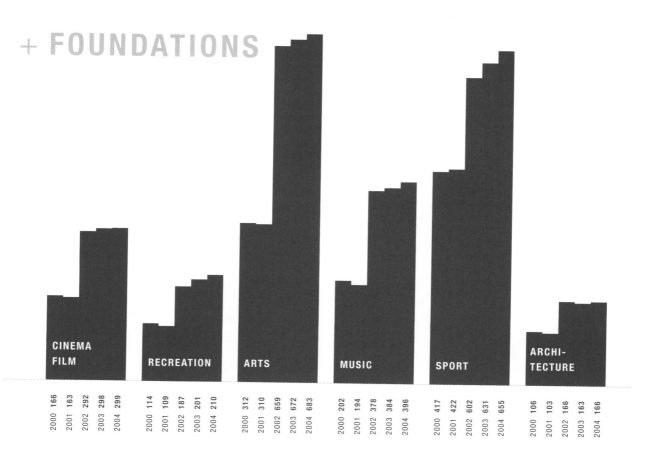

CINEMA FILM

2000	166
2001	163
2002	292
2003	298
2004	299

RECREATION

2000	114
2001	109
2002	187
2003	201
2004	210

ARTS

2000	312
2001	310
2002	659
2003	672
2004	683

MUSIC

2000	202
2001	194
2002	378
2003	384
2004	396

SPORT

2000	417
2001	422
2002	602
2003	631
2004	655

ARCHI-TECTURE

2000	106
2001	103
2002	166
2003	163
2004	166

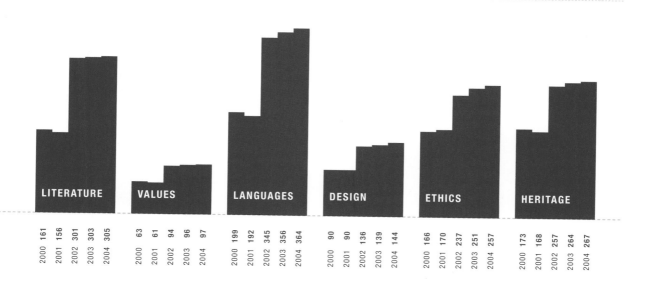

LITERATURE

2000	161
2001	156
2002	301
2003	303
2004	305

VALUES

2000	63
2001	61
2002	94
2003	96
2004	97

LANGUAGES

2000	199
2001	192
2002	345
2003	356
2004	364

DESIGN

2000	90
2001	90
2002	136
2003	139
2004	144

ETHICS

2000	166
2001	170
2002	237
2003	251
2004	257

HERITAGE

2000	173
2001	168
2002	257
2003	264
2004	267

389

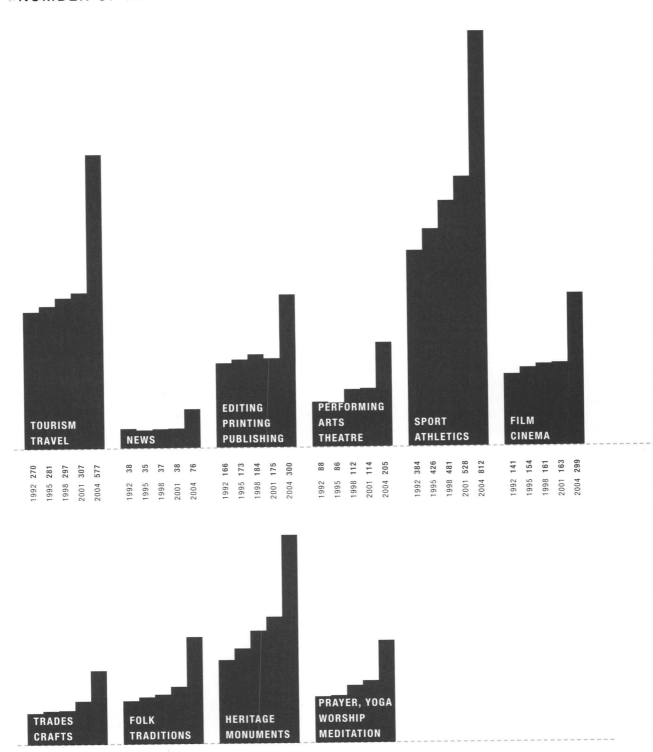

TOURISM TRAVEL

1992	270
1995	281
1998	297
2001	307
2004	577

NEWS

1992	38
1995	35
1998	37
2001	38
2004	76

EDITING PRINTING PUBLISHING

1992	166
1995	173
1998	184
2001	175
2004	300

PERFORMING ARTS THEATRE

1992	88
1995	86
1998	112
2001	114
2004	205

SPORT ATHLETICS

1992	384
1995	426
1998	481
2001	528
2004	812

FILM CINEMA

1992	141
1995	154
1998	161
2001	163
2004	299

TRADES CRAFTS

1992	62
1995	66
1998	67
2001	85
2004	144

FOLK TRADITIONS

1992	85
1995	92
1998	97
2001	112
2004	208

HERITAGE MONUMENTS

1992	163
1995	185
1998	219
2001	246
2004	405

PRAYER, YOGA WORSHIP MEDITATION

1992	90
1995	98
1998	113
2001	118
2004	199

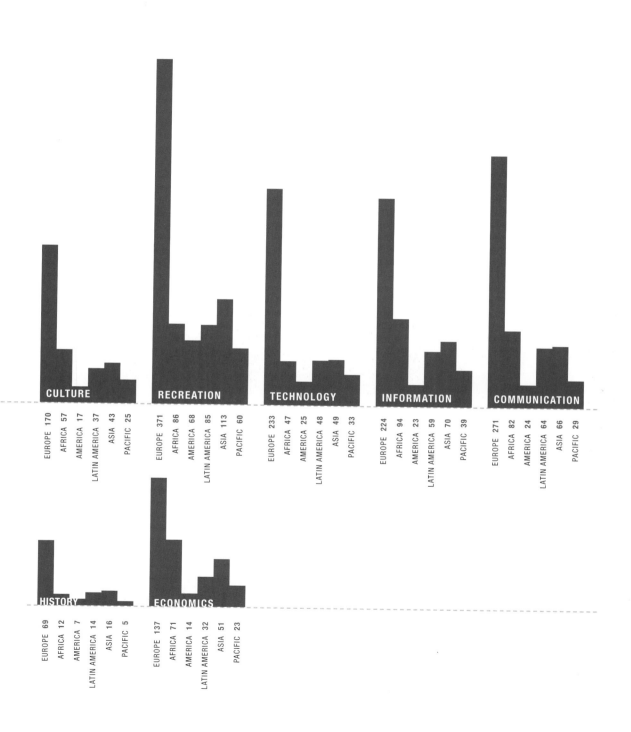

CULTURE

EUROPE 170
AFRICA 57
AMERICA 17
LATIN AMERICA 37
ASIA 43
PACIFIC 25

RECREATION

EUROPE 371
AFRICA 86
AMERICA 68
LATIN AMERICA 85
ASIA 113
PACIFIC 60

TECHNOLOGY

EUROPE 233
AFRICA 47
AMERICA 25
LATIN AMERICA 48
ASIA 49
PACIFIC 33

INFORMATION

EUROPE 224
AFRICA 94
AMERICA 23
LATIN AMERICA 59
ASIA 70
PACIFIC 39

COMMUNICATION

EUROPE 271
AFRICA 82
AMERICA 24
LATIN AMERICA 64
ASIA 66
PACIFIC 29

HISTORY

EUROPE 69
AFRICA 12
AMERICA 7
LATIN AMERICA 14
ASIA 16
PACIFIC 5

ECONOMICS

EUROPE 137
AFRICA 71
AMERICA 14
LATIN AMERICA 32
ASIA 51
PACIFIC 23

	ASSETS (BLN)	FISCAL YEAR END DATE	GIVE INTERNATIONALLY	GIVE TO CULTURE	GIVE EXPLICITLY INTERNATIONALLY TO CULTURAL ORGS/PEOPLE (EXCLUDING GRANTS TO EDUCATION-RELATED ORGS/PEOPLE)
UNITED STATES (1)					
FORD FOUNDATION (NY)	11.62 $	2005	X	X	X
J. PAUL GETTY TRUST (CA)	9.62 $	2005	X	X	X
WILLIAM AND FLORA HEWLETT FOUNDATION (CA)	8.52 $	2006	X	X	*_
ANDREW W. MELLON FOUNDATION (NY)	5.59 $	2005	X	X	*_
JOHN D. AND CATHERINE T. MACARTHUR FOUNDATION	5.49 $	2005	X	X	*_
ROCKEFELLER FOUNDATION (NY)	3.42 $	2005	X	X	X
SMITHSONIAN	2.27 $	2006	X	X	*_
SOROS FOUNDATION NETWORK (US + HUNGARY) OPEN SOCIETY INSTITUTE	859 MLN $	2006	X	X	*_
EUROPE (2)					
FONDAZIONE CARIPLO (ITALY)	9.6 €		X	X	
ROBERT BOSCH STIFTUNG (GERMANY)	5.2 €		X	X	
CALOUSTE GULBENKIAN FOUNDATION (PORTUGAL)	3.08 €	2005	X	X	
AGA KHAN FOUNDATION NETWORK (SWITZERLAND)	1.11 €	2006	X	X	
SOROS FOUNDATION NETWORK (US + HUNGARY) OPEN SOCIETY INSTITUTE	859 MLN €	2006	X	X	
BRITISH MUSEUM (BRITAIN)	565 MLN €	2007	X	X	
EUROPEAN CULTURAL FOUNDATION (NETHERLANDS)	12.95 MLN €	2006	X	X	
PRINCE CLAUS FUND (NETHERLANDS)	3.50 MLN €	2006	X	X	
FONDAZIONE MONTE DEI PASCHI DI SIENA (ITALY)	11 €			X	
COMPAGNIA DI SAN PAOLO (ITALY)	7.8 €			X	
FONDAZIONE CARIVERONA (ITALY)	5.9 €			X	
FONDAZIONE CASSA DI RISPARMIO DI TORINO (ITALY)	5.7 €			X	
GARFIELD WESTON FOUNDATION (UK)	3.5 €			X	
FONDAZIONE CASSA DI RISPARMIO DI PADOVA E ROVIGO (ITALY)	3.7 €			X	
PRUSSIAN CULTURAL HERITAGE FOUNDATION (GERMANY)				X	
COMPAGNIA DI SAN PAOLO DI TORINO (ITALY)			X	X	
VOLKSWAGEN STIFTUNG (GERMANY)	2.3 €	2002	X	X	X
THE LEVERHULME TRUST (UK)	26.7 MLN £	2002		X	
FONDAZIONE CASSA DI RISPARMIO DI ROMA (ITALY)				X	
FONDAZIONE CASSA DI RISPARMIO DI VERONA VICENZA BA (ITALY)				X	
FONDAZIONE CASSA DI RISPARMIO DI FIRENZE (ITALY)				X	
FONDAZIONE CASSA DI RISPARMIO CUNEO (ITALY)				X	
ESMEE FAIRBAIRN FOUNDATION (UK)				X	

	ASSETS (BLN)	FISCAL YEAR END DATE	GIVE INTERNATIONALLY	GIVE TO CULTURE	GIVE EXPLICITLY INTERNATIONALLY TO CULTURAL ORGS/PEOPLE (EXCLUDING GRANTS TO EDUCATION-RELATED ORGS/PEOPLE)
JAPAN (3)					
SASAKAWA PEACE FOUNDATION	82.09 YEN	2006	X	X	
TOYOTA FOUNDATION	29.5 YEN	2003	X	X	
SUMITOMO FOUNDATION			X	X	
MITSUBISHI FOUNDATION	20.03 YEN	2006		X	
ISHIBASHI FOUNDATION			X	X	X
CANADA (4)					X
VANCOUVER FOUNDATION				X	X
J.W. MCCONNELL FOUNDATION				X	
THE WINNIPEG FOUNDATION				X	X
THE CALGARY FOUNDATION	299.4 MLN $ CAD	2006		X	
CHINA (5)					
THE SOONG CHING-LING FOUNDATION				X	
HONG KONG (6)					
HONG KONG JOCKEY CLUB CHARITIES TRUST	25.6 MLN $ HK			X	
LI KA SHING FOUNDATION			X	X	
SHAW FOUNDATION HONG KONG LTD			X	X	
TIN KA PING FOUNDATION			X	X	
INDIA (7)					
CONCERN INDIA FOUNDATION	127 MLN	2006		X	X
INDIA FOUNDATION FOR THE ARTS				X	
SIR RATAN TATA TRUST	27.9 MLN $ US	2006		X	
BIRLA FOUNDATION				X	

*_ ONLY GIVES INTERNATIONALLY FOR CULTURE RELATED TO UNIVERSITIES AND/OR TO STUDENTS/EDUCATION

(1) US FOUNDATIONS ARE THE TOP 10 FOUNDATIONS IN TERMS OF INTERNATIONAL GIVING

(2) EUROPEAN FOUNDATIONS ARE THE TOP 10 FOUNDATIONS BY ASSETS IN 6 EU COUNTRIES (BELGIUM, FRANCE, GERMANY, ITALY, SWEDEN, AND THE UK)

(3) JAPANESE FOUNDATIONS ARE RANDOMLY SELECTED FROM A LIST OF THE TOP 12 FOUNDATIONS IN JAPAN AS RECOGNIZED BY THE JAPANESE FOUNDATION CENTER, IN TERMS OF FOUNDATION ASSETS IN 1999

(4) CANADIAN FOUNDATIONS THAT HAVE AT LEAST $10 MILLION CAD IN ASSETS. THEY ARE ORDERED IN DECREASING TOTAL ASSET SIZE, AS PER THEIR MOST RECENT REGISTERED CHARITY INFORMATION RETURN WITH THE CANADA REVENUE AGENCY, USUALLY FOR 2004. ALL FIGURES ARE IN CANADIAN DOLLARS

(5) MAJOR CHINESE FOUNDATIONS AS NOTED BY ASIANPHILANTHROPY.ORG

(6) MAJOR HONG KONG FOUNDATIONS AS NOTED BY ASIANPHILANTHROPY.ORG

(7) MAJOR INDIAN FOUNDATIONS AS NOTED BY ASIANPHILANTHROPY.ORG

5. PRIVATE SECTOR SPONSORSHIP SELECT COUNTRIES

	MAIN LAW WHICH OUTLINES TAX DEDUCTIONS TO PRIVATE SPONSORS OF ARTS AND CULTURE	GOVERNMENT SCHEME TO PROMOTE BUSINESS SPONSORSHIP IN THE ARTS AND CULTURE	MAIN SECTORS ATTRACTING PRIVATE SPONSORSHIP	ESTIMATED VALUE OF PRIVATE SPONSORSHIP GENERATED PER YEAR (AS OF 2007 UNLESS SPECIFIED)
AUSTRIA	SPONSORS' ORDINANCE (1987). REGIONAL LEGISLATION	SOME REGIONS REQUIRE ADDITIONAL CONTRIBUTIONS FROM LOCAL COMMUNITIES AND PRIVATE SOURCES	FINE ARTS AND MUSIC	43 MILLION EUROS
BELGIUM (FLEMISH)	BELGIAN LAW MAKES NO LEGAL PROVISION FOR GENUINE CORPORATE TAX DEDUCTION FOR INVESTMENT IN CULTURE	PPP PROGRAM (ONLY ATTRACTIVE FOR CULTURAL PROJECTS WITH A DEGREE OF COMMERCIAL PROFITABILITY)	CONCERTS AND FESTIVALS OF CLASSICAL MUSIC, ART EXHIBITIONS	54.30 MILLION EUROS 1999
CANADA	NO LAW TO ENCOURAGE PRIVATE SPONSORSHIP OF CULTURE AND THE ARTS	INFORMATION NOT AVAILABLE	MEDIA, LIBRARIES AND THE PERFORMING ARTS	47.9 MILLION CAD
FINLAND	NO SINGLE LAW TO ENCOURAGE PRIVATE SPONSORSHIP OF CULTURE AND THE ARTS BUT SERIES OF TAX BREAKS TO ENCOURAGE BUSINESS SPONSORSHIP OF THE ARTS	NO	INFORMATION NOT AVAILABLE	10 MILLION EUROS
FRANCE	LAW ON THE DEVELOPMENT OF SPONSORSHIP (1987), MECENAT LAW (2003)	PROJECTS LAUNCHED BY THE MINISTRY OF CULTURE TO ATTRACT PRIVATE SPONSORSHIP	FINE ARTS AND MUSIC	183 MILLION EUROS 1999
GERMANY	NO SINGLE LAW TO ENCOURAGE SPONSORSHIP OF CULTURE AND THE ARTS, BUT SERIES OF TAX BREAKS, SUMMARIZED IN A DIRECTIVE OF THE MINISTRY OF FINANCE (BMF-SPONSORING-ERLASS 1998)	INCENTIVES MAINLY IN THE LOCAL GOVERNMENT LEVEL	FINE ARTS AND MUSIC	500 MILLION EUROS 2004
GREECE	TAX EXEMPTIONS FOR CULTURAL SPONSORSHIP (1990)	INFORMATION NOT AVAILABLE	MUSIC	22.4 MILLION EUROS 1999

	MAIN LAW WHICH OUTLINES TAX DEDUCTIONS TO PRIVATE SPONSORS OF ARTS AND CULTURE	GOVERNMENT SCHEME TO PROMOTE BUSINESS SPONSORSHIP IN THE ARTS AND CULTURE	MAIN SECTORS ATTRACTING PRIVATE SPONSORSHIP	ESTIMATED VALUE OF PRIVATE SPONSORSHIP GENERATED PER YEAR (AS OF 2007 UNLESS SPECIFIED)
ITALY	LAW 342/2000 ALLOWING DEDUCTION ON DONATIONS AND SPONSORSHIP	INFORMATION NOT AVAILABLE	CULTURAL HERITAGE, MUSICAL AND PERFORMING ARTS, EXHIBITIONS AND CULTURAL EVENTS	205.70 MILLION EUROS 1999
NETHERLANDS	NO, BUT DIFFERENT TAX INCENTIVE SCHEMES RELEVANT FOR THE ARTS, MEDIA AND HERITAGE	CULTURAL SPONSORSHIP CODE	FINE ARTS AND MUSIC	50 MILLION EUROS
SAN MARINO	THERE ARE NO SPECIFIC LAWS ENCOURAGING INVESTMENTS IN THE CULTURAL SECTOR BY PRIVATE INDIVIDUALS. TAX LAW N.91 OF 1984 AND SUBSEQUENT AMENDMENTS ESTABLISH THAT DONATIONS BY INDIVIDUALS IN THE CULTURAL FIELD ARE INCLUDED IN DEDUCTIBLE LIABILITIES.	NO	CONCERTS, MUSIC AND DANCE FESTIVALS, ART EXHIBITIONS, FINE AND PERFORMING ARTS, PUBLICATION OF LITERATURE, THEATER PERFORMANCES, CULTURAL HERITAGE	180,000 EUROS 2005
SPAIN	ACT ON TAX EXEMPTIONS FOR NON-PROFIT-MAKING ORGANIZATIONS AND ON SPONSORSHIP (2002)	INFORMATION NOT AVAILABLE	CLASSICAL MUSIC AND PAINTING	59.7 MILLION EUROS 1999
SWEDEN	NO LAW TO ENCOURAGE PRIVATE SPONSORSHIP	CULTURE AND BUSINESS FORUM	HALF OF ALL SPONSORSHIP GOES TO MUSEUMS AND ART GALLERIES AND THE REST TO THEATER AND DANCE	SEK 93 BILLION 2002
SWITZERLAND	NO SINGLE LAW TO ENCOURAGE SPONSORSHIP OF CULTURE AND THE ARTS BUT SERIES OF TAX BREAKS AND PARLIAMENTARY DISCUSSIONS ABOUT NEW REGULATIONS	NO, EXCEPT ON THE LOCAL LEVEL	COMPANIES DEVELOP CORPORATE IDENTITY BY ORGANIZING THEIR OWN CONCERTS OR THEATER TOURS. THEY ALSO COMMISSION OR DEVELOP PROJECTS WITH CULTURAL INSTITUTIONS OR ARTISTS	320 MILLION EUROS 2004
UNITED KINGDOM	NO LAW TO ENCOURAGE PRIVATE SPONSORSHIP OF CULTURE AND THE ARTS	BUSINESS SPONSORSHIP INCENTIVE SCHEME	EXHIBITIONS, DANCE, MUSIC, THEATER, FESTIVALS, HERITAGE	GBP 452.1 MILLION 2004/2005

CULTURAL INGOS & FOUNDATIONS

Globalization shapes an emergent transnational civil society, where international NGOs (INGOs), foundations and similar organization are active across national boundaries. While these organizations operate in many areas, they are also present in the field of culture. Some have existed for many decades, e.g., International PEN, an association of writers with 145 centers in 104 countries (its strap line is 'Promoting literature, defending freedom of expression'). In Europe, there is the European Cultural Foundation, established by the Swiss writer Denis de Rougemont in 1954, and the European Forum for the Arts and Heritage (EFAH), set up in 1992 to be the voice of and, the arts and culture sector vis à vis the European Institutions. Other bodies are more recent, such as the International Network for Cultural Diversity, set up in 1998 to advance the worldwide movement that led to the adoption of the UNESCO cultural diversity convention in 2005. A special case is the International Federation of Arts Councils and Cultural Agencies set up in the year 2000 'to benefit artists, arts organisations and communities worldwide,' whose members are mostly 'arm's-length' bodies supported by government.

Cultural INGOs and foundations contribute to cultural innovation, exchange and dissemination. They are involved in funding, implementation, facilitating partnerships, and creating collaborative and community initiatives. The Council of Europe (Teneva, 2002) has suggested the following roles for cultural INGOs:

1. In a democratic framework, civil society is increasingly important in the field of culture for it provides the necessary mechanisms for inciting change.
2. INGOs play a significant role in the reconstructing of the democratic state and the building of a pluralistic civil society.
3. Corporate philanthropy and sponsorship is important for the development of a strong third sector, especially in the arts.
4. INGOs are critical to the process of cultural policy elaboration, necessitating an effective bottom-up communication in this process.
5. The arts play a significant role in social inclusion.

While many INGOs and foundations that work internationally often support cultural causes as part of their larger mandates, there are only a handful of INGOs and international foundations that focus solely or primarily on culture.

WHAT DO WE KNOW
ABOUT CULTURAL INGOS AND FOUNDATIONS?

The number of such bodies has grown considerably in recent years. For instance, INGOs specific to the field of culture (unspecified) have grown from 669 in 2000 to 1,423 in 2004, and arts INGOs grew from 312 to 683 in the same period (see data point 1).

Entities in the US remain the chief international funder in the realm of culture. While direct cross-border giving from the US has actually weakened (between 2002 and 2004, it fell by 3 per cent), grants to US-managed international and global programs increased (by 49 per cent between 2002 and 2004). Of the top US foundations that give both culturally and internationally, the Ford Foundation is the largest (in terms of asset size, $11.6 billion in 2005), followed by the J. Paul Getty Trust (with $9.62 billion in assets in 2005), the William and Flora Hewlett Foundation ($8.52 billion in assets in 2006), the Andrew W. Mellon Foundation ($5.59 billion in assets in 2005), the John D. and Catherine T. MacArthur Foundation ($5.49 billion in assets in 2005), and the Rockefeller Foundation (with $3.42 billion in assets in 2005).[1]

In Europe, according to a study carried out by the Fitzcarraldo Foundation for the Network of European Foundations for Innovative Cooperation (NEFIC), the territorial scope of grants given by EU foundations shows a strong partiality towards programs within the foundations' own country, followed by those in Central and Eastern Europe, and then to programs in other EU countries. Arts and culture grant-making by EU foundations to the US, Africa, and Latin America represented the smallest portion of overall grants. Most foundations surveyed in the study pointed to financial constraints as the primary obstacle to implementing international programs. Structural constraints as well as historical, cultural, and legal issues were also cited as obstacles.

Data on the philanthropic sector outside the US and the EU are sparse. Japanese foundations engage primarily in international education and student-exchange programs (Asia Pacific Philanthropy Consortium, 2006). In 2002, there were over 3,000 registered foundations in Korea. Almost all Chinese foundations are fundraising and/or operating institutions and rarely give internationally. Hong Kong has the largest local concentration of foundations in China. Similar to patterns in Japan, the majority of grant-making foundations in Hong Kong give grants for educational programs. Hong Kong foundation grants often go to support activities in mainland China, with only a few foundations with grant-making activities benefiting Southeast Asia and the rest of the world. India has an estimated number of over 80,000 grant-making organizations, funding domestic programs and activities almost exclusively.

WHAT ARE THE ISSUES?

A Council of Europe conference held in 2001 identified three main issues relevant to the needs and demands of arts and culture organizations (Teneva, 2002). First is the need to build successful arts and business partnerships. This can be done through the development of education opportunities, capacity building, identification of good practice, increased private sector involvement, utilization of boards and trustees to attract business sponsorship, and building business networks to support the arts. The second issue is the interface between culture and policy. Cultural organizations can implement a bottom-up approach in cultural policy elaborations by achieving a consensus within the cultural sector about policies, implementation of a communication portal for the efficient transfer of information relevant to culture and policy (e.g., yearly reports), creating a cultural policy think-tank, and the mobilization of artists to proactively engage with policy concerns. The third requirement relates to the role of arts and culture in the social inclusion processes. Arts foundations need to be further integrated through cross-sectoral cooperation between the state and civil society through the development of formal education programs and training, distribution of literature documenting the arts as a tool for social inclusion, and formation of a lobby of prominent artists for arts promotion.

The 2005 UNESCO Convention on the Protection and Promotion of the Diversity of Cultural Expressions picks up on these issues and puts significant emphasis on INGOs and foundations as part of a wider civil society. Implicitly or explicitly, reference to civil society and its institutions is made in several articles of the Convention. In particular Article 11 acknowledges the fundamental role of civil society in protecting and promoting the diversity of cultural expressions, and calls on parties to encourage the active participation of civil society in their efforts to achieve the objectives of the Convention. Article 6 states that parties to the Convention may adopt measures aimed at protecting and promoting the diversity of cultural expressions within their territory that, among others, include measures aimed at encouraging nonprofit organizations to develop and promote the free exchange and circulation of ideas, cultural expressions and cultural activities, goods and services, and to stimulate both the creative and entrepreneurial spirit in their activities. Articles 12 and 15 encourage partnerships with INGOs for the enhancement of capacities to protect and promote the diversity of cultural expressions.

[1] Information gathered from organizations' annual reports.

EMPLOYMENT + PROFESSIONS

GLOBAL CREATIVE CLASS % OF TOTAL WORKFORCE

REPORTED IN THE WORK OF RICHARD FLORIDA (2005)   INCLUDING TECHNICIANS   EXCLUDING TECHNICIANS

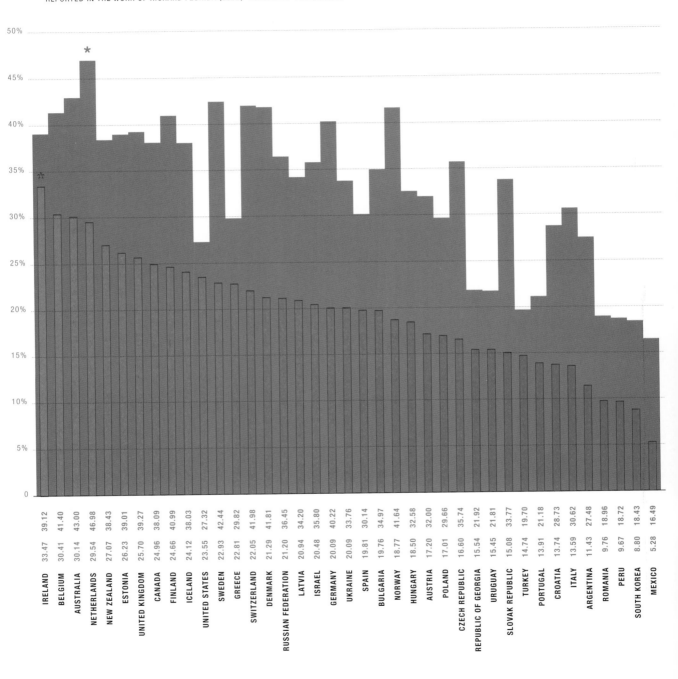

Country	Including	Excluding
IRELAND	33.47	39.12
BELGIUM	30.41	41.40
AUSTRALIA	30.14	43.00
NETHERLANDS	29.54	46.98
NEW ZEALAND	27.07	38.43
ESTONIA	26.23	39.01
UNITED KINGDOM	25.70	39.27
CANADA	24.96	38.09
FINLAND	24.66	40.99
ICELAND	24.12	38.03
UNITED STATES	23.55	27.32
SWEDEN	22.93	42.44
GREECE	22.81	29.82
SWITZERLAND	22.05	41.98
DENMARK	21.29	41.81
RUSSIAN FEDERATION	21.20	36.45
LATVIA	20.94	34.20
ISRAEL	20.48	35.80
GERMANY	20.09	40.22
UKRAINE	20.09	33.76
SPAIN	19.81	30.14
BULGARIA	19.76	34.97
NORWAY	18.77	41.64
HUNGARY	18.50	32.58
AUSTRIA	17.20	32.00
POLAND	17.01	29.66
CZECH REPUBLIC	16.60	35.74
REPUBLIC OF GEORGIA	15.54	21.92
URUGUAY	15.45	21.81
SLOVAK REPUBLIC	15.08	33.77
TURKEY	14.74	19.70
PORTUGAL	13.91	21.18
CROATIA	13.74	28.73
ITALY	13.59	30.62
ARGENTINA	11.43	27.48
ROMANIA	9.76	18.96
PERU	9.67	18.72
SOUTH KOREA	8.80	18.43
MEXICO	5.28	16.49

2. CULTURAL EMPLOYMENT IN SELECT COUNTRIES

COUNTRY	CULTURAL EMPLOYMENT AS % OF TOTAL: **CULTURAL INDUSTRIES**	CULTURAL EMPLOYMENT AS % OF TOTAL: **CULTURAL OCCUPATIONS**	**GROWTH** OR **DECLINE** OF CULTURAL EMPLOYMENT
EUROPEAN UNION 2002 – 2004	**2.5**% CULTURAL INDUSTRIES, OCCUPATIONS; **3.1**% CULTURAL INDUSTRIES AND OCCUPATIONS INCLUDING CULTURAL TOURISM[1]		+ **1.85**% COMPARED TO – **0.04**% IN TOTAL EMPLOYMENT
UNITED STATES	**7.0**% 2005	**10.5**% 2006[2]	1998 – 2005: + **9.1**% INDUSTRIES, COMPARED TO + **5.5**% IN TOTAL DOMESTIC INDUSTRIES
AUSTRALIA 2001	**5.1**%[3]	**3.1**%	1996 – 2001: + **11**% CULTURAL INDUSTRIES, COMPARED TO + **9**% IN EMPLOYMENT IN INDUSTRIES OVERALL
CANADA	**4.5**% 2005	**0.8**% 2001 ARTISTS ONLY[7]	1991 – 2001: + **29**% COMPARED TO + **10**% TOTAL EMPLOYMENT (OCCUPATIONS – ARTISTS ONLY)
NEW ZEALAND 2001	**4.8**% CULTURAL INDUSTRIES[4]	**3.2**% CULTURAL OCCUPATIONS	1996 – 2001: OCCUPATIONS AND INDUSTRIES COMBINED + **8.5**%
SINGAPORE 2000	**2.2**%[5]	NO DATA	NO DATA
JAPAN 1996 – 2001	**3.2**% CREATIVE INDUSTRIES	NO DATA	+ **7.9**% COMPARED TO – **7.9**% IN INDUSTRIES OVERALL
HONG KONG 2002	**3.7**% CREATIVE INDUSTRIES[6]	NO DATA	1997 – 2002: + **3.7**% AVERAGE PER YEAR IN INDUSTRIES
TAIWAN 2000	**3.6**% CULTURAL CREATIVE INDUSTRIES	NO DATA	NO DATA
BRAZIL 2003	**4.0**% CULTURAL SECTOR	NO DATA	NO DATA

[1] ACCORDING TO EUROSTAT: "CULTURAL EMPLOYMENT COVERS BOTH CULTURAL OCCUPATIONS IN THE WHOLE ECONOMY AND ANY EMPLOYMENT IN DIMENSION, SUCH AS LIBRARIANS, WRITERS, PERFORMING ARTISTS, ARCHITECTS, ETC. THE OCCUPATION IS DEFINED AS A SUBSET OF THE ISCO CLASSIFICATION. ALL THESE OCCUPATIONS ARE TAKEN INTO ACCOUNT, WHATEVER THE MAIN ACTIVITY OF THE EMPLOYER. CULTURAL ACTIVITIES ARE DEFINED AS A SUBSET OF THE NACE CLASSIFICATION, AND INCLUDE PUBLISHING, MOTION PICTURE AND VIDEO ACTIVITY, WHOLESALE AND RETAIL OF CULTURAL GOODS. IN THESE ACTIVITIES, ALL EMPLOYMENT IS TAKEN INTO ACCOUNT, WHATEVER THE OCCUPATION (ARTISTIC, TECHNICAL, ADMINISTRATIVE, MANAGERIAL), BECAUSE THEY ARE ALL REQUIRED FOR THE OPERATION OF THE 'CULTURAL INDUSTRY'." THEREFORE, FIGURES FOR INDUSTRIES ALONE OR OCCUPATIONS ALONE ARE NOT AVAILABLE FOR THE EU OVERALL.

[2] 2006 FIGURES ARE LIKELY INFLATED IN COMPARISON TO OTHER COUNTRIES BECAUSE SOME CULTURAL CATEGORIES ARE COMBINED WITH OTHER NON-CULTURAL FIELDS (FOR EXAMPLE, ARCHITECTURE IS COMBINED WITH ENGINEERING). A 2003 REPORT ON U.S. CULTURAL INDUSTRIES PLACED THE CONTRIBUTION OF CULTURAL EMPLOYMENT TO TOTAL EMPLOYMENT AT 2.5%.

[3] AUSTRALIA: ANOTHER REPORT SHOWED COPYRIGHT INDUSTRIES AS 3.8% OF TOTAL (1999 – 2000).

[4] NEW ZEALAND: IN ANOTHER REPORT (2000 – 2001): 3.6% COPYRIGHT INDUSTRIES (+)19.2% (1996–7 THRU 2000–1) COMPARED WITH (+)20% IN EMPLOYMENT OVERALL.

[5] SINGAPORE: 2000: OR 3.8% INCLUDING CULTURAL DISTRIBUTION INDUSTRIES. ANOTHER REPORT SHOWED COPYRIGHT INDUSTRIES AS 3.4% OF TOTAL (ALSO 2000).

[6] HONG KONG: ANOTHER REPORT SHOWED CREATIVE INDUSTRIES AS 5.3% IN 2002; AND ANOTHER REPORT SHOWED COPYRIGHT INDUSTRIES TO BE 5.9% IN 2002.

[7] CANADA: ACCORDING TO SOURCE, THESE FIGURES ARE BASED ON CENSUS DATA, AND THEY ARE THOUGHT BY STUDY AUTHORS TO BE A LOW ESTIMATE "BECAUSE OF THE FREQUENCY OF MULTIPLE JOB-HOLDING AMONG ARTISTS AND THE MAY TIMING OF THE CENSUS" (EXECUTIVE SUMMARY P.4). ARTISTS IN MAJOR CITIES REPRESENT 1% OF THE WORKFORCE IN MAJOR CITIES.

COUNTRY	#1 CULTURAL INDUSTRY[1]	#1 CULTURAL OCCUPATION	#2 CULTURAL INDUSTRY	#2 CULTURAL OCCUPATION	#3 CULTURAL INDUSTRY	#3 CULTURAL OCCUPATION
UNITED STATES 2003	**PUBLISHING 0.5%** OF ALL EMPLOYMENT	NO DATA	**INDEPENDENT ARTISTS, WRITERS, PERFORMERS** (**0.5%** OF ALL EMPLOYMENT)	NO DATA	**ADVERTISING** (**0.3%** OF ALL EMPLOYMENT)	NO DATA
AUSTRALIA[2] 1996 – 2001	**DESIGN** (**25%** OF CULTURAL) **+20%**	2001: **PUBLISHING + PRINTING** (**17%** OF CULTURAL)[3]	**NEWSPAPER, BOOK, STATIONERY RETAIL** (**14%** OF CULTURAL); **+9.9%**	**DESIGNERS + RELATED WORKERS** (**15%** OF CULTURAL)[4]	**NEWSPAPER PRINTING** OR **PUBLISHING** (**9%** OF CULTURAL); **−2.6%**	**MUSICIANS, ACTORS, RELATED WORKERS** (**10.9%** OF CULTURAL)[5]
CANADA 1996 – 2001	NO DATA	**MUSICIANS + SINGERS** (**24%** OF ARTISTS)[6]	NO DATA	**WRITERS** (**16%** OF ARTISTS)	NO DATA	**ARTISANS + CRAFTPERSONS** (**15%** OF ARTISTS) **+ PRODUCERS, DIRECTORS, CHOREOGRAPHERS + RELATED** (**15%**)
CHILE 2004	**TOURISM** (**67%** OF CULTURAL EMPLOYERS, **68%** OF EMPLOYEES)	NO DATA	**PUBLISHING** (**11%** OF CULTURAL EMPLOYERS, **13%** OF EMPLOYEES)	NO DATA	**CULTURAL RECREATION** (**5%** OF CULTURAL EMPLOYERS, **6%** OF EMPLOYEES)[7]	NO DATA
NEW ZEALAND 1996 – 2001	**SOFTWARE + COMPUTERS** (**34%** OF CULTURAL); **+90.4%**[8]	**EARLY CHILDHOOD TEACHER**[9] (**19%** OF CULTURAL); **+39%**	**PUBLISHING** (**18.3%** OF CULTURAL)[10]	**GRAPHIC DESIGNER** (**8%** OF CULTURAL) **+35%**	**TV, RADIO** (**9%** OF CULTURAL)[11]	**LIBRARIAN** (**7%** OF CULTURAL); **+10%**
JAPAN[12] 2001 – 2004	**COMPUTER SOFT-WARE** (**38.3%** OF CREATIVE)	NO DATA	**ARCHITECTURAL DESIGN SERVICES** (**16.3%** OF CREATIVE)	NO DATA	**NPOs** (**6.8%** OF CREATIVE); **+5.6%**	NO DATA
HONG KONG 2002	**IT-RELATED** (**29.7%** OF CULTURAL); **+22.7%** AVERAGE PER YEAR 1997 – 2002	NO DATA	**PUBLISHING** (**18.8%** OF CULTURAL)	NO DATA	**ADVERTISING** (**17%** OF CULTURAL)	NO DATA
BRAZIL 2003	**EDUCATION + TEACHING** (**17%** OF CULTURAL)	NO DATA	**BOOK, JOURNAL, MAGAZINE RETAIL** (**12%** OF CULTURAL)	NO DATA	**EDITING + PUBLISHING** (**11%** OF CULTURAL)	NO DATA

[1] FOR EACH INDUSTRY AND OCCUPATION, THE % OF TOTAL CULTURAL EMPLOYMENT COMPRISED, AND ITS GROWTH (+) OR DECLINE (−) RATE, ARE GIVEN WHEN AVAILABLE.

[2] AUSTRALIA: 1999 – 2002: FILM AND VIDEO.

[3] AUSTRALIA: FOR DATA ABOVE, (+) (−) NOT AVAILABLE. 2001 -GRAPHIC DESIGNER (15% OF CULTURAL); #1 OCCUPATION AMONG ARTISTS ONLY (2001); MUSICIAN (13% OF CULTURAL, (+)12% FROM 1993).

[4] AUSTRALIA: FOR DATA ABOVE, (+) (−) NOT AVAILABLE. #2 OCCUPATION AMONG ARTISTS ONLY (2001) -VISUAL ARTIST 9%, UP FROM 6% IN 1987.

[5] AUSTRALIA: FOR DATA ABOVE, (+) (−) NOT AVAILABLE. #3 OCCUPATION AMONG ARTISTS ONLY (2001) -WRITER 7%, UP FROM 3% IN 1987.

[6] CANADA: THOUGH MUSICIANS AND SINGERS MADE UP THE LARGEST % OF ARTISTS IN CANADA OVERALL, THE MOST POPULATED ARTISTIC OCCUPATIONS IN TORONTO, VANCOUVER, AND MONTREAL WERE IN THE CATEGORY OF PRODUCERS, DIRECTORS, CHOREOGRAPHERS, AND RELATED.

[7] CHILE: INCLUDES MUSEUMS, LIBRARIES, GARDENS, ZOOS, ETC.

[8] NEW ZEALAND: IN ANOTHER REPORT, "OTHER CULTURAL INDUSTRIES" WAS BY FAR THE MOST POPULATED CATEGORY: 46% OF CULTURAL; (+)0%. ASIDE FROM THESE "OTHER" CATEGORIES, #1 INDUSTRY WAS INTEREST GROUPS (11% OF CULTURAL); (+)30%.

[9] NEW ZEALAND: "OTHER CULTURAL OCCUPATIONS" CATEGORY SCORED HIGHER THAN ANY ONE OCCUPATIONAL CATEGORY: 45% OF CULTURAL; (+)7%.

[10] IN ANOTHER REPORT: PRESCHOOL EDUCATION (11% OF CULTURAL); (+)29%

[11] NEWSPAPER, BOOKS, STATIONERY (8% OF CULTURAL); (+)7%.

[12] 1996 – 2001 JAPAN: COMPUTER SOFTWARE (31% OF CREATIVE INDUSTRIES); (+)47%. ARCHITECTURE AND ENGINEERING SERVICES (27.5% OF CREATIVE INDUSTRIES); (−)9%. PUBLISHING (9% OF CREATIVE INDUSTRIES); (−)5%.

4. **QUALITY OF LIFE** OF ARTISTS IN SELECT COUNTRIES

TABLE (ADAPTED FROM UNESCO, 2004) COMPARING AND CONTRASTING EMPLOYMENT REGIMES AND SOCIAL BENEFITS SYSTEMS OF ARTISTS AROUND THE WORLD

COUNTRY	RIGHTS AND "PROFESSIONAL" STATUS	SICKNESS AND MATERNITY	EMPLOYMENT INJURY
BULGARIA	YES	YES	AVAILABLE TO EMPLOYEES OF COMPANIES
BELGIUM	YES	NO DATA	AVAILABLE TO EMPLOYEES OF COMPANIES
NORWAY	IN SELECTED CULTURAL OCCUPATIONS	AVAILABLE TO EMPLOYEES OF COMPANIES	AVAILABLE TO EMPLOYEES OF COMPANIES
PERU	NO DATA	YES	IN SELECTED CULTURAL OCCUPATIONS
DENMARK	IN SELECTED CULTURAL OCCUPATIONS	AVAILABLE TO EMPLOYEES OF COMPANIES	IN SELECTED CULTURAL OCCUPATIONS
FRANCE	IN SPECIAL CASES	YES	NO DATA
LITHUANIA	YES	AVAILABLE TO EMPLOYEES OF COMPANIES	AVAILABLE TO EMPLOYEES OF COMPANIES
NETHERLANDS	YES	YES	NO DATA
PHILIPPINES	YES	YES	NO DATA
UNITED STATES	YES	AVAILABLE TO EMPLOYEES OF COMPANIES	AVAILABLE TO EMPLOYEES OF COMPANIES
BRAZIL	YES	AVAILABLE TO EMPLOYEES OF COMPANIES	AVAILABLE TO EMPLOYEES OF COMPANIES
CUBA	NO	AVAILABLE TO EMPLOYEES OF COMPANIES	AVAILABLE TO EMPLOYEES OF COMPANIES
FINLAND	NO	YES	AVAILABLE TO EMPLOYEES OF COMPANIES
LATVIA	NO/IMPROVING	AVAILABLE TO EMPLOYEES OF COMPANIES	AVAILABLE TO EMPLOYEES OF COMPANIES
ITALY	YES	YES	NO DATA
SERBIA	YES	AVAILABLE TO EMPLOYEES OF COMPANIES	AVAILABLE TO EMPLOYEES OF COMPANIES
ECUADOR	NO DATA	AVAILABLE TO EMPLOYEES OF COMPANIES	AVAILABLE TO EMPLOYEES OF COMPANIES
UKRAINE	YES	NO DATA	NO DATA
MALAWI	NO	NO DATA	NO DATA
SWITZERLAND	NO DATA	AVAILABLE TO EMPLOYEES OF COMPANIES	AVAILABLE TO EMPLOYEES OF COMPANIES

* THOUGH VERY LITTLE INFORMATION IS READILY AVAILABLE ABOUT THE RIGHTS TO WORK, PROFESSIONAL STATUS, AND EMPLOYMENT BENEFITS AND
REGIMES WHICH CULTURAL PROFESSIONALS ENJOY IN VARIOUS COUNTRIES, UNESCO HAS MADE AVAILABLE SOME DATA (COLLECTED FROM COUNTRY
WEBSITES) ABOUT THESE ISSUES. THIS TABLE IS THUS ADAPTED FROM ONE THAT UNESCO HAS PRODUCED. THE ORIGINAL TABLE GAVE MUCH GREATER DETAIL

HEALTH CARE PROTECTION	OLD AGE, INVALIDITY, SURVIVORS	UNEMPLOYMENT
YES	YES	YES
YES	YES	YES
YES	YES	YES
YES	YES	YES
IN SELECTED CULTURAL OCCUPATIONS	NO	YES
YES/IMPROVING	YES/IMPROVING	YES
AVAILABLE TO EMPLOYEES OF COMPANIES	IN SPECIAL CASES	AVAILABLE TO EMPLOYEES OF COMPANIES AND IN SPECIAL CASES
NO DATA	AVAILABLE TO EMPLOYEES OF COMPANIES	YES
YES	YES	NO
AVAILABLE TO EMPLOYEES OF COMPANIES	AVAILABLE TO EMPLOYEES OF COMPANIES	YES
AVAILABLE TO EMPLOYEES OF COMPANIES	YES	AVAILABLE TO EMPLOYEES OF COMPANIES
YES	YES	YES
YES	IN SPECIAL CASES	AVAILABLE TO EMPLOYEES OF COMPANIES
AVAILABLE TO EMPLOYEES OF COMPANIES	YES	AVAILABLE TO EMPLOYEES OF COMPANIES AND IN SPECIAL CASES
NO DATA	YES	NO DATA
YES	IN SELECTED CULTURAL OCCUPATIONS	IN SELECTED CULTURAL OCCUPATIONS
AVAILABLE TO ALL PUBLIC EMPLOYEES	AVAILABLE TO EMPLOYEES OF COMPANIES	RECEIVE SPECIAL GOVERNMENT ARTIST STATUS WHEN EMPLOYEES OF COMPANIES
YES	NO DATA	AVAILABLE TO EMPLOYEES OF COMPANIES AND UNION/TRADE ASSN MEMBERS
YES	AVAILABLE TO EMPLOYEES OF COMPANIES	AVAILABLE TO EMPLOYEES OF COMPANIES
AVAILABLE TO EMPLOYEES OF COMPANIES	AVAILABLE TO THOSE WHO HAVE PAID IN	YES

ABOUT THE CATEGORIES PRESENTED ABOVE (WHEN DATA WERE AVAILABLE). IN THIS ADAPTATION, THE AIM IS *NOT* TO QUANTIFY OR EVALUATE THE BENEFITS AND THE RIGHTS WHICH CULTURAL PROFESSIONALS HAVE IN THESE COUNTRIES, BUT TO SIMPLY NOTE *WHETHER* AND *UNDER WHAT CIRCUMSTANCES* THESE INDIVIDUALS RECEIVE *SOME* TYPE OF BENEFITS OR RIGHTS IN THESE CATEGORIES.

CULTURAL EMPLOYMENT + PROFESSIONS

The growth of the cultural industries worldwide has spawned a corresponding expansion in cultural employment. This has in turn spurred regional and national economies and provided opportunities for people to make a living using their cultural talents. Yet cultural employment has grown far more quickly in developed nations, a trend accentuated by the tendency of cultural professionals to 'cluster' in global cultural 'hotspots' (cf. chapters by Scott and Greffe in this volume; see also Addison, 2006; Florida, 2005). The result is often a 'winner takes all' (Addison, 2006) scenario that makes it difficult for developing nations to attract and keep their cultural talent. Nonetheless, many have suggested that cultural industries may hold the key to advancement for developing nations who successfully invest in cultural talent and thereby attract creative individuals to their soil (see chapter by Isar in this volume).

The rapidly changing cultural economy also presents new challenges to cultural workers. Compared to workers in other fields, cultural workers are more likely to be independent or to work in small enterprises, to maintain multiple jobs, and to engage in temporary or part-time work. These differences often mean unconventional, yet professionalized, careers—increased flexibility and creativity on the one hand, decreased job security and stability on the other.

WHAT IS CULTURAL EMPLOYMENT?

There is no single definition of cultural employment, as researchers have tailored measures to the differing landscapes of various societies. Employment may be thought of in terms of either industries or occupations. Cultural industries are fields of cultural production which involve workers whose activities may or may *not* be creative or artistic in nature (such as all workers involved in the fashion industry), while cultural occupations refer to specific artistic and cultural roles and professional titles which individuals may don. These occupations may be found in both cultural and non-cultural industries—for example, web designers often work for companies whose products or services are non-cultural. Additionally, many cultural professionals must supplement creative endeavors with work which is non-cultural.

Definitions of cultural industries and occupations have therefore ranged from very narrow to quite broad. Some include only the 'fine arts' markets, or 'upstream' aspects of the cultural production continuum; these generate creativity, original ideas, and innovation (Addison, 2006). Richard Florida's (2005) 'global creative class' (see data point 1) is broad and includes any and all professional work that involves creativity, such as scientific pursuits and inventions, in addition to cultural contributions. Applied aspects of cultural work, including 'new media' industries such as digital reproduction of music, or advertising, may be considered 'downstream' activities, or those which involve the skilled *execution* of cultural innovations, their replication, or distribution.

Many, but not all, cultural occupations are professions in the traditional sense. In other words, they require specialized knowledge and skills, allow workers significant autonomy, and benefit society as a whole, rather than just an individual or corporation. Some may be considered part of the professional elite who receive recognition for their contributions on a global scale—a benefit to which access may vary in part based upon how far 'up' or 'downstream' individuals find themselves in the cultural production continuum.

Finally, many cultural professionals are also entrepreneurs, as discussed in the chapter in this volume by Tom Aageson. A cultural entrepreneur may be an artist or cultural worker who works on a freelance or contract basis, or someone who invests in their own cultural micro-business. The term also refers to major actors who bring arts and culture to society on a large scale, such as brokers and philanthropists for civic and national-level arts.[1]

TRENDS IN CULTURAL EMPLOYMENT (see data points 2 and 3)

- Between 2002 and 2004 in the EU, cultural employment made up 2.5 per cent of the cultural industries (3.1 per cent if including cultural tourism).
- In the US in 2005, employment in the cultural industries was 7 per cent, however, this figure is likely inflated because some cultural categories are combined with non-cultural occupation categories (e.g., architecture is categorized alongside engineering).
- After the US, Australia has the highest percentage of cultural employment at 5.1 per cent in 2005. In fact, cultural employment overall grew 11 per cent in Australia between 1996 and 2001. In that same time period, the top cultural occupations were publishing and printing, design related work, and music and acting.
- Canada experienced the highest growth in employment in the cultural industries, with a growth rate of 29 per cent between 1991 and 2001. Top cultural occupations in this time period were music and acting, writing, and artisanal and craft work.
- In Asian countries, cultural employment accounts for 2.2 per cent in Singapore, 3.2 per cent in Japan, 3.7 per cent in Hong Kong, and 3.6 per cent in Taiwan.
- Cultural employment in Brazil in 2003 was 4 per cent for the whole cultural sector.

WHAT ARE THE ISSUES?

Scott and others have provided much evidence of the 'clustering effect' and its negative impact upon nations who lack cultural centers. Nonetheless, support for the notion that purposive efforts to stimulate cultural employment are important strategies for economic development in under-resourced countries comes from the fact that many countries have shown greater growth in cultural industries than in the economy overall in recent years (as shown in the indicator suite).

Several contributors to this volume have observed that in today's cultural market, quality is as important to competitiveness as low cost of products. This has led to the rise of a 'workshop' model of production in which workers collaborate in order to uniquely serve a client, as opposed to a 'chain' model of linear production. These authors suggest that one set of implications of this trend is that many cultural professionals are relegated to 'artisan' status: they must produce more units for a given financial return than 'fine artists,' and it is more difficult to protect intellectual property rights in such a scenario. Though society has valued upstream 'artists' more highly than downstream 'artisans' since the Renaissance, a 'commercial art bias' in today's global market increasingly forces artists to package their work into functional and marketable products; there exists therefore much overlap between artists and artisans. As shown in the indicator suite, downstream positions such as those in advertising, digital media, and design comprise an increasingly prominent portion of the cultural employment available worldwide (see chapter by Friel and Santagata in this volume; and Addison, 2006).

Clearly, individuals and cultural production teams who want to succeed in the global cultural market need networking and connecting abilities, specialized training in a discrete field which can produce functional objects, virtuosity in defining the characteristics of cultural products, and creativity in developing new products. Across the board, cultural workers are highly educated in comparison to other careers; this fact has been documented in Canada, New Zealand, and throughout the EU. Students often travel internationally to learn cultural occupational skills at top schools in global cultural centers with close ties to local cultural industries (Addison, 2006; Florida, 2005). Migration to key centers of cultural production also allows professionals to be 'in the mix' of new technologies and innovative strategies, which may be key to career success for such individuals in today's global market (Addison, 2006).

Cultural workers must therefore invest significant resources in education and entrepreneurial endeavors in order to access employment opportunities, yet cultural industries and occupations do not always sufficiently nurture cultural talent. Income levels of cultural workers relative to the general workforce vary greatly: Those who worked in arts and culture in New Zealand in 1996 and 2001 were most often of European descent and tended to make more than the median income level for the workforce overall. Artists in Canada in 2001, by contrast, earned on average 26 per cent *less* than other workers, with a substantial number of individuals making poverty wages. Yet education levels among cultural professionals were high in both countries—in Canada, they were double that of the general workforce.

In Hong Kong, 98 per cent of cultural establishments are small or medium enterprises (these have grown to 4.1 per cent 1999-2004). Cultural employers in Chile, on average, employed approximately 18 workers in 2004, indicating a similar tendency toward small enterprises. Such entrepreneurial careers may often be characterized by part-time work, side jobs, and temporary work, though this varies depending upon the specific cultural occupation. In New Zealand, for example, part-time work rates in cultural fields were about the same as in the workforce overall; however, certain types of performers, visual artists, and writers and critics averaged much higher levels of part-time work.

POLICY IMPLICATIONS AND RECOMMENDATIONS

Government policies, political repression and upheaval, and the forces of democratization impact upon artist mobility and the ability of countries to retain cultural professionals (Addison, 2006). As shown in the indicator suite, employment benefit regimes and rights of cultural professionals vary by country. European Union countries, Latin American countries such as Peru and Cuba, the Philippines, and others lead in establishing quality of life supports for cultural workers and professionals (see data point 4). Florida has argued that although the United States boasts great cultural resources, restrictive visa policies and other policies may undercut its continued leadership in the global cultural economy. Singapore, the UK, Argentina, Brazil, and Hong Kong, on the other hand, are examples of countries that have made intentional efforts to *invest* in cultural industries as a way to employ their populaces and grow their economies. This is very much in line with both Friel and Santagata (see their chapter in this volume), who reason that nations who want to capitalize on their cultural workforce must upgrade the status of artisans to artists, recognize intellectual property rights, and work to bridge the aesthetics of these two segments of the arts market. As many contributions to the literature have observed, cultural activities and facilities can provide important urban renewal strategies, the mobility of artists ought to be supported by national governments (even in poor countries where artists are nonetheless globally mobile), and poor countries in particular must improve the climate for small business in general, if their cultural industries are to succeed.

Endnotes

[1] Leon Botstein, American conductor (American Symphony Orchestra, Jerusalem Symphony Orchestra), President of Bard College, and Leon Levy Professor in Arts and Humanities, serves as a prime example of a high-profile cultural entrepreneur. Botstein has worked beyond his own art to raise the quality and prestige of Bard, has brought about the construction of a landmark concert hall for the university designed by architectural giant Frank Gehry, and has been called a 'leading advocate of progressive education' (Wikipedia, 2007) in the arts and in the public education system.

GOVERNMENT EXPENDITURE ON CULTURE + RECREATION

% OF TOTAL GOVERNMENT SPENDING COUNTRIES SORTED BY HUMAN DEVELOPMENT INDEX (LOW TO HIGH)

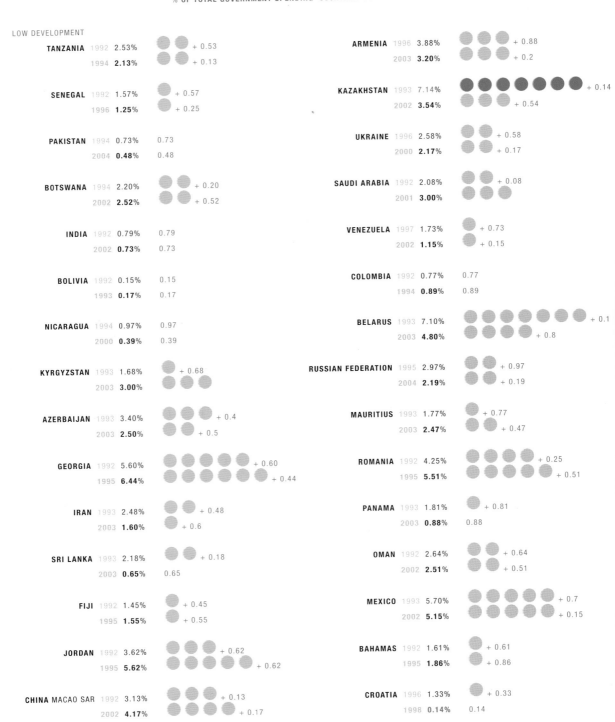

LOW DEVELOPMENT

TANZANIA	1992 2.53%	+ 0.53
	1994 **2.13%**	+ 0.13
SENEGAL	1992 1.57%	+ 0.57
	1996 **1.25%**	+ 0.25
PAKISTAN	1994 0.73%	0.73
	2004 **0.48%**	0.48
BOTSWANA	1994 2.20%	+ 0.20
	2002 **2.52%**	+ 0.52
INDIA	1992 0.79%	0.79
	2002 **0.73%**	0.73
BOLIVIA	1992 0.15%	0.15
	1993 **0.17%**	0.17
NICARAGUA	1994 0.97%	0.97
	2000 **0.39%**	0.39
KYRGYZSTAN	1993 1.68%	+ 0.68
	2003 **3.00%**	
AZERBAIJAN	1993 3.40%	+ 0.4
	2003 **2.50%**	+ 0.5
GEORGIA	1992 5.60%	+ 0.60
	1995 **6.44%**	+ 0.44
IRAN	1993 2.48%	+ 0.48
	2003 **1.60%**	+ 0.6
SRI LANKA	1993 2.18%	+ 0.18
	2003 **0.65%**	0.65
FIJI	1992 1.45%	+ 0.45
	1995 **1.55%**	+ 0.55
JORDAN	1992 3.62%	+ 0.62
	1995 **5.62%**	+ 0.62
CHINA MACAO SAR	1992 3.13%	+ 0.13
	2002 **4.17%**	+ 0.17

ARMENIA	1996 3.88%	+ 0.88
	2003 **3.20%**	+ 0.2
KAZAKHSTAN	1993 7.14%	+ 0.14
	2002 **3.54%**	+ 0.54
UKRAINE	1996 2.58%	+ 0.58
	2000 **2.17%**	+ 0.17
SAUDI ARABIA	1992 2.08%	+ 0.08
	2001 **3.00%**	
VENEZUELA	1997 1.73%	+ 0.73
	2002 **1.15%**	+ 0.15
COLOMBIA	1992 0.77%	0.77
	1994 **0.89%**	0.89
BELARUS	1993 7.10%	+ 0.1
	2003 **4.80%**	+ 0.8
RUSSIAN FEDERATION	1995 2.97%	+ 0.97
	2004 **2.19%**	+ 0.19
MAURITIUS	1993 1.77%	+ 0.77
	2003 **2.47%**	+ 0.47
ROMANIA	1992 4.25%	+ 0.25
	1995 **5.51%**	+ 0.51
PANAMA	1993 1.81%	+ 0.81
	2003 **0.88%**	0.88
OMAN	1992 2.64%	+ 0.64
	2002 **2.51%**	+ 0.51
MEXICO	1993 5.70%	+ 0.7
	2002 **5.15%**	+ 0.15
BAHAMAS	1992 1.61%	+ 0.61
	1995 **1.86%**	+ 0.86
CROATIA	1996 1.33%	+ 0.33
	1998 **0.14%**	0.14

ESTONIA	1992	5.52%	+ 0.52
	1996	**5.59%**	+ 0.59
BAHRAIN	1996	0.70%	+ 0.7
	2000	**0.63%**	+ 0.63
HUNGARY	1992	4.11%	+ 0.11
	1994	**3.63%**	+ 0.63
KUWAIT	1992	2.26%	+ 0.26
	1999	**4.26%**	+ 0.26
CZECH REPUBLIC	2002	2.78%	+ 0.78
	2003	**2.66%**	+ 0.66
CYPRUS	1992	0.54%	0.54
	1994	**0.72%**	0.72
PORTUGAL	1993	2.23%	+ 0.23
	2003	**2.50%**	+ 0.5
SLOVENIA	1992	2.90%	+ 0.9
	1993	**4.37%**	+ 0.37
SOUTH KOREA	1992	1.40%	+ 0.4
	2002	**1.31%**	+ 0.31
GREECE	1995	1.40%	+ 0.4
	2003	**1.26%**	+ 0.26
ISRAEL	1993	3.68%	+ 0.68
	2003	**3.09%**	+ 0.09
GERMANY	1993	2.94%	+ 0.94
	2003	**2.32%**	+ 0.32
SPAIN	1992	2.98%	+ 0.98
	1995	**3.19%**	+ 0.19
UNITED KINGDOM	1993	2.71%	+ 0.71
	2003	**2.18%**	+ 0.18
ITALY	1993	2.18%	+ 0.18
	2003	**2.12%**	+ 0.12

FRANCE	1995	1.83%	+ 0.83
	2002	**1.97%**	+ 0.97
DENMARK	1994	4.38%	+ 0.38
	2004	**4.41%**	+ 0.41
AUSTRIA	1995	2.57%	+ 0.57
	2003	**2.50%**	+ 0.5
BELGIUM	1993	1.67%	+ 0.67
	2003	**2.56%**	+ 0.56
LUXEMBOURG	1993	4.43%	+ 0.43
	2003	**4.60%**	+ 0.6
FINLAND	1993	3.39%	+ 0.39
	2003	**3.20%**	+ 0.2
NETHERLANDS ANTILLES	1993	1.83%	+ 0.83
	2003	**1.47%**	+ 0.47
NETHERLANDS	1995	2.89%	+ 0.89
	2003	**2.72%**	+ 0.72
UNITED STATES	1993	1.19%	+ 0.19
	2003	**1.42%**	+ 0.42
JAPAN	1993	0.42%	0.42
	2003	**0.41%**	0.41
SWEDEN	1995	4.89%	+ 0.89
	2003	**2.66%**	+ 0.66
IRELAND	1995	1.42%	+ 0.42
	2002	**1.92%**	+ 0.92
AUSTRALIA	1992	3.88%	+ 0.88
	2002	**2.87%**	+ 0.87
ICELAND	1994	5.69%	+ 0.69
	2004	**5.35%**	+ 0.35
NORWAY	1993	3.82%	+ 0.82
	2003	**2.77%**	+ 0.77

HIGH DEVELOPMENT

407

2. GOVERNMENT EXPENDITURE ON EDUCATION

% **OF TOTAL GOVERNMENT SPENDING** COUNTRIES SORTED BY HUMAN DEVELOPMENT INDEX (LOW TO HIGH)

LOW DEVELOPMENT

CHAD	1994	21.7%	+ 1.7		**AZERBAIJAN**	1993	3.4%	3.4
	2001	**25.0%**	+ 5.0			2003	2.5%	2.5
COTE D'IVOIRE	1996	20.3%	+ 0.3		**GEORGIA**	1992	24.5%	+ 4.5
	1998	**11.8%**	+ 1.8			1995	**10.2%**	+ 0.2
TANZANIA	1992	7.7%	7.7		**IRAN**	1993	20.0%	
	1994	**7.5%**	7.5			2003	**4.1%**	4.1
SENEGAL	1992	31.4%	+ 1.4		**DOMINICAN REPUBLIC**	1992	17.0%	+ 7.0
	1996	**30.1%**	+ 0.1			1996	**24.1%**	+ 4.1
KENYA	1993	38.0%	+ 8.0		**SRI LANKA**	1993	15.0%	+ 5.0
	2003	**41.4%**	+ 1.4			2003	**13.1%**	+ 3.1
LESOTHO	1992	5.8%	5.8		**FIJI**	1992	24.6%	+ 4.6
	2001	**7.7%**	7.7			2002	**29.4%**	+ 9.4
BANGLADESH	1996	18.5%	+ 8.5		**SAINT VINCENT + THE GRENADINES**	1993	25.6%	+ 5.6
	2000	**16.5%**	+ 6.5			2003	**25.6%**	+ 5.6
PAKISTAN	1994	11.6%	+ 1.6		**JORDAN**	1992	19.8%	+ 9.8
	2004	**16.8%**	+ 6.8			1995	**21.3%**	+ 1.3
BOTSWANA	1994	23.0%	+ 3.0		**CHINA** MACAO SAR	1992	9.6%	9.6
	2002	**27.4%**	+ 7.4			2002	**12.2%**	+ 2.2
INDIA	1992	15.5%	+ 5.5		**KAZAKHSTAN**	1993	29.1%	+ 9.1
	2002	**16.1%**	+ 6.1			2002	**25.1%**	+ 5.1
HONDURAS	1992	31.7%	+ 1.7		**UKRAINE**	1996	23.2%	+ 3.2
	1997	**35.2%**	+ 5.2			2000	**27.3%**	+ 7.3
BOLIVIA	1992	8.1%	8.1		**SAUDI ARABIA**	1992	18.4%	+ 8.4
	1993	**9.0%**	9.0			2001	**26.4%**	+ 6.4
REPUBLIC OF MOLDOVA	1992	40.1%	+ 0.1		**THAILAND**	1992	30.6%	+ 0.6
	2002	**28.5%**	+ 8.5			2002	**33.3%**	+ 3.3
NICARAGUA	1994	16.6%	+ 6.6		**VENEZUELA**	1997	36.4%	+ 6.4
	2000	**15.4%**	+ 5.4			2002	**43.2%**	+ 3.2
KYRGYZSTAN	1993	19.1%	+ 9.1		**COLOMBIA**	1992	24.8%	+ 4.8
	2003	**25.1%**	+ 5.1			1994	**21.0%**	+ 1.0

BRAZIL	1993	14.8%	+ 4.8
	2003	**17.3%**	+ 7.3
RUSSIAN FEDERATION	1995	20.8%	+ 0.8
	2004	**18.7%**	+ 8.7
MAURITIUS	1993	19.9%	+ 9.9
	2003	**19.0%**	+ 9.0
MALAYSIA	1992	30.2%	+ 0.2
	1995	**30.3%**	+ 0.3
ROMANIA	2002	22.6%	+ 2.6
	2003	**21.4%**	+ 1.4
PANAMA	1993	28.7%	+ 8.7
	2003	**24.6%**	+ 4.6
TRINIDAD + TOBAGO	1993	19.3%	+ 9.3
	2003	**23.7%**	+ 3.7
OMAN	1992	14.4%	+ 4.4
	2002	**20.8%**	+ 0.8
MEXICO	1993	35.8%	+ 5.8
	2002	**36.9%**	+ 6.9
BAHAMAS	1992	22.8%	+ 2.8
	1995	**22.1%**	+ 2.1
COSTA RICA	1992	29.4%	+ 9.4
	2002	**32.6%**	+ 2.6
CROATIA	1996	11.6%	+ 1.6
	1998	**11.3%**	+ 1.3
ESTONIA	1992	34.1%	+ 4.1
	1996	**27.8%**	+ 7.8
ARGENTINA	1993	4.9%	4.9
	1998	**6.0%**	6.0
HUNGARY	1992	22.2%	+ 2.2
	1994	**21.4%**	+ 1.4
KUWAIT	1992	11.6%	+ 1.6
	1999	**22.0%**	+ 2.0
MALTA	1992	29.6%	+ 9.6
	1996	**27.7%**	+ 7.7

CZECH REPUBLIC	1995	19.5%	+ 9.5
	2003	**19.1%**	+ 9.1
CYPRUS	1992	16.3%	+ 6.3
	1994	**20.4%**	+ 0.4
PORTUGAL	1993	29.4%	+ 9.4
	2003	**28.8%**	+ 8.8
SLOVENIA	1992	19.8%	+ 9.8
	1993	**24.3%**	+ 4.3
SOUTH KOREA	1992	24.2%	+ 4.2
	2002	**21.6%**	+ 1.6
GREECE	1995	20.4%	+ 0.4
	2003	**17.8%**	+ 7.8
ISRAEL	1993	22.8%	+ 2.8
	2003	**23.1%**	+ 3.1
GERMANY	1993	19.0%	+ 9.0
	2003	**17.9%**	+ 7.9
NEW ZEALAND	1992	26.3%	+ 6.3
	1994	**26.1%**	+ 6.1
SPAIN	1992	20.0%	
	1996	**22.9%**	+ 2.9
UNITED KINGDOM	1993	17.9%	+ 7.9
	2003	**17.2%**	+ 7.2
ITALY	1993	25.3%	+ 5.3
	2003	**23.7%**	+ 3.7
FRANCE	1995	21.0%	+ 1.0
	2002	**20.0%**	
DENMARK	1994	21.9%	+ 1.9
	2004	**23.3%**	+ 3.3
AUSTRIA	1995	27.6%	+ 7.6
	2003	**27.8%**	+ 7.8
BELGIUM	1995	30.3%	+ 0.3
	2003	**26.9%**	+ 6.9
LUXEMBOURG	1993	25.4%	+ 5.4
	2003	**24.1%**	+ 4.1

HIGH DEVELOPMENT >

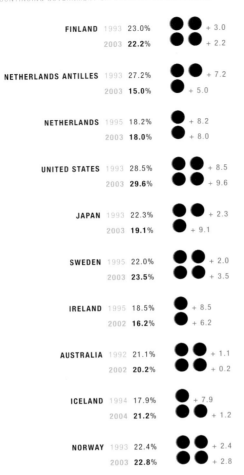

FINLAND	1993	23.0%		+ 3.0
	2003	**22.2%**		+ 2.2
NETHERLANDS ANTILLES	1993	27.2%		+ 7.2
	2003	**15.0%**		+ 5.0
NETHERLANDS	1995	18.2%		+ 8.2
	2003	**18.0%**		+ 8.0
UNITED STATES	1993	28.5%		+ 8.5
	2003	**29.6%**		+ 9.6
JAPAN	1993	22.3%		+ 2.3
	2003	**19.1%**		+ 9.1
SWEDEN	1995	22.0%		+ 2.0
	2003	**23.5%**		+ 3.5
IRELAND	1995	18.5%		+ 8.5
	2002	**16.2%**		+ 6.2
AUSTRALIA	1992	21.1%		+ 1.1
	2002	**20.2%**		+ 0.2
ICELAND	1994	17.9%		+ 7.9
	2004	**21.2%**		+ 1.2
NORWAY	1993	22.4%		+ 2.4
	2003	**22.8%**		+ 2.8

HIGH DEVELOPMENT

PUBLIC SPENDING ON CULTURE BY SECTOR

AS % OF TOTAL PUBLIC SPENDING ON CULTURE

1%

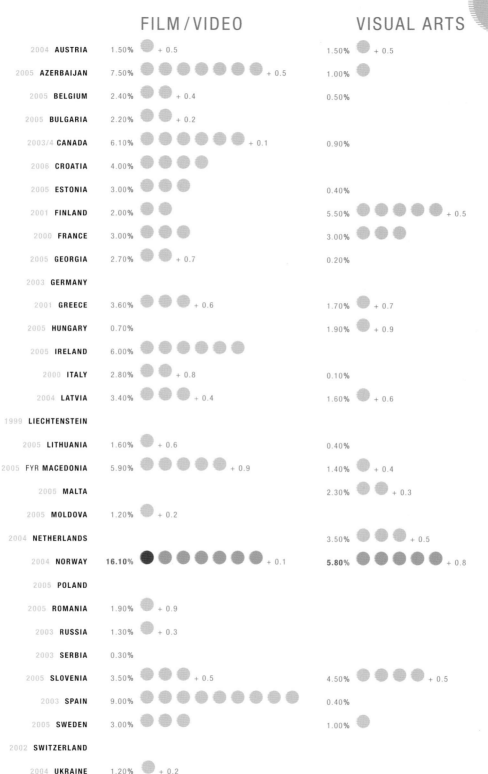

		FILM/VIDEO	VISUAL ARTS
2004	AUSTRIA	1.50% + 0.5	1.50% + 0.5
2005	AZERBAIJAN	7.50% + 0.5	1.00%
2005	BELGIUM	2.40% + 0.4	0.50%
2005	BULGARIA	2.20% + 0.2	
2003/4	CANADA	6.10% + 0.1	0.90%
2006	CROATIA	4.00%	
2005	ESTONIA	3.00%	0.40%
2001	FINLAND	2.00%	5.50% + 0.5
2000	FRANCE	3.00%	3.00%
2005	GEORGIA	2.70% + 0.7	0.20%
2003	GERMANY		
2001	GREECE	3.60% + 0.6	1.70% + 0.7
2005	HUNGARY	0.70%	1.90% + 0.9
2005	IRELAND	6.00%	
2000	ITALY	2.80% + 0.8	0.10%
2004	LATVIA	3.40% + 0.4	1.60% + 0.6
1999	LIECHTENSTEIN		
2005	LITHUANIA	1.60% + 0.6	0.40%
2005 FYR	MACEDONIA	5.90% + 0.9	1.40% + 0.4
2005	MALTA		2.30% + 0.3
2005	MOLDOVA	1.20% + 0.2	
2004	NETHERLANDS		3.50% + 0.5
2004	NORWAY	**16.10%** + 0.1	**5.80%** + 0.8
2005	POLAND		
2005	ROMANIA	1.90% + 0.9	
2003	RUSSIA	1.30% + 0.3	
2003	SERBIA	0.30%	
2005	SLOVENIA	3.50% + 0.5	4.50% + 0.5
2003	SPAIN	9.00%	0.40%
2005	SWEDEN	3.00%	1.00%
2002	SWITZERLAND		
2004	UKRAINE	1.20% + 0.2	

RADIO / TV

PERFORMING ARTS*

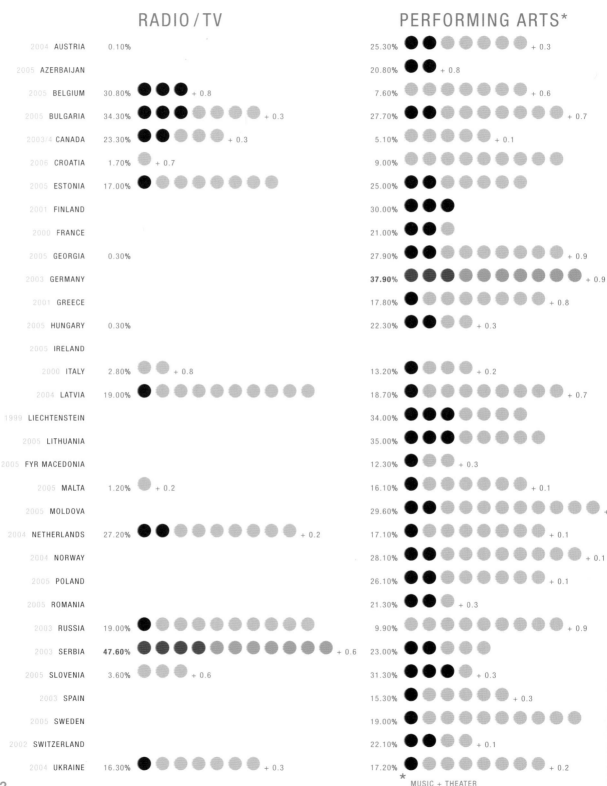

		RADIO/TV	PERFORMING ARTS*
2004	AUSTRIA	0.10%	25.30% + 0.3
2005	AZERBAIJAN		20.80% + 0.8
2005	BELGIUM	30.80% + 0.8	7.60% + 0.6
2005	BULGARIA	34.30% + 0.3	27.70% + 0.7
2003/4	CANADA	23.30% + 0.3	5.10% + 0.1
2006	CROATIA	1.70% + 0.7	9.00%
2005	ESTONIA	17.00%	25.00%
2001	FINLAND		30.00%
2000	FRANCE		21.00%
2005	GEORGIA	0.30%	27.90% + 0.9
2003	GERMANY		**37.90%** + 0.9
2001	GREECE		17.80% + 0.8
2005	HUNGARY	0.30%	22.30% + 0.3
2005	IRELAND		
2000	ITALY	2.80% + 0.8	13.20% + 0.2
2004	LATVIA	19.00%	18.70% + 0.7
1999	LIECHTENSTEIN		34.00%
2005	LITHUANIA		35.00%
2005	FYR MACEDONIA		12.30% + 0.3
2005	MALTA	1.20% + 0.2	16.10% + 0.1
2005	MOLDOVA		29.60% +
2004	NETHERLANDS	27.20% + 0.2	17.10% + 0.1
2004	NORWAY		28.10% + 0.1
2005	POLAND		26.10% + 0.1
2005	ROMANIA		21.30% + 0.3
2003	RUSSIA	19.00%	9.90% + 0.9
2003	SERBIA	**47.60%** + 0.6	23.00%
2005	SLOVENIA	3.60% + 0.6	31.30% + 0.3
2003	SPAIN		15.30% + 0.3
2005	SWEDEN		19.00%
2002	SWITZERLAND		22.10% + 0.1
2004	UKRAINE	16.30% + 0.3	17.20% + 0.2

* MUSIC + THEATER

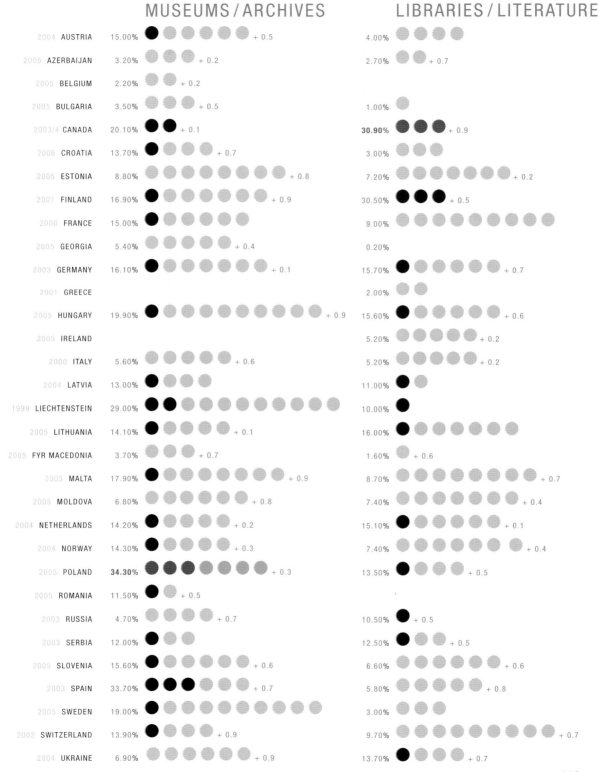

MUSEUMS / ARCHIVES   LIBRARIES / LITERATURE

		MUSEUMS / ARCHIVES	LIBRARIES / LITERATURE
2004	AUSTRIA	15.00% ●●●●● + 0.5	4.00% ●●●●
2005	AZERBAIJAN	3.20% ●●● + 0.2	2.70% ●● + 0.7
2005	BELGIUM	2.20% ●● + 0.2	
2005	BULGARIA	3.50% ●●● + 0.5	1.00% ●
2003/4	CANADA	20.10% ●● + 0.1	30.90% ●●● + 0.9
2006	CROATIA	13.70% ●●● + 0.7	3.00% ●●
2005	ESTONIA	8.80% ●●●●●●●● + 0.8	7.20% ●●●●●●● + 0.2
2001	FINLAND	16.90% ●●●●●●● + 0.9	30.50% ●●● + 0.5
2000	FRANCE	15.00% ●	9.00% ●●●●●●●●●
2005	GEORGIA	5.40% ●●●● + 0.4	0.20%
2003	GERMANY	16.10% ●●●●● + 0.1	15.70% ●●●●●● + 0.7
2001	GREECE		2.00% ●●
2005	HUNGARY	19.90% ●●●●●●●●●● + 0.9	15.60% ●●●●●● + 0.6
2005	IRELAND		5.20% ●●●●● + 0.2
2000	ITALY	5.60% ●●●●● + 0.6	5.20% ●●●●● + 0.2
2004	LATVIA	13.00% ●●●●	11.00% ●●
1999	LIECHTENSTEIN	29.00% ●●●●●●●●●●	10.00% ●
2005	LITHUANIA	14.10% ●●●●● + 0.1	16.00% ●●●●●●
2005	FYR MACEDONIA	3.70% ●●● + 0.7	1.60% ● + 0.6
2005	MALTA	17.90% ●●●●●●●● + 0.9	8.70% ●●●●●●●● + 0.7
2005	MOLDOVA	6.80% ●●●●●● + 0.8	7.40% ●●●●●●● + 0.4
2004	NETHERLANDS	14.20% ●●●● + 0.2	15.10% ●●●●●● + 0.1
2004	NORWAY	14.30% ●●●●● + 0.3	7.40% ●●●●●●● + 0.4
2005	POLAND	34.30% ●●●●●●● + 0.3	13.50% ●●●● + 0.5
2005	ROMANIA	11.50% ● + 0.5	
2003	RUSSIA	4.70% ●●●● + 0.7	10.50% ● + 0.5
2003	SERBIA	12.00% ●●●	12.50% ●●● + 0.5
2005	SLOVENIA	15.60% ●●●●● + 0.6	6.60% ●●●●●● + 0.6
2003	SPAIN	33.70% ●●●●● + 0.7	5.80% ●●●●● + 0.8
2005	SWEDEN	19.00% ●●●●●●●●	3.00% ●●●
2002	SWITZERLAND	13.90% ●●● + 0.9	9.70% ●●●●●●●●● + 0.7
2004	UKRAINE	6.90% ●●●●● + 0.9	13.70% ●●● + 0.7

413

4. GOVERNMENT EXPENDITURE
ON CULTURE
IN % BY LEVEL OF GOVERNMENT

CENTRAL GOVERNMENT

REGIONAL/PROVINCIAL GOVERNMENT

LOCAL/MUNICIPAL GOVERNMENT

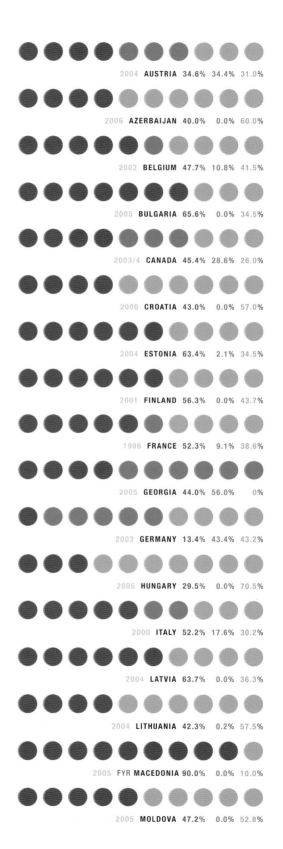

2004 **AUSTRIA** 34.6% 34.4% 31.0%

2006 **AZERBAIJAN** 40.0% 0.0% 60.0%

2002 **BELGIUM** 47.7% 10.8% 41.5%

2005 **BULGARIA** 65.6% 0.0% 34.5%

2003/4 **CANADA** 45.4% 28.6% 26.0%

2000 **CROATIA** 43.0% 0.0% 57.0%

2004 **ESTONIA** 63.4% 2.1% 34.5%

2001 **FINLAND** 56.3% 0.0% 43.7%

1996 **FRANCE** 52.3% 9.1% 38.6%

2005 **GEORGIA** 44.0% 56.0% 0%

2003 **GERMANY** 13.4% 43.4% 43.2%

2005 **HUNGARY** 29.5% 0.0% 70.5%

2000 **ITALY** 52.2% 17.6% 30.2%

2004 **LATVIA** 63.7% 0.0% 36.3%

2004 **LITHUANIA** 42.3% 0.2% 57.5%

2005 FYR **MACEDONIA** 90.0% 0.0% 10.0%

2005 **MOLDOVA** 47.2% 0.0% 52.8%

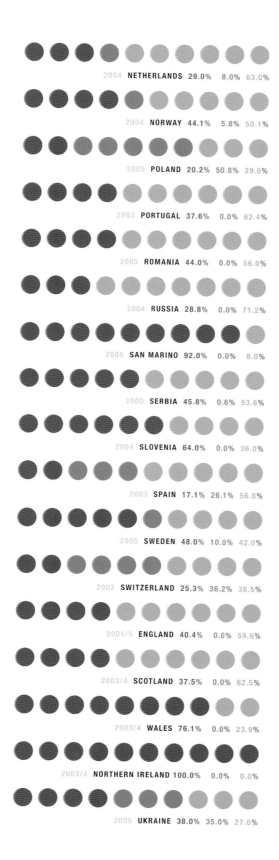

2004 **NETHERLANDS** 29.0% 8.0% 63.0%

2004 **NORWAY** 44.1% 5.8% 50.1%

2005 **POLAND** 20.2% 50.8% 29.0%

2003 **PORTUGAL** 37.6% 0.0% 62.4%

2005 **ROMANIA** 44.0% 0.0% 56.0%

2004 **RUSSIA** 28.8% 0.0% 71.2%

2005 **SAN MARINO** 92.0% 0.0% 8.0%

2000 **SERBIA** 45.8% 0.6% 53.6%

2004 **SLOVENIA** 64.0% 0.0% 36.0%

2003 **SPAIN** 17.1% 26.1% 56.8%

2005 **SWEDEN** 48.0% 10.0% 42.0%

2002 **SWITZERLAND** 25.3% 36.2% 38.5%

2004/5 **ENGLAND** 40.4% 0.0% 59.6%

2003/4 **SCOTLAND** 37.5% 0.0% 62.5%

2003/4 **WALES** 76.1% 0.0% 23.9%

2003/4 **NORTHERN IRELAND** 100.0% 0.0% 0.0%

2005 **UKRAINE** 38.0% 35.0% 27.0%

GOVERNMENT EXPENDITURES ON CULTURE AND EDUCATION

Governments play a significant role in financing the provision of culture and education. Their interventions represent a variety of policy stances that are reflected in expenditure and subsidy patterns. Most countries provide subsidies to encourage local, regional and national cultural production and distribution. Others invest in both culture and education in order to attain more competitive positions in global markets. A shrinking number of countries, including the US, give priority to the play of market forces and limit government's role. All nations, however, find that the forces of globalization connect cultures across national boundaries and thereby impact patterns of funding and expenditure.

One example of a major cultural influence on different regions is what has become known as 'Americanization,' which refers more specifically to the American entertainment industries and less to the American subsidized art and culture fields (see Wyszomirski's chapter in this volume). However, the United States is not the only globally pervasive cultural force. Japan and Europe (in all its diversity) also exert cultural influence. Many regard these processes as a threat to indigenous cultures and thus call for cultural protection in the form of tariffs as well as non-tariff barriers.

Policy analysts in most countries argue that government ought to intervene in the cultural marketplace because of market failure: the market does not result in an efficient allocation of resources. Culture, they suggest, has certain characteristics of a public good. The same argument has been established and is no longer contested even in the US as regards education. Education expenditure thus takes place largely in the public sector for all countries in the analysis.

CONCEPTS AND DATA

Expenditure data are taken for the United Nations National Account Statistics. Availability of data reflects national statistical resources and capacities, which implies that government spending in developing countries is much less documented. The United Nations National Accounts are organized differently for individuals and for governments. For example, data on cultural and recreational spending for the public sector always includes religion. This is not the case for the private sector. Differences and trends that emerge may well, at least in part, be influenced by such issues, particularly in countries where spending on religious activities is substantial. This needs to be kept in mind when comparing household versus government cultural spending.

PATTERNS AND TRENDS

Data point 1 shows that countries vary significantly in the extent to which governments engage in cultural spending—a pattern that applies to developed as well as developing countries, and to market economies as well as to economies in transition.

The majority of the developed world has shown a tendency to decrease the share of culture, recreation, and religion in government spending, as Figure 1 shows. It also appears that, at least for the Group of 8 leading industrialized nations (G8), there is a trend towards convergence. Those countries with relatively high expenditures on culture, recreation, and religion are tending to reduce it (e.g., Germany or the UK) and those with relatively low spending in the sector are increasing it (US).

Developing countries are split in terms of their spending trends. Some governments, like that of India, Pakistan, and Nicaragua, have decreased their share of cultural expenditures. Others are spending more on culture than previously. Botswana, Kyrgyzstan, and Mauritius belong in this category.

Spending on education is less volatile than spending on culture (see data point 2). Developed countries in particular don't appear to have changed their expenditure patterns by much over the period under review. Further, with few exceptions, developed countries spend in between 17 and 27 per cent of their overall budget on education. This range is notably larger for developing countries. Azerbaijan, for instance, reportedly spends only 2.5 per cent of its budget on education versus Kenya's 41.4 per cent.

In some cases, the argument could be made that public expenditure on education crowds out private expenditure. However, one has to keep in mind that the data only show spending in relation to the total government budget. For a more complete analysis,

Figure 1

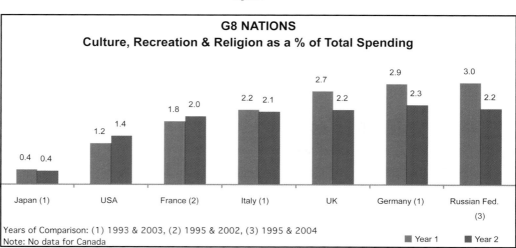

G8 NATIONS
Culture, Recreation & Religion as a % of Total Spending

Japan (1): 0.4 / 0.4
USA: 1.2 / 1.4
France (2): 1.8 / 2.0
Italy (1): 2.2 / 2.1
UK: 2.7 / 2.2
Germany (1): 2.9 / 2.3
Russian Fed. (3): 3.0 / 2.2

Years of Comparison: (1) 1993 & 2003, (2) 1995 & 2002, (3) 1995 & 2004
Note: No data for Canada

■ Year 1   ■ Year 2

Source: United Nations, National Account Statistics (2005)

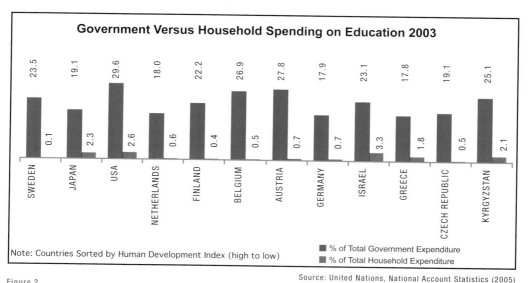

Government Versus Household Spending on Education 2003

	SWEDEN	JAPAN	USA	NETHERLANDS	FINLAND	BELGIUM	AUSTRIA	GERMANY	ISRAEL	GREECE	CZECH REPUBLIC	KYRGYZSTAN
% of Total Government Expenditure	23.5	19.1	29.6	18.0	22.2	26.9	27.8	17.9	23.1	17.8	19.1	25.1
% of Total Household Expenditure	0.1	2.3	2.6	0.6	0.4	0.5	0.7	0.7	3.3	1.8	0.5	2.1

Note: Countries Sorted by Human Development Index (high to low)

■ % of Total Government Expenditure
■ % of Total Household Expenditure

Figure 2

Source: United Nations, National Account Statistics (2005)

total nominal spending may be included as well. Figure 2 provides a comparison of private versus public spending on education in 2003.

In terms of education, the questions of quality and equity emerge. Increasingly, public education competes with private education. Wealthier families may opt to send their children to a private school, resulting in an educational gap as private schools are often better funded. This poses a challenge to ensure that disadvantaged communities are not trapped in a 'vicious cycle' of poverty. The United States, for instance, has been struggling to raise standardized test scores at publicly funded schools as income inequality has increased (US Department of Education, 2006).

A key policy issue as regards public expenditure is the kind of culture to be supported. Guidelines are difficult to set, given the broad spectrum of activities and the diversity of stakeholders involved. Most countries consider that there ought to be efforts for the protection of cultural heritage. This happens also at the regional and international levels, e.g., through UNESCO's World Heritage Fund. Some developing countries, including the Seychelles, include the potential for economic development through culture in their guidelines on cultural policy (OCPA, n.d.). Cultural diversity is another issue in this framework. Some nations, such as Canada, have included cultural diversity in their cultural policy objectives (ERICArts, n.d.).

Data point 3 illustrates, by country, trends in support of certain cultural activity types over others. Norway ranks highest in government spending on film/video and the visual arts, followed by Spain and Finland. Comparatively, Serbia spends significantly on radio/TV, Germany on the performing arts, Poland on museums/archives, and Canada on libraries and literature.

Countries vary in terms of their policy structures regarding cultural issues. Whereas some nations emphasize national identity and a cross-provincial master plan for cultural development, others focus on local culture and cultural diversity within the state. The former concept is being followed by Japan, where the

local governments are largely charged with the implementation of cultural property protection policies from the national government. Thailand's cultural policy on the other hand is structured in a way that provincial bodies of cultural policy report to local governors rather than the national ministry directly. The American model also shows a minority of cultural policy-making and funding decisions taken at the national level. Rather, US cultural policy is being developed among various partners at the local and city level (see Wyszomirski's chapter in this volume).

As data point 4 shows for selected countries, the role of central, regional/provincial and local municipal government in cultural funding varies significantly. It ranges from exclusive central government funding, as in the case of Northern Ireland or Macedonia, to an emphasis on local funding, as in The Netherlands or Hungary.

417

TRADE

GROSS VALUE ADDED CULTURAL/CREATIVE INDUSTRIES

IN US$ THOUSANDS

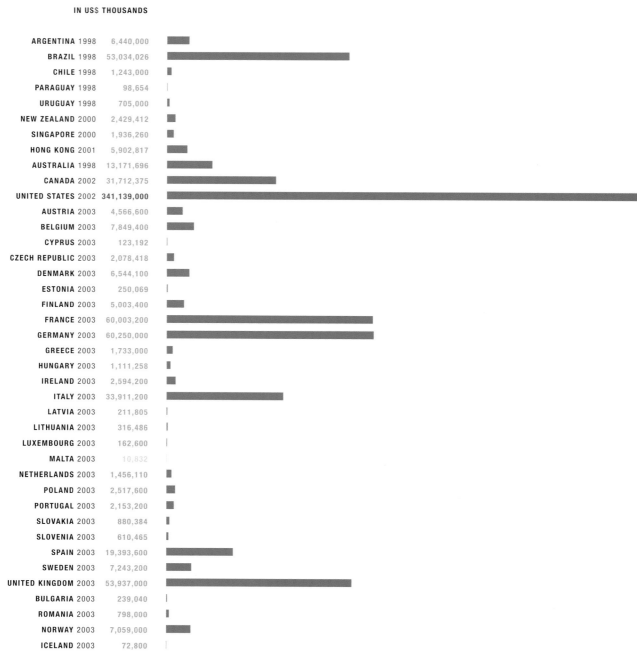

ARGENTINA 1998	6,440,000	
BRAZIL 1998	53,034,026	
CHILE 1998	1,243,000	
PARAGUAY 1998	98,654	
URUGUAY 1998	705,000	
NEW ZEALAND 2000	2,429,412	
SINGAPORE 2000	1,936,260	
HONG KONG 2001	5,902,817	
AUSTRALIA 1998	13,171,696	
CANADA 2002	31,712,375	
UNITED STATES 2002	341,139,000	
AUSTRIA 2003	4,566,600	
BELGIUM 2003	7,849,400	
CYPRUS 2003	123,192	
CZECH REPUBLIC 2003	2,078,418	
DENMARK 2003	6,544,100	
ESTONIA 2003	250,069	
FINLAND 2003	5,003,400	
FRANCE 2003	60,003,200	
GERMANY 2003	60,250,000	
GREECE 2003	1,733,000	
HUNGARY 2003	1,111,258	
IRELAND 2003	2,594,200	
ITALY 2003	33,911,200	
LATVIA 2003	211,805	
LITHUANIA 2003	316,486	
LUXEMBOURG 2003	162,600	
MALTA 2003	10,832	
NETHERLANDS 2003	1,456,110	
POLAND 2003	2,517,600	
PORTUGAL 2003	2,153,200	
SLOVAKIA 2003	880,384	
SLOVENIA 2003	610,465	
SPAIN 2003	19,393,600	
SWEDEN 2003	7,243,200	
UNITED KINGDOM 2003	53,937,000	
BULGARIA 2003	239,040	
ROMANIA 2003	798,000	
NORWAY 2003	7,059,000	
ICELAND 2003	72,800	

CULTURAL CONTRIBUTION TO GDP BY INDUSTRY 2002

ARTS + ANTIQUES TRADE **DESIGN** **ADVERTISING** ARCHITECTURE VIDEO, FILM + PHOTOGRAPHY
MUSIC + THE VISUAL + PERFORMING ARTS **PUBLISHING / WRITTEN MEDIA** **RADIO + TV BROADCASTING**

UNITED STATES

| 0.06% | 3.95% | 6.11% | 5.60% | 11.45% | 8.88% | 34.14% | 29.82% |

CANADA

| 3.00% | 3.00% | 8.00% | 3.00% | 10.00% | 7.00% | 52.00% | 14.00% |

UNITED KINGDOM

| 1.19% | 13.35% | 12.00% | 9.00% | 5.00% | 9.00% | 36.00% | 15.00% |

AUSTRALIA

| 0.44% | 2.00% | 14.00% | 5.00% | 14.00% | 6.00% | 39.00% | 20.00% |

FRANCE

| 1.04% | 0.80% | 30.00% | 6.00% | 13.00% | 9.00% | 28.00% | 12.00% |

419

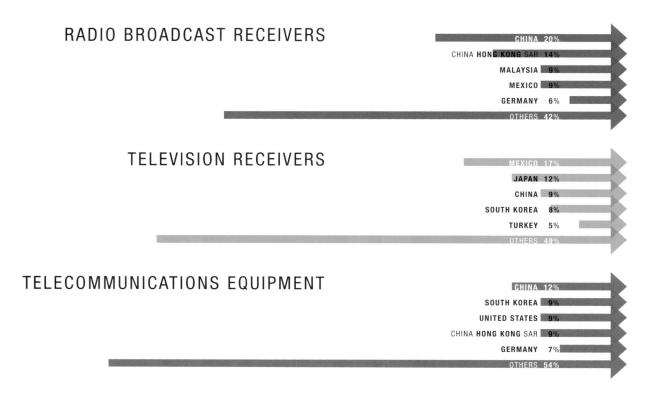

RADIO BROADCAST RECEIVERS

CHINA 20%
CHINA **HONG KONG** SAR 14%
MALAYSIA 9%
MEXICO 9%
GERMANY 6%
OTHERS 42%

TELEVISION RECEIVERS

MEXICO 17%
JAPAN 12%
CHINA 9%
SOUTH KOREA 8%
TURKEY 5%
OTHERS 49%

TELECOMMUNICATIONS EQUIPMENT

CHINA 12%
SOUTH KOREA 9%
UNITED STATES 9%
CHINA **HONG KONG** SAR 9%
GERMANY 7%
OTHERS 54%

4. TOP 5 **TRADEBLOCKS** FOR **EXPORT** OF **CULTURAL GOODS**

IN $US BILLIONS 1993 + **2003**

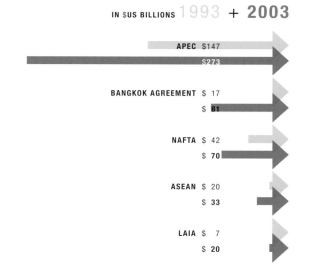

APEC $147
$273

BANGKOK AGREEMENT $ 17
$ 81

NAFTA $ 42
$ 70

ASEAN $ 20
$ 33

LAIA $ 7
$ 20

TOP **IMPORTERS** 2003

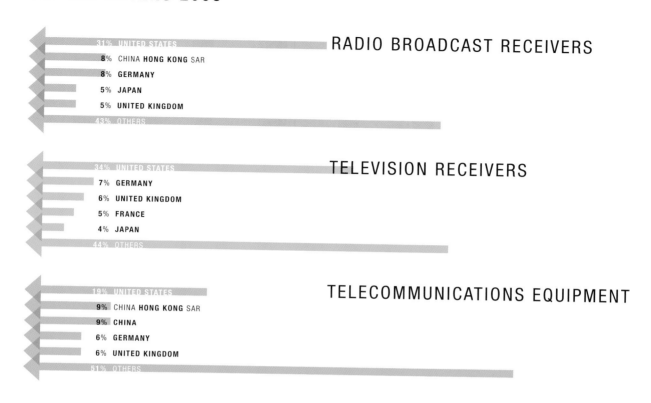

RADIO BROADCAST RECEIVERS

31% UNITED STATES
8% CHINA **HONG KONG** SAR
8% GERMANY
5% JAPAN
5% UNITED KINGDOM
43% OTHERS

TELEVISION RECEIVERS

34% UNITED STATES
7% GERMANY
6% UNITED KINGDOM
5% FRANCE
4% JAPAN
44% OTHERS

TELECOMMUNICATIONS EQUIPMENT

19% UNITED STATES
9% CHINA **HONG KONG** SAR
9% CHINA
6% GERMANY
6% UNITED KINGDOM
51% OTHERS

TOP 5 **TRADEBLOCKS** FOR **IMPORT** OF **CULTURAL GOODS**

1993 + **2003**

$124.47 **APEC**
$254.18

$ 60.30 **NAFTA**
$130.03

$ 10.62 **BANGKOK AGREEMENT**
$ 37.59

$ 16.26 **ASEAN**
$ 21.75

$ 10.06 **LAIA**
$ 18.01

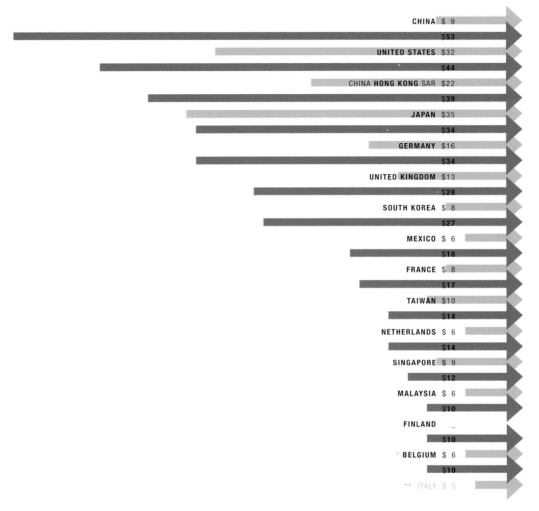

CHINA $ 9
$53

UNITED STATES $32
$44

CHINA **HONG KONG** SAR $22
$39

JAPAN $35
$34

GERMANY $16
$34

UNITED **KINGDOM** $13
$28

SOUTH KOREA $ 8
$27

MEXICO $ 6
$18

FRANCE $ 8
$17

TAIWAN $10
$14

NETHERLANDS $ 6
$14

SINGAPORE $ 9
$12

MALAYSIA $ 6
$10

FINLAND —
$10

* BELGIUM $ 6
$10

** ITALY $ 5

* THE 1993 VALUE OF BELGIUM INCLUDES LUXEMBOURG

** ITALY WAS IN TOP 15 IN 1993, BUT NOT IN 2003

TOP 15 **IMPORTERS** OF **CULTURAL GOODS** 1993 + **2003**

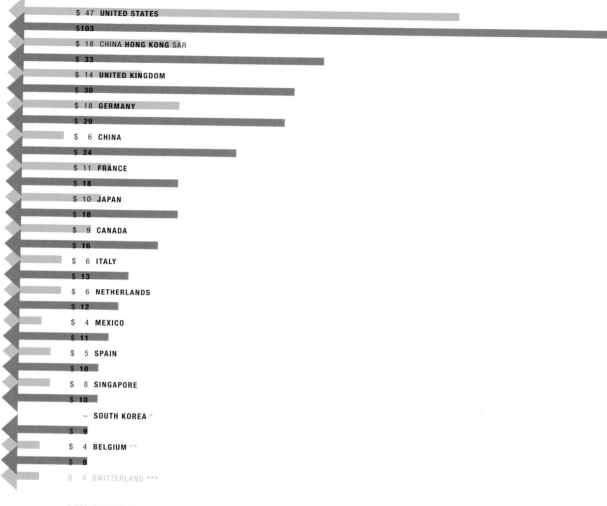

$ 47	**UNITED STATES**	
$103		
$ 18	CHINA **HONG KONG** SAR	
$ 33		
$ 14	**UNITED KINGDOM**	
$ 30		
$ 18	**GERMANY**	
$ 29		
$ 6	**CHINA**	
$ 24		
$ 11	**FRANCE**	
$ 18		
$ 10	**JAPAN**	
$ 18		
$ 9	**CANADA**	
$ 16		
$ 6	**ITALY**	
$ 13		
$ 6	**NETHERLANDS**	
$ 12		
$ 4	**MEXICO**	
$ 11		
$ 5	**SPAIN**	
$ 10		
$ 8	**SINGAPORE**	
$ 10		
–	**SOUTH KOREA** *	
$ 9		
$ 4	**BELGIUM** **	
$ 9		
$ 4	SWITZERLAND ***	

* REPUBLIC OF KOREA WAS NOT IN TOP 15 IN 1993

** THE 1993 VALUE OF BELGIUM INCLUDES LUXEMBOURG

*** SWITZERLAND WAS IN TOP 15 IN 1993, BUT NOT IN 2003

TRADE

As various chapters in this volume show, different terms are used for the components of the cultural economy. Thus UNESCO posits that the 'cultural industries' consist of goods and services that 'combine the creation, production and commercialization of contents which are intangible and cultural in nature.' UNESCO includes in its definition industries such as 'publishing, music, audiovisual technology, electronics, video games and the Internet' (UNESCO, 2006). In his chapter in this volume, Pratt uses a broader definition of the cultural economy that is inclusive of the social aspect of these industries, namely the wider web of social and economic activities that produce cultural products and services. One might also define the cultural economy in terms of intellectual property rights, as does the UK's Department for Culture, Media and Sport (DCMS): 'those industries which have their origin in individual creativity, skill and talent and which have a potential for wealth and job creation through the generation and exploitation of intellectual property.' While definitions remain unsettled, it is nevertheless necessary to locate the cultural in the context of the global economy, in particular the transnational movement of goods and services. This is the purpose of this suite.

THE CULTURAL ECONOMY

As data point 1 shows, in terms of size, measured as gross value added, the United States' cultural economy stands out, followed by Germany, France, the United Kingdom, Canada, Brazil, Italy and Spain. Everywhere it is recognized that the cultural industries have an enormous economic potential. In New Zealand the cultural sector contributes about 3.1 per cent of the GDP with a growth rate of 9 per cent, well above the general rate of the economy. In the European Union, the cultural economy contributes 5.4 per cent to the region's GDP. The role of the cultural economy is also increasing over time. From 1999 to 2003 countries such as Lithuania and the Czech Republic experienced 67.8 per cent and 56 per cent respectively in growth in the value added to their GDPs by this sector. On average the 25 European Union countries experienced growth of 6.6 per cent during this four-year period.

Among the five MERCOSUR countries (Brazil, Argentina, Uruguay, Venezuela, and Paraguay) Brazil's cultural economy is the largest in terms of gross value added: it represents 12.5 per cent of the country's GDP. Uruguay follows with 7.3 per cent. These data, however, are based on a broader definition of what constitutes the cultural economy, and are not measured according to the UN or OECD definitions. Among OECD countries, using a narrower definition, the range is from 0.2 per cent of GDP (Malta) to 3.4 per cent (France).

Data point 2 considers the value added of the cultural economy to the GDP in five countries (US, UK, France, Canada and Australia). In all five countries, publishing and print media play the largest role, ranging from 28 per cent in France to 52 per cent in Canada. In all but one case radio and TV broadcasting comes in second.

Import and export of cultural goods and services is largely dominated by OECD countries and China, and depending on the goods involved, Malaysia, Korea, and Turkey (data point 3). Specifically, global trade in cultural entertainment and media plays a key part in China's dominance as an exporter. The United States emerges as the single most important importer of cultural goods. In terms of exporters there have been significant shifts over the years as some countries have stepped into the market and others reduce their role. Between 1993 and 2003 Japan dropped from being the leading exporter of these cultural goods, with a total of 35.4 billion U.S. dollars in 1993 to 34.4 billion in 2003. Most notable was China's step up from 9 to 53 billion over this period, a 489 per cent increase. With respect to the world's importers, over this ten-year period the United States, Hong Kong, the United Kingdom, and Germany have consistently been in the top four positions.

WHAT ARE THE KEY TRADE ISSUES?

The increasing value of the cultural economy in many countries and the rapidly growing trade in cultural goods and services have important implications for economic development, cultural expression and cultural diversity. The issues include imbalances between North and South and how to ensure market access for producers and consumers in low income countries. Global concentrations in the import and export of cultural goods and services is demonstrated in figures that reveal that regions such as Africa and Latin America represent less than 4 per cent of the world's trade in cultural products. What is more, many segments of the market for cultural goods in services are oligopolistic, dominated by a few large transnational corporations (see indicator suite in Transnational Corporations).

The growth of the value added of cultural industries and the rise of countries like China as lead cultural exporters suggest that the cultural economy can drive significant economic development. While some countries (e.g., New Zealand, Canada), regions (Catalonia) and cities (London, Paris) realize this potential, a study on the role of culture in European Union economies concludes that 'the role of the cultural and creative sector within this context [of economic development] is still largely ignored.' This study goes on to point out:

> Indeed, the move to measure the socio-economic performance of the sector is a relatively recent trend. Moreover, the exercise is a contentious one. For many, the arts are a matter of enlightenment or entertainment. That leads to the perception that the arts and culture are marginal in terms of economic contribution and should therefore be confined to the realms of public intervention. This may explain to a large extent the lack of statistical tools available to measure the contribution of the cultural sector to the economy whether at the national or international level, in particular compared to other industry sectors. (MKW Wirtschaftsforschung, 2006)

The EU cultural economies study, undertaken by the firm KEA European Affairs, succeeds in making a strong case for the prioritization of the creative industries based on their sustained high economic performance within EU countries. The KEA study and the resulting next steps in terms of cultural policy are highlighted in the text box in this volume by Nicolas Gyss.

GLOBAL BRANDS

TOP 20 GLOBAL BRANDS

		2005 VALUE IN $M	2006 VALUE IN $M	% CHANGE
01.	GOOGLE	37,445	66,434	+77%
02.	GENERAL ELECTRIC	55,834	61,880	+11%
03.	MICROSOFT	62,039	54,951	-11%
04.	COCA-COLA	41,406	44,134	+7%
05.	CHINA MOBILE	39,168	41,214	+5%
06.	MARLBORO	38,510	39,166	+2%
07.	WAL-MART	37,567	36,880	-2%
08.	CITI	31,028	33,706	+9%
09.	IBM	36,084	33,572	-7%
10.	TOYOTA	30,201	33,427	+11%
11.	McDONALDS	28,985	33,138	+14%
12.	NOKIA	26,538	31,670	+19%
13.	BANK OF AMERICA	28,155	28,767	+2%
14.	BMW	23,820	25,751	+8%
15.	HEWLETT-PACKARD	19,732	24,987	+27%
16.	APPLE	15,975	24,728	+55%
17.	UPS	21,829	24,580	+13%
18.	WELLS FARGO	n.a.	24,284	n.a.
19.	AMERICAN EXPRESS	18,780	23,113	+23%
20.	LOUIS VUITTON	19,479	22,686	+16%

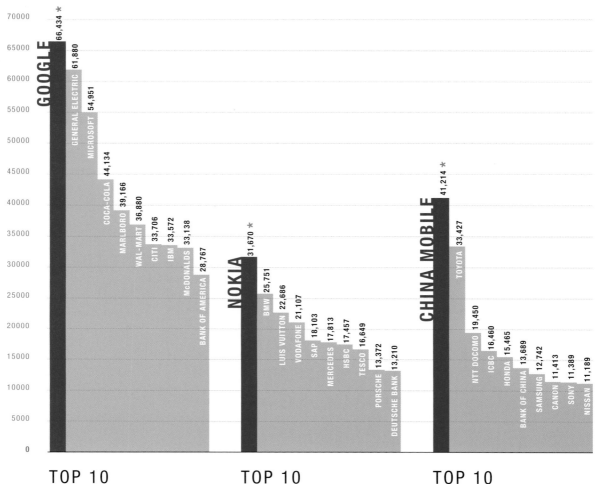

TOP 10

NORTH AMERICAN

BRANDS 2006

IN $M

TOP 10

EUROPEAN

BRANDS 2006

INCLUDING UK, IN $M

TOP 10

ASIAN

BRANDS 2006

IN $M

BY CATEGORY: MOBILE COMMUNICATION FAST FOOD LUXURY GOODS APPAREL

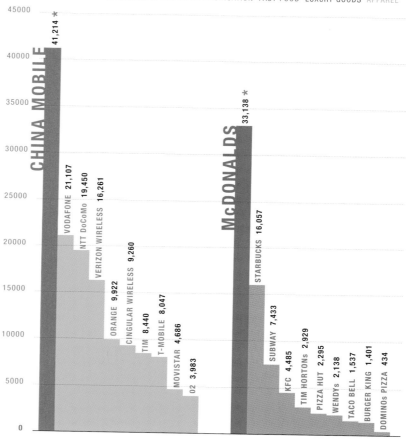

TOP 10
MOBILE
COMMUNICATION
BRANDS 2006
IN $M

TOP 10
FAST FOOD
BRANDS 2006
IN $M

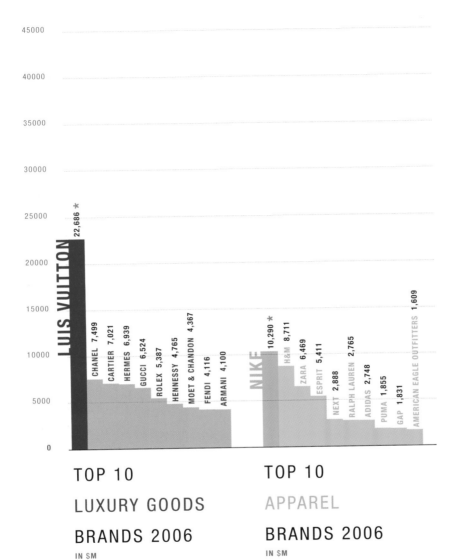

45000

40000

35000

30000

25000

22,686 *

20000

LUIS VUITTON

15000

10000
CHANEL 7,499
CARTIER 7,021
HERMES 6,939
GUCCI 6,524
ROLEX 5,387
HENNESSY 4,765
MOET & CHANDON 4,367
FENDI 4,116
ARMANI 4,100

10,290 *
H&M 8,711
NIKE
ZARA 6,469
ESPRIT 5,411
NEXT 2,888
RALPH LAUREN 2,765
ADIDAS 2,748
PUMA 1,855
GAP 1,831
AMERICAN EAGLE OUTFITTERS 1,609

5000

0

TOP 10

LUXURY GOODS

BRANDS 2006

IN $M

TOP 10

APPAREL

BRANDS 2006

IN $M

GLOBAL BRANDS

Branding is an important marketing principle that helps determine corporate strategies for product development, marketing and over market positioning (cf. in particular Ichikawa chapter in this volume). Brand performance has become an increasingly significant issue for global corporations as well as regions and cities that try to market themselves as cultural capitals and economically as well as culturally vital centers.

WHAT IS GLOBAL BRANDING?

There are several consultancies and organizations that rank global brands. Interbrand and *Business Week* have been rating global brands for six years with a method that Interbrand developed and used to assess brands for nearly twenty years. Millward Brown Optimor, a global marketing research organization whose brand rankings are published by *The Financial Times*, evaluates global brands with its Brandz Top 100 method that incorporates consumer data into brand assessments and valuations.

Methods of calculating brand rankings differ. Interbrand determines brand value by calculating the net present value of the expected earnings for the year to come. Brands must have a minimum value of US$2.7 billion, 'achieve about one third of their earnings outside of their home country, have publicly available marketing and financial data, and have a wider public profile beyond their direct customer base (Interbrand, 2006).' Millward Brown Optimor utilizes a more holistic method and incorporates consumer brand perception as well as financial measures. Estimated earnings at net present value, contribution to the parent-business and prospects for growth are the three primary financial indicators that are measured.

WHAT DO WE KNOW ABOUT GLOBAL BRANDING?

Using the Millward Brown Optimor ratings, in 2006 there were some noticeable swings in global brands (see data point 1). Google leaped from seventh place in 2005 to first place in 2006, with a brand value increase of US$28.9 billion, a 77 per cent increase from the 2005 value. Other significant leaps were Apple's 55 per cent improvement to place it sixteenth and Hewlett Packard's 27 per cent change to move it to fifteenth place. Microsoft experienced the largest decrease in brand value, falling 11 per cent to third place from first. IBM followed with a 7 per cent decrease.

Analysis of regional brands reveals certain market tendencies (see data point 2). The top ten North American brands are dominated by the presence of Google, food and beverage brands and financial brands. In contrast the leading European brands represent the automobile, communications and financial industries. Asian brands tend to be representative of the same industries as the European brands.

Within certain cultural industries little change occurred in the last year (see data point 3). The fast food sector continues to be dominated by American companies McDonalds and Starbucks, in first and second place respectively. McDonalds' brand value increased by 14 per cent, while the brand value of Starbucks displayed an impressive 45 per cent jump. The leading companies in the mobile phone sector similarly showed no change in positions from 2005 to 2006. This sector is led by the Chinese company China Mobile, followed by the UK company Vodafone. Lastly, the apparel industry showed no noticeable changes in the

last year, with Nike, H&M and Zara still holding the top three respective positions. Interbrand attributes their strong brand hold in the apparel industry to their 'style-conscious, low-cost chains' (Interbrand, 2006).

WHAT ARE THE ISSUES?

Global businesses have a strong interest in creating brand qualities that differentiate their brands from others. Brand-driven shareholder creation is a concept that posits that high shareholder returns are correlated with brand performance (Dorffer, 2006). This concept, promoted by Millward Brown Optimor, emphasizes understanding the customer, aligning marketing indicators with business return measurements, and the importance of measuring brands as intangible assets.

Despite different cultural tastes and preferences, brands are still able to cross borders. Google's operations in China are one example of a brand component that has been tailored for the local market. The Beijing office of Google China, which opened in the Fall of 2005, announced in January 2006 that it would comply with China's censorship laws and modify its search engine content accordingly. Google's motto 'Don't be evil' appeared to many to contradict the operational decisions made in China. The company's stock fell and protests and debate erupted in the United States. Even the US Congress took an interest in the matter. Google is just one example of the power that brands have in the global economy, but it also effectively illustrates that along with increased market visibility global brands face the possibility of being scrutinized by a wider audience. Indeed, there is increased recognition of sustainable brand values and corporate social responsibility.

In addition to the increased visibility and accountability that global brands may experience, the Internet and other technological developments increasingly play an important part in the success of a company to develop and market a global brand. Online branding has added a new component to marketing which previously focused on newspapers, magazine, television and radio as the primary communication outlets. Siegmund (2003), of the Center on Global Brand Leadership at the Columbia Business School, points out that the interactive nature of the Internet and its ability to reach relevant specific markets are two advantages to online branding.

1. RICHARD FLORIDA'S **GLOBAL CREATIVITY INDEX**

THE GLOBAL CREATIVITY INDEX IS DERIVED FROM THREE SEPARATE INDICES GENERATED BY RICHARD FLORIDA (2005) AND IRENE TINAGLI.
THE TALENT INDEX, TECHNOLOGY INDEX, AND TOLERANCE INDEX ARE ALL EQUALLY WEIGHTED TO CREATE THE CREATIVITY INDEX,
WITH COUNTRY RESULTS NORMALIZED ON A SCALE FROM 0 TO 1.

COUNTRIES SORTED BY CREATIVITY INDEX (HIGH TO LOW)

STANDARDIZED CREATIVITY SCORE

0.808	SWEDEN
0.766	JAPAN
0.684	FINLAND
0.666	UNITED STATES
0.637	SWITZERLAND
0.613	DENMARK
0.612	ICELAND
0.611	NETHERLANDS
0.595	NORWAY
0.577	GERMANY
0.548	CANADA
0.528	AUSTRALIA
0.526	BELGIUM
0.525	ISRAEL
0.517	UNITED KINGDOM
0.465	SOUTH KOREA
0.462	FRANCE
0.459	NEW ZEALAND
0.438	AUSTRIA
0.414	IRELAND
0.382	CZECH REPUBLIC
0.371	GREECE
0.365	SPAIN
0.360	ESTONIA
0.339	RUSSIAN FEDERATION
0.335	ITALY
0.296	UKRAINE
0.291	SLOVAK REPUBLIC
0.282	HUNGARY
0.280	CROATIA
0.275	BULGARIA
0.262	LATVIA
0.240	URUGUAY
0.239	POLAND
0.234	PORTUGAL
0.230	CHINA
0.219	GEORGIA
0.199	ARGENTINA
0.186	TURKEY
0.185	CHILE
0.177	INDIA
0.164	MEXICO
0.159	BRAZIL
0.132	PERU
0.131	ROMANIA

2. EUROPE'S **SUMMARY INNOVATION INDEX** 2006

COUNTRIES SORTED BY SUMMARY INNOVATION INDEX (HIGH TO LOW)

STANDARDIZED SII SCORE

0.73	SWEDEN
0.69	SWITZERLAND
0.68	FINLAND
0.63	DENMARK
0.61	JAPAN
0.59	GERMANY
0.54	LUXEMBOURG
0.54	UNITED STATES
0.53	UNITED KINGDOM
0.49	NETHERLANDS
0.49	ICELAND
0.48	BELGIUM
0.48	FRANCE
0.48	IRELAND
0.48	AUSTRIA
0.36	NORWAY
0.35	SLOVENIA
0.34	CZECH REPUBLIC
0.34	ESTONIA
0.34	ITALY
0.31	SPAIN
0.30	CYPRUS
0.30	MALTA
0.27	LITHUANIA
0.26	HUNGARY
0.25	CROATIA
0.23	PORTUGAL
0.23	SLOVAK REPUBLIC
0.22	GREECE
0.22	LATVIA
0.22	POLAND
0.21	BULGARIA
0.19	ROMANIA
0.08	TURKEY

CREATION, INNOVATION + PROTECTION

3. NOTABLE **ART SCHOOLS** # OF **FACULTY** # OF **STUDENTS** % OF INTERNATIONAL STUDENTS

188 UNIVERSIDADE DE SAO PAULO (2007)
1,314 **3.7%** INTERNATIONAL STUDENTS

494 RHODE ISLAND SCHOOL OF DESIGN (2005)
2,258 **13.0%** INTERNATIONAL STUDENTS

560 SCHOOL OF THE ARTS INSTITUTE CHICAGO (2005)
2,588 **17.3%** INTERNATIONAL STUDENTS

207 CALIFORNIA INSTITUTE OF THE ARTS (2004)
1,242 **15.0%** INTERNATIONAL STUDENTS

487 ART CENTER COLLEGE OF DESIGN (2005)
1,628 **18.0%** INTERNATIONAL STUDENTS

500 CHINA ACADEMY OF ART (2007)
7,000 **1.9%** INTERNATIONAL STUDENTS

253 TOKYO NATIONAL UNIVERSITY OF FINE ARTS (2006)
3,174 **3.3%** INTERNATIONAL STUDENTS

373 AKADEMIE DER BILDENDEN KUNST WIEN (2007)
996 **29.4%** INTERNATIONAL STUDENTS

56 ECOLE NATIONALE SUPERIEURE DES BEAUX-ARTS (2005-06)
564 **19.9%** INTERNATIONAL STUDENTS

178 UNIVERSITÄT DER KÜNSTE BERLIN (2007)*
4,500 **17.8%** INTERNATIONAL STUDENTS

160 KONINKLIJKE ACADEMIE VAN BEELDENDE KUNSTEN, DEN HAAG (2007)
1,000 **15.0%** INTERNATIONAL STUDENTS

NOTE: THE DISTINCTION BETWEEN FULL-TIME AND PART-TIME FACULTY COULD NOT BE VERIFIED IN MOST CASES - NUMBERS MAY INCLUDE ONE OR BOTH CATEGORIES
* # OF FACULTY AT THE UNIVERSITAET DER KUENSTE BERLIN IS FULL-TIME ONLY, NO DATA FOR PART-TIME INSTRUCTORS

OF **TRADEMARKS** + **PATENTS** HELD BY TOP 15 FORTUNE 500 GLOBAL COMPANIES IN RANKED ORDER **2006**

OF PATENTS   # OF TRADEMARKS

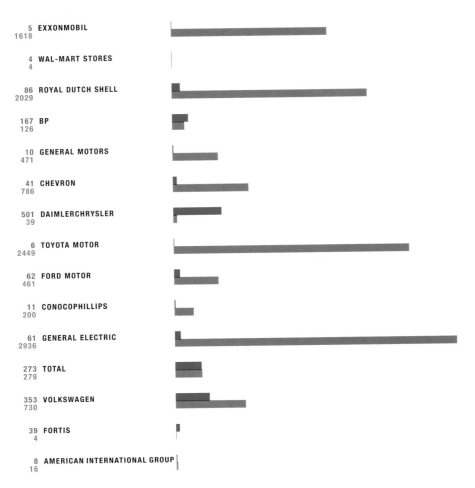

	# OF PATENTS	# OF TRADEMARKS
EXXONMOBIL	5	1618
WAL-MART STORES	4	4
ROYAL DUTCH SHELL	86	2029
BP	167	126
GENERAL MOTORS	10	471
CHEVRON	41	786
DAIMLERCHRYSLER	501	39
TOYOTA MOTOR	6	2449
FORD MOTOR	62	461
CONOCOPHILLIPS	11	200
GENERAL ELECTRIC	61	2936
TOTAL	273	279
VOLKSWAGEN	353	730
FORTIS	39	4
AMERICAN INTERNATIONAL GROUP	8	16

## 5

PCT PATENT APPLICATIONS

BY COUNTRY **2006**

49555	UNITED STATES	35%	3403	SWITZERLAND	2%
26906	JAPAN	19%	3123	SWEDEN	2%
16929	GERMANY	12%	2723	ITALY	2%
5935	SOUTH KOREA	4%	2532	CANADA	2%
5902	FRANCE	4%	2139	AUSTRALIA	1%
5045	UNITED KINGDOM	3%	1915	FINLAND	1%
4393	NETHERLANDS	3%	1725	ISRAEL	1%
3910	CHINA	3%	9165	ALL OTHERS	6%

NOTE: THE PATENT COOPERATION TREATY (PCT) IS AN INTERNATIONAL PATENT LAW TREATY,
CONCLUDED IN 1970. IT PROVIDES A UNIFIED PROCEDURE FOR FILING PATENT APPLICATIONS TO
PROTECT INVENTIONS IN EACH OF ITS CONTRACTING STATES. A PATENT APPLICATION FILED UNDER
THE PCT IS CALLED AN INTERNATIONAL APPLICATION OR PCT APPLICATION.

TOP COUNTRIES **PCT INTERNATIONAL APPLICATIONS**

OF **PCT APPLICATIONS** FILED IN 2005

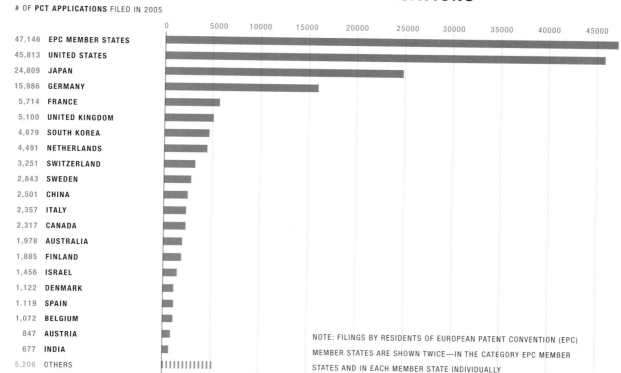

47,146	EPC MEMBER STATES	
45,813	UNITED STATES	
24,809	JAPAN	
15,986	GERMANY	
5,714	FRANCE	
5,100	UNITED KINGDOM	
4,679	SOUTH KOREA	
4,491	NETHERLANDS	
3,251	SWITZERLAND	
2,843	SWEDEN	
2,501	CHINA	
2,357	ITALY	
2,317	CANADA	
1,978	AUSTRALIA	
1,885	FINLAND	
1,456	ISRAEL	
1,122	DENMARK	
1.119	SPAIN	
1,072	BELGIUM	
847	AUSTRIA	
677	INDIA	
5,206	OTHERS	

NOTE: FILINGS BY RESIDENTS OF EUROPEAN PATENT CONVENTION (EPC)
MEMBER STATES ARE SHOWN TWICE—IN THE CATEGORY EPC MEMBER
STATES AND IN EACH MEMBER STATE INDIVIDUALLY

TOP 20 **COUNTRIES** OR **REGIONAL OFFICES** FILING

PATENTS WORLDWIDE TOTAL # OF PATENTS FILED IN 2004: **1,599,000**

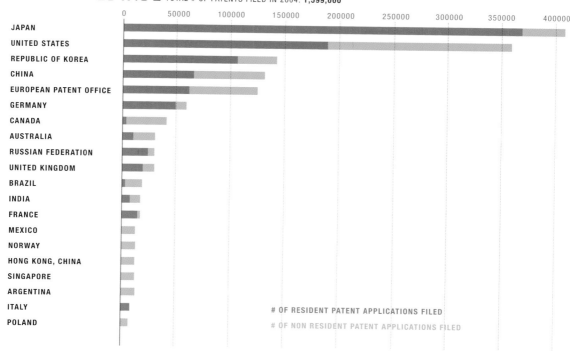

JAPAN
UNITED STATES
REPUBLIC OF KOREA
CHINA
EUROPEAN PATENT OFFICE
GERMANY
CANADA
AUSTRALIA
RUSSIAN FEDERATION
UNITED KINGDOM
BRAZIL
INDIA
FRANCE
MEXICO
NORWAY
HONG KONG, CHINA
SINGAPORE
ARGENTINA
ITALY
POLAND

OF RESIDENT PATENT APPLICATIONS FILED
OF NON RESIDENT PATENT APPLICATIONS FILED

8. WORLDWIDE
PATENT FILINGS

PATENT APPLICATIONS FILED BY NON RESIDENTS

PATENT APPLICATIONS FILED BY RESIDENTS

9. # OF **PCT**
INTERNATIONAL
APPLICATIONS

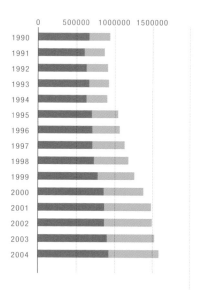

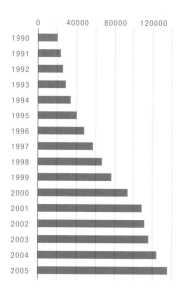

10. **PATENT APPLICATION**
PER CAPITA 2006

PATENT APPLICATIONS PER 10,000 PEOPLE

4.56	**SWITZERLAND**	
3.64	**FINLAND**	
3.44	**SWEDEN**	
2.68	**NETHERLANDS**	
2.53	**ISRAEL**	
2.10	**JAPAN**	
2.05	**GERMANY**	
1.64	**UNITED STATES**	
1.24	**SOUTH KOREA**	
1.04	**AUSTRALIA**	
0.93	**FRANCE**	
0.83	**UNITED KINGDOM**	
0.78	**CANADA**	
0.46	**ITALY**	
0.03	**CHINA**	

163 **BERNE CONVENTION** FOR THE PROTECTION OF LITERARY AND ARTISTIC WORKS (1886)

|||||||||||||||||||||||||||||||||||||||||||

30 **BRUSSELS CONVENTION** RELATING TO THE DISTRIBUTION OF PROGRAM-CARRYING SIGNALS TRANSMITTED BY SATELLITE, THE "SATELLITE CONVENTION" (1974)

||||||||

13 **FILM REGISTER TREATY** ON THE INTERNATIONAL REGISTRATION OF AUDIOVISUAL WORKS (1989)

|||

35 **MADRID AGREEMENT** CONCERNING THE INTERNATIONAL REGISTRATION OF MARKS (1891)

||||||||||

46 **NAIROBI TREATY** ON THE PROTECTION OF THE OLYMPIC SYMBOL (1981)

||||||||||||

171 **PARIS CONVENTION** ON THE PROTECTION OF INDUSTRIAL PROPERTY (1883)

|||||||||||||||||||||||||||||||||||||||||||||

14 **PATENT LAW TREATY** (2000)

|||

76 **PHONOGRAM CONVENTION** FOR THE PROTECTION OF PRODUCERS OF PHONOGRAMS AGAINST UNAUTHORIZED DUPLICATION OF THEIR PHONOGRAMS (1971)

|||||||||||||||||||

86 **ROME INTERNATIONAL CONVENTION** FOR THE PROTECTION OF PERFORMERS, PRODUCERS OF PHONOGRAMS AND BROADCASTING ORGANIZATIONS (1961)

||||||||||||||||||||||

146 **SINGAPORE TREATY**

||||||||||||||||||||||||||||||||||||

38 **TRADEMARK LAW TREATY**

||||||||||

63 **WCT**

|||||||||||||||

61 **WPPT**

|||||||||||||||

CREATION, INNOVATION

+ PROTECTION
Research suggests that creativity and innovation, in cultural expression as in many other domains, emerges at the crossroads of social, cultural and political forces, and more frequently at the margins and boundaries rather than at the center of systems, be they political entities, organizations or professions (Brown and Duguid, 2002). Creativity is embedded in social, cultural, and political phenomena and is related to specific configurations in terms of structure, power and meaning.

Creativity involves a basic tension. On the one hand, creativity appears as a highly idiosyncratic act in which latent and manifest talents, expertise and serendipity combine in often seemingly unpredictable ways. Yet alongside this image of the artist as the lonely, accidental genius kissed by the muse is the view that both the likelihood that creativity will emerge and that creative acts will be recognized and in turn lead to innovation and sustained change are closely linked to the organization of economy and society as well as patterns in the cultural domain itself (National Bureau of Economic Research, 2006).

Today, the notion of creativity can designate forms of virtual reality in which actors are free to make choices and play roles normally unavailable to them—seemingly dissociated from the social world of everyday life. The technological products made available to individuals can turn many into 'creators' themselves: from the personal computer and digital camera to the cell phone, humankind inhabits an increasingly networked world in which communication and personal expression and development reign supreme.

Yet what are the standards of creativity, and how do we know if something is truly novel? Do the creators themselves care about standards, or are creative acts more play for entertainment than work inspired by the muse, and more about escaping the status quo than changing it?

In recognition of the dilemma with respect to origin, attempts have been initiated to protect specialized knowledge and innovation via intellectual property (IP) rights. These rights create a legal claim of ownership for innovation of, among others, a specific manner of artistic expression. Different forms of IP rights include patents, copyrights, trademarks, industrial design rights, and trade secrets.

FACETS OF CREATIVITY
Richard Florida's Global Creativity Index (see data point 1) hints at 'the ability of a country to harness and mobilize creative talent for innovation, entrepreneurship, industry formation, and long-run prosperity' (Florida, 2005). It is closely correlated with the European Innovation Index (data point 2), which is based on similar principles.

Intellectual property rights are a set of exclusive rights granted to the inventor of 'creations of the mind' (World Intellectual Property Organization, 2007). This may constrain others from using the creation and enable the inventor to charge a fee for distribution.

Piracy, officially known as copyright infringement, refers to a violation of the above-described exclusive rights of the 'owner' of intellectual property. The most-cited example of piracy is the sharing of audiovisual material via the Internet. In many (mostly lesser developed) countries one can also find stores openly selling pirated products.

Both the Creativity Index and the Innovation Index used in this suite point towards great creative potential in Western Europe, the United States, and Japan. Sweden holds the top rank for both indices. Creativity also appears to be highly correlated with economic output and with the United Nations' Human Development Index (Florida, 2005).

Further, the United States and Japan are the worldwide leaders in terms of protection indicators. In 2006, the US applied for 49,555 patents compared to Japan at 26,906 (see data point 5). Together, the two countries account for 54% of applications worldwide. When looking at patent applications per capita, the pattern changes significantly: Switzerland, Finland and Sweden dominate this category (see data point 10). It is important to note that these developed nations' dominance does not necessarily mean that developing nations have less IP to protect, but rather that the intellectual capital in those nations does not have the mindset that leads to a need for protection. Traditional and indigenous knowledge, for instance (see indicator suite on Traditional & Indigenous Knowledge in this volume), has traditionally been excluded from IP rights.

As discussed below, there is a strong negative correlation between development and national piracy rates. The simple correlation coefficient between Human Development Index Rank 2006 and piracy rate is 0.79. This may reflect attempts of individuals and businesses to bypass licensing fees that may prevent them from access to products.

Universities and schools are a major driving force for innovation in arts and culture. Schools vary greatly in size of student body, faculty, endowment, as well as the percentage of international students. Public investment in art education may be regarded as an indicator of the value that a society places on artistic creation.

Internationally renowned art schools vary widely in terms of size and student body. Schools in Asia stand out as the largest in terms of student populations (see data point 3). At the same time, they have lower percentages of foreign students than the European and North American schools. Out of the 106 international students at Tokyo National University of the Arts in 2006, 41 were from Korea, 21 from China, 8 from the United States, and 4 from Germany. Three out of the top nine US art schools are located in California: California Institute of the Arts, Art Center College of Design, and the University of California, Los Angeles.

Data point 4 also indicates that distinct differences exist among the largest transnational corporations who gain by protecting their intellectual properties. In particular, automobile companies have great numbers of trademarks protecting their work, with most of them originating from the developed world. DaimlerChrysler and Deutsche Telekom AG rank among the highest to obtain trademarks among their peers. Discrepancies are not quite as wide when looking at patents. However, Western nations' corporations dominate this field as well.

Proponents of intellectual property rights justify their existence via the economic analysis that deferred profits give incentives for innovation. Basically, the argument is the following: For most intellectual property, the initial innovative or creative process constitutes the bulk of production costs. Later multiplication is relatively cheap. The price of an additional copy of computer software, for instance, is really just a blank CD and the writing process. The research that has gone into developing that software, on the other hand, can be very expensive. Hence if the producer does not charge a premium price for the product (higher than marginal cost of production), R&D costs are not recuperated, making the business unprofitable and discouraging investment.

Opponents of intellectual property rights, on the other hand, argue that, among other negative side-effects, intellectual property rights are counter-productive for international development. Ruth L. Gana argues that if developing nations are excluded from new technology via excessive fees, they are trapped in a vicious cycle of poverty (Benthall, 1999). Also, since a lot of IP is non-rivalrous in consumption in certain cases the argument is made that innovations should be made available to the general public at low cost. This is most visibly the case in pharmaceuticals—Brazil and Thailand recently decided to break established patents of HIV drugs and instead produce them generically (Cohen, 2007).

Intellectual property rights and the lack of enforcement thereof in certain countries have led to an increasing number of international disputes. China has curtailed its piracy rate in recent years. However, given the size of its population, it is still a cause for concern for major producers of intellectual property around the world. The United States has repeatedly accused China of inadequate enforcement of IP obligations (Mandigora, 2007) and losses from piracy in China are estimated at $5.4 billion in 2006 (Business Software Alliance, 2007).

DISSEMINATION + STORAGE

1. **NOTABLE MUSEUMS** COLLECTION SIZE + # OF ANNUAL VISITORS

COLLECTION SIZE*   ANNUAL # VISITORS

THE SMITHSONIAN 2006
136,900,000   **23.2** MILLION VISITORS

BRITISH MUSEUM 2006
6,500,000   **4.9** MILLION VISITORS

THE STATE HERMITAGE 2004
3,000,000   **2.5** MILLION VISITORS

THE METROPOLITAIN MUSEUM OF ART 2006
2,000,000   **4.0** MILLION VISITORS

POLO MUSEALE FIORENTINO - UFFIZI GALLERY 2006
250,000   **5.0** MILLION VISITORS

JAPAN NATIONAL MUSEUM 2006
119,792   **3.0** MILLION VISITORS

THE GETTY MUSEUM & VILLA 2006
111,695   **1.5** MILLION VISITORS

THE TATE GALLERIES 2004–2005
64,765   **6.2** MILLION VISITORS

THE LOUVRE 2003
35,000   **5.7** MILLION VISITORS

EL MUSEO DEL PRADO 2005
8,500   **1.9** MILLION VISITORS

MUSEE D'ORSAY 2006
4,000   **3.0** MILLION VISITORS

* FIGURE BASED ON # OF PIECES

2. # OF UNESCO REGISTERED **MUSEUM ARCHIVES** BY REGION **AS OF 2005**

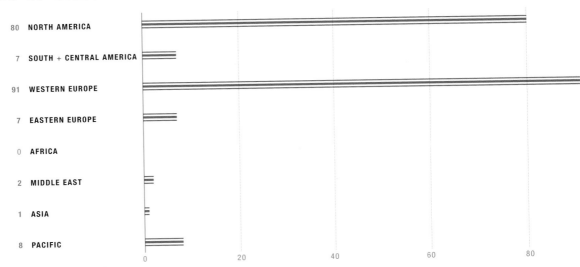

80	**NORTH AMERICA**	
7	**SOUTH + CENTRAL AMERICA**	
91	**WESTERN EUROPE**	
7	**EASTERN EUROPE**	
0	**AFRICA**	
2	**MIDDLE EAST**	
1	**ASIA**	
8	**PACIFIC**	

0   20   40   60   80

★ 150,000,000 THE BRITISH LIBRARY 2007

134,000,000 THE LIBRARY OF CONGRESS 2007

34,510,159 NATIONAL LIBRARY OF RUSSIA 2005

23,730,000 NATIONAL LIBRARY OF CHINA 2003

23,500,000 DEUTSCHE NATIONALBIBLIOTHEK 2007

15,000,000 VERNADSKY NATIONAL LIBRARY OF UKRAINE 2005

13,000,000 BIBLIOTHEQUE NATIONALE DE FRANCE 2005

8,500,000 BIBLIOTECA NACIONAL BRASIL 2006

8,300,000 NATIONAL LIBRARY OF BELARUS 2007

8,000,000 BIBLIOTHECA ALEXANDRINA 2007

3. LARGEST NATIONAL LIBRARIES

OF ITEMS HELD

★ 15,555,533 HARVARD UNIVERSITY 1

12,025,695 YALE UNIVERSITY 11

9,985,903 UNIVERSITY OF CALIFORNIA BERKELEY 4

9,277,042 COLUMBIA UNIVERSITY 7

8,064,896 UNIVERISTY OF CALIFORNIA LOS ANGELES 14

7,911,834 UNIVERSITY OF WISCONSIN MADISON 16

7,644,371 CORNELL UNIVERSITY 12

7,363,549 UNIVERSITY OF CHICAGO 9

7,135,000 UNIVERSITY OF OXFORD 10

7,000,001 UNIVERSITY OF CAMBRIDGE 2

6,639,850 UNIVERSITY OF WASHINGTON SEATTLE 17

6,495,597 PRINCETON UNIVERSITY 8

5,760,065 UNIVERSITY OF PENNSYLVANIA 15

3,648,821 JOHN HOPKINS UNIVERSITY 20

3,149,836 UNIVERSITY OF CALIFORNIA SAN DIEGO 13

2,782,406 MASSACHUSETTS INSTITUTE OF TECHNOLOGY 5

2,000,342 UNIVERSITY OF TOKYO 19

4. TOP RANKED UNIVERSITIES + THEIR LIBRARY COLLECTION 2007

5. DISTRIBUTION OF

RECORDS IN WORLDCAT

BY FIVE-YEAR PERIODS 1975–2005

WORLDCAT IS THE WORLD'S LARGEST BIBLIOGRAPHIC DATABASE, BUILT AND MAINTAINED COLLECTIVELY BY LIBRARIES THAT PARTICIPATE IN THE OCLC GLOBAL COOPERATIVE. CREATED IN 1971, WORLDCAT CATALOGS THE CONTENT OF MORE THAN 50,000 LIBRARIES IN MORE THAN NINETY COUNTRIES. AS OF MAY 2007, IT CONTAINED MORE THAN 1 BILLION RECORDS REFERENCING PHYSICAL AND DIGITAL ITEMS IN MORE THAN 360 LANGUAGES. WORLDCAT ITSELF IS NOT DIRECTLY PURCHASED BY LIBRARIES, BUT SERVES AS THE FOUNDATION FOR MANY OTHER FEE-BASED OCLC SERVICES (SUCH AS RESOURCE SHARING AND COLLECTION MANAGEMENT)

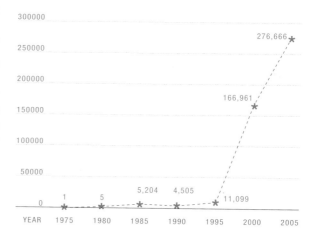

YEAR	1975	1980	1985	1990	1995	2000	2005
	1	5	5,204	4,505	11,099	166,961	276,666

## 6

WIKIPEDIA: # OF EDITS PER MONTH* + NEW ARTICLES PER DAY

IN THOUSANDS *IN ALL LANGUAGES

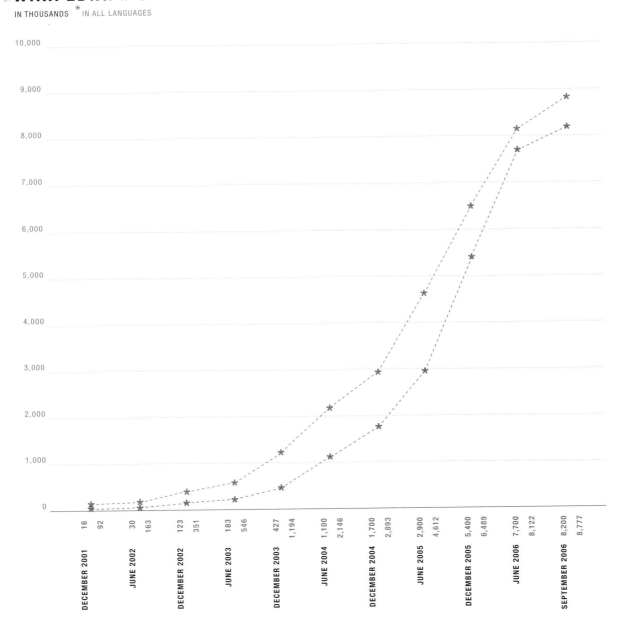

| | 16 | 30 | 123 | 183 | 427 | 1,100 | 1,700 | 2,900 | 5,400 | 7,700 | 8,200 |
| | 92 | 163 | 351 | 546 | 1,194 | 2,146 | 2,893 | 4,612 | 6,489 | 8,122 | 8,777 |

DECEMBER 2001 JUNE 2002 DECEMBER 2002 JUNE 2003 DECEMBER 2003 JUNE 2004 DECEMBER 2004 JUNE 2005 DECEMBER 2005 JUNE 2006 SEPTEMBER 2006

GOOGLE

18.7 MILLION SEARCH HOURS PER MONTH

37 MILLION SEARCH MINUTES PER DAY

112 MILLION SEARCHES PER DAY

YAHOO

7.1 MILLION SEARCH HOURS PER MONTH

14 MILLION SEARCH MINUTES PER DAY

42 MILLION SEARCHES PER DAY

AOLSEARCH

15.5 MILLION SEARCH HOURS PER MONTH

31 MILLION SEARCH MINUTES PER DAY

93 MILLION SEARCHES PER DAY

MSNSEARCH

5.4 MILLION SEARCH HOURS PER MONTH

11 MILLION SEARCH MINUTES PER DAY

32 MILLION SEARCHES PER DAY

OVERTURE

0.8 MILLION SEARCH HOURS PER MONTH

2 MILLION SEARCH MINUTES PER DAY

5 MILLION SEARCHES PER DAY

INFOSPACE

1.1 MILLION SEARCH HOURS PER MONTH

2 MILLION SEARCH MINUTES PER DAY

7 MILLION SEARCHES PER DAY

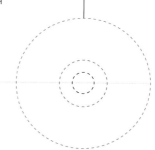

ALTAVISTA

0.8 MILLION SEARCH HOURS PER MONTH

2 MILLION SEARCH MINUTES PER DAY

5 MILLION SEARCHES PER DAY

ASK

2.3 MILLION SEARCH HOURS PER MONTH

5 MILLION SEARCH MINUTES PER DAY

14 MILLION SEARCHES PER DAY

NETSCAPE

0.7 MILLION SEARCH HOURS PER MONTH

1 MILLION SEARCH MINUTES PER DAY

4 MILLION SEARCHES PER DAY

LOOKSMART

0.2 MILLION SEARCH HOURS PER MONTH

1 MILLION SEARCHES PER DAY

EARTHLINK

0.4 MILLION SEARCH HOURS PER MONTH

1 MILLION SEARCH MINUTES PER DAY

3 MILLION SEARCHES PER DAY

LYCOS

0.2 MILLION SEARCH HOURS PER MONTH

1 MILLION SEARCHES PER DAY

DISSEMINATION & STORAGE
Ongoing innovation and greater availability of new and 'superior' knowledge exert pressure on existing knowledge, information and practices. The 'cult of innovation' so characteristic of modern societies on the one hand, and the need to store, preserve and disseminate relevant knowledge and information on the other, both pose great challenges.

The Internet and digital media are growing rapidly in terms of usage and accessibility. Lower access costs—information can be retrieved without commuting—appear to be driving an 'information boom,' which provides highly specialized and detailed information on virtually any topic. To learn about issues in Ugandan agriculture, Mayan archeological sites or paintings shown in the world's major museums one no longer needs to physically be there, as the information is increasingly available on the Internet. Clearly, this creates opportunities for scholarship but also makes research prone to a greater degree of misinformation and bias.

EXPLANATION OF CONCEPTS
Storage of knowledge is the preservation of that which is acknowledged as important to society. This can take many forms including audiovisual information, art, and architecture. The term 'storage' implies an institutionalization—explicitly representing knowledge in a way that will be meaningful for future generations. Dissemination ensures both accessibility to and outreach efforts directed at stored knowledge. Traditionally, this process was embodied in museums, monuments and libraries. Increasingly, digital media are used and the Internet and electronic databases play a significant role.

Storage and dissemination of knowledge are fundamentally interconnected with heritage and preservation (see relevant suite). In some ways it is difficult to differentiate between cultural heritage and knowledge. For example, preserving a part of the Berlin Wall can be regarded as a visual, tangible way of storing information, conceptually similar to written documentation in a library.

The idea behind open source information is that it is accessible and modifiable by a large number of people. In the case of Wikipedia, anybody with access to the Internet can view and potentially edit articles. This means that information is subject to bias and lack of knowledge, yet at the same time, the very process opens up new opportunities for peer review, and may, in the medium to long terms, strengthen the quality of the information presented.

WHAT ARE THE TRENDS?
The world's major museums are concentrated in the industrially developed world. Ranked by number of visitors, the Smithsonian in Washington, DC tops the list (see data point 1).

With the growth of the Internet, electronic storage of knowledge is booming. Open content databases contribute to this trend: Wikipedia is growing exponentially with the input from Internet users around the world (see data point 6). This is a major break with traditional encyclopedias for which data were assembled by the publisher in a centralized fashion.

The major brick-and-mortar libraries of the world are national collections or those of major universities. Ranking libraries according to size is difficult: items held range from journals and research papers to encyclopedias. The US Library of Congress is, for instance, the largest library in the world, while the British Library holds the largest number of items (see data point 3). Libraries differ vastly with respect to languages of holdings: works held in the Bibliotheca Alexandrina in Alexandria, Egypt are 48 per cent English, 42 per cent Arabic, 5 per cent French, and 3 per cent German. The German National Library, on the other hand, focuses solely on works in German or translations to and from German.

The largest university research collection is held by the University of California at its 10 campuses (see data point 4). Harvard University is home to the largest single-campus library among the top schools. But even brick-and-mortar libraries are moving towards electronic storage. Columbia University, for instance, boasts more than 500 electronic databases, 45,000 e-journals, 450,000 e-books, and 645,000 e-images (Columbia University, 2007).

With the growth of open content databases, the question of reliability has become a critical issue, as Internet users around the world can access and modify information on Wikipedia. As a result, many articles have been found to be inaccurate or deliberately misleading. In response, major universities, including UCLA and the University of Pennsylvania, have banned open source databases in citations (Daniels & Johnson, 2007). Wikipedia was also blocked by the Republic of China several times for undisclosed reasons.

Storage and dissemination involve judgment on what is deemed worthy of preservation and promotion. The world's museums can only record and store so much. This brings up the question of costs in terms of maintaining existing collections versus adding and expanding holdings. Particularly in times of high artistic productivity and booming art markets, the pressure on museum policies in terms of buying and selling objects can be significant.

With the combined effects of globalization, growing media hunger for innovation (cf. chapter by Wyszomirski in this volume) and the growth of cultural fusions, the limitations of storage become increasingly significant. If a cultural movement is only a fad, should it be recorded? And how can the line between the temporary and the permanent be drawn in meaningful ways?

World organizations such as UNESCO can provide some guidance pertaining to which types of cultural knowledge ought to be preserved and how. Since the establishment of the 2003 Convention for the Safeguarding of the Intangible Cultural Heritage, UNESCO has targeted 'intangible' and 'living' cultural knowledge among its preservation efforts. Intangible cultural knowledge is primarily comprised of oral traditions, performing arts, social practices and rituals, knowledge and craftsmanship, among others. Based on the Convention, UNESCO has designated ICH on every continent in the world and continues to expand the list. Another example is UNESCO's Memory of the World Register, which aims to identify documentary heritage of world significance via an international advisory committee. National governmental bodies also participate in this effort, such as Japan's Cultural Properties Department of the Agency for Cultural Affairs, which identifies, preserves, and ensures utilization of cultural properties. Again, this reflects the blur between cultural heritage and knowledge.

TRADITIONAL +

INDIGENOUS KNOWLEDGE

1. TOP 20 **COUNTRIES** WITH HIGHEST # OF WORLD BANK REGISTERED
INDIGENOUS KNOWLEDGE PRACTICES AS OF 2007

INDIA	39
BURKINA FASO	25
SRI LANKA	21
TANZANIA	19
KENYA	15
CAMEROON	14
MALI	12
GHANA	11
NIGERIA	11
ETHIOPIA	10
EASTERN AFRICA REGION	9
HONDURAS	7
MOZAMBIQUE	7
UGANDA	7
ZIMBABWE	7
NIGER	6
SENEGAL	6
CONGO	4
AFRICA REGION	3
BENIN	3

2. # OF WORLD BANK REGISTERED

INDIGENOUS KNOWLEDGE PRACTICES BY DOMAIN AS OF 2007

Domain	Count
AGRICULTURE	136
HEALTH, NUTRITION AND POPULATION	39
EDUCATION	27
SOCIAL PROTECTION	19
ENVIRONMENT	13
PRIVATE SECTOR DEVELOPMENT	10
TELECOMMUNICATIONS AND INFORMATICS	5
PUBLIC SECTOR DEVELOPMENT	3
FINANCE	2
URBAN DEVELOPMENT	1

3. COLLECTION OF **GENETIC PLANT MATERIAL**: # OF ACCESSIONS OF PLANT GENETIC RESOURCES TRADITIONAL TO REGIONS BY MEMBER INSTITUTE

AS OF 2006

140189 **ICARDA**
|||||||||||||||||||||||||||||||||| INTERNATIONAL CENTER FOR AGRICULTURAL RESEARCH IN THE DRY AREAS

120527 **CIMMYT**
||||||||||||||||||||||||||||||| CENTRO INTERNACIONAL DE MEJORAMIENTO DE MAIZ Y TRIGO

114865 **ICRISAT**
|||||||||||||||||||||||||||||| INTERNATIONAL CROPS RESEARCH INSTITUTE FOR THE SEMI-ARID TROPICS

108272 **IRRI**
||||||||||||||||||||||||||| INTERNATIONAL RICE RESEARCH INSTITUTE

72262 **CIAT**
|||||||||||||||||| CENTRO INTERNACIONAL DE AGRICULTURA TROPICAL

52845 **AVRDC**
||||||||||||| WORLD VEGETABLE CENTER

27596 **IITA**
||||||| INTERNATIONAL INSTITUTE OF TROPICAL AGRICULTURE

20177 **ILRI**
|||||| INTERNATIONAL LIVESTOCK RESEARCH INSTITUTE

15061 **CIP**
|||| CENTRO INTERNACIONAL DE LA PAPA

14759 **WARDA**
|||| THE AFRICA RICE CENTER

1785 **ICRAF**
| THE WORLD AGROFORESTRY CENTRE

1240 **INIBAP**
| BIOVERSITY INTERNATIONAL

4. FORMS OF AUTHORIZATION FOR UTILIZATIONS OF **FOLKLORE EXPRESSIONS** # OF COUNTRIES 2002

SURVEY QUESTION: **ARE EXPRESSIONS OF FOLKLORE IN YOUR COUNTRY REGARDED AS**:

PART OF NATIONAL HERITAGE **34**

PROPERTY OF INDIGENOUS OR OTHER LOCAL COMMUNITIES **16**

PROPERTY OF LOCAL ARTISTS **16**

NONE **3**

SURVEY QUESTION: **DO "EXPRESSIONS OF FOLKLORE," EITHER AS DESCRIBED IN THE MODEL PROVISIONS, OR AS THE TERM IS UNDERSTOOD IN YOUR COUNTRY, RECEIVE SPECIFIC LEGAL PROTECTION AS INTELLECTUAL PROPERTY IN YOUR NATIONAL LAWS OR REGULATIONS (WHETHER THE LAWS OR REGULATIONS ARE RELATED TO INTELLECTUAL PROPERTY OR NOT)?**

YES **36%**

NO **51%**

NO RESPONSE **13%**

TRADITIONAL & INDIGENOUS

KNOWLEDGE
Throughout history, communities around the world have generated knowledge that is passed on from generation to generation. Often this knowledge has been the cornerstone of food security, health, natural resource management, and education systems, hence critical to the communities' livelihoods. In many instances, indigenous knowledge still provides the most affordable means of medical treatment and sufficient agricultural yields. Roughly 80 per cent of the developing world's population depends on indigenous knowledge for health care purposes (WHO, 2002). This knowledge, much of which is tacit and not easily codified, reflects the cultural identity of the communities who have created it (Gorjestani, 2002). Moreover, it has also served in many cases as the basis for modern Western medicines and treatments. As such, indigenous knowledge is a critical component of the cultural capital of these communities, and could therefore contribute significantly towards their sustainable and long-term development (cf. the chapter by Ryan, Keane & Cunningham in this volume).

WHAT IS INDIGENOUS/TRADITIONAL KNOWLEDGE?
Although the term 'indigenous knowledge' is used increasingly all over the world, there is no single definition. This may be largely due to the fact that indigenous knowledge spans an immensely diverse set of subjects. There are, however, common elements among these definitions that have been captured by two leading scholars:

> Indigenous knowledge is local knowledge—knowledge that is unique to a given culture or society. Indigenous knowledge contrasts with the international knowledge system generated by universities, research institutions and private firms. It is the basis for local-level decision making in agriculture, health care, food preparation, education, natural-resource management, and a host of other activities in rural communities (Warren, 1991)

> Indigenous knowledge is (…) the information base for a society, which facilitates communication and decision-making. Indigenous information systems are dynamic, and are continually influenced by internal creativity and experimentation as well as by contact with external systems. (Flavier et al., 1995)

Even UNESCO has been unable to offer a single clear definition but summarizes the major characteristics of indigenous knowledge in the following manner:
• Locally bound, indigenous to a specific area
• Culture- and context-specific
• Non-formal knowledge
• Orally transmitted, and generally not documented
• Dynamic and adaptive
• Holistic in nature
• Closely related to survival and subsistence for many people worldwide

WHAT ARE THE TRENDS?
Only recently have international agencies begun to collect data on indigenous knowledge and practices. The data in this suite indicate that the main arena of indigenous knowledge is agriculture (see data point 2). Moreover, the data mostly reside in the Global South, and in particular, India (see data point 1). Asia and Africa certainly dominate in the number of accessions to plant genetic resources, identified to be traditional to the region. And yet, according to survey data, most nations feel that their knowledge has not been properly protected from outside users.

The international community has mobilized to help protect indigenous knowledge and recognize the wealth that it represents for humanity. This is being done in the domain of intellectual property rights (cf. chapter by Sundara Rajan in this volume), and by stepping up the efforts made by multi-lateral organizations. Both the World Bank and the United Nations have sought ways to incorporate indigenous knowledge in their work.

WHAT ARE THE ISSUES?
The main issue of international concern regarding indigenous knowledge is that is has failed to be protected in the past. Many claim that indigenous knowledge has been used by Western nations in their health and daily functions, yet they make no effort to recognize the fact that the intellectual property in question belongs elsewhere. It is of utmost significance for the international community to begin tracking those elements of knowledge and practice that are indigenous to certain portions of the world and grant them access to the international property rights system that is supposed to protect them.

Because of the failure to protect much indigenous knowledge is lost. In many cases, this is due wholly to the introduction of foreign technologies that offer better short-term results (World Bank, 2007). Thus old practices are forgotten and there is increasing dependency on technology from other regions (see chapters by Reis and Davis, and Dhamija in this volume).

NEWS

₁. SOURCES OF NEWS + INFORMATION
USED BY ADULT INTERNET USERS

IN SELECT COUNTRIES WORLDWIDE **MAY 2007**
(% OF RESPONDENTS)

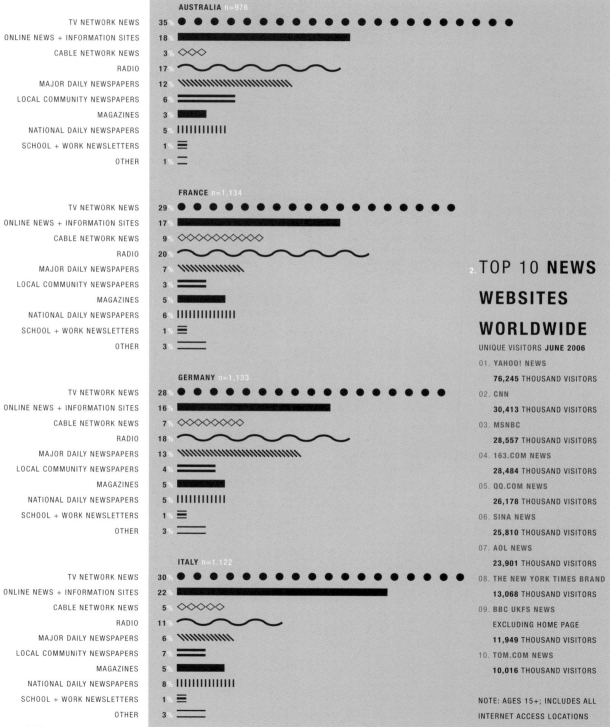

AUSTRALIA n=976

TV NETWORK NEWS	35%
ONLINE NEWS + INFORMATION SITES	18%
CABLE NETWORK NEWS	3%
RADIO	17%
MAJOR DAILY NEWSPAPERS	12%
LOCAL COMMUNITY NEWSPAPERS	6%
MAGAZINES	3%
NATIONAL DAILY NEWSPAPERS	5%
SCHOOL + WORK NEWSLETTERS	1%
OTHER	1%

FRANCE n=1,134

TV NETWORK NEWS	29%
ONLINE NEWS + INFORMATION SITES	17%
CABLE NETWORK NEWS	9%
RADIO	20%
MAJOR DAILY NEWSPAPERS	7%
LOCAL COMMUNITY NEWSPAPERS	3%
MAGAZINES	5%
NATIONAL DAILY NEWSPAPERS	6%
SCHOOL + WORK NEWSLETTERS	1%
OTHER	3%

GERMANY n=1,133

TV NETWORK NEWS	28%
ONLINE NEWS + INFORMATION SITES	16%
CABLE NETWORK NEWS	7%
RADIO	18%
MAJOR DAILY NEWSPAPERS	13%
LOCAL COMMUNITY NEWSPAPERS	4%
MAGAZINES	5%
NATIONAL DAILY NEWSPAPERS	5%
SCHOOL + WORK NEWSLETTERS	1%
OTHER	3%

ITALY n=1,122

TV NETWORK NEWS	30%
ONLINE NEWS + INFORMATION SITES	22%
CABLE NETWORK NEWS	5%
RADIO	11%
MAJOR DAILY NEWSPAPERS	6%
LOCAL COMMUNITY NEWSPAPERS	7%
MAGAZINES	5%
NATIONAL DAILY NEWSPAPERS	8%
SCHOOL + WORK NEWSLETTERS	1%
OTHER	3%

₂. TOP 10 **NEWS** **WEBSITES** **WORLDWIDE**

UNIQUE VISITORS **JUNE 2006**

01. YAHOO! NEWS
   76,245 THOUSAND VISITORS
02. CNN
   30,413 THOUSAND VISITORS
03. MSNBC
   28,557 THOUSAND VISITORS
04. 163.COM NEWS
   28,484 THOUSAND VISITORS
05. QQ.COM NEWS
   26,178 THOUSAND VISITORS
06. SINA NEWS
   25,810 THOUSAND VISITORS
07. AOL NEWS
   23,901 THOUSAND VISITORS
08. THE NEW YORK TIMES BRAND
   13,068 THOUSAND VISITORS
09. BBC UKFS NEWS
   EXCLUDING HOME PAGE
   11,949 THOUSAND VISITORS
10. TOM.COM NEWS
   10,016 THOUSAND VISITORS

NOTE: AGES 15+; INCLUDES ALL
INTERNET ACCESS LOCATIONS

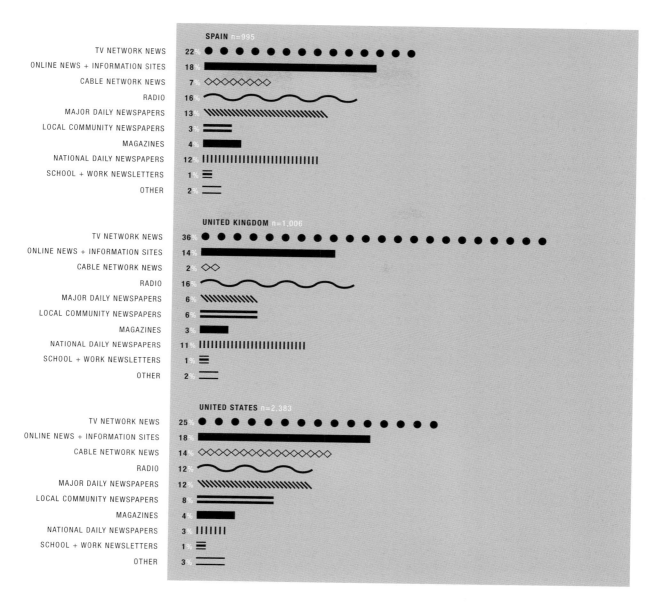

SPAIN n=995

TV NETWORK NEWS	22%
ONLINE NEWS + INFORMATION SITES	18%
CABLE NETWORK NEWS	7%
RADIO	16%
MAJOR DAILY NEWSPAPERS	13%
LOCAL COMMUNITY NEWSPAPERS	3%
MAGAZINES	4%
NATIONAL DAILY NEWSPAPERS	12%
SCHOOL + WORK NEWSLETTERS	1%
OTHER	2%

UNITED KINGDOM n=1,006

TV NETWORK NEWS	36%
ONLINE NEWS + INFORMATION SITES	14%
CABLE NETWORK NEWS	2%
RADIO	16%
MAJOR DAILY NEWSPAPERS	6%
LOCAL COMMUNITY NEWSPAPERS	6%
MAGAZINES	3%
NATIONAL DAILY NEWSPAPERS	11%
SCHOOL + WORK NEWSLETTERS	1%
OTHER	2%

UNITED STATES n=2,383

TV NETWORK NEWS	25%
ONLINE NEWS + INFORMATION SITES	18%
CABLE NETWORK NEWS	14%
RADIO	12%
MAJOR DAILY NEWSPAPERS	12%
LOCAL COMMUNITY NEWSPAPERS	8%
MAGAZINES	4%
NATIONAL DAILY NEWSPAPERS	3%
SCHOOL + WORK NEWSLETTERS	1%
OTHER	3%

3. SELECT INTERNATIONAL **NEWS OUTLETS**:

SALES + EMPLOYEES 2005/2006

BBC WORLD UK	$967.2 MILLION	1,782 EMPLOYEES
AL JAZEERA QATAR	NO DATA	400 EMPLOYEES
CNN USA	$794.0 MILLION	2,200 EMPLOYEES
DEUTSCHE WELLE GERMANY	$337.4 MILLION	1,499 EMPLOYEES
TV5MONDE FRANCE	$ 29.2 MILLION	322 EMPLOYEES

447

TV AND ONLINE NEWS

Television and the Internet are the prime sources for news in terms of access and use. Online news is reclaiming a portion of the audience that print media lost to television news, but it is also growing of its own accord via news portals.

The advent and subsequent rapid growth of the Internet present an ongoing challenge to the business model of established media corporations. On the one hand, the Internet has allowed media corporations to reverse the trend of overall declining readerships as they are now able to reach larger potential audiences, generate additional revenue through advertising, and promote their print product. Online sites have also enabled TV news networks to post programs after they have been broadcast. Although established news providers (print media and television) including *The New York Times*, CNN, and *Business Week* were the first to create online news sites, Internet-based portals like Yahoo soon followed suit and now see the highest rates of usage by those seeking online news. Today, all major newspapers and weeklies maintain websites, as do many radio and television stations, yet continued problems in pricing and charging for online news and shifts in the market for advertising are affecting the revenue situation of all news providers.

CONCEPTS

TV news refers to the broadcast of information regarding current events through the medium of television. The majority of news stories are pre-recorded reports edited and pieced together by the television networks, while live reports are presented by reporters on the scene, often with the help of a studio reporter. Producers determine what stories are included or excluded, and thereby influence the outcome of a newscast. Thus, news is invariably shaped by individuals and consequently informed by their culture.

Online news describes the production and dissemination of current events via the Internet and is rooted in the tradition of print media, which had dominated the mass media market before technological advances helped make radio and television the primary media.

WHAT DO WE KNOW?

The indicator suite shows the wide and expanding reach of TV and, more prominently, online news. In terms of sales, the most prominent television news companies have been CNN, the BBC and Al Jazeera, with Deutsche Welle and TV5Monde not far behind (see data point 3). Founded in 1980 by Ted Turner, CNN is a private news network based in Atlanta with 36 bureaus and more than 900 affiliates worldwide that presently maintains networks in four different languages. Al Jazeera is an Arabic-language television channel that began broadcasting in 1996 with a $150 million grant from the Emir of Qatar. Al Jazeera is the most frequently viewed news channel in the Middle East, with its exclusive interviews and footage rebroadcast by Western media.

BBC, Deutsche Welle (DW-TV) and TV5Monde are public broadcasting networks. BBC aired its first TV bulletin in 1954, and now serves more than 200 countries worldwide. DW-TV is available globally via satellite and cooperates with Germany's Foreign Service on matters of public diplomacy (Auswaertiges Amt Deutschland, 2007). TV5Monde is the only digital, global French language network, broadcasting 24 hours a day, 365 days

a year, to more than 25 million households in 203 countries worldwide, making it the third largest global network in terms of subscribers (TV5Monde, 2007).

About 76 million unique Internet users accessed Yahoo.com in June 2006, making it the largest source for news online, followed by CNN (30.4 million), and MSNBC (see data point 2).

WHAT ARE THE ISSUES?

The formation of giant media conglomerates has changed the market structure of the broadcasting industry into an oligopoly, in which a few firms could potentially control the majority of the market (Klinenberg, March/April 2007). This could give these firms significant power not only in determining what to broadcast, when and where, but also to control pricing policies, and thereby access. At the same time, rapidly changing technologies and political realities continue to create new media environments that are more open and more diversified than in the past. Innovation rather than market consolidation appears to drive how new news media are forming.

CNN, Al Jazeera, and BBC have all been charged with biased reporting. Conservatives have accused CNN's reporting of enforcing a liberal position, whereas international journalists have criticized CNN for leniency in reporting on Bush's War on Terror. Similarly, Al Jazeera has been deemed by officials of the Bush Administration in the United States as 'hateful propaganda' from the Arab world, while many Arab critics chide its admonishment of authoritarian regimes in the Middle East. The call for more balanced reporting and the view that the broadcasting conglomerates perpetuate Western influence around the world has inspired the growth of alternative news outlets, many initiated as government entities (see table on next page). As a result, the landscape of governmental broadcasting, which until recently remained reminiscent of Cold Ward realities, is changing to reflect emerging geopolitical realities.

Independently of questions of ownership, the impact of globalization on how news and information is recoded, produced and disseminated remains a contested issue. Some argue that the so-called 'CNN effect' (resulting from expedited news travel via the Internet and 24-hour international television news) has deflated the quality of news reporting, and now provides unsound policy platforms by prompting public figures and governments to act hastily in order to put on the appearance of effective leadership. In this view, the media function alternately or simultaneously as (1) policy agenda setting agents, (2) impediments to the achievement of desired policy goals, and (3) accelerants to decision making (Livingston, 1997). Aware of the public's instant and easy access to information about current events, including strategic decisions and actions, political leaders may act to appease public criticism and response, thereby catering their decisions to the segment of the population who can afford television and Internet access.

NETWORK+HQ	LAUNCHED	OWNER(S)	FUNDER(S)	LANGUAGES	EMPLOYEES	ANNUAL BUDGET
PRESS TV Tehran	JULY 2007	Islamic Republic of Iran Broadcasting	Iranian Government	English, Persian	**400** (2007)	**250** billion Rials
FRANCE 24 Paris	DEC 2006	Groupe TF1 & France Télévisions	French Government	French, English, Arabic	**390** (2006)	**80** million Euros
RUSSIA TODAY Moscow	DEC 2005	TV Novosti	Russian Government	English, Russian, Arabic	**700** (2007)	Unknown
teleSUR Caracas	JULY 2005	Pan-Latin American TV network	$10 million (USD) provided by the countries that jointly own the network: Venezuela (51% share), Argentina (20%), Cuba (19%), and Uruguay (10%), and in April 2006 Bolivia's President Evo Morales agreed to buy a 5% stake. Nicaragua followed in March 2007 and Ecuador in August.	Spanish	**160** (2006)	**$10** million USD

TELEVISION

BRAZIL:

REALITY TV	$15,000
SITCOMS	$20,000
DRAMAS	$30,000
TV MOVIES	$45,000

MEXICO:

REALITY TV	$15,000
SITCOMS	$20,000
DRAMAS	$35,000
TV MOVIES	$40,000

AUSTRALIA:

REALITY TV	$20,000
SITCOMS	$30,000
DRAMAS	$50,000
TV MOVIES	$75,000

JAPAN:

REALITY TV	$20,000
SITCOMS	$30,000
DRAMAS	$40,000
TV MOVIES	$60,000

CANADA:

REALITY TV	$ 30,000
SITCOMS	$ 50,000
DRAMAS	$ 85,000
TV MOVIES	$125,000

HUNGARY:

REALITY TV	$10,000
SITCOMS	$15,000
DRAMAS	$25,000
TV MOVIES	$30,000

CZECH REPUBLIC:

REALITY TV	$10,000
SITCOMS	$15,000
DRAMAS	$20,000
TV MOVIES	$25,000

POLAND:

REALITY TV	$20,000
SITCOMS	$25,000
DRAMAS	$45,000
TV MOVIES	$50,000

RUSSIA:

REALITY TV	$25,000
SITCOMS	$40,000
DRAMAS	$60,000
TV MOVIES	$75,000

AUSTRIA:

REALITY TV	$15,000
SITCOMS	$20,000
DRAMAS	$30,000
TV MOVIES	$40,000

BELGIUM:

REALITY TV	$15,000
SITCOMS	$20,000
DRAMAS	$35,000
TV MOVIES	$45,000

SCANDINAVIA:

REALITY TV	$15,000
SITCOMS	$30,000
DRAMAS	$40,000
TV MOVIES	$50,000

NETHERLANDS:

REALITY TV	$15,000
SITCOMS	$25,000
DRAMAS	$50,000
TV MOVIES	$75,000

SPAIN:

REALITY TV	$20,000
SITCOMS	$35,000
DRAMAS	$70,000
TV MOVIES	$90,000

ITALY:

REALITY TV	$ 30,000
SITCOMS	$ 40,000
DRAMAS	$ 75,000
TV MOVIES	$100,000

FRANCE:

REALITY TV	$ 30,000
SITCOMS	$ 50,000
DRAMAS	$ 80,000
TV MOVIES	$100,000

UNITED KINGDOM:

REALITY TV	$150,000
SITCOMS	$100,000
DRAMAS	$140,000
TV MOVIES	$150,000

GERMANY:

REALITY TV	$ 40,000
SITCOMS	$ 75,000
DRAMAS	$150,000
TV MOVIES	$200,000

2. TOP 10 COUNTRIES: TOTAL HOURS OF **TV FORMAT PROGRAMMING**: IMPORTED AND EXPORTED

← IMPORTED AND EXPORTED →

IMPORTED	EXPORTED
01. GERMANY 2002 – **1,523** HOURS 2003 – **1,827** HOURS 2004 – **1,742** HOURS	**01. UNITED KINGDOM** 2002 – **3,010** HOURS 2003 – **3,666** HOURS 2004 – **3,795** HOURS
02. FRANCE 2002 – **1,326** HOURS 2003 – **1,562** HOURS 2004 – **1,812** HOURS	**02. NETHERLANDS** 2002 – **1,762** HOURS 2003 – **2,480** HOURS 2004 – **2,569** HOURS
03. ITALY 2002 – **1,132** HOURS 2003 – **1,737** HOURS 2004 – **1,692** HOURS	**03. UNITED STATES** 2002 – **1,758** HOURS 2003 – **1,952** HOURS 2004 – **2,236** HOURS
04. SPAIN 2002 – **1,103** HOURS 2003 – **1,184** HOURS 2004 – **1,338** HOURS	**04. AUSTRALIA** 2002 – **1,021** HOURS 2003 – **957** HOURS 2004 – **718** HOURS
05. AUSTRALIA 2002 – **634** HOURS 2003 – **695** HOURS 2004 – **991** HOURS	**05. SWEDEN** 2002 – **261** HOURS 2003 – **343** HOURS 2004 – **558** HOURS
06. POLAND 2002 – **656** HOURS 2003 – **619** HOURS 2004 – **805** HOURS	**06. FRANCE** 2002 – **275** HOURS 2003 – **317** HOURS 2004 – **340** HOURS
07. UNITED KINGDOM 2002 – **677** HOURS 2003 – **625** HOURS 2004 – **633** HOURS	**07. NORWAY** 2002 – **35** HOURS 2003 – **106** HOURS 2004 – **482** HOURS
08. NETHERLANDS 2002 – **467** HOURS 2003 – **601** HOURS 2004 – **579** HOURS	**08. DENMARK** 2002 – **155** HOURS 2003 – **220** HOURS 2004 – **202** HOURS
09. BELGIUM 2002 – **393** HOURS 2003 – **370** HOURS 2004 – **821** HOURS	**09. ITALY** 2002 – **144** HOURS 2003 – **165** HOURS 2004 – **191** HOURS
10. DENMARK 2002 – **570** HOURS 2003 – **393** HOURS 2004 – **470** HOURS	**10. ARGENTINA** 2002 – **141** HOURS 2003 – **132** HOURS 2004 – **182** HOURS

3. TV FORMAT PROGRAMMING HOURS
BY SELECT GENRE

01. GAME SHOW
2002 – **6,754** HOURS
2003 – **7,138** HOURS
2004 – **7,655** HOURS

02. REALITY TV
2002 – **2,958** HOURS
2003 – **3,848** HOURS
2004 – **3,608** HOURS

03. SCRIPTED TV
2002 – **625** HOURS
2003 – **731** HOURS
2004 – **928** HOURS

04. MAGAZINE/STUDIO-BASED
2002 – **850** HOURS
2003 – **1,019** HOURS
2004 – **877** HOURS

05. VARIETY
2002 – **642** HOURS
2003 – **754** HOURS
2004 – **717** HOURS

06. HOME IMPROVEMENT
2002 – **82** HOURS
2003 – **115** HOURS
2004 – **256** HOURS

07. MAKEOVER
2002 – **14** HOURS
2003 – **48** HOURS
2004 – **215** HOURS

4. GLOBAL MARKET POTENTIAL FOR CABLE TV
BY REGION 2007

35.1% ASIA

25.8% EUROPE

23.2% NORTH AMERICA + THE CARIBBEAN

7.4% AFRICA + THE MIDDLE EAST

7.1% LATIN AMERICA

1.3% OCEANA

5. SELECT WORLD CITIES: **CABLE TV MARKETS** BY REGION **2007***

% OF THE COUNTRY

		%		
OCEANA	NOUMEA **NEW CALEDONIA**	76.7%	$	17 MILLION
	PAPEETE **FRENCH POLYNESIA**	52.2%	$	16 MILLION
	AUCKLAND **NEW ZEALAND**	38.0%	$	223 MILLION
	MELBOURNE **AUSTRALIA**	28.9%	$	1,134 MILLION
	SYDNEY **AUSTRALIA**	29.3%	$	1,150 MILLION
NORTH AMERICA + THE CARIBBEAN	PORT-AU-PRINCE **HAITI**	70.4%	$	59 MILLION
	HAVANA **CUBA**	52.9%	$	116 MILLION
	SANTO DOMINGO **DOMINICAN REPUBLIC**	64.7%	$	230 MILLION
	SAN JUAN **PUERTO RICO**	23.0%	$	106 MILLION
	MONTREAL **CANADA**	25.5%	$	1,667 MILLION
	TORONTO **CANADA**	29.9%	$	1,956 MILLION
	LOS ANGELES **UNITED STATES**	8.2%	$	6,216 MILLION
	NEW YORK **UNITED STATES**	22.8%	$	17,171 MILLION
LATIN AMERICA	LIMA **PERU**	56.1%	$	565 MILLION
	SANTIAGO **CHILE**	64.1%	$	682 MILLION
	BOGOTA **COLOMBIA**	45.4%	$	822 MILLION
	BUENOS AIRES **ARGENTINA**	12.2%	$	375 MILLION
	MEXICO CITY **MEXICO**	28.4%	$	1,821 MILLION
	SAO PAULO **BRAZIL**	13.4%	$	1,241 MILLION
EUROPE	MOSCOW **RUSSIA**	30.2%	$	1,355 MILLION
	MADRID **SPAIN**	28.8%	$	1,745 MILLION
	ROME **ITALY**	25.4%	$	2,663 MILLION
	PARIS **FRANCE**	70.3%	$	8,333 MILLION
	LONDON **UNITED KINGDOM**	35.0%	$	4,300 MILLION
	BERLIN **GERMANY**	20.3%	$	3,298 MILLION
ASIA	SEOUL **SOUTH KOREA**	48.9%	$	2,878 MILLION
	MAHARASHTRA STATE **INDIA**	17.3%	$	3,685 MILLION
	YOKOHAMA **JAPAN**	6.8%	$	2,013 MILLION
	TOKYO **JAPAN**	16.8%	$	4,968 MILLION
	CHONGQING **CHINA**	10.1%	$	4,605 MILLION
	BEIJING **CHINA**	11.9%	$	5,441 MILLION
	SHANGHAI **CHINA**	14.3%	$	6,529 MILLION
AFRICA + THE MIDDLE EAST	JIDDAH **SAUDI ARABIA**	37.3%	$	746 MILLION
	KARACHI **PAKISTAN**	38.4%	$	849 MILLION
	JOHANNESBURG **SOUTH AFRICA**	31.5%	$	981 MILLION
	CAIRO **EGYPT**	59.6%	$	1,208 MILLION
	ISTANBUL **TURKEY**	38.4%	$	1,225 MILLION

* BASED ON POTENTIAL MARKET DEMAND

TELEVISION

Television is a major vehicle for the flow of information on a transnational scale. To a large extent, TV flows, their content, as well as access to them, both reflect and perpetuate global power structures in terms of corporate and national interests. The result is an imbalanced amalgamation of perspectives that favors the developed world and excludes many voices, viewers and listeners in the Global South. This pattern, frequently referred to as 'media imperialism,' claims that Western economic dominance has created media markets which export cultural beliefs, especially through the TV and film mediums, to other regions. However, this idea seems to oversimplify the complex relationships that audiences around the world have with TV as a medium, and underestimate the growing presence of regional media broadcasting centers (see chapter by Curtin in this volume).

WHAT IS THE TELEVISION INDUSTRY?

Television is a system for transmitting, receiving, and reproducing audio and visual information from one place to another via wires and radio waves. Considered the most powerful medium of mass communication and a valued entertainment source, television is a major worldwide industry. The technology of television has become increasingly sophisticated and is now a very different industry than its original form of black and white reception. Newer technologies include digital, as opposed to analog, cable television, liquid crystal display (LCD) screens, high definition and plasma/flat panel TVs as well as projection systems.

WHAT DO WE KNOW ABOUT TV AND GLOBALIZATION?

Certain durable goods are often used as economic indicators of household poverty rates in a given country or area. Among the durable goods measured by Euromonitor International (2007) are black and white TV, cable TV, color and satellite TV systems. These key economic statistics illustrate the global importance the television industry now holds as a cultural industry and TVs as predictors of wider consumer trends. Global trends show that in many places, cable TV ownership is increasing at the greatest rate, with slightly more moderate increases observed in the cases of color and satellite TVs while black and white TV ownership is declining.

The data suite supports the growing scope and scale of the industry as well as several other emerging trends such as the following:

- *Television formats* are sales of TV show concepts or outlines to other countries where they are adapted to a different cultural, political and economic context. The global market for TV format sales between countries is growing, with the three largest suppliers of formats being the UK, the Netherlands and the US. The top consumers or importers of formats are Germany, France, and Italy (see data point 2).
- Price points vary considerably for US-produced TV formats by country and by genre with countries such as the Czech Republic, Brazil, Mexico, and Hungary paying the lowest amounts and countries such as Germany, UK, Canada and France paying the highest amounts (see data point 1).
- Game shows followed by reality TV have the most programming hours (see data point 3).
- Cable TV markets are most lucrative in the world's cities (see data point 5). The top cities in terms of cable TV market worth, by region, are Sydney, Australia; New York, US; Mexico City, Mexico; Paris, France; Shanghai, China; and

Istanbul, Turkey. The countries where the urban markets were more evenly spread throughout several cities as opposed to concentration within just the capital are Argentina, the United States, China, Brazil and India.

WHAT ARE THE ISSUES?

Unequal access and control of content are among the most critical issues. As television and radio programs are developed and aired by networks, they not only provide information, but also inculcate certain viewpoints and opinions. Those located in developing parts of the world have fewer options for information access and largely consume what others produce, thereby perpetuating a culture of hegemony, i.e., typically Western popular culture; thus, television functions as a reflection and medium of dominant paradigms and power imbalances. The West dominates world television with respect to volume of broadcast stations and sales of TV formats (concepts or outlines for shows which are then adapted to a local context); this critical control of content and access in many areas of Latin America, Africa, Asia and the Pacific can subtly affect regional cultures over a sustained period of time.

Television formats purchases reduce the costs of producing a show or TV movie in-country. However, formats do not assist in expanding the local television industry, creating jobs or stimulating local creativity. Reality TV is a particularly popular and influential type of TV format used in replications in other countries. Reality shows also happen to be the least expensive genre of television show available. Also, many reality shows involve a public participation component that is usually in the form of SMS mobile-phone texting. SMS 'voting' is low cost and extremely accessible to individuals all over the world while the sheer volume of 'voters' is creating large amounts of revenue for phone companies and TV broadcasting companies (Levine, 2003). The reality show trend is truly global with various derivations of familiar Western TV show themes such as *Big Brother* and *Dancing with the Stars* in countries such as South Africa, India, and China, throughout Eastern and Western Europe, Israel, and Nigeria. While the concept of reality TV shows is Western in origin, many countries are appropriating reality TV and inserting their own cultural elements to include local beliefs, languages and relevant political issues into the show's context (Brennan, 2004).

Data points 4 and 5 illustrate the worldwide scale of potential cable TV markets, which is largest in the regions of Asia, Europe, North America and the Caribbean. In many areas of the world, this growing market is being supplied by the companies and providers at the forefront of technological innovation such as in the use of digital cable over analog. For instance, in Africa, the digital cable audience grew by 139,000 subscribers to 793,000 for the year and now accounts for 62 per cent of the total number of subscribers on the continent, establishing a solid platform for the roll-out of interactive television (iTV) services. While many of the big providers are headquartered in South Africa, there are also a small number of emerging indigenous broadcasters such as Frontage Satellite Television (FSTV) in Nigeria (Africa News, 2005). However, digital technology, while exhibiting consistent decreases in user fees, is still quite expensive, especially in terms of monthly fees, which can tend to limit market access to economically developing countries. Developed countries found in Europe and North America are projected to have significant increases in digital television ownership (see figure next page).

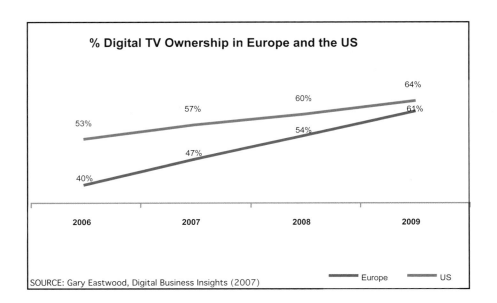

% Digital TV Ownership in Europe and the US

64%

60%

57%

53%

61%

54%

47%

40%

2006   2007   2008   2009

Europe   US

SOURCE: Gary Eastwood, Digital Business Insights (2007)

RADIO INDUSTRY

1. GLOBAL REVENUE FOR SATELLITE GROUND EQUIPMENT

INCLUDES GATEWAYS, NOCS, SATELLITE NEWS GATHERING EQUIPMENT,
FLYAWAYS, VSATS, DBS DISHES, SATELLITE RADIOS, SATELLITE PHONES

US$ BILLIONS

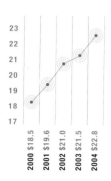

2000	$18.5
2001	$19.6
2002	$21.0
2003	$21.5
2004	$22.8

2. RADIO ADVERTISING EXPENDITURES

SELECT COUNTRIES US$ MILLIONS 2000-2009

*ESTIMATED

	AUSTRALIA	BRAZIL	CANADA	FRANCE	GERMANY	CHINA	INDIA	ITALY	JAPAN	SOUTH KOREA	UK	USA	RUSSIA	SOUTH AFRICA
2000	523	263	837	890	912	192	41	565	1,879	206	825	20,819	45	192
2002	536	152	901	887	740	267	59	482	1,667	226	763	19,423	115	226
2004	632	207	998	976	769	402	54	658	1,629	214	846	20,364	250	304
2006	689	322	1,168	1,016	827	569	84	687	1,600	228	790	20,892	366	359
2007*	720	338	1,241	1,025	837	663	125	725	1,587	235	797	21,211	439	405
2008*	756	355	1,313	1,044	847	813	181	769	1,574	242	812	21,541	527	450
2009*	767	373	1,389	1,063	857	930	190	810	1,559	249	826	22,402	622	496

3. RADIO FRANCE INTERNATIONALE BREAKDOWN OF LISTENERS BY REGION 2006

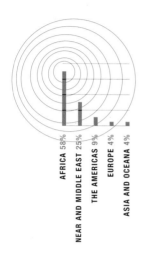

AFRICA 58%
NEAR AND MIDDLE EAST 25%
THE AMERICAS 9%
EUROPE 4%
ASIA AND OCEANA 4%

4. AUDIENCE SIZES AND ANNUAL EXPENDITURES MAJOR INTERNATIONAL RADIO SERVICES

2006 EXPENDITURES
OF LISTENERS
*THIS FIGURE INDICATES HOW MANY PEOPLE CAN RECEIVE DW-RADIO

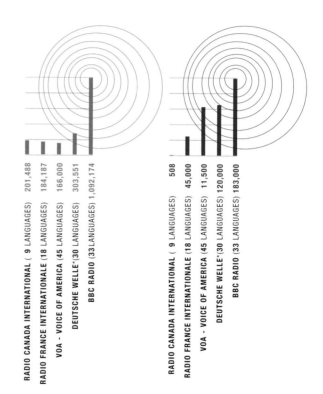

RADIO CANADA INTERNATIONAL (9 LANGUAGES) 201,488
RADIO FRANCE INTERNATIONALE (18 LANGUAGES) 184,187
VOA - VOICE OF AMERICA (45 LANGUAGES) 166,000
DEUTSCHE WELLE*(30 LANGUAGES) 303,551
BBC RADIO (33 LANGUAGES) 1,092,174

RADIO CANADA INTERNATIONAL (9 LANGUAGES) 508
RADIO FRANCE INTERNATIONALE (18 LANGUAGES) 45,000
VOA - VOICE OF AMERICA (45 LANGUAGES) 11,500
DEUTSCHE WELLE*(30 LANGUAGES) 120,000
BBC RADIO (33 LANGUAGES) 183,000

5. DECLINE IN TRADITIONAL MEDIA USAGE DUE TO INCREASES IN NEW FORMS 2006 (% OF RESPONDENTS, N=58 IN 25 COUNTRIES)

NEW METHODS INCLUDE INTERNET, BLOGS, VIRAL MARKETING, SEARCH

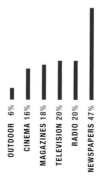

OUTDOOR 6%
CINEMA 16%
MAGAZINES 18%
TELEVISION 20%
RADIO 20%
NEWSPAPERS 47%

RADIO Radio broadcasting, prior to the advent of television, was the primary means for news and communication over long distances worldwide. While television has succeeded in usurping radio broadcasting as the primary source of information in most parts of the developed world, this is not the case in every context. In many parts of the developing world radio continues to play a prominent role in information dissemination, especially where individual TV ownership is low, where the market for cable TV providers is restricted and where electricity is scarce or unavailable.

Radio is a system that conveys information between various points by relying on the wireless transmission of electromagnetic waves through space. Shortwave radio, operating at frequencies between 3 and 30 MHz, can reach longer distances than AM/FM radio, but varies greatly in regard to quality of sound. International broadcasting typically broadcasts over shortwave in a range of frequencies and languages. Not subject to local regulation, shortwave radio can add to political diversity in countries with limited freedom of information; by the same token, it can also serve as a tool of political propaganda. Satellite radio is a recent technological advance that is also becoming increasingly popular and, in some ways, revitalizing the industry especially in developed countries where TV has overshadowed radio. Satellite radio is a digital radio signal broadcast by a communications satellite that allows for much greater geographical coverage than with the traditional terrestrial signals. Mobile technologies used in conjunction with satellite radio technology allow listeners to roam large distances, potentially over a whole continent, while maintaining access to the same radio stations. However, the majority of satellite radio services are accessed through individual paid subscriptions.

WHAT DO WE KNOW ABOUT THE RADIO INDUSTRY?

The radio industry has declined 20 per cent due to the increase in consumption of other forms of information dissemination media (see data point 5). However, the industry data shown in this suite illustrate a divergence in market patterns between the developed and the developing worlds, making it difficult to draw common and universally-applicable conclusions.

- Globally, revenue for satellite ground equipment used for satellite radio broadcasting has increased dramatically from US$18.5 billion in 2000 to US$25.2 billion in 2005. However, much of this revenue is most likely being generated in the US and Western Europe (see data point 1).
- Radio advertising expenditures show divergent trends by country, with projected increases (from 2000 – 2009) in Canada, the US, China, Italy, Russia and South Africa and decreases or stagnation in Brazil, Germany, Japan, South Korea, and the UK (see data point 2).
- While satellite radio subscriptions are increasing in the US, terrestrial radio still accounts for the vast majority of the industry with 282.2 million people per week versus 13.6 million satellite subscriptions per week. Internet radio ranks second after terrestrial with 29 million people per week (see table at left).
- Some of the largest internationally broadcast radio services around the world are funded by government and as part of compulsory fees. In terms of audience size, BBC Radio (UK) ranks the largest followed by Deutsche Welle (German), Voice of America (US), Radio France Internationale and finally Radio Canada International. VOA regularly broadcasts content in 45 languages, BBC in 33, Deutsche Welle in 30, and Radio France and Canada in 18 and 9 languages respectively (see data point 4).
- Projected radio advertising expenditures for 2006-2011 in the US show a marginal increase when compared to projected Internet advertising spending (see figure below).

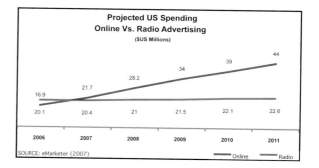

Projected US Spending Online Vs. Radio Advertising ($US Millions)

SOURCE: eMarketer (2007)

USA WEEKLY RADIO AUDIENCE BY TECHNOLOGY 2007

	Audience in Millions
Terrestrial radio	**282.8**
Internet radio*	**29**
Satellite radio subscribers	**13.6**
Podcasting**	**7.1**
Mobile phone audio streaming	**4.1**
High-definition	**0.3**

* ages 12+

** data estimated based on Los Angeles, San Francisco, Seattle, St. Louis, Chicago, Boston, Washington, DC, Miami, Dallas and Atlanta markets.

Source: eMarketer (2007)

WHAT ARE THE ISSUES?

Unequal access and control of content are critical issues. As radio programs are developed and aired by broadcasters, they not only provide information, but also inculcate certain viewpoints and opinions. Those located in developing countries have fewer options for information access and largely consume what others produce. This can contribute to the hegemony of Western popular culture; and thus, radio can function as a reflection and medium of dominant paradigms and power imbalances. Foreign government-funded radio broadcasts in particular have invested heavily in crafting content and 'messaging' for particular regions of the world. Voice of America, BBC and Radio France Internationale all have highly crafted region-specific broadcasts which put forth content that supports their regional political interests, most notably in Africa, the Middle East, and parts of Asia.

Satellite radio services represent the forefront of technological advances within the radio industry through exponentially increasing the geographical scope of access to potential listeners. This form of radio utilizes a high-caliber satellite whose transmission is only restricted by the curvature of the earth's surface. Consequently, only two or three satellites are necessary to provide uniform access to an entire continent. However, like other forms of radio media, the content and access rights to satellite radio are being dictated by a small number of primarily US-owned corporations. In fact, the only two satellite radio providers in the US, XM Satellite Radio and Sirius, are currently negotiating with the FCC towards a potential merger which would result in the reduction of control of the North American market to one single provider (Orol and Nolter, 2007). Worldspace, another US-based company, is the leading worldwide provider of satellite radio outside North America with services offered in over 130 countries, including India and China, Africa, the Middle East, and Western Europe. Worldspace service plans range from US$5-$10/month, and approximately half of all channels offered consist of Western broadcasts such as BBC and Fox News with the remaining channels developed by regional or national-level third parties (WorldSpace, n.d.). An exception to the American satellite radio industry oligopoly is MobaHO!, a Tokyo-based satellite radio service catering to the Japanese market by offering over 40 channels since October 2004 (MobaHO!, n.d.).

PRINT MEDIA

1. THE WORLD'S **BIGGEST NEWSPAPER MARKETS**

BY COPIES SOLD DAILY **2006**

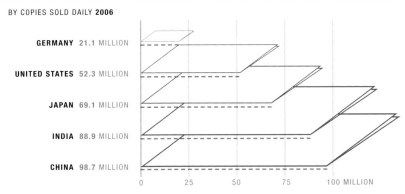

GERMANY 21.1 MILLION
UNITED STATES 52.3 MILLION
JAPAN 69.1 MILLION
INDIA 88.9 MILLION
CHINA 98.7 MILLION

0   25   50   75   100 MILLION

2. WORLD **NEWSPAPER** PAID **CIRCULATION TRENDS** BY REGION **2006**

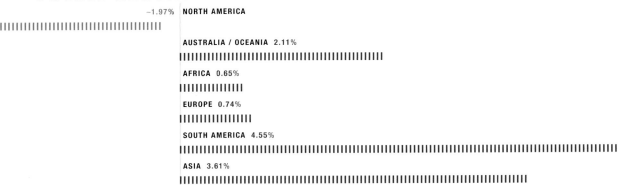

−1.97% **NORTH AMERICA**

AUSTRALIA / OCEANIA 2.11%

AFRICA 0.65%

EUROPE 0.74%

SOUTH AMERICA 4.55%

ASIA 3.61%

3. **NEWSPAPER CIRCULATION GROWTH TRENDS** IN MAJOR MARKETS **2002 – 2006** / 2006 ONLY

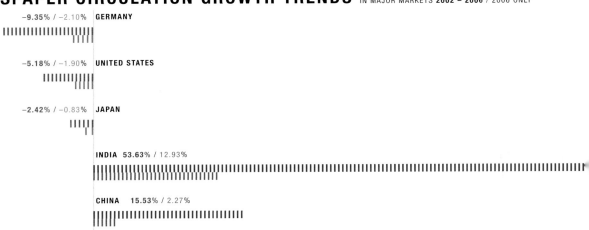

−9.35% / −2.10% **GERMANY**

−5.18% / −1.90% **UNITED STATES**

−2.42% / −0.83% **JAPAN**

INDIA 53.63% / 12.93%

CHINA 15.53% / 2.27%

4. THE WORLD'S 50 LARGEST NEWSPAPERS

01.	YOMIURI SHIMBUN	JAPAN	14,246,000
02.	THE ASAHI SHIMBUN	JAPAN	12,326,000
03.	MAINICHI SHIMBUN	JAPAN	5,635,000
04.	NIHON KEIZAI SHIMBUN	JAPAN	4,737,000
05.	CHUNICHI SHIMBUN	JAPAN	4,571,000
06.	BILD	GERMANY	4,220,000
07.	THE SUN	UNITED KINGDOM	3,461,000
08.	SANKEI SHIMBUN	JAPAN	2,665,000
09.	USA TODAY	UNITED STATES	2,603,000
10.	CANAKO XIAOXI	CHINA	2,530,000
11.	THE CHOSUN ILBO	SOUTH KOREA	2,428,000
12.	TOKYO SPORTS	JAPAN	2,425,000
13.	DAILY MAIL	UNITED KINGDOM	2,411,000
14.	THE JOONGANG ILBO	SOUTH KOREA	2,200,000
15.	TIMES OF INDIA	INDIA	2,131,000
16.	THE MIRROR	UNITED KINGDOM	2,117,000
17.	THE DONG-A ILBO	SOUTH KOREA	2,100,000
18.	NIKKAN SPORTS	JAPAN	1,987,000
19.	HOKKAIDO SHIMBUN	JAPAN	1,947,000
20.	THE WALL STREET JOURNAL	UNITED STATES	1,821,000
21.	SPORTS NIPPON	JAPAN	1,791,000
22.	PEOPLE'S DAILY	CHINA	1,773,000
23.	NEW YORK TIMES	UNITED STATES	1,673,000
24.	YANGTSE EVENING NEWS	CHINA	1,650,000
25.	GUANGZHOU DAILY	CHINA	1,600,000
26.	DAINIK BHASKAR	INDIA	1,570,000
27.	YUKAN FUJI	JAPAN	1,559,000
28.	YANGCHENG EVENING NEWS	CHINA	1,500,000
29.	THE HANKOOK ILBO	SOUTH KOREA	1,500,000
30.	JAGARAN	INDIA	1,500,000
31.	SHIZUOKA SHIMBUN	JAPAN	1,474,000
32.	LOS ANGELES TIMES	UNITED STATES	1,396,000
33.	HOCHI SHIMBUN	JAPAN	1,390,000
34.	SANKEI SPORTS	JAPAN	1,368,000
35.	XINMIN EVENING NEWS	CHINA	1,218,000
36.	MALAYALA MANORAMA	INDIA	1,214,000
37.	CHUTIAN METRO DAILY	CHINA	1,213,000
38.	THAI RATH	THAILAND	1,200,000
39.	THE MAEIL BUSINESS NEWSPAPER	SOUTH KOREA	1,110,000
40.	ZEITUNGSGRUPPE WAZ	GERMANY	1,064,000
41.	THE WASHINGTON POST	UNITED STATES	1,049,000
42.	GUJARAT SAMACHAR	INDIA	1,041,000
43.	NISHI-NIPPON SHIMBUN	JAPAN	1,033,000
44.	HINDUSTAN TIMES	INDIA	1,032,000
45.	NANFANG CITY NEWS	CHINA	1,030,000
46.	NEUE KRONEN ZEITUNG	AUSTRIA	1,018,000
47.	CHICAGO TRIBUNE	UNITED STATES	1,016,000
48.	DAILY TELEGRAPH	UNITED KINGDOM	1,003,000
49.	THE KOREA ECONOMIC DAILY	SOUTH KOREA	1,000,000
50.	BEIJING EVENING NEWS	CHINA	980,000

5. THE WORLD'S 50 LARGEST MAGAZINES

01.	READER'S DIGEST	UNITED STATES	12,078,000
02.	BETTER HOMES AND GARDENS	UNITED STATES	7,605,000
03.	FAMILY CIRCLE	UNITED STATES	4,634,000
04.	WOMEN'S DAY	UNITED STATES	4,205,000
05.	TIME	UNITED STATES	4,112,000
06.	LADIES' HOME JOURNAL	UNITED STATES	4,101,000
07.	KAMPIOEN	NETHERLANDS	3,756,000
08.	PEOPLE	UNITED STATES	3,625,000
09.	PLAYBOY	UNITED STATES	3,215,000
10.	NEWSWEEK	UNITED STATES	3,183,000
11.	READERS	CHINA	3,000,000
12.	COSMOPOLITAN	UNITED STATES	2,993,000
13.	MAXIM	UNITED STATES	2,541,000
14.	BOSOM FRIEND	CHINA	2,500,000
15.	GLAMOUR	UNITED STATES	2,407,000
16.	REDBOOK	UNITED STATES	2,387,000
17.	MARTHA STEWART LIVING	UNITED STATES	2,341,000
18.	O, THE OPRAH MAGAZINE	UNITED STATES	2,269,000
19.	BILD AM SONNTAG	GERMANY	2,164,000
20.	U.S. NEWS & WORLD REPORT	UNITED STATES	2,026,000
21.	NATIONAL ENQUIRER	UNITED STATES	1,788,000
22.	VERSION FEMINA	FRANCE	1,767,000
23.	FEMME ACTUELLE	FRANCE	1,710,000
24.	MEN'S HEALTH & SPORTS	UNITED STATES	1,678,000
25.	SHAPE	UNITED STATES	1,668,000
26.	IN STYLE	UNITED STATES	1,665,000
27.	ENTERTAINMENT WEEKLY	UNITED STATES	1,641,000
28.	WOMAN'S WORLD	UNITED STATES	1,640,000
29.	PRIMA	FRANCE	1,529,000
30.	BILD DER FRAU	GERMANY	1,478,000
31.	BA XIAO SHI YI WAI	CHINA	1,400,000
32.	SAGA MAGAZINE	UNITED KINGDOM	1,206,000
33.	NEUE POST	GERMANY	1,173,000
34.	LOVE	CHINA	1,150,000
35.	PLEINE VIE	FRANCE	1,122,000
36.	WESTWORLD	CANADA	1,119,000
37.	READER'S DIGEST	CANADA	1,107,000
38.	DER SPIEGEL	GERMANY	1,086,000
39.	FREIZEIT REVUE	GERMANY	1,049,000
40.	STERN	GERMANY	1,042,000
41.	NOTRE TEMPS	FRANCE	1,029,000
42.	READER'S DIGEST	GERMANY	1,001,000
43.	PRONTO	SPAIN	962,000
44.	VAR BOSTAD	SWEDEN	934,000
45.	NON NO	JAPAN	920,000
46.	CLAUDIA	POLAND	911,000
47.	READER'S DIGEST	UNITED KINGDOM	907,000
48.	DAS NEUE BLATT	GERMANY	902,000
49.	LIZA	RUSSIA	900,000
50.	SHANGHAI STYLE	CHINA	900,000

PRINT MEDIA

The term 'print media' refers to newspapers, periodicals, journals, magazines, printed mail, signs, and other ink-press forms. Although this industry profits vastly from globalization, it is also facing challenges from increased demand and competition of new print media forms, primarily created by the Internet. A generational shift in readership ensures that the print media industry will continually need to address changing preferences and demographics in an increasingly globalized world.

WHAT ARE THE TRENDS?

The indicator suite on print media illustrates the following:

- Fewer than 70 per cent of the top 100 most circulated newspapers worldwide originate in Asia, with Japan claiming the top 5 ranked newspapers (see data point 4).
- *Reader's Digest* magazine has the largest global circulation of 12.1 million, followed by *Better Homes and Gardens*, *Family Circle*, *Women's Day*, and *Time*—all demonstrating the global reach of US magazines (see data point 5).
- The Middle East, South America, and Africa are absent from the top 50 circulated world newspapers. *Jang*, from Pakistan, is the most circulated Asian newspaper, ranking 70th worldwide (WAN, 2007).

In recent years, according to UNESCO (2005), international trade in newspapers and periodicals increased by an average of 2.1 per cent annually, with growth rates in high-income countries (between 1.8 per cent and 3.4 per cent) lower than in low-income countries (between 12.3 per cent and 14.3 per cent). Conversely, nearly 93 per cent of all exported newspapers and periodicals come from high-income countries and a near 67 per cent of all newspapers and periodicals traded worldwide were traded in Europe alone.

Defying competition from online sources, printed newspaper circulation increased by 2.3 per cent in 2006. This number jumps to 4.61 per cent when including free daily newspapers. Total world circulation of daily newspapers, paid-for and free, stands at 556 million. Average daily readership is estimated at more than 1.4 billion. Sales increased in all regions except for North America (see data point 2). Significant increases were also reported in advertising and classified revenues (Bundesverband Deutscher Zeitungsverleger, 2007).

China, India, Japan, the United States and Germany are the world's largest national markets for newspapers (see data point 1). When looking at circulation per capita, Japan, Norway, Colombia, Finland, and Sweden top the list.

Out of the largest markets, India stands out with an impressive circulation growth rate of 13 per cent (see data point 3). Germany, Japan and the United States have actually decreased circulation in recent years. India also leads in terms of advertising revenue growth, which was 23.18 per cent in 2006 (WAN, 2007).

WHAT ARE THE ISSUES?

Changing readership demographics and associated news preferences are some of the primary issues affecting the print media industry. Newspaper readers tend to be increasingly more representative among older adults (European Information Service, 2005), as younger readers choose alternative news sources. This generational gap further contributes to the declining growth in the sector in much of the developed world, as well as to growth limits in Africa, Asia and Latin America. Indeed, there is an emerging consensus among experts that future growth will not come from the declining print media sector, but come from the Internet and the electronic advertising options it offers (Middle East Company News Wire, 2005).

A major concern for analysts in the media industry is the concentration of market power. Globalization forces have enabled corporations to transcend borders and acquire stakes in foreign media, thus creating oligopolies. Rupert Murdoch, head of News Corp, for instance, is a major player in the media industries of Europe, Asia, Australia, and the United States. Branches of News Corp include The New York Post, MySpace, and satellite broadcasters in Asia and Europe. Recently, the company acquired the flagship news source Dow Jones & Co, publisher of the Wall Street Journal (Perez-Pena & Sorkin, 2007). News Corp has been accused of conservative political propaganda many times over, most notably via the US news channel Fox News.

To attract new advertisers, media companies are 'branding' publications and creating niche products. In order to streamline production, more and more newspapers, such as *The New York Times* and *The Boston Globe*, are outsourcing to freelance journalists, designers, editors and presses. Some critics have complained that outsourcing and commodification of print media have caused a 'tabloidization' of the industry, and reduced its capacity as a watch-dog of public affairs.

With the movement towards non-traditional print formats by both readers and advertisers, printers and media companies are crossing over in order to retain and capture new clientele (Middle East Company News Wire, 2005). By 2003, about 60 per cent of all publishers and printers were involved in some sort of cross-media by maintaining websites, creating PDFs, etc. (Core, 2003). As costs and losses rise, print media companies that cannot compete by changing their services and streamlining their production are at an increased risk of folding.

The central questions for the print media sector increasingly surround the possible replacement of traditional media products and processes with new technologies, models, outlets, and ways of distribution. This will clearly challenge current business models first and foremost, and with it the oligopolies of print media conglomerates that account for a large share of global newspaper and magazine production and distribution. These questions guide the industry as it moves forward, searching for new and sustainable business model approaches as technologies and reader preferences continue to change.

Finally, the World Association of Newspapers (WAN, 2007) acknowledges a global threat to the freedom of press. Between November 2006 and June 2007, 59 journalists were killed worldwide and many others were prosecuted legally. Iraq stands out as the most dangerous country for journalists during that time with 26 deaths. Nevertheless, death threats to investigative reporters are common in many countries.

BOOKS

1. GLOBAL **PUBLISHING MARKET VALUE** 2006

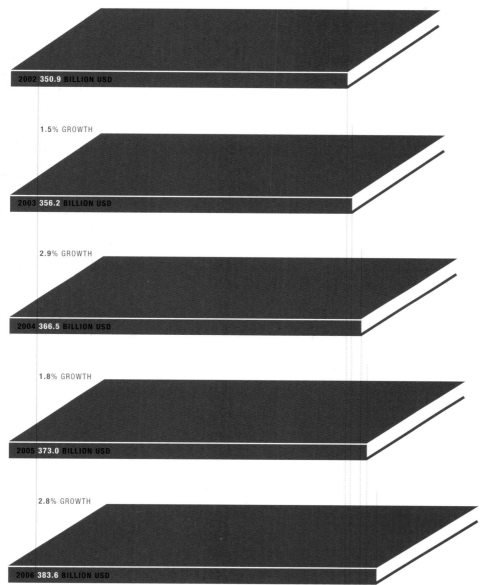

2002 **350.9** BILLION USD

1.5% GROWTH

2003 **356.2** BILLION USD

2.9% GROWTH

2004 **366.5** BILLION USD

1.8% GROWTH

2005 **373.0** BILLION USD

2.8% GROWTH

2006 **383.6** BILLION USD

01. UNITED STATES
2002 **106,500** MILLION USD
2003 **109,200** MILLION USD
2004 **112,900** MILLION USD
2005 **113,200** MILLION USD
2006 **115,200** MILLION USD

02. ASIA-PACIFIC
2002 **77,800** MILLION USD
2003 **79,300** MILLION USD
2004 **82,400** MILLION USD
2005 **85,300** MILLION USD
2006 **88,800** MILLION USD

03. JAPAN
2002 **45,500** MILLION USD
2003 **44,400** MILLION USD
2004 **44,500** MILLION USD
2005 **44,900** MILLION USD
2006 **45,300** MILLION USD

04. GERMANY
2002 **37,800** MILLION USD
2003 **37,300** MILLION USD
2004 **36,700** MILLION USD
2005 **37,100** MILLION USD
2006 **37,500** MILLION USD

05. UNITED KINGDOM
2002 **29,200** MILLION USD
2003 **29,400** MILLION USD
2004 **30,000** MILLION USD
2005 **30,600** MILLION USD
2006 **31,200** MILLION USD

06. FRANCE
2002 **24,358** MILLION USD
2003 **24,424** MILLION USD
2004 **24,660** MILLION USD
2005 **24,698** MILLION USD
2006 **24,815** MILLION USD

2. COMPOSITION OF POTENTIAL WORLDWIDE **BOOK MARKET***

USD MILLIONS + % **2006**

EUROPE 1,543	NORTH AMERICA + CARIBBEAN 1,543	ASIA + OCEANIA 2,019	AFRICA 238	MIDDLE EAST 247	LATIN AMERICA 495
25%	25%	34%	4%	4%	8%

* THIS STUDY USES 'POTENTIAL' AS AN INDICATOR FOR THE REAL MARKET. NUMBERS ARE VERY CLOSE TO ACTUAL FIGURES.

07. CHINA

2002 **12,000** MILLION USD
2003 **13,100** MILLION USD
2004 **14,700** MILLION USD
2005 **16,100** MILLION USD
2006 **17,500** MILLION USD

08. ITALY

2002 **11,400** MILLION USD
2003 **11,600** MILLION USD
2004 **11,800** MILLION USD
2005 **12,000** MILLION USD
2006 **12,200** MILLION USD

09. CANADA

2002 **10,700** MILLION USD
2003 **11,000** MILLION USD
2004 **11,300** MILLION USD
2005 **11,400** MILLION USD
2006 **11,600** MILLION USD

10. SPAIN

2002 **9,100** MILLION USD
2003 **9,300** MILLION USD
2004 **9,600** MILLION USD
2005 **10,000** MILLION USD
2006 **10,400** MILLION USD

11. NETHERLANDS

2002 **6,059** MILLION USD
2003 **6,063** MILLION USD
2004 **6,217** MILLION USD
2005 **6,312** MILLION USD
2006 **6,405** MILLION USD

12. BELGIUM

2002 **3,538** MILLION USD
2003 **3,566** MILLION USD
2004 **3,627** MILLION USD
2005 **3,694** MILLION USD
2006 **3,756** MILLION USD

3. US **BOOK EXPORT** + **IMPORT** 1970 – 2004

Year	US BOOK IMPORT	US BOOK EXPORT
1970	92.0 MILLION USD	174.9 MILLION USD
1975	147.6 MILLION USD	269.3 MILLION USD
1980	306.5 MILLION USD	518.9 MILLION USD
1985	564.2 MILLION USD	591.2 MILLION USD
1990	855.1 MILLION USD	1415.1 MILLION USD
1995	1184.5 MILLION USD	1779.5 MILLION USD
2000	1590.5 MILLION USD	1877.0 MILLION USD *
2004	* 1934.4 MILLION USD	1740.5 MILLION USD

4. WORLDWIDE **MARKET** FOR **BOOKS**

INCLUDING FUTURE PROJECTIONS 2001 – 2011

2001	6,098.40 MILLION USD
2002	6,047.82 MILLION USD
2003	5,999.28 MILLION USD
2004	5,952.88 MILLION USD
2005	5,934.61 MILLION USD
2006	6,075.08 MILLION USD
2007	6,246.79 MILLION USD
2008	6,424.33 MILLION USD
2009	6,607.94 MILLION USD
2010	6,797.83 MILLION USD
2011	6,994.27 MILLION USD

5. ASIA-PACIFIC **PUBLISHING MARKET SEGMENTATION** BY COUNTRY 2006

- 51% JAPAN
- 20% CHINA
- 13% REST OF REGION
- 8% SOUTH KOREA
- 8% INDIA

BOOKS The international book publishing market is becoming increasingly dominated by a handful of transnational corporations formed through mergers and acquisitions. This process of concentration began in the 1980s, driven by greater economies of scale in publishing and later with the incorporation of other types of media (e.g., music, movies, and television). A process of diversification and decentralization is simultaneously occurring due to innovations in information technology that create new opportunities and threats, raising questions regarding intellectual property rights and information flows, and which have changed the access and usage of books around the world.

A survey of 1,324 exhibitors and publishers from 86 countries carried out at the 2007 Frankfurt Book Fair highlighted the latest challenges facing the book industry (Frankfurt Book Fair, 2007). Some 53 per cent of those surveyed identified digitization as the biggest issue facing writers, book publishers and sellers. Other challenges cited were increasing globalization (24 per cent), user-generated content (22 per cent) and the ongoing battle over territorial rights (15 per cent). Despite this outlook, only 11 per cent thought traditional book forms would become obsolete in fifty years' time. Yet the survey does confirm that the book itself, and the publishing industry at large, is undergoing a revolutionary process that challenges once common definitions of what constitutes a book, its purpose, cultural relevance and form.

WHAT DO WE KNOW ABOUT BOOKS?

Books represented approximately 19 per cent of US$11.3 billion in trade of cultural goods in 2002, directly behind recorded media, the leading category. Books and other print media grew 3.7 per cent between 1994 and 2002, with slower growth in high-income countries (between 1.8 per cent and 3.4 per cent from 1994 to 2002), and higher rates in low-income countries (12.5 per cent on average). Despite this large increase, the share of low-income countries in the global book trade remains small. About 87 per cent of all book exports in 2002 came from high-income countries, with 53 per cent from Europe alone (UNESCO, 2005).

The book trade occurs mainly between Europe and North America, with slow but increasing involvement by Asia, and limited participation by Africa. The top book producers at the end of the twentieth century were the UK, Germany, the US, Spain, and Japan with between 111,000 and 56,000 books produced each year (UNESCO, 2005). Losses due to illegal copying of copyrighted books exceeded US$15.8 billion in 2005, with copyright infringements most prevalent in Russia, China, and South Korea (*Publishers Weekly*, 2006b).

In 2005, US book sales reached $25.1 billion and book publishers spent about $232 million on advertising (*Publishers Weekly*, 2006a, c). In Japan, approximately 65,500 books were published per year by the end of the twentieth century; in China, a rapidly emerging market for books, over 100,000 new titles were published, representing a tenfold increase over the past decade (Goff, 2006). Worldwide, used-book sales increased heavily, thanks in part to the proliferation of websites that sell them; for instance, Internet sales of used trade books rose 33 per cent in 2004 (Bakkum, 2006).

The indicator suite on books highlights that:
- The worldwide market for books is expected to grow in coming years, from the current amount of US$6,246.79 million to approximately US$6,994.27 million by 2011 (see data point 4).
- Global publishing market value increased from US$350.9 billion in 2002 to US$383.6 billion in 2006—a 9.3 per cent increase (see data point 1).
- The top ten countries and regions with the largest market value in 2006 were the United States, the Asia-Pacific region, Japan, Germany, UK, France, China, Italy, Canada and Spain (see data point 1).
- The United States dominates the global publishing world, and as such, the number of book exports have consistently outshined book imports since the 1970s (see data point 3). From 1985 to 1990, exports experienced a dramatic increase of 139.4 per cent (from $591.2 million to $1,415.1 million). The first year that book imports ($1,934.4 million) into the US outgrew book exports ($1,740.5 million) was 2004.
- In the Asia-Pacific region, the publishing market is dominated by Japan (51 per cent), followed by China (20 per cent), India and South Korea (both 8 per cent), and then the remainder of

Table 1: TOP 5 PUBLISHING HOUSES

company (parent corp)	year of data	# of employees	sales (millions)	NY Times bestsellers 2006	# of imprints	books published per year	# of countries with imprints	2004 US market share
Random House (bertelsmann)	2005	5,395	2,164.90	43	100	9000	15	16.50%
Penguin Group (Pearson)	2005	953	848	138	41 UK only	4000	15	11.20%
HarperCollins (News Corp.)	2007	1,425	1,310	128 2007	44	n/a	4	11.40%
Simon & Schuster (Viacom)	2007	1,500	14,320*	111	8	1800	5	7.90%
Hachette Livre (Lagardere)	was aquired by Lagardere group in 2006 from Time Warner - limited data	31,324**	11,219***	71	10	5000	13	n/a

* Sales turnover for CBS Corp. Publishing accounted for 6% of revenues in 2006.
** 2006 figure for Lagardere
*** 2006 Lagardere media sales contribution (of which 98.3% is Hachette Livre)

SOURCE: Company websites and annual reports.

the region's countries (13 per cent) (see data point 5).

- Asia is clearly emerging as a new competitor in the book publishing industry, challenging to offset the current domination of US and European publishers. 2005 projections of latent demand of the worldwide book market by regions positioned Asia & Oceana at 34 per cent, followed by North America & Caribbean, 25 per cent; Europe, 25 per cent; Latin America, 8 per cent; Middle East, 4 per cent; and Africa, 4 per cent in terms of potential industry revenues (see data point 2).

WHAT ARE THE ISSUES?

The world's book industry is dominated by an oligopoly of five publishing houses—all transnational corporations—that pose challenges to book production, access and dissemination (see Table 1). Some experts fear that concentration will lead to 'dumbing down' and sensationalist pushing of select bestsellers. However, e-books, print-on-demand, small presses, and independent-publishing options are opening alternatives to authors (and readers).

E-books are an expanding market (Table 2) that offers new opportunities for preserving, updating, and disseminating texts. At the same time, e-books and digitization present new challenges to the book industry, libraries and archives, since information in the Web age is tied to a boundless space that can be easily copied and altered, often without regard to ownership and copyrights. The ongoing Google Library project (see text box on this topic, in chapter by Goggin) to scan millions of books from libraries in the US and the UK in order to increase access to printed materials illustrates this issue. Some view this and similar projects as expanding the possibilities of human knowledge, while others see them as the replacement of the traditional book with no regard for creativity and ownership.

Similarly, issues such as piracy can disrupt and threaten the book industry where definitions and practices of intellectual property vary across nations. In many developing countries, piracy of books, especially textbooks, is common practice with local presses and individuals. Textbook piracy is most pronounced in Asia, where, the number of college attendees is increasing, the use of English in education is widespread, and less expensive and high quality printing services abound. Lower prices in developing countries create flows of illegal copies back into richer countries via the Web.

Many developing countries rely on book imports, which bring with them elements of outside cultures into local contexts. Book shortages, lack of infrastructure, illiteracy, few local publishers and the prevalence of English books exacerbate inequities between developing and developed countries. In this light, books are both tools for cultural enrichment, education and empowerment, and tools for sustaining the global socioeconomic and political hierarchies; thus, ownership and control of the publishing industry are key indicators of how books are distributed, made available, used and read.

Table 2: **WORLDWIDE E-BOOK REVENUES, 2004 & 2005**
(US$ millions and % increase vs. prior year)

2004	**$ 9.7**
2005	**$11.9** (23%)

SOURCE: International Digital Publishing Forum (April 2006).

FILM

1. TOP **FILM PRODUCTION STUDIOS**:
% GLOBAL MARKET SHARE 2007

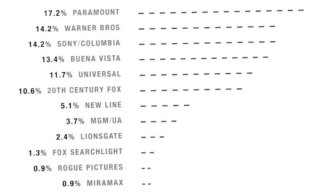

17.2%	PARAMOUNT	– – – – – – – – – – – – – – – – –
14.2%	WARNER BROS	– – – – – – – – – – – – – –
14.2%	SONY/COLUMBIA	– – – – – – – – – – – – – –
13.4%	BUENA VISTA	– – – – – – – – – – – – –
11.7%	UNIVERSAL	– – – – – – – – – – –
10.6%	20TH CENTURY FOX	– – – – – – – – – –
5.1%	NEW LINE	– – – – –
3.7%	MGM/UA	– – – –
2.4%	LIONSGATE	– – –
1.3%	FOX SEARCHLIGHT	– –
0.9%	ROGUE PICTURES	– –
0.9%	MIRAMAX	– –

2. LEADING **ONLINE VIDEO CONTENT** CATEGORIES:
US USERS SECOND HALF 2006 FIRST HALF 2007

49%	62%	**NEWS CLIPS**	
47%	36%	**MUSIC VIDEOS**	
33%	38%	**MOVIE TRAILERS**	
26%	33%	**TV SHOWS**	
21%	29%	USER GENERATED VIDEOS	
20%	25%	**MOVIES**	
11%	21%	**SPORTS CLIPS**	
9%	8%	OTHER	

3. MOVIE DOWNLOAD RENTAL + SALES REVENUES
PROJECTED FOR 2011 STUDIO + CONTENT PROVIDER SHARE OF REVENUES + **TOTAL REVENUES**

UNITED STATES	$530	MILLION USD
	$720	MILLION USD
WESTERN EUROPE	$405	MILLION USD
	$572	MILLION USD

530   720

405   572

4. WORLD **BOX OFFICE REVENUE** BY MARKET SHARES **2006**

OTHER **5%**   ASIA-PACIFIC **15%**   EUROPE **33%**   NORTH AMERICA **47%**

5. WORLDWIDE **ONLINE FILM REVENUES** BY REGION **2002 – 2005** & PROJECTED **2010** IN USD

INCLUDES REVENUES FROM ONLINE DVD SALES, DOWNLOADS, STREAMING AND SUBSCRIPTIONS

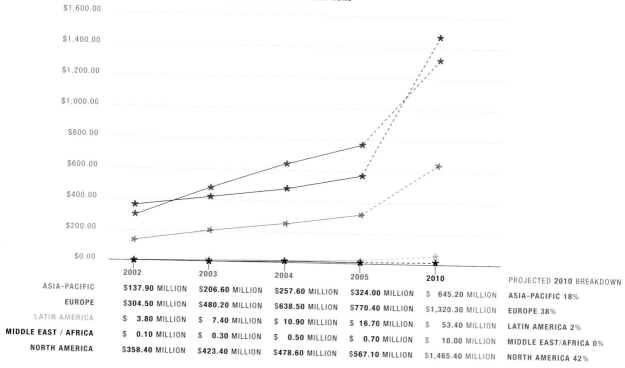

	2002	2003	2004	2005	2010	PROJECTED 2010 BREAKDOWN
ASIA-PACIFIC	$137.90 MILLION	$206.60 MILLION	$257.60 MILLION	$324.00 MILLION	$ 645.20 MILLION	ASIA-PACIFIC 18%
EUROPE	$304.50 MILLION	$480.20 MILLION	$638.50 MILLION	$770.40 MILLION	$1,320.30 MILLION	EUROPE 38%
LATIN AMERICA	$ 3.80 MILLION	$ 7.40 MILLION	$ 10.90 MILLION	$ 16.70 MILLION	$ 53.40 MILLION	LATIN AMERICA 2%
MIDDLE EAST / AFRICA	$ 0.10 MILLION	$ 0.30 MILLION	$ 0.50 MILLION	$ 0.70 MILLION	$ 10.00 MILLION	MIDDLE EAST/AFRICA 0%
NORTH AMERICA	$358.40 MILLION	$423.40 MILLION	$478.60 MILLION	$567.10 MILLION	$1,465.40 MILLION	NORTH AMERICA 42%

6. **NATIONALLY PRODUCED FILMS** VERSUS **PRODUCTION IN ANOTHER COUNTRY** BY SELECT COUNTRY **2000 – 2005** # OF FILMS

SOUTH KOREA

		NATIONAL	FOREIGN
NATIONAL	2000	62	277
	2002	82	192
	2004	74	194
	2005	83	213

UNITED KINGDOM

		NATIONAL	FOREIGN
NATIONAL	2000	51	39
	2002	41	43
	2004	28	47
	2005	42	36

GERMANY

		NATIONAL	FOREIGN
NATIONAL	2000	60	28
	2002	62	55
	2004	82	39
	2005	91	55

JAPAN

		NATIONAL	FOREIGN
NATIONAL	2000	282	362
	2002	293	347
	2004	310	339
	2005	356	375

SPAIN

		NATIONAL	FOREIGN
NATIONAL	2000	64	34
	2002	80	57
	2004	92	41
	2005	89	53

FRANCE

		NATIONAL	FOREIGN
NATIONAL	2000	111	60
	2002	106	94
	2004	130	73
	2005	126	114

AUSTRALIA

		NATIONAL	FOREIGN
NATIONAL	2000	22	8
	2002	24	9
	2004	19	12
	2005	19	12

ITALY

		NATIONAL	FOREIGN
NATIONAL	2000	87	16
	2002	97	33
	2004	97	41
	2005	59	27

FILM The global film industry is dominated by a small number of transnational corporations. This 'entertainment complex' is commonly referred to as 'Hollywood' (Coe, 2001; Currah, 2006) and while only one of the top five film production companies' corporate headquarters is located in Hollywood (Paramount), all five are located in the greater Los Angeles area: Burbank, CA (Warner Bros. and Buena Vista/Disney Corporation), Culver City, CA (Sony Pictures), and Universal City, CA (Universal Studios). However, this hegemony is increasingly challenged by changes in technology, the growing reach of the Internet, as well as the rise of several distinct and thriving regional film centers, most notably Bollywood (India), Nollywood (Nigeria), and Dubai.

WHAT DO WE KNOW ABOUT THE FILM INDUSTRY?

The indicator suite on Film highlights global trends in the creation and distribution of film media in their various forms, with special attention to the growth in digitized and online movies. While Internet access to films has helped to further equalize regional levels of film media consumption, creation and distribution are still primarily dominated by the US. Data point 1 illustrates that the only company with a substantial share of the market outside of the US is Lion's Gate, located in Vancouver, Canada. European movie-making remains fragmented into relatively small national markets, although European studios are becoming increasingly transnational, including joint productions. Even within the US, the studios are spatially concentrated in and around Los Angeles with only two studios located in New York City. Other trends featured in the suite are:

- Online movie downloads grew 5 per cent from the end of 2006 to the first half of 2007. This growth, while significant, is still outpaced by increased downloading of news clips (13 per cent growth) and TV shows (8 per cent) (see data point 2).
- Downloads of movie trailers have grown by 5 per cent as well, which may indicate continued growth in full movie downloads given the trend in decreasing movie theater sales (see data point 2).
- Movie download rental and sales revenue projections for 2011 show that the US is predicted to surpass Europe by close to 150 million USD (see data point 3).
- Worldwide box office revenue for 2006 supports the trend in US dominance in terms not just of production but also of cultural consumption with 47 per cent of the market share as opposed to Europe's 33 per cent and Asia's 15 per cent (see data point 4).
- Nationally-produced films as opposed to foreign or jointly-produced films vary by country and over time. In terms of increases in national film production and sheer volume, Japan stands out with 356 films produced in-country in 2005 (this list excludes the US). Contrastingly, the UK, Italy and Australia show decreases in nationally-produced films and increases or stabilization in foreign or joint production (see data point 6).

WHAT ARE THE ISSUES?

Digitization has been one of the most significant technological advances of recent years, allowing for expanded global access to films through the Internet as seen in several of the data points found in this suite. Digitized movie theaters are an even newer trend that can be found in localized markets mostly in Asia and the US. The digitization of movie screens also may be characterized as an attempt by the film industry to combat declining movie theater ticket sales (see table below). The decline in theater audiences seems to be primarily attributable to the rising numbers in online film consumption. There are also other emerging mediums that are keeping people away from the theaters such as access to movies on mobile phones and iPods. Deemed the 'fourth screen,' mobile phones have the potential to target huge segments of the population in most parts of the world. While many phone companies and Apple (with the video iPod) are increasing memory and resolution for better viewing capacity, the size of the screens has kept most consumers to viewing and downloading short films or TV shows (BBC News, 2007).

CHANGE IN CINEMA ATTENDANCE FOR SELECT MARKETS:

2005-2005	MARKET	% CHANGE
	US	- 8.70%
	EU States	-11.40%
	Brazil	-21.70%
	Australia	-10.20%
	Japan	- 5.70%
	South Korea	5.80%

SOURCE: European Audiovisual Observatory, FOCUS – World Film Market Trends 2006

Piracy, illegal reproductions and downloads have most adversely affected Hollywood. By contrast, Bollywood and Nollywood, though also affected, have chosen to combat falling revenue in different ways. Average production costs and times in India and Nigeria are much lower than in the US, requiring smaller absolute revenue to generate a profit. Nollywood films are produced within a month (McLaughlin, 2005), and new movies are available on video or DVD within a week of release (Ruigrok, 2006). Additionally, Bollywood works closely with the music industry, releasing movies and soundtracks together to generate increased revenue.

The Motion Picture Association of America estimates that piracy cost the global film industry US$18.2 billion in 2005 alone (BBC News, 2006). However, the major organizations and companies supporting the worldwide crackdown on intellectual property rights as they pertain to the major creative industries such as film and music tend to be Western and more specifically American (cf. chapter by Pinter in this volume).

France and Canada have been instrumental in renewing the very old international debate over protection as a means to limit and protect against the infiltration of 'foreign,' i.e., American, music and film. Uganda and Ghana have felt that Nollywood's proliferation into their countries has undermined their own fledging film markets (McLaughlin, 2005). In the music industry the backlash is not quite as strong against US dominance, but many countries have regulations reserving certain percentages of radio and TV airtime for national artists.

There is an increasing connection between the prolific Bollywood film industry, which produces more than 1,000 films per year, and the city of Dubai in terms of production, screenings, events and consumption (Akhil, 2007). For instance, the International Indian Film Academy (IIFA) awards were held in Dubai in 2006. Additionally, many film production companies, such as the state-of-the-art 22 million sq. ft. Dubai Studio City facility are cropping up in the city and heavily marketing their services to Bollywood filmmakers. Thus, while Hollywood appears to dominate the film industry in terms of market share, other regional film centers are increasingly becoming important players.

MUSIC

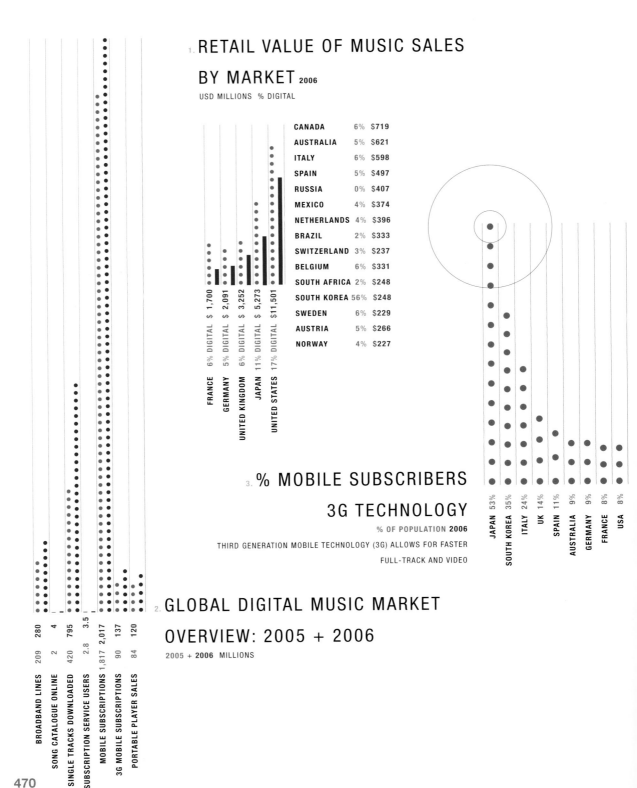

1. RETAIL VALUE OF MUSIC SALES BY MARKET 2006

USD MILLIONS   % DIGITAL

CANADA	6%	$719
AUSTRALIA	5%	$621
ITALY	6%	$598
SPAIN	5%	$497
RUSSIA	0%	$407
MEXICO	4%	$374
NETHERLANDS	4%	$396
BRAZIL	2%	$333
SWITZERLAND	3%	$237
BELGIUM	6%	$331
SOUTH AFRICA	2%	$248
SOUTH KOREA	56%	$248
SWEDEN	6%	$229
AUSTRIA	5%	$266
NORWAY	4%	$227

FRANCE 6% DIGITAL $ 1,700
GERMANY 5% DIGITAL $ 2,091
UNITED KINGDOM 6% DIGITAL $ 3,252
JAPAN 11% DIGITAL $ 5,273
UNITED STATES 17% DIGITAL $11,501

3. % MOBILE SUBSCRIBERS 3G TECHNOLOGY

% OF POPULATION 2006

THIRD GENERATION MOBILE TECHNOLOGY (3G) ALLOWS FOR FASTER FULL-TRACK AND VIDEO

JAPAN 53%
SOUTH KOREA 35%
ITALY 24%
UK 14%
SPAIN 11%
AUSTRALIA 9%
GERMANY 9%
FRANCE 8%
USA 8%

2. GLOBAL DIGITAL MUSIC MARKET OVERVIEW: 2005 + 2006

2005 + 2006 MILLIONS

BROADBAND LINES	209 280
SONG CATALOGUE ONLINE	2 4
SINGLE TRACKS DOWNLOADED	420 795
SUBSCRIPTION SERVICE USERS	2.8 3.5
MOBILE SUBSCRIPTIONS	1,817 2,017
3G MOBILE SUBSCRIPTIONS	90 137
PORTABLE PLAYER SALES	84 120

4. MUSIC INDUSTRY COMPARISON

BY SECTOR VALUE
2005 + 2006

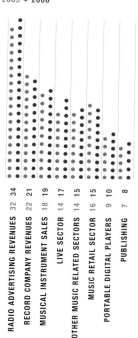

RADIO ADVERTISING REVENUES 32 34
RECORD COMPANY REVENUES 22 21
MUSICAL INSTRUMENT SALES 18 19
LIVE SECTOR 14 17
OTHER MUSIC RELATED SECTORS 14 15
MUSIC RETAIL SECTOR 16 15
PORTABLE DIGITAL PLAYERS 9 10
PUBLISHING 7 8

BELGIUM: SUPERMARKETS 15 14 9
WHOLESALE/INDEPENDENTS 15 13 12
RETAILERS 18 18 23
MULTIPLES 44 45 45
FRANCE: MAIL ORDER/INTERNET 4 4 4
CHAINS 18 17 18
HYPERMARKET/SUPERMARKETS 38 37 36
SPECIALISTS 36 39 40
GERMANY: DIRECT MAIL 14 14 11
INTERNET 9 15 18
SPECIALIST/DEPARTMENT STORES 33 28 26
LARGE CHAINS 39 39 37
UK: INTERNET 6 9 11
CHAINS/MULTIPLES 18 17 12
SUPERMARKETS 18 23 25
MUSIC SPECIALISTS 49 45 46
US: INTERNET 3 6 9
TAPE/RECORD CLUB 4 4 11
OTHER STORE 51 54 33
RECORD STORE 37 33 36

6. % OF TOTAL MUSIC SALES

BY GENRE FOR SELECT COUNTRIES
2002 + 2004 + 2006

AUSTRALIA: DANCE 6 3 4
CLASSICAL 4 4 5
ROCK/POP 76 80 80
FRANCE: COMPILATIONS 26 18 23
INTERNATIONAL 22 25 23
FRENCH SONGS 34 35 33
GERMANY: CLASSICAL 7 8 8
ROCK 16 19 18
POP 44 38 37
UK: R&B 7 9 9
POP 30 30 24
ROCK 31 30 41
US: RAP/HIP-HOP 14 12 11
COUNTRY 11 13 13
ROCK 25 24 34

MUSIC

Music is an integral part of human culture, reflecting deeply cultural, often religious or spiritual roots, evolving in many ways and directions. Today, the music industry is undergoing a complex and often contradictory process of consolidation, reorganization, contraction and expansion at the same time. Control of the music industry is continually narrowing to just a few major transnational corporations. This trend has been a recurrent theme throughout the volume and the data suites for industries such as film, radio and TV. Because of the profound influence of popular music on national and regional cultures, concern over Western, in particular American, dominance in global media is growing. While the US continues to lead the world in production and music-generated revenue, new technologies such as the Internet are creating previously unimaginable possibilities in relation to the music distribution and consumer access.

WHAT DO WE KNOW ABOUT THE MUSIC INDUSTRY?

The top five music industry conglomerates accounted for close to US$13.5 billion in sales revenue for 2006 (see table below). Four out of the five conglomerates are located in the US, with the fifth based in the UK. This picture of a highly concentrated industry has major implications for the rest of the world's music artists, consumers, producers and disseminators.

Digital music downloading from the Internet is widespread as shown in the case of Japan (see figure on next page); such downloads challenge the market power of the major music corporations.

The Music Industry Data Suite highlights emerging global music industry trends:

- Music sales data, ranked by market, shows that the US leads by far, followed by Japan, the UK, Germany, France and Canada. In terms of the percentage of digital sales by market, the rankings are the same, except that France has a slightly higher portion of digital sales than Germany (see data point 1).
- Locations for music purchases have been shifting significantly in many countries due to increased digital downloads as compared to store purchases. Data point 5 depicts trends by country such as increases in US music purchases over the Internet as well as through mail-based tape/music clubs. In the UK, purchases in music specialty shops and chain stores/multiplexes have decreased while supermarkets and the Internet as sources of music have increased. Germany

shows similar market trends to the UK while France has seen an increase in music purchases at chains and specialty shops, decreases at supermarkets and stagnation in terms of Internet sales.
- Musical genres, despite increasing global spread of Western-style music, differ greatly by country. In France, sales of international music and compilation albums are growing while in Australia rock and pop music are by far the most popular. Germany and the UK have both seen a decline in pop and an increase in rock. Conversely, R&B music is growing in popularity in the UK yet doesn't rank as a top selling genre in Germany. Finally, the US industry, which makes up the greatest share of the world music market, is showing an uptake in rock and country music with a slight decline in sales of rap and hip-hop (see data point 6).
- Mobile subscribers to the new technology 3G, which allows for faster downloading of full music track and video online content, is on the rise, particularly in parts of Asia (see data point 3). As of 2006, the global digital music market has been dominated by mobile subscriptions, which account for more than double the revenue as compared to the second largest type of downloads, single tracks (see data point 2).

WHAT ARE THE ISSUES AROUND MUSIC AND GLOBALIZATION?

Digitalization (i.e., the electronic construction of sound and video through binary codes) of music content has profoundly changed the industry. We now can listen to and watch music and movies on digital players, including computers, mobile telephones and hand-held devices. We are able to access and download music files through a variety of sites on the Internet, which has had crucial effects on record stores around the world. Music has instead become a stream of information to be accessed and played anywhere and at any time. However, increased access to music files on the mostly-unregulated Internet has exacerbated questions of intellectual property rights, corporate control of art and consumer rights.

The proliferation of piracy and illegal downloads has created a revenue crisis in recent years. Because of the immediate and potentially crippling impacts of this issue, the industry is collaborating with national governments to crack down on illegal file sharing. Technological and marketing innovation has also helped

THE TOP MUSIC INDUSTRY CONGLOMERATES BY SALES		
	SALES (USD millions)	# OF EMPLOYEES
UNIVERSAL MUSIC GROUP (New York, USA)	$5,794.80	1,050
EMI GROUP PLC (London, UK)	$3,548.20	5,458
WARNER MUSIC GROUP CORP. (New York, USA)	$3,516.00	4,000
WARNER/CHAPPELL MUSIC, INC. (Los Angeles, USA)	$ 607.00	542
SONY/BMG MUSIC PUBLISHING (New York, USA)	$ 441.00 (est.)	575

SOURCE: Hoovers.com (as of 2006).

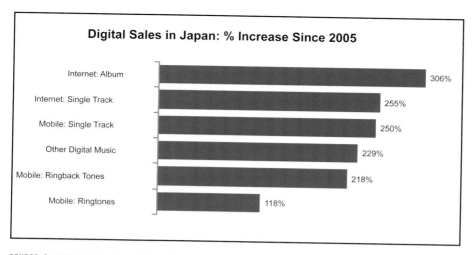

Digital Sales in Japan: % Increase Since 2005

Internet: Album	306%
Internet: Single Track	255%
Mobile: Single Track	250%
Other Digital Music	229%
Mobile: Ringback Tones	218%
Mobile: Ringtones	118%

SOURCE: Recording Industry Association of Japan (2007).

to bring the music industry out of near ruin in 2005 through the success of legal purchased downloads. The Recording Industry Association of America (RIAA) is leading the fight against piracy through a number of high profile and controversial court cases against file sharers. Their efforts have been successful in stemming Peer-2-Peer networks and illegal sharing in the US and much of Western Europe (RIAA, n.d.). However, in many parts of the world it remains incredibly difficult to control piracy, such as in China where 90 per cent of all CDs are pirated (*Cultures and Globalization, volume 1*). Transnational corporations (mostly US-based) have been the most active in the piracy, debate, and while many proclaim that they seek to speak for and protect artists, artists themselves have been relatively silent in the debate. Recently, a few big-name artists such as Radiohead, Madonna and Nine Inch Nails have come up with their own innovative solutions to the digital online music downloading question. All three artists have chosen to capitalize on their large fan bases, utilizing direct access through technology to essentially circumvent the major music label companies. Radiohead in particular is pioneering a new approach to sales and pirated downloads by making their newest album available online with no restrictions, simply asking consumers to pay what they determine the music is worth. Unofficial sources suggest that at this early date, on average consumers are paying US$10.17 per copy of the album (NPR, 2007).

SPORTS

1. MOST WATCHED **SPORTS EVENTS WORLDWIDE** 2006

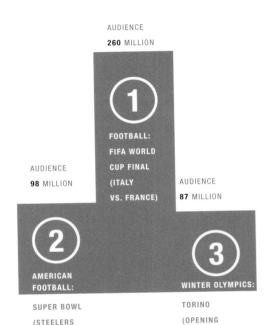

AUDIENCE
260 MILLION

1
FOOTBALL:
FIFA WORLD
CUP FINAL
(ITALY
VS. FRANCE)

AUDIENCE
98 MILLION

2
AMERICAN
FOOTBALL:
SUPER BOWL
(STEELERS
VS. SEAHAWKS)

AUDIENCE
87 MILLION

3
WINTER OLYMPICS:
TORINO
(OPENING
CEREMONY)

4. FOOTBALL: CHAMPIONS LEAGUE FINAL (ARSENAL VS. BARCELONA)
   AUDIENCE **86** MILLION
5. FORMULA ONE: BRAZILIAN GRAND PRIX
   AUDIENCE **83** MILLION
6. NASCAR: DAYTONA 500
   AUDIENCE **20** MILLION
7. BASEBALL: WORLD SERIES GAME 5
   AUDIENCE **19** MILLION
8. GOLF: US MASTERS (FINAL DAY)
   AUDIENCE **17** MILLION
9. TENNIS: WIMBLEDON MEN'S SINGLES FINAL
   AUDIENCE **17** MILLION
10. BASKETBALL: NBA FINALS GAME 6
    AUDIENCE **17** MILLION
11. CYCLING: TOUR DE FRANCE (FINAL STAGE)
    AUDIENCE **15** MILLION
12. GOLF: US OPEN (FINAL DAY)
    AUDIENCE **10** MILLION
13. GOLF: RYDER CUP (FINAL DAY)
    AUDIENCE **6** MILLION
14. COMMONWEALTH GAMES: MELBOURNE (OPENING CEREMONY)
    AUDIENCE **5** MILLION
15. CRICKET: ICC CHAMPIONS TROPHY (FINAL)
    AUDIENCE **3** MILLION

2. TOP EARNING **GOLFERS** 2006

OFF COURSE
ON COURSES
IN US$

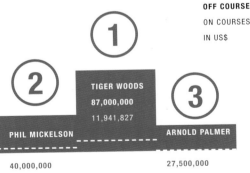

1
TIGER WOODS
87,000,000
11,941,827

2
PHIL MICKELSON
40,000,000
4,256,505

3
ARNOLD PALMER
27,500,000
42,850

4. VIJAY SINGH	20,000,000	4,811,026
5. GREG NORMAN	22,500,000	127,202
6. MICHELLE WIE	19,500,000	735,224
7. ERNIE ELS	14,500,000	3,866,435
8. JIM FURYK	9,100,000	8,886,084
9. JACK NICKLAUS	17,500,000	180,167
10. RETIEF GOOSEN	12,000,000	4,024,184

OFF COURSE – OFF COURSE INCLUDES ESTIMATES FROM ENDORSEMENTS,
BONUSES, APPEARANCES, FEES, CORPORATE OUTINGS, ETC.

3. HIGHEST PAID **MALE ATHLETES** + **FEMALE ATHLETES** IN US$ 2007

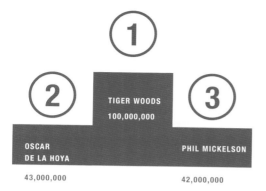

	MEN	
1.	TIGER WOODS	100,000,000
2.	OSCAR DE LA HOYA	43,000,000
3.	PHIL MICKELSON	42,000,000
4.	KIMI RAIKKONEN	42,000,000
5.	MICHAEL SCHUMACHER	36,000,000
6.	DAVID BECKHAM	33,000,000
7.	KOBE BRYANT	33,000,000
8.	SHAQUILLE O'NEAL	32,000,000
9.	RONALDINHO	31,000,000
10.	MICHAEL JORDAN	31,000,000

	WOMEN	
1.	MARIA SHARAPOVA	23,000,000
2.	MICHELLE WIE PROJECTED	19,000,000
3.	SERENA WILLIAMS	14,000,000
4.	ANNIKA SORENSTAM	10,000,000
5.	DANICA PATRICK	5,000,000

5. GLOBAL **CORPORATE SPONSORSHIP** TOP 10 SPORTS CATEGORIES IN US$ 2006

1.	FOOTBALL SOCCER	$1,811,490,000
2.	VENUES	$1,219,000,000
3.	MOTORSPORT FORMULA ONE	$ 634,066,000
4.	AMERICAN FOOTBALL	$ 260,000,000
5.	BASEBALL	$ 130,000,000
6.	CRICKET	$ 114,000,000
7.	BASKETBALL	$ 100,000,000
8.	MOTORCYCLE RACING	$ 90,000,000
9.	ATHLETICS	$ 75,000,000
10.	MOTORSPORT OTHER	$ 60,000,000

4. 25 MOST VALUABLE **FOOTBALL CLUBS** 2006

BY WORTH IN BRITISH POUNDS

1.	MANCHESTER UNITED	740 MILLION POUND
2.	REAL MADRID	528 MILLION POUND
3.	ARSENAL	466 MILLION POUND
4.	BAYERN MUNCHEN	427 MILLION POUND
5.	AC MILAN	420 MILLION POUND
6.	JUVENTUS	289 MILLION POUND
7.	INTER MILAN	282 MILLION POUND
8.	CHELSEA	274 MILLION POUND
9.	BARCELONA	273 MILLION POUND
10.	SCHALKE 04	240 MILLION POUND
11.	LIVERPOOL	231 MILLION POUND
12.	LYON	175 MILLION POUND
13.	NEWCASTLE	132 MILLION POUND
14.	TOTTENHAM	124 MILLION POUND
15.	ROMA	114 MILLION POUND
16.	HAMBURG	112 MILLION POUND
17.	MAN CITY	106 MILLION POUND
18.	B DORTMUND	101 MILLION POUND
19.	AJAX	100 MILLION POUND
20.	CELTIC	94 MILLION POUND
21.	EVERTON	84 MILLION POUND
22.	MARSEILLE	80 MILLION POUND
23.	WEST HAM UNITED	79 MILLION POUND
24.	RANGERS	75 MILLION POUND
25.	ASTON VILLA	71 MILLION POUND

6. GLOBAL TOP 15 **CORPORATE SPONSORSHIP DEALS**

TOTAL VALUE OF DEAL IN US$ 2006

1.	CITIGROUP FINANCIAL: NEW YORK METS	$ 400,000,000
2.	MOTOROLA: NFL	$ 200,000,000
3.	VISA: FIFA PARTNER 2007 – 2014	$ 200,000,000
4.	AMERICAN: AMERICAN AIRLINES CENTER	$ 195,000,000
5.	EMIRATES: FIFA PARTNER 2007 – 2014	$ 195,000,000
6.	NIKE: BARCELONA	$ 189,000,000
7.	U OF PHOENIX: CARDINALS STADIUM	$ 154,000,000
8.	RED BULL: RED BULL RACING	$ 150,000,000
9.	NIKE: BRAZILIAN FOOTBALL FEDERATION	$ 144,000,000
10.	ADIDAS: JAPAN FOOTBALL ASSOCIATION	$ 140,000,000
11.	BANK OF AMERICA: BANK OF AMERICA STADIUM	$ 126,000,000
12.	LUCAS OIL: INDIANAPOLIS COLTS STADIUM	$ 122,000,000
13.	CISCO: OAKLAND ATHLETICS STADIUM	$ 120,000,000
14.	VODAFONE: VODAFONE MCLAREN MERCEDES	$ 120,000,000
15.	ANHEUSER-BUSCH: DRINKS-BEER EXCLUSIVE	$ 100,000,000

SPORTS Sport is a culturally and politically complex phenomenon, and one that is becoming increasingly lucrative, as the lines between sports and entertainment are blurring. Like many other cultural phenomena, sports are affected by globalization in practice (e.g., the rise of soccer as the pre-eminent global sport), in organizations (e.g., the rise of 'super-clubs' such as Manchester United and global spectacles like the Olympics), and in structure (e.g., more dominant sports crowding out less popular, niche sports in terms of media attention).

Culturally, sport is a vehicle for expressing ideals of health and beauty through exercise, and, in an international context, even peace and human understanding—the Olympic movement as the clearest manifestation of this. Because sport is also a locus of group identity, we also have 'sports nationalism' and the instrumentalization of sports by politics, e.g., the perverted 1936 Olympics, the 1978 Soccer World Cup in Argentina, and the partially boycotted 1980 and 1984 Olympics.

WHAT ARE SPORTS?

Sports are organized game playing, regulated by rules, permitted equipment, and objectives. While some sports are cooperative and have no clear winners or losers, most involve competition, typically between two opposing teams or individuals playing against each other with varying mechanisms for keeping score, and determining a winner. Historically, sports have a complex heritage: linked to the celebration of youth and healthy exercise on the one hand, their competitive elements used to represent a country, region, city or a distinct group of people playing for the glory of winning on the other—linking sport to various forms of cultural identity.

THE SCALE AND RISE OF GLOBAL SPORTS

Globally, the Olympics, the Football FIFA World Cup and the American Super Bowl are the most watched sporting events, all well attended and followed by audiences throughout the world

(see data point 1). The globalization of football (soccer) is linked to the spread of the British Empire and later to the migration of British people to commonwealth countries. Between 1850 and 1930, the British successfully introduced competitive football to the United States, Canada, Mexico, South America, South Africa, Brazil, China, Singapore, Sudan, Russia, Austria, Hungary, Greece, Italy and Portugal (Goldblatt, 2004). Although the British are largely responsible for the global spread of the game, its origins lie in China (10,000 BC), further highlighting the evolution and globalization of the sport (Goldblatt, 2004).

Today, the globalization of sports is highly dependent on revenues from broadcasting and corporate sponsorship (see data points 5 and 6). In 2005, FIFA, the International Football Association, received roughly CHF$750 million (approximately US$670 million) in events related revenue, including broadcasting rights for the 2006 Soccer World Cup and the qualifying matches (FIFA, 2005). The revenue generated from broadcast partnerships for the Olympic Games has grown significantly: in 1996, the Atlanta Games generated US$898 million, whereas in Athens in 2004 the sum was almost US$1.5 billion, and projected revenue for the 2008 games in Beijing is roughly US$1.7 billion (*Cultures & Globalization Vol. 1*, and IOC, 2007).

TV audiences worldwide are also growing. Event management has become more responsive to corporate sponsors. An interesting observation emerges from a study conducted by *The Independent* in 2007: most organizations vastly overstate the size of their TV audience. The National Football League in the US, for instance, reports that a billion people watched the Super Bowl in 2006. The real number was less than a tenth of that (98 million). FIFA claimed an audience of 715.1 million when the real number was 260 million ('Why FIFA's claim,' March 2007).

Football, undoubtedly the world's most popular sport, is geographically concentrated in Europe. Ranked according to market

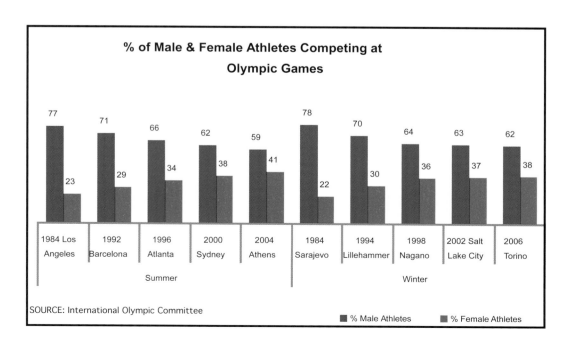

% of Male & Female Athletes Competing at Olympic Games

	1984 Los Angeles	1992 Barcelona	1996 Atlanta	2000 Sydney	2004 Athens	1984 Sarajevo	1994 Lillehammer	1998 Nagano	2002 Salt Lake City	2006 Torino
% Male Athletes	77	71	66	62	59	78	70	64	63	62
% Female Athletes	23	29	34	38	41	22	30	36	37	38

Summer / Winter

SOURCE: International Olympic Committee

■ % Male Athletes　■ % Female Athletes

value, all top 25 teams are based in Europe (see data point 4). Recently there have been attempts to market football in areas where other sports are dominant, most notably with David Beckham's move to the Los Angeles Galaxy in 2007. This is expected to boost the sport's popularity in the United States.

Regardless of popularity, however, only two football players make it into the top ten highest paid athletes list: David Beckham and Ronaldinho (see data point 3). The top three male athletes compete in three different (individual) sports and are all US citizens. The highest paid female athletes also compete in individual sports (tennis, golf and race car driving). With increased corporate sponsorship, it is not surprising that the highest earning golf athletes make most of their money off-field (see data point 2).

WHAT ARE THE ISSUES?

Ongoing gender discrepancies between male and female athletes continue to challenge the field of sports, particularly with regards to participation in international sporting events. Historically, women participate at lower levels than men, although their participation rate has increased, as shown by the data on participating athletes in past Olympic games (see graphic). While the percentage of women athletes in the Olympics has grown to 40 per cent for the summer games in 2004, some countries have no female athletes participating in any of the Olympic games (International Working Group on Women in Sports, n.d.).

Related to participation rates for men and women are compensation differentials. In tennis, for instance, a debate is ongoing about financial discrimination against women in major tournaments. Opponents of equal pay argue that men play longer (five sets) than women (three sets) in most tournaments and should therefore receive more prize money. Nevertheless, all Grand Slam tournaments other than Wimbledon have instituted equal pay policies. Media coverage is biased towards male athletes, as well: seven of the ten most watched television events in 2006 were male-only (see data point 1).

When sports such as football acquire loyal communities of fans, issues of identity formation and identity politics arise. These may range from local hooliganism to international conflict, as with the so-called Soccer War between Honduras and Nicaragua. In such instances, sport is the conduit through which underlying conflicts crystallize.

The globalization of sports like football has brought about a mismatch between input markets and revenue markets. While players in major football clubs are increasingly internationally recruited, and now represent around half of the players in major European leagues, the major revenue source through ticket sales remains local, and grounded in deep-seated loyalties. As broadcasting revenue increases relative to ticket sales, football clubs are turning into commercial franchises, void of their original cultural roots in particular cities or regions, and the support of local fans. In other words, the globalization of sports will make some sports such as football more lucrative from a commercial perspective, but less relevant in terms of local identity.

POPULAR SPORTS WORLDWIDE

Football (soccer)
Ice Hockey
Baseball
Cricket
Rugby
Table Tennis
Wrestling
Kickboxing
Other Sports
No Information

SOURCE: National Geographic Society, June 2006.

VIDEO GAMES

VIDEO GAME CONSOLE SALES SOFTWARE + HARDWARE WORLDWIDE

BY BRAND IN US$ MILLIONS 2002 – 2006

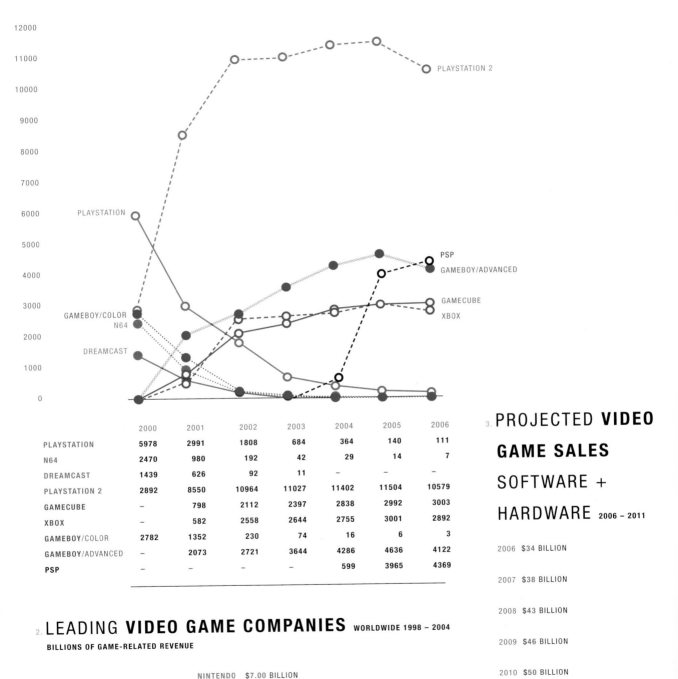

	2000	2001	2002	2003	2004	2005	2006
PLAYSTATION	5978	2991	1808	684	364	140	111
N64	2470	980	192	42	29	14	7
DREAMCAST	1439	626	92	11	–	–	–
PLAYSTATION 2	2892	8550	10964	11027	11402	11504	10579
GAMECUBE	–	798	2112	2397	2838	2992	3003
XBOX	–	582	2558	2644	2755	3001	2892
GAMEBOY/COLOR	2782	1352	230	74	16	6	3
GAMEBOY/ADVANCED	–	2073	2721	3644	4286	4636	4122
PSP	–	–	–	–	599	3965	4369

3. **PROJECTED VIDEO GAME SALES** SOFTWARE + HARDWARE 2006 – 2011

2006	$34 BILLION
2007	$38 BILLION
2008	$43 BILLION
2009	$46 BILLION
2010	$50 BILLION
2011	$54 BILLION

2. **LEADING VIDEO GAME COMPANIES** WORLDWIDE 1998 – 2004

BILLIONS OF GAME-RELATED REVENUE

NINTENDO	$7.00 BILLION
SONY	$4.50 BILLION
EA	$1.80 BILLION

4. WORLDWIDE GAME REVENUES

BY SECTOR **2000**, **2005** + **2010** PARTIALLY PROJECTED **IN US$** MILLIONS
* INCLUDES SALES + RENTALS

CONSOLE HARDWARE

2000	$ 4,791													
2005	$ 3,894											
2010	$ 5,771															

CONSOLE SOFTWARE *

2000	$ 9,451																									
2005	$13,055																																			
2010	$17,164																																														

HANDHELD HARDWARE

2000	$ 1,945						
2005	$ 3,855	||||||||||
2010	$ 1,715					

HANDHELD SOFTWARE *

2000	$ 2,872								
2005	$ 4,829													
2010	$ 3,113										

PC SOFTWARE *

2000	$ 5,077															
2005	$ 4,313											
2010	$ 2,955										

INTERACTIVE TV

2000	$ 81		
2005	$ 786	||
2010	$ 3,037	|||||||

BROADBAND

2000	$ 70		
2005	$ 1,944	|||||
2010	$ 6,352	||||||||||||||||

MOBILE

2000	$ 65		
2005	$ 2,572	||||||
2010	$11,186	|||||||||||||||||||||||||||||

5. TOP SELLING VIDEO + COMPUTER GAMES 2004

TOP SELLING VIDEO GAMES BY UNITS SOLD

RANK + GAME	PLATFORM	RATING
01. GRAND THEFT AUTO: SAN ANDREAS	PS2	M
02. HALO 2	XBX	M
03. MADDEN NFL 2005	PS2	E
04. ESPN NFL 2K5	PS2	E
05. NEED FOR SPEED: UNDERGROUND 2	PS2	E
06. POKEMON FIRE RED	GBA	E
07. NBA LIVE 2005	PS2	E
08. SPIDER-MAN 2	PS2	T
09. HALO	XBX	M
10. ESPN NFL 2K5	XBX	E
11. POKEMON LEAF GREEN	GBA	E
12. MADDEN NFL 2005	XBX	E
13. NCAA FOOTBALL 2005	PS2	E
14. FABLE	XBX	M
15. MVP BASEBALL 2004	PS2	E
16. NFL SREET	PS2	E
17. TONY HAWK'S UNDERGROUND 2	PS2	T
18. METAL GEAR SOLID 3: SNAKE EATER	PS2	M
19. MARIO BROTHERS 3: MARIO 4	GBA	E
20. NEED FOR SPEED: UNDERGROUND	PS2	E

TOP SELLING COMPUTER GAMES BY UNITS SOLD

RANK + GAME	RATING
01. THE SIMS 2	T
02. DOOM 3	M
03. WORLD OF WARCRAFT	T
04. HALF-LIFE 2	T
05. THE SIMS 2 SPECIAL EDITION	T
06. THE SIMS DELUXE	T
07. BATTLEFIELD VIETNAM	T
08. CALL OF DUTY	T
09. ROLLER COASTER TYCOON 3	E
10. ZOO TYCOON: COMPLETE COLLECTIONS	E
11. CITY OF HEROES	T
12. UNREAL TOURNAMENT 2004	M
13. THE SIMS: MAKIN' MAGIC EXPANSION PACK	T
14. AGE OF MYTHOLOGY	T
15. FAR CRY	M
16. HALO: COMBAT EVOLVED	M
17. STAR WARS: KNIGHT OF THE OLD REPUBLIC	T
18. FLIGHT SIMULATOR 2004: CENTURY OF FLIGHT	E
19. ZOO TYCOON 2	E
20. ROME: TOTAL WAR	T

RATINGS: THE ENTERTAINMENT SOFTWARE RATING BOARD (ESRB) LABELS GAMES ACCORDING TO CONTENT. THIS IS A VOLUNTARY PROCESS BUT ALMOST ALL GAME PUBLISHERS IN THE US AND CANADA SUBMIT THEIR GAMES FOR RANKING.

E – EVERYONE (CONTENT SUITABLE FOR AGES 6 AND OLDER), **T** – TEEN (CONTENT SUITABLE FOR AGES 13 AND OLDER), **M** – MATURE (CONTENT SUITABLE FOR AGES 17 AND OLDER)

VIDEO GAMES The origins of interactive visual games go back over half a century to the patent known as the Cathode-Ray Tube Amusement Device in 1947. Since then, with the introduction of the personal computer in the 1980s, the market has expanded exponentially and devices and games have become increasingly sophisticated. Today, producers of gaming hardware and software are looking at increasingly global markets, and tailor their products to appeal to different cultures at regional levels. This diffusion of products brings opportunities and challenges, most notably issues of cultural sensitivity and cultural fusion. As audiovisual products, video games are exempt from certain World Trade Organization free trade regulations. However, the growth of the market makes practices of protection and banning increasingly political issues as well (cf. the chapter by Toby Miller in this volume).

The pace has picked up in recent decades and several major corporations are fighting for market share in the growing video games market. While Microsoft's Xbox 360 and Sony's PlayStation 3 fight for market share among the video gaming community, the Nintendo Wii is the latest attempt to expand beyond traditional market segments by using motion sensors in its control system to simulate physical games and sports such as tennis and bowling.

EXPLANATION OF CONCEPTS

Video games in this suite refer to interactive games that are played via specialized computer-chip game consoles, including portable systems such as the GameBoy Advance and PSP. The term is increasingly also used for computer games, which are treated separately from this analysis. Computer games are games that can be played on PCs or laptops that are not designed exclusively for gaming purposes.

Video games are thought to have different psychological effects from movies because of the active role of the player. When watching a movie portrayal of a killer, one does not actively take action and kill, which is the case for games—hence the issue of rating (Anderson et al., 2007). This is done on a voluntary basis in the United States. However, most retailers have a policy not to carry unrated games or games that are rated 'adults only.' The organization that is in charge of rankings on a national level in North America is the Entertainment Software Rating Board (ESRB). Ratings go from EC (early childhood—3 years and older) to AO (adults only—18 years and older) (Entertainment Software Rating Board, 2007). Other countries employ similar rating scales but differ in their tolerance of violence and sexual content. Germany, for instance, is less tolerant of violence in games than the United States, and one minister there has called for laws that would punish gamers with up to one year imprisonment for cruel actions in video games (Entertainment Consumers Association, 2007).

WHAT ARE THE TRENDS?

Contrary to stereotypical public perceptions of the video games market, young males do not constitute the bulk of consumers. In fact, women over the age of 18 make up about 28 per cent of gamers while boys aged 6-17 make up only 21 per cent (Entertainment Software Association, 2005). Demographics are expected to further diffuse with new products targeting non-traditional gamers. Sony's PlayStation 2 thus far has been the single best-selling console in terms of both hardware and software (see

data point 1). However, it has reached the maturity stage and the next generation game consoles (the PlayStation 3, the Xbox 360, and the Nintendo Wii) are expected to take over the market.

From 1998 to 2000, Nintendo was the leading video game company with a revenue of US$7 billion in that time period (see data point 2). Sony and EA Games followed with revenues of US$4.5 billion and US$1.8 billion. The largest market for games is Asia Pacific, followed by the United States (PricewaterhouseCoopers, June 2007). However, Europe, the Middle East, and Africa are expected to catch up—growth rates in these regions are expected to outweigh that in the United States in the foreseeable future.

WHAT ARE THE ISSUES?

Content is the biggest point of contention. Critics underline profanity, violence, and sexual content. The popularity of controversial games like Grand Theft Auto (GTA): San Andreas (best-selling game in the US in 2004) sparked widespread debate. The player can start gang wars, randomly kill helpless civilians, and steal cars in GTA. Curiously, however, the most serious threat to sales to the game was not about violence: it was recalled after a hidden sex scene (known as 'Hot Coffee') was unlocked by a hacker. The game was later re-released in two versions: one with the controversial scene, rated 'adults only' (AO), and one without the scene, rated 'mature' (M) (Deci, 2007). Several high-profile politicians in the United States including New York Senator Hillary Clinton used the Hot Coffee controversy to call for content regulation in the video game market (Deci, 2007). Regarding the link between violence and violent games, reference is often made to the Columbine High School shooting: the killers were known to have been fans of the shooting game Doom. Even those who are skeptical of a causal link between violent games and violent behavior, such as Jonathan Freedman (2002), acknowledge that the two are positively related:

> Those who are exposed to more violence in the media and/or who prefer more violence in the media tend to be more aggressive than those who are exposed to or prefer less violence.

Yet, it seems unclear whether video games cause violent behavior or if violent personalities simply have a tendency to play those games. Scientific studies on the subject are numerous and vary in opinion. Anderson et al. (2007) conclude that violent video games cause more violence in gamers while Freedman (2002) refutes the argument, pointing out that most studies are inconclusive and a lot of data are misinterpreted.

Political issues also arise with respect to content, typically around stereotyping and cultural simplification for the sake of gaming action. For example, a recently released Hezbollah game in which the gamer battles Israeli troops has sparked controversy for teaching children 'that hatred and violence are positive attributes' ('Hezbollah,' August 16, 2007). War games have long been biased and stereotypical, but certain political perspectives seem to be more acceptable than others.

As for software, piracy is a problem for game publishers. Particularly in developing countries, piracy rates are high (see indicator suite on Creation, Innovation & Protection).

FASHION

1. FASHION WEEK EVENTS AROUND THE WORLD

NAME	YEAR ESTABLISHED	# OF EXHIBITORS 2007/08
NEW YORK FASHION WEEK	1943	**76** DESIGNERS
PARIS FASHION WEEK	N/A	**79** DESIGNERS
LONDON FASHION WEEK	1983 BRITISH FASHION COUNCIL ESTABLISHED	**49** DESIGNERS (CATWALK), **200** DESIGNERS (EXHIBI
MILAN FASHION WEEK	1958 CAMERA NAZIONALE DELLA MODA ITALIANA ESTABLISHED	**104**
HONG KONG FASHION WEEK	1968	**1500** +
JAPAN FASHION WEEK **TOKYO**	1985 SINCE 2003 IN TOKYO	**41** HOUSES, **43** BRANDS
COPENHAGEN FASHION WEEK	1964	**17** DESIGNERS
FASHION WEEK IN **MOSCOW**	1994	**60** DESIGNERS
JOHANNESBURG FASHION WEEK	2007	**18** DESIGNERS
THE **ASIA PACIFIC** FASHION WEEK **SYDNEY**	1995	**73** COLLECTIONS
BELGRADE FASHION WEEK	1985	**58** SERBIAN DESIGNERS, **35** INTERNATIONAL
SAO PAULO FASHION WEEK	1997	**57**
ICELAND FASHION WEEK **REYKJAVIK**	2000	**36 – 42** DESIGNERS
LAKME INDIA FASHION WEEK **NEW DEHLI**	2000	**14** INDIAN DESIGNERS
BANGKOK FASHION WEEK	2005	**30** + DESIGNERS

2. HONG KONG FASHION WEEK EXHIBITORS:

MAJOR EXPORT MARKETS

DURING FIRST 11 MONTHS OF 2006, HONG KONG'S TOTAL EXPORTS OF CLOTHING AND ACCESSORIES INCREASED **3.4%** TO ABOUT USD **25.8** BILLION

EUROPE	**49%**
ASIA PACIFIC	**26%**
AMERICAS	**25%**
UNITED STATES	**22%**
OTHER EUROPE	**18%**
JAPAN	**9%**
GERMANY	**7%**
FRANCE	**7%**
ITALY	**7%**
UNITED KINGDOM	**7%**
CHINESE MAINLAND	**5%**
HONG KONG	**4%**
OTHER ASIA PACIFIC	**4%**
AUSTRALIA	**3%**
SPAIN	**3%**
CANADA	**2%**
TAIWAN	**1%**

3. HOUSES OF **HAUTE COUTURE** 2007

*HAUTE COUTURE IS A TERM LEGALLY PROTECTED IN FRANCE

HOUSE NAME	DATE ESTABLISHED	COMPANY/OWNER
CHANEL	1909	PRIVATE – **WERTHEIMER FAMILY**
CHRISTIAN DIOR	1946	PUBLIC – **GROUPE ARNAULT SAS**
GIVENCHY	1952	PUBLIC – **LVMH GROUP**
JEAN LOUIS SCHERRER	1962	PUBLIC – **FRANCE LUXURY GROUP**
EMANUEL UNGARO	1965	PRIVATE – **MOUNIR MOUFARRIGE**, PRESIDENT
CHRISTIAN LACROIX	1987	PUBLIC – **LVMH GROUP**
JEAN PAUL GAULTIER	1977	PUBLIC/PRIVATE – **HERMÈS INTERNATIONAL** (OWNS 35%)
DOMINIQUE SIROP	2003	PRIVATE
ADELINE ANDRÉ	1981	PRIVATE
FRANK SORBIER	1991	PRIVATE
CORRESPONDENT MEMBERS (FOREIGN)		
ELIE SAAB	2003	PRIVATE – **OWNED BY DESIGNER**
GIORGIO ARMANI	2005 IN PARIS	PRIVATE – **GIORGIO ARMANI SPA**
VALENTINO	1960	PRIVATE – **VALENTINO FASHION GROUP SPA**

4. TOP FASHION LABELS SALES AND REVENUES IN USD BY ONLINE SEARCH VOLUME

THE NORTH FACE	ANNUAL SALES	$ 34.4	MILLION EST.	101 THOUSAND SEARCHES
BURBERRY	2006 SALES	$ 1,292.3	MILLION	103 THOUSAND SEARCHES
JUICY COUTURE		N/A: SUBSIDIARY TO LIZ CLAIBORNE		107 THOUSAND SEARCHES
EDDIE BAUER	2006 SALES	$ 1,013.5	MILLION	109 THOUSAND SEARCHES
LACOSTE	ANNUAL SALES	$ 4.15	MILLION	109 THOUSAND SEARCHES
PUMA	2006 SALES	$ 3,125.7	MILLION	116 THOUSAND SEARCHES
JOES JEANS	2006 SALES	$ 4,526.4	MILLION	118 THOUSAND SEARCHES
PRADA	PRIVATE	SALES N/A		120 THOUSAND SEARCHES
CHANEL	PRIVATE	SALES N/A		122 THOUSAND SEARCHES
BABY PHAT	ANNUAL SALES	$ 2.8	MILLION EST.	150 THOUSAND SEARCHES
ADIDAS	2006 SALES	$13,303.8	MILLION	175 THOUSAND SEARCHES
GUCCI	2007 REVENUE	$ 2,901.3	MILLION	190 THOUSAND SEARCHES
NEW BALANCE	2005 SALES	$ 1,540.0	MILLION	210 THOUSAND SEARCHES
NIKE	2007 SALES	$16,325.9	MILLION	337 THOUSAND SEARCHES
LOUIS VUITTON	2006 SALES	$20,193.2	MILLION	526 THOUSAND SEARCHES

5. WOMEN'S

TOP **FASHION MAGAZINES**

2005 CIRCULATION NUMBERS

VOGUE 214,348

CONDE NAST PUBLICATIONS INC.

12 COUNTRIES + REGIONAL EDITIONS

ELLE 208,132

LAGARDÈRE ACTIVE MEDIA

45 COUNTRIES + REGIONAL EDITIONS

HARPER'S BAZAAR 735,000

HEARST CORPORATION

22 COUNTRIES + REGIONAL EDITIONS

INSTYLE 916,857

TIME WARNER

7 COUNTRIES + REGIONAL EDITIONS

FASHION

The fashion industry encompasses the creation and marketing of new styles and forms of clothing and accessories, combining artisanal creation and franchising for conspicuous consumption as a signifier of socio-economic class as well as the expression of individual style and cultural inventiveness. Today's fashion industry began in Europe, notably in France, with craftsmen and tailors catering to the needs of royalty and later the urban middle class and the elite. By the mid-twentieth century, several of the French fashion houses became internationally recognized fashion labels, creating global brands such as Louis Vuitton, Hermès, and Cartier (Thomas, 2007), followed by various other designers, notably Lancetti and Karl Lagerfeld for Versace.

WHAT IS THE FASHION INDUSTRY?

The fashion industry goes together with the wider luxury goods sector. Luxury goods constitute a US$157 billion industry encompassing high fashion clothes, accessories, jewelry, fragrance, and cosmetics (Thomas, 2007). However, fashion is still deeply rooted in creativity, artistic design and local culture and place. While branding frequently leads to a degree of design homogenization to appeal to diverse buyer cultures around the world, there also exists a growing emphasis on local designers and innovation, in particular in Asia, Latin America and Central and Eastern Europe.

WHAT DO WE KNOW ABOUT GLOBALIZATION IN THE FASHION INDUSTRY?

Major phenomena illustrated by the indicator suite are the enormous increases in demand and the shifts in buyer profiles for high fashion goods. The rapid increase in wealth around the world and the expansion of the middle classes in many countries has transformed the structure of the fashion industry. Thomas (2007) estimates that by 2011, China will be the world's most important luxury market. Brand name cultivation and mass media marketing to sell an image of luxury are now top priorities for the big companies in the fashion and luxury goods market (cf. chapter by Ichikawa in this volume). This and other trends are quantified in the indicator suite:

- The emergence of an emphasis on local designers in new regional fashion centers is seen in the creation of numerous fashion weeks since 1985 including Tokyo, Moscow, Johannesburg, Sydney, Belgrade, Sao Paolo, Iceland, New Delhi, and Bangkok (see data point 1).
- Fashion weeks have become attractive events for host cities. For example, London Fashion Week for the February 2007 shows generated US$24 million in media coverage, US$40 million in orders, and over US$100 million in revenue for the city.
- There has been a significant decline in haute couture houses from 106 at the end of World War II to only 10 in 2007 (see graph below), indicating supply-side concentrations through mergers and acquisitions.
- Cross-fertilization between Eastern and Western fashion is happening with greater frequency due to the loosening of trade restrictions and greater mobility of creative talent. The top four export markets for Hong Kong Fashion Week are Europe (49 per cent), Asia Pacific (26 per cent), the Americas (25 per cent) and the US (22 per cent) (see data point 2).
- Of the ten designated haute couture houses in 2007, all of which were previously private or family owned, five have

become public corporations (see data point 3).
- The top fashion labels by online search volume are mostly public companies that have concentrated on mass media marketing to the wider global audience. The top five brands are Louis Vuitton, Nike, New Balance, Gucci and Adidas (see data point 4).

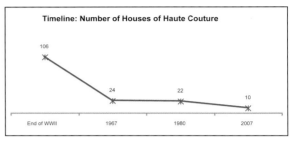

Timeline: Number of Houses of Haute Couture

106 — End of WWII
24 — 1967
22 — 1980
10 — 2007

SOURCE: C. Jeammet (March 2007)

WHAT ARE THE ISSUES SURROUNDING THE FASHION INDUSTRY?

The Decline of Haute Couture

'Haute couture' is a French term meaning 'high tailoring.' To be designated as a haute couture fashion house many criteria must be met and approved by La Chambre Syndicale de la Haute Couture, which falls under the French Department of Industry. The steep decline in haute couture houses over the past 60 years has corresponded with a rise of 'democratic fashion' or fashion tailored to a wider and more global audience. Street fashion and irreverent design are now what sell on a wider scale. Of the top five fashion labels selling online, three are sportswear companies. Many privately owned fashion houses have gone public and this has often resulted in pressure for ever increasing shareholder returns and the outsourcing of production to cut costs (Thomas, 2007). Lower priced, high-volume sales have replaced low-volume, high-ticket sales.

The Great or Not-So-Great Divide: Mass Retail Marketing and 'High Fashion'

Today's fashion brand names can be generally divided between the luxury market, encompassing high-end fashion retail, and the mass market retail names such as H&M, Zara, or Gap (cf. chapter by Ichikawa in this volume). Interestingly, both rely equally on global image and marketing schemes in order to attain their sales objectives, the only difference being the markets they are targeting. Few exceptions aside, both groups are made up of mostly public companies with supply chains tending to be off-shore. While there are still differences in quality and associated status between types of fashion goods, mass retail and the high fashion sectors within the industry are remarkably more similar than in the past.

Counterfeiting of Luxury Goods

Luxury brands are among the most counterfeited products today. The World Customs Organization states that the fashion industry loses up to US$9.7 billion per year to counterfeiting—and most profits fund illicit activities such as drug trafficking, human trafficking and terrorism (Thomas, 2007).

Fashion Industry Ethics?

While it is valued for the creative production of high-quality goods that are aesthetically pleasing, the fashion industry is not without its share of controversy and ethical questioning. From concern over the health of fashion models and the image they portray, to racial discrimination within the industry, to labor practices and the environment, these questions are all increasingly posed, especially as the fashion giants' profit margins grow. 'Ethical Fashion' is a burgeoning movement which aims to incorporate socially responsible values into the fashion industry. This includes looking at the supply sources and people behind the clothes as well as taking into account the environmental footprint that the industry leaves behind (BBC News, n.d.).

ADVERTISING INDUSTRY

1. WORLDWIDE PRODUCT
PLACEMENT SPENDING:
% MARKET SHARE 2006
% CHANGE OF
MARKET SHARE 2005-2006

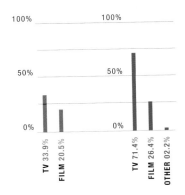

2. TOP 20 ADVERTISING CATEGORIES BY SPENDING 2006

USD MILLIONS

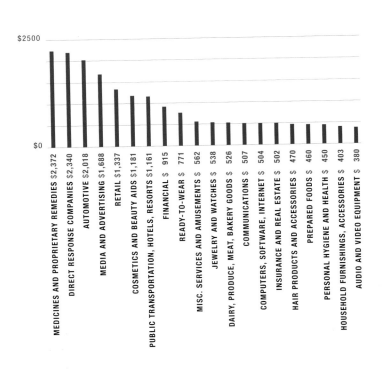

3. GLOBAL ONLINE
ADVERTISING SPENDING
+ PROJECTIONS 2002-2011

USD MILLIONS

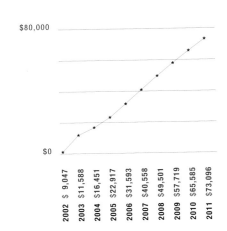

4. TOP ADVERTISING COMPANIES RANKED BY REVENUE 2006

USD MILLIONS *ESTIMATED

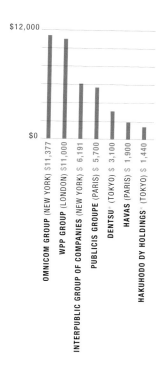

$12,000

$0

OMNICOM GROUP (NEW YORK) $11,377
WPP GROUP (LONDON) $11,000
INTERPUBLIC GROUP OF COMPANIES (NEW YORK) $ 6,191
PUBLICIS GROUPE (PARIS) $ 5,700
DENTSU* (TOKYO) $ 3,100
HAVAS (PARIS) $ 1,900
HAKUHODO DY HOLDINGS (TOKYO) $ 1,440

5. GLOBAL ADVERTISING SPENDING AND PROJECTIONS FOR VIDEO GAMES 2006-2011

USD MILLIONS EXCLUDES MOBILE GAMES

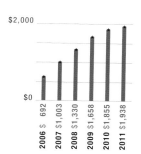

$2,000

$0

2006 $ 692
2007 $1,003
2008 $1,330
2009 $1,658
2010 $1,855
2011 $1,938

6. FASTEST GROWING ADVERTISING MARKETS BY COUNTRY: 2006

% CHANGE 2005-2006

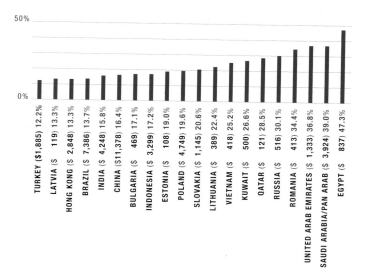

50%

0%

TURKEY ($1,885) 12.2%
LATVIA ($ 119) 13.3%
HONG KONG ($ 2,848) 13.3%
BRAZIL ($ 7,386) 13.7%
INDIA ($ 4,248) 15.8%
CHINA ($11,378) 16.4%
BULGARIA ($ 469) 17.1%
INDONESIA ($ 3,299) 17.2%
ESTONIA ($ 108) 19.0%
POLAND ($ 4,749) 19.6%
SLOVAKIA ($ 1,145) 20.6%
LITHUANIA ($ 389) 22.4%
VIETNAM ($ 418) 25.2%
KUWAIT ($ 500) 26.6%
QATAR ($ 121) 28.5%
RUSSIA ($ 516) 30.1%
ROMANIA ($ 413) 34.4%
UNITED ARAB EMIRATES ($ 1,333) 36.8%
SAUDI ARABIA/PAN ARAB ($ 3,924) 39.0%
EGYPT ($ 837) 47.3%

ADVERTISING

Globalization is integrating not just trade, investment and financial markets. It is also integrating consumer markets. …Economic integration has accelerated the opening of consumer markets with a constant flow of new products. There is fierce competition to sell to consumers worldwide, with increasingly aggressive advertising.

On the social side local and national boundaries are breaking down in the setting of social standards and aspirations in consumption. Market research identifies "global elites" and "global middle classes" who follow the same consumption styles, showing preferences for "global brands"... [T]he consumer receives a flood of information through commercial advertising. An average American, it is estimated, sees 150,000 advertisements on television in his or her lifetime. And advertising is increasing worldwide, faster than populations or incomes. Global advertising spending, by the most conservative reckoning, is now $435 billion.
(United Nations Development Programme, 1998)

The scenario depicted by the United Nations Development Program in its 1998 Human Development Report has not changed in recent years; rather global advertising has intensified as countries and corporations look to foreign markets for new buyers and consumers (cf. chapter by Scott in this volume). With the advent of the Internet, and more recently social networking and online social worlds, advertising has truly become global. Through increased product placement on billboards, taxis, films, TV series and through 'spam' e-mails, ads have become seemingly inescapable. This raises issues of privacy, safety and standards of products, mass commercialization of culture, and corporate influence on our tastes and preferences.

TRENDS IN GLOBAL ADVERTISING

Advertising is a growing global business that utilizes all types of media outlets and channels from radio, television, mobile phones, the Web, print media, and films to billboards and au-

tomobiles in order to target potential markets and consumers. According to ZenithOptimedia (www.zenithoptimedia.com), worldwide ad spending reached US$434,528 million in 2006 and is projected to increase to US$519,593 million by 2009. North America spends the most on advertising—more than half of the world total in 2006 (see table below). While Western and free-market economies dominate the global advertising field, it is interesting to note that Egypt, Saudi Arabia, and the United Arab Emirates were the top three emerging advertising markets in 2006, followed by Eastern European and Central Asian countries (see data point 6).

There exists some variation of spending in terms of the types of media outlets utilized for advertising. In 2005, the US, Brazil, Australia, Mexico and India dominated ad spend via television outlets, while the US, France, Italy, Japan and Spain were the top countries to utilize film (PQ Media LLC, 2006). As domestic advertising has become saturated, companies have looked overseas to sell their products, and increasingly to the Internet to reach target audiences. Indeed, global online advertising has grown from US$9,047 million in 2002 to $40,558 million in 2007—almost a 250 per cent increase over a five-year period (see data point 3). By 2011, global online advertising is expected to reach US$73,096 million. Online video games are also a growing market for advertisers, with a projected spend of US$1,938 million by 2011, a 180 per cent increase from only US$692 million in 2006 (see data point 5).

In 2006, the top advertising companies, by revenue, were Omnicom Group in New York, WPP Group based in London, Interpublic Group of Companies also in New York, Publicis Group in Paris, and Dentsu in Tokyo (see data point 4). Medicine and proprietary remedies was the top category for advertising by industry with spending at US$2,372 million, followed by direct response companies (US$2,340 million) and automotive (US$2,018 million), followed by media and advertising (US$1,668) (see data point 2).

WHAT ARE THE ISSUES?

Advertising is viewed in the business world as necessary for eco-

WORLD FORECAST OF TOTAL ADVERTISING SPEND

	2004 ($m)	2005 ($m)	2006 ($m)	2007 ($m)	2008 ($m)
NORTH AMERICA	168,250	173,271	182,209	189,878	197,369
EUROPE	104,567	108,448	113,010	117,726	122,657
ASIA-PACIFIC	78,802	83,162	88,819	95,420	101,816
LATIN AMERICA	15,546	18,021	19,754	21,090	22,244
AFRICA, MIDDLE EAST, OTHERS	18,160	21,206	24,581	28,043	32,190
WORLD	385,324	404,108	429,373	452,157	476,276

SOURCE: Screen Digest: 127, April 2006

nomic growth and financial stability, but it invariably imposes certain social costs by encouraging consumption. For the consumer, advertisements serve multiple purposes, from learning about the latest trends in fashion to learning about new technology or innovative medicines to treat deadly diseases. Yet, advertising can also be confusing and serve to misinform rather than inform the public when so-called 'ad wars' between companies, or even political candidates, send mixed messages about the safety of a product or the qualities and experience of a politician. In recent decades, governments have made efforts to regulate the content and reach of advertising in the public interest. This was seen in 1991 when the Swedish government banned advertising to children under twelve, and with the 1998 World Health Organization Framework Convention on Tobacco Control, which requires all 168 signatory countries to ban tobacco advertising (FCTC, n.d.).

While the common perception of advertisements conjures up images of benign television ads or billboard placements, more often than not we are increasingly exposed to covert advertising or 'guerilla promotions' (Levinson, 1984) influencing tastes, preferences, styles, and values via mass communication and infiltration of the Internet. Examples of this type of advertising are spam e-mails (or bulk e-mails), banner and pop-up ads on web pages, promotional encounters in public places, buses and taxis covered in brand messages or icons, and intentional product placement in feature films (for instance, the placement of luxury items in the James Bond movies). Thus, advertising or brand placement in major media, such as films, reflects a form of what Scott (cf. his chapter in this volume) describes as 'the ever-increasing incursion of sign-value into the sphere of productive activity.' The embedded nature of cultural aesthetics in consumer products arouses suspicion and critiques of the global advertising industry as fueling a consumer economy that privileges some cultures over others and perpetuates the domination of a few transnational cultural corporations.

Technology has given consumers some options and advantages. The recent development of TiVo and DVRs allows viewers to watch and record programs so as to fast forward through commercials. As well, Internet movie rental services such as Netflix, and the increasing sales of television series in box sets, allow viewers to bypass commercial advertisements. The advertising industry is adapting to this with more product placement on the Internet, in television shows and films, thus again leaving consumers little hope of escaping some form of advertisement in their home or in public spaces.

ARCHITECTURE + DESIGN

1. INTERNATIONAL UP-AND-COMING ARCHITECTS FORBES LIST 2007

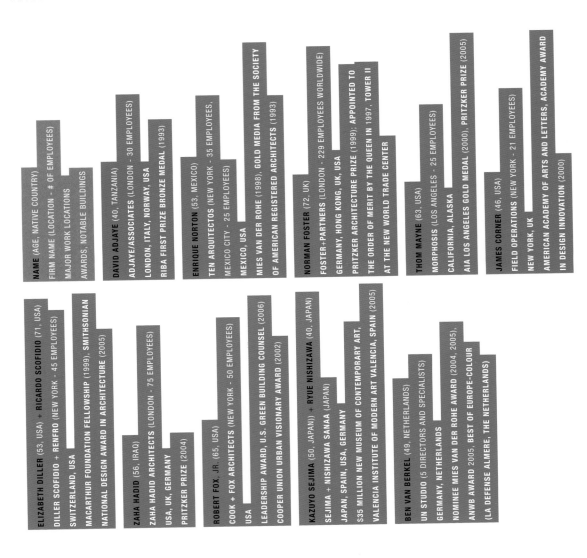

NAME (AGE, NATIVE COUNTRY)
FIRM NAME (LOCATION - # OF EMPLOYEES)
MAJOR WORK LOCATIONS
AWARDS, NOTABLE BUILDINGS

DAVID ADJAYE (40, TANZANIA)
ADJAYE/ASSOCIATES (LONDON - 30 EMPLOYEES)
LONDON, ITALY, NORWAY, USA
RIBA FIRST PRIZE BRONZE MEDAL (1993)

ENRIQUE NORTON (53, MEXICO)
TEN ARQUITECTOS (NEW YORK - 35 EMPLOYEES,
MEXICO CITY - 25 EMPLOYEES)
MEXICO, USA
MIES VAN DER ROHE (1998), GOLD MEDIA FROM THE SOCIETY
OF AMERICAN REGISTERED ARCHITECTS (1993)

NORMAN FOSTER (72, UK)
FOSTER+PARTNERS (LONDON - 229 EMPLOYEES WORLDWIDE)
GERMANY, HONG KONG, UK, USA
PRITZKER ARCHITECTURE PRIZE (1999); APPOINTED TO
THE ORDER OF MERIT BY THE QUEEN IN 1997, TOWER II
AT THE NEW WORLD TRADE CENTER

THOM MAYNE (63, USA)
MORPHOSIS (LOS ANGELES - 25 EMPLOYEES)
CALIFORNIA, ALASKA
AIA LOS ANGELES GOLD MEDAL (2000), PRITZKER PRIZE (2005)

JAMES CORNER (46, USA)
FIELD OPERATIONS (NEW YORK - 21 EMPLOYEES)
NEW YORK, UK
AMERICAN ACADEMY OF ARTS AND LETTERS, ACADEMY AWARD
IN DESIGN INNOVATION (2000)

ELIZABETH DILLER (53, USA) + RICARDO SCOFIDIO (71, USA)
DILLER SCOFIDIO + RENFRO (NEW YORK - 45 EMPLOYEES)
SWITZERLAND, USA
MACARTHUR FOUNDATION FELLOWSHIP (1999), SMITHSONIAN
NATIONAL DESIGN AWARD IN ARCHITECTURE (2005)

ZAHA HADID (56, IRAQ)
ZAHA HADID ARCHITECTS (LONDON - 75 EMPLOYEES)
USA, UK, GERMANY
PRITZKER PRIZE (2004)

ROBERT FOX, JR. (65, USA)
COOK + FOX ARCHITECTS (NEW YORK - 50 EMPLOYEES)
USA
LEADERSHIP AWARD, U.S. GREEN BUILDING COUNSEL (2006)
COOPER UNION URBAN VISIONARY AWARD (2002)

KAZUYO SEJIMA (50, JAPAN) + RYUE NISHIZAWA (40, JAPAN)
SEJIMA + NISHIZAWA SANAA (JAPAN)
JAPAN, SPAIN, USA, GERMANY
$35 MILLION NEW MUSEUM OF CONTEMPORARY ART,
VALENCIA INSTITUTE OF MODERN ART VALENCIA, SPAIN (2005)

BEN VAN BERKEL (49, NETHERLANDS)
UN STUDIO (5 DIRECTORS AND SPECIALISTS)
GERMANY, NETHERLANDS
NOMINEE MIES VAN DER ROHE AWARD (2004, 2005),
ANWB AWARD 2005, BEST OF EUROPE-COLOUR
(LA DEFENSE ALMERE, THE NETHERLANDS)

2. GLOBAL INTERIOR DESIGN MARKET: ACTUAL AND PROJECTED EARNINGS
USD MILLIONS

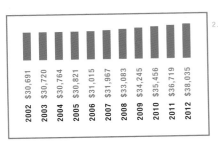

2002	$30,691
2003	$30,720
2004	$30,764
2005	$30,821
2006	$31,015
2007	$31,967
2008	$33,083
2009	$34,245
2010	$35,456
2011	$36,719
2012	$38,035

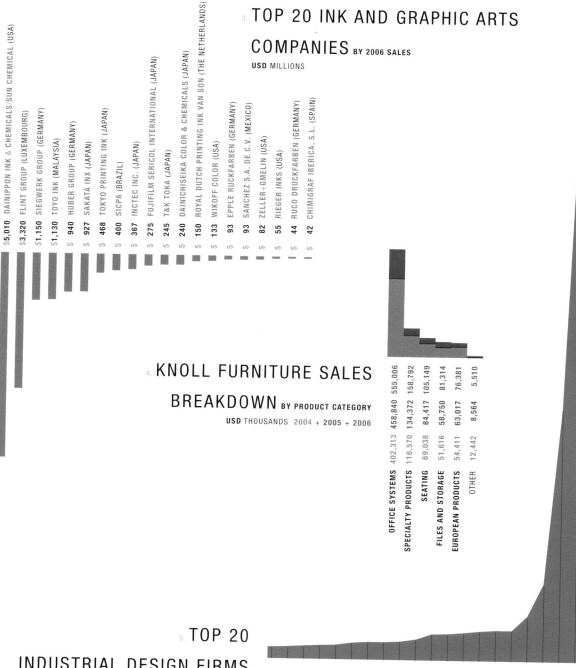

TOP 20 INK AND GRAPHIC ARTS
3.

COMPANIES BY 2006 SALES

USD MILLIONS

- $5,010 DAINIPPON INK & CHEMICALS/SUN CHEMICAL (USA)
- $3,320 FLINT GROUP (LUXEMBOURG)
- $1,150 SIEGWERK GROUP (GERMANY)
- $1,130 TOYO INK (MALAYSIA)
- $ 940 HUBER GROUP (GERMANY)
- $ 927 SAKATA INX (JAPAN)
- $ 468 TOKYO PRINTING INK (JAPAN)
- $ 400 SICPA (BRAZIL)
- $ 367 INCTEC INC. (JAPAN)
- $ 275 FUJIFILM SERICOL INTERNATIONAL (JAPAN)
- $ 245 T&K TOKA (JAPAN)
- $ 240 DAINICHISEIKA COLOR & CHEMICALS (JAPAN)
- $ 150 ROYAL DUTCH PRINTING INK VAN SON (THE NETHERLANDS)
- $ 133 WIKOFF COLOR (USA)
- $ 93 EPPLE RUCKFARBEN (GERMANY)
- $ 93 SANCHEZ S.A. DE C.V. (MEXICO)
- $ 82 ZELLER+GMELIN (USA)
- $ 55 RIEGER INKS (USA)
- $ 44 RUCO DRUCKFARBEN (GERMANY)
- $ 42 CHIMIGRAF IBERICA, S.L. (SPAIN)

KNOLL FURNITURE SALES
4.

BREAKDOWN BY PRODUCT CATEGORY

USD THOUSANDS 2004 + 2005 + 2006

OFFICE SYSTEMS	402,313	458,840	555,006
SPECIALTY PRODUCTS	116,570	134,372	158,792
SEATING	69,038	84,417	105,149
FILES AND STORAGE	51,616	58,750	81,314
EUROPEAN PRODUCTS	54,411	63,017	76,381
OTHER	12,442	8,564	5,510

TOP 20
5.

INDUSTRIAL DESIGN FIRMS

BY SALES **2006** **USD** MILLIONS

- $ 14.6 FLIAD & ASSOCIATES
- $ 15 STELLAR
- $ 16.7 BAKER AND ASSOCIATES
- $ 17.3 HDR ARCHITECTURE
- $ 17.9 INGENIUM GROUP
- $ 21.5 WARE MALCOMB
- $ 22.1 MERRICK & CO.
- $ 22.4 STV GROUP
- $ 23.4 KLINGSTUBBINS
- $ 25.9 STANTEC
- $ 30.3 BURNS & MCDONNELL
- $ 31.5 THE BENHAM COS.
- $ 35 M+W ZANDER
- $ 37.5 CLARK, RICHARDSON & BISKUP
- $ 38 URS CORP.
- $ 38.5 GHAFARI ASSOCIATES
- $ 56.4 SSOE
- $ 99 CARTER & BURGESS
- $326.7 CH2M HILL
- $839.9 JACOBS ENGINEERING GROUP

ARCHITECTURE & DESIGN

Globalization has greatly impacted architecture and design in a number of ways —from the spread of influences to commissioning systems, and patterns of competition and collaborations. As globalization has exponentially increased the speed of cultural exchange related to design and architecture, styles, themes, buildings and design products are simultaneously being diversified and universalized in locations around the world. The notion that the modern city (rather than the nation-state) is the central point of exchange of ideas, trade, art and design has become, in many instances, a rallying cry for modern architecture (cf. indicator suite on Global Cities).

Designs begin conceptually at the local level and then, through the vehicles of transnational corporations such as IKEA, Target, Alessi, Nike, Swarovski, BMW, Hermès and Knoll, become commercial products sold in world markets. Much of industrial, furniture, and even graphic design business models have followed this pattern of local design becoming global. Conversely, the Internet and the advent of desktop publishing have allowed for smaller, individual designers to produce their furniture, objects, posters and graphics with low costs as well as access to a large virtual audience.

WHAT DO WE KNOW ABOUT DESIGN AND ARCHITECTURE?

Design as a broad term may encompass a wide variety of industries; however this data suite concentrates primarily on the interior, industrial, furniture, ink and graphic design fields. The Architecture and Design indicator suite shows considerable geographical diversity among architects. However, the majority of top architects and designers are primarily located in North America, Europe and Asia. The following trends are also observed:

- Design firms dealing in engineering, architecture and contract work based on annual sales data are primarily US-based companies, with 13 firms out of the top 20, and the rest based either in Canada or Western Europe (see data point 5).
- Every person/firm named on the Forbes List of International Up-And-Coming Architects has done projects in multiple country sites, thus illustrating the increasing globalization of the field (see data point 1).
- The global interior design industry is projected to increase by US$7,344 million during the period of 2007-2012 (see data point 2).
- Of the top 20 ink and graphic design companies in 2006, the largest company in terms of sales was based in the US at US$5,010 million as compared to the second highest ranked company in Luxembourg with US$3,320 million in sales (see data point 3).

WHAT ARE THE ISSUES?

Global cities around the world are using public and private investments in architecture as part of policies and programs aimed at urban revitalization, notably to help stake out a distinctive local identity as well as to increase the city's strategic position in the global economy. Architecture is used to help 'brand' a city by linking its name to a particular building or other architectural feature. The Eiffel Tower in Paris has long been a case in point, as are the Sydney Opera House, the Guggenheim Museum in Bilbao, Spain, or the Petronas Tower in Kuala Lumpur, Malaysia.

Industrial furniture and graphic design forms are evolving at a rapid pace as a result of globalization. Cultural visual ideals as well as perceptions of art and function are inexorably linked to design work. However, the branding and import of industrial, mass-produced design products by transnational corporations has exposed lower socio-economic groups to 'high' design such as that of Target and IKEA. Conversely, design concepts that can be efficiently mass-produced and will appeal to the largest number of consumers, across culture, gender, religious and age barriers, can often be found to be void of any cultural context.

Technological advances such as the Internet and home computer graphics programs have greatly altered information and access to design work for both creators and consumers. This access and lack of capital costs allows for additional freedom of expression for designers and enhanced levels of innovation. While most mass-marketed graphic, industrial and furniture designs tend to take a Western approach to the visualization of culture, increased access is allowing designers with outside worldviews to explore non-Western mediums. Reza Abedini is an influential figure in the Iranian graphic arts resurgence that focuses on cultivating a contemporary Iranian visual culture. While political difficulties can present a barrier to cultural exchange between the West and Iran, Abedini's website is easily accessible to consumers and designers around the world. In 2006, his work earned him the honor to be the first graphic designer to receive the Prince Claus Award ('A man apart,' 2007).

Architecture and design works are increasingly focused on the central idea of the global city as a creative space, inspiration and showcase for cosmopolitan architects and designers. In the summer of 2007, the Tate Modern art museum in London presented an exhibition entitled 'Global Cities' featuring Cairo, Istanbul, Johannesburg, London, Los Angeles, Mexico City, Mumbai, São Paulo, Shanghai and Tokyo. Using data from the 2006 International Architectural Biennale in Venice, the exhibit highlighted the globalizing nature of architecture and form in creating the identity of a city, and featured internationally recognized and background-diverse architects such as Nigel Coates, Zaha Hadid, Herzog & de Meuron, and Rem Koolhaas (Tate Modern, n.d.).

The crucial lack of cultural specificity in many recently imported global architectural works is well-articulated in the words of Juhani Pallasmaa (2007), former dean of architecture at the Helsinki University of Technology:

> Architecture continues to possess the capacity to root us in our domicile, to enrich and dignify our daily life, to still further express values of life that give us genuine satisfaction and joy. Yet, as contemporary architects distribute their signature images around the world, the very task and understanding of architecture is distorted. Instead of being a means of structuring and articulating the lived human world, the art of architecture presents itself as an instrument of mental manipulation and vulgar business, tragically both historical and distant (in this, as well, architectural journalism also needs to reassess its ethical role).

This statement reminds us that many of the greatest names in international architecture and their 'name-branded' works that dot the globe use techniques not entirely dissimilar to some of the marketing tactics used by the most successful transnational companies which also contribute to cultural homogenization and the elimination of a 'sense of place.'

ART AUCTIONS + GALLERIES

1. GLOBAL **ART AUCTION SALES** VOLUME IN USD BILLIONS **1997 – 2006**

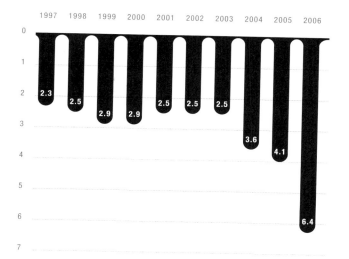

1997: 2.3
1998: 2.5
1999: 2.9
2000: 2.9
2001: 2.5
2002: 2.5
2003: 2.5
2004: 3.6
2005: 4.1
2006: 6.4

4. **AUCTION SALES**
TURNOVER BY COUNTRY **2006**

UNITED STATES	45.9%
UNITED KINGDOM	26.9%
OTHER COUNTRIES	7.2%
FRANCE	6.4%
CHINA	4.9%
GERMANY	2.9%
ITALY	2.8%
NETHERLANDS	1.1%
SWEDEN	1.1%
SPAIN	0.8%

2. SOTHEBY'S **NET AUCTION SALES** BY YEAR

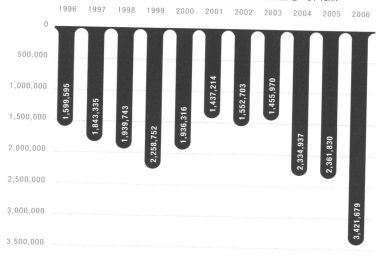

1996: 1,599,595
1997: 1,843,335
1998: 1,939,743
1999: 2,258,752
2000: 1,936,316
2001: 1,437,214
2002: 1,552,703
2003: 1,455,970
2004: 2,334,937
2005: 2,361,830
2006: 3,421,679

3. SOTHEBY'S **AUCTION SALES** BY YEAR **BY REGION** *SALES FOR JANUARY THROUGH JULY 2007 ONLY

2005 NORTH AMERICA **45**% — UNITED KINGDOM **36**% — CONTINENTAL EUROPE **11**% — ASIA **8**%

2006 NORTH AMERICA **50**% — UNITED KINGDOM **33**% — CONTINENTAL EUROPE **9**% — ASIA **8**%

2007* NORTH AMERICA **45**% — UNITED KINGDOM **42**% — CONTINENTAL EUROPE **7**% — ASIA **6**%

5. GLOBAL **AUCTION** **SALES** TURNOVER

BY FINE ART CATEGORY **2006**

PAINTING   75.7%

DRAWING / WATERCOLOR   11.1%

SCULPTURE   7.9%

PRINT   2.6%

PHOTOGRAPHY   2.2%

OTHER MEDIA   0.5%

6. **ART.COM** INC.

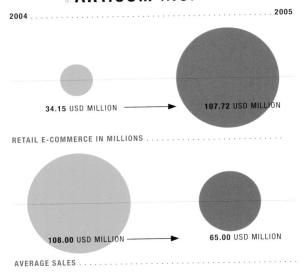

2004 2005

34.15 USD MILLION ⟶ **107.72** USD MILLION

RETAIL E-COMMERCE IN MILLIONS ....

108.00 USD MILLION ⟶ **65.00** USD MILLION

AVERAGE SALES ....

7. 100 TOP SELLING **ART AUCTION PIECES** BY PERIOD **2002, 2004, 2006** TOTAL SALES TURNOVER

2002 – USD **590.4** MILLION   20TH **CENTURY 76.3**%   19TH **CENTURY 19.4**%   17TH / 18TH **CENTURY 4.3**%

2004 – USD **835.3** MILLION   20TH **CENTURY 72.2**%   19TH **CENTURY 22.2**%   17TH / 18TH **CENTURY 5.6**%

2006 – USD **1,373.0** MILLION   20TH **CENTURY 86.2**%   19TH **CENTURY 11.5**%   17TH / 18TH **CENTURY 2.3**%

GLOBAL PERFORMANCE ART

INTERNATIONAL **PHILHARMONIC TOUR LOCATIONS**

ISRAEL PHILHARMONIC (2007):

NEW YORK **UNITED STATES**
SAN FRANCISCO **UNITED STATES**
LOS ANGELES **UNITED STATES**
TOKYO **JAPAN**
OSAKA **JAPAN**
NAGOYA **JAPAN**
HIROSHIMA **JAPAN**
FUKUOKA **JAPAN**
KITA KYUSHU **JAPAN**
SALZBURG **AUSTRIA**
LEIPZIG **GERMANY**
BERN **SWITZERLAND**
FRANKFURT **GERMANY**
LJUBLJANA **SLOVENIA**
LINZ **AUSTRIA**
TORINO **ITALY**
MILANO **ITALY**
FIRENZE **ITALY**
BRUSSELS **BELGIUM**
AMSTERDAM **NETHERLANDS**
PARIS **FRANCE**
COPENHAGEN **DENMARK**
BONN **GERMANY**
LUXEMBOURG **LUXEMBOURG**
BARCELONA **SPAIN**

VIENNA PHILHARMONIC (2006-07):

BONN **GERMANY**
SALZBURG **AUSTRIA**
BUDAPEST **HUNGARY**
OSLO **NORWAY**
MOSKVA **RUSSIA**
VALENCIA **SPAIN**
MADRID **SPAIN**
NEW YORK **UNITED STATES**
PARIS **FRANCE**
AMSTERDAM **NETHERLANDS**
BERLIN **GERMANY**
VIENNA **AUSTRIA**
MILANO **ITALY**
ZARAGOZA **SPAIN**
FIRENZE **ITALY**
WARSAW **POLAND**

LONDON PHILHARMONIC (2007):

MADRID **SPAIN**
LUXEMBOURG **LUXEMBOURG**
DUBLIN **IRELAND**
FRANKFURT **GERMANY**

NEW YORK PHILHARMONIC (2007):

WARSAW **POLAND**
BUDAPEST **HUNGARY**
VIENNA **AUSTRIA**
FRANKFURT **GERMANY**
HAMBURG **GERMANY**
BERLIN **GERMANY**
PARIS **FRANCE**
LUXEMBOURG **LUXEMBOURG**
NEW YORK **UNITED STATES**
TOKYO **JAPAN**
OSAKA **JAPAN**
KOBE **JAPAN**
SEOUL **SOUTH KOREA**
TAEGU **SOUTH KOREA**

BERLIN PHILHARMONIC (2007-08):

MARSEILLE **FRANCE**
SALZBURG **AUSTRIA**
BERN **SWITZERLAND**
NEW YORK **UNITED STATES**
BOSTON **UNITED STATES**
PARIS **FRANCE**
VIENNA **AUSTRIA**
STUTTGART **GERMANY**
FRANKFURT **GERMANY**
ESSEN **GERMANY**
BREMEN **GERMANY**
RIGA **LATVIA**
TALLIN **ESTONIA**
HELSINKI **FINLAND**
STOCKHOLM **SWEDEN**

OPERA COMPANY **CONDUCTORS + DIRECTORS**

NAME + COUNTRY OF ORIGIN	OPERA COMPANY	LOCATION	LENGTH OF CURRENT TENURE

ANTONIO PAPPANO, MUSIC DIRECTOR _ _ _ _ _ _ **ROYAL OPERA** _ _ _ _ _ _ _ _ _ _ LONDON, UNITED KINGDOM _ _ _ 2002 – PRESENT

UNITED KINGDOM - BORN TO ITALIAN PARENTS

PREVIOUS CONDUCTING AND DIRECTING – NORSKE OPERA IN OSLO, COVENT GARDEN, ENGLISH NATIONAL OPERA, SAN FRANCISCO OPERA, LYRIC OPERA OF CHICAGO, THÉATRE DU CHÂTELET, AND BERLIN STAATSOPER.

GERARD MORTIER, DIRECTOR _ _ _ _ _ _ _ _ _ **OPÉRA NATIONAL DE PARIS** _ _ _ _ PARIS, FRANCE _ _ _ _ _ _ _ _ _ 2001 – PRESENT

FRANCE

PREVIOUS CONDUCTING AND DIRECTING – THÉATRE ROYAL DE LA MONNAIE À BRUXELLES, FESTIVAL DE SALZBOURG, RUHRTRIENNALE 2002-2004 FESTIVAL.

SEIJI OZAWA, CONDUCTOR _ _ _ _ _ _ _ _ _ _ **WIENER STAATSOPER** _ _ _ _ _ _ _ VIENNA, AUSTRIA _ _ _ _ _ _ _ _ 2002 – PRESENT

CHINA - BORN TO JAPANESE PARENTS   VIENNA STATE OPERA

PREVIOUS CONDUCTING AND DIRECTING – BOSTON SYMPHONY ORCHESTRA, LA SCALA IN MILAN, THE MET, OPÉRA NATIONAL DE PARIS, COVENT GARDEN OPERA LONDON, SALZBURG FESTIVAL.

MARCELO LAMBARDERO, ARTISTIC DIRECTOR _ _ **TEATRO COLÓN** _ _ _ _ _ _ _ _ _ _ BUENOS AIRES, ARGENTINA _ _ _ 2005 – PRESENT

ARGENTINA

PREVIOUS CONDUCTING AND DIRECTING – BEGAN HIS CAREER AT THE TEATRO COLÓN. STUDIED AT THE INSTITUTO SUPERIOR DE ARTE, TEATRO COLÓN, AND HAS BEEN A SINGER AND STAGE DIRECTOR THERE SINCE 1992.

ROBERTO ABBADO, CONDUCTOR _ _ _ _ _ _ _ _ **TEATRO ALLA SCALA** _ _ _ _ _ _ _ MILAN, ITALY*

ITALY

PREVIOUS CONDUCTING AND DIRECTING – ROYAL LIVERPOOL PHILHARMONIC, MONTREAL SYMPHONY, THE BOSTON SYMPHONY, PHILADELPHIA ORCHESTRA, CHICAGO SYMPHONY, LOS ANGELES PHILHARMONIC, ORCHESTRE NATIONAL DE FRANCE, BUDAPEST PHILHARMONIC, SYDNEY SYMPHONY ORCHESTRA, AND ON.

MICHAEL BODER, GUEST CONDUCTOR _ _ _ _ _ _ **STAATSOPER UNTER DEN LINDEN** _ _ _BERLIN, GERMANY*

SEPTEMBER SHOW PHAEDRA   BERLIN STATE OPERA

GERMANY

PREVIOUS CONDUCTING AND DIRECTING – COLOGNE, HAMBURG, STUTTGART, MUNICH, BERLIN, DRESDEN, THE ROYAL OPERA HOUSE, COVENT GARDEN IN LONDON.

SIR RICHARD ARMSTRONG _ _ _ _ _ _ _ _ _ _ _ **OPERA AUSTRALIA** _ _ _ _ _ _ _ _ SYDNEY, AUSTRALIA*

UNITED KINGDOM

PREVIOUS CONDUCTING AND DIRECTING – THE ROYAL OPERA, WELSH NATIONAL OPERA, SCOTTISH OPERA, LONDON PHILHARMONIC, BBC SYMPHONY ORCHESTRA, BOURNEMOUTH SYMPHONY ORCHESTRA.

* CONDUCTS WORLDWIDE

3. OPERA COMPANY **CORPORATE SPONSORS** ONLY INCLUDES PRIMARY OR FIRST LISTED **2006/2007**

TOP CORPORATE SPONSOR	OPERA COMPANY	LOCATION	SPONSOR DESCRIPTION
SKY & ARTSWORLD	**ENGLISH NATIONAL OPERA**	LONDON, ENGLAND	BRITISH SATELLITE TELEVISION CHANNEL FEATURING PROGRAMMING RELATED TO THE ARTS
ERNST AND YOUNG	**OPÉRA NATIONAL DE PARIS**	PARIS, FRANCE	INTERNATIONAL BUSINESS AND ACCOUNTING CONSULTING FIRM
LEXUS	**WIENER STAATSOPER** VIENNA STATE OPERA	VIENNA, AUSTRIA	CAR COMPANY
HEWLETT-PACKARD & ORACLE	**TEATRO ALLA SCALA**	MILAN, ITALY	COMPUTER EQUIPMENT AND SOFTWARE COMPANY
AUSTRALIA POST & MAZDA	**OPERA AUSTRALIA**	SYDNEY, AUSTRALIA	MAIL SERVICES AND CAR COMPANY
BMW NIEDERLASSUNG BERLIN	**BERLIN STATE OPERA**	BERLIN, GERMANY	CAR COMPANY
HOTEL PANAMERICANO	**TEATRO COLÓN**	BUENOS AIRES, ARGENTINA	LUXURY HOTEL IN BUENOS AIRES

4. **SEATING CAPACITY** + **TICKET PRICES** OF OPERA HOUSES IN USD **2007**

SYDNEY OPERA HOUSE
THE OPERA THEATRE ONLY
TICKETS $ 44 – $ 191   1,547 SEATS

BERLIN STATE OPERA
TICKETS $ 22 – $ 109   1,600 SEATS

OPÉRA NATIONAL DE PARIS
TICKETS $177 – $ 218   2,156 SEATS

ROYAL OPERA HOUSE
TICKETS $ 14 – $1,210   2,268 SEATS

ENGLISH NATIONAL OPERA
NOT INCLUDING BOX SEATS
TICKETS $ 30 – $ 168   2,358 SEATS

TEATRO COLÓN
NOT INCLUDING BOX SEATS
TICKETS $ 14 – $ 70   2,367 SEATS

TEATRO ALLA SCALA
TICKETS $ 16 – $ 231   2,800 SEATS

1. THE PULITZER PRIZE IN INTERNATIONAL REPORTING 2000 – 2007

YEAR	JOURNALIST	NEWS ORGANIZATION	TOPIC
2000	MARK SCHOOFS	THE VILLAGE VOICE	AIDS CRISIS IN AFRICA
2001	IAN JOHNSON	WALL STREET JOURNAL	THE FALUN GONG MOVEMENT IN CHINA
2002	BARRY BEARAK	NEW YORK TIMES	WAR-TORN AFGHANISTAN
2003	KEVIN SULLIVAN AND	WASHINGTON POST	MEXICO'S CRIMINAL JUSTICE SYSTEM
	MARY JORDAN		
2004	ANTHONY SHADID	WASHINGTON POST	THE AMERICAN INVASION OF IRAQ
2005	KIM MURPHY	LOS ANGELES TIMES	RUSSIA'S FIGHT AGAINST TERORISM AND THE ECONOMY
2006	JOSEPH KAHN AND	NEW YORK TIMES	CHINA'S LEGAL SYSTEM
	JIM YARDLEY		
2007	STAFF	WALL STREET JOURNAL	THE EFFECTS OF CHINA'S BOOMING ECONOMY

2. ACADEMY AWARD TITLES FOR BEST PICTURE AND BEST FOREIGN FILM 1996 – 2007

	BEST PICTURE			BEST FOREIGN LANGUAGE FILM	
YEAR	TITLE	GROSS BOX OFFICE SALES IN USD	YEAR	TITLE	GROSS BOX OFFICE SALES IN USD
1996	THE ENGLISH PATIENT	$ 231,976,425 WORLDWIDE 1997	1996	KOLYA	$ 1,094,819 US + ITALY TOTAL 1997
1997	TITANIC	$1,835,300,000 WORLDWIDE 2003 DEC.	1997	CHARACTER	$ 1,998,013 US + NETHERLANDS 1997
1998	SHAKESPEARE IN LOVE	$ 132,972,868 WORLDWIDE 1999 SPRING	1998	LIFE IS BEAUTIFUL	$ 86,699,868 US + EUROPE 1998/1999
1999	AMERICAN BEAUTY	$ 356,296,601 WORLDWIDE	1999	ALL ABOUT MY MOTHER	$ 19,011,865 WORLDWIDE 1999 – 2002
2000	GLADIATOR	$ 445,935,611 WORLDWIDE 2001 APR.	2000	CROUCHING TIGER, HIDDEN DRAGON	$157,290,122 WORLDWIDE 2002
2001	A BEAUTIFUL MIND	$ 181,578,593 US + UK 2002 SPRING	2001	NO MAN'S LAND	$243,957,453 WORLDWIDE 2001
2002	CHICAGO	$ 306,776,732 WORLDWIDE 2004	2002	NOWHERE IN AFRICA	$ 48,093,334 WORLDWIDE 2003
2003	THE LORD OF THE RINGS: THE RETURN OF THE KING	$1,118,888,979 WORLDWIDE 2004	2003	THE BARBARIAN INVASIONS	$ 9,721,905 WORLDWIDE 2003
2004	MILLION DOLLAR BABY	$ 138,032,154 WORLDWIDE 2005 SPRING	2004	THE SEA INSIDE	$ 22,745,806 WORLDWIDE 2004/2005
2005	CRASH	$ 65,924,931 WORLDWIDE 2005/2006	2005	TSOTSI	$ 3,753,598 WORLDWIDE 2006
2006	THE DEPARTED	$ 166,935,430 WORLDWIDE 2006/2007	2006	THE LIVES OF OTHERS	$ 33,777,957 WORLDWIDE 2006/2007

3. ACADEMY AWARD BEST FOREIGN FILM NOMINEES BY REGION 1956 – 2007

REGION	1956 – 1959	1960 – 1969	1970 – 1979	1980 – 1989	1990 – 1999	2000 – 2007
AFRICA	–	1	1	1	1	3
ASIA + THE PACIFIC	2	4	2	3	7	4
EASTERN EUROPE	1	12	9	9	8	3
WESTERN EUROPE	17	27	32	30	27	18
LATIN AMERICA + THE CARIBBEAN	–	4	2	4	5	4
MIDDLE EAST	–	1	4	1	1	1
NORTH AMERICA	–	–	–	2	–	2

4. NOBEL PRIZE IN LITERATURE RECIPIENTS BY REGION 1901 – 2006

67 RECIPIENTS **WESTERN EUROPE**

11 RECIPIENTS **EASTERN EUROPE**

9 RECIPIENTS **NORTH AMERICA***

8 RECIPIENTS **LATIN AMERICA + THE CARIBBEAN**

5 RECIPIENTS **ASIA + THE PACIFIC**

3 RECIPIENTS **AFRICA****

2 RECIPIENTS **MIDDLE EAST**

* ALL FROM THE UNITED STATES   ** TWO WHITE SOUTH AFRICAN AUTHORS

5. PRITZKER PRIZE WINNERS 1995 – 2006

YEAR	NAME	NATION OF ORIGIN	WORK LOCATIONS	NOTABLE WORK
1995	TADAO ANDO	JAPAN	JAPAN, SPAIN MAIN OFFICE SITE OSAKA, JAPAN	ROKKO HOUSING PROJECT
1996	JOSÉ RAFAEL MONEO	SPAIN	SPAIN, USA BASED IN MADRID, SPAIN	NATIONAL MUSEUM OF ROMAN ART, MÉRIDA
1997	SVERRE FEHN	NORWAY	NORWAY, SWEDEN AND DENMARK BASED IN OSLO, NORWAY	NORWEGIAN PAVILION, THE BRUSSELS WORLD EXHIBITION
1998	RENZO PIANO	ITALY	WORLDWIDE BASED IN GENOA, ITALY AND PARIS, FRANCE	CENTRE GEORGE POMPIDOU, PARIS
1999	SIR NORMAN FOSTER	GREAT BRITAIN	WORLDWIDE BASED IN LONDON, UNITED KINGDOM	WORLD'S LARGEST AIRPORT, HONG KONG
2000	REM KOOLHAAS	NETHERLANDS	WORLDWIDE TEACHES AT HARVARD UNIVERSITY, USA	THE KUNSTHAL, ROTTERDAM
2001	JACQUES HERZOG AND PIERRE DE MEURON	SWITZERLAND	WORLDWIDE BASED IN BASEL, SWITZERLAND	THE CONVERSION OF THE GIANT BANK SIDE POWER PLANT ON THE THAMES RIVER, LONDON TO A NEW GALLERY OF MODERN ART FOR THE TATE MUSEUM
2002	GLENN MURCUTT	AUSTRALIA	WORLDWIDE SOLE PRACTITIONER IN SYDNEY, AUSTRALIA	ENVIRONMENTALLY SENSITIVE MODERNIST HOUSES
2003	JØRN UTZON	DENMARK	WORLDWIDE RETIRED TO MAJORCA, SPAIN	THE SYDNEY OPERA HOUSE
2004	ZAHA HADID	IRAQ	WORLDWIDE BASED IN LONDON, UNITED KINGDOM	ROSENTHAL CENTER FOR CONTEMPORARY ART, CINCINNATI, OHIO
2005	THOM MAYNE	UNITED STATES	WORLDWIDE BASED IN LOS ANGELES, USA	THE NEW YORK OLYMPIC VILLAGE FOR THE 2012 GAMES
2006	PAUL MENDES DA ROCHA	BRAZIL	BRAZIL BASED IN SAO PAULO, BRAZIL	BRAZILIAN SCULPTURE MUSEUM SAO PAULO'S FINE ARTS MUSEUM, PATRIARCH PLAZA

ROLF SCHOCK LAUREATES 1993 – 2005

YEAR	NAME	COUNTRY OF ORIGIN	DESCRIPTION
1993	RAFAEL MONEO	SPAIN	ARCHITECTURE INTEGRATING CLASSICAL AND MODERN DESIGN
1995	CLAES OLDENBURG	UNITED STATES	MONUMENTAL SCALE SCULPTURE
1997	TORSTEN ANDERSON	SWEDEN	CONCEPTUAL PAINTINGS + SCULPTURE
1999	JACQUES HERZOG AND PIERRE DE MEURON	SWITZERLAND	ARTISTIC ARCHITECTURAL ACHIEVEMENTS
2001	GUISEPPE PENONE	ITALY	USING PREDOMINANTLY WOOD AS WORKING MATERIAL; THEMES OF MANKIND AND NATURE
2003	SUSAN ROTHENBERG	UNITED STATES	PAINTING WITH THEMES OF ANIMALS AND GEOMETRIC SHAPES
2005	KAZUYO SEJIMA AND RYUE NISHIZAWA	JAPAN	ARCHITECTURE THAT IS ECONOMICAL BUT TRANSLUCENT IN FORM

DESIGN + ADVERTISING AWARDS BY TOP RECIPIENTS AND # OF WINNING AGENCIES 2002 – 2007

2002 _ TOTAL WINNING AGENCIES	10
BUD LIGHT ALCOHOLIC BEVERAGE	3
VOLKSWAGEN CARS	4
REEBOK SPORTS APPAREL	4
STELLA ARTOIS ALCOHOLIC BEVERAGE	4
LEVI'S APPAREL	8

2003 _ TOTAL WINNING AGENCIES	25
SPRINT PCS TELECOM	4
FOX SPORTS NET MEDIA	5
NSPCC NON-PROFIT	5
JOHN SMITH'S ALCOHOLIC BEVERAGE	6
BBC MEDIA	9

2004 _ TOTAL WINNING AGENCIES	6
STREAMLIGHT LIGHTING	3
MTV MEDIA	4
SONY/SONY PLAYSTATION ELECTRONIC GAMES	8
HONDA/HONDA UK CARS	10
GUARDIAN NEWS MEDIA	14

2005 _ TOTAL WINNING AGENCIES	11
STELLA ARTOIS ALCOHOLIC BEVERAGE	3
LYNX 24-7 TOILETRIES	4
TBS NETWORK MEDIA	5
HONDA CARS	6
CHANNEL 4 MEDIA	9

2006 _ TOTAL WINNING AGENCIES	11
3 TELECOM	2
VODAPHONE TELECOM	2
SONY ELECTRONICS	2
FIVE MEDIA	4
THINK! ROAD SAFETY PUBLIC SERVICE	3

2007 _ TOTAL WINNING AGENCIES	7
DOVE TOILETRIES	2
HONDA CARS	2
SKITTLES FOOD	4
COMBOS PRETZELS FOOD	5

THE GLOBAL ARTS MARKET

The global arts market, as examined in this suite, refers primarily to the fine arts, including music, theater, painting, sculpture, drawing, architecture and design (see also text box on the arts market boom in this volume). Arts markets have long existed as local, regional or national-level entities that appeal to a specific audience's experiences, beliefs, historical context and language. Particular genres (e.g., paintings, writing) and particular art objects (e.g., African masks, Chinese vases, Japanese prints) have long transcended national boundaries to form international markets. As Halle and Tiso point out in this volume many segments of the market for visual arts remain national or regional in nature or are concentrated in a few urban centers of two regions, North America and Europe, and thus not truly 'global.'

However, many segments of the arts market are rapidly transcending these barriers. Like other markets, the supply and demand for the arts is undergoing a process of globalization driven by economic opportunities, socio-cultural change and technological innovations that bring up complex policy issues in terms of fair trade, cultural diversity, access to information and knowledge as well as cultural sovereignty. What is more, the expansion of the global economy, and fortunes made in the growing economies of China and Russia in particular have increased demand for fine art, especially paintings, resulting in a significant rise in prices for twentieth century as well as contemporary art. The global fine art market grew over 52 per cent in 2006, hitting US$6.4 billion (Reuters, 2007).

WHAT DO WE KNOW ABOUT THE GLOBAL ARTS MARKET?

Current trends in the global arts market include buyers' preferences for contemporary art over the old masters as well as Asian art. The US currently dominates both auction sales turnover (by 45 per cent) as well as number of galleries represented at Art Basel. Also, there is a continued trend of involvement in and support of the arts by the private sector, notably through corporate sponsors. The following points highlight additional emerging patterns within the global arts market:

- From 2005 to 2006, the number of art works sold at auction for over US$1 million nearly doubled and total revenue increased to $2.7 billion from $1.4 billion, in large part due to the frequency of high-ticket sales (Artprice, 2006).
- The global arts market is dominated by European artists, and traded mostly in Europe and the United States: 72 per cent of international art auctions, measured by yearly turnover, are located in the US and the EU; only 5 per cent of the total number of international art auctions take place outside of the US and Europe (see indicator suite on Art Auctions and Galleries, data point 4).

Among other art forms, the following facts and trends stand out:
- Many of the most recognized opera companies are funded through corporate sponsors whose primary areas of business include everything from television media to selling cars to investment banking and computer software (see indicator suite on Global Performance Art, data point 3). However, the majority of companies still rely heavily on public grants (see English National Opera graph, next page).
- Opera conductors and directors tend to be nationals of the country in which they have a permanent conductorship position. However, most conductors have worked with companies all over the world throughout their careers, frequently serving as guest conductors (see indicator suite on Global Performance Art, data point 2).

TOP TEN GROSSING ARTISTS AT AUCTION - 2006

Artist Name	Name and Date of Work	Selling Price (USD)	Auction House
PICASSO, Pablo	"Dora Maar au chat" (1941)	$ 85 000 000	Sotheby's (New York)
KLIMT, Gustav	"Portrait of Adele Bloch-Bauer II" (1912)	$ 78 500 000	Christie's (New York)
GAUGUIN, Paul	"L'homme à la hache" (1891)	$ 36 000 000	Christie's (New York)
van GOGH, Vincent	"L'Arlésienne, Madame Ginoux" (1890)	$ 36 000 000	Christie's (New York)
KLIMT, Gustav	"Birch Forest" (1903)	$ 36 000 000	Christie's (New York)
KIRCHNER, Ernst Ludwig	"Berliner Strassenszene/Bäume" (1913-1914)	$ 34 000 000	Christie's (New York)
CÉZANNE, Paul	"Nature morte aux fruits et pot de gingembre" (c.1895)	$ 33 000 000	Sotheby's (New York)
TURNER, William	"Giudecca, La Donna della Salute and San Giorgio" (prior to 1851)	$ 32 000 000	Christie's (New York)
PICASSO, Pablo	"Le repos" (1932)	$ 31 000 000	Christie's (New York)
KLIMT, Gustav	"Apple Tree I" (1912)	$ 29 500 000	Christie's (New York)

SOURCE: Artprice.com, "Art market trends" (2006).

ENGLISH NATIONAL OPERA: BREAKDOWN OF FUNDING SOURCES

Arts Council Grants	**53**%
Box Office Income	**28**%
Sponsorship & Supporters	**10**%
Exploitation Income	**7**%
Other Grants	**1**%

SOURCE: English National Opera (2007).

• The major philharmonic orchestras' tours tend to cluster in the same regions of the world, namely North America, Western Europe and Asia, with the heaviest concentration of performances in Western Europe (see indicator suite on Global Performance Art, data point 1).

WHAT ARE THE ISSUES?

The role of the 'market' is frequently debated and has been since Adorno in the 1930s and Pierre Bourdieu in the 1970s, plus many others. Several contributors to this volume explore the complex role of the market economy in the creation and consumption of art and cultural goods (see introduction and chapters by Cunningham et al. and Scott). The chapter by Halle and Tiso compares the market-based example of galleries in New York's Chelsea district to the traditional state-sponsored French model for the cultivation of high art, and show that the market can indeed stimulate innovation and new talent, and provide a public good through its quasi-museum spectator role while still maintaining a competitive edge among buyers from around the world.

Increased access to information is contributing to the ongoing shifts in global arts markets in terms of who the buyers are and what and how they are purchasing art work. Artprice is one of several on-line auction databases which are helping to inform consumers and standardize price levels in a relatively volatile market. Artprice and many others, including the largest auction houses, Sotheby's and Christie's, have included online, real time auction bidding services, which has been a step forward in terms of global access to the art buying process.

There is a growing concern that the huge surge in global arts market turn-over is a bubble ready to burst once stock markets decline and the world economy slows, as happened in the 1980s. However, art markets can be fairly insulated against short-term economic cycles and respond more to long-term expansions and contractions of wealth. Another potentially protective characteristic of the globalizing arts market today compared to the arts market of the 1980s is the growing diversity of demand and the type of buyer. An increasing number of high net worth individuals from Asia and Russia and the Middle East are already significantly contributing to art auction sales (Pogrebin, 2007).

Finally, the awards system in the arts is also changing. There is a distinct 'economy of prestige' which is increasingly globalized (see text box by James English in Introduction of this volume). Still, many of the most prestigious art awards, prizes and fellowships have been founded and are administered by North American or European institutions and their recipients have traditionally been representative of these regions as well (see indicator suite on Prizes and Competitions, data points 1 thru 7). However, new awards are being created and/or gaining additional international recognition that have helped to fill the gap in terms of the cultivation of artistic achievements in Africa, the Middle East, Asia and Latin America. Some examples of these awards are the Aga Khan Award for Architecture (honoring Islamic architecture and community projects), the Golden Pen of Freedom Award (mostly given to Asian and African journalists for freedom of the press), the Filmfare Awards (honoring Bollywood artists), and the Tezuka Osamu Cultural Prize (honoring Japanese Manga comic book artists). These awards represent not only different regions but also different artistic genres related to their local cultural context, connecting the local to the global.

THE INTERNET

1. WORLD **INTERNET USAGE** BY REGION **2007**
AS OF JANUARY 11, 2007

40%

30%

20%

10%

0%

NORTH AMERICA 21%   EUROPE 29%   ASIA 35%

LATIN AMERICA +
CARIBBEAN 8%   AFRICA 3%   MIDDLE EAST 2%

2. WORLD **INTERNET USAGE GROWTH** 2002 – 2006

OCEANIA/AUSTRALIA 2%

DECEMBER **2000** – 361 MILLION USERS   AUGUST **2001** – 513 MILLION USERS   SEPTEMBER **2002** – 587 MILLION USERS   DECEMBER **2003** – 719 MILLION USERS   DECEMBER **2004** – 817 MILLION USERS   DECEMBER **2005** – 1,018 MILLION USERS   DECEMBER **2006** – 1,093 MILLION USERS

3. TOP TEN **LANGUAGES**
USED IN THE WEB AS OF JAN. 2007

30%	**ENGLISH**	3%	**PORTUGUESE**
14%	**CHINESE**	3%	**KOREAN**
8%	**SPANISH**	3%	**ITALIAN**
8%	**JAPANESE**	3%	**ARABIC**
5%	**GERMAN**	18%	REST OF WORLD
5%	**FRENCH**		LANGUAGES

4. AVERAGE # OF **BLOGS**
CREATED PER DAY WORLDWIDE

OCTOBER	2006	97,500 BLOGS	|||||||||||||||||||||||
NOVEMBER	2006	91,000 BLOGS	||||||||||||||||||||||
DECEMBER	2006	83,750 BLOGS	|||||||||||||||||||||
JANUARY	2007	89,500 BLOGS	||||||||||||||||||||||
FEBRUARY	2007	113,600 BLOGS	||||||||||||||||||||||||||

5. TOP 10 COUNTRIES IN **INTERNET USAGE** VERSUS

% **INTERNET PENETRATION** AS OF NOV. **2006**

INTERNET PENETRATION IS THE RATIO BETWEEN THE SUM OF INTERNET USERS IN A COUNTRY AND THE TOTAL POPULATION ESTIMATE OF THAT COUNTRY

			SOUTH KOREA
UNITED STATES	209,025 THOUSAND USERS	69.9% INTERNET PENETRATION	
CHINA	123,000 THOUSAND USERS	9.4% INTERNET PENETRATION	1. NAVER.COM
JAPAN	86,300 THOUSAND USERS	67.2% INTERNET PENETRATION	2. YAHOO!
GERMANY	50,616 THOUSAND USERS	61.3% INTERNET PENETRATION	3. DAUM.NET
INDIA	40,000 THOUSAND USERS	3.6% INTERNET PENETRATION	4. CYWORLD.COM
UNITED KINGDOM	37,600 THOUSAND USERS	62.5% INTERNET PENETRATION	5. NATE.COM
SOUTH KOREA	33,900 THOUSAND USERS	67.0% INTERNET PENETRATION	6. INTERNET AUCTION
ITALY	30,764 THOUSAND USERS	52.0% INTERNET PENETRATION	7. GOOGLE
FRANCE	29,521 THOUSAND USERS	48.4% INTERNET PENETRATION	8. EMPAS.COM
BRAZIL	25,900 THOUSAND USERS	14.1% INTERNET PENETRATION	9. YOUTUBE
			10. GMARKET.COM.KR

6. TOP **WEBSITES** GLOBALLY + BY COUNTRIES RANKED ACCORDING TO THE TOP 10 BY INTERNET USAGE AS OF SEPT. **2007**

GLOBAL
1. YAHOO!
2. MSN
3. GOOGLE
4. YOUTUBE
5. WINDOWS LIVE
6. MYSPACE
7. BAIDU.COM
8. ORKUT
9. WIKIPEDIA
10. WWW.QQ.COM

UNITED STATES
1. YAHOO!
2. GOOGLE
3. MYSPACE
4. YOUTUBE
5. MSN
6. FACEBOOK
7. eBAY
8. WINDOWS LIVE
9. CRAIGSLIST.ORG
10. WIKIPEDIA

CHINA
1. BAIDU.COM #1 CHINESE
   SEARCHING ENGINE
2. WWW.QQ.COM
3. CHINA.COM.CN #1 CHINESE
   NEWS PORTAL
4. SOHU.COM.CN
5. 163.COM #1 CHINESE
   VIDEO PORTAL
6. TAOBAO.COM
7. GOOGLE CHINA
8. TOM.COM
9. YAHOO! CHINA
10. 56.COM #2 CHINESE
   VIDEO PORTAL

JAPAN
1. YAHOO! JAPAN
2. GOOGLE JAPAN
3. FC2.COM
4. MIXI.JP
5. YOUTUBE
6. RAKUTEN.COM.JP
7. LIVEDOOR
8. GOOGLE
9. GOO.NE.JP SEARCH ENGINE
10. WIKIPEDIA

GERMANY
1. GOOGLE GERMANY
2. eBAY GERMANY
3. GOOGLE
4. YAHOO!
5. YOUTUBE
6. WIKIPEDIA
7. GMX.NET
8. MSN
9. STUDIVERZEICHNIS.COM
10. SPIEGEL ONLINE

INDIA
1. YAHOO!
2. ORKUT SOCIAL NETWORK
3. GOOGLE INDIA
4. GOOGLE
5. REDIFF.COM INDIA LTD.
6. MSN
7. YOUTUBE
8. NAUKRI.COM
9. BLOGGER
10. WINDOWS LIVE

ITALY
1. GOOGLE ITALY
2. YAHOO!
3. GOOGLE
4. YOUTUBE
5. MSN
6. WINDOWS LIVE
7. LIBERTO.IT
8. eBAY ITALY
9. ALICE
10. MYSPACE

FRANCE
1. GOOGLE FRANCE
2. SKYROCK
3. MSN
4. YAHOO!
5. WINDOWS LIVE
6. FREE.FR
7. GOOGLE
8. DAILYMOTION.COM
9. ORANGE.FR
10. YOUTUBE

BRAZIL
1. ORKUT
2. GOOGLE BRAZIL
3. MSN
4. UNIVERSO ONLINE
5. YAHOO!
6. GOOGLE
7. YOUTUBE
8. TERRA.COM.BR
9. WINDOWS LIVE
10. GLOBO.COM

7. **BLOG POSTS** WORLDWIDE

BY LANGUAGE 4TH QUARTER 2006

5%	OTHER		
1%	FARSI	3%	ITALIAN
1%	GERMAN	3%	SPANISH
2%	FRENCH	8%	CHINESE
2%	PORTUGUESE	36%	ENGLISH
2%	RUSSIAN	37%	JAPANESE

THE INTERNET

The Internet is a complex system of interconnected computer networks, largely created via fiber-optic broadband cables and receivers. As the latest step in the evolutionary sequence from the telegraph to telephone, radio, television and the computer, the Internet is expanding and revolutionizing the world of communication. According to the International Internet Society (2007), it is 'at once a world-wide broadcasting capability, a mechanism for information dissemination, and a medium for collaboration and interaction between individuals and their computers without regard for geographic location.' In this way, Friedman (2006) argues that the Internet has been instrumental in 'flattening' the world by facilitating greater connectivity of the local to the global, bringing emerging economies into the forefront as major economic competitors, and creating opportunities for growth and development unlike ever before. Yet many would challenge such optimism and point to serious issues relating to the Internet's role in contributing to a digital divide, the proliferation of misinformation, increased threats to privacy, greater availability of pornography, etc.

WHAT DO WE KNOW ABOUT THE INTERNET?

As of October 2007, currently over 1.2 billion people worldwide are characterized as 'Internet users' (Internet World Stats, 2007). As the Internet continues to grow and spread, its uses become more varied, and with significant commercial potential. In addition, the use of blogs, chat rooms and now virtual worlds has played an important role in developing new participatory forms of communication across multiple divides (cf. indicator suite on the Cultural Commons). The indicator suite on the Internet demonstrates:

- Worldwide Internet growth increased by 202 per cent between December 2000 and 2006 (see data point 2).
- Regions with the largest Internet usage are Asia (35 per cent), Europe (29 per cent) and North America (21 per cent) (see data point 1).
- The top three countries in terms of number of people using the Internet are the United States (209,025), China (123,000), and Japan (86,300) (see data point 5).
- The top three emerging countries in terms of Internet use are China (with only a 9.4 per cent penetration rate), India (3.6 per cent) and Brazil (14.1 per cent) (see data point 5).
- The top three languages of the Internet overall are English, Chinese and Spanish, which account for 50 per cent of web pages online; however, the languages which largely dominate the blogging world are Japanese (37 per cent of all blogs), English (36 per cent) and Chinese (8 per cent) (see data point 7).
- In March 2006, web sites which received the highest number of unique visitors (in thousands) were MSN-Microsoft sites (538,578,000 visitors), Google sites (495,788,000) and Yahoo! sites (480,228,000) (see data point 6).
- As of September 1, 2007, Yahoo! and Google were the most visited web portals in the US, Japan, Germany, India, Italy, France and Brazil (where Orkut—a social networking site run by Google—is most commonly used). Yet lesser known and nationally-based web search engines also ranked the highest in other countries, such as Baidu in China and Naver in South Korea (see data point 6).
- The total number of blogs online is uncertain, but in July 2007 Technorati.com (a blog search engine) claimed to track almost 89.4 million blogs daily (Sifry, 2007), with approximately 113,000 new blogs created each day (see table below).
- About two-thirds of bloggers are women, of which 58 per cent are between the ages of 13 and 19 (see Blogs data suite, *Cultures and Globalization, volume 1*).

NUMBER OF BLOGS CREATED PER DAY WORLDWIDE

January 2004-2007	
January 2004	7,300
January 2005	40,000
January 2006	67,000
January 2007	113,600

SOURCE: Technorati.com

WHAT ARE THE ISSUES?

Concerns regarding the Internet center on access, privacy, censorship, and ownership. The open nature of the Internet makes it a potent instrument for creative expression and the widespread sharing of knowledge and information. By the same token, these very capacities entail critical issues about intellectual property rights and the public domain (cf. indicator suite and digest on the Cultural Commons).

Today, the Internet reaches nearly 18.9 per cent of the world's population. However, this reach is uneven, with heavy concentrations in the industrialized countries in Asia, Europe and North America. This global digital divide is the result of unequal access to computers, Internet network technology, literacy as well as computer literacy, and costs associated with purchasing and owning computers that can connect to the Internet. Worldwide, the Netherlands and South Korea have the largest broadband penetration (Internet World Stats, 2007), but elsewhere, and for the nearly 3 billion people that live on less than two dollars a day, access to the Internet remains elusive (Shah, 2006).

In August 2006, a Brazilian judge ordered Google to release information on select individuals believed to be using its social networking service, Orkut, to traffic drugs and child pornography. Google refused on the basis that the location of Google's servers in the United States is not subject to Brazilian law. This refusal by Google to work with the Brazilian government contrasts starkly with Google's cooperation with the Chinese government to censor its content of Google-China and demonstrates the strategic thinking of major Internet corporations when deciding on whether to protect or deny the right to privacy and freedom of speech online.

A pressing issue connected to access and regulation of the Internet is the use of cyberspace for pornography. This reflects a growing international governance and law enforcement problem that is often tied to human trafficking and crime. According to Family Safe Media (http://www.familysafemedia.com), approximately 4.2 million websites (12 per cent of all online content) are pornographic. The United States has by far the largest number of pornographically related web pages, followed by Germany (see table below). With Internet pornography sales in 2006 estimated at US$97.06 billion, it is not a problem likely to go away anytime soon.

NUMBER OF PORNOGRAPHIC WEB PAGES BY COUNTRY

country	porn pages
UNITED STATES	244,661,900
GERMANY	10,030,200
UNITED KINGDOM	8,506,800
AUSTRALIA	5,655,800
JAPAN	2,700,800
THE NETHERLANDS	1,883,800
RUSSIA	1,080,600
POLAND	1,049,600
SPAIN	852,800

Source: Family Safe Media, (n.d.)

INDICATOR SUITE # CULTURES AS A SYSTEM OF SITES + MOVEMENTS

GLOBAL SITES + EVENTS

31. **GLOBAL CULTURAL CENTERS + CITIES**

NEW YORK/LOS ANGELES

TOKYO

SINGAPORE

SÃO PAULO/RIO DE JANEIRO

JOHANNESBURG

BEIJING/SHANGHAI

LONDON

BERLIN

PARIS

32. **GLOBAL EVENTS**

MOVEMENTS + FLOWS

33. **EDUCATIONAL EXCHANGE**

34. **CULTURAL TOURISM**

35. **GLOBAL CONCERT TOURS**

GLOBAL CULTURAL CENTERS + CITIES

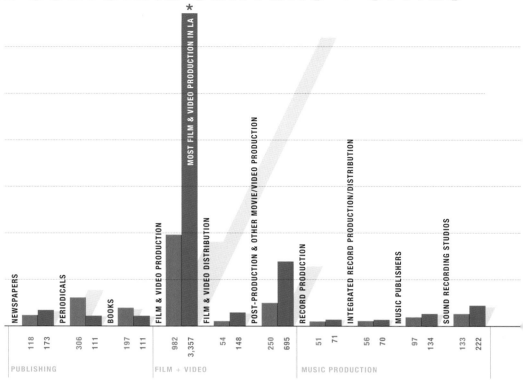

*
MOST FILM & VIDEO PRODUCTION IN LA

NEWSPAPERS	PERIODICALS	BOOKS	FILM & VIDEO PRODUCTION	FILM & VIDEO DISTRIBUTION	POST-PRODUCTION & OTHER MOVIE/VIDEO PRODUCTION	RECORD PRODUCTION	INTEGRATED RECORD PRODUCTION/DISTRIBUTION	MUSIC PUBLISHERS	SOUND RECORDING STUDIOS	

118 173 | 306 111 | 197 111 | 982 3,357 | 54 148 | 250 695 | 51 71 | 56 70 | 97 134 | 133 222

PUBLISHING   FILM + VIDEO   MUSIC PRODUCTION

2. ESTIMATED % BREAKDOWN OF

CULTURAL ESTABLISHMENTS IN NY + LA 2004 NOTE: THESE FIGURES DO NOT INCLUDE NONPROFITS OR SELF

ESTIMATED TOTAL # OF CULTURAL BUSINESSES 15,630
NEW YORK COUNTY (MANHATTAN)

%	Category
5.01%	PUBLISHING
8.23%	FILM + VIDEO
2.36%	MUSIC PRODUCTION
1.71%	BROADCASTING
13.75%	LIBRARIES + EDUCATION
6.47%	ARCHITECTURE
20.57%	**APPLIED DESIGN**
6.37%	ADVERTISING
16.40%	PERFORMING ARTS
3.83%	ART DEALERS + MUSEUMS
5.36%	TOURISM
9.19%	INDEPENDENT ARTISTS/WRITERS

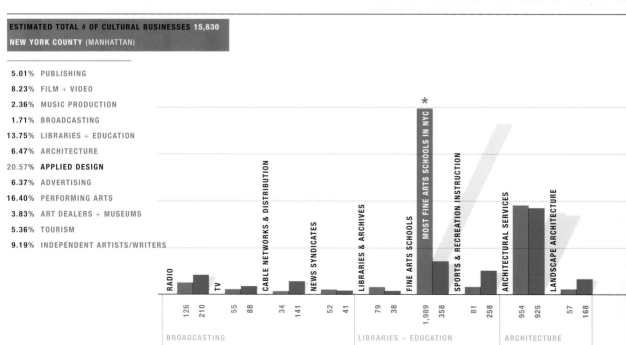

*
MOST FINE ARTS SCHOOLS IN NYC

RADIO	TV	CABLE NETWORKS & DISTRIBUTION	NEWS SYNDICATES	LIBRARIES & ARCHIVES	FINE ARTS SCHOOLS	SPORTS & RECREATION INSTRUCTION	ARCHITECTURAL SERVICES	LANDSCAPE ARCHITECTURE

126 210 | 55 88 | 34 141 | 52 41 | 79 38 | 1,989 358 | 81 258 | 954 925 | 57 168

BROADCASTING   LIBRARIES + EDUCATION   ARCHITECTURE

NEW YORK + LOS ANGELES

ESTIMATED # OF **CULTURAL ESTABLISHMENTS** IN
NEW YORK (MANHATTAN) + **LOS ANGELES COUNTIES** 2004

NEW YORK CITY # OF FIRMS

LOS ANGELES # OF FIRMS

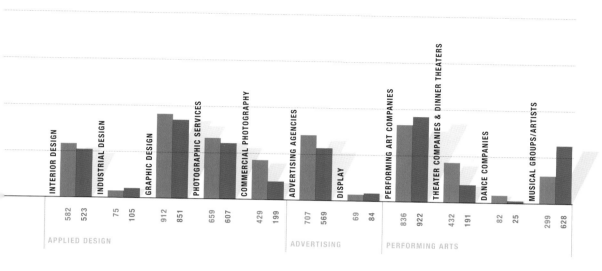

	APPLIED DESIGN				ADVERTISING		PERFORMING ARTS			
INTERIOR DESIGN	INDUSTRIAL DESIGN	GRAPHIC DESIGN	PHOTOGRAPHIC SERVICES	COMMERCIAL PHOTOGRAPHY	ADVERTISING AGENCIES	DISPLAY	PERFORMING ART COMPANIES	THEATER COMPANIES & DINNER THEATERS	DANCE COMPANIES	MUSICAL GROUPS/ARTISTS
582	75	912	659	429	707	69	836	432	82	299
523	105	851	607	199	569	84	922	191	25	628

EMPLOYED BUSINESSES, AND THEREFORE MAY BE UNDER-COUNTED

ESTIMATED TOTAL # OF CULTURAL BUSINESSES 12,130
LOS ANGELES COUNTY

2.96%	PUBLISHING
18.98%	FILM + VIDEO
2.45%	MUSIC PRODUCTION
2.17%	BROADCASTING
2.96%	LIBRARIES + EDUCATION
4.94%	ARCHITECTURE
13.10%	APPLIED DESIGN
4.66%	ADVERTISING
13.49%	PERFORMING ARTS
1.40%	ART DEALERS + MUSEUMS
4.93%	TOURISM
27.97%	INDEPENDENT ARTISTS/WRITERS

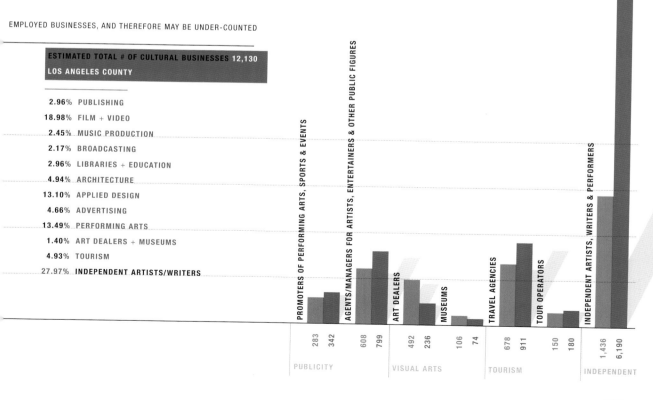

★ MOST INDEPENDENT ARTISTS, WRITERS & PERFORMERS IN LA

PUBLICITY		VISUAL ARTS		TOURISM		INDEPENDENT
PROMOTERS OF PERFORMING ARTS, SPORTS & EVENTS	AGENTS/MANAGERS FOR ARTISTS, ENTERTAINERS & OTHER PUBLIC FIGURES	ART DEALERS	MUSEUMS	TRAVEL AGENCIES	TOUR OPERATORS	INDEPENDENT ARTISTS, WRITERS & PERFORMERS
283	608	492	106	678	150	1,436
342	799	236	74	911	180	6,190

509

CULTURAL EMPLOYEES IN
NY COUNTY (MANHATTAN) + LA COUNTY 2004

EMPLOYEES IN NY COUNTY
OF AN ESTIMATED **220,735** TOTAL OF CULTURAL WORKERS
23% **PUBLISHING** BOOKS, NEWSPAPERS, PERIODICALS + DIRECTORIES
5% **FILM & VIDEO**
3% **MUSIC PRODUCTION** + **RECORDING**
13% TV + RADIO **BROADCASTING**
1% INTERNET SERVICES + **WEB** SEARCH PORTALS
3% **LIBRARIES**/ARCHIVES, ART SCHOOLS + SPORTS **EDUCATION**
4% **ARCHITECTURE**
6% **APPLIED DESIGN**
13% **ADVERTISING**
21% **PERFORMING ARTS**
4% **ART** DEALERS + MUSEUMS
3% **TOURISM** AGENTS + OPERATORS
1% **INDEPENDENT ARTISTS + PERFORMERS**

MOST FILM & VIDEO EMPLOYEES IN LA

MOST PUBLISHING EMPLOYEES IN NYC *

MOST BROADCASTING EMPLOYEES IN NYC *

MOST ADVERTISING EMPLOYEES IN NYC *

MOST PERFORMING ARTS EMPLOYEES IN NYC *

Category	NYC	LA
PUBLISHING	15,432	47,972
FILM & VIDEO	86,285	11,597
MUSIC PRODUCTION	5,625	5,990
BROADCASTING	21,811	29,667
WEB	3,842	1,176
LIBRARIES + EDUCATION	4,962	6,720
ARCHITECTURE	9,284	9,799
APPLIED DESIGN	13,285	13,277
ADVERTISING	15,811	28,351
PERFORMING ARTS	20,992	46,899
VISUAL ARTS	3,250	8,804
TOURISM	7,257	7,219
OTHER	14,429	3,264

HIGHEST ESTIMATED # OF ACTORS IN NYC WORKING OUTSIDE THE CREATIVE INDUSTRY

4. THE EMBEDDEDNESS OF NYC'S
CULTURAL INDUSTRIES

ESTIMATED # OF CREATIVE WORKERS IN NYC
OUTSIDE OF THE CREATIVE INDUSTRIES

% CREATIVE WORKERS IN NON-CREATIVE INDUSTRIES

12.21% ARCHITECTS
12.70% ART DIRECTORS
14.42% FINE ARTISTS
18.33% MULTI-MEDIA ARTISTS + ANIMATORS
51.02% COMMERCIAL + INDUSTRIAL DESIGNERS
63.63% FASHION DESIGNERS
33.21% GRAPHIC DESIGNERS
34.02% INTERIOR DESIGNERS
26.17% SET + EXHIBIT DESIGNERS
33.52% ACTORS
13.35% PRODUCERS + DIRECTORS
54.93% DANCERS
78.52% **CHOREOGRAPHERS**
41.08% MUSICIANS + SINGERS
27.55% EDITORS
12.81% WRITERS + AUTHORS
6.06% PHOTOGRAPHERS
12.32% FILM + VIDEO EDITORS

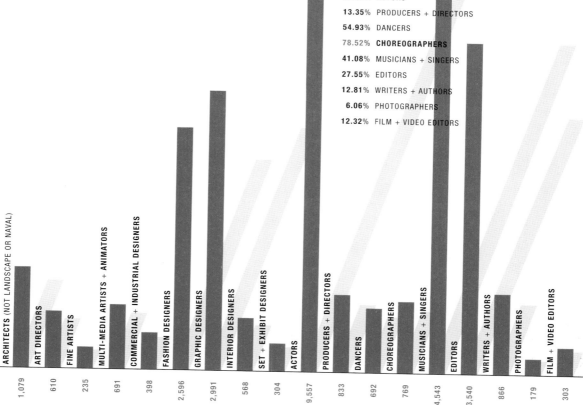

ARCHITECTS (NOT LANDSCAPE OR NAVAL)	ART DIRECTORS	FINE ARTISTS	MULTI-MEDIA ARTISTS + ANIMATORS	COMMERCIAL + INDUSTRIAL DESIGNERS	FASHION DESIGNERS	GRAPHIC DESIGNERS	INTERIOR DESIGNERS	SET + EXHIBIT DESIGNERS	ACTORS	PRODUCERS + DIRECTORS	DANCERS	CHOREOGRAPHERS	MUSICIANS + SINGERS	EDITORS	WRITERS + AUTHORS	PHOTOGRAPHERS	FILM + VIDEO EDITORS
1,079	610	235	691	398	2,596	2,991	568	304	9,557	833	692	769	4,543	3,540	866	179	303

5. TOP 15 **PUBLIC CULTURAL CORPORATIONS**

HEADQUARTERED IN **NEW YORK CITY** AS OF FEBRUARY 2007

COMPANY NAME	INDUSTRY	SALES ($MIL.)	# OF EMPLOYEES
VERIZON COMMUNICATION INC.	TELECOMMUNICATIONS SERVICES, COMPUTER/INTERNET SERVICES, MEDIA	75,112.00	250,000
TIME WARNER INC.	MEDIA (TV + PRINT), COMPUTER SOFTWARE, LEISURE, CABLE/INTERNET PROVIDER, MOTION PICTURE + VIDEO PRODUCTION	43,652.00	87,850
NEWS CORPORATION	MEDIA (TV + PRINT), COMPUTER SOFTWARE, LEISURE, CABLE/INTERNET PROVIDER, MOTION PICTURE + VIDEO PRODUCTION	25,327.00	47,300
AMERICAN EXPRESS COMPANY	FINANCIAL SERVICES, MEDIA	24,267.00	65,800
CONSOLIDATED EDISON INC.	ENERGY, TELECOMMUNICATIONS SERVICES	11,690.00	14,537
OMNICOM GROUP INC.	GLOBAL ADVERTISING	10,481.10	62,000
THE INTERPUBLIC GROUP OF COMPANIES INC.	GLOBAL ADVERTISING + MARKETING	6,274.30	43,000
THE McGRAW-HILL COMPANIES INC.	PUBLISHING	6,003.60	19,600
IAC/INTERACTIVE CORP	CATALOG AND MAIL-ORDER RETAIL (ONLINE CONGLOMERATE)	5,753.70	28,000
BARNES & NOBLE, INC.	BOOK RETAIL + PUBLISHING	5,103.00	39,000
SONY BMG MUSIC ENTERTAINMENT	MUSIC RETAIL + RECORDING	5,000.00	10,000
THE HEARST CORPORATION	PRINT MEDIA + PUBLISHING	4,550.00	17,016
BLOOMBERG L.P.	SYNDICATED NEWS SERVICE, TV + PUBLISHING	4,100.00	8,200
WARNER MUSIC GROUP CORP.	MUSIC RETAIL + RECORDING	3,516.00	4,000
THE NEW YORK TIMES COMPANY	PUBLISHING, INTERNET, TV	3,372.80	11,965

TOP 15 **PUBLIC CULTURAL CORPORATIONS**

HEADQUARTERED IN **LA COUNTY** (INCLUDING LONG BEACH + SANTA ANA) **AS OF FEBRUARY 2007**

COMPANY **NAME**	INDUSTRY	SALES ($MIL.)	# OF **EMPLOYEES**
THE WALT DISNEY COMPANY	MEDIA, MOTION PICTURE + VIDEO PRODUCTION, COMPUTER SOFTWARE, LEISURE, RETAIL, TV BROADCASTING, PUBLISHING, TELECOMMUNICATIONS SERVICES	34,285.00	133,000
THE DIRECTV GROUP INC.	TELECOMMUNICATIONS SERVICES	13,164.50	9,200
KB HOME	CONSTRUCTION, ENGINEERING + ARCHITECTURAL SERVICES	9,441.70	6,700
AECOM TECHNOLOGY CORPORATION	CONSTRUCTION + ARCHITECTURAL SERVICES	3,300.00	26,000
LIVE NATION INC.	LEISURE + ENTERTAINMENT, MEDIA, PRODUCER + PROMOTER OF LIVE ENTERTAINMENT	2,936.80	3,000
QUICKSILVER INC.	SPORTS RETAIL + APPAREL, MOTION PICTURE + VIDEO PRODUCTION, INTERNATIONAL SPORTING EVENTS	2,362.30	7,875
UNIVISION COMMUNICATIONS INC.	TV, MUSIC, RADIO BROADCASTING (MOSTLY TO SPANISH-SPEAKING AUDIENCE)	2,166.60	4,219
WILLIAM LYON HOMES	CONSTRUCTION, INTERIOR DESIGN SERVICES	1,856.00	977
ACTIVISION, INC.	COMPUTER SOFTWARE, ENTERTAINMENT SOFTWARE + GAME PUBLISHING	1,468.00	2,149
METRO-GOLDWYN-MAYER, INC.	MEDIA, MOTION PICTURE + VIDEO PRODUCTION, CABLE SUBSCRIPTION SERVICES	1,430.00	1,440
THQ, INC.	COMPUTER SOFTWARE, ENTERTAINMENT SOFTWARE + GAME PUBLISHING	806.60	1,600
GEMSTAR- TV GUIDE INTERNATIONAL, INC.	MEDIA, PUBLISHING, CABLE + SATELLITE SERVICES	604.20	1,780
UNITED ONLINE, INC.	INTERNET + ONLINE SERVICE PROVIDERS, MEDIA CONTENT PROVIDERS	525.10	900
DREAMWORKS ANIMATION SKG INC.	MEDIA, ANIMATION, MOTION PICTURE + VIDEO PRODUCTION	462.30	1,280
ENTRAVISION COMMUNICATIONS CORPORATION	TV, MUSIC, RADIO BROADCASTING (MOSTLY TO SPANISH-SPEAKING AUDIENCE)	281.00	1,148

TOP 20 **CULTURAL INDUSTRY CORPORATIONS**

HEADQUARTERED IN TOKYO AS OF FEBRUARY 2007 LISTED BY PRIMARY INDUSTRY ACTIVITIES ONLY

COMPANY NAME	INDUSTRY	SALES ($MIL.)	# OF EMPLOYEES
HITACHI, LTD	CONSUMER ELECTRONICS, COMPUTER HARDWARE	80,450.80	306,876
SONY CORPORATION	CONSUMER ELECTRONICS, AUDIO & VIDEO EQUIPMENT, TV, MOTION PICTURE & VIDEO PRODUCTION	63,541.20	158,500
TOSHIBA CORPORATION	CONSUMER ELECTRONICS, COMPUTER HARDWARE, TELECOMMUNICATIONS EQUIPMENT	53,945.20	172,000
MITSUBISHI ELECTRIC CORPORATION	CONSUMER ELECTRONICS, TELECOMMUNICATIONS EQUIPMENT	31,712.50	97,661
KDDI CORPORATION	TELECOMMUNICATIONS & WIRELESS SERVICES	27,150.50	12,373
SOFTBANK CORP.	FINANCIAL, TELECOMMUNICATIONS SERVICES, INTERNET CONTENT & SERVICE PROVIDERS	9,428.10	14,182
PIONEER CORPORATION	CONSUMER ELECTRONICS, TELECOMMUNICATIONS EQUIPMENT	6,347.60	38,826
CASIO COMPUTERS CO., LTD.	CONSUMER ELECTRONICS, TELECOMMUNICATIONS EQUIPMENT	4,934.90	12,673
SEGA SAMMY HOLDINGS INC.	ENTERTAINMENT & GAMES SOFTWARE, LEISURE/ENTERTAINMENT, TOYS & GAMES	4,704.80	6,416
FUJI TELEVISION NETWORK, INC.	TELEVISION CABLE & BROADCAST NETWORKS, FILM & VIDEO, ADVERTISING & MARKETING, TV BROADCASTING	4,432.70	1,354
NIPPON TELEVISION NETWORK, CORP.	TELEVISION CABLE & BROADCAST NETWORKS, FILM & VIDEO, ADVERTISING & MARKETING, TV BROADCASTING	3,325.10	2,869
TOKYO BROADCASTING SYSTEM, INC.	TELEVISION CABLE & BROADCAST NETWORKS, FILM & VIDEO, ADVERTISING & MARKETING, TV BROADCASTING	2,805.50	1,226
KONAMI CORPORATION	ENTERTAINMENT & GAMES SOFTWARE, LEISURE/ENTERTAINMENT	2,231.50	12,218
WILLCOM, INC.	TELECOMMUNICATIONS & WIRELESS SERVICES	1,783.60	875
YAHOO JAPAN CORPORATION	INTERNET AND WEB SEARCH SERVICES PROVIDERS	1,095.10	1,713
SQUARE ENIX CO., LTD.	ENTERTAINMENT & GAMES SOFTWARE	1,058.50	3,050
SHOCHIKU CO., LTD.	MOTION PICTURE & VIDEO PRODUCTION, ADVERTISING & MARKETING	836.20	1,458
UNIDEN CORPORATION	TELECOMMUNICATIONS & WIRELESS SERVICES	729.10	19,496
SKY PERFECT COMMUNICATION INC.	TELECOMMUNICATIONS, TV & CABLE BROADCAST NETWORKS	700.10	468
RAKUTEN, INC.	INTERNET RETAIL CONGLOMERATE	204.30	4,075

GLOBAL CULTURAL CENTERS + CITIES
TOKYO

2. ESTIMATED % OF **CULTURAL ESTABLISHMENTS** IN JAPAN 2004

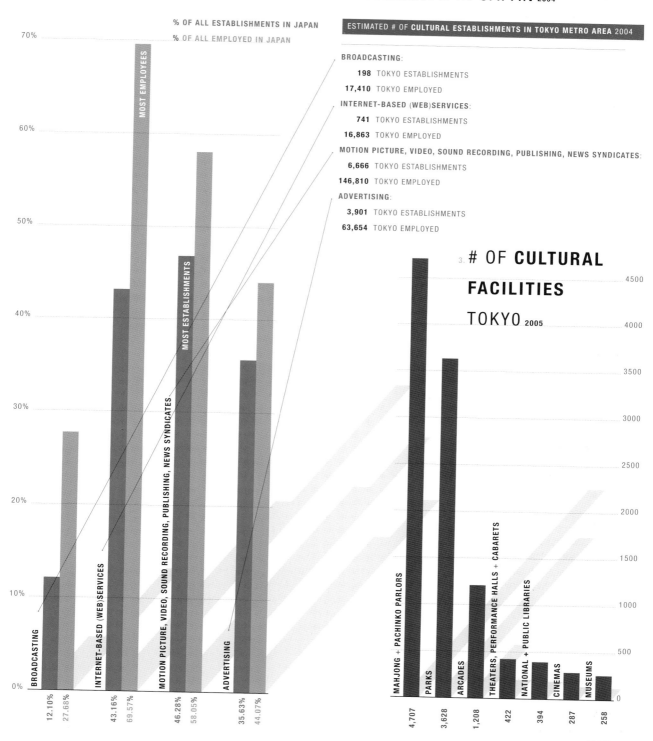

% OF ALL ESTABLISHMENTS IN JAPAN
% OF ALL EMPLOYED IN JAPAN

MOST EMPLOYEES

MOST ESTABLISHMENTS

70%

60%

50%

40%

30%

20%

10%

0%

BROADCASTING — 12.10% — 27.68%
INTERNET-BASED (WEB)SERVICES — 43.16% — 69.57%
MOTION PICTURE, VIDEO, SOUND RECORDING, PUBLISHING, NEWS SYNDICATES — 46.28% — 58.05%
ADVERTISING — 35.63% — 44.07%

ESTIMATED # OF **CULTURAL ESTABLISHMENTS IN TOKYO METRO AREA** 2004

BROADCASTING:
198 TOKYO ESTABLISHMENTS
17,410 TOKYO EMPLOYED

INTERNET-BASED (WEB)SERVICES:
741 TOKYO ESTABLISHMENTS
16,863 TOKYO EMPLOYED

MOTION PICTURE, VIDEO, SOUND RECORDING, PUBLISHING, NEWS SYNDICATES:
6,666 TOKYO ESTABLISHMENTS
146,810 TOKYO EMPLOYED

ADVERTISING:
3,901 TOKYO ESTABLISHMENTS
63,654 TOKYO EMPLOYED

3. # OF **CULTURAL FACILITIES** TOKYO 2005

4500
4000
3500
3000
2500
2000
1500
1000
500
0

MAHJONG + PACHINKO PARLORS — 4,707
PARKS — 3,628
ARCADES — 1,208
THEATERS, PERFORMANCE HALLS + CABARETS — 422
NATIONAL + PUBLIC LIBRARIES — 394
CINEMAS — 287
MUSEUMS — 258

PUBLIC CULTURAL CORPORATIONS HEADQUARTERED IN SINGAPORE

AS OF FEBRUARY 2007

LISTED BY PRIMARY + SECONDARY INDUSTRY ACTIVITIES ONLY; A MAJORITY OF THESE COMPANIES' CULTURAL ENDEAVORS ARE SECONDARY ACTIVITIES

COMPANY NAME	INDUSTRY	SALES ($MIL.)	# OF EMPLOYEES
FRASER AND NEAVE, LIMITED	PUBLISHING	2,527.30	15,134
CREATIVE TECHNOLOGY LTD.	CONSUMER ELECTRONICS	1,127.50	7,780
STARHUB LTD.	TELECOMMUNICATIONS	942.9	2,800
WANT WANT HOLDINGS LTD.	MOTION PICTURE & VIDEO	688.1	20
SINGAPORE PRESS HOLDINGS LIMITED	NEWSPAPER PUBLISHING, INTERNET CONTENT, TV	649	3,540
THAKRAL CORPORATION LTD.	CONSUMER ELECTRONICS, FILM & VIDEO	241.7	1,000
HAW PAR CORPORATION LIMITED	ENTERTAINMENT/LEISURE	72.3	442
FIRST LINK INVESTMENTS CORPORATION LIMITED	CONSUMER ELECTRONICS	27.5	950
GENERAL MAGNETICS LIMITED	FILM & VIDEO	13.3	N/A

NOTE: MANY OF THESE COMPANIES ARE SIMILAR TO THE LIKES OF GENERAL ELECTRIC (USA). THEIR PRIMARY ACTIVITIES AND HOLDINGS ARE IN INDUSTRIAL PRODUCTION (I.E., MINING) AND MANUFACTURING, HOWEVER, THEY MAY OWN THE LARGEST NEWSPAPER OR LARGEST TV STATION IN SINGAPORE.

2. # OF **MAJOR ART COMPANIES**

1995 2000 **2005**

ARTS COMPANIES REFER TO COMPANIES REGISTERED WITH THE ACCOUNTING AND CORPORATE REGULATORY
AUTHORITY AND INCLUDE PERFORMING ARTS COMPANIES, COMMERCIAL ART GALLERIES, ART AUCTIONEERS,
ARTS CONSULTANTS AND MANAGERS

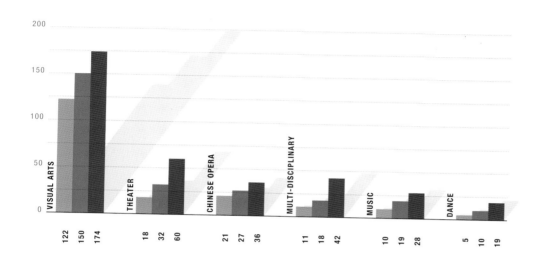

VISUAL ARTS	THEATER	CHINESE OPERA	MULTI-DISCIPLINARY	MUSIC	DANCE
122 150 174	18 32 60	21 27 36	11 18 42	10 19 28	5 10 19

3. ESTIMATED # OF **CREATIVE ESTABLISHMENTS + EMPLOYEES IN SINGAPORE** BY SERVICE INDUSTRY 2004

PUBLISHING SERVICES:

848 SINGAPORE ESTABLISHMENTS
5,845 SINGAPORE EMPLOYED

MOTION PICTURE, RADIO & TV:

513 SINGAPORE ESTABLISHMENTS
6,682 SINGAPORE EMPLOYED

TELECOMMUNICATIONS:

535 SINGAPORE ESTABLISHMENTS
15,067 SINGAPORE EMPLOYED

IT SERVICES:

3,798 SINGAPORE ESTABLISHMENTS
24,143 SINGAPORE EMPLOYED

OTHER INFORMATION SERVICES:

69 SINGAPORE ESTABLISHMENTS
1,645 SINGAPORE EMPLOYED

COMMUNITY + SOCIAL ACTIVITIES:

7,541 SINGAPORE ESTABLISHMENTS
124,664 SINGAPORE EMPLOYED

ARTS, ENTERTAINMENT + RECREATION:

2,673 SINGAPORE ESTABLISHMENTS
22,914 SINGAPORE EMPLOYED

PERSONAL HOUSEHOLD + OTHER:

12,909 SINGAPORE ESTABLISHMENTS
47,678 SINGAPORE EMPLOYED

NOTE: SINGAPORE GOVERNMENT DEFINES
ALL ACTIVITIES WITHIN MANUFACTURING,
RETAIL TRADE, TRANSPORT AND
COMMUNICATION, BUSINESS, REAL ESTATE,
COMMUNITY, SOCIAL AND PERSONAL
ACTIVITIES AS 'SERVICE' INDUSTRIES.
ONLY FINANCIAL AND GOVERNMENT
SERVICES ARE EXCLUDED.

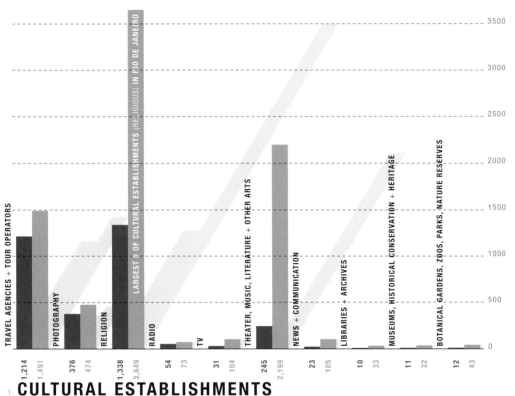

TRAVEL AGENCIES + TOUR OPERATORS

PHOTOGRAPHY

RELIGION

LARGEST # OF CULTURAL ESTABLISHMENTS (RELIGIOUS) IN RIO DE JANEIRO

RADIO

TV

THEATER, MUSIC, LITERATURE + OTHER ARTS

NEWS + COMMUNICATION

LIBRARIES + ARCHIVES

MUSEUMS, HISTORICAL CONSERVATION + HERITAGE

BOTANICAL GARDENS, ZOOS, PARKS, NATURE RESERVES

| 1,214 | 376 | 1,338 | 54 | 31 | 245 | 23 | 10 | 11 | 12 |
| 1,491 | 474 | 3,649 | 73 | 104 | 2,199 | 105 | 33 | 32 | 43 |

1. CULTURAL ESTABLISHMENTS

SÃO PAULO # OF ESTABLISHMENTS BY SECTOR 2007 (OF 206,937 TOTAL)   RIO DE JANEIRO **# OF ESTABLISHMENTS BY SECTOR 2003** (OF 201,422 TOTAL)

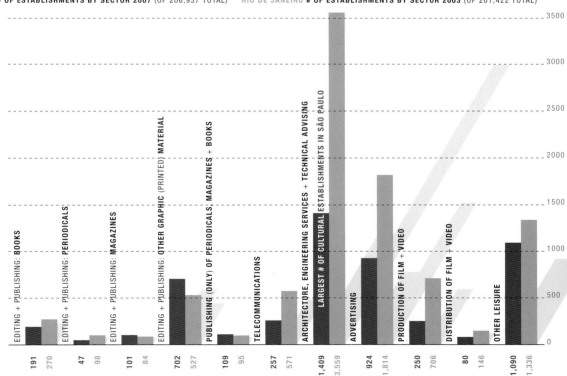

EDITING + PUBLISHING: BOOKS

EDITING + PUBLISHING: PERIODICALS

EDITING + PUBLISHING: MAGAZINES

EDITING + PUBLISHING: OTHER GRAPHIC (PRINTED) MATERIAL

PUBLISHING (ONLY) OF PERIODICALS, MAGAZINES + BOOKS

TELECOMMUNICATIONS

ARCHITECTURE, ENGINEERING SERVICES + TECHNICAL ADVISING

LARGEST # OF CULTURAL ESTABLISHMENTS IN SÃO PAULO

ADVERTISING

PRODUCTION OF FILM + VIDEO

DISTRIBUTION OF FILM + VIDEO

OTHER LEISURE

| 191 | 47 | 101 | 702 | 109 | 257 | 1,409 | 924 | 250 | 80 | 1,090 |
| 270 | 98 | 84 | 527 | 95 | 571 | 3,559 | 1,814 | 706 | 146 | 1,336 |

SÃO PAULO + RIO DE JANEIRO

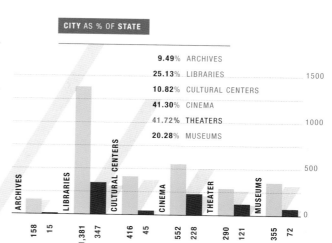

2. CULTURAL INSTITUTIONS

SÃO PAULO

STATE OF SÃO PAULO # OF **INSTITUTIONS** 2003
CITY OF SÃO PAULO # OF **INSTITUTIONS** 2003

CITY AS % OF **STATE**

9.49%	ARCHIVES
25.13%	LIBRARIES
10.82%	CULTURAL CENTERS
41.30%	CINEMA
41.72%	THEATERS
20.28%	MUSEUMS

ARCHIVES: 158 / 15
LIBRARIES: 1,381 / 347
CULTURAL CENTERS: 416 / 45
CINEMA: 552 / 228
THEATER: 290 / 121
MUSEUMS: 355 / 72

HIGHEST # OF CULTURAL INSTITUTIONS ARE SITES OF HISTORIC, CULTURAL, RELIGIOUS + ARTISTIC RELEVANCE

3. # OF **CULTURAL INSTITUTIONS**

RIO DE JANEIRO

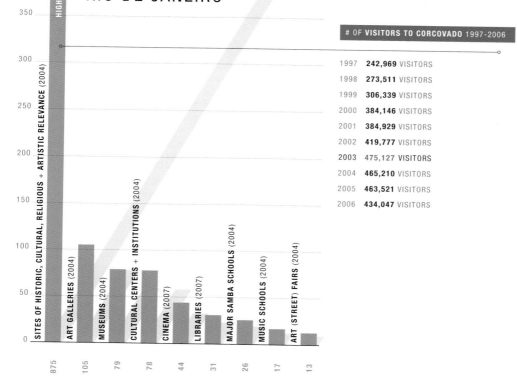

OF **VISITORS TO CORCOVADO** 1997-2006

1997	**242,969**	VISITORS
1998	**273,511**	VISITORS
1999	**306,339**	VISITORS
2000	**384,146**	VISITORS
2001	**384,929**	VISITORS
2002	**419,777**	VISITORS
2003	475,127	VISITORS
2004	**465,210**	VISITORS
2005	**463,521**	VISITORS
2006	**434,047**	VISITORS

SITES OF HISTORIC, CULTURAL, RELIGIOUS + ARTISTIC RELEVANCE (2004): 875
ART GALLERIES (2004): 105
MUSEUMS (2004): 79
CULTURAL CENTERS + INSTITUTIONS (2004): 78
CINEMA (2007): 44
LIBRARIES (2007): 31
MAJOR SAMBA SCHOOLS (2004): 26
MUSIC SCHOOLS (2004): 17
ART (STREET) FAIRS (2004): 13

1. CULTURAL INDUSTRY CORPORATIONS BASED IN JOHANNESBURG

AS OF AUGUST 2007

COMPANY NAME	INDUSTRY	SALES ($MIL.)	# OF EMPLOYEES
NASPERS	MEDIA COMPANY INCLUDING ELECTRONIC AND PRINT MEDIA AND TELEVISION	2,516.20	12,545
MIH HOLDINGS LIMITED*	INTERNET AND TELEVISION SERVICES INCLUDING CABLE AND DIGITAL SATELLITE TV	1,876.67 * *	SEE NASPERS
SAPPI LIMITED	FINE PAPER PRODUCER	4,941.00	15,618 * * *
STEINHOFF INTERNATIONAL HOLDINGS LIMITED	FURNITURE AND OTHER FURNISHINGS MANUFACTURING, PRODUCTION AND DISTRIBUTION	5,016.30	50,000
CLASSIC FM	RADIO BROADCASTING STATIONS	2,842.42	24
INDEPENDENT NEWS AND MEDIA (SOUTH AFRICA) (PTY) LTD.	PRINT MEDIA	2,478.33	140

* A SUBSIDIARY OF NASPERS

* * CONVERTED FROM SA RAND TO USD ON 8/8/07 AT HTTP://WWW.OANDA.COM/CONVERT/CLASSIC; CURRENCY RATE USED: 1 USD/7.05523 ZAR

* * * NUMBER OF EMPLOYEES AS OF 2005

2. MAJOR MEDIA ESTABLISHMENTS BASED IN JOHANNESBURG 2007

JOHANNESBURG IS THE HEADQUARTERS OF SOUTH AFRICA'S MEDIA INDUSTRY

TYPE	ESTABLISHMENTS	TYPE	ESTABLISHMENTS
DAILY NEWSPAPER	THE SOWETAN	NATIONAL WEEKLIES	THE MAIL & GUARDIAN
	THE DAILY SUN		THE SUNDAY INDEPENDENT
	BUSINESS DAY		THE FINANCIAL MAIL
	THE STAR		THE DAILY SUN
	THE CITIZEN		THE SABC
	BEELD	TELEVISION	E.TV
	NOVA		M-NET
	THE SUNDAY TIMES		MULTICHOICE
	CITY PRESS	RADIO STATIONS	94.7 HIGHVELD
	SUNDAY WORLD		94.2 JACARANDA
	RAPPORT		5FM
			702
			CLASSIC FM
			SAFM
			METRO FM
			YFM
			RADIO 2000
			KAYA FM

3. NASPERS

ORGANIZATIONAL TREE

MIH GROUP

SOUTH AFRICA
PAY-TELEVISION
M-NET
SUPERSPORT
INTERNET 6%

INTERNATIONAL
PAY-TELEVISION 57%
SUB-SAHARAN AFRICA
GREECE + CYPRUS
INTERNET
CHINA, THAILAND, RUSSIA
TECHNOLOGY 1%
IRDETO, ENTRIA, MEDIAZONE
PRINT MEDIA
CHINA, BRAZIL

MEDIA24 GROUP

SOUTH AFRICA
NEWSPAPERS + MAGAZINES 25%
PRINTING + DISTRIBUTION 6%
PUBLISHERS + AGENTS
PRIVATE EDUCATION 3%
DIGITAL

4. CULTURAL ATTRACTIONS

AUG. 2007

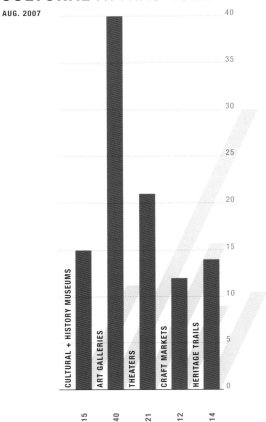

CULTURAL + HISTORY MUSEUMS — 15
ART GALLERIES — 40
THEATERS — 21
CRAFT MARKETS — 12
HERITAGE TRAILS — 14

CHINESE CULTURAL CORPORATIONS BASED IN BEIJING

BEIJING BASED **COMPANIES + OVERVIEW**:	**KEY INFORMATION**:	**KEY NUMBERS**:		**TOP COMPETITORS**:
BAIDU WHICH MEANS A 'HUNDRED TIMES,' IS THE SECOND LARGEST CHINESE-LANGUAGE INTERNET SEARCH ENGINE WITH AN INDEX OF SOME 1.2 BILLION PAGES. IT ALSO HOSTS A SERIES OF SERVICES, INCLUDING NEWS, MP3, AND IMAGE SEARCH.	COMPANY TYPE: PUBLIC - NASDAQ (GM): BIDU SINGLE LOCATION	FISCAL YEAR-END 2006 SALES (MIL.) 2006 NET INCOME (MIL.) 2005 EMPLOYEES	DEC. $107.4 $ 38.7 1307	- SINA - SOHU.COM - TOM ONLINE
KONGZHONG ONE OF THE LEADING PROVIDERS OF INTERACTIVE ENTER-TAINMENT SERVICES FOR WIRELESS DEVICES IN CHINA. IT OFFERS GAMES, PICTURES, KARAOKE, ELECTRONIC BOOKS, MOBILE PHONE PERSONALIZATION FEATURES, INSTANT MESSAGING, AS WELL AS NEWS AND OTHER MEDIA CONTENT. KONGZHONG IS THE TOP WVAS (WIRELESS VALUE ADDED SERVICES) PROVIDER TO CHINA MOBILE AND CHINA NETCOM.	COMPANY TYPE: PUBLIC - NASDAQ (GM): KONG [ADR] HEADQUARTERS	FISCAL YEAR-END 2006 SALES (MIL.) 2006 NET INCOME (MIL.) 2005 EMPLOYEES	DEC. $106.8 $ 24.7 855	- SINA - SOHU.COM - TOM ONLINE
NETEASE THE COMPANY'S WEB PORTAL OFFERS ONLINE COMMUNICATION AND E-COMMERCE SERVICES, AS WELL AS CONTENT CHANNELS TARGETING USERS IN MAINLAND CHINA. NETEASE IS ALSO ACTIVE IN ONLINE GAME DEVELOPMENT, WITH POPULAR TITLES SUCH AS WESTWARD JOURNEY ONLINE II AND FANTASY WESTWARD JOURNEY.	COMPANY TYPE: PUBLIC - NASDAQ (GS): NTES [ADR]	FISCAL YEAR-END 2006 SALES (MIL.) 2006 NET INCOME (MIL.) 2005 EMPLOYEES	DEC. $277.3 $159.3 1601	- SINA - SOHU.COM - TOM ONLINE
SOHU SOHU.COM (SOHU MEANS 'SEARCH FOX') OPERATES CHINA'S LEADING WEB PORTAL AND OFFERS COMMUNICATION TOOLS SUCH AS E-MAIL AND INSTANT MESSAGING, AND MORE THAN 30 CONTENT CHANNELS COVERING NEWS, SPORTS, BUSINESS, AND OTHER TOPICS. SOHU ALSO OPERATES WEB-SITES DEVOTED TO ALUMNI COMMUNITIES, GAMING, AND REAL ESTATE.	COMPANY TYPE: PUBLIC - NASDAQ (GS): SOHU HEADQUARTERS	FISCAL YEAR-END 2006 SALES (MIL.) 2006 NET INCOME (MIL.) 2005 EMPLOYEES	DEC. $134.2 $ 25.9 1634	- BAIDU.COM - SINA
TOM ONLINE IS VYING WITH SOHU.COM AND SINA FOR SOME CYBERSPACE. THE COMPANY OPERATES A CHINESE INTERNET PORTAL, AS WELL AS WIRE-LESS SERVICES FIRM BEIJING LEI TING (LTWIJI). TOM ONLINE PROVIDES MESSAGING SERVICES AS WELL AS DOWNLOADABLE NEWS HEADLINES, SPORTS INFORMATION, GAMES, AND RING TONES THROUGH ITS WIRELESS OPERATIONS. TOM ONLINE ALSO EARNS REVENUE THROUGH ADVERTISING, COMPUTER HARDWARE SALES, E-COMMERCE FEES, AND E-MAIL SERVICES. THE COMPANY IS THE INTERNET HOLDINGS OF HONG KONG-BASED MEDIA FIRM TOM GROUP LIMITED (PREVIOUSLY TOM.COM).	COMPANY TYPE: PUBLIC - NASDAQ (GS): TOMO [ADR]	FISCAL YEAR-END 2005 SALES (MIL.) 2006 NET INCOME (MIL.) 2005 EMPLOYEES	DEC. $172.1 $ 45.0 1037	- NET EASE - SINA - SOHU
XINHUA FINANCE MEDIA UNLIMITED XINHUA FINANCE MEDIA, A SUB-SID-IARY OF XINHUA FINANCE, IS A BUSINESS SERVICES PROVIDER, BUSINESS PUBLISHER, AND BROADCASTER IN CHINA. ITS CORE ADVERTISING AND MARKETING RESEARCH BUSINESS PLACES PRINT, TV, AND BILLBOARD ADS FOR SUCH GLOBAL CLIENTS AS MINDSHARE AND CARAT. XINHUA ALSO PUBLISHES PRINT PERIODICALS, PRODUCES AND BROADCASTS TELEVISION AND RADIO SHOWS.	COMPANY TYPE: PUBLIC - NASDAQ (GM): XFML [ADR]	FISCAL YEAR-END 2006 SALES (MIL.) 2006 NET INCOME (MIL.) 2005 EMPLOYEES	DEC. $ 59.0 $ 3.3 623	- AMERICAN ASSOCIATION OF ADVERTISING AGENCIES - CNN - REUTERS
HUI CONG INTERNATIONAL INFORMATION CO. PRODUCES BUSINESS INFOR-MATION IN CHINA, PRINTS TRADE JOURNALS, OFFERS MARKET RESEARCH SERVICES, PROVIDES TELEVISION ADVERTISEMENT MARKETING, AND PRO-VIDES BUSINESS INFORMATION ONLINE. THE COMPANY BOASTS MORE THAN 20 BRANCHES, 1 MILLION CLIENTS, AND 10 MILLION INFORMATION USERS.	COMPANY TYPE: PRIVATE-ASSOCIATION SINGLE LOCATION	N/A		N/A

2. CHINESE CULTURAL CORPORATIONS BASED IN SHANGHAI

AS REPORTED ON HOOVERS.COM

SHANGHAI BASED COMPANIES + OVERVIEW:	KEY INFORMATION:	KEY NUMBERS:		TOP COMPETITORS:
ACOM INTERNATIONAL INC. THE COMPANY OPERATES CHINA'S LARGEST – IN TERMS OF REVENUE AND AIRTIME – TV DIRECT SALES BUSINESS. IT AIRS PROGRAMS THAT ARE, ON AVERAGE, FIVE TO TEN MINUTES IN LENGTH ON FOUR NATIONWIDE CHINA CENTRAL TELEVISION (CCTV) CHANNELS, 28 NATIONAL SATELLITE TV CHANNELS, FOUR INTERNATIONAL SATELLITE CHANNELS OPERATING IN CHINA, AND EIGHT LOCAL CHANNELS.	COMPANY TYPE: PUBLIC - NYSE: ATV [ADR]	FISCAL YEAR-END 2006 SALES (MIL.) 2006 NET INCOME (MIL.) 2005 EMPLOYEES	DEC. $196.5 $ 3.9 1768	- ALIBABA - AVON - E-BAY
SHANDA INTERACTIVE ENTERTAINMENT LIMITED ONE OF THE LARGEST OPERATORS OF ONLINE GAMES IN CHINA, SHANDA INTERACTIVE ENTERTAINMENT NETWORK OFFERS POPULAR CHINESE GAMES SUCH AS THE LEGEND OF MIR II AND THE WORLD OF LEGEND (ALSO KNOWN AS WOOOL) THROUGH ITS SHANDA NETWORKING BUSINESS.	COMPANY TYPE: PUBLIC - NASDAQ (GS): SNDAQ	FISCAL YEAR-END 2006 SALES (MIL.) 2006 NET INCOME (MIL.) 2005 EMPLOYEES	DEC. $211.9 $ 67.8 2392	- ELECTRON ARTS - SONY ONLINE ENTERTAINMENT - TOM ONLINE
SINA CORPORATION THIS COMPANY OFFERS THE WORLD A NEW WEB LANGUAGE – CHINESE. SINA CORPORATION (PREVIOUSLY SINA.COM) OPERATES FOUR CHINESE-LANGUAGE WEB PORTALS SERVING CHINA, HONG KONG, TAIWAN, AND CHINESE SPEAKERS IN NORTH AMERICA, AND HAS MORE THAN 200 MILLION REGISTERED USERS. SINA ALSO OFFERS SUBSCRIPTION-BASED CONTENT, SINA MOBILE (WIRELESS SERVICES), SINA E-COMMERCE (ONLINE SHOPPING), AND SINA.NET (SEARCH, E-MAIL, BUSINESS LISTINGS, MARKETING, AND E-COMMERCE TO BUSINESS AND GOVERNMENT AGENCIES.	COMPANY TYPE: PUBLIC - NASDAQ (GS): SINA	FISCAL YEAR-END 2006 SALES (MIL.) 2006 NET INCOME (MIL.) 2005 EMPLOYEES	DEC. $212.9 $ 39.9 1900	- NETEASE - SOHU.COM - YAHOO
THE9 LIMITED THE EXPRESS TRAIN TO ONLINE GAMING IN CHINA IS CALLED THE9. ITS GAMING WEB SITE OFFERS UP MASSIVELY MULTIPLAYER ONLINE ROLE-PLAYING GAMES (MMORPGs). THE9 HAS AN EXCLUSIVE LICENSE TO OPERATE WORLD OF WARCRAFT (WOW), A 3-D MMORPG DEVELOPED BY BLIZZARD ENTERTAINMENT (THE GAME STUDIO OF VIVENDI GAMES), IN CHINA.	COMPANY TYPE: PUBLIC - NASDAQ (GM): NCTY SINGLE LOCATION	FISCAL YEAR-END 2006 SALES (MIL.) 2006 NET INCOME (MIL.) 2005 EMPLOYEES	DEC. $126.3 $ 40.0 854	- NETEASE.COM - SHANDA INTERACTIVE ENTERTAINMENT LIMITED - SINA

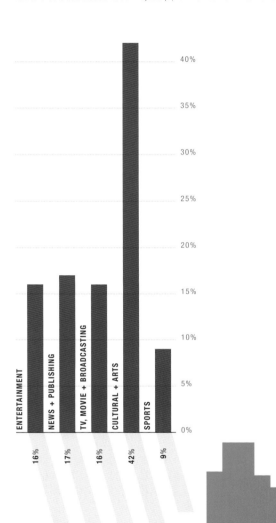

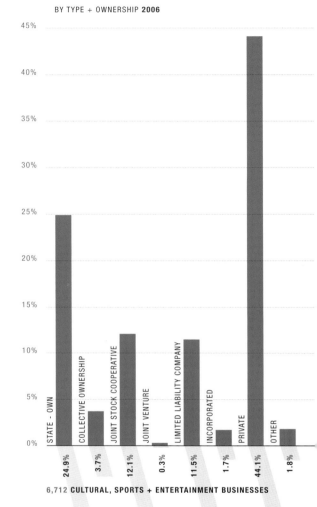

3. BEIJING: **CULTURAL**, **SPORTS** + **ENTERTAINMENT BUSINESS**

TOTAL # OF BUSINESSES 2006 = **6,850** (6,712 DOMESTIC + 138 FOREIGN)

ENTERTAINMENT — 16%
NEWS + PUBLISHING — 17%
TV, MOVIE + BROADCASTING — 16%
CULTURAL + ARTS — 42%
SPORTS — 9%

4. BEIJING: BREAKDOWN OF **DOMESTIC BUSINESS**

BY TYPE + OWNERSHIP **2006**

STATE - OWN — **24.9%**
COLLECTIVE OWNERSHIP — **3.7%**
JOINT STOCK COOPERATIVE — **12.1%**
JOINT VENTURE — **0.3%**
LIMITED LIABILITY COMPANY — **11.5%**
INCORPORATED — **1.7%**
PRIVATE — **44.1%**
OTHER — **1.8%**

6,712 CULTURAL, SPORTS + ENTERTAINMENT BUSINESSES

5. SHANGHAI: # OF **CINEMAS + THEATERS + PERFORMANCE GROUPS** 2000 - 2005

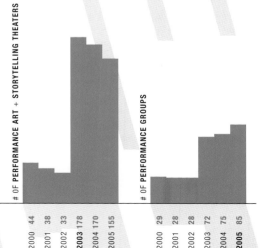

OF CINEMAS
2000 242
2001 273
2002 273
2003 238
2004 225
2005 193

OF PERFORMANCE ART + STORYTELLING THEATERS
2000 44
2001 38
2002 33
2003 178
2004 170
2005 155

OF PERFORMANCE GROUPS
2000 29
2001 28
2002 28
2003 72
2004 75
2005 85

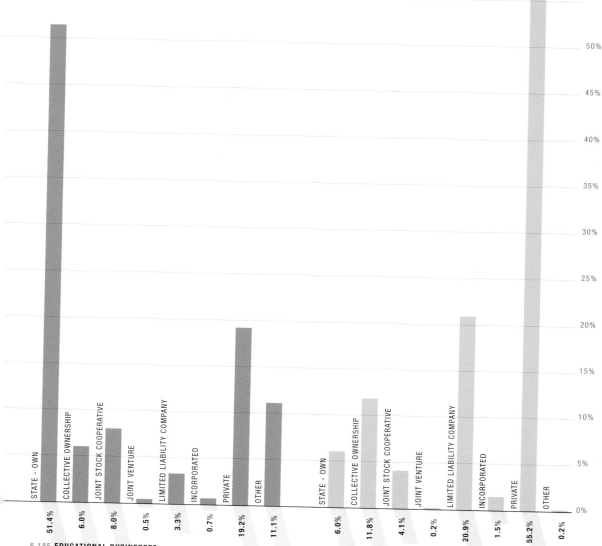

STATE - OWN **51.4%**
COLLECTIVE OWNERSHIP **6.0%**
JOINT STOCK COOPERATIVE **8.0%**
JOINT VENTURE **0.5%**
LIMITED LIABILITY COMPANY **3.3%**
INCORPORATED **0.7%**
PRIVATE **19.2%**
OTHER **11.1%**

6,185 **EDUCATIONAL BUSINESSES**

STATE - OWN **6.0%**
COLLECTIVE OWNERSHIP **11.8%**
JOINT STOCK COOPERATIVE **4.1%**
JOINT VENTURE **0.2%**
LIMITED LIABILITY COMPANY **20.9%**
INCORPORATED **1.5%**
PRIVATE **55.2%**
OTHER **0.2%**

8,287 **ARCHITECTURAL BUSINESSES**

525

GLOBAL CULTURAL CENTERS + CITIES

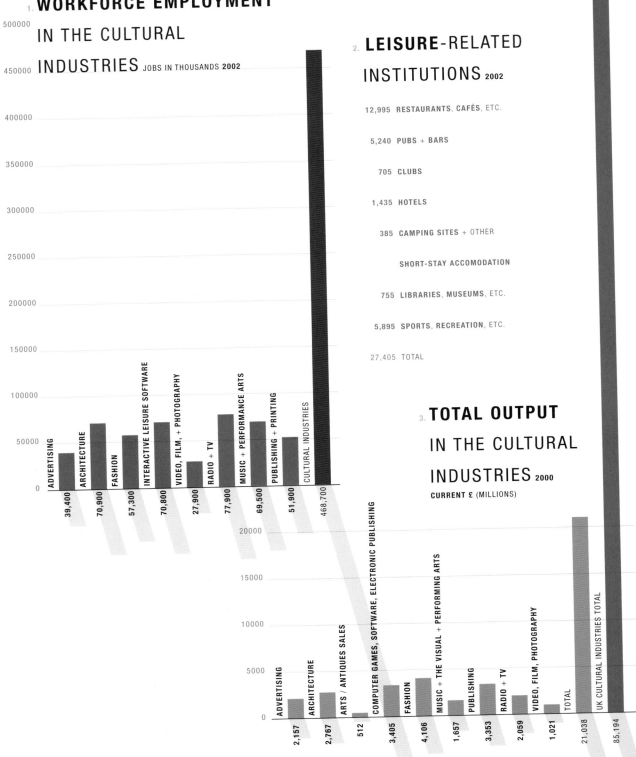

1. WORKFORCE EMPLOYMENT IN THE CULTURAL INDUSTRIES JOBS IN THOUSANDS 2002

- ADVERTISING — 39,400
- ARCHITECTURE — 70,900
- FASHION — 57,300
- INTERACTIVE LEISURE SOFTWARE — 70,800
- VIDEO, FILM, + PHOTOGRAPHY — 27,900
- RADIO + TV — 77,900
- MUSIC + PERFORMANCE ARTS — 69,500
- PUBLISHING + PRINTING — 51,900
- CULTURAL INDUSTRIES — 468,700

2. LEISURE-RELATED INSTITUTIONS 2002

- 12,995 RESTAURANTS, CAFÉS, ETC.
- 5,240 PUBS + BARS
- 705 CLUBS
- 1,435 HOTELS
- 385 CAMPING SITES + OTHER SHORT-STAY ACCOMODATION
- 755 LIBRARIES, MUSEUMS, ETC.
- 5,895 SPORTS, RECREATION, ETC.
- 27,405 TOTAL

3. TOTAL OUTPUT IN THE CULTURAL INDUSTRIES 2000 CURRENT £ (MILLIONS)

- ADVERTISING — 2,157
- ARCHITECTURE — 2,767
- ARTS / ANTIQUES SALES — 512
- COMPUTER GAMES, SOFTWARE, ELECTRONIC PUBLISHING — 3,405
- FASHION — 4,106
- MUSIC + THE VISUAL + PERFORMING ARTS — 1,657
- PUBLISHING — 3,353
- RADIO + TV — 2,059
- VIDEO, FILM, PHOTOGRAPHY — 1,021
- TOTAL — 21,038
- UK CULTURAL INDUSTRIES TOTAL — 85,194

LONDON

4. AVERAGE WEEKLY **HOUSEHOLD** **EXPENDITURE** ON **RECREATION + CULTURE**[1]

£ PER WEEK **2001/02**

1 DATA ARE USUALLY AGGREGATED OVER MORE THAN ONE YEAR, BUT BECAUSE OF THE MOVE TO THE NEW COICOP CLASSIFICATION FOR EXPENDITURE, THESE DATA RELATE ONLY TO THE 2001/02 SURVEY. IN CONSEQUENCE SAMPLE SIZES ARE SMALL AND DATA SHOULD BE TREATED WITH CAUTION.
2 EXCLUDES TAKE-AWAY MEALS EATEN AT HOME

	LONDON	UNITED KINGDOM
AUDIO-VISUAL, PHOTOGRAPHIC + INFORMATION EQUIPMENT	10.5	8.0
- AUDIO EQUIPMENT AND ACCESSORIES, CD PLAYERS	3.6	3.0
- TV, VIDEO + COMPUTERS	6.0	4.5
- PHOTOGRAPHIC + CINEMATOGRAPHIC EQUIPMENT	1.0	0.5
- OPTICAL INSTRUMENTS, BINOCULARS, TELESCOPES, MICROSCOPES	–	0.1
OTHER MAJOR DURABLES FOR RECREATION + CULTURE	0.5	1.5
OTHER RECREATIONAL ITEMS + EQUIPMENT, GARDENS + PETS	7.1	9.5
- GAMES, TOYS + HOBBIES	2.1	2.1
- COMPUTER SOFTWARE + GAMES	0.5	1.0
- EQUIPMENT FOR SPORT, CAMPING + OPEN-AIR RECREATION	0.7	1.0
- HORTICULTURAL GOODS, GARDEN EQUIPMENT AND PLANTS ETC.	2.2	2.6
- PETS + PET FOOD	1.5	2.7
RECREATIONAL + CULTURAL SERVICES	18.1	16.3
- SPORTS ADMISSIONS, SUBSCRIPTIONS + LEISURE CLASS FEES	6.5	5.0
- CINEMA, THEATER + MUSEUMS ETC.	2.2	1.7
- TV, VIDEO, SATELLITE RENTAL, CABLE SUBSCRIPTIONS, TV LICENSES	5.0	4.7
- MISCELLANEOUS ENTERTAINMENT	1.1	0.9
- DEVELOPMENT OF FILM, DEPOSIT FOR FILM DEVELOPMENT, PASSPORT PHOTOS	0.5	0.4
- GAMBLING PAYMENTS	2.8	3.7
NEWSPAPERS, BOOKS + STATIONERY	7.4	6.2
- BOOKS, DIARIES, ADDRESS BOOKS, CARDS ETC.	4.5	3.3
- NEWSPAPERS	1.8	1.8
- MAGAZINES + PERIODICALS	1.1	1.0
PACKAGE HOLIDAYS	9.5	12.5
- PACKAGE HOLIDAYS - UNITED KINGDOM	0.7	0.7
- PACKAGE HOLIDAYS - ABROAD	8.8	11.7
EATING AWAY FROM HOME	22.0	15.0
- RESTAURANT + CAFÉ MEALS	15.4	10.9
- TAKE-AWAY FOOD + SNACK FOOD[2]	6.6	4.1

5. **TOP TOURIST ATTRACTIONS** 2001

BY # OF VISITORS

315 THOUSAND	MUSEUM OF LONDON
317 THOUSAND	BRITISH LIBRARY EXHIBITION GALLERIES
400 THOUSAND	PHOTOGRAPHERS GALLERY
410 THOUSAND	NATIONAL MARITIME MUSEUM
441 THOUSAND	SERPENTINE GALLERY
638 THOUSAND	IMPERIAL WAR MUSEUM
838 THOUSAND	SAINT PAUL'S CATHEDRAL
907 THOUSAND	LONDON ZOO
910 THOUSAND	ROYAL ACADEMY
986 THOUSAND	WESTMINSTER ABBEY
1,012 THOUSAND	TATE BRITAIN
1,270 THOUSAND	NATIONAL PORTRAIT GALLERY
1,353 THOUSAND	SCIENCE MUSEUM
1,446 THOUSAND	VICTORIA + ALBERT MUSEUM
1,696 THOUSAND	NATURAL HISTORY MUSEUM
2,019 THOUSAND	TOWER OF LONDON
3,552 THOUSAND	TATE MODERN
3,850 THOUSAND	BRITISH AIRWAY LONDON EYE
4,801 THOUSAND	BRITISH MUSEUM
4,919 THOUSAND	NATIONAL GALLERY

## 6

15 NOTABLE CULTURAL CORPORATIONS HEADQUARTERED IN LONDON

AS OF AUGUST 2007 ADAPTED FROM HOOVERS.COM

COMPANY **NAME**/TYPE/STOCK EXCHANGE LISTING/PRIMARY INDUSTRIES	SALES ($MIL)	# EMPLOYEES	DESCRIPTION
BT GROUP PLC PUBLIC NYSE:BT; LONDON:BTA TELECOMMUNICATIONS	39,600.70	106,200	UK'S LEADING TELECOMMUNICATIONS CARRIER.
REED ELSEVIER GROUP PLC PRIVATE (JOINT VENTURE - UK & DUTCH) PUBLISHING (PERIODICALS, MAGAZINES + BOOKS), ADVERTISING	10,018.20	36,800	THE FIRM'S LEGAL PUBLISHING OPERATIONS FALL UNDER THE LEXISNEXIS BANNER, OFFERING ONLINE, CD-ROM, AND HARD COPY LEGAL, CORPORATE, AND GOVERNMENT INFORMATION. ITS ELSEVIER UNIT PUBLISHES SCIENTIFIC, TECHNICAL, AND MEDICAL INFORMATION.
BRITISH SKY BROADCASTING GROUP PLC PUBLIC NYSE:BSY; LONDON:BSY TELECOMMUNICATIONS, CABLE + SATELLITE SERVICES, CABLE TV + BROADCAST SERVICES	9,119.80	11,216	BRITISH SKY BROADCASTING GROUP (BSKYB) IS THE UK'S #1 PAY-TV PROVIDER. HOLDS BROADCAST RIGHT TO LEADING FOOTBALL (SOCCER) LEAGUES IN ENGLAND AND SCOTLAND. TO BOOST BRAND AWARENESS, BSKYB BROADCASTS THREE CHANNELS - SKY NEWS, SKY SPORTS NEWS, AND SKY TRAVEL. RUPERT MURDOCH'S NEWS CORP. OWNS 38% OF BSKYB, AND MURDOCH'S SON IS CEO.
BRITISH BROADCASTING CORPORATION PRIVATE - GOVERNMENT TV + RADIO BROADCASTING, TV + RADIO STATIONS, MEDIA + TELECOMMUNICATIONS	6,966.70	25,377	THE DOMINANT BROADCASTER IN THE UK. THE BBC WORLD SERVICE BROADCASTS RADIO PROGRAMMING IN MORE THAN 30 LANGUAGES AND SUBSIDIARY BBC WORLDWIDE OFFERS INTERNATIONAL TV CHANNELS (BBC PRIME, BBC AMERICA), PROGRAM DISTRIBUTION, AND MAGAZINE PUBLISHING.
EMI GROUP PLC PUBLIC LONDON:EMI MUSIC PRODUCTION + DISTRIBUTION, MEDIA (MUSIC)	3,541.00	5,458	EMI GROUP IS THE #3 MAJOR RECORD COMPANY (BEHIND UNIVERSAL MUSIC GROUP AND SONY BMG). DISTRIBUTES CDS, VIDEOS, AND OTHER MUSIC FORMATS PRIMARILY THROUGH IMPRINTS CAPITOL, EMI RECORDS, AND VIRGIN. ITS EMI MUSIC PUBLISHING, THE WORLD'S LARGEST MUSIC PUBLISHER, HANDLES THE RIGHTS TO OVER A MILLION SONGS.
INFORMA PLC PUBLIC LONDON:INF PUBLISHING (PERIODICALS, MAGAZINES + BOOKS)	2,034.80	7,593	INFORMA (FORMERLY T&F INFORMA) PUBLISHES ACADEMIC, SCIENTIFIC, BUSINESS, AND PROFESSIONAL INFORMATION THROUGH MORE THAN 2,000 ELECTRONIC AND PRINT PUBLICATIONS. ITS PRODUCTS INCLUDE NEWSLETTERS, MAGAZINES, CD-ROMS, AND RESEARCH REPORTS. THE COMPANY ALSO PUBLISHES ABOUT 40,000 BOOK TITLES.
CHANNEL FOUR TELEVISION CORPORATION PRIVATE - GOVERNMENT TV + RADIO BROADCASTING, TV + RADIO STATIONS, MEDIA	1,538.60	889	THIS TV CHANNEL BROADCASTS AN ECLECTIC MIX OF PROGRAMMING, SUCH AS BIG BROTHER AND JAMIE'S SCHOOL DINNERS. THE COMPANY ALSO FINANCES AND DISTRIBUTES FILMS, SELLS TELEVISION PROGRAMS INTERNATIONALLY, OPERATES FOUR DIGITAL TV CHANNELS, AND PROVIDES STUDIO AND PRODUCTION SERVICES.

UNITED BUSINESS MEDIA PLC
PUBLIC
LONDON:UBM
PUBLISHING (PERIODICALS, MAGAZINES
+ BOOKS), ADVERTISING

1,447.30   5,000   AN INFORMATION CLEARINGHOUSE. THE COMPANY'S HOLDINGS INCLUDE HIGH-TECH PUBLISHER CMP MEDIA (INFORMATIONWEEK, GAME DEVELOPER, WINDOWS DEVELOPER NETWORK) AND PR NEWSWIRE.

DAWSON HOLDINGS PLC
PUBLIC
LONDON:DHN
DISTRIBUTION (PRINT MEDIA)

1,406.80   3,026   THE UK'S #3 PRINT MEDIA DISTRIBUTOR (BEHIND #1 WH SMITH AND #2 JOHN MENZIES).

GUARDIAN MEDIA GROUP PLC
PRIVATE
PUBLISHING (MAGAZINES +
PERIODICALS), MEDIA, TV + RADIO
BROADCASTING

1,371.30   7,107   THE COMPANY'S INTERESTS INCLUDE NATIONAL NEWSPAPERS (THE GUARDIAN, THE OBSERVER), REGIONAL NEWSPAPERS (MANCHESTER EVENING NEWS, READING EVENING POSTS), REGIONAL RADIO STATIONS, ONLINE SITES, AND WEEKLY SHOPPER MAGAZINES (AUTOTRADER, BIKE TRADER).

ARUP GROUP LIMITED
PRIVATE - GOVERNMENT
ARCHITECTURAL + ENGINEERING
SERVICES

929.80   6,732   PROVIDES ENGINEERING, ARCHITECTURAL, AND PLANNING SERVICES WORLDWIDE, FOCUSING ON BUILDING, INFRASTRUCTURE, AND CONSULTING PROJECTS. ARUP GROUP'S SERVICE OFFERINGS RANGE FROM ACOUSTICS ENGINEERING (ARUP WORKED ON THE SYDNEY OPERA HOUSE) TO WIND ENGINEERING. ARUP GROUP WORKS IN MORE THAN 30 COUNTRIES WORLDWIDE.

M&C SAATCHI PLC
PUBLIC
LONDON AIM:SAA
ADVERTISING

723.50   880   M&C SAATCHI PROVIDES CREATIVE ADVERTISING AND MARKETING SERVICES TO SUCH CLIENTS AS REUTERS, THAMES WATER, ROYAL BANK OF SCOTLAND, BRITISH AIRWAYS AND GLAXOSMITHKLINE. THE FIRM HAS 13 OFFICES AROUND THE WORLD.

SCI ENTERTAINMENT GROUP PLC
PUBLIC
LONDON:SEG
COMPUTER SOFTWARE DEVELOPMENT
+ SOFTWARE PUBLISHING (ENTERTAIN-
MENT + GAMES)

325.20   900   DESIGNS, LICENSES, AND MARKETS COMPUTER GAME SOFTWARE THROUGH ITS SCI GAMES SUBSIDIARY. THE COMPANY'S GAMES ARE DESIGNED TO BE PLAYED ON SONY PLAYSTATION 2, MICROSOFT XBOX, NINTENDO GAMECUBE, PCS, AND HANDHELD PLATFORMS.

ARSENAL HOLDINGS PLC
PRIVATE
PROFESSIONAL SPORTS TEAM + CLUB

268.70   312   ARSENAL HOLDINGS OWNS AND OPERATES ARSENAL FOOTBALL CLUB, ONE OF THE TOP SOCCER TEAMS IN THE ENGLISH PREMIER LEAGUE. ARSENAL ALSO OWNS THE TEAM'S HOME GROUND AT EMIRATES STADIUM WHERE IT HAS HOSPITALITY OPERATIONS AND RETAIL OUTLETS. MOST OF THE COMPANY'S REVENUE COMES FROM TICKET SALES AND BROADCASTING.

THE SANCTUARY GROUP
PUBLIC
LONDON:SPG
MEDIA (MUSIC), MUSIC PRODUCTION,
TALENT AGENCY + MUSICIAN
PROMOTER

269.80   556   THE SANCTUARY GROUP PROVIDES A BEVY OF PRODUCTS AND SERVICES RELATED TO MUSIC AND MUSICIANS. THE COMPANY'S RECORD PRODUCT DIVISION CONSISTS OF MORE THAN 20 RECORD LABELS AND PRODUCES CDS, DVDS, MUSIC DOWNLOADS, AND RINGTONES.

1. EMPLOYMENT
IN BERLIN's CULTURAL ECONOMY 2005

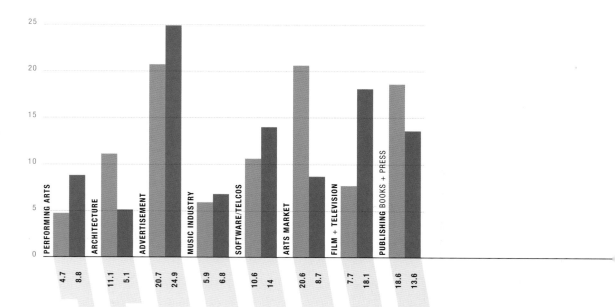

PERFORMING ARTS	4.7 / 8.8
ARCHITECTURE	11.1 / 5.1
ADVERTISEMENT	20.7 / 24.9
MUSIC INDUSTRY	5.9 / 6.8
SOFTWARE/TELCOS	10.6 / 14
ARTS MARKET	20.6 / 8.7
FILM + TELEVISION	7.7 / 18.1
PUBLISHING BOOKS + PRESS	18.6 / 13.6

2. REVENUE GENERATED 2005
PER EMPLOYEE BY SECTOR

THOUSANDS OF EUROS

29.4	PERFORMING ARTS
64.3	ARCHITECTURE
36.2	ADVERTISEMENT
76.2	MUSIC INDUSTRY
237.3	SOFTWARE/TELCOS
103.3	ARTS MARKET
70.4	FILM + TELEVISION
39.1	PUBLISHING BOOKS + PRESS

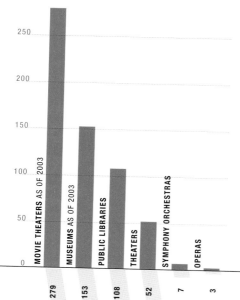

3. CULTURAL INSTITUTIONS 2004

250	
200	
150	
100	
50	
0	

MOVIE THEATERS AS OF 2003 — 279
MUSEUMS AS OF 2003 — 153
PUBLIC LIBRARIES — 108
THEATERS — 52
SYMPHONY ORCHESTRAS — 7
OPERAS — 3

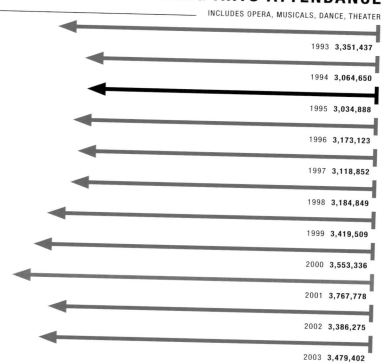

4. PERFORMING ARTS ATTENDANCE

INCLUDES OPERA, MUSICALS, DANCE, THEATER

1993 3,351,437
1994 3,064,650
1995 3,034,888
1996 3,173,123
1997 3,118,852
1998 3,184,849
1999 3,419,509
2000 3,553,336
2001 3,767,778
2002 3,386,275
2003 3,479,402

GLOBAL CULTURAL CENTERS + CITIES

1. PARIS-BASED **CULTURAL INDUSTRY CORPORATIONS** PUBLIC + PRIVATE

AS OF AUGUST 2007

COMPANY NAME	INDUSTRY	**SALES** USD MILLIONS	# OF **EMPLOYEES**
VIVENDI	MEDIA AND TELECOMMUNICATIONS	26,444.0	37,014
PPR S.A.	LUXURY GOODS, FRAGRANCE, FASHION	23,656.2	78,453
LVMH MOET HENNESSY LOUIS VUITTON S.A.	LUXURY GOODS	20,193.2	64,253
PUBLICIS GROUPE S.A.	ADVERTISING + MEDIA SERVICES	5,790.8	39,936
HERMES INTERNATIONAL	FASHION + ACCESSORIES	1,998.6	6,825
EURO DISNEY S.C.A.	TOURISM, RESTAURANTS, SHOPS + LIVE ENTERTAINMENT	1,295.8	12,250
EDITIS	PUBLISHING COMPANY	919.1	2,300
S.T. DUPONT S.A.	LUXURY GOODS, FINE PENS, FRAGRANCE, FASHION, ETC.	101.2	846
GAMELOFT S.A.	VIDEO GAME DEVELOPMENT + PUBLISHING	90.3	1,950
STE NOUV EXPL RENOV RENAIS THEATRE PARIS	THEATRICAL PRODUCTIONS + SERVICES	7.3	82
NEXTRADIO TV	TELEVISION + RADIO MEDIA	47.4	4
HI-MEDIA S.A.	INTERNET MARKETING DESIGN	29.3	82
LAGARDERE S.C.A.	MAGAZINE PUBLISHING + AEROSPACE	18.5	48,245
CHRISTIAN DIOR S.A.	HIGH FASHION	17.2	63,683
ROISSY FILMS	INDEPENDENT FILM + TV DISTRIBUTION	9.1	16
NRJ GROUP	MEDIA, TELEVISION, INTERNET, MOBILE PHONES	5.7	10
AGENCE FRANCE-PRESSE	INTERNATIONAL NEWS AGENCY	NO FIGURES AVAILABLE	
MONDADORI FRANCE	MAGAZINE PUBLISHING		
GROUPE ZANNIER S.A.	CHILDREN'S FASHION		
AGNÉS B	FASHION, COSMETICS + ACCESSORIES		
SIPA PRESS	PHOTOGRAPHY + STORY PUBLISHING		
PATHÉ	FILM PRODUCTION + DISTRIBUTION		

PARIS

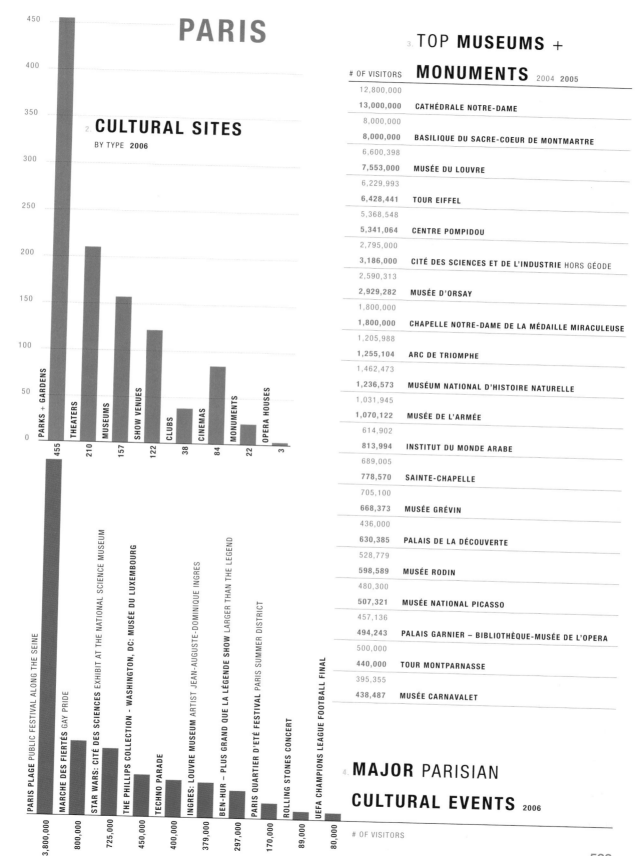

2. CULTURAL SITES
BY TYPE 2006

Type	Count
PARKS + GARDENS	455
THEATERS	210
MUSEUMS	157
SHOW VENUES	122
CLUBS	38
CINEMAS	84
MONUMENTS	22
OPERA HOUSES	3

3. TOP MUSEUMS + MONUMENTS 2004 2005

OF VISITORS

2004	2005	
12,800,000	13,000,000	CATHÉDRALE NOTRE-DAME
8,000,000	8,000,000	BASILIQUE DU SACRE-COEUR DE MONTMARTRE
6,600,398	7,553,000	MUSÉE DU LOUVRE
6,229,993	6,428,441	TOUR EIFFEL
5,368,548	5,341,064	CENTRE POMPIDOU
2,795,000	3,186,000	CITÉ DES SCIENCES ET DE L'INDUSTRIE HORS GÉODE
2,590,313	2,929,282	MUSÉE D'ORSAY
1,800,000	1,800,000	CHAPELLE NOTRE-DAME DE LA MÉDAILLE MIRACULEUSE
1,205,988	1,255,104	ARC DE TRIOMPHE
1,462,473	1,236,573	MUSÉUM NATIONAL D'HISTOIRE NATURELLE
1,031,945	1,070,122	MUSÉE DE L'ARMÉE
614,902	813,994	INSTITUT DU MONDE ARABE
689,005	778,570	SAINTE-CHAPELLE
705,100	668,373	MUSÉE GRÉVIN
436,000	630,385	PALAIS DE LA DÉCOUVERTE
528,779	598,589	MUSÉE RODIN
480,300	507,321	MUSÉE NATIONAL PICASSO
457,136	494,243	PALAIS GARNIER – BIBLIOTHÈQUE-MUSÉE DE L'OPERA
500,000	440,000	TOUR MONTPARNASSE
395,355	438,487	MUSÉE CARNAVALET

4. MAJOR PARISIAN CULTURAL EVENTS 2006

OF VISITORS

Event	# of Visitors
PARIS PLAGE PUBLIC FESTIVAL ALONG THE SEINE	3,800,000
MARCHE DES FIERTÉS GAY PRIDE	800,000
STAR WARS: CITÉ DES SCIENCES EXHIBIT AT THE NATIONAL SCIENCE MUSEUM	725,000
THE PHILLIPS COLLECTION - WASHINGTON, DC: MUSÉE DU LUXEMBOURG	450,000
TECHNO PARADE	400,000
INGRES: LOUVRE MUSEUM ARTIST JEAN-AUGUSTE-DOMINIQUE INGRES	379,000
BEN-HUR – PLUS GRAND QUE LA LÉGENDE SHOW LARGER THAN THE LEGEND	297,000
PARIS QUARTIER D'ETÉ FESTIVAL PARIS SUMMER DISTRICT	170,000
ROLLING STONES CONCERT	89,000
UEFA CHAMPIONS LEAGUE FOOTBALL FINAL	80,000

GLOBAL CULTURAL CENTERS & CITIES

In every period of human history cities have been centers of information, communication, economic activities and trade as well as loci of political power and cultural influence. The distinct urban cultures of cities like New York, Paris, Tokyo, and Rio de Janeiro, to name but a few, have long given them strong transnational influence as centers of cultural distinction, creativity and innovation.

The term 'global city,' first coined by Saskia Sassen (1991), emerged from the ways in which under globalization certain cities take on a multitude of characteristics and roles linking them to other global metropolises. It is therefore not the scale of urban agglomerations themselves that matters for global city status, but the multi-functionality of cities as global centers of trade, commerce, politics, and culture that sets them apart (Scott, 2001). The table below illustrates some of the multiplicities that characterize the world's most significant cities. It is interesting to note that while there are select cities (e.g., Paris, New York, London, and Tokyo) which occupy the top slots in multiple categories, the last column indicates that lesser known Asian and African cities will gain prominence in years to come.

What sets the current period apart from the nineteenth century, when many of today's global cities became more transnational, is the change in global connectedness. Innovations in technology and the Internet make it possible for connections to happen at greater speed and with greater volume and frequency, resulting in complex flows of goods, services, capital, people, and information. While some have theorized that greater global connectivity signals a kind of 'death of geography' in a digital age, Andy Pratt and Allen Scott (cf. their chapters in this volume) maintain that 'place matters even more' with regard to the specialization of the creative industries in cities or city-regions, which help to concentrate local culture, aesthetics, knowledge, infrastructure and inputs while simultaneously creating links to new consumers and producers worldwide. This effect can be seen in the monopoly of Hollywood, now threatened by the emerging film industries of Bollywood and Nollywood (cf. the digest on Film in this volume). Indeed, in recent years, this specialization can also be seen through trends in city branding and product differentiation strategies, and the efforts of international organizations, such as UNESCO, to promote the cultural industries unique to select cities (see UNESCO's Creative Cities Network, next page).

RANK	LARGEST URBAN AGGLOMERATION 2006 millions	GROSS METROPOLITAN PRODUCT GDP in $US billions	CITIES WITH OVER 1 MILLION FOREIGN-BORN % of pop.	MOST EXPENSIVE CITIES Ranked	NO. OF FORTUNE GLOBAL 500 COMPANIES 2006	# OF INGO & IGO SECRETARIATS BASED IN CITY 2004	FASTEST GROWING URBAN AREA Av. annual growth 2006 to 2020
1	Tokyo (35.53)	Tokyo (1,191)	Dubai (83%)	Moscow	Tokyo (52)	Brussels (3088)	Beihai, China (10.58%)
2	Mexico City (19.24)	New York (1,133)	Toronto (44.9%)	London	Paris (27)	Paris (1965)	Ghaziabad, India (5.20%)
3	Mumbai (18.84)	Los Angeles (639)	Hong Kong (38%)	Seoul	New York (24)	London (1569)	Sana'a, Yemen (5.00%)
4	New York (18.65)	Chicago (460)	Miami (36.5%)	Tokyo	London (23)	Washington DC (1107)	Surat, India (4.99%)
5	São Paulo (18.61)	Paris (460)	Los Angeles (34.7%)	Hong Kong	Beijing (15)	New York (1092)	Kabul, Afghanistan (4.74%)
6	Delhi (16.00)	London (452)	Riyadh (34%)	Copenhagen	Seoul (9)	Geneva (962)	Bamako, Mali (4.45%)
7	Calcutta (14.57)	Osaka/Kobe (341)	Sydney (31.2%)	Geneva	Toronto (8)	Rome (874)	Lagos, Nigeria (4.44%)
8	Jakarta (13.67)	Mexico City (315)	San Francisco (29.5%)	Osaka	Madrid (7)	Tokyo (463)	Faridabad, India (4.44%)
9	Buenos Aires (13.52)	Philadelphia (312)	Melbourne (28.5%)	Zürich	Zürich (7)	Vienna (451)	Dar es Salaam, Tanza
10	Dhaka (13.09)	Washington DC (299)	New York (27.9%)	Oslo	Houston (6)	Strasbourg (407)	Chittagong, Banglade

SOURCES: Union of International Associations, 2005; Migration Policy Institute (n.d.); City Mayors, 2007; Fortune, 2006.

CITIES OF CRAFT AND FOLK ART
Aswan, Egypt; Santa Fe, New Mexico, USA

CITIES OF DESIGN
Berlin, Germany; Buenos Aires, Argentina;
Montreal, Canada

CITY OF GASTRONOMY
Popayan, Colombia

CITY OF LITERATURE
Edinburgh, UK

CITIES OF MUSIC
Bologna, Italy; Seville, Spain

SOURCE: UNESCO, 2007

Despite the argument that greater connectivity creates opportunities for new competitors to usurp the positions of traditionally prominent cities, globalization does not necessarily speed up the process by which such competitors may arise for it also can serve to perpetuate the domination (through market concentration) of some locations (e.g., the North) over others (e.g., the South). In this way, Reis and Davis (cf. their chapters in this volume) argue, greater connectivity and technology sometimes gives the 'appearance' of new opportunities.

Globalization intensifies diversity and differentiation among populations, producing polymorphous and variegated urban cultures. Such cultures can enrich and strengthen cities, but they can also exclude and be a source of social and cultural divisions at the regional and global levels. Managing these issues and the potential conflicts they harbor goes beyond the capacity of conventional urban planning. The pluralistic, diverse, outward looking and competitive global city requires a new 'multi-cultural literacy' (UN-Habitat, 2004: 6), with a greater role allocated to civil society as a participating actor, and information technology as a new way of communicating with diverse constituencies to achieve greater social accountability of urban planning and governance.

The importance of 'cities' in examining flows of information, knowledge, labor, cultural goods and services highlights the limitations of using the nation-state as the central unit of analysis to learn about global processes, especially with respect to the global cultural economy. Yet, examining cities requires the availability of consistent and comparable statistics, which currently is difficult to amass across such diverse entities. Not only are better statistics needed for learning about cities in general, but more data equally distributed across cities of the North and Global South is essential for furthering understanding about the present and potential changes globalization may have on these locations for years to come.

CITIES HIGHLIGHTED IN THE INDICATOR SUITES
The indicator suite on Global Cultural Centers and Cities attempts to demonstrate the scale and scope of the cultural industries in select cities through the number of establishments, employment, major creative corporations and sectors for each location, significant tourist sites, numbers of cultural institutions, and other unique city features (see individual city indicator suites for more details and data):

NEW YORK & LOS ANGELES
(For statistics on numbers of cultural institutions, see last year's volume.)
- The estimated total number of cultural business establishments is 15,630 for New York and 12,130 for Los Angeles.
- The top three industry sectors for cultural establishments in New York are Applied Design (20.57 per cent), Performing Arts (16.40 per cent) and Libraries & Education (13.75 per cent); whereas in Los Angeles the top three sectors are Independent Artists & Writers (27.97 per cent), Film & Video (18.98 per cent) and Performing Arts (13.49 per cent).
- Of 220,735 creative workers, a majority in New York tend to be employed in Publishing (23 per cent), Performing Arts (21 per cent), Broadcasting (13 per cent) and Advertising (13 per cent); however, this contrasts sharply with that of Los Angeles, where of a total of 218,422 creative workers, almost 40 per cent are employed in the Film & Video industry, followed by Broadcasting and Publishing (both at 10 per cent).
- In New York, 78.57 per cent of choreographers, 63.63 per cent of fashion designers, and 54.93 per cent of dancers are employed in non-creative establishments.
- According to Hoovers.com (an industry and company watch database), the top three public cultural corporations in New York are Verizon Communications, Time Warner and News Corporation. By 2008, this order is expected to change with New Corporation's, recent acquisition of Dow Jones. In Los Angeles, the top three cultural corporations are Walt Disney, DIRECTV Group, and KB Home.

LONDON
- Of a total of 468,700,000 creative workers, 16.62 per cent are employed in Radio and Television as well as in Architecture, and 15.11 per cent are employed in establishments concentrated on Interactive Leisure Software.
- The total output of creative industries in London in 2000 was £21,038 million.
- The top five cultural corporations in London (according to Hoovers.com) are BT Group, Reed Elsevier Group, British Sky Broadcasting Group, EMI Group and Informa plc.
- The breakdown of leisure related institutions in London in 2002 was: restaurants & cafes (12,995), sports & recreation (5,895), pubs/bars (5,240) and hotels (1,435).
- The top tourist attractions (by number of visitors) in London in 2001 were the National Gallery, British Museum, British Airways London Eye, Tate Modern, and Tower of London.

TOKYO & SINGAPORE
- In Japan, there are 123,774 cultural establishments total. Of that, Tokyo is the location of 46.28 per cent of motion picture, video, publishing and news syndicate businesses, as well as 44.07 per cent of advertising establishments, 43.16 per cent of Internet-based services and 27.68 per cent of broadcasting establishments.
- In Singapore, information technology services comprise the largest segment of cultural establishments (3,798) followed by 848 establishments in publishing, motion picture, radio

and television. There are approximately 7,541 establishments related to community and social activities.

- Tokyo is known as the center of production and sales of global consumer electronics, and indeed, in February 2007, hoovers.com listed Hitachi, Sony, Toshiba and Mitsubishi Electric as the top corporations by sales, headquartered in Tokyo. Major Tokyo corporations are also found in television, cable and broadcasting; film and video; telecommunications; and book and video game publishing.
- In Singapore, the measure of the creative sector can be traced to the number of large firms that are involved in the creative industries as secondary activities. For example, Fraser & Neave Ltd. is the top corporation based in Singapore whose primary activities are in the beverage industry; however, this company also owns the *Singapore Times*, the top newspaper for the country.
- In 2005, Tokyo had 4,707 Mahjong & Pachinko parlors, 3,628 parks, 1,208 video arcades, 422 theaters or performance halls, 394 libraries, 287 cinemas and 258 museums.

BEIJING & SHANGHAI

- The types of business that comprise the 6,850 cultural, sports or entertainment establishments in Beijing are related to culture and the arts (42 per cent), followed by television, film and broadcasting (16 per cent), news and publishing (17 per cent), entertainment (16 per cent) and sports (9 per cent).
- 44 per cent of domestic cultural businesses in Beijing are privately owned, and 25 per cent are owned by the state. This situation is reversed with regards to education, where 52 per cent of educational organizations are state-owned, and 19 per cent are privately owned.
- In Shanghai in 2005, there were 236 cinemas, 160 theater groups and 85 performance art groups.
- Internet, online gaming, social networking and entertainment services constitute a majority of the sectors covered by top cultural corporations in both Beijing and Shanghai. In Beijing, Baidu (a Chinese-language Internet search engine company with a net income of US$107.4 million) is the top cultural corporation, and in Shanghai it is Acorn International (a television direct sales business with a net income in 2006 of US$196.5 million).
- Another indication of the growing IT, Internet and entertainment sectors is the types of large foreign companies establishing satellite offices in both cities. Sony, Microsoft, Hilton, Apple, Nike, Dell and Pepsi rank as the largest foreign corporations in Beijing, while IBM and Intel are laying roots in Shanghai.

RIO DE JANEIRO & SÃO PAULO

- Of 206,937 establishments in São Paulo, roughly 4.2 per cent are cultural, whereas in Rio de Janeiro the number of cultural establishments accounts for 8.7 per cent of 201,422 businesses.
- In São Paulo in 2003, there were 15 cultural archives, 347 libraries, 45 cultural centers, 228 cinemas, 121 theaters, and 72 museums. As a whole, the metropolitan area accounts for 25 per cent of all libraries in the state of São Paulo, as well as 41 per cent of all cinemas and theaters, and 20 per cent of all museums.
- In 2004 in Rio de Janeiro, there were 875 sites of historic, cultural or religious relevance; 105 art galleries, 79 museums, 778 cultural centers, and 13 art (street) fairs. In 2007, Rio de Janeiro had 44 cinemas, 31 libraries, 26 major samba

schools (or *blocos*) and 17 music schools.

- Rio de Janeiro city invests in the local Carnival as a tourist attraction and to support the city's vibrant cultural traditions. Although investment in recent years has not returned to 2003 figures, investment has steadily risen from 22,381,000 (Reals$) in 2004 to 23,095,000 in 2007 (approximately US$13 million each year) (Portal Oficial da Prefeitura da Cidade do Rio de Janeiro, 2007).
- In 2007, Johannesburg had 15 cultural and history museums, 40 art galleries, 21 theaters, 12 craft markets and 13 heritage trails.
- Naspers is the most significant cultural corporation head-quartered in Johannesburg. As a major multinational media conglomerate and holding company, Naspers received 72 per cent of its revenues from South Africa. In 2006, its sales reached US$2,516.2 million.
- Over 75 per cent of Naspers revenues come from pay television services and print media (Hoovers.com).

PARIS & BERLIN

- Of 25,780 cultural firms in Berlin 20.7 per cent are related to Advertising, 20.6 per cent in the Arts Market, and 18.6 per cent in Publishing; and of 199,183 workers in cultural firms, the top three sectors for employment are Advertising (24.9 per cent), Film and Television (18.1 per cent), and Software and Technology (14 per cent).
- Workers in the Software and Technology sector in Berlin generate by far the largest amount of revenue compared to any of the other cultural sectors (€237.3 thousand in 2005).
- In 2004, there were 279 cinemas, 153 museums, 108 public libraries, 52 theaters, 7 symphony orchestras and 3 opera institutions in Berlin.
- Luxury goods items, media and entertainment are the major activities of some of the largest cultural corporations in Paris. Vivendi is the largest with sales of US$26,444 million in 2006, followed by PPR SA (formerly Pinault-Printemps-Redoute) with sales of US$23,656.2 million and LVMH Moet Hennessy Louis Vuitton SA with sales of US$20,193.2 million.
- The top visited museums and monuments in Paris in 2004 were: the Cathedral of Notre Dame, the Sacré-Cœur Basilica (Basilica of the Sacred Heart), the Louvre, the Eiffel Tower, and the Pompidou Center.
- In Paris, 2006, there were 455 parks and gardens, 210 theaters, 157 museums, 122 show venues, 84 cinemas, 38 clubs, 22 monuments and 3 opera houses.

CAIRO, TEHRAN & DUBAI

The Middle Eastern cities of Cairo, Tehran and Dubai possess great significance as centers of Arab culture and religion, as well as geopolitical and economic influence. Attempts to cover these cities in the same detail as the others were hindered by a lack of sufficient or recent data, however, some points of interest are detailed below:

- Tehran is the site of 38 per cent of Iran's professional, cultural and technical training facilities (Tehran Municipality Amarnameh 1384, Statistical Report 2005-2006).
- A majority of culturally significant sites and institutions in Tehran surround religion or nature. In 2005-2006, there were 1,091 mosques; 1,001 parks and gardens; 232 religious

ceremony halls; and 167 cultural institutions, organizations, places, and gyms. There were also 27 museums, 84 cinemas and 58 galleries (Tehran Municipality, n.d.).

- In Dubai, there are 29 art societies and galleries, 12 movie theaters, 11 media foundations, 10 cultural centers, unions and associations, 6 foreign cultural centers, and 3 music groups and orchestras (Dubai Cultural Council, n.d.).
- In 2003 in Cairo, there were 2,748 mosques, of which 2,300 were built with government funds; 423 sports clubs, groups and recreation centers; 310 libraries; 183 churches and 43 cultural centers (Cairo Governate, 2003; Egypt's Information Portal, 2003).

1. NOTABLE **PILGRIMAGES** # OF VISITORS

		0	10,000,000	20,000,000	30,000,000

60,000,000 **ALLAHABAD 2003** HINDUISM, INDIA

5,000,000 **MECCA 2006** ISLAM, SAUDI ARABIA

5,000,000 **LOURDES YR. AVERAGE** CATHOLICISM, FRANCE

3,822,240 **VATICAN/HOLY SEE 2004 AVERAGE** CATHOLICISM, ITALY

1,500,000 **KURUKSHETRA 2006** HINDUISM, INDIA

1,500,000

200,000 **MOUNT FUJI YR. AVERAGE** SHINTO/BUDDHISM, JAPAN

179,944 **SANTIAGO DE COMPOSTELA 2004** CHRISTIANITY, SPAIN

50,000 **LUMBINI 2007** BUDDHISM, NEPAL

0	1,000,000	2,000,000	3,000,000

NOTABLE INTERNATIONAL FILM FESTIVALS

FESTIVAL NAME:	LOCATION:	AUDIENCES:	# OF FILMS SHOWCASED:	DURATION:
TORONTO INTERNATIONAL FILM FESTIVAL 2006	TORONTO, CANADA	900,000	400	10 DAYS
CANNES FILM FESTIVAL 2007	CANNES, FRANCE	34,000	1,049	10 DAYS
VENICE FILM FESTIVAL 2007	VENICE, ITALY	–	51	10 DAYS
BERLIN INTERNATIONAL FILM FESTIVAL 2007	BERLIN, GERMANY	180,000	–	10 DAYS
SUNDANCE FILM FESTIVAL 2007	PARK CITY, UTAH, USA	–	122	10 DAYS
SHANGHAI INTERNATIONAL FILM FESTIVAL 2007	SHANGHAI, CHINA	300,000	164	9 DAYS
INTERNATIONAL FILM FESTIVAL ROTTERDAM 2007	ROTTERDAM, NETHERLANDS	367,000	635	12 DAYS
MOSCOW INTERNATIONAL FILM FESTIVAL 2007	MOSCOW, RUSSIA	–	83	10 DAYS
DONOSTIA-SAN SEBASTIÁN INTERNATIONAL FILM FESTIVAL 2007	SAN SEBASTIÁN, SPAIN	–	83	10 DAYS
LOCARNO INTERNATIONAL FILM FESTIVAL 2006	LOCARNO, SWITZERLAND	–	170	10 DAYS
KARLOVY VARY INTERNATIONAL FILM FESTIVAL 2005	KARLOVY VARY, CZECH REPUBLIC	142,500	242	9 DAYS
MAR DEL PLATA INTERNATIONAL FILM FESTIVAL 2007	MAR DEL PLATA, ARGENTINA	–	347	11 DAYS
TRIBECA FILM FESTIVAL 2006	NEW YORK, USA	–	169	13 DAYS
RAINDANCE FILM FESTIVAL 2006	LONDON, UNITED KINGDOM	–	86	A WEEK

NOTABLE MUSIC FESTIVALS OVER 100,000 VISITORS + WELL RECOGNIZED

FESTIVAL NAME:	LOCATION:	AUDIENCES:	# OF ARTISTS OR PERFORMANCES:	DURATION:
CLASSICAL				
SCHLESWIG-HOLSTEIN MUSIC FESTIVAL 2007	SCHLESWIG-HOLSTEIN, GERMANY	–	184	35 DAYS
SALZBURG FESTIVAL 2005	SALZBURG, AUSTRIA	238,463	212	40 DAYS
MOSTLY MOZART 2007	NEW YORK, USA	–	35	25 DAYS
THE COLMAR INTERNATIONAL FESTIVAL 2007	COLMAR, FRANCE	–	–	13 DAYS
OPERA				
BAYREUTH FESTIVAL 2007	BAYREUTH, GERMANY	6,000	–	35 DAYS
ROCK				
SUMMERFEST 2007	MILWAUKEE, USA	892,005	–	11 DAYS
EUROCKÉENNES DE BELFORT 2006	MALSAUCY, FRANCE	100,000	–	3 DAYS
OXEGEN 2008	COUNTY KILDARE, IRELAND	80,000*	–	3 DAYS
FUJI ROCK FESTIVAL 2005	NAEBA, JAPAN	100,000	–	3 DAYS
JAZZ				
THE MONTREAL INTERNATIONAL JAZZ FESTIVAL 2007	MONTREAL, CANADA	250,000	3,000	11 DAYS
THE NEW ORLEANS JAZZ & HERITAGE FESTIVAL 2007	NEW ORLEANS, USA	400,000*	–	6 DAYS
MONTREAUX JAZZ FESTIVAL 2004	MONTREAUX, SWITZERLAND	220,000	4,000	16 DAYS
WORLD				
FESTIVAL IN THE DESERT 2007	ESSAKANE, MALI	4,000	30	3 DAYS
TECHNO				
LOVE PARADE 2006	BERLIN, GERMANY	1,500,000*	1,500	1 DAY
EXIT 2005	NOVI SAD, SERBIA	150,000	–	4 DAYS
MUSIC AND MORE				
GLASTONBURY 2006	PILTON, ENGLAND	150,000	700	3 DAYS
EDINBURGH INTERNATIONAL FESTIVAL 2005	EDINBURGH, UNITED KINGDOM	360,000	1,940	3 WEEKS
VIENNA FESTIVAL 2006	VIENNA, AUSTRIA	50,000*	167	5 WEEKS
BURNING MAN 2005	BLACK ROCK DESERT, USA	35,567	32	1 DAY
COACHELLA VALLEY MUSIC AND ARTS FESTIVAL 2007	COACHELLA VALLEY, USA	180,000	123	3 DAYS

* YEARLY AVERAGE

4. INTERNATIONAL BOOK FAIRS 2007

BOOK EXPO CANADA
ATTENDANCE: **2517**
AUTHOR ATTENDANCE: **645**
PUBLIC ATTENDANCE: **PROFESSIONALS ONLY**
GROWTH IN THE PAST YEAR: **15%**
LOCAL EXHIBITORS: **2298 CA / 50 US**
FOREIGN EXHIBITORS: **73**
SPONSORSHIP / ORGANIZER: **REED EXPO; CANADIAN PUBLISHERS COUNCIL**

BOOK EXPO AMERICA
ATTENDANCE LAST YEAR: **37,041**
PUBLIC ATTENDANCE: **PROFESSIONALS ONLY**
GROWTH IN THE PAST YEAR: **36%**
EXHIBITORS: **1,679**
FOREIGN EXHIBITORS: **28 COUNTRIES REPRESENTED**
EXHIBITION SPACE (SQ.FT): **257,077**
SPONSORSHIP / ORGANIZER: **REED EXPO**

GUADALAJARA BOOK FAIR
PUBLIC ATTENDANCE LAST YEAR: **525,000**
PROFESSIONAL ATTENDANCE: **16,740**
FOREIGN ATTENDANCE: **39 COUNTRIES**
GROWTH IN THE PAST YEAR: **PUBLIC 6% / PROFESSIONAL 9%**
EXHIBITORS: **2,045**
FOREIGN EXHIBITORS: **1,444**
PRESS: **1,523 JOURNALISTS**

RIO DE JANEIRO BOOK FAIR
ATTENDANCE LAST YEAR: **630,000**
GROWTH: **30% EVERY YEAR**
YEAR FOUNDED: **1983**
SPONSORSHIP / ORGANIZER: **EMBRATEL, LIGHT, PETROBAS**

BUENOS AIRES BOOK FAIR
ATTENDANCE: **1,000,000**
FOREIGN ATTENDANCE: **58 COUNTRIES**
GROWTH IN THE PAST 10 YEARS: **# OF EXHIBITORS HAS DOUBLED**
EXHIBITORS: **1,521**
YEAR FOUNDED: **1975**
EXHIBITION SPACE (M²): **45,000**

FRANKFURT BOOK FAIR
ATTENDANCE LAST YEAR: **286,621**
FOREIGN ATTENDANCE: **113 COUNTRIES**
PUBLIC ATTENDANCE: **101,328**
GROWTH IN THE PAST YEAR: **0.6%**
EXHIBITORS: **7,272**
FOREIGN EXHIBITORS: **4,029**
PRESS: **1,200 JOURNALISTS, 25% INTERNATIONAL**

LONDON BOOK FAIR
ATTENDANCE: **14,314**
PUBLIC ATTENDANCE: **PROFESSIONALS ONLY**
EXHIBITORS: **1,996**
FOREIGN EXHIBITORS: **1,129**
EXHIBITION SPACE (M²): **32,000**
SPONSORSHIP / ORGANIZER: **REED EXPO**

LEIPZIG BOOK FAIR
DURATION: **4 DAYS**
ATTENDANCE: **127,500**
EXHIBITORS: **2,348**
FOREIGN EXHIBITORS: **360 COUNTRIES REPRESENTED**
EXHIBITION SPACE (M²): **20,000**
SPONSORSHIP / ORGANIZER: **LEIPZIGER MESSE GMBH, PROJECT TEAM BUCHMESSE**

PARIS BOOK FAIR
DURATION: **6 DAYS**
ATTENDANCE: **165,000**
EXHIBITORS: **1,200**
FOREIGN EXHIBITORS: **25 COUNTRIES REPRESENTED**
EXHIBITION SPACE (M²): **55,000**
SPONSORSHIP / ORGANIZER: **SNE**

GENEVA BOOK FAIR
DURATION: **5 DAYS**
ATTENDANCE: **120,000**
EXHIBITORS: **300**
SPONSORSHIP / ORGANIZER: **SALON INTERNATIONAL DU LIVRE**

BOLOGNA BOOK FAIR
ATTENDANCE LAST YEAR: **4,701**
PUBLIC ATTENDANCE: **PROFESSIONALS ONLY**
EXHIBITORS: **1,300**
FOREIGN EXHIBITORS: **66 COUNTRIES REPRESENTED**
EXHIBITION SPACE (M²): **20,000**
SPONSORSHIP / ORGANIZER: **BOLOGNAFIERE**

THESSALONIKI BOOK FAIR
ATTENDANCE LAST YEAR: **70,000**
PUBLIC ATTENDANCE: **OPEN TO PUBLIC, BUT LARGELY PROFESSIONAL**
GROWTH IN PAST YEAR: **40%**
EXHIBITORS: **400 PUBLISHERS**
FOREIGN EXHIBITORS: **47 COUNTRIES REPRESENTED**
EXHIBITION SPACE (M²): **12,000**

GOTEBORG BOOK FAIR

ATTENDANCE: **102,000**

FOREIGN ATTENDANCE: **20 COUNTRIES**

PUBLIC ATTENDANCE: **OPEN TO PUBLIC**

EXHIBITORS: **850**

EXHIBITION SPACE (M²): **12,195**

YEAR FOUNDED: **1985**

AVERAGE VISIT TIME: **6 HRS. 40 MINS.**

BALTIC BOOK FAIR

ATTENDANCE: **55,400**

PUBLIC ATTENDANCE: **OPEN TO PUBLIC**

GROWTH IN PAST 5 YEARS: **40% INCREASE IN ATTENDANCE**

EXHIBITORS: **375**

FOREIGN EXHIBITORS: **248**

SPONSORSHIP / ORGANIZER: **LITEXPO, LITHUANIAN PUBLISHERS ASSOCIATION**

BEIJING BOOK FAIR

FOREIGN ATTENDANCE: **48 COUNTRIES**

PUBLIC ATTENDANCE: **PROFESSIONALS ONLY**

GROWTH IN THE PAST YEAR: **20% MORE BOOTH SPACE**

EXHIBITORS: **1,501**

FOREIGN EXHIBITORS: **1,000**

EXHIBITION SPACE (M²): **26,000**

YEAR FOUNDED: **1993**

DELHI WORLD BOOK FAIR

ATTENDANCE LAST YEAR: **1,000,000**

FOREIGN ATTENDANCE: **18 COUNTRIES REPRESENTED**

GROWTH: **30% BETWEEN 2005 - 2006**

EXHIBITORS: **13,000**

EXHIBITION SPACE (M²): **38,000**

SPONSORSHIP / ORGANIZER: **NATIONAL BOOK TRUST INDIA**

CAIRO BOOK FAIR

ATTENDANCE: **3,000,000**

PUBLISHER ATTENDANCE: **632 PUBLISHERS, UP 20% FROM 2006**

FOREIGN ATTENDANCE: **32 COUNTRIES, UP 25% FROM 2006**

YEAR FOUNDED: **1969**

JERUSALEM BOOK FAIR

FOREIGN ATTENDANCE: **40 COUNTRIES**

PUBLISHER ATTENDANCE: **1,200 PUBLISHERS**

YEAR FOUNDED: **1963** BIENNIAL

ABU DHABI BOOK FAIR

ATTENDANCE LAST YEAR: **400,000**

FOREIGN ATTENDANCE: **46 COUNTRIES** 29 NON-ARABIC

PUBLISHER ATTENDANCE: **406 PUBLISHERS**

EXHIBITION SPACE (M²): **28,512**

YEAR FOUNDED: **1990**

SPONSORSHIP / ORGANIZER: **HYDRA PROPERTIES, IPIC, DAMAS**

SEOUL BOOK FAIR

ATTENDANCE: **230,000**

PUBLIC ATTENDANCE: **OPEN TO PUBLIC ON SELECTED DAYS**

LOCAL EXHIBITORS: **388**

FOREIGN EXHIBITORS: **81**

SPONSORSHIP / ORGANIZER: **KOREAN PUBLISHERS ASSOCIATION, MINISTRY OF CULTURE AND TOURISM**

TOKYO INTERNATIONAL BOOK FAIR

LOCAL ATTENDANCE LAST YEAR: **54,370**

FOREIGN ATTENDANCE: **1,348**

LOCAL EXHIBITORS: **168 FROM 30 COUNTRIES AND REGIONS**

FOREIGN EXHIBITORS: **558 COUNTRIES REPRESENTED**

YEAR FOUNDED: **1993**

SPONSORSHIP / ORGANIZER: **REED EYPO**

HONG KONG BOOK FAIR

ATTENDANCE: **686,590**

PUBLIC ATTENDANCE: **OPEN TO PUBLIC**

EXHIBITORS: **434**

FOREIGN EXHIBITORS: **15 COUNTRIES REPRESENTED**

EXHIBITION SPACE (M²): **33,161**

SPONSORSHIP / ORGANIZER: **HONG KONG TRADE DEVELOPMENT COUNCIL**

TAIPEI BOOK FAIR

ATTENDANCE LAST YEAR: **440,000**

FOREIGN ATTENDANCE: **41 COUNTRIES**

PUBLIC ATTENDANCE: **PROFESSIONALS ONLY**

GROWTH IN PAST YEAR: **5% INCREASE IN EXHIBITORS**

EXHIBITORS: **500**

FOREIGN EXHIBITORS: **115 COUNTRIES REPRESENTED**

YEAR FOUNDED: **2005**

CAPE TOWN BOOK FAIR

ATTENDANCE LAST YEAR: **49,000**

FOREIGN ATTENDANCE: **21 COUNTRIES**

PUBLIC ATTENDANCE: **OPEN TO PUBLIC**

GROWTH IN PAST YEAR: **FLOOR SPACE DOUBLED**

EXHIBITORS: **349**

FOREIGN EXHIBITORS: **35 COUNTRIES REPRESENTED**

EXHIBITION SPACE (M²): **10,000**

PRESS: **260 JOURNALISTS**

5. TRENDS IN 'BIENNIALIZATION' GROWTH OF HOLDING BIENNALES WORLDWIDE

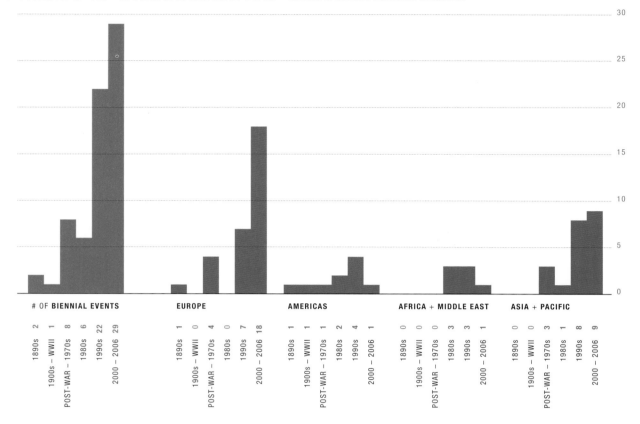

# OF **BIENNIAL EVENTS**						**EUROPE**						**AMERICAS**						**AFRICA + MIDDLE EAST**						**ASIA + PACIFIC**					
2	1	8	6	22	29	1	0	4	0	7	18	1	1	1	2	4	1	0	0	0	3	3	1	0	0	3	1	8	9
1890s	1900s – WWII	POST-WAR – 1970s	1980s	1990s	2000 – 2006	1890s	1900s – WWII	POST-WAR – 1970s	1980s	1990s	2000 – 2006	1890s	1900s – WWII	POST-WAR – 1970s	1980s	1990s	2000 – 2006	1890s	1900s – WWII	POST-WAR – 1970s	1980s	1990s	2000 – 2006	1890s	1900s – WWII	POST-WAR – 1970s	1980s	1990s	2000 – 2006

6. NOTABLE **LIVE CHARITY CONCERTS WORLDWIDE**

LIVE EARTH – CONCERT TO COMBAT GLOBAL CLIMATE CHANGE **LARGEST GLOBAL ENTERTAINMENT EVENT EVER HELD** JULY 7TH, 2007 – LASTED 24 HOURS

MAJOR CONCERTS	BROADCASTING CHANNELS	LEADING BROADCASTERS	# OF ARTISTS	# OF AUDIENCE	# OF COUNTRIES/ TERRITORIES REACHED	FRIENDS OF LIVE EARTH PROGRAM
8	**500**	**11**	**> 100**	**2 BILLION**	**213**	**10,413**
NEW YORK	TV	NBC (USA)			178 COUNTRIES	
LONDON	RADIO	SHANGHAI MEDIA GROUP + CTV (CHINA)			35 TERRITORIES	
JOHANNESBURG	INTERNET	BBC (UNITED KINGDOM)				
RIO DE JANEIRO	WIRELESS	PRO SIEBEN (GERMANY)				
SHANGHAI		TVGLOBO (BRAZIL)				
TOKYO		FUJI TV + NHK (JAPAN)				
SYDNEY		SOUTH AFRICA BROADCAST COMPANY				
HAMBURG		FOXTEL (AUSTRALIA)				
		PREMIERE RADIO NETWORK				
		XM + SIRIUS SATELLITE RADIO				
		WORLD SPACE SATELLITE RADIO				

# PUBLICATIONS	# OF MAJOR PARTNERS		MAIN ORGANIZERS
91	**31**		**2**
SHORT FILMS: 60	OFFICIAL ONLINE PARTNERS:	SUPPORTING PARTNERS:	KELVIN WALL
PSAS: 30	MSN	AISO.NET	AL GORE
BOOKS: 1	OFFICIAL PARTNERS:	EARTHLAB FOUNDATION	
	SMART	EBAY	
	PHILIPS	EVITE	
	PEPSI	GLOBALIZATION PARTNERS INTERNATIONAL	
	ESURANCE	NATIONAL GEOGRAPHIC	
	STONY	VISIBLE STRATEGIES	
	VERISIGN	TWITTER	
	ABSOLUT	KEEN	
	CAMPAIGN PARTNERS:	GIBSON GUITAR	
	THE ALLIANCE FOR CLIMATE PROTECTION	AUDE	
	THE CLIMATE GROUP	INTELSAT	
	I COUNT	BRAND NEUTRAL	
	AVAAZ	IGNITION	
	CONTROL ROOM	EMPIRE STATE BUILDING	
	INTERNATIONAL NGO PARTNERS	ONDAH	
	WWF - THE LARGEST	COMMUNITY ENERGY INC.	

GLOBAL EVENTS The growth and spread of festivals and symbolic events mirrors trends of globalization, and the simultaneous homogenization and localization of cultures and forms of creativity and presentation. The cultural significance of celebrations, festivals, and sites lies in their ability to promote unity, share knowledge, confirm values and beliefs, evoke emotional response, and reinforce identity (cf. chapters by Klaic and Miguez in this volume). Many global festivals and cultural events around the world surround religion, the arts (music, cinema and media) as well as place-specific themes and histories. With the advent of the Internet, more and more events are becoming transnational, having been promoted, accessed and experienced in and out of cyberspace. Increasingly, global media events are organized around fund-raising and awareness-building campaigns that focus on specific problems and issues such as poverty or climate change.

WHAT DO WE KNOW ABOUT GLOBAL EVENTS?

Global and local events attract visitors and media attention, often having a significant impact on the local economy (cf. indicator suite on Sports in this volume). Like cultural institutions (e.g., the Guggenheim Museum in Bilbao, Spain), such events can push a city onto the world map of the arts (e.g., the Documenta in Kassel, Germany) and even help 'brand' a city or place with a certain identity (e.g., the Hayes Literary Festival in the UK, or the Salzburg Festival in Austria).

The origins of major events lie in religious pilgrimages, and they remain among the largest gatherings worldwide. The Kumbh Mela in India remains the largest such gathering in the world. Although traditionally held every twelve years over a two-month period, it is the 'half Mela' (held very six years) in Allahabad which receives the largest numbers, estimated at 60,000,000 visitors (see data point 1).

Like the Kumbh Mela, many significant events in Asia, the Middle East and Europe take place at sites and cities of religious symbolism, such as Lumbini (the birthplace of Gautama Buddha, the founder of Buddhism), Santiago de Compostela in Spain (the burial place of St. James), or Lourdes (the site in France where the Virgin Mary allegedly appeared to a young girl). In 2006, some 50,000 people made the annual visit to Mecca (the haj), with similar numbers to Lourdes; both rank as the second largest pilgrimages taken after the Kumbh Mela (see data point 1).

Clearly, art events are of more recent origin, and typically receive more media attention than religious events. Frequently located in Europe or North America, notable film and music festivals have become iconic of their host cities (see data points 2 and 3). The Toronto Film Festival remains the largest in the world with an audience of 900,000. However the Cannes Film Festival remains one of the most prestigious, showcasing the largest number of films (1,049 films total in 2007). Independent or alternative film and music festivals tend to take place in less prominent cities or more obscure locations. For instance, the Sundance Film Festival, the largest independent film competition, takes place in Park City, Utah. 'Burning Man,' a techno music and arts festival, takes place in the middle of the Nevada desert in the United States, while the most important festival of World music (the 'Festival in the Desert') occurs in Essakane, Mali, which, because of its remote location, has the fewest number of visitors.

International book fairs play an important role in the field of publishing. As the oldest book fair, the Frankfurt Book Fair remains one of the most significant fairs in trade-books worldwide, noted in 2007 by its ability to draw the largest number of international representatives from over 113 countries (cf. textbox on the Frankfurt Book Fair in this volume). The Cairo Book fair attracted 3 million attendees, and the Delhi World Book Fair boasted 13,000 exhibitors in 2007 (see data point 4).

Biennales represent another significant global event, referring to large-scale exhibitions held periodically to showcase international contemporary art which simultaneously act as a vehicle to establish the cultural positioning of a city or location (Asian Art Archive, 2007; cf. chapters by Halle and Tiso in this volume). The first biennale to take place was the Venice Biennale in 1895, which to this day remains the most prominent and prestigious with its components of art, architecture, music, theater, and dance. The 2005 51st Venice Biennale received 915,000 visitors, the largest figure for any biennale of that year. Before World War II, biennales were typically held in Europe or North America. Afterwards and into the 1970s, they were inaugurated in Asia and the Pacific, followed by the Middle East in the 1980s (see data point 5). Almost 65 per cent of all biennales are initiated by national governments as a form of location branding, to increase the number of tourists and to boost a local economy (Asian Art Archive, 2007).

NOTABLE BIENNALES: NUMBER OF ARTISTS

Kassel Documenta (2007)	**450**
Havana (2006)	**121**
São Paulo (2007)	**118**
Venice (2005)	**96**
Singapore (2007)	**95**
Shanghai (2006)	**94**
Sydney (2006)	**85**
Berlin (2007)	**76**
Paris (2006)	**35**

Source: Asian Art Archive (2007)

World festivals include more traditional and long-standing events along with newer, more alternative celebrations that embrace 'fringe' and other non-mainstream forms of expression, along with transnational movements, and increasingly rely upon technology and the Internet to promote large-scale global event broadcasts. The recent Live Earth concerts to combat global warming, held simultaneously in eight major cities worldwide, constituted the largest global entertainment and charity event to date, having attracted an estimated audience of 2 billion across 178 countries and 35 territories (see data point 6). Indeed, Live Earth attracted the largest online audience to date for a live concert event. More than 55 million concert videos were streamed on MSN, Live Earth's online partner, demonstrating the power of the Internet, wireless and satellite radio to promote and enable many to experience a global event. Currently, an even larger worldwide live concert, World Peace One, is under preparation for its show in December 2007.

WHAT ARE THE ISSUES?

Large-scale international exhibitions, events, and festivals face the task of organizing and making coherent the great diversity of styles, conceptions, and approaches that exist around the world (Weinberg and Pratt Brown, 2006). Who decides what is worthy of display and celebration in these international festivals is a contentious issue. Likewise, the question of who can attend and participate in global events highlights the fact that many global festivals and events reinforce art and creativity as the realm of a wealthy elite, while other, usually more local and often religious events provide opportunities for all to participate in expression and celebration.

Thus, global events and festivals highlight issues surrounding cultural diversity as well as organizational capacity. Some charge that globalization has caused a Westernization of world cultures, and a decline of local ceremonies, customs, festivals, and other symbolic traditions. The domination of many large-scale events and festivals by certain Western influences may point to commodification and commercialization trends (cf. chapter by Scott in this volume). At the same time, while such homogenization trends are occurring, changes in communication technologies make it possible for local and regional cultural realities to be reaffirmed, even rekindled, and given global visibility through festivals and similar events.

EDUCATIONAL EXCHANGE

1a. EDUCATION EXCHANGE: FLOWS OF STUDENTS

AT THE TERTIARY LEVEL 2004

TOP 5 SENDING COUNTRIES AND TOP 5 DESTINATION COUNTRIES.

ARAB STATES, CENTRAL + EASTERN EUROPE, CENTRAL ASIA, EAST ASIA + THE PACIFIC

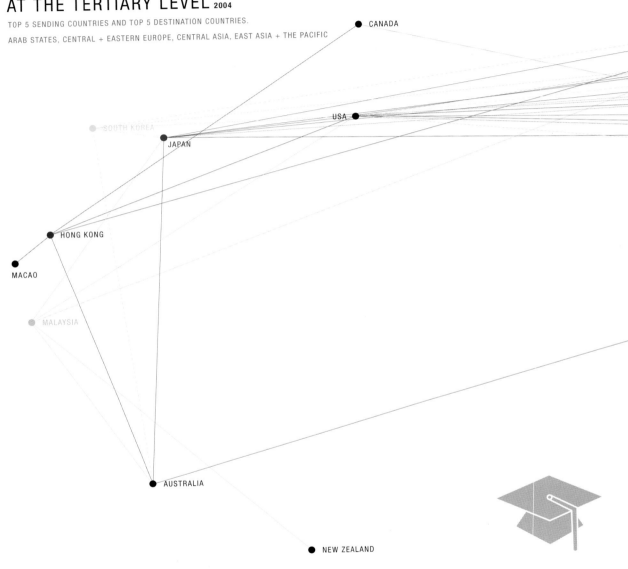

#1 SENDING COUNTRY	MOROCCO	ALGERIA	TUNISIA	LEBANON	SYRIA
# OF TOTAL STUDENTS	51,503	24,356	13,983	11,286	10,385
#1 DESTINATION	FRANCE 32,802	FRANCE 22,250	FRANCE 9,748	FRANCE 4,671	JORDAN 2,279
#2 DESTINATION	GERMANY 8,305	UK 452	GERMANY 1,849	USA 2,179	FRANCE 2,237
#3 DESTINATION	BELGIUM 2,579	GERMANY 304	CANADA 635	GERMANY 976	GERMANY 1,207
#4 DESTINATION	USA 1,835	SWITZERLAND 266	USA 341	ITALY 577	SAUDI ARABIA 668
#5 DESTINATION	NETHERLANDS 1,664	BELGIUM 255	SWITZERLAND 276	UK 575	ARMENIA 630

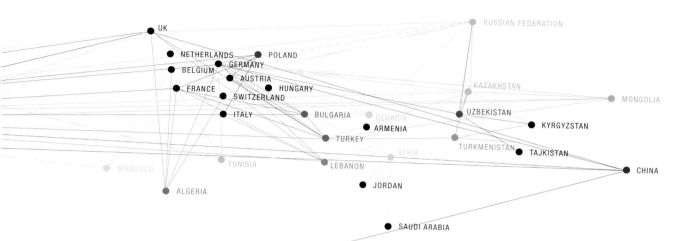

TURKEY

52,048

- - - - - - - - - - - - - -

GERMANY 27,582
USA 11,398
FRANCE 2,273
UK 1,960
AUSTRIA 1,820

RUSSIAN FEDERATION

34,473

- - - - - - - - - - - - - -

GERMANY 11,462
USA 5,532
FRANCE 2,597
KAZAKHSTAN 2,177
UK 1,878

POLAND

28,786

- - - - - - - - - - - - - -

GERMANY 15,417
FRANCE 3,270
USA 2,913
AUSTRIA 1,172
ITALY 1,002

UKRAINE

25,188

- - - - - - - - - - - - - -

GERMANY 7,618
RUSSIAN FED. 6,841
USA 2,004
POLAND 1,809
HUNGARY 1,005

BULGARIA

24,619

- - - - - - - - - - - - - -

GERMANY 12,116
USA 3,734
FRANCE 2,905
AUSTRIA 1,588
TURKEY 948

KAZAKHSTAN

27,356

- - - - - - - - - - - - - -

RUSSIAN FED. 20,098
KYRGYZSTAN 3,635
GERMANY 876
TURKEY 781
USA 538

UZBEKISTAN

17,163

- - - - - - - - - - - - - -

KYRGYZSTAN 9,856
RUSSIAN FED. 2,430
KAZAKHSTAN 1,783
TAJKISTAN 1,277
GERMANY 520

GEORGIA

6,679

- - - - - - - - - - - - - -

GERMANY 3,000
RUSSIAN FED. 1,357
ARMENIA 932
USA 373
FRANCE 275

MONGOLIA

4,567

- - - - - - - - - - - - - -

GERMANY 1,400
USA 711
JAPAN 689
KAZAKHSTAN 569
TURKEY 309

TURKMENISTAN

4,530

- - - - - - - - - - - - - -

RUSSIAN FED. 1,385
TURKEY 1,293
KAZAKHSTAN 719
KYRGYZSTAN 418
TAJKISTAN 303

CHINA

343,126

- - - - - - - - - - - - - -

USA 87,943
JAPAN 76,130
UK 47,738
AUSTRALIA 28,309
GERMANY 25,284

SOUTH KOREA

95,885

- - - - - - - - - - - - - -

USA 52,484
JAPAN 23,280
GERMANY 5,488
AUSTRALIA 3,915
UK 3,482

JAPAN

60,424

- - - - - - - - - - - - - -

USA 40,835
UK 6,395
AUSTRALIA 3,172
GERMANY 2,547
FRANCE 2,337

MALAYSIA

40,884

- - - - - - - - - - - - - -

AUSTRALIA 16,094
UK 11,806
USA 6,483
JAPAN 1,841
NEW ZEALAND 831

HONG KONG

34,199

- - - - - - - - - - - - - -

AUSTRALIA 13,165
UK 10,577
USA 7,353
CANADA 1,852
MACAO 746

TOP 5 SENDING COUNTRIES AND TOP 5 DESTINATION COUNTRIES.

LATIN AMERICA + THE CARIBBEAN, NORTH AMERICA + WESTERN EUROPE, SOUTH AND WEST ASIA, SUB-SAHARAN AFRICA

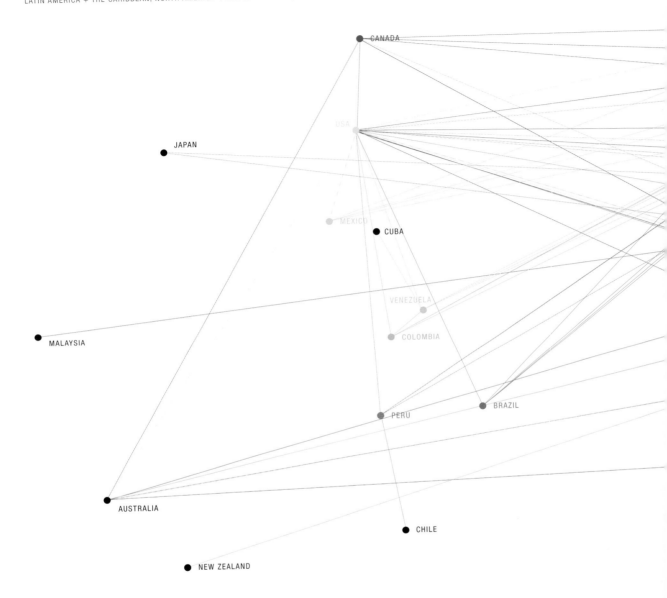

	MEXICO	BRAZIL	COLOMBIA	PERU	VENEZUELA
#1 SENDING COUNTRY					
# OF TOTAL STUDENTS	21,661	19,619	16,090	9,715	9,569
	- - - - - - - - - - - - - - -	- - - - - - - - - - - - - - -	- - - - - - - - - - - - - - -	- - - - - - - - - - - - - - -	- - - - - - - - - - - - - - -
#1 DESTINATION	USA 13,329	USA 7,799	USA 7,533	USA 3,771	USA 5,575
#2 DESTINATION	UK 1,973	GERMANY 1,801	FRANCE 1,754	GERMANY 902	CUBA 847
#3 DESTINATION	FRANCE 1,452	PORTUGAL 1,760	VENEZUELA 1,206	CHILE 722	PORTUGAL 595
#4 DESTINATION	GERMANY 977	FRANCE 1,759	GERMANY 988	ITALY 687	SPAIN 488
#5 DESTINATION	SPAIN 937	UK 1,110	SPAIN 797	FRANCE 498	FRANCE 405

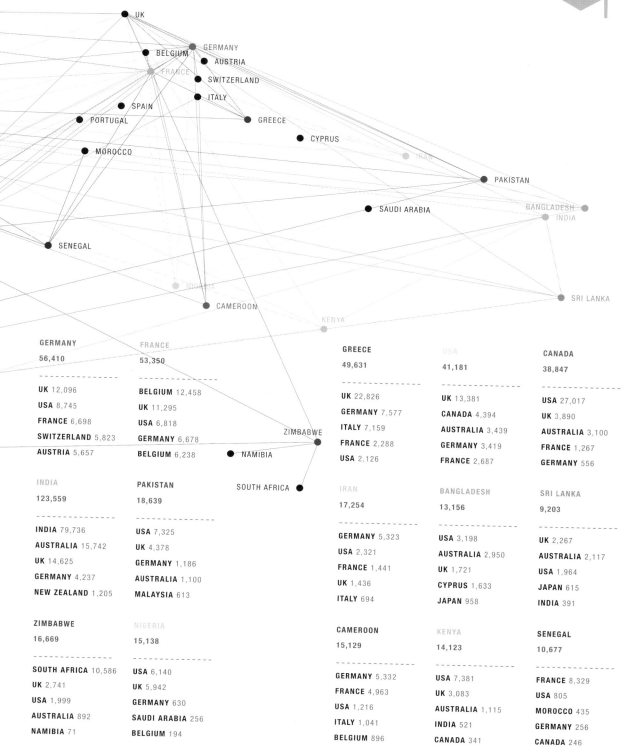

UK

GERMANY
BELGIUM
AUSTRIA
FRANCE
SWITZERLAND
ITALY
SPAIN
PORTUGAL
GREECE
CYPRUS
MOROCCO
IRAN
PAKISTAN
SAUDI ARABIA
BANGLADESH
INDIA
SENEGAL
SRI LANKA
NIGERIA
CAMEROON
KENYA
ZIMBABWE
NAMIBIA
SOUTH AFRICA

GERMANY
56,410

- - - - - - - - - - - - - -

UK 12,096
USA 8,745
FRANCE 6,698
SWITZERLAND 5,823
AUSTRIA 5,657

FRANCE
53,350

- - - - - - - - - - - - - -

BELGIUM 12,458
UK 11,295
USA 6,818
GERMANY 6,678
BELGIUM 6,238

GREECE
49,631

- - - - - - - - - - - - - -

UK 22,826
GERMANY 7,577
ITALY 7,159
FRANCE 2,288
USA 2,126

USA
41,181

- - - - - - - - - - - - - -

UK 13,381
CANADA 4,394
AUSTRALIA 3,439
GERMANY 3,419
FRANCE 2,687

CANADA
38,847

- - - - - - - - - - - - - -

USA 27,017
UK 3,890
AUSTRALIA 3,100
FRANCE 1,267
GERMANY 556

INDIA
123,559

- - - - - - - - - - - - - -

INDIA 79,736
AUSTRALIA 15,742
UK 14,625
GERMANY 4,237
NEW ZEALAND 1,205

PAKISTAN
18,639

- - - - - - - - - - - - - -

USA 7,325
UK 4,378
GERMANY 1,186
AUSTRALIA 1,100
MALAYSIA 613

IRAN
17,254

- - - - - - - - - - - - - -

GERMANY 5,323
USA 2,321
FRANCE 1,441
UK 1,436
ITALY 694

BANGLADESH
13,156

- - - - - - - - - - - - - -

USA 3,198
AUSTRALIA 2,950
UK 1,721
CYPRUS 1,633
JAPAN 958

SRI LANKA
9,203

- - - - - - - - - - - - - -

UK 2,267
AUSTRALIA 2,117
USA 1,964
JAPAN 615
INDIA 391

ZIMBABWE
16,669

- - - - - - - - - - - - - -

SOUTH AFRICA 10,586
UK 2,741
USA 1,999
AUSTRALIA 892
NAMIBIA 71

NIGERIA
15,138

- - - - - - - - - - - - - -

USA 6,140
UK 5,942
GERMANY 630
SAUDI ARABIA 256
BELGIUM 194

CAMEROON
15,129

- - - - - - - - - - - - - -

GERMANY 5,332
FRANCE 4,963
USA 1,216
ITALY 1,041
BELGIUM 896

KENYA
14,123

- - - - - - - - - - - - - -

USA 7,381
UK 3,083
AUSTRALIA 1,115
INDIA 521
CANADA 341

SENEGAL
10,677

- - - - - - - - - - - - - -

FRANCE 8,329
USA 805
MOROCCO 435
GERMANY 256
CANADA 246

549

2. TOP **15 SENDING COUNTRIES** 2004

OF STUDENTS

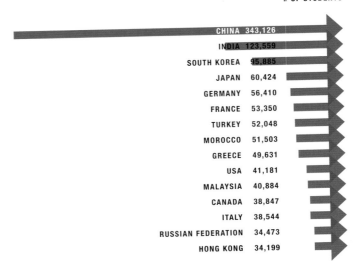

CHINA	343,126
INDIA	123,559
SOUTH KOREA	95,885
JAPAN	60,424
GERMANY	56,410
FRANCE	53,350
TURKEY	52,048
MOROCCO	51,503
GREECE	49,631
USA	41,181
MALAYSIA	40,884
CANADA	38,847
ITALY	38,544
RUSSIAN FEDERATION	34,473
HONG KONG	34,199

3. TOP **15 RECEIVING COUNTRIES** 2004

OF STUDENTS

572,509	USA
300,056	UK
260,314	GERMANY
237,587	FRANCE
166,954	AUSTRALIA
107,030	JAPAN
75,786	RUSSIAN FEDERATION
64,046	SWITZERLAND
49,979	SOUTH AFRICA
40,641	ITALY
40,033	CANADA
32,469	SWEDEN
31,101	AUSTRIA
27,731	MALAYSIA
26,359	NEW ZEALAND

TOP RECEIVING COUNTRIES

BY REGION 2004   # OF STUDENTS

ARAB STATES: JORDAN	15,816
LEBANON	13,930
SAUDI ARABIA	12,199
MOROCCO	6,393
ALGERIA	4,677
CENTRAL + EASTERN EUROPE: RUSSIAN FEDERATION	75,786
CZECH REPUBLIC	10,338
UKRAINE	15,622
TURKEY	12,729
HUNGARY	12,226
CENTRAL ASIA: KYRGYZSTAN	16,249
KAZAKHSTAN	8,690
ARMENIA	3,346
TAJIKISTAN	2,208
AZERBAIJAN	1,991
EAST ASIA + THE PACIFIC: AUSTRALIA	166,954
JAPAN	107,030
MALAYSIA	27,731
NEW ZEALAND	26,359
MACAO	14,627
LATIN AMERICA + THE CARIBBEAN: CUBA	13,705
CHILE	5,211
ARGENTINA	3,261
VENEZUELA	2,472
URUGUAY	2,100
NORTH AMERICA + WESTERN EUROPE: USA	572,509
UK	300,056
GERMANY	260,314
FRANCE	237,587
SWITZERLAND	64,046
SOUTH + WEST ASIA: INDIA	7,738
IRAN	1,791
PAKISTAN	389
BANGLADESH	385
SUB-SAHARAN AFRICA: SOUTH AFRICA	49,979
CAMEROON	1,529
TOGO	1,307
SENEGAL	1,295
MALI	1,221

MOROCCO: FRANCE	32,802
GERMANY	8,305
BELGIUM	2,579
USA	1,835
NETHERLANDS	1,664
OTHER	4,318
TURKEY: GERMANY	27,582
USA	11,398
FRANCE	2,273
UK	1,960
AUSTRIA	1,820
OTHER	7,015
KAZAKHSTAN: RUSSIAN FEDERATION	20,098
KYRGYZSTAN	3,635
GERMANY	876
TURKEY	781
USA	538
OTHER	1,428
CHINA: USA	87,943
JAPAN	76,130
UK	47,738
AUSTRALIA	28,309
GERMANY	25,284
OTHER	77,722
MEXICO: USA	13,329
UK	1,973
FRANCE	1,452
GERMANY	977
SPAIN	937
OTHER	2,993
GERMANY: UK	12,096
USA	8,745
FRANCE	6,698
SWITZERLAND	5,823
AUSTRIA	5,657
OTHER	17,391
INDIA: USA	79,736
AUSTRALIA	15,742
UK	14,625
GERMANY	4,237
NEW ZEALAND	1,205
OTHER	8,014
ZIMBABWE: SOUTH AFRICA	10,586
UK	2,741
USA	1,999
AUSTRALIA	892
NAMIBIA	71
OTHER	380

TOP SENDING COUNTRIES

IN REGION BY TOP DESTINATIONS **2004**

OF STUDENTS ▷

OF STUDENTS: AUSTRALIA USA UK

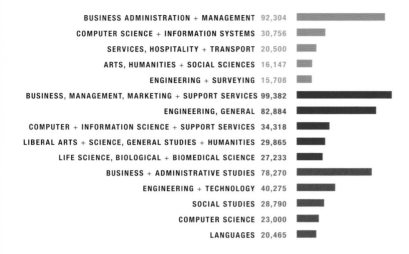

BUSINESS ADMINISTRATION + MANAGEMENT 92,304

COMPUTER SCIENCE + INFORMATION SYSTEMS 30,756

SERVICES, HOSPITALITY + TRANSPORT 20,500

ARTS, HUMANITIES + SOCIAL SCIENCES 16,147

ENGINEERING + SURVEYING 15,708

BUSINESS, MANAGEMENT, MARKETING + SUPPORT SERVICES 99,382

ENGINEERING, GENERAL 82,884

COMPUTER + INFORMATION SCIENCE + SUPPORT SERVICES 34,318

LIBERAL ARTS + SCIENCE, GENERAL STUDIES + HUMANITIES 29,865

LIFE SCIENCE, BIOLOGICAL + BIOMEDICAL SCIENCE 27,233

BUSINESS + ADMINISTRATIVE STUDIES 78,270

ENGINEERING + TECHNOLOGY 40,275

SOCIAL STUDIES 28,790

COMPUTER SCIENCE 23,000

LANGUAGES 20,465

INTERNATIONAL STUDENTS IN HIGHER EDUCATION

COMPARISON OF MAJOR ENGLISH SPEAKING DESTINATIONS BY TOP FIVE SOURCE MARKETS:

AUSTRALIA, UK, CANADA, USA, NEW ZEALAND: (% CHANGE) + 2003 + 2004

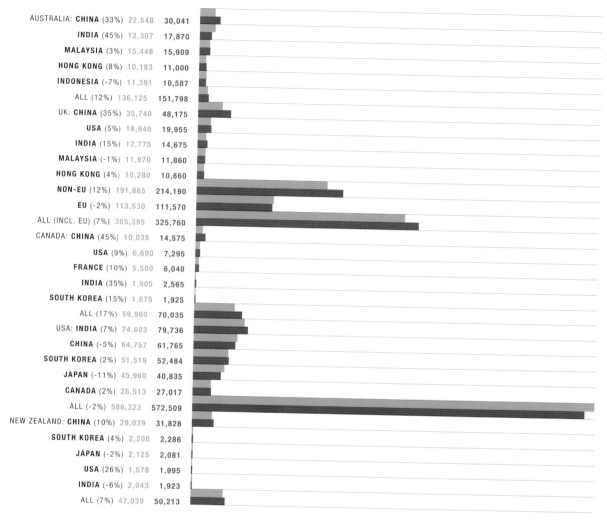

	2003	2004
AUSTRALIA: **CHINA** (33%)	22,548	**30,041**
INDIA (45%)	12,307	**17,870**
MALAYSIA (3%)	15,448	**15,909**
HONG KONG (8%)	10,183	**11,000**
INDONESIA (-7%)	11,391	**10,587**
ALL (12%)	136,125	**151,798**
UK: **CHINA** (35%)	35,740	**48,175**
USA (5%)	18,940	**19,955**
INDIA (15%)	12,775	**14,675**
MALAYSIA (-1%)	11,970	**11,860**
HONG KONG (4%)	10,280	**10,660**
NON-EU (12%)	191,865	**214,190**
EU (-2%)	113,530	**111,570**
ALL (INCL. EU) (7%)	305,395	**325,760**
CANADA: **CHINA** (45%)	10,035	**14,575**
USA (9%)	6,690	**7,295**
FRANCE (10%)	5,500	**6,040**
INDIA (35%)	1,905	**2,565**
SOUTH KOREA (15%)	1,675	**1,925**
ALL (17%)	59,960	**70,035**
USA: **INDIA** (7%)	74,603	**79,736**
CHINA (-5%)	64,757	**61,765**
SOUTH KOREA (2%)	51,519	**52,484**
JAPAN (-11%)	45,960	**40,835**
CANADA (2%)	26,513	**27,017**
ALL (-2%)	586,323	**572,509**
NEW ZEALAND: **CHINA** (10%)	29,039	**31,828**
SOUTH KOREA (4%)	2,200	**2,286**
JAPAN (-2%)	2,125	**2,081**
USA (26%)	1,578	**1,995**
INDIA (-6%)	2,043	**1,923**
ALL (7%)	47,039	**50,213**

NEW ZEALAND STATISTICS ARE FOR FULL-FEE STUDENTS ATTENDING A TERTIARY ORGANIZATION.

THEY INCLUDE STUDENTS DOING NON-HIGHER EDUCATION STUDY.

8. TOP 3 **UNIVERSITIES** BY REGION: **INTERNATIONAL STUDENT BODY**

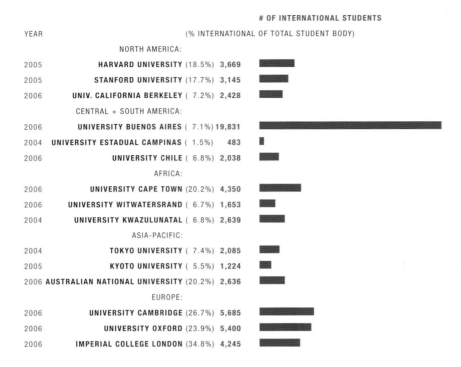

OF INTERNATIONAL STUDENTS

YEAR		(% INTERNATIONAL OF TOTAL STUDENT BODY)
	NORTH AMERICA:	
2005	**HARVARD UNIVERSITY** (18.5%)	3,669
2005	**STANFORD UNIVERSITY** (17.7%)	3,145
2006	**UNIV. CALIFORNIA BERKELEY** (7.2%)	2,428
	CENTRAL + SOUTH AMERICA:	
2006	**UNIVERSITY BUENOS AIRES** (7.1%)	19,831
2004	**UNIVERSITY ESTADUAL CAMPINAS** (1.5%)	483
2006	**UNIVERSITY CHILE** (6.8%)	2,038
	AFRICA:	
2006	**UNIVERSITY CAPE TOWN** (20.2%)	4,350
2006	**UNIVERSITY WITWATERSRAND** (6.7%)	1,653
2004	**UNIVERSITY KWAZULUNATAL** (6.8%)	2,639
	ASIA-PACIFIC:	
2004	**TOKYO UNIVERSITY** (7.4%)	2,085
2005	**KYOTO UNIVERSITY** (5.5%)	1,224
2006	**AUSTRALIAN NATIONAL UNIVERSITY** (20.2%)	2,636
	EUROPE:	
2006	**UNIVERSITY CAMBRIDGE** (26.7%)	5,685
2006	**UNIVERSITY OXFORD** (23.9%)	5,400
2006	**IMPERIAL COLLEGE LONDON** (34.8%)	4,245

9a. **HARVARD UNIVERSITY:** TOTAL # OF **INTERNATIONAL STUDENTS** 2006

BY REGION OF ORIGIN: TOP 3 GRADUATE FIELDS OF STUDY

INSUFFICIENT UNDERGRAD DATA

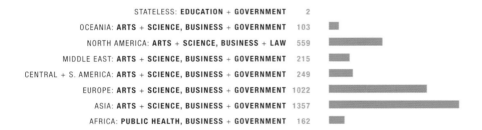

STATELESS: **EDUCATION + GOVERNMENT**	2
OCEANIA: **ARTS + SCIENCE, BUSINESS + GOVERNMENT**	103
NORTH AMERICA: **ARTS + SCIENCE, BUSINESS + LAW**	559
MIDDLE EAST: **ARTS + SCIENCE, BUSINESS + GOVERNMENT**	215
CENTRAL + S. AMERICA: **ARTS + SCIENCE, BUSINESS + GOVERNMENT**	249
EUROPE: **ARTS + SCIENCE, BUSINESS + GOVERNMENT**	1022
ASIA: **ARTS + SCIENCE, BUSINESS + GOVERNMENT**	1357
AFRICA: **PUBLIC HEALTH, BUSINESS + GOVERNMENT**	162

9b. **UNIVERSITY BUENOS AIRES:** TOTAL # OF **INTERNATIONAL STUDENTS**

2006 **BY REGION OF ORIGIN** TOP UNDERGRADUATE FIELDS OF STUDY

INSUFFICIENT GRAD DATA

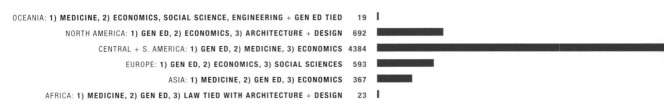

OCEANIA: **1) MEDICINE, 2) ECONOMICS, SOCIAL SCIENCE, ENGINEERING + GEN ED TIED**	19
NORTH AMERICA: **1) GEN ED, 2) ECONOMICS, 3) ARCHITECTURE + DESIGN**	692
CENTRAL + S. AMERICA: **1) GEN ED, 2) MEDICINE, 3) ECONOMICS**	4384
EUROPE: **1) GEN ED, 2) ECONOMICS, 3) SOCIAL SCIENCES**	593
ASIA: **1) MEDICINE, 2) GEN ED, 3) ECONOMICS**	367
AFRICA: **1) MEDICINE, 2) GEN ED, 3) LAW TIED WITH ARCHITECTURE + DESIGN**	23

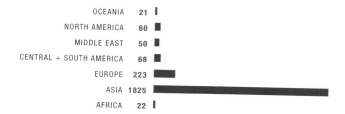

UNIVERSITY OF TOKYO: TOTAL # OF **INTERNATIONAL STUDENTS**

2004 **BY REGION OF ORIGIN**

Region	#
OCEANIA	21
NORTH AMERICA	60
MIDDLE EAST	50
CENTRAL + SOUTH AMERICA	68
EUROPE	223
ASIA	1825
AFRICA	22

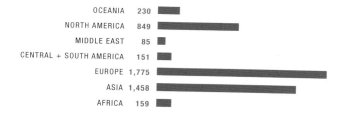

CAMBRIDGE UNIVERSITY: TOTAL # OF **INTERNATIONAL STUDENTS**

2004 **BY REGION OF ORIGIN**

Region	#
OCEANIA	230
NORTH AMERICA	849
MIDDLE EAST	85
CENTRAL + SOUTH AMERICA	151
EUROPE	1,775
ASIA	1,458
AFRICA	159

EDUCATIONAL EXCHANGE Educational exchange is the movement and placement of students across national borders to study in countries other than their own. Indeed, the 'internationalization of tertiary education' and the globalization of university systems are clearly evident in the rising numbers of students who study abroad (UNESCO, 2006). The indicator suite on Educational Exchange shows that many of the world's emerging economies are taking the lead in sending students abroad to take advantage of educational opportunities; at the same time, host countries and universities are recognizing the advantages of receiving international students, as they contribute a growing share of higher education funding.

Tracking and analyzing educational exchange data is critical in our increasingly globalized world. As companies in developing countries compete in the global economic landscape, their workers require not only the quality education their competitors boast, but also the necessary cultural and linguistic skills. Some countries, including Sweden, South Africa, the United Kingdom and Ireland, have developed policies to attract more international students to improve their global competitiveness as well as the funding base for higher education (Atlas, n.d.). Sending countries have their own needs, too, and approach the system of educational exchange frequently through the lens of national interest.

WHAT DO WE KNOW ABOUT EDUCATIONAL EXCHANGE?
According to the UNESCO Global Education Digest the number of students studying in countries other than their own increased 43 per cent between 1999 and 2004 from 1.7 to 2.5 million. Based on population growth estimates and increases in the wealth of developing nations, approximations indicate that the numbers of educational exchange students will double by 2015 and then double again by 2025.

Most notable are the trend data for China. Chinese students studying overseas represent 14 per cent of the world's total number of exchange students. In 2004, nearly 350,000 of its citizens were overseas pursuing tertiary education. Furthermore, while there are noticeable trends in the destinations of the world's leading sending nations, India, with the second largest number of students abroad, sends nearly 65 per cent of its students to the US.

CHINA		INDIA	
Top Sending Country of **EAST ASIA & THE PACIFIC**		Top Sending Country of **SOUTH & WEST ASIA**	
Top 5 Destinations		Top 5 Destinations	
USA	**26**%	USA	**65**%
Japan	**22**%	Australia	**13**%
UK	**14**%	UK	**12**%
Australia	**8**%	Germany	**3**%
Germany	**7**%	New Zealand	**1**%
Other	**23**%	Other	**6**%

SOURCE: UNESCO, Global Education Digest 2006

Only 26 per cent of Chinese students, however, pursue university education in the US, and the distribution of destinations is more balanced, with Japan for example receiving 22 per cent and the UK receiving 14 per cent of Chinese students.

Clearly, educational exchange reflects global cultural and economic relationships. While the US is the primary destination for a majority of Mexico's undocumented immigrants, typically of lower socio-economic status, American universities are also overwhelmingly the principal hosts for Mexico's educated citizens from the more privileged economic classes. Over 60 per cent of Mexico's students studying abroad are in the United States (see data point 5). Similar regional trends are found elsewhere. For example, 65 per cent of Zimbabwe's students studying outside of the country are in neighboring South Africa and 74 per cent of Kazakhstan's education exchange students study in universities in the Russian Federation.

Students from sub-Saharan Africa are by far the most mobile. Nearly 6 per cent of students from this region are studying in another nation. This compares to the .4 per cent of North American students who leave their countries of origin to study elsewhere. Limited opportunities to quality university education are very likely the primary impulse that sends sub-Saharan Africans to study abroad.

Among the world's regions, North America and Western Europe dominate for receiving international students (see data points 1 through 4). The United States, United Kingdom, Germany and France respectively are the top host countries for international students. The US received nearly 573,000 students from abroad during 2004—almost twice the number the UK received. Interestingly, we see a 5 per cent decrease from 2003 to 2004 of Chinese students going to the US while during the same period the UK experienced a 35 per cent increase of Chinese students enrolling in their universities—very likely as a result of stricter visa policies in the US under the Patriot Act of 2002.

Analysis of the top 500 universities, as ranked by the Institute of Higher Education, reveals that the leading European universities have a larger representation of international students than any other region. International students comprise nearly 35 per cent of the student body of Imperial College London, compared to 18.5 per cent at Harvard University, 20.2 per cent at the University of Cape Town, and 20.2 per cent at the Australian National University (see data point 8). However, a 2007 *Newsweek* ranking concludes that the top three 'global universities' are Harvard, Stanford and Yale. In fact the highest ranking European university, Oxford, comes in at eighth place. *Newsweek*'s ranking included variables that considered openness, diversity, percentages of international students and faculty, research, published articles, library holdings, and faculty-to-student ratios (Institute of Higher Education, 2005).

WHAT ARE THE ISSUES?
A critical issue is the *brain drain* inherent in the loss of human capital that occurs when students choose not to return home after receiving an education abroad. Brain drain is a real problem affecting many parts of the developing world in particular. UNDP estimates that 'Ethiopia lost 75 per cent of its skilled workforce between 1980 and 1991' (Dervis, 2007) UNDP administrator Kemal Dervis also estimates that during nearly the

last two decades some 20,000 professionals have been leaving Africa annually. The Middle East and other areas affected by political instability are also facing brain drain problems. The International Monetary Fund ranks Iran as one of the countries facing the highest brain drain, with estimates of 150,000 leaving annually.

The benefits of international education exchange are multiple and apply to both sending and receiving countries. Sweden, South Africa, the UK and Ireland are countries that recognize the need for explicit policies to attract international students. All four have partnered with the Institute of International Education through the Atlas of Student Mobility, to actively state their higher education internationalization policies. South Africa trains its university advisors in credit evaluation to help facilitate credit transfer and actively promotes outreach to other African countries. The UK, as part of the Prime Minister's Initiative, has even created an Education UK brand that universities can use when marketing their programs. Ireland is creating a new statutory agency, Education Ireland, to coordinate policy for this purpose. As Richard Levin, President of Yale University, states (Levin, 2006):

> The bottom line: the flow of students across national borders—students who are disproportionately likely to become leaders in their home countries—enables deeper mutual understanding, tolerance and global integration.

CULTURAL TOURISM

1. AUSTRALIA: CULTURAL TOURISM, INTERNATIONAL VISITORS

AVERAGE ANNUAL VISITS 1999-2003

THOUSANDS OF VISITORS

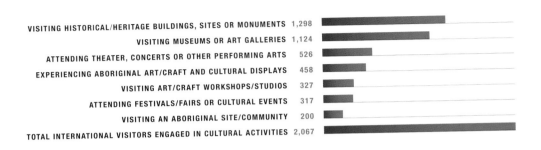

VISITING HISTORICAL/HERITAGE BUILDINGS, SITES OR MONUMENTS	1,298
VISITING MUSEUMS OR ART GALLERIES	1,124
ATTENDING THEATER, CONCERTS OR OTHER PERFORMING ARTS	526
EXPERIENCING ABORIGINAL ART/CRAFT AND CULTURAL DISPLAYS	458
VISITING ART/CRAFT WORKSHOPS/STUDIOS	327
ATTENDING FESTIVALS/FAIRS OR CULTURAL EVENTS	317
VISITING AN ABORIGINAL SITE/COMMUNITY	200
TOTAL INTERNATIONAL VISITORS ENGAGED IN CULTURAL ACTIVITIES	2,067

2. MEXICO: STATES BY ARCHEOLOGICAL HISTORICAL SIGNIFICANCE + TOP 10 STATES RECEIVING VISITORS TO ARCHEOLOGICAL SITES

THOUSANDS OF VISITORS 2007

BAJA CALIFORNIA

SONORA

CHIHUAHUA

COAHUILA

BAJA CALIFORNIA SUR

DURANGO

NUEVO LEON

SINALOA

TAMAULIPAS

ZACATECAS

NAYARIT

YUCATAN

TABASCO

QUINTANA ROO

CAMPECHE

CHIAPAS

ARCHEOLOGICAL SITES

HISTORICAL MONUMENTS

CAVE PAINTINGS

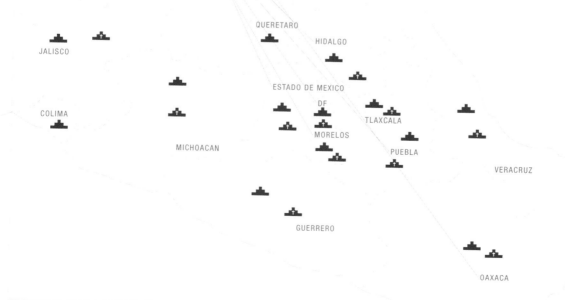

TOTAL VISITORS

MEXICO: 2,794,500

YUCATAN: 1,772,900

QUINTANA ROO: 976,400

OAXACA: 647,900

MORELOS: 597,000

VERACRUZ-LLAVE: 588,700

CHIAPAS: 467,100

PUEBLA: 251,200

HIDALGO: 225,300

DISTRITO FEDERAL: 162,900

QUERETARO

HIDALGO

JALISCO

ESTADO DE MEXICO

COLIMA

DF

TLAXCALA

MICHOACAN

MORELOS

PUEBLA

VERACRUZ

GUERRERO

OAXACA

₃ FRANCE: TOP 10 CULTURAL SITES ₂₀₀₅

MILLIONS OF VISITORS

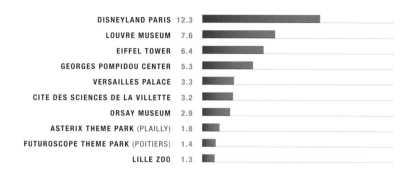

DISNEYLAND PARIS	12.3
LOUVRE MUSEUM	7.6
EIFFEL TOWER	6.4
GEORGES POMPIDOU CENTER	5.3
VERSAILLES PALACE	3.3
CITE DES SCIENCES DE LA VILLETTE	3.2
ORSAY MUSEUM	2.9
ASTERIX THEME PARK (PLAILLY)	1.8
FUTUROSCOPE THEME PARK (POITIERS)	1.4
LILLE ZOO	1.3

₄ MOST VISITED SITES IN INDIA ₂₀₀₅

THOUSANDS OF VISITORS

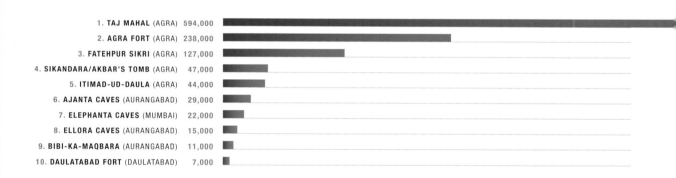

1. TAJ MAHAL (AGRA)	594,000
2. AGRA FORT (AGRA)	238,000
3. FATEHPUR SIKRI (AGRA)	127,000
4. SIKANDARA/AKBAR'S TOMB (AGRA)	47,000
5. ITIMAD-UD-DAULA (AGRA)	44,000
6. AJANTA CAVES (AURANGABAD)	29,000
7. ELEPHANTA CAVES (MUMBAI)	22,000
8. ELLORA CAVES (AURANGABAD)	15,000
9. BIBI-KA-MAQBARA (AURANGABAD)	11,000
10. DAULATABAD FORT (DAULATABAD)	7,000

TOP 10 AMUSEMENT/THEME PARK CHAINS

WORLDWIDE 2003

MILLIONS OF VISITORS (ESTIMATED)

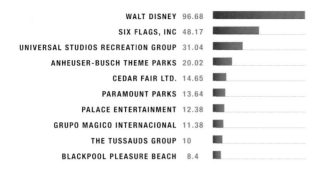

WALT DISNEY	96.68	
SIX FLAGS, INC	48.17	
UNIVERSAL STUDIOS RECREATION GROUP	31.04	
ANHEUSER-BUSCH THEME PARKS	20.02	
CEDAR FAIR LTD.	14.65	
PARAMOUNT PARKS	13.64	
PALACE ENTERTAINMENT	12.38	
GRUPO MAGICO INTERNACIONAL	11.38	
THE TUSSAUDS GROUP	10	
BLACKPOOL PLEASURE BEACH	8.4	

1. A MAUSOLEUM BUILT UNDER MUGHAL EMPEROR SHAH JAHAN IN MEMORY OF HIS FAVORITE WIFE, MUMTAZ MAHAL. UNESCO CALLS IT 'THE JEWEL OF MUSLIM ART IN INDIA AND ONE OF THE UNIVERSALLY ADMIRED MASTERPIECES OF THE WORLD'S HERITAGE.'

2. A WALLED PALATIAL CITY, THE FORT IS ALSO KNOWN AS LAL QILA, FORT ROUGE AND THE RED FORT OF AGRA.

3. BUILT IN HONOR OF SUFI SAINT SALIM CHISTI IN 157 BY MUGHAL EMPEROR AKBAR. A COMPLEX OF MONUMENTS AND TEMPLES, WHICH INCLUDES ONE OF THE LARGEST MOSQUES IN INDIA, THE JAMA MASJID.

4. MAUSOLEUM OF MUGHAL EMPEROR AKBAR THE GREAT.

5. A MAUSOLEUM BUILT ENTIRELY OF PURE MARBLE. MANY OF THE DESIGN ELEMENTS FORESHADOW THE TAJ MAHAL.

6. ROCK-CUT CAVE MONUMENTS DATING FROM THE SECOND CENTURY BCE, CONTAINING PAINTINGS AND SCULPTURE CONSIDERED TO BE MASTERPIECES OF BOTH BUDDHIST RELIGIOUS ART AND UNIVERSAL PICTORIAL ART.

7. THE 'CITY OF CAVES,' ON AN ISLAND OFF MUMBAI, CONTAINS A COLLECTION OF ROCK ART LINKED TO THE CULT OF SHIVA.

8. BUILT BETWEEN THE 5TH CENTURY AND 10TH CENTURY, 35 CAVES EXCAVATED OUT OF THE VERTICAL FACE OF THE CHARANANDRI HILLS COMPRISED OF BUDDHIST, HINDU AND JAIN CAVE TEMPLES AND MONASTERIES.

9. BUILT IN THE LATE 17TH CENTURY, THE MONUMENT'S NAME TRANSLATES LITERALLY TO 'TOMB OF THE LADY' BUT HAS EARNED THE NICKNAME 'POOR MAN'S TAJ' BECAUSE IT WAS MADE TO RIVAL THE TAJ MAHAL.

10. THE AREA OF A VILLAGE WHICH INCLUDES THE HILL-FORTRESS OF DEVAGIRI.

TOP 10 TRAVEL AGENCIES BY SALES 2005

6.

$ MILLIONS USD: AS LISTED ON HOOVERS.COM

TUI AG (GERMANY)	$18,135
BCD TRAVEL (USA)	$12,000
CARNIVAL CORPORATION (ENGLAND)	$11,839
CARLSON WAGONLIT TRAVEL, INC. (USA)	$11,500
ROYAL CARIBBEAN CRUISES (FRANCE)	$ 5,230
MYTRAVEL GROUP (USA)	$ 5,163
FIRST CHOICE HOLIDAYS PLC (ENGLAND)	$ 4,574
SABRE HOLDINGS CORPORATION (USA)	$ 2,824
KUONI TRAVEL HOLDING LTD (SWITZERLAND)	$ 2,804
TRAVELPORT	$ 2,616

TOP TOUR OPERATORS 2006

7.

$ MILLIONS USD: AS LISTED ON HOOVERS.COM

COMPANY NAME	HEADQUARTERS	SALES ($MIL)	EMPLOYEES
Q H TOURS LIMITED	MASCO, NEW WALES, AUSTRALIA	10,464.30	34,832
THOMAS COOK AKTIENGESELLSCHAFT	OBERURSEL (TAUNUS), HESSEN, GERMANY	9,359.70	24,628
TUI UK TRANSPORT LIMITED	LONDON, ENGLAND	2,429.80	850
CLUB MEDITERRANEE S.A.	PARIS, FRANCE	1,917.40	20,333
REWE TOURISTIK GMBH	KOLN, NORDRHEIN-WESTFALEN, GERMANY	1,719.10	262
JETAIR NV	OOSTENDE, WEST-VLAANDEREN, BELGIUM	796.70	495
KUONI TRAVEL LIMITED	DORKING, ENGLAND	630.50	495
THOMAS COOK NEDERLAND BV	HOOFDDORP, NOORD-HOLLAND, THE NETHERLANDS	596.80	1,061
GRAND CIRCLE CORPORATION	BOSTON, MA, USA	577	3,000
THOMAS COOK RETAIL LIMITED	PETERBOROUGH, ENGLAND	564.10	8,504
LOTUS INTERNATIONAL LIMITED	LONDON, ENGLAND	437.30	450
L'TUR TOURISMUS AG	BADEN-BADEN, BADEN WUERTTEMBERG, GERMANY	409	129
THE GLOBESPAN GROUP PLC	EDINBURGH, SCOTLAND	407.40	197
MAUPINTOUR LLC	LAS VEGAS, NV, USA	400	95
THOMAS COOK SIGNATURE LIMITED	PETERBOROUGH, ENGLAND	389.90	768
VIKING LINE ABP	MARIEHAMM, FINLAND	382.70	2,886
MYTRAVEL NORWAY AS	OSLO, NORWAY	338.80	115
JALPAK INTERNATIONAL (EUROPE) BV	AMSTERDAM, NOORD-HOLLAND, THE NETHERLANDS	324	504
TRAVEL 2 LIMITED	LONDON, ENGLAND	317	456
AIRTOURS HOLIDAYS LIMITED	ROCHDALE, ENGLAND	294.10	1,000
THOMSON HOLIDAYS LIMITED	LONDON, ENGLAND	294.10	1,000
OY AURINKOMATKAT - SUNTOURS LIMITED AB	HELSINKI, UUSIMAA, FINLAND	281.40	292
THE MARK TRAVEL CORPORATION	MILWAUKEE, WI, USA	266.40	1,700

TOP 10 TRAVEL-RELATED WEBSITES
AMONG USA, HONG KONG + AUSTRALIAN INTERNET USERS 2006
% MARKET SHARE

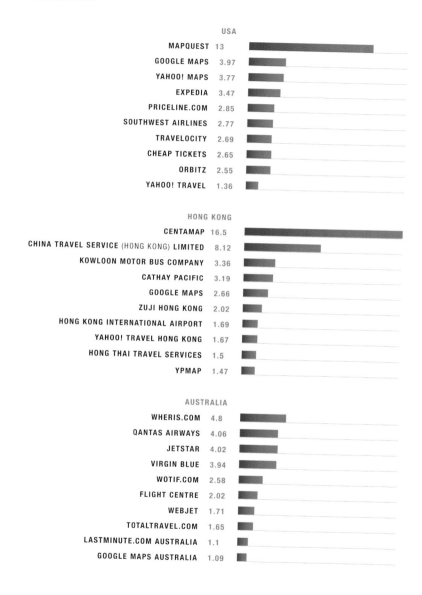

USA

MAPQUEST	13
GOOGLE MAPS	3.97
YAHOO! MAPS	3.77
EXPEDIA	3.47
PRICELINE.COM	2.85
SOUTHWEST AIRLINES	2.77
TRAVELOCITY	2.69
CHEAP TICKETS	2.65
ORBITZ	2.55
YAHOO! TRAVEL	1.36

HONG KONG

CENTAMAP	16.5
CHINA TRAVEL SERVICE (HONG KONG) LIMITED	8.12
KOWLOON MOTOR BUS COMPANY	3.36
CATHAY PACIFIC	3.19
GOOGLE MAPS	2.66
ZUJI HONG KONG	2.02
HONG KONG INTERNATIONAL AIRPORT	1.69
YAHOO! TRAVEL HONG KONG	1.67
HONG THAI TRAVEL SERVICES	1.5
YPMAP	1.47

AUSTRALIA

WHERIS.COM	4.8
QANTAS AIRWAYS	4.06
JETSTAR	4.02
VIRGIN BLUE	3.94
WOTIF.COM	2.58
FLIGHT CENTRE	2.02
WEBJET	1.71
TOTALTRAVEL.COM	1.65
LASTMINUTE.COM AUSTRALIA	1.1
GOOGLE MAPS AUSTRALIA	1.09

9. TOP 10 TRAVEL-RELATED WEBSITES IN GERMANY + FRANCE

RANKED BY UNIQUE VISITORS: MARCH **2007**

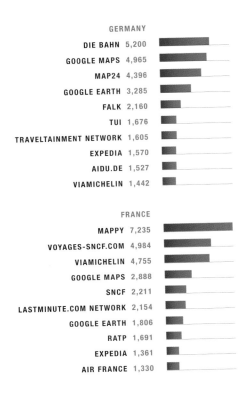

GERMANY

DIE BAHN	5,200
GOOGLE MAPS	4,965
MAP24	4,396
GOOGLE EARTH	3,285
FALK	2,160
TUI	1,676
TRAVELTAINMENT NETWORK	1,605
EXPEDIA	1,570
AIDU.DE	1,527
VIAMICHELIN	1,442

FRANCE

MAPPY	7,235
VOYAGES-SNCF.COM	4,984
VIAMICHELIN	4,755
GOOGLE MAPS	2,888
SNCF	2,211
LASTMINUTE.COM NETWORK	2,154
GOOGLE EARTH	1,806
RATP	1,691
EXPEDIA	1,361
AIR FRANCE	1,330

CULTURAL TOURISM

As the international tourism industry contributes to globalization and in turn seizes the opportunities thus created and provided, it is important to examine the advantages and disadvantages for the world's cultural and environmental heritage. What is now known as 'cultural tourism' allows more and more people everywhere to improve their awareness and appreciation of the world's museums, monuments, natural wonders, etc. However, at the same time, it is a threat to the integrity of the cultures and sites themselves (cf. chapter by Throsby in this volume; also the indicator suite on Heritage Preservation). In the context of this tension, this indicator suite looks at some of the world's top tourist destinations and cultural sites, as well as some of the key players, such as tour agencies, that seek to capture market shares in this rapidly growing part of the cultural economy.

WHAT IS CULTURAL TOURISM?

Cultural tourism is the component of tourism oriented towards the arts and cultural sites of a particular country or region. Its destinations may include museums, archeological sites, theme parks, monuments, natural and environmental sites, even zoos. It may be defined in a range of ways and may often play a variety of roles in the cultural economy. Cultural tourism may be just a piece of a complex cultural industry such as in the case of the Brazilian Bahian Carnival explored in Paolo Miguez's chapter in this volume. Or, conversely, cultural tourism destinations based on events may be initiated for the primary purpose of 'branding the city' in an effort to attract additional cultural tourism dollars as seen with many global artistic festivals (see chapter by Klaic in this volume).

Regardless of how it is defined or its relation to the existing cultural industries, there appears to be consensus that cultural tourism is growing significantly in volume as middle class markets emerge around the world, particularly in Asia, where the market is projected to continue to develop rapidly.

WHAT DO WE KNOW ABOUT CULTURAL TOURISM?

Trends in tourism statistics reveal that in 2005, France, Spain and the US were the top three tourist destinations (UNWTO, 2007). France led with a reported 76 million international tourist arrivals, with Spain following with 55.6 million and the US with 49.4 million. China was the fourth most visited country and is projected by the World Tourism Organization to take the lead by 2020. Other countries that are predicted to move into the top ten are the Russian Federation, Hong Kong and the Czech Republic. Regionally, Europe attracts the most international tourists with 54 per cent of the market, and Asia and the Pacific are in second place with 19 per cent of the market.

A closer look at the most visited destinations shows that in France, the top ten cultural sites are theme parks, museums, and major historical and architectural sites (see data point 3). Disneyland Paris is the most visited cultural site with just over 12 million visitors in 2005. The Louvre Museum follows with 7.6 million visitors. In the US, the Smithsonian Institution reports the most visitors with 34 million in 2000, followed by the National Air and Space Museum with 9 million. Australia defines cultural tourism slightly differently in that visits to aboriginal communities are included in the analysis of visits by international tourists: 458,000 people visited art/craft and cultural displays in aboriginal communities between 1999 and 2003 (see data point 1).

Theme parks are one of the recurring types of popular cultural attractions reported. In the Asian/Pacific Rim region, Disneyland Tokyo was the leading amusement park in 2005, attracting 13 million visitors (Amusement Business, 2006). Globally, Walt Disney is the leading amusement park chain for attendance and revenues with seven parks around the world. Premier Parks/Six Flags came in second place, with Universal Studios third (see data point 5).

WHAT ARE THE ISSUES?

Tourism is one of the world's leading industries. International tourist arrivals are estimated to increase to 1.6 billion a year by 2020, with travelers spending more than US$2 trillion, as compared to US$445 billion currently. The economic, social and even political impact that tourism can have is significant; and as UNESCO indicates, there is a need for clearly articulated policies and strategies for maximizing the benefits and minimizing the costs of this impact.

One of the contested issues is the potentially negative impact cultural tourism can have on culture itself, as expressed in UNESCO's Plan of Action for International Co-operation on Tourism Management in Heritage Cities (n.d.: Point 6):

> The right balance should be struck between the issue of valorizing of the heritage as a means to generate both welfare opportunities for the host community—which bears the costs of tourist exploitation—and the financial means needed to preserve and promote the heritage itself; and the imperative of conservation of the physical integrity, value, and symbols embodied in the heritage for the future generations and the collective memory.

In response, local and national government agencies as well as international bodies like the World Tourism Organization are creating policies for sustainable tourism in order to mitigate negative impacts. For example, the 2007 International Seminar on Sustainable Development of Tourism in Central and Eastern Europe concluded that some of the primary challenges policy needs to address are:

* reducing the seasonality of demand,
* maintaining and enhancing community prosperity in the face of change,
* minimizing resource use and the production of waste, and
* conserving and giving value to natural and cultural heritage (UNWTO, 2007: 8-11).

At the same time, many developing countries are also recognizing that cultural tourism can play an important role in reducing poverty. In Tanzania tourism comprises 16 per cent of GDP and is thought to provide approximately 200,000 jobs in the country (UNWTO and Tanzania Tourist Board, July 2006). Recognizing its potential to be a catalyst of economic development the country has created a cultural tourism program that identifies the top destinations as well as the heritage tourism of some 120 ethnic groups across Tanzania.

GLOBAL CONCERT TOURS

1. GLOBAL CONCERT TOURS MARKET 2004 + 2005

GLOBAL CONCERT TOURS	2004	2005	% CHANGE
GROSS US BILLIONS	2.6	2.6	0.3%
ATTENDANCE MILLIONS	54.5	53.8	− 1.3%
CAPACITY MILLIONS	71.3	68.8	− 3.5%
SHOWS	14,301	15,679	9.6%
SELLOUT SHOWS	3,758	4,903	30.5%

2a. TOP GROSSING CONCERT TOURS 2001-2002 + 2003-2004

TOTAL GROSS IN MILLIONS

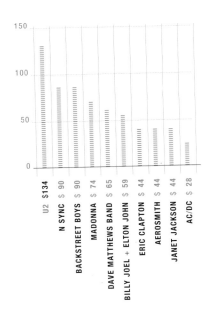

U2 $134
N SYNC $ 90
BACKSTREET BOYS $ 90
MADONNA $ 74
DAVE MATTHEWS BAND $ 65
BILLY JOEL + ELTON JOHN $ 59
ERIC CLAPTON $ 44
AEROSMITH $ 44
JANET JACKSON $ 44
AC/DC $ 28

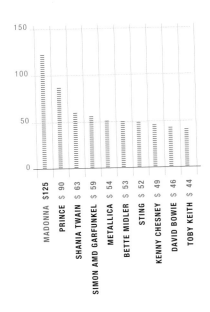

MADONNA $125
PRINCE $ 90
SHANIA TWAIN $ 63
SIMON AMD GARFUNKEL $ 59
METALLICA $ 54
BETTE MIDLER $ 53
STING $ 52
KENNY CHESNEY $ 49
DAVID BOWIE $ 46
TOBY KEITH $ 44

TOP GROSSING CONCERT TOURS 2003-2004

TOTAL ATTENDANCE TOTAL CAPACITY # OF SHOWS # OF SELLOUT SHOWS

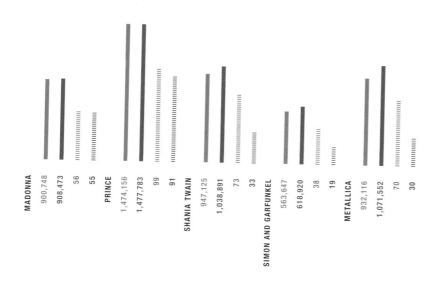

MADONNA 900,748 908,473 56 55
PRINCE 1,474,156 1,477,783 99 91
SHANIA TWAIN 947,125 1,038,891 73 33
SIMON AND GARFUNKEL 563,647 618,920 38 19
METALLICA 932,116 1,071,552 70 30

TOP GROSSING CONCERT TOURS 2003-2004

TOTAL ATTENDANCE TOTAL CAPACITY # OF SHOWS # OF SELLOUT SHOWS

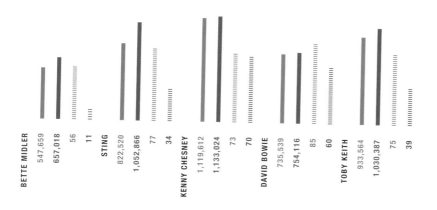

BETTE MIDLER 547,659 657,018 56 11
STING 822,520 1,052,866 77 34
KENNY CHESNEY 1,119,612 1,133,024 73 70
DAVID BOWIE 735,539 754,116 85 60
TOBY KEITH 933,564 1,030,387 75 39

3. TOP 10 GROSSING CONCERT VENUES 2004

WITH CAPACITY OF 10,001-15,000 SEATS

TOTAL GROSS $ IN THOUSANDS **TOTAL ATTENDANCE** IN THOUSANDS

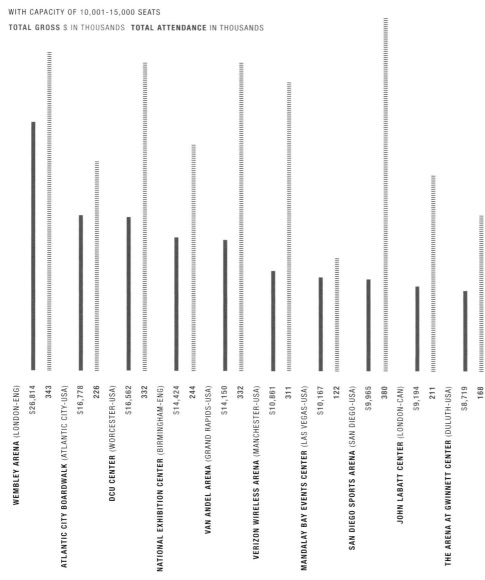

WEMBLEY ARENA (LONDON-ENG)
$26,814
343

ATLANTIC CITY BOARDWALK (ATLANTIC CITY-USA)
$16,778
226

DCU CENTER (WORCESTER-USA)
$16,562
332

NATIONAL EXHIBITION CENTER (BIRMINGHAM-ENG)
$14,424
244

VAN ANDEL ARENA (GRAND RAPIDS-USA)
$14,150
332

VERIZON WIRELESS ARENA (MANCHESTER-USA)
$10,861
311

MANDALAY BAY EVENTS CENTER (LAS VEGAS-USA)
$10,167
122

SAN DIEGO SPORTS ARENA (SAN DIEGO-USA)
$9,965
380

JOHN LABATT CENTER (LONDON-CAN)
$9,194
211

THE ARENA AT GWINNETT CENTER (DULUTH-USA)
$8,719
168

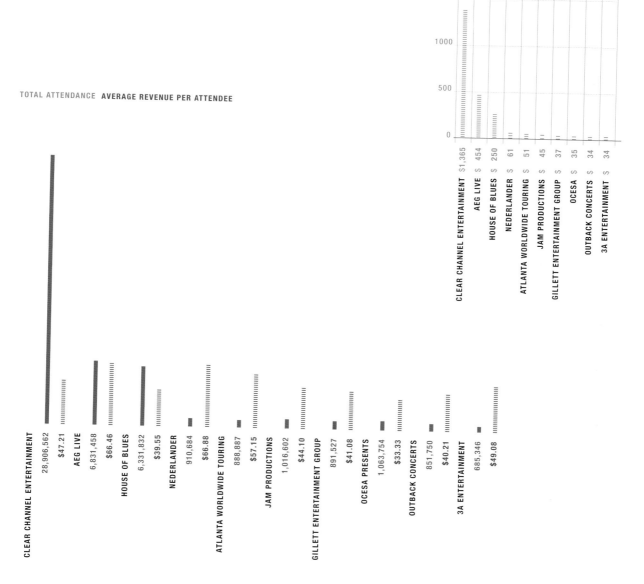

TOTAL ATTENDANCE **AVERAGE REVENUE PER ATTENDEE**

CLEAR CHANNEL ENTERTAINMENT
28,906,562
$47.21

AEG LIVE
6,831,458
$66.46

HOUSE OF BLUES
6,331,832
$39.55

NEDERLANDER
910,684
$66.88

ATLANTA WORLDWIDE TOURING
888,887
$57.15

JAM PRODUCTIONS
1,016,602
$44.10

GILLETT ENTERTAINMENT GROUP
891,527
$41.08

OCESA PRESENTS
1,063,754
$33.33

OUTBACK CONCERTS
851,750
$40.21

3A ENTERTAINMENT
685,346
$49.08

CLEAR CHANNEL ENTERTAINMENT $1,365
AEG LIVE $ 454
HOUSE OF BLUES $ 250
NEDERLANDER $ 61
ATLANTA WORLDWIDE TOURING $ 51
JAM PRODUCTIONS $ 45
GILLETT ENTERTAINMENT GROUP $ 37
OCESA $ 35
OUTBACK CONCERTS $ 34
3A ENTERTAINMENT $ 34

5. LIVE NATION INTERNATIONAL TOURS + EVENTS 2004-2006

2004 2006 **2006**

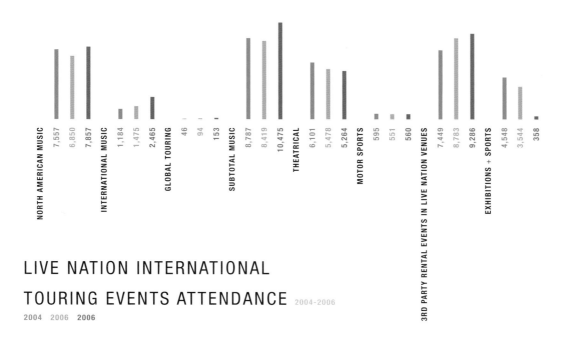

NORTH AMERICAN MUSIC
7,557
6,850
7,857

INTERNATIONAL MUSIC
1,184
1,475
2,465

GLOBAL TOURING
46
94
153

SUBTOTAL MUSIC
8,787
8,419
10,475

THEATRICAL
6,101
5,478
5,264

MOTOR SPORTS
595
551
560

3RD PARTY RENTAL EVENTS IN LIVE NATION VENUES
7,449
8,783
9,286

EXHIBITIONS + SPORTS
4,548
3,544
358

LIVE NATION INTERNATIONAL TOURING EVENTS ATTENDANCE 2004-2006

2004 2006 **2006**

701,000
2,428,000
2,914,000

TOTAL EVENTS 2004-2006

2004 2006 **2006**

27,480
26,775
25,943

TOP 10 SPORTS + ENTERTAINMENT PROMOTERS AS OF JULY 2007

COMPANY NAME	LOCATION	SALES US$ MIL	EMPLOYEES
01. **LIVE NATION**, INC	BEVERLY HILLS, CA, USA	3,691.60	3,000
02. **MECCA BINGO** LTD.	MAIDENHEAD, ENGLAND	516.90	6,647
03. **WORLD WRESTLING ENTERTAINMENT**, INC	STAMFORD, CT, USA	262.90	460
04. **CENTER OPERATING COMPANY** L.P.	DALLAS, TX, USA	156	1,625
05. **SMG MANAGEMENT**	PHILADELPHIA, PA, USA	141	580
06. **HOLIDAY CO**, LTD	TAIPEI CITY, TAIPEI, TAIWAN	140.30	20
07. **PALACE SPORTS & ENTERTAINMENT**, INC	AUBURN HILLS, MI, USA	134.40	1,400
08. **RTL SHOP** GMBH	KOLN, NORDRHEIN-WESTFALEN, GERMANY	105.40	90
09. **LINCOLN CENTER FOR THE PERFORMING ARTS**, INC	NEW YORK, NY, USA	101.70	525
10. **OLYMPIA ENTERTAINMENT**, INC	DETROIT, MI, USA	96	1,000

## 7

CONCERT + EVENT TICKETING: INTERACTIVE CORP + TICKETMASTER
AS LISTED ON HOOVERS.COM

	TOTAL REVENUES	EMPLOYEES	SUBSIDIARIES	EXAMPLE SUBSIDIARIES	GLOBAL OFFICE LOCATIONS
INTERACTIVE CORP-IAC (NEW YORK, NY)	2006: $6.3 BILLION	20,000 FULL-TIME	268	HSN, TRAVELSMITH, CORNERSTONE BRANDS, TICKETMASTER, LENDING TREE, MATCH.COM, ASK. COM, CITYSEARCH, EXCITE	ARGENTINA, AUSTRALIA, BRAZIL, CANADA, CHINA, COLOMBIA, DENMARK, ENGLAND, EGYPT, FINLAND, FRANCE, GERMANY, IRELAND, ITALY, JAPAN, MEXICO, NETHERLANDS, NEW ZEALAND, NORTHERN IRELAND, NORWAY, PORTUGAL, SCOTLAND, SINGAPORE, SPAIN, SWEDEN, TURKEY, VENEZUELA
TICKETMASTER	2005: $950.2 MILLION	10,405	3	RESERVE AMERICA, TICKETWEB, ADMISSION	AUSTRALIA, BRAZIL, CANADA, CHILE, CHINA, DENMARK, FINLAND, GERMANY, IRELAND, MEXICO, NETHERLANDS, NEW ZEALAND, NORWAY, SPAIN, SWEDEN, TURKEY, UNITED KINGDOM

8. TOP 10 CONCERTS JULY 2006 + 2007

AGGREGATED FROM BILLBOARD MAGAZINE'S WEEKLY BOXSCORE

HEADLINING ARTISTS 2006	JULY GROSS REVENUES	JULY TOTAL ATTENDANCE	CONCERT PROMOTERS
BON JOVI	45,266,095	649,785	WEST/AEG LIVE
MADONNA	27,033,065	157,472	THE NEXT ADVENTURE
TIM MCGRAW AND FAITH HILL	20,130,442	253,752	LIVE NATION, JACK UTSICK PRESENTS N.E., BEAVER PRODS.
KENNY CHESNEY	16,246,814	276,143	AEG LIVE
DAVE MATTHEWS BAND	15,080,057	347,117	LIVE NATION, HOUSE OF BLUES CANADA
BONNAROO MUSIC FESTIVAL	14,731,723	80,681	SUPERFLY PRODS.
TAKE THAT	11,204,720	167,967	KENNEDY STREET ENTERTAINMENT
CELINE DION	9,768,790	72,167	AEG LIVE
ANDREA BOCELLI	9,017,088	65,389	LIVE NATION, CLASSIC ENTERTAINMENT
TOM PETTY AND THE HEARTBREAKERS	6,017,405	120,969	LIVE NATION, JAM PRODS.

HEADLINING ARTISTS 2007	JULY GROSS REVENUES	JULY TOTAL ATTENDANCE	CONCERT PROMOTERS
THE POLICE	43,751,190	379,939	THE NEXT ADVENTURE (A LIVE NATION COMPANY)
DOWNLOAD FESTIVAL	20,179,520	70,000	LIVE NATION-UK
TIM MCGRAW AND FAITH HILL	17,122,132	177,332	LIVE NATION
ROGER WATERS	15,150,513	173,214	ANDREW HEWITT CO./BILL SILVA PRESENTS, LIVE NATION
KENNY CHESNEY	13,467,014	207,429	EAGLES STADIUM OPERATOR, THE MESSINA GROUP/AEG LIVE; LIVE NATION; UNITED CONCERTS
JUSTIN TIMBERLAKE	11,626,801	136,252	CONCERTS WEST/AEG LIVE
CELINE DION	8,014,166	57,979	CONCERTS WEST/AEG LIVE
GWEN STEFANI	5,416,794	113,400	LIVE NATION
BRYAN ADAMS	4,693,997	67,359	LIVE NATION-UK
AEROSMITH	4,229,577	47,000	LIVE NATION-UK

GLOBAL CONCERT TOURS

Although often considered as a single coherent industry with shared objectives and interests, the music industry is actually an amalgamation of rather distinct fields such as recording and publishing, merchandising, music video production, promotion, and live music production (Williamson and Cloonan, 2007). This indicator suite on global concert tours attempts to break down one segment of the overall global music universe (see related indicator suites on music and festivals). Accounting for almost 13 per cent of the global music industry (Lopes, n.d.), concert tours play a significant role in generating revenue for musicians, songwriters, music labels and producers, as well as the burgeoning concert promotion industry. While the Internet, piracy and online broadcasting of music have challenged record sales, concert tours have grown in importance for promoting musicians, bands and orchestras at the global level. Indeed, tours have become an essential vehicle for creating and sustaining artistic popularity, and hence sales. Both the organizers of tour venues and the concert promoters help keep the music industry economically vibrant in the face of increasing digitization.

WHAT ARE GLOBAL CONCERT TOURS?

Since the 1990s, and with the growth of MTV and music videos, concert tours have become large-scale enterprises, lasting for several months or even years, seen by hundreds of thousands or millions of people, and worth millions of dollars in ticket revenues. Indeed, popular music concert tours have become spectacles, incorporating the use of stage lighting and special effects, backup stage performers, elaborate costumes, film, video and even pyrotechnics. In this way, concerts provide exposure to the public and serve as an integral promotional outlet for musicians or albums, resulting in increased revenues, not necessarily for the artist alone, but for the music label, ticket seller and concert promoter as well.

TRENDS AND ISSUES

From 2004 to 2005, although global concert tours grew only .3 per cent (see data point 1), concert tour shows grew 9.6 per cent and sellout shows grew 30.5 per cent. The top grossing concert tour from 2001 and 2002 was U2's 'Elevation' tour which reached US$134 million (see data point 2a). In 2003 to 2004, Madonna's 'Re-invention' tour grossed US$125 million, and in 2006, Madonna's 'Confessions' tour became the highest grossing concert tour by a female artist with US$195 million total in revenues (Waddell, 2006). Of all the top ten grossing concerts in July 2006 and July 2007, top artists represented countries from North America or Europe alone (see data point 8).

In 2004, of the leading venues for global concert tours, the top ten were dominated by sites in England, the United States and Canada (see data point 3). Wembley Arena in London received the largest gross revenues of US$26,814,000 as a concert venue, while the San Diego Sports Arena in the US had the largest number of concert attendees for that year (380,000).

In 2004, Clear Channel was the leading concert promoter (see data point 4), with its concert promotion division fueled by its subsidiary, Live Nation. During this year, Clear Channel promoted the most concerts and had more sellout shows than any other concert promoter or their main rival, House of Blues (see graph below). At the end of 2004, Live Nation was spun-off of Clear Channel Entertainment and became an independent corporation.

Today's global concert industry has experienced increasing market concentration, dominated by a handful of concert promoters and ticket sellers—the most formidable being Live Nation and Ticketmaster. As in 2004, Live Nation remains the leading concert promoter worldwide with revenues of US$3,692 million in 2006 (see data point 6). In July 2006 and 2007, Live Nation promoted at least half of the top 20 concerts for those months (see data point 8). International touring events promoted by Live Nation have increased in attendance from 701,000 attendees in 2004 to 2,914,000 in 2006 (see data point 5). Indeed, Live Nation as a brand name has become synonymous with not only the live musical acts which they promote, but with the venues they own and the numerous event promotion businesses which they have acquired over recent years. In 2006 alone, Live Nation owned/operated 131 venues in North America and Europe, and acquired 7 major events promotion companies, the most notable being House of Blues, no longer a main competitor and yet one

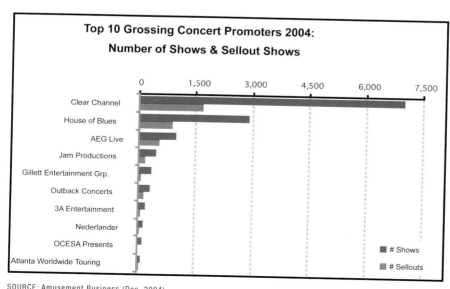

Top 10 Grossing Concert Promoters 2004: Number of Shows & Sellout Shows

SOURCE: Amusement Business (Dec. 2004)

of the most recognizable names in the live music venue business in North America (Live Nation, 2006 Annual Report).

Ticketmaster is the global leader in ticket sales worldwide, not only for concerts, but also for most entertainment, sports and cultural events. As a subsidiary of Interactive Corp. (IAC), based in New York, Ticketmaster's reach extends well into North America, Latin America, Europe, and parts of Asia (namely China) (see data point 7). Through their 6,500 ticket centers, the Ticketmaster outlets sell approximately 1,000,000 tickets for events each year. In 2005, Ticketmaster's total revenues reached US$950.2 million, a majority of that acquired via the markup value of tickets through various service fees (see data point 7).

It is estimated that between 1996 and 2003, ticket prices rose 8.9 per cent in the United States (compared to 2.3 per cent of inflation), with similar increases in Europe ('Winners take all in rockonomics,' 2006). Some concert goers and artists, such as the band Pearl Jam in 1994, have complained that the markup price of tickets has made it economically unfeasible to attend, making concerts an increasingly elitist activity. Yet, if the attendance and rising popularity of concerts for artists such as Madonna is any indication, it is clear that concert tours for popular music artists will continue to grow as a significant revenue generator for musicians, ticket sellers and concert promoters. In fact, the recent US$100 million deal between Madonna and Live Nation for rights to three albums, concert promotion and merchandising indicates that artists with star-power and concert promoters are entering into a new realm of music-making where record labels and music companies may find themselves increasingly bypassed ('Madonna nears deal to leave record label,' 2007).

INDICATOR SUITE

CULTURES AS A POLITICAL SYSTEM

REGULATORY FRAMEWORKS + POLICY

36. INTERNATIONAL STANDARDS

37. NATIONAL + REGIONAL CULTURAL POLICY

38. INTERNATIONAL REGULATORY FRAMEWORKS

INTERNATIONAL STANDARDS

1. ISO **ANNUAL PRODUCTION** OF STANDARDS 1998-2006

	0	200	400	600	800	1000	1200	1400
1058 YEAR 1998								
961 YEAR 1999								
986 YEAR 2000								
813 YEAR 2001								
889 YEAR 2002								
995 YEAR 2003								
1247 YEAR 2004								
1240 YEAR 2005								
1338 YEAR 2006								

2. ISO ANNUAL PRODUCTION: # **OF NEW PAGES**

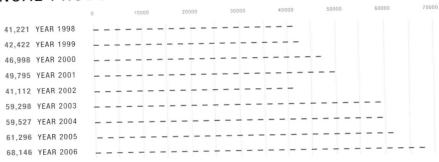

	0	10000	20000	30000	40000	50000	60000	70000
41,221 YEAR 1998								
42,422 YEAR 1999								
46,998 YEAR 2000								
49,795 YEAR 2001								
41,112 YEAR 2002								
59,298 YEAR 2003								
59,527 YEAR 2004								
61,296 YEAR 2005								
68,146 YEAR 2006								

3. TOP 15 COUNTRIES PER # OF ALLOCATED ISMN IDENTIFIERS AS OF 2003

ISMN: INTERNATIONAL STANDARD MUSIC NUMBER IS A TEN-CHARACTER ALPHANUMERIC IDENTIFIER

	0	100	200	300	400
GERMANY 504					
UNITED KINGDOM 209					
FINLAND 121					
CANADA 103					
FRANCE 96					
AUSTRALIA 93					
SPAIN 90					
CROATIA 90					
LITHUANIA 84					
SWEDEN 75					
DENMARK 67					
NORWAY 59					
CZECH REPUBLIC 53					
POLAND 51					
ITALY 45					

4. # OF **ISSN RECORDS** BY TYPE YEAR 2004 YEAR 2005 YEAR 2006

ISSN: INTERNATIONAL STANDARD SERIAL NUMBER IS AN EIGHT-DIGIT NUMBER WHICH IDENTIFIES ALL
PERIODICAL PUBLICATIONS, INCLUDING ELECTRONIC SERIALS

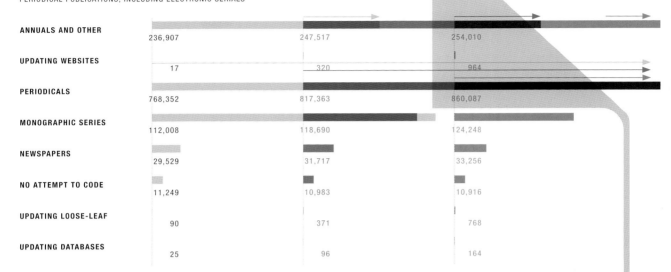

	YEAR 2004	YEAR 2005	YEAR 2006
ANNUALS AND OTHER	236,907	247,517	254,010
UPDATING WEBSITES	17	320	964
PERIODICALS	768,352	817,363	860,087
MONOGRAPHIC SERIES	112,008	118,690	124,248
NEWSPAPERS	29,529	31,717	33,256
NO ATTEMPT TO CODE	11,249	10,983	10,916
UPDATING LOOSE-LEAF	90	371	768
UPDATING DATABASES	25	96	164

5. TOTAL # OF **RECORDS IN THE ISSN REGISTER** 2001-2006

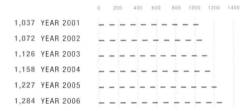

0   200   400   600   800   1000   1200   1400

1,037	YEAR 2001
1,072	YEAR 2002
1,126	YEAR 2003
1,158	YEAR 2004
1,227	YEAR 2005
1,284	YEAR 2006

6. ALLOCATION OF **ISSN RECORDS** BY REGION YEAR 2001 YEAR 2006

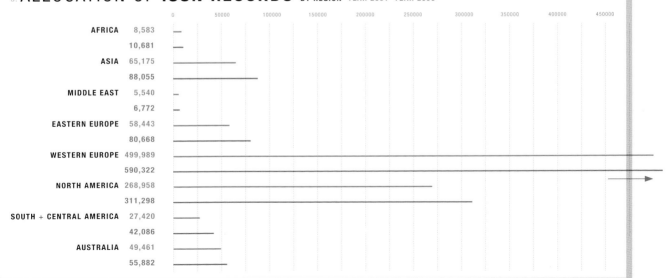

0   50000   100000   150000   200000   250000   300000   350000   400000   450000

AFRICA	8,583
	10,681
ASIA	65,175
	88,055
MIDDLE EAST	5,540
	6,772
EASTERN EUROPE	58,443
	80,668
WESTERN EUROPE	499,989
	590,322
NORTH AMERICA	268,958
	311,298
SOUTH + CENTRAL AMERICA	27,420
	42,086
AUSTRALIA	49,461
	55,882

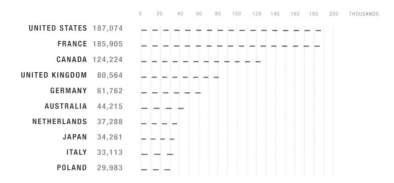

		0	20	40	60	80	100	120	140	160	180	200	THOUSANDS
UNITED STATES	187,074												
FRANCE	185,905												
CANADA	124,224												
UNITED KINGDOM	80,564												
GERMANY	61,762												
AUSTRALIA	44,215												
NETHERLANDS	37,288												
JAPAN	34,261												
ITALY	33,113												
POLAND	29,983												

INTERNATIONAL STANDARDS International standards are developed by a range of international organizations. By definition, international standards are intended for universal, worldwide use either by direct application or through their adaptation to local conditions. The adoption of international standards results in the creation of national standards that are all substantially the same as international standards are in technical content, but may have: a) editorial differences as to appearance, use of symbols and measurement units (e.g., substitution of a point for a comma as the decimal marker) and b) differences resulting from governmental regulations or industry-specific requirements caused by fundamental climatic, geographical, technological, or infrastructural factors, or safety requirements that a given standard-setting authority considers appropriate.

International standards are one way of overcoming technical and other barriers in international commerce caused by differences among technical regulations and standards developed independently and separately by nations or companies. International standards help prevent or overcome problems of incompatibility by avoiding transaction costs in transnational business and technology development. They also help lower developmental costs for new products and services. For consumers, they allow greater comparability.

Behind the economic-technical rationale for international standards there is a significant cultural dimension. Indeed, the cultural influence of international standards is immense, as they have profound impacts on human and organizational behavior. They are often rather subtle forces of globalization in the sense that they shape everyday behavior and penetrate virtually all aspects of human endeavor. Standards are part of the increasingly global social organization of rationalized modernity, and contribute, in the name of efficiency, to greater similarities across cultures.

STANDARD-SETTING ORGANIZATIONS

In the fields of education and culture, UNESCO has been the main agency for standard-setting for over sixty years. Indeed, standard-setting represents one of the main constitutional functions of UNESCO. The instruments used by UNESCO to establish and oversee are conventions, declarations, and recommendations (see digest on International Regulatory Frameworks). Outside the field of culture, there are a relatively small number

of organizations that serve as the main holders and producers of these kinds of international standards: the International Organization of Standardization (ISO), the International Electrotechnican Commission (IEC), the Codex Alimentarius, the International Telecommunication Union (ITU), the International Labor Organization (ILO), the World Wide Web Consortium (W3C), and the Internet Corporation for Assigned Names and Numbers (ICANN). While these organizations do not deal explicitly with the cultural industries, many of their policies, particularly in relation to technology, dissemination and labor practices, are cross-cutting and, either directly or indirectly, impact the cultural industries. With the exception of the W3C and ICANN, members of these organizations are nations who also belong to the United Nations. W3C membership is composed of organizations. Among W3C member organizations, ISO is by far the largest, containing the greatest numbers of standards, and is the most well-known for setting standards. ISO also sets international standards in conjunction with other organizations, indicated in the serial number that is assigned to the specific standard.

ICANN was created in 1998 to oversee a number of Internet-related tasks previously performed directly on behalf of the US government by other organizations, notably the Internet Assigned Numbers Authority (IANA). Through a memorandum of understanding with the US government, ICANN aims 'to transition management of the Domain Name System (DNS) from the U.S. government to the global community' (ICANN, n.d.). This will allow for input on future Internet governance policy issues from nations around the world.

The IEC is an international standards organization that prepares and publishes international standards for all electrical, electronic and related technologies—collectively known as 'electrotechnology.' IEC standards cover a vast range of technologies from power generation, transmission and distribution to home appliances and office equipment, semiconductors, fiber optics, batteries, solar energy, nanotechnology and marine energy to mention just a few. The IEC also manages conformity assessment schemes that certify whether equipment, systems or components conform to its International Standards (IEC, n.d.).

The ITU is an international organization established to standardize and regulate international radio and telecommunications. It was founded as the International Telegraph Union in Paris on May 17, 1865. Its main tasks include standardization, allocation of the radio spectrum, and organizing interconnection arrangements between different countries to allow international phone calls (ITU, n.d.).

The primary goal of the ILO is to promote opportunities for women and men to obtain decent and productive work, in conditions of freedom, equity, security and human dignity. In working towards this goal, the organization seeks to promote employment creation, strengthen fundamental principles and rights at work (workers' rights), improve social protection, and promote social dialogue as well as provide relevant information, training and technical assistance (ILO, n.d.).

The W3C is the main international standards organization for the World Wide Web (W3). It is arranged as a consortium where member organizations maintain full-time staff for the purpose of working together in the development of standards for the W3. As of March 2007, the W3C had 441 members (W3C, n.d.).

TRENDS IN STANDARD-SETTING

As globalization has increased the number and speed of global transactions, a need for standards is evermore present. The data in this suite illustrate that ISO standards and the number of pages associated with these standards have been steadily rising over recent years. Since the last book, the number of standards has risen by almost 1,000, while the number of pages has risen by over 10 per cent since 2005. The figure on the next page depicts a timeline detailing the implementation of major international standards, many of which have only recently been instituted. This serves as an additional indicator illustrating the correlation, in many cases, of the rise of globalization with the need/creation of internationally recognized standards.

Organizations other than those mentioned above that create standards concerning cultural goods are the International ISMN Agency (International Standard Music Number) and the holders of the ISSN (International Standard Serial Number). In both instances, the data indicate that Western European nations are the main upholders of both of these standards, and that the number of allocated standards has risen over the years. This may be related to globalization's effect on the World Wide Web, which has become the common dissemination network across the world. As users are file-sharing various cultural goods, it is logical for the number of standards that serve as unique identifiers of a piece of work to increase over time.

Lastly, it should be noted that both the increase in file-sharing and the increase in media capacity have precipitated additional standards to be created, and/or the frequency of enforcement to increase. Data in this suite indicate recent adoptions of standards for musical or text works, which were formerly not necessary. Standards for audio-visual work were only put into place in 2003.

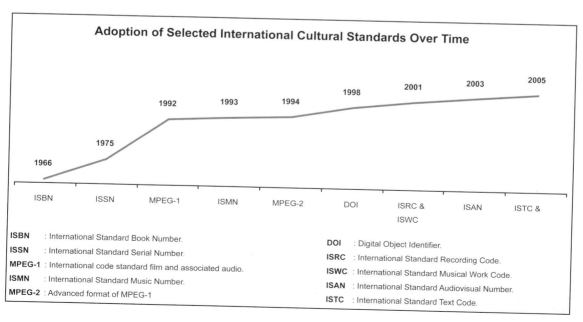

Adoption of Selected International Cultural Standards Over Time

1966 — ISBN
1975 — ISSN
1992 — MPEG-1
1993 — ISMN
1994 — MPEG-2
1998 — DOI
2001 — ISRC & ISWC
2003 — ISAN
2005 — ISTC &

ISBN : International Standard Book Number.
ISSN : International Standard Serial Number.
MPEG-1 : International code standard film and associated audio.
ISMN : International Standard Music Number.
MPEG-2 : Advanced format of MPEG-1

DOI : Digital Object Identifier.
ISRC : International Standard Recording Code.
ISWC : International Standard Musical Work Code.
ISAN : International Standard Audiovisual Number.
ISTC : International Standard Text Code.

NATIONAL +

REGIONAL CULTURAL

POLICY

1. CULTURALLY LEAST CONNECTED COUNTRIES + THE ORGANIZATIONS CONNECTING THEM

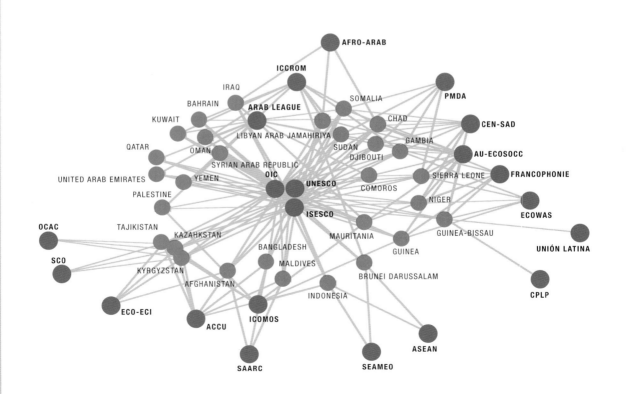

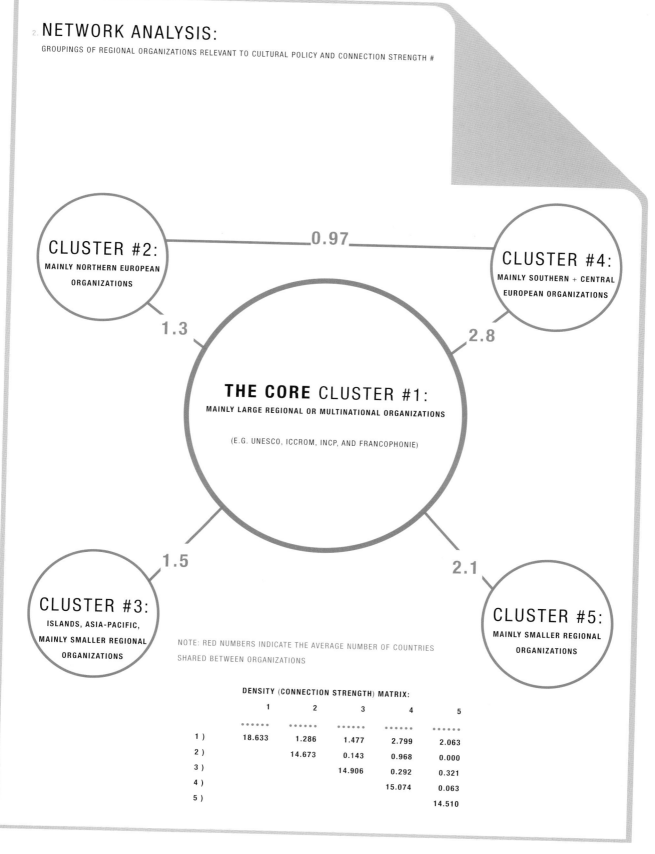

NETWORK ANALYSIS:

GROUPINGS OF REGIONAL ORGANIZATIONS RELEVANT TO CULTURAL POLICY AND CONNECTION STRENGTH #

CLUSTER #2:
MAINLY NORTHERN EUROPEAN ORGANIZATIONS

0.97

CLUSTER #4:
MAINLY SOUTHERN + CENTRAL EUROPEAN ORGANIZATIONS

1.3

2.8

THE CORE CLUSTER #1:
MAINLY LARGE REGIONAL OR MULTINATIONAL ORGANIZATIONS

(E.G. UNESCO, ICCROM, INCP, AND FRANCOPHONIE)

1.5

2.1

CLUSTER #3:
ISLANDS, ASIA-PACIFIC, MAINLY SMALLER REGIONAL ORGANIZATIONS

CLUSTER #5:
MAINLY SMALLER REGIONAL ORGANIZATIONS

NOTE: RED NUMBERS INDICATE THE AVERAGE NUMBER OF COUNTRIES
SHARED BETWEEN ORGANIZATIONS

DENSITY (CONNECTION STRENGTH) MATRIX:

	1	2	3	4	5
1)	18.633	1.286	1.477	2.799	2.063
2)		14.673	0.143	0.968	0.000
3)			14.906	0.292	0.321
4)				15.074	0.063
5)					14.510

CLUSTER #1:
MAINLY LARGE MULTINATIONAL
ORGANIZATIONS

CLUSTER #2:
MAINLY NORTHERN EUROPEAN
ORGANIZATIONS

THE CORE CLUSTER #1 MAINLY LARGE MULTINATIONAL ORGANIZATIONS:

_INTERNATIONAL NETWORK ON CULTURAL POLICY INCP

_INTERNATIONAL COUNCIL ON MONUMENTS AND SITES (ICOMOS)

_FRANCOPHONIE

_COMMUNITY OF SAHEL-SAHARAN STATES (CENSAD)

_UNION LATINA

_ECONOMIC COMMUNITY OF WEST AFRICA STATES (ECOWAS)

_ISLAMIC EDUCATIONAL, SCIENTIFIC AND CULTURAL ORGANIZATION (ISESCO)

_ORGANIZATION OF IBEROAMERICAN STATES FOR EDUCATION, SCIENCE AND CULTURE (OEI)

_AFRICAN UNION: ECONOMIC, SOCIAL AND CUTURAL COUNCIL (AU-ECOSOCC)

_THE PROGRAMME FOR MUSEUM DEVELOPMENT IN AFRICA (PMDA)

_ORGANIZATION OF AMERICAN STATES (OAS)

_INTERNATIONAL CENTER FOR THE STUDY OF THE PRESERVATION AND RESTORATION OF CULTURAL PROPERTY (ICCROM)

_UNESCO, OFICINA REGIONAL DE CULTURA PARA AMERICA LATINA Y EL CARIBE (ORCALC)

_PARLAMENTO LATINOAMERICANO-PARLATINO

_ARAB LEAGUE

_ORGANIZATION OF THE ISLAMIC CONFERENCE (OIC)

CLUSTER #2 MAINLY NORTHERN EUROPEAN ORGANIZATIONS:

_EUREGIO MAAS-RHEIN

_GROSSREGION SAAR-LOR-LUX

_BALTIC COOPERATION

_SISTEMA DE INTEGRACION CENTROAMERICANA (SICA)

_BARENTS REGIONAL COUNCIL

_TAALUNIE

_ARCTIC COUNCIL

CLUSTER #3:
MAINLY ISLANDS, ASIA-PACIFIC
SMALLER REGIONAL
ORGANIZATIONS

CLUSTER #4:
MAINLY SOUTHERN EUROPEAN
ORGANIZATIONS

CLUSTER #5
MAINLY SMALLER REGION
ORGANIZATIONS

CLUSTER #3 **MAINLY ISLANDS, ASIA-PACIFIC, SMALLER REGIONAL ORGANIZATIONS:**

_**SHANGHAI COOPERATION ORGANIZATION** (SCO)

_**PACIFIC ISLANDS FORUM SECRETARIAT** (PIF)

_**SOUTH ASIAN ASSOCIATION FOR REGIONAL COOPERATION** (SAARC)

_**SECRETARIAT OF THE PACIFIC COMMUNITY/SOUTH PACIFIC COMMISSION** (SPC)

_**ASIA/PACIFIC CULTURAL CENTER FOR UNESCO** (ACCU)

_**GEORGIA, UKR, AZ, MOL** (GUAM)

_**ORGANIZATION OF CENTRAL ASIAN COOPERATION** (OCAC)

_**ECONOMIC COOPERATION ORGANIZATION CULTURAL INSTITUTE** (ECO-ECI)

CLUSTER #4 **MAINLY SOUTHERN EUROPEAN ORGANIZATIONS:**

_**CENTRAL EUROPEAN INITIATIVE** (ECI)

_**VISEGRAD GROUP**

_**ALPS ADRIA**

_**EUROPEAN UNION**

_**COUNCIL OF MINISTERS - SOUTHEAST EUROPE** (COMSEE)

_**QUADRILATERALE**

_**PLATFORM CULTURE - CENTRAL EUROPE** (CCE)

_**BLACK SEA ECONOMIC COOPERATION** (BSEC)

_**COUNCIL OF EUROPE** (COE)

CLUSTER #5 **SMALLER REGIONAL ORGANIZATIONS:**

_**ASSOCIATION OF SOUTHEAST ASIAN NATIONS** (ASEAN)

_**COMMUNITY OF PORTUGUESE-SPEAKING COUNTRIES** (CPLP)

_**AFRO-ARAB CULTURAL INSTITUTE**

_**SOUTHERN AFRICAN DEVELOPMENT COMMUNITY** (SADC)

_**SOUTHEAST ASIAN MINISTERS OF EDUCATION ORGANIZATION** (SEAMEO)

_**EUROREGION CULTURELLE**

-**EAST AFRICAN COMMUNITY** (EAC)

NATIONAL REGIONAL CULTURAL POLICY

Many of the issues local and national cultural policy-makers face have become trans-national level for a variety of reasons. The production and consumption of cultural goods and services increasingly transcend national borders (UNESCO, n.d.). Culture is thus closely linked to trade policies or environmental issues. International and regional organizations provide expanding platforms for agenda-setting, cooperation, and trade. Among the goals these organizations pursue are, next to the promotion of trade in cultural goods and services, the preservation of cultural heritage, and accompanying diffusion of technical expertise and best practices. In the field of development, the case is that the strengthening of the national and regional cultural economy contributes to social and economic advancement; at the same time, the feasibility of locally tailored approaches to preserve unique cultural values, knowledge and know-how continues to be debated.

A number of regional organizations have cultural issues on their agenda, albeit typically not as a main priority. Well-known examples include the African Union, the Arab League, and the European Union. Many other regional bodies devote resources to cultural cooperation. International bodies vary widely in terms of how many member states they comprise, how active they are, financial resources, and the broader legitimacy they enjoy.

NOTES ON DATA

Included in this suite are transnational organizations that include cultural topics or issues as part of their agenda. In some cases, this may be misleading, as meetings may be dominated by other topics such as regional economy or political trends. Further, the scope of issues that culture comprises makes comparisons difficult. While some organizations focus entirely on preservation, others attempt to shape cultural development in order to achieve policy goals in other areas.

A number of organizations allow for observer status in addition to membership as a criterion for participation. Observers can generally attend meetings but not actively take part in discussions or votes. The Organization of the Islamic Conference, for instance, includes five countries as well as several international organizations and other institutions that were granted observer status.

In addition to regional organizations and agreements, many countries establish bilateral agreements on culture. For example, Bangladesh has engaged in forty such agreements (APRCCN, n.d.).

WHAT ARE THE ISSUES?

As several chapters in this volume have shown, the place of cultural goods and services in international trade is a contested issue. Negotiations during the Uruguay Round of the GATT resulted in an implicit exemption of cultural goods and services from regulations governing international markets. Many national governments have argued that if the cultural sector were left entirely in the hands of the market, a range of cultural values, practices and patrimonies could be eroded or be completely eliminated. Thus far, the trade exception has been applied to audiovisual goods and services.

A related point of contention, also highlighted in various chapters in this volume, is the enforcement of intellectual property (IP) rights. Protection is aimed at supporting innovation and the innovator. Economically developed countries, including the United States, demand stronger enforcement of IP protection from developing countries, not just for music or audiovisual products but also for pharmaceuticals and biotechnology. Developing countries argue that the United States did not enforce IP rights during earlier stages of its own economic development and that these demands are therefore inequitable (Lohr, 2002).

WHAT ARE THE TRENDS?

There is no clear distinction between developing and developed countries in terms of membership in regional organizations. (A shortcoming here is the lack of data on levels of participation, activity, and actual influence.) There are, however, regional differences. Northwest African countries are generally more involved in cultural cooperation than southeastern African nations (see figure).

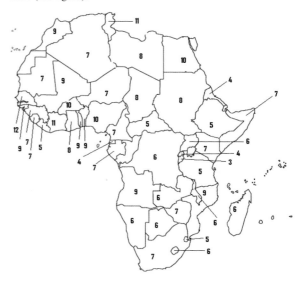

Number of memberships in regional organizations relevant to cultural policy of selected African countries, (SOURCE: UNESCO, 2007; Culturelink Network, 2007; Observatory of Cultural Policy in Africa, 2007).

The following diagram compares the average number of memberships of countries across continents:

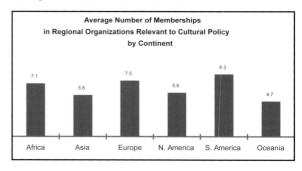

(SOURCE: UNESCO, 2007; Compendium of Cultural Policies and Trends in Europe, 2007; Culturelink Network, 2007; Observatory of Cultural Policy in Africa, 2007).

A core-periphery analysis shows that larger, politically established and physically interconnected countries tend to be more involved in cultural cooperation. This 'core' group includes Austria, South Africa, and Japan. On the other hand, island nations, those whose political legitimacy is challenged, and economically struggling countries tend to be more culturally isolated. This 'periphery' group includes Antigua and Barbuda, the Maldives, and Rwanda.

Further, certain groups of countries display similar patterns. One example of a cluster that results from a network analysis is the following: Cook Islands, Fiji, Kiribati, Marshall Islands, Micronesia (Federated States of), Nauru, Niue, Palau, Papua New Guinea, Samoa, Solomon Islands, Tonga, Tuvalu, Vanuatu. All of these are small island nations in the Pacific Ocean who all independently display similar patterns of cultural cooperation.

In addition to cultural ties on a governmental level, there is steadily increasing cooperation on an organizational and professional level (Council of Europe/ERICarts, 2007). Non-governmental organizations (see indicator suite on INGOs) and educational institutions organize cross-cultural events. These data are not included in the present suite but may significantly enhance the connections between governments.

INTERNATIONAL

REGULATORY

FRAMEWORKS

1. WTO MEMBERS' GATS **COMMITMENTS ON CULTURAL SERVICES** AS OF 2005

(#)= TOTAL NUMBER OF COUNTRIES IN EACH REGION

AFRICA (52)

3	**RADIO/TV PRODUCTION + TRANSMISSION**	---
5	**MOTION PICTURE/VIDEO PRODUCTION + DISTRIBUTION**	
2	**SOUND RECORDING**	—
5	**LIBRARY, ARCHIVES + MUSEUMS**	
9	**ENTERTAINMENT: THEATER, LIVE BANDS, + CIRCUSES**	....

AMERICAS (35)

4	**RADIO/TV PRODUCTION + TRANSMISSION**	---
4	**MOTION PICTURE/VIDEO PRODUCTION + DISTRIBUTION**	
2	**SOUND RECORDING**	—
4	**LIBRARY, ARCHIVES + MUSEUMS**	
15	**ENTERTAINMENT: THEATER, LIVE BANDS, + CIRCUSES**	....

ARAB WORLD (21)

1	**RADIO/TV PRODUCTION + TRANSMISSION**	--
3	**MOTION PICTURE/VIDEO PRODUCTION + DISTRIBUTION**	
1	**SOUND RECORDING**	—
1	**LIBRARY, ARCHIVES + MUSEUMS**	
2	**ENTERTAINMENT: THEATER, LIVE BANDS, + CIRCUSES**	.....

ASIA + PACIFIC (47)

4	**RADIO/TV PRODUCTION + TRANSMISSION**	---
12	**MOTION PICTURE/VIDEO PRODUCTION + DISTRIBUTION**	
6	**SOUND RECORDING**	——
3	**LIBRARY, ARCHIVES + MUSEUMS**	
4	**ENTERTAINMENT: THEATER, LIVE BANDS, + CIRCUSES**	....

EUROPE (5)

1	**RADIO/TV PRODUCTION + TRANSMISSION**	--
7	**MOTION PICTURE/VIDEO PRODUCTION + DISTRIBUTION**	
1	**SOUND RECORDING**	—
4	**LIBRARY, ARCHIVES + MUSEUMS**	
10	**ENTERTAINMENT: THEATER, LIVE BANDS, + CIRCUSES**	....

2. # OF **WTO COUNTRIES** WITH GATS COMMITMENTS IN CULTURAL SECTORS

BY SECTOR AS OF 2005

13 **RADIO/TV PRODUCTION + TRANSMISSION**

12 **SOUND RECORDING**

40 **ENTERTAINMENT: THEATER, LIVE BANDS, + CIRCUSES**

31 **MOTION PICTURE/VIDEO PRODUCTION + DISTRIBUTION**

17 **LIBRARY, ARCHIVES + MUSEUMS**

3. GATS COMMITMENTS IN CULTURAL AND OTHER SERVICES

ORIGINAL MEMBERS   FIRST SIX ACCESSIONS   AS OF 2005

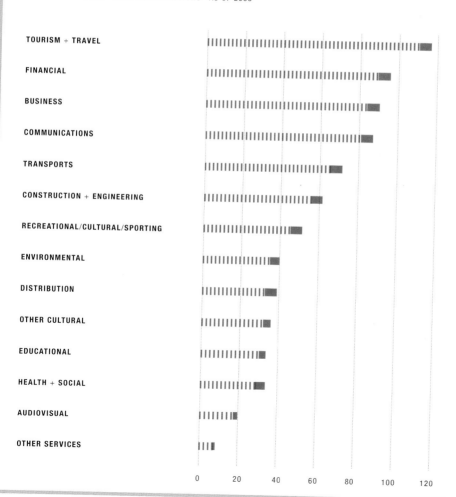

4. CHANGE IN THE # OF **PUBLISHED ARTICLES** AVAILABLE ON **GOOGLE SCHOLAR**

RELATED TO SELECT UNESCO CONVENTIONS: 2000 - PRESENT

YEAR **2000**

18 ARTICLES RELATED TO **CPPD**

26 ARTICLES RELATED TO **CPW**

1 ARTICLES RELATED TO **CSI**

YEAR **2001**

24 ARTICLES RELATED TO **CPPD**

14 ARTICLES RELATED TO **CPW**

3 ARTICLES RELATED TO **CSI**

YEAR **2002**

25 ARTICLES RELATED TO **CPPD**

29 ARTICLES RELATED TO **CPW**

0 ARTICLES RELATED TO **CSI**

YEAR **2003**

20 ARTICLES RELATED TO **CPPD**

25 ARTICLES RELATED TO **CPW**

1 ARTICLES RELATED TO **CSI**

YEAR **2004**

32 ARTICLES RELATED TO **CPPD**

34 ARTICLES RELATED TO **CPW**

16 ARTICLES RELATED TO **CSI**

YEAR **2005**

49 ARTICLES RELATED TO **CPPD**

30 ARTICLES RELATED TO **CPW**

11 ARTICLES RELATED TO **CSI**

YEAR **2006**

55 ARTICLES RELATED TO **CPPD**

35 ARTICLES RELATED TO **CPW**

12 ARTICLES RELATED TO **CSI**

YEAR **2007**

10 ARTICLES RELATED TO **CPPD**

18 ARTICLES RELATED TO **CPW**

7 ARTICLES RELATED TO **CSI**

UNESCO CONVENTION ON THE PROTECTION + PROMOTION OF THE DIVERSITY OF CULTURAL EXPRESSIONS

PHASE 1			PHASE 2				
INSTRUMENT DEPOSITED AT UNESCO	NATIONAL LEGISLATIVE/EXECUTIVE PROCESS:						
	COMPLETED	SUBTOTAL	ADVANCED	INITIATED	TARGET COUNTRIES	SUBTOTAL	TOTAL
AFRICA							
BURKINA FASO	SOUTH AFRICA	10	CONGO	GUINEA	ANGOLA	22	32
CAMEROON				GABON	BENIN		
DJIBOUTI					BOTSWANA		
MADAGASCAR					C.AFRICAN REP. NIGER		
MALI					IVORY COAST NIGERIA		
MAURITIUS					GAMBIA UGANDA		
NAMIBIA					GHANA RWANDA		
SENEGAL					KENYA SWAZILAND		
TOGO					LESOTHO TANZANIA		
					MALAWI CHAD		
AMERICAS					MOZAMBIQUE ZAMBIA		
BOLIVIA	URUGUAY	9	BRAZIL	ARGENTINA	COLOMBIA CUBA	16	25
CANADA	VENEZUELA		PARAGUAY	CHILI	COSTA RICA HAITI		
ECUADOR	STE-LUCIA			CUBA	GUATEMALA JAMAICA		
GUATEMALA					NICARAGUA DOMINICAN REPUBLIC		
MEXICO					PANAMA TRINIDAD + TOBAGO		
PERU					SALVADOR		
ARAB WORLD							
		0	JORDAN?	TUNISIA	ALGERIA, EGYPT, LEBANON,	8	8
ASIA/OCEANIA					MAURITANIA, MOROCCO, SYRIA		
INDIA		1	CHINA		BANGLADESH, CAMBODIA, KOREA,	10	11
					INDONESIA, NEW ZEALAND, PHILIPPINES,		
EUROPE					SRI LANKA, THAILAND, VIETNAM		
EU MEMBERS		19			EU MEMBERS	19	38
AUSTRIA			GERMANY	BELGIUM	GREECE		
BULGARIA*			ARMENIA?	ICELAND	HUNGARY		
DENMARK			CYPRUS	ITALY	IRELAND		
SPAIN			PORTUGAL	LATVIA	NETHERLANDS		
ESTONIA			UNITED KINGDOM		POLAND		
FINLAND					CZECH REPUBLIC		
FRANCE							
LITHUANIA					OTHER EUROPEAN COUNTRIES		
LUXEMBOURG					GEORGIA		
MALTA					SWITZERLAND		
SLOVAKIA					RUSSIA		
SLOVENIA					UKRAINE		
SWEDEN							
ROMANIA*	* EUROPEAN UNION MEMBER STATES AS OF JANUARY 2000						
OTHER EUROPEAN COUNTRIES							
ALBANIA							
BELARUS							
CROATIA							
MOLDOVA							
MONACO							
35	4	39	10	10	55	75	114

35	39	39	49	59	114		114

FREQUENCY OF SUPPORT FOR **UNESCO** **CONVENTIONS** BY MEMBERS

OF YEARS   AVERAGE # OF COUNTRIES SIGNING EACH YEAR SINCE ADOPTED TO PRESENT

# of Years	Convention	
59	AFI	‖‖‖
1		‖‖‖
57	AI	‖‖‖
2		‖‖‖‖‖
55	UCCA	‖‖‖
2		‖‖‖‖‖
55	P3	‖‖‖
1		‖‖‖
53	CPC	‖‖‖
2		‖‖‖‖‖
53	PCP	‖‖‖
2		‖‖‖‖‖
49	CEO	‖‖
1		‖‖‖
49	CIEP	‖‖
1		‖‖‖
47	CDE	‖‖
2		‖‖‖‖‖
46	ICP	‖‖‖
2		‖‖‖‖‖
45	PIC	‖‖
1		‖‖‖
37	CMPP	‖‖‖‖‖‖‖‖‖‖‖‖‖‖‖‖‖‖‖‖‖‖‖‖‖‖‖‖‖‖‖‖‖‖
3		‖‖‖‖‖‖‖
36	CPPP	‖‖‖‖‖‖‖‖‖‖‖‖‖‖‖‖‖‖‖‖‖‖‖‖‖‖‖‖‖‖‖‖‖
2		‖‖‖‖‖
36	CWI	‖‖‖‖‖‖‖‖‖‖‖‖‖‖‖‖‖‖‖‖‖‖‖‖‖‖‖‖‖‖‖‖‖
4		‖‖‖‖‖‖‖‖‖‖
36	UCC	‖‖‖‖‖‖‖‖‖‖‖‖‖‖‖‖‖‖‖‖‖‖‖‖‖‖‖‖‖‖‖‖‖
2		‖‖‖‖‖
36	P1-SR	‖‖‖‖‖‖‖‖‖‖‖‖‖‖‖‖‖‖‖‖‖‖‖‖‖‖‖‖‖‖‖‖‖
1		‖‖‖
36	P2	‖‖‖‖‖‖‖‖‖‖‖‖‖‖‖‖‖‖‖‖‖‖‖‖‖‖‖‖‖‖‖‖‖
1		‖‖‖
35	CPW	‖‖‖‖‖‖‖‖‖‖‖‖‖‖‖‖‖‖‖‖‖‖‖‖‖‖‖‖‖‖‖‖
5		‖‖‖‖‖‖‖‖‖‖‖‖

33 CDP ||||||||||||||||||||||||||||||||||||||||||||||||||||||||||||||||||||||
1 |||
33 CRSL ||||||||||||||||||||||||||||||||||||||||||||||||||||||||||||||||||||||
1 |||
31 ICRS ||||||||||||||||||||||||||||||||||||||||||||||||||||||||||||||||||
0
31 PAI ||||||||||||||||||||||||||||||||||||||||||||||||||||||||||||||||||
3 |||||||
29 CRS ||||||||||||||||||||||||||||||||||||||||||||||||||||||||||||||
0
28 MCA ||||||||||||||||||||||||||||||||||||||||||||||||||||||||||||
0
28 CRSE ||||||||||||||||||||||||||||||||||||||||||||||||||||||||||||
2 |||||
26 RCR ||||||||||||||||||||||||||||||||||||||||||||||||||||||
1 |||
25 PCW ||||||||||||||||||||||||||||||||||||||||||||||||||||||
3 |||||||
24 CRSA ||||||||||||||||||||||||||||||||||||||||||||||||||||
1 |||
20 PCW 6-7 ||||||||||||||||||||||||||||||||||||||||||
2 |||||
18 CTV ||||||||||||||||||||||||||||||||||||||
1 |||
10 CRQ ||||||||||||||||||||||
4 |||||||||
8 SPHC ||||||||||||||||||||
6 ||||||||||||||
6 CPU ||||||||||||||
2 |||||
4 CSI ||||||||||
20 ||||||||||||||||||||||||||||||||||||||||||||
2 ICD |||||
29 |||||||||||||||||||||||||||||||||||||||||||||||||||||||||||||
2 CPPD |||||
32 ||||||||||||||||||||||||||||||||||||||||||||||||||||||||||||||||||||

UNESCO CONVENTIONS

CODE	RATIFIED CONVENTIONS	YEAR OF ADOPTION

Code	Convention	Year
AFI	- Agreement for Facilitating the International Circulation of Visual and Auditory Materials of an Educational, Scientific and Cultural character with Protocol of Signature and model form of certificate provided for in Article IV of the above-mentioned Agreement	1948
AI	- Agreement on the Importation of Educational, Scientific and Cultural Materials, with Annexes A to E and Protocol annexed	1950
P3	- Protocol 3 annexed to the Universal Copyright Convention concerning the effective date of instruments of ratification or acceptance of or accession to that Convention	1952
UCCA	- Universal Copyright Convention, with Appendix Declaration relating to Article XVII and Resolution concerning Article XI	1952
CPC	- Convention for the Protection of Cultural Property in the Event of Armed Conflict with Regulations for the Execution of the Convention	1954
PCP	- Protocol to the Convention for the Protection of Cultural Property in the Event of Armed Conflict	1954
CEO	- Convention concerning the Exchange of Official Publications and Government Documents between States	1958
CIEP	- Convention concerning the International Exchange of Publications	1958
CDE	- Convention against Discrimination in Education	1960
ICP	- International Convention for the Protection of Performers, Producers of Phonograms and Broadcasting Organizations	1961
PIC	- Protocol Instituting a Conciliation and Good Offices Commission to be Responsible for Seeking the Settlement of any Disputes which may Arise between States' Parties to the Convention against Discrimination in Education	1962
CMPP	- Convention on the Means of Prohibiting and Preventing the Illicit Import, Export and Transfer of Ownership of Cultural Property	1970
CPPP	- Convention for the Protection of Producers of Phonograms against Unauthorized Duplication of their Phonograms	1971
CWI	- Convention on Wetlands of International Importance especially as Waterfowl Habitat	1971
P1-SR	- Protocol 1 annexed to the Universal Copyright Convention concerning the application of that Convention to the works of stateless persons and refugees	1971
P2	- Protocol 2 annexed to the Universal Copyright Convention concerning the application of that Convention to the works of certain international organizations	1971
UCC	- Universal Copyright Convention as revised on 24 July 1971, with Appendix Declaration relating to Article XVII and Resolution concerning Article XI.	1971
CPW	- Convention concerning the Protection of the World Cultural and Natural Heritage	1972
CDP	- Convention relating to the Distribution of Programme-Carrying Signals Transmitted by Satellite	1974
ICRS	- International Convention on the Recognition of Studies, Diplomas and Degrees in Higher Education in the Arab and European States bordering on the Mediterranean	1976
PAI	- Protocol to the Agreement on the Importation of Educational, Scientific and Cultural Materials, with Annexes A to H	1976
CRS	- Convention on the Recognition of Studies, Diplomas and Degrees in Higher Education in the Arab States	1978
MCA	- Multilateral Convention for the Avoidance of Double Taxation of Copyright Royalties, with model bilateral agreement and additional Protocol	1979
RCR	- Regional Convention on the Recognition of Studies, Certificates, Diplomas, Degrees and other Academic Qualifications in Higher Education in the African States	1981
PCW	- Protocol to amend the Convention on Wetlands of International Importance especially as Waterfowl Habitat	1982
PCW 6-7	- Protocol to amend Articles 6 and 7 of the Convention on Wetlands of International Importance especially as Waterfowl Habitat	1987
CTV	- Convention on Technical and Vocational Education	1989
CRQ	- Convention on the Recognition of Qualifications concerning Higher Education in the European Region	1997
SPHC	- Second Protocol to the Hague Convention of 1954 for the Protection of Cultural Property in the Event of Armed Conflict	1999
CPU	- Convention on the Protection of the Underwater Cultural Heritage	2001
CSI	- Convention for the Safeguarding of the Intangible Cultural Heritage	2003
CPPD	- Convention on the protection and promotion of the diversity of cultural expressions	2005
ICD	- International Convention against Doping in Sport	2005

FREQUENCY OF SUPPORT FOR **UNESCO**

CONVENTIONS BY MEMBERS

PROPORTION (%) OF UNESCO MEMBERSHIP SIGNING TO PRESENT

%	Convention
19.8%	AFI
51.6%	AI
52.1%	UCCA
27.1%	P3
60.9%	CPC
49.5%	PCP
26.6%	CEO
24.5%	CIEP
49.0%	CDE
44.8%	ICP
17.2%	PIC
58.9%	CMPP
39.6%	CPPP
80.2%	CWI
33.9%	UCC
19.8%	P1-SR
21.9%	P2
95.8%	CPW
15.6%	CDP
9.9%	CRSL
6.3%	ICRS
51.6%	PAI
7.3%	CRS
4.2%	MCA
24.0%	CRSE
10.9%	RCR
43.8%	PCW
10.4%	CRSA
19.8%	PCW 6-7
7.8%	CTV
22.4%	CRQ
23.7%	SPHC
7.3%	CPU
40.6%	CSI
30.2%	ICD
32.8%	CPPD

TIMELINE OF **UNESCO TREATIES** ADOPTED

TREATY

Years: 1948 1949 **1950** 1951 1952 1953 1954 1955 1956 1957 1958 1959 **1960** 1961 1962 1963 1964 1965 1966 1967 1968 1969 **1970** 1971 1972 1973 1974 1975 1976 1977 1978 1979 **1980** 1981 1982 1983 1984 1985 1986 1987 1988 1989 **1990** 1991 1992 1993 1994 1995 1996 1997 1998 1999 **2000** 2001 2002 2003 2004 2005 2006 2007

TREATY	# OF COUNTRIES RATIFIED	FREQUENCY OF RATIFICATION PER YEAR
AFI	38	1.5
AI	99	0.5
UCCA	100	0.5
P3	52	1.0
CPC	117	0.4
PCP	95	0.5
CEO	51	0.9
CIEP	47	1.0
CDE	94	0.5
ICP	86	0.5
PIC	33	1.3
CMPP	113	0.3
CPPP	76	0.4
CWI	154	0.2
UCC	65	0.5
P1-SR	38	0.9
P2	42	0.8
CPW	184	0.1
CDP	30	1.1
CRSL	19	1.7
ICRS	12	2.5
PAI	99	0.3
CRS	14	2.0
MCA	8	3.5
CRSE	46	0.6
RCR	21	1.2
PCW	84	0.3
CRSA	20	1.2
PCW 6-7	38	0.5
CTV	15	1.2
CRQ	43	0.2
SPHC	45	0.1
CPU	14	0.4
CSI	78	0.0
CPPD	58	0.0
ICD	63	0.0

REGULATORY FRAMEWORKS Five UN System entities are carrying out standard-setting work that impacts on the issues raised throughout this volume (UNESCO, UNCTAD, WIPO, ILO and UNDP; see chapter 7) as is to some extent the European Union. In addition, the World Trade Organization, by virtue of its mandate, is also a party to the contemporary tension between two sometimes seemingly contradictory objectives, and the economic, political and social forces behind them: on the one hand, the expansion of international trade in cultural goods and services within the global free trade regime and on the other, the need to protect and promote cultural diversity in the face of hegemonic market forces.

UNESCO was the specialized agency of the UN System set up to deal with culture under the mandate to 'contribute to peace and security by promoting collaboration among the nations through education, science and culture in order to further universal respect for justice, for the rule of law and for the human rights and fundamental freedoms which are affirmed for the peoples of the world, without distinction of race, sex, language or religion, by the Charter of the United Nations,' (UNESCO, 2002).

By virtue of its constitution, UNESCO (a) collaborates in the work of advancing the mutual knowledge and understanding of peoples, through all means of mass communication, and to that end recommends such international agreements as may be necessary to promote the free flow of ideas by word and image; (b) gives fresh impulse to popular education and to the spread of culture; and (c) maintains, increases and diffuses knowledge (www.unesco.org).

A major part of UNESCO's work is the process of creating, negotiating, implementing and governing international agreements in terms of a regulatory framework for education, science, and culture. This regulatory framework built by UNESCO has achieved great scope and complexity since the 1950s, and now spans a wide range of academic, educational, cultural and artistic aspects—from a Universal Copyright Convention (1952), and the Convention Against Discrimination in Education (1960), to the Convention on the Protection and Promotion of the Diversity of Cultural Expressions (2005).

As the indicator suite shows, UNESCO's regulatory framework continues to expand and 'thicken' in terms of the number of conventions, yet at a slower pace than in the 1960s and 1970s. Only five treaties have been adopted since 1990, as opposed to 12 in the 1970s alone (see data point 8). There is also a slow-down in the way countries become signatories of treaties once negotiated and accepted. Only nine of the over 30 treaties are signed by at least half of member states; the majority of treaties are signed by between a quarter and half of UNESCO members, and twelve by less than one in five (see data point 7). As result, a major problem of the international regulatory framework is its 'patchy' structure and unevenness by which member states become signatories and parties of treaties through ratification and, ultimately, implementation at national levels.

UNESCO's panoply of standard-setting instruments in the field of culture is particularly well-known. To date, the most popular of these has been the 1972 Convention Concerning the Protection of the World Cultural and Natural Heritage. But this primacy may well be challenged by the 2005 UNESCO Convention on the Protection and Promotion of the Diversity of Cultural Expressions—which pertains directly to the topic of the present volume. Unlike many of the other recently adopted conventions the 'Cultural Diversity Convention' has already achieved both a high number of ratifications (see data point 5) in a relatively short period of time, and significant scholarly attention (see data point 4). The point of departure for the elaboration of this instrument was the Universal Declaration on Cultural Diversity, which UNESCO adopted in 2001, specifically Article 8 of the Declaration, which sets out a key principle concerning the specific nature of cultural goods and services, one that now meets with near-universal approval in the international system:

> In the face of present-day economic and technological change, opening up vast prospects for creation and innovation, particular attention must be paid to the diversity of the supply of creative work, to due recognition of the rights of authors and artists and to the specificity of cultural goods and services which, as vectors of identity, values and meaning, must not be treated as mere commodities or consumer goods.

Both the Declaration and the Convention are important additions to the framework of principles enunciated and promoted by the United Nations System. The Convention, however, was opposed by consecutive US administrations and, irrespective of an emerging transnational consensus, continues to be criticized by those who believe that cultural goods and services should in fact be treated as commodities like any other. While most observers see the Convention as a 'quantum leap' forward towards a more comprehensive system of global cultural governance based on fundamental principles, some therefore question the very assumptions underlying it, while still others fear that this convention, like others, may find only limited actual support by governments in terms of policymaking and regulation in the arena of culture.

The WTO's main aim is to ensure free and fair trade (see also indicator suite on Trade); in terms of the cultural economy, the cultural goods and services are regulated as part of the General Agreement on Trade in Services (GATS). This agreement entered into force in 1995, and was borne out of the Uruguay Round of negotiations to stimulate international trade by reducing barriers and protective policies at national levels. As data point 1 shows, the coverage of the Agreement remains rather patchy across regions, and overall 'undersubscribed' (see data point 2) relative to the total WTO membership.

CULTURES + GLOBALIZATION SERIES 2:
REFERENCES - INDICATOR SUITES + DIGESTS
*Numerals below correspond to graphics displayed in the indicator suite layouts

VALUES, PARTICIPATION, CONSUMPTION

CULTURAL VALUES

1-2, 4, 6-7   Pew Global Attitudes Project. (2003). Views of a changing world. Available from http://pewglobal.org/datasets/

3 + 5   World Values Survey. (1999-2004). World Values Survey. Available from http://www.worldvaluessurvey.org

DIGEST: CULTURAL VALUES

Berger, P.L. (1997). Four faces of global culture. National Interest, 49: 23-29.

Inglehart, R., Basáñez, M., & Menéndez Moreno, A. (1998). Human values and beliefs: Across-cultural sourcebook of political, religious, sexual, and economic norms in 43 societies: Findings from the 1990-1993 World Values Survey. Ann Arbor: University of Michigan Press.

Van Deth, J.W., & Scarborough, E. (Eds.). (1995). The impact of values. New York: Oxford University Press.

CULTURAL PARTICIPATION

1   Nielsen/NetRatings. (n.d.). Global index chart. Retrieved January 29, 2007, from http://www.nielsen-netratings.com/resources.jsp?section=pr_netv&nav=1

2   Nielsen/NetRatings. (n.d.). Internet audience metrics. Retrieved January 31, 2007, from http://www.nielsen-netratings.com/resources.jsp?section=pr_netv&nav=1

3   Australian Bureau of Statistics. (2004). Arts & culture in Australia: A statistical overview Retrieved November 28, 2006, from http://www.abs.gov.au/AUSSTATS/abs@.nsf/DetailsPage/4172.02004%20(Reissue)?OpenDocument

Australian Council for the Arts.(2003). Some Australian arts statistics. Retrieved November 28, 2006, from http://www.australiacouncil.gov.au/publications/arts_sector/some_australian_arts_statistics

Choo, K.Y. (2001, October). Changes in Korean people's use of time during 1981-2000. Paper presented at the International Association for Time Use Research 2001 Conference, Oslo, Norway. Retrieved from http://www.ssb.no/english/about_ssb/conference/iatur_2001/papers.html

National Statistical Office of Thailand. (n.d.). Average time of participants 15 years and older by activity Available from http://web.nso.go.th/eng/stat/timeuse/time_content.htm

Social & Cultural Planning Office of the Netherlands. (2004). Trends in time: The use and organization of time in the Netherlands, 1975-2000. Retrieved November 29, 2006, from http://www.scp.nl/english/publications/books/9037701965/Trends_in_time.pdf

Statistics Canada. (2005). Overview of time use of Canadians. Retrieved November 28, 2006, from http://www.statcan.ca/bsolc/english/bsolc?catno=12F0080X

Statistics Finland. (n.d.). Culture and mass media. Retrieved November 28, 2006, from http://statfin.stat.fi/statweb/start.asp?LA=en&DM=SLEN&lp=catalog&clg=culture_and_mass_media

Statistics of South Africa. (2001). A survey of time use: How South African men & women spend their time. Retrieved November 29, 2006, from http://www.statssa.gov.za/publications/statsabout.asp?PPN=TimeUse&SCH=2364

UK National Statistics Office. (2005). Time use survey. Retrieved November 29, 2007, from http://www.statistics.gov.uk/cci/nugget.asp?id=7

US Bureau of Labor Statistics. (2005). U.S. time use survey 2005. Retrieved November 29, 2006, from http://www.bls.gov/news.release/archives/atus_07272006.pdf

4   EuroStat. (n.d.). Comparable time use statistics. Retrieved November 28, 2006, from http://epp.eurostatec.europa.eu/portal/page?_pageid=1073,1135281,1073_1135295&_dad=portal&_schema=PORTAL&p_product_code=KS-CC-05-001

5 + 6   European Commission. (2002). Eurobarometer survey on Europeans' participation in cultural activities. Retrieved January 30, 2007, from http://forum.europa.eu.int/Public/irc/dsis/edtcs/library?l=/public/culture&vm=detailed&sb=Title

7 + 8   European Commission. (2003). Eurobarometer July 2003: The new Europeans and culture. Retrieved January 9, 2007, from http://ec.europa.eu/culture/eac/sources_info/studies/eurobarometer_en.html

9   Yearbook of Statistics Singapore. (2006). Latest statistical news. Retrieved January 8, 2007, from www.singstat.gov.sg

10   Instituto Nacional de Estadistica Geografia e Informatica. (n.d.). Estadistica [translated into English from Spanish]. Retrieved January 19, 2007, from http://www.inegi.gob.mx/inegi/default.aspx

11   Australian Bureau of Statistics. (2006). Arts & culture in Australia: A statistical overview, 2004. Retrieved June 28, 2007, from http://www.abs.gov.au/AUSSTATS/abs@.nsf/DetailsPage/4172.02004%20(Reissue)?OpenDocument

12 + 13   World Values Survey. (1999-2004). World Values Survey. Available from http://www.worldvaluessurvey.org

14   International Intelligence on Culture, Cultural Capital Ltd. and Hong Kong Policy Research Institute. (2005). Hong Kong arts and cultural indicators research report. Retrieved January 8, 2007, from http://www.hkadc.org.hk/en/infocentre/research/report_200510

15   Japan Ministry of Internal Affairs and Communications Statistics Bureau. (2001). Survey on time use & leisure activities. Retrieved January 9, 2007, from http://www.stat.go.jp/English/data/shakai/

Bourdieu, P. (1984). Distinction: A social critique of the judgment of taste. Cambridge, MA: Harvard University Press.

Bourdieu, P., & Passeron, J. (1977). Reproduction education, society and culture. Beverly Hills, CA: Sage.

DiMaggio, P., & Mukhtar, T. (2004). Arts participation as cultural capital in the United States, 1982-2002:Signs of decline? Poetics, 32: 169-194.

Lewis, J., & Miller, T. (2003). Critical cultural policy studies: A reader. Oxford, England: Blackwell.

CULTURAL CONSUMPTION

1

United Nations. (2006). National account statistics 2005: Main aggregates and detailed tables. New York: United Nations Publications.

Europa. (n.d.). Audiovisual and media Retrieved June, 26, 2007 from http://europa.eu/scadplus/leg/en/lvb/l24109.htm

HERITAGE + THE CULTURAL COMMONS

HERITAGE PRESERVATION

1-3

UNESCO (United Nations Educational, Scientific and Cultural Organization). (n.d.). World heritage list. Retrieved July 6, 2007, from http://whc.unesco.org/en/list

4

UNESCO World Heritage Committee. (1999). Item 14 of the Provisional Agenda, Twenty-Third Session: Marrakesh, Morocco. Retrieved July 12, 2007, from http://whc.unesco.org/archive/1999/whc-99-conf209-18e.pdf

UNESCO World Heritage Committee. (2000). Item 13 of the Provisional Agenda, Twenty-Fourth Session: Cairns, Australia. Retrieved July 12, 2007, from http://whc.unesco.org/archive/2000/whc-00-conf204-15reve.pdf

UNESCO World Heritage Committee. (2006). Statement of accounts of the World Heritage Fund for 2004-2005, Annex I, Thirtieth Session: Vilnius, Lithuania. Retrieved July 12, 2007, from http://whc.unesco.org/archive/2006/whc06-30com-15e.pdf

5

UNESCO. (n.d.). List of the masterpieces of the oral and intangible heritage of humanity. Retrieved July 8, 2007, from http://www.unesco.org/culture/ich/index.php?pg=00107

6

WMF (World Monuments Fund). (n.d.). 100 most endangered sites. Retrieved July 8, 2007, from http://www.worldmonumentswatch.org/

7

Ethnologue. (n.d.). Nearly extinct languages. Retrieved July 18, 2007, from http://www.ethnologue.com/nearly_extinct.asp

8   UNESCO World Heritage Committee. (2007). Budget of the World Heritage Center, Thirty-First Session: Christchurch, Zambia. Retrieved July 12, 2007, from http://whc.unesco.org/en/ statutorydoc/searchDocuments=&meeting=31COM

9   Hatton, B. (2007, July 7). 7 new Wonders of the World chosen. Forbes. Retrieved July 20, 2007, from http://www.forbes.com/feeds/ap/2007/07/07/ap3891659.html

New7Wonders Foundation turns sights on natural monuments. (2007, July 8). Sofia News Agency. Retrieved July 20, 2007, from http://www.novinite.com/view_news.php?id=82739

New7Wonders. (n.d.). The New7Wonders Foundation and campaign. Retrieved July 20, 2007, from http://www.new7wonders.com/index.php?id=7

Owen, J. (2007). Photo gallery: New 7 Wonders vs. Ancient 7 Wonders [online exclusive]. Retrieved July 20, 2007, from National Geographic Web site: http://news.nationalgeographic. com/news/2007/07/photogalleries/seven-wonders/index.html?source=G1915

10   UNESCO. (n.d.). New inscribed properties. Retrieved July 20, 2007, from http://whc.unesco. org/en/newproperties/

DIGEST: HERITAGE PRESERVATION

ARCH Foundation. (n.d.). Introduction. Retrieved July 24, 2007, from http://www.arch.at/

BBC News. (2007, July 7). Global vote picks seven wonders. Retrieved July 9, 2007, from http://news.bbc.co.uk/2/hi/europe/684267.stm

Inside N7W. (n.d.). New 7 Wonders. Retrieved July 10, 2007, from http://www.new7wonders. com/index.php?id=39

Isar, Y.R. (2004). Tangible and intangible heritage: Are they really Castor and Pollux? In INTACH Vision 2020 (Proceedings of the conference INTACH 2020 organized by the Indian National Trust for Art and Cultural Heritage, November 2004). New Delhi, India: INTACH.

Kurin, R. (2004, May). Intangible cultural heritage in the 2003 UNESCO Convention. Museum International, 221-222.

Lowenthal, D. (1985). The past is a foreign country. Cambridge, England: Cambridge University Press.

Telegraph.co.uk. (2007, July 9). New Seven Wonders of the World announced. Retrieved July 15, 2007, from http://www.telegraph.co.uk/travel/main.jhtml?xml=/travel/2007/07/09/ etsevenwonders109.xml

Smith, N. (2007, July 8). New Seven Wonders chosen. Sunday Times. Retrieved July 15, 2007, from http://www.timesonline.co.uk/tol/news/world/article2043145.ece

UNESCO. (n.d.). Intangible heritage. Retrieved from http://portal.unesco.org/culture/en/ev.php-URL_ID=2225&URL_DO=DO_TOPIC&URL_SECTION=201.html

Viejo Rose, D. (2007). Conflict and the deliberate destruction of cultural heritage. In H. K. Anheier & Y. R. Isar (Eds.), Conflicts and tensions: The Cultures and Globalization Series, Vol. 1. London: Sage

1-2

Vara, V. (2006, October 2). MySpace has large circle of friends, but rivals' cliques are growing too.

Wall Street Journal. Retrieved June 5, 2007, from http://online.wsj.com

3

Trendcatching. (n.d.). MySpace usage statistics. Retrieved June 5, 2007, from http://www.trendcatching.com/2006/05/myspace_usage_s.html

4

Athena. (n.d.). Table of contents. Retrieved June 20, 2007, from http://un2sg4.unige.ch/athena/html/athome.html

E-book.com.au. (n.d.). Free books. Retrieved June 20, 2007, from http://www.e-book.com.au/freebooks.htm#2%20-%20free%20digital%20libraries%20website

Infomotions, Inc. (2007). Alex Catalogue of Electronic Texts. Retrieved June 20, 2007, from http://www.infomotions.com/alex/

Internet Public Library. (n.d.). About the Internet Public Library. Retrieved October 30, 2007, from http://www.ipl.org/div/about/

Ockerbloom, J.M. (2007). The Online Books Page. Retrieved June 20, 2007, from http://digital.library.upenn.edu/books/

Project Gutenberg. (2006). Advanced search: Language. Retrieved June 18, 2007, from http://www.gutenberg.org/catalog/world/search

Project Gutenberg. (n.d.). Main page. Retrieved June 20, 2007, from http://www.gutenberg.org/wiki/Main_Page

University of Virginia Library. (n.d.). EText Center. Retrieved June 20, 2007, from http://etext.lib.virginia.edu/

5-6

YouTube. (2007). Most viewed (all time): All. Retrieved June 12, 2007, from http://www.youtube.com/browse?s=mp&t=a&c=0&l=JP

7-9

OECD (Organisation for Economic Co-operation and Development). (2006). OECD information technology outlook 2006. Retrieved June 12, 2007, from http://213.253.134.29/oecd/pdfs/browseit/9306051E.PDF

10

Alexa. (2007). Activeworlds. Retrieved June 5, 2007, from http://www.alexa.com/data/details/traffic_details?url=activeworlds.com

Alexa. (2007). Moove online. Retrieved June 5, 2007, from http://www.alexa.com/data/details/traffic_details?url=Moove.com

Alexa. (2007). Second Life. Retrieved June 5, 2007, from http://www.alexa.com/data/details/traffic_details?url=secondlife.com

Alexa. (2007). There.com. Retrieved June 5, 2007, from http://www.alexa.com/data/details/traffic_details?url=There.com

Statsaholic. (2007). Website traffic graphs for Kaneva.com. Retrieved June 5, 2007, from http://www.statsaholic.com/kaneva.com

11

Active Worlds. (n.d.). Retrieved May 15, 2007, from Wikipedia Web site: http://en.wikipedia.org/wiki/Active_Worlds

Bray, D., & Konsynski, B. (2007). Virtual worlds, virtual economies, virtual institutions. Retrieved June 19, 2007, from Scribd database.

Castellanos, M. (2007, June 19). Virtual world meets reality. Retrieved May 17, 2007, from CBS News Web site: http://www.cbsnews.com/stories/2007/05/07/tech/gamecore/main2767869. shtml?source=RSSattr=GameCore_2767869

Dotsoul. (n.d.). Retrieved May 17, 2007, from Wikipedia Web site: http://en.wikipedia.org/ wiki/Dotsoul

Groovenet. (n.d.). There Philippines. Retrieved June 13, 2007, from http://www.groovenet. ph/there

Herrmann, J. (2005, December 20). Is this reality virtual, or is it one of endless possibilities? Florida Times-Union. Retrieved May 15, 2007, from http://www.jacksonville.com/community/cc/ herrmann/stories/122005/122005115219.shtml

Jana, R., & McConnon, A. (2007, April 13). Digital surburbia. BusinessWeek. Retrieved May 15, 2007, from http://www.businessweek.com

Kaneva, Inc. (n.d.). Retrieved May 15, 2007, from Wikipedia Web site: http://en.wikipedia. org/wiki/Kaneva%2C_Inc

MacMillan, D. (2006, April 16). Big spenders of Second Life. BusinessWeek. Retrieved from http://www.businessweek.com

MacMillan, D. (2006, May 1). Virtual land, real money. BusinessWeek. Retrieved from http:// www.businessweek.com

MindArk. (n.d.). About MindArk. Retrieved June 19, 2007, from http://www.mindark.com/

Moove. (n.d.). Retrieved May 17, 2007, from Wikipedia Web site: http://en.wikipedia.org/ wiki/Moove

Moove online. (n.d.). What is moove online? Retrieved May 15, 2007, from http://www.moove. com/info_moove_online.htm

PRAVDA On-Line. (2007, June 1). Virtual world to be created in China. Retrieved June 3, 2007, from http://english.pravda.ru/news/world/01-06-2007/92601-china_virtual-0

Second Life. (2007). What is Second Life? Retrieved May 15, 2007, from http://secondlife.com/ whatis/

Second Life. (n.d.). Retrieved May 15, 2007, from Wikipedia Web site: http://en.wikipedia. org/wiki/Secondlife

Techcrunch. (2007, March 16). Kaneva: A place for (3D) friends. Message posted to http://www. techcrunch.com/2007/03/16/kaneva-a-place-for-3d-friends/

There. (n.d.). Your brand in There. Retrieved May 1, 2007, from http://www.there.com/ yourBrandVirtualRealEstate.html

There (Internet service). (n.d.). Retrieved May 15, 2007, from Wikipedia Web site: http:// en.wikipedia.org/wiki/There.com

Walsh, T. (2006, September 29). 'There' to get thin avatar chat client, new terrain, broadcast TV. Retrieved June 7, 2007, from Clickable Culture Web site: http://www.secretlair.com/index.php?/ clickablecultureentry/there_to_get_thin_avatar_chat_client_new_terrain_broadcast_tv/

Boynton, R. (2004, January 25). The tyranny of copyright? New York Times Magazine, 40-45.

Creative Commons. (n.d.). Learn more. Retrieved June 21, 2007, from
http://creativecommons.org/learnmore/

Drache, D., & Froese, M. (2006). Globalization, world trade and the cultural commons: Identity, citizenship and pluralism. New Political Economy, 11(3): 361-382.

Gordon-Murnane, L. (2005). Generosity and copyright: Creative commons and creative commons search tools. Searcher, 13(7).

Lessig, L. (2004). Free culture: How big media uses technology and the law to lock down culture and control creativity. Retrieved October 16, 2007, from University of Oslo Web site: http://www.jus.uio.no/sisu/free_culture.lawrence_lessig/portrait.pdf

Ostrom, E., & Hess, C. (2001, November). Artifacts, facilities, and content: Information as a common-pool resource. Paper presented at the Conference on the Public Domain, Duke Law School, Durham, North Carolina. Retrieved from Duke Law School Web site: http://www.law.duke.edu/pd/papers/ostromhes.pdf

Roush, W. (2007, July/August). Second Earth. Technology Review.
Retrieved October 16, 2007, from
https://www.technologyreview.com/Infotech/18888/

CORPORATIONS + ORGANIZATIONS

TRANSNATIONAL CULTURAL CORPORATIONS

1 Forbes. (2007). The Global 2000. Retrieved August 8, 2007, from
http://www.forbes.com/lists/2007/18/biz_07forbes2000_The-Global-2000_IndName_14.html

2 CNNMoney.com (2007). Fortune Global 500. Retrieved August 8, 2007, from
http://money.cnn.com/magazines/fortune/global500/2007/industries/145/1.html

3 Hoovers. (2007). Global cultural companies [search by industry]. Retrieved August 8, 2007, from
www.hoovers.com

4A Time Warner. (2006). 2006 annual report. Retrieved August 15, 2007, from
http://ir.timewarner.com/annuals.cfm?ptype=1

Time Warner. (2006). 2006 earnings releases. Retrieved August 15, 2007, from
http://ir.timewarner.com/archives.cfm?ptype=1

Time Warner. (2007). 2007 corporate profile book. Retrieved August 15, 2007, from
http://www.timewarner.com/corp/aboutus/fact_sheet.html

4B Disney. (2006). 2006 annual report. Retrieved August 15, 2007, from
http://corporate.disney.go.com/investors/fact_books.html

Disney. (2006). 2006 fact book. Retrieved August 15, 2007, from
http://corporate.disney.go.com/investors/fact_books.html

4C News Corporation. (2006). 2006 annual report. Retrieved August 15, 2007, from http://www.newscorp.com/Report2006/AnnualReport2006/HTML2/news_corp_ar2006_0003.htm

News Corporation. (2007). Filmed entertainment. Retrieved August 15, 2007, from http://www.newscorp.com/operations

4D Comcast. (2007). Comcast Cable Networks. Retrieved August 15, 2007, from http://www.comcast.com/corporate/about/pressroom/comcastcablenetworks/comcastcablenetworks.html

Comcast. (2007). Comcast reports 2006 results and outlook for 2007. Retrieved August 15, 2007, from http://www.cmcsk.com/phoenix.zhtml?c=118591&p=irol-newsArticle&ID=956792&highlight='%20target

Oligopoly Watch. (2004). Oligopoly brief: Comcast. Retrieved August 15, 2007, from http://www.oligopolywatch.com/2004/05/02.html

4E Vivendi. (2006). Vivendi 2006 annual report. Retrieved August 15, 2007, from http://www.vivendi.com/corp/en/regulated_information/financial_reports.php

DIGEST: TRANSNATIONAL CULTURAL CORPORATIONS

Dunning, J.H. (2006). Globalization: Economic opportunities, social challenges. Transnational Corporations, 15(3).

Economist. (2006, January 21). Old media. Economist, p. 9. Retrieved September 10, 2007, from Expanded Academic ASAP database.

Economist. (2007, August 2). Rupert gets his trophy. Retrieved September 10, 2007, from http://www.economist.com/business/displaystory.cfm?story_id=9581285

Hannaford, S. (2007). Defining the new oligopoly. Retrieved August 20, 2007, from Oligopoly Watch Web site: http://www.oligopolywatch.com/stories/2003/04/17/definingTheNewOligopoly.html

Time Warner (company profile). (2007). Retrieved April 28, 2007, from www.hoovers.com

World Public Opinion. (2006, January 11). 20 nation poll finds strong global consensus: Support for free market system, but also more regulation of large companies. Retrieved June 28, 2007, from http://www.worldpublicopinion.org/pipa/articles/btglobalizationtradera/154.php?nid=&id=&pnt=154&lb=btgl

CULTURAL INGOS + FOUNDATIONS

1-3 Union of International Associations (Ed.). (2005-2006). Yearbook of international organizations (Vol. 5). Munich: K.G. Saur Verlag Gmbh.

4 Aga Khan Foundation. (2007). Annual report 2006. Retrieved August 23, 2007, from http://www.akdn.org/akf/AKF_AR_2006_lowres.pdf

Andrew W. Mellon Foundation. (2006). Summary of grants and contributions, 2005. Retrieved August 23, 2007, from http://www.mellon.org/news_publications/annual-reports-essays/grants/

APPC (Asia Pacific Philanthropy Consortium). (2006). Grant making foundations in China. Retrieved August 23, 2007, from Philanthropy and the Third Sector in Asia and the Pacific Web site: http://www.asianphilanthropy.org/grant/local/china/china.html

APPC. (2006). K.K. Birla Foundation. Retrieved August 23, 2007, from Philanthropy and the Third Sector in Asia and the Pacific Web site: http://www.asianphilanthropy.org/grant/local/india/birla.html

APPC. (2006). Sir Robert Ho Tung Charitable Fund. Retrieved August 23, 2007, from Philanthropy and the Third Sector in Asia and the Pacific Web site: http://www.asianphilanthropy.org/grant/local/hongkong/roberthotung.html

APPC. (n.d.). Local grantmaking foundations. Retrieved August 23, 2007, from Philanthropy and the Third Sector in Asia and the Pacific Web site: http://www.asianphilanthropy.org/index.html

British Museum. (2007). Annual report 2006-2007. Retrieved August 23, 2007, from http://www.thebritishmuseum.ac.uk/the_museum/about_us/management_and_governance/annual_reports_and_accounts.aspx

Calgary Foundation. (2007). Financial statements of the Calgary Foundation. Retrieved August 23, 2007, from http://www.thecalgaryfoundation.org/documents/AuditedStatements2007_000.pdf

Calouste Gulbenkian Foundation. (2006). Annual report 2005. Retrieved August 23, 2007, from http://www.gulbenkian.org/english/report2005.asp

Canadian Jewish News. (2000). Retrieved August 23, 2007, from http://www.cjnews.com/pastissues/00/may25-00/front5.htm

China Children and Teenagers' Fund. (n.d.). [Translated into English from Chinese]. Retrieved August 23, 2007, from http://www.cctf.org.cn/

China Population Information and Research Center. (n.d.). Retrieved August 23, 2007, from http://www.cpirc.org.cn/en/eindex.htm

Community Chest of Hong Kong. (n.d.). [Translated into English from Chinese]. Retrieved August 23, 2007, from http://www.commchest.org/

Compagnia di San Paolo. (2007). Report 2006. Retrieved August 23, 2007, from http://www.compagnia.torino.it/english/rapporto_annuale/2006.html

Concern India Foundation. (n.d.). Retrieved August 23, 2007, from http://www.concernindia.org/

Ente Cassa di Risparmio di Firenze. (n.d.). [Translated into English from Italian]. Retrieved August 23, 2007, from http://www.entecarifirenze.it/online/html/asp/index.asp

Esmée Fairbairn Foundation. (2007). Annual report and accounts 2006. Retrieved August 23, 2007, from http://www.esmeefairbairn.org.uk/

European Cultural Foundation. (2007). Annual report 2006. Retrieved August 23, 2007, from http://www.eurocult.org/key-documents/

European Foundation Centre. (2007). Knowledge resources on and for funders. Retrieved August 23, 2007, from www.efc.be/projects/eu/research

Fletcher, A. (n.d.). Charity begins at home: Solid foundations can benefit family and society. Asiaweek. Retrieved August 23, 2007, from http://www.asiaweek.com/asiaweek/96/0308/feat6.html

Fondation Lucie et André Chagnon. (2004). Home page [translated into English from French]. Retrieved August 23, 2007, from http://www.fondationchagnon.org/

Fondazione Cariplo. (2007). A long term benchmark for assets conservation. Retrieved August 23, 2007, from http://www.fondazionecariplo.it/portal/page36.do?link=oln212.redirect&seu169a.oid.set=199#

Fondazione Cariverona. (n.d.). [Translated into English from Italian]. Retrieved August 23, 2007, from http://www.fondazionecrverona.org/home1.php3

Fondazione Cassa di Risparmio Cuneo. (2000). Informazioni [translated into English from Italian]. Retrieved August 23, 2007, from http://www.fondazionecrc.it/informazioni.html

Fondazione Cassa di Risparmio di Padova e Rovigo. (n.d.). [Translated into English from Italian]. Retrieved August 23, 2007, from http://www.fondazionecariparo.it/

Fondazione Cassa di Risparmio di Roma. (n.d.). [Translated into English from Italian]. Retrieved August 23, 2007, from http://www.fondazionecrroma.it/opencms/opencms/fondazione

Fondazione Cassa di Risparmio di Torino. (2007). Fondazione CRT. Retrieved August 23, 2007, from http://www.fondazionecrt.it/fondazioneEng.html

Fondazione Cassa di Risparmio di Verona Vicenza BA. (n.d.). Solidarietà Internazionale. Retrieved August 23, 2007, from http://www.fondazionecrverona.org/Attivita/Int_Effett/Index_ Int_Effet_Lev2.Php3?Kmacro=G&Kzona=VR&Ksettore=79

Fondazione Monte dei Paschi di Siena. (2007). Financial statement 2006 [translated into English from Italian]. Retrieved August 23, 2007, from http://www.fondazionemps.it/eng/bilancio. asp?id=7

Ford Foundation. (2007). Trust 2006 report. Retrieved August 23, 2007, from http://www. fordfound.org/about/financial2.cfm

Foundation Center. (2007). Top 100 U.S. foundations by asset size. Retrieved August 23, 2007, from http://foundationcenter.org/findfunders/topfunders/top100assets.html

Foundations in Canada. (n.d.). Retrieved August 23, 2007, from Wikipedia Web site: http:// en.wikipedia.org/wiki/Foundations_in_Canada

Garfield Weston Foundation. (2007). Garfield Weston Foundation 2006 annual report and accounts. Retrieved August 23, 2007, from http://www.garfieldweston.org/report/Balance Sheet.aspx

Hartley, C., & Holly, K. (2002). The international foundation directory (11th ed.). London: Europa Publications.

Hewlett Foundation. (2006). Annual report 2005. Retrieved August 23, 2007, from http://www.hewlett.org/AboutUs/AnnualReports/2005annualreport.htm

Hong Kong Jockey Club Charities Trust. (n.d.). [Translated into English from Chinese]. Retrieved August 23, 2007, from http://www.hkjc.com

Hongkong Bank Foundation. (2006). The Hongkong Bank Foundation. Retrieved August 23, 2007, from http://www.hongkongbankfoundation.org.hk/foundation/

India Foundation for the Arts. (2005). Annual report 2004-05. Retrieved August 23, 2007, from http://www.indiaifa.org/images/AnnualReport04-05.pdf

Ishibashi Foundation. (2001). Ishibashi Foundation. Retrieved August 23, 2007, from http://www. ishibashi-foundation.or.jp/ishibashi_web_e/index_top_e.html

J. Paul Getty Trust. (2007). 2006 report. Retrieved August 23, 2007, from http://www.getty. edu/about/governance/trustreport/trust_report.pdf

J.W. McConnell Family Foundation. (2006). Home page. Retrieved August 23, 2007, from http://www.mcconnellfoundation.ca/default.aspx?page=1&lang=en-US

John D. and Catherine T. MacArthur Foundation. (n.d.). International program: Global security and sustainability. Retrieved August 23, 2007, from http://www.macfound.org/site/c.lkLXJ8MQKrH/b.929441/k.74BD/International_Grantmaking.htm

Leverhulme Trust. (n.d.). Welcome to the Leverhulme Trust website. Retrieved August 23, 2007, from http://www.leverhulme.ac.uk/

Li Ka Shing Foundation. (n.d.). Mr. Li Ka-shing. Retrieved August 23, 2007, from http://www.lksf.org/eng/about/likashing/index.shtml

Mitsubishi Foundation. (n.d.). The Mitsubishi Foundation. Retrieved August 23, 2007, from http://www.mitsubishi-zaidan.jp/mzd000e.htm

Prince Claus Fund. (2007). Annual report 2006. Retrieved August 23, 2007, from http://www.princeclausfund.org/en/who_we_are/facts_and_figures/annualreport2006.shtml

Prussian Cultural Heritage Foundation. (n.d.). Budget figures [translated into English from German]. Retrieved August 23, 2007, from http://www.hv.spk-berlin.de/english/wir_ueber_uns/haushaltsdaten.php

Robert Bosch Stiftung. (2006). Profile. Retrieved August 23, 2007, from http://www.bosch-stiftung.de/content/language1/html/index.asp

Rockefeller Foundation. (2006). 2005 annual report. Retrieved August 23, 2007, from http://www.rockfound.org/about_us/2005rfar.pdf

Sasakawa Peace Foundation. (2007). Statement of financial position. Retrieved August 23, 2007, from http://www.spf.org/e/profile/statement.html

Shaw Foundation Hong Kong Ltd. (2006). Introduction. Retrieved August 23, 2007, from http://www.shawprize.org/en/organization/introduction.html

Sir Ratan Tata Trust. (2006). Annual report 2005-2006. Retrieved August 23, 2007, from http://www.srtt.org/downloads/SRTTAnnualReport2005-06.pdf

Smithsonian Institution. (2007). Annual report 2006. Retrieved August 23, 2007, from http://www.si.edu/opa/annualrpts/06report/index.htm

Soong Ching-Ling Foundation (n.d.). [Translated into English from Chinese]. Retrieved August 23, 2007, from http://www.sclf.org/

Soros Foundation Network. (2007). 2006 annual report. Retrieved August 23, 2007, from http://www.soros.org/resources/articles_publications/publications/annual_20070731

Sumitomo Foundation. (2007). The Sumitomo Foundation. Retrieved August 23, 2007, from http://www.sumitomo.or.jp/e/index.htm

Tin Ka Ping Foundation. (n.d.). Retrieved August 23, 2007, from http://www.tinkaping.org/

Toyota Foundation. (2007). The Toyota Foundation. Retrieved August 23, 2007, from http://www.toyotafound.or.jp/etop.htm

Winnipeg Foundation. (n.d.). Your centre for community philanthropy. Retrieved August 23, 2007, from http://www.wpgfdn.org/

Vancouver Foundation. (n.d.). About us. Retrieved August 23, 2007, from http://www.vancouverfoundation.bc.ca/AboutVancouverFoundation/Statistics.shtml

Volkswagen Stiftung. (2007). Wir Stiften Wissen [Translated into English from German]. Retrieved August 23, 2007, from http://www.volkswagen-stiftung.de/

Western Unix Trade Association. (1995). Soon Ching Ling Foundation. Retrieved August 23, 2007, from http://www.wuta.com/Wuta/soong.html#A01

Wyatt, W. (2007, March 5). Top European foundations: Larger and meaner. Retrieved August 23, 2007, from http://www.watsonwyatt.com/news/press.asp?ID=17125

5

Council of Europe/ERICarts. (n.d.). Private sector sponsorship: Laws, schemes and targets. Retrieved June 20, 2007, from http://www.culturalpolicies.net/web/comparisons-tables.php?aid=41&cid=46&lid=en

DIGEST: CULTURAL INGOS + FOUNDATIONS

APPC. (2006). Philanthropy and the Third Sector in Asia and the Pacific: Grantmaking foundations in Hong Kong. Retrieved August 23, 2007, from Philanthropy and the Third Sector in Asia and the Pacific Web site: http://www.asianphilanthropy.org/grant/local/hongkong/hksar.html

APPC. (2006). Philanthropy and the Third Sector in Asia and the Pacific: Grantmaking foundations in India. Retrieved August 23, 2007, from Philanthropy and the Third Sector in Asia and the Pacific Web site: http://www.asianphilanthropy.org/grant/local/india/india.html

APPC. (2006). Philanthropy and the Third Sector in Asia and the Pacific: Grantmaking foundations in Korea. Retrieved August 23, 2007, from Philanthropy and the Third Sector in Asia and the Pacific Web site: http://www.asianphilanthropy.org/grant/local/korea/korea.html

Council on Foundations. (2006). International grantmaking update. Retrieved August 23, 2007, from http://www.cof.org/Council/newsletter.cfm?ItemNumber=7951&navItemNumber=2198

Fondazione Fitzcarraldo. (2003). Cultural cooperation in Europe: What role for foundations? Retrieved August 23, 2007, from http://www.fitzcarraldo.it/ricerca/pdf/CulturalCooperation_Final%20Report.pdf

Japan Foundation Center. (n.d.). An outlook of Japanese grant-making foundations. Retrieved August 23, 2007, from http://www.jfc.or.jp/eibun/bun/e_bun1.html

Teneva, K. (2002). Culture & civil society: A promising relationship or a missed opportunity? [Conference report, November 9-10, 2001]. Seminar organized by the Red House Centre for Culture and Debate, the Soros Centre for the Arts—Sofia, Bulgaria, the Ministry of Culture, and the Council of Europe. Retrieved from the Red House Centre for Culture and Debate Web site: http://www.redhouse-sofia.org/engl/projects/p_conferences/culture_civil_society2.html

EMPLOYMENT + PROFESSIONS

EMPLOYMENT + PROFESSIONS

1

Florida, R. (2005). The flight of the creative class. New York: HarperCollins.

2

Australia Bureau of Statistics. (2004). Work in selected culture and leisure activities, Australia, April 2004 (Corrigendum). Retrieved May 8, 2007, from http://www.abs.gov.au/Ausstats/abs@.nsf/lookupMF/D86A9FF41EC1D574CA2568A900139430

Bureau of Economic Analysis, United States Department of Commerce. (2006). Table 6.8D. Persons engaged in production by industry. Retrieved June 28, 2007, from http://www.bea.gov/bea/dn/nipaweb/TableView.asp#Mid

Bureau of Labor Statistics, Department of Labor, USA. (2006). Table 11. Employed persons by detailed occupation, sex, race, and Hispanic or Latino ethnicity. Retrieved June 28, 2007, from http://www.bls.gov/cps/cpsaat11.pdf

Chun-hung, N.G., Hui, D., Mok, P., Ngai, F., Wan-kan, C., & Yuen, C. (2004). A study on Hong Kong creativity index (interim report). Retrieved May 7, 2007, from http://ccpr.hku.hk/HKCL-InterimReport.pdf

European Commission. (2006, October). The economy of culture in Europe. Retrieved March 20, 2007, from http://ec.europa.eu/culture/eac/sources_info/studies/economy_en.html

European Union Eurostat. (2002). Cultural employment in Europe, 2002. Retrieved March 9, 2007, from http://europa.eu/rapid/pressReleasesAction.do?reference=STAT/04/68&format=HTML&aged=1&language=EN&guiLanguage=en

Hill Strategies Research Inc. (2006, March 29). Artists in large Canadian cities. Retrieved March 9, 2007, from http://www.hillstrategies.com/resources_details.php?resUID=1000160

Hollister, V., & Throsby, C.D. (2003). Don't give up your day job: An economic study of professional artists in Australia. Sydney: Australia Council for the Arts.

IBGE (Instituto Brasileiro de Geografia e Estatística). (2003). Cadastro central de empresas 2003 [translated into English from Portuguese]. Retrieved April 20, 2007, from http://www.ibge.gov.br/home/estatistica/economia/cadastroempresa/2003/defaulttab_.shtm

Ministry of Public Management, Home Affairs, Posts and Telecommunications, Japan. (n.d.). Establishment and enterprise census. Retrieved February 26, 2007, from http://www.soumu.go.jp/english/

New Zealand Ministry for Culture and Heritage. (2006). 2006 cultural indicators for New Zealand. Retrieved May 7, 2007, from http://www.stats.govt.nz/analytical-reports/cultural-indicators-2006.htm

OECD (Organisation for Economic Co-operation and Development). (2006, August 23). International measurement of the economic and social importance of culture. Retrieved June 28, 2007, from http://www.oecd.org/dataoecd/26/51/37257281.pdf

UNESCO (United Nations Educational, Scientific and Cultural Organization). (2003). Economic contributions of Singapore's creative industries. Retrieved March 9, 2007, from http://portal.unesco.org/culture/fr/file_download.php01033f66c875d9196bb30e5e22b3e3feMICA+-+Economic+Contribution+Singapore+2003.pdf#search+%22%22creative%20industries%22%20Australia%20statistics%22

3

Australia Bureau of Statistics. (2004). Work in selected culture and leisure activities, Australia, April 2004 (Corrigendum). Retrieved May 8, 2007, from http://www.abs.gov.au/Ausstats/abs@.nsf/lookupMF/D86A9FF41EC1D574CA2568A900139430

Chun-hung, N.G., Hui, D., Mok, P., Ngai, F., Wan-kan, C., & Yuen, C. (2004). A study on Hong Kong creativity index (interim report). Retrieved May 7, 2007, from Center for Cultural Policy and Research at the University of Hong Kong Web site: http://ccpr.hku.hk/HKCL-Interim Report.pdf

European Commission. (2006, October). The economy of culture in Europe. Retrieved March 20, 2007, from http://ec.europa.eu/culture/eac/sources_info/studies/economy_en.html

European Union Eurostat. (2002). Cultural employment in Europe, 2002. Retrieved March 9, 2007, from http://europa.eu/rapid/pressReleasesAction.do?reference=STAT/04/68&format=HTML&aged=1&language=EN&guiLanguage=en

Hill Strategies Research Inc. (2006, March 29). Artists in large Canadian cities. Retrieved March 9, 2007, from http://www.hillstrategies.com/resources_details.php?resUID=1000160

Hollister, V., & Throsby, C.D. (2003). Don't give up your day job: An economic study of professional artists in Australia. Sydney: Australia Council for the Arts.

IBGE. (2003). Cadastro central de empresas 2003 [translated into English from Portuguese]. Retrieved April 20, 2007, from http://www.ibge.gov.br/home/estatistica/economia/cadastroempresa/2003/defaulttab_.shtm

Instituto Nacional de Estadísticas y el Consejo Nacional de la Cultura y las Artes, Chile. (2004). Anuario de cultura y tiempo libre: Creación, patrimonio, recreación y medios de comunicación 2004 [translated into English from Spanish]. Retrieved May 18, 2007, from http://www.ine.cl/canales/chile_estadistico/encuestas_consumo_cultural/pdf/cutura2004.pdf

Ministry of Public Management, Home Affairs, Posts and Telecommunications, Japan. (n.d.). Establishment and enterprise census. Retrieved February 26, 2007, from http://www.soumu.go.jp/english/

New Zealand Ministry for Culture and Heritage. (2007). 2006 cultural indicators for New Zealand. Retrieved May 7, 2007, from http://www.stats.govt.nz/analytical-reports/cultural-indicators-2006.htm

OECD. (2006, August 23). International measurement of the economic and social importance of culture. Table USA.1. Retrieved June 28, 2007 from http://www.oecd.org/dataoecd/26/51/37257281.pdf

UNESCO. (2004, September 9). Condition de l'artiste [table comparing and contrasting employment regimes and social benefit systems of artists around the world]. Retrieved April 5, 2007, from http://portal.unesco.org/culture/fr/ev.php-URL_ID=22643&URL_DO=DO_TOPIC&URL_SECTION=201.html

4

DIGEST: EMPLOYMENT + PROFESSIONS

Aageson, T.H. (2008). Cultural entrepreneurs: Producing cultural value & wealth. In H. K. Anheier & Y.R. Isar (Eds.), Cultural economy: The Cultures and Globalization Series, Vol. 2. Thousand Oaks, CA: Sage.

Addison, T. (2006). The international mobility of cultural talent (Research Paper No. 2006/108). Helsinki, Finland: United Nations University–World Institute for Economic Development Research.

Australia Bureau of Statistics. (2004). Work in selected culture and leisure activities, Australia, April 2004 (Corrigendum). Retrieved May 8, 2007, from http://www.abs.gov.au/Ausstats/abs@.nsf/lookupMF/D86A9FF41EC1D574CA2568A900139430

Catching on to 'Japan cool.' (2007). Asia Times. Retrieved May 25, 2007, from http://www.atimes.com/atimes/Japan/IE03Dh01.html

European Commission. (2006, October). The economy of culture in Europe. Retrieved March 20, 2007, from http://ec.europa.eu/culture/eac/sources_info/studies/economy_en.html

Florida, R. (2005). The flight of the creative class. New York: HarperCollins.

Greffe, X., & Sato, N. (2008). Cultural value logics in a global economy: Linking artists and artisans. Unpublished manuscript.

Hollister, V., & Throsby, C. D. (2003). Don't give up your day job: An economic study of professional artists in Australia. Sydney: Australia Council for the Arts.

IBGE. (2003). Cadastro central de empresas 2003 [translated into English from Portuguese]. Retrieved April 20, 2007, from http://www.ibge.gov.br/home/estatistica/economia/ cadastroempresa/2003/defaulttab_.shtm

King, B. (2007). SXSW Day 6: Gilberto Gil wants to free digital culture [electronic version]. Technology Review, 1. Retrieved July 20, 2007, from Web site: http://www.technologyreview. com/blog/editors/17562/

Moisés, J. Á., & Albuquerque, R. C. d. (1998). Pesquisa economia da cultura—resumo. Rio de Janeiro: Fundação João Pinheiro.

Ministry of Public Management, Home Affairs, Posts and Telecommunications, Japan. (2006). Establishment and enterprise census. Retrieved February 26, 2007, from http://www.soumu. go.jp/english/

Wikipedia. (2007, July 20). Leon Bolstein. Retrieved August 2, 2007, from http://en.wikipedia. org/wiki/Leon_Botstein

Yoshimoto, M. (2003). The status of creative industries in Japan and policy recommendations for their promotion. Tokyo: NLI Research.

CULTURAL PRODUCTION + DISSEMINATION

GOVERNMENT CULTURAL EXPENDITURES

1-4

United Nations. (2006). National account statistics 2005: Main aggregates and detailed tables. New York: United Nations Publications.

DIGEST: GOVERNMENT CULTURAL EXPENDITURES

ERICarts. (n.d.). Canada: General objectives and principles of cultural policy. Retrieved July 19, 2007, from http://www.culturalpolicies.net/web/canada.php?aid=33

OCPA (Observatory on Cultural Policies in Africa). (n.d.). Retrieved July 19, 2007, from http://www.ocpanet.org/

US Department of Education. (2006). National Assessment of Educational Progress 2006: Comparing private schools and public schools using hierarchical linear modeling. Retrieved July 19, 2007, from http://nces.ed.gov/nationsreportcard/pdf/studies/2006461.pdf

TRADE

1

Australian Bureau of Statistics. (2004). Arts & culture in Australia: A statistical overview. Retrieved January 12, 2007, from http://www.abs.gov.au/AUSSTATS/abs@.nsf/Latestproducts/ Contents12004%20(Reissue)?opendocument&tabname=Summary&prodno=4172.0&issue=2004 %20(Reissue)&num=&view=

Centre for Cultural Policy Research. (2003). Baseline study on Hong Kong creative industries. Retrieved January 12, 2007, from http://ccpr.hku.hk/Baseline_Study_on_HK_Creative_ Industries-eng.pdf

Culture, Tourism and the Centre for Education Statistics. (2004). Economic contribution of culture in Canada. Retrieved January 12, 2007, from http://www.statcan.ca/english/research/81-595-MIE/81-595-MIE2004023.pdf

European Commission. (2006). The economy of culture in Europe. Retrieved March 20, 2007, from http://ec.europa.eu/culture/eac/sources_info/studies/economy_en.html

Hong, T.M., Choo, A., & Ho, T. (2003). Economic contribution of Singapore's creative industries, Economic Survey of Singapore. Retrieved January 12, 2007, from UNESCO Web site: http://portal.unesco.org/culture/fr/file_download.php/01033f66c875d9196bb30e5e22b3e3feMICA+-+Economic+Contribution+Singapore+2003.pdf#search=%22%22creative%20industries%22%20Australia%20statistics%22

New Zealand Institute of Economic Research. (2002). Creative industries in New Zealand. Retrieved January 12, 2007, from UNESCO Web site: http://portal.unesco.org/culture/en/file_download.php/f10ce71cc883f9674c2271851d47beaaNZ+-+Creative+Industries+New+Zealand.pdf

OECD. (n.d.). International measurement of the economic and social importance of culture. Retrieved January 12, 2007, from http://www.oecd.org/dataoecd/26/51/37257281.pdf

WIPO (World Intellectual Property Organization). (2006). Study on the economic importance of industries and activities protected by copyright and related rights in the MERCOSUR countries and Chile. Retrieved January 12, 2007, from http://www.wipo.int/freepublications/en/copyright/889/wipo_pub_889_1.pdf

2
Gordon, J.C., & Beilby-Orrin, H. (2006, August). International measurement of the economic and social importance of culture statistics directorate. Retrieved February 13, 2007, from OECD Web site http://www.oecd.org/dataoecd/26/51/37257281.pdf

3
UNCTAD (United Nations Conference on Trade and Development). (n.d.). Retrieved February 18, 2007, from http://stats.unctad.org/Handbook/TableViewer/tableView.aspx

4-5
UNCTAD. (n.d.). Retrieved February 14, 2007, from http://stats.unctad.org/Handbook/

DIGEST: TRADE

DCMS (United Kingdom Government Department for Culture, Media and Sport). (n.d.). Creative industries. Retrieved June 9, 2007, from http://www.culture.gov.uk/what_we_do/Creative_industries

European Commission. (2006, October). The economy of culture in Europe. Retrieved March 20, 2007, from http://ec.europa.eu/culture/eac/sources_info/studies/economy_en.html

Gordon, J.C., & Beilby-Orrin, H. (2006, August). International measurement of the economic and social importance of culture statistics directorate. Retrieved February 13, 2007, from OECD Web site: http://www.oecd.org/dataoecd/26/51/37257281.pdf

MKW Wirtschaftsforschung. (2006). Study on the economy of culture in Europe. Retrieved January 12, 2007, from http://www.cultural-economy.eu/2006.php?lang==en

New Zealand Trade and Enterprise. (2006). Developing creative industries in New Zealand. Retrieved June 9, 2007, from http://www.nzte.govt.nz/section/11756.aspx

UNCTAD. (2006). Handbook of statistics. Retrieved February 8, 2007, from http://stats.unctad.org/Handbook/ReportFolders/ReportFolders.aspx?CS_referer=&CS_ChosenLang=en

UNESCO. (2005). International flows of selected cultural goods and services, 1994-2003. Defining and capturing the flows of global cultural trade. Retrieved October 24, 2007, from http://portal.unesco.org/en/ev.php-URL_ID=31230&URL_DO=DO_TOPIC&URL_SECTION=201.html

UNESCO. (2006). Developing countries losing out in cultural trade. Retrieved June 9, 2007, from http://portal.unesco.org/en/ev.php-URL_ID=31230&URL_DO=DO_TOPIC&URL_SECTION=201.html

UNESCO. (2006). What is the market structure of cultural industries? Retrieved June 9, 2007, from http://portal0.unesco.org/culture/admin/ev.php?URL_ID=18671&URL_DO=DO_TOPIC&URL_SECTION=201&reload=1181699571&PHPSESSID=0 c6c873a50dc18d715780ead6c4eaa63

GLOBAL BRANDS

1-3

Millward Brown Optimor. (2006). Brandz top 100 most powerful brands. Retrieved April 30, 2007, from http://www.millwardbrown.com/Sites/optimor/Media/Pdfs/en/BrandZ/BrandZ-2006-Top100Brands.pdf

DIGEST: GLOBAL BRANDS

Dorffer, C. (2006). Brand-driven shareholder value creation (Millward Brown Optimor white paper). Retrieved June 9, 2007, from http://www.millwardbrown.com/Sites/Optimor/Media/Pdfs/en/WhitePapers/6771C393.pdf

Global brands scorecard. (2006). Retrieved June 9, 2007, from Finfacts Ireland, Business and Finance Portal Web site: http://www.finfacts.ie/brands.htm

Interbrand. (2006). Best global brands 2006. Retrieved June 9, 2007, from http://www.ourfishbowl.com/images/surveys/BGB06Report_072706.pdf

Millward Brown Optimor. (2006). Brandz top 100 most powerful brands. Retrieved April 30, 2007, from http://www.millwardbrown.com/Sites/optimor/Media/Pdfs/en/BrandZ/BrandZ-2006-Top100Brands.pdf

Siegmund, M. (2003, January). The secret of successful online branding. Retrieved June 9, 2007, from Center on Global Brand Leadership of the Columbia Business School Web site: http://www.globalbrands.org/research/working/Online_Branding.pdf

Thompson, C. (2006, April 23). Google's China problem, and China's Google problem. New York Times. Retrieved June 9, 2007, from http://www.nytimes.com/2006/04/23/Magazine/23google.html?ex=1181880000&en=a0414d6cebf7ec1a&ei=5070

CREATION, INNOVATION + PROTECTION

1

Florida, R. (2005). The flight of the creative class. New York: HarperCollins.

2

Pro Inno Europe, Inno Metrics. (2006). European innovation scoreboard 2006: Comparative analysis of innovation performance. Retrieved on July 25, 2007, from http://www.proinno-europe.eu/doc/EIS2006_final.pdf

3

Akademie der Bildenen Kuenste Wien. (n.d.). [Translated into English from German]. Retrieved August 13, 2007, from http://www.akbild.ac.at/Portal/akademie/uber-uns/berichte/jahresabschlus-2005

Akademie der Bildenen Kuenste Wien. (n.d.). [Translated into English from German]. Retrieved August 9, 2007, from https://campus.akbild.ac.at/akbild_online/webnav.in

Art Center College of Design. (2007). 07-08 catalog. Retrieved August 13, 2007, from http://www.artcenter.edu/accd/pdf/catalog_cover_015.pdf

Berlin University of the Arts. (n.d.). Retrieved July 26, 2007, from Wikipedia Web site: http://en.wikipedia.org/wiki/Universit%C3%A4t_der_K%C3%BCnste_Berlin

California Institute of the Arts. (n.d.). About CalArts. Retrieved August 13, 2007, from http://www.calarts.edu/aboutcalarts

China Academy of Art. (n.d.). China Academy of Art. Retrieved August 9, 2007, from http://www.caa.edu.cn/setting/international/20031118/57_4.htm

China Academy of Art. (n.d.). Retrieved August 9, 2007, from Wikipedia Web site: http://en.wikipedia.org/wiki/China_Academy_of_Art

Koninklijke Academie van Beeldende Kunsten. (n.d.). English information. Retrieved August 9, 2007, from http://www.kabk.nl/English/introduction/-/nl

Koninklijke Academie van Beeldende Kunsten. (n.d.). International students. Retrieved August 9, 2007, from http://www.kabk.nl/international_students/index.xml

Ministère de la Culture et de la Communication. (2007). Beaux Arts de Paris L'Ecole Nationale Supérieure: Livret de l'Etudiant 2007-2008. [Translated into English from French]. Retrieved August 13, 2007, from http://www.ensba.fr/download/pdf/Ensba_LivreEtudiant.pdf

Rhode Island School of Design. (n.d.). Admissions: Facts + figures. Retrieved August 9, 2007, from http://www.risd.edu/factsfigures.cfm

Rhode Island School of Design. (n.d.). RISD: About RISD. Retrieved August 9, 2007, from http://www.risd.edu/aboutrisd.cfm

School of the Arts Institute Chicago. (n.d.). At a glance. Retrieved August 9, 2007, from http://www.saic.edu/about/glance/index.html

Tokyo National University of Fine Arts and Music. (2006). Tokyo Geijutsu Daigaku 2006. Retrieved August 14, 2007, from http://www.geidai.ac.jp/english/about/pdf/H18gaiyou_E.pdf

Tokyo National University of Fine Arts and Music. (n.d.). Retrieved August 9, 2007, from Wikipedia Web site: http://en.wikipedia.org/wiki/Tokyo_National_University_of_Fine_Arts_and_Music

Universidade de São Paulo. (n.d.). Anuário Estatístico [Translated into English from Portuguese]. Retrieved August 14, 2007, from http://sistemas.usp.br/anuario/

Universitaet der Kuenste Berlin. (2007). The Berlin University of the Arts [Translated into English from German]. Retrieved August 9, 2007, from http://www.udk-berlin.de/sites/content/themen/universitaet/index_ger.html

University of the Arts London. (n.d.). International students. Retrieved July 26, 2007, from http://www.arts.ac.uk/international.htm

Fortune Global 500. (2006). Retrieved August 7, 2007, from CNNMoney Web site: http://money.cnn.com/magazines/fortune/global500/2006/full_list/index.html

WIPO. (n.d.). Madrid Express structured search. Retrieved August 7, 2007, from http://www.wipo.int/ipdl/en/search/madrid/search-struct.jsp

WIPO. (2006). WIPO patent report 2006. Retrieved August 7, 2007, from http://www.wipo.int/ipstats/en/statistics/patents/pdf/patent_report_2006.pdf

4

5-11

Benthall, J. (1999). Critique of intellectual property. Anthropology Today, 15(6): 1-3.

Brown, J.S., & Duguid, P. (2002). Creativity versus structure: A useful tension. In E.B. Roberts (Ed.), Innovation driving product, process and market change. San Francisco: MIT Sloan Management Review.

Business Software Alliance. (2007). 2006 global software piracy study. Retrieved August 13, 2007, http://w3.bsa.org/globalstudy/2006study.cfm

Cohen, J. (2007, May). AIDS drugs: Brazil, Thailand override big pharma patents. Retrieved August 9, 2007, from Science Web site: http://www.sciencemag.org/cgi/content/full/316/5826/816?rss=1

Florida, R. (2005). The flight of the creative class. New York: HarperCollins.

Landry, C. (2000). The creative city: A toolkit for urban innovators. London: Comedia, Earthscan Publications Ltd.

Mandigora, G. (2007). The recent US–China intellectual property dispute. Retrieved August 9, 2007, from Trade Law Center for South Africa Web site: http://www.tralac.org/scripts/content.php?id=6450.

National Bureau of Economic Research. (2006, March). New Ideas About New Ideas Conference. Retrieved August 9, 2007, from http://www.nber.org/~sewp/newideas.html

Rogers, E.M. (2003). Diffusion of innovations (5th ed.). New York: Free Press.

WIPO. (2007). What is intellectual property? Retrieved August 9, 2007, from http://www.wipo.int/about-ip/en/

DISSEMINATION + STORAGE

1

British Museum. (n.d.). The British Museum publication scheme. Retrieved August 10, 2007, from http://www.thebritishmuseum.ac.uk/the_museum/about_us/foi_publication_scheme.aspx

Hermitage Museum. (n.d.). Hermitage projects. Retrieved August 10, 2007, from http://www.hermitagemuseum.org/html_En/13/hm13_2_009.html

Hermitage Museum. (n.d.). Visitor information. Retrieved August 10, 2007, from http://www.hermitagemuseum.org/html_En/02/hm2_1.html

Louvre. (2007). Les finances du musée du Louvre. Retrieved August 10, 2007, from http://www.louvre.fr/media/repository/ressources/sources/pdf/RA03finances_v2_m56577569830541188.pdf

Louvre. (2007). La fréquentation du musée du Louvre. Retrieved August 10, 2007, from http://www.louvre.fr/media/repository/ressources/sources/pdf/RA03frequentation_v2_m56577569830541189.pdf

Louvre. (n.d.). Overview. Retrieved August 10, 2007, from http://www.louvre.fr/llv/oeuvres/alaune.jsp?bmLocale=en

Metropolitan Museum of Art. (n.d.). Frequently asked questions. Retrieved August 10, 2007, from http://www.metmuseum.org/visitor/faq_hist.htm

Metropolitan Museum of Art. (2006). Annual report for the year 2005-2006. Retrieved August 10, 2007, http://www.metmuseum.org/annual_report/2005_2006/report_2005_2006.asp

Ministerio de Industria, Turismo, y Comercio. (2006). Los visitantes del Museo del Prado en el año 2005 [translated into English from Spanish]. Retrieved August 10, 2007, from http://www.iet.tourspain.es/informes/documentacion/FronturFamilitur/Informe_anual_2005_museo_prado.pdf

Musée d'Orsay. (n.d.). Retrieved August 10, 2007, from http://www.musee-orsay.fr/ORSAY/orsaygb/html.nsf/By+Filename/mosimple+edito+index?OpenDocument

Polo Museale Fiorentino. (n.d.). Welcome. Retrieved August 10, 2007, from http://www.polomuseale.firenze.it/english/benvenuto.asp

Smithsonian. (n.d.). About the Smithsonian. Retrieved August 10, 2007, from http://www.si.edu/about/

Staatliche Museen zu Berlin. (n.d.). Locations. Retrieved August 10, 2007, from http://www.smb.spk-berlin.de/e/loc/m.html

Tate Online. (n.d.). Home page. Retrieved August 10, 2007, from http://www.tate.org.uk/

Tokyo National Museum. (2005). Outline of the Independent Administrative Institution National Museum. Retrieved August 10, 2007, http://www.tnm.jp/en/organization/pdf/NATMUS_gaiyou_jpn_eng_2006.pdf

UNESCO. (2005). UNESCO archive portal. Retrieved August 10, 2007, from http://www.unesco.org/cgi-bin/webworld/portal_archives/cgi/page.cgi?d=1&g=Archives/Academia_and_culture/Museums/index.shtml

Biblioteca Nacional Brasil. (n.d.). Home page [translated into English from Portuguese]. Retrieved August 14, 2007, from http://www.bn.br/site/default.htm

Bibliotheca Alexandrina. (n.d.). Collection overview. Retrieved August 14, 2007, from http://www.bibalex.org/Libraries/Presentation/Static/15120.aspx

Bibliotheque Nationale de France. (n.d.). La BnF en chiffres [translated into English from French]. Retrieved August 14, 2007, from http://www.bnf.fr/pages/zNavigat/frame/connaitr.htm?ancre=chiffres.htm

British Library. (n.d.). Facts and figures. Retrieved August 14, 2007, from http://www.bl.uk/aboutus/quickinfo/facts/index.html

Deutsche Nationalbibliothek. (2007). Die Deutsche Nationalbibliothek im Überblick. [translated into English from German]. Retrieved August 14, 2007, from http://www.ddb.de/wir/ueber_dnb/dnb_im_ueberblick.htm

Library of Congress. (2007). Fascinating facts. Retrieved August 14, 2007, from http://www.loc.gov/about/facts.html

National Library of Belarus. (n.d.). Collections. Retrieved August 14, 2007, from http://www.nlb.by/eng/default.asp?item=2&id=9

National Library of China. (n.d.). Introduction of National Library of China. Retrieved August 14, 2007, from http://www.nlc.gov.cn/en/aboutus/history.htm

National Library of Russia. (2006). Figures for the year 2005. Retrieved August 14, 2007, from http://www.nlr.ru/eng/nlr/facts/

2

3

Vernadsky National Library of Ukraine. (n.d.). The Vernadsky National Library of Ukraine. Retrieved August 14, 2007, from http://www.nbuv.gov.ua/eng/

4

Association of Research Libraries. (2006). ARL statistics 2004-05. Retrieved August 6, 2007, from http://www.arl.org/bm~doc/arlstat05.pdf

Bodleian Library at Oxford University. (2004). Statistical factsheet No. 26. Retrieved August 6, 2007, from http://www.bodley.ox.ac.uk/users/mh/facts/facts26.htm

University of California Libraries. (2007). About the UC Libraries. Retrieved August 6, 2007, from http://libraries.universityofcalifornia.edu/about/

University of Cambridge Library. (2007). Cambridge University Library annual report 2006-2006. Retrieved August 6, 2007, from http://www.lib.cam.ac.uk/About/annual_report_2005-6.pdf

University of Tokyo. (n.d.). Major collection. Retrieved August 6, 2007, from http://www.lib.u-tokyo.ac.jp/koho/guide/coll/collection-e.html

5

Lavoie, B.F., Silipigni Connaway, L., & O'Neill, E.T. (2006). Mapping Worldcat's digital landscape. Retrieved August 6, 2007, from http://www.ala.org/ala/alcts/alctspubs/librestechsvc/LRTS_51n2Lavoie.pdf

Online Computer Library Center. (n.d.). WorldCat. Retrieved August 6, 2007, from http://www.oclcpica.org/dasat/index.php?cid=100655&conid=0&sid=37d631d15e0159c861f29598613ebf6

6

Wikimedia. (2007). Wikipedia statistics: Edits per month. Retrieved August 6, 2007, from http://stats.wikimedia.org/EN/TablesDatabaseEdits.htm

Wikimedia. (2007). Wikipedia statistics: New articles per day. Retrieved August 6, 2007, from http://stats.wikimedia.org/EN/TablesArticlesNewPerDay.htm

7

1 Cog. (n.d.). Don't say 'search engine'—say 'Google.' Retrieved August 6, 2007, from http://www.1cog.com/search-engine-statistics.html

DIGEST: DISSEMINATION + STORAGE

Columbia University. (2007). Fast facts about Columbia University Libraries. Retrieved August 13, 2007, from http://www.columbia.edu/cu/lweb/about/facts.html

Daniels, L., & Johnson, A. (2007). The word on Wikipedia: Trust but verify. Retrieved August 14, 2007, from MSNBC Web site: http://www.msnbc.msn.com/id/17740041/

UNESCO. (n.d.). Memory of the world. Retrieved November 16, 2007, from http://portal.unesco.org/ci/en/ev.php-URL_ID=1538&URL_DO=DO_TOPIC&URL_SECTION=201.html

UNESCO. (n.d.). What is intangible cultural heritage? Retrieved November 16, 2007, from http://www.unesco.org/culture/ich/index.php?pg=00002

Visiting Arts. (n.d.). Japan cultural profile. Retrieved August 10, 2007, from http://www.culturalprofiles.net/japan/Units/2915.html

TRADITIONAL + INDIGENOUS KNOWLEDGE

1-2

World Bank. (n.d.). IK practices database. Retrieved August 5, 2007, from http://www4.worldbank.org/afr/ikdb/search.cfm

3   SINGER (System-Wide Information Network for Genetic Resources). (n.d.). Overview of holding institutes. Retrieved August 5, 2007, from http://www.singer.cgiar.org/overview/inst. php?reqid=1179210725.588

4   WIPO. (n.d.). Final report on national experiences with the legal protection of expressions of folklore. Retrieved August 5, 2007, from http://www.wipo.int/documents/en/meetings/2002/igc/ pdf/grtkfic3_10.pdf

DIGEST: TRADITIONAL + INDIGENOUS KNOWLEDGE

Flavier, J.M., et al. (1995). The regional program for the promotion of indigenous knowledge in Asia. In D.M. Warren, L. J. Slikkerveer, & D. Brokensha (Eds.), The cultural dimension of development: Indigenous knowledge systems (pp. 479-487). London: Intermediate Technology Publications.

Gorjestani, N. (2002). Indigenous knowledge for development: Opportunities and challenges. Retrieved August 13, 2007, from World Bank Web site: http://www.worldbank.org/afr/ik/ikpaper_ 0102.pdf

World Bank Group. (2007). Learning about IK. Retrieved August 13, 2007, from http:// go.worldbank.org/5JABIFGJX0

Warren, D. M. (1991). Using indigenous knowledge in agricultural development: World Bank Discussion Paper No. 127. Washington, DC: World Bank.

WHO (World Health Organization). (2002, June). Fact sheet No. 271. Retrieved August 13, 2007, from http://www.who.int/medicines/organization/trm/factsheet271.doc

CULTURAL INDUSTRIES + FIELDS

NEWS (OFFLINE, ONLINE)

1   Harris Interactive, Inc. (2007, June 11). Harris poll. Retrieved August 31, 2007, from eMarketer database.

2   comScore Networks, Inc. (2006, August). World metrix. Retrieved August 30, 2007, from eMarketer database.

3   Al Jazeera. (n.d.). About us. Retrieved November 26, 2007, from http://english.aljazeera.net/NR/ exeres/650457A1-0CDF-4D37-A11A-80D01D01AABB.htm

BBC & CNN (company profiles). (2005, 2006). Retrieved August 31, 2007, from http://www. hoovers.com

Deutsche Welle. (2007, May). Background. Retrieved August 30, 2007, from http://www.dw-world.de/dw/article/0,2144,822473,00.html

TV5 Monde. (2007). Présentation. Retrieved August 30, 2007, from http://www.tv5.org/TV5Site/ tv5monde/presentation.php

Ahlers, D., & Hessen, J. (2005). Traditional media in the digital age: Data about news habits and advertiser spending lead to a reassessment of media's prospects and possibilities. Nieman Reports, 59(3): 65-69.

Auswaertiges Amt Deutschland. (2007). Welcome to the Federal Foreign Office [translated into English from German]. Retrieved August 31, 2007, from http://www.auswaertiges-amt.de/diplo/en/AAmt/AA/Kommunikation.html

Carvajal, D. (2006, January 8). All-news television spreading its wings. International Herald Tribune. Retrieved August 31, 2007, from http://www.iht.com/articles/2006/01/08/business/tv09.php

CJR. (2003, November/December). Canned news: What does it mean when local TV news isn't local? Columbia Journalism Review. Retrieved August 31, 2007, from http://cjrarchives.org/issues/2003/6/

France 24. (n.d.). About France 24. Retrieved September 25, 2007, from http://www.france24.com/france24Public/en/page-footer/about-france-24.h

Klinenberg, E. (2007, March/April). Breaking the news. Mother Jones Magazine. Retrieved September 25, 2007, from http://www.motherjones.com/news/feature/2007/03/breaking_the_news.html

Livingston, S. (1997). Clarifying the CNN effect: An examination of media effects according to type of military intervention. Retrieved September 25, 2007, from http://www.ksg.harvard.edu/presspol/research_publications/papers/research_papers/R18.pdf

Palser, B. (2005). TV news meets cyberspace: Will freewheeling Internet users watch online shows? American Journalism Review, 27(4): 74.

PRAVDA On-Line. (2005, July 28). The US Congress approved transmissions to Caracas if the messages of Telesur are 'anti-American.' Retrieved October 16, 2007, from http://english.pravda.ru/world/americas/28-07-2005/8646-telesur-0

Press TV. (n.d.). About us. Retrieved September 25, 2007, from http://www.presstv.ir/aboutus.aspx

Russia Today. (2007). Corporate profile. Retrieved September 25, 2007, from http://www.russiatoday.ru/corporate_profile

TelesurTV. (2007). Concepto: Un canal para la integración. Retrieved September 25, 2007, from http://www.telesurtv.net/secciones/concepto/index.php

TV5 Monde. (2007). Présentation. Retrieved August 30, 2007, from http://www.tv5.org/TV5Site/tv5monde/presentation.php

UN (United Nations). (2006, December 18). TV5Monde to expand relationship with United Nations after signing four-year renewed agreement with international organization of La Francophonie. Retrieved November 27, 2007, from http://www.un.org/News/Press/docs/2006/pi1757.doc.htm

TV

1

Variety. (2005). Global price guide. Retrieved July 23, 2007, from http://www.variety.com/article/VR1117930314.html?categoryid=2075&cs=1

2-3

Fey, C., Schmitt, D., & Bisson, G. (2005, April). The global trade in television formats. London: Screen Digest Limited.

4-5

Parker, P. (2006). The 2007-2012 world outlook for digital color televisions. Retrieved July 23, 2007, from www.marketresearch.com [Academic database].

DIGEST: TV

Africa News. (2005, October 27). Nigeria: Rise and rise of pay-TV stations. Retrieved November 16, 2007, from LexisNexis database.

Brennan, S. (2004, January 6). Reality TV goes global. Nielsen Entertainment News Wire. Retrieved November 16, 2007, from AllBusiness database.

Euromonitor International. (2007). Possession of household durables. Retrieved November 16, 2007, from Global Market Information database.

Levine, J. (2003, March 17). Sex, money and videotape. Forbes. Retrieved November 16, 2007, from http://www.forbes.com/forbes/2003/0317/088_print.html

RADIO

1

Satellite Industry Association. (2007, April). World satellite ground equipment revenues ($ billions). Wireless Satellite & Broadcasting Newsletter, 17(4): 1. Retrieved July 23, 2007, from TableBase database.

2

Haymarket Business Publications Ltd. (2007, March 30). World Media 2007: Australia. Campaign: 14. Retrieved July 23, 2007, from TableBase database.

Haymarket Business Publications Ltd. (2007, March 30). World Media 2007: Brazil. Campaign: 15. Retrieved July 23, 2007, from TableBase database.

Haymarket Business Publications Ltd. (2007, March 30). World Media 2007: Canada. Campaign: 16. Retrieved July 23, 2007, from TableBase database.

Haymarket Business Publications Ltd. (2007, March 30). World Media 2007: France. Campaign: 17. Retrieved July 23, 2007, from TableBase database.

Haymarket Business Publications Ltd. (2007, March 30). World Media 2007: Germany. Campaign: 19. Retrieved July 25, 2007, from TableBase database.

Haymarket Business Publications Ltd. (2007, March 30) World Media 2007: Greater China. Campaign: 21. Retrieved July 25, 2007, from TableBase database.

Haymarket Business Publications Ltd. (2007, March 30). World Media 2007: India. Campaign: 22. Retrieved July 25, 2007, from TableBase database.

Haymarket Business Publications Ltd. (2007, March 30). World Media 2007: Italy. Campaign: 23. Retrieved July 25, 2007, from TableBase database.

Haymarket Business Publications Ltd. (2007, March 30). World Media 2007: Japan. Campaign: N/A. Retrieved July 25, 2007, from TableBase database.

Haymarket Business Publications Ltd. (2007, March 30). World Media 2007: Russia. Campaign: 33. Retrieved July 25, 2007, from TableBase database.

Haymarket Business Publications Ltd. (2007, March 30). World Media 2007: South Africa. Campaign: 36. Retrieved July 25, 2007, from TableBase database.

Haymarket Business Publications Ltd. (2007, March 30). World Media 2007: South Korea. Campaign: 37. Retrieved July 25, 2007, from TableBase database.

Haymarket Business Publications Ltd. (2007, March 30). World Media 2007: UK. Campaign: 41. Retrieved July 25, 2007, from TableBase database.

Haymarket Business Publications Ltd. (2007, March 30). World Media 2007: US. Campaign: 42. Retrieved July 25, 2007, from TableBase database.

3   Radio France Internationale. (2006). RFI en bref: Les chiffres cles [translated into English from French]. Retrieved September 28, 2007, from http://www.rfi.fr/pressefr/articles/072/article_30.asp

4   BBC. (2007). Annual report and accounts 2006/2007. Retrieved September 28, 2007, from http://www.bbc.co.uk/annualreport/executive/

Deutsche Welle. (2006). Revenue and expenditure account. Retrieved September 28, 2007, from http://www.goethe-bytes.de/popups/popup_pdf/0,,2367595,00.pdf

Deutsche Welle. (2007, June). DW-Radio: A success story in many languages. Retrieved September 28, 2007, from http://www.dw-world.de/dw/article/0,2144,822475,00.html

Radio Canada. (2006). CBC/Radio-Canada annual report 2005-2006. Retrieved September 27, 2007, from http://www.cbc.radio-canada.ca/annualreports/2005-2006/pdf/AR0506_e.pdf

Radio France International. (2006-2007). Radio France International annual report 2006-2007. Retrieved September 28, 2007, from http://www.rfi.fr/pressefr/images/093%5Craport_actgivite2007.pdf

Voice of America. (n.d.). About VOA. Retrieved September 28, 2007, from Voice of America Web site: http://www.voanews.com/english/About/FastFacts.cfm

5   ICOM (International Communications Agency Network, Inc.). (2006). Retrieved September 28, 2007, from eMarketer database.

DIGEST: RADIO

MobaHO! (n.d.). Online-customer center. Retrieved October 6, 2007, from http://www.mobaho.com/english/support/mobaho.html

Orol, R., & Nolter, C. (2007). FCC to review satellite radio merger. Daily Deal/The Deal. Retrieved October 6, 2007, from LexisNexis database.

WorldSpace. (n.d.). About WorldSpace. Retrieved October 6, 2007, from http://www.worldspace.com/about/index.html

1-2   IFABC (International Federation of Audit Bureaux of Circulations). (2007). Top publications of the world. Retrieved August 28, 2007, from http://www.ifabc.org/top50.asp

3   WAN (World Association of Newspapers). (2007). World press trends: Global newspaper circulation, advertising on the upswing. Retrieved August 29, 2007, from http://www.wan-press.org/print.php3?id_article=14362

4   WAN. (2007). Publicis eyes more digital acquisitions, keeps goals. Retrieved August 29, 2007, from http://www.wan-press.org/print.php3?id_article=14363

5   WAN. (2007). Tendances mondiales de la presse: Hausse gobale de la diffusion et de la publicité dans les journaux [translated into English from French]. Retrieved August 29, 2007, from http://www.wan-press.org/print.php3?id_article=14364

DIGEST: PRINT MEDIA

Bundesverband Deutscher Zeitungsverleger. (2007, June 22). Trends in der Presse Weltweit: Auflagen und Anzeigeneinnahmen steigen [translated into English from German]. Retrieved August 29, 2007, from http://www.bdzv.de/bdzv_intern+M56256966a54.html

Core, E. (2003). Crossing into cross-media: Printers looking to expand and retain their clientele are learning to manage and reformat content for a variety of media beyond the printed page. Graphic Arts Monthly, 75(4): 46-49.

European Information Service. (2005, September 21). Publishing commission opens consultation on digital challenges. European Report, No. 2990.

Kubota, C. (2005, July 6). Japanese newspapers cling to power against Internet. Retrieved October 24, 2007, from Monsters and Critics Web site: http://tech.monstersandcritics.com/news/printer_1031210.php

Middle East Company News Wire. (2005, January 17). What is the future of Middle East publishing? Retrieved October 24, 2007, from AME Info Web site: http://www.ameinfo.com/52350.html

Perez-Pena, R., & Sorkin, A. (2007, August 1). Dow Jones deal gives Murdoch a coveted prize. New York Times. Retrieved October 24, 2007, from http://www.nytimes.com/2007/08/01/business/media/01dow.html

UNESCO. (2005). International flows of selected cultural goods and services, 1994-2003. Defining and capturing the flows of global cultural trade. Retrieved October 24, 2007, from http://portal.unesco.org/en/ev.php-URL_ID=31230&URL_DO=DO_TOPIC&URL_SECTION=201.html

WAN. (2005). World press trends. Retrieved June 10, 2006, from http://www.wan-press.org/article7321.html

WAN. (2007). World press trends: Global newspaper circulation, advertising on the upswing. Retrieved August 29, 2007, from http://www.wan-press.org/print.php3?id_article=14362

BOOKS

1 Datamonitor. (2006, November). Global publishing: Industry profile. Retrieved September 14, 2007, from http://dbic.datamonitor.com/industries/profile/ ?pid=0DE874EA-B8A0-4AD4-8B37-F3C35D07F89A

2 Parker, P. (2005). The 2006-2011 world outlook for printing and binding of general and trade books. Retrieved September 6, 2007, from http://www.marketresearch.com [Academic database].

3 Greco, R., Rodriguez, C., & Wharton, R.M. (2007). The culture and commerce of publishing in the 21st century. Palo Alto, CA: Stanford University Press.

4 Parker, P. (2005). The 2006-2011 world outlook for printing and binding of general and trade books. Retrieved September 6, 2007, from http://www.marketresearch.com [Academic database].

5 Datamonitor. (2006, November). Publishing in Asia-Pacific: Industry profile. Retrieved September 13, 2007, from Datamonitor Business Information Center [now MarketLine] database.

DIGEST: BOOKS

Bakkum, B. (2006, March 9) 'Pre-owned' books gain popularity (used books sales and forecast) [brief article]. The Writer.

Frankfurt Book Fair. (2007, October 8). Frankfurt Book Fair survey reveals the challenges facing the book industry worldwide. Retrieved October 10, 2007, from http://www.frankfurt-book-fair. com/en/index.php?content=/en/presse_pr/pressemitteilungen/details/16110/content.html

Goff, P. (2006, February 8). A new chapter for literature. South China Morning Post.

International Digital Publishing Forum. (2006, April). Industry eBook sales statistics 2005. Retrieved October 9, 2007, from eMarketer database.

Publishers Weekly. (2006a, March 6). Book ad spending up. Retrieved from http://www. publishersweekly.com/article/CA6312334.html?q=Book+ad+spending+up%2E

Publishers Weekly. (2006b, February 20). Piracy losses top $600 million. Retrieved from http://www.publishersweekly.com/article/CA6308611.html

Publishers Weekly. (2006c, March 13). US book sales hit $25.1 billion. Retrieved from http://www.publishersweekly.com/article/CA6315256.html?q=US+book+sales+hit+%2425%2E1 +billion%

2E UNESCO. (2005). International flows of selected cultural goods and services, 1994-2003. Defining and capturing the flows of global cultural trade. Retrieved October 24, 2007, from http://portal.unesco.org/en/ev.php-URL_ID=31230&URL_DO=DO_TOPIC&URL_ SECTION=201.html

FILM

1 Box Office Mojo. (n.d.). Studio market share. Retrieved September 14, 2007, from http://www. boxofficemojo.com/studio/

2 Are Internet television ratings low? (2007, September 17). Retrieved September 18, 2007, from eMarketer database.

3 Casting the big movie download roles. (2007, September 7). Retrieved September 14, 2007, from eMarketer database.

4   Screen Digest Cinema Intelligence. (2006). Global box office marks recovery: Gains in all major markets, only UK suffers slight decline. Retrieved September 14, 2007, from TableBase database.

5   Informa Media Group. (2003, October). Film on the Internet. Retrieved March 19, 2007, from eMarketer database.

6   European Audiovisual Observatory. (2006). Focus 2006: World Film Market trends. Retrieved September 17, 2007, from http://www.obs.coe.int/oea_publ/market/focus.html

DIGEST: FILM

Akhil, S. (2007, March 17). Bollywood through the ages: The cinema. The Age. Retrieved October 16, 2007, from LexisNexis database.

BBC News. (2006, June 29). FBI break up film piracy ring. Retrieved March 28, 2007, from http://news.bbc.co.uk/2/hi/entertainment/5128070.stm

Coe, N.M. (2001). A hybrid agglomeration? The development of a satellite-Marshallian industrial district in Vancouver's film industry. Urban Studies, 38: 1753-1775.

Currah, A. (2006). Hollywood versus the Internet: The media and entertainment industries in a digital and networked economy. Journal of Economic Geography, 6: 439-468.

McLaughlin, A. (2005, December 20). Africans, camera, action: 'Nollywood' catches world's eye. Christian Science Monitor. Retrieved April 28, 2006, from http://www.csmonitor.com

Ruigrok, I. (2006, February). Under the spell of Nollywood. Current Affairs. Retrieved March 28, 2006, from http://www.krachtvancultuur.nl/en/current/2006/february/nollywood.html

Sunshine duo make mobile movie. (2007, February 13). BBC News. Retrieved April 28, 2007, from http://news.bbc.co.uk/2/hi/technology/6355517.stm

MUSIC

1   IFPI (International Federation of the Phonographic Industry). (2007, May). Music market data 2006. Retrieved August 30, 2007, from http://www.ifpi.org/content/library/music%20market%20sales%20data%202006.pdf

2-3   IFPI. (2007). Recording industry in numbers. Retrieved August 30, 2007, from http://87.84.226.196/mro/publications/

4   IFPI. (n.d.). The broader music industry. Retrieved August 30, 2007, from http://www.ifpi.org/content/library/the-broader-music-industry.pdf

5-6   IFPI. (2007). Recording industry in numbers. Retrieved August 30, 2007, from http://87.84.226.196/mro/publications/

DIGEST: MUSIC

NPR. (2007, October 11). Fans take up Radiohead on pay-what-you-like offer. NPR News Blog. Retrieved October 11, 2007, from http://www.npr.org/blogs/news/2007/10/fans_take_up_radiohead_on_payw_1.html

RIAA (Recording Industry Association of America). (n.d.). Piracy: Online and on the street. Retrieved October 11, 2007, from http://www.riaa.com/physicalpiracy.php

SPORTS

1

Why Fifa's claim of one billion TV viewers was a quarter right. (2007, March). Independent. Retrieved August 27, 2007, from http://sport.independent.co.uk/football/news/article2314154.ece

2

The Golf Digest 50. (2007). Golf Digest. Retrieved August 24, 2007, from http://www.golfdigest.com/rankings/2006/GolfDigest50_gd2006

3

Celebrity 100: Female athletes. (2007). Forbes. Retrieved August 23, 2007, from http://www.forbes.com/2007/06/12/07celebrities_Female_Athletes_slide.html?thisSpeed=10000

The world's top earning athletes. (2007). Forbes. Retrieved August 23, 2007, from http://www.forbes.com/sportsbusiness/2007/10/25/sports-tiger-woods-biz-sports-cz_kb_1026athletes.html

4

Richest soccer teams. (2007). Forbes. Retrieved August 23, 2007, from http://www.forbes.com/2007/03/29/soccer-valuations-beckham-biz-services-cx_pm_07soccer_0329soccer_land.html

5-6

Buying up the bleachers: Stadium-naming deals top $1.4 billion amid solid gains for sponsorship overall. (2007). Brandweek. Retrieved August 22, 2007, from TableBase database.

DIGEST: SPORTS

FIFA (Fédération Internationale de Football Association). (2005). Financial report 2005. Retrieved November 27, 2007, from http://fifa.com/

Goldblatt, D. (2004) . Football yearbook: 2004/5. London: Dorling Kindersley Ltd.

IOC (International Olympic Committee). (2007). Global broadcast revenue. Retrieved November 27, 2007, from http://www.olympic.org/uk/organisation/facts/revenue/broadcast_uk.asp

IOC. (n.d.). Olympic Games. Retrieved May 5, 2007, from http://www.olympic.org/uk/games/index_uk.asp

International Working Group on Women in Sports. (n.d.). Retrieved May 18, 2007, from http://www.canada2002.org/e/progress/index.htm

Why Fifa's claim of one billion TV viewers was a quarter right. (2007, March). Independent. Retrieved August 27, 2007, from http://sport.independent.co.uk/football/news/article2314154.ece

VIDEO GAMES

1

DFC Intelligence. (2005). Leading video game companies worldwide 1998-2004. Retrieved August 17, 2007, from eMarketer database.

Informa Media Group. (2004). The dynamics of games (4th ed.). Retrieved August 17, 2007, from eMarketer database.

Kagan Research. (2007, April 13). US video game software sales by console 2006 (% market share). Retrieved August 17, 2007, from eMarketer database.

2   DFC Intelligence. (2005). Leading video game companies worldwide 1998-2004. Retrieved August 17, 2007, from eMarketer database.

3   Verna, P. (2007). Video game advertising: Getting to the next level. Retrieved August 16, 2007, from eMarketer database.

4   Informa Telecoms & Media. (2005). The dynamics of games (5th ed.). Retrieved August 17, 2007 from eMarketer database.

5   Entertainment Software Association. (2005). 2005 sales, demographics and user data. Retrieved August 17, 2007, from http://www.theesa.com/files/2005EssentialFacts.pdf

DIGEST: VIDEO GAMES

Anderson, C., Gentile, D., & Buckley, K. (2007). Violent video games' effects on children and adolescents. New York: Oxford University Press.

Deci, T.J. (2007). All Media Guide 2007. Retrieved August 20, 2007, from AllGame Beta Web site: http://www.allgame.com/cg/agg.dll?p=agg&sql=1:48058

Entertainment Consumers Association. (2007). GamePolitics.com. Retrieved August 21, 2007, from http://gamepolitics.com/2006/12/06/in-wake-of-rampage-german-minister-wants-jail-time-for-violent-game-creators-and-distributors/

Entertainment Software Association. (2005). 2005 sales, demographics and user data: Essential facts about the computer and video game industry. Retrieved August 17, 2007, from http://www.theesa.com/files/2005EssentialFacts.pdf

Entertainment Software Rating Board. (2007). Game ratings and descriptor guide. Retrieved August 20, 2007, from http://www.esrb.org/ratings/ratings_guide.jsp

Freedman, J. (2002). Media violence and its effect on aggression: Assessing the scientific evidence. Toronto: University of Toronto Press.

Hezbollah videogame: War with Israel. (2007, August 16). Reuters. Retrieved August 20, 2007, from http://www.cnn.com/2007/WORLD/meast/08/16/hezbollah.game.reut/index.html?iref=mpstoryview

In the wake of rampage, German minister wants jail time for violent game creators, distributors and players. (2007). Retrieved August 21, 2007, from GamePolitics Web site: http://gamepolitics.com/2006/12/06/in-wake-of-rampage-german-minister-wants-jail-time-for-violent-game-creators-and-distributors

PricewaterhouseCoopers. (2007, June 22). Global entertainment and media outlook: 2005-2009. Retrieved August 21, 2007, from eMarketer database.

FASHION

1   About Jo'Burg Fashion Week. (2007, July). Retrieved August 20, 2007, from http://www.joburgfashionweek.co.za/

Beck's Fashion Week: About us. (n.d.). Retrieved August 20, 2007, from http://www.belgradefashionweek.com/english/onama.php

Calendario Oficial Da Moda Brasileira. (n.d.). Retrieved August 20, 2007, from http://www.spfw.

com.br/index.php?form_action=english_home

Camera Nazionale Della Moda Italiana: History. (n.d.). Retrieved August 20, 2007, from http://www.cameramoda.it/eng/areaistituz/storia.php

Cumming-Bruce, N. (2005, August 11). Thailand struts onto runway of world fashion. International Herald Tribune. Retrieved August 20, 2007, from http://www.iht.com/articles/2005/08/10/business/thai.php

Emling, S. (2006, October 3). Big 4 fashion week gets new company. International Herald Tribune. Retrieved August 18, 2007, from http://www.iht.com/articles/2006/10/03/features/Rweeks.php

Fashion world readies for first India fashion week. (2000, August 14). Times of India. Retrieved August 20, 2007, from http://timesofindia.indiatimes.com/articleshow/2745579.cms

Federation Francaise de la Couture. (n.d.). Mode a Paris. Retrieved September 11, 2007, from http://www.modeaparis.com/

Fortini, A. (2006, February 8). How the runway took off: A brief history of the fashion show. Slate. Retrieved August 17, 2007, from http://www.slate.com/id/2135561

The history of Copenhagen Fashion Week. (n.d.). Retrieved August 20, 2007, from http://www.copenhagenfashionweek.com/18343/CFW%20History

Hong Kong Fashion Week Fall/Winter. (n.d.). Retrieved August 20, 2007, from http://hkfashionweekfw.tdctrade.com/index.htm

Iceland Fashion Week. (2003, July 17). Retrieved August 20, 2007, from http://www.visitreykjavik.is/default.asp?cat_id=17&module_id=220&element_id=497

London Fashion Week. (n.d.). Retrieved August 20, 2007, from http://www.londonfashionweek.co.uk

Mercedes-Benz Fashion Week. (n.d.). Retrieved August 21, 2007, from http://www.mbfashionweek.com/newyork/

Our mission: Fashion Week in Moscow. (n.d.). Retrieved August 20, 2007, from http://www.fashionweekinmoscow.com/aboutus/mission.php

Paris fashion shows. (n.d.). Retrieved August 18, 2007, from http://www.parisfashionshows.net/

Rosemount Australian Fashion Week. (n.d.). Retrieved August 20, 2007, from http://afw.com.au/home.asp

Tokyo International Forum. (n.d.). Japan Fashion Week in Tokyo 2006. Retrieved August 20, 2007, from http://www.t-i-forum.co.jp/english/magazine/vol52_fashion.html

2   Hong Kong Fashion Week for Fall/Winter 2007and World Boutique, Hong Kong 2007. (n.d.). Retrieved August 20, 2007, from http://hkfashionweekfw.tdctrade.com/survey2007/main.htm

3   Jeammet, C. (2007, March). Haute couture: Une appellation réduite à 10 maisons. France 3. Retrieved August 20, 2007, from http://cultureetloisirs.france3.fr/mode/defilesparisiens/103405-fr.php?page=2

4   Joes, Inc. (2006). Form 10-K: Innovo Group Inc–INNO. Retrieved September 12, 2007, from http://phx.corporate-ir.net/phoenix.zhtml?c=84356&p=irol-sec

Joes, Inc. (company profile). (n.d.). Retrieved September 12, 2007, from www.hoovers.com

VNU Business Media. (2006, April). Stylophane apparel brand popularity index. Apparel, 47(8): 1543-2009. Retrieved August 20, 2007, from TableBase database.

5

Clark, N. (2006, April 6). Couture clash. Media Analysis, 19. Retrieved August 20, 2007, from LexisNexis database.

Elle Worldwide network: 45 editions. (n.d.). Retrieved September 12, 2007, from http://www.i-g-a.com/networks.asp?cdn=1&cdt=508

Hearst Corporation. (n.d.). Harper's Bazaar. Retrieved September 12, 2007, from http://www.hearstcorp.com/magazines/property/mag_prop_hb_2000.html

Take Pride in America public service announcements take off. (2006, January 27). FunOutdoors. Retrieved September 12, 2007, from http://www.funoutdoors.com/node/view/1422

TimeWarner. (n.d.). Time Inc. Retrieved September 12, 2007, from http://www.timewarner.com/corp/businesses/detail/time_inc/index.html

Vogue. (n.d.). Cover archive. Retrieved September 12, 2007, from http://www.vogue.co.uk/CoverArchive/

DIGEST: FASHION

BBC News. (n.d.). Blast, art and design: What is ethical fashion? Retrieved September 11, 2007, from http://www.bbc.co.uk/blast/art/articles/what_is_ethical_fashion.shtml

BBC News. Girls under 16 should not model. (2007, July 11). Retrieved September 12, 2007, from http://news.bbc.co.uk/2/hi/uk_news/6290284.stm

Jeammet, C. (2007, March). Haute couture: Une appellation reduite a 10 maisons [translated from French into English]. Retrieved August 20, 2007 from France3.fr website: http://cultureeloisirs.france3.fr/mode/defilesparisiens/103405-fr.php?page=2

Thomas, D. (2007, August 20). Deluxe: How luxury lost its luster [excerpt]. NPR. Retrieved September 11, 2007, from http://www.npr.org/templates/story/story.php?storyId=13799348

ADVERTISING

1

PQ Media, LLC. (2007, March). Seen on TV, sold online. Retrieved September 20, 2007, from eMarketer database.

2

Publishers Information Bureau/TNS Media Intelligence. (2007, March 5). Top advertising categories. Retrieved September 19, 2007, from TableBase database.

3

PricewaterhouseCoopers and Wilkofsky Gruen Associates. (2007, June 20). Global entertainment and media outlook: 2007-2011. Retrieved September 20, 2007, from eMarketer database.

4

VNU Business Media. (2007, April 16). 24th annual agency report cards. Adweek (48): 18. Retrieved September 19, 2007, from TableBase database.

5

ABI Research. (2007, April). Console and handheld online gaming. Retrieved September 20, 2007, from eMarketer database.

6

Haymarket Business Publications Ltd. (2007, March 30). World Media 2007: Eastern Europe. Campaign: 14. Retrieved July 23, 2007, from TableBase database.

FCTC (Framework Convention Alliance for Tobacco Control). (n.d.). The WHO framework convention for tobacco control: A public health movement. Retrieved October 10, 2007, from http://www.fctc.org/

Levinson, J. (1984). Guerrilla marketing. Boston: Houghton Mifflin.

PQ Media, LLC. (2006). Top five countries worldwide ranked by paid product placement spending for select media 2005 (millions). Retrieved October 10, 2007, from eMarketer database.

United Nations Development Programme. (1998). Human development report 1998. Retrieved October 10, 2007, from http://hdr.undp.org/reports/global/1998/en/

ZenithOptimedia. (2007). Global facts and forecasts: Advertising expenditure forecasts (October 2007). Retrieved October 10, 2007, from http://www.zenithoptimedia.com/gff/index.cfm?id=77

ARCHITECTURE + DESIGN

1

Adjaye Associates. (n.d.). Adjaye Associates. Retrieved September 28, 2007, from http://www.adjaye.com

Field Operations. (n.d.). Studio: People. Retrieved September 28, 2007, from http://www.fieldoperations.net

Foster and Partners. (n.d.). Team. Retrieved September 28, 2007, from http://www.fosterandpartners.com/Team/SeniorPartners/Default.aspx

Lerer, L. (2007, March 14). Tastemakers: Architecture. Retrieved from Forbes Web site: http://www.forbes.com/forbeslife/2007/03/13/tastemaker-architecture-design-forbeslife-cx_ll_0314architecture.html

Morphosis. (n.d.). People. Retrieved September 28, 2007, from http://www.morphosis.net

Sheridan, J. (2007, September 18). Medium size firms hit happy medium. Retrieved September 28, 2007, from eOCULUS Web site: http://www.aiany.org/eOCULUS/newsletter/?p=824

Ten Arquitectos. (n.d.). Firm profile. Retrieved September 28, 2007, from http://www.ten-arquitectos.com

University of British Columbia. (n.d.). University Boulevard Architectural Design Competition, Stage 1: Short list of architectural teams. Retrieved September 28, 2007, from http://www.universitytown.ubc.ca/archcomp/shortlist.php

UNStudios. (n.d.). Studio: Directors and specialists. Retrieved September 28, 2007, from http://www.unstudio.com/studio/directors-and-specialists

2

Parker, P. (2006). The 2007-2012 world outlook for interior design services. Retrieved September 28, 2007, from www.marketresearch.com [Academic database].

3

Rodman Publishing Corp. (2007, August). The international rankings: Ink and graphic arts sales. Ink World, 13(8): 25. Retrieved September 28, 2007, from TableBase database.

4

Knoll. (2006). 2006 annual report. Retrieved September 28, 2007, from http://media.corporate-ir.net/media_files/irol/66/66169/2006_KnollAnnualReport.pdf

5

Reed Business Information. (2007, July). Industrial report: Demand for specialty factories spurs industrial sector recovery. Building Design & Construction, 48(9): 53. Retrieved September 28, 2007, from TableBase database.

A man apart. (2007, May). Creative Review, 46. Retrieved October 9, 2007, from LexisNexis database.

Pallasmaa, J. (2007, June). On history and culture. Architectural Record, 195(6): 105. Retrieved October 9, 2007, from LexisNexis database.

Tate Modern. (n.d.). Global cities. Retrieved October 9, 2007, from http://www.tate.org.uk/modern/exhibitions/globalcities/form.shtm

Worldview: Perspectives on architecture and urbanism from around the globe. (n.d.). Retrieved October 9, 2007, from http://worldviewcities.org

GLOBAL ARTS MARKET

ART AUCTIONS + GALLERIES

1 Global art auction sales volume in dollars for 1997 to 2005. (2006, February). Institutional Investor Americas, 40(2). Retrieved August 15, 2007, from RDS Business Reference Suite database.

2-3 Sotheby's. (n.d.). About us. Retrieved August 13, 2007, from http://www.sothebys.com/

4-5 Artprice. (2006). 2006 art market trends/tendances du marche de l'art. Retrieved August 15, 2007, from http://img1.artprice.com/pdf/trends2006.pdf

6 E-Business profile: Art.com Inc., 2004 & 2005. (2006, May). Retrieved August 14, 2007, from eMarketer database.

7 Artprice. (2002). Art market trends 2002. Retrieved August 15, 2007, from http://web.artprice.com/AMI/AMI.aspx?id=NzMwMTAwMTEyMDUzOTk=

Artprice. (2004). 2004 art market trends/tendances du marche de l'art. Retrieved August 15, 2007, from http://press.artprice.com/pdf/Trends2004.pdf

Artprice. (2006). 2006 art market trends/tendances du marche de l'art. Retrieved August 15, 2007, from http://img1.artprice.com/pdf/trends2006.pdf

GLOBAL PERFORMANCE ART

1 Berliner-philharmoniker. (n.d.). Berlin Philharmonic concerts on tour. Retrieved May 1, 2007, from http://www.berliner-philharmoniker.de/en/konzertreisen/

Israel Philharmonic Orchestra. (n.d.). Calendar. Retrieved May 1, 2007, from http://www.ipo.co.il/list/list.asp

New York Philharmonic. (n.d.). New York Philharmonic 2007-2008 season. Retrieved May 1, 2007, from http://nyphil.org/attend/season/index.cfm?page=eventsByMonth&dateRequest=9/01/2007&seasonNum=7

Wiener Philharmoniker. (n.d.). Weiner Philharmoniker tours. Retrieved May 1, 2007, from http://www.wienerphilharmoniker.at/index.php?set_language=en&cccpage=concerts_tour

Opera Australia's Oz Opera. (n.d.). Retrieved August 30, 2007, from http://www.opera-australia. org.au/opera/oaweb.nsf/Wf-company?readform&loc=lookups/111-OZOPERA?opendocument

Opera National de Paris. (n.d.). Direction Gerard Mortier. Retrieved August 20, 2007, from http://www.operadeparis.fr/Biographie.asp?id=227

Pittsburg Symphony Orchestra. (n.d.). Roberto Abbado. Retrieved August 20, 2007, from http://www.pittsburghsymphony.org/pghsymph.nsf/bios/Roberto+Abbado

Royal Opera House. (n.d.). About the music conductor, Antonio Pappano. Retrieved August 20, 2007, from http://info.royaloperahouse.org/Opera/index.cfm?ccs=613

Teatro Colón. (n.d.). Actualidad 2005: Marcelo Lombardero, director de Ópera del Teatro Colón. Retrieved August 20, 2007, from http://www.musicaclasicaargentina.com/2criticasjea17.htm

Weiner Staatsoper. (n.d.). Organisation: Seiji Ozawa. Retrieved August 30, 2007, from http://www.staatsoper.at/Content.Node2/home/haus/178_1.php

Australia Post. (n.d.). Retrieved August 30, 2007, from http://www.auspost.com.au/

English National Opera. (n.d.). Company principles. Retrieved August 30, 2007, from http://www.eno.org/about/index.php

Opera Australia. (n.d.). Opera Australia sponsorship. Retrieved August 30, 2007, from http://www.opera-australia.org.au/opera/oaweb.nsf/Wf-company?readform&loc=lookups/111-SPONSORSINTRO?opendocument

Oracle. (n.d.). Products and services. Retrieved August 30, 2007, from http://www.oracle.com/products/index.html

SkyArts Channel 267. (n.d.). Retrieved August 30, 2007, from http://www.skyarts.co.uk/Default.aspx

Teatro Alla Scala. (n.d.). Credits. Retrieved August 30, 2007, from http://www.teatroallascala.org/public/LaScala/EN/index.html

Teatro Colón. (n.d.). Retrieved August 30, 2007, from http://www.teatrocolon.org.ar/inicioing.htm

Weiner Staatsoper. (n.d.). Sponsors. Retrieved August 30, 2007, from http://www.staatsoper.at/Content.Node2/home/haus/7780.php#

Berlin Staatsoper. (n.d.). Retrieved September 5, 2007, from http://www.lares-lexicon.com/installations/berlinconsultants.html

English National Opera. (n.d.). Prices and seating plan. Retrieved September 5, 2007, from http://www.eno.org/book/seating_plans.php

Neilan, T. (2007). Q and A: Buenos Aires music. New York Times. Retrieved September 2, 2007, from http://query.nytimes.com/gst/fullpage.html?sec=travel&res=9C0DE2DE1239F93BA1575BC0A9629582

Opéra National de Paris. (n.d.). Billetterie en ligne. Retrieved September 5, 2007, from http://www.operadeparis.fr/Saison-2007-2008/Operas.asp#

Opéra National de Paris. (n.d.). Palais Garnier. Retrieved September 5, 2007, from http://www.fsz.bme.hu/opera/par_garnier.html

Royal Opera House. (n.d.). Auditorium seating plans and prices. Retrieved September 5, 2007, from http://info.royaloperahouse.org/Tickets/Index.cfm?ccs=167&cs=202&login=0

Royal Opera House. (n.d.). Select your own seat. Retrieved September 5, 2007, from http://esales roh.org.uk/tickets/reserve.aspx?perfid=1440#

Sydney Opera House. (n.d.). Il trittico. Retrieved September 5, 2007, from http://www. sydneyoperahouse.com/sections/whats_on/boxoffice/event_details.asp?EventID=1962&sm =1&ss=1

Sydney Opera House. (n.d.). Retrieved September 5, 2007, from http://www.sydneyopera house.com/

Teatro alla Scala. (n.d.). Retrieved September 5, 2007, from http://www.teatroallascala.org/ public/LaScala/EN/index.html

This is theatre. (n.d.). The London Coliseum. Retrieved September 5, 2007, from http://www. thisistheatre.com/londontheatre/coliseumtheatre.html

Weiner Staatsoper. (n.d.). Tickets. Retrieved September 5, 2007, from https://tickets.staatsoper-berlin.de/applet/applet.jsp

PRIZES + COMPETITIONS

1   Pulitzer Prizes. (n.d.). Retrieved August 30, 2007, from http://www.pulitzer.org/

2   Academy of Motion Picture Arts and Sciences. (n.d.). The Official Academy Awards Database. Retrieved August 30, 2007, from http://www.oscars.org/awardsdatabase/index.html

IMDb: The Internet Movie Database. (n.d.). Retrieved August 30, 2007, from http://www.imdb. com/title/tt0116209/business

3   Academy of Motion Picture Arts and Sciences. (n.d.). The Academy of Motion Picture Arts and Sciences Awards Database. Retrieved August 20, 2007, from http://awardsdatabase.oscars.org/ ampas_awards/DisplayMain.jsp?curTime=1186530383687

4   Nobel Prize.org. (n.d.). All Nobel laureates in literature. Retrieved August 30, 2007, from http://nobelprize.org/nobel_prizes/literature/laureates/

5   Pritzker Architecture Prize. (n.d.). Retrieved August 20, 2007, from http://www.pritzkerprize. com/main.htm

6   Royal Swedish Academy of Sciences. (n.d.). Retrieved August 20, 2007, from http://www.kva. se/KVA_Root/eng/awards/search_laureates/search.asp

7   D&AD Awards. (n.d.). Retrieved August 20, 2007, from http://www.dandad.org/awards/ awards-archive.asp

DIGEST: GLOBAL ARTS MARKET

Artprice. (2006). 2006 art market trends/tendances du marché de l'art. Retrieved August 15, 2007, from http://img1.artprice.com/pdf/trends2006.pdf

Artprice. (n.d.). Retrieved August 14, 2007, from http://www.artprice.com/

Asahi Shimbun's Osamu Tezuka Culture Awards. (n.d.). Retrieved September 10, 2007, from http://www.jai2.com/tezaward.htm

Pogrebin, R. (2007, August 29). Volatile markets? Art world takes stock. New York Times. Retrieved August 23, 2007, from http://www.nytimes.com/2007/08/29/arts/design/29mark. html?_r=2&8dpc&oref=slogin&oref=slogin

Reuters. (2007, May 22). Global fine arts market. Retrieved August 23, 2007, from http://www.reuters.com/article/consumerproducts-SP-A/idUSL2233405520070323

THE INTERNET

THE INTERNET

1-3   Internet World Stats. (2007). Internet World Stats: Population and usage statistics. Retrieved June 5, 2007, from http://www.internetworldstats.com/stats.htm

4   Technorati. (2007, April). The state of the blogosphere. Retrieved September 1, 2007, from eMarketer database.

5   Internet World Stats. (2007). Internet World Stats: Population and usage statistics, top 20 countries with the highest number of Internet users. Retrieved June 5, 2007, from http://www. internetworldstats.com/top20.htm

6   Alexa. (n.d.). Alexa: Top sites. Retrieved September 1, 2007, from http://www.alexa.com

7   Technorati. (2007, April). The state of the blogosphere. Retrieved September 1, 2007, from eMarketer database.

DIGEST: THE INTERNET

Family Safe Media. (n.d.). Pornography statistics [Graphic representation showing the estimated number of pornographic Web pages by country]. Retrieved from http://www.familysafemedia. com/pornography_statistics.html

Friedman, T. (2006). The world is flat [updated and expanded]: A brief history of the twenty-first century. New York: Farrar, Straus and Giroux.

International Internet Society. (2007). A brief history of the Internet. Retrieved October 3, 2007, from http://www.isoc.org/internet/history/brief.shtml

Internet World Stats. (2007). Internet usage statistics: The big picture [Graphic representation showing countries with the highest broadband and DSL penetration]. Retrieved October 24, 2007, from http://www.internetworldstats.com/dsl.htm

Shah, A. (2006, November 24). Poverty facts and stats. Retrieved October 3, 2007, from http://www.globalissues.org/TradeRelated/Facts.asp

Sifry, D. (2007, April 5). The state of the blogosphere. Retrieved October 3, 2007, from http://technorati.com/weblog/2007/04

GLOBAL SITES + EVENTS

GLOBAL CULTURAL CENTERS & CITIES

NEW YORK + LOS ANGELES

1-3 U.S. Census Bureau. (2007). County business patterns. Retrieved February 5, 2007, from http://www.census.gov/prod/www/abs/cbptotal.html

4 Center for an Urban Future. (2005, December). Creative New York. Retrieved February 1, 2007, from http://www.nycfuture.org

5-6 Hoovers. (n.d.). Cultural corporations [search by industry]. Retrieved February 14, 2007, from http://www.hoovers.com

TOKYO

1 Hoovers. (n.d.). Creative or cultural corporations [search by industry]. Retrieved April 24, 2007, from http://www.hoovers.com

2 Ministry of Public Management, Home Affairs, Posts & Telecommunications (n.d.). Establishment & enterprise census. Retrieved February 26, 2007, from http://www.soumu.go.jp/english/

3 Tokyo Metropolitan Government. (n.d.). Tokyo statistical yearbook. Retrieved August 27, 2007, from http://www.toukei.metro.tokyo.jp/tnenkan/2005/tn05qyte0520g.htm

SINGAPORE

1 Hoovers. (n.d.). Public creative corporations [search by industry]. Retrieved March 28, 2007, from http://www.hoovers.com

2 Singapore Ministry of Information, Communication and the Arts. (2000). Renaissance City report: Culture and the arts in Renaissance Singapore. Retrieved March 28, 2007, from http://www.mica.gov.sg/mica_business/b_creative.html

3 Singapore Department of Statistics. (2004). Economic survey series. Retrieved March 28, 2007, from http://www.singstat.gov.sg/pdtsvc/pubn/business.html#esssvc

SÃO PAULO + RIO DE JANEIRO

1 Secretaria Municipal de Planejamento (cidade de São Paulo). (n.d.). Mapas e dados [translated into English from Portuguese]. Retrieved August 21, 2007, from http://sempla.prefeitura.sp.gov.br/mapasedados.php

2   Fundação Seade. Guia cultural do estado de São Paulo. (2003). Cultura [translated into English from Portuguese]. Retrieved August 13, 2007, from http://www.investimentos.sp.gov.br/portal. php/informacoes/qualidade/cultura

3   Portal Oficial da Prefeitura da Cidade do Rio de Janeiro. (n.d.). Armazém de dados [translated into English from Portuguese]. Retrieved August 13, 2007, from http://www.armazemdedados.rio. rj.gov.br/arquivos/2143_fluxoereceita_carnaval_verao_07.XLS

JOHANNESBURG

1   Classic FM (company profile). (2007). Retrieved August 7, 2007, from www.hoovers.com

Hoovers. (n.d.). Public creative corporations [search by industry]. Retrieved August 13, 2007, from http://www.hoovers.com

Independent News & Media PLC. (n.d.). Group profile. Retrieved August 7, 2007, from http://www.inmplc.com/main.php?menu=menu2&mb=cp

Naspers. (2007). Annual report. Retrieved August 7, 2007, from http://www.naspers.co.za/Financials/naspers_ar2007/downloads/naspers_ar2007_english.pdf

Naspers (company profile). (n.d.). Retrieved August 7, 2007, from http://www.hoovers.com

SAPPI (company profile). (n.d.). Retrieved August 7, 2007, from www.hoovers.com
Steinhoff International Holdings. (n.d.). People centre. Retrieved August 7, 2007, from http://www.steinhoffinternational.com/peo_home.htm

2   Joburg. (n.d.). Media. Retrieved August 13, 2007, from City of Johannesburg Web site: http://www.joburg.org.za/business/communication.stm

3   Naspers (company profile). (n.d.). Retrieved August 7, 2007, from www.hoovers.com

4   Davie, L. (2007, August 7). Joburg is SA's culture capital. Retrieved August 13, 2007, from City of Johannesburg Web site: http://www.joburg.org.za/2007/aug/aug7_theatres.stm

Joburg. (n.d.). Museums. Retrieved August 13, 2007, from City of Johannesburg Web site: http://www.joburg.org.za/whatson/museums.stm

BEIJING + SHANGHAI

1-2   Hoovers. (n.d.). Cultural corporations [search by industry]. Retrieved July 8, 2007, from http://www.hoovers.com

3-4   Bureau of Statistics, Beijing. (2005). Economics investigation. Retrieved June 6, 2007, from http://www.bjstats.gov.cn/jjpcsj/index.htm

5   Bureau of Statistics, Shanghai. (2006). Shanghai statistics yearbook. Retrieved June 5, 2007, from http://www.stats-sh.gov.cn/2004shtj/tjnj/tjnj2006.htm

LONDON

1   Greater London Authority Economics. (2004, April). London's creative sector: 2004 update. Retrieved July 31, 2007, from http://www.creativelondon.org.uk/server.php?show=nav.009004001

2   Office for National Statistics. (2007). Focus on London 2007. Retrieved July 31, 2007, from http://www.statistics.gov.uk/focuson/london/default.asp

3   Greater London Authority Economics. (2004, April). London's creative sector: 2004 update. Retrieved July 31, 2007, from http://www.creativelondon.org.uk/server.php?show=nav.009004001

4-5   Office for National Statistics. (2003). Focus on London 2003. Retrieved July 31, 2007, from http://www.statistics.gov.uk/StatBase/Product.asp?vlnk=10527

6   Hoovers. (n.d.). Cultural corporations [search by industry]. Retrieved August 2, 2007, from http://www.hoovers.com

BERLIN

1-2   Berliner Senatsverwaltung für Wirtschaft. (2007). Technologie und Frauen 2007 [translated into English from German]. Retrieved August 2, 2007, from http://www.berlin.de/sen/waf/register/kulturwirtschaft.html

3   Press and Information Office of the State of Berlin. (2006). Berlin: Basic information. Retrieved August 2, 2007, from http://www.berlin.de/imperia/md/content/rbm-skzl/fifawm/factsheetwmenglisch.pdf

4   Statistisches Landesamt Berlin. (2003). Das Neue Amt für Statistik Berlin-Brandenburg [translated into English from German]. Retrieved August 2, 2007, from http://www.statistik-berlin.de

PARIS

1   Hoovers. (n.d.). Cultural industry corporations [search by industry]. Retrieved August 17, 2007, from http://www.hoovers.com

2-4   Paris Convention and Visitors Bureau. (2007). Tourism in Paris 2006: Key figures. Retrieved August 17, 2007, from http://pro.parisinfo.com/uploads/ch/iffres_cles_2007_2.pdf

DIGEST: GLOBAL CULTURAL CENTERS + CITIES

Cairo Governorate. (2003). Description in figures 2003 [translated into English from Arabic]. Retrieved July 9, 2007, from http://www.idsc.gov.eg/Periodicals/WasfMisr/cai.pdf

City Mayors. (2007). Urban statistics. Retrieved October 9, 2007, from http://www.citymayors.com/sections/rankings_content.html

Dubai Cultural Council. (n.d.). [Translated into English from Arabic]. Retrieved July 9, 2007, from http://www.dubaiculturalcouncil.net/ar/

Egypt's Information Portal. (2003, March). Educational, cultural, & youth services in Egypt [translated into English from Arabic]. Retrieved July 9, 2007, from http://www.idsc.gov.eg/Docs/DocsDetails.asp?rIssueCategory=3&MainIssues=10&DocID=51

Fortune. (2006). Fortune Global 500. Retrieved October 9, 2007, from http://money.cnn.com/magazines/fortune/global500/2006/cities/

Migration Policy Institute. (n.d.). Global city migration map [interactive map showing percentage of foreign born in cities with 1 million or more foreign residents]. Retrieved October 9, 2007, from http://www.migrationinformation.org/DataHub/gcmm.cfm

National Research Council. (2003). Cities transformed: Demographic change and its implications in the developing world. Panel on Urban Population Dynamics. Washington, DC: National Academies Press Portal.

Oficial da Prefeitura da Cidade do Rio de Janeiro. (n.d.). Armazém de dados [translated into English from Portuguese]. Retrieved August 13, 2007, from http://www.armazemdedados.rio.rj.gov.br/

Sassen, S. (1991). The global city. Princeton, NJ: Princeton University Press.

Scott, A.J. (Ed.). (2001). Global city regions: Trends, theory, policy. Oxford, England: Oxford University Press.

Tehran Municipality. (n.d.). Life in Tehran [translated into English from Persian]. Retrieved July 9, 2007, from http://www.tehran.ir

Tehran Municipality Amarnameh. (1384). Statistical report 2005-2006 [translated into English from Persian]. Retrieved July 9, 2007, from http://www.tehran.ir

UNESCO (United Nations Educational, Scientific, and Cultural Organization). (2007). Creative Cities Network. Retrieved October 9, 2007, from http://portal.unesco.org/culture/en/ev.php-URL_ID=24544&URL_DO=DO_TOPIC&URL_SECTION=201.html

UN-Habitat. (2004). The state of the world's cities 2004/2005. London: Earthscan.

Union of International Associations. (2005). Yearbook of international organizations: Guide to global civil society networks 2005-2006 (Vol. 5). Munich: K.G. Saur.

GLOBAL EVENTS

1

Buddha Dharma Education Association Inc. (2001). Buddhist pilgrimage Chan Khoon San. Retrieved August 14, 2007, from http://www.urbandharma.org/pdf/buddhistpilgrimage.pdf

Catholic Association. (n.d.). Lourdes. Retrieved July 25, 2007, from http://www.catholicassociation.co.uk/lourdes/introlourd.shtml

Kurukshetra ready and waiting for 15 lakh pilgrims. (2006, March 26). The Hindu. Retrieved July 25, 2007, from http://www.hindu.com/2006/03/29/stories/2006032914930400.htm

Ministry of Hajj, Kingdom of Saudi Arabia. (n.d.). Hajj and Umrah statistics. Retrieved July 25, 2007, from http://www.hajinformation.com/main/l.htm

Millions bathe at Hindu festival. (2007, January 3). BBC News. Retrieved August 14, 2007, from http://news.bbc.co.uk/2/hi/south_asia/6226895.stm

Nepal Tourism Board. (n.d.). Rural tourism: Lumbini. Retrieved July 25, 2007, from http://www.welcomenepal.com/trpap/areas_lumbini.html

Record Vatican crowds continue a year after pope's death. (2006). Catholic News Service. Retrieved August 14, 2007, from http://www.catholicnews.com/data/stories/cns/0601684.htm

Vatican: The Holy See. (2007, June 6). Holy See Press Office: World Youth Day. Retrieved August 14, 2007, from http://www.vatican.va/news_services/press/documentazione/documents/giornate-mondiali/giornata-mondiale-gioventu_elenco_en.html

World Youth Day. (n.d.). Retrieved August 14, 2007, from Wikipedia Web site: http://en.wikipedia.org/wiki/World_Youth_Day

2

Berlin International Film Festival. (n.d.). The Berlinale: A festival profile. Retrieved July 31, 2007, from http://www.berlinale.de/en/das_festival/festivalprofil/profil_der_berlinale/index.html

Donostia–San Sebastián International Film Festival. (n.d.). The way it was 2006. Pictures 2006. Retrieved July 31, 2007, from http://www.sansebastianfestival.com/2006/asi_in/asi_09_00.htm

Festival de Cannes. (n.d.). Who we are. Retrieved July 31, 2007, from http://www.festival-cannes.com/en/about/whoWeAre

Film Festival Locarno. (n.d.). Locarno 2006: The complete selection. Retrieved July 31, 2007, from http://jahia.pardo.ch/jahia/Jahia/home/2007/cache/offonce/lang/en/pid/19?cnid=929

International Film Festival Rotterdam. (2007). Annual report 2006/2007. Retrieved July 31, 2007, from http://professionals.filmfestivalrotterdam.com/eng/the_festival/annual_report.aspx

International Film Festival Rotterdam. (n.d.). Retrieved July 31, 2007, from Wikipedia Web site: http://en.wikipedia.org/wiki/International_Film_Festival_Rotterdam

Karlovy Vary International Film Festival. (2006). A brief festival history. Retrieved July 31, 2007, from http://www.kviff.com/en/brief-festival-history/

Mar del Plata Film Festival. (2006). Program. Retrieved July 31, 2007, from http://www.mardelplatafilmfest.com/22/programacion_secciones_e.php

Moscow International Film Festival. (2007). Film catalogue. Retrieved July 31, 2007, from http://www.moscowfilmfestival.ru/29/eng/moscow/films/

Raindance Film Festival. (2007). Festival. Retrieved July 31, 2007, from http://www.raindance.co.uk/festival/

Shanghai International Film Festival. (n.d.). Retrieved July 31, 2007, from http://www.siff.com/Article/ShowArticle.asp?ArticleID=86

Skillings, P. (2007). The 2007 Tribeca Film Festival guide. Retrieved July 31, 2007, from http://manhattan.about.com/od/artsandculture/a/tribecafilm2006.htm/

Toronto International Film Festival. (2007). Retrieved July 31, 2007, from http://www.torontointernationalfilmfestival.ca/

Venice Film Festival. (n.d.). Retrieved July 31, 2007, from http://www.labiennale.org/en/news/cinema/en/68442.html

2007 Sundance Film Festival. (n.d.). Retrieved July 31, 2007, from Wikipedia Web site: http://en.wikipedia.org/wiki/2007_Sundance_Film_Festival

3

Boucher, J. (2007, May 1). Celebrities rock Coachella Valley Music Festival. Los Angeles Times. Retrieved August 14, 2007, from http://www.latimes.com

Bumbershoot. (2007). Retrieved July 27, 2007, from Wikipedia Web site: http://en.wikipedia.org/wiki/Bumbershoot

Burning Man. (n.d.). Burning Man timeline. Retrieved August 14, 2007, from http://www.burningman.com/whatisburningman/about_burningman/bm_timeline.html#2005

Coachella Valley Music and Arts Festival. (2007). Retrieved July 27, 2007, from Wikipedia Web site: http://en.wikipedia.org/wiki/Coachella_Valley_Music_and_Arts_Festival

Colmar International Festival. (n.d.). Home. Retrieved August 15, 2007, from http://www.festival-colmar.com/index.php?lang=en

Edinburgh International Festival. (n.d.). About the festival. Retrieved July 25, 2007, from http://www.eif.co.uk/G8_About_the_Festival.php?PHPSESSID=8e2a1a99dc444151 62bdb48ec6c1ce63

Edinburgh International Festival Society. (2006). Review 2005. Retrieved July 25, 2007, from http://www.eif.co.uk/_cms/files/EIF_2005_Annual_Review.21.pdf

Eurockéennes. (2007). Retrieved July 26, 2007, from Wikipedia Web site: http://en.wikipedia.org/wiki/Eurock%C3%A9ennes

EXIT. (2007). Retrieved July 26, 2007, from Wikipedia Web site: http://en.wikipedia.org/wiki/EXIT_%28festival%29

Festival au Desert. (2007, January 20). Desert discs. Retrieved July 25, 2007, from http://www.festival-au-desert.org/doc/press/Economist%2001%2020%2007.jpg

Festival au Desert. (n.d.). Retrieved July 25, 2007, from http://www.festival-au-desert.org/index.cfm?w=296

Festival International de Jazz de Montreal. (n.d.). Rapport du Président. Retrieved July 25, 2007, from http://www.montrealjazzfest.com/Fijm2007/motPresident_en.aspx#rapport

Glastonbury Festival. (2007). Glastonbury Festival. Retrieved July 26, 2007, from Wikipedia Web site: http://en.wikipedia.org/wiki/Glastonbury_Festival

Internet FAQ archive. (n.d.). How can I get tickets to the Bayreuth Festival? Retrieved August 15, 2007, from http://www.faqs.org/faqs/music/wagner/general-faq/section-15.html

Fuji Rock Festival. (2007). Retrieved July 27, 2007, from Wikipedia Web site: http://en.wikipedia.org/wiki/Fuji_Rock_Festival

Lincoln Center for the Performing Arts. (n.d.). Mostly Mozart Festival. Retrieved August 15, 2007, from http://www.lincolncenter.org/load_screen.asp?screen=Mostly%20Mozart%20Festival

Montreaux Jazz Festival. (n.d.). Concerts and tickets. Retrieved August 14, 2007, from http://www.montreuxjazz.com/concerts/program_en.aspx?id=2&d=4

New Orleans Jazz & Heritage Festival. (n.d.). Retrieved July 27, 2007, from http://www.nojazzfest.com/

Oxegen. (2007). Retrieved July 26, 2007, from Wikipedia Web site: http://en.wikipedia.org/wiki/Oxegen

Salzburg Festival. (n.d.). Facts and figures. Retrieved July 25, 2007, from http://www.salzburgfestival.at/eckdaten.php?lang=en

Schleswig-Holstein Musik Festival. (2007). The festival. Retrieved August 15, 2007, from http://www.shmf.de/inhalt.asp?ID=14870&Zeit=21:36:40&BesucherID=136340

Summerfest. (n.d.). Retrieved July 25, 2007, from http://www.summerfest.com/index.html

2Camels.com. (n.d.). Love Parade. Retrieved July 25, 2007, from http://www.2camels.com/love-parade.php

Vienna Festival. (n.d.). Retrieved August 14, 2007, from http://www.festwochen.or.at/index.php?id=49&L=1&detail=

Woodstock Oxfordshire. (2007). Retrieved July 27, 2007, from Wikipedia Web site: http://en.wikipedia.org/wiki/Woodstock

4 Cairo International Book Fair. (n.d.). 2007 CIBF highlights. Retrieved August 7, 2007, from http://www.sis.gov.eg/VR/book/english/html/news4.htm

Canadian Business Map. (n.d.). Retrieved August 15, 2007, from commercecan.ic.gc.ca/scdt/bizmap/interface2.nsf/vDownload/ISA_2731/$file/X_3121750.DOC

Frankfurt Book Fair. (n.d.). eServices & catalogues. Retrieved August 1, 2007, from http://www.frankfurt-book-fair.com/en/index.php?content=https%3A//e.book-fair.com/frameset.aspx%3FsetCultureInfo%3Den-US

Geneva Book Fair highlights. (n.d.). New York Jewish Times. Retrieved August 15, 2007, from http://www.nyjtimes.com/Entertainment/Books/GenevaBookFairHighlights.htm

Guadalajara International Book Fair. (n.d.). Preliminary 2007 statistics. Retrieved August 7, 2007, from http://www.fil.com.mx/ingles/i_info/i_info_num.asp

Hong Kong Book Fair. (n.d.). Previous fair information. Retrieved August 7, 2007, from http://hkbookfair.tdctrade.com/chi/previous/summary.htm

Kolkata Book Fair. (2007). Retrieved August 7, 2007, from Wikipedia Web site: http://en.wikipedia.org/wiki/Calcutta_Book_Fair

Leipzig Book Fair. (n.d.). Welcome to the Leipzig Book Fair. Retrieved August 15, 2007, from http://www.leipziger-messe.de/LeMMon/buch_web_eng.nsf

London Book Fair. (n.d.). Exhibitor list. Retrieved August 1, 2007, from http://www.londonbookfair.co.uk/page.cfm/Action=OSite/OSiteID=3/t=m

Syndicat National de l'Edition. (n.d.). Paris Book Fair and other activities. Retrieved August 15, 2007, from http://www.sne.fr/english/parisbookfair_origins.htm

5 Asia Art Archive. (2006). All you want to know about international biennials. Retrieved August 14, 2007, from http://www.aaa.org.hk/onlineprojects/bitri/en/index.asp

Berlin Biennale. (n.d.). The 4th Berlin Biennale. Retrieved August 7, 2007, from http://www.berlinbiennale.info//index.php?option=com_content&task=blogcategory&id=40&Itemid=83

Biennale de Paris. (n.d.). Experience a Biennale. Retrieved August 7, 2007, from http://www.biennaledeparis.org/archives/2004/en/index.htm

Biennale of Sydney. (2007). Retrieved August 7, 2007, from Wikipedia Web site: http://en.wikipedia.org/wiki/Biennale_of_Sydney

CubaNow.net. (n.d.). Section of Cuban thinking, culture, politics and art. Retrieved August 7, 2007, from http://www.cubanow.net/global/loader.php?&secc=12&item=876&cont=show.php

District Varanasi. (n.d.). Introduction. Retrieved August 14, 2007, from http://varanasi.nic.in/intro/intro.html

Documenta Kassel. (n.d.). d11 2002. Retrieved August 7, 2007, from http://www.documenta12.de/d11.html?&L=1

International Congress and Convention Association. (n.d.). ICCA publishes country and city rankings 2006. Retrieved August 15, 2007, from http://www.iccaworld.com/npps/story.cfm?ID=1305

Venice Biennale. (n.d.). La Biennale di Venezia. Retrieved August 7, 2007, from http://www.labiennale.org/en/

World Peace One. (n.d.). World peace one-ten. Retrieved August 8, 2007, from http://worldpeaceone.com/WP12007/home.html

6   Live Earth breaks world-wide audience records. (2007, July 23). Retrieved August 8, 2007, from Live Earth Web site: http://www.liveearth.org/?p=237

DIGEST: GLOBAL EVENTS

Asian Art Archive. (2007). All you want to know about international art biennales. Retrieved October 2, 2007, from http://www.aaa.org.hk/onlineprojects/bitri/en/intro.asp

Documenta. (n.d.). Platform 5_Documenta 11. Retrieved October 2, 2007, from http://www.documenta12.de/archiv/d11/data/english/index.html

UNESCO. (n.d.). Cultural diversity. Retrieved October 2, 2007, from http://portal.unesco.org/culture/en/ev.php-URL_ID=2450&URL_DO=DO_TOPIC&URL_SECTION=201.html

Weinberg, A.D., & Pratt Brown, A. (2006). Whitney Biennial 2006: Foreword. Retrieved October 2, 2007, from http://www.whitney.org/www/2006biennial/overview_forward.php

MOVEMENTS + FLOWS

EDUCATIONAL EXCHANGE

1-5   UNESCO Institute for Statistics. (2006). Global education digest. Retrieved March 11, 2007, from http://www.uis.unesco.org/TEMPLATE/pdf/ged/2006/GED2006.pdf

6   Australian Education International. (2006, May). Research snapshot: International students enrollment by fields of study. Retrieved March 23, 2007, from http://aei.dest.gov.au/AEI/MIP/Statistics/Default.htm

Institute of International Education Network. (2006). Report on international educational exchange: Fields of study, international students. Retrieved March 23, 2007, from http://opendoors.iienetwork.org/?p=89194

UK Higher Education Statistics Agency. (2006). What subjects do international students study? Retrieved April 2, 2007, from http://www.hesa.ac.uk

7   Australian Education International. (2005). International students in higher education: Comparison of major English speaking destinations for the top five source markets. Number 3. Retrieved April 2, 2007, from http://aei.dest.gov.au/AEI/MIP/Statistics/Default.htm

8   Institute of Higher Education. (2005). Top 500 world universities. Retrieved March 20, 2007, from http://ed.sjtu.edu.cn/rank/2005/ARWU2005TOP500list.htm

Kyoto University. (2006). Student data. Retrieved March 20, 2007, from http://www.kyoto-u.ac.jp/english/euni_int/e01_data/students2005.htm

Top universities. (2006). University profiles. Retrieved March 20, 2007, from http://www.topuniversities.com/

University of Cape Town. (2006). Statistics. Retrieved March 20, 2007, from http://www.uct.ac.za/about/intro/statistics/

University of KwaZulu-Natal. (2006). 2004 international student enrolment [1] at the University of KwaZulu-Natal. Retrieved March 20, 2007, from http://www.ukzn.ac.za/ukzninternational/statistics.html

University of KwaZulu-Natal. (2006). Retrieved March 20, 2007, from Wikipedia Web site: http://en.wikipedia.org/wiki/University_of_KwaZulu_Natal

University of Tokyo. (2006). International students. Retrieved March 20, 2007, from http://www.u-tokyo.ac.jp/stu04/e08_02_e.html

University of Tokyo. (2006). International students. Retrieved March 20, 2007, from http://www.u-tokyo.ac.jp/res03/d03_02_02_e.html

University of Witwatersrand. (2006). Facts. Retrieved March 20, 2007, from http://web.wits.ac.za/AboutWits/WitsToday/WitsFacts.htm

9A   Harvard University. (2006). Harvard University Factbook 2005-2006. Retrieved March 20, 2007, from http://vpf-web.harvard.edu/budget/factbook/current_facts/2006OnlineFactBook.pdf

Top universities. (2006). University profiles. Retrieved March 20, 2007, from http://www.topuniversities.com/

9B   Top universities. (2006). University profiles. Retrieved March 20, 2007, from http://www.topuniversities.com

Universidad de Buenos Aires. (2006). Censo de estudiantes [translated into English from Spanish]. Retrieved March 20, 2007, from http://www.uba.ar/institucional/censos/Estudiantes2004/censo-estudiantes.pdf

9C   Top universities. (2006). University profiles. Retrieved March 20, 2007, from http://www.topuniversities.com

University of Tokyo. (2006). International students. Retrieved March 20, 2007, from http://www.u-tokyo.ac.jp/stu04/e08_02_e.html

University of Tokyo. (2006). International students. Retrieved March 20, 2007, from http://www.u-tokyo.ac.jp/res03/d03_02_02_e.html

9D   Cambridge University. (2006). Cambridge University Reporter. Retrieved March 20, 2007, from http://www.admin.cam.ac.uk/reporter/2004-05/special/19/studentnumbers2005.pdf

Top universities. (2006). University profiles. Retrieved March 20, 2007, from http://www.topuniversities.com

DIGEST: EDUCATIONAL EXCHANGE

Atlas of International Student Mobility. (n.d.). FAQs. Retrieved March 20, 2007, from http://www.atlas.iienetwork.org/?p=54855

Atlas of International Student Mobility. (n.d.). Promotional activities and policies. Retrieved March 20, 2007, from http://atlas.iienetwork.org/page/85685/

Australian Education International. (2005, October). International students in higher education: Comparison of major English speaking destinations. Research Snapshot, Number 3.

Australian Education International. (2006, May). International students enrollments by field of study. Research Snapshot, Number 10.

Committee for Economic Development. (2006). Education for global leadership: The importance of international studies and foreign language education for US economic and national security.

Retrieved May 20, 2007, from http://www.ced.org/docs/report/report_foreignlanguages.pdf

Dervis, K. (2007). Keynote address presented at the International Labour Organization 11th African Regional Meeting. Retrieved from the UNDP Web site: http://content.undp.org/go/newsroom/2007/april/dervis-ilo-african-meeting-20070425.en?categoryID=593043&lang=en

Harrison, F. (2007, January 8). Huge cost of Iranian brain drain. BBC News. Retrieved May 20, 2007, from http://news.bbc.co.uk/2/hi/middle_east/6240287.stm

Institute of Higher Education. (2005). Academic ranking of world universities 2005. Retrieved March 20, 2007, from http://ed.sjtu.edu.cn/ranking2005.htm

Kelo, M., Teichler, U., & Wächter, B. (2006). Toward improved data on student mobility in Europe: Findings and concepts of the Eurodata study. Journal of Studies in International Education, 10: 194.

Levin, R. (2006, August 21-28). The world's most global universities. Newsweek International. Retrieved March 11, 2007, from http://www.msnbc.msn.com/id/14320413/site/newsweek/page/0/

The complete list: The top 100 global universities. (2007). Newsweek International. Retrieved March 11, 2007, from http://www.msnbc.msn.com/id/14321230/site/newsweek/

Tsiko, S. (2007, May 2). Africa's brain drain. Gibbs Magazine. Retrieved May 20, 2007, from http://www.gibbsmagazine.com/Brain%20Drain%20in%20Africa.htm

UNESCO Institute for Statistics. (2006). Global education digest. Retrieved March 11, 2007, from http://www.uis.unesco.org/TEMPLATE/pdf/ged/2006/GED2006.pdf

CULTURAL TOURISM

1 Hossain, A., Heaney, L., & Carter, P. (2005). Cultural tourism in regions of Australia. Retrieved April 1, 2007, from http://www.culturaldata.gov.au/__data/assets/pdf_file/58356/Cultural_tourism_in_regions_of_Australia.pdf

2 Guerrero, A.B. (n.d.). Perspectiva educativa ambiental del turismo cultural y alternativo en Mexico [translated into English from Spanish]. Retrieved April 8, 2007, from http://www.inegi.gob.mx/inegi/contenidos/espanol/prensa/contenidos/articulos/ambientales/turismo.pdf

3 Institut National de la Statistique et des Études Économiques. (2006). France in facts and figures: Most popular cultural and recreational sites. Retrieved April 1, 2007, from National Institute for Statistics and Economic Studies Web site: http://www.insee.fr/en/ffc/chifcle_fiche.asp?tab_id=337

4 India Ministry of Tourism. (2005). India tourism statistics 2005. Retrieved April 5, 2007, from http://tourism.gov.in/ITS2005.pdf

5 Top 10 amusement/theme park chains worldwide. (2003). Amusement Business, 115(51): 14. Retrieved April 12, 2007, from TableBase database.

6 Hoovers. (n.d.). Travel companies [search by industry]. Retrieved April 12, 2007, from http://www.hoovers.com

7 Hoovers. (n.d.). Top tour operators [search by industry]. Retrieved April 5, 2007, from http://www.hoovers.com

8 Hitwise. (2007). Monthly category report: Travel. Retrieved April 8, 2007, from http://www.hitwise.com/resources/reports-and-webinars.php

9   Nielsen/NetRatings. (2007). Top 10 travel-related websites in Germany & France ranked by unique visitors: March 2007. Retrieved May 17, 2007, from eMarketer database.

DIGEST: CULTURAL TOURISM

Amusement business. (2006, January 8). Retrieved April 2, 2007, from TableBase database. ICOMOS (International Council on Monuments and Sites). (n.d.). Charter for cultural tourism. Retrieved May 28, 2007, from http://www.icomos.org/tourism_charter.html

UNESCO. (n.d.). Cultural tourism. Retrieved May 28, 2007, from http://portal.unesco.org/culture/en/ev.php-URL_ID=11408&URL_DO=DO_TOPIC&URL_SECTION=201.html

UNESCO. (n.d.). Culture tourism and sustainable development. Retrieved May 28, 2007, from http://www.unesco.org/culture/tourism/html_eng/cities3.shtml

UNESCO. (n.d.). World heritage list. Retrieved May 28, 2007, from http://whc.unesco.org/en/list

UNWTO (United Nations World Tourism Organization) and Tanzania Tourist Board. (2006, July). Tanzania cultural tourism programme. Retrieved May 28, 2007, from http://www.unwto.org/regional/africa/events/morocco/pres06.pdf

UNWTO. (2007, March 1). International seminar: Sustainable development of tourism in Central and Eastern Europe. Retrieved November 28, 2007, from http://www.unwto.org/regional/europe/PDF/2007/lithuania/presentations/summary_report_vilnius.pdf

UNWTO. (2007). Tourism highlights. Retrieved May 28, 2007, from http://www.world-tourism.org/facts/menu.html

GLOBAL CONCERT TOURS

1   Global concert tours market by gross revenue, attendance, venue capacity, number of shows, and number of sellout shows in dollars, units, and percent change for 2004 and 2005. (2006). Amusement Business, 118(3). Retrieved April 1, 2007, from TableBase database.

2A   Global top 25 concert tours in 2004 ranked by total gross in US dollars, with each tour's total attendance, total capacity, number of shows and number of sellouts. (2004). Amusement Business, 116(29). Retrieved April 1, 2007, from TableBase database.

The year in touring 2001. (2001). Amusement Business 113(51). Retrieved April 1, 2007, from TableBase database.

2B-2C   Global top 25 concert tours in 2004 ranked by total gross in US dollars, with each tour's total attendance, total capacity, number of shows and number of sellouts. (2004). Amusement Business, 116(29). Retrieved April 1, 2007, from TableBase database.

3   Top concert venues. (2004). Amusement Business, 116(29). Retrieved April 1, 2007, from EBSCO Host database.

4   Global top 20 concert promoters by all-promotion total gross, sole-promotion total gross, total attendance, number of shows, and number of sellout shows in dollars and units for the year ending November 2004. (2005). Amusement Business, 118(6). Retrieved April 3, 2007, from TableBase database.

5   Thomson Financial. (2006). Live Nation SEC Filing Form 10-K: Annual report. Retrieved April 24, 2007, from Thomson Financial Web site: http://phx.corporate-ir.net/phoenix.zhtml?c=194146&p=irol-YXJkLmNvbS9WwvZmlsa W5nLnhtbD9yZXBvPXRlbmsmaXBhZ2U9NDcxNDgzNiZhdHRhY2g9T04=

6   Hoovers. (2007). Sports and entertainment promoters [search by industry]. Retrieved April 24, 2007, from http://www.hoovers.com

7   Interactive Corp-IAC (company profile). (2007). Retrieved April 1, 2007, from http://www.hoovers.com

Ticketmaster (company profile). (2007). Retrieved April 1, 2007, from http://www.hoovers.com

Ticketmaster. (n.d.). About Ticketmaster. Retrieved April 1, 2007, from http://www.ticketmaster.com/h/about_us.html

8   Billboard Boxscore. (2006, July). Billboard Magazine. Retrieved April 3, 2007, from Gale Expanded Academic ASAP database.

DIGEST: GLOBAL CONCERT TOURS

Live Nation. (2006). 2006 annual report. Retrieved October 17, 2007, from http://phx.corporate-ir.net/phoenix.zhtml?c=194146&p=irol-reports

Lopes, G. (n.d.). The broader music industry. Retrieved October 17, 2007, from International Federation of the Phonographic Industry Web site: http://www.ifpi.org/content/section_views/index.html

Madonna nears deal to leave record label. (2007). New York Times: Media and Advertising. Retrieved October 17, 2007, from http://www.nytimes.com/2007/10/11/business/media/11madonna.html?8br

Waddell, R. (2006, December 14). Stones' bigger bang is top-grossing tour of 2006. Billboard Magazine. Retrieved October 17, 2007, from http://billboard.com/bbcom/news/article_display.jsp?vnu_content_id=1003521640

Williamson, J., & Cloonan, M. (2007). Rethinking the music industry. Popular Music, 26(2): 305-322.

Winners take all in rockonomics. (2006). BBC News. Retrieved October 17, 2007, from http://news.bbc.co.uk/1/hi/business/4896262.stm

REGULATORY FRAMEWORKS + POLICY

INTERNATIONAL STANDARDS

1-2   ISO (International Organization for Standardization). (1998-2006). Annual reports. Retrieved February 9, 2007, from http://www.iso.org/iso/en/aboutiso/annualreports/index.html

ISO. (2007). ISO in figures for the year 2006. Retrieved February 9, 2007, from http://www.iso.org/iso/en/aboutiso/isoinfigures/archives/January2007.pdf

3   International ISMN Agency (International Standard Music Number). (1995-2002). Number of allocated ISMN identifiers in comparison. Retrieved February 9, 2007, from http://www.ismn-international.org/agencies/statistics.html

4   ISSN International Centre. (2006). Number of records per type. Retrieved February 9, 2007, from http://www.issn.org/files/active/1/NUMBER%20OF%20RECORDS%20PER%20TYPE_2006.pdf

5

ISSN International Centre. (2006). Total number of records in the ISSN Register. Retrieved February 9, 2007, from http://www.issn.org/files/active/1/TOTAL%20NUMBER%20OF%20RECORDS%20IN%20THE%20ISSN%20REGISTER_2006.pdf

6

ISSN International Centre. (2006). Number of records from countries with an ISSN National Centre. Retrieved February 9, 2007, from http://www.issn.org/files/active/1/NUMBER%20OF%20RECORDS%20PER%20TYPE_2006.pdf

7

ISSN International Centre. (2006). Number of records from countries with an ISSN National Centre. Retrieved February 9, 2007, from http://www.issn.org/files/active/1/NUMBER%20OF%20RECORDS%20PER%20TYPE_2006.pdf

DIGEST: INTERNATIONAL STANDARDS

ICANN (Internet Corporation for Assigned Names and Numbers). (n.d.). Fact sheet. Retrieved October 9, 2007, from http://www.icann.org/general/fact-sheet.html

IEC (International Electrotechnical Commission). (n.d.). About the IEC. Retrieved November 28, 2007, from http://www.iec.ch

ILO (International Labor Organization). (n.d.). About the ILO. Retrieved November 28, 2007, from http://www.ilo.org/global/About_the_ILO/lang--en/index.htm

ITU (International Telecommunications Union). (n.d.). Telecommunications Standardization Sector (ITU-T). Retrieved November 28, 2007, from http://www.itu.int/ITU-T/index.html

Office of International Standards and Legal Affairs of UNESCO. (2007). Volume II: Conventions, recommendations, declarations and charters adopted by UNESCO (1948-2006). Paris: UNESCO; and Leiden, Netherlands: Martinus Nijhoff Publishers.

UNESCO (United Nations Educational, Scientific and Cultural Organization). (2007, March 9). Monitoring of the implementation of UNESCO's standard-setting instruments: Part II, model guidelines. Retrieved November 28, 2007, from http://unesdoc.unesco.org/images/0014/001498/149861e.pdf#page=7

W3C (World Wide Web Consortium). (n.d.). W3C activities. Retrieved November 28, 2007, from http://www.w3.org/Consortium/activities

Yusuf, A.A. (Ed.). (2007). Standard-setting at UNESCO: Normative action in education, science and culture (Vol. 1). Paris: UNESCO; and Leiden, Netherlands: Martinus Nijhoff Publishers.

NATIONAL + REGIONAL CULTURAL POLICY

1-2

African Union. (n.d.). Member states. Retrieved July 2, 2007, from http://www.africa-union.org/root/AU/memberstates/map.htm

African Union. (n.d.). Statutes of the Economic, Social and Cultural Council of the African Union. Retrieved July 2, 2007, from http://www.africa-union.org/ECOSOC/STATUTES-En.pdf

Alps-Adria Working Community. (2007). Homepage. Retrieved July 25, 2007, from http://aalib.izum.si/

Arctic Council. (n.d.). The Arctic Council. Retrieved July 20, 2007, from http://www.arctic-council.org

Asia/Pacific Cultural Centre for UNESCO. (n.d.). About ACCU. Retrieved July 25, 2007, from http://www.accu.or.jp/en/about/index.shtml

Baltic Cooperation. (n.d.). Welcome to the Baltic Cooperation Forum. Retrieved July 5, 2007, from http://www.baltic-cooperation.eu/UNIQ118531677421026/lang1/doc4143A.html

Barents Regional Council. (2007). Barents Regional Council. Retrieved July 5, 2007, from http://www.beac.st/default.asp?id=132

Black Sea Economic Cooperation. (2007). About BSEC. Retrieved July 10, 2007, from http://www.bsec-organization.org/main.aspx?ID=About_BSEC

Black Sea Economic Cooperation. (2007). Area of cooperation: Culture. Retrieved July 10, 2007, from http://www.bsec-organization.org/areas_of_cooperation.aspx?ID=Culture

Central European Initiative. (2007). Central European Initiative. Retrieved July 10, 2007, from http://www.ceinet.org/main.php?pageID=16

Community of Portuguese-Speaking Countries. (n.d.). CPLP's basic principles. Retrieved June 29, 2007, from http://www.cplp.org

Council of Europe/ERICarts. (n.d.). International cultural cooperation in Europe: Organisation and trends. Retrieved July 10, 2007, from http://www.culturalpolicies.net/web/comparisons-public-bodies.php?aid=27&cid=44&lid=en

Council of Europe/ERICarts. (n.d.). Public bodies responsible for national cultural policy developments. Retrieved July 10, 2007, from http://www.culturalpolicies.net/web/comparisons-tables.php

Council of Ministers of Culture of Southeast Europe. (n.d.). Charter of the Council of Ministers of Culture of Southeast Europe. Retrieved July 10, 2007, from http://www.norden.org/internationellt/sk/CharterFinal310305.pdf

European Union. (n.d.). Europe in action: Cultural cooperation. Retrieved July 2, 2007, from http://ec.europa.eu/culture/portal/action/cooperation/coop_en.htm

Government of Slovenia. (2007). Regional cooperation: Central European Initiative. Retrieved July 20, 2007, from http://www.mzz.gov.si/en/foreign_policy/regional_cooperation/?type=98

GUAM (Georgia, Ukraine, Azerbaijan, Moldova). (2007). GUAM Organization for Democracy and Economic Development. Retrieved July 12, 2007, from http://www.guam.org.ua/211.0.0.1.0.0.phtml

International Centre for the Study of the Preservation and Restoration of Cultural Property. (2007). ICCROM member states. Retrieved June 29, 2007, from http://www.iccrom.org/eng/00about_en/00_01govern_en/memstates_en.shtml

International Centre for the Study of the Preservation and Restoration of Cultural Property. (2007). What is ICCROM? Retrieved June 29, 2007, from http://www.iccrom.org/eng/00about_en/00_00whats_en.shtml

International Council on Museums and Sites. (2007). National committees list. Retrieved July 2, 2007, from http://www.international.icomos.org/list_cn.htm

International Network on Cultural Policy. (2007). About us. Retrieved June 29, 2007, from http://incp-ripc.org/about/index_e.shtml

International Network on Cultural Policy. (2007). Member countries. Retrieved June 29, 2007, from http://incp-ripc.org/members/index_e.shtml

Islamic Educational, Scientific and Cultural Organization. (2007). In focus. Retrieved July 15, 2007, from http://www.isesco.org.ma/English/Charter.html

Islamic Educational, Scientific and Cultural Organization. (2007). Membership of ISESCO. Retrieved July 15, 2007, from http://www.isesco.org.ma/membres/IndexEng.htm

Nordic Council of Ministers. (2007). Culture news. Retrieved June 29, 2007, from http://www.norden.org/kultur/uk/index.asp?lang=6

Organisation of Iberoamerican States for Education, Science and Culture. (n.d.). Presentación [translated into English from Spanish]. Retrieved July 2, 2007, from http://www.oei.es/acercaoei.htm

Organisation Internationale de la Francophonie. (n.d.). Membres. Retrieved July 12, 2007, from http://www.francophonie.org/oif/membres.cfm

Taalunie (Dutch Language Union). (2007). About us. Retrieved July 12, 2007, from http://taalunieversum.org/en/about_us

UNESCO. (n.d.). International Network of Observatories in Cultural Policies. Retrieved July 20, 2007, from http://www.unesco.org/culture/development/observatories/html_eng/members.shtml

UNESCO. (n.d.). Member states. Retrieved July 20, 2007, from http://erc.unesco.org/portal/UNESCOMemberStates.asp?language=en

Visegrad Group. (n.d.). Welcome! Retrieved July 2, 2007, from http://www.visegradgroup.eu/main.php

DIGEST: NATIONAL + REGIONAL CULTURAL POLICY

APRCCN (Asia-Pacific Regional Center of the Culturelink Network). (n.d.). Bangladesh: Cultural policy & law. Retrieved July 24, 2007, from http://www.culturelink.or.kr/policy_bang.html#8.%20INTERNATIONAL%20%20%20CULTURAL%20CO-OPERATION

Council of Europe/ERICarts. (2007). Compendium of cultural policies and trends in Europe (8th ed.). Bonn, Germany: ERICarts.

Lohr, S. (2002, October 14). New economy: The intellectual property debate takes a page from 19th-century America. New York Times. Retrieved July 31, 2007, from http://query.nytimes.com/gst/fullpage.html?res=9C07E4D8103AF937A25753C1A9649C8B63

UNESCO. (n.d.). What co-operation strategies should be adopted at the international level? Retrieved July 23, 2007, from http://portal.unesco.org/culture/en/ev.php-URL_ID=18696&URL_DO=DO_TOPIC&URL_SECTION=201.html

INTERNATIONAL REGULATORY FRAMEWORKS

1-3

Van Grasstek, C. (n.d.). Treatment of cultural goods and services in international trade agreements. Retrieved April 7, 2007, from UNESCO Bangkok Web site: http://www.unescobkk.org/fileadmin/user_upload/culture/Cultural_Industries/Singapore_Feb_05/Treatment_of_cultural_goods_and_services_GRASSTEK.pdf

4

GoogleScholar.com. (n.d.). [Search for number of hits for each convention listed]. Retrieved April 7, 2007, from http://scholar.google.com

5

Coalition for Cultural Diversity. (2006). UNESCO convention ratification campaign: State of play of the ratification campaign. Retrieved April 7, 2007, from http://www.cdc-ccd.org/Anglais/Liensenanglais/frameratifications_eng.htm

UNESCO. (n.d.). Culture. Retrieved July 7, 2007, from http://portal.unesco.org/culture/en/ev.php-URL_ID=34603&URL_DO=DO_TOPIC&URL_SECTION=201.html

DIGEST: INTERNATIONAL REGULATORY FRAMEWORKS

UNESCO. (2002). Constitution of the United Nations Cultural, Scientific and Cultural Organization (Article 1). Retrieved from http://unesdoc.unesco.org/images/0012/001255/125590e.pdf#page=7

UNESCO. (2005). Convention on the Protection and Promotion of the Diversity of Cultural Expressions. Retrieved August 10, 2007, from http://portal.unesco.org/culture/en/ev.php-URL_ID=33232&URL_DO=DO_TOPIC&URL_SECTION=201.html

INDEX

Abdykalykov, Aktan, 158
Achbar, Mark, 54, 64
Actoz, 142
Adbusters, 62
Adorno, T.W., 43, 44, 49, 309
advertising
  and broadcasting, 222
  fashion industry, 256
  and games, 229
  Internet, 59
aesthetic value, 16, 31, 163–4
  and capitalism, 309–10
  and fashion industry, 256–7
  and industrialization, 308
Afghanistan, 61
Africa, 123–32, 227
  access to global culture, 20
  consumerism and culture, 125
  creative/cultural industries, 110
  cultural diversity, 124–6
  film production, 95, 129–31
    pirating, 131
  Film and Television Festival
    (FESPACO), 130
  governments and local repression,
    125–6
  hierarchies of race and place,
    131–2
  Internet access and use,
    60, 192
  investment and indigenous culture,
    124–5
  local cultural businesses, 114
  multinational corporations and
    cultural diversity, 124–6
  Organization of African Unity
    (Nairobi 1992), 110
  power elites and indigenous
    culture, 125
  publishing, 99, 126–8
    dependent on school
      textbooks, 127
    desk-top publishing, 128
    and indigenous cultures,
      126–7
    profit motive, 126
  telephone, mobile and Internet
    use, 243
  text messaging, 53
  views of African culture, 20, 124,
    128–30, 132
    in Hollywood films, 129–30

African Books Collective (ABC), 127
African Publishers Network
  (APNET), 127
agglomerations, 47–8, 145, 316
  and competition, 315
  and distribution, 319
  see also corporations
Aid to Artisans, 158, 274
Al Jazeera, 63
ALADI (Latin American Integration
  Association), 186
Alam, Shahidul, 97, 106
Albania, 181
Ali Hasan of Varanasi, 137
Álvarez, Luciano, 194
Amazon, 90
American Association of
  Publishers, 249
Amin, A., 4–5, 11
Amman Festival, 262
Anderson, Benedict, 53, 64
Anderson, C., 23, 25, 144, 146,
  191, 198
Anna Lindh Foundation for
  Euro-Mediterranean
  Cooperation, 268
anti-copyright movements,
  74, 75–6, 86
Apple, 89, 192, 245
Argentina, 45, 57, 187, 189, 194
Armory Show, 293, 294
art, 157, 160
  auction sales, 296–7, 302–4
  as business, 163–4
  and crafts, 136–7, 275
  intrinsic value of, 30, 31, 40,
    163–4, 171
Art Basel, 293–5
art fairs, 293–5
art galleries, 103–4, 292–5,
  299–303
artisans and designers, 277–8
Arts and Crafts, 276
arts education, 32
arts festivals/exhibitions, 18, 157,
  260–8
  'alternative' (unofficial)
    festivals, 265
  economic expectations, 260–2
  film festivals, 264–5
  and ICT use, 266
  and local economies, 260–1, 266

arts festivals/exhibitions *cont.*
  music festivals, 265, 266, 267
  need for policies, 268
  and Olympic Games, 263
  performing arts, 264, 266
  politically inspired, 260
  prestige of, 263–4
  programming, 264
  and sponsorship,
    261, 265–6
  and subsidies, 261, 263
  and tourism, 261
arts groups, 96–7
  income and quality, 31–2
  and new technologies, 32
Asia
  art market, 296
  growth of media, 215
  Internet access and use,
    60, 192
  media liberalisation, 148–9
  text messaging, 53, 64
  see also Central Asia; China; East
    Asia; India; Japan; Korea;
    South Asia
Asia Society, 288, 289
Asia-Europe Foundation, 268
Asong, Linus, 128
Atwood, Margaret, 62
auction houses: art sales, 296–7,
  302–4
Australia
  Aboriginal Arts Board, 287, 288
  Aboriginal Arts and Crafts Pty Ltd,
    287–8
  arts and crafts centers, 288
  arts festivals, 262
  creative industries contribution to the
    economy, 45
  government cultural policies,
    105, 288
  indigenous art, 18, 284–90
    cultural origins, 285, 286, 287
    demand for, 284–5
    markets, 285–9
      breakthrough: international,
        287–9
      domestic, 286–7
      public sector, 287
      tourists, 286
    New York: Dreamings exhibition
      (1988), 288–9

Australia *cont.*
New York: private collectors and philanthropy, 289
Papunya Tula Artists Pty Ltd, 287, 288
styles, 286
subsidies, 287, 288
turnover, 284
indigenous languages, 286
Internet usage, 192
mobile technolgy and economy, 23
Second Life residents, 236
telephone, mobile and Internet use, 243
Austria, 170, 250
Authors Guild, 249
authors/artists
and business, 93
and computer use, 32
and copyright, 70, 71, 72, 76–8, 80, 86–7
economic rights, 31–2, 69, 70, 77, 86–7
and Internet, 32
and market considerations, 163
permanent relationship with work, 77–8
Avignon Festival, 261

Baalbek International Festival, 262
Babelsberg film studios, 175
Bahia Carnival, 270–3
and Bahia culture, 270–1
business carnival, 271–2
challenges of, 272
indicators of, 271
Balkans *see* Southeastern Europe
Bangladesh, 97
Barbados, 102
Bardon, Geoffrey, 287, 290
Baudrillard, J., 308, 322
Bauhaus, 276, 309
BBC, 88, 222
BBC World, 63
Becker, H.S., 44, 49
Beijing: Dashanzi art district, 304–5
Belarus
piracy, 175
Belgium, 170, 236
Benetton, 254
Benjamin, Walter, 309, 322
Benkler, Yochai, 23–4, 26, 87, 89, 91
Berne Convention for the Protection of Literary and Artistic Works, 72, 73, 74, 77, 79
Beshkempir, 158

BitTorrent, 241, 246
blocos, 270, 271, 272, 273
blogging, 246
Bogotá Festival, 262
Bollywood, 57, 220–1
books, 58–9, 90, 99, 169–70
book fairs, 248–50
Bordieu, P., 307, 322
Bosnia and Herzegovina, 179, 180, 181
Bradford v. Sahara, 221
Brazil
Bahia Carnival, 270–3
business structure, 187
copyright and piracy, 189, 190
creative and economic advance, 21, 22, 187
creative/cultural industries, 22
contribution to the economy, 45
film and television production, 57
literacy: *Reading Agents*, 190
mobile technolgy use, 192
music sales, 194
Second Life residents, 236
Brickhill, Paul, 99, 106
British Council, 93
broadband, 60, 152, 244
Brown, Doug, 33, 40
Browne, S., 102, 106
Buckman, John and Jan, 88
Bulgaria, 175, 180, 181
business: expansionist tendencies, 216–17
business plans, 104
businesses *see* agglomerations; corporations; cultural enterprises; cultural entrepreneurs

Cahen, Claude, 137
Cairo, 223
Festival, 262
Cameroon, 128
CAN (Andean Nations Community), 186
Canada
at the Frankfurt Book Fair, 250
broadband Internet, 60
copyright law, 73, 77, 111
creative industries' contribution to the economy, 45
'cultural exception', 111
cultural policies, 105
cultural trade, 57, 62
immigration from Caribbean, 187, 193
magazines and national culture, 59
regulating global cultural flow, 62
Second Life residents, 236

Canclini, Nestor García, 56
Cantor Fitzgerald, 230
capital, internally-financed, 102, 104
capitalism
and aesthetic value, 309–10
rise of, 217
CARICOM (Caribbean Community), 186
Carioca Carnival, 270
Castronova, Edward, 236, 238
Caves, R., 16, 26, 65, 205, 210, 313, 322
CCTV, 145, 149
censorship, 71, 78–9
Central Asia, 155–62
art, 157, 160
arts festivals/exhibitions, 157
copyright, 159
cultural diversity, 155
cultural entrepreneurship, 105–6
cultural identities, 156, 159
cultural management, 159
educational campaigns, 156
film and film festivals, 157–8, 161
with Western studios, 158
funding for the arts, 159
new markets for cultural products, 157, 160
nomadic and sedentary people, 155
participation in culture, 159–60
regional links, 160
Shamanist traditions, 157
Soviet era, 155–6, 158
sustainable development, 159
traditional crafts, 158, 161
training and employment, 159
video-art, 157
Central and Eastern Europe, 172–7
cinemas: ownership and management, 174–5
cultural diversity, 176
cultural economy and market economy, 172
cultural organizations, 173
employment in cultural industries, 173
ethnic conflicts, 176
film production, 175
mass and subcultures, 176
multiculturalism, 176
national cultures, 176
piracy, 175
privatization, 174, 175
state protection, 172–3

Central and Eastern Europe *cont.*
   transition from Soviet system,
      172–3, 176–7
   video businesses, 175
Center National de la
   Cinématographie, 319
Chamberlin, E., 308, 322
Chanel, 256, 258
Charman, Sue, 90, 91
Chartrand, Harry, 201, 210
Chattopadhya, Kamaladevi, 138
Chicago, 308
Chile, 45, 189
China, 146
   appeal of Korean culture, 151
   art, 302, 304–5
   arts festivals, 262, 265
   crafts, 139, 279
   creative and economic advance,
      19, 21, 23
   creative/cultural industries, 199
   cultural economy restrictions, 143
   East Asian pop culture, 141
   expansion of cultural markets, 61
   fashion industry, 255, 258
   film production, 144
      expansion, 57, 217
   growth of media, 215
   imports of Hollywood films, 223
   Internet use, 23, 60, 244
   telephone, mobile and Internet use,
      243, 244
   television, 57, 142, 145
      and Korean Wave, 149, 151
   text messaging, 23, 53
   video games, 142
Chios, 319, 320
Christian groups and games, 229
Christie's, 296, 302, 303, 304
Christopherson, Susan, 218, 219, 226
citizenship and community, 56
clusters
   of producers, 145, 208, 312–14
   of skills, 218–19
CNN, 63
Coca-Cola, 229
Colombia, 189, 190, 194
   Bogotá Festival, 262
computers
   and pollution, 232
   use by authors/artists, 32
   see also Internet
Connor, Steven, 30, 40
consumerism, 124, 125, 182, 183
consumers, 35–7
   co-creation, 24–5, 242
   and cultural choices, 317
   culture as private good, 36–7

consumers *cont.*
   culture as public good, 37
   and feedback, 47
convergence, 151, 152, 164, 192
copyleft, 74, 86
copyright/intellectual property rights
   (IPR), 43, 54, 55, 67–80
   and anti-copyright movements,
      74, 75–6, 86
   and authors/artists, 86–7
   and Bollywood films, 221
   in broadcasting and films,
      223, 224
   and censorship, 71, 78–9
   and consumer choice, 69
   'core' and 'total', 205
   and corporations, 70, 71, 75
   and Creative Commons, 89–90
   and cultural diversity, 74–5
   and cultural exception, 111, 311
   and cultural value, 71–2, 76
   and developing world, 73, 113
   and digital media, 68–9
   dispute settlement, 73
   and 'employment rule', 70, 71
   enforcement and regulation, 68–9
   favouring developed world, 113
   favouring large distributors, 87
   fostering creativity, 86
   and free culture, 86–7, 89–90
   harmonization, 74–5
   and human rights, 76–8
   international copyright law, 72–4
      cultural implications, 74–6
   as moral rights, 76–7, 80
   new policy approach, 76–8
   as obstacle to knowledge, 68
   role in free market, 90
   in software industry, 71
   and value of cultural exchange, 68
corporations, 16, 46, 62, 145, 316
   and competition, 315
   control of the cultural economy, 47
   controlling cultural trade, 70
   and copyright, 70, 71, 75
   and cultural diversity, 124–6
   and diversification, 316
   in music production, 33
   sponsorship of festivals, 265–6
Corral, Milagros del, 111
cosmopolitanism, 42, 56, 141
Costa Rica, 189
Cowan, Tyler, 19, 26
crafts
   and art, 136–7, 275
   Central Asia, 158, 161
   China, 139, 279
   in developing countries, 278–9

crafts *cont.*
   and economic development, 158
   India, 17–18, 135–40
   industrial revolution, 275–6
   and local cultures, 274, 275
   low costs and wages, 279
   marketing, 102
   neglect of, 274
   quality of, 274, 279
   quantity produced, 279–80
   transition to soft industrial design,
      277–8, 279–80
      collective trademarks, 281–2
      cultural districts, 280–1
Creative Commons, 85, 88, 89–90, 91,
   189, 312
'creative economy' in developing
   countries (UNCTAD), 116, 117
'Creative Economy for
   Development', 117
creative migration (film production),
   218–19, 224
creative/cultural industries, 16–17, 19,
   21–2, 44, 56–7
   classification, 208–9
   and competition, 16
   contribution to the economy, 45
   definitions, 6–8, 205–7, 207
   in developing countries, 38–9,
      109–10
      income from cultural
         economy, 47
   and economic growth,
      16–17, 20–1
   and global economy, 98
   and government policy, 7, 56
   and innovation, 17
   new prominence of, 37
   organizational form, 46
   as political lobbyists, 71
   regional uses of the term, 22
   social networks, 24–5
creativity
   and copyright, 86
   creative class, 111
   and cultural entrepreneurs,
      93–4, 94, 99–100
   definitions, 204
   value of, 152
Croatia, 179, 180, 181
Crouching Tiger Hidden Dragon, 145
cultural capital, 98, 104
cultural commons, 55, 62–3
   and government policies, 61–2
cultural districts, 280–1
cultural diversity, 33, 42, 55–7,
   74, 111
   Africa, 124–6

cultural diversity *cont.*
  Australia, 284–90
  Central Asia, 155
  Central and Eastern Europe, 176
  and copyright law, 74–5
  cultural entrepreneurs, 123, 124
  Europe, 167–8, 168–9
  and fashion industry, 259
  and film production, 219–23
  and homogeneity, 74, 75
  and human rights, 62
  and international
    communications, 33
  source of creativity and quality, 167
  various meanings of, 167
cultural economy
  as anthropological/socialogical
    construct, 29
  competitive model, 15, 16, 19–21
  as concept, 3–4, 43–4
  contemporary scene, 310–12
  definitions and characteristics, 43–6,
    46–7, 49, 307
  and economic development, 317–19
  economic growth model, 143–5
  growth model, 15, 16–17, 21–2
  innovation or creative economy
    model, 15, 17, 19, 23–4
  Keynsian/neo-Marxist analysis, 17
  location, 47–8
  production-based model, 44, 45
  as proportion of total economy,
    310–11
  Schumpterian conceptions, 17, 18
  welfare/subsidy model, 15, 16,
    17–18
cultural enterprises, 96–8, 101–5
  diversity of, 97
  essentials for starting, 104
  finance, 101–6
  government cultural policies, 104–5
  local, 95, 97, 99, 102–3, 103–4
  network of small companies, 46
  and sustainability, 101
cultural entrepreneurs, 18, 92–6, 98–
    100, 105–6
  and access to markets, 95
  creativity and innovation of, 99–100
  detrimental to cultural diversity,
    123, 124
  focussing on consumption, 123
  and innovation, 92, 93–4, 98
  mission-driven, 100
  and new markets, 95
  origins of concept, 96
  promoting Euro-American
    culture, 124
  pursuit of profit, 123

cultural entrepreneurs *cont.*
  role and characteristics, 98–100
  suppressing cultural identity, 124
  taking risks, 94, 96, 101
  training for, 106, 114–15
  understanding creativity, 94
  vision of, 92, 93, 104
cultural exception, 21, 111, 167, 311
cultural exchange, 55
  and global economics, 67
  in history, 67, 135, 141
  sending and receiving texts, 143
  speed of, 227
cultural flow, 60–2, 70
  and copyright, 71
  and dissent, 63
  impeded by copyright law, 87
  regulation of, 61–2
cultural goods and cultural
    exception, 167
cultural identity, 33, 56–7, 62, 156,
    159, 185
  and global culture flows, 61
  and international
    communications, 33
  and magazines, 59
cultural press, 159
cultural products, 54, 73
  driving global growth, 86
  and economic value, 70
  rapid turnover, 46
  short life of, 46
  transferability and adaptation,
    142, 143
  work process, 46
cultural sustainability, 101
cultural tourism, 36, 57, 151, 206, 286
  and arts festivals, 261
  Australia, 286
  Korea, 151
cultural trade, 35, 54–5, 60
  controlled by corporations, 70
  disparities, 192
  exports, 56–7
  and local businessess, 105
  and new markets, 95
  as proportion of global economy, 94
  as proportion of GNP, 60
  as proportion of world trade, 70
cultural value, 30
  distribution, 34
  and economic value, 16–17, 19,
    30, 32–4, 35, 37–8, 40, 42,
    76, 308, 309
  and traditional culture, 75
culture
  and communication, 3
  definitions of, 3, 15, 43, 52, 204

culture *cont.*
  as 'goods/products', 73
  as private good, 36–7
  as public good, 17, 37
  'residual, dominant, emergent'
    (Williams: *Culture*), 15, 26
Cunningham, S., 16, 26
Cyworld, 242, 247
Czech Republic
  languages, 176

Dakar Plan of Action, 110
Darfur is Dying, 229
Denmark, 105
deregulation, 37
design, 17, 276, 308, 309
  and artisans, 277–8
developing countries
  and copyright, 73, 113
  creative/cultural industries, 38–9,
    109–10
  cultural trade, 112
  disparities, 192
  economic importance of crafts,
    278–9
  expansion of cultural markets, 61
  and fashion industry, 257
  fostering creative/cultural
    industries, 116
  losing out, 38
  ownership in the cultural
    economy, 47
  recasting global economy
    (1970s), 109
  rising educational standards, 60–1
digital media, 53, 54, 241–8
  blogging, 246
  and book publishing, 248–9
  and contemporary cultural dynamics,
    242–3
  contribution to cultural economy,
    241–2
  and copyright, 68–9
  and cultural diversity, 242
  and cultural products, 242
  and dissent, 53–4
  economic impact, 245
  global access and use, 243–5
  global variations in use, 242–3
  in Korea, 151–2
  and language groups, 242
  mobile media and wireless, 247–8
  novelty of, 241
  peer-to-peer (p2p) networks,
    245–6
  significant for cultural dynamics of
    globalization, 242–3
  social networking sites, 246–7

digital media cont.
  and transformation of traditional
    media, 241
  see also Internet; text messaging
Digital Millennium Copyright Act (USA),
  74, 87
dissent, 52, 53, 54, 63, 64
DMB (Digital Media Broadcasting), 152
Dominican Republic, 189
Downs, Anthony, 63, 65
Drik, 97
Dubai, 296, 297
Dubrovnik, 261

East Asia, 141–6
  consumers: knowledge of cultural
    products, 144
  copyright infringement, 144
  cosmopolitanism in cities, 141
  cultural economy as economic
    growth model, 143–5
  cultural exchange, 141, 142
  cultural flow to the West, 146
  cultural products
    importing and exporting, 142
    transferability and adaptation,
      142, 143
  cultural/creative industries, 22
  film production, 144
    and traditional cultures, 145
  government cultural policy,
    141, 146
  imitation, 144
  international co-production, 144
  outsourcing, 143–4
  regional production, 141
  television
    formats, 144
    transferability and adaptation, 142
  traditional cultures, 145
  transfer of technologies, 141
  video games, 142
  video outlets, 144
  Western dominance in cultural
    flow, 141
  see also China; Japan; Korea
economic sociology, 43, 44
economic sustainability, 101
economic value
  aesthetic value, 30, 31, 40
  and cultural value, 32–4, 35,
    37–8, 76
  techniques of assessment, 39
economics, 4–5
economy and cultural economy, 42–3,
  44–6, 48
Ecuador, 45, 189
Edinburgh Festival, 261

education and social change, 60–1
educational campaigns: Central
  Asia, 156
Egypt, 57, 137
Electronic Arts, 230, 231–2
elitism, 17
Ellis, S., 143, 147
emails, 53
Emerson, Jed, 101, 106
EMI, 88
employment conditions in the media,
  113–14
employment in cultural economy, 310
English, James, 5, 11
environmental sustainability, 101
ESA (Entertainment Software
  Association), 233
Ethiopia, 243
Eurasia Foundation, 158
Europe, 163–71
  art as business, 163–4
  art and economics dichotomy,
    163–4, 171
  challenges of globalization, 163–4
  collaborative creativity, 164
  contempoary art market, 296
  copyright, 170
  'creative industries': use of term,
    7, 8, 22
  cultural diversity, 167–8, 168–9
  cultural economy
    performance and employment,
      168
  cultural exception, 21, 167
  cultural policies of business sector, 166
  cultural protection and promotion,
    61–2
  cultural trade, 57
  culture and markets, 21
  decreasing cultural centrality, 21
  distrust of cultural industries, 164
  domestic consumption, 164
  film production, 170
  government funding, 163, 164, 165,
    167–8
  growth of media, 215
  individualization, 164
  industialization, 308
  Internet usage, 192
  moveable heritage, 170
  national cultures, 163, 170
  new cultural companies, 165
  publishing, 169–70
  role of cultural producers, 165
  sponsorship from business, 165–6
  telephone, mobile and Internet use, 243
  see also Central and Eastern
    Europe; Southeastern Europe

European Union
  Cultural Capital scheme, 264
  cultural policy, 169
  Culture 2000 program, 167
  media co-production, 199
  Media Plus Program, 319
  share of selected sectors in total
    employment, 180
  share of selected sectors in total
    value added, 179
  study on the economy of culture in
    Europe (2006), 168–9
  Television Without Frontiers,
    111, 167
evaluation, 30

Fabindia, 139
Fair Trade, 258
fashion industry, 253–9
  advertising, 256
  and aesthetics, 256–7
  brands, 253–4, 258
  in China, 258
  conglomerates, 254, 255, 257
  and consumers, 258
  creation process, 254–5
  and cultural diversity, 259
  and culture, 256
  designers, 254
  distribution, 256
  and education, 259
  and emerging countries, 257
  and environment, 258
  haute couture, 254, 256
  impact of globalization, 253–4
  and intellectual property rights,
    257–8
  marketing, 254, 258
  production, 255–6
  retailers, 254
Fekete, John, 30, 40
fields: definition, 207
film production, 57–8, 95, 129–31
  centers of production,
    217, 218–20
  clustering of skills, 218–19, 224
  and cultural diversity, 219–23
  distribution, 217–18, 220
  and distribution, 57–8
  diverification, 316
  early years, 217, 220
  expansion of companies, 217
  film festivals, 157–8, 161, 264–5
  pirating, 131
  TRIPS, 167
Flickr, 241
Florida, Richard, 8, 11, 98, 107, 111,
  119, 204

Food Force, 229
Ford Foundation, 114
formal and informal economies, 46
Fortune magazine, 231, 232
France
    at the Frankfurt Book Fair, 250
    contempoary art market,
        296, 297
    copyright law, 73
    creative industries
        contribution to the economy, 45
    cultural exception, 111, 167, 168
    cultural trade, 57, 163
    film production, 130, 319
    government funding, 165
    music festivals, 267
    new cultural companies, 165
    newspapers, 64
    publishing, 169, 170
    Second Life residents, 236
Frankfurt Book Fair, 249–50
Frankfurt School, 42, 43, 109,
    309, 320
free culture, 85–90
    and copyright laws, 86–7, 89–90
Free Software Foundation, 86
freedom of expression, 59, 62
freedom of the press, 71
Frieze (London), 293, 294
Full Spectrum Warrior, 229

Gadiesh, O., 143, 147
Galliano, John, 254
games, 20, 142, 227–38
    and advertising, 229
    and Christian groups, 229
    console sector, 230, 233, 234–5
    expos, 233–4
    growth rates, 233, 234
    makers and players, 228–9
    markets, 229, 231
    MMOGs (Massively Multiplayer
        Online Games), 235–7
    and pollution, 232
    with social/political messages, 229–
        30
    theorizing, 228–9
    and US military, 229
Gantchev, Dimiter, 113
García Canclini, Nestor, 185,
    87, 188, 198
Gareeva, Raisa, 105–6
Garnham, N., 22, 26, 44, 50
GATS (General Agreement on Trade in
    Services), 55, 167
GATT (General Agreement on Tariffs
    and Trade), 56, 59, 64, 69, 87,
    149, 167

German, Alexei, 173
Germany, 45, 62, 170, 236, 308
Ghana, 95
Ghiyath-ud-Din, 136
Gil, Gilberto, 270
Gilberto, Joao, 270
Gilmore, James H., 152, 154
Gilroy, Paul, 1, 12
Glasgow, 264
'global': meaning of, 292–3
Global Alliance for Cultural
    Diversity, 112
global citizenship, 55–7, 63–4
Global Conflict: Palestine, 230
global cultural economy
    characteristics, 54–6
    cultural flow, 60–2
        and dissent, 63
        regulation of, 61–2
    definition, 52
global inequalities, 47, 109
global literature, 33
global markets, 33, 54
    and local industries, 95
    and music, 33
global media growth, 215–16
'Global South Creative Economy Expo'
    (Shanghai 2008), 117–18
'globalization': definition, 3
Gnutella, 245
Goethe: *Weltliteratur*, 33
Golden Mask festival, 266
Google, 24, 87
Google Books Library Project, 248–9
    and copyright, 249
government cultural policies, 37–8, 43,
    105–6
    in broadcasting and films, 222, 223
    control of media, 311
    and creativity as driving force, 38
    and cultural commons, 61–2
    and cultural industries, 56
    private sector investment, 37
    urban/regional development, 317–19
Grand Theft Auto, 230, 231
Grauso, Mario, 257
Great Exhibition (1851), 276
Great Silk Road, 155
Greece, 167, 170, 179, 180, 181
Grokster, 245
Guardian newspaper, 246
Gucci Group, 255, 257
Guild of Handicrafts, 276

H&M, 254, 256, 258
Habermas, Jurgen, 53, 63, 65
Hague system for industrial
    designs, 112

Haiti, 243
Hall, Stuart, 34, 40, 57, 65
hallyu see Korea, Korean Wave
handicraft *see* crafts
Hartley, John, 200, 210, 286, 290
Harvey, David, 216, 217, 225
haute couture, 254, 256
Hengdian World Studios, 144
Hero, 145
Hesmondhalgh, David, 207, 210
Hewism, Robert, 6
Holden, John, 18–19, 26
Hollywood
    and Bollywood, 220, 221
    cultural exchange and
        adaptation, 142
    development as film center,
        218–19, 220
    outsourcing, 146
homogeneity and diversity, 42
Hong Kong
    contempoary art market,
        296, 297, 304
    'creative industries', 22
    film production, 143, 217, 218
    telephone, mobile and Internet
        use, 243
    television, 141, 142, 143, 144
Honolulu, 95
House of Flying Daggers, 145
Howkins, John, 116
HSX (Hollywood Stock Exchange), 230
human rights and moral rights, 76–8
Hungary, *175*
Hyde, Lewis, 30, 41

Ibermedia, 194
ICCI (International Center on Creative
    Industries), 117
ICT (information and communication
    technology), 33–4, 151
    access and use, 244–5
    and aesthetic value, 31
    and arts festivals/exhibitions, 266
    and authors/artists, 32–3
    and content, 69–70
    and copyright, 76
    and cultural businesses, 32
    and cultural diversity, 33
    and cultural flow, 70
    and cultural value, 33–5
    demand for cultural goods, 36–7
    and dissent, 53–4, 63, 64
    driving globalization, 67
    enabling mass production, 46
    and global citizenship, 55–7, 63–4
    and individualization, 164
    interactive consumption, 36–7, 57

ICT (information and communication technology) cont.
in music, 32
and new artforms, 32, 33
ownership, 53, 54
and political power, 53–4, 63, 63–4
and social change, 63
and social and political choices, 89
and value creation, 30–1, 32–3
in world economy, 69
see also digital media; Internet; text messaging
Idris, Kamil, 112
ILO (International Labour Organization), 22, 108, 113–15, 118
crafts development, 274
'Small Enterprise Development and Job Creation in the Cultural Sector', 114
IMF (International Monetary Fund), 125, 149
imitation, 144, 221
India
crafts, 17–18, 135–40
arteliers, 137
and arts, 136–7
and consumerism, 136
cottage industry sector, 138
economic importance of, 279
and education, 139
and globalization, 138–40
guilds, 137
history, 136–7
and industrialization, 137–8
regional styles, 137
subsidies, 138
transfers of capital, 136
Varanasi weavers, 135, 136, 138, 139
creative and economic advance, 19, 21
Creative Future for entrepreneurs, 93–4
expansion of cultural markets, 61
fashion industry, 255
film production, 57–8, 199
Bollywood, 220–1
expansion: studio system, 217
and globalization, 220
growth of media, 215
Handicrafts Development, 135
industrialization, 137
Internet use, 60
new technologies and exploitation of the weak, 136
radio, 222
revenues from crafts, 279

India cont.
social disparities, 136
Weavers Studio: local cultural enterprises, 100–1
individual and community, 124, 164
Indonesia, 246, 278–9
industrial districts, 48
industrialization, 137–8, 275–6, 308–9
information flow, 47
Innis, Harold, 53, 65
Intellectual Property Association, 189
Intergovernmental Conference on Cultural Policies (Stockholm 1998), 111
International Convention fro the Protection of Performers, Producers of Phonograms and Broadcasting Organisations, 114
international cultural policies, 38–9
agencies, 108–19
policy-making process, 115
'International Forum on Creative Economy for Development', 117–18
international organizations, 54–5
craft development projects, 274
International Young Creative Entrepreneur awards, 93
Internet
access and use, 23, 59–60, 191, 192, 244–5
variations, 243–4
advertising, 59
and authors/artists, 32
books online, 90
broadband, 60
and copyright, 34, 35, 68
and cosmopolitanism, 56
'cultural commons', 35, 55
cutltural value, 34–5
and global citizenship, 55–6
and knowledge, 88, 89
and magazine publishing, 59
mobile, 247
music, 68, 88, 89
copyright, 245
downloading, 88
music-sharing sites, 241, 245
piracy, 190
and niche interests, 90
Open Access, 88
piracy, 34, 190
publishing, 88
research online, 88, 89
use of English, 192
user-generated content, 87
and value creation, 34

Internet Relay Chat (IRC), 244
Iran, 136, 137, 279
Istanbul Festival, 262–3
Italy, 165, 167, 170, 236, 250
ITC (International Trade Center)
economic importance of crafts, 279
Ito, Joichi, 90
ITU (International Telecommunications Union), 244

Jacobs, Marc, 254
Jamaica, 95, 193
Japan
anime and computer games, 141, 143
arts festivals, 262
and Asian popular culture, 148
consumer of Canadian cultural products, 62
copyright law, 19
fashion industry, 255, 258
film production and distribution, 57
games, 231, 234
information technology and economic growth, 69
manga, 143, 151
mobile phone use, 247
Second Life residents, 236
television, 142, 143
exports, 144
Jenkins, Henry, 23–4, 26
journals online, 88
Journey to the West, 142
Jurassic Park, 149

Kazaa, 245
Kazakhstan, 156, 158, 160
KEA European Affairs, 168
Keane, Michael, 286, 290
Khudoinazarov, Bakhtiar, 158
Killer, 158
Kingdom, John, 108, 120
Klein, Naomi, 54, 66
Kluge, John W., 289
Kong, L. et al., 22, 26
Korea, 21, 143
arts festivals, 262
broadband use, 60
broadcasting
appeal of Korean dramas, 150–1
imports and exports, 150
outsourced broadcasting, 149
SBS (Seoul Broadcasting System), 149
competition from Hollywood, 149
digital media, 151–2

Korea *cont.*
    economic crisis (late 90s), 149–50
    film production, 141
    games, 142, 143, 231
    government cultural policies, 149
    Hallyu tourism, 151
    Internet use, 152
    Korean Wave, 148–53
        rise of, 148–9
        expansion, 150–1
        convergence, 151–2, 152–3
        future, 152
        chaebols (family-owned
            conglomerates), 149, 150
    mobile phone use, 153, 243, 247
    telephone, mobile and
        Internet use, 243
    TV dramas, 141
Kyrgyz Republic, 156, 158, 160

LA Electronic Entertainment Expo,
    233, 234–5
Lagerfield, Karl, 258
languages
    Australia, 286
    and digital media, 242
Latin America and Caribbean,
    22, 185–98
    audio-visual sectors, 194
    book publishing, 194, 195
    business structure, 187
    *Centro Regional para el Fomento del
        Libro en América Latina y el
        Caribe* (CERLALC), 110
    copyright and piracy,
        188, 189–90
    cultural exchanges, 186–7
    cultural exports, 192, 194
    cultural identities, 185
    cultural rights, 185–6
    digital music business, 188
    economic indicators, 187
    immigration, 187
    Internet access and use, 191, 192
    literacy, 187, 190–1
    markets, 187, 188, 194, 195
    media market share, 194
    mobile technology use, 192
    multiculturalism, 188–9
    music
        digital market, 191
        sales, 193, 194
    opportunities and threats, 195–7
    patchwork of cultures, 186
    poverty, 187
    publishing trade, 189
    socio-economic standing, 185, 187
    television, 57, 187–8, 194, 195

Latin-American Parliament, 186
Latvia, 105, 175
Leadbeater, Charles, 23
Lebanon, 262
Lee, Ang, 145, 146
Legend of Mir, 142
Lessig, Lawrence, 58, 86,
    87, 89, 91
Lille, 264
Linden Lab, 236, 237, 238
literacy, 60–1, 187, 190–1
Lithuania, 175
LiveJournal, 231, 232
local cultures, 62
logic of accumulation, 216–18
London, 296, 297, 310
Los Angeles, 310, 318
Los Angeles Olympic Games, 263
Lothal, 135
Lotman, Yuri M., 142, 147
Lowenstein, Douglas, 233
Luna Papa, 158, 161
luxury industry, 254, 255, 257
LVMH, 255

Macedonia, 179, 180, 181
McLuhan, Marshall, 53, 66
Madrid system for trademarks, 112
magazines, 59
Magnatune, 88
Malaysia, 23
Maldives, 135
Mali, 279
'managerial revolution', 217
Manchester, 319
manga, 143, 151
Mann, Michael, 292–3, 306
Maori, 23
Marithé & François Girbaud, 256
market forces in film production and
    television, 223
markets, 6, 8–9, 52, 104
    books, 90
    competition, 46
    forms and regulation, 46
    and inequalities, 47
    niche marketing, 308
    ownership in Anglo-American
        market, 61
Markusen, Ann, 206–7, 211
Marx, Karl, 4, 217
mass production
    and cultural value, 309–10
mastiha, 319–20
Maugham, W. Somerset, 312
media capital, 223
    forces of socio-cultural variation,
        219–23

media capital *cont.*
    logic of accumulation, 216–18
    trajectories of creative migration,
        218–19
media imperialism, 215, 216
Megaw, J.V.S. and M.Ruth, 286, 290
Mellander, C., 98, 107
Mercosur, 186
Metcalfe, Bob, 89
Meteor Garden, 142
Mexico, 150, 243
    business structure, 187
    copyright and piracy, 189, 190
    economy, 187
    film and television production, 57
    music sales, 194
    publishing, 195
*Mexico City Declaration on Cultural
    Policies* (1982), 109
Middle East, 192
Miège, B., 44, 50
Miller, Toby, 285, 291
Mir Ali Shir, 136
MMOGs (Massively Multiplayer Online
    Games), 235–7
mobile technology, 23, 53–4, 64
    use, 243, 244
    see also text messaging
Moldova
    Internet use, 181
Montenegro, 180, 181
Moore, Michael, 54
Morocco, 255
Morris, William, 276
Mosco, Vincent, 228, 232, 239
Mota da Silva, Denise, 186–7, 198
Mugabe, Robert, 126
multiculturalism, 188–9
Mumbai, 57–8, 218, 220–1
Murdoch, Rupert, 24, 87, 215, 247
Murray, C., 9, 12
music
    axé music, 271
    classical music festivals, 265, 267
    and copyright law, 68
    and global markets, 33
    on the Internet, 64, 68, 88, 89
    Magnatune, 88
    marginal groups, 316
    music-sharing sites, 241, 245
    and p2p, 245, 246
    Papaya Music, Central America, 195
    piracy, 189, 190
    pop music festivals, 265
    production and artistic value, 33
    production system, 45
    profits, 64
    reggae music, 193

music cont.
use of new technologies, 32
world music, 33, 95, 265
My Wife is a Gangster, 145
Myer, R., 285, 291
Myers, Fred, 284, 287, 288, 291
MySpace, 24, 87, 242, 246, 247
Mystic Maritime Museum, 103–4

Nagina, 136
Naples, 281, 282
Napster, 241, 245
national cultures, 95, 163, 170
National System of Innovation, 115
Nepal, 92
Netease, 142
Netherlands, 236, 250, 263–4
networks, 104, 151, 164, 313
new artforms, 32, 33
New International Economic Order
(NIEO), 109, 115
new markets for cultural products
Central Asia, 157, 160
New Mexico Community Fund, 103
new technologies *see* digital media;
ICT (information and
communication technology);
Inernet
New World Information and
Communication Order
(NWICO), 109
New York
arts festivals, 263, 264
Chelsea art galleries, 292–3,
299–302
and auction houses, 299
content, 299–301
free admission, 298
opportunities for artists, 298
small galleries, 298
success of, 302
contemporary art market, 296, 297
Dreamings exhibition (1988),
288–9
employment in cultural
economy, 310
market for Australian indigenous
art, 288–9
New Zealand, 151
news, 63, 242
newspapers, 59, 64, 222
and blogs, 246
NICL (New International Division of
Cultural Labour), 228
Nigeria, 125
film production, 95, 130–1, 132
radio, 222
video films, 222

Nintendo, 230
NL: a Season of Dutch Arts in the
Berkshires, 263–4
Nobel Prize, 5, 6
Nomads, 158, 161
North America, 192
see also Canada; USA
Ntumazah, Ndeh, 128
Nyamnjoh, F.B., 127, 128, 134

Odegard, Stephanie, 92
Olinda, 270
Omirbaev, Darejan, 158
Onyeani, Chika, 131
open access, 88
open archives, 88
open knowledge, 89
open source software, 86
ownership and control, 47
Oxford Internet Institute survey, 244

Pacific Community Fund, 103
Pakistan
economic importance of crafts, 279
Pan African Booksellers Association
(PABA), 127
Pan African Writers (PAWA), 127
Pandemic, 229
Papaya Music, 195
Papua New Guinea, 243
Paraguay, 189, 194
Paris, 290, 308, 318
Parsons, T., 44, 50
participation in culture, 159–60
'Partnership for Technical Assistance
for Enhancing the Creative
Economy in Developing Countries'
(Shanghai 2005), 117
Patent Cooperation Treaty, 112
Patron Publishing House, 128
Paz, Octavio, 186
peer-to-peer (p2p) networks, 245–6
performing arts, 264, 266
Peru, 95, 102, 189, 279
Pesce, Mark, 23
Pew Internet & American Life surveys,
244
Philippines, 278–9
Phillips de Pury, 299
photography: *Drik*, 97
Pine, B. Joseph, 152, 154
piracy, 131, 175, 189, 190
PlayStation, 230–1
Poiret, Paul, 256
Poland, 175, 176, 279
Polanyi, K., 4, 44, 51
political power and ICT, 53, 63
Polo, Mark, 141

Portugal, 170
potters, 95
Potts, J., 16, 24, 26
Pratt, A.C., 44, 51, 310, 323
print media, 64, 70
prizes, 5–6
Procter and Gamble, 257
profits/not-for-profit sector, 47, 110
Program-Related/Mission-Related
Investments (PRI/MRI), 102–3
Public Library of Science, 35
public service broadcasting, 222
publishing, 58–9, 70, 99, 126–8
and digital media, 248–9
and Google Books Library, 248–9
number of books, 90
online, 88
Putumayo, 95

QPS (Quadruple-Play-Service), 151
Quemain, Alain, 294–5, 306

radio, 222
Raise the Red Lantern, 145
RAND Corporation: report, 38
Recife, 270
Red Tape Recording Studios, 319
regulation, 46
of film and broadcast media, 222,
223, 224
research online, 88, 89
Resistance: Fall of Man, 229
Richemont Group, 255
Ricupero, Rubens, 115, 116
Ring, The, 146
Rio de Janeiro Carnival, 262
Robinson and Halie, 36–7, 41
Rocha, Glauber, 270
Rock Start, 231
Romania, 175, 179, 180, 181
Rudaki, 136
Rugmark, 92
Ruskin, John, 276, 308
Russia, 173, 174, 175, 176
Russian Academy of Sciences, 172
Rwanda, 53

Sahara Media Entertainment, 221
Salzburg Festival, 261
Santa Fe, USA, 98
Santos, Edna dos, 116
Saudi Arabia, 23, 256
SBS, 149
Scher, Phillip, 95, 107
Schumpeter, Joseph A., 96, 107
Scott, Allen J., 219, 226
Second Life, 230, 235–7, 236, 238
Second World, 230

sectors: definition, 208
Serbia, 179, 180, 181
Shah, Darshan, 100–1
Shall We Dance, 146
Shanda, 142
Shanghai, 117
'sharing economy', 85
Sheffield, 319
Shilp Gurus, 135
Shim, Doobo, 149, 154
Shiraishi, Saya, 148, 154
Short Message Service (SMS) *see* text
    messaging (SMS)
SICA (System of Centro-American
    Integration), 186
sign-value in productive activity, 307–8
Singapore, 22, 151, 266
Skinner, B.F., 137
Slovakia, 175, 176
Smith, Adam, 4
Smith, Terry, 284, 291
social entrepreneurs, 96
social networks, 24, 241, 242, 245–6,
    246–7
    and copyright, 68
social sustainability, 101
soft industrial design, 277–8, 279–80
    collective trademarks, 281–2
    cultural districts, 280–1
Soja, E.W., 314
Sony, 230, 231
Sotheby's, 296, 302, 303, 304
South Africa, 22, 57, 127, 128
South Asia
    child labour, 92
    crafts, 135–40
    cultural/creative industries, 22
Southeastern Europe, 178–84
    consumers and participation, 181
    cultural consumerism, 182, 183
    cultural/creative industries:
        emergence of, 178, 179–80
    Internet use, 181
    local and global interactions, 182–3
    markets and aesthetics, 181–2
    role of local agents, 178–9
    share of selected sectors in total
        employment, 180
    share of selected sectors in total
        value added, 179
    transition to capitalism, 178–9
Soviet Union, 155–6, 158
Soyinka, W., 125, 134
Spain, 165, 167, 236, 250
Special Unit for South-South
    Cooperation, 117–18
sponsorship, 103, 165–6, 261, 265–6
Stallman, Richard, 86

Star TV, 215–16
Storper, Dan, 100
Storper, Michael, 218, 219, 226
subsidized arts, 16, 18–19, 165
    broadcasting and films, 223–4
    Central Asia, 159
    radio, 222
Sundara Rajan
    Mira T., 75, 81
sustainability, 101, 159
Sweden, 98, 310
Switzerland, 236, 250
    Art Basel, 293, 294, 295
Syria, 137

Taiwan, 141, 142, 143, 262
Tajikistan, 156, 158
Tashkent, 157
Tatu group, 176
Taylor, E.W., 4
Technorati, 246
telephone use, 60, 243
television
    broadband, 60
    and copyright/intellectual property
        rights (IPR), 58
    downloading and peer-sharing, 246
    expansion of companies, 217
    formats, 143, 144
    most ubiquitous medium, 58
    spending and profits, 58
Tennis for Two, 228
text messaging (SMS), 53, 247
textile crafts, 279
Thailand, 151
Theater of the Oppressed, 262
Theyskens, Olivier, 257
Thompson, Kristin, 220, 226
Thrift, N., 4–5, 11
Throsby, David, 54, 66
Timberland, 258
Time magazine, 152
Todd, Emmanuel, 60, 66
Tokyo Game Show, 233, 234
Tomlinson, John, 216, 226
Tortilleria Editorial, 195
TPS (Triple-Play-Service), 151
trade and cultural value, 35
Trade Related Intellectual Property
    Rights Agreement, 54, 55
Treaty of Amsterdam, 169
Treaty of Maastricht, 165, 168
Trinidad-Tobago, 95
trio eléctrico, 270, 273
TRIPS (Agreement on Trade-Related
    Aspects of Intellectual Property
    Rights), 58, 69, 72–3, 74, 75, 87,
    167, 311

Tunisia, 243, 255
Turin International Training Center, 114
Turkey, 243, 262–3, 279
Turkmenistan, 156
TVB, 141, 144

UCC (user created content), 152
Ugbomah, Eddie, 129, 130
UK
    copyright/intellectual property rights
        (IPR) law, 77
    creative/cultural industries, 200
        contribution to the economy, 45
    cultural policies, 7, 8, 105
    employment in cultural
        economy, 310
    funding of the arts, 7, 8, 165
    immigration from Caribbean,
        187, 193
    industialization, 308
    performance targets for cultural
        organizations, 38
    public service broadcasting, 222
    quitting UNESCO (1984-5), 109
    regulating global cultural flow, 62
    Second Life residents, 236
    telephone, mobile and Internet
        use, 243
*UK Creative Industries Mapping
    Document*, 45
Ukraine, 175
UN Special Unit for South-South
    Cooperation, 108
UNCTAD (United Nations Conference
    on Trade and Development), 21,
    22, 39, 108, 115–17
    conference (Sao Paulo 2004), 115
    crafts development, 274
    forum (Salvador de Bahia 2005),
        116–17, 118
    UNCTAD X conference (Bangkok
        2000), 115
UNDP (United Nations Development
    Program), 39, 117
UNESCO (United Nations Educational,
    Scientific and Cultural
    Organization), 42, 55, 108, 109–
    12
    *Convention on the Protection of the
        Diversity of Cultural
        Expressions*, 167
    *Convention on the Protection and
        Promotion of the Diversity of
        Cultural Expressions*, 22, 38–9,
        56, 62, 109, 112
    Convention on the Protection and
        Promotion of the Diversity of
        Cultural Expressions, 10, 311

UNESCO (United Nations Educational, Scientific and Cultural Organization) *cont.*
and copyright/intellectual property rights (IPR), 110, 111
crafts development, 274
cultural diversity, 111
Cultural Diversity Convention (2007), 22, 38–9
cultural trade disparities, 192
development of creative/cultural industries, 110–11
Flows of Selected Cultural Goods and Services (1994-2003), 94
Medium-Term Plan (1989), 110
Medium-Term Strategy (1996-2001), 110–11
Medium-Term Strategy (2002), 111
'Place and Role of Cultural Industries in the Cultural Development of Societies' (Montreal 1980), 109
support of arts festivals, 268
survey of crafts in international markets, 278–9
UNIDO (United Nations Industrial Nations Development Organization), 139
Uniqlo, 258
United Arab Emirates, 23
Universal Declaration on Cultural Diversity (2001), 111
urban development, 308–9, 314, 318–19
Uruguay, 45, 194
Manos del Uruguay, 196
US Trade Representative (USTR), 71
USA
American Assembly: report on the arts (1997), 203
arts organizations, 199
BLS (Bureau of Labor Statistics), 206
broadband Internet use, 60
Center for an Urban Future, 205, 210
competitors with American popular culture, 199
copyright industries, 205
copyright/intellectual property rights (IPR) law, 19, 72, 73, 74, 75
dispute with France and Canada, 73
corporate growth and profits, 62
creative industries, 208
contribution to the economy, 45, 57
use of term, 22
cultural trade, 57, 61
development of broadcasting, 222
diversity as function of competition, 62

USA *cont.*
dominance of international communications technology, 227
employment in cultural economy, 310
film production
expansion: studio system, 217
and exports, 95
and foreign competition, 316
views of Africa, 129
games, 229, 231, 234
GSA (General Services Administration), 201
immigration from Latin America and Caribbean, 187, 193
information technology and economic growth, 69
lobbying by creative/cultural industries, 71
local creative economy, 199–210
AFTA (Americans for the Arts), 202
arts and city economies, 201–2
arts impact studies, 201–2
broadening concept of arts/culture, 203
cultural tourism, 206
decentralization policies, 202–3
definitional approaches, 203–9, 204
classification schemes, 207–9, 208
copyright approach, 205
non-profit and commercial arts, 205
occupations and employment, 206–7
overall grouping, 203–4
product and production structure, 207
products and services, 204–5
negative public impacts, 202
non-profit arts, 205, 208–9
old public patronage, 201, 201–2
magazine publishing: dispute with Canada, 59
market for visual art, 286
markets for cultural products, 61
and multinational corporations, 315
music production and exports, 95
NALAA (National Assembly of Local Arts Agencies), 201–2
NASAA (National Assembly of State Arts Agencies), 202, 205–6, 211
National Endowment for the Humanities, 289
NEA (National Endowment for the Arts), 201, 206, 211
PCAH (President's Commission for the Arts and Humanities), 203
public support of the arts, 38
quitting UNESCO (1984-5), 109

USA *cont.*
San Diego Foundations report (2006), 204, 211
Second Life residents, 236
subsidized arts, 199, 200
telephone, mobile and Internet use, 243
television
and copyright/intellectual property rights (IPR), 58
profits from, 58
urban growth, 308–9
see also New York
user-generated content, 87, 242
Uzbekistan, 105–6, 150, 156

valorization, 30
value
crisis of, 29, 30–1
and cultural economy, 29–30
definition of, 29–30
economic and cultural, 29, 30
and technological change, 30–1
value chain, 29
value creation, 31–2
and authors/artists, 31–2
value distribution
Internet, 34–5
value and globalization
consumption, 35–7
culture as private good, 36–7
culture as public good, 37
cultural trade, 35
government cultural policies, 37–8
ICT (information and communication technology), 32–3
international cultural policy, 38–9
Veloso, Caetano, 270
Venezuela, 45, 57, 187, 189
Venice Biennale (2005), 157, 160
video, 244
video-sharing sites, 241
video/audio production, 190
Vietnam
economic importance of crafts, 279
vision, 99, 100
of cultural entrepreneurs, 92, 93, 104

Walker and Rasamimanana, 129, 134
Weavers Studio, 100–1
weaving, 92, 95, 100–1, 135, 138–9
Wedding Banquet, 145
West Africa, 57
What is Love All About?, 149
WiBro (Wireless Broadband), 152
Wiener Werkstätte, 276

Williams, Raymond, 15, 26
Winter Sonata, 150
WIPO (World Intellectual Property
    Organization), 22, 72, 74, 87, 108,
    110, 112–13, 118, 189
  Creative Industries Division,
    112–13
  *Guide on Surveying the Economic
    Contribution of the Copyright-
    Based Industries*, 113
  Internet Treaties, 74
Wireless Access Protocol (WAP), 247

World Bank, 39, 102,
    125, 274
World Heritage List, 30
World Internet Survey, 245
World of Legend, 142
world music, 33, 95, 265
World Summit on the Information
    Society, 248
World Wide Web *see* Internet
WTO (World Trade Organization),
    42, 54, 57, 59, 63, 69, 73,
    75, 87, 167

Wu, John, 146
Xbox, 130, 231

Yimou, Zhang, 146
YouTube, 24, 87, 241
Yukihito, Tabata, 305

Zambia, 114
Zara, 254
Zhang Yimou, 145
Zhou, Yi Ping, 117
Zimbabwe, 99, 126